ROOTS OF REVOLUTION

Franco Venturi was born in 1914 and lived in Turin where his father Lionello was Professor of History of Art. In 1932, when Lionello refused to take the oath of loyalty to Fascism, the Venturi family emigrated to Paris where Franco attended the Faculty of Arts and became militant in the anti-Fascist group Giustizia e Libertà headed by Carlo Rosselli. His first work as an historian was *La Jeunesse de Diderot* (1939), the starting point of his research on the *Encyclopédie*. He participated actively in the Italian Resistance. From 1947 to 1949 he lived in the Soviet Union, where he prepared his best-known work on Russian populism, *Roots of Revolution*. Venturi contributed not only to work on the French and Italian Enlightenment, but also more generally to a conceptualization of the Enlightenment as a European and Atlantic exchange of ideas, as utopia and reform, as the will to transform the world through politics and economics. This is the theme of his last unfinished masterwork, *Settecento riformatore*. He died in 1994.

ALSO BY FRANCO VENTURI

Dei delitti e delle pene. Con una raccolta di lettere e documenti relativi alla nascita dell'opera e alla sua fortuna nell'Europa del Settecento. A cura di Franco Venturi

Le Vrai système, ou le Mot de l'énigme métaphysique et morale (with Jean Thomas)

Dalmazzo Francesco Vasco, 1732–1794

Esuli russi in Piemonte dopo il '48

Genova a metà del Settecento

Jeunesse de Diderot, 1713–1753.

Le Origini dell'Enciclopedia

ROOTS OF REVOLUTION

A History of the Populist and Socialist Movements in 19th Century Russia

Franco Venturi

With a revised author's introduction, *Russian Populism*

Translated from the Italian by Francis Haskell

Introduced by Sir Isaiah Berlin

PHOENIX
PRESS

5 UPPER SAINT MARTIN'S LANE
LONDON
WC2H 9EA

To my Father and Mother

A PHOENIX PRESS PAPERBACK

Roots of Revolution first published in Great Britain
by Weidenfeld & Nicolson in 1960
'Russian Populism' first published in English
by Chicago University Press in 1982
This paperback edition published in 2001
by Phoenix Press,
a division of The Orion Publishing Group Ltd,
Orion House, 5 Upper St Martin's Lane,
London WC2H 9EA

Copyright © 1952, 1972 by Antonello Venturi

A CIP catalogue record for this book
is available from the British Library.

Printed and bound in Great Britain by
Clays Ltd, St Ives plc

ISBN 1 84212 253 3

CONTENTS

INTRODUCTION

PROFESSOR FRANCO VENTURI'S work on the Russian Populist movement is the fullest and most authoritative account in any language of a decisive phase in the history of the Russian revolutionary movement. In the face of every temptation Professor Venturi has preserved a calm impartiality of judgment which has caused him to be recognized, in the West and the Soviet Union alike, as a leading authority on Russian revolutionary history, a fact almost without precedent in our day. Professor Venturi has had unusual opportunities to consult primary sources not easily accessible to Western scholars, and has embodied the results of his exhaustive research in a clear and tranquil narrative that orders and explains a confused mass of events and ideas which no Western scholar has hitherto successfully disentangled and assessed. The author's intellectual and historical grasp of his subject is both greater and more minute than that of his predecessors in this field, and his book can therefore fail to interest only three groups of critics: those who look on all history through the eyes of the victors, and for whom accounts of movements that failed, of martyrs and minorities, seem without interest as such; those who think that ideas play little or no part in determining historical events; and finally those who are convinced that the Russian revolution was simply the result of the application of Marxist ideas imported from the West, and possessed no significant roots in the Russian past. I find it difficult to think that anyone but the most impervious fanatic could emerge from reading these objective and convincing pages with these heresies unimpaired. Russian Populism, more fortunate than many Western movements, has at last found its historian.

Russian Populism is the name not of a single political party, nor of a coherent body of doctrine, but of a widespread radical movement in Russia in the middle of the nineteenth century. It was born during the great social and intellectual ferment which followed the death of Tsar Nicholas I and the defeat and humiliation of the Crimean War, grew to fame and influence during the 'sixties and 'seventies, and reached its culmination with the assassination of Tsar Alexander II, after which it swiftly declined. Its leaders were men of very dissimilar origins, outlooks and capacities; it was not at any stage more than a loose congeries of small independent groups of conspirators or their sympathizers, who sometimes united for common action, and at other times operated in isolation. These groups tended to differ both about ends and about means. Nevertheless they held certain fundamental

vii

beliefs in common, and possessed sufficient moral and political solidarity to entitle them to be called a single movement. Like their predecessors, the Decembrist conspirators in the 'twenties, and the circles
that gathered round Herzen and Belinsky in the 'thirties and 'forties, they
looked on the government and the social structure of their country as
a moral and political monstrosity—obsolete, barbarous, stupid and odious
—and dedicated their lives to its total destruction. Their general ideas were
not original. They shared the democratic ideals of the European radicals of
their day, and in addition believed that the struggle between social and economic classes was the determining factor in politics; they held this theory not
in its Marxist form (which did not effectively reach Russia until the 'seventies)
but in the form in which it was taught by Proudhon and Herzen, and before
them by Saint-Simon, Fourier and other French socialists and radicals
whose writings had entered Russia, legally and illegally, in a thin but steady
stream, for several decades.

The theory of social history as dominated by the class war—the heart of
which is the notion of the coercion of the 'have-nots' by the 'haves'—was
born in the course of the Industrial Revolution in the West; and its most
characteristic concepts belong to the capitalist phase of economic development. Economic classes, capitalism, cut-throat competition, proletarians and
their exploiters, the evil power of unproductive finance, the inevitability of
increasing centralization and standardization of all human activities, the
transformation of men into commodities and the consequent 'alienation'
of individuals and groups and degradation of human lives—these notions are
fully intelligible only in the context of expanding industrialism. Russia, even
as late as the 'fifties, was one of the least industrialized states in Europe.
Nevertheless, exploitation and misery had long been amongst the most
familiar and universally recognized characteristics of its social life, the
principal victims of the system being the peasants, both serfs and free, who
formed over nine-tenths of its population. An industrial proletariat had
indeed come into being, but by mid-century did not exceed 2 or 3 per cent
of the population of the Empire. Hence the cause of the oppressed was still
at that date overwhelmingly that of the agricultural workers who formed
the lowest stratum of the population, the vast majority being serfs in
state or private possession. The Populists looked upon them as martyrs
whose grievances they were determined to avenge and remedy, and as
embodiments of simple uncorrupted virtue, whose social organization (which
they largely idealized) was the natural foundation on which the future of
Russian society must be rebuilt. The central Populist goals were social justice
and social equality. Most of them were convinced, following Herzen,
whose revolutionary propaganda in the 'fifties influenced them more
than any other single set of ideas, that the essence of a just and equal society
existed already in the Russian peasant commune—the *obshchina*, organized
in the form of a collective unit called the *mir*. The *mir* was a free association

of peasants which periodically redistributed the agricultural land to be tilled; its decisions bound all its members, and constituted the corner-stone on which, so the Populists maintained, a federation of socialized, self-governing units, conceived along lines popularized by the French socialist Proudhon, could be erected. The Populist leaders believed that this form of cooperation offered the possibility of a free and democratic social system in Russia, originating as it did in the deepest moral instincts and traditional values of Russian, and indeed all human, society, and they believed that the workers (by which they meant all productive human beings), whether in town or country, could bring this system into being with a far smaller degree of violence or coercion than had occurred in the industrial West. This system, since it alone sprang naturally from fundamental human needs and a sense of the right and the good that existed in all men, would ensure justice, equality and the widest opportunity for the full development of human faculties. As a corollary of this, the Populists believed that the development of large-scale centralized industry was not 'natural', and therefore led inexorably to the degradation and dehumanization of all those who were caught in its tentacles: capitalism was an appalling evil, destructive of body and soul; but it was not inescapable. They denied that social or economic progress was necessarily bound up with the Industrial Revolution. They maintained that the application of scientific truths and methods to social and individual problems (in which they passionately believed), although it might, and often did, lead to the growth of capitalism, could be realized without this fatal sacrifice. They believed that it was possible to improve life by scientific techniques without necessarily destroying the 'natural' life of the peasant village, or creating a vast, pauperized, faceless city proletariat. Capitalism seemed irresistible only because it had not been sufficiently resisted. However it might be in the West, in Russia 'the curse of bigness' could still be successfully fought, and federations of small self-governing units of producers, as Fourier and Proudhon had advocated, could be fostered, and indeed created, by deliberate action. Like their French masters, the Russian disciples held the institution of the state in particular hatred, since to them it was at once the symbol, the result, and the main source of injustice and inequality—a weapon wielded by the governing class to defend its own privileges—and one that, in the face of increasing resistance from its victims, grew progressively more brutal and blindly destructive. The defeat of liberal and radical movements in the West in 1848–9 confirmed them in their conviction that salvation did not lie in politics or political parties: it seemed clear to them that liberal parties and their leaders had neither understood nor made a serious effort to forward the fundamental interests of the oppressed populations of their countries. What the vast majority of peasants in Russia (or workers in Europe) needed was to be fed and clothed, to be given physical security, to be rescued from disease, ignorance, poverty and humiliating inequalities. As for political rights, votes, parliaments, republican forms, these were meaningless and useless to ignorant, barbarous, half-naked and starving men; such programmes merely mocked their misery. The Populists shared with the nationalistic Russian Slavophils (with whose political ideas they had otherwise little in common) a loathing of the rigidly class-conscious social pyramid of the West that was complacently accepted, or fervently believed in, by the conformist bourgeoisie and the bureaucracy to whom this bourgeoisie looked up.

The satirist Saltykov, in his famous dialogue between a German and a Russian boy, immortalized this attitude when he declared his faith in the Russian boy, hungry and in rags, stumbling in the mud and squalor of the accursed, slave-owning Tsarist régime, because he had not, like the neat, docile, smug, well-fed, well-dressed German boy, bartered away his soul for the sixpence that the Prussian official had offered him, and was consequently still capable, if only he was allowed to do so (as the German boy no longer was), of rising one day to his full human height. Russia was in darkness and in chains, but her spirit was not captive; her past was black, but her future promised more than the death in life of the civilized middle classes in Germany or France or England, who had long ago sold themselves for material security and had become so apathetic in their shameful, self-imposed servitude that they no longer knew how to want to be free.

The Populists, unlike the Slavophils, did not believe in the unique character or destiny of the Russian people. They were not mystical nationalists. They believed only that Russia was a backward nation which had not reached the stage of social and economic development at which the Western nations (whether or not they could have avoided this) had entered upon the path of unrestrained industrialism. They were not, for the most part, historical determinists; consequently they believed that it was possible for a nation in such a predicament to avoid this fate by the exercise of intelligence and will. They saw no reason why Russia could not benefit by Western science and Western technology without paying the appalling price paid by the West. They argued that it was possible to avoid the despotism of a centralized economy or a centralized government by adopting a loose, federal structure composed of self-governing, socialized units both of producers and of consumers. They held that it was desirable to organize, but not to lose sight of other values in the pursuit of organization as an end in itself; to be governed primarily by ethical and humanitarian and not solely by economic and technological—'ant-hill'—considerations. They declared that to protect human individuals against exploitation by turning them into an industrial army of collectivized robots was self-stultifying and suicidal. Ideas of the Populists were often unclear, and there were sharp differences among them, but there was an area of agreement wide enough to constitute a genuine movement. Thus they accepted, in broad outline, the educational and moral lessons, but not the state worship, of Rousseau. Some of them—indeed perhaps the majority—shared Rousseau's belief in the goodness of simple men, his conviction that the cause of corruption is the crippling effect of bad institutions, his acute distrust of all forms of cleverness, of intellectuals and specialists, of all self-isolating *côteries* and factions. They accepted the anti-political ideas, but not the technocratic centralism, of Saint-Simon. They shared the belief in conspiracy and violent action preached by Babeuf and his disciple Buonarroti, but not their Jacobin authoritarianism. They stood with Sismondi and Proudhon and Lamennais and the other originators of the notion of the welfare state, against, on the one hand, *laissez faire*, and, on the other, central authority, whether nationalist or socialist, whether temporary or permanent, whether preached by List, or Mazzini, or Lassalle, or Marx. They came close at times to the positions of Western Christian socialists, without, however, any religious faith, since like the French Encyclopaedists of the previous century, they believed in 'natural' morality and scientific truth. These were some of the beliefs that held them together. But they were divided by differences no less profound.

The first and greatest of their problems was their attitude towards the peasants in whose name all that they did was done. Who was to show the peasants the true path to justice and equality? Individual liberty is not, indeed, condemned by the Populists, but it tends to be regarded as a liberal catchword, liable to distract attention from immediate social and economic tasks. Should one train experts to teach the ignorant younger brothers—the tillers of the soil, and, if need be, stimulate them to resist authority, to revolt and destroy the old order before the rebels had themselves fully grasped the need or meaning of such acts? That is the view of such dissimilar figures as Bakunin and Speshnev in the 'forties; it was preached by Chernyshevsky in the 'fifties, and was passionately advocated by Zaichnevsky and the Jacobins of 'Young Russia' in the 'sixties; it was preached by Lavrov in the 'seventies and 'eighties, and equally by his rivals and opponents—the believers in disciplined professional terrorism—Nechaev and Tkachev, and their followers who include—for this purpose alone—not only the Socialist-Revolutionaries but also some of the most fanatical Russian Marxists, in particular Lenin and Trotsky.

Some among them asked whether this training of revolutionary groups might not create an arrogant *élite* of seekers of power and autocracy, men who would, at best, believe it their duty to give the peasants not what the peasants asked for but what they, their self-appointed mentors, thought good for them, namely, that which the masses ought to ask for, whether they in fact did so or not. They pushed the question further, and asked whether this would not, in due course, breed fanatical men who would pay too little heed to the actual wants of the vast majority of the Russian population, intent on forcing upon them only what they—the dedicated order of professional revolutionaries, cut off from the life of the masses by their own special training and conspiratorial lives—had chosen for them, ignoring the hopes and protests of the people itself. Was there not a terrible danger here of the substitution of a new yoke for the old, of a despotic oligarchy of intellectuals in the place of the nobility and the bureaucracy and the Tsar? What reason was there for thinking that the new masters would prove less oppressive than the old? This was argued by some among the terrorists of the 'sixties—Ishutin and Karakozov, for example—and even more forcibly by the majority of the idealistic young men, who 'went among the people' in the 'seventies and later, with the aim not so much of teaching others as of themselves learning how to live, in a state of mind inspired by Rousseau (and perhaps by Nekrasov or Tolstoy) at least as much as by more tough-minded social theorists. These young men, the so called 'repentant gentry', believed themselves to have been corrupted not merely by an evil social system but by the very process of liberal education which makes for deep inequalities and inevitably lifts scientists, writers, professors, experts, civilized men in general, too high above the heads of the masses, and so itself becomes the richest breeding-ground of injustice and class oppression; everything that obstructs understanding between individuals or groups or nations, that creates and keeps in being obstacles to human solidarity and fraternity, is *eo ipso* evil; specialization and university education build walls between men, prevent individuals and groups from 'connecting', kill love and friendship, and are among the major causes responsible for what, after Hegel and his followers, came to be called the 'alienation' of entire orders or classes or cultures. Some among the Populists contrived to ignore or evade this problem. Bakunin, for example, who, if he was not a Populist himself, influenced Populism profoundly, denounced faith in intellectuals and experts as liable to lead to the most ignoble of tyrannies—the rule of scientists and pedants—but would not face the problem of whether the revolutionaries had come to teach or to learn. It was left unanswered by the terrorists of the 'People's Will' and their sympathizers. More sensitive and morally scrupulous thinkers—Chernyshevsky and Kropotkin, for example, felt the oppressive weight of the question, and did not attempt to conceal it from themselves; yet whenever they asked themselves by what right they proposed to impose this or that system of social organization on the mass of peasants who had grown up in a wholly different way of life, that might embody far profounder values of its own, they gave no clear reply. The question became even more acute when it was asked (as it increasingly came to be in the 'sixties) what was to be done if the peasants actually resisted the revolutionaries' plans for their liberation? Must the masses be deceived, or, worse still, coerced? No one denied that in the end it was the people, and not the revolutionary *élite*, that must govern, but in the meanwhile how far was one allowed to go in ignoring the majority's wishes, or in forcing them into courses which they plainly loathed? This was by no means a merely academic problem. The first enthusiastic adherents of radical Populism— the missionaries who went 'to the people' in the famous summer of 1874— were met by mounting indifference, suspicion, resentment and sometimes active hatred and resistance, on the part of their would-be beneficiaries who, as often as not, handed them over to the police. The Populists were thus forced to define their attitude explicitly, since they believed passionately in the need to justify their activities by rational argument. Their answers, when they came, were far from unanimous. The activists, men like Tkachev, Nechaev, and in a less political sense, Piasarev, whose admirers came to be known as Nihilists, anticipated Lenin in their contempt for democratic methods. Since the days of Plato, it had been argued that the spirit was superior to the flesh, and those who know must govern those who do not. The educated cannot listen to the uneducated and ignorant masses. The masses must be rescued by whatever means were available, if necessary against their own foolish wishes, by guile, or fraud, or violence if need be. But it was only a minority in the movement who accepted this division and the authoritarianism that it entailed: the majority were horrified by the open advocacy of such Machiavellian tactics, and thought that no end, however good, could fail to be destroyed by the adoption of monstrous means.

A similar conflict broke out over the attitude to the state. All Russian Populists were agreed that the state was the embodiment of a system of coercion and inequality, and therefore intrinsically evil; neither justice nor happiness were possible until it was eliminated. But in the meanwhile what was to be the immediate aim of the revolution? Tkachev is quite clear that until the capitalist enemy had been finally destroyed, the weapon of coercion —the pistol torn from his hand by the revolutionaries—must on no account be thrown away, but must itself be turned against him. In other words the machinery of the state must not be destroyed, but must be used against the inevitable counter-revolution; it cannot be dispensed with until the last enemy has been—in Proudhon's immortal phrase—successfully liquidated, and mankind consequently has no further need of any instrument of coercion. In this doctrine he was followed by Lenin more faithfully than mere adherence to the ambivalent Marxist formula about the dictatorship of the proletariat seemed to require. Lavrov, who represents the central stream of Populism, and reflect all its vacillations and confusions, characteristically advocated not indeed the immediate or total elimination of the state but its systematic reduction to something vaguely described as the 'minimum'. Chernyshevsky, who is the least anarchistic of the Populists, conceives of the state as the organizer and protector of the free associations of peasants or workers, and contrives to see it at once as centralized and decentralized, a guarantee of order and efficiency, and of equality and individual liberty too.

All these thinkers share one vast apocalyptic assumption: that once the reign of evil—autocracy, exploitation, inequality—is consumed in the fire of the revolution, there will arise naturally and spontaneously out of its ashes a natural, harmonious, just order, needing only the gentle guidance of the enlightened revolutionaries to attain to its proper perfection. This great Utopian dream, based on simple faith in regenerated human nature, was a vision which the Populists shared with Godwin and Bakunin, Marx and Lenin. Its heart is the pattern of sin and fall and resurrection—of the road to the earthly paradise the gates of which will only open if men find the one true way and follow it. Its roots lie deep in the religious imagination of mankind, and there is therefore nothing surprising in the fact that this secular version of it had strong affinities with the faith of the Russian Old Believers—the dissenting sects—for whom, since the great religious schism of the seventeenth century, the Russian state and its rulers, particularly Peter the Great, represented the rule of Satan upon earth; this persecuted religious underground provided a good many potential allies whom the Populists made efforts to mobilize.* There were deep divisions among the Populists; they differed about the future rôle of the intellectuals, as compared with that of the peasants; they differed about the historical importance of the rising class of capitalists, gradualism versus conspiracy, education and propaganda versus terrorism and preparation for immediate risings. All these questions were interrelated and they demanded immediate solutions. But the deepest rift among the Populists arose over the urgent question of whether a truly democratic revolution could possibly occur before a sufficient number of the oppressed had become fully conscious—that is, capable of understanding and analysing the causes of their intolerable condition. The moderates argued that no revolution could justly be called democratic unless it sprang from the rule of the revolutionary majority. But in that event, there was perhaps no alternative to waiting until education and propaganda had created this majority—a course that was being advocated by almost all Western socialists—Marxist and non-Marxist alike—in the second half of the nineteenth century. Against this the Russian Jacobins argued that to wait, and in the meanwhile to condemn all forms of revolt organized by resolute minorities as irresponsible terrorism or, worse still, as the replacement of one despotism by another, would lead to catastrophic results: while the revolutionaries procrastinated, capitalism would develop rapidly; the breathing space would enable the ruling class to develop a social and economic base incomparably stronger than that which it possessed at present; the growth of a prosperous and energetic capitalism would create opportunities of employment for the radical intellectuals themselves: doctors, engineers, educators, economists, technicians, and experts of all types would be assigned profitable tasks and positions, nor would their new bourgeois masters (unlike the existing régime) seek to force them into any kind of political conformity; the intelligentsia would obtain special privileges, status and wide opportunities for self-expression—harmless radicalism would be tolerated, a good deal of personal liberty permitted—and in this way the revolutionary cause would lose its most valuable recruits. Once those whom

* Professor Venturi is exceptionally illuminating on the rôle played by some of these sectarians—Martyanov, Kelsiev, Shchapov, for example, as well as such odd figures as Khudyakov and Tolstoy's friend, Bochkarev. His pages on their part in the revolutionary movement, and particularly on their influence on the peasants to whom they spoke in the familiar religious language that was natural to them, contain rare and valuable information.

insecurity and discontent had driven into making common cause with the oppressed had been partially satisfied, the incentive to revolutionary activity would be weakened, and the prospects of a radical transformation of society would become exceedingly dim. The radical wing of the revolutionaries argued with great force that the advance of capitalism, whatever Marx might say, was not inevitable; it might be so in Western Europe, but in Russia it could still be arrested by a revolutionary *coup*, destroyed in the root before it had had time to grow too strong. If recognition of the need to awaken the 'political consciousness' of the majority of the workers and peasants (which by this time, and partly as a result of the failure of the intellectuals in 1848, had been pronounced absolutely indispensable to the revolution both by Marxists and by the majority of the Populist leaders) was tantamount to the adoption of a gradualist programme, the moment for action would surely be missed; in place of the Populist or socialist revolution would there not arise a vigorous, imaginative, predatory, successful capitalist régime which would succeed Russian semi-feudalism as surely as it had replaced the feudal order in Western Europe? And then who could tell how many decades or centuries might elapse before the arrival, at long last, of the revolution? And when it did arrive, who could tell what kind of order it would, by that time, install— resting upon what social basis?

All Populists were agreed that the village commune was the ideal embryo of those socialist groups on which the future society was to be based. But would the development of capitalism not automatically destroy the commune? And if it was maintained (although perhaps this was not explicitly asserted before the 'eighties) that capitalism was already destroying the *mir*, that the class struggle, as analysed by Marx, was dividing the villages as surely as the cities, then the plan of action was clear: rather than sit with folded hands and watch this disintegration fatalistically, resolute men could and must arrest this process, and save the village commune. Socialism, so the Jacobins argued, could be introduced by the capture of power to which all the energies of the revolutionaries must be bent, even at the price of postponing the task of educating the peasants in moral, social and political realities; indeed, such education could surely be promoted more rapidly and efficiently after the revolution had broken the resistance of the old régime. This line of thought, which bears an extraordinary resemblance, if not to the actual words, then to the policies pursued by Lenin in 1917, was basically very different from the older Marxist determinism. Its perpetual refrain was that there was no time to lose. Kulaks were devouring the poorer peasants in the country, capitalists were breeding fast in the towns. If the government possessed even a spark of intelligence, it would make concessions and promote reforms, and by this means divert educated men whose will and brain was needed for the revolution into the peaceful paths of the service of the reactionary state; propped up by such liberal measures, the unjust order would continue and be strengthened. The activists argued that there was nothing inevitable about revolutions: they

were the fruit of human will and human reason. If there were not enough of
these, the revolution might never take place at all. It was only the insecure
who craved social solidarity and communal life; individualism was always a
luxury, the ideal of the socially established. The new class of technical
specialists—the modern, enlightened, energetic men celebrated by liberals
like Kavelin and Turgenev, and at times, even by the radical individualist
Pisarev—were for the Jacobin Tkachev 'worse than cholera or typhus', for
by applying scientific methods to social life they were playing into the hands
of the new, rising capitalist oligarchs and thereby obstructing the path to
freedom. Palliatives were fatal when only an operation could save the
patient: it merely prolonged his disease and weakened him so much that in
the end not even an operation could save him. One must strike before these
new, potentially conformist, intellectuals had grown too numerous and too
comfortable and had obtained too much power, for otherwise it would be too
late: a Saint-Simonian *élite* of highly paid managers would preside over a
new feudal order—an economically efficient but socially immoral society,
inasmuch as it was based on permanent inequality.

The greatest of all evils was inequality. Whenever any other ideal came
into conflict with equality, the Russian Jacobins always called for its sacrifice
or modification; the first principle upon which all justice rested was that of
equality; no society was equitable in which there was not a maximum degree of
equality between men. If the revolution was to succeed, three major fallacies
had to be fought and rooted out. The first was that men of culture alone
created progress. This was not true, and had the bad consequence of inducing
faith in *élites*. The second was the opposite illusion—that everything must be
learnt from the common people. This was equally false. Rousseau's Arcadian
peasants were so many idyllic figments. The masses were ignorant, brutal,
reactionary and did not understand their own needs or good. If the revolution
depended upon their maturity, or capacity for political judgment or organization, it would certainly fail. The last fallacy was that only a proletarian majority
could successfully make a revolution. No doubt a proletarian majority might
do that, but if Russia was to wait until it possessed one, the opportunity of
destroying a corrupt and detested government would pass, and capitalism
would be found to be too firmly in the saddle. What then must be done?
Men must be trained to make the revolution and destroy the present system and
all obstacles to social equality and democratic self-government. When this
was achieved, a democratic assembly was to be convened, and if those who
made the revolution took care to explain the reasons for it, and the social
and economic situation that made it necessary, then the masses, benighted
though they might be today, would assuredly, in the view of the Jacobins,
grasp their condition sufficiently to allow themselves to be—indeed to welcome the opportunity of being—organized into the new free federation of
productive associations. But supposing they were still, on the morrow of a
successful *coup d'état*, not mature enough to see this? Herzen did indeed ask

this awkward question again and again in his writings in the late 'sixties. The majority of the Populists were deeply troubled by it. But the activist wing had no doubt of the answer: strike the chains from the captive hero, and he will stretch himself to his full height and live in freedom and happiness for ever after. The views of these men were astonishingly simple. They believed in terrorism and more terrorism to achieve complete, anarchist, liberty. The purpose of the revolution, for them, was to establish absolute equality, not only economic and social, but 'physical and physiological': they saw no discrepancy between this bed of Procrustes and absolute individual freedom. This order would be imposed in the beginning by the power and authority of the state, after which, the state, having fulfilled its purpose, would swiftly 'liquidate' itself. Against this, the spokesmen of the main body of the Populists argued that Jacobin means tended to bring about Jacobin consequences: if the purpose of the revolution was to liberate, it must not use the weapons of despotism that were bound to enslave those whom they were designed to liberate: the remedy must not prove more destructive than the disease. To use the state to break the power of the exploiters and to impose a specific form of life upon a people, the majority of whom had not been educated to understand the need for it, was to exchange the Tsarist yoke for a new, not necessarily less crushing one— that of the revolutionary minority. The majority of the Populists were deeply democratic; they believed that all power tended to corrupt, that all concentration of authority tended to perpetuate itself, that all centralization was coercive and evil, and, therefore, that the sole hope of a just and free society lay in the peaceful conversion of men by rational argument to the truths of social and economic justice and democratic freedom. In order to obtain the opportunity of converting men to this vision, it might indeed be necessary to break the existing obstacles to free and rational intercourse—the police state, the power of capitalists or of landowners—and to use force in the process, whether mass mutiny or individual terrorism. But this concept of temporary measures presented itself to them as something wholly different from leaving absolute power in the hands of any party or group, however virtuous, once the power of the enemy had been broken. Their case is the classical case, during the last two centuries, of every libertarian and federalist against Jacobins and centralizers: it is Voltaire's case against both Helvétius and Rousseau; that of the left wing of the Gironde against the Mountain; Herzen used these arguments against the doctrinaire communists of the immediately preceding period—Cabet and the disciples of Babeuf; Bakunin denounced the Marxist demand for the dictatorship of the proletariat as something that would merely transfer power from one set of oppressors to another; the Populists of the 'eighties and 'nineties urged this against all those whom they suspected of conspiring (whether they realized this or not) to destroy individual spontaneity and freedom, whether they were *laissez faire* liberals who allowed factory owners to enslave the masses, or radical collectivists who were ready to do so themselves; whether they were promoters of capitalist combines

a*

or Marxist advocates of centralized authority; indeed they looked upon the entrepreneurs (as Mikhailovsky wrote to Dostoevsky in his celebrated criticism of his novel *The Possessed*) as the more dangerous—as brutal, amoral 'social Darwinists', profoundly hostile to variety and individual freedom and character. This, again, was the main political issue which, at the turn of the century, divided the Russian Socialist-Revolutionaries from the Social-Democrats; and over which, a few years later, both Plekhanov and Martov broke with Lenin: indeed the great quarrel between the Bolsheviks and the Mensheviks (whatever its ostensible cause) turned upon it. In due course Lenin himself, two or three years after the October revolution, while he never abandoned the central Marxist doctrine, expressed his bitter disappointment with those very consequences of it which his opponents had predicted—bureaucracy and the arbitrary despotism of the party officials; and Trotsky accused Stalin of this same crime. The dilemma of means and ends is the deepest and most agonizing problem that torments the revolutionary movements of our own day in all the continents of the world, not least in Asia and Africa. That this debate took so clear and articulate a form within the Populist movement makes its development exceptionally relevant to our own predicament.

All these differences occurred within the framework of a common revolutionary outlook, for, whatever their disagreements, all Populists were united by an unshakable faith in the revolution. This faith derived from many sources. It sprang from the needs and outlook of a society still overwhelmingly pre-industrial, which gave the craving for simplicity and fraternity, and the agrarian idealism which derives ultimately from Rousseau—a reality which can still be seen in India and Africa today, and which necessarily looks Utopian to the eyes of social historians born in the industrialized West. It was a consequence of the disillusionment with parliamentary democracy, liberal convictions and the good faith of bourgeois intellectuals that resulted from the fiasco of the European revolutions of 1848–9, and from the particular conclusion drawn by Herzen that Russia, which had not suffered this revolution, might find her salvation in the undestroyed, natural socialism of the peasant *mir*. It was deeply influenced by Bakunin's violent diatribes against all forms of central authority, and in particular the state; and by his vision of men as being by nature peaceful and productive, and rendered violent only when they are perverted from their proper ends, and forced to be either gaolers or convicts. But it was also fed by the streams that flowed in a contrary direction: by Tkachev's faith in a Jacobin *élite* of professional revolutionaries as the only force capable of destroying the advance of capitalism helped on its fatal path by innocent reformists and humanitarians and careerist intellectuals, and concealed behind the repulsive sham of parliamentary democracy; even more by the passionate utilitarianism of Pisarev, and his brilliant polemics against all forms of idealism and amateurishness, and in particular the sentimental idealization of the simplicity and beauty of peasants in general, and of Russian peasants in particular, as beings touched by grace, remote from the corrupting influences of the decaying West. It was supported by the appeal which these 'critical realists' made to their compatriots to save themselves by self-help and hard-headed energy—a kind of neo-Encyclopaedist campaign in favour of natural science, skill and professionalism, directed against the humanities, classical learning, history and other forms of 'sybaritic' self-indulgence. Above all it contrasted 'realism' with the literary culture which had lulled the best men in Russia into a condition where corrupt bureaucrats, stupid and brutal landowners and an obscurantist Church could exploit them or let them rot, while aesthetes and liberals looked the other way.

But the deepest strain of all, the very centre of the Populist outlook, was the individualism and rationalism of Lavrov and Mikhailovsky. With Herzen they believed that history followed no predetermined pattern, that it possessed 'no libretto', that neither the violent conflicts between cultures, nations, classes (which for Hegelians constituted the essence of human progress) nor the struggles for power by one class over another (represented by Marxists as being the motive force of history) were inevitable. Faith in human freedom was the cornerstone of Populist humanism; the Populists never tired of repeating that ends were chosen by men, not imposed upon them, and that men's wills alone could construct a happy and honourable life—a life in which the interests of intellectuals, peasants, manual workers and the liberal professions could be reconciled; not indeed made wholly to coincide, for that was an unattainable ideal; but adjusted in an unstable equilibrium, which human reason and constant human care could adjust to the largely unpredictable consequences of the interaction of men with each other and with nature. It may be that the tradition of the Orthodox Church with its conciliar and communal principles and deep antagonism both to the authoritarian hierarchy of the Roman Church, and the individualism of the Protestants, also exercised its share of influence. These doctrines and these prophets and their Western masters—French radicals before and after the French revolution, as well as Fichte and Buonarroti, Fourier and Hegel, Mill and Proudhon, Owen and Marx, played their part. But the largest figure in the Populist movement, the man whose temperament, ideas and activities dominated it from beginning to end, is undoubtedly that of Nikolai Gavrilovich Chernyshevsky and his immediate allies and followers. The influence of his life and teachings, despite a multitude of monographs, still await its interpreter.

Nicholas Chernyshevsky was not a man of original ideas. He did not possess the depth, the imagination or the brilliant intellect and literary talent of Herzen, nor the eloquence, the boldness, the temperament or the reasoning power of Bakunin, nor the moral genius and unique social insight of Belinsky. But he was a man of unswerving integrity, immense industry and a capacity rare among Russians for concentration upon concrete detail. His deep, steady, lifelong hatred of slavery, injustice and irrationality did not express itself in large theoretical generalizations, or the creation of a sociological or metaphysical system, or violent action against authority. It took the form of slow, uninspired, patient accumulation of facts and ideas—a crude, dull but powerful intellectual structure on which one might found a detailed policy of practical action appropriate to the specific Russian environment which he desired to alter. Chernyshevsky was in greater sympathy with the concrete, carefully elaborated socialist plans, however mistaken they might be, of the Petrashevsky group (to which Dostoevsky had belonged in his youth crushed by the government in 1849), than to the great imaginative constructions of Herzen, Bakunin and their followers.

A new generation had grown up during the dead years after 1849. These young men had witnessed vacillation and outright betrayals on the part of liberals which had led to the victories of the reactionary parties in 1849. Twelve years later they saw the same phenomenon in their own country, when the manner in which the peasants had been emancipated in Russia seemed to them to be a cynical travesty of all their plans and hopes. Such men as these found the plodding genius of Chernyshevsky, his attempts to work out specific solutions to specific problems in terms of concrete statistical data; his constant appeals to facts; his patient efforts to indicate attainable, practical, immediate ends rather than desirable states of affairs to which there was no visible road; his flat, dry, pedestrian style, his very dullness and lack of inspiration, more serious and, ultimately, more inspiring than the noble flights of the romantic idealists of the 'forties. His relatively low social origin (he was the son of a parish priest) gave him a natural affinity with the humble folk whose condition he was seeking to analyse, and an abiding distrust, later to turn into fanatical hatred, of all liberal theorists, whether in Russia or the West. These qualities made Chernyshevsky a natural leader of a disenchanted generation of socially mingled origins, no longer dominated by good birth, embittered by the failure of their own early ideals, by government repression, by the humiliation of Russia in the Crimean War, by the weakness, heartlessness, hypocrisy and chaotic incompetence of the ruling class. To these tough-minded, socially insecure, angry, suspicious young radicals contemptuous of the slightest trace of eloquence or "literature", Chernyshevsky was a father and confessor, as neither the aristocratic and ironical Herzen nor the wayward and ultimately frivolous Bakunin could ever become.

Like all Populists, Chernyshevsky believed in the need to preserve the peasant commune and to spread its principles to industrial production. He believed that Russia could profit directly by learning from the scientific advances of the West, without going through the agonies of an industrial revolution. 'Human development is a form of chronological unfairness', Herzen had once characteristically observed, 'since late-comers are able to profit by the labours of their predecessors without paying the same price'; 'History is fond of her grandchildren', Chernyshevsky repeated after him, 'for it offers them the marrow of the bones, which the previous generation had hurt its hands in breaking.' For Chernyshevsky history moved along a spiral, in Hegelian triads, since every generation tends to repeat the experience not of its parents, but of its grandparents, and repeats it at a 'higher level'. But it is not this historicist element in his doctrine that bound its spell upon the Populists. They were most of all influenced by his acute distrust of reforms from above, by his belief that the essence of history was a struggle between the classes, above all by his conviction (which derives nothing, so far as we know, from Marx, but draws upon socialist sources common to both) that the state is always the instrument of the dominant class, and cannot, whether it consciously desires this or not, embark on those necessary reforms the success of which would end its own domination. No order can be persuaded to undertake its own dissolution. Hence all attempts to influence the Tsar, all attempts to evade the horrors of revolution, must (he concluded in the early 'sixties) remain necessarily vain. There was a moment in the late 'fifties when, like Herzen, he had hoped for reforms from above. The final form of the Emancipation, and the concessions which the government had made to the landowners, cured him of this illusion. He pointed out with a good deal of historical justification that the liberals, who hoped to influence the government by Fabian tactics, thus far merely succeeded in betraying both the peasants and themselves: first they compromised themselves with the peasants by their relations with their masters; after that, the governing class found little difficulty, whenever this suited their convenience, in representing them as false friends to the peasants and turning the latter against them. This had occurred in both France and Germany in 1849. Even if the moderates withdrew in time, and advocated violent measures, their ignorance of conditions and blindness to the peasants' and workers' actual needs usually led them to advocate utopian schemes which in the end cost their followers a terrible price.

Chernyshevsky had evolved a simple form of historical materialism, according to which social factors determined political ones, and not *vice versa*. Consequently he held with Fourier and Proudhon that liberal and parliamentary ideals merely evaded the central issues: the peasants and the workers needed food, shelter, boots; as for the right to vote, or to be governed by liberal constitutions, or to obtain guarantees of personal liberty, these meant little to hungry and half-naked men. The social revolution must come first: appropriate political reforms would follow of themselves. For Chernyshevsky the principal lesson of 1848 was that the Western liberals, the brave no less than the cowardly, had demonstrated their political and moral bankruptcy, and with it that of their Russian disciples—Herzen, Kavelin, Granovsky, and the rest. Russia must pursue her own path. Unlike the Slavophils, and like the Russian Marxists of the next generation, he maintained with a wealth of economic evidence that the historical development of Russia, and in particular the peasant *mir*, were in no sense unique, but followed the social and economic laws that governed all human societies. Like the Marxists (and the Comtian positivists), he believed that such laws could be discovered and stated; but unlike the Marxists, he was convinced that by adopting Western techniques, and educating a body of men of trained and resolute wills and rational outlook, Russia could 'leap over' the capitalist stage of social development, and transform her village communes and free cooperative groups of craftsmen into agricultural and industrial associations of producers who would constitute the embryo of the new socialist society. Technological progress did not, in his view, automatically break up the peasant commune: 'savages can be taught to use Latin script and safety matches'; factories can be grafted on to workers' *artels* without destroying them; large-scale organization could eliminate exploitation, and yet preserve the predominantly agricultural nature of the Russian economy.*

Chernyshevsky believed in the decisive historical rôle of the application of science to life, but unlike Pisarev, did not regard individual enterprise, still less capitalism as indispensable to this process. He retained enough of the Fourierism of his youth to look upon the free associations of peasant communes and craftsmen's *artels* as the basis of all freedom and progress. But at the same time, like the Saint-Simonians, he was convinced that little would be achieved without collective action—state socialism on a vast scale. These incompatible beliefs were never reconciled; Chernyshevsky's writings contain statements both in favour of and against the desirability of large-scale industry. He is similarly ambivalent about the part to be played (and the part to be avoided) by the state as the stimulator and controller of industry, about the function of managers of large collective industrial enterprises, about the relations of the public and private sectors of the economy, and about the political sovereignty of the democratically elected parliament and its relation to the state as the source of centralized economic planning and control.

The outlines of Chernyshevsky's social programme remained vague or inconsistent, and often both. It is the concrete detail which, founded as it was on real experience, spoke directly to the representatives of the great popular masses, who had at last found a spokesman and interpreter of their own needs and feelings. His deepest aspirations and emotions were poured into *What is to be done?*, a social utopia which, grotesque as a work of art, had a literally epoch-making effect on Russian opinion. This didactic

---

* Professor Venturi very aptly quotes Populist statistics (which seem plausible enough) according to which the number of peasants to that of landowners in the 'sixties was of the order of 234:1, while the land owned by them stood to that of their masters in the ratio of $1:11\frac{1}{2}$, and their incomes were 97·5:2·5; as for industry, the proportion of city workers to peasants was 1:100. Given these figures it is perhaps not surprising that Marx should have declared that his prognosis applied to the Western economies, and not necessarily to that of the Russians, even though his Russian disciples ignored this concession, and insisted that capitalism was making enormous strides in Russia, and would soon obliterate the differences that divided it from the West. Plekhanov (who stoutly denied that Chernyshevsky had ever been a Populist) elaborated this theory, and Lenin acted upon it, with results that mankind will not easily forget.

novel described the 'new men' of the free, morally pure, cooperative socialist commonwealth of the future; its touching sincerity and moral passion bound their spell upon the imaginations of the idealistic and guilt-stricken sons of prosperous parents, and provided them with an ideal model in the light of which an entire generation of revolutionaries educated and hardened itself to the defiance of existing laws and conventions, and acceptance of exile and death with sublime unconcern. Chernyshevsky preached a naïve utilitarianism. Like James Mill, and perhaps Bentham, he held that basic human nature was a fixed, physiologically analysable, pattern of natural processes and faculties, and that the maximization of human happiness could therefore be scientifically planned and realized. Having decided that imaginative writing and criticism were the only available media in Russia for propagating radical ideas, he filled the *Contemporary*, a review which he edited together with the poet Nekrasov, with as high a proportion of direct socialist doctrine as could be smuggled in under the guise of literature. In this work he was helped by the violent young critic Dobrolyubov, a genuinely gifted man of letters (which Chernyshevsky was not) who, at times, went even further in his passionate desire to preach and educate. The aesthetic views of the two zealots were severely practical. Chernyshevsky laid it down that the function of art was to help men to satisfy their wants more rationally, to disseminate knowledge, to combat ignorance, prejudice and the anti-social passions, to improve life in the most literal and narrow sense of these words. Driven to absurd consequences, he embraced them gladly. Thus he explained that the chief value of marine paintings was that they showed the sea to those who, like, for instance, the inhabitants of central Russia, lived too far away from it ever to see it for themselves; and he maintained that his friend and patron Nekrasov, because by his verse he moved men to greater sympathy with the oppressed than other poets had done, was for that reason the greatest Russian poet, living or dead. His earlier collaborators, civilized and fastidious men of letters like Turgenev and Botkin found this grim fanaticism increasingly difficult to bear. Turgenev could not long live with this art hating and dogmatic schoolmaster. Tolstoy despised his dreary provincialism, his total lack of aesthetic sense, his intolerance, his wooden rationalism, his maddening self-assurance. But these very qualities, or, rather, the outlook of which they were characteristic, helped to make him the natural leader of the 'hard' young men who had succeeded the idealists of the 'forties. Chernyshevsky's harsh, flat, dull, humourless, grating sentences, his preoccupation with concrete economic detail, his self-discipline, his passionate dedication to the material and moral good of his fellow men, the grey, self-effacing personality, the tireless, devoted, minute industry, the hatred of style or of any concessions to the graces, the unquestionable sincerity, the combination of brutal directness, utter self-forgetfulness, indifference to the claims of private life, innocence, personal kindness, pedantry, moral charm, capacity for self-sacrifice, created the image that later became the prototype of the Russian revolutionary hero and martyr. More than any other publicist he was responsible for drawing the final line between 'us' and 'them'. All his life he preached that there must be no compromise with 'them', that the war must be fought to the death and on every front; there were no neutrals; that, so long as this war was being fought, no work could be too trivial too repulsive or too tedious for a revolutionary to perform. His personality and outlook set its seal upon two generations of Russian revolutionaries; not least upon Lenin, who admired him devotedly.

In spite of his emphasis on economic or sociological arguments, the basic approach, the tone and outlook of Chernyshevsky and of the Populists generally, is moral, and at times indeed, religious. These men believed in socialism not because it was inevitable, nor because it was effective, not even because it alone was rational, but because it was just. Concentrations of political power, capitalism, the centralized state, trampled upon the rights of men and crippled them morally and spiritually. The Populists were stern atheists, but socialism and orthodox Christian values coalesced in their minds. They shrank from the prospect of industrialism in Russia because of its brutal cost, and they disliked the West because it had paid this price too heartlessly. Their disciples, the Populist economists of the 'eighties and 'nineties, Danielson and Vorontsov,* for example, for all their strictly economic arguments against the possibility of capitalism in Russia (some of which seem a good deal sounder than their Marxist opponents have represented them as being), were in the last analysis moved by moral revulsion from the sheer mass of suffering that capitalism was destined to bring, that is to say, by a refusal to pay so appalling a price, no matter how valuable the results. Their successors in the twentieth century, the Socialist-Revolutionaries, sounded the note which runs through the whole of the Populist tradition in Russia: that the purpose of social action is not the power of the state, but the welfare of the people; that to enrich the state and provide it with military and industrial power, while undermining the health, the education, the morality, the general cultural level of its citizens, was feasible but wicked. They compared the progress of the United States, where, they maintained, the welfare of the individual was paramount, with that of Prussia, where it was not. They committed themselves to the view (which goes back at least to Sismondi) that the spiritual and physical condition of the individual citizen matters more than the power of the state, so that if, as often happened, the two stood in inverse ratio to one another, the rights and welfare of the individual must come first. They rejected as historically false the proposition that only powerful states could breed good or happy citizens, and as morally unacceptable the proposition that to lose oneself in the life and welfare of his society is the highest form of self-fulfilment for the individual. Belief in the primacy of human rights over other claims is the first principle that separates pluralist from centralized societies,

* Who wrote under the pseudonyms of Nikolay ——on and V.V. respectively.

and welfare states, mixed economies, 'New Deal' policies, from one-party governments, 'closed' societies, 'five-year plans', and, in general, forms of life built to serve a single goal that transcends the varied goals of differing groups or individuals. Chernyshevsky was more fanatical than his followers in the 'seventies and 'eighties, and believed far more strongly in organization, but even he neither stopped his ears to the cries for immediate help which he heard upon all sides, nor believed in the need to suppress the wants of individuals who were making desperate efforts to escape destruction, in the interests of even the most sacred and overmastering purpose. There were times when he was a narrow and unimaginative pedant, but at his worst he was never impatient nor arrogant, nor inhumane, and was perpetually reminding his readers and himself that in their zeal to help, the educators must not end by bullying their would-be beneficiaries, that what 'we'—the rational intellectuals—think good for the peasants may be not what they themselves want, and that to ram 'our' remedies down 'their' throats is not permitted. Neither he nor Lavrov, nor even the most ruthlessly Jacobin among the proponents of terror and violence, ever took cover behind the inevitable direction of history as a justification of what would otherwise have been patently unjust or brutal. If violence was the only means to a given end, then there might be circumstances in which it was right to employ it; but this must be justified in each case by the intrinsic moral claim of the end—an increase in happiness, or solidarity, or justice, or peace, or some other universal human value that outweighs the evil of the means, never by the view that it was rational and necessary to march in step with history, ignoring one's scruples and dismissing one's own 'subjective' moral principles because they were necessarily provisional, on the ground that history herself transformed all moral systems and retrospectively justified only those principles which survived and succeeded.

The mood of the Populists, particularly in the 'seventies, can fairly be described as religious. This group of conspirators or propagandists saw itself, and was seen by others, as constituting a dedicated order. The first condition of membership was the sacrifice of one's entire life to the movement, both to the particular group and party, and to the cause of the revolution in general. But the notion of the dictatorship of the party or of its leaders over individual lives—in particular over the beliefs of individual revolutionaries—is no part of this doctrine, and is indeed contrary to its entire spirit. The only censor over the individual's acts is his individual conscience. If one has promised obedience to the leaders of the party, such an oath is sacred, but it extends only to the specific revolutionary objectives of the party and not beyond them, and ends with the completion of whatever specific goals the party exists to promote—in the last resort, the revolution. Once the revolution has been made, each individual is free to act as he thinks right, since discipline is a temporary means and not an end. The Populists did indeed virtually invent the conception of the party as a group of professional conspirators with no private lives, obeying a total discipline—the core of the 'hard' professionals, as against mere sympathizers and fellow-travellers; but this sprang from the specific situation that obtained in Tsarist Russia, and the necessity, and conditions for effective conspiracy, and not from belief in hierarchy as a form of life desirable or even tolerable in itself. Nor did the conspirators justify their acts by appealing to a cosmic process which sanctified their every act, since they believed in freedom of human choice and not in determinism. The later Leninist conception of the revolutionary party and its dictatorship, although historically it owed much to these trained martyrs of an earlier day, sprang from a different outlook. The young men who poured into the villages during the celebrated summer of 1874, only to meet with non-comprehension, suspicion and often outright hostility on the part of the peasants, would have been profoundly astonished and indignant if they had been told that they were to look upon themselves as the sacred instruments of history, and that their acts were therefore to be judged by a moral code different from that common to other men.

The Populist movement was a failure. 'Socialism bounced off people like peas from a wall', wrote the celebrated terrorist Stepnyak Kravchinsky to his fellow revolutionary Vera Zasulich in 1876, two years after the original wave of enthusiasm had died down. 'They listen to our people as they do to the priest'—respectfully, without understanding, without any effect upon their actions. 'There is noise in the capitals/The prophets thunder/A furious war of words is waged/But in the depths, in the heart of Russia,/There all is still, there is ancient peace.' These lines by Nekrasov convey the mood of frustration which followed the failure of the sporadic efforts made by the revolutionary idealists in the late 'sixties and early 'seventies, peaceful propagandists and isolated terrorists alike—of whom Dostoevsky painted so violent a picture in *The Possessed*. The government caught these men, exiled them, imprisoned them, and by its obstinate unwillingness to promote any measures to alleviate the consequences of an inadequate land reform drove liberal opinion towards sympathy with the revolutionaries. They felt that public opinion was on their side, and finally resorted to organized terrorism. Yet their ends always remained moderate enough. The open letter which they addressed to the new Emperor in 1881 is mild and liberal in tone. 'Terror', said the celebrated revolutionary Vera Figner many years later, 'was intended to create opportunities for developing the faculties of men for service to society.' The society for which violence was to blast the way was to be peaceful, tolerant, decentralized and humane. The principal enemy was still the state.

The wave of terrorism reached its climax with the assassination of Alexander II in 1881. The hoped-for revolution did not break out. The revolutionary organizations were crushed, and the new Tsar decided upon a policy of extreme repression. In this he was, on the whole, supported by public opinion, which recoiled before the assassination of an Emperor who had, after all, emancipated the peasants, and who was said to have been meditating other liberal measures. The most prominent leaders of the movement were executed or exiled; lesser figures escaped abroad, and the most gifted of those who were still free—Plekhanov and Akselrod—gradually moved towards Marxism. They felt embarrassed by Marx's own concession that Russia could in principle avoid passing through a capitalist stage even without the aid of a communist world revolution—a thesis which Engels conceded far more grudgingly and with qualifications—and maintained that Russia had in fact already entered the capitalist stage. They declared that, since the development of capitalism in Russia was no more avoidable than it had been in its day in the West, nothing was to be gained by averting one's face from the 'iron' logic of history, and that for these reasons, so far from resisting industrialization, socialists should encourage it, indeed profit by the fact that it, and it alone, could breed the army of revolutionaries which would be sufficient to overthrow the capitalist enemy—an army to be formed out of the growing city proletariat, organized and disciplined by the very conditions of its labour.

The vast forward leap in industrial development made by Russia in the 'nineties seemed to support the Marxist thesis. It proved attractive to revolutionary intellectuals for many reasons: because it claimed to be founded on a scientific analysis of the laws of history which no society could hope to evade; because it claimed to be able to 'prove' that, although much violence, misery and injustice—exploitation, pauperization, conflicts between classes, nations, interests—were bound to occur as the pattern of history inexorably unfolded itself, yet the story would have a happy ending. Hence the conscience of those who felt guilty because they acquiesced in the miseries of the workers, or at any rate did not take active—that is, violent—steps to alleviate or prevent them, as Populist policy had demanded, felt assuaged by the 'scientific' guarantee that the road, covered though it might be with the corpses of the innocent, led inevitably to the gates of an earthly paradise. According to this view the expropriators would find themselves expropriated by the sheer logic of human development, although the course of history might be shortened, and the birth pangs made easier, by conscious organization, and above all an increase in knowledge (that is, education) on the part of the workers and their leaders. This was particularly welcome to those who, understandably reluctant to continue with useless terrorism which merely led to Siberia or the scaffold, now found doctrinal justification for peaceful study and the life of ideas, which the intellectuals among them found far more congenial than bomb-throwing.

The heroism, the disinterestedness, the personal nobility of the Populists, was often admitted by their Marxist opponents. They were regarded as worthy forerunners of a truly rational revolutionary party, and Chernyshevsky was sometimes accorded an even higher status and was credited with insights of genius—an empirical and unscientific, but instinctively correct, approach to truths of which only Marx and Engels could provide the demonstration, armed as they were with the instrument of an exact science to which neither Chernyshevsky, nor any other Russian thinker of his day, had yet attained. Marx and Engels grew to be particularly indulgent to the Russians: they were praised for having done wonders for amateurs, remote from the West and using home-made tools; they alone in Europe had, by 1880, created a truly revolutionary situation in their country; but it was made clear, particularly by Kautsky, that this was no substitute for professional methods and the use of the new machinery provided by scientific socialism. Populism was written down as an amalgam of unorganized moral indignation and utopian ideas in the muddled heads of self-taught peasants, well-meaning university intellectuals* and other social casualties of the confused interim between the end of an obsolescent feudalism and the beginning of the new capitalist phase in a backward country. Marxist historians still tend to describe it as a movement compounded of systematic misinterpretation of economic facts and social realities, noble but useless individual terrorism, and spontaneous or ill-directed peasant risings—the necessary but pathetic beginnings of real revolutionary activity, the prelude to the real play, a scene of naïve ideas and frustrated practice destined to be swept away by the new revolutionary, dialectical science heralded by Plekhanov and Lenin.

What were the ends of Populism? Violent disputes took place about means and methods, about timing, but not about ultimate purposes. Anarchism, equality, a full life for all, these were universally accepted. It is as if the entire movement—the motley variety of revolutionary types which Professor Venturi describes so well and so lovingly—Jacobins and moderates, terrorists and educators, Lavrists and Bakuninists, 'troglodytes', 'recalcitrants' and 'country folk', members of 'Land and Liberty' and of 'The People's Will', were all dominated by a single myth: that once the monster was slain, the sleeping princess—the Russian peasantry—would awaken and without further ado live happily for ever after.

This is the movement of which Professor Venturi has written the history, the fullest, clearest, best written and most impartial account of a particular stage of the Russian revolutionary movement in any language. Yet if the movement was a failure, if it was founded on false premises and was so easily extinguished by the Tsarist police, has it a more than historical interest—that of a narrative of the life and death of a party, of its acts and its ideas? On this Professor Venturi discreetly, as behoves an objective historian, offers no direct opinion. He tells the story in chronological sequence; he explains what occurs; he describes origins and consequences; he illuminates the relations of various groups of Populists to one another, and leaves moral and political speculation to others. His work is not an apologia either for Populism or its opponents. He does not praise or

---

* Professor Venturi's account both of peasant risings and, still more, of the student movements out of which Populism, properly so called—the *Narodnik* groups of 1876–8— wholly sprang, are among the most original and valuable contributions to our knowledge of what the author likes to regard as a kind of Russian Carbonarism.

condemn, and seeks only to understand. Success in this task plainly needs no further reward. And yet one may, at moments, wonder whether Populism should be dismissed quite as easily as it still is today, both by communist and bourgeois historians. Were the populists so hopelessly in error? Were Chernyshevsky and Lavrov—and Marx who listened to them—totally deluded?

Was capitalism in fact inevitable in Russia? The consequences of accelerated industrialization prophesied by the neo-Populist economists in the 'nineties, namely a degree of social and economic misery as great as any undergone in the West during the Industrial Revolution, did occur, both before, and, at an increasing tempo, after the October revolution. Were they avoidable? Some writers on history consider this type of question to be absurd as such. What happened, happened. We are told that if we are not to deny causality in human affairs, we must suppose that what took place can only have done so precisely as it did; to ask what might have happened if the situation had been different is the idle play of the imagination, not worthy of serious historians. Yet this academic question is not without acute contemporary relevance. Some countries such, for example, as Turkey, India, and some states in the Middle East and Latin America, and even Yugoslavia, have adopted a slower tempo of industrialization and one less likely to bring immediate ruin to backward areas before they can be rehabilitated, and have done so in conscious preference to the forced marches of collectivization upon which, in our day, the Russians, and after them the Chinese, have embarked. Are these non-Marxist governments inescapably set upon a path to ruin? For it is Populist ideas which lie at the base of much of the socialist economic policy pursued by these and other countries today.

When Lenin organized the Bolshevik revolution in 1917, the technique that he adopted, *prima facie* at least, resembled those commended by the Russian Jacobins, Tkachev and his followers who had learnt them from Blanqui or Buonarroti, more than any to be found in the writings of Marx or Engels at any rate after 1851. It was not, after all, full-grown capitalism that was enthroned in Russia in 1917. Russian capitalism was a still growing force, not yet in power, struggling against the fetters imposed upon it by the monarchy and the bureaucracy, as it had done in eighteenth-century France. But Lenin acted as if the bankers and industrialists were already in control. He acted and spoke as if this was so, but his revolution succeeded not by taking over the centres of finance and industry (which history should already have undermined) but by a seizure of strictly political power by a determined and trained group of professional revolutionaries, precisely as had been advocated by Tkachev. If Russian capitalism had reached the stage, which, according to Marxist historical theory, it had to reach before a proletarian revolution could be successful, the seizure of power by a determined minority, and a very small one at that—a mere *Putsch*—could not, *ex hypothesi*, have retained it long. And this indeed is what Plekhanov said over and over again in his bitter denunciations of Lenin in 1917: ignoring his argument that much may be permitted in a backward country, provided that the results were duly saved by orthodox Marxist revolutions successfully carried out soon after in the industrially more advanced West. These conditions were not fulfilled; Lenin's hypothesis proved historically irrelevant; yet the Bolshevik revolution did not collapse. Could it be that the Marxist theory of history was mistaken? Or had the Mensheviks misunderstood it, and concealed from themselves the anti-democratic tendencies which had always been implicit in it? In which case were their charges against Mikhailovsky and his friends, after all, wholly just? By 1917 their own fears of the Bolshevik dictatorship rested upon the same basis. Moreover, the results of the October revolution turned out to be oddly similar to those which Tkachev's opponents had prophesied that his methods must inevitably produce: the emergence of an *élite*, wielding dictatorial power, designed in theory to wither away once the need for it had gone; but, as the Populist democrats had said over and over again, in practice more likely to grow in aggressiveness and strength, with a tendency towards self-perpetuation which no dictatorship seems able to resist. The Populists were convinced that the death of the peasant commune would mean death, or at any rate a vast setback, to freedom and equality in Russia; the Left Socialist-Revolutionaries, who were their direct descendants, transformed this into a demand for a form of decentralized, democratic self-government among the peasants, which Lenin adopted when he concluded his temporary alliance with them in October 1917. In due course the Bolsheviks repudiated this programme, and transformed the cells of dedicated revolutionaries—perhaps the most original contribution of Populism to revolutionary practice—into the hierarchy of centralized political power, which the Populists had steadily and fiercely denounced until they were themselves finally, in the form of the Socialist-Revolutionary party, proscribed and annihilated. Communist practice owed much, as Lenin was always ready to admit, to the Populist movement; for it borrowed the technique of its rival and adapted it with conspicuous success to serve the precise purpose which it had been invented to resist.

ISAIAH BERLIN

OXFORD, *November* 1959

REVISED AUTHOR'S INTRODUCTION, RUSSIAN POPULISM

My plan—or, better, my desire—to study the history of the 19th-century Russian revolutionary movement dates back to the 1930s. In Leningrad and Moscow, a long silence about populist and libertarian movements began with the death of Kirov. In the world outside Russia, everything invited or forced one to look for the roots of socialist ideas and of the nihilist revolts. They were roots that inevitably led back to those who generation after generation had fought against czarist autocracy, passionately trying to predict, interpret, and change the fate of their own country. After the war, an unforeseen opportunity—a three-year stay in Moscow between 1947 and 1950—opened the doors of the Lenin Library to me; that institution housed the documents and memoirs of Russian revolutionaries as well as the texts of the vast Russian historiography of the 1920s and early 1930s concerning the movement. The Lenin Library's door was a narrow one in those days; it did not lead to a catalog (as a result, one had to reconstruct the bibliography solely on the basis of reviews, journals, and notes on the books), or to the archives containing manuscripts and documents (which were completely inaccessible to me then).[1] But it would be in poor taste, in fact unjust, to complain about the narrowness of that door, which at that time was closed to so many scholars, to so many Russians, for whom it was also a vital necessity to study the true relationship between their past and their present, between the revolutionary movement and the Stalinist dictatorship. For them it was even more difficult than for me, a foreigner, to form their own ideas about this relationship, engulfed as they were in the silence, isolation, and monotony of official historiography.

Perhaps that solitude was not without some benefits. At that time a wide gulf separated the populists from the Marxists, social democrats, and revolutionary socialists. It was impossible to study the period that followed the end of *Narodnaya Volya* in Moscow in the forties, and the first years of the new century were even more inaccessible. The populist era was practically the last period in the history of the Russian revolutionary movement about which it was possible to obtain texts and documents—perhaps not all, but at least in sufficient number. Then began the silence, so deep and impenetrable that even today, almost thirty years after Stalin's death, it has not been definitively broken. Despite some interesting exceptions, in the Soviet Union the beginning of the 20th century remains one of the less investigated and discussed periods of Russian history.

Later, after reading Marc Bloch, I saw how this break between the 19th and 20th centuries could change into something positive. It is not the historical generation immediately following, not the children who will understand what their fathers wanted and did. Some detachment is necessary for one generation to understand another above and beyond the immediate legacy. Historic continuity is anything but uniform, and it requires that one stand back. Instead, in Russia, the social democrats starting with Plekhanov, then the Bolsheviks and Mensheviks from Lenin to Dan, as well as the revolutionary socialists—that is, all the movements that dominated Russia during the 20th-century revolutions—tended naturally to consider the populists as a legacy either to deny or to use, to spend or to hoard. The image of the generation of Herzen and Chernyshevsky, of Bakunin and of Zhelyabov, was profoundly changed by this process of assimilation, which was not historical but was largely political. Then Stalin's dictatorship began, and broke this continuity of the Russian intelligentsia and the revolutionary movement. In 1950, passionate discussions had become strict erudition at best; the legacy had been reduced to a few sentences of Lenin's, perpetually repeated; and an absolute silence had fallen over those revolutionaries, like the men of the *Narodnaya Volya*, who had tried more intensely than others to unite and hold together thought and action.

It was time to try to find the historical reality, to return to the sources. The first thing to do, obviously, was to cut unhesitatingly the dead and formal bond that in Soviet historiography apparently still united these men with the age of great political discussions, of Plekhanov, Lenin, Martov, and Chernov. Only one of these men had remained; this was Lenin, of course, and he too had been reduced to a pure and simple symbol and guarantor of a political and ideological continuity that in reality was becoming exhausted. To understand the populists, the first thing to do was to leave Lenin aside. How Lenin understood Herzen, Chernyshevsky, and the *Narodnaya Volya* is an interesting topic, but it mainly serves to understand Lenin and the Bolsheviks. A generation later, in 1950, his ideas seemed removed from the context in which they were born, far from the era of the Russian revolutions, transformed into a pure symbol of a continuity that was rhetorically and artificially reaffirmed. In order to understand the populists, it was better to replace this political symbolism with simple silence, in the midst of which the true words and the echo of the facts behind the 19th-century Russian revolutionary movement could be heard. Thus, in the book I wrote then, I deliberately mentioned Lenin only once, to thank the library in Moscow that bears his name.

In another matter it was necessary to react to the enforced antihistorical situation that had been created in the Soviet Union. The entire 19th-century revolutionary movement after the Decembrists and before the Marxists—that is, the Russian populist movement—was no longer seen as a whole. It was not seen as a trend that, despite all the internal differences and conflicts, had its own unity and continuity and could be regarded as a single human event in its birth, development, decline, and tragic end. As often happens, official ideology had replaced this view with a last judgment, placing the evil on one side and the good on the other, obscuring the former in darkness and silence and blending the latter in the strained and indistinct light of an ideological paradise. In this division, the good were called revolutionary democrats and included Herzen (with the usual reservations and distinctions) and especially Belinsky, Chernyshevsky, and Dobrolyubov, along with a certain number of followers and imitators. The bad were Bakunin, Lavrov (with the extenuating circumstances of his case), Mikhailovsky, and, above all, the men from the *Narodnaya Volya*. In this vast historical novel, the characters of the 1860s were the heroes, those of the 1870s the antiheroes.[2] The motivation for these verdicts is of little interest. But it is important to know why such judgments were made. Even today, after such a long time, it is not easy to find the reasons.

The discussion of the *Narodnaya Volya* which took place in 1930 and 1931, with I. A. Teodorovich and V. I. Nevsky as protagonists, is vivid and of great interest, and filled with elements that strongly reflected the tense political situation of those years. In fact, it was the most interesting historiographical and ideological debate provoked by the collectivization of the peasants, which was then taking place.[3] Teodorovich's ideas had been derived from the populist movement, but later he had become a Marxist. Nevsky had been part of the group of men who, with Lenin, had carried out and guided the October revolution. In the debate one could hear the voices of the survivors of the 19th-century revolutionary movement, of the populist members of the 'Society of Those Condemned to Forced Labor and Deportation,' as well as the hoarse and monotonous voices of cold-blooded builders of the new state ideologies of convenience. Even today, in looking over all their works, one is struck by the tragic, unreal air of the debate among the survivors, mere shadows on the brink of the abyss. A few years later, in 1935–36, all the men, institutions, journals, publishers, and ideas had vanished. The primary cause, or at least the most obvious one, was the will of Stalin. He did not want anyone, for any reason, to talk about revolutionaries who were capable of using bombs and revolvers, of carrying out partisan actions and coups de main. As Stalin explained to A. A. Zhdanov, who told the city committee of the Leningrad Communist Party on February 25, 1935, 'If we bring up our young on the men of the *Narodnaya Volya*, we will bring up terrorists.'[4] The security measures adopted by Stalin thus dealt with both the dead and the living, and were applied with equal ruthlessness against the memory of revolutionary populism and against the historians and scholars who had studied it. As a result, the editing of the works of Bakunin, Lavrov, Mikhailovsky, and Tkachev was stopped; the journal *Katorga i Ssylka* ceased publication; and Nevsky and Teodorovich, Steklov and Gorev, accompanied and followed by a great many others, disappeared. The official theory was expressed by E. Yaroslavsky, who in 1937 addressed the new generations, saying that 'the young members of the

Party and of the Komsomol do not always know or sufficiently appreciate the significance of the struggle that for decades our party carried on against this, overcoming the influence of populism, annihilating it as the worst of the enemies of Marxism and of the whole cause of the proletariat.'[5]

As we have seen, the burden of immediate political necessity had been decisive in the mid-1930s in bringing about the sharp tear that Stalin made in Russia's historical fabric. At the same time, as we find from Zhdanov's conversation quoted above, the dictator had decided to cut short any reconsideration of the origins of the Bolshevik party itself. In his eyes, the whole history of the party before 1917 was nothing but insignificant 'prehistory' clearly unworthy of study.[6]

More than just making a clean cut, however, it was also necessary to know where to insert the knife and how to separate the good men from the bad. Considerations of security and public order were no longer adequate. Inevitably, the choice was ideological. By expunging the revolutionary element in the 19th century from Bakunin to the *Narodnaya Volya*, one risked showing only the more democratic and reformist elements, from Belinsky to Herzen, from Chernyshevsky to Dobrolyubov. Obviously baptizing them 'democratic revolutionaries' was not enough to change their nature. For when these men were authentic revolutionaries, as they often managed to be, they were revolutionaries in a different sense, contrary to the 'revolution from above' that Stalin was carrying out in those years. How could this contradiction be remedied?

The problem was solved for about twenty years, starting in 1935, by the most diverse methods, from pure and simple censorship of texts to forced interpretations, and by the continuous attempt to make the images of these men coincide with the icons that official ideology had established for them. This division between the 'democratic revolutionaries' and the populists occasionally took ridiculous forms, as when there was an attempt to separate Herzen and Ogarev, two men who during their lifetimes had been inseparable friends and companions. But despite all the difficulties and uncertainties, by these methods the democratic revolutionaries were preserved from the silence and scorn that were destined to fall on their followers in the 1870s. The works of the populists were printed, occasionally in editions whose new research and additions made them quite valuable (consider the works of Chernyshevsky). Despite all the restrictions, their ideas continued to be expressed openly in Russia.

To what, in the final analysis, was their at least partial survival due? Clearly there are practical reasons: how could one rid Russian literature of men like them? Herzen, whose every page contradicted the dictatorship, was especially difficult to eliminate. Yet we must not forget that these were the years when Russian literature was deprived even of Dostoevsky. One would think that an operation even more difficult than the one that would have had to be carried out on Herzen's living body. In fact, the reasons for this choice were not purely those of opportunity and convenience. There was something in the democratic revolutionaries that resisted any attempt at annihilation. The national problem, the problem of the bond between the revolutionary movement and Russian history, was continually raised in their work. Socialists in a particular country could not help wondering about the origins of socialism in that country. The ossification of Marxism required the circulation of a different and perhaps older blood. Devoid of true populistic content and of the real problems that Herzen and Chernyshevsky had posed in discussing the peasants and the original economic and political development of Russia, often reduced to empty formulae, Russian socialism nevertheless emerged and took the place left by the declining internationalism of the twenties. Thus, Chernyshevsky replaced Marx as the putative father of socialism in Russia. It was an inconvenient position, but it responded to a real need, and created the first rough outline of a new relationship between Russian tradition and the Soviet state, a very different relationship from what the Marxists and internationalists thought they had achieved in the 1917 revolution.

In the 1930s and 1940s this reemergence of the past took a negative form, of jealous guardedness and petty nationalism. When not denied altogether, the international ties of the populists and of the Russian revolutionaries were greatly obscured. The intent was to defend their originality and their autonomy, but it was a useless, vain, and wrong defense on a historic plane, and it hampered or even prevented the investigation and understanding of the deep bonds that united the populists with 19th-century Europe.

In this case, I concluded, while trying to break this artificial and suffocating isolation, that perhaps the best way was to affirm unhesitatingly, right from the first lines of the book I was writing, that I was dealing with a page in the history of the European socialist movement, that at every opportunity I would try to tie up the historical threads that had been dropped or broken by the official Soviet historiography of those years.

Even in the isolation and silence of Moscow between 1948 and 1950, there was still a faint echo of the 1920s' interrupted dialogue on Russia's revolutionary past. Until 1935, that discussion had been too lively to prevent the recognition of a few but obvious signs of some people's silent desire to resume and pursue it. I was aware that B. P. Kozmin was continuing his work in Moscow. He had produced some of the most important books and articles that I had read in the Lenin Library. Research on the true situation of the peasants in the 19th century had not been entirely stopped. To realise this, one only had to read the works of Druzhinin. As much as possible, I followed the forthright and patient work of Levin, Valk, Oksman, and others, men who, despite the adverse circumstances, were trying to keep the true tradition of historical and philological studies alive in the Soviet Union. The situation in which these men were working became clearer to me day by day, in all its tragedy: I gradually discovered the impossibility of finding a number of great books, I saw whole collections of writers, memorialists, and historians with the names of the editors and annotators barbarically defaced and erased. The truth was evident; Russian historiography had been devastated in the 1930s and 1940s.

It was equally clear to me what needed to be done: to report as fully as possible, quoting texts and documents as widely as possible, demonstrating their true voice, freeing them from their later petrification and ideological incrustations; to recount the events of populism. I was increasingly convinced that in populism lay the roots, the deepest and truest origins, of contemporary Russia.

This conclusion aroused in me considerable admiration and enthusiasm for that generation of revolutionaries, as well as a keen interest in the Soviet scholars of the 1920s who had tried so vigorously to make known and bring to life the experiences of the thinkers and rebels of 19th-century Russia, and who, like the works they studied, had been overcome by the dark storm of the 1930s. When I presented the completed book to Italian readers in 1952, I concluded in the *Notiziario Einaudi* of June 30:

As I progressed in my work I was caught by an increasing sense of admiration for those who, in extremely difficult circumstances, wished to pursue the 'narrow path' they had chosen to its very end. That consequential spirit, which one of them claimed was the distinctive characteristic of Russian history, proved to be a source of energy, a force that swept the weaker men uninterrupted toward absurdity, but led the best men to that complete dedication that is the dominant characteristic of all populism. Thus it is not, I hope, psychological complacency that drove me to gather the details of the lives of so many obscure characters. It was the only way I could reach the individual without being distracted by outlines, could stress the truly original element of Russian populism. And I hope this will excuse me for having written two overly lengthy volumes.

These volumes, entitled *Il populismo russo*, were published by Einaudi in 1952. The discussion they aroused in Italy centered on the basic points and, because of the esoteric nature of these themes, was more historiographic than historical, concentrating more on principles, methods, and conclusions than on facts, research, and doubts. Was it proper to write the history of a movement like populism, while subordinating all the elements of social, political, economic, literary, and ideological history of the era in which it took place? Or, above all, should one insert it into a more complex reality until it simply became part of a global view of 19th-century Russia? I clearly favored the first alternative over the second. Aldo Garosci, writing under the pseudonym of Aldo Magrini, said in the *Mondo* (September 20, 1952) that I was right, while Giuseppe Berti, in the May and July 1953 issues of *Rinascita*, said that I was wrong. Garosci also mentioned the problem of what of the great political tradition of the Russian intelligentsia had survived and what had been buried. He concluded by asking (this was 1952, in the era of extreme Stalinism) why the ideals of the 19th-century revolutionaries had failed to transform Russia or had 'ceased to operate effectively'—'even if they certainly remained as inspiring myths and as the ideal culmination of something that, in part, reminds us more of what the populists were combating than of what they liked.' In the Russian silence, czarism seemed to reacquire its rights.

Berti, on the other hand, was convinced that only economic evolution, only facts and figures on the transformation of Russian life, could make a Western reader understand the reality of this country; these were more significant than interpretations given by the revolutionaries and more effective than the revolutionaries' stated desire to change or overturn that reality. 'A history of populism without a deep examination of the profound economic and class distinctions that occurred in Russian campaigns *after* the reforms, from 1861 to 1881 (distinctions that were to determine the entire resulting evolution of the *narodnichestvo*), such a history lacks a basis for judgment.' This is an affirmation to which many historians, even non-Marxists, would readily subscribe, perhaps modifying it in various degrees. Yet even Berti, one of the greatest and most acute experts on revolutionary events in the modern world, relied on the internal logic of the movements, the conflicts of ideas and desires, the tragedies that resulted, when he related the history of the Communist International and recounted the function and origins of the Italian Communist Party and its relationship with parties in other countries.

I do not wish to deny the possibility of writing the history of a society like that in Russia after the peasant reforms of 1861. But to understand a movement like populism, it was necessary to disentangle it completely from all the general, sociological explanations that, in Russia and elsewhere, had shrouded it, stifling its most active and creative elements.

The most powerful confirmation I have had of this approach came from Andrea Caffi, an Italian well known to Russia since the first decades of the century. He was a participant in and witness of the age of the Russian revolutions, a companion and friend of the survivors of 19th-century populism, and in 1952, in Paris, was living out the last years of a free and talented existence.[7] He wrote to me that complete detachment from the legends and traditions of the century was correct; that even if it was difficult, the attempt to establish a relationship between Russia and Europe was indispensable. He corrected me on many specific points (and naturally I paid scrupulous attention to his suggestions in the second edition); he said he had discussed my book with his friends from the publishing house of Gallimard, with A. Camus and especially with B. Parrain, and he made me feel how useful it could be to bring to light the great age of the 19th-century intelligentsia and make it more widely known.

The comments of some of the Italian readers of *Il populismo russo* convinced me—though little persuasion was needed—of how little this era was known. For example, Giovanni Spadolini wrote in the December 12, 1952, issue of the *Gazzetta del popolo*, 'It is strange that the Populist movement—so genuinely Russian, so adherent to the conditions and mentality of the Russian proletariat, so completely traditional and nostalgic in spirit—should have Western philosophical origins and declare a clear derivation from Proudhon's and Blanc's classic themes (not to mention the influence of classical German philosophy on Bakunin).'

But Leo Valliani responded to such statements, defending the writing of the history of political movements without then being obliged to write a total history. He affirmed that

the spirit that moved the Russian populists is not a measure of the backwardness of an immense semifeudal country, but rather expresses the ideological assimilation of the more radical and restless tendencies of European society on the part of a rather thin stratum of revolutionary intellectuals who consider their country, Russia, as a prison to be transformed, through the removal of the bars, into a superior social community, conforming to the most generous ideals of Western socialism. . . . Is this a spirit of disunity that leads to more extreme desires just because one is forced to remain in the dream world? No, on the contrary, the characteristic of populism is its unlimited faith in Russia's capacity to achieve more rapid and especially more direct progress than that allowed by the dominant skepticism of other European countries. . . . Although it developed under political, social, and economic conditions that were far behind those in the West, the Russian revolutionary movement was no less socialistic in its ideology and in its plans than the movements that were expressed at the same time in the First International and in the Paris Commune itself. . . . But while in the West socialism deliberately represented a class schism in the heart of the nation, in Russia populism spontaneously succeeded in detaching the active and educated forces of the country from the czars. . . . Populism could be considered, both in thought and in the material struggle, as the conscience (even if it was not the authorized representative) of the great national aspirations. Herein lies the reason for its intimate resistance, for its resurrection with its forces multiplied many times, only twenty years after the tragic end of the Narodnaya Volya. [*Lo spettatore italiano*, no. 6, June 1953]

It was 1953, the year Stalin died and Beria was eliminated. The problem of determining the value of the moral and political tradition that the Russian intelligentsia had managed to create through so many struggles and so many difficulties returned. It went beyond the circle of scholars and, in Italy as elsewhere, became everyone's problem. The evidence gathered in *Il populismo russo* succeeded in persuading at least some people, as we have seen in the examples quoted above, of the clarity of the message that was emerging after the revolution, the war, the dictatorship. Armanda Guiducci then wrote:

The most painful thing to establish is how, for a large number of Western men of culture, most of the works of Dobrolyubov, devoted to showing the discrepancy between the intelligentsia's task and its real position, are not at all outdated. Nor are Tkachev's violent satires on the pride of intellectuals and his struggle to make them acquire such a clear social conscience that any general praise of progress is repulsed as a means of hiding reality (optimism was then called 'positivism'). Nor are Lavrov's ideas on the responsibility of the intellectual class and his conviction that every society, even tomorrow's, that lacked the active and critical participation of cultured men was destined to be tyrannical. [*Il pensiero critico*, nos. 7–8, December 1953]

These themes of the ethical purpose of populism were particularly strongly felt in Italy during those years. And, though there were significant differences, something similar could be said about Germany.[8] On the other hand, two attempts to place the history of the 19th-century revolutionary movement in an entirely political and economic context came from England and America. A review in the *Times Literary Supplement* (June 12, 1953) took up the problems of the formation and function of the educated elite in backward countries from a perspective presented by the English historian Hugh Seton-Watson in his well-known works *The Decline of Imperial Russia, 1854–1914*, *The East European Revolution*, and *The Russian Empire, 1801–1917*. It said, 'The Russian revolutionary movement started from the *intelligentsia*. The word is Russian, and the phenomenon first appeared in Russia. But later developments in other countries of southern and eastern Europe and of Asia have shown that it is in no sense peculiarly Russian. The *intelligentsia* is a product or modern education. . . . The educated Russian shared the most advanced culture of contemporary Europe. He could not fail to see the contrast between this culture and the state of his own country. Material backwardness, social oppression and lack of freedom filled him with shame.' The students who came from nonprivileged classes; the children of the preachers; and those who came from oppressed nations such as the Poles, the Ukrainians, and the Jews, thus joined in the opposition movement. 'Ideal and personal motives combined to place the majority of the *intelligentsia* in opposition to the régime and caused them to prefer the revolutionaries to the Government. Certain flowers and weeds grow only in certain soils. Had not the *intelligentsia* as a group been alienated from the régime, the professional revolutionary conspirators, a small minority drawn from its ranks, could never have appeared.'

Thus, Seton-Watson viewed populism as a particularly significant example of the formation of modern revolutionary elites. The English historian was trying to observe objectively, in its final results and in its typical elements, a process that in the book he was reviewing had been studied from within, from the viewpoint of the consciences of those who had been faced with the dilemma of either forming a limited and active group or expanding into the masses. They were men who had hesitated over that choice, struggling with themselves and with the external conditions that alternately induced or forced them to withdraw into an elite group or to mix with the entire Russian population. It was not the dramatic element in this choice, nor the desperate attempt to find a way out of the dilemma in which their numbers, their condition, and their ideas enclosed them, but the fatal formation of an intelligentsia and of a party of professional revolutionaries that was at the center of Seton-Watson's analysis. He was too good a historian to stop at this purely sociological view; fundamentally, he was more interested in the political than in the ethical function of populism. He was especially attracted by the paradigm that the revolutionary movement seemed to establish even in countries like Yugoslavia and China. The article in the *Times Literary Supplement* concluded, 'This is not to deny the specific features of the Russian movement. Indeed, because it was the first movement on this pattern, it greatly influenced the leaders of others. Chernyshevsky, Bakunin, Ishutin, Tkachev and A. D. Mikhailov are unquestionably Russian. Those who study them should . . . examine both those features which unite them to the stream of European thought and action, and those which distinguish them.'

One had to go far back in Russian history to find these specific traits, going back to the influence of religion, whether orthodox or of the schismatic sects. Thus one returned to those dilemmas and moral and ideological problems which the desire to reach the roots of modern revolutions had initially seemed to place in the background in the English historian's analysis. But the fundamental, inevitable question remained. What part had Russian populism played in the birth and development of modern theories of elites?

Equally important for those who were studying 19th-century revolutionary Russia from the perspective of the middle of the 20th century was the other problem, posed by Alexander Gerschenkron in the *American Historical Review* of October 1953: What was the relationship between populism and the economic backwardness of Russia? What was its value and its importance in the theory of economic development? 'The populists clearly saw the advantages inherent in Russia's being a late-comer upon the modern historical scene. They saw and stressed the possibility of adopting the results of foreign experience without incurring the heavy cost of experimentation, of errors and detours. Both Herzen and Chernyshevski found very felicitous phrases to express the essence of this situation.' Thus, according to the American scholar, the awareness of economic backwardness had been the starting point for the whole populist movement. But Gerschenkron added that the populists had quickly distorted their intuition and had soon affirmed paradoxically that 'the preservation of the *old* rather than the easy adoption of the *new* constituted the "advantages of backwardness." The result was a tragic surrender of realism to utopia. Here is perhaps the main reason for the decline of populism. When the rate of industrial growth leapt upward in the middle of the eighties, after the government had committed itself to a policy of rapid industrialization, the divorce between the populist utopia and the economic reality became too great and the movement proved unable to survive the repressions which followed Alexander the Third's advent to the throne.'

Gerschenkron thought that from the political viewpoint, too, Russian backwardness was the key element for understanding the radicalism of the populists. Both 'the absence of constitutional government and the late start of economic development' explained the rise of the intelligentsia and the contradictions in the revolutionary movement that accompanied it, always oscillating between a spirit of dedication and conspiratorial machiavellianism, between anarchy and exultation of the Jacobin state. Populism could and should be seen, not as one chapter in the history of socialist movements, but 'as a chapter in the history of ideologies in conditions of backwardness.' Viewed from this angle, 'the story of Russian populism may acquire a note of actuality and may serve better to emphasize the great dangers that are inherent in unduly prolonged periods of economic and political backwardness.'[9] These were ideas that Gerschenkron was then developing in that series of essays that have made him, as is well known, the most incisive historian of modern Russian economics, as well as one of the most inspired theorists on the problems of backwardness and development.[10]

After reading his works, the very problem of Russian populism was transformed for me and, I believe, for others, Gerschenkron's interpretation has become a starting point in the discussion that has taken place on this subject in the last fifteen years. His contribution to that discussion has been so rich and complex that it has persuaded me to postpone the debate until we examine more closely what has recently been written on the Slavophiles and Herzen, on Chernyshevsky and Mikhailovsky. The only general element that emerges from this very fruitful dialogue concerns the function of ideas and political ideals in the historical process that we are studying. Is an idea that seems to look back in time—that apparently goes back to the past, that seems to prefer what has been and to exclude what is to come—in itself destined to have a negative effect, does it really constitute a utopian brake on economic and social development? Or does it represent, at least occasionally, an attempt to *reculer pour mieux sauter*, a fruitful attempt to conserve what had been precious in the past to transmit it to the future? History is not made by only looking ahead, but, I would say, by looking both forward and back. Is not socialism itself—the idea of a community and of equality of goods, of an economy based on solidarity—a remnant from the past that has been conserved and transformed into an ideal for the future? And were not socialism and communism, not just populism, ideas that were originally consciously opposed to economic development? Let us open again the old and very basic book of Filippo Buonarroti, the book through which 18th-century communist ideas were transmitted to the 19th century and to, among others, the Russian populists. In fact, without opening it, let us look at the cover of this venerated book. Under the title, *Conspiration pour l'égalité dite de Babeuf*, is the author's motto: *Eas enim optimas esse leges putandum est quibus non divites sed honesti prudentesque homines fiant*. It is taken from Diodorus of Sicily, book 2, chapter 5. It would be difficult to find a more explicit declaration against economic development. The populist's idea of the *obshchina*, their desire for revolution and for peasant equality, were no less involved in the same direction. Because of this, I believe Russian populism should also be considered as a page in the history of European socialism. Along with the movement itself, one should consider and study the ideas of the past that it transmitted to the future, the utopian elements that it undoubtedly contained (but how can one be detached from the past without projecting it outside of time and space and making it timeless and utopian?), and the stimuli toward a modern economy that were certainly not lacking (Chernyshevsky thought about the use of machinery in his *obshchina*, which had been transformed into an agrarian cooperative). Only such a union of past and future, like every other socialist ideal, would have allowed the establishment of deep contacts with the masses in Russia and elsewhere. Only in this way could they be brought to live and struggle in a modern industrial society (here, too, not liberalism but socialism was to become the political ideal of the proletariat). When Marxism arrived, even in St. Petersburg, it was attractive for the element of socialism that it contained, not for its analysis of the development of capitalism or for its justification of primitive accumulation or of free trade. The reason for all this seems evident: it was only through socialism that the workers could see the defense of their own interests, of their own way of being and living. And why deny this to the peasants? They saw in Russia, in populist socialism, a defense of their own interests as well as of their own traditions. As for the internal history of populism, is it truly possible to note, as Gerschenkron maintains, that as we gradually move through the 1860s and 1870s there is a step backward, even a reversal of tendencies, an obscuring of the consciousness that the populists originally had of the advantages of economic backwardness, a fall to the pure and simple extolling of the past? Is the *Narodnya Volya* really a regression compared to Herzen? Were not the *Narodnovolcy* the most clear-sighted and lucid judges of Russia's economic structure, of the fundamental importance that the state had had in its development? These debates and those years seemed to mark progress, not regression. Gerschenkron knows about these matters better than most, but it is still useful to recall them in discussing his interpretation of Russian populism.

In the mid-1950s in the Soviet Union, the debate moved from less general questions to a discussion of these problems. There was no longer a forced silence in response to questions from the West. Research on these themes was reappearing even in Moscow and Leningrad. It would be useful to describe in detail how this occurred. It is not easy to tell when the change arose from a political directive from above, derived from the party's and the government's preparation for the Twentieth Congress (February 1956), and when it was a matter of a persistent drive on the part of Soviet scholars. Evidently both elements were present, but in what amounts and with what timing? In any case, we cannot say that Sedov, one of the most active promoters of this debate, was wrong when about ten years later he wrote that 'the process of liberation from the ideas and concepts that had been fixed for two decades was long and difficult.'[11]

It was quite natural that in 1956 the most comprehensive and recent bibliography of populism during the 1870s and 1880s received its impetus from this discussion.[12] Also in 1956, a polemic on the origins and character of populism began to appear in historical journals. It is particularly interesting to note that among the most active participants in this debate right from the start were a historian of the student movement, Tkachenko, and a scholar who had specialized in problems of youth in the Stalinist period, Sedov. Already in 1956, writings of men who in later years were among the most active scholars of populism, such as Itenberg and Pirumova, were being published. In 1957, after over twenty years during which he had restricted himself to detailed, erudite contributions, B. P. Kozmin published his first important work, *The Russian*

Section of the First International. In January 1958, under the direction and initiative of M. V. Nechkina, the 'Group for the Study of the Revolutionary Situation in Russia from 1859 to 1861' was established. And in the same year the first book since the 1930s on populism as a whole appeared. It was written by Sh. M. Levin,[13] who remarked in the introduction, 'On the whole, this work was already completed several years ago.'[14] Like other writings that appeared around that time, this book had not evolved through urging from above, after the Twentieth Congress. Nevertheless, it saw the light thanks to the fact that censorship had become somewhat more lenient.

But along with the old wood that came to life again, the first crop of populist historiography during the 1950s also contained some less sound and tasty fruit. There were attempts to present ideas and views of the Stalinist era in a new form, not without some appropriate concessions and 'updating.' In this area, it was often a matter, not of a complete break or of a profound renewal, but of a thaw that carried with it much mud and silt.

One of the first exercises in updating was carried out on *Il populismo russo*, my work. It was the year (1955) of the Tenth International Historical Congress, held in Rome, where for the first time Soviet historians were full participants. In issue number 8 of the journal *Vosprosy istorii*, which was distributed then, along with a summary in Italian, was a review of my book by S. A. Pokrovsky. It dealt with the problem of the relationship between the 19th-century revolutionary movements in Russia and the West. But it was not presented in order to invite further research in this area (this became Itenberg's task in an article in the same journal, no. 9, the next year). Rather, his purpose was to take pleasure in the fact that a Western scholar had 'rejected the preconceived and widespread viewpoint in reactionary literature on the would-be contrast between Western and Eastern culture' (from the Italian summary). It was balm to the wound of the traditional Russian and Soviet sense of inferiority, not a clear and precise confirmation that Stalinist nationalism, extending even into the field of historical research, had cut the ties between the Soviet Union and the rest of the world. Similarly, Pokrovsky confirmed that in the book he was reviewing no gap had been created between the 'revolutionary democrats' and the 'populists,' but he did not face the discussion on this essential element, on this crux of the historiographical period that was ending. Some other old themes were again being hammered in: the Slavophiles should be considered purely and simply as reactionaries; the ideas of the Russian liberals could all be explained according to their class situation; any true libertarian element was nonexistent in the ideas of Herzen, who would never have rejected the Jacobin tradition; Chernyshevsky never had illusions about reform, he had always demanded the confiscation of all land belonging to the nobles; populism of the 1870s had a 'progressive function' (and this was the main concession made regarding concepts of the Stalinist era), but it could not be considered a socialist movement because of this; nor should one forget that Tkachev, Bakunin, and Lavrov had actually taken steps backward and not forward compared with Belinksy, Herzen, and Chernyshevsky. Their ideas were and remained 'petit-bourgeois.' Any attempt to establish a deep relationship between the revolutionary populists and 1917 was and remained profoundly wrong. 'The Great October Socialist Revolution was carried out by the working class, allied with the poorest peasants, under the guidance of the Communist party that was fighting under the banner of Marxism.' Simple and easy. This was why Pokrovsky expressed 'his regret for the fact that the book lacked a critique of the theory and tactics of populism.'

Nevertheless, his review was interesting not only for what it said but also for what it did not say. He did not quote any other Russian books; those of the 1920s still could not be mentioned, and the more recent ones did not yet exist. He let it be understood that a book on the history of populism was also needed in Russia, as it was no longer a forbidden topic, but he hastened to warn readers against the temptation of accepting the approach of the 'essential work' he had examined.

The contradictions in such a controlled updating were even more evident when, in 1957, S. A. Pokrovsky himself published a little book called *Falsifiers of the History of Russian Political Thought in Contemporary Bourgeois Reactionary Literature* (published by the Academy of Sciences of the USSR Institute of Law). The tenth, and last, chapter was entitled 'The Progressive Scholars of the West Study the History of Russian Revolutionary Thought.' There were only a few of these progressive scholars: Vernell M. Oliver (for his article in *Journal of Negro History*, October 1953, on Russian radicals and the American Civil War), Armand Coquart (for his work on Pisarev which came out in Paris in 1946), and the author of *Il populismo russo*. According to Pokrovsky, the limited size of this group had an explanation: 'The falsifying literature and the activity of the authors who serve the imperialist reaction are born partly from an attempt to paralyze the influence of progressive literature that arises in Western Europe and in America as a result of the profound interest that world progressive environments have in Soviet culture' (p. 173).

But before observing more closely this conspiracy of the imperialist falsifiers of history against one of the few progressive historians of Russian populism who flourished in the West (it must have been a very effective conspiracy since only three men had managed to evade it), one should again ask what drove even such reserved and conservative reviewers as Pokrovsky to deal with populism, to discuss its nature and its recurrent interest. In his book Pokrovsky concluded that 'Franco Venturi's work was serious scientific research. One could and should debate much with the author, but one could not remain indifferent to his essential work [*opera capitale*]. Its appearance is clear evidence of a reawakening of interest in the traditions of Russian revolutionary thought' (p. 179).

This last allusion actually had little to do with Western historians, whether imperialist or progressive. The rediscovery of Russian revolutionary tradition at the end of the 1950s was mainly a Soviet phenomenon. In historiographical research, as in literary and artistic research, one referred back to the 1920s, and from there one moved further back. One did not look exclusively or particularly toward Marxism, which remained an area in which discussion was difficult, but toward populism and the great debate between Westerners and Slavophiles in the early 19th century. There was a predominantly moral element in this aspect of the anti-Stalinist revolt before the Khrushchev era. In the *narodniki* one found a model of purity and energy, a return to origins and to principles, beyond the machiavellianism, the drama, and the compromises of the 1930s and 1940s. From Herzen to the *Narodnaya Volya*, every historian sought a source of inspiration that could persuade him of the importance and justice of the struggle of the intelligentsia, who were decisive men capable of any sacrifice. The updating and the concessions of official historiography were only one external and more visible aspect of a deep current that was leading the Soviet intelligentsia to reconsider its own origins and its own values. And in this, an encounter with populism was inevitable. As a result, the discussion on this aspect of past life expanded extraordinarily in those years.[15]

On closer observation, one can see that in the West, too, a growing number of scholars and historians were inquiring into the moral roots and populist origins of the intelligentsia and of the Russian revolution. This was partly in response to the work in Russia and partly because of a kind of parallel in the situations on both sides of the Iron Curtain, which was gradually being lifted at that time. In 1955 an important collection edited by Ernest J. Simmons, entitled *Continuity and Change in Russian and Soviet Thought*, was published. Though it dealt with more general problems, it particularly discussed populism.[16] In 1958 James H. Billington's book on Mikhailovsky was published. Among the many figures in 19th-century Russia who anxiously inquired into the interdependence and contrasts between moral and material progress, Mikhailovsky was one of the most significant theoreticians.[17] In 1961 Martin Malia's book, *Alexander Herzen and the Birth of Russian Socialism, 1812–1855*, was published. Here the moral concerns took on more psychological forms.[18] A subdued but very perceptive comment on these reemerging ethical and philosophical concerns in those years came from George L. Kline.[19] A stronger voice was Isaiah Berlin's in an article called 'Russian Populism' published in *Encounter* in July 1960, which, in an enlarged and more complete form, became the introduction to the English translation of *Il populismo russo* published in London the same year.[20] In his contribution to *Continuity and Change in Russian and Soviet Thought*, Berlin had already touched on a central problem in his discussion entitled 'Herzen and Bakunin on Individual Liberty.'[21] The libertarian seed at the core of Herzen's ideas, and from which so much of populism had derived its origin and its strength, was pointed out as one of the most original and forceful elements in 19th-century political thought, not only in Russia but in all of Europe. 'As an acute and prophetic observer of his time he is comparable perhaps to Marx and Tocqueville, as a moralist he is more interesting and original than either' (p. 478). Herzen alone had managed to create and live a morality that did not depend on a tendency to consider all human actions in relation to their historical background, on messianism, on the abstractions and the nightmares of postrevolutionary Europe. In comparison, Bakunin's thought and action seemed to be profoundly immersed in the morass and dangers of his century. Herzen was seen as the creator of the ideas and modes of feeling of the intelligentsia. In Bakunin lay the seeds of all the contradictions of the revolutionary movement.

Thus, somewhat paradoxically and with deliberate, forced simplification, yet with great vigor, Berlin tried to return to the purest source of the revolt and of liberty in 19th-century Russia, after a century of tragic events, defeats, dictatorship, and oppression. In true Russian fashion, he was taking to their logical conclusion things that had been implicit in many of the attitudes and hopes of the intellectuals of the post-Stalinist period. In another essay on the 1840s, entitled 'The Admirable Decade,' Berlin may have risked being too pleased about this rediscovery of the values of tradition and the anecdotes and peculiarities of this reviving tradition of the intelligentsia, but when he was confronted with the problems of revolutionary populism, he faced them with strength, without hesitation. 'In spite of the emphasis on economic and sociological arguments, the basic approach, the tone and outlook of Chernyshevsky and of the the populists generally is moral, and at times indeed religious. These men believed in socialism not because it was inevitable, but because it was just.'[22] The populists had been aware of the danger that their voluntary position, which always maintained the tension of utopia in their struggle, might lead to the formation of an elite of revolutionaries who would impose socialism from above, or of fanatics who might place a new yoke on the Russian peasants in place of the old one, 'a despotic oligarchy of intellectuals in place of the nobility and bureaucracy of the czar' (p. xii). The whole debate, all the internal conflicts in the populist movement, testified to the depth of feeling about this central issue. The nihilistic as well as the anarchistic attitudes, the popular movement as well as the varied forms of the clandestine organization, had been attempts to respond to the question that every revolutionary felt was essential and central. Chernyshevsky's hard realism, his bleak but honest pragmatism, had been decisive in the orientation of the attitudes of revolutionary youth. 'He was a man of unswerving integrity, immense industry and capacity, rare among Russians for concentration upon concrete detail.' His practical energy, his social position (as we know, he was the son of a parish priest), his moral strength had made him 'a natural leader of a disenchanted generation of socially mingled origins, no longer dominated by good birth, embittered by the failure of their own ideals, by government repression, by the humiliation of Russia in the Crimean War, by the weakness, heartlessness, hypocrisy and chaotic incompetence of the ruling class' (p. xx). A generation was thus turned into a movement that was deeply convinced that 'Russia could leap over the capitalist stage of social development and transform the village communes and free cooperative groups of craftsmen into agricultural and industrial associations of producers who would constitute the embryo of the new socialist society' (p. xxii).

Twenty years of attempts and defeats, of struggles and sacrifices, from 1861 to 1881, during which these ideas were tested against reality, would profoundly mark the destiny of modern Russia, not only for what they succeeded in doing and creating (a party of professional revolutionaries, a new relationship between the intelligentsia and the revolution, a profound faith in socialism), but also because of what the defeat prevented them from accomplishing. The leap into the world of liberty and justice, above and beyond the long and painful road of capitalism and industrialization, was not realized. Yet, concludes Berlin, even after such a long time lag, after the victory and triumph of Marxist ideas in Russia, after the disdainful silence of the Stalinist era, it was still necessary to return to studying and understanding the populists. One should do so, not only because their vision of the evolution of a modern economy influenced events in 20th-century Russia, not only because populist concepts appeared in underdeveloped countries of the modern world, but above all because the fears and struggles of those first Russian revolutionaries with the problems of the relationship between the elite and the populace, between the revolutionary dictatorship and the mass of workers, had a worrying immediacy in the Soviet Union between the 1950s and 1960s. Thus Berlin did not hesitate to write,

The populists were convinced that the death of the peasant commune would mean death, or, at any rate, a vast setback, to freedom and equality in Russia; the Left Socialist-Revolutionaries, who were their direct descendants, transformed this into a demand for a form of decentralized, democratic self-government among the peasants, which Lenin adopted when he concluded his temporary alliance with them in October 1917. In due course the Bolsheviks repudiated this programme and transformed the cells of dedicated revolutionaries—perhaps the most original contribution of populism to revolutionary practice—into the hierarchy of centralized political power, which the Populists had steadily and fiercely denounced. . . . Communist practice owed much, as Lenin was always ready to admit, to the Populist movement; for it borrowed the technique of its rivals and adapted it with conspicuous success to serve the precise purpose which it had been invented to resist. [P.xxx]

The discussion that followed these words, and the presentation of the English version of *Il populismo russo*, failed to confirm Pokrovsky's prediction about the desires of the 'falsifiers of history serving the imperialistic reaction' to 'suffocate and paralyze' progressive Western historians with the intention of preventing a broader knowledge of the 19th-century Russian revolutionary movement. The discussion was long and animated. Why, asked many of the participants (and Berlin had noted the same in his introduction), had this book been accepted both by the Soviets and by people from the West? And this especially in the years of cold, or even cultural, war?[23] Did history really have the power to overcome the conflicts of differing ideology and politics and to offer a common ground on which the Russians, who were emerging from the

Stalinist experience, could meet Westerners who were shedding the results of the Cold War? Despite everything, the author of this book was and is convinced that one should have and one must answer in the affirmative. Naturally the limitations of Clio's clarifying capacity are evident, but her work should not be considered ineffectual because of this. One cannot expect her to be the remedy to all ills. Nevertheless, she always serves and will serve to arouse energy, to recreate a desire for truth that is capable of going beyond any ideological and political barrier. A detailed account, as precise as possible, of the events of the 19th-century Russian revolutionary movement could serve as a reminder and a measure for the Soviets who were beginning to understand the principles and roots of the society in which they lived. At the same time, it could be an indispensable means of showing Westerners the decades of struggles, of sacrifices, of moral victories, and of practical defeats of Russia in the past. In the midst of so many economic explanations, of so many fatalistic and sociological interpretations, a historical account of a political movement once again demonstrated its effectiveness.

But on closer examination, was this Soviet and Western acceptance based on a misunderstanding? After Pokrovsky's comments came those of M. V. Nechkina, which were much more comprehensive and open.[24] In the numerous studies on populism that appeared in Russia at the beginning of the 1960s, there was never a lack of favorable comment on *Il populismo russo* and its English translation. The acknowledgments almost became a ritual. In the West, too, in the thinking and research that was developing at an extraordinary pace in those same 1960s, *Il populismo russo* had often appeared as a useful departure point. But was this not a purely formal and academic convergence in which the Soviets and Westerners often meant different things even when they used similar or identical words?

The point of rupture was indicated by Leonard Schapiro. Russia and the West differed less in their interpretation of populism than in the importance attributed to this movement in the formation of Bolshevism, in the preparation for the 1917 revolution. Schapiro, a well-known expert on modern Russian history, wrote in the July 28, 1960 issue of *The Listener,*

Professor Berlin notes that Venturi's work has been acclaimed both in the West and in the Soviet Union, and attributes this unusual fact to the 'calm impartiality' with which the book is written. It would indeed be a remarkable thing if this were the reason, since impartial scholarship does not usually command Communist admiration if its conclusions disagree with party shibboleths. [In this Schapiro was both right and wrong: right if he was referring to the state organs of cultural politics and wrong if he was referring to the numerous Soviet scholars who were sensitive, because of their experiences, to the demands of philological and documentary rigor.] But Sir Isaiah is not quite right. Venturi has been criticized in the Soviet Union for hinting that the psychological type of the Bolshevik was engendered in the nineteenth century. Bolshevik kinship with such conspiratorial fanatics of revolution as Tkachev is indeed fairly obvious. But it is contrary to the aura of pure democracy with which modern Soviet convention demands that Lenin be surrounded. Moreover the fact that Venturi is more often than not praised by Soviet writers is due, in my opinion, not to his impartiality, but to his, quite incidental, acceptance of the current Soviet view of the liberals, which was also that of the populists—cowardly, selfish, indifferent to the suffering of the masses. . . . It is this blind spot which leads the Soviet critics to label his work as 'progressive'—the highest term of praise.

Let us temporarily leave aside the problem of Russian liberalism; we shall return to it as it deserves more detailed discussion. What counts more, and what was becoming more evident from Schapiro's words as well as from all the discussion in the 1960s on Russian populism, was the desire of Soviet scholars as well as English ones to characterize the relationships, to understand the link between the Russian revolutionary movement and October 1917.

Every day in Russia it was becoming more evident that in order to exorcize and remove this problem, and in order to set one's conscience at rest with history, it no longer sufficed to repeat the traditional formulae of orthodoxy. Had the populists not been utopians, petit bourgeois? Had Lenin not been a scientific and Marxist revolutionary? This obviously meant the a priori denial of a problem that continually presented itself before anyone who attempted to reconstruct a biography of Lenin, or his formation, or who studied the establishment of a professional revolutionary party in St. Petersburg, or who discussed the formulae and the reality of Russian economic development in the 20th century. From biography to economics, everything seemed to pose the question of the relationship between populism and Bolshevism. The pure and simple methods of censorship and silence were no longer enough, even if the works of the Russian Jacobin, Tkachev, edited by B. P. Kozmin, which ceased to be published during the 1930s, had not been taken up again in the 1960s, or if the whole dispute between the Mensheviks and the Bolsheviks on this theme remained 'off limits' for Soviet historiography. But how could one avoid reconsidering what Lenin had written on Chernyshevsky and on the revolutionaries of the *Narodnaya Volya*? How could one remain silent about Bakunin, how could one pretend that Nechaev had never existed? How could one not pose the question of how the workers' movement in St. Petersburg had really been born? And aside from the stereotyped formulae, what had the discussions between the populists and the Marxists at the end of the century signified? It was a discussion that was fundamental, as we know, for Lenin's formation and for all trends among the Russian intelligentsia in those years. Something similar was taking place on the other side of the ocean. There, too, the usual and current interpretation of the roots of Bolshevism appeared increasingly unsatisfactory and false. The interpretation was entirely pragmatic and political, based on the cynicism and revolutionary machiavellianism of conspiracies and plots, first of the Jacobins and then of the Leninists.

In the May 6, 1961 issue of *National Review*, Stefan F. Possony used *The Roots of Revolution*, as it is called in English, as a starting point for his revolutionary genealogy of communism, showing the prophets of the revolution as having almost biblical descent. But the fathers and grandfathers of Bolshevism ended up multiplying, so that for a genealogist like him, they included not only Nechaev and Tkachev, but also Filippo Buonarroti and Babeuf, the Carbonari and Mazzini. Nothing remained but the increasingly firmly rooted conviction that history, at least the history of revolutionary movements, drew its roots and its raison d'être from the techniques of the conspiracy and from the idea of a perpetually renewed plot of which the Russians (and perhaps the Italians) had for generations seemed to be masters. This was the ultimate limit of a conception that had reached the point of absurdity. On the other hand, A. J. P. Taylor stressed the fact that during the czarist empire, the spirit of 1848 had survived, while it had disappeared or been transformed in European countries. Thus he stressed a fact of undoubted importance, that is, the difference in the rhythm of development of revolutionary ideas in Russia and elsewhere (*Observer*, July 3, 1960).

James Joll emphasized the importance of not deviating from a rigorous historical view. Even the relationship between the *Narodnaya Volya* and Lenin, which undoubtedly existed and was important, could be understood, not by contriving derivations and genealogies, but only by studying each man and each era in itself for what each had thought, said, and done.

There is a great temptation for a historian writing about Russia in the nineteenth century to see everything in relation to the upheaval of 1917, which is still the more important historical influence of our times today. The movements of the past century tend to be judged by the extent to which they contributed to the October Revolution and their success or failure is assessed by many writers according to their role in ultimately helping or hindering the success of Lenin and Trotsky. So it is salutary and refreshing when a historian looks at Czarist Russia for its own sake and analyses its vivid and vigorous intellectual life without reference to what was to come after. [*Spectator*, July 8, 1960]

Yet another English commentator concluded that the dramatic, moral, and historical value of the populists would have been lost if these men had been placed in a pantheon of revolutionaries or if they had been transformed into examples and models of the excellence or inadequacy of one ideology or another. 'The history of this movement is above all a record of individuals,' W. S. Merwin concluded, 'many of whom would have been remarkable in any circumstance, faced with confusion and injustice, surrounded by suffering, devoting themselves, always at considerable risk, to an effort to discover what, in such a situation, is the duty of a man, what he can live for and, if necessary, die for, what he can really accomplish for those around him. In the main, the populists were struggling to create values in a world without them, and any such attempt, it seems, is quite likely to fail. But if the account of it is ever really irrelevant, then surely everything else is too' (*Nation*, September 23, 1961).

Thus, the figures of the Russian populists, freed from the outlines and formulae to which they had often been reduced by their followers and their enemies, gradually reached the concerns, the questioning of the subsequent later century; they offered their experience to anyone who was again faced with the problems of nihilism and liberty, of dictatorship and socialism. The 1960s were a decade of intense work in these areas. The burden of the past was heavy, as we have seen, and not only in Russia. But it is the task of historians to help bear this weight, and despite many difficulties and many restrictions they seem to have carried out their duty to a considerable extent. It is certainly worth observing their work closely.

The thaw in Russia had just begun, and the first shift needed was among the great frozen blocks of quotations from Lenin and Marx. These were in great disorder and confusion after the disappearance of the 'great simplifier,' who even in this corner of Soviet ideology had placed everything in rigid and elementary order with obsessive monotony. It was not difficult to discover that, in order to fabricate such a picture, it had been necessary to dismember Lenin's sentences, removing them from their political and chronological context, isolating them and thus making them say whatever was wanted. One example will suffice. In an essay written between 1901 and 1902, 'What Is to Be Done?' Lenin had included a few very fundamental pages on the function of theory in all revolutionary movements, 'Without revolutionary theory there cannot be a revolutionary movement.' This affirmation was particularly important for a party such as the recently formed Russian social democratic one, which was faced with truly exceptional problems. With a full awareness of the dreadful task that lay before the Russian revolutionaries and of their responsibility toward the world socialist movement, and with poorly disguised pride arising from the exceptional situation, Lenin went on to say that 'the tasks of the Russian social democracy are greater than any faced by other social democratic parties in the world.' 'Later we will discuss the political and organizational tasks that are imposed by the need to free the whole population from the yoke of czarism. Here we want to discuss the fact that the fighting function of the avant-garde can only be taken on by a party guided by avant-garde theory. To understand what this means in concrete terms, one need only recall the predecessors of Russian social democracy, Herzen, Belinsky, Chernyshevsky, and the extraordinary group of revolutionaries of the 1870s, one only need consider the universal function that Russian literature is now acquiring, one need only. . . . but we do not need other examples'[25] These words alone would be sufficient to show how the moral and ideological tension of populism was still alive in the young Lenin. In the Stalinist era these words were constantly subjected to the anthological method: some men cut Chernyshevsky's quotations, others removed the revolutionaries from the *Narodnaya Volya*. Each took the piece that served him best.

Is it worth recalling these sad events? It is essential, if no less sad, to recollect that in the 1960s in the Soviet Union, Lenin's deleted phrases, once returned to the world, often provided protection or cover for those who planned to study the populists. Behind the shield of Lenin, in whom the relationship with the

19th-century revolutionaries was still alive and personal, the Soviet scholars of the 1960s were able to return, though against the trend of the times, to 'the predecessors of social democracy,' to 'Russian socialism,' to the very origins of the revolutionary movement in their country. Lenin's words were made use of, as they had been in the Stalinist era. But at that time they had been used for suppression and prevention. Twenty years later, they were at least occasionally used to reestablish contacts with the past.

But the bust of Lenin remained Janus-faced in the Soviet Union. If one side encouraged and supported the historians in their effort to get away from Stalinism, the other hindered open discussion of the populists' ideas, of their conception of Russia's economic development, and of their vision of peasant socialism. Lenin's words were interpreted in a great variety of ways, as happens when one looks in old texts for support and proof of one's own ideas rather than seeking historical reality, and when one treats the words as an authority rather than as a stimulus for research. Those who wish to know this work of orientation (I do not think it is worth a detailed description, yet only in detailed exposition would it acquire value and significance) should see the bibliography already mentioned which accompanies the miscellany in honor of the eightieth birthday of B. P. Kozmin, and also the review by S. S. Volk and S. K. Mikhailova in *Sovetskaya istoriografiya revolyutsionnogo narodnichestva 70-kh-nachala 80-kh godov XIX veka* (Soviet historiography of revolutionary populism of the seventies and eighties in the 19th century).[26] The authors rightly concluded, after quoting numerous articles and scientific conferences on Lenin and populism, that 'after having reestablished a comprehensive evaluation that is favorable to populism, scholars gradually moved to investigate it in detail and more deeply' (p. 147).

We too must follow the Soviet historians on this path, noting an important preliminary ideological readjustment, that is, along with and beyond Lenin, the return to Marx and his ideas about the 19th-century Russian revolutionary movement. In 1947, almost without any introduction or explicit justification, a precious little volume was published: *Perepiska K. Marksa i F. Engelsa a russkimi politicheskimi deyatelyami* (The correspondence of K. Marx and F. Engels with Russian political men). Twenty years later the Marxist-Leninist Institute collected notes, letters, and documents of any kind that gave evidence of the relationship between Marx and Engels and revolutionary Russia. These documents were published in a fundamental volume which provided a vivid picture of the great interest, doubts, and problems that Russian populism had evoked when Marx and Engels saw it arise at the same time as the revolution of 1848 and develop before their eyes during the 1860s and 1870s.[27] It is a pity that Soviet editors have not yet lost the habit of only providing translated texts without bothering to also provide the original French, German, and English. Above all, it is a pity that they did not want to be more complete in their collection. Why give only a fragment of the four outlines of the letter Marx sent to Vera Zasulich on March 8, 1881? These documents vividly demonstrated his hesitations, his doubts about the central problem of populism, that is, about the affirmation that Russia could have had, thanks to its backwardness and to the peasant *obshchina*, an economic development that was substantially different from that in Western Europe, avoiding capitalism and moving directly to socialist forms of life and production. In the definitive version of this letter, Marx admitted that this was possible provided that the *obshchina* freed itself from the social environment in which it was forced to exist and which prevented its development. Thus, Marx ended up accepting Chernyshevsky's ideas. Taking advantage of Western Europe's experience with capitalism, Russia could make the traditional peasant communities the basis for her socialism. This was 1881, and for twenty years the populist movement had posed the question of how to detach the *obshchina* from the czarist world in order to lead it to the socialist world. These were passionate questions to which Marx did not reply in 1881, despite the insistent and repeated inquiries from the most diverse trends of Russian populism.[28] The Gordian knot of the Russian revolution had not been cut. Some years earlier, discussing the problem with Mikhailovsky, Marx had already left the matter open, refusing to prophesy or to descend into an empty philosophy of history.[29] While preparing to write to Zasulich in 1881, in his notes and outlines, he continually returned to the idea that only a revolution in Russia could save the *obshchina*.[30] But in the letter that he actually sent, he did not go beyond the simple possibility of a socialist development in a country like Russia, where capitalism had not yet broken the ancient peasant community traditions.

It was Engels, in discussion with N. F. Danielson, who in the 1890s affirmed with increasing clarity that capitalism had already won in Russia and that the country had already started on the road that the West had followed previously. Through a concise and very interesting discussion, the populist hypothesis was discarded. In the foreground, there emerged with increasing clarity the idea that Marx had seemed to accept in 1882 when he and Engels (who probably was the real author) signed the introduction to the second Russian edition of the *Communist Manifesto*. The idea was that the revolution, which alone could save the *obshchina*, could only be realized if the example and the initiative for social transformation that went beyond capitalism were to come from the West. Those who arrived late on the historical scene had the advantage of benefiting not only from the technical and economic experience of the more advanced capitalist countries but also and especially from the socialist revolution that had matured in the meantime. 'If the Russian revolution serves as a sign for the proletariat revolution in the West, so that they complement each other, then the present Russian *obshchina* will be the starting point for socialist development.'[31]

After 1882, Engels spent a decade developing this point of view. The Western European model became the center of his view of Russia's future as he further discarded the hypothesis, which Marx had accepted, of the possibility of socialist development in the world of the Russian peasants. There was a large element of historical fatalism, and full acceptance of the consequences that this triumph of the capitalist way must bring. As Engels wrote, 'History is the most cruel of all the goddesses, and she drives her chariot through heaps of corpses, not only during wars but also in periods of 'peaceful' economic development. And we are fools enough not to find the courage in ourselves to make progress a reality unless we are forced to it by suffering that seems almost intolerable.'[32] The populist ideas seemed more and more like illusions in Engels's polemic, which was not without a renewed sense of superiority mixed with scorn for those who sought a different road to economic and social development in Russia. 'In a land like yours,' Engels wrote to Plekhanov on February 26, 1895, 'where modern large-scale industry is grafted onto the primitive peasant communities and where all the intermediate stages of civilization are present, in a land surrounded intellectually by a more or less effective Chinese wall desired by despotism, one should certainly not be surprised that ideas take shape in the most unexpected and extraordinary ways.'[33] And, as Engels well knew, this situation was creating a new form of fanaticism and ideological superstition. As he said, 'The works of Marx were being interpreted in the most diverse and contradictory ways, almost as if they were quotations of the classics or of the New Testament.'[30] What for the populists had been a desire to fulfill their moral convictions through practical solutions now risked being changed into a total acceptance of Russia's development according to the capitalist and proletariat model. In vain, Danielson confronted Engels with the physical, biological, and demographic limits beyond which Russia could not go in its efforts to industrialize (and this limit will be a heavy burden on the rhythm of Russia's development in the subsequent decades, as Gerschenkron has stressed). In vain, faced with history which passed over heaps of corpses, the populists stressed everyone's right to rebel and protest (and this was an essential element of Russia's development in the 20th century). But with the great drive toward industrialization at the end of the 19th century, Marx's doubts seemed to vanish into the past momentarily, while a new and rigid view of bourgeois development was taking shape.

One cannot say that the recent Soviet discussions on this first encounter and clash between populism and Marxism, engaging though they are, went very far. The return to Marx has often dealt with his relationship with the Russian revolutionaries of the 1860s and 1870s, rather than with those who fought for his ideas.[35] The books of Reuel and Polevoy seemed to revive interest in the problems of grafting Marxism onto the trunk of the 19th-century Russian revolutionary movement. However, the clear separation between the history of populism and the history of Marxism, and the desire not to mix the two or even to juxtapose or compare them, again led to silence.[36] Not even the renewed interest in Plechanov seems to have led to a deeper investigation into these questions.[37] The important publication of a broad selection of populist economic texts, in 1958, can be considered a significant sign, but nevertheless it was not followed by the expected debates.[38]

In the last decade, more significant contributions have come from America and England. Studies by Salomon M. Schwarz, Leopold Haimson, D. W. Treadgold, Arthur P. Mendel, J. L. H. Keep, S. H. Baron, J. Frankel, and A. Walicki, to mention only a few, again discuss the question of the relationship between populism and Marxism.[39] Despite their considerable value, it must be said that these books often risk perpetuating the deep division and separation established in Russia between the history of social democracy and the history of the previous revolutionary movement. In the name of political formulae and ideological forms, they risk severing the profound psychological and political unity between the various phases of the struggle against czarist absolutism.

From the standpoint of our particular interests, the studies of Richard Pipes have special importance. Pipes reexamined the relationship between the young Lenin and the populist and Jacobin tradition. In a brilliant and penetrating investigation into the history of words and their rapid change in the last decades of the 19th century, he has presented the precise meaning of the terms *narodnik* and *narodnichestvo*.[40] In his 'semantic inquiry,' Pipes has confirmed that these terms were coined and became established only in the mid 1870s and that then they designated only a part, a trend, in the Russian revolutionary movement, the part that maintained that 'the intellectuals should not lead the people in the name of abstract, bookish, imported ideas but adapt themselves to the people as it was, promoting resistances to the government in the name of real, everyday needs' (p. 445). The meaning of the term soon broadened, but there is no doubt—and it is to Pipes's credit that he stresses this—that the Russian Marxists were the first to give it a more general meaning, and to make it synonymous with all Russian revolutionary trends that did not accept their new ideas. Thus the semantic investigation leads to the same conclusions as the ideological one, and emphasizes the great importance of the discussions of Marx, Engels, and their followers which we have already mentioned. It is certainly not the first time in the history of ideas and political movements that a baptism comes from the adversaries. But why should one deduce from this, as Pipes does, that the use of the word *narodnichestvo* 'had no historical justification'? Pipes probably does not take sufficient account of the weight that traditions, ideas, and sentiments formed in the 1850s and 1860s had during the 1870s. To me it seems impossible to maintain that in the mid 1870s the *narodniki* supported 'the commune or artel not so much because Herzen or Chernyshevsky had done so, but because they were the institution they actually encountered in the villages and therefore considered them "popular"' (as Pipes asserts, p. 452).

The ideas and passions aroused by Herzen and Chernyshevsky in their followers who 'went to the people' were too important for the young men to discover the *obshchina* by themselves and with their own eyes. In reality they saw it through the colors and the problems that their masters—not just Herzen and Chernyshevsky, but also Bakunin, Lavrov, and Tkachev—had taught them to look for. And it is this continuity and this tradition that constitute, beyond all internal differences, the character and the unity of the populist movement to which the Marxists and the social democrats contributed in the 1890s, leaving the mark of their definition. On closer observation, a return to the events of the 1860s and 1870s is not just legitimate, but essential. Among other things, the term *narodnichestvo* has the advantage of recalling how, through the discussions of the 1880s and 1890s, the existing great revolutionary hope was transformed. This was the hope that Russia would avoid passing through a capitalist phase, a hope that, despite many doubts, was upheld by Karl Marx himself.[41]

Like the Soviet scholars of the sixties, we too must set aside these 'comprehensive evaluations' to begin to 'investigate in detail and more deeply.' First of all, how and when were the ideas born that later characterized the whole populist movement? How did that ideology start to crystallize? The most important answers do not come from historians of the political movements but from historians of the world of the Russian peasants, that is, from those who saw the problem from the viewpoint of the villages, not from the viewpoint of the intelligentsia. Pierre Pascal, the scholar whose investigations go back to the protopope Avvakum, Pugachev, and Dostoevsky, in collecting his articles (or *'esquisses,'* as he calls them), in a book entitled *Civilisation paysanne en Russie* has helped us understand the tragedy of the Russian peasants. He describes their conflict with the modern industrial world, their tenacious defense of their traditions, their forms of life, their interests as compared with those of the nobles, the bureaucrats, and the organizers from the cities.[42] In these pages we observe the intelligentsia's discovery, between the 18th and 19th centuries, of the autonomous existence of the Russian people. We can feel the peasant *obshchina* still pulsating and surviving tenaciously in the years immediately before Stalinist collectivization.[43] We live next to 'la paysanne du nord' in her hard but productive and dignified labor (pp. 45 ff.). We are directly in touch with the traditional organization of solidarity in the village through his 'Entr'aide paysanne en Russie' (pp. 63 ff.). We experience life in a small, isolated village in the province of Nizhni Novgorod in 1926–28 ('Mon village, il y a quarante ans,' pp. 75 ff.). And in his last essay, 'Esénine—poète de la campagne russe,' we too are carried away in the frightful storm which momentarily seemed to exalt and give universal value to the Russian peasant world, only to crush its ancient traditions and deny its deepest and truest values. It is a tragedy that was expressed with the greatest purity and despair by the poet Esenine. Here he is, like the village within him, where he continues to live even when he takes part in the events of the city. He too is caught up

in this great turbulence of unanimity, with all the Russian people. Only those who, like them, have lived through it can understand their conduct and their works at this time. It is not merely a throne which crumbles, it is not a monarchy which is going to be replaced by a parliamentary regime, it is not such and such reforms which are going to be enacted: the jurists and professors can believe that if they like. The Russian people themselves feel otherwise, have other ambitions. . . . It is an immense revolt against all the iniquities, the oppressions, the cruelties, the hypocrisies, against the great scandal of the war, an immense aspiration toward the happiness of all men. The mighty will be cast down from their throne and the poor shall be exalted. Peace to all the universe! [Pp. 121 ff.]

Better than anyone else, Pierre Pascal has revealed to us what immense, explosive power lay at this time in Russia in the revolutionary encounter between secular peasant aspirations and the intelligentsia's profound desire for a moral renewal, in the populist charge that the 19th century had passed on to the 20th century.

More recent investigations into the history of the Russian village seem to confirm and add specifics to Pierre Pascal's view, from the detailed and accurate history by Jerome Blum[44] to the excellent collection of articles by Wayne S. Vucinich entitled *The Peasant in Nineteenth-Century Russia*.[45] The reality of peasant life in 19th-century Russia is described and studied from the social standpoint by Mary Matossian, while Terence Emmons has reexamined the question of the emancipation of 1861. Donald W. Treadgold raises the question of religion in Russian village life. Among other historians, John S. Curtiss has written about the military, Francis M. Watters about the *obshchina*, Reginald E. Zelnik about the transformation of the peasants into workers, Michael Petrovich about Russian historiography on peasant problems, and Donald Fanger about *The Peasant in Literature*. Nicholas V. Riasanovsky provides a conclusion in *The Problem of the Peasant*; it is a carefully arranged and precise little encyclopedia on what has been written and said about the Russian village from the age of Alexander I to that of Nicholas II. Of particular importance, on the other hand, are the studies on the permanence and the revival of the peasant *obshchina* after the 1917 revolution. In this area, it is enough to cite the works of Moshe Lewin and D. J. Male.[46]

It has been the task of Michael Confino, the Israeli historian, to create a new basis for discussing the results of the agronomic, economic, and social transformations, ordered from above, that came from the West and were imposed on the Russian peasant world by state machinery and world market demands. Confino's first work was *Domaines et seigneurs en Russie vers la fin du XVIIIe siècle. Etude de structures agraires et de mentalités économiques*.[47] In it he made a precise study of the rise and development of new methods of administration that seemed to promise a renewal of all noble estates during Catherine's reign. But these conflicted with the harsh realities of serfdom, of diffidence, of the resistance of a village threatened by a progress that might make the working and living conditions of a *muzhik* even harsher. The final phase of this development, which coincided with the beginning of the new century, was one of crushed hopes, disillusionment, and stasis. The Russian nobles, shaped by military discipline and by service to the absolute state, had brought to the villages, not a spirit of enterprise, but an aura of officialdom and bureaucracy, of being judges and tutors. The peasants had responded, exceptionally but dangerously, by revolting, and generally by the daily defense of the unwritten laws of their village community. In the long run, the nobles maintained and even aggravated the rule of serfdom, while the peasant ended up preserving and often imposing his own techniques, his own mentality, and his own traditional life-style on the landlord.

In his second work, *Systèmes agraires et progrès agricole. L'assolement triennal en Russie au XVIIIe–XIXe siècles*, Michael Confino used a technical investigation (the effects of triple crop rotation) to penetrate all aspects of peasant reality in modern Russia.[48] In his work, we see the Russian triangle—the landlord, the *obshchina*, and the state—being gradually modified and transformed, driven by technical reality and its requirements, by the search for new land, by the exhaustion of fields, by demographic changes, by the variation in market opportunities, but it still remains the immovable basis of social relationships both before and after the reforms of 1861. With great difficulty and only in part, the landlord manages to replace triple rotation with extensive agriculture. The *obshchina* continues to regulate, balance, and maintain stable village life, imposing its own techniques and its own mentality. The state, even when it manages to carry out reforms as fundamental as those of 1861, cannot avoid defending the interests of the nobles and trying to control the peasant *obshchina* without being able to break it down or change it. Only the industrialization of the late 19th and early 20th centuries provided a way out of this situation. However, industrialization was a weighty instrument, difficult to manage, burdensome for all Russian society, and was far from producing all the effects of which it was capable when Russia entered in the era of its modern revolutions.

It should not surprise us that, before industrialization, a movement was born that sought not only the breakdown of the Russian triangle but that wished to do this by supporting the peasant *obshchina*. The landlords had to be eliminated, and what about the state? Doubts about this past problem made some revolutionaries seek the complete destruction of the state while others wanted its transformation and utilization.

Thus, by following Michael Confino in his *étude d'économie et de sociologie rurales*, we seem to truly return to the terrain where populism was born. Observing the movement, so to speak, close to the ground, we see it arise when the ideas and technical knowledge imported from the West fail to transform local reality and seem to make life even more burdensome for the peasants, at first evoking a defensive and diffident reaction toward foreigners and hostility for anything that threatens traditions, and eventually, fairly quickly, bringing the belief that only by going to the peasant's side, only by accepting and making the village traditions one's own, would it be possible to introduce foreign ideas and techniques to everyone's advantage. Thus the justification of serfdom and of the landlord's control over the village was replaced by a defense of Russian agronomic traditions, of the *mir*, of the periodic redistribution of land, of the lack of enclosures, of the spirit of solidarity and equality that dominated the Russian village.[49]

This process was anything but linear. Rather, it was a continual regermination of similar ideas at the most varied times and in varied forms, from the age of Catherine to that of Nicholas I. It is a remarkable fact that as far back as 1789, a man like Radishchev, in a series of notes and sketches on the situation in the regions around St. Petersburg, could reach the conclusion that the period redistribution of land, with the intention of assuring every peasant plots of similar yield, 'was a bad thing for agriculture, but good for equality.'[50] In discussing annual redistribution, Radishchev remarked, 'Who in our time would have thought that in Russia we are realizing what the finest legislators sought in ancient times and what more modern ones think of, and from which arises the great Russian agriculturalist's love for his own hearth?'[51]

Naturally such opinions were continually and vigorously contradicted by those who looked at the peasants in the West, the 'farmers' or *fermiers*, as a model of what should be followed and imitated in Russia. Everything in the present agrarian system must be changed, they thought, and certainly the *obshchina* could not escape this total condemnation. But how was this change to be achieved? The *muzhik's* resistance was deep and invincible. Faced with this resistance, the ruling class had a persistent need to find the reason for the peasants' obstinate desire to maintain their traditional forms. At the same time there was a temptation to yield to it, accepting reality and justifying it before the West. Even the famous statesman P. D. Kiselev, talking about the state peasants who during the 1830s and 1840s were the object of his activities as a reformer, concluded: 'It is true that the periodic redistributions are a nuisance, but one can only change this usage by instituting individual ownership, which also has its inconveniences; it eliminates the marvelous advantage of communal ownership, thanks to which there are no proletarians among the peasants of the state, and each family has its share in the village's assets.'[52]

Nor could these landlords and state officials, wrestling with the Russian economic situation between the 18th and 19th centuries, avoid one question that was continually posed by the reality surrounding them. Did the roots of backwardness lie in the regime of peasant serfdom or in the collective responsibility of the *mir*, in the *obshchina*, and in the redistribution of land? What were the relationships between one aspect and the other of this single reality? All the discussion between the economist Tengoborsky and the young Ogarev, Herzen's friend, was based on this problem that was discussed in a variety of forms until 1861.[53] Even after his detailed and lucid historical investigation, Confino seems to hesitate before such a question. 'Did the peasant neglect his work because of the fact that the plots pass from hand to hand or was it because he was conscious of working for others, without being recompensed or rewarded for his labor?' and the 'morcellement des terres,' the cause of poor yields, was it due to the communal regime of the village or rather, as Confino maintains, to the 'historical circumstances of the formation of the *terroirs* and the evolution of seigneurial land ownership'? Undoubtedly 'this symbiosis of communal practices and of rules of organization was at the heart of the ambivalence that one notices in the attitude of the landlords toward the rural commune.'[54]

That ambivalence and ambiguity were crystallized into an ideology of the *obshchina* and the *mir* as soon as these truths about peasant life were ideally detached and isolated from the context of landlords and serfs in which they had been placed, and were inserted into a more general historical, religious, political, and social view. We have already found Radishchev regarding the *obshchina* as the solution to the lengthy search for a more just society. In the Decembrists, and especially in Pestel, there is a return and development of the desire to see the Russian village from the point of view of economic initiative and improvement, on one hand, and security for all on the other. The liberation of the peasants, which the provisional republican government would have assured, would rest on this double principle. The recent excellent edition of Pestel's *Russkaya pravda* allows us to follow closely the development of these ideas by the head of the Southern Society.[55]

Other studies on the Decembrists allow us to observe other moments and aspects of this discussion. For example, in the early 1820s, S. I. Turgenev tried to raise the nobles' desire for agrarian modernization to a political and not just a technical level, trying to explain to them that the abolition of slavery was the foremost problem, that to achieve this it was even worth accepting and supporting the autocratic government, and that from this fundamental reform a more liberal and just regime would necessarily arise. Thus the reality of the Russian peasants forced an alliance between the tradition of enlightened despotism and the newer and more lively tradition of liberalism. Power and the state became the pivot point, the central element in the vision of those who were not resigned to conservatism and a standstill. There arose a 'statist' view, in contrast with the 'popular' view, of the past and the future of Russia.[56]

One function of the Slavophiles in the 1830s and 1840s was to insert the popular elements—the *obshchina*, the *mir*, the whole peasant world—into a vision that was no longer enlightened, statist, or liberal, but religious and romantic. This grafting was often contrived and imprecisely executed, and produced abundant but flaccid fruits on the communal spirit, on the innate Christianity of the Russians, and on the purity and health of the peasant community which was uncontaminated by egoism, violence, foreign influence, and by the city and the state. All these ideas led to a reactionary rhetoric, conservative and even nationalistic.[57] But the first generation of Slavophiles had a historical function that was far from such tasks of propaganda and the defense of czarism. Even the Soviet historians, after decades of massive and monotonous condemnation, began to discuss these opinions and to try to get a better idea of what really had been the function of men such as Kireevsky, Khomyakov, and Aksakov in the history of Russia. There is a particularly interesting discussion of this in the pages of *Voprosy literatury*, which began with a brilliant article by Aleksandr Yanov, published in issue number 5 in 1969. In the Slavophile movement he sees a first positive response to the sense of inferiority caused in the 18th century by contrast with the West, by the conviction that became crystallized in the early 19th century that a true culture and literature did not exist in Russia. The Slavophiles countered this negation with a real religion of the Russian people, the peasants. If the destiny of the Slavophiles was to become reactionaries, this was not because of their initial ideas, which were anything but reactionary, but because they did not understand that the roots of despotism in their country lay in the very Russian people they idealized. Despite this, it was the Slavophiles who posed the problem of what could and should be drawn from the national reality in order to achieve the more liberal world of which they dreamed. It was they who pointed the way, the hopes for Russia's liberation. Once despotism had been removed, all progress would be assured. Thus, they were comparing Utopia with autocracy, and it was this utopian, religious attitude of theirs that led them away from liberty. Their reactionary fate did not derive from the feudal and aristocratic character of their ideas but from their abstract democratic attitude, their adoration of the Russian people.

Again in *Voprosy literatury*, through the words of S. A. Pokrovsky, the echo of the past years, of the stalinist era, replied to Yanov, showing that the sense of inferiority and the fear of the West have not disappeared from present-day Russia, and that their present form is just the same: a feeling of bitter nationalistic vindication (no. 5 [1969], pp. 117 ff.). Others contributed to this debate, including B. Egorov (no. 5, pp. 128 ff.), A. Dementev (no. 7, pp. 116 ff.), and I. Ivanov (no. 7, pp. 129 ff.). Ivanov rightly emphasized the fact that the Slavophiles were so convinced of the meekness of the Russian peasant, so persuaded that he neither intended to nor knew how to rebel, that one could conclude that it was possible and desirable to introduce and establish the freedom of the press in Russia. Ivanov insisted that the Slavophiles were actually opposed to the savage methods of combating barbarity, to revolutions, and to despotism. It is in this attitude that the deepest root of the renewed Soviet interest in these figures lies. It is an interest in men who were distant from the Russia of today, 19th-century romantics who for decades seemed to have been scorned and left in oblivion. An extensive movement of return toward ancient Russia, to the religion of their fathers, leads men to see the past differently and to consider and again appreciate values that seemed to have been destroyed or buried. (To be convinced of this, one only need observe the new attitude toward medieval Russian art or read the works of Pasternak or of Solzhenitsyn, or just see Tarkovsky's film on Andrei Rublev.) But, more significantly, one can see how this profound and varied movement extant in Russia today, eventually turns, as in the 1830s and as in the period of the development of Slavophilism, against an adversary, an enemy who is both feared and loathed, that is, against the despotic and bureaucratic state.

Another contributor to this debate, L. Frizman, stresses that the Slavophiles were a very small minority amid a great sea of reactionary nobles in the age of Nicholas I (no. 7, p. 148). Did not the utopian element that undoubtedly existed in the Slavophiles' ideas derive from this unequal struggle against the reality that overwhelmed them? As utopias go, writes E. Maimin, was not the idea of giving Western political forms to Russia in 1905 and 1917 also utopian? It is evident that today some profound and unexpected echoes are responding to the revived and subdued voice of the 19th-century Slavophiles. In the early 1960s, *Vosprosy literatury* had included an impassioned discussion on revolutionary populism. At the end of the decade, in 1969, there was a return to the more distant first origins of the intelligentsia, to an aspect that had remained in the shadows for many years; there was a return to the relationship between Russia and the Western world, from where there reemerged the ever-present problem of the despotic and bureaucratic state.

The discussion we have examined has another remarkable aspect. It quite clearly admits that outside Russia the Slavophiles and their historical significance had been discussed at length, well before it was decided to reopen the debate in the Soviet Union. As in the case of populism, there had been approximately a fifteen-year delay. Therefore, naturally, N. V. Riasanovsky's book, *Russia and the West in the Teachings of the Slavofiles: A Study of Romantic Ideology*, was recalled.[58] There was also mention, though perhaps not enough, of the work by Andrei Walicki, undoubtedly the most searching and intelligent investigation of these problems.[59] Other works named include the studies by Eberhard Müller, *Russischer Intellekt in Europäischer Krise. Ivan Kireevskij, 1806–1856*; the work by Peter K. Christoff, *An Introduction to Nineteenth Century Russian Slavophilism: A Study in Ideas, Vol. 1: A. S. Xomjakof*; and the revised and enlarged second edition of Robert Stupperich's work, *Jurij Samarin und die Anfänge der Bauernbefreiung in Russland*.[60] If to these we add the works published in recent years on the ever fascinating problem of the continual reflection and intertwining of the Western image of Russia and of the idea that Russia had about herself (e.g., that of Dieter Groh, or the more restricted and specialized but very useful work by Karsten Goehrke), and if from the Soviet side we add the detailed and clear, though somewhat dull and handbookish, work by N. A. Cagolov, we have before us the main elements of the recent rich discussion on the formation, among the Slavophiles of the 1830s and 1840s, of the ideological terrain in which populism set down its roots.[61]

Despite all the uncertainty, contradictions, and romantic vagueness, there is no doubt about the function and importance of men such as Kiereevsky, Khomyakov, and Koshelev. The feelings of rivalry, envy, love, and hate that the Western world had aroused in the Russians for centuries grew deeper, causing a painful awareness of the cost, mainly on a moral plane, of the works of Peter, Catherine, and Alexander. It also brought an awareness of the effort required to build a strong and powerful state modeled on the Western pattern but at the same time responding to Russia's deep need for expansion and power. After a century in which Russia struggled to follow Western Europe, to imitate and use her, there developed a profound disillusionment, an insurmountable repulsion toward the Europe that had come out of the French Revolution. The forms and opinions through which this disillusionment was expressed were taken from the West itself, from Saint-Simon and Thierry, from Louis Blanc and Carlyle, from Schelling and from the German romantics. But Russia's withdrawal into herself, the return to Russian tradition, cannot be explained exclusively by cultural influences and a simple repetition of forms. It is something deeper and less clear that was mingled with a growing distrust in Russia's capacity to become completely European, to reach the West on an economic, political, technical, and intellectual plane, and the fear of still being too weak and young to be able to accept the examples coming from outside her borders. This movement resulted in Russia seeking refuge not so much in Christianity (too universal to serve as a protection or shelter) as in the church; after all, the church really was local and Russian. And if orthodoxy became the religious utopia of this disillusionment and isolation, the people, the *narodnost*, and the traditional forms of the Russian village became its political and social utopea. They, too, developed slowly and uncertainly at the end of the 1830s. Eberhard Müller is right in saying that for a long time the *narodnost* remained a very problematic concept, not a certainty and a faith.[62] The same applies to the *obshchina* and the *mir*, which in the writings of the first Slavophiles are not real elements to be observed, studied, and understood, but rather a possible incarnation of a religious and social community with a mystic and orthodox content. It was only when Haxthausen joined in that the debate among the Slavophiles about the *obshchina* deepened. What a strange fate for the German baron who came to be considered the discoverer of the Russian peasant community. He did observe and describe it, and in doing so made no small contribution to bringing down to earth the Russians' discussions in the 1840s about the origin and nature of the *mir*. (He never used the word *obshchina* and is responsible for the fact that in the West the structure of the Russian village is generally referred to by the first and not the second of these words.)

Haxthausen was well aware of the fact that he was not dealing with an exclusively or typically Russian reality. He had come from Westphalia and had studied the agrarian regimes of Western Germany before studying Prussia and Russia. At least since the age of von Möser the problem of the mark, the primitive Germanic community, had been the subject of lively discussion among historians and agronomists in those regions. In his eyes, the Russian situation demonstrated a particularly remarkable and perfect survival of forms that had disappeared elsewhere.[63]

It was Slavophiles who gave Haxthausen's 'discovery' a national value, and by doing so assimilated it and made it their own. Their views of the *obshchina* were anything but unanimous. Some considered it an excellent element of Russian life, while others saw it as an obstacle to the country's economic improvement. These conflicting views reflected the debates on these subjects that had taken place earlier among the Russian nobility.[64] In the *obshchina*

Khomyakov saw the expression of orthodoxy, the cornerstone of Russian society, the seed of a better world in the future. Koshelev replied that it really was a matter of the survival of the youth of the Russian people. Such youth had long since vanished in the West. Self-administration was an illusion, as personal experience had already proved (in elections the strongest and the richest win and the spirit of unanimity is soon destroyed). Land is worked more effectively if it belongs to the peasant. Furthermore, the community spirit was dangerous. Should artisans, too, place their income in a communal account? And the landlords, 'should they join the *obshchina*? There would be nothing left to do but hand over our land, forests, fields, etc., to it. With the principle of the *obshchina* we will either reach the point of general collective property, that is, the end of all property, or we will do nothing but perpetuate the subdivision of the country into classes.' It was not the *obshchina* but the soil's fertility and the amount of available labor that had always determined the fate of Russian agriculture. Only someone like Haxthausen who had not lived in Russia could speak enthusiastically about the peasant communities, concluded Koshelev.

Khomyakov countered these remarks with his historic, aesthetic, and above all moral and religious view of the *obshchina*, without confronting the economic and technical problems that his friend had raised.[65] It was in this contrast between ideology and technology, between the religious ideal and economic needs, that the vision of the Russian village became crystallized during the 1840s and 1850s and greatly influence the reforms of 1861.[66]

If this is the terrain from which populism was born, the revolutionary seed was sowed there by Herzen. The value and significance of his words—in 1848 and during the years of disillusionment, despair, and difficult recovery that followed the revolutionary period—have naturally continued to attract attention and arouse discussion in Russia and abroad.[67] Even in the past decade it has been possible to observe how Herzen remains a sensitive index, a barometer of the Russian intelligentsia's position; they regard him not only as their founder but also as an ever present secret adviser in times of doubt, difficulty, and the tragedies of daily existence. The edition of Herzen's works, begun in 1954 and completed in 1965 (the dates somehow seem symbolic),[68] can be considered a true monument to him. In its pages, Herzen's lucid, penetrating thought seems to be continually freeing itself from the rigid academic forms in which it was edited, to continue an ongoing dialogue on the problems of revolution and liberty. Its publication was followed by the appearance of photocopied editions (rare in Russian editorial policy) of the periodicals Herzen published, *Polyarnaya zvezda* and *Kolokol*.[69] The Soviet scholars who participated in these publications collected their observations, *trouvailles*, and reflections in a miscellany.[70] The volume begins with one of Herzen's previously unpublished thoughts, edited and commented upon by Oksman; it shows extremely clearly how aware Herzen was of his own role and that of the Occidentalists. On May 24, 1862, he wrote:

Only the powerful thought of the West, the last expression of its long historical development, could have stirred to life the germ that slumbered in the breast of the patriarchal
order of the Slavic people. The *artel* [the workers' association] and the rural commune,
the division of products and of fields, the communal assembly and the union of villages
in self-governing arrondissements, all this will serve to establish our future regime of
national liberty. But these establishments are nothing more than scattered stones, and
without Western thought the edifice of our future would never have more than its
foundations.[71]

Herzen reached this conclusion after considerable hesitation and vacillation.
For him, as for the Slavophiles, disillusionment with the West had been one of
the most powerful forces driving him to seek a reason to live in and have hopes
for Russia. Herzen's disillusionment was not rooted in the pettiness and mean-
ness of the age of Louis Philippe. His wound was caused by the defeat of the
Parisian workers in June 1848, the impossibility of France's becoming an
active supporter of Poland and Italy, and the fact that France had become an
open enemy of Mazzini's Roman republic. In Herzen's eyes the West had
proved itself incapable of living up to the very ideals it had created. Would
Russia be able to make them live again and to develop them on her own soil?
Even in his worst moments of desperation, Herzen did not lose faith in the
people and the intellectuals of his country.

The most important documents in this dialogue between Herzen and the
West have been studied by Michel Cadot, an expert on the relationship
between Russia and the West during the early 19th century. Cadot's edition of
Jules Michelet's *Légendes democratiques du Nord*, which includes much previously unknown material, is a substantial contribution to the understanding of
the world in which Herzen's ideas were maturing.[72] However, what has not
been adequately discussed, either in Russia or abroad, is the political tangle in
Herzen's ideas at the height of the revolution when, in a unique way, he tried
to unite his admiration for Proudhon with his hope in Blanqui. The problems
and contradictions of the populism and socialism of the 1860s and 1870s were
already germinating during Herzen's intense experiences in Rome, Paris,
Geneva, and then, when he was defeated, in Nice. The theme of his disillusionment is central to the work of Vera Piroschkow.[73] We can gather what
Herzen's activities were in those years only indirectly from the first pages of
Eberhard Reissner's work.[74] Lampert, who has provided us with a vivid
portrait of Herzen, does not treat the burning political and social issues of the
1848 revolution or Herzen's participation in it.[75] So let us look at the most
important book on Herzen published in some time, by Martin Malia. In its
pages there is certainly at least a partial answer to the questions we have
asked.[76] It is only partial because the author's perspective is psychological
rather than historical. The title promises *The Birth of Russian Socialism*. But to
understand Russian socialism we are taken through the young Herzen's rebellion against his father and his family, the stress under which he developed—in
effect, a kind of historical psychoanalysis. This is always a difficult, uncertain,

and unreliable method to apply, even to a man like Herzen, who wrote so much and so confessionally. Would it not be better to understand the political problems of the 1848 revolution, observing and comprehending the meaning and significance of the replies Herzen tried to give day by day, month by month? Naturally, Malia tries to do this, but his psychological method leads him to explain Herzen through Herzen rather than to see his concrete actions. There is a grave risk of imprisoning a character in a closed, individual, and often impenetrable existence. The biographical method—used very effectively by Malia in following an individual's activity in his world—is as fruitful as the psychological method is uncertain; the latter fatally detaches the individual from his own actions and from his own environment. Thus, for Malia, Herzen's 'crucial year' is 1847, when Herzen left Russia for good, rather than 1848 or 1849 when he was seeking a way out of the contradictions of the European and Parisian revolution. Malia concentrates more on Herzen's travels and adventures than on his books and pamphlets, his discussions and ideas, which really were what Herzen lived for in those years. The relationship between the revolution of 1848 and those of 1789 and 1793, the problem of the French state, the profound influence of Proudhon, and Herzen's understanding of Blanqui's will to insurrection, these were at the 'birth of Russian socialism' more than Herzen's personal drama and his extraordinary psychology. Moreover, we can taste the fruits of that psychology directly in every page of Herzen's marvelous writings which give us immediate contact with his moral, political, and intellectual experiences. But the historian must look for the political experiences through the political and social logic of Herzen's era.

Herzen wrote with a mastery and originality unequaled by any of his contemporaries and friends who, in those decisive years, were creating the new populist, radical, and socialist ideas of the Russian intelligentsia. He surpassed Bakunin, whose letters from his youth are nevertheless so vivid as to make us regret that they have not been published again in the Soviet Union. He was unequaled by Belinsky, who along with Herzen was the greatest contributor to the formation of the intelligentsia's mentality. It is interesting to observe how political and academic bias and censorship in the Soviet Union have often divided this group of friends in recent historical research. Belinsky, entrusted to historians of literature, is separated from Bakunin, who has only recently and partially emerged from the shadows where his later anarchic ideas had placed him, and from Herzen, who has ascended to the heavens of the great men and thus is often prevented from continuing the very human dialogue that he had held with these and other friends in St. Petersburg and Moscow.[77]

If we want to relive and participate in the intensity of the feelings that bore the seed of later populist protests and revolt, we must open the works of Julian Gregorovich Oksman. For example, let us consider his work devoted to the famous letter Belinsky wrote to Gogol on July 3, 1847, or his essay on the continuity and detachment between Belinsky and the political traditions of the Decembrists.[78] Here a psychological incentive is certainly not lacking, even if it is restricted by the rigid integrity of philological and historical research. In these pages we find the authentic tradition of the intelligentsia, where liberty is conquered with difficulty, is always threatened, and is worth defending by any means, including a double or aesopian language. For both Oksman and Herzen, Belinsky's letter to Gogol is, in Herzen's words, not only 'something ingenious' but also 'his testament.' Oksman recognizes its power and its historical importance through the effect it had on his friends, on Bakunin (who used the letter as a starting point for a speech in Paris on November 29, 1847, which caused him to be exiled from France), on Herzen who spoke of it in an unforgettable way in *My Past and Thoughts* ('I felt a lump in my throat and remained silent for a long time . . .'), on I. S. Turgenev ('Belinsky's letter to Gogol is my whole religion'), on N. I. Sazonov, and on P. V. Annenkov. Not only is Belinsky's political position with respect to his contemporaries established, but it is also defined in comparison with his predecessors, like the Decembrist exile N. I. Turgenev whose book *La Russie et les russes*, published in early 1847, had no small influence on the formulation of Belinsky's 'minimal program.'

This is a theme that Oksman takes up again and develops in his essay 'Belinsky and the Political Traditions of the Decembrists.' Here too the problem is both difficult and subtle. How and to what extent did the echo of an ill-fated and defeated struggle for liberty, like that of the Decembrists, reach a new generation during Nicholas I's age of repression and tyranny? How did it reach people like the young Belinsky, who continued on the road without daring to look back or to question those who had preceded them, and who, like Belinksy, sometimes ended up condemning them for their past failures, for their historical deficiencies? When Oksman talks about Gogol, and also when he follows the difficult legacy of the Decembrists, in both cases the conclusion he suggests seems evident. The message of liberty, he tells us, does not let itself be submerged, and the request for democracy, even if limited or partial, and even if it is smothered, still forms the seed for a deep renewal of revolutionary will.

Outside the Soviet Union such problems were certainly less pressing, even in the 1960s. In the West the door was opened wider (and a sacred text assures us that this is not always an advantage). There was a broader perspective in placing these distant and hidden conflicts, which were emerging from underground in the Russia of Nicholas I, into their correct historical place in the midst of a Europe that was undergoing the 1848 revolution. If Edward J. Brown's book on Stankevich suffers from too much political and ideological detachment, others by Scheibert, Lampert, Schapiro, and Pomper managed to achieve a sounder historical reconstruction.[79]

The first years of Alexander II's reign, the liberation of the peasants, and the beginning of the age of reform substantially confirmed Herzen's and Belinsky's intuition. Liberty was revolutionary in Russia. Each reform would raise the problem of a complete transformation of Russian society. In one decade, conventionally called the 1860s, though it was actually the period from 1854 to 1864, there was a movement from a timid emergence of liberalism and Slavophilism in the early part of the century to the formation of a socialist and revolutionary movement which in later decades could not be eradicated from Russian lands. What was the reason for such an important change?

For decades, people had continued to look back at the 1860s in times of crisis, in periods of uncertainty in Russian society. It was natural, too, that even a century later, between 1954 and 1964, Soviet writers (consider Pasternak) and historians emerging from the despotism of the Stalinist era should look back to the age of reform, the end of peasant servitude, the development of the student movement and of the first *Zemlya i Volya*, and this tempestuous dawn of liberty. What could they tell us about such an important period in their country?

One must admit that on the level of economic and social history the answer has been inadequate. It has been tirelessly repeated that capitalism had developed sufficiently in Russia to lead fatally to the dissolution of feudal bonds. This was just repetition of an ancient chorus, and did not restate the problems of Russian society in the middle of the last century. It did not bring an understanding of the details of the process of industrialization in Russia. Nor did it ask what the real situation was at the beginning of the reign of Alexander II. The answers in this area did not come from Soviet historians but from across the ocean, from American scholars such as Emmons and especially from Alexander Gerschenkron, in the pages of his economic history of Russia written for the *Cambridge Economic History* (vol. 6, 1965) and later included in his volume *Continuity in History and Other Essays*.[80] Halfway, so to speak, between the Americans and the Russians are the French scholars, with a *Recueil d'articles et de documents*, organized by R. Portal and entitled *Le Statut des paysans libérés du servage. 1861–1961*.[81] The traditional interpretation has not been expressly questioned, but in itself the material presented in this work is so rich, especially Confino's contribution, as to cause one to seriously reconsider the very bases of the problem.

The Russians too have contributed to the debate, and not insignificantly. Among communist historians, the idea of the passage from feudalism to capitalism had generally been accompanied by the affirmation that this transformation, even if required by the changed economic situation, had to find its own driving force in the revolt of the peasant masses, in the revolutionary drive of the *muzhiki*, who rebeled against the burden of their lords and masters. This brought about the studies, including some very valuable ones, on the peasant movements, uprisings, and repression by the state. But in the 1930s and 1940s a significant obstacle evidently arose in the Soviet Union. Even the finest scholars (like Ignatovich, for example) who came from the prerevolutionary period, or who carried on the great tradition of peasant history which is one of the cornerstones of Russian historiography, evidently had to mark time. In those Stalinist years one could still study and investigate the revolts of the *muzhiki* in the archives. But a reinterpretation of the facts or reflection on the nature, character, and value of these obscure rebellions was certainly not encouraged. Stalin, convinced as he was that the populists should be abandoned in silence, was equally convinced that the only acceptable peasant revolts were those that had come from above. The situation in rural Russia after the collectivization in 1929 certainly did not invite close study of the rebellions and revolts that had accompanied the reforms of 1861. Soon there developed one of those dissociated and contradictory situations so common in the intellectual life of the Soviet Union. On one hand, the moving force behind the reforms had been the rebellious peasants; on the other, it was better not to look too closely at these village movements. The revolutionary myth was hovering over reality without illuminating it or penetrating it.

The situation was even more peculiar if we recall that Alexander II, too, had preferred revolutions from above rather than from below. It was he who had promulgated this expressive and typical formula. In fact, the process through which the 1861 reforms were carried out, their consequences in later decades, and their function in the development of industrialization in the country all seemed to confirm what the men of the *Narodnaya Volya* had clearly foreseen. The state had played a decisive role in this process. The revolution from above not only represented a defensive reaction by the emperor and the nobles, it responded to a profound need of the whole social life in Russia, where transformation could only come from above, through the machinery of the state. This was simply because the classes and groups that were capable of moving the Russian giant toward the modern world were too weak economically and too impotent socially. Thus in a historiographical plan, it is natural that the best and most careful research was directed, not at the buried truths of the 19th-century Russian villages, but rather at understanding the plans and reality that had preceded or accompanied the first ten years of Alexander II's reign. One only need consider the now classic works of Druzhinin and Zayonchkovsky. The latter undertook to explode the myths of the peasant revolt, which in the Soviet Union had often fallen into a pattern of retrospective revolutionary rhetoric, and to clear the field of the grave methodological errors that had spoiled these studies. But, above all, he faced a task that could no longer be deferred, that of providing a history of the politics of the Russian state during the second half of the 19th century.

Some of Zayonchkovsky's battles have been won, and he can even allow himself some irony, for example, when he describes the methods by which statistics on the 19th-century peasant movements were, and, we fear, are, constructed.

Unfortunately, we do not have precise data on the breadth of the peasant movement. The method for their computation has not been given in detail, and the figures concerning it recall the 'statistical' method which consists of summing two phenomena of completely different dimensions (following the principle: 'One camel plus one chicken'). Thus a peasant uprising in which thousands of people took part is considered as one unit, and at the same time the refusal to do forced labor by a handful of peasants also counts as one unit. . . . The second defect found in the historiography of the peasant movement lies in the constant effort to augment the dimensions of the uprisings (letting oneself be guided by the principle: 'the more uprisings, and more important the research'). Unfortunately, this tendency became very widespread, especially in the work of minor historians, but not only among them.[82]

In reading these statistics and skimming the numerous documents published recently on the peasant movement in Russia (a collection under this very title and composed of large and basic volumes was published about twenty years ago under the direction of Druzhinin[83]), we are faced with the thought of what the French historians of the *Annales* school might make of it. Meanwhile, some advances have been made toward the use of the tools of anthropology in the interpretation of the dreams, hopes, and utopias of the *muzhiki*.[84] But this line of inquiry, though suggestive, is obviously not the road to understanding of the age of reform under Alexander II. In the center of the picture, even in Soviet historiography, lies the political problem.

Here is the standard form, repeated thousands of times, used in the Soviet Union to define the problem: 'revolutionary situation in Russia between 1859 and 1861.' A group of historians, following the initiative of the Academy of Sciences of the USSR and directed by M. V. Nechkina, undertook a study of this theme. With great care they collected an impressive amount of material, debates, and conclusions published, at least in part, in five volumes in a large and important miscellany which came out between 1960 and 1970.[85] Every aspect of these three years was examined, from the problems of the czar's government to the peasant movement, from the development of the first clandestine organization to the mood of the intelligentsia. All this was held together by the idea of the 'revolutionary situation' which Russia had experienced on the eve of and at the time of the application of the manifesto for the liberation of the serfs. Naturally, the formula comes from Lenin, who long since had matured it and expressed it in its clearest and most definitive form in his article, 'Failure of the Second International,' published in the journal *Kommunist* in June 1915:

What are the signs of a revolutionary situation? We will not be mistaken if we point them out in these three elements: 1) the impossibility of the dominant classes maintaining their dominion unchanged, one crisis or another among those who are in high positions, a crisis in the politics of the dominant class that creates a division through which the discontent and wrath of the oppressed classes erupts. For the revolution to take place, it is usually not enough for 'those who are on the bottom not to accept it anymore,' but it is necessary that those who are above 'can no longer live as before'; 2) the intensification beyond the normal level of the needs and the difficulties among the oppressed classes; 3) an increase, due to the causes mentioned, of the activity of the masses, who in peaceful times let themselves be preyed upon without protesting, and who in times of turmoil, as in any crisis situation, are driven to make their own protests, as much as 'those who are above.'[86]

As an example of such a revolutionary situation, Lenin mentions Germany in the 1860s and 'the years 1859–61 and 1879–80 in Russia.'

Soviet superstition had transformed this simple example into a true procrustean bed. How could one make the revolutionary situation terminate in 1861 when it was evident that the crises of the ruling class and popular discontent had augmented and deepened after 1861, all through 1862, and in 1863? (As we know, that was the year when a revolution actually did occur, though it was not the revolution of the Russian peasants, but of the most important nation oppressed by czarism, that is, Poland.) The distortion caused by this erroneous chronology became even more serious if one considered what, from the revolutionary point of view, was the most important element and the one that left the biggest mark in the future. This was the emergence and the consolidation of a true party intent on interpreting and leading the peasant revolt and defeating the Russian autocracy. The more closely one observed this process of the formation of the first *Zemlya i Volya*, the more evident it was that it had not reached a point of consolidation and did not become a true secret society until the final months of 1861. The height of its operation was in 1862 and continued into 1863. The numerous attempts to make it exist and function before the manifesto of February 19, 1861 merely created a series of hypotheses and suppositions that could not stand up to a critical examination of the facts. The book by Ya. I. Linkov, which came out in 1964, marked the end of these vain attempts to make Herzen and Chernyshevsky the heads of a mysterious conspiracy, when in fact their function was to be the creators of the revolutionary and populist animus in 19th-century Russia. Linkov put an end to the conspiratorial theory that had been superimposed on a historic reality, made, in fact, of free initiative, profound revolts, and desperate individual research in the midst of the contradictions in the situation created in Russia in the decade between 1854 and 1864.[87]

Naturally, this end was precarious and provisional, so that there was no lack of backsliding. The temptation to replace the free creation of new ideas and new political forces with organizations, plots, and conspiracies continued even in the most recent Soviet historiography. A hard, dry, gray cement still tends to imprison and immobilize men as free as Herzen, or those young men who created the customs, morality, and psychology of the Russian revolutionary. What they left within the solidified Soviet ideology seems like fossil remains. To find them alive one first has to crack the enveloping rock. It is necessary to do so, for example, in reading the volume by N. N. Novikova called *Revolyutsionery 1861 goda* (The revolutionaries of 1861). Even this very obvious title is taken from Lenin. And a real Leninist obsession induces the author, in discussing the relationship between the Velikoruss group and the developing *Zemlya i Volya*, to use arguments of the following kind against the historian Linkov: 'In this case Ya. I. Linkov does not contradict our opinion but that of V. I. Lenin, who called the members of the Velikoruss "leaders of the democratic movement" and linked them to the names of Chernyshevsky,

Dobrolyubov, and their companions.'[88] And to think that Novikova carried out considerable research even—and this is rare in the Soviet Union—in private archives. But nothing stands up, everything gives way before a generic definition, a journalistic mention, a simple list of examples which Lenin compiled by chance.

An overall view of the work carried out in Russia on the period of the first 'revolutionary situation' (naturally shifting its chronology, as many, in fact most, Soviet scholars did more or less silently) establishes first of all that the new material gathered is important. One need only consider the academic edition of Herzen's works, completed in 1965; or the editions of the works of Dobrolyubov, of N. A. Serno-Solovevich, of Ogarev; or the patient reprinting of the recollections and memoirs of Panteleyev, Sleptsov, Shelgunov, Mikhailov, and many others; or the very complete research that has been done on the Polish revolution of 1863 and the participation in it by the men of the Zemlya i Volya. One need only list the titles from the veritable library created in the past fifteen years about the first decade of Alexander II's reign to realize how much interest and what results have come from work on these problems. Men and facts put so much pressure on the preconceived outlines, deforming them, distorting them until one would expect to see them broken down. Is the monotonous repetition of the classic quotations in the introductions and conclusions of so much of this research really any guarantee that these traditional outlines have not been broken down in the minds of those who confronted them with the problems and results of their own research. It remains a formal compliance with an ideological ritual which already is devoid of substance.

The main problem of the 1860s had been the relationship between the reviving desire for liberty and the need that was developing for equality and then for social revolution. These two ideas and these two aspirations had arisen together during the Crimean War and after the death of Nicholas I. They took on dozens of different forms in the debates between Herzen and Chicherin, Herzen and Kavelin, Chernyshevsky and Turgenev, Herzen and Chernyshevsky, Herzen and Dobrolyubov, Ogarev and Serno-Solovevich, Bakunin and the Polish revolutionaries, and others in every aspect of that period. If that era were to be judged solely on the fervor with which liberty and equality were experienced and discussed, it undoubtedly would merit the Leninist definition of the 'revolutionary situation.'

In the Soviet Union, the greatest temptation was to date the split between the liberals and socialists further back than it had actually occurred. There was a further temptation to establish a much deeper and wider division between them than had actually existed. By contrast, in the West the greatest temptation was often to try to establish a Russian liberal tradition quite separate from the populist and revolutionary tradition and to set it apart from the revolutionary tradition as distinctly as possible. In 1957, Victor Leontovitsch began this trend with his Geschichte des Liberalismus in Russland.[89] The next year George Fischer continued it with his study, Russian Liberalism: From

Gentry to Intelligentsia.[90] The historiographic and juridical aspect, a very important element of Russian liberalism, was examined by Klaus Detlev Grothusen in *Die historische Rechtsschule Russlands. Ein Beitrag zur russichen Geistesgeschichte in der zweiten Hälfte des 19. Jahrhunderts.*[91] This trend reached its culmination in a brilliant little book by Leonard Schapiro, *Rationalism and Nationalism in Russian Nineteenth-Century Political Thought.*

The result of all these efforts, which have brought to light a whole world that had been buried under the ruins of the Russian revolutions, seems very clear: once an insurmountable gap had been established between the liberals and the Russian revolutionaries (that is, between Chicherin and Herzen), the liberalism of the czarist era increasingly clearly revealed its conservative character, and it seemed better suited to the renewed attempt at enlightened despotism that was one of the main aspects of the reign of Alexander II. In fact, these liberals desired a state of law more than political liberty. They believed more in the state machinery, in laws, and in the courts than in a constitution or an open political struggle. They emphasized judicial guarantees more than freedom of the press. And we must not forget that they too lived, not only in the age of Alexander II, but also in the age of Napoleon III and Bismarck. Thus, to use again the particularly important and characteristic example of Chicherin, if Chizhevsky had been able to consider him a 'classical liberal'[92] and Leontovitsch could speak of him as a man of 'liberaler Konservatismus,'[93] it was not by chance that George Fischer found in the German but not in the British tradition the suitable word to express his thoughts and called him a 'Rechtsstaat liberal.'[94] Schapiro concluded by saying that Chicherin, 'one of the most outstanding intellects of the Russian nineteenth century,' had been 'too liberal to be welcomed by the conservatives, and too conservative to be accepted by the liberals. The unity and consistency of his thought justify the application to him of the epithet which Viasemsky chose for Pushkin—liberal conservative.'[95] One can understand, after reading such opinions, why Richard Pipes concluded that the theme to be studied in 19th-century Russia was the conservative trend rather than the liberal.[96]

Fortunately, this historical separation between liberty and revolution, between liberalism and populism (of which both Westerners and Russians are guilty), was made unreal by the life of the 1860s, by the incontrovertible fact that liberalism, Slavophilism, radicalism, and populism were born in the same social world, the world of the intelligentsia. The men of both tendencies were not cold adversaries and enemies, but passionate friends who suffered deeply in the conflicts, clashes, and differences that arose between them. This is made abundantly clear in the relationship between Herzen, Chicherin, Chernyshevsky, and Dobrolyubov. It is not just by chance that their differences have been so thoroughly studied in recent years. Against every forced division between those who live and suffer together there is always a man of genius, Alexander Ivanovich Herzen, who evades all academic labels or classification related to party politics. To anyone who opens the new and accurate

edition of his complete works, the explanations, often repeated in Soviet literature, of his 'liberal illusions' must seem weak and vain. Herzen is the last man
in the world to become an icon or a portrait of 'socialist realism.' In every
page, he repeatedly poses the question of the relationship between liberty and
revolution.

Something similar could be said although on a different level, of Ogarev,
who finally emerged from the limbo where he had been left for years, or of
Dobrolyubov, who with his deep and passionate moralism played an important part in separating the liberals from the radicals. The same could also be
said of Chernyshevsky, the key figure for understanding the birth of the revolutionary movement in Russia, who is finally, though slowly, being freed from
the icon where he too had been placed. He speaks to us especially in his *Letters
without an Address*, about his last hope and that of his companions, about their
last effort to show a democratic and liberal way out of the crisis caused by the
emancipation of the peasants. In his young friends and followers, Nikolai and
Aleksander Serno-Solovevich, we already see the consolidation of the revolutionary party when the doors were closed to all other developments. (And for
them, and for Chernyshevsky, the doors were prison doors.) These young men,
also, were too strong to remain perpetually deformed and mutilated by the
reaction. Their desire for liberty (even in a liberal and constitutional form, as
with Nikolai Serno-Solovevich, for example) stands out clearly in their writing, even when the Soviet presenters wish to see it as little as possible.

Despite all these rediscoveries, and despite the need for a general view of this
whole period, a history of the ten years from 1854 to 1864, of the great drama
of the reform and the birth of the revolutionary movement, has still not
appeared in Russia. Clearly, this period must have attracted the passionate
attention of the Soviets. It contained a crisis after a long period of dictatorship; reforms imposed from above; a desire to give life to a *Rechtsstaat*, without arriving at liberty and democracy; repeated attempts to use old tools to
confront new problems; and a new sense of futility and fatigue deriving from
this policy of administering the reforms just as absolutism had been administered before. Finally came the explosion of rage, of nihilism, of bile, as Herzen
called it, before the doors that had opened briefly but were now closed, the disappointed hopes. How could all this drama of the 1860s not have interested
the Russians a century later? They were undergoing a crisis that, though
certainly different, had many points common with the 19th-century one. It
was not a matter of taking the passions of the present back to the past; that
had already been overdone in Soviet historiography during the Stalinist age.
One should not yield to the temptation of again painting Herzen and
Chernyshevsky, Dobrolyubov and Serno-Solovevich in one's own image. One
had to achieve more complete and objective historical research. There had
been a step in this direction, and it had produced good results. Nevertheless,
if a more integral historical view did not develop, it was because the basic
problem was not solved. On the political level, liberty had not won, and on the

historical level the interweaving in the relationship between liberalism, socialism, and populism had not been examined and fully unraveled. The outlines of
the 'revolutionary democracy' of the 1860s, of the 'revolutionary situation' of
1859–61, were weakened, stretched, and deformed, but they were not abandoned. A historical view in which Herzen and Kavelin, Chernyshevsky and
Chicherin, Alexander II and Zaichnevsky each had his own function (no
longer classed as elect or reprobate) seemed to emerge slowly, but it did not
achieve the required clarity and firmness.

Both inside and outside the Soviet Union, what has remained vivid and
poignant is the sense of bitterness and disappointment caused by the destruction of so many hopes, of so many illusions born in the years of preparation
for Alexander II's reforms, of so many sacrifices engulfed and annihilated by
the great Russian state machine. The 'revolutionary situation,' seen as a whole
and in its development, again took on the appearance that it had had in the
eyes of the most sensitive and passionate of its contemporaries, that is, the
form of a failed revolution. It was no great consolation to affirm that there had
been figures like Chernyshevsky, who had had the intelligence and the lucidity
to foresee such a failure. What was more important historically was to observe,
in a case as interesting as this one, whether disappointment had aroused the
revolt, and whether a new revolutionary will had emerged from the failure.
The men of the first *Zemlya i Volya* had briefly hoped that a *jacquerie* would
arise from the disappointment experienced by the great peasant masses once
they had recognized the injustices and the deception that existed to their own
detriment, when they had understood that liberty obtained from above was
that of the lords and of the state, not that of the people and of the villages. Yet
it was the revolutionaries of those first clandestine organizations who were
forced to acknowledge that the peasant movements diminished between 1861
and 1863 and that this last date had not marked, as they had hoped, the
beginning of a general revolt.

Then, in 1863, the revolutionary intellectuals, ready for any sacrifice just in
order to stand with the Poles in their revolt against the czarist state, had to
recognize that the Polish insurrection had only served to unleash the most
violent forms of nationalism and reaction in Russia. The students of those
years who had hoped for a life in an entirely new culture soon had to accept
the only path that seemed open to them: they had to abandon the lecture halls,
cultivate individual detachment, and deny all culture. This was the situation,
the terrain in which the Russian nihilism of the 1860s took root. The first
person to realize its importance and its danger was Herzen ('Very dangerous!!!'
was the title of his first call of alarm). It then spread, taking on the most
diverse and contradictory forms, absorbing elements of Schopenhauer's
philosophy, of French radicalism from the last years of the Second Empire,
and of Darwinism and positivist science. Yet deep down, from the first *Zemlya
i Volya* to the tragic failure of Nechaev's *Narodnaya Rasprava*, it preserved an
element of powerless rage, of disillusioned protest when confronted with the

failed revolution from which this nihilism had been born and had developed.

In order to truly understand the bitter ferment, the first thing to do, as Vittorio Strada has suggested, is to reconsider Herzen's writings, which after a hundred years are still extraordinarily vivid and penetrating in their analysis of the state of mind of the protesters of a century ago.[97] The other way, followed more frequently in the past decade, leads to a close examination of the writings of the major nihilists of those times, of Pisarev as well as of the most important journal of that tendency, the *Russkoe slovo*. Again, the international situation in which this ferment developed has not been sufficiently considered in Russia. The results of A. Coquart's research, published in Paris in 1946, have not been sufficiently appreciated in Moscow and Leningrad (for example, in matters regarding the relationship between Pisarev's and Carl Vogt's ideas). One parallel in particular—that is, the simultaneous discussion of Darwin's ideas in America and in Europe—has been omitted. Regarding the social effects of this debate, and the elitist and racist consequences it may have produced, Robert Hofstadter's *Social Darwinism in American Thought* seems essential. Only in this way can B. P. Kozmin's valuable ideas and observations on Pisarev and his era have a less restricted and esoteric meaning, and almost become symbols or signs of an internal dialogue in the Russian and Soviet intelligentsia which has continued uninterrupted for a century.

Already in 1929, Kozmin had opened a wide path to an intelligent reconsideration of these problems in his article 'D. I. Pisarev and Socialism,' recently reprinted in a posthumous collection of his essays.[98] From the suffocating sense of the impossibility of achieving the revolution, which dominated the Russian intellectuals of the 1860s, Kozmin had gone back to the results of the failure of the 1848 revolution, thus expanding the Russian drama of the age of reforms to all of Europe. In this light, the function of the intellectuals—of the 'proletariat of thought,' as Pisarev called them—had seemed all the more essential. This was not an exclusively Russian concept, and naturally it could be found in the West. But while in the West the proletariat of thought had turned its attention to the working class, in Russia the situation had soon proved profoundly different. In Russia, the proletariat of thought was poorer and less powerful than anywhere else. It tried futilely to open the way to cooperatives, to mutual aid, to any kind of defense organization, as it was even more defenseless than the peasants themselves. 'The peasant had his house, a little plot of land'; the proletariat of thought had none of this.[99] All attempts to impose itself, to make itself indispensable, seemed to fail. Before the young intelligentsia lay an abyss. *Hic Rhodus, hic salta*. In fact, having exhausted efforts to save itself alone, or to dream of systems as a ruling class, to regard itself as an elite, in the early 1870s the proletariat of thought ended up carrying out its 'go to the people' movement. As Kozmin concluded, 'This was why that trend in our social thought, represented by Pisarev, really had only one short-lived victory, despite the brilliant victories recorded in the second half of the 1860s. Then they had to give the initiative to the adversary, to

populism, which looked to the peasants. After this date, Pisarev had many
attentive readers, but he no longer had anyone to exalt him and follow him
with enthusiasm.'[100]

In an essay written in 1941 but not published before it was included in the
collection mentioned, Kozmin had tried to find a reconfirmation of his interpretation of nihilism in the reactions and polemics of the populist writer
Saltykov-Shchedrin.[101] The true enemies of the proletariat of thought, of the
young Russian revolutionaries of the 1860s, he said, were not the liberals but
the absolutism and the despotism of the czar. Chernyshevsky had said so in his
Letters without an Address. Herzen had not tired of repeating this. But these
truths could not be stated in the Stalinist era. Nevertheless, as the recent
publisher of his works points out, Kozmin had not accepted the Stalinist interpretation which had become an axiom of Soviet historiography in the 1940s
and which on close examination was nothing but 'a transposition to the field of
study of the thesis that considered social democracy in Western Europe as the
basic enemy of communism.'[102] For Kozmin, deep inside every phase of the
whole Russian revolutionary movement, including nihilism, lay the problem of
the relationship between liberty and revolution.

In recent years, studies on the nihilist period and on Pisarev have multiplied.
This is evident from the two books by F. Kuznetsov and by L. E. Varustin on
the *Russkoe slovo*, the main journal of this trend. We also see that, though the
time since the 1920s has not passed in vain, the mark of the Stalinist period has
not disappeared. In these two books, but especially in the first, there is a
striking element of naiveté. The authors seem to rediscover the men and the
Europe of the 19th century, almost as if they were very distant and unusual
people and lands. They are carried away by the radicalism, the drive, the
extremism of their compatriots of a hundred years before, without sufficiently
investigating the side of them that is darker, stranger, and more disquieting.
The division—or, as it was then called, the 'schism'—between 'nihilists,' that
is, between the readers of Pisarev and those of Saltykov-Shchedrin, is ex-
tenuated by the effort to reconcile posthumously the contenders of a common
progressive faith.

Something of this too normal, too positive view also remains perhaps in
works that are nevertheless considered among the best recent books on the
Russian revolutionary movement between the end of the Polish insurrection
and the 1866 assassination attempt. These works are R. V. Filippov's *The
Populist Revolutionary Organization of N. A. Ishutin and I. A. Khudyakov
(1863–66)*, published in Petrozavodsk in 1964, and the book by E. S.
Vilenskaya, *The Revolutionary Underground in Russia (The 1860s)*, published
in Moscow in 1965. The authors' research is in depth, and they have clarified
numerous complicated questions, exploding long-standing myths and retriev-
ing men and facts that had fallen into oblivion. What does not reappear is the
atmosphere of the 'underground.' One wonders if the authors, especially
Vilenskaya, actually asked themselves what might have been the ideas that

drove Khudyakov to the people and what put a revolver in Karakozov's hand. Filippov speaks of 1865 as a 'phase of tormented uncertainty and tactical research.'[103] Was it really only tactical? The author adds, 'One need only imagine the political atmosphere in Russia in 1864–65 to understand how natural was the fact that some leaders of Ishutin's group began to develop a conspiratorial mentality.'[104] Natural? The desire to create a close group of revolutionaries and terrorism are not so easily explained. The conspiracy's choice of the name 'Inferno' and expectation of completely abnormal behavior from its members were facts that stirred the imagination of contemporaries and became a basis for wild tales, but it must not be rejected and set aside.

Soviet scholars in the 1960s tried to explain the explosion of the conspiratorial mentality not only through the depressed situation in the 1860s but also by attributing particular weight and value to political elements that were foreign to the world of the populists and which then penetrated their movement, adding 'liberal' elements or even reviving clandestine Polish groups. Filippov and Vilenskaya and especially T. F. Fedosova have turned their attention to the existence of contact between Ishutin and Khudyakov's organization and elements of the ruling class who were dissatisfied with the policies of Alexander II, and also with Polish conspirators who were trying to pursue the conflict after the defeat of the 1863 insurrection.[105] The alleged witnesses are undoubtedly important. Vilenskaya has shown that Karakozov's trial was greatly distorted by internal quarrels within the emperor's entourage. Fedosova has stressed the importance of the clandestine Polish Committee and of its Siberian ramifications during this whole period of the Russian 'underground.' But still, these historians do not manage to find the meeting point between the tactical and organizational elements and the evolution of the ideas inside the revolutionary movement in those years.

Filippov is certainly correct in emphasizing the populist and socialist character of Ishutin and Khudyakov's organization. He is also right in pointing out how the need for liberty was deeply rooted in these young men's feelings. In fact, liberty was potentially anarchical, Proudhonian, and federalistic, since, as Filippov rightly indicates, the spread of Bakunin's ideas seemed to begin with the Muscovite ferment in the 1860s. Nevertheless, another liberty existed, a constitutional or democratic one. It reached the young men from outside, like the remains of the liberal ideas or linked with the Polish desire for independence. Ishutin and Khudyakov tended to solve the problems that were urgently put to them on a tactical and practical plane, not an ideological one. They were and remained socialists, and together they soon were prepared to use any means (conspiracy, assassination attempts, a conquest of power, an alliance with the liberals or with national movements) just to realize an ideal that the whole world around them seemed to negate and repudiate. The situation made them have doubts about the peasant revolt. Yet the people were the only social force capable of giving life to socialism. All means began to seem good as long as they destroyed this contradiction. 'This was the tragedy of populism,' concludes Vilenskaya. 'In fact, the idea of creating a "party" that would undertake the functions that the previous revolutionary generation had attributed to the popular masses contained the intuition, as yet unconscious, that the peasant could not win the struggle against autocracy without the guidance and organizational power of another class. And since this other class did not exist in Russia in the 1860s, there was nothing left for the revolutionaries but to shift the people's task to a 'party' and add considerable conspiratorial tactics to the idea of the peasant socialist revolution.'[106]

As we can see, the Marxist scheme provides the deus ex machina of this populist tragedy. But we must concentrate on this drama, which actually had no hope or faith in the proletarian messiah, if we want to understand the deep conflicts that lay in the hearts of these young men. Were the tensions and contradictions not deeply scarred by the corrosive acid of the nihilistic ideas and atmosphere of those years, as Filippov seems to maintain? There is explicit evidence of the hostility against Pisarev, of the polemic against the model of Bazarov presented by Turgenev in *Fathers and Sons*. Yet in Ishutin and Khudyakov's organization there was no lack of the cynicism, violence, and desperation against which Herzen had reacted and which led to the tragic events of Nechaev's life.

In the Soviet Union, after so many discussions and polemics in the 1920s, silence has fallen on Nechaev. It is the embarrassed silence of one who, having set out to look for the most genuine sources of the thoughts and inspiration of the Russian revolutionary movements, suddenly finds himself face to face with a monstrous product of that source. *Toute proportion gardée*, Soviet historians sometimes react to Nechaev as they do to Stalin, repeating rituals of condemnation with varying degrees of vigor, thus trying to ward off his possible reappearance, without really trying to investigate the nature of and reasons for his actions and his power. And, unlike Stalin's case, one actually could let silence fall on Nechaev who was studied so much in the past and on whom an entire curious little library of books has been written. Like those who have sinned and suffered much, he too could be accorded the oblivion applied to cases that are considered closed.

This could have happened if two men, Tkachev and Bakunin, whose intellectual and political background were very different from Nechaev's and whose lives crossed his, had not appeared to keep his memory alive. For both these revolutionaries, the episode of the young workman who became the violent, arrogant organizer of the *Narodnaya Rasprava*, the People's Summary Justice, did not pass without leaving deep marks. The history of their relationship still remains one of the most basic and revealing elements in the more intimate life of the Russian revolutionary movement between the 1860s and 1870s. If one adds that Nechaev left his mark on the entire evolution of the student movement during that period, as well as on events in Russian emigration, on Herzen's environment, on Herzen's daughter Natalia, and on Ogarev, one must conclude that it is impossible to try to reconstruct the development from

Nechaev's conspiracy to the 'go to the people' movement without recalling this disturbing figure. This was the first example of an element coming from the common people and penetrating the revolutionary intelligentsia, bringing a profound desire for action and at the same time momentarily breaking down moral and political bases. Nechaev is a *revenant* who cannot be exorcised.

The previously unknown documents on Nechaev published by Michael Confino are impressive. They confirm the criminal and abnormal characteristics that Nechaev was known to have and that were inextricably linked with an exceptional capacity for action and an even greater gift of making people listen to him and follow him. Above all, they are impressive because of the political and moral problems they pose. Here is Bakunin, one of the most famous revolutionaries of his times, a man who had seen the 1848 revolution and Siberia, who had literally gone around the world. And he let himself be conquered by an uncultured and violent boy, so much so as to see in him the incarnation of the Russian revolution that he was then theorizing and preaching about. Confino identifies the psychological and personal reasons for this attitude: Bakunin's incipient and premature old age, the vulnerability of his revolutionary passion in a time of historic calm, on the very eve of the tempest of the Franco-Prussian war and of the Commune. More significant are the roots and moral and ideological conclusions of this encounter and these clashes. No one has expressed them more clearly than Bakunin himself in a letter to Nechaev dated June 2, 1870, at a time when his enthusiasm was waning and a break between the two men began to emerge as the only logical outcome of their increasingly deep disagreements. This long letter deserves to remain one of the fundamental documents of the whole history of the Russian revolutionary movement.[107]

Ten years later, Bakunin was in the same situation in which Herzen had found himself before the first manifestations of nihilism. There was the additional aggravation that now the new Nechaevian incarnation of nihilism also seemed a consequence of his own thought, of his own weaknesses and hopes.

The *Revolutionary Catechism* that Bakunin had circulated along with his own written appeals, and which so many historians (including myself) attributed to him, now seems to be the fruit of Nechaev's despair, resentment, and desire for revenge and abuse. 'Votre catéchisme—un catéchisme d'*abrek*' (that is, a Georgian bandit's catechism), he writes in a phrase that seems to attribute the paternity and all the responsibility for the famous document to the young Russian. Whatever Bakunin's part in the writing, if there was any (and perhaps the question will always remain unresolved), the important fact is that now Bakunin repudiated the work, considering it foreign and unacceptable. In it, he had finally recognized a terrible urge for fanaticism and violence that was not even enlightened by a vision of a free and better world, but rather was darkened by a fiercely close and cruel concept of society. 'Your cruelty full of abnegation, [the Russian text is more expressive and profound: *samootverzhen-*

noe izuverstvo], your extreme fanaticism—you wish to make them . . . the rule of life for the community.' It was a desire for 'the total negation of the nature of man, and of society.'

Only religious fanatics and ascetics can dream of conquering nature; that is why I was astonished—but not too much so and not for long, to find in you a sort of mystic, pantheistic idealism. . . . Yes, my dear friend, you are not a materialist like the rest of us poor sinners, but an idealist, a prophet, a sort of monk of the revolution; your hero should not be Babeuf, nor even Marat, but one such as Savonarola. . . . In your way of thinking you are more like a Jesuit than like us. . . . You are a fanatic—therein lies your enormous and characteristic force, and there too is the cause of your blindness; but blindness is a great and deadly weakness, blind energy wanders and stumbles and, the more powerful it is, the greater and more inexorable its failures.'[108]

The foundations of Bakunin's thought were the Enlightenment and Rousseau, and reacted against Nechaev's fanaticism and machiavellianism; once the monstrous plant that had overgrown them had been painfully torn out and discarded, the bare foundations reappeared. Bakunin knew he had nourished the plant, but now he wanted to be freed from it. It was not just a matter of the more conspicuous aspects of Nechaev's mind, his continual deception, his indifference to evil and to crime itself. Bakunin wanted to deny, to shake off Nechaev's political substance. He reaffirms that only a 'spontaneous, popular, and social' revolution is admissible and desirable. 'It is my profound conviction that any other revolution is dishonest, harmful, and fatal to liberty and to the people.' The single goal of the revolutionary movement must be 'to awaken the spontaneous forces of the people, to make them cohere and to organize them.' Any attempt to replace them, to act in their name, to deceive them was damaging and futile. In Russia, only *l'idéal populaire* (we could call it populism) had the right to call itself revolutionary. Any conspiracy, any plot, any artificial device would only falsify and distort the profound movement of the country.

Yet, a few months earlier, Bakunin had seen in Nechaev an incarnation of this *révolution populaire (narodnaya revolyutsya)*. In addition to recognizing him for his energy and his violence, he had accepted not only his positive aspects but also his negative ones. Was it not perhaps Bakunin himself who for decades had wanted the unleashing of the 'evil passions,' the only ones capable of overturning the present society and of destroying the modern state? Had he not looked hopefully at the great and the petty bandits in the Russian popular world? And now, why protest against this *abrek*, this Russian boy who, in his eyes, had become a desperate Georgian bandit? Like Herzen ten years earlier, Bakunin had recognized in the first exponents of the Russian revolution, not only a spirit of dedication and a willingness for sacrifice, but also those profound distortions, those inevitable wounds that society and the Russian state had inflicted on their personalities. Now, faced with the figure of Nechaev, Bakunin too was faced with the reality of his country. Here fanaticism and cruelty were born and grew side by side, along with dedication and sacrifice. The people's revolution in Russia would be terrible, the explosion of the desire for liberty and of the dreadful passions would be tragic. Like Herzen, Bakunin eventually envisioned Russia pervaded with and soaked in mud 'from the infinite and multiform Russian mire. The Russian world—state, privileged class, and people at the same time—is a horrible world. The Russian revolution will be horrible certainly. He who fears the horrors and the slime, let him distance himself from this world and from this revolution, but he who wishes to serve it, let that one, knowing where he is going, strengthen his nerves and be ready for everything' (pp. 651–53). For everything? Was this not precisely what Nechaev had said and done? In the final analysis, the problem became a moral one.

The Russian revolution would have been aroused and helped by the 'proletariat of thought.' Bakunin does not use this expression, but he alludes to the phenomenon, describing it as 'an enormous mass of educated and thinking people who are at the same time deprived of every job, of every career, of every way out . . . three-fourths at least of the university youth, the seminarians, the sons of peasants and bourgeois, the sons of petty functionaries and of ruined nobles. . . .' The people were 'the revolutionary army.' From the proletariat of thought would come the general staff. But what guarantee would they give of truly desiring the liberation of the people? This guarantee could only come from the morality of those dedicated to it. 'It is necessary to organize and truly *moralize* this world.' In itself, the proletariat of thought was no better than the society around it. 'There is in this world little enough of moral sense, with the exception of a small number of iron natures, eminently moral, formed according to Darwinian law in the midst of filthy oppression and infinite misery.' It was not difficult to imagine what the vast majority would have done if they had found themselves 'in a situation which permits them to exploit and oppress the people. One can affirm with certainty that they would exploit and oppress them in all tranquility' (p. 657). Only virtue, only morality could enable them to avoid the danger of falling into the surrounding mud. Adopting jesuitical means in the revolutionary movement meant preparing them to become 'excellent spies and lackeys of power.' Only the struggle against the state, only the ideal of liberty could help them avoid fatally substituting themselves for the government that the revolution was to defeat. Thus, in the heart of every action one had to insert 'the self-determination of the people on a base of absolute equality, of complete and multiform human liberty.' Only such a high and true ideal could dominate the harsh reality of the future revolution.

'Imagine yourself in the middle of the triumph of the spontaneous revolution in Russia.' By now every barrier, every obstacle has been overcome. 'It is general anarchy.' And it really is not an idyll. 'The horrible mud that has accumulated in enormous quantities in the depths of the people mounts to the surface.' The competition among the new men who have just come from the heart of the country is unleashed. 'Audacious, intelligent, dishonest, and ambitious . . . they confront, struggle with, and destroy one another.' The only ones who can give meaning to this spontaneous anarchy are the revolutionaries. "Strong in their thought which expresses the essence of the instincts, desires and needs of the people; strong in their clearly understood goal amidst the crowd of men struggling with no goal and no plan,' these men would eventually establish the 'collective dictatorship' of their secret organization. 'This dictatorship is not tainted by cupidity, vanity, or ambition, because it is impersonal and imperceptible and because it does not procure for the men who belong to its groups, nor for any groups, any advantages, or honors, or any official recognition of power.' In reality, such men are only strong in their energy and in their mind (pp. 661–63). Thus, right from the start they must be the best, the most lucid, and invariably the most ready to sacrifice themselves for the people, 'the strongest, the most passionate, inflexibly and invariably devoted' (p. 665). Fatally, such men were few, but what counted was their excellence and their total dedication.

Yet how could such a nucleus, such a secret society, have arisen if it adopted trickery and deceit? Undoubtedly, the terrible struggle that was taking place in Russia and the struggle that would have to be faced on the day of the revolution did not allow them to spare any means or blows—provided, as Bakunin says, they were directed solely against the enemy. Inside the secret society, principles of the purest equality and the most perfect liberty had to prevail. 'Equal rights among all the members and unconditional and absolute solidarity . . . absolute sincerity . . . mutual fraternal confidence. . . . The nervous, fearful, vain, and ambitious are excluded from the society. . . . In adhering to the society, each member condemns himself forever to public anonymity and insignificance. . . . Each decision of the general meeting is absolute law. . . . Each member has the right to know everything . . .' (pp. 669–71). Thus Bakunin made a definitive break with Nechaev's hierarchical conception, with any Carbonaro-type secrecy, with any centralization of Jacobin origin. He was the first of the Russian revolutionaries to base everything on democracy and on internal fraternity, both elements united and joined with the maximum energy and decision in the external struggle. Everything was permitted against the enemy—secrecy, violence, assassination attempts, and conspiracies. But within the fraternity of those dedicated to bringing about a different and better world, rights were sacred and duties absolute.

This solution often recurs in the history of the Russian revolutions. In 1870, it had at least one great and inestimable merit, that of arousing the energies of the revolutionaries and taxing them to the utmost. Everything would depend on them. All political and moral responsibility fell on their shoulders. Anyone who accepted such a terrible challenge was certainly an exceptional man, as Bakunin had foreseen. In reality, as he had said, few responded to the appeal. But from those men came the populism of the 1870s, from the followers of Natanson and of Chaikovsky to the second *Zemlya i Volya* to the *Narodnaya*

Volya. It was on the basis of morality that they recruited supporters, reacting with the strength and purity of youth against the machiavellianism, the aberrations, the hidden and overt fears, and the nihilism of Nechaev. At the beginning of the 1870s a few dozen youths were able to recreate a limpid atmosphere in a world (they too were aware of it) floundering in slime. Though slowly and from afar, Bakunin's appeals reached them. Some of the pages of his *Statism and Anarchism* became the fundamental documents of their movement. They felt that these pages corresponded closely to their deepest needs.[109]

Initially they were unaffected by the ideas of men like Tkachev, who had briefly been allied with Nechaev and who later, with great lucidity and intelligence, had criticized the ideas of Bakunin and the populists. Tkachev and others had observed these ideas from a viewpoint that was machiavellian, not in the negative sense, but in that it reminded everyone of the inevitable problem of power and the state. They said that the secret and omnipresent dictatorship in which Bakunin saw the future of the revolution would lead to the development of a sort of church with a power similar to that of a party or government, and affirmed that the internal organization of the revolutionary movement would not remain free and egalitarian but would fatally change into a conspiracy and a plot. Tkachev, the Jacobin and supporter of Blanqui, was thus going against the current, and in some ways he remains in that position in the Soviet Union, where his ideas have been surrounded by a preoccupied silence which was broken only briefly in the 1920s with the publications of scholars who saw in him an element of the internal debate of the revolutionary movement that could not be ignored.

Thus, it was not in Tkachev that the young men of the 'go to the people' movement found what they were seeking. Rather, they found it in the populist theorists and writers, in the theories of progress that were then being elaborated, in a view of history that fully expressed their rejection of the world around them and their hope for a profound socialist transformation. They found it in minor writers such as D. A. Sleptsov who now continued writing, on a different and enduing level, the 'literature of denunciation' which had flourished ten years before, providing continuous sustenance for the young men as they drew closer to the people and explored the villages. They found it in men like Nekrasov and Saltykov-Shchedrin. But, above all, their guides were the ethnographers, who opened the Russian peasant world to them, and thinkers such as Lavrov and Mikhailovsky who were able to enlarge on the meaning of the debt that these young men felt they owed to the people, opposing positivism and scientism of the nihilistic sort, to create a new morality founded on the desire for a free and pluralistic society.

Even the minor writers of this populist trend have continued to attract the attention of Soviet scholars. In some recent works on the poetry and literature of populism, one finds the same enthusiasm for the rediscovery of this movement that we already observed in the research on its political aspects. However, not much work has been done on the thinkers, philosophers, and economists of the 1870s.[110] The collection of Lavrov's works that appeared in 1965 is certainly useful, but its new sociological covering conceals a return to traditional themes and interpretations.[111] Sedov's article on Mikhailovsky and B. S. Itenberg's contribution on him in his essay on revolutionary populism are important symptoms of a rebirth of interest in Mikhailovsky, who had seemed buried under the old party condemnations. But we still must look outside Russia to find a real discussion of his ideas.[112]

Undoubtedly, recent Soviet research on the revolutionary populists of the 1870s, from the 'go to the people' movement to the *Narodnaya Volya*, has been fuller and more important. In fact, this is one of the brightest chapters in recent Soviet historiography. After a hiatus of many years, the documents published in the past were taken up again and unknown ones were sought in the archives. Even a complete and valuable review of the archive sources regarding revolutionary populism was published, a rare thing in the USSR, which it would be futile to seek for other political trends of the 19th and 20th centuries.[113] Some syntheses that reexamine all the fundamental aspects of the movement have been published.[114] In the second edition of *Il populismo russo* the reader can find many additions and corrections that I have been led to make in the thirty-year-old text after reading numerous Soviet articles and studies that are impossible to list here, but from which there is much to be drawn and to learn.

What historical nourishment can we gain from this rich harvest? Apart from enthusiasm for the rediscovery of the past that had been obliterated in the Stalinist era, apart from admiration for the heroism of the revolutionary populists, what fruits have Soviet historians reaped from this research?

First of all, it seems evident that they were more able to insert populism into the history of Russia than they had been earlier. In this, P. A. Zayonchkovsky has been very effective, doing as much to clarify the second revolutionary crisis of the late 1870s as he did to explain the first one during Alexander II's reforms. His book on this subject is one of the best to have come out of Russia in recent years. In his introduction to the text he successfully breached party interpretations of this crisis, clearing the field of nonexistent major peasant movements and reestablishing a true perspective on the final duel fought between the government and the revolutionaries of the *Narodnaya Volya* at the end of the czar's reign, a duel that seems even more tragic as we realize that it was not accompanied or aroused by mass movements.[115] Zayonchkovsky, in extending his research in the archives and reconstructing the day-to-day government policies, has definitely demonstrated how extraordinarily effective the populist revolutionaries were, what their influence was on the evolution of the czarist situation at that time. Of course the *Narodnaya Volya* was defeated, but the desire for liberty and justice that it had brought to the very heart of the Russian state could not be cast aside. Historians such as N. Troitsky and B. V. Vilensky have illustrated other aspects of the Russian state structure of that period, especially the character and function of lawyers and the judiciary.

There still remains a wide area for investigation, that of the liberal, moderate, and reactionary movements and their effective weight in the 'revolutionary situation' at the end of Alexander II's reign. But Soviet scholars seem to be well on their way to an understanding of the political value, the actual force of revolutionary populism during that period in Russian history.

We cannot say the same about the relationship between the second *Zemlya i Volya* and the *Narodnaya Volya* and the world revolutionary movement of that time. It was the epoch of the great historical development of socialism toward politics, from Proudhonian and Bakuninist anarchism, through the Paris Commune, toward the creation of great social democratic movements and parties, and toward the constitution of the Second International. Leo Valiani has presented this development, in which the Russian movement was one of the most significant elements, with special thoroughness.[116] But there are still too many obstacles in the Soviet Union that prevent a historical view such as the one Valiani has presented. The conflicts between Bakunin and Marx are still too much part of the local mythology to permit a broader and more detached perspective. The recent interest in Bakunin that has been shown in Russia is certainly a positive sign, but for now we must admit that the study of the passage from the First to the Second International lies mainly in non-Russian hands (consider the Institute of Social History in Amsterdam). It is not that Soviet writings do not discuss the links between the Russian, English, German, French, Italian, and Polish movements. (The books of Itenberg, who was one of the first to publicize this internationalization of the history of populism, are sufficient evidence.) But they treat only the links, relationships, and influences, all of which are useful and require study but do not pose or solve the problem of the European role in what happened in Russia, or of the Russian contribution to the more general evolution and configuration of socialism in the 1870s and 1880s.

In less than a decade, the young revolutionary populists rejected without difficulty, almost naturally, the calls of the constitutionalists and the liberals. Having vigorously condemned Jacobin and conspiratorial ideas as well, they plunged into direct social action, without intermediaries, among the peasant masses and the workers in the cities. Through the 'go to the people' movement, through the formation of the first groups in the villages and factories, above all through their experience in the clandestine struggle—the blows that fell on them, the arrests, the succession of defeats, the trials—after a few years, and faced with the problem of politics, they more or less completely abandoned the anarchic ideal and recognized the need for a centralized organization. At the end of this development the *Narodnaya Volya* gave a particularly deep and thoughtful form to these conclusions, pointing out the exceptional and specific function of the state in the evolution of the economy and of modern Russian society. They formed a real clandestine party, capable of gathering and directing the most efficient and active forces of the revolutionary generation of the 1870s.

Did they represent a step backward, then? Or a continuous pendulum motion between the anarchic ideal and the reality of the struggle? The history of populism itself seems to demonstrate how superficial and inadequate such explanations are. There was no return to Nechaev and to Tkachev. The Executive Committee of the *Narodnaya Volya* no longer had anything in common with Ishutin's Hell. In fact, through the 'go to the people' movement and the organizations that came out of it, Russia found a road toward democratic thought and action, at the same time reconfirming the socialist ideal that lay at the root of the whole populist movement. The needs of politics and liberty were felt in the very heart of populism, and by now they were far from and different from the aspirations of the age of reform. The anarchic ideal increasingly became a desire for autonomy in the villages and in the workers' organizations. Slowly and with difficulty, Proudhonian federalism gave way to an ideal of liberty, of local self-administration as opposed to a centralized and bureaucratic state. Protest became an organized and conscious struggle against autocracy. Internally, the need for clandestine action and terrorism imposed an extraordinary discipline on the populist party, but this did not prevent struggles between trends based on clear and explicit ideas and desires. The moral ferment that had moved the young populists in the early 1870s brought exceptional loyalty and frankness to their organizations. For a moment it seemed that what Bakunin had hoped for, that is, a free party, was truly realized even in the midst of the harshest battles and the greatest oppression.

This germination of a democratic will in Russian populism has particularly attracted the attention of Soviet historians in recent years. Let us take only one example, and one of the best, that of the book by G. G. Vodolazov, *Ot Chernyshevskogo k Plekhanovu* (From Chernyshevsky to Plekhanov), published by the University of Moscow in 1969. According to Vodolazov, what distinguishes Russia is the fusion between revolutionary democracy and socialism. Economic backwardness explains this brief unification of two political elements that elsewhere had manifested themselves at different chronological times. The best expressions of Russian populism and socialism were those in which both elements were present. However, when they appeared separately, decadence and corruption followed. The supreme expression of Chernyshevsky's thought came in *Letter without an Address*, 'a last attempt to improve the life of the people while avoiding bloodshed . . . an attempt by an intelligent and wise revolutionary leader. He always sought a way to avoid the peasant revolution. He called for an end to serfdom because it was an obstacle to economic life.'[117] He was not listened to, and his politics of authentic and thorough reform were rejected. Nevertheless, a great debate emerged in the 1860s and left deep traces in Russia's later history. Chernyshevsky knew how to combat liberalism. Though its optimism eventually prevented access to the root of the problem, Chernyshevsky never failed to take advantage of all the legal possibilities. Vodolazov adds that one must not exaggerate the repressive character of the censorship of those days, 'if only because in the years after

Chernyshevsky's death the concept of the possibilities of censorship expanded considerably' (p. 53). The creator of populist policies was really 'neither a liberal nor an unreasonable revolutionary' (p. 41). His ideas conflicted entirely with those of men like Tkachev and Nechaev, who intended to 'drive the people to paradise with a stick' (p. 79). Russian socialism was not born of such despotic dreams as theirs, but from the germination of a new popular awareness. Dobrolyubov represented the beginning of the reawakening in the darkness. Pisarev indicated what science and knowledge could bring to this democratic process. For him 'self-education' was 'liberation' (p. 116). Of course, he started from disillusionment; reform and revolution seemed to lead to nothing and to evil. Where had the French Revolution led? But this sense of disillusionment had to be overcome. When did revolutions ever lead where one intended? From the republic of virtue had come Bonapartism (p. 85). The Russian revolutionary movement was able to go beyond this disillusionment and these defeats. Populism maintained faith in the socialist ideal that had been maturing. The discussions of the 1870s dealt with the means, not the ultimate goals of the whole movement (p. 128). From the polemics of that era, from the experience of the revolutionaries in this decisive period, it became increasingly apparent that 'a socialism that is not democratic is not socialism.' Russian Jacobinism seemed increasingly clearly like a 'communism for the barracks, as Marx and Engels called it' (p. 146). Lavrov's followers, in contributing to the criticism of Tkachev, drew closer to the central line of the development of socialism as a whole.

What were the roots of the fanaticism, of the voluntarism that played such a large role in the history of Russian socialism? Vodolazov looks for the answer to this fundamental question in the very heart of the populist idea, that is, in the hope and the possibility of skipping the capitalist phase of economic development. 'The objective possibility of accelerating the development process of certain countries (using the results from more developed countries) made the function of the conscious element more important.'[118] This was the function of the parties, of the intelligentsia. The intelligentsia occasionally ended up presenting itself as truly providential for the Russian people. Nevertheless the history of revolutionary populism demonstrated how it wanted and knew how to keep the 'conscious element' and its own fundamental democratic will united. According to Vodolazov, the union of the two was the essential element in all of Russian socialism.

Following this route, Vodolazov saw in Plekhanov the logical and natural outcome of all populism. This era, too, in the history of European socialism flowed into the age and life of the Second International. Such a Marxist conclusion nevertheless seems too simple among so many internal differences; it offers a too conventional and easy unravelling of the drama of Chernyshevsky, Bakunin, Tkachev, and of the *Zemlya i Volya* and the *Narodnaya Volya*.

A sense of dissatisfaction with the explanations given about populism in the past seems to pervade the most recent historiography both in Russia and in

America. In the United States, Richard Wortman especially has stressed the moral and psychological questions.[119] In the USSR, in an introduction for V. A. Tvardovskaya's book *Socialist Thought in Russia between the 1870s and 1880s*, M. Ya. Gefter, one of the most lively scholars studying this problem, has expressed similar doubts and has urged research on something new, though still clearly stating the problem in terms of political history. 'One of the greatest difficulties of the Marxists lies in the need to explain why the utopianism [of the populists] that had undergone serious defeats in the ideological duel with proletarian socialism, not only did not die an obscure and quiet death . . . but was transformed in 1905 into the ideal of millions of peasants who were reawakening, and became the direct ideology of peasant democracy in Russia.[120] In more ideological and less directly political forms, others in the Soviet Union have expressed a need to discuss again the history of Russian socialism, that is, of the socialism that developed in Russia before, alongside, and in a different way from Marxist socialism.[121] As we have seen, twenty or thirty years ago, this interest in the local roots of socialism arose from the nationalistic end of the Stalinist era and brought upon itself all the crude contradictions of that period. At present the experience of revolutionary populism is often observed because in it one can see a democratic experience, because there is a search for a relationship between the popular masses and the intelligentsia.

The inevitable problem, the obligatory conclusion of this renewed interest is always the same: a historical confrontation with Marxism. As Soviet historiography gradually advances, taking up and reconsidering, one hopes, the relationship between the Mensheviks, the Bolsheviks, and the revolutionary socialists, it will be faced with the questions that are already *in nuce*, as we have seen, in the history of populism and of the whole revolutionary movement, from Herzen to the *Narodnaya Volya*. I am personally convinced that there is only one way out of the Marxist difficulty. One must understand that for the past two centuries socialist thought and movements in all Europe have been too rich and varied to be monopolized by only one trend, even if the trend is Marxism. Every attempt to establish in the context of socialism a so-called scientific trend that is considered authentic, and opposed to other utopian and false trends, is not only historically wrong but eventually leads to a voluntary mutilation and distortion of all socialist thought. By now, Soviet historians are also faced with a similar problem. Democracy and socialism, intelligentsia and the people, backward or advanced economic development, these are some of the many points one cannot escape if one wants to understand what populism was historically and how it affected modern Russian history.

Franco Venturi, 1972
Translated by Fausta Serge Walsby and Margaret O'Dell

Notes

1 In an article entitled 'Recent Soviet Historiography of Russian Revolutionary Populism,' John E. Bachman writes: 'Venturi's post-war research was based on extensive materials from Soviet archives, and he received considerable aid from Soviet historians' (*Slavic Review* [December 1970], p. 602, n. 10). *Utinam,* as the ancients said, or 'wishful thinking,' as we say.

2 A lively and critical description of the situation, especially from the standpoint of literary history, can be found in A. Belkin, 'Narodniki i revolyutsionnoye demokraty' [Revolutionary populists and democrats], in *Vosprosy literatury,* 1960, no. 2, pp. 116 ff. In response, in the same issue of the journal, p. 142, Ya. Elsberg pointed out that the position of the Stalinist age had had 'the great merit' of having fought 'against the socialist revolutionary critics (V. Chernov, Ivanov-Razumnik and others).' A few issues later, B. Meilach also praised such merits (no. 10, p. 87). On the fate of one of the two adversaries indicated, see *The Memoirs of Ivanov-Razumnik,* with a short introduction by G. Janovsky, trans. from the Russian and annotated by P. S. Squire (London: Oxford University Press, 1965).

3 See V. I. Chesnokov, 'V. I. Nevsky kak istorik revolyutsionnogo dvizheniya v Rossii' [V. I. Nevsky as historian of the revolutionary movement in Russia], report on a doctoral thesis (Voronezh: Izdatelstvo voronezhskogo universiteta, 1966).

4 These words are taken from the archives and quoted by M. G. Sedov, 'Sovetskaya literatura o teoretikakh narodnichestva' [Soviet literature on the theoreticians of populism], in *Istoriya i istoriki. Sbornik statey* [History and historians, a collection of articles] (Moscow: Nauka, 1965), p. 257.

5 E. M. Yaroslavsky, *Razgrom narodnichestva* [The downfall of populism] (Moscow, 1937), pp. 79–80; quoted in Sedov, pp. 256–57.

6 Sedov, 'Sovetskaya literatura,' p. 257.

7 See Andrea Caffi, *Critica della violenza* (Milan: Bompiani, 1966), and *Scritti politici* (Florence: La Nuova Italia, 1970).

8 See Peter Scheibert, 'Wurzeln der Revolution,' *Jahrbücher für Geschichte Osteuropas,* no. 3 (October 1962), pp. 323 ff.

9 This review is reproduced in Alexander Gerschenkron, *Continuity in History and Other Essays* (Cambridge, Mass.: Harvard University Press, 1968), pp. 454 ff.

10 In addition to the volume cited, see Alexander Gerschenkron, *Economic Backwardness in Historical Perspective* (Cambridge, Mass.: Harvard University Press, 1962).

11 M. G. Sedov, *Geroichesky period revolyutsionnogo narodnichestva* [The heroic period of revolutionary populism] (Moscow: Mysl, 1966), p. 38.

12 'Literatura po istorii revolyutsionnogo narodnichestva 70–80 godov XIX veka vyshedshaya v 1956–1964' [Literature on the history of revolutionary populism in the 1870s–1880s which appeared between 1956 and 1964], in *Obshchestvennoe dvizhenie v poreformennoy Rossii. Sbornik statey k 80-letiyu so dnya rozhdeniya B. P. Kozmina* [The social movement in Russia in the years following the reform of 1861. A collection of articles commemorating the 80th birthday of B. P. Kozmin] (Moscow: Nauka, 1966), pp. 370 ff.

13 Sh. M. Levin, *Obshchestvennoe dvizhenie v Rossii (60–70-e gody XIX veka)* [The social movement in Russia in the 1860s–1870s] (Moscow: Soc. Ek.-Lit., 1958).

14 Ibid., p. 11.

15 For an initial and partial orientation, see N. Ja. Kraineva and P. V. Pronina, *Trudy Instituta istorii Akademii Nauk SSSR, 1936–1965* [The work of the Institute of History of the Academy of Sciences of the USSR, 1936–1965], 4 vols. (Moscow, 1965). However, a considerable part of the discussion can be found in the publications of the different universities of the USSR, as well as in a variety of journals. A mechanical and simplified view of the relationship between intellectuals and the state in the Soviet Union makes Bachman's informative article, 'Recent Soviet Historiography' (see n. 1 above), unpersuasive.

16 Ernest J. Simmons, ed., *Continuity and Change in Russian and Soviet Thought* (Cambridge, Mass.: Harvard University Press, 1955). The volumes of the *Harvard Slavic Studies* (1953 ff.) of those same years are also characteristic.

17 James H. Billington, *Mikhailovsky and Russian Populism* (Oxford: Oxford University Press, 1958).

18 Martin Malia, *Alexander Herzen and the Birth of Russian Socialism, 1812–1855* (Cambridge, Mass.: Harvard University Press, 1961).

19 See the three-volume anthology inspired by him, *Russian Philosophy*, ed. J. M. Edie, J. L. Scanlan, and M.-B. Zeldin, with the collaboration of George L. Kline (Chicago: Quadrangle Books, 1965). (Vol. 1 is devoted to the beginnings of philosophy in Russia, to the Slavophiles and to the occidentalists; vol. 2 is devoted to the nihilists, populists, and critics of religion and culture; vol. 3 deals with pre-revolutionary philosophy and theology, philosophers in exile, Marxists, and communists); see also George L. Kline, *Religious and Anti-Religious Thought in Russia* (Chicago: University of Chicago Press, 1968).

20 *The Roots of Revolution: A History of the Populist and Socialist Movements in Nineteenth Century Russia*, trans. from the Italian by Francis Haskell, with an introduction by Isaiah Berlin (London: Weidenfeld & Nicolson, 1960). The American edition was published by Alfred E. Knopf. In 1966 a paperback edition was published by Grosset & Dunlap, in New York.

21 In Simmons, *Continuity and Change*, pp. 473 ff.

22 Berlin, 'Introduction,' *Roots of Revolution*, p. xxiv.

23 'One of the few recent historical works that have been favorably received both in the Soviet Union and the West,' wrote Geoffry Barraclough in the *Manchester Guardian* of July 1, 1960.

24 Regarding the book *Il movimento decabrista e i fratelli Poggio* [The Decembrist movement and the Poggio brothers] (Turin: Einaudi, 1971). The review appeared in *Voprosy istorii*, no. 3, pp. 156 ff.

25 *Chto delat?* [What is to be done?] *Complete Works*, 4th ed. (Moscow, 1946), 5:342. I cite Lenin's works in this edition because it was typical of the Stalinist era. See the fine edition of *What Is to Be Done?* edited by Vittorio Strada (Turin: Einaudi, 1971).

26 *Sovetskaya istoriografiya klassovoy borby i revolyutsionnogo dvizheniya* [Soviet historiography of the class struggle and the revolutionary movement in Russia], ed. A. L. Shapiro (Leningrad: LGU, 1967), 1:142 ff.

27 *K. Marks, F. Engels i revolyutsionnaya Rossiya* [K. Marx, F. Engels and revolutionary Russia] (Moscow: Izd. politicheskoy literatury, 1967).

28 Ibid., pp. 433–34.

29 Letter to the editor of *Otechestvennye zapiski* (1877), in ibid., pp. 77 ff.

30 The Russian translation of Marx's sketches can be found in K. Marx and F.

Engels, *Sochineniya* [Works] (Moscow: Gos. Izd. politicheskoy literatury, 1961), 19:400 ff.

31 *K. Marks, F. Engels i revolyutsionnaya Rossiya*, p. 89. The preface is dated January 21, 1882.

32 Ibid., p. 646, letter to Danielson on February 24, 1893.

33 Ibid., p. 723.

34 Ibid., p. 656, letter to I. A. Gurvich, dated May 24, 1893.

35 See, for example, S. S. Volk, *Karl Marks i russkie obshchestvennye deyateli* [Karl Marx and the political men of Russia] (Leningrad: Nauka, 1969).

36 A. L. Reuel, *Russkaya ekonomicheskaya mysl 60-70-kh godov XIX veka i marksizm* [Russian economic thought of the 1860's–1870's and Marxism] (Moscow: Gos. izd. politicheskoy literatury, 1956). Yu. Z. Polevoy, *Zarozhdenie marksizma v Rossii* [The rise of Marxism in Russia] (Moscow: Akademiya nauk SSSR, Institut istorii, 1959).

37 On this, see the bibliography in V. V. Micurov and Yu. M. Kritsky, *Rossiyskiye rabochiye i social-demokraticheskoye dvizhenie 70-ch-nachala 90-ch gg. XIX v. v sovestskoy istoriograficheskoy literature* [The Russian workers' and social democratic movement from the seventies to the beginning of the nineties of the 19th century in Soviet historiography], in *Sovetskaya istoriografiia klassovoy borby*, pp. 200 ff.

38 *Narodnicheskaya ekonomicheskaya literatura. Izbrannye proizvedeniya* [Populist economic literature: selected works], ed. N. K. Karataev (Moscow: Izd. soc.-ekon. literatury, 1958).

39 Salomon M. Schwarz, 'Populism and Early Russian Marxism on Ways of Economic Development of Russia (The 1880s and 1890s),' in *Continuity and Change in Russian and Soviet Thought*, pp. 40 ff.; Leopold Haimson, *The Russian Marxists and the Origins of Bolshevism* (Cambridge, Mass.: Harvard University Press, 1955); Donald Treadgold, *Lenin and His Rivals: The Struggle for Russia's Future, 1898–1906* (London, 1955); Arthur P. Mendel, *Dilemmas of Progress in Zarist Russia: Legal Marxism and Legal Populism* (Cambridge, Mass.: Harvard University Press, 1961); J. L. H. Keep, *The Rise of the Social Democracy in Russia* (Oxford: Clarendon Press, 1963); S. H. Baron, *Plekhanov, the Father of Russian Marxism* (London: Routledge & Kegan Paul, 1963); Jonathan Frankel, *Vladimir Akimov, or the Dilemmas of Russian Marxism: 1895–1903* (Cambridge: Cambridge University Press, 1969); and Andrzei Walicki, *The Controversy over Capitalism: Studies in the Social Philosophy of the Russian Populists* (Oxford: Clarendon Press, 1969).

40 Richard Pipes, 'The Origins of Bolshevism: The Intellectual Evolution of the Young Lenin,' in *Revolutionary Russia* (Cambridge, Mass.: Harvard University Press, 1968), and 'Narodnichestov: A Semantic Inquiry,' in *Slavic Review* 23, no. 3 (September 1964): 441 ff.

41 See Andrzei Walicki, 'Russia,' in *Populism: Its Meanings and National Characteristics*, ed. Ghita Ionescu and Ernest Gellnern (London: Weidenfeld & Nicolson, 1969), pp. 62 ff. See now the first volume of the fundamental biogaphy by Richard Pipes, *Struve: Liberal on the Left, 1870–1905* (Cambridge, Mass.: Harvard University Press, 1970), certainly the most important book on the relationship between populism and Marxism in Russia at the turn of the century. Of great interest is Vittoria Strada's discussion of the relationship between populism

and Marxism in the introduction of his edition of Lenin's *What Is to Be Done?* (see n. 25 above).

42 Pierre Pascal, *Civilisation paysanne en Russie. Six esquisses* (Lausanne: Editions de l'Age d'Homme, 1969).

43 'La Commune paysanne après la révolution,' an article published in *La Révolution prolétarienne* (November 1, 1928), and collected in ibid., pp. 29 ff.

44 Jerome Blum, *Lord and Peasant in Russia from the Ninth to the Nineteenth-Century* (Princeton, N.J.: Princeton University Press, 1961), esp. pp. 277 ff., 'The Last 150 Years of Serfdom.'

45 Wayne S. Vucinich, *The Peasant in Nineteenth-Century Russia* (Stanford, Calif.: Stanford University Press, 1968).

46 Moshe Lewin, *La Paysannerie et le pouvoir soviètique. 1928–1930* (Paris and The Hague: Mouton, 1966); and D. J. Male, *Russian Peasant Organization before Collectivization* (Cambridge: Cambridge University Press, 1971).

47 Michael Confino, *Domaines et seigneurs en Russie vers la fin du XVIIIe siècle. Etudes de structures agraires et de mentalité économiques* (Paris: Institut d'ètudes slaves de l'Université de Paris, 1963).

48 Michael Confino, *Systèmes agraires et progrès agricole* (Paris and The Hague: Mouton, 1969).

49 Ibid., pp. 295 ff. For a similar and parallel shift from the defense of slavery in the English colonies, based on the affirmation of its superiority over the peasant and the modern worker in general, to the use, by liberals and socialists, of a similar criticism of the capitalist world, see the interesting article by E. Bickerman, 'Pouchkine, Marx et l'Internationale exclavagiste,' in *La Nouvelle Clio*, no. 8 (September 1950), pp. 416 ff.

50 Confino, *Systèmes agraires*, p. 296. See A. L. Shapiro, 'Zapiski o peterburgskoy guberniy A. N. Radishcheva' [Notes on the governorship of St. Petersburg of A. N. Radishchev], in *Istoricheskiy archiv* 5 (1950): 253, n.d. See A. N. Radishchev, *Polnoye sobranie sochineniy* [Complete works] (Moscow and Leningrad: Akademiya nauk, 1952), 3:549, n. 4.

51 Shapiro, 'Zapiski,' p. 273; and Radischchev, *Polnoye sobranie sochineniy*, p. 132.

52 Quoted by Confino, *Systèmes agraires*, p. 300.

53 Ibid., pp. 331 ff. and 355 ff.

54 Ibid., p. 356.

55 *'Russkaya pravda' P. I. Pestelya i sochineniya ey predshestvuyushchiya* ['Russian Law' by P. I. Pestel and the writings that precede it], ed. M. V. Nechkina (Moscow: Glavnoye archivnoye upravleniye, 1958). See S. S. Volk, *Istoricheskiye vzglyady dekabristov* [The historical conceptions of the Decembrists] (Moscow and Leningrad: Akademiya nauk SSSR, 1958), pp. 347 ff.; Hans Lemberg, *Die nationale Gedankenwelt der Dekabristen* (Köln and Graz: Böhlau, 1963); B. E. Syroechkovsky, *Iz istoriy dvizheniya dekabristov* [From the history of the Decembrists] (Moscow: MGU, 1969), pp. 14ff.

56 V. V. Pugachev, 'Sergei Ivanovich Turgenev,' in *Uchenye zapiski*, of the State University of Gorky, no. 58, Historical-Philosophical Series, 1963, pp. 299 ff.

57 Nicholas V. Riasanovsky, *Nicholas I and Official Nationality in Russia: 1825–1855* (Berkeley and Los Angeles: University of California Press, 1959); and Edward C. Thaden, *Conservative Nationalism in Nineteenth Century Russia* (Seattle: University of Washington Press, 1964).

58 N. V. Riasanovsky, *Russia and the West in the Teachings of the Slavofiles: A Study of Romantic Ideology* (Cambridge, Mass.: Harvard University Press, 1952).

59 Andrei Walicki, *W kręgu konserwatywnej utopii. Stuktura i przemiany rosyjskiego słowianofilstwa* [In the world of conservative utopias. Structure and development of Russian Slavophilism] (Warsaw: Państwowe wydawnictwo naukowe, 1964). An Italian translation of this work has been published by Einaudi.

60 Eberhard Müller, *Russischer Intellekt in Europäischer Krise. Ivan Kireevskij, 1806–1856* (Cologne: Böblau, 1966); Peter K. Christoff, *An Introduction to Nineteenth Century Russian Slavophilism: A Study in Ideas,* vol. 1, *A. S. Xomjakof* ('s-Gravenhage: Mouton, 1961); Robert Stupperich, *Jurij Samarin und die Anfänge der Bauernbefreiung in Russland* (Wiesbaden: O. Harrassowitz, 1969).

61 Alexander Von Schelting, *Russland und Europa im russischen Geschichtsdenken* (Bern: A. Frank, 1948); Dieter Groh, *Russland und Europa. Ein Beitrag zur europäischen Geistesgeschichte* (Neuwier: Herman Lucherhand, 1961); Karsten Goehrke, *Die Theorie über Entstehung und Entwicklung des Mir* (Wiesbaden: O. Harrassowitz, 1964); N. A. Cagolov, *Ocherki russkoy ekonomicheskoy mysli perioda padeniya krepostnogo prava* [Essays on Russian economic thought during the final period of the servitude of the serfs] (Moscow: Akademiya nauk SSSR, Institut ekonomiki, 1956). To these works one can add the anthology edited by Dmitrij Tschizewskij and Dieter Groh, *Europe und Russland. Teste zum Problem des westeuropäischen und russischen Selbstverständnisses* (Darmstadt: Wissenschaftliche Buchgesellschaft, 1959).

62 Muller, *Russischer Intellekt,* p. 31.

63 Goehrke, *Theorie über Entstehung und Entwicklung des Mir,* pp. 14 ff. See what Haxthausen wrote later (not without being influenced, in turn, by the Slavophile ideologies of the fifties) in the pamphlet *De l'abolition par voie législative du partage égal et temporaire des terres dans les communes russes* (Paris: A. Frank, 1858), p. 11: 'For my part, I know the communal constitution of several countries in Europe, either by having seen them close at hand or having made them the object of study, but I never knew a single one that was worth those of the Russian countryside,' and on p. 14 he added that 'one must not imagine this communal organization of the equal division of arable land to be something particular or unique to Russia.' For Germany, one had only to recall what Tacitus had written, and he adds: 'I found even in 1834, in the Hochwald of Treves, communes [*Geherberschafts-gemeinden*] where they divided the land anew among the members of the communes every thirteen years. The land taxes and the ordnance survey have made this state of things impossible to maintain. One can imagine the complaints and resistance of these folk when they are obliged to a final definitive division of the common property.' For Haxthausen's interpretation of Tacitus, see his study, *Über die Agrarverfassung in den Fürstenthümern Paderborn und Corvey und deren Conflicte in der gegenwärtigen Zeit* (Berlin: G. Reimer, 1828), pp. 95 ff.

64 The fundamental documents of this debate (it is too bad they are not more accessible and easily available for consultation) are: the letter of A. I. Koshelev to A. S. Khomyakov, dated March 16, 1848, published in N. Kolyupanov, *Biografiya Aleksandra Ivanovicha Kosheleva* [The biography of A. I. Koshelev], ed. O. F. Kosheleva (Moscow: Kushnerev, 1889–92), vol. 2, app., pp. 103 ff.; the reply of A. S. Khomyakov, published in *Russkiy arkhiv* (1878); and the response of Koshelev, inserted in the book cited here, by Kolyupanov, pp. 106 ff.

65 See Christoff, *An Introduction*, pp. 202 ff., and 'A. S. Khomiakov on the Agricultural and Industrial Problem in Russia,' in *Essays in Russian History: A Collection Dedicated to George Vernadsky* (Hamden, Conn.: Archon Books, 1964), pp. 131 ff.

66 N. M. Druzhinin, 'Krestyanskaya obshchina v ocenke A. Gakstgauzena i ego russkikh sovremennikov' [The peasant community in the opinion of A. Haxthausen and his Russian contemporaries], in *Ezhegodnik germanskoi istorii* (Moscow: Nauka, 1969), pp. 28 ff.; and Druzhinin, 'A. Gakstgauzen i russkie revolyutsionnye demokraty' [A. Haxthausen and the Russian democratic revolutionaries], *Istoriya SSSR*, 1967, no. 3, pp. 69 ff.

67 For what was published in the fifties, see F. Venturi, 'Testi e studi herzeniani,' *Rivista storica italiana*, 1959, no. 4, pp. 395 ff. More recently, of particular note is the little volume by A. I. Volodin, *Gertsen* (Moscow: Mysl, 1970).

68 A. I. Herzen, *Sobranie sochineniy v tridstati tomakh* [Works in thirty volumes] (Moscow: Akademiya nauk SSSR, 1954–55).

69 *Polyarnaya zvezda* [Polar star], 9 vols. including nn., indexes, ed. M. V. Nechkina and E. L. Rudnitskaya (1966–68); and *Kolokol* [The bell], 10 vols., ed. M. V. Nechkina (Moscow: Akademiya nauk SSSR, 1963).

70 *Problemy izuchenya Gertsena* [Problems in the study of Herzen] (Moscow: Akademiya nauk SSSR, 1963).

71 Ibid.

72 Jules Michelet, *Légendes démocratiques du Nord, nouvelle édition augmentée de fragments inédits, avec introduction, notes et index par Michel Cadot*, Faculté des lettres et sciences humaines de l'Université de Clermont Ferrand, 2d ser., no. 28 (Paris: Presses Universitaires de France, 1968), esp. pp. 387 ff. See also the vast study by Cadot, *La Russie dans la vie intellectuelle française. 1839–1856* (Paris: Fayard, 1967), esp. pp. 330 ff., in which Cadot discusses the ideas about Russian peasants commonly held in France during that period, and pp. 381 ff., about Russia's past. Above all, see pp. 461 ff., the chapters entitled, 'La Pologne, la Russie et le panslavisme' and 'La Russie, l'europe et la révolution.'

73 Vera Piroschkow, *Alexander Herzen. Der Zusammenbruch einer Utopie* (Munich: Anton Pustet, 1961).

74 Eberhard Reissner, *Alexander Herzen in Deutschland* (Berlin: Akademie-Verlag, 1963), chap. 1, 'Alexander Herzaen in der Kritik der deutschen Offentlichkeit der 50er Jahre.'

75 E. Lampert, *Studies in Rebellion* (London: Routledge & Kegan Paul, 1957).

76 See Malia, *Alexander Herzen and the Birth of Russian Socialism* (see n. 18 above), pp. 335 ff., 'The Crucial Year, 1847,' and pp. 369 ff., 'The Revolution of 1848.'

77 The collection of Bakunin's letters edited by Yu. M. Steklov, broken off in 1935, has become a bibliographic rarity and is not to be found. The Soviet reader has not been offered any choice of the youthful works of Bakunin, contrary to what has occurred for considerably less significant writers of the thirties and forties. Nevertheless, on the renewal of interest in Bakunin in Russia, see here pp. lxxxvi ff. As for Belinsky, the most characteristic work to have appeared in Russia is by V. S. Nechaeva, *V. G. Belinsky, zhizn i tvorchestvo* [V. G. Belinsky. Life and works], in 4 vols. The first appeared in 1949, the second in 1954, the third (concerning the years 1836–41) in 1961, and the fourth (1842–48) in 1967, in Moscow, edited by the Academy of Sciences of the USSR. Unquestionably competent and useful, this

biography is often weak in presenting the moral and political problems in the life and activities of Belinsky. On the vast literature on him, as on his writer friends, we refer the reader to K. D. Muratova, *Istoriya russkoy literatury XIX veka. Bibliograficheskii ukazatel* [History of Russian literature of the 19th century. Bibliographical indicator] (Moscow and Leningrad: Akademiya nauk SSSR, 1962).

78 Yu. G. Oksman, *Pismo Belinskogo k Gogolyu kak istoricheskiy dokument* [The letter from Belinsky to Gogol as an historical document], in *Ot 'Kapitanskoy dochki' k 'Zapiskam okhotnika.' Pushkin. Ryleev. Kolcov. Belinsky. Turgenev. Issledovnaiya i materialy* [From 'The Captain's Daughter' to 'A Sportsman's Notebook.' Pushkin. Ryleev. Koltsov. Belinsky. Turgenev. Research and materials] (Saratov: Knizhnoye Izdatelstvo, 1959), pp. 203 ff; Oksman, 'Belinsky i politicheskiye traditsiy dekabristov' [Belinsky and the political traditions of the Decembrists], in *Dekabristy v Moskve. Sbornik Statey* [The Decembrists in Moscow. A collection of articles] (Moscow: Moskovsky rabochii, 1963), pp. 185 ff.

79 Peter Scheibert, *Vom Bakunin zu Lenin. Geschichte der Russischen revolutionären Ideologien. 1840–1895*, vol. 1, *Die Formung des radikalen Denkens in der Auseinandersetzung mit Deutschem Idealismus und Französischem Bürgertum* (Leiden: E. J. Brill, 1956); Edward J. Brown, *Stanchievich and His Moscow Circle, 1830–1840* (Stanford, Calif.: Stanford University Press, 1966); Lampert (n. 75 above); L. Schapiro, *Rationalism and Nationalism in Russian Nineteenth-Century Political Thought* (New Haven, Conn.: Yale University Press, 1967); and Philip Pomper, *The Russian Revolutionary Intelligentsia* (New York: Thomas Y. Crowell, 1970). On the problem of the intelligentsia, see the collection of articles edited by Richard Pipes, *The Russian Intelligentsia* (New York: Columbia University Press, 1961); Allen McConnel, 'The Origin of Russian Intelligentsia,' *South and East European Journal* 8, no. 1 (1964): 1 ff.; Daniel F. Brower, 'The Problem of Intelligentsia,' *Slavic Review* 26 (December 1967): 1163 ff. An English version of Belinsky's letter to Gogol can be found in Marc Raeff, *Russian Intellectual History: An Anthology, with an Introduction by Isaiah Berlin* (New York: Harcourt, Brace & World, 1966), pp. 252 ff.

80 Gerschenkron, *Continuity in History*, pp. 140 ff.

81 R. Portal, *Le Statut des paysans liberés du servage. 1861–1961* (Paris and The Hauge: Mouton, 1963).

82 P. A. Zayonchkovsky, *Otmena krepostnogo prava v Rossiy. Izdaniye trete pererabotannoye i dopolnennoye* [The abolition of peasant serfdom in Russia. Third edition revised and completed] (Moscow, 1968). The first two editions of this work appeared in 1954 and 1960. A comparison between them is very instructive for understanding the evolution of Soviet historiography in the last fifteen years. A still classic work is that by P. A. Zayonchkovsky, *Provedenie v zhizn krestyanskoy reformy 1861 g.* [The application of the peasant reform of 1861] (Moscow, 1958).

83 N. M. Druzhinin, ed., *Krestyanskoye dvizhenie v Rossii v XIX–nachale XX veka* [The peasant movement in Russia in the 19th century and at the beginning of the 20th century] (Moscow: Mysl). Here is how it is divided, with indication of the date of publication: 1796–1825 (1961), 1826–49 (1961), 1850–56 (1962), 1857–May 1861 (1963), June 1861–69 (1964), 1870–80 (1968), 1881–89 (1960), 1890–1900 (1959), 1901–May 1907 (not published), June 1907–July 1914 (1966). See also the recent investigation by N. M. Druzhinin, *Byvshie udelnye krestyane posle reformy*

1863 g. (1863–1883) [The ex-peasants of the appanage after the reforms of 1863 (1863–1883)], in '*Istoricheskiye zapiski,*' no. 85 (1970), pp. 159 ff.

84 Kirill Vasilevich Chistov, *Russkiye narodnye socialno-utopicheskiye legendy XVII–XIX vv.* [The popular social-utopian legends of Russia in the 17th to 19th centuries] (Moscow: Nauka, 1967).

85 *Revolyutsionnaya situaciya v Rossiy v 1859–1861 gg.* [The revolutionary situation in Russia between 1859 and 1861] (Moscow: Akademiya nauk SSSR, Institut istoriy, 1960–).

86 Lenin, *Sochineniy* [Works], 4th ed. (Moscow, 1948), 21:189–90.

87 Ja. I. Linkov, *Revolyutsionnaya borba A. I. Gercena i N. P. Ogareva i taynoe obshchestvo 'Zemlya i Volya' 1860-ch gg.* [The revolutionary struggle of A. I. Herzen and N. P. Ogarev and the secret society 'Land and Liberty' in the 1860s] (Moscow: Nauka, 1964).

88 N. N. Novikova, *Revolyutsionery 1861 goda* [The revolutionaries of 1861] (Moscow: Nauka, 1968).

89 Victor Leontovitch, *Geschichte des Liberalismus in Russland* (Frankfurt am Main: Vittorio Klostermaan, 1957). See especially pt. 3, *Entwicklung der politischen Freiheit. 1856–1914*, pp. 233 ff. The author himself explains how the inspiration came to him from *Storia del liberalismo europeo* by Guido De Ruggiero, even if he then admits immediately that the tasks facing Russian liberalism were very different from those that this political trend had to face in the West.

90 George Fischer, *Russian Liberalism: From Gentry to Intelligentsia* (Cambridge, Mass.: Harvard University Press, 1958).

91 Klaus Detlev Grothusen, *Die historische Rechtsschule Russlands. Ein Beitrag zur russischen Geistesgeschichte in der zweiten Hälfte des 19. Jahrhunderts* (Giessen: Justus Liebig-Universität, 1962). See esp. the two chapters devoted to Kavelin (pp. 90 ff.) and to Chicherin (pp. 120 ff.). From a sociological standpoint, one can add Klaus Von Beyme, *Politische Soziologie im Zaristischen Russland* (Wiesbaden: Otto Harrassowitz, 1965) (the pages on Chicherin, Mikhailovsky, etc., are of interest).

92 D. Tschizewskij, *Hegel bei den Slaven* (Darmstadt, 1961), p. 311.

93 Leontovitsch, p. 246.

94 Fischer, *Russian Liberalism*, p. 67.

95 Schapiro, *Rationalism and Nationalism*, p. 90 (see n. 79 above).

96 Richard Pipes, 'Russian Conservatism in the Second Part of the Nineteenth Century' (paper presented at the XIIIth International Congress of Historical Sciences, Moscow, 1970).

97 Vittorio Strada, *Leggendo 'Padri e figli,'* in *Tradizione e rivoluzione nella letteratura russa* (Turin: Einaudi, 1969), pp. 14 ff.

98 B. P. Kozmin, *Literatura i istoriya. Sbornik statey* [Literature and history. A collection of articles], ed. E. S. Vilenskaya (Moscow: Khudozhestvennaya literatura, 1969), pp. 243 ff.

99 Ibid., p. 236.

100 Ibid., p. 327.

101 'Politicheskaya napravlennost ocherka Shchedrina Kapluny' [The political significance of Shchedrin's essay 'The Capons]', in ibid., pp. 328 ff.

102 Ibid., p. 357, and see p. 510n.

103 R. V. Filippov, *Revolyutsionnaya narodnicheskaya organizatsiya N. A. Ishutina–I.*

A. Khudyakova (1863–1866) [The populist revolutionary organization of N. A. Ishutin and I. A. Khudyakov (1863–1866)] (Petrozavodsk: Karelskoye knizhnoye izdatelstvo, 1964), p. 40.

104 Ibid., p. 71.

105 T. F. Fedosova, 'Polsky Komitet v Moskve i revolyutsionnoye podpole 1863–1866' [The Polish Committee in Moscow and the revolutionary underground, 1863–1866], in *Revolyutsionnaya rossiya i revolyutsionnaya Polska (Vtoraya polovina XIX veka). Sbornik statey pod red. V. A. Dyakova, I. S. Millera, N. P. Mitinoi* [Revolutionary Russia and revolutionary Poland (second half of the 19th century), a collection of articles edited by V. A. Dyakov, I. S. Miller, N. P. Mitina] (Moscow: Nauka, 1967), pp. 125 ff.

106 Ibid., pp. 464–65.

107 Michael Confino, 'Bakunin et Nečaev. Les débuts de la rupture. Introduction à deux lettres inédites de Michel Bakunin. 2 et 9 juin 1870,' in *Cahiers du monde russe et soviétique*, 7, no. 4 (1966): 625 ff. See now the definitive edition of all the documentation in *Michel Bakounine et ses relations avec Sergej Nečaev. 1870–72. Ecrits et matériaux. Introduction et annotations de Arthur Lehning* (1971), in *Archives Bakounine*, ed. A. Lehning, A. J. C. Rüter, and P. Scheibert (Leyden: E. J. Brill, for the International Institute of Social History of Amsterdam, 1961 ff).

108 Confino, 'Bakunin et Nečaev,' pp. 633–35.

109 *Gosudarstvennost i anarchiya* [Statism and anarchism] was included in the definitive edition of the *Archives Bakounine*. Needless to say, this whole collection is indispensable also for the history of the Russian revolutionary movement from the sixties to the seventies.

110 Purely as an example, see vol. 32 of *Literaturnoye nasledstvo*, which came out in 1963, devoted entirely to D. A. Sleptsov, with an introductory article by K. I. Chukovsky; the numerous and important articles by E. Bushkanec in *Russkaya literatura*; the discussion on populism that took place in the pages of *Voprosy literatury* in 1960 and 1961; the book by N. V. Osmakov, *Poeziya revolyutsionnogo narodnichestva* [The poetry of revolutionary populism] (Moscow: Akademiya nauk SSSR, 1961); the interesting studies by E. Taratuta on Stepnyak-Kravchinsky; the article by V. F. Zacharina, 'Revolutsionnaya propagandistskaya literatura 70-ch godov XIUX veka' [The literature of propaganda of the 1870s], *Istoricheskiye zapiski*, vol. 71 (1962); the ed. of V. G. Bazanov and O. B. Alexseeva of the *Agitatsionnaya literatura russkikh revolyutsionnykh narodnikov* [The propaganda literature of the Russian revolutionary populists] (Leningrad: Nauka, 1970); M. S. Goryachkina, *Khudozhestvennaya proza narodnichestva* [The literature of populism] (Moscow: Nauka, 1970), and *Russkaya literatura i narodnichestvo* [Russian literature and populism] (Leningrad: LGU, 1971); and V. F. Zacharina, *Golos revolyutsionnoy Rossiy. Literatura revolyutsionnogo podpolia 70-kh godov. 'Izdaniya dlya naroda'* [The voice of revolutionary Russia. The literature of the revolutionary underground of the 1870s. 'The editions for the people'] (Moscow, 1971).

111 P. L. Lavrov, *Filosofiya i sociologiya* [Philosophy and sociology], 2 vols., ed. by I. S. Knizhnik-Vetrov and A. F. Okulov (Moscow: Mysl, 1965). See the definitive edition of the Lavrov documents collected by Boris Sapir, *Vpered: 1873–1877. From the Archives of Valerian Nikolaevich Smirnov*, 2 vols. (Dordrecht: D. Reidel, 1970).

112 M. G. Sedov, *K. voprosu ob obshchestvenno-politicheskikh vzglyadakh N. K.*

Mikhailovskogo [On the question of the social and political ideas of N. K. Mikhailovsky], in *Obshchestvennoye dvizhenie v poreformennoy Rossii. Sbornik statey k 80-letiyu so dnya rozhdeniya B. P. Kozmina* [The social movement in Russia after the reform of 1861. A collection of articles for the 80th birthday of B. P. Kozmin] (Moscow: Nauka, 1965), pp. 179 ff.; and B. S. Itenberg, *Dvizhenie revolyutsionnogo narodnichestva. Narodnicheskiye kruzhki i 'khozdenie v narod' v 70-ch godakh XIX v.* [The movement of revolutionary populism. The populist groups and the 'go to the people' movement of the seventies of the 19th century] (Moscow: Nauka, 1965), pp. 104 ff.; Billington (see n. 17 above); Mendel (see n. 39 above); F. B. Randall, 'N. K. Mikhailovskij's What Is Progress?' in *Essays in Russian and Soviet History in Honor of Geroid Tanquary Robinson, Edited by John Shelton Curtiss* (Leyden: E. J. Brill, 1963); Pomper, pp. 107 ff., contains a particularly clear and persuasive exposition on the contrast between nihilism and Mikhailovsky's ideas between 1861 and 1870. This vast bibliography, though it does not pretend to be complete, will to some extent make up for a weakness of which *Il populismo russo (The Roots of Revolution)* has often been accused, that is, the lack of a specific discussion of Mikhailovsky's ideas. In fact, Mikhailovsky always refused to participate in the revolutionary movement and organization and therefore can legitimately be excluded from a book that discusses only revolutionary populism. Nevertheless, there is no doubt about his influence on young men who were preparing to go to the people, and on the whole movement of the seventies. (But then why not discuss Saltykov-Shchedrin and many others?) I had to resist the temptation to make this book into a history of Russian culture and society in the latter half of the 19th century, even if, admittedly, it is particularly difficult to make a division between revolutionary populism and the general movement of thought of that era and one easily runs the risk of being unjust when dealing specifically with Mikhailovsky. See the discussion of this if R. V. Filippov, *Iz istorii narodnicheskogo dvizheniya v pervom etape 'khozhdeniya v narod' (1863–1864)* [From the history of the populist movement in the first stage of the 'go to the people' movement (1863–1864)] (Petrozavodsk: Karelskoe knizhnoe izdatelstvo, 1967), pp. 99 ff. On problems that are parallel and related to those posed by the figure of Mikhailovsky, see the interesting studies of E. L. Rudnitskaya, 'Nikolai Nozhin,' in *Revolyutsionnaya situaciya v Rossiy v 1859–1861 gg.* [The revolutionary situation in Russia between 1859 and 1861] (Moscow: Akademiya nauk SSSR, Institut istoriy, 1962), 2:444 ff.; V. I. Taneev, *Detstvo, yunost, mysli o budushchem* [Childhood, youth, thoughts on the future], ed. M. P. Bastin (Moscow: Akademiya nauk SSSR, Institut filologiy, 1959); P. S. Skurinov, *Kritika pozitivizma V. I. Taneevym* [The criticism of V. I. Taneev of positivism] (Moscow: MGU, 1965); and A. P. Kazakov, *Teoriya progressa v russkoy sociologii kontsa XIX veka (P. L. Lavrov, N. K. Mikhailovsky, M. M. Kovalevsky)* [The theory of progress in Russian sociology at the end of the 19th century (P. L. Lavrov, N. K. Mikhailovsky, M. M. Kovalevsky)] (Leningrad: LGU, 1969); and Walicki, *The Controversy over Capitalism.*

113 *Revolyutsionnoye narodnichestvo 70-ch godov XIX veka. Sbornik dokumentov i materialov v dvuch tomakh* [Revolutionary populism of the 1870s. A collection of documents and materials in two volumes], ed. S. N. Valk, S. S. Volk, B. S. Itenberg, and S. M. Levin (Moscow: Nauka, 1964–65), 2:391–444.

114 R. V. Filippov, *Iz istoriy revolyutsionno-demokraticheskogo dvizheniya v Rossiy v*

kontse 60-kh–nachale 70-kh godov XIX veka [The history of the democratic revolutionary movement in Russia at the end of the 1860s and at the beginning of the 1870s] (Petrozavodsk: Gosudarstvennoye Izdatelstvo Karelskoy SSSR, 1962); 'Ideologiya Bolshogo obshchestva propagandy (1869–1874); [The ideology of the great society of propaganda (1869–1874)], in ibid., 1963; N. A. Troitsky, *Bolshoe obshchestvo propagandy (1871–1874). (Tak nazyvaemye 'Chaikovsky')* [The great society of propaganda (1871–1874). The so-called followers of Chaikovsky] (Saratov: Izdatelstvo saratovskogo universiteta, 1963); Itenbereg; S. S. Volk, *Narodnaya Volya. 1879–1882* [The will of the people. 1879–1882] (Moscow: Nauka, 1966); Sedov, *Geroichesky period revolyutsionnogo narodnichestva;* Filippov, *Iz istoriy narodnicheskogo dvizheniya*; and N. A. Troitsky, 'Nekotorye voprosy istoriografiy revolyutsionnogo narodnichestva 70-kh godov' [Some historiographical problems on the populist revolutionary movement in the seventies], *Istoriograficheskiy sbornik*, 1971, no. 3, pp. 70 ff.

115 P. A. Zayonchkovsky, *Kriziz samoderzhaviya na rubezhe 1870–1880 godov* [The crisis of autocracy between the seventies and eighties of the 19th century] (Moscow: MGU, 1964). See M. I. Kheyfec, *Vtoraya revolyutsionnaya situaciya v Rossiy (konets 70-kh i nachalo 80-kh godov XIX v.). Krizis pravitelstvennoy politiki* [The second revolutionary situation in Russia (end of the 1870s and beginning of the 1880s). The crisis in government policy] (Moscow: MGU, 1963).

116 Leo Valiani, 'Dalla I alla II Internazionale,' in *Questioni di storia del socialismo* (Turin: Einaudi, 1958), pp. 168–263.

117 G. G. Vodolazov, *Ot Chernyshevskogo k Plekhanovu* [From Chernyshevsky to Plekhanov] (Moscow: MGU, 1969), p. 39; following quotations are also from this volume.

118 G. G. Vodolazov, 'Osobennosti razvitiya socialisticheskoy mysli v Rossii v otrazhenii russkoy zhurnalistiki 60-70-ch godov XIX v. Aztoreferat dissertacii na soiskaniye uchenoy stepeni kandidata istoricheskikh nauk' [Details on the development of socialist thought reflected in the Russian pampleteering of the 1860s and 1870s. Author's report on the dissertation for the title of candidate in historical sciences] (Moscow: MGU, Fakultet zhurnalistiki, 1967), p. 19.

119 Richard Wortman, *The Crisis of Russian Populism* (Cambridge: Cambridge University Press, 1967).

120 M. Ya. Gefter, preface to V. A. Tvardovskaya, *Sotsialisticheskaya mysl Rossiy na rubezhe 1870–1880-kh godov* [Russian socialist thought between the 1870s and 1880s] (Moscow: Nauka, 1969), p. 6.

121 See, for example, *Idei sotsializma v russkoy klassicheskiy literature* [The ideas of socialism in classical Russian literature], ed. N. I. Prutskov (Leningrad: Nauka, 1969).

AUTHOR'S NOTE: While correcting the proofs of this second edition, I received the valuable bibliography compiled for the Institute of History of the Academy of Sciences of the USSR by N. Ya. Krayneva and P. V. Pronina, under the editorship of B. S. Itenberg. It is entitled *Narodnichestvo v rabotach sovetskikh issledovateley* [Populism in the studies of Soviet researchers between 1953 and 1970] (Moscow, 1971). I also received an interesting essay by M. G. Vandalkovskaya, *M. K. Lemke—istorik russkogo revolyutsionnogo dvizheniya* [M. K. Lemke—historian of the Russian revolutionary movement] (Moscow: Nauka, 1972).

PREFACE

◆◆◆

IN WRITING this book I have tried to write one chapter of the story of the European Socialist movement. It is not a history of Russia in the nineteenth century, nor of the thought and literature of the period. I have examined Russia's internal and external problems, and the ideals and beliefs of her subjects, only in so far as they touch on the formation and development of Populism. The rise of those ideas which guided the movement have been discussed in some detail in the chapters on men such as Herzen, Bakunin and Chernyshevsky. But the core of the book consists in the account of the conspiracies and struggles through which Populism expressed itself.

It is true that even when, in the 'seventies, Populism lived a life of its own, distinct from that of the intelligentsia which had given it birth, it was still accompanied by a current of political and economic thought which reflected its problems. Revolutionary Populism, as it came to be called, went hand in hand with legal Populism. Interesting though the latter is, I have not discussed it in this book. To make such a study would in fact involve a re-examination of the whole cultural situation of Russia at the time. Rather have I tried to show the inner life of a political movement in violent conflict with the world in which it operated.

Still less have I considered Populism as reflected in literature. So important was the rôle of literature in the life of the nation during the nineteenth century, and so many its links with the development of society, that the history of Russia has been seen entirely in terms of her great novelists, Turgenev, Tolstoy and Dostoevsky. By deliberately confining myself to the story of revolutionary Populism I hope at least to show how mistaken such an attitude can be and how important it is to make those distinctions in Russian history which we so naturally do in the history of France or Italy. It is just as unsatisfactory to try to understand 'nihilism' by reading only the novels of Turgenev as to explain the fortunes of the republican party under the July Monarchy by referring to Balzac. Dostoevsky can teach us very little about Nechaev. Indeed the very political function of nineteenth-century Russian literature, familiar to its contemporaries and so much discussed today, can only be explained historically if we first examine the Populist movement in its own right, clearly distinguishing it from novels and other forms of literature.

On the other hand I have paid special attention to the links between Russian Populism and the contemporary Socialist movements of

Western Europe. Herzen and Bakunin in 1840, Chernyshevsky in 1860, Ishutin in 1866, and in the 'seventies Tkachev and Lavrov, *Zemlya i Volya* and *Narodnaya Volya*—these are Russia's reactions to the problems of romantic socialism and the rise and inner conflicts of the First International. Such actions may indeed have been very much conditioned by local circumstances, but they are incomprehensible if divorced from the forces which gave rise to them. I have already stated that I am concerned with a section of the European Socialist movement, and to stress this I have again and again referred to the bonds between Russian Populism and events in Italy during these years.

As regards the time-span of the book, I think that there can be no doubt about the starting date. The 1848 revolution crystallized Populist ideology in the minds of Herzen, Bakunin, Chernyshevsky and a few other Russian 'Westerners' of the 'forties, and though its roots and ramifications must be sought among the Decembrists and Slavophils and the entire intellectual and social history of Russia, all these earlier elements came to a head around 1848.

On the other hand my final date, 1st March 1881—the assassination of Alexander II by the Executive Committee of *Narodnaya Volya*—may seem more arbitrary. *Narodnaya Volya* survived the repression, though weakened and, so to speak, exhausted. In later years, after reaction and hesitation, political movements such as that of the Socialist-Revolutionaries were confessedly inspired by Populist theories. The year 1881 therefore marks a break, but not the end of Russian Populism. And yet historically speaking we can say that a period came to an end in that year. The Socialist-Revolutionaries came into being in an entirely new political atmosphere. They were a great party, whereas the history of nineteenth-century Populism had been one of conspiracies and of relatively small groups. And above all the later Russian revolutionary movement no longer had a single aim and plan of action which was basically shared by all its participants. Between 1848 and 1881 Russian socialism was Populist. Later it was to become socialist-revolutionary, social-democratic, Menshevik, Bolshevik, anarchist. Hence this book is concerned with the revolutionary movement during a phase when it was no longer liberal, as it had been with the Decembrists, but not yet split into differing and sometimes conflicting components. It deals with the fundamental breeding-ground from which later, in changed circumstances, were to arise the forces that led to the revolution of 1917. And I hope to convince the reader that it is indispensable to study this breeding-ground if we are to understand the later development of Russian socialism. For it was between 1848 and 1881 that the ideas and psychological characteristics which shaped the upheaval of 1917 came into being. And so I hope that these dates are less arbitrary than they may seem at first sight.

As for the question of terminology: Populism is the translation of the Russian word *narodnichestvo*. This is derived from *narod* (people) and was first used around 1870. At about the same time the word *narodnik* (Populist) first came into being. Hence it was only when the movement became organized and active that it found a name for itself. Before that it had been described as Socialist, Communist, Radical, Nihilist. Though each one of these terms describes one aspect or phase of Populism, none of them suggests the various features common to all the personalities and currents of opinion in a movement comparable to conservatism, liberalism, etc. Strictly speaking, therefore, I should have spoken of 'pre-Populism' before 1870; but I have avoided the use of a terminology that would merely have been pedantic and have followed the current Russian practice of extending the word Populism to cover the whole period.

I have tried to incorporate in the English edition certain corrections of factual errors which escaped me in preparing the original Italian edition and which some kind friends and reviewers have brought to my notice. I also like to think that the bibliographical note on the Populist movement contained at the end of this volume is more up to date and takes into account the recent rapid growth of interesting and valuable publications on the subject which have appeared both in the Soviet Union and in other countries.

Finally I have been lavish in my use of quotations from memoirs, statutes of revolutionary organizations and other important sources. It is up to the reader to judge the value of the book as history; it should at least have a certain value as a collection of documents concerned with a movement that has still been insufficiently studied.

It is a pleasure to thank the libraries whose books I consulted as the basis for this work: the Vsesoyuznaja biblioteka imeni V. I. Lenina and the Gosudarstvennaya publichnaya istoricheskaya biblioteka of Moscow, the Gosudarstvennaya publichnaya biblioteka imeni M. E. Saltykova-Shchedrina of Leningrad; the Biblioteca Vittorio Emanuele, the Biblioteca dell'Istituto Pontificio Orientale and the Biblioteca apostolica Vaticana of Rome; the Bibliothèque Nationale and the library of the École nationale des langues orientales vivantes of Paris; the library of the International Instituut voor Sociale Geschiedenis of Amsterdam; the Bibliothèque publique et universitaire of Geneva, and the British Museum, London.

Of the many friends I should in fairness thank for their help in this work I will mention only my wife Gigliola who has taken an active part in every stage of its production.

TURIN, *January 1960*

1. HERZEN

HERZEN WAS THE true founder of Populism. He was inspired by his precocious attempt to bring Socialism to the Russia of Nicholas I; by his enthusiastic participation in the intellectual life of Moscow before the 1848 revolution; by his support for this revolution in Italy and France. In fact Populism first expressed itself in the life of a man, rather than in an ideology. Despite many writings of political insight and literary distinction, Herzen's most important work was his autobiography—*My Past and Thoughts*. The personal element remained a feature of Russian Populism, and the movement always fathered personalities rather than dogma. When the established Populism of the 'sixties at length required a doctrine, Herzen was almost forgotten, for he had only his experiences as critic and political explorer to bequeath to the new generation.

This neglect was responsible for the sad and embittered close of Herzen's remarkably free and intelligent life. Yet his experiences had to be constantly relived by the Populists as they set out to rediscover his ideas and appraise the various positions he maintained. And in 1881, when Populism had completed its first stage, and its significance was debated and assessed, Herzen reappeared clearly as the 'eponymous hero', the true creator of the movement.[1]

In his memoirs and other writings, where autobiography constantly intrudes on politics, Herzen often looks back to the world, still eighteenth century in character, of his early youth. Within his own family circle he had been able to meet the last elderly representatives of the Voltairian fashion of Catherine II's time. They were the survivors of the aristocratic enlightenment —the patina on an age in which the Russian nobility had tried to justify its existence by providing itself with a social conscience. And they were the representatives of the neo-classicism, which, in building St Petersburg and countless country houses, had created the first modern civilization of that country. Herzen was always critical of this society; he soon moved away from it, striving with all the ardour of youth to raise a barrier between himself and the preceding generation. Ideologically this barrier took the form of Saint-Simonism. However, Herzen was imbued with the eighteenth-century spirit, and when he returned to it in later life he felt that he was recovering his youth, that time 'which is the fullest, the best, the most "our own"'.[2]

Herzen's early experiences were of great importance to him because they had their counterpart in the history of his country. The revolt of 14th

1+

December 1825, and its suppression, crystallized the longing for a free and enlightened Russia which had inspired the noblest spirit of the eighteenth century. The final outburst of that spirit was the revolt of the Decembrists. Suppression of the revolt put a stop to such activities, but at the same time turned them into a legend of early promise, unfulfilled.

Herzen was a boy at the time, but he fully sensed the importance of what had happened. 'The stories of the revolt and the trial, and the horror which seized Moscow, shook me deeply. A new world opened for me and became the centre of my spiritual life. The execution of Pestel and his comrades woke me for ever from my youthful dreams.'[3]

His first reaction was to continue the work of those martyrs; to dedicate himself completely to the cause for which they had fallen. One night on the Sparrow Hills, the range which dominates the bend of the Moscow river and overlooks the whole city, he and Ogarev vowed to sacrifice their 'entire lives to the struggle which the Decembrists had begun'.[4] Twenty-six years later, he wrote that 'the scene may appear artificial and theatrical; in reality, as our lives have shown, it was deeply and religiously sincere'.[5]

This was no boast. The deep feeling aroused in him by the Decembrist movement was his initiation into political life.

Yet this feeling was a 'childish liberalism', an urge to prolong a cause which he was soon to realize was already dead. Later, though he still admired the movement as a spiritual impulse, as a great force of enthusiasm and a legend, he was conscious of the break between the glorious past and his new work. At the height of his career, his sense of historical justice and his deep reverence spurred him to reprint his memories of these fathers of the revolution; to reforge the links, after thirty years of rule by Nicholas I, with the men of 14th December. But he was inspired by esteem, rather than by a wish to bind himself to what was still relevant in that movement. The Decembrists were to remain a remote example for him—an example which he did much to create.

But can we accept as accurate the picture that he gives us in his autobiography of his relations with the Decembrists? To answer this we must know whether the Decembrist movement contained the origins of Populism. Herzen himself scarcely admits the debt. But as we examine these origins, we may still feel that it exists.

The idea of 'sacrifice' played such an important part in the ideology of the Decembrists that it must have influenced Populism, in which the conception of 'obligations' towards the people, and 'sacrificing oneself for the people' was so much discussed. The secret societies behind the attempted rising on 14th December were largely aristocratic. Many members belonged to great families who owned large numbers of serfs; yet their main policy was the liberation of the peasantry. Although they disputed the means, they were all agreed on the final intention. They must therefore have seemed like men who were ready to sacrifice themselves, out of conviction, for a cause that was not their own. On hearing of the plot, Count Rostopchin raised himself on his deathbed and exclaimed that 'hitherto revolutions had been made by peasants who wanted to become gentlemen; now gentlemen tried to make a revolution so as to become cobblers'.[6] (Rostopchin was a great representative of the old order—as Governor of Moscow he is said to have set fire to the city to thwart Napoleon, whom he regarded first and foremost as a general of the French Revolution.) The Count grasped, with the intuition that comes from hatred, one of the most important aspects of the Decembrist revolutionaries—the attempt to impose on themselves (even before imposing them on others) fundamental social reforms. True, there had been a precedent on the night of 4th August 1789. But the situations differed. In Russia there had been no 'great fear'; the nobles did not have to sacrifice immediately things which in any case they risked losing later. Besides, even in the French Revolution that gesture remained as a striking example of generosity. The effort of the Russian rebels to follow their convictions against their interests must have seemed still more spectacular.[7]

Later historians, notably Pokrovsky, have tried to prove that the nobility would in fact have profited by the end of serfdom. They maintain that the economic conditions at the time—increasing internal markets for agricultural produce and a growing international trade—actually pointed that way. But although the matter certainly throws light on one aspect of the politics of 1825, we cannot discuss it here. However, it does not affect the idea of sacrifice for the people, which we want to emphasize, and which the Decembrists adopted more definitely than did many other contemporary or similar movements in Europe. The wish to establish a bridge between the enlightened élite and the peasantry by means of sacrifice was to prove full of promise for the future. This connection was designed to take place outside the authority of the absolutist State, and, indeed, was aimed against it.

The same can be said of the relationship between political and economic problems within the Decembrist movement. This conspiracy which combined constitutional and military features, similar in so many respects to the Spanish, Neapolitan and Piedmontese movements of the time, found itself faced with exceptional social problems. The fate of millions depended on the way in which the peasants would be freed. The discussions within the secret societies were naturally concerned with constitutional forms and the social structure of the State, with the problems of liberalism and constitutionalism which had come to the fore in the French Restoration. But these discussions always ended by raising the question of deeper changes; and so turned a liberal movement into something of a social revolution.

In other words, the Decembrists reconsidered not only the political problems of the French Restoration but the social ones of the Revolution. We find, especially in Pestel, a return to the atmosphere of the preceding century; the same books are read and discussions take the same form. This was partly because eighteenth-century Russian culture had never suffered a violent break—neither a revolution, nor a real Napoleonic occupation, nor a restoration—and partly because the conditions against which the Decembrists fought did not allow them to stop at liberalism. It was this that led the more decided among them to the idea of a republic in a world of more or less constitutional monarchies, and it was this that led them willy-nilly to re-examine the problem of the 'Agrarian Law'.

The Decembrists then began to lay the foundations for the controversy which was to become the central issue for Herzen and all the Russian intelligentsia—should the serfs be freed 'with land' or 'without land'? In the first case they would be granted reasonably large properties; in the second, they would become manual workers or tenants. Each solution had its supporters within the various groups, and the discussion which often led to the changing of initial standpoints lasted for years. On the whole this was the most important controversy (during the first part of the last century) concerned with the social structure of the Russian countryside.[8]

The discussion was also conducted from the point of view of practical economics. An attempt was made to adapt the theories of the English and French economists to the Russian situation. It was suggested that the solution should be left to natural economic forces, which would of themselves divide the land without the intervention of the law. But the peasant problem in Russia was too fundamental for such a solution; so a return was made to the eighteenth-century debates on the origin and basis of property. The proposed land reform raised the whole problem of the distribution of property and the achievement of equality. The situation resembled that of France during the Revolution, though on a very different scale. In Russia, where much of the land was periodically redistributed among the members of the agrarian communities (*obshchina*), there arose for the first time the problem of relations between the wish for equality and primitive agrarian collectivism; between the land reform and the *obshchina*; between the ideas of a small enlightened minority and the traditions of the Russian village.

The personal development of Pestel himself, who was to become one of the boldest and most decided of the conspirators, gives us an interesting reflection of this rapid deepening of Decembrist ideas. Between 1819 and 1820, under the influence of Sismondi's *Nouveaux principes d'économie politique*, Pestel wrote a series of short notes on economic and administrative problems. The question of the peasants was already pre-eminent, but he still thought in terms of freeing them without land. 'The worst solution', he wrote, 'would be to give the land to the peasants. Agriculture is not a question of the number of hands, but of capital and culture, and the peasants have neither one nor the other.' He considered, too, the position of farmers whom he called the 'capitalists of the peasant classes'. But above all he considered the problem of economic development, as much from the agricultural as from the industrial point of view.[9]

However, a few years later, when completing and discussing the 'Russian

Law' which he and his followers must have considered as the fundamental document of the conspiracy, he gave pride of place to equal distribution and agrarian collectivism.[10]

About property, there exist two fundamental and contradictory opinions. Some say, 'The Almighty has created the human race and has granted the earth to it for sustenance. Nature itself produces everything that can serve to support man. For this reason the earth is the common property of the entire human race and not of private owners. It cannot, therefore, be divided among a few men to the exclusion of others . . . It was on this basis that the famous Roman Agrarian Law was founded, which established the frequent division of land among all citizens.' Others object that 'Work is at the origin of all property, and that the man who cultivates the land and farms its different products must have exclusive right of possession'. They add that 'great expense is necessary to make agriculture prosper, and so the man who agrees to make this expense should own the land as his private property'.

How could these contradictory opinions be resolved? Pestel had no intention of accepting either of these theories. He envisaged the Russia which would emerge from the revolution as a country where both could be applied equally. He maintained the right to life contained in the first theory, but admitted the right of earning reward contained in the second. 'We must consider granting the necessities of life to everyone; at the same time we must create plenty. Every human being has an indisputable natural right to the first; the second belongs only to him who succeeds in obtaining it through his own work.'

In practice, the solution was to divide the land in each district into two identical parts.

The first of these will constitute common land, the other private land. Common land will belong collectively to the entire community of each district, and will be inalienable. It may be neither sold nor pawned; it will be used to obtain the necessities of life for all citizens without exception, and will belong to each and all. Private land, on the other hand, will belong either to the State or to private persons who will own it in complete freedom, and will have the right to do with it what they think best. These lands will be thus used as private property and to create plenty.[11]

Semevsky, one of the best-informed writers on Russia's peasant history, tries to trace the origins of this plan to a brochure of the French revolutionary period by the Abbé Antoine de Cournaud; to the writings of Charles Hall; even to the influence of the Carbonari and other groups.[12] But there is no point in trying to specify a relationship which is both deeper and more general. Pestel's words are the result of his own thought—the thought of a man who has pondered long on the theories of the entire French eighteenth century; on the work of Mably and the Physiocrats.

Pestel made a fresh contribution to the debate by linking the 'Agrarian Law' to the traditional customs of the Russian village. 'At first sight', he said, 'it may seem that such a plan could only be introduced with great difficulty, but it is worth remembering that such plans would meet greater obstacles in other countries than in Russia. Here public opinion views them with great favour; from the earliest times a similar division of land into two parts has been practised.'[13] (Landlord property had always existed alongside the *obshchina*.) He added that in any case the common lands would have to be periodically redistributed according to the traditional rules of agrarian collectivism.[14]

In this way egalitarian ideas found a link with the situation as it actually existed in Russia. The *obshchina*, detached from the feudal society of which it formed a part, was to become the basis of a social order founded on the universal right of humanity to the necessities of life.

The 'Russian Law' was thus not utopian; it was a proposal for land reform based on institutions already in existence and influenced by European achievements. It was through this that a bond remained with less bold and less revolutionary schemes of the other Decembrists. They, too, were aware of the various changes in Europe during the last decades, and the possible consequences of abolishing serfdom. They saw that to give freedom without land was to sow the fatal seed of pauperism and a proletariat. In 1809, Speransky, the reforming minister of Alexander I, said that 'The lot of the peasant who pays his *redevances*, and who has in return his own strip of land, is incomparably better than that of those poor wretches—the English, French and American workers.' And the Decembrists often referred to his words and plans.[15]

So fear of creating a labouring class and a proletariat made the Decembrists reject freedom 'without land', and turn away from the example of England. Nor did the simple distribution of strips according to the French precedent seem to be the best solution. For that too might soon lead to a class of agricultural labourers.[16]

For this reason the Decembrists turned again and again to the *obshchina*, looking upon it as a guarantee of stability and security. However, N. Muraviev and I. Yakushkin, two of the leaders, maintained that at a second stage the communal properties also would have to be divided. But soon Yakushkin admitted that these were in fact a guarantee against poverty. Socially, too, the communal properties would check excessive individualism by creating a collective spirit: 'Each action of a single man within them is guided by the spirit of the entire community.'[17] In a French version of the 'Russian Law', Pestel himself speaks of the 'principe de solidarité' which would have inspired the agricultural communities.[18]

The Decembrists thus resumed the discussion on the feasibility of dividing the common land—a discussion which had already been amply developed throughout Europe during the eighteenth century. In Russia itself there had been no lack of defenders of the agrarian communities; but praise had come from the ranks of the conservatives. The periodical redistribution of the land, and the assumed absence of poverty and labourers, had seemed to them proofs of the excellence of the Russian property system—including, of course, its corner-stone, serfdom. These defenders of the ancient tradition of the Fatherland against western influence had been the first to eulogize the *obshchina*. Among them was Shcherbatov, perhaps Rostopchin, and most important of all, Boltin.[19]

The agrarian communities were beginning to assume another meaning. They were to continue even after the abolition of serfdom, and Pestel's *principe de solidarité* would protect Russia from the evils that Sismondi had taught them to see in Western Europe. No longer did the *obshchina* seem a mere feature of the Russian tradition, but an answer to the experiences of the West. Pestel did not just accept Sismondi's criticisms of the society which had emerged from the French and industrial revolutions; he provided a plan which was already Socialist in character.

But the Decembrist revolt was quelled and Pestel was executed. His 'Russian Law', which had been literally buried in the ground, was unearthed during the investigation, and was one of the facts which convinced Nicholas I of the seriousness of the conspiracy. Indeed, the Tsar considered the document so dangerous that he would not allow it to be shown even to the full Committee of Inquiry. The 'Law' remained sealed in the archives until the end of the last century, and was not printed until after the revolution of 1905.

But the seed of Socialism contained in it still thrived among some of the Decembrists. They continued to ponder (in Siberia) the ideas which had so excited them when planning the conspiracy. Perhaps the most important of these exiles was N. A. Bestuzhev, one of the few Decembrists who had studied economics. Others were N. I. Turgenev and M. F. Orlov who escaped deportation and death, and who were later closely associated with the young Herzen.

Bestuzhev was a convinced free-trader, who had always fought against every form of monopoly and protection. He expressed his opinions in a work published in 1831 *On Free Trade and Economic Activities*.[20] But in examining the situation in France, England and the United States he developed his criticism of monopoly much further, probably under Sismondi's influence. He now took a pessimistic view of the concentration of capital and the rise of the proletariat. Later he began to take an interest in the problem of land ownership, which he followed in the few French books which he managed to obtain in Siberia. He read the *Histoire parlementaire de la Révolution française* by Buchez and Roux. From it he absorbed the ideas of Claude Fauchet, who maintained the right of all men to the land and discussed at length the Spartan agrarian laws and the 'Jubilee years' of the Bible. So, to some extent, Bestuzhev reached the same conclusions as Pestel.

Which is the more useful for agriculture, great estates or small properties? There is the example of England, where constant subdivisions have allowed a few great capitalists to own nearly all the land. On the other hand there is the example of

France, where subdivisions have doubled production. Again, there is the example of Russia, where regular subdivisions have until now avoided a landless proletariat. So what can be done? Divide the land into private properties? With what results? Or consider that the land belongs to the State, as in Russia? But can land belong to anyone?[21]

Pestel's ideas (like Herzen's) were crystallized by the 1848 revolution. They became a defence of Russian tradition against Western Europe, and a eulogy of the seeds of collectivism and democracy which were to be found in Russia's rural life. Discussing N. I. Turgenev's book *La Russie et les Russes*, which had appeared in France in 1847, Bestuzhev wrote in February 1850,

Let us examine the proletariat. This exists throughout Europe because the land is the inalienable property of private owners. In time, the right to dispose of this property concentrates the land into a few hands. We see that even in the wealthiest countries, the number of owners is scarcely a thousandth of the population; everyone else becomes part of a landless proletariat. Without even mentioning England, let us look at France. The land holdings distributed after the revolution of '89, less than a century later, have been so divided by legacies, marriages and so on, that half now belong to the monopolists, and the other half no longer give any return. Again, we see the same in the possessions of our nobles, where half belong to the great estates and the other half are mortgaged to the banks. In my opinion land, air, water—of which we are incapable of making even an atom—cannot belong to us. Thus God said through Moses: 'The earth is mine and you are only guests on it.' This was confirmed by the agrarian laws of Catherine II, for with us there can be no proletariat; everyone, however poor, always has the right to a piece of land to support him, if he has the strength and the will to obtain it. An *obshchina* is in fact social Communism in practice, in which the land is a means for work; whereas the French Communists do not provide the means, but demand the right. The right to work, without the means, leads to starvation.[22]

It is the last remark that gives these ideas their historical interest. First Pestel, then Herzen believed that the 'social Communism' of the Russian *obshchina* was a direct answer to the problems of economic development in Western Europe. Now even Bestuzhev had moved from free trade and the ideas of Sismondi, to a form of Populist Socialism.

A similar change of outlook took place in other Decembrists. After the revolution of 1848, M. A. Fonvizin, who had been brought up on Montesquieu, Rousseau and Raynal, wrote an article, *On Socialism and Communism*, in which he called himself a Christian Socialist.[23]

This brief consideration of the development of political controversy before 14th December 1825 has been necessary for our history. It is true that Herzen and the Populists probably knew only a fraction of these ideas—that they saw the Decembrists primarily as models of self-sacrifice and heroism in the struggle for freedom. But this little-known fragment of Russian political thought provides a link which joins the traditional feudal system (where the Tsar was overlord of all the land, where the government administered a very large portion of it, where the peasant *obshchina* was a regular feature), to later theorizing on what Bestuzhev was to call 'social Communism'.

Herzen himself was later to hint at this feature of the Decembrist movement: 'Pestel le premier montrait la terre, la possession foncière et l'expropriation de la noblesse comme la base la plus sûre pour asseoir et enraciner la révolution.'[24] And in 1858 he was to say: 'Pestel va directement à son but, à la réorganisation complète et radicale du gouvernement sur des bases non seulement républicaines, mais socialistes.'[25]

The violent suppression of the Decembrist movement meant that its spirit of social revolution could not develop—indeed, it had later to be re-created from other sources. For decades no renewal of the movement was possible, and the destruction of the *élite*, which had gradually been formed during the eighteenth and early nineteenth centuries, profoundly affected the reign of Nicholas I. Count Uvarov, the Emperor's Minister of Public Instruction, said it was his ambition to delay Russia's intellectual development by fifty years, lest the country be ruined by following too quickly the example of Western Europe. Nicholas I's suppression of the Decembrists had gone far towards achieving this ambition.

Herzen recalled vividly the terrible years which followed the crushing of the secret societies: 'À la vue de la Russie officielle on n'avait que le désespoir au cœur.' And yet, he added, 'à l'intérieur il se faisait un grand travail, un travail sourd et muet, mais actif et non interrompu'.[26] Elsewhere he said that 'the eager, hopeful spirit of Alexander I's time grew calmer, sadder and more serious. The torch which feared to shine above ground, burnt below, lighting the depths.'[27]

One of the earliest and most important indications of this 'travail sourd et muet' was the formation in the early 'thirties of a small group of young men inspired by the ideas of Saint-Simon, and led by Herzen, Ogarev and Sazonov.

> I remember the room with five *arshin*
> The bed and the chair and the table with the tallow candle
> And us three, sons of the Decembrists
> Pupils of the new world
> Of Fourier and Saint-Simon.
> We swore to devote all our lives
> To the people and its liberation
> The foundation we set was Socialism.
> And to achieve our sacred ends
> We had to create a secret society
> And spread it secretly, step by step.

Ogarev has described here all the essential features of the group—the romantic, almost religious atmosphere, the feeling that they were the sons of the Decembrists and the attempt to spread the ideas of Fourier and Saint-Simon.

1*

In a short imaginative essay called 'The Crowd', Ogarev, explained the motive of his political activities and the 'sacred aims' mentioned in his poetry. Watching the colourful crowd that swarmed in Moscow's Red Square, and leaning on the railing outside the church of St Basil, he discusses with a friend the fate of the masses,

To lead this crowd just for a minute!—Don't tell me, Waldemar, that it's not possible . . . Surely in their intelligent faces, in their great capacity to understand and act, and in the quickness of their minds, there are enough elements to create a harmonious whole—to give humanity a shining example of social life and a picture of man's great destiny. Believe me, Waldemar, nature does not distribute her gifts uselessly, nor does she pointlessly mark people's faces with distinctive features. This hope reconciles me to humanity.[28]

The July revolution in Paris and the Polish revolt of 1831 were powerful incitements to the group. New ideas reached them from France and encouraged action. 'Our first step in the world of thought', said Ogarev, later, 'was not a search for the abstract, but a clash with concrete society—a clash which roused in us the thirst for analysis and criticism. At the ages of fourteen, fifteen, sixteen, under the influence of Schiller, Rousseau and 14th December, we studied mathematics and the natural sciences. We wanted something definite, although we were uncertain of what we sought.'[29]

It is difficult to determine exactly how much the young men knew of Saint-Simon. They may have known more of what was written about the cult of Saint-Simon than of what he actually did. Herzen, for instance, quotes from Olinde Rodrigues, and mentions chiefly the pamphlets and trials of Saint-Simon's followers.

It was probably the criticism of the 'Enlightenment', the philosophy of history and the dawning of a new era in organic science and religion, which first struck Herzen and his friends. Such matters are discussed in some of Herzen's writings at the end of 1832, called *On the Place of Man in Nature*. Even later he was to write mainly of the religious aspect of Saint-Simonism, and of the 'réhabilitation de la chair'.

But although this was the most obvious effect of Saint-Simonism on Herzen, the desire for 'palingenesis' was already modified by his critical spirit. He said that if Saint-Simon's ideology was to be a new Christianity, it ran the risk common to all religions, of moving from 'pure foundations' and a 'great and exalted' vision to 'obscure mysticism'. As early as 1833, the development of Saint-Simonism confirmed his doubts. Writing to Ogarev, he said,

What you say is true. We are right to be interested in it. We feel (and I wrote this to you two years ago when the idea was still original) that the world is waiting for a renewal; that the revolution of '89 is broken, and that a new era must be brought about through *palingenesis*. European society must be given new foundations, based more firmly on right, on morality and on culture. This is the actual meaning of our experiences—this is Saint-Simonism. But I don't refer to its decadence, as I call its religious form (Enfantin etc.).[30]

For these reasons Herzen did not give up his investigation of the Socialist doctrine of Fourier and others. ('Its oddity', he said, 'is justified by its ends.') But he did not confine himself to their theories. He was consumed by the desire for knowledge and had great plans for reading—Michelet, Vico, Montesquieu and Herder; Roman law and the political economy of Say and Malthus; all these he mentioned to Ogarev.[31]

Then what made Herzen look to Saint-Simonism for the heart of his romantic vision? It was something even more important for his future development than Socialism. It was his break with the French Revolution—his criticism of democracy which he himself was to develop after 1848, but which he had already found in origin in Saint-Simon. It is strange that even as early as this we find a trace of Hébert's spirit in Herzen's political ideas; a spirit whose origin it is difficult to trace, but which probably derives from, or at least is similar to, the earliest roots of Saint-Simon's conceptions. It is not by chance that the hero of the French Revolution who then most often appeared in his writings was the cosmopolitan Anacharsis Cloots.[32]

But these political investigations within the framework of romantic culture were abruptly interrupted by the arrest of Herzen and his circle on 21st July 1834. The group had spread, and its members had planned to publish a review. Their political and social ideas had by now clearly distinguished them from other contemporary philosophical groups.

Herzen remained in prison until April of the following year. He was condemned to exile, first at Perm and then at Vyatka in the north-east of European Russia.

His isolation fostered the religious and sentimental aspects of his romanticism. His criticism of Saint-Simon's followers for distorting the doctrines of their master (a criticism which had been the most personal contribution of his youth) gave way to a form of romanticism akin to Christianity. In order to live more intensively, and to escape from the mean provincial atmosphere of his surroundings, he became introspective. It was not by chance that he here began the autobiography which he was to continue throughout his life.

Romantic introspection led him, as it led many of his contemporaries and friends, to resignation and a willingness to accept real existence as rational. However, this reconciliation with the world did not have the doctrinaire violence which showed later in Bakunin and Belinsky.[33] In Herzen a religious wish for interior peace predominated, because he realized that powerless, alone and cut off from the familiar society of his Moscow friends he could achieve nothing.

Politically this reconciliation expressed itself in a few *Scattered Notes on Russian Legislation* written at Vyatka in 1836. In these he gave a more favourable judgment than he had yet done, or would ever do again, on the civilizing work of the Tsarist State. The government, he thought, had already carried out a task of enlightenment and education, which could be continued in the future. He saw both good and bad, and continued to criticize the privileges of the nobility and the serfdom of the peasants; but he surveyed it all with the mild eye of the reformer. These notes only deserve mention because at the very moment of reconciliation with the world they contained a hint of what would become Herzen's first interest—peasant Socialism. In examining the Russian situation more calmly, he observed the periodical redistribution of the fields in the peasant communities. He mentioned his ideas on the subject in a note 'This is the *lex agraria*—the Jubilee Year'.[34]

This was no more than a hint. To pursue it further Herzen had to reconquer a world less private and more in touch with social reality. He was to do this when he left Vyatka and rejoined the intellectual centres of Moscow and St Petersburg. The truth which he rediscovered after discarding his religious romanticism he called 'realism'.

At Vladimir in 1838, Herzen could still write that 'present-day German philosophy [Hegel] is very comforting; a fusion of thought, revelation, and the conceptions of idealism and theology'.[35] This was similar to the point of view expressed by Bakunin, who wrote at that time a number of long letters in which Hegelianism and pietism were combined. During the next ten years Herzen rid himself of these 'comforting harmonies', and found in politics as well as in philosophy their true contradictions.

His contact with the capital was short. Almost at once he was sent back to the provinces, to Novgorod, for having dared to criticize in a private letter the administration of public order in St Petersburg. But this short contact again brought him face to face with the problem of the State and its function in Russia. He returned to the researches on Peter the Great which he had begun in his earlier years. He was inspired no longer by youthful admiration, but by a wish to interpret history in the light of his knowledge of both the Russian sources and the great contemporary French historians—Thierry, Michelet and Guizot. His attempts to understand Peter the Great convinced him that the period which that Tsar had initiated was now closing. 'His epoch ends with us. We complete the great task of humanizing the old Russia. After us will come an epoch of organic development, concerned with the substance, not the form, and therefore purely human in character.'[36]

Thus his youthful ideas of *palingenesis* were being transformed into a belief in the start of a new historical epoch—an epoch ripe for development, and ready to replace the oppressive age of Nicholas I. It was Herzen's duty to prepare himself.

His acceptance of the idea that Russia should be Europeanized—a process which he viewed as the starting point of the new epoch—brought him into violent conflict with the two most active exponents of Russian Hegelianism, Belinsky and Bakunin. In 1837 these had accepted the correctness of Hegel's theories on the political as well as on the philosophical plane, and had extolled the absolutist State as the incarnation of 'objective reason'. They had reached this paradoxical conclusion in a desperate search for 'reality', at a time when the government aimed to deprive the intellectuals of all political action. Herzen spoke of 'a renunciation of the rights of the intellect, an incomprehensible and unnatural suicide'.

Belinsky continued to defend his theories until the beginning of 1840, in open conflict with Herzen and with others who believed in freedom. Belinsky violently maintained that the conscience of the Russian people had always found complete expression in the actions of the Tsar—the incarnation of Russian civilization and freedom. But this violence, which seemed to Herzen a form of suicide, contained an element of salvation, for it revealed the same political spirit which made Belinsky's contemporaries believe in French utopias. Belinsky had merely constructed the strangest and most intellectual of all utopias—the absolutism of the Russian emperors. He could not, of course, hold this position for long. Soon he too was to grow interested in Western theories, and find in them the satisfaction which he had vainly sought in conforming to absolutism. Eventually, whilst Herzen and Ogarev devoted themselves more and more to the study of Hegel and German philosophy, Belinsky began to explore more modern social theories. From the combination of these philosophical and political enthusiasms was born the Westernism of the 'forties.

This Westernism was in direct opposition to the Slavophil tendencies which (chiefly in Moscow) were developing into a political movement. Belinsky's 'absolutist period' had itself been an extreme reaction against the Slavophils; a defence of the function of the Russian State against the supporters of the purely nationalist spirit of the Church and the village. Just as Belinsky had absurdly tried to see the reign of Nicholas I as an enlightened despotism, so the Slavophils took an equally romantic view of the Russian people. The Slavophils looked back a long time—to Frederick II and Herder, to the German culture of the end of the eighteenth century and beginning of the nineteenth. They had been deeply influenced by the German intellectual atmosphere and were, in fact, its tardy product.

But their discussion could not remain bound to the tradition of Peter the Great and the romantic idealization of the Russian past. Such a form would have been sterile and impractical; on one hand an official apology of absolutism, on the other, a sentimental reaction against it. It could only have been an academic discussion on the philosophy of Russia's history and spirit, and on the institutions in which they expressed themselves. It was the function of the exceptionally lively culture of the 'forties to widen the discussion. This widening led at least some of the Westerners to conceive a development rather than a rejection of absolutism; while the Slavophils tried to understand better the people and the past about which they spoke so much.

Herzen himself, a man of sparkling intelligence, played no small part in this change; he alone was to emerge with a complete and effective political outlook.

In 1842 he was able to return to Moscow, which he now made the centre of his activities. He was at last free from provincial exile; free also from the administrative career which he had curiously combined with his life as an exile, and which had become almost too successful. He embarked on a second youth, more mature but as enthusiastic and as interested in European culture as the first. He was quickly ridding himself of the load of resignation, boredom and vague religion piled upon him by his years of solitude. In his diary he has left a wonderful record of this liberation from romantic dreams —of this rebirth of more concrete political and philosophical interests. And it is a record of a spiritual process which he shared with all contemporary Europe—a Europe which was moving towards the revolution of 1848.

At first the ideal of the Slavophils seemed to embody the very ideas and emotions which Herzen was then rejecting. 'Impossible to speak with them; they are as stupid and harmful as the pietists.'[37] Two years later in 1844 he produced an historical analogy to the Slavophil ideal.

Slavophilia has its parallels in the history of modern Western literature. There is the appearance in Germany after the Napoleonic wars of national and romantic tendencies, which rejected as too general and cosmopolitan the ideas which had developed from Leibnitz and Lessing to Herder, Goethe and Schiller. Though the rise of this neo-romanticism was natural, it was a scholarly phenomenon which took no account of either reality or the masses. It was not hard to guess that after ten years it would be forgotten. Slavophilia plays exactly the same role. It has no roots in the people; it is a purely literary disease.[38]

This encouraged Herzen to study the German roots of Slavophil culture, and to settle his own accounts with idealistic philosophy. He followed the activities of left-wing Hegelianism in Berlin, and its new developments in Ruge's *Deutsche Jahrbücher*. He read Feuerbach. But his main help was a personal reflection on Hegel. 'There is nothing more absurd', he wrote, 'than the German opinion—shared by all the tribe—of Hegel as an arid reasoner, a hard-boiled dialectician like Wolff. In fact, all his work is penetrated by the power of poetry, and he himself, carried away (partly against his will) by his own genius, expresses speculative thoughts with great energy and enunciates impressive truths. How powerful is his destruction of all the decoration which adorns truth! What brilliant insight, penetration and percipience.'[39] It was here that he sought the kernel of Hegel's thought. The 'philosophy of history' he found the frailest part of the system, an artificial construction which concealed rather than revealed history.

He was struck by Hegel's admitting the existence of an external spirit above human events. Hegel remained, as he then wrote, 'the Columbus of philosophy and humanity'. But what was the point, he asked,

. . . of the two concentric circles which he uses to define the human spirit: history, the record of that spirit, its realization, its truth, its essence, and the spirit apart as a thing in itself? These two circles may have the same radius, but sometimes a circle whose radius is spirit itself assumes an incomprehensible infinite length . . . At other times, again, we come across a single circle while Hegel always thinks there are two. In all this there is a tautological duplication which makes truth so complicated that it can be called the most extravagant repetition of the century.[40]

The problem therefore was to free historical development from the theology with which Hegel had enshrouded it. But this could only be achieved by giving first place to practical action rather than theory. 'Hegel has hinted at, rather than developed, the idea of action . . . He explores the regions of the spirit, he talks of art and science, but forgets action, which is, however, woven into all historical events.'[41]

Because of his doubts Herzen did not try to re-elaborate Hegel's philosophy so as to include this new problem. It proved the limit beyond which he was no longer really Hegelian. Instead of reconsidering the dialectic, he recognized the flaw in the system as originating in Germany's own historical development where science had been separated from life, and philosophy from politics. But the despised world of action had had its revenge. 'The realm of the practical is not inarticulate; when the time came its voice was raised.'[42] The time came with the death of Goethe and Hegel.

'Buddhists of science', was what Herzen called the men who insisted on contemplation at a time which should now be devoted to action.

They halt at every moment as if it was the truth, mistake every partial determination for the final determination. They need judgments and ready-made rules, and every time they pause, imagine with ludicrous credulity that they have reached the absolute end and are ready to relax.[43]

What remained for him of Hegel's philosophy was the belief in development, the interpretation of the dialectic not as a philosophy of history but as a movement which had its own intrinsic value. This made him say later that the 'embryology of history differs from the development of the dialectic of the spirit'. On yet another occasion he described Hegel's philosophy as the 'algebra of revolution'.[44]

These conclusions were thus parallel to those being reached simultaneously by the Hegelian left-wing in Germany. Herzen welcomed the symptoms of this political and social awakening. '*Se muove, se muove*' (*sic*), he wrote in Italian, reading the *Deutsche Jahrbücher*. 'Germany is moving towards political emancipation.' But he added that Germany continued to reveal 'its characteristically closed system of thought, made up simultaneously of depth and quietism'.[45] As a sign of the reaction against this political quietism, an article in the review signed by a Frenchman, Jules Elysard, especially pleased him. He did not yet know that this was Bakunin's pseudonym.[46]

His deep political passion, his complete and revolutionary rejection of the entire official world of the Russian Empire, could only be echoed by a man who, like himself, had really had personal experience of the Russian situation. By extolling the passion for destruction, Bakunin expressed some of Herzen's own feelings. German culture, however alive, could no longer satisfy him.

And so to oppose this German idealism Herzen turned to eighteenth-century France. Although Saint-Simon had taught him to look upon this period as consisting of purely negative and destructive forces, he and the young Hegelians in Germany were now rediscovering it. 'We have forgotten the eighteenth century . . . Yet this stage of development was immensely important, and brought about essential benefits.'[47] This led him back to his scientific studies—to a defence of the scientific method from Bacon to the Encyclopaedists, and to the rediscovery in the English and French eighteenth century of a political and social force which he could not find in Romanticism and German philosophy. He saw in the Encyclopaedists the men who had achieved the vision which had begun to torment him at Vyatka, when he wrote: 'Thought without action is a dream.' He now felt that for years he had been merely dreaming. He drew on Voltaire and Diderot as stimulants to action and to 'realism' as well as to the reappraisal of the Socialist ideas which had so excited him in Moscow in 1831.

Belinsky had reached a very similar conclusion after his 'absolutist' phase. As a reaction against Hegelianism (which had led to his paradoxical apology for Tsarism) he had embraced the socialist theories that came from Paris in the works of Cabet, Fourier, Leroux and Proudhon. He thus discovered Socialism ten years after Herzen. But these ten years had been fruitful for both of them. Russian Socialism in the 'forties had had a thorough grounding in the philosophy of Hegel, and this gave it a very special character. It was no longer the romantic urge for a *palingenesis*, but was, or at least aimed to be, the search for philosophical and political truth.

One of the roots of this Socialism before 1848 lay in the interpretation that many of these authors had put on Hegel's philosophy. Both for Belinsky and for Bakunin—though in different ways—it seemed to be an explanation of the course of individual human lives rather than of history itself. 'A metaphysic of mind and will' as Annenkov has ably defined it in his remarkable essay *The Remarkable Decade of 1838 to 1848*.[48] The smallest details of private life—love, hate, tastes, dislikes—seemed to be symptoms and in some ways revelations of the 'Idea'. This metaphysic of psychology had an obviously religious character. It was partly derived from earlier Russian thinkers, who had tried to apply to individual human destinies the complicated mythology of masonry and gnostic mysticism which dominated Russian lodges. It was really a sort of renovated pietism, but 'although it contained many fantastic elements, it was certainly superior to the methods [of psychological understanding] which dominated their contemporaries' (Annenkov).[49] Such examinations of conscience, which were made with eyes reverently raised towards Hegel's Idea, helped to form the intellectuals who in the 'forties brought about the first spiritual flowering after the Decembrists.

This rather personal application of Hegelianism had an important result. With a few exceptions (principally, of course, Belinsky's and Bakunin's apologies for absolutism) when the intellectuals wanted to abandon the world of 'beautiful souls' and Hamlet-like doubts, they now looked for reality within themselves. They made an effort to undergo a spiritual revival and take up a position independent of authority in considering the ethical relations of the intellectual towards the people; they did not try to apply the philosophy of history to peoples, groups and classes. In short, they preferred a 'metaphysic of mind and will' to 'the metaphysic of politics' so popular in the Hegelian left-wing in Germany and Poland.

French Socialism of the early nineteenth century, which was closely related to problems of psychology and morals (see for instance Fourier and Leroux), naturally satisfied them. The novels of George Sand often constituted a link between French and Russians. We can follow this assimilation of French utopian ideas from the early discussions of Belinsky's group in St Petersburg to Petrashevsky's circle. These ideas were absorbed by men who were looking chiefly for a truth to guide their lives. They left the job of constructing a philosophy of history, designed to include Russia, to the Slavophils (those conservative followers of German philosophy).

Although Belinsky took part in the socialist movement, he was also a true psychologist with a prophetic insight into the themes likely to promote fruitful discussion among his readers and widen intellectual controversy. Like Bakunin, he trusted his own instincts, defended creative passion, and sought both within and beyond French Socialism for the means to develop the Russian intelligentsia.[50] His contemporaries admired the seriousness of his work, the ruthless logic to which he subjected his own ideas, a process which in many other writers was in danger of becoming a game or theological speculation. For him, as Herzen was to say, 'les vérités, les résultats n'étaient ni des abstractions, ni des jeux d'esprit, mais des questions de vie ou de mort'.[51]

But for Herzen Socialism meant a return to the ideas of his younger days, a continuation and criticism of his early apprenticeship to Saint-Simon. Once again, as had happened ten years earlier, he found himself unable wholly to accept the French books which he was eagerly reading.

Of course, the Saint-Simonists and Fourierists have made the most important prophecies for the future, but *something* is missing. Fourier, despite his colossal foundations, is terribly prosaic, too concerned with petty details. Luckily his pupils have substituted their own works for his. Saint-Simon's pupils have destroyed their master. People will remain unmoved as long as prophecies are made in this way. Communism, of course, is nearer the masses, but at the moment it seems largely a negation, a storm-cloud loaded with thunder-bolts which, like the judgment of God, will destroy our absurd social system unless men repent.[52]

By Communism of course Herzen meant the legacy of Babeuf, and the Swiss Communist Movement led by Weitling. 'His words sometimes have the power of prophecy. He has excellently defined his position as regards the Liberals. Some of his ideas are absurd (for example, the theory of theft) but there are also striking truths.'[53] Bakunin's association with this movement made Herzen scrutinize it even more closely. But Weitling's predictions were not enough.

Communism was the problem, not its solution. Only in Socialism was there an answer to Communist negation. Thus Considérant's social analysis greatly interested him. 'His examination of contemporary life is excellent and fills one with fear and shame.'[54] But of all the Socialist writers, it was Proudhon who most attracted his attention. 'I have at last read', he noted in his diary,

his article on property; an excellent work, better than anything else that has yet been written on the subject. Of course, his main thesis is not new to anyone who has pondered and deeply felt the problem, but it is all very well developed with keen insight and is powerfully expressed. He completely repudiates property, but recognizes private ownership. This is not just his own idea, but the logical and inevitable end of a process of reasoning which is used to demonstrate the criminal and absurd impossibility of the right to property and the necessity of ownership.[55]

A year later he read *De la création de l'ordre dans l'humanité* by Proudhon —'the man who wrote about property'. The reading of it brought back his main doubts about the whole of the current French Socialist movement. It seemed to him like the scattered fragments of some future Socialist doctrine, or a collection of material for some eventual creative work, rather than a system which could already withstand attack and criticism. His exploration of German philosophy and his reflections on Hegel and Feuerbach clearly showed him the ingenuousness—the 'niaiserie'—to be found in these French writers. 'We must look beyond this and consider it as we do a bad habit to be put up with in a worthy man, and then move on.'[56]

Herzen's general reflections on French Socialism are of great interest. Starting from the Communist tradition and seeing in it a denial of existing society, a demand which was close to the hearts of the masses but not a solution, he looked for an answer in the work of those writers who had made the most profound analyses of society. So he moved with growing certainty towards a form of Proudhonism and began to judge it critically in the light of his own experience and his own philosophical ideas.

Thus fortified, he directed his attention to the contemporary Russian situation. He no longer found it possible to continue his projected studies of the age of Peter the Great, or his attempted revaluation of the function of the State in the history of his country's civilization. He concentrated more and more on the peasants and the life of the Russian people.

His attention was drawn to them by the plans for reform, which the government was considering. They were very cautious plans, it is true; still, for the first time since the intransigent reaction that had followed the Decembrist revolt, the official world was reviewing the problem of serfdom. Herzen had no illusions. 'It's a *false* liberation of the serfs', he said, adding, 'Ne réveillez pas le chat qui dort.'[57]

Official interest was only one symptom of the renewed interest in this problem throughout society. Even the Slavophil movement, which he had first looked upon as composed mainly of neo-romantics and pietists, now appeared to him to be an important example of the current preoccupation. It was no longer enough to criticize their religious position and see in Slavophilia just one more product of the countless philosophies of history. For now the controversy was to become much more detailed and much more political. Moscow was the natural centre of the Slavophils, and it was the spirit of Moscow, as opposed to that of St Petersburg, which they wished to represent. Herzen lived and worked in their capital, and there established that complex relationship made up of love and hatred, opposition and support, which was to continue in various forms throughout his life, and which finally led him to Populism.

The Slavophil movement was a symptom of political regeneration, chiefly because it tried to give content and meaning to *narodnost*, which was one of the passwords of the reign of Nicholas I. The word itself, derived from *narod*, meaning both 'people' and 'nation' (like the German *Volk*), had been taken from *Volkstum*, and had a similar political intonation, one of reaction against the French Revolution, against the subsequent national and at the same time liberal movements. At this time, i.e. in 1843, Uvarov, the Minister of Public Instruction under Nicholas I, proclaimed the official trinity of autocracy, orthodoxy and *narodnost*, whose natural synthesis, it was claimed, lay in the first of these—autocracy. The absolutist system thus found it necessary to deck itself out with Christianity and nationalism, as if looking for its lawful foundation in religion and the people.

Such camouflage was best admired from a distance. It was a typical directive of despotism, as great a danger because of those who reject it as because of those who take it seriously and try to give it effective meaning, which was just what the Slavophils were aiming to do. They wanted to make use of sentiment to bring back the Church to life, and to feel themselves close to the Russian people—the peasants, and popular traditions as distinct from the State. They exalted patriarchal forms of life and rejected modern systems which were less national in character.

But, as Herzen noted, even if 'the Government had raised the banner of *narodnost*, it would never permit the movement to advance. One more move, one more thought, and even the Slavophils would have been lost.'[58] Herzen was looking beyond the fanaticism and the eclectic and reactionary features of the Slavophil movement, which even in these years he never tired of emphasizing; and beyond the official slogans. He was searching for the living force which had inspired its ideas.

He admired the personal characteristics of some of the Slavophil writers; he regarded Aksakov, Khomyakov, Kireyevsky and Samarin as men who were genuinely searching for truth and believed they had found it. This was not only because of his respect for them as individuals but, above all, because of that delicate consideration that so often inspired his judgment. 'It's impossible not to appreciate such people, even if our opinions are diametrically opposed.'[59]

Ivan Kireyevsky he looked upon as a man 'who had felt intensely the nature of the current Russian problem, and who had struggled through blood and tears to a solution—an impossible solution, but a less repugnant one than the pietistic optimism of Aksakov'.[60] Of all the Slavophils it was Kireyevsky who was to have the greatest influence on him.

But though personal respect might delay his break with the Slavophil group and might lead him to assume a less extreme position than Belinsky, it could never in itself have profoundly affected his development. There was, moreover, a far stronger bond: it was the Slavophils who suggested to him a field of investigation—the Russian village. Although this had not been outside his interests, it would not have assumed such political importance, had it not been for the vague, persistent, penetrating preaching of the Slavophils.

These men, who declared themselves to be representatives of the mediaeval Russian tradition, and who repudiated Peter the Great because he had created a state which he intended to be modern, emphasized the importance of the collective elements in the Russian village. Hating the contemporary world, they exalted the most primitive aspects of the peasant communities, the systems of land tenure and distribution.

It must be emphasized that their conceptions were vague and expressed in philosophical and religious terms. Yet it was not without reason that Khomyakov could boast in 1857 that as from 1839 the Slavophils had concentrated their attention on the *obshchina* as 'giving birth to a new spiritual movement'.[61] And Samarin was to say in 1847 that 'the answer to the most urgent problem of the West (i.e. Socialism) lies in the oldest customs of the Slavs'.[62]

But Herzen was right when he in turn noted that the Slavophils were only interested in these problems (and especially the relations between the Russian peasants and Western Socialism) because even in Russia Socialism had already been discussed. Had not he himself spoken of the theories of Saint-Simon at the beginning of the 'thirties? But the function of the Slavophils in the development of Russian Socialism must not be considered merely in this light. They really did help to transform Socialism from an intellectual reflection of the problems of the West to a question which was closely related to the peasants in their own country. This is certainly not what they intended, but thanks to Herzen, their opponent, this is what they achieved. By keeping alive the discussion on the earliest forms of agrarian communities in Russia, which had begun in the eighteenth century and had already assumed such importance for the Decembrists, these supporters of a backward and patriarchal country life prepared the ground for Herzen's Populism.[63]

During the first years after his return to Moscow, Herzen was still inclined to criticize even the social aspect of the Slavophil ideology. Horrified by the position of the Russian peasant, he wrote,

Our Slavophils speak of the communal principle, of the fact that we have no proletariat, of the constant subdivision of the land. These are all useful aspects, but they are derived partly from a neglected opportunity of economic development. For instance, among the Bedouins, the right to property does not have the egoistic character which it does in Europe. But they (the Slavophils) forget their complete lack of self-respect and stupid submission to all oppression. Is it surprising that among our peasants, the right to property has not developed in the direction of individual tenure, when we remember that his strip of land is not his own, and when even his wife, son and daughter do not belong to him? What is the property of a slave? His position is even worse than that of a proletarian. He is a *thing*, a mere tool to cultivate the fields whose master can do everything except kill him, by the same token as under Peter, in certain places, it was forbidden to pull down oak trees. Give him the legal right to self-defence. Only then will he be a man. Twelve million people *hors la loi . . . Carmen horrendum.*[64]

The communal features of Russian peasant life thus seemed to him to be the result of a neglected historical development. He did not then suggest, as he did later, that for this very reason they might be developed along Socialist lines. But he did, even at this stage, argue that the opportunity for further development lay along the road of complete liberation from all forms of slavery. Only civil liberties could justify the preservation of these communal features at some later stage.

Thus the Slavophils had a similar function to that fulfilled in Russia a generation earlier by the followers of Sismondi, or a generation earlier still by the Physiocrats. Both these philosophies had been first regarded as providing new justifications for old realities: as the explanation and apology for the landed estates of the nobility, for the relative lack of industrial development, and, sometimes, even for the serfdom of the peasants. Now, Slavophilia was putting a similar interpretation on the German philosophy of history, its deep attraction for the primitive, for origins, for the 'people' outside the limits of politics. But similar attempts at justification—when made by people who seriously believed in them and who were honestly convinced by these Western ideas—always ended by providing ammunition for their opponents: first to the enlightened Radishchev, then to the more radical Decembrists, and now to Herzen.

It is unlikely, however, that these matters would have played such an important part in their lives, but for the arrival among the Slavophils of a Prussian investigator, Haxthausen, who had pursued his researches among such traces of collectivism as still survived in certain parts of Prussia, and who now undertook a systematic and patient study of the Russian village, its traditions and customs in the various regions of Nicholas I's Empire. Enthusiastic about his 'discovery', he proclaimed it to the world in three huge volumes.[65]

Even this aspect of Russian life was destined to be 'discovered' by a foreigner. The Russians had naturally studied the question of the *obshchina* long before him and had done so in the light of modern socializing tendencies for they needed to see the reflection in Europe of their own problems. Only then could they consider them as a whole. In the eighteenth and nineteenth centuries, for instance, a great part of the discussion between Westerners and patriots had been no more than an echo of the impressions of English, French and German travellers and writers. Haxthausen's book now served a similar function by promoting discussion on the collectivist aspects of Russian agrarian organization.[66]

Herzen met him in Moscow in 1843.

I was amazed by his clear picture of the life of our peasants and the power of our landlords, rural police and the administration in general. He looks upon the peasant communities as an important element which has survived from the most distant antiquity, and which must be developed in the light of present-day requirements. He thinks that the individual liberation of the serfs, with or without land, would be harmful. It would only bring isolated and weak families face to face with the terrible severity of the rural police, *das Beamtenwesen ist grässlich in Russland.*

This was a defence of patriarchal life against the interference of the modern State. But the kernel of this particular defence lay not in the nobility, but in the peasant community. And it was this that attracted Herzen's attention, even though he was not convinced by Haxthausen's theory. He wondered whether the *obshchina* itself would be able to resist for long the power of the *Beamtenwesen*. 'The position of an *obshchina*', he wrote then, 'depends on whether the landlord is rich or poor, is in government service or not, lives in St Petersburg or the country, administers his land in person or through a steward. The whole matter is so variable and uncertain that all development is stultified.'[67]

Confronted with the ideas of Haxthausen, Herzen saw that only by the *obshchina* playing its part in the evolution of the Russian State and society would its eventual retention and development be justified. His apologia for patriarchalism was gradually changing into a Populist vision of the future of the Russian countryside.[68]

But this vision was to take shape only after contact with the West, and the failure of the 1848 revolution. Before he emigrated, Herzen was chiefly concerned to counter the Slavophils and help to create a feeling of spiritual and political independence in opposition to the official world. He thought that everything else should give way to this. The antithesis of people and government which the Slavophils had proclaimed as part of their philosophy was entirely theoretical, incapable of active political development, unlikely to inspire deeper research into Russia's past. It was an idealization of Russia's origins based on an unhistorical myth. It merely helped to inspire the ethnographic research which accompanied the rise of Populism, and which played such an important part in Russian culture, without ever creating a political movement.[69] The most important feature of Russian life in the 'forties lay in the rise of the intelligentsia. Belinsky had wielded great authority because he knew how to lead a movement whose banner was 'Westernism'. Herzen too, in the years immediately before his emigration, with his 'realism', his scientific outlook and his enlightenment, forged the political conscience of the intellectuals of his own generation; he endowed them with a deep feeling of independence towards authority and the State, and this constituted their true *raison d'être*.

Herzen, at this time, established his position as a writer, under the name of Iskander, a pseudonym that he retained all his life. In 1845 he abandoned pamphlets and 'letters' on philosophical problems for his first important literary work, the novel *Who is to blame?*, which was followed by three short stories and the curious philosophical *conte On the works of Doctor Krupov. On mental illnesses in general and especially their spread by epidemics.*

These works are distinguished by an intelligent and subtle (sometimes too subtle) balance between thought and feeling. Discussion and autobiographical confession are inextricably mixed. The lucid style suffused with poetry is the by-product of a sharp, biting intelligence. He adopted this literary form from a desire for spiritual and social clarity, and the need to build new and truer relations between himself and other men. In his autobiography—written in his maturity—he was to be less restrained; here he was more acute.

Belinsky, after reading *Who is to blame?*, wrote him an enthusiastic letter which is worth quoting because it reveals the very uncertainty with which the critic expressed himself.

In artistic natures, intelligence becomes talent [i.e. genius, in the eighteenth-century meaning of the word], creative fantasy; so in their work as poets they are extra-ordinarily, enormously intelligent but are often limited as people, almost stupid (Pushkin, Gogol). In you, as in all natures which are primarily thoughtful and con-scious, talent and fantasy have themselves become intelligence, but they are given life and fire, and encouraged by humanistic tendencies, which for you are neither intrinsic nor extrinsic, but co-essential with your nature. You have very great intel-ligence, so great, in fact, that I don't see why one man should have so much. You also have great talent and fantasy, but you do not possess that pure original talent which generates everything from itself and makes use of intelligence as an inferior function. No, your talent, the devil knows, is a bastard or rather is related to your nature as intelligence is to artistic nature.[70]

And he implored him to write much and thus reveal the nature of his talent to himself.

These literary works of Herzen did indeed reveal something of great importance. For in them was revealed the long process of spiritual enquiry, the concealed illumination of a personality in search of 'truth'—all the combined psychological and religious analysis—that formed the kernel of philosophical discussions which lasted more than a decade. All this was not incorporated in a system of philosophy but found its true outlet in literature. Herzen's stories were among the early, though certainly not among the ripest,

fruits of the great Russian literary harvest of the last century. His books were
not yet masterpieces, but from the work which was created as a by-product of
Iskander's thinking, Belinsky could guess that something really great was
emerging—the world of the new Russian literature. The decisive step was
not Herzen's, but before leaving Russia he had helped in no small measure
to create a new intellectual and artistic world.

Politically, his last years in Russia were less fruitful. He discussed with
growing eagerness the possibility of leaving Russia and making direct
contact with the Western world, and when he finally decided to emigrate,
it was chiefly because he felt himself caught in a blind alley.

This was the hazard implicit in the entire 'Western' movement to which he
belonged, and which in Moscow was becoming associated more and more
with him and with the historians Granovsky and Kavelin, and writers such
as Botkin, Korsh, Ketcher, and others. Annenkov, who took part in this
movement, has explained better than anyone the fundamental reasons for the
political impotence and internal dissolution of this group. 'They had no
complete, thought-out, political formula. They paid attention to problems as
they arose, and they criticized and examined only contemporary phenomena.'
They began in fact by opposing the vague mythology of the Slavophils; but
they did not want to pursue the struggle into the larger arena of principles
either concerning Russia's internal affairs or about her cultural relations with
the rest of Europe. They did not want to become the prisoners of a philosophy
of history. But this 'good conscience' of the Westerners, as Annenkov said,
left them in the last analysis 'with empty hands'.[71] In other words, this group
of men, who, with the notable exception of Herzen, represented the germ of
mid-century Russian Liberalism, was in its enforced detachment from all
political activity, on the one hand, too conscious of the moral issues involved
to collaborate in any way with the government of Nicholas I; and, on the
other, too learned and too exhausted by the effort of escaping from the
myths and metaphysics of romanticism to create new, active and effective
political ideals. And so it gradually withdrew more and more into historical
research, literary criticism and the study of customs. The inefficacy of Russian
Liberalism, even after the Crimean War, has at least one of its roots in this
period of the late 'forties. This retreat into research, however, had one
important result. It inspired the reconsideration of the problem of the
Russian State and the reforms of Peter the Great (the problem that had
interested Herzen). In so doing it opened up a way of escape from the blind
alley of the Slavophils to a conception of history which, though it created
the myth of the continuity and progressive function of the State, nevertheless
established with Granovsky, Kavelin, Chicherin and especially Solovev the
foundations of modern Russian historiography.[72]

But Herzen was no more an historian than he was a novelist. The practical
politician in him felt the impossibility of developing a Liberalism which was
based on a study of history. In newspaper articles and private conversations

he gave support and publicity to Granovsky's first lectures in Moscow. Here was the intellectual atmosphere that he planned to develop according to his own convictions. But though he tried repeatedly, because he was bound by sentiment and friendship to this group of Russian friends, he eventually decided with reluctance that it was impossible to bring the standard of the debates up to the necessary level.

We know little of the earliest discussions in 1846, chiefly because we lack the documents. The account given by Herzen in *My Past and Thoughts* is of the greatest human interest, but is given more from a personal than a political angle.[73] The letters and accounts of others are only fragmentary.

Nevertheless the probable problems discussed can be summarized under three headings.

First, there was the position to be taken up *vis-à-vis* the masses. This discussion ran parallel (though in Russia it was more taken up with custom and moral problems) to the one occurring in Berlin at the same time among the Hegelian left-wing thinkers on the relationship between the intellectuals and the 'crowd'. They considered once more the problem of *narodnost*. Granovsky said that he felt some sympathy for the position of the Slavophils. By so doing, he denied or at any rate limited the results of the discussions that had been held with them. Belinsky sought to give *narodnost* a meaning nearer to 'patriotism' as this was understood in Western Europe. Botkin intelligently summed up all these ideas, saying,

Slavism has not yet produced a practical man—instead we have either a gypsy like Khomyakov or a muddle-headed aristocrat like Aksakov or a monk like Kireyevsky. And they are the best. But for all this, the Slavophils have pronounced one true word *narodnost*, nationality. This is their great merit. Generally in their criticism they are entirely right, but as soon as they turn to the positive side they show their limitations—ignorance and a suffocating patriarchalism—ignorance of the simplest principles of political economy, intolerance, obscurantism, etc.[74]

In this mixture of comprehension and criticism, Botkin confessed that the Westerners had not solved or even faced the problem of the relations between the intelligentsia and the people, which the romantic Slavophils did at least recognize as fundamental.

The second, and much more important, question was the function of the bourgeoisie in Russia's future political life. This was a reaction against the Socialism which had inspired men's minds in the early 'forties; a symptom of maturity, following the youthful and enthusiastic utopianism of those years. But for Herzen, it inevitably represented an abandonment of those very ideas which he was now trying to formulate. The Westerners were in fact being more and more influenced by the history of France and the function of the *tiers état*. Their vision of Russia's future political life was inspired by the conception of the bourgeoisie which Guizot, Thierry, etc. had reached by different approaches. It was naturally Granovsky, the historian, who criticized most incisively the utopianism of the Westerners. 'Socialism', he said, 'is extraordinarily harmful, because it teaches men to try and solve the problems of political life, not in the political arena which it despises, but on the side; and this leads to the destruction both of Socialism and of politics.'[75] But the discussion on the bourgeoisie was more generally expressed in *boutades* such as Botkin's, who said that 'the working class, of course, had all his sympathy', but for all that he could not refrain from adding, 'Would to heaven we had a bourgeoisie on our side!'[76]

The discussion more often involved the clash of different ideals than any examination of the situation. But by gradually covering new ground, it began to anticipate future problems. The members of the group were, in fact, beginning to wonder, though still in a very confused fashion, whether they were faced with a bourgeois period or one in which Socialist ideals could be realized.

The third problem with which Herzen's memoirs are concerned was philosophical in character. In this fight against romanticism he had now reached a position more and more akin to that of Voltaire and Diderot. These were the two chief names in the fiercest discussion that he had with Granovsky, who wanted to retain his faith in the immortality of the soul and in a form of spiritualism which was not easily defined but which had strong emotional roots. It is not therefore surprising that Feuerbach soon became the touchstone on which the Westerners divided.

Because of this atmosphere, Herzen felt that his departure from Moscow in 1847 represented a sort of liberation. Later he looked back to this formative period in Russia and the fruitful Moscow discussions, but in retrospect these years were covered by a veil, as if the debates had been too far removed from reality and too exclusively literary in tone. He found the atmosphere of Moscow in the 'forties 'doctrinaire'. He had fought the Slavophil philosophy of history and that of his own friends, but his struggle seemed to meet with no success. The intellectual parties were hardening into a sort of sclerosis; the Slavophils and Westerners seemed to be looking back more and more to the past, the former to the Russia of the Middle Ages, the latter to that of Peter the Great. 'It is time', Herzen answered, 'for the world to forget those periods of its past which are not necessary; or rather to remember them but only as periods that are over and no longer exist.'[77]

This desire for liberation coloured all his ideas when he left for Paris. It even affected his views about Russia's future which he found, because it was a country not overburdened with the weight of past history so dear to the doctrinaire, full of glorious promise. As early as 1844 he noted in his diary Goethe's lines dedicated to America, which he found even more applicable to Russia.

> *Dich stört nicht im Innern*
> *Zu lebendiger Zeit*
> *Unnutzes Erinnern*
> *Und vergeblicher Streit.*[78]

These lines were Herzen's formula of liberation.

When his friends received his first letters—really articles and published as such—they were more embittered than surprised. Herzen not only continued his criticism of all forms of Westernism, which was already deliberately bourgeois in character, but accentuated it.

As a description of France in the period preceding the revolution, the letters are noteworthy for their clarity. They do not yet carry his ideas any further, but they constitute—once he had made contact with Western Europe—a condensation of them. The France of Louis-Philippe, on the point of collapse, was certainly not likely to win his approval. What really interested him in Paris in 1847 was the alignment of forces opposing the existing régime, and a realization of the extent to which democratic and Socialist ideas were gaining ground.

He regarded the rule of the bourgeoisie as doomed. 'It has neither a great past nor any future. It was momentarily valuable as a negation, a transition, a contradiction . . . Offspring of the elegant nobility and the rude populace, the bourgeoisie combines the worst defects of each, yet has lost the qualities of both.'[79] Against it there had already arisen a combination of aristocrats and people, idealists and proletarians—all those, in fact, who did not want to submit to 'political economy', and were looking for a solution of the social problem, which no past revolution had succeeded in providing. For this reason he said that, after so many upheavals, Europe was still only at the beginning of the real problem.

Herzen's first contact with Paris confirmed his Socialist aspirations, even though he did not find the new political force which he had sought for twenty years. Around him were

generous indignation, *pia desideria* and criticisms which do not constitute a political doctrine, let alone one for the people. There is nothing that bears less relation to the people's own desires. The people demand ready solutions, doctrines, faith; need a banner, well-defined objects for which to strive. But those who were daring in criticism were utterly uncreative. All the fantastic utopias of the last twenty years have been put forward for the approval of the people, who possess a genuine tact which makes them listen and then shake their head. They do not believe in abstract utopias which are not carefully worked out and efficient, national, full of religion and poetry.[80]

Thus lack of faith in the immediate possibilities of Socialism, together with a radical distrust in the vitality and future of the bourgeoisie which held power, coloured these letters, as they do all his writings 'before the storm', and was a forewarning of the deep disillusionment he experienced when the revolution of 1848 failed.

Towards the end of 1847 he went to Italy, and there participated in the first act of the European revolution. His observations are vivid but journalistic, profound only in patches. His judgment was influenced by admiration for the Roman people and for the formation of the Civic Guard, and by a growing appreciation of the strength of individuality which he grew to love in every aspect of Italian life. 'Italy is more than Rome. It is every little town and each one different. Granovsky, my friend, we did not really understand Italy. We were mistaken about it in detail, as, on a larger scale, we were mistaken about France.'[81] He was struck in this early phase of the *Risorgimento* by the complexity of the Italian revival, and in that ferment, so different from the canalized movement in a centralized State like France, Herzen placed his sympathies and his hopes.[82]

When he returned to France, the struggle between the *Assemblée Nationale* and the clubs was at its height. In this (influenced also by what he had seen in Italy) he recognized a conflict of ideologies and classes, a decisive struggle between the traditional centralism of French politics and the new forces which the revolution had begun to bring to light. Herein lies the originality of his point of view.

This allowed him to grasp the essential nature of the struggle between Lamartine and Blanqui. He saw France make a supreme effort to cross the boundaries imposed in 1793 and to carry on the revolution where Robespierre had left off. In his eyes 15th May was a continuation, half a century later, of the 9th Thermidor. But this time the revolutionaries were no longer influenced as Robespierre had been, by faith in the Assembly, no longer ready, if need be, to die for it, no longer, therefore, incapable of appealing to the masses. This time the revolutionaries were to march *against* the Assembly. 'The people of Paris were prepared to do what Robespierre never dared[83] . . . That is why', he added,

the conservatives and the liberals of the old school fight with such fury against Barbès, Blanqui, Raspail; that is why on 15th May the Assembly and the Executive Commission, which detest each other, fell into each other's arms. Even the Monarchists took up arms to save the Republic and the National Assembly. For, by saving those, they saved the principle of Monarchy, irresponsible power, constitutional order, the abuses of the capital, and finally, the Pretenders to the Throne. On the other side was the Republic, not of Lamartine but of Blanqui; a Republic not of words but of deeds; universal suffrage not merely applied pettily and stupidly for the election of a despotic Assembly, but for the whole administration; the liberation of man, the commune and the department from submission to a strong government using bullets and chains as methods of persuasion.[84]

This is one of Herzen's finest passages of political analysis. It shows that his Socialism was now definitely leaving behind the realm of Utopias and romantic visions, and entering the political field.

But on 15th May the revolutionary uprising had been defeated. Why? To understand this Herzen returned to the origin of the movement, the days that immediately followed 24th February. Within a few weeks, the revolution had seemed to him to be on the defensive, or even in retreat. It had not been sufficiently prepared. 'Lamartine and the men of the "National" at the head of the movement were a great misfortune for France.'[85] No one, in fact, had known how to profit from the period that immediately followed 24th

February, during which, according to Herzen, it would have been possible to perform miracles. The republican party proved to be too small; the elections had been carried out in the most unfortunate manner at the worst possible time.

Politically defeated on 15th May the revolutionary movement was socially routed during the early days of June. The party, which Herzen himself described as of 'the Communists and Socialists and with them the Paris workmen',[86] was definitely crushed. For him, as for so many European Socialists, these events were notable for their revelation of the proletariat. In 1847 it had seemed to him, though only for a short time, a model of dignity and humanity, and immediately brought to mind a comparison with the Russian serfs—a comparison which scarcely flattered the latter in a moral or material sense.[87] Now the Parisian workman appeared in a new light, as a member of the revolutionary proletariat. 'Despite the fact that he has had no opportunity for education, and that he has been weighed down by work and anxiety about his daily bread, he has the energy which comes from deeply felt thought, and has so far excelled the bourgeois that they can no longer understand him and feel with terror and hatred that this young fighter, his hands hardened with work, seems to be the dark and threatening prophet of their own downfall.' He traced the origin of the proletariat to the revolt of Lyons, observed the formation under Louis-Philippe of its 'serious, austere' character, which had made it become 'the one class in France to enjoy a wide range of political ideas, because it stood apart from the closed circle which held the accepted ideas of the time. As a class it was unique because its fellow in misfortune—the poor peasantry—groaned under the burden of the *status quo* in contrast to the multifarious activities of the industrial workers.'[88]

The June days were decisive for him. They signalized the heartfelt break (which he was later to try in vain, for political reasons, to hide or to heal) with the entire liberal bourgeois world. The discussions about this problem two years earlier in Moscow, the ideas of the friends he had left in Russia, were now illuminated by a terrible light. 'The days of June have no precedent in the past', he wrote to Moscow. 'The terror, after the insurrection, is horrible. It is a retrograde terror, coloured by all the fear of the French bourgeoisie, the stupidest class of the entire European population, to whom Cavaignac is a genius, because he did not recoil from Civil War. And Thiers also is a genius, because he has no sense of honour. All defenders of the bourgeoisie, like you, have been splashed by the mud.'[89] And in another letter he said that the terror of 1793 was grandiose compared to that which broke out in the three months of siege against the Parisian workmen. His constantly repeated references to the June days are among the most moving in Herzen's kaleidoscopic diary of the 1848 revolution.[90]

There was a single ray of hope: 'France and even Europe may perish in the struggle, but the social factor will prevail over these decadent forms which Europe is unwilling to renounce.'[91] He felt that the people were still a repository of strength. He was to say later, 'After the June days I saw that the revolution was defeated, but I still believed in it; I had faith in the miraculous vitality of the survivors, in their moral influence.'[92]

He viewed the 1848 revolution as in all its essential elements (ideological and social) a Socialist revolution, foiled from the beginning by immature ideas and impotent men.

He had little faith in Louis Blanc, who remained aloof from the central political movement and withdrew from the Luxembourg Commission, leaving himself no freedom of action and acknowledging the authority of Lamartine's government. 'He became a preacher of Socialism; he had a great influence on the workers, but he had no real political authority.'[93] 'In reality', he concluded, 'Louis Blanc never understood Socialism; his well-known book *De l'Organisation du Travail* and a few brilliant phrases established his reputation.'[94] He considered the *ateliers nationaux* a mere expedient adopted by a government terrified of unemployment. In the Luxembourg Commission he saw only 'the earliest Christian Church in Ancient Rome', and in Louis Blanc, 'the first priest and preacher in the new church, and its sessions no more than the solemn liturgies of an adolescent Socialism'.[95]

Herzen had much more respect and admiration for Blanqui. At one moment he suggested the need for a temporary dictatorship, to fill the gap between the monarchy and the republic. But what drew him to Blanqui, apart from his political vision and his revolutionary passion, was the certainty that he would not hesitate when confronted with the traditional ideas which were suffocating the democrats.

Blanqui is the revolutionary of our time. He has understood that nothing can be merely readjusted, but that the primary task is to pull down the existing structure. Gifted with remarkable eloquence, he roused the masses; all his words were an indictment of the old world. They loved him less than Barbès, but they preferred to listen to him.[96]

Nevertheless, Herzen's deepest sympathies were for Proudhon. His own day-to-day view of the revolution was deeply influenced, as he himself has admitted, by 'the excellent periodicals' of Proudhon and Thoré—the *Peuple* and the *Vraie République*. And, as disappointments piled up and his confidence in the revolution grew smaller, Proudhon's activities assumed greater importance in his eyes. For nearly a year he supported him materially and collaborated politically with him, urging him on to more active policies.[97] In August 1849 he gave him the financial means to create *La Voix du Peuple*, reserving the right to contribute and in some respects to direct its foreign policy. Proudhon's fight against Louis Napoleon was 'a real poem of anger and scorn'.[98] It was Proudhon who made him aware of the terrible danger implicit in President Napoleon's rise to power; Proudhon who inspired him with growing distrust of the traditional democrats, who while apparently regaining vitality by their opposition to Napoleon were, in fact, growing daily more impotent, not only in their immediate policies but also in their historical function.

Herzen's participation in the demonstration of 13th June—which forced him to flee to Geneva—was a last effort, the fulfilment of a duty. His failure confirmed his negative opinion of the 'Mountain'. 'The democratic current', he wrote from Geneva, in September, 'or the party of movement, was defeated because it was not worthy of success; because it has always made mistakes; because it has always been afraid of being revolutionary in the true sense; because it attacked the Throne merely in order to gain power itself.'[99]

But was the revolution really over? Herzen did not think so. Encouraged (as were so many European revolutionaries) by the hope of a strengthening of the movement, he turned his attention to the peasants. In June 1851 he wrote,

Those workmen who can think for themselves do not look for ties with the professional revolutionaries or with newspaper editors, but with the peasants. Since the brute hand of the police has closed the clubs and electoral committees, the workers' platform has gone to the country. Their propaganda therefore operates more freely and goes far deeper than club gossip. A great storm is brewing among the peasants. They know nothing of the constitution or the separation of powers, but they look greedily at the rich landlord, at the lawyer, at the usurer; and they see that however much they work, their money goes into the hands of others, and so they listen to the workmen . . . will be a true revolution of the masses.[100]

Then, when the *coup d'état* of 2nd December broke out in France, one last possibility seemed open—the hope that always exists in times of violent reaction; that it would not be capable of settling the problems raised by the revolution. But when this, too, came to nothing, at least initially, his experiences of the 1848 revolution were at last complete. He could now draw his conclusions and appreciate where his twofold reaction to the France of Louis-Philippe and the Second Republic had led him: a reaction which had been produced by the individualist revolt against State centralism on the one hand and the Socialist revolt against the rule of the bourgeoisie on the other.

Both the individualism, which had been one of the features of Russian culture of the 'thirties and 'forties, and the instinctive revolt against the State in the name of the people which was part of the Slavophil programme now showed him that in monarchies as in republics, in absolutist as in Jacobin theory, a single evil had to be fought, a single symptom of decadence—that purely exterior *order* which had, in fact, triumphed in June.[101]

He constantly looked back to try to understand the nature of the instinct for freedom and independence which he had felt stirring in Russian culture, and which he had sought but never found in contemporary Frenchmen apart from Proudhon. He never succeeded in defining it because it was primarily an enhanced capacity for self-knowledge in which self-deception played no part and which enabled him to scrutinize real people instead of shadows. So Herzen did not turn to theories of anarchy like Bakunin, but concentrated his efforts against the ideology of the modern State, against the Jacobin tradition, against what he called the 'democratic orthodoxy'.[102]

He wished to strike at this ideology, because he recognized it as one more variety of the abstract speculations and religions which he had overcome in order to arrive at his 'realism', another of those shadows of the past which he wanted to banish with the light of reason. He has left us a very vivid account of his struggle and of how he achieved the 'unhappiness of knowledge'.

Every man carries deep within himself a permanent revolutionary tribunal, an implacable Fouquier-Tinville and—most important—a guillotine. Sometimes the judge is fast asleep and the guillotine rusty; then the false, the past, the romantic, the weak, raise their heads . . . There is no way out: either condemn and go ahead, or reprieve and stop half-way. People are afraid of logic and when they unenthusiastically bring to the tribunal the Church, the State, the family, morality, good and evil, they still try to save fragments of the past. They throw over Christianity, but keep the immortality of the soul, idealism, providence . . . Reason is implacable, like the Convention; it is pitiless and without hypocrisy.[103]

All his charges against the 'choristers of the revolution', the 'professional revolutionaries', and those who wished to revive the past have this same tone of implacability, and are pitiless, just as he was pitiless with himself.

The 'Montagnard' democrats of 1848 seemed to him the most convincing example of what happens when the internal guillotine refuses to function. They thought they were republicans, but in fact they merely followed the traditions of the monarchical State; they thought they were atheists, but really they were priests of a religion of their own invention, and slaves of a set of out-of-date symbols; they thought they were revolutionaries and in reality they were only conservatives.

A Republic, as they understand it, is an abstract and unattainable idea, the result of purely theoretical thinking, an apotheosis of the existing régime, the transfiguration of what already exists.[104]

Presented in this lucid and forthright manner, these ideas were to have a deep influence on the entire Russian Populist movement, so suspicious of all generic democratic ideas, so responsive to individual motives for revolt against the State, and therefore instinctively opposed to the Jacobin tradition.

In the light of this criticism, his own political ideal was now clarified. 'Government is not an end, but a necessity; not a sacrosanct institution to be served by Levites, but a bank, a chancellery of the nation's affairs'—in other words, the maximum of freedom, the minimum of Napoleonic centralization. This was where the revolution had led him.

But Herzen was convinced that the Republic could only be attained after 'a revolutionary dictatorship, which must not invent new civil codes or create a new order, but must smash all monarchist relics in the Commune, the Department, the Tribunals and the Army. It will unmask all the actors of the old order, will strip them of their cloaks, their uniforms and their epaulettes, of all the symbols of power which moves people so intensely.'[105]

This revolt had by now acquired a precise social content. Just as the defeat of 15th May had not made him lose faith in a revolution which would go beyond that of the Jacobins, so the June days had only confirmed his faith in Socialism. In this perspective, even his criticisms of traditional forms found their historical justification. He saw how alive the religion of the Jacobins had been in 1793, when they had known what they wanted. Their descendants were, however, uncertain; for behind their Republic stood Socialism.

The régimes of France and other European States do not correspond to their slogans of liberty, equality and fraternity. Any actual realization of these ideals would be a denial of present European life, and would mean its destruction.[106]

One may regret the aristocracy, one may pity the old world, but it stands condemned because it has found within itself its own limits: 'The workman no longer wants to work for others.'[107] Every republic which did not appreciare this fact was condemned to die.

The revolution of 1848 thus left Herzen certain of one thing—Europe would be saved only by an internal Socialist revolution. 'But can the exhausted European organism support such a crisis and find the energy for a rebirth? Who knows? Europe is very old; its energies are not sufficient to sustain its own ideas, nor has it sufficient will-power to achieve its ends . . . Its past is rich, it has lived long, and in the future its heirs can be America on one hand and the Slavs on the other.'[108]

For this reason he concentrated attention on Russia to which he wished to hand on the benefit of his experience. His pessimistic view of the future of France and of Europe in general made him recall the sweeping condemnations and prophecies of the Slavophils. Were they right when they spoke of the corruption of the West? As before, he rejected an idea which they had reached by comparing a primitive, unhistorical Russia with the rest of Europe. It was now the future which had to be considered. Russia could contribute a solution to the problems which were exhausting Western Europe. So his hope in the future of Russia grew, as his other hopes collapsed.

As early as 1849 he said that this was the most suitable moment 'to raise a Russian voice'.[109] In May of that year he tried to establish a printing press in Paris. He prepared an appeal to the Russians to explain his ideas. 'France', he said, 'frightened of the future, immersed in a sort of stupor, now rejects all that has been gained by the blood and toil of the last seventy years.' For this reason the people of Europe turned more and more to Russia; the conservatives in the hope of finding realized there their ideal of a strong government, the revolutionaries because they had imbibed of the ideas of the

2+

Russian émigrés Bakunin, Sazonov and Herzen himself. It was time, there-fore, for a free voice to be heard, for printing works which could not be published in Russia.[110] He noted that the French were beginning to read Haxthausen's book, and that the relations between the Russian agrarian communities and Western Socialism were interesting a public which was inclining to the view 'that the Russians were Socialists by tradition'.[111]

He tried several times to establish links with the Polish émigrés, in order to give an international character to his opposition to Nicholas I. But the reaction which followed 13th July 1849 and the Bonapartism which he encountered among the Poles put an end to these early approaches. His plan to create a Russian centre abroad, to print books and newspapers, was only to be resumed in London some years later.

When the Russian government tried to compel him to return to his country, he refused. 'I remain here, not only because it disgusts me to put on hand-cuffs again as soon as I cross the frontier, but so as to be able to work. One can live anywhere as long as one does nothing, but for me there is only one aim here—our aim.'[112]

Despite the failure of his efforts to raise a Russian voice, hope in the great future of his country made him believe, even in the worst phase of European reaction, that his work as an émigré could be useful and important. He determined to make known his political conclusions to other Russians, and Russia itself to other peoples. 'Europeans must know their neighbour', he said. 'Now they only fear her, but we must make them know what they fear.'[113]

Russia's lack of traditions, which he had already noted as a promise for the future, and which he had found expressed in Goethe's lines, now seemed even more valuable since his experience of French politics.

Nous sommes moralement plus libres que les européens, et ce n'est pas seulement parce que nous sommes affranchis des grandes épreuves à travers lesquelles se développe l'occident, mais aussi parce que nous n'avons point de passé qui nous maîtrise. Notre histoire est pauvre, et la première condition de notre vie nouvelle a été de la renier entièrement [i.e. through Peter the Great]. Il ne nous est resté de notre passé que la vie nationale, le caractère national, la cristallisation de l'état: tout le reste est élément d'avenir.[114]

By now, this idea of freedom began to be more clearly defined in Herzen's mind. Russia was free from traditions and therefore, he wrote, 'Je ne vois pas que la Russie doive nécessairement subir toutes les phases du développe-ment européen.'[115] This implied that Western Socialism imported into Russia would find in the agrarian communities such favourable ground for development that the period of bourgeois revolutions could be avoided.

He wrote to Mazzini, 'Je ne crois en Russie à aucune autre révolution qu'à une guerre de paysans', and he referred to Pugachev. This was the revolution which was to strike 'le despotisme glacial de Pétersbourg'.[116] It would destroy all the bonds that tied the rural community to the noble and the State. It would retain the periodical redistribution of the land, thus insuring against the formation of a proletariat and hunger. It would develop internal self-administration.

Pourquoi la Russie perdrait-elle maintenant sa commune rurale, puisqu'elle a pu la conserver pendant toute la période de son développement politique, puisqu'elle l'a conservée intacte sous le joug pesant du tzarisme moscovite, aussi bien que sous l'autocratie à l'européenne des empereurs?[117]

But was Russia capable of achieving such a revolution? Here, too, his answer was not intended as a prophecy. He was merely pointing the way to the crossroads at which the Socialist tendencies of Western Europe and the possibilities which he believed to exist in the Russian countryside itself could meet.

Two factors, however, encouraged an affirmative answer to his question: the strength of the Russian peasant, who had retained his humanity through many despotisms, together with a feeling of independence and remoteness from authority; and above all the spiritual and intellectual life of modern Russia. He then wrote one of his finest pieces to explain to those who had been defeated in Western Europe in the struggles of 1848 what was implied by 'the development of revolutionary ideas in Russia'.

And for the future revolutionaries, for those who would refuse to be 'des révolutionnaires incomplets',[118] Herzen wrote,

The people suffer much, their life is burdensome, they harbour deep hatreds, and feel passionately that there will soon be a change . . . They are waiting not for ready-made works but for the revelation of what is secretly stirring in their spirits. They are not waiting for books but for apostles—men who combine faith, will, conviction and energy; men who will never divorce themselves from them; men who do not necessarily spring from them, but who act within them and with them, with a dedicated and steady faith. The man who feels himself to be so near the people that he has been virtually freed by them from the atmosphere of artificial civilization; the man who has achieved the unity and intensity of which we are speaking—he will be able to speak to the people and must do so.[119]

Herzen went on to say that few would find the necessary capacity, and seemed to relax into pessimism himself; but this paragraph contained the ideal which was to animate the Populists.

The fundamental elements of Russian Populism—distrust of all democracy; belief in a possible autonomous development of Socialism in Russia; faith in the future possibilities of the *obshchina*; the need to create revolutionaries who could dedicate themselves to the people—these were the principles Herzen clung to after his experiences in 1848, the ideals he had created for the next generation.[120]

2. BAKUNIN

BAKUNIN WAS BORN only two years after Herzen. Yet so great is the contrast between their political development that the two men appear to belong to different generations. Herzen had found in his own family and in the world of his early youth a direct link with the culture of the Enlightenment and the Decembrist revolt. Bakunin, on the other hand, had to cover all this ground by himself. Herzen was a 'son of the Decembrists', as Ogarev was to say; Bakunin was a son of the age of Nicholas I and the atmosphere of fear and concealed enthusiasms which oppressed the 'thirties. Confirmation of this lies in the weary and difficult road through philosophy and religion which Bakunin (a man born for spontaneous action) had to travel in order to reach the world of politics. His progress is a good example of the significant rift in Russian life occasioned by the suppression of 14th December 1825.[1]

It is all the more remarkable in view of the fact that Bakunin too was a son of the enlightened aristocracy which, during the reign of Catherine, had looked to Europe for inspiration.[2] As a young man his father had been sent to the Russian Legation in Florence and had studied at the University of Padua. He had also—so the family said—personally taken part in the storming of the Bastille and, perhaps, in the proclamation of the Parthenopean Republic.[3] At the age of forty he had married a young girl of the Muravev family, some of whose members were among the most famous leaders of the Decembrists. But all this had left him no more than a liberal yet timid aristocrat, more and more isolated within the confined life of the provincial gentry —the patriarchal administrator of his great estates in the Tver region. He wrote poetry about the charms of his existence and expressed his satisfaction with Russian life, including peasant serfdom, which he too complacently contrasted with the 'freedom of homeless wage-earners in other countries, of enlisted serfs in the wretched slavery of other men's houses'.[4] He was, in fact, fully convinced that democracy was best left to the small republics of antiquity, and that in any case it was essential not to be drawn into conspiracies or secret societies.

The son passed the early years of his life in this sheltered society of culture and good intentions. And for a long time he devoted his energies to transforming this world, in an attempt to create a spiritual centre within it based on the ideals which aroused his enthusiasm. Many years passed before he could break away from it.

In 1845, in a letter which harked back to his early life with his brothers and sisters, he wrote to them from Paris: 'Everything or nothing: that is my motto, my battlecry, and I will not go back on it. As you see, my friends, I haven't changed. But what of you? I am frightened of asking you. Your wretched captivity—you are surrounded by such a petty world, enclosed within such narrow bounds . . .'5

He was to spend ten years of his life trying to change, and finally escape from, this world, and the process left its mark on him. Later he was to live like a *barin*, whose easy-going and impractical habits revealed the Russian provincial gentleman beneath the bohemian and the revolutionary.

He was the eldest son and he began his career in the traditional manner by entering an officer cadets' school in St Petersburg. He was unable to adapt himself to the life and as a punishment he was sent to a small garrison in Lithuania. In 1831, writing to his parents about the Polish revolt, he said: 'No, the Russians are not French. They love their country, they revere their Emperor. His will is their law.'6 In general, his letters at this time faithfully reflect the *mondaine* life of the capital—fatherland, religion, fine sentiments. The Bakunin of later years can only be recognized in his passion for music, and even this he loved because it roused his spirits.

Nevertheless, alone, in his small garrison, he began to write that 'his mind was boiling and seeking nourishment', and that 'the powerful forces of his spirit, beating in vain against the cold and unbearable obstacles of the physical world, induced melancholy in him'.7 Fired by the desire to live more intensely, inspired by a patriotic and romantically religious passion, he sought in the general situation of the world an explanation of his disquiet. He abused the tradition of the eighteenth century—whose last ageing representatives he had known in the capital—and came to the conclusion: 'No, we do not yet belong to the nineteenth century, we are still between one century and the next—a tormenting situation, an interregnum between two lots of ideas.'

When, at the age of twenty, he began to visualize a way of escape, his words took on a more personal tone and reflected the increasing maturity which his isolation in Lithuania had effected. 'Concentration of energy in the will is the only way. When we are able to say: *ce que je veux, Dieu le veut*, then at last we shall be happy, and our suffering over.'8 Here, for the first time, we can recognize the true Bakunin beneath the uniform of the young officer.

In St Petersburg he at last found tranquillity in the study of German philosophy and happiness in the awareness of his own growing personality. He said that having met Stankevich 'at this time of our life, prevented our not losing all faith in the high destiny of mankind'.9 Stankevich—together with a few friends—provided him, by flinging him into philosophical speculation, with the means of escape from the world in which he had been born. 'There's only one real misfortune that can afflict a man, one real disaster— that is to lose the will, the desire, the energy for activity, and to have no purpose in life. When that happens he not only can but *must* shoot himself.'[10] So he wrote on 14th December 1835 to one of Stankevich's friends, A. P. Efremov, by now a friend of his own.

In a generation in which so many, with varying degrees of romanticism, made 'the beautiful soul' their ideal, Stankevich really was one.[11] He lived up to his ideals (derived at first from Schelling and later from Hegel) with a freshness, an innocence and a modesty worthy of the German romantics. He was one of the few men in Russia who really understood idealistic philosophy. His mind was able to draw sustenance from it far removed from the sophistical justification of ideas and sentiments, which had little or nothing to do with philosophy.[12] In an autobiographical letter of real beauty, written before he moved on from Schelling to Hegel, he told his friend Granovsky, who was planning to devote his life to the study of history, just what philosophy had meant to him, and what he ought to look for in history. With great delicacy and subtlety he explained how he himself discovered the world of poetry and philosophy via aesthetics, and how he now wished to integrate his spiritual world. He ended by drawing up a programme of studies for himself, telling his young friend that 'reading is only useful when it is undertaken with a set purpose, to solve a problem'.[13]

No one of his generation has described with such simplicity and sincerity as Stankevich the revelation of the world of the spirit bequeathed to him by the Germans, the change in his entire being, which he felt when plunging into Kant or Fichte. No one else had such a natural gift for teaching himself philosophy. Despite the religious feeling which he put into his philosophical reading, he always had an end in view. He felt the need to find in poetry or in history support, nourishment and proof of the truth which he thought he had discovered within himself. The philosophy of Hegel, to which he became passionately devoted, was in his latter years to add a more reflective note to this thirst for truth.

With all this, Stankevich remained a typical Russian idealist of the 'thirties. The desire for an escape from concrete reality was so strong that the dazzling light of the truth which he had discovered turned it into a mere 'spectre',[14] utterly petty and devoid of meaning. There is, of course, in such an attitude an element, not just of instinctive religious feeling, but also of mysticism. But he wished to remain a philosopher, and so, when complete detachment had been achieved, he inevitably reconsidered the problem of 'reality', i.e. the reconquest of the practical and living outer world, which had so abruptly lost all meaning in his eyes.

Not even his adherence to Hegel could completely mend this early break with the world. The problem re-arose at every occasion, even over the most trivial questions of daily life. He said one day that he himself and his young idealist friends were all men of the *enges Gewissen*, or 'finicky conscience'— and the use of this casuistical metaphor to translate the term is most appropriate. He accepted the Hegelian criticism of this state of mind, which he found in the *Encyclopaedia of Theological Sciences* by Rosenkranz, which he was then reading: 'It comes from the need for an ethical harmony which scrutinizes every action from every possible angle. The trouble is that a conscience of this kind finds so many angles, indeed, an infinity of them and ends up', he said, referring to Bakunin, 'by plunging ahead without noticing anything, and thereby performing immoral actions.'[15] This was an exact description of the state of mind of these young idealists.

In April 1835 Bakunin had written him a letter setting out his aspirations, and when Stankevich replied that these corresponded to his own, they met in October of the same year and laid the foundations of a firm friendship. It was Stankevich who pointed out to Bakunin, when he settled in Moscow, the particular importance of Kant. But Bakunin was reluctant and, despite his yearning for truth, he protested his small understanding of philosophical language and, in general, his limited acquaintance with abstractions.[16] It was Stankevich who gently guided him, and who gave him advice on how to read works of philosophy and how to meditate on them.

After some hesitation, Bakunin plunged into philosophy with all the force of his personality. Yet it was not in Kant but in Fichte that he found what he was looking for. Besides, Stankevich, his guide to idealistic reading, had told him that 'Kant is useful as an introduction to the modern systems',[17] and Bakunin had no intention of waiting too long before entering the temple. The year 1836 was his Fichtian year.

They read simultaneously, but in different towns, the *Bestimmung des Menschen*, and from afar Stankevich wrote of the impression that this work had made on him: 'It has led me to a terrible, unhealthy state of mind, made up of indecision and utter doubt. I am in anguish, and can see no way of escaping.' Fichte had so far cut him off from the outside world that he began to doubt of its very existence. 'All the consoling things of life, action, art, knowledge, love—everything has lost its significance for me. I myself do not know why.'[18] But his balanced mind soon recovered, and from Fichte he passed to 'a better understanding of Hegel'.[19]

The same longing for detachment also attracted Bakunin. He was looking for a single truth, to which he could utterly devote himself. He wanted to stop being Hamlet 'as we all are',[20] and to regard the 'artificial'[21] moral life of society as remote and petty. He wanted to destroy within himself 'individual, family and national egoism',[22] and to consider man happy only when 'he never loses sight of the Absolute'.[23] All this Bakunin looked for and found in Fichte. 'This is the road for me. It may be sad and lonely, but it is worthy of me.'[24]

Returning to Fichte some years later, when reading a biography of the philosopher, Bakunin wrote, 'Here is the true hero of our time. I have always loved him deeply, and have envied his extraordinary power, his indifference to circumstance and opinion and his capacity for moving tirelessly and directly towards the ends that he has set himself, guided by the knowledge of truth and the blessing of God. I possess similar qualities, but I still have to develop my powers.'[25]

Before leaving for Berlin in 1837, Stankevich had time to help him in his study of Hegel. This convinced Bakunin—as it had already convinced Stankevich (for whom the Fichtian period had been much less important)—that what was required was not to raise the earth towards the heavens like a Titan, but rather to seek God in history. The problem of 'reality' after so much romantic enthusiasm occupied the next stage of his life. Hegel helped him to bring to an end 'the time of our stormy youth and of freedom, when we were consumed by enthusiasm, the time when the word "reality" had not yet been spoken among us'.[26]

From about half-way through 1837, Hegelian terminology begins to predominate in his letters. The Absolute—which he had originally wanted to master and affirm—colours all his thoughts. There is even a danger of it leading not to a deeper understanding of things but rather investing everything with an absolute value, and assigning the value of category and truth to every phenomenon, and every feeling. Bakunin no longer sought consolation, but justification. The general religious phraseology of his Fichtian phase now became more personal, detailed, casuistic and finicky.

Stankevich was now abroad. Bakunin remained at the centre of a small group of philosophers in Moscow. He read and re-read Hegel, growing more and more convinced by his ideas, and preaching them to others. An expression of Hegel's ideas, not original, it is true, but proving his knowledge of the philosopher, is to be found in two articles of these years, of which only one was published—in 1840. From Hegel he at last succeeded in finding a reconciliation with reality, which was neither religious abandon nor an absorption in empirical problems. It was an attempt to give expression to the impulses within himself, which could no longer be expressed as infinite love or a vague and powerful religious feeling.

Together with Belinsky who was, during these years, largely under his influence, he then applied his philosophy to the political world around him, as Herzen had done. In so doing, he wished to convince himself that he had escaped from mere vague aspirations and the dreams of 'beautiful souls' into history and life. By his effort of concentration, his quasi-religious repudiation of the world and the illumination he had gained from Hegel, he felt able to understand and explain the bleak oppressive political reality of Nicholas I. It was by such strange and complicated means that Bakunin finally reached his real goal, the problem of politics.

For the time being he had reached a dead end; but the various roads which all these young Moscow philosophers—Stankevich, Belinsky, Bakunin, Botkin and Granovsky—had taken to escape from an apology for absolutism show the importance that this paradox had assumed for them. The controversy between 1837 and 1840 was enlarged into a discussion, which is the

Russian version—complicated by personal and religious problems—of the contemporary discussion in Germany among the Young Hegelians.

Once again Stankevich showed the balanced nature of his thought, ironically noting the conclusion which his friends had reached. He was too sincere in his search for 'a clear faith, a friend to reason',[27] to allow himself to be deceived now. Their Hegelianism rang false to him. Without entering the discussion on the philosophy of history, he criticized the assumption on which they based their theories. He rebelled against the idea of taking, as they did, a poet like Schiller, and turning him into a symbol—romantic sentimentality —so as to make him the butt of all they rejected and hated. 'The news of the literary works and ideas of our friends are scarcely comforting', he wrote to Granovsky. 'If they do not understand what reality means, I suppose that they will at least respect what Hegel himself has said . . . Let them read what he says about Schiller in the *Aesthetic*, . . . let them read the *Logic*: that reality in the sense of immediacy, external existence, is only contingent, whereas the true reality is only reason and spirit.'[28] This was a good answer on the philosophical plane. But it did not take account of the fact that Bakunin and Belinsky were facing a new problem, that of practical political activity. And the explanation of this they were beginning to seek in Hegel.

Even Stankevich himself, in the latter years of his life, had to face similar problems, though in another form. He wished to preserve the personal, individual element, the originality of the Self, which he feared was being lost in Hegel's philosophy of history. This reaction took the form of a defence of the traditional idea of the soul. 'If it is true that Hegel denies the immortality of the soul, we will throw him over.'[29] His psychological interests, which had led him to philosophy, now made him hesitate when faced with having to accept the consequences of the dialectic.

Besides, Feuerbach and other recent German philosophical works suggested to him this very problem of the justification of all practical activity. In 1840 he wrote from Rome to Bakunin, and told him of his doubts. 'The Idea is the life of the Absolute: as soon as we have reached the Idea, we no longer need any Science. Bearing life within itself, effortlessly, it becomes contemplation, bliss; Science disappears.' Having followed the Hegelian vision to its end, what then remained to be done? 'From the Idea we can build life', he answered, 'and thus the Idea inevitably becomes action, recognizes its own work, and is satisfied with it.' He goes on to say that he has read the work of August Cieszkowski, the Polish Hegelian, *Prolegomena zur Historiographie*. 'This divides history into three periods: Art, Science (and we are at the end of this period) and Action. The division is false, because it is not based on history. But this last thought—that Science must turn into Action, must melt in it—is correct . . . We now feel the need to bind these categories more closely together, to combine philosophy and feeling not only in the head but in the blood, the body, the whole being.'[30]

2*

This was in some ways Stankevich's philosophical testament; in it he too tried to find an approach to the practical world.

Belinsky's reaction, on the other hand, was less philosophical than Stankevich's, but no less interesting. He had visited Bakunin and had understood his exceptional quality (he said that he had the nature of a lion)—but he saw also all his negative sides: 'his monstrous pride', his frivolity and incapacity to listen to others. This analysis of Bakunin the man also implied a criticism of the philosophy that he had built up from Fichte and Hegel. He seemed to see reflected in his character as in a mirror that desire for the Absolute, which rendered the pettiness of his personality futile, while his idealistic asceticism in contrast to the outside world made him lose the sense of things around him. This was why Belinsky criticized him. 'You have never loved individual subjects and images.' For Belinsky, the critic of poetry and literature, the lover and inspirer of men, this was a mortal, unforgiveable sin. His relations with Bakunin are characterized by this admiration for the energy which he felt in him, and by a sincere hatred aroused by his inability to appreciate the individual. 'I respect you, but I cannot love you', he said. For Belinsky, the rebellion against Bakunin was also a rebellion against Idealism.

The first break came about the defence which he felt compelled to make of small, simple things, of that paltry reality which ought not to require philosophical justification.

I told Bakunin that one could reason from the philosophical point of view about God and about art, but about the merits of cold veal, one must speak simply. He replied that this was a revolt against idealism, that I was ruining myself, that I would become a good fellow in the sense of *bon vivant, bon camarade*, etc. I want to abandon the pretence of being a great man. I want to be like everyone else.[31]

Belinsky's whole defence of the individual, beginning with himself, marked the beginning of a new life. He was no longer dominated by the notion that he must sacrifice everything to the Idea, throwing his dignity to the winds and committing 'suicide' to maintain the philosophical values of the State of Nicholas I.

So, Belinsky did not create a philosophy of action. He gave up struggling with Hegel's dialectic, but, anguished and sensitive, he made his mark on the Russian life of the 'forties by his strong sense of 'subjects and individual imaginations'. With this revolt against Bakunin began his St Petersburg phase, the most fruitful of his brief period of activity. Before going abroad Bakunin was able to observe the effects of German philosophy on less gifted men than himself, Stankevich and Belinsky, men who did not surrender their whole hearts to it. In old age he was filled with horror by the character of Granovsky, for instance, an intelligent, peaceful and moderate Hegelian. 'There was not a drop of the blood in him that really loved humanity, as there was in Diderot or in Danton. He lived and died in a state of sentimental humanitarianism. What a vast difference there is between him and our Diderot: that rough realist Vissarion Belinsky. Compared to the giant Stankevich, Granovsky was a good young man, and nothing more.'[32]

Granovsky was, in fact, to develop, on the historical plane, the 'reconciliation with absolutism' that had been made by Bakunin and Belinsky. In opposition to the Slavophils, he extolled the figure of Peter the Great, and in general the function of enlightened absolutism in Russian history. For Granovsky, the Hegelian reconciliation with reality was to be the point of departure for his own liberal, historical ideas.

When he finally went abroad in 1840, Bakunin had broken with everyone. He felt isolated. His political conceptions remained those of a conservative by philosophical choice; his ideas were those of a convinced Hegelian. Yet he felt profoundly dissatisfied. He was now in agreement with no one. His anxiety was expressed in personal quarrels, which grew increasingly complicated, and in polemics, which now lost all theoretical meaning, and degenerated into conflicts of temperament. Belinsky said that Bakunin was not 'one of us'; Granovsky said that in his presence he felt *unheimlich*. Bakunin's philosophy failed to dominate the minds of his friends. For years he had wanted to study in Berlin and at last, helped financially by Herzen, he was able to leave Russia.

Strange as it may seem, Hegelian orthodoxy helped him—once in Germany —to abandon all philosophy. In the meantime, it brought him into direct contact with the discussions of the Hegelian Left, which he had scarcely been aware of in Russia. His very desire for the Absolute prevented him searching for a philosophical ladder to help him from speculation to action, an abstract justification for practical activity. His philosophy collapsed once it had fulfilled its purpose ('Hegel's philosophy either kills or strengthens weak characters', Stankevich had said).[33] There remained his detachment from the surrounding world, and above all the wish to give an absolute value to the new direction of his life. He disdained as worthless anything not directed to this end. The rest could now be dismissed with the eternal justification that 'grey is the theory and green the tree of life'.[34]

There is little important evidence of Bakunin's inner development during his early years in Germany. He still owed much to Hegelian philosophy.

God preserve us from any wretched compromise. Better to be logically abstract than stick to the concrete world. Being logical in the abstract soon leads to a knowledge of one's own one-sidedness. Compromise leads nowhere.[35]

There is, in fact, no gradual progress from his political orthodoxy to his revolutionary ideas of 1842. All the concentrated inner life of his preceding years had prepared him for a leap. While his Moscow friends and the young Hegelians in Germany were still discussing the need to round off classical German philosophy by practical action, and to establish within the Hegelian system the relations between politics and philosophy, Bakunin had already made the leap. He was already becoming the living example of practical action, and, to use Herzen's expression, of its 'vendetta with philosophy'.

When Herzen read, in Moscow, the article 'Die Reaction in Deutschland. Ein Fragment von einem Franzosen', he was enthusiastic. He found in it the political passion which he was looking for in Moscow, and which Bakunin in one bound had found in Germany.

The article was aimed mainly at those who wanted a compromise between the existing world and the revolution. He referred the compromisers to the logic of Hegel, the laws of Solon, and to the example of the Jews in Poland, who in the last war had supported first the Poles and then the Russians, and in the end had been hanged by both.

His article was an act of faith in the revolution which, by destroying the existing world, would open the doors to the world of the spirit. It would affect the field of philosophy too, by exploding theories in the name of practical action. The end of the article—the most famous phrase of the work, often subsequently quoted—reveals its real meaning: 'The passion for destruction is at the same time a creative passion.'

It is a brilliant phrase, which demonstrates his intransigence, but which loses its political meaning when it is removed from its context—

The people, the poorer classes, whose rights are recognized in theory, but who until now, because of their origins and position, have been deprived of property, condemned to ignorance and therefore (in actual practice) to slavery—these classes, the true people, everywhere grow menacing . . . men everywhere are enthralled by the promise of a future which is synonymous with freedom. Even over Russia, of which we know so little and which is perhaps destined to a great future, clouds are gathering. The air is sultry and heavy with storms.[36]

His revolutionary passion and his bold confrontation of the world had at last developed a content, and it was a social content.

He was so taken by his new ideal that he gradually broke off his connections with Russia, to which he decided not to return. His farewell to Turgenev, the future novelist, whom he met in Berlin during the first phase of his stay in Germany, and who was the last Russian whom he tried to convert to his Hegelian religion, was a sort of symbol of the deeper break with his friends, with Moscow and with Russia.[37] In November 1842 he was already so certain of his political ideal that he himself encouraged Ruge to draw the ultimate practical conclusions in his fight against orthodox Hegelianism. In the autumn of that year he left Berlin for Dresden, and decided to devote all his energies to political work with the German Socialist groups. At Dresden he met the poet Herwegh, and together they emigrated to Switzerland to create a nucleus of Socialists and Radicals.[38] It was Herwegh who first introduced Bakunin to Weitling and the latter's Communist group, the first with which he established contact.

Weitling had recently published *The Guarantees of Liberty and Harmony*— 'a really important work', wrote Bakunin to Ruge. He was interested not so much in Weitling's purely utopian theories or political ideas as in the evidence of the proletarian state of mind. 'Reading the book one sees that he describes exactly what a proletarian feels, what he could not fail to feel.'

Bakunin was faced with a new world, and he began to try to understand it passively, which was his natural state of mind, he once said, when coming across something unknown and radically new. He listened in silence, convinced that 'negation is the only nourishment, the fundamental condition of every live life'.[39]

When Bakunin began to consider the artisans, the proletariat that he had met through Weitling, it is very likely he had already, instinctively, assimilated the anarchical tendencies of this vociferous German revolutionary. Indeed they closely resemble his own later ideas. But this was not the aspect that he now stressed. He questioned the value of the very essence of Weitling's teaching and the Communism contained in it. And he finally came to the conclusion: 'His is not a free society, a really live union of free people, but a herd of animals, intolerably coerced and united by force, following only material ends, utterly ignorant of the spiritual side of life.'[40]

Yet Communism posed a problem which was implicit in the very structure of society. 'Communism does not spring from theories but from the people's instinct, and this is never mistaken.'[41] 'We are on the eve of a great revolution . . . which will not be merely political in character, but concerned with principles and religion.'[42] Under the old banner of liberty, equality and fraternity, democracy was beginning a new struggle, inspired by the workers' will for freedom. Weitling's preaching was merely a symptom. His Communism was merely a mistaken solution of a living and fundamental problem. 'True Communism' to counter this vulgar and despotic variety had still to be found.

When Weitling's movement was crushed, Bakunin, who was indirectly involved in the persecution, had to leave the city. After a brief stay in Switzerland he joined Ruge and the other German émigrés in Paris. There he continued his researches into 'true Communism', which in Switzerland he had for a moment thought of embracing—not only intellectually but by becoming a workman and thus proving his own freedom of action. But this notion was transitory, and was due chiefly to the increasing difficulties of his economic situation.

In Paris, where he remained for some years—and which he originally liked so much that he said he would stay there for ever—his life was entirely devoted to reading and discussing philosophical and political ideas. He had an exceptionally large and lively circle of acquaintances and friends, and was in constant touch with the German émigrés. He also had personal contacts with Proudhon, Louis Blanc, Marrast, George Sand, Michelet—in fact the centre of what was to comprise the Left in 1848.[43]

He was at first especially interested in Communist undercurrents. He got to know Cabet, and in October 1844 he wrote to his friend Solger[44] that 'he was studying political economy and was a Communist with all his heart'.[45] In a letter of September of the same year Engels includes him among the Communists, and it was Bakunin who had first introduced Engels to a workmen's meeting. The impression made on him by Weitling's group had evidently been strong, despite the reserves expressed in the article published in Zurich.

During this period Bakunin was specially close to the group which was trying, at the end of 1844, to transform the *Vorwärts*, the German paper published in Paris, into an organ of émigré Socialism. The leaders were Ruge, Marx, Herwegh and Heine. But here too he felt something in the atmosphere that prevented him putting his whole heart into the work. He felt the same narrowness and artificiality that had made him unable to accept Weitling's utopia.

These gentlemen are strangers to the fundamental demands of human dignity and freedom. Rather sad, isn't it? . . . From this point of view the French Communists are more progressive, human, proud and free. They are full of dignity and self-respect, and so they appreciate dignity and freedom in others.[46]

In any case Marx encouraged Bakunin to expand his political ideas. Some years later, in 1871, Bakunin was to say:

Marx was then far more extremist than I was. At that time I had no ideas on political economy, and my Socialism was purely instinctive. Although younger than I, Marx was already an atheist, a doctrinaire materialist and a conscious Socialist . . . We met often enough for me to appreciate his knowledge and his serious and passionate devotion to the cause of the proletariat, although it was always mixed with personal vanity.[47]

Marx, in his turn, was interested in the Russians who had attached themselves to the German émigrés in Paris. Bakunin was the only political personality among them. But in 1844 others were to be found with him: Sazonov, who had with Herzen founded the Saint-Simonist group in Moscow; and also G. M. Tolstoy, a colourful aristocrat (related to the Decembrist, Ivashov) from the Kazan region. He promised Marx that he would sell his possessions and give him the proceeds. Though he did not do this, he retained his progressive views, and later provided Belinsky with the financial means to edit the *Sovremennik*.[48] Marx said that these Russians were drawn to the world of Communist sects entirely out of curiosity, out of 'gluttony'. In fact, as Bakunin was soon to show, this was not the only reason. But their relations at first were dominated by Marx's feeling of superiority towards the Russians. This was one reason why Bakunin turned to the French and the Poles, loosening his ties with the German émigrés. But he took this step mainly because he had found in Marx's more scholarly theories the same denial of a 'free society' which had disenchanted him from the ideas of Weitling.

Looking back on this period of his life many years later, he concluded that Marx was a great thinker, but that 'Proudhon understood and had a far greater feeling for freedom . . . It's very likely that in theory Marx can construct an even more rational system of freedom than Proudhon, but he lacks the instinctive feeling for it. As a German and a Jew, he is authoritarian from head to foot.'[49]

'True Communism' Bakunin found not in Marx, but in Proudhon. Bakunin's attitude to the Frenchman's political and social conceptions was similar to Herzen's towards the ideas of the Russian Slavophils at this time. He accepted some of his central perceptions, but he wanted to strip them of their covering and above all to criticize them in the light of his previous philosophical experiences. This was to be a slow process, which Bakunin could consider completed only when he had formulated his anarchism, which was merely (as he himself claimed) Proudhon's system 'enlarged, developed and freed of all its metaphysical, idealist and doctrinaire decoration'.[50]

We have too little evidence about the relations between Proudhon and Bakunin in these Paris years to be able to reconstruct the stages of this elaboration. Besides, their influences were reciprocal, for Bakunin, with Marx and Grün, was one of those who aroused Proudhon's interest in the Hegelian dialectic. But we know what this meant for Bakunin. In his discussions with Proudhon he used the dialectic chiefly as an instrument to seek 'reality', to extract the political kernel from a complex system, and to discover in it a Socialism free of the despotic elements of which he had been conscious in the Communism of Weitling and the German émigrés.

His journalistic activities in Germany and Switzerland, and his personal contact with the Hegelian Left and Communist sects, soon attracted the attention of the Tsarist police. At the end of 1844 he was condemned by the Senate 'for having had criminal relations abroad with a group of disaffected elements, and for not having submitted to the orders of His Majesty's Government to return to Russia—to deprivation of his rights and dignities, and, ordered, on return to Russia, to be deported to forced labour in Siberia, and the confiscation of all his goods (if he had any)'.[51] This sentence, published in the Paris press (through the Russian Embassy), brought his attention back to his own country. In January 1845 he sent an open letter of protest to the newspaper La Réforme to expound his views on the situation. Another Russian émigré, Golovin, had been sentenced to the same penalties by the Senate, and had also publicly protested, claiming the rights of the Russian nobility and appealing to a hypothetical 'charter' granted in ancient times by the Emperors to the aristocracy. It was Golovin's intervention which led to Bakunin's letter.

It was not true, he wrote, that there existed in Russia an opposition consisting of the nobility and the constitutional bodies. The Senate had no autonomy. Russian despotism was complete.

Aristocratie bien pitoyable et bien ridicule, qui, parfaitement étrangère à toutes les questions du siècle, à tous ces grands intérêts de l'humanité qui se débattent hors de son sein, ne sait parler dans ses réunions que des occupations, des gestes et des paroles de la famille impériale et des calembours du Grand-Duc Michel.

He followed up this attack on the nobility and absolutism with a brief but effective description of the forces which really were opposing despotism. This was the first time that a Russian revolutionary had spoken in this way to European democrats, and that the forces and problems of what was later to become Russian Populism had been singled out and publicly described.

Il faut dire cependant que, parmi ces nobles Russes et surtout parmi les jeunes gens, il y en a déjà un assez grand nombre qui ont des tendances plus élevées. Ceux-là gémissent de l'abaissement où ils se trouvent plongés avec les autres et dont ils se sentent solidaires, quoique pour leur compte ils n'en soient nullement coupables. Ceux-là suivent avec amour les progrès de la civilisation et de la liberté en Europe, et se donnent toutes les peines du monde pour se rapprocher du peuple, chose extrêmement difficile, parce qu'ils en sont séparés par un abîme. Ils tâchent de conserver et de cultiver en eux-mêmes, et d'allumer dans les autres, le feu sacré des grands et des nobles instincts. Ils se cherchent mutuellement dans cette nuit profonde, dans cette atmosphère empoisonnée par l'esclavage, la délation et la crainte, qui les enveloppent et les isolent. Ah! Monsieur, il faut avoir vécu en Russie pour bien comprendre toute l'influence qu'ont sur le développement intellectuel et moral d'un homme la position où il se trouve et le monde qui l'entoure! Dieu veuille que ces jeunes gens ne succombent pas! Car ceux d'entre eux qui auront résisté jusqu'à la fin aux nombreuses entraves qui les enchaînent pourront peut-être encore être utiles à notre patrie. Mais ils agiront alors non 'comme', mais 'quoique' nobles. Car je vous le répète, Monsieur, la noblesse russe, comme telle, est complètement démoralisée, impuissante et morte.

Pour moi, je m'en plains pas . . . Je crois que pour des pays malheureux et opprimés, comme la Russie et la Pologne, il n'y a pas d'autre salut que la démocratie.

Ne pensez pas, Monsieur, que la démocratie soit impossible dans ma patrie. Pour mon compte, je suis intimement persuadé qu'elle est l'unique chose qui y soit sérieusement réalisable, et que toutes les autres formes politiques, quelque nom qu'elles prennent, seraient aussi étrangères et odieuses au peuple russe que le régime actuel.

Car le peuple russe, Monsieur, malgré le terrible esclavage qui le déprime, et malgré les coups de bâton qui pleuvent sur lui de tous les côtés, a des instincts et des allures parfaitement démocratiques. Il n'est point corrompu lui, il n'est que malheureux. Il y a dans sa nature demi-barbare quelque chose de si énergique et de si large, une telle abondance de poésie, de passion et d'esprit, qu'il est impossible de ne pas être convaincu, en le connaissant, qu'il a encore une grande mission à remplir dans ce monde. Tout l'avenir de la Russie réside en lui, dans cette masse si innombrable et si imposante d'hommes qui parlent la même langue et qui seront bientôt, j'espère, animés par le même sentiment et par la même passion. Car le peuple russe avance, Monsieur, malgré toute la mauvaise volonté du gouvernement. Des insurrections partielles et très graves de paysans contre leur seigneurs— insurrections qui se multiplient d'une manière effrayante—ne le prouvent que trop. Le moment n'est pas éloigné, peut-être, où elles se confondront dans une grande révolution et, si le gouvernement ne se dépêche pas d'émanciper le peuple, il y aura beaucoup de sang repandu.

On dit que l'empereur Nicolas y pense. Plût à Dieu! car s'il parvenait réellement à émanciper les paysans d'une manière franche et large, ce serait un véritable bienfait, qui lui ferait pardonner bien de choses, et il a beaucoup de choses a se faire pardonner, son règne n'ayant été marqué, jusqu'à présent, que par l'avilissement de tout ce qu'il y a eu encore de noble indépendance et de bons éléments en Russie . . .

Bakunin had thus not shed his doubts regarding the young Russian intellectuals, his former friends. He knew their weaknesses, but he also knew that, apart from those to be found in the Tsar and the peasant masses, the only fertile political seeds lay in them.

Between the peasants and the Tsar, however, he oscillated, hesitating between a revolution from below and a radical reform from above. These hesitations lasted for more than twenty years, and were shared by most of his generation. Revolutionary Populism could come into being only after these doubts had been overcome, as they were, first by the young intellectuals who were growing up in Russia during the 'sixties, and only later by Bakunin himself. Until then, hope in a dictatorship of the Tsar, acting for the people against the nobles, was to remain one of the two poles of his political vision. The other was his great hope that the isolated revolts of the serfs might one day turn into a revolution.

The arrival in Paris of Herzen, and of Belinsky in July 1847, finally rekindled Bakunin's interest in the problems of Russia. This had never been completely abandoned, but merely lapsed when the Western Socialist movements had taken first place in his attention.

From a distance Herzen had read and admired Bakunin's articles. After reading his protest in *La Réforme*, he had noted in his diary 'This is the language of a free man, a language that to us sounds like that of a savage. We are not used to it. We are used to allegories and to bold words *intra muros*.'[52]

Despite this distant admiration, when he reached Paris even he was stunned by Bakunin's ideas and mode of speaking. He found him absorbed in the world revolution and the problems of France, and quite incapable of understanding the importance of the intellectual movements in Russia, which were the only possible substitutes for a free political life there. Bakunin asked Herzen for news of the Government and politics. Herzen told him of Granovsky's lectures, and the university and literary world. Herzen in fact was still preoccupied with the world in which he had until then taken part, that of the Russian intelligentsia. He himself had helped to develop it along political lines, but it was certainly not yet a political party. Bakunin, since he had left, had covered much ground alone, but at the price of losing for many years any chance of influencing Russian life. They could no longer understand each other. It was now Herzen's turn to free himself from the doctrinaire ways of thought in Moscow.

The discussion was rekindled by the arrival of Belinsky. Bakunin maintained that Belinsky ought to remain in Paris and no longer dissipate his energies in St Petersburg in the daily and frequently unsuccessful struggle to express his ideas. In Russia, he was stifled by the censorship, constantly threatened with the possibility of police intervention. From this point of view, Bakunin was certainly right. Only death saved Belinsky from persecution.

What then was the point of such a life? In Paris he could have been at the centre of the Russian refugees.[53] But Belinsky stuck to his decision to return to St Petersburg, convinced that only there could he be of use. He said that Bakunin was 'like a German, was born mystical, idealist, romantic, and will die like that, because you don't change your nature by throwing over philosophy'.[54] This was not just a clash of differing temperaments. Ever since 1846 Belinsky had been exchanging his Socialist ideas for a more realistic outlook and was less influenced by French utopias, and concentrated more on the problem of freeing the serfs and the liberty of the press. Bakunin and Herzen opposed him (as well as Annenkov and Botkin, who were both in Paris at this time) not only with their Socialist ideas but also with their conception of the part of the bourgeoisie in Russian history. They argued that Russia must be freed from the danger of becoming bourgeois, of falling into a similar social situation to that of the France of Louis Philippe. Belinsky agreed with his friends' criticisms of the situation in France, but could not agree with the drastic conclusions they drew from them. He said that 'Russia's development began when the nobility was being changed into the bourgeoisie. Poland was the best example of the power of a State which had no bourgeoisie with rights of its own.' He wished to continue working in St Petersburg, and he believed that he could develop the social movements and the intelligentsia which had made such progress in the 'forties, because he had a short-term programme and one more capable of immediate fulfilment. He wanted to remain at the head of the 'Westerners', the men who later became Liberals. Herzen and Bakunin, on the other hand, hoping for a direct transition from a Russia still dominated by the nobility to Socialism, were then beginning to lay the ideological foundations of Populism. This was the precise point at which the Westerners and the Populists parted ways at the end of the 'forties.

Bakunin found in this a confirmation of the theory that he had already expressed in his first article on Russia; he was now more certain than ever that it would be a difficult process to transform Russian intellectuals into active revolutionaries. Opposed to him he saw Belinsky, who refused to emigrate, and he realized that Annenkov and Botkin maintained their reforming and liberal ideas more firmly than ever.

Years earlier this conviction had made him look for another way of influencing the situation in Russia. In the article protesting against his sentence he had already hinted at the need for Poland to move along the road to democracy. On his journey between Switzerland and Paris he had visited Lelewel, the democratic Polish historian living in Brussels; he had then tried to establish political ties with the Polish émigrés. In February 1846 the *Constitutionnel* published an article by him on the persecution of Catholics in Lithuania and White Russia. He claimed, among other things, that 'the oppression of Poland is a disgrace to my country, and its liberation may perhaps mean the liberation of Russia'.[55] Thus the national problem in the Russian Empire would provide that striking force against Tsarism which the intellectual movements of the educated classes seemed unable to bring about.

Here, too, Bakunin was trying to move forward alone, surrounded by the greatest difficulties. He was the first Russian after the Decembrists to try to make a political alliance with the Polish Nationalists. Few were to put their trust in him, especially since the Russian Embassy in Paris started the rumour that he was a Tsarist agent, a slander that pursued him for the rest of his life. Throughout 1846 he was very discouraged by these early failures. Political discussions between him, a Russian revolutionary, and the Poles, who looked at all problems from their own nationalist point of view, were often difficult, sometimes impossible. But at last in 1847 he was able to make a great speech at a meeting to commemorate the revolt of 1830.

This speech shows how his desire to make contact with the Polish émigrés had given birth to his vision of an Eastern European revolution. Such hopes were to grow during the two following years. As early as September 1847 he wrote to Herwegh: 'We can feel the storm approaching. Believe me, things will soon go well. Life will soon begin for us, we will work together in the generous and stormy way which is so necessary for us.'[56] He felt 1848 drawing near. He thought that even in Russia 'the peasants will no longer wait for freedom from the Tsar. Their growing revolts show that they are tired of waiting.'[57] So he told the Poles that an agreement between Russia and Poland was a great step forward, a cause to which it was right to dedicate themselves wholeheartedly. Once Nicholas I's empire had been overthrown, such a reconciliation would mean the freeing of all the Slavs and the real end to tyranny in Europe.[58]

These public assertions led to his expulsion from France at the request of the Russian Embassy. It was in Brussels, to which he now fled, that he began his real work of organization and conspiracy among the democratic émigrés, who were gathering there on the eve of the 1848 revolution. He began to work among the Poles, who at first received him well.

Shortly before his arrival in Brussels, a 'Democratic Society for the Union of all Countries' had been formed, made up of Belgian democrats and Communists together with representatives of the various refugees. Marx and Engels (as German Communists) were members of this Society, and at one of its meetings Marx made his famous speech on free trade, before being sent by the group to London to get in touch with the *Fraternal Democrats*, a Chartist organization, but internationalist in character. These

contacts led to the demand for a Communist programme, which Marx and
Engels then formulated in the *Manifesto*. In Brussels, Bakunin soon clashed
with the Marxists, even more violently than he had done some years earlier
in Paris.

Vanity, malice, quarrels, haughtiness in theory, timidity in practice, high minded
thoughts on life, activity and simplicity, and in practice complete absence of life,
action or simplicity. Self-conscious and thoughtful workmen and a disgusting
playing with them. 'Feuerbach is bourgeois', and the word 'bourgeoisie' becomes
an epithet boring to the point of nausea through repetition—and they themselves,
from head to foot, are little provincial petty bourgeois. In a word, lies and stupidity,
stupidity and lies. Impossible to breathe freely in such a society. I keep away from
them, and have explicitly stated that I won't enter their Communist union of
workmen, and that I won't have anything to do with them.[59]

Instead, he wanted to establish close relations with the Poles. But in the
clannish and embittered atmosphere of the emigration, Bakunin could not
do what he wanted. The insinuations that he was a Tsarist agent made the
problem still more difficult. The suspicion he met with almost suffocated him.
He was unable to ally himself with any movement which he considered of
any vitality. The Polish question—involving religious and social, national
and international problems—he saw in all its complexity in the struggles of
these little émigré groups. 'Separately, they are nearly all good Poles. Together,
as a party, they are worthless.' Even among the best he did not find one of
those 'powerful new chords, whose vibrations can set in motion the hearts of
the new generation and make them leap with joy'.[60] Lelewel, despite his age,
was one of the most remarkable characters. It is possible indeed that it was
Lelewel who suggested to him (perhaps on his first short visit to Brussels in
1844) the Slav *obshchina* as a possible seedbed for Socialism. There is no
exact evidence of this in Bakunin's letters, but he is to be found explaining
to another émigré the 'enormous difference between the agrarian community
and the *phalanstery*'. By this he probably meant that he saw in the Slav
obshchina characteristics of liberty and autonomy, which were absent from
the Fourierist organization.

His last months in Brussels caused him growing disappointment in the
'Democratic Society' in which he had at first placed such great hopes. But
it allowed him to make another speech, in which—in the name of the
Decembrists and the fallen Poles—he repeated his ideas of a new union
between Russia and Poland, both freed from the Tsarist yoke.[61] He was
also able to forge a few personal links which were to be useful when the
revolution of 1848 broke out.

'The days following the February revolution were the happiest of Bakunin's
life', Herzen wrote later.[62] He at once returned to Paris and to the men who
had fought on the barricades and who were now organizing the demonstrations
to establish the provisional government. Caussidière, the Republican prefect
of police, is reported to have said of him, 'Quel homme, quel homme!

On the first day of the revolution he is a real treasure, on the next he ought to be shot.' Bakunin lived in the *Caserne de Tournon*, near the Luxembourg, together with the Republican Guard, which was then being formed, and the workmen who had collected there. Three years later, locked up in the Peter-Paul fortress in St Petersburg, he was to tell his royal confessor of the profound impression that had been made on him by meeting these men.

I assure Your Majesty that in no other class or place have I ever found such noble self-denial, such an instinctive sense of honour, such cordial delicacy of expression, such lovable gaiety combined with so much heroism, as in these simple uneducated men, who always were and always will be a thousand times better than their leaders.[63]

But though his imagination was captured by the human aspects of the revolution, his mind soon turned to Eastern Europe, where he would have the chance to have his say and put his desire for action into practice. On 13th March *La Réforme* published an article by him on the European significance of the February revolution. 'All practical people of the old régime have now become utopian, and yesterday's utopia is the only thing that is reasonable and feasible.' This utopia was for him pure, unconditional democracy for France and the whole of Europe.

Democracy excludes conquest, but the victory of the revolutionary principle in Europe is a question of life or death for France . . . The revolutionary movement will only stop when Europe, the whole of Europe *including Russia*, is changed into a democratic federal republic. I am a Russian, and my spirit belongs to Russia. This revolution, destined to save all people, will also save Russia. Of this I am convinced.[64]

He promised to expand his ideas on the revolution in the Slav countries in a subsequent article, but this was never written. With a little money, given him by Flocon, and with two passports in his pocket, he went to the duchy of Pomerania hoping to find there, with the Poles, a base for his activities in the East. He was arrested in Berlin, probably at the request of the Russian Government, but he was soon afterwards released.

His journey across Germany in April 1848 was rapid, but this did not prevent him from giving a vivid description of a German world 'in confusion, but without a real revolution'. He was struck by the lack of a central organization in the movement. The German revolution seemed to be incoherent and fragmentary. And of its social character he wrote: 'Now, it is not the kings and princes who are strong, but the bourgeoisie, which is desperately antagonistic to the republic, because it brings in its wake social problems and the triumph of democracy.' Yet,

only the republic can get rid of the dead and benighted German union and bring real unity—the ideal of every German—*Deutsche Einheit*. You cannot imagine the amount of nonsense that has been spoken about this. What is alive in Germany is the proletariat and the peasants. There will be a terrible revolution, a real flood of barbarians, which will wipe the ruins of the old world off the face of the earth.

Then the fortunes of the good, amiable Bürger will be bad, terrible. The symptoms of this revolution can be seen everywhere: scarcity of money, fewer buyers, factories stopping work, the number of unemployed workmen increasing daily. The democratic revolution will begin here within two or three months at the latest. The leaders are gradually organizing their forces and trying to bring about a unified revolutionary movement of the whole of Germany.[65]

In spite of his doubts about so many aspects of Germany—and especially the nationalism apparent in her relations with the Danes and her uncertain attitude towards the Poles and Slavs—Bakunin retained this faith in German democracy until the last possible moment. The bitter anti-German feelings of his later years sprang from his disappointment at the collapse of these great hopes.

He stayed only a few days in Berlin. Passing through Leipzig he met Ruge again who, some years earlier, had turned him towards democratic ideas. He told him that he feared for the future of the revolution in France. When he had left Paris, the reaction was already beginning to make itself felt. Bakunin was not alone in this judgment, which was shared by many Socialist leaders in France. But he probably saw more clearly than they did the international consequences of the situation. The failure to help Italy and Spain was its most dangerous symptom. He told Ruge that the French understood nothing of the German revolution, and still less of the Slav one. This view of the situation encouraged him more than ever to devote his activities to the Slav world, and to aim especially at Russia. He was convinced that only if the revolution spread to Eastern Europe could it triumph in the West and in France.[66]

At Breslau, where he stayed for some time seeking agreement with the Poles who were meeting there, his plans came to nothing. Once again contacts with the émigrés proved difficult. Prussian policy, which for a short time had favoured the Polish movement, began to turn against it, especially when it assumed a distinctly peasant tendency directed against the aristocracy.

In May 1848 the Slav congress at Prague at last gave him the chance to express his ideas. His policy consisted of a noble attempt to swim against the tide by encouraging the Slav national movement to adopt policies which should not merely avoid conflict with, but actually support, the democratic revolutions in France, Germany, Austria, Hungary and Italy. He thus tried to counteract the influence of the conservative forces, which were making use of these young political movements and playing on their national rivalries.

References to Bakunin's Panslavism of these years are usually vague, and conceal a lack of understanding of his political activities.[67] Panslavism is like an expandable portmanteau that can be made to contain almost anything, and into it Bakunin put his own policies, convinced that the idea of a federation would have encouraged the Slavs to take part in the great struggle which the revolution was waging throughout Europe.

His policy, therefore, has its Machiavellian element in the desire to use, without much belief in its value, the banner of nationalism for revolutionary ends. The expression 'Revolutionary Panslavism' can be accepted as a description of his policy, only if it is remembered that Bakunin himself put the emphasis on the adjective and not on the noun. It may also be true that later in this complicated game, Bakunin was carried away and eventually overwhelmed by 'the demoniac force of Nationalism', as he once described it; and that he did not succeed in dragging it into the field of an internationalism which he conceived of as a free alliance and a collaboration of democratic forces. But this only means he, too, felt weighed down by the destiny of 1848, in which the national and social elements were so entangled that neither of them could develop until everyone had realized the extent of the failure.

When he reached Prague in June he at once expressed these ideas in his negotiations with the other participants at the Congress and in newspaper articles. The Slavs, he said, had been oppressed for too long to become the means of oppressing other people. Only a Slav federation 'from the Adriatic to the Black Sea and from the White Sea to Siberia' would guarantee freedom for them all and range them alongside the other democracies. The federation, as he envisaged it, was to give to a 'Slav Council' absolute authority in foreign affairs and in the maintenance of freedom within each of the federated nations. The social programme was to be one of democratic equality without any specific connection with Socialism. In his observations, Bakunin clearly explained that it was his aim to prevent the growing nationalist movements from degenerating into internal Slav wars or wars directed against other people. 'Respect and love for the freedom of others is in their eyes the basic condition of their own freedom.'[68]

It must be remembered that he expounded these ideas at the Congress of Prague, which had been called to oppose the German Congress of Frankfurt, with the aim (as far as some of its organizers were concerned) of supporting the Hapsburg monarchy against the Hungarians. It is not therefore surprising that Bakunin's views did not prevail and that neither they nor their author took first place at the Congress. He was well aware that he was swimming against the tide, and so he tried to restrict his aims to the recall of the Croat troops from Italy, and the union of at least a few Slav nationalities within the nucleus of a federation without for the moment counting on Russia. He then began to create a political organization to achieve these ends. This was a secret society 'The Slav Friends', made up of a few people who shared his ideas, chiefly spokesmen of the Slovak, Croat and Serb movements.

When the Prague rebellion broke out owing to provocation from the Austrian troops and the revolt of small groups of 'democratic Czechs', Bakunin plunged himself body and soul into the struggle and its direction, although he had probably had no part in preparing it. But he had no faith in its timeliness or chances of success.

The Slav Congress was broken off, and on his return to Berlin in July Bakunin resumed his activities as soon as he had put an end to the slander that he was a Tsarist agent. This time the charge was especially dangerous as it was quoted by Marx in the *Neue Rheinische Zeitung* and Bakunin had to get guarantees to refute it. Further persecution by the Prussian police, once more incited by Russia, forced him to keep moving round Germany, while he prepared his *Appeal to the Slavs*, which he published at Leipzig in December 1848.[69]

In it he repeated, with greater effect and more openly, the ideas that he had tried in vain to impose on the Congress of Prague. The Slavs, he said, had united against German policy, which denied their right to existence. But now they must link their own fortunes to those of the revolutionary movement in Germany. The Slavs had ancient rivalries with the Hungarians, but now they must side with revolutionary Hungary, and realize that any help given to the Austrian Emperor would only increase the extent of their own oppression. Of course, he went on, Russia was a great Slav country, but Nicholas I's policy was against the interests of European democracy, and the Slavs must therefore not only refuse to rely on him, but must openly fight against him. He concluded with an appeal for a 'general federation of European republics' rather than for a specifically Slav federation which he scarcely mentioned.[70]

'This is a critical moment in the existence of the Slavs. Everyone must do his duty, and then God's will may be done. Much love is needed to take the right line at this difficult time', he wrote in a letter.[71] It was indeed a sense of duty which guided him whilst writing his *Appeal to the Slavs*. Even in its wording, this pamphlet made the smallest possible concession to the nationalist forces which he felt to be the greatest enemy, but which must now be deflected so as to benefit the revolution.

Such a clear standpoint gave him the right to implore the German democrats, too, to examine their consciences. He had again allied himself with Ruge, 'a German patriot, but not a teutomane', who had protested against 'the young German freedom' in Poland, Prague, Italy and against 'all his compatriots who were Francophobes, Danophobes, Slavophobes: in fact all "phobes" except tyrannophobes'.[72] The attack which Engels now launched against his *Appeal* must have convinced him of the real strength of nationalist feeling among the German revolutionaries. In the *Neue Rheinische Zeitung* of 15th and 16th February, Engels wrote an article called 'Democratic Panslavism' in which, among other things, he specifically denied any right of autonomous existence to the Slav countries and, in general, any future for them. Bakunin must have drawn the conclusion that it was very difficult to make an alliance with the German revolutionaries.

Quite apart from this, Germany's internal situation already seemed badly compromised by lack of courage among the leaders. Not that this made him despair. As Herzen had done when the revolution began to collapse in France, so now in Germany Bakunin looked chiefly to the peasants, hoping for a renewal of the movement there. Until then, he said, the democratic leaders had believed it possible to move the peasants 'with abstract political phrases, either constitutional or republican. They did not want to rouse the so-called "evil passions" of the people.' This had led to the reaction. But by now the peasants would have understood this. 'The "evil passions" will unleash the peasants' war, and this cheers me, because I am not afraid of anarchy, but long for it with all my heart. Only this can uproot us from the accursed mediocrity in which we have been vegetating for so long.' Even the reaction itself might be of some use. It would at last concentrate men's minds, and make people realize that the time for talk was over. 'Now, thank God, they're beginning to organize and create secret societies.'[73] Later, in his *Confession* he said that the German democrats' most serious mistake was to have spread their propaganda in the towns instead of in the villages. Yet, he added, it would not have been difficult to arouse the revolutionary spirit of the peasants, especially in Germany where there still survived so many relics of the feudal system.

This review of the revolutionary situation helped to make his plans for its resumption much clearer in 1849. Basing himself on Dresden and relying on a new movement in Germany, he would at the same time direct a Slav organization concentrated in Bohemia, rather than Poland, in which he had now lost hope. In the social sphere the movement was to take on a more popular character. As he wrote in an early draft of his *Appeal to the Slavs*, the social problem and the class struggle in France—and in other countries where they had got entangled with the question of nationality—had shattered the hopes of 1848. 'The reactionaries would have been too stupid if they had not been able to turn this situation to their advantage', and so they had 'preached a bourgeois crusade against the proletariat.' The bourgeoisie, for its part, had disarmed the people, thus depriving itself of weapons with which to defend freedom. The only hope now was an insurrection of the people alone organized by the most determined revolutionaries.

The exact plans for action that Bakunin deduced from this analysis are uncertain. Our only evidence comes from the statements he made in prison, and especially the *Confession* to Nicholas I, written in the Peter-Paul fortress. This last, though extremely interesting from the psychological point of view, is not historically reliable, being a sort of photographic negative of Bakunin's personality. It reflects the exhaustion, doubt and diffidence that influenced his actions, and above all the more questionable elements of his ideology. These were burnt to ashes by his consuming desire to affirm the social and national freedom of the Slavs, but, in prison, they were consciously used by him to deceive and enlist the sympathies of his royal gaoler.

In the *Confession* even his Panslavism reveals only its negative aspects, and is coloured by his distrust of the Germany of 1848, and of France and Europe in general. Absent, too, is the vigour which had once led him to believe in a

spontaneous initiative of the Slavs, which alone could have led to an
intensification of the revolution in the West. He ends by extolling the pure
destructive force of the Russian Empire and the brutal and utterly negative
destruction of a world that had been unable to resurrect itself through
revolution.

So his hesitations between a peasant revolution from below and radical
reforms from above—whose origins we noticed in an article of some years
earlier—returned. For a time he wanted to substitute Russian conquest on
the Emperor's initiative for the revolution which had not succeeded through
the spontaneous initiative of the people.

Letters to his family from prison conclusively prove that Bakunin did not
really believe in the ideas contained in his *Confession*, but remained faithful
to his revolutionary tenets. What he wrote for Nicholas I was only the
shadow of his political ideology, an expression of his disappointment at the
failure of 1848. The *Confession*, therefore, must be read critically, not only
in its details, which can be checked by other documents, but also as regards
some of the ideas, which is sometimes difficult. This is especially true of his
views on the revolution in Germany and Bohemia in 1849.

It is true that these views were dominated by a growing distrust of legal
and parliamentary methods. By August 1848 he had taken up a position
parallel to that of Proudhon and Herzen, though it was expressed with a
violence entirely his own. In a letter to Herwegh he praised Proudhon, and
continued:

I am not much interested in parliamentary debates. The time for parliamentary
life, constituent and national assemblies is over . . . I don't believe in constitutions
and laws. Even the best constitution would not satisfy me. We need something
else—impetus, life, a new world, without laws and therefore free.[74]

As he was to say in his *Confession*, he wanted a republic, but not a parliamentary one. It was to be dominated rather by a 'strong dictatorial power
with the exclusive task of raising and educating the popular masses. In other
words it must be a power which is free in character and spirit, yet which lacks
parliamentary forms; it must publish books whose content is free, yet it
must not allow freedom of the press; it must be surrounded by people thinking as it does and must derive enlightenment from their advice, and strength
from their free cooperation; but it must be limited by no one and nothing.'[75]

As can be seen, the anarchist terminology which he had used to fight
parliamentary institutions—and which certainly corresponded to his deepest
feelings—in fact describes a programme which can be described as Blanquist
rather than anarchist.

The revolutionary government with unlimited revolutionary authority was to sit in
Prague. The nobility and hostile clergy were to be driven out, the Austrian administration burnt to ashes, the employees driven out, except a few among the most
important and competent who would be used for advice and also to run a library

of statistics at Prague. All the clubs, newspapers and every expression of garrulous anarchy were to be subjected to a single dictatorial power. All young men and any others of use were to be divided into categories according to their character, capability and addresses, and then spread throughout the country to give it a revolutionary organization and a temporary army. The popular masses were to be divided into two sections: one, lightly armed, to stay at home and protect the new order and, if necessary, to take part in the partisan war. The young and anyone capable of carrying arms, factory workers and unemployed artisans and a large part of the educated bourgeois youth were to form the regular army, not *Freischaren*, but a regular army, trained with the help of former Polish officers, and even Austrian soldiers and junior officers, promoted according to their capacity and zeal to the various commissioned ranks. The expense would have been enormous, but I hoped that this could have been partly met out of confiscated goods and out of vouchers like those granted by Kossuth . . . This was my plan.[76]

Though he thus devoted most of his powers to the secret organization which was to prepare this revolution in Bohemia, Bakunin did not forget the one that was the final end of his activities, which had always been aimed at Russia. He now began to collect his ideas on the situation there, and he eventually dictated a work which was called *Russische Zustände. Ein Bild aus der Jetztzeit*,[77] and was published at Leipzig in the summer of 1849. This was a description of Russia's social and political conditions made for Europeans 'who knew almost nothing of them'.[78] But it was chiefly a vision of Russia's future—a complete formulation of his revolutionary Populism—that sprang from the vivid contrast between his many experiences in Europe and his view of conditions in Russia.

He had begun to collect notes on foreign policy, which included comments of some interest on the links between Prussia and Russia. He showed the difficulties of solving the Polish problem, and once more explained why he had lost his hopes of a revolution in Poland. But he soon left his first draft to turn to an inquiry into Russia's internal situation—the army, the peasants and the aristocracy. His observations on the soldiers were chiefly dictated by the immediate purpose of encouraging Europe 'not to despise nor to fear'[79] the Russian army. His highly coloured picture of its weaknesses must have seemed strange to the German and European reader, but that it contained some truth can be seen by considering not that year's expedition to Hungary, but the Crimean War some time later.

Of far greater interest are his remarks on the peasants. Attacking the theories which described them as slaves utterly subjected to the Tsar, Bakunin emphasized the proofs they had given of independent and revolutionary spirit. This was shown especially in the development of religious sects and the great peasant movements of Stenka Razin and Pugachev in the seventeenth and eighteenth centuries, that had continued sporadically ever since.

In Russia it is a question not merely of abolishing slavery and of establishing the freedom of the individual, but also of the right to land. The peasants speak openly of this. They do not say, 'our landlord's property', but *our* property. So the *social* nature of the Russian revolution is already determined. It has its roots in the very character of the people and in the organization of the *obshchina*. Land belongs to the *obshchina*; the individual peasant merely has the right to use it. Hereditary right is concerned only with the noble's property; not with the strips of land. Every twenty to twenty-five years there is a redistribution. To interfere with this organization, even with the best intentions, would certainly not be allowed. It would be a sentence of death for any landlord or noble.[80]

As can be seen, Bakunin was now convinced of the importance of the *obshchina*, which, by virtue of the traditional and collective ownership of the land by the peasants, would give a social character to the future Russian revolution. The importance of these agrarian communities in Slav life may first have been suggested to him by Lelewel. His discussions with Herzen in Paris had confirmed this view. Yet his appreciation of it was probably chiefly derived from his own reflections on the situation in Russia prompted perhaps by reading Haxthausen's book, which he had quoted in the first draft of this work.

He then gave a brief and lively picture of the intellectual situation.

Contemporary Russian literature is entirely concerned with noting and depicting the shameful and unbearable conditions of the nation. It is a period like that undergone by Germany at the time of Boerne, a time of self-consciousness and unhealthy self-flagellation. As a result of all this the young aristocrats are convinced that they are worthless and have no future—both because of and despite the fact that they are aristocrats—and that Russia's strength and future lie enclosed within the people. This is the dogma of present-day Russia.[81]

The belief commonly held in Europe that the movement which had developed for example at Moscow had sprung from the nobles' opposition to governmental centralization was a great mistake. 'Moscow is in fact the centre of discontent—but discontent of the radical youth who despise a government career and resort to the people.'[82]

The movement to go to the people, of which Bakunin here speaks, was conceived of as a sacrifice, imposed by the situation and at the same time as a voluntary gesture. The aristocracy in fact recognized its failure and, at the same time, renounced its chances of forming a new ruling class. So the intelligentsia would give rise, not to a bourgeoisie, but to a revolutionary movement.

At this very time Herzen was urging the revolutionaries to destroy the false civilization within themselves and to dedicate themselves entirely to the cause of the people. Bakunin was already beginning to turn this renunciation into a theory, giving it an absolute value. He was thus formulating his own brand of anarchism. His view of the future of the intelligentsia corresponded in fact to the ideas he had formed of the function of the revolutionaries in the Europe of 1849. Experience had shown him the substantial nature of the various obstacles which stood in the way of democratic revolution throughout Europe; those obstacles which he, like so many others, had thought could be quickly overcome by the fire of enthusiasm aroused by 1848. Now what was needed was complete dedication to a negative, destructive function. The true revolutionaries would be those who destroyed the old world, leaving the task of building 'to others, better, more intelligent, fresher than we are'.[83]

His revolutionary programme for Bohemia and this opinion of Russia completed the researches into 'true Communism' which he had begun in Switzerland after his meeting with Weitling.

He too—like Herzen and so many of the Socialists before 1848—had started with a combination of great interest in and strong opposition to Communism. By Communism he meant the specific tradition of Babeuf, Buonarroti and the movements that drew their inspiration from them in the 'thirties and 'forties, especially those of Cabet and Weitling. Opposition, especially at first, was due to the vulgarity, violence and tyranny which these Socialists could not fail to perceive in the Communist ideas. Their own romanticism, a deeper and more complex knowledge of economics and a critical view of Jacobinism turned them against tendencies of this kind. Communism remained for them a direct expression of the proletarian state of mind; a symptom that revealed the social situation; a prophecy but not a solution. Bakunin, too, had shared this attitude. Though once—and only once—he had proclaimed himself a Communist, he constantly developed this attitude, opposing Weitling and Marx, and moving towards Proudhon.

In the years before 1848 Marx too had been critical of simple traditional Communism, which he called utopian. But after the *German Ideology* he had stifled his doubts. He ceased openly attacking the myth of traditional Communism, and found an outlet in the study of social reality, economic development, etc. He left unplanned the organization of the future city and adopted Communism as the ultimate end of the evolution of history, which was his only interest. And in 1848 he was entirely engaged in acting practically to accelerate the process and bring it to its final fruition.

Faced with these fundamental problems of nineteenth-century Socialism, Bakunin had shown both to others and to himself the wonderful breadth of his untrammelled temperament—a temperament that had been able to absorb all his preceding experiences, stripped of the formulas and doctrines that had clothed them. But, as Belinsky noticed, he could change theories, but not his nature; and this included the tendency to rationalize his passions and most intimate feelings. His words can nearly always be interpreted either as the reaction of a rebel, faced with a petty world—for instance, the liberal German bourgeoisie and its nationalism—or as the germ of a complete negation of laws and government.[84]

That this was chiefly a personal reaction and the assertion of his will is proved by the fact that when he descended to the level of programmes Bakunin thought in terms of a revolutionary dictatorship. He eventually accepted the methods of the French Revolution and of Babeuf, which he developed along lines parallel to those of Blanqui. His early anarchism only emphasized the negative, entirely destructive value which he assigned to this revolutionary dictatorship.

We have seen that Herzen also—though in different ways and though he did not take part in conspiracies or in the drafting of detailed plans—underwent a similar development. He too looked upon Blanqui as the real revolutionary of the time, because he was capable of adopting methods indispensable for the destruction that was needed.

Thus Herzen, and even more Bakunin, achieved a momentary fusion of Communist and Socialist elements. In both men we can see reflected a characteristic stage of the revolution during those years, made up of the confluence of the traditions of Babeuf and Saint-Simon, of Fourier and Proudhon. Disappointment at the defeat of 1848 and hope in a revival of the revolution led them to believe in a dictatorship of the Blanqui type as the only means of destroying the obstacles which had blocked the way in 1848. But for both of them the content of this future revolution was no longer the Communist ideal, but that of the Socialists of the 'thirties and 'forties, especially of Proudhon. When their temporary adherence to Blanqui came to an end, Herzen found himself once more a Populist and Bakunin an anarchist.

In both men these ideas were united to an increased distrust of the reviving energies of Western Europe and pessimism as regards the fate of France and Germany. And so they turned their attention to Russian problems and derived from their experiences a new vision of the Russian peasant masses, the *obshchina* and the capacity for revolution and liberty contained in the Russian village and the life of the intelligentsia.

From this vision—fraught with pessimism in Herzen, with exaltation in Bakunin—was born Populism, as a belief in a revolution of the peasants supported by a ruling class, by that fraction of the intelligentsia which was capable of defending the interests and traditions of the peasants and voluntarily fusing with them.

Arrested for his participation in the revolt of Dresden in May 1849—in which he had shown exceptional sang-froid and resolution after a last attempt to urge his Prague followers to organize a concerted rising—Bakunin was condemned to death on 14th January 1850, together with two companions. He was then handed over to Austria in July of the same year. There he was again condemned to death in May 1851 by a military tribunal, and a few days later was handed over to Russia. And so began his long years of prison and Siberia.

3. THE PEASANT PROBLEM AND SOCIALISM IN THE 'THIRTIES AND 'FORTIES

HERZEN AND BAKUNIN more fully than anyone else of their generation understood the problems of Russian society and their relationship to spiritual and physical changes in the rest of Europe. But both of them, in different ways, had been exiles in their own country even before they crossed its frontiers and plunged into the revolution of 1848. And it was only then that their ideas began to crystallize. Only spiritual and actual separation from their country enabled them to gain a complete picture of Russian problems. But, for this very reason, in order to trace the roots of the Populist movement, it will now be necessary to return to Russia: to the daily and growing conflict between peasants, nobles and the State in the empire of Nicholas I; to the slow infiltration of Socialist ideas into the intelligentsia; and finally to the formation of movements which began to assimilate these ideas.

The debate, which had been so intensively pursued among the Decembrists on the fate of the Russian countryside, on serfdom and on the traditional forms of land holdings, did not come to an end with the suppression of the rising of 1825. The problems raised by the existing state of affairs were too serious for this to be possible. But the debate henceforth was no longer free, allowing of open comparison between Russia and other countries. It was transferred to the higher ranks of the State bureaucracy and the Emperor's leading councillors. It was no longer illuminated by general ideas, but rather by the lively realization that something had to be done, if only to check the immediate dangers and difficulties of the situation. And so it merely led to a series of plans, which were conceived without imagination and seldom put into execution. These plans were often drawn up in a muddled way, dictated by the contradictory desire to stabilize the existing situation and at the same time to remove or conceal its worst defects; to demonstrate the power of absolutism (and thus in some ways continue the tradition of Peter the Great and of Catherine II) and yet simultaneously to use despotism for the conservative purpose of arresting change. Yet even in the bureaucratic literature and the timid efforts at reform made during the time of Nicholas I the problems stand out clearly, and explain the aspirations and modes of thought of those freer spirits who were toying with programmes very similar to those of the Populists.[1]

The Emperor had had compiled a complete review of the situation which

63

was based on the facts that had come to light at the trial of the Decembrists. He himself frequently consulted this list of criticisms, proposals and plans. But the land problem, although it always remained present in his mind and preoccupied high government circles, was, so to speak, placed in the archives and discussed only in private. None the less various reasons compelled the government to take action: there was the example of other countries, especially Austria and Prussia; the general economic development; the financial difficulties of the nobles which had been brought about by their mounting debts and by their inability to obtain from their estates sufficient revenue to meet their needs; the increase in population; above all—as is shown by the researches of the Third Section which Nicholas established at this time—the fear of peasant disorders.

All other considerations might be shelved—for fifty years perhaps, as his minister Uvarov hoped—but this last factor demanded immediate attention. The setting up in 1826 of a committee to prepare various reforms can be regarded as a counter-attack against the Decembrist movement. But the later bureaucratic efforts of the 'thirties and 'forties were undertaken chiefly because the ruling classes thought that the situation in the country was deteriorating. As early as 1832 an inspecting Senator drew up a report, which came to the following conclusion:

I have closely observed the spirit of the peasant classes and, in general, of the lowest ranks of the population, and have noticed a vast change in their attitude. They have grown bolder, more independent, less submissive, and at the same time poorer. They have stopped revering, as they once did, officials and the representatives of constituted authority.[2]

The Senator, with his hurried generalizations, showed that he too was affected by that general fear of the peasant masses, which is one of the characteristic features of the period. However, the statistics of peasant disorders directed against nobles and officials, though varying in scale and content in different parts of the Empire, show that he was not completely mistaken. Even the plain figures are significant. Between 1826 and 1829, there had been eighty-eight disturbances; between 1830 and 1834, sixty; between 1835 and 1839, seventy-nine; between 1840 and 1844, a hundred and thirty-eight; between 1845 and 1849, two hundred and seven.[3] We must remember that the criteria of the police in listing these risings varied greatly and were very unreliable. They grouped together small local disorders and serious risings which shook whole districts; acts of insubordination, so-called merely because of petty-minded notions of order held by the local authorities, and genuine revolts. But even bearing this in mind, the significance of the trend is obvious. Symptoms of insubordination in the countryside rapidly increased during the two decades that preceded the revolution of 1848. There are other factors to confirm this conclusion. On an average, seven landowners were murdered by the peasants every year. Yet between 1835 and

1843, four hundred and sixteen people were deported to Siberia for attempts on the lives of landlords.[4] Flights of peasants from the nobles' estates to avoid taxes and ill-treatment were frequent, and sometimes took place on a huge scale. Entire villages disappeared in search of other lands and freedom, often making for the Caucasus. In the 'forties this phenomenon became even more serious. In the department of Kursk twenty thousand peasants made preparations for flight, and were only persuaded to remain by the arrest of the first to leave (and even they tried for a time to resist the troops).

No full detailed examination of these uprisings of the 'thirties and 'forties has been made from material in the archives, which is often too incomplete to give an exact idea of their nature. Nevertheless, investigation of the most important of them shows that the causes varied widely, depending, for instance, on the type of land on which the peasant worked, i.e. whether it belonged to a noble, to the State lands, or to the private lands of the Crown. Lack of land was one reason for discontent, though not the most usual. More frequently the conflicts concerned the use of forests and pasture-lands, and especially the size of the *corvées* and the payment of dues in cash. The imposition of extra, more or less illegal taxes also led to protests and clashes. In these cases, the peasants' struggle to defend their rights was transformed particularly easily into a general protest against all the officials of the State and their abuses.[5]

A detailed map of these disorders has not, as far as I am aware, been made. But they appear to have been especially serious in the western regions of the empire and in the territory around the Urals, i.e. the districts in which they were aggravated by problems of nationality.[6] Particularly threatening disturbances (though here due to a specific cause) took place both in the countryside and in the towns during the cholera epidemic of 1830 to 1832.[7]

In view of the widely varying nature of these demonstrations, we cannot deduce from them any very detailed indications of the real state of mind of the peasant masses. They are chiefly significant as a symptom. But if, for the purposes of history, we must carefully sift the facts in our possession to gauge their exact importance, politically the conclusions were already apparent to the authorities as early as 1834, when the chief of police, Benkendorf, wrote:

Every year, the idea of freedom spreads and grows stronger among the peasants owned by the nobles. In 1834 there have been many examples of peasants' insubordination to their masters. And the enquiries show that nearly all these cases do not derive from ill-treatment or abuses, but purely from the idea of obtaining the right to freedom.

Benkendorf was certainly exaggerating. That the serfs were inspired by the idea of liberty was all too obvious, but that they rebelled with the specific purpose of obtaining their emancipation cannot generally be proved. Rarely were their hopes as high as this. Rather, inspired by the idea of freedom they

3+

sought in individual cases to defend their right to life, their customs and their traditions which clearly conflicted with the oppressive conditions in which they were forced to live. Naturally, the growing impoverishment of many of them, the constant famines of these years, and the general economic conditions which made serfdom less and less bearable only served to strengthen such an attitude. Even Benkendorf knew this, and pointed out that the various movements had no connection with each other. But, he continued:

A difficult situation may arise—war, diseases, famine, or people with the fatal idea of taking advantage of these circumstances to damage the government. And then giving freedom to the nobles' peasants may easily provoke grave disturbances.[8]

And so the chief of the police, by raising the bugbear of a peasant revolt, advised the Emperor to use all his immense power to 'solve this difficult problem, which can no longer be postponed'. The secret committee established at the beginning of the following year 1835 'to inquire into the means of bettering the situation of the peasants of the different categories' was one answer to this demand. It gave birth to an important enquiry, reformed the administration of the State's property (about half the peasants in Russia depended directly on the State), and suggested various other plans. But its real significance lay in the demonstration of one fact: the extraordinary power held by Nicholas I, the most despotic of contemporary European sovereigns, was in fact extremely limited when it came to tampering with the foundation of Russia's social structure. The reasons for this were many, but in the last analysis they were all summed up in one psychological factor: the fear that any attempt at reform would end in revolution.

In 1825 Nicholas I had decimated the enlightened nobility on the Senate Square in St Petersburg, and he continued to persecute the men, families and ideas which could in any way be connected with what had been the only bold and independent expression of public opinion during his reign. So that now, when it came to even the smallest interference with the rights of the provincial landed nobility, he found no support and no possibility of creating any movement which might aim at reforms. He was faced with a nobility whose only interest was the retention of all its exclusive rights.

Tradition, intellectual limitations and self-interest precluded him from relying on the peasants themselves for support. Although some day—to be postponed as long as possible—they would have to be transformed from slaves into 'free farmers', in the hateful words of Alexander I, this was the one step which Nicholas would never take. Yet this step was the only one theoretically possible; although it would involve impairing the interests of the nobility, the peasants alone could provide the necessary social foundation for his empire. The bureaucracy was corrupt and lacked initiative, the middle classes were divided among themselves and imbued with reactionary ideas. Yet though the possibility of such a step was purely theoretical, even the idea aroused the imagination of those who looked back to the tradition of Peter the Great and enlightened despotism, to a crowned dictator, who could, by liberating the serfs, will the transformation of Russia. These were the lines on which the embryonic intelligentsia was thinking in the transitional years between the 'thirties and 'forties: Herzen, for instance, in exile; Bakunin and Belinsky 'reconciling themselves with reality'; and with them, little by little, those intellectual and social forces which, within two decades, were to form the new public opinion. These were the independents who were one day to allow Nicholas's successor, Alexander II, to carry out the peasant reform and escape from the dilemma: rigid conservatism or the danger of having to rely on the peasants themselves.

The committee which was created in 1835 brought to light—a dim, opaque light it is true—all the different aspects of the various conflicting forces which were to delay for so long the emancipation of the serfs in Russia, the last country in Europe where this measure was adopted. The fundamental contradiction between these forces was reflected in the committee's plans, in the enquiry that it promoted, in the difficulties that it met with and even in its composition.

Its members, six at first, represented the higher bureaucracy which had been formed under Alexander I and Nicholas I. They themselves were convinced that as far as the peasant problem was concerned they ought to follow the example set by the Austrian empire and Prussia ever since the eighteenth century. They had no doubt of the need to abolish the existing régime through the gradual intervention of the State in the relations between nobles and serfs. Indeed, P. D. Kiselev, who was soon to become the central figure of this committee and leader of all attempts at agrarian reform during the reign of Nicholas I, actually came from the society from which the Decembrists had sprung. Indeed he had had direct relations with them, which he was now careful to conceal. Had it been possible to achieve from above only a fraction of what the friends of his youth had tried to take by storm; had it been possible to obtain as a concession what they had tried to impose on the Emperor—this would have been the right moment. And Kiselev worked hard to this end. The fact that his efforts led to such limited results was only one more proof of the weakness of Nicholas I's despotism; strong only when it remained quite static, and weak as soon as it tried to take action.

The first plan suggested by Kiselev and Speransky (Alexander I's reforming minister who now, at the end of his life, collaborated for the last time in the effort to bring about some modification in the social conditions of the Russian countryside) was based on the idea of leaving the nobles and State in entire possession of their land, none of which was to be given to the peasants. The peasants were to be freed of their obligation not to leave the land which they farmed, but were to continue paying their original dues in work, cash or kind. New contracts were to be made only in individual cases and by permission of the landlord and were then to be guaranteed and controlled by the State. The plan was discussed over a long period; the committee itself was reorganized; another one was created, and eventually a reform in the system of State property was accomplished and a law enacted in 1842 which allowed, but did not compel, the nobles to draw up new contracts with their peasants, changing their status from 'serfs' to peasants 'with limited obligations' (*vremenno-obyazannye*).

Throughout these discussions, Kiselev had tried to make the State take the lead by arranging new contracts with the peasants on the property it owned. With this start, he thought that he could alter the relations between private landlords and the serfs, either by drawing up an inventory of the nobles' property—thus indirectly intervening in determining the amount of dues—or by finally insisting on the duty of landlords to make contracts with their peasants. This would have meant that peasants were legally free, even though they would still have been subjected to the jurisdiction of the landlord and to collective responsibility as regards taxes, etc.

In the event, he only succeeded in creating a new administrative machine for State lands and in somewhat modifying the legal position of those who cultivated them. But his plan to extend these reforms by various changes regarding the property of the nobles failed. In 1846 another of Nicholas I's councillors, Perovsky, Minister of the Interior, tried with only very limited success to introduce 'inventories', a measure which in Hungary, for instance, had been in use since 1760.

This is not the place to enter in greater detail into these plans and the few reforms which were actually put into practice. What is of particular interest is the fact that Kiselev, and the few who shared his ideas, met with twofold opposition: from below as well as from above.

It was not, of course, that the peasants themselves or any social force organized in their name could oppose these schemes, which in any case were usually considered in secret committees. In the great majority of cases the peasants did not even know of the changes which were being planned. Though the State peasants had derived some improvement from it, the serfs of private landlords were hardly affected by the law of 1842. Of about ten million 'souls' only twenty-four thousand became peasants 'with limited obligations'.

The opposition was of another kind and far more deep-seated. It made itself felt even in the offices where the plans were being drawn up. 'The unfortunate idea—almost universally held among peasants on private estates—that they belong to the landlords but that the land belongs to them, is one of the fundamental obstacles standing in the way of the desired end of introducing improvements in their conditions. It is capable of exciting their spirits and giving rise to serious disturbances.' So said a report drawn up in 1835.[9]

This state of affairs, although not referred to, was fully apparent to all concerned with the proposed reforms. Would the peasants be content with emancipation of their persons but without being granted the land that they farmed? The same question was asked a few years later in 1842 by the French Ambassador in St Petersburg, Auguste-Casimir Périer, when he wrote to his Minister of Foreign Affairs, Guizot:

The greatest obstacle lies in the moral grossness or, at least, utter ignorance of the population. Almost everywhere the peasants think that, because they are serfs, they alone have a true right to own the land. Often an owner who wishes to move peasants from one department to another meets that terrible force of inertia, backed up by the following words which constitute the Russian serf's entire code: 'Our life belongs to you, you can take it. But you have no right to move us from the land which belongs to us.' This dangerous prejudice is rooted in the souls of millions of people, nor can it be removed merely by laws. It will have to be the task of civilization, of moral improvement, and for this nothing has yet been done.

The French chargé d'affaires repeated this two years later:

La grande difficulté de l'affranchissement consiste dans cette idée innée chez le paysan qu'il est inséparable de la terre, dans ce sens que la terre lui appartient bien plus qu'il n'appartient à la terre.[10]

Associated with the peasant's idea of his natural right to the land was that of complete liberation from the taxes which oppressed all the serfs. In this connection, Perovsky, Nicholas I's Minister of the Interior, wrote in 1845:

According to popular ideas, freedom consists . . . in a complete lack of all authority and submission. Anyone who denies that this is the peasants' theory, is either dishonest or he does not know Russia. It is easy to realize the truth of what I am saying, not only as regards distant provinces and departments on the borders of the Empire, but in the capital itself. Hundreds of thousands of peasants who live there either temporarily or permanently think of liberty only in these terms, despite their greater intellectual development.[11]

In fact, the authorities well knew that they were faced with the same situation that Pestel and the more radical Decembrists had considered from the opposite point of view. The abolition of serfdom in Russia contained within itself the germs of a social revolution. Kiselev, too, perfectly understood this. Any transference of the nobles' property to the peasants, as for example had occurred on a small scale in 1803 in certain regions of the empire, would lead, he wrote in 1839, 'to the destruction of the independence of the nobility and to the formation of a democracy arising out of serfdom'.[12]

And, yet, if the authorities wanted to carry out some reform, it was obviously not possible to wait for 'the moral improvement' in which lay Périer's only hopes. Some political means had to be found of fighting those 'dangerous prejudices'. They had refused to transform the serfs into a class of labourers because it was considered impossible and dangerous both in the short and the long run. They had turned down any step which would lead to the peasants owning the lands belonging to the nobles and the State. Some middle way had to be found. Besides, for Kiselev and for the bureaucrats of Nicholas I, a reasonable compromise was not only a necessity but their political ideal—the conversion into small change of their wish to continue in some way or other the tradition of enlightened despotism.

Some of Kiselev's colleagues on the committee, and at first he himself, were convinced that this middle way should be sought by hastening the process of social differentiation among the peasants themselves, i.e. by undermining the economic basis of that elementary conception of equality which the peasants associated with their ideas on land ownership. These elementary ideas of equality had been given substance in the tradition of periodical redistributions of the land, and in the collective paying of taxes and feudal dues. They had also been recognized by the laws of the State which under Catherine II, especially, had aimed at assuring a sufficient acreage of farming land to those peasants who were employed on the State's properties.

The enquiry of 1836 had shown how much this spirit of equality, latent in the very forms of serfdom and peasant tradition, had in fact been undermined by the rise of a group of richer farmers who began to have considerable influence on the entire life of the *obshchina*. These farmers, for instance, tipped the scales of periodical redistribution in their own favour and, in various ways, subjected the community of poorer peasants to their own control. But the enquiry had also shown how deeply these traditional forms were rooted. The assiduous inspectors were often shocked by the disorder, the vulgarity and the violence which prevailed in the meetings of the *mir*, and also by its many obvious injustices. Nevertheless it was in the *obshchina* and the *mir* that the peasants expressed those ideas on land ownership which had so impressed and irritated Kiselev and Périer. It was through these organizations, the only ones at its disposal, that peasant society defended itself. The communities naturally differed from district to district, reflecting the entire range of peasant life. Self-administration in the villages was less active in the centre of Russia than in the north, where for centuries life had been freer. It was most independent in Siberia (where there was no serfdom) and generally in those parts of the country which were richest and which had been most recently colonized. Yet, despite all this variety, there was one common factor; the *obshchina* represented the tradition and ideal of the peasant masses. How then could it be broken?

As early as 1826 Speransky had once again suggested the plan which had naturally occurred to many of those who had examined the Russian agrarian problem since the time of Catherine II. This was to establish legal rights of succession on the land farmed by the peasants. Speransky saw the inevitable social consequences of such a step. The number of labourers without land would rise, and the equality which prevailed in the villages, and still more in the minds of the peasants, would be destroyed. 'The inequality of fate is entirely natural. It exists everywhere, even in the present situation of the peasants who belong to the State and landlords.'[13] This inequality should therefore be confirmed and developed. But he proposed retaining the *obshchina* and only gradually moving towards its internal differentiation, by indirect measures such as displacing the population, etc. Other reformers, both then and later, proposed similar plans with the same end in view.

These plans clearly suggest that their authors realized more and more as time went on the magnitude of the obstacle with which they were faced. As will be remembered, some of the Decembrists—among them the boldest, those who had most appreciated the need to introduce a rural economy more akin to that of Western Europe—had ended by postponing the task of dismembering the collectivist organization of the village. Speransky's plan of 1826 still reflects the reforming period of Alexander I. The plans of the 'thirties are far less determined. Their authors no longer had the courage to formulate a distinct line of action. And yet the need to create free labour and a class of peasant holders grew ever more urgent if Russia was to go on competing in the international markets. The general economic development of the country emphasized this need. During this time social differences within the Russian village were of themselves increasing rather than diminishing and it was only the energies of the would-be reformers which were beginning to weaken. Kiselev, who in 1836 proposed yet another plan for this purpose, after the enquiry which he had promised, ended by persuading himself that 'the present situation is not all that bad . . . The State should try not to liquidate the *obshchina* but rather to control it, and subject it to a reorganized State hierarchy, capable of turning the *mir* into the basis of government administration of the village.'[14] In other words, the forces of despotism were not aiming to introduce either large- or small-scale changes in the social structure, but rather to bring the *obshchina* under their own protection. They wanted to absorb within the administration the communal organizations which already existed, confining the principle of individual property only to regions which were newly colonized. This was making the best of a bad situation, by using the *obshchina* as a conservative element of society, an institution which would prevent the formation of a large class of peasant proletarians which, as Kiselev said, must be avoided for political reasons.

'Kiselev thus consciously and openly broke with the whole tradition of the previous thirty years', the historian N. M. Druzhinin justly observed.[15] He returned instead to the earlier tradition of Catherine II's ministers who had tried to regulate the rights and duties of these peasant associations and to control and balance them within the organization of the absolutist State as a whole. But the very fact that such a policy was resumed at the end of the 'thirties showed the government's weakness. The State tried to gain a closer control over the *obshchina*, because it was not in a position to transform it. New laws were devised to govern it because the effect of a possible reform was feared. The greatest of these fears was of the final consequences of those 'dangerous prejudices' which the *obshchina* harboured.

The *obshchina* thus showed its double nature; on one hand it was bound to the entire social structure, born of the feudal conception of the granting of the land by the landlord, whether noble or the State, and of the spirit of equality which naturally accompanied uniformity of dues whether in money or kind; and, on the other hand, it was bound to those ideas and customs which such a position had rooted in the minds of the peasants themselves.

The peasants had derived their own theories from their position as serfs, thinking that the land had been assigned to them permanently and that they themselves ought to redistribute it so that the burdens attached to it should fall equally on all. Thus anyone who considered the *obshchina* to be an institution typical of serfdom could only conclude that it must be abolished, either by reducing all the peasants to manual labourers or by creating a class of richer peasants by means of rights of succession. So argued the various 'liberal' reformers. On the other hand, anyone who looked at the *obshchina* from the peasants' point of view would immediately realize that it incorporated their ideals and contained the germs of peasant Socialism. The Slavophils began to think in this way at the end of the 'thirties, and were followed by Herzen, Bakunin and the Socialists of the coming decades.

Between the Liberals and these first Populists stood the force of conservatism, which succeeded in retaining serfdom practically untouched throughout the reign of Nicholas I and enabled the State to exert a more minute control over the peasant communities. Such was the result of the silent resistance from below and of the opposition which expressed itself more in the fears of the reformers than in the revolts of the subjects.

More obvious and immediate were the effects of opposition from above, which showed itself in the nobility's resistance to any reform. Memories of Paul I's violent end, which were reviving among the nobility and even among the diplomatic corps at St Petersburg, underlined the weak position of the autocrat when faced with the nobility.

There is no doubt that the strength of this aristocratic reaction was exaggerated in Western Europe, if only because of the easy parallel with the situation in France during the last decades of the old régime. The resistance of the nobles was proportionate to the weakness of the autocracy, to which was attributed a greater desire for reform than it ever really cherished. None the less in the 'forties the symptoms of this reaction were obvious:

L'empereur a rencontré une opposition à laquelle il eut été dangereux de ne pas céder . . . La noblesse n'oubliera pas facilement cette chaude alarme et ne sera pas aisément rassurée contre le retour de velléités semblables,

said the French Ambassador, not without reason.[16] Indeed Nicholas soon tried to strengthen the position of the landed nobility through a series of financial measures, loans, etc.

The nobles aimed at defending their traditional rights against encroachments by the State. Yet, on closer inspection, it is not difficult to see that they too were prevented from abolishing serfdom, though in the 'forties a growing number of them recognized that such a step might be advantageous—by the same obstacle which had stopped the Tsarist State. Baron Haxthausen, the Prussian authority on Russia's agrarian situation, summed up the situation as follows:

Serfdom has become unnatural, and it will soon be impossible to maintain, still less to retain for the future. Intelligent people recognize this. But the most important problem is to dissolve the relationship without unleashing a social revolution.[17]

This fear grew more intense during the years that preceded the revolution of 1848. Further rumours of government action against serfdom—culminating in a law of 1847 which allowed peasants to redeem themselves in the event of their landlord's property being auctioned, and the growing number of local acts of insubordination—encouraged ever more widespread fear and reaction among the nobility. The aristocracy grew still more alarmed by the revolt of Galicia in 1846. This was of the greatest importance for the history of Eastern Europe, for it showed—though only on a small scale—that an absolutist monarchy such as the Austrian would dare to use a peasant *jacquerie* for its own ends. Because of these fears, the nobility knew that it could look to the Emperor for support. Nicholas himself said 'that he would never have allowed such disorders from below. He wanted the solution to be reached from above'. And he added, 'I am sure that now the Austrians will find it difficult to restore order among the people, because although a people's army may be useful in a specific instance, it is very dangerous, leading to insubordination and disorders. And then Communism is at hand.'[18] And so, although at this time he carried out a few reforms in Poland and the south-eastern territories (i.e. near Galicia), Nicholas I neither dared nor wanted to extend these timid ventures to Russia itself.

The revolution of 1848 in Europe put an end to all reforming tendencies. One of the leading representatives of the Slavophils, Kireyevsky, clearly expressed the opinions of the nobility: 'It is to be hoped that the government will not excite the people with false rumours of emancipation; that it will not introduce any new law, until matters in the West calm down and are settled; that it will not, for example, make inventories of the nobles' possessions. For all this only disturbs men's spirits by filling them with unattainable hopes.'[19] Such advice was scarcely necessary. The European revolution of 1848 inaugurated the reaction in Russia which lasted until the Crimean War and which constituted Nicholas I's ideal of government.[20]

The foregoing examination of the Emperor's policy towards the peasants will have helped to make clear the reasons for this ideal, and what were the contrasting forces which immobilized all Nicholas's activities in the social field. And yet, his reforming tendencies had met with a response in the educated classes. It was from among them that there was arising the force which would one day allow an advance to be made in the peasant problem.

3*

It was here that were being considered the problems which Nicholas I had not even succeeded in raising. We must now turn to the intelligentsia.

Besides Herzen and Bakunin, and the groups which were forming round them in Moscow and St Petersburg, we come across isolated thinkers who were trying to find individual, personal solutions to the same problems and who were reacting individually to those same stresses which led the more important intellectual groups towards Proudhon, Leroux and Fourier.

V. S. Pecherin in the 'thirties was the first of these. His fragmentary memoirs, poems and a few letters provide interesting evidence of his feeling of isolation, and of his need to look for his own road in his own way. But above all, he expresses horror at the Russia of Nicholas I:

I fled from Russia as one flees from a city with the plague. No reflection was needed. The plague spares no one, let alone anyone with a weak constitution. I foresaw, I was convinced, that had I remained in Russia with my weak and soft character, I would inevitably have become the vilest of loyal subjects or would have ended in Siberia for no reason. I fled, without a thought, to save my human dignity.[21]

In other words, his flight was personal, not political, and his pilgrimage was religious, not fundamentally social. This in itself reveals one aspect of Russian Socialism at this time. Pecherin also was impressed by Lamennais as Bakunin had been. Like all his contemporaries, he cherished a cult for George Sand: 'Her novels were intoxicating poems, sacred hymns in which she sang of the appearance of a new revelation.'[22] A few years later, in 1843, Bakunin wrote to his sisters, 'George Sand is not only a poetess but a prophet who has a revelation to offer. Hers is an apostolic religious nature.'[23] Pecherin, like Bakunin, approached Communism from a sort of religious Socialism. He read Buonarroti's The Conspiracy of Equality, which was shown to him by a Polish émigré, Bernacki, later the friend of Bakunin and Herzen. Pecherin tells us how he had anxiously sought this book at Zurich with no success, and then, trembling with excitement, found it one day in a second-hand bookshop in Liège.

But this sensitive and educated man was not destined to become a conspirator or a political writer. He found his truth not in the Communist tradition, against which he finally reacted with all his soul, but in that religious element which was contained in romantic Socialism. After having explored the world of utopias and European refugees, in 1840 he was finally converted to Catholicism. He became a Redemptorist in England, where Herzen met him and found him wholly withdrawn into himself. But his adventures were not yet over. Summoned to Rome in 1859 he fled from it, inspired by a feeling similar to that which had made him flee from Russia as a young man. He lived in Dublin as chaplain of a hospital and developed sympathy for Populist ideas, and for the new life in Russia generally, after the emancipation of the serfs.

Of far greater interest was the experience of Ogarev in the 'forties—

although this also is an example of a personal rather than a political situation. Herzen's young friend, who had sworn with him on the Sparrow Hills to dedicate his life to the cause of freedom, was by nature sensitive and weak, in some respects not unlike Pecherin. He, too, was particularly concerned with the problems of conduct and his attitude to the surrounding world. Yet he devoted his life to social problems and was one of the creators of the psychology of Populism.

The peasant problem continued to preoccupy Ogarev's mind throughout his life. In his autobiographical fragments he said that he had grown up 'with the serf's hatred of the life of his landlord'.[24] In the 'forties, on returning from exile—to which he had been condemned for joining Herzen in creating a Saint-Simonist group—his political activity took the direction of making a life for himself which was 'consonant with truth', and writing a few articles which revealed, even under the censorship, his opposition to the existing agrarian structure.[25] But above all he studied, with a romantic rather than methodical impulse, those subjects—among them economics and medicine—which he thought would be of use for practical measures of reform among the peasants. He began among the many serfs on his own estates. He freed them and gave them such advantageous working conditions that many years later their families still remembered him as a benefactor.[26] He was convinced that only industrial development could really better conditions in the countryside, and so he began to organize a factory. Unlike so many other similar undertakings on the property of nobles, the work in this factory was done not by serfs but by paid workers. At the same time, he built residential farm schools designed to give a 'general technical education'.

All this was intended only as the basis of a far greater project, about which we have only indirect information. It appears to have been aimed at transforming his property into a Socialist colony. It would be interesting to know exactly what were the ideas which guided him in this plan.[27] Though it is possible that he was directly influenced by current French utopias, he mainly saw in this 'attempt at practical action' a vision of peasant Socialism. In any case these ventures were already inspired by that psychological and moral outlook which, in 1856, made him emigrate to work with Herzen in London. There he formulated with—and sometimes before—his friend some of the typical standpoints of Populism in the 'sixties. In a letter of 1843 or 1844 we already find, though in religious terminology, what was later to be his and Herzen's idea of the movement 'to go to the people'. He spoke of his desire to live 'in der Wahrheit' and he added, 'What is the man to do who feels himself overcome by grief at his own position, brought about through heredity and not through work? He must become a proletarian.'[28] At the same time he wrote to a friend that 'he did not wish to be rich, that he wished to turn to the people and work with them'.[29]

More and more he began to reflect on the problems of Russian peasant society. He had himself been able to observe on his own estates the importance of social differences within it, and he had concluded that the *obshchina* represented equality only in name. 'I do not know what else one can call an equality of taxation where abilities are unequal; an equality of land holdings where work and capital are unequal. Our *obshchina* means only equality of slavery.'[30]

Like Herzen, he began to speak of the *obshchina* as a principle of Socialism only when he was abroad. In Russia, they had both looked critically at this traditional institution. Herzen had continued in his diary the discussion which he had had with Haxthausen; Ogarev had made his attitude plain in the above quotations, which came from a plan for the reorganization of his own property.

All this shows that both men looked upon the *obshchina* not so much as a complete and satisfactory institution for regulating social relations within the village but as an ideal by means of which aspirations for equality could be given a foothold in the world of the Russian peasant. It might, they thought, also serve as a possible point of contact between Russia and Socialism. Only at a distance could they carry through this process of idealization which removed the *obshchina* from the feudal life in which it had been contained and turned it into the political and revolutionary myth of Populism.

Ogarev's attempts to create a Socialist colony on his own estates had already led him in this direction. These ventures were in fact another form of the dissatisfaction with the various French utopias which Herzen and Bakunin had also experienced. Ogarev did not remain a Saint-Simonist, nor did he become a Fourierist. In his wish for 'practical action' in the Russian countryside a new seed was contained.[31]

Lack of materials prevents further discussion of his plans. However, one interesting letter survives concerning his ambitions. This was written to Ogarev (probably in 1844) by Sazonov, the third of the three founders of the Saint-Simonist group. Sazonov had emigrated, Ogarev had met him in 1842 in Germany, and he now wrote to him from Paris, where he had settled.

The letter is possibly the first in a long dispute. Ogarev was 'a repentant noble' as the type came to be called, sensitive to his social position as to a sin, his mind already seething with the ideas that were later to lead to the movement 'to the people'. Sazonov countered with common sense and stressed the need to use his wealth for his own good and that of others. As if to prove this point of view, and emphasize his realism, he gave his friend a picture of the Communist and Socialist movements of the time. He not only spoke of Proudhon ('if not the most acute, at least the most talented'), of Louis Blanc, Cabet and Weitling, but also of the German émigrés Ruge, Marx and Herwegh.

These latter came to Paris intending to work stubbornly and systematically. They had all already shown though in different ways, their capacity for action. They went to Switzerland, already affected by Socialism and Communism, but not yet converted to these theories. Here, in a foreign and new country, deprived of the support of the daily activities to which they were used, isolated and angry, they have entirely abandoned themselves to extremist theories, forgetting the national spirit which they ought to have represented and which, perhaps, was looking to them for salvation.

Sazonov concluded from the experiences of the young German émigrés that 'even if there is some truth in Communism, yet all discussion about it should be put off to the distant future. At this moment such discussions would greatly hinder the development of civilization.' This contention was indistinguishable from that of Granovsky and all the Western liberals in Moscow. However vague and insubstantial, Ogarev's plans at least showed the possibility of developing in a different direction; and he himself worthily followed them up from 1856 onwards.

Among the Westerners in St Petersburg, V. A. Milyutin, one of the youngest writers in the review edited by Belinsky, was another man who, in 1847, tried to compare Russian problems and Western Socialist theories, no longer from the angle of religion or personal conduct but rather from that of political economy. His articles are among the most interesting examples of the growing political trend of the intelligentsia as the 1848 revolution drew near, a trend which was stifled by the subsequent reaction until after the Crimean War.[32]

Milyutin's family ties give a special character to this effort of reasoned Socialism, which he began to expound in the pages of *Otechestvennye Zapiski* and the *Sovremennik*. He had grown up in St Petersburg in an old aristocratic family, which for some time had devoted itself to industry. He had been chiefly influenced by his mother, who was the sister of Kiselev, the man who had been most active in the attempt to reform serfdom. His two brothers, who were brought up with him, were later to be among the most prominent politicians of the Liberal bureaucracy of the reign of Alexander II. One was the Minister for War, the other played a very active part in bringing about the peasant reforms.

V. A. Milyutin was a convinced Westerner. He wrote an article on the proletariat and destitution in France and England, attacking those who looked upon these features of Western civilization as proof of its decadence.

The terrible situation of the French working classes is the occasion for the most unfounded attacks on the West. Its present situation reveals only confusion and the clash of opinions and interests. But we are not prepared to realize that this clash of interests is a sign not of disintegration but of life, that it does not reveal the corruption of society but its maturity, its vitality, its energy.[33]

Socialist literature itself was proof of the West's earnest desire to solve these problems. Sismondi and Proudhon confirmed the fact that 'in the social sciences generally and even in political economy' a situation of 'breaking point and crisis'[34] had been reached. He saw in this proof that there had come into being a desire (which transcended the mere scientific study of economic phenomena) to transform the very foundations of society. This tendency seemed to him the most vital element in Western thought, and for this reason he was both a Westerner and a Socialist.

But, like Herzen, Ogarev, and even Bakunin, he found none of the existing Socialist theories satisfactory. They represented, he said, something more important than a pure and simple rejection of classical political economy. For this reason he admitted their fundamental importance, linked as they were to real problems—the proletariat, destitution and the situation in the English and French countryside. The new Socialist utopias were the sign that men 'felt and foretold'[35] a new vision. They no longer bore any resemblance to the utopias of earlier centuries, because they had arisen *after* political economy. They derived their historical justification from the attempt to criticize these old utopias. But they had to be freed from the remaining elements of utopianism, mysticism, and dreams; they must be made rational and positive. It was essential to study and to understand reality, to discover its tendencies and forces, 'to transform this dream by bringing it nearer to life'. 'The Utopia through itself, and by virtue of the very energies for development contained in it, thus passes into science.'[36]

This is not the place to dwell on the criticisms of the various Socialist systems drawn up by Milyutin. In philosophy he admired Comte, in economies he was specially influenced by Proudhon, whose ideas on workers' movements, strikes, etc., he fully accepted. He gave a detailed description of these phenomena in England and France and brought them home to the Russian public. But strikes, he thought, were no solution. Milyutin's articles (written under the censorship of Nicholas I and therefore in the most general terms) show his interest in Louis Blanc's organization of labour, and above all, perhaps, in Fourierism, even though none of these movements fully satisfied him.

Sismondi's criticisms of the capitalist system were at the very basis of his social beliefs. But, as he said, 'Sismondi, though he was an ardent defender of the poorer classes, was at the same time an aristocrat by birth and sympathies . . . As a man and a thinker, he was enraged by all forms of injustice and was on the side of the victim. But as representative of a caste, he could not entirely free himself from a few one-sided ideas which he had absorbed in his youth. Sismondi did not understand the real meaning of the needs of his time, and he thought that he could confine himself to a few half measures when, in fact, what was needed was a radical reform of the economic structure.'[37] Milyutin's estimate of Sismondi obviously reflects the effort which the Russian 'aristocrats' at this time were making to carry out to the very end the policies that the Swiss economist had suggested.

There was another reason for his interest in Sismondi. Although he was chiefly concerned to understand and to make known to his compatriots the problems raised by industrial development, Milyutin always paid special attention to agricultural problems, which for Russia were of far greater importance. His descriptions of the rural situation in France, England and Ireland in fact served to point out the various possibilities which would arise after emancipation of the serfs in Russia, if this should ever take place. His barely hinted conclusions show that his Socialism, when faced with Russia's agrarian problems, was assuming a Populist character. He maintained that the two fundamental tendencies of modern agricultural economy were on the one hand the transference of land to the peasants through the abolition of the nobles' privileges, and, on the other, the increasingly obvious economic advantages to be derived from large farms. How could these two contradictory tendencies be reconciled? Only by association—the union of peasants in cooperatives. 'The right to land can be very widely distributed but the land itself must remain indivisible and single.' For this reason, he sympathized with Fourierism. Probably he saw in the *phalanstery* the prototype of large peasant farms. In other words, he sought elsewhere, and by other means, what his contemporaries were searching for in the *obshchina*.

The religious, moral and social problems which had been variously raised by Pecherin, Ogarev and Milyutin found a centre at the end of the 'forties in the groups which formed round Petrashevsky in St Petersburg.[38]

The strange, circumscribed society of the Petrashevskists was very different from the world of Herzen and Bakunin. Its spirit was no longer in direct touch with the rest of Europe; its members no longer travelled in France, Italy and Germany. They lacked the wide and balanced culture of those others who, despite all the difficulties imposed by the censor, had expressed themselves in reviews and newspapers under their direct or indirect control. Nor was it like the world of the Slavophils, men generally of great learning, capable of elaborating systems, of a theological nature it is true, but nevertheless grandiose in conception; a society which had perhaps aimed to confine itself to old Muscovy, but had done so deliberately in the grand manner, and certainly not out of necessity.

The Petrashevskists were also mostly gentry, but very few of them were rich. Many indeed were very poor and were forced by necessity to work in government service. Their attitude and conduct lack the width of Moscow, and reflect rather the narrowness of the bureaucratic capital of Nicholas I's great empire. Among their leading exponents only one had personal knowledge of Europe. The others greedily absorbed its culture from afar, enclosed in an atmosphere which stifled them. Theirs was a mass of mistaken ambitions and readiness for sacrifice, of immense hope and small means, of petty passions and great ideals. Such is our impression today as we read their memoirs and fragmentary writings.

Saltykov-Shchedrin, the author, was a member of the group for a short time during his youth and was exiled to Vyatka for publishing an article whose Socialist spirit was very like that of the Petrashevskists. He has left us a satirical and pathetic picture of the state of mind which dominated this group. It was composed, he said, of men who had begun 'to read without knowing the alphabet, to walk without knowing how to stand upright'. They were 'like moral hunchbacks, made up of contradictions', who ended by creating round themselves an atmosphere of 'despotism'. Why? Because life 'had given desires and not the means to realize them, and so they built up utopias without knowing how to lead people to them'.[39]

It is easy to see, therefore, why their contemporaries have left us such an unfavourable and often contradictory judgment of them. The Moscow Slavophils were violently critical, chiefly, though not only, out of conservatism. They were provoked by the Western origins of 'Nordic Communism', as Khomyakov called it, as well as by its subversive character.[40] Herzen, when he heard of them a few years later, was concerned with the unhealthy character which he thought he detected in them. Bakunin, who came across some of the Petrashevskists in Siberia ten years later, had a similar impression. As for Western Europe, it knew very little of them in 1848 and 1849.[41]

Yet their work was by no means fruitless. Dostoevsky, who took part in the movement, said later that the Socialists (i.e. of the 'sixties and 'seventies when he was writing) had sprung from the Petrashevskists 'who had sown many seeds'.[42] This psychologically true impression is confirmed by the historically more exact evidence of D. D. Akhshamurov, another of the Petrashevskists. 'Our small group carried within itself the seeds of all the reforms of the 'sixties.'[43] Petrashevsky's group was placed at the crossing of two roads. One was to lead the intelligentsia to play a political part; the other pointed to the creation of a more specifically revolutionary movement. The group itself harboured elements of both these trends.

Such was indeed their intention, as Petrashevsky himself clearly said. They hoped 'to put themselves at the head of the intellectual movement of the Russian people',[44] and they aimed to follow the example of Voltaire[45] and the French Encyclopaedists. They began with weekly meetings, at which they discussed a wide variety of problems, sometimes impromptu, and then, more and more usually, after a short reading.

A number of other groups were formed round the nucleus started by Petrashevsky. They met less regularly and were less coherently organized, and they ended by representing different political tendencies. From the very first Petrashevsky himself and his immediate followers felt an intense desire to propagate their ideas; they looked for disciples in the most varying surroundings: at meetings of the nobility, among the lower middle classes and in the schools. Petrashevsky was a true hunter of men. In the field of literature alone he was able to attract two young men, Dostoevsky and Saltykov-Shchedrin, and, indirectly, a student called Chernyshevsky. Their proselytism spread beyond the capital, and they ended by having followers in other cities such as Reval, Moscow, etc. When the movement was eventually defeated, it had grown so much that it had become the base for all Westerners then in Russia who were not just liberals or moderates. Ogarev himself, for example, went to their meetings for a short time, and was involved in their persecution.

Their propaganda was carried out by means of pamphlets written by members of the group. These were read and commented on at their meetings, and above all in a library which Petrashevsky had succeeded in collecting by the most varied means, and from which his friends borrowed books. Its catalogue has been published,[46] and is of the greatest interest. It contains most of the French Socialists before 1848 and, to a far smaller extent, those of the revolution itself. The collection, too, shows their concern with propaganda, and contains many works of popularization. All the different trends are represented, most frequently those of the Fourierists, but also many of the works which had by then been published by Proudhon, the Christian Socialists, Flora Tristan, Leroux, Pecqueur, Raspail, Vidal, Villegardelle, Louis Blanc. The Communists, too, were represented with Cabet, Dézamy, Engels (*Die Lage der arbeitenden Klasse in England*) and Marx (*La misère de la philosophie*). Besides these and a large number of books by economists and planners, there was a very full collection of works on the most varying political, legal and social problems, chiefly French, but including a number of books published in the West on Russia and Poland; as well as studies of other European countries, including Italy. The library reveals a deep interest in social theories and a passion—which might be called journalistic—for life in Europe around 1848.

As the movement grew, its members felt the urge to develop fuller means of propaganda than manuscripts and discussions on books. Some proposed printing abroad and thus creating an émigré centre out of reach of Nicholas I's censorship, such as Herzen and Golovin were beginning to plan. Others suggested a clandestine printing press in Russia itself. But these remained plans for the future, though it seems that a start was made of putting the second proposal into effect.

Eventually they decided to create a genuine secret society starting from the groups already in existence. The leaders of the various groups discussed the possibility of doing this. Speshnev, who had adopted Communist ideas, proposed setting up a 'central committee' made up of representatives of the various groups. He said that there were three possible ways to act—the 'Jesuitical' (i.e. a conspiracy), propaganda and insurrection. He did not conceal the fact that his sympathies were with the last, and he said that, united, they would be able to try all three possibilities which seemed open to them. A first sketch of this 'central committee' seems to have been drawn up but their efforts in this direction were soon halted by the arrests which began in April 1849.

But it was not only repression which stopped them. Even in the discussions before the movement came to an end, its members had felt the weight of the terrible disparity between their projects and the means available to implement them. It was true, one of them said, that, had there broken out 'a political upheaval' in Russia, such a society could be of great importance. But it was objected that it was very unlikely that this would occur. He agreed that they would have to 'wait for twenty years'.[47] And so, naturally, this prospect made them turn back to the desire for intellectual leadership, which had been at the root of all their activities—the spreading of Socialist propaganda within the various groups of Russian society, which was their real *raison d'être*. Petrashevsky himself did not encourage transforming the groups which he had set in motion into a secret society. So they reached the fringes of true conspiracy but could not move beyond and remained enclosed within the very world from which they had sprung.

At the beginning of 1845 yet another obstacle had come to light in the discussions of the group. Constant clashes between different ideas and personalities showed that they did not constitute a united movement but rather a collection of different trends, divided not only as to choice of means but also as to ideals. The central core was Fourierist, and Petrashevsky was its strongest personality. Others, for example the brothers Debu, had tried to draw Fourier's *phalanstery* ever closer to the Russian *obshchina*. Yet others, grouped around Speshnev, proclaimed themselves Communists. Many called themselves Liberals, as a sign of their strong but generalized sense of revolt against the prevailing situation in Russia. The 'central committee' itself thus came to be looked upon as a meeting of 'different representatives of different opinions who, each separately, should organize a special committee to represent their own tendencies'.[48] The Socialist and Fourierist elements remained the strongest and most active. Their purpose, they said, was to unite 'in the first place the Socialists, and then all people with progressive ideas'.[49] But this did not prevent internal controversies and ideological conflicts; indeed it encouraged them. And of all their activities it is these internal controversies which are of the greatest historical importance.

It is not difficult to see why Mikhail Vasilevich Petrashevsky became a follower of Fourier. His mentality was strikingly similar to that of the French Utopian. He, too, combined the mind of a dreamer with a craving for detailed analysis carried to the point of pedantry. In both men eccentricity was married to extreme stubbornness. In the writings of Fourier, he was to find suitable nourishment. 'When I read his works for the first time, I seemed to be reborn. I bowed down in front of the greatness of his genius. Just as if I had previously been not a Christian but a pagan, I destroyed all my other idols, and made him my only god.'[50]

So he looked to Fourier not only for a solution to political and economic problems but rather for a whole conception of life, both personal and social. In general, he looked upon the French Socialists as continuing the work of the eighteenth-century philosophers who, as he said—characteristically drawing up a catalogue—'had tried to bring man into correct relationship with (1) himself, (2) society (other people), (3) the whole of humanity,

(4) nature; and', he added, 'Socialism is the attempt to solve these problems'.[51] In fact, like so many of his contemporaries, he was looking to Socialism for a solution of religious problems.

But he gradually narrowed this wide conception into one that included primarily social, administrative and judicial problems. In face of the actual situation in Russia, his Socialism broke up into a series of reforms ranging from the individual private life of each citizen to the position of peasant relationships, from the introduction of freedom to the reform of the judicial system.

He tried to expound these reforming ideas in *A Pocket Dictionary of Foreign Words used in Russian*. Publication was begun in 1844, and the second and final section was supervised by him. He tricked the censorship and succeeded in making known—though in a somewhat veiled manner—some of the leading ideas of Fourier and other Socialists like Villegardelle, Owen, Saint-Simon, etc. His presentation of these ideas in itself implied an attack—indirect, but obvious enough for anyone who could read between the lines—against serfdom and lack of freedom in Russia. The *Dictionary* was eventually withdrawn from circulation. Herzen took it to Paris, when he emigrated in 1847, as a rarity and as a symptom of the change that was taking place.

Petrashevsky also tried to put his Fourierism to practical use, explaining it in person to the peasants on his poverty-stricken estate in the region of St Petersburg. He built a large communal house for them with collective services, to replace the wretched huts in his village. One night he found it in ashes. It had probably been burnt down by the peasants themselves.[52]

He then tried to stimulate discussion on landed property in Russia, and explained to an assembly of nobles the advantages which would have accrued by allowing merchants to own land and peasants on condition of changing them from serfs to peasants 'with limited obligations'. The price of land, for instance, would increase. But this drew on him both the suspicions of the authorities, and the bitter criticisms of his friends, who accused him of abandoning his Socialist principles. So he gave up these attempts, more and more convinced that only propaganda carried out by the groups around him and a widespread diffusion of Fourier's ideas could bring about the reforms that he desired.

He therefore vigorously expounded his Fourierism at the meetings which periodically took place in his house. He continued preaching it even in prison and before the Committee of Inquiry. Even in his will, written in his cell, he bequeathed a third of the sum obtained from selling his property to Victor Considérant, 'leader of the Fourierists, for the formation of a *phalanstery*'.[53]

On 7th April 1849 he organized a banquet in Fourier's honour. This marked the culmination of the movement. In a speech he recalled that he was 'one of the oldest propagators of Socialism in our backward country. Our mission as Fourierist Socialists in Russia is not as easy as may appear at first sight. Though fate has spared us the difficulties of discovery, and though we have a pole star in the doctrines of Fourier, yet inevitably when putting these doctrines into practice we are faced with difficulties—local obstacles so to speak—which neither our master nor his best interpreters in the West could in any way foresee . . . We must remember that we are placed on the barbarous soil of our country, and that our entire social life is a result of oriental barbarism and patriarchalism. The mind of the Russian people has not yet woken up. And we, not only as Socialists but merely as men who have thrown over prejudices and who know how to look truth in the face, cannot hope simply because of these qualities to win the support of the masses for our convictions.'[54]

And so at this banquet he proposed a toast to 'a knowledge of reality'. This was the fruit of his experiences all these years. With his eyes firmly fixed on Fourierism as 'a pole star', he himself had personally made a great effort to understand the situation in Russia, and he invited his friends to do the same and thus prepare the ground for the introduction of their ideals.

We must not turn away from the reality which surrounds us with a smile of derision. But we must look at it carefully, study it in detail, and enable all its vital elements to reach the full development that we desire.

At the heart of the situation was the problem of the peasants. For some time he had been convinced that there was only one possible way of really abolishing serfdom. This was to free the peasants 'with the land that they farmed, with no recompense for the nobles'.[55] As the Committee of Inquiry later said when summing up a plan of his which has since been lost, 'Such an emancipation would have given the peasant the lion's share of the land.'

By discussing this problem, reading Haxthausen, and 'studying reality' he found in Russia itself a situation to which his Fourierism could be applied. In the statement that he made in prison he was to write that, faced with the agrarian reform, 'with this complete and entire change of our social life, I thought of the *phalanstery* as its key and as its touchstone'.[56] The peasants should not only be given all the land that they cultivated, but should organize their work in large farms which were to combine—as he said, using one of Fourier's phrases, the 'ménage morcelé' and the 'ménage associé'—private ownership and collective organization. And so, quite naturally, he thought of the comparison between the *phalanstery* which he envisaged for the Russian countryside of the future and the *obshchina*. Indeed, this was the word with which he translated Fourier's fundamental idea into Russian. Socialism would show how to 'reorganize work in the *obshchina*'.[57]

And so it was for this reason, quite apart from any other psychological problem, such as the search for a different system of morality, and quite apart from all his other strange qualities, that Fourier assumed such great importance for him and for his friends. Fourier alone, unlike all other

French Socialist thinkers, could influence the one true Socialist movement existing in Russia at this time.

Fourierism, in fact, had a double aspect. It acted as a criticism of the entire system of capitalism, and also as a model for a new organization. Though both these aspects were assimilated by the Russian Fourierists, it was naturally the second that attracted the majority. A. P. Beklemishev, for example, wrote in 1848 a detailed and interesting study on 'The advantages of a community as compared with dispersal of the different kinds of work'. This proposed the *phalanstery* as a model for landowners wishing to transform their farms. In prison, Petrashevsky too emphasized this reforming and conciliatory aspect of Fourierism, and tried to show the advantage for landowners—and even for the Emperor himself—of creating large farms to be worked by collective labour. But these moves were merely tactical. He was in fact convinced that the chance of achieving his aims was indissolubly linked to a complete reform of social relationships, as well as to the confiscation of the nobles' lands for the benefit of the peasants.

He had found in Fourier's *phalanstery* the Utopia by means of which the peasant *obshchina* could be removed from its feudal ties and could become a germ of peasant Socialism. Herzen too had reached the same conclusion for different reasons. It was not for nothing that Petrashevsky always insisted on 'the function of theory as a guide for practice'.[58] The Socialist ideas that he had so enthusiastically studied were to change the *obshchina* into a *phalanstery*.

On the other hand, some of his followers reached a more specifically Populist conclusion. They saw in the Russian countryside an element of Socialism which was already in existence. While Petrashevsky insisted on the collective organization of labour, they turned mainly to the periodical redistribution of land holdings, and glorified the communal tradition in Russian peasant life. They, too, claimed that the *obshchina* had stood in the way of the destitution which had afflicted the West, as well as the expropriation of peasants which would have turned them into proletarians. For example, in his *Exposition of Socialist Systems* written in prison, Yastrzhembsky explained that in Russia 'the peasants, although they are serfs, are not poverty stricken, because serfdom is, though in a primitive way, a kind of association . . . As for factory workers, when their wages fall too sharply, they all return to the countryside. And so in Russia it can really be claimed that there is no proletariat or destitution.'[59] N. Ya. Danilevsky reached the same conclusion. He, too, was implicated in the trial and, with Petrashevsky, was the greatest expert on Fourier's system in the movement.

As far as we can judge from the documents which survive, the leading representatives of what can be called the 'Populist wing' of the Petrashevskists were the brothers K. and I. M. Debu, descendants of the Frenchman Desbout, who had settled in Russia in the eighteenth century. The first was one of Petrashevsky's most trusted supporters, and was to have been a member of the projected 'central committee' of the Society. After them came N. S. Kashkin, the son of a Decembrist. He, too, was a convinced Fourierist, but was specially concerned with agricultural problems. A dozen years later he came into contact with M. Serno-Solovevich, one of the founders of *Zemlya i Volya*. Both were fully occupied in trying to make the most of the agrarian reform brought about by Alexander II.[60]

Dostoevsky too—if we are to believe a memoir writer of the time[61]—was convinced even at this time that 'We must look to the life and age-old organization of our people, to the *obshchina* and to the *artel*'. It is more likely, however, that this is a reflection of Dostoevsky's later views, when he came back from Siberia and developed a sympathy for the Slavophils.[62] At this stage he was for a radical emancipation of the serfs, and was under the influence of the most decided and politically minded of the Petrashevskists, Speshnev, Durov, etc. In his deposition he claimed to be strongly opposed not only to the Slavophils—as did all his companions—but also to Fourierism.

There is no social system in the West so derisory, so unpopular and so ridiculed as that of Fourier. It is already dead, and its followers do not understand that they are only living dead. In the West and in France at this moment, every system, every theory is dangerous for society, for the starving proletarians reach out for any plan out of sheer desperation, and are prepared to use it as their banner . . . But for us in Russia, in St Petersburg, it is absolutely obvious that Fourierism can only exist in the uncut pages of books, or in a tender innocent soul as an idyll or a poem in twenty-four cantos.[63]

He was of course here defending himself against charges which were to lead to the death penalty. But this defence probably corresponds to his fundamental ideas. It is true that, as a writer, he was interested in the psychology of Fourier, who gave him some ideas for his future novels. But his political views were more urgent and less utopian. What he wanted was less censorship and fewer constraints for the people. Above all Dostoevsky was not in 1849 (or indeed later) a man with the mentality of a politician. The year 1848 interested him as a drama, and what attracted him most in Socialism was the fact that it was 'a science in ferment, chaos, alchemy rather than chemistry, astrology rather than astronomy', though he thought that 'from the present chaos something powerful will emerge, something reasonable and beneficial for the public good, just as chemistry emerged from alchemy, and astronomy from astrology'.[64] He felt the same stimulus that at this time drove Bakunin to look for 'true Communism' and Herzen towards 'Russian Socialism', and made Milyutin say that it was time to move from utopia to science. But his impulses took an imaginative form. The documents on Dostoevsky's participation in this movement are highly expressive of a general state of mind, but they do not give us an exact picture of it. Their importance is mainly psychological.

Next to the orthodox and Populist Fourierists was the small group of Communists led by N. A. Speshnev, the man whom Dostoevsky called his

'Mephistopheles'. He had proposed a tighter organization, and had spoken of a 'central committee'. He, more than any of his companions, hoped for a peasant revolt. This, he thought, would lead to a dictatorship which could then establish Russian agriculture in large collective farms.

N. A. Speshnev was certainly 'a man remarkable from many points of view',[65] as Bakunin was to say when he met him in Siberia in 1859. Unlike the other Petrashevskists, he was rich, and owned about five hundred souls in the department of Kursk. In 1839 he fled, first to Helsingfors and then abroad, with a beautiful Polish girl, who apparently poisoned herself for love of him. He was in Switzerland at the time of the war of the *Sonderbund*, in which he may have taken part on the side of the Democrats. He then lived in Paris, Vienna and Dresden, in contact with the Polish émigrés and the French Socialists. Leroux invited him to collaborate on the *Revue Indépendante*. In December 1847 he was back again in St Petersburg, and there, despite his temperamental reserve, began to attract followers among the groups who were associated with Petrashevsky. He explained to them that 'Socialism is not a new form of political economy but a new form of politics.' This was the title which he gave to a work which he wrote at this time, but which has since been lost.[66] He was very probably under the direct influence of Dézamy (and so of Babeuvism) and also of Weitling, whom he met in Switzerland, besides the writings of the German émigrés in Paris (Marx, Engels, etc.). In any case, he always called himself a Communist, in contrast to Socialists of all other tendencies, especially the Fourierists.

This controversy between Socialists and Communists was often complicated by personal feelings, for example Petrashevsky's claim that Speshnev was dominated by pride and acted out of 'dépit de la vie'.[67]

From a political point of view the conflict was chiefly between the men who wanted a slow diffusion of ideas, a gradual adaptation of Fourierism to the situation of Russia, and those who—like Speshnev—emphasized the need for a conspiracy, a 'purely political'[68] movement. He did not worry too much about the means employed. This is probably what he meant when he spoke of a 'Jesuit' model,[69] or when he maintained the need for a dictatorship. This suggestion led to violent clashes of opinion, and one day Petrashevsky said, 'I would be the first to raise my hand against the dictator.'[70]

But Speshnev continued to maintain that this was the only way to solve the peasant problem which, as he said, 'was the most important of all, the one from which we must begin'.[71]

In November 1848 he met, at one of Petrashevsky's evening discussions, someone who strengthened these convictions. The person in question was the manager of some gold-mines in Siberia, and was a strong man of decided character. He gave Speshnev and a few others a detailed account of how in 1842 he had had to suppress a serious revolt among the peasants of the State properties in the department of Perm. A world of hidden struggles suddenly opened up before them. Dostoevsky, who was there, merely noted that

Chernosvitov, the man who told them this, 'spoke the Russian language exactly as Gogol wrote it'. But Speshnev's conclusion belonged to politics rather than literature. It confirmed his ideas that such revolts were the only means of bringing about a true revolution. This is one of the few occasions where we have exact information about a link between peasant revolts and the rise of a revolutionary movement in the Russian intelligentsia of the 'forties.

The 'central committee' which Speshnev proposed on this occasion was tied to his hopes of getting into contact with the most active centres of popular discontent, especially in the Urals. Action 'à la Pugachev'[72] was needed. Chernosvitov had told him that the State peasants in the department of Perm had revolted because of a rumour that they were to be sold to the nobles or to the administration of the Crown property. They wanted to stay as they were. So they combined loyalty to the Tsar with hatred for the greedy and corrupt local officials, as well as for the entire administration which had been reorganized by Kiselev's reforms. The peasants shared these feelings and so did the 'better educated' serfs who worked in the mines of the Urals. 'There are many highly educated men among them, engineers and competent surveyors. In general they are sufficiently developed to be able to absorb ideas which go far beyond their daily lives.'[73] Chernosvitov also spoke much of Siberia, in whose future the Petrashevskists had great hopes. He too thought that some day it ought to be freed in some way from the control of St Petersburg.

We do not know what political conclusions Speshnev arrived at as a result of these conversations apart from the necessity for a revolution. He may have seen his ideas of nationalizing land and industry in a new light. Russian Fourierism had constantly studied the large traditional estates of the nobles in relation to an ideal model of the *phalanstery*. So now Speshnev's Communism harboured a comparison between the situation of the State peasants, who represented about half the rural population, and the ideas which, either directly or indirectly, he absorbed from Babeuf.

Besides this more immediate practical aspect, the discussions between Socialists and Communists within the Petrashevskist groups are of great theoretical importance.

Danilevsky laid the foundations for these discussions when he said that Fourier maintained that 'Science must discover the laws of the harmonious organization of the relations between men . . . In other words, the laws of human happiness.' Whereas Communists, he claimed, had merely taken to its logical extreme the idea of equality which had been born in the Age of Enlightenment: 'Man does not desire equality, but freedom and happiness. Yet none of those who advance the theory of equality has shown or even tried to show that it necessarily brings happiness. This would certainly be difficult to prove.'[74]

Most Russian Fourierists were motivated by the desire to improve their own situation and that of the peasants. They did not call for an egalitarian revolt, but for reforms, radical reforms. Petrashevsky said that 'Communists are Socialists by sentiment . . . Horrified by the terrible contrasts between misery and extravagant wealth . . . they see in the destruction of private property the abolition of all evils.'[75] Petrashevsky saw, too, in Fourierism the 'scientific', reasoned and complex answer to this instinctive and utopian Communism.

So when one of Speshnev's followers, Timkovsky, one day proposed to Petrashevsky that an agreement between the two movements could be reached, based on the idea that in future the Russian countryside ought to be run partly in Socialist and partly in Communist organizations, Petrashevsky answered with a long letter that is the most important contribution to this debate.[76]

The problem of organizing work, which is the fundamental problem of social life, has been more carefully worked out by the Fourierists than by any other Socialists. They have scrutinized human nature more closely than anyone, and have considered man—the living unit of social life—not in the abstract, as an idea, as do most Communists, but as he is. Social life has been adapted to man not man to arbitrary forms of social life. Fourierism leads gradually and naturally to what Communism wishes to impose immediately and forcibly. Communism wishes to direct all the forces of society simultaneously to changing society, without regard to means. Fourierism wishes to employ the energies which are not indispensable for maintaining the existence of society itself.

For these reasons he rejected any compromise, and continued to maintain his own point of view.

No reply of Speshnev or his followers survives.[77] Just when the problems were becoming more clearly defined, discussion was suppressed. For a time they hoped that the rejection of even the smallest reforms from above and the growing reaction of Nicholas I would lead to more serious peasant revolts which would turn into a revolution.

This was their last hope, and when it failed nothing remained but to resign themselves to prison and Siberia.

4. THE KOLOKOL

WHEN HERZEN reached London at the end of August 1852, he had plumbed the lowest depths of a depression which had been growing steadily since the defeats of 1848. Fate had struck him down and destroyed his family. The intellectual excitement, which had inspired him during the revolution and the reaction, was now gone, leaving him with a feeling of disenchantment and guilt. In his ablest pamphlets he had set forth his political conclusions in detail: his violent criticisms of *Montagnard* democracy and his dark prophecies about the fate of Western Europe. 'The comedy is over, *Fuimus*', he had written at the beginning of the year.[1] As soon as he reached England he said to Ruge:

Battus le 13 Juin, nous nous dispersâmes pleins d'espérances. Depuis ce temps tout a péri, la France est devenue une caverne de brigands et un peuple de laquais. Heureux celui qui s'est sauvé avec les siens. Moi, au contraire, j'ai tout perdu, j'ai perdu dans un naufrage ma mère et un de mes fils, j'ai perdu ma femme. Battu, même dans mon foyer, après des épreuves terribles, amères—je me traîne sans occupation ni but, d'un pays dans un autre.[2]

He was cut off from all contact with his friends in Moscow. He was almost the only Russian to have fled, and had as yet no ties with refugees from other countries. He had come to London with no plans for action and with no confidence in himself or in others.

Of one thing only he was certain: Russia could be one of the centres and possibly even the very centre of the revival which one day was bound to come. The threads now had to be taken up again. In Russia they had been snapped not by an unsuccessful revolution but by a preventive counter-revolution which, however oppressive, might have left men less bitter than the experiences that he himself had undergone in the West. And so his aims must at first be modest; no preaching of Socialist and revolutionary principles, but concentration on the two permanent features of the Russian situation: the awakening of the intelligentsia and the problem of the peasants. The important thing, he said, as early as the beginning of 1853, was that there was 'a movement and not a status quo'.[3]

'I am not the venerable Osip', he said, referring to Mazzini, and he refused to adopt the rôle of 'the dervish of the Italian revolution', as Omodeo had called Mazzini—the untiring preacher of his principles, even during the worst phases of reaction; the organizer of plots and revolutions, even when

their success seemed most remote. It was not only the very different conditions in Italy and Russia which influenced Herzen's decision, but also his
entire political outlook which combined Socialism with criticism of democracy, and was centred on Russia because he had lost faith in the West.

When a revolutionary movement eventually arose in Russia, with Chernyshevsky and the new generation of *Zemlya i Volya*, Herzen was bitterly
blamed for the standpoint he adopted in 1853. His policy did in fact play an
extremely important rôle during the time of reforms, but later it seemed to
be a repudiation of those principles which he himself had expounded in his
writings of 1848.

In fact, however, there was no question of repudiation. Rather, his ideas
had developed. They had been libertarian and Socialist in face of the modern
Jacobin State and now, at a time of reaction and slow revival, they became
liberal and reforming. His experiences of 1848 had made him lose enthusiasm for, but not faith in, violent revolution, as he once explained when
quarrelling with the new generation. His ends remained the same, but he no
longer believed in the means which had inspired him during the revolution.

In London he soon made contacts with the international émigrés, whom
he always looked upon with a mixture of human sympathy and ironical
amusement. The latter was reserved for the French, the leaders of the
Montagne, whom for a long time he had privately considered unworthy of
victory. His only real friends were the Italians, Mazzini and Saffi, and a few
Poles, especially Worcell.

He only really hated one group: the German supporters of Marx, and he
wrote one of the most virulent passages in his memoirs about them. He
disagreed with them over the various attempts that were being made to create
a common, democratic and Socialist organization, and which were later to
lead to the formation of the First International. It is true that underlying this
conflict were two different political conceptions. But the more immediate
cause was the ghost of Bakunin, who was incarcerated in the Peter-Paul
fortress in St Petersburg. When an English newspaper circulated the old
rumour that Bakunin was a Tsarist agent, various circumstances led Herzen
to believe (without reason) that Marx had inspired it. Bakunin's name was
a sort of sounding board for the different estimates each held of the possibility of revolution in the Slav countries. Disputes on this subject between
the Russian and German Socialists had already been very violent in 1848.
Herzen was inspired by his hopes in Russia, which Marx continued to
attack while, by implication at least, he took up a favourable attitude
towards Turkey.

Support came first from the Poles. When Worcell, at the beginning of
1853, sounded the chances of the Polish émigrés backing the creation of a
London printing press with Cyrillic type—the first indispensable tool for
Russian propaganda—Herzen was enthusiastic. He saw that this might give
him the chance of achieving what in 1849 he had vainly attempted to do in

Paris, and he threw himself into this venture with all his energy, money and talent.

The first page of this 'Free Russian Press in London' was dated 21st February 1853.[4] It was a call *To our brothers in Russia.* As Herzen explained in a letter, the intention was to break the silence which had descended on the Empire of Nicholas I after 1848, and to penetrate its curtain of fear. This had become so great that the government did not even need to use handcuffs; a mere threat was enough to reduce the boldest members of the intelligentsia to morose silence. 'In our country there is not even any persecution', he wrote. 'Who, for instance, has been thrown into prison or deported since 1848?'[5] True there had been the Petrashevskists, whom he often quoted in his letters of this time, as a proof that some action at least had been attempted while Europe was in ferment. But they, he added, had attempted an organization. Much less was now being asked: merely that free men should begin to think and to write once more. He himself was prepared to print in London anything that they sent. It was much less difficult to send a manuscript than they imagined. The barrier was far less effective than they believed. 'Why are we silent? Could it be that we have nothing to say?'[6]

Herzen had hit the nail on the head. The response to his *Du développement des idées révolutionnaires en Russie* showed him how terrified the Moscow intellectuals were. His friend Granovsky accused him of having exposed all the ablest members of the intelligentsia to danger by speaking openly of their ideas and by revealing the true political significance of their intellectual activities—such as their discussions on the Slavophils and the *obshchina*; and by claiming that 'le mutisme encourage le despotisme' and rebuking them for their silence.[7] The intellectuals sought refuge in an ivory tower of culture and in the literary forms farthest removed from life. This is exemplified in the *Sovremennik* for 1852 or 1853, the same review which had been edited by Belinsky and which had published Herzen's first creative writings.[8]

The 'Free Russian Press' was aimed at this apathetic state of mind. At first it seemed to meet with no response. But when the situation slowly began to change, the first symptoms of revival were precisely those which Herzen had helped to arouse.

During the Crimean War individual writers once again began to discuss Russia's general problems and suggest reforms. Their ideas were circulated in manuscripts, whose number greatly increased as the movement which followed the war and the change of reign developed. Although this political literature still lacked self-confidence, it was none the less significant. Herzen later collected some of these works with a view to writing the history of this revival. He published them in the first small volumes in the series which he called *Voices from Russia.* They began to appear in 1856, and kept in step with the spread of ideas in liberal circles, showing that the intelligentsia had now resumed its function, which had been interrupted in 1849.[9]

Apart from this appeal, the other works published by Herzen in London during 1853 dealt with the peasant problem. St George's Day was drawing near, he said, in a pamphlet addressed to 'the Russian nobility'—St George's Day when the peasants of mediaeval days had had the right to change their landlord. Indeed they had been free to do this until, at the end of the sixteenth century, they had been tied to the land which they farmed. Here for the first time the emancipation of the serfs, which was to be carried out less than ten years later, was openly raised within a broad perspective and sincerely discussed.

Herzen appealed to the nobles, or at least to a minority of them, to abandon their privileges. Only thus could they win their own freedom.

You can't be a free man and own household serfs, whom you buy like chattels and sell like a flock of sheep. You can't be a free man and have the right to whip peasants and send your household serfs to be flogged. You can't even talk of human rights when you own human souls.

What then held back the nobles who already appreciated this fundamental aspect of human dignity? Fear; fear of the Tsar who, through the slavery of the serfs, made the nobles themselves into slaves; and fear of a peasant revolt, which had put an end to all earlier efforts at reform. 'What has happened to the various committees, meetings, plans and proposals for reforms?'[10] Postponement, said Herzen, could lead to only one thing: the peasants would end by rising in earnest. He said to the nobles:

We still believe in you. You have given us pledges in the past and our hearts have not forgotten. [He was referring to the Decembrists.] And so we do not turn directly to our unhappy brothers to disclose to them strength of which they are unaware; to show them the means—which they do not yet guess at; to explain your weakness— which they do not suspect; and tell them 'Up brothers, it's time to take up axes. It's no longer the time for *corvées* and domestic slavery. We must fight for sacred liberty. The landlords have exploited us enough; they have had enough of our daughters; they have broken enough sticks on the backs of our grandfathers. Up, lads, straw, straw for the landlord's house so that it will be warmed up for the last time!'[11]

So powerful was this threat of a *jacquerie* that many of those landlords who were most keen on reforms could not forgive Herzen—all the more so as this was not just a threat but also a moral condemnation, anticipating the Populist spirit of the 'sixties and 'seventies. 'The *pugachevshchina* is a terrible thing but we must speak frankly: if the emancipation of the peasants cannot be obtained in any other way, then even that would not be too great a price. Terrible crimes bring with them terrible consequences.'[12] And he clearly saw where all this would lead.

Our people do not know the word Socialism, but its meaning is close to the soul of the Russian who lives out his days in the peasant *obshchina* and the workmen's *artel*. Socialism is the bridge between Russia and the revolution. Floods of this kind cannot be stopped by customs officers or whips . . . Stand aside if you do not want to drown; or swim with the current.

Herzen's intention was to show the more intelligent and cultivated members of the nobility where this current was flowing, and how they could escape. He claimed that the only possible solution was 'emancipation with land'. The nobles themselves ought to propose this, not only out of a spirit of sacrifice, but simply because it was in their interest. Let them follow the example given by the French aristocracy on 4th August 1789.

Herzen was thus thinking in terms of a movement to be led by the intellectuals and the enlightened nobility, directed against serfdom and the Tsar, who was its mainstay. As he wrote shortly afterwards, the most active forces in Russia were the 'anarchist' element in the aristocracy and the 'Communist' element in the people.[13] Freedom and land were the fundamental passwords.

Herzen continued to speak on these lines until 1855, when Nicholas I died. In 1853 he published another pamphlet, *Sacred Property*, taking as his motto Pugachev's prophecy: 'I am not yet the real crow, but only a small crow; the real one is still flying in the sky.'[14] He summed up the history of the relations between the peasants and the State in Russia—a history of oppression and revolt—so as to warn reformers against the idea of applying to the Russian countryside 'the points of view of Liberalism and the religion of property'. These were contrary to the feelings of the people. Only land granted to the peasants in their traditional collective holdings could lead to a real reform.

Just imagine the European agrarian structure [and he was thinking chiefly of England] with the absolutism of St Petersburg. Just imagine twenty million proletarians looking for work on the nobles' land, in a country where there is no respect for the law, where the entire administration is corrupt and under the influence of the nobles; and where a human being is nothing and personal influence everything.[15]

Russia's situation would then be worse than Ireland's. Nor did he share the hopes of those who looked upon this peasant proletariat as a possible revolutionary force for the future. 'To be starving and a proletariat is by no means enough to make a revolutionary.' The State would merely be able to destroy him the more easily. Only the *obshchina* could protect the peasants as it had already done in the past. 'The *obshchina* will save the Russian people.' But this of course was possible only if the *obshchina* could be freed from the power of the landlord, whom Haxthausen had idyllically considered its protector and governor. In fact, the *obshchina* was entirely independent, not only from the economic but also from the administrative point of view, and its only relations with the landlord were those involved in serfdom.

Between the peasants on the one hand, and the landlords and the State on the other, there was a gulf. Constituted authority, as conceived by the peasants, was just a 'Union of *obshchinas* in larger groups, and the grouping of these into an entire people, a land (res publica)'.[16] The existing State, they thought, was merely superimposed on this simple social arrangement of the countryside.

As Herzen said at a great international meeting held in London in November 1853, to celebrate the 23rd anniversary of the Polish revolt of 1830—the first public acknowledgment of the position he had won for himself among the émigrés—'Russia is a land of contradictions and extremes. There is Communism below, despotism above, and between them—unsure of itself— is the nobility, fearing a jacquerie from below, and banishment and forced labour from above.'[17] He explained that Russian despotism did not correspond to the popular idea of constituted authority, nor was it the apotheosis of modern ideas on legitimate monarchy. It was a dictatorship without solid traditional ties—'a preventive Bonapartism'.[18] These words vividly and powerfully summed up his many-sided experiences of the West and his theories about the situation in Russia.

When the Crimean War broke out he adopted a reasoned attitude, convinced that none of the powers then marching against Russia really wanted to destroy or even seriously injure Nicholas I's 'dictatorship'. He wrote a manifesto for the Russian soldiers, deliberately aimed at those who were stationed in Poland, because they alone could be reached through his Polish contacts. But the main reason was that, in so doing, he was linking his activities, however small, to those of his comrades—men fighting for a cause which was parallel if not identical to his own. He did not wish to take part in the manœuvres of the great powers. To the Russian soldiers who were occupying Poland he wrote:

You are defending the Tsar and not the people—a Tsar who has left half Russia in peasant serfdom; who presses into service innumerable recruits, and has them beaten to death. A Tsar who allows officers to flog his soldiers; and policemen to beat civilians; and anyone who is not a peasant, to beat a peasant. By defending him, you will defend all the evils of Russia. By fighting for him, you will fight for the rights of the landlords, for flogging and for slavery, for thefts which officials do not even trouble to conceal and for the daily plunder of the landlords.

Police records show that this appeal had a fairly wide circulation. It corresponded to the feelings of many of the peasant recruits in this war, during which, as will be seen, the hope of immediate emancipation grew rapidly. Mazzini specially admired this pamphlet, and reprinted it in the Italia del Popolo on 11th April 1854.[19]

Apart from this first limited attempt to reach Russia, Herzen's work during the Crimean War was aimed at making Russian internal problems better known to the English and to the growing number of people who wished to know something about the country. He reiterated that Russia would develop along different lines to the West, as it had already passed through its 'revolutionary embryology during its European period',[20] which had opened with Peter the Great. Russia would soon be faced with those social problems which, in a different form, were of such concern to Europe.

His pessimism about the West made him, at least at the beginning of the war, overestimate Russia's potentialities. She was strong, he thought, not through her own forces but through the weakness of others. 'This war', he said in February 1854, 'will be a majestic and martial introduction of the Slavs into world history, and at the same time a funeral march of the old world.'[21] The events of the war, however, soon showed him that the empire of Nicholas I was much weaker than he had imagined. As a reaction, his hopes in the living forces of Russia and in the possibility that they would triumph against the weak empire of Nicholas I grew stronger.

Thanks to the support which he had found among the English Chartists, he had an opportunity for saying this at a meeting in London on 27th February 1855, which included all the émigré leaders: Louis Blanc, Victor Hugo, Marx, Mazzini, Kossuth and Worcell.[22] After speaking of the Decembrists and the Petrashevskists, he said that the important thing now was to unite the desire for personal liberty which was stirring in Russia with the collective tradition of the peasants. 'This sums up the whole function of Socialism.' Nor would Russia have to traverse all the ground covered by other countries, 'History is really unfair, and to those who join late it gives the reward that comes from experience.'[23] This phrase, which Chernyshevsky was to repeat almost word for word a few years later, symbolized the inspiration of the early Populists at a time when the era of reforms was dawning. Events themselves, they thought, would give these reforms a social content. And from this the Russian Socialist movement would come into being.

A few days after this meeting, Nicholas I died. 'We are drunk, we have gone mad, we have become young again', Herzen wrote in a letter when he heard the news. And even later, he enjoyed describing the immense delight he had felt. The three terrible decades were at last over. One idea obsessed him: to take up once again the threads which had been broken by the Emperor when he came to the throne and destroyed the Decembrist movement. Herzen wanted to concentrate his activities under the old banner of the Decembrists, to draw his inspiration from them and thus directly associate the present situation with the only true revolutionary venture of the first part of the century. The very name of the review *Pole Star* which he now printed on his 'Free Russian Press' was to commemorate the periodical which some of the most typical Decembrists had started in the 'twenties. On the cover he put the heads of the five who had been condemned to death, and as a motto he chose Pushkin's line 'Long live reason'.

This was not merely a return to his youth or the desire to honour the memory of his forefathers. His main hopes were still chiefly based on the spirit of independence and on the initiative of the intelligentsia, and so he emphasized the liberal Decembrist roots rather than the Socialist elements. Immediate practical considerations also suggested this policy. Herzen realized that his activities had as yet met with a feeble, or unfavourable, response in Russia. His Socialism was too far removed from an intelligentsia which was only slowly beginning to awaken. During the Crimean War a few had secretly been convinced that only a Russian defeat could revive interest in internal problems, but such feelings had remained purely negative. And now all hopes were centred on the new Emperor, Alexander II, and they were still hopes rather than demands. A reforming public opinion, and not a revolutionary movement, was coming into being.

Herzen's two years of activity in London had convinced him that the doctrinaire views of his Moscow friends were even more narrowly and obstinately held than he had at first believed. Granovsky had not approved of Herzen's appeal to the nobility, arguing that it was wrong to speak badly of Peter the Great, and thus emphasizing the difference between his own liberalism derived from history, and Herzen's ideas. This made Herzen realize that 'his friends represented an unhappy, tired and noble generation which had suffered, but not a young force, not a hope, not a youthful, ringing salute to the future'.[24] At the beginning of his activities in London he had said that he did not write exclusively for them, but 'for the young'.[25] This attitude was strengthened whenever he received a letter showing the profound effect of his words on minds which were then opening to problems of Russian life. 'J'avoue que j'ai pleuré à chaudes larmes en les lisant.'[26] But he could not put too great hopes in these symptoms of a deeper awakening.

He found it impossible to break with his Moscow friends, the Westerners, both for personal reasons (always so important for him) and because he felt that despite everything the movement would be reborn through this group and that they would eventually express the chief demands of Russian society. This is in fact what did occur as soon as Alexander II came to the throne.

From the objective point of view this permanent tie was a mistake. It brought constant disappointments, and renewed vain hopes that the liberals whose ideas had been formed in the 'forties would change with the new epoch. Only in 1863 did these hopes finally disappear. But in 1855 this misapprehension was based on the belief that, with the change of reign, the intelligentsia and the liberal nobility would not take revolutionary action against the Tsar. Their function should be that of guide—a sign-post to the State and the Emperor—to bring about at last the fundamental reform of peasant serfdom.

Herzen now published a letter to Alexander II, to explain the situation clearly to him. The writer was a Socialist, the recipient was a despot; between them there was only one piece of common ground: a programme to include freedom for the intellectuals and land for the peasants. Turning to the intelligentsia Herzen wrote: 'We have no system, no doctrine; we appeal alike to the Europeans [i.e. the Westerners] and the Panslavs [i.e. Slavophils]. Only those who confine themselves to justifying the autocracy must be

4+

excluded.' The combined forces of the intellectuals were not merely useful, but absolutely essential, to bring about freedom and reform.

This position made Herzen a real power in Russia, and the true guide to public opinion for about five years. His works were read in the Winter Palace and the smallest provincial towns, in Moscow and in Siberia—where the first number of the *Pole Star* reached the exiled Decembrists as a first word of encouragement and greeting after thirty years of exile.

Herzen thus brought himself into perfect harmony with the situation in Russia. The period between 1855 and 1857 was characterized by a rapid intellectual development and by uncertainty on the part of the authorities. 'Public opinion then made giant strides. Russian literature grew ten years in two years', as Herzen said. Yet the Tsar remained uncertain. The war went on and, even when the armistice had been signed, there were foreign problems to solve. This lack of decision in internal politics, even when he could concentrate all his attention on them, is generally attributed to Alexander II's unpreparedness, and to the scarcity of competent high officials after the thirty years of Nicholas I's reign. All this is true, but it does not touch the heart of the problem. In actual fact, when Alexander II came to the throne he found himself in the same situation as his father, condemned to paralysis whenever he wished to interfere with Russia's social and political foundations. He was allowed, rather than compelled, to move by public opinion, which assured him its support and shared his responsibility, and even prepared the series of plans and practical proposals which were the basis of the peasant reforms. The bureaucracy was incapable, even on the technical plane, of taking such a step. Alexander II, after his first long period of uncertainty, eventually showed himself sufficiently open-minded to realize that he needed this public support and that without it he could not move towards the abolition of serfdom. He therefore extended some measure of freedom to opinion.

And so even the obstacles which were placed in the way of books and articles from London were due more to the traditional fears of the police and to the bureaucratic practices of the previous reign than to any deliberate desire to stop them. Besides, a new opportunity now occurred to enable such books to exert a profound influence. The prohibition which Nicholas I had placed on all travel abroad was cancelled. A torrent of people began to move between London, Paris, Germany and Russia. It was enough to circulate the publications of the 'Free Russian Press' in Europe for them to reach Russia itself in travellers' suitcases.

From 1855 to 1857 Herzen aimed at hastening the development of public opinion. He did this by setting all problems in wider perspective, by turning back to the Decembrists, and by explaining in every possible way (and chiefly through his Memoirs) the trends of thought during the thirty years of Nicholas I's reign. In so doing he linked the new generation to its predecessor. At the same time he issued warnings against the dangers of the immediate situation. He said that it was too similar to what he himself had seen in Rome, when it had seemed that Pius IX was becoming a liberal. Too many figures were still missing from this revival. Bakunin and Petrashevsky were still in Siberia, even though the surviving Decembrists had been finally reprieved. But above all, the key problem, that of the peasants, was still untouched.

His rôle as a constructive observer enabled him to make an exact estimate of the new position of the intelligentsia. Moscow had now lost the eminence it had gained in the 'forties. The entire movement was centred in the capital. In September 1856 he told Turgenev that even he, Herzen, who came from Moscow, was far more loved in St Petersburg than in Moscow. He was astounded, but it confirmed his impression that the reforms could come only from the centre, from the capital, from the Tsar.

The more typical liberals, such as Kavelin and Chicherin, thought that if Herzen wanted to have any influence on the situation he should tone down his attacks still further and give up preaching Socialism. Herzen published their views in his *Voices from Russia*, but he was careful not to follow them. The example of 1848, of those spurious victories which had been so easily won by public opinion, had impressed themselves too powerfully on his mind for him to throw over his own position of independence.

In his letter, Kavelin told Herzen that the war had made the intelligentsia liberal and not revolutionary and that the state of mind of the 'thinking portion of the Russian population' could be summed up as follows: 'We are contrite rather than angry. Even in the boldest conversations I have not once heard anyone mention the need for secret societies, for revolution and for limiting the absolutist power or anything of the kind.' This was certainly true, at least in general, although during these two years of waiting, a few small groups of young men who did not share these ideas were beginning to spring up, as we shall see. But these were only small symptoms and as yet of no importance. Any initiative from above, such as the promise of a peasant reform, would be enough to make them vanish.

The most serious feature of the state of mind described by Kavelin lay elsewhere, in his assertion that no one wished to limit the power of the autocracy. These liberals were certainly not constitutionalists. As far as they were concerned, being liberal meant only the creation of free public opinion, capable of influencing the monarch by means of the press and ideas, but not by means of political organizations. They rejected not only conspiracies but any legal organization which might give effect to their own political ideas. They were not so much liberals as supporters of an enlightened despotism, and as there was not much illumination to be found in the autocrat himself and in the group of high officials that he had inherited from his father, they kept it all to themselves. They showed, in fact, the typical pride of the Russian intelligentsia, which was then in full flower and inspired by the sense of its own importance.

Characteristically it was the Slavophils who defined most clearly what was actually happening. They said that in Russia, by tradition (they generally had to be sustained by a more or less mythical tradition before committing themselves), 'power' had always resided in the Tsar, and 'opinion' in the people, and that these two forces should be completely independent. Though utterly absurd from the constitutional point of view, this theory does in fact reflect the actual position of these two forces as they groped for each other in the twilight which succeeded the shadows of Nicholas I's reign.

The reason for this liberalism of 'opinion' only, which did not touch the structure of the absolutist State, naturally lay in Russia's social system. Only the nobles could have thought of organically limiting the power of Alexander II. They had done this, or rather tried to do it, at the time of the Decembrists. At that time the constitutional problem had, together with the problem of the peasants, been at the heart of their discussions and their activities. But in 1856 it was the great mass of the nobles which was chiefly threatened by reforms. A large number of them were not so much opposed to the future reforms of Alexander II as frightened of them. Thirty years of Nicholas I had attached them to the preservation of their privileges and had made them hope that the *status quo* would continue indefinitely. Some of them, of course, felt differently, and some even understood, as Herzen had explained in 1853, that reform would in fact have benefited them too. But these were a disorganized minority. They had lost all autonomy and had become more and more bound up with the intelligentsia, who had now inherited the function the nobles held in 1825. Thirty years after the Decembrists any constitutionalism backed by the nobles could amount to no more than a mixture of social conservatism, confirmation of privileges, and peasant serfdom. Real reform could only be achieved from above, by the Emperor and by the government, urged on by an increasingly lively public opinion.

Herzen therefore devoted all his energies to rousing the intelligentsia, though he was well aware of the dangers latent in this situation. He did everything possible to convince the wavering educated classes and at least some of the nobility and high government officials that the nobles' conservatism could only be successfully defeated if an economic programme favourable to the peasants were adopted, and if the emancipation assured the peasants the land which they farmed. Conditions in Russia prevented any further move. When Kavelin told Herzen that it was no use thinking that in Russia there were people who shared the ideas of Mazzini and Kossuth, he was compelled to admit that Kavelin was right; as he had to again when Kavelin told him that it was useless to be an 'anarchist', when 'only the government could do anything'. Herzen laid more stress on the social aspect of the plan for reform. While Kavelin condemned the *obshchina* as 'a half-wild social germ . . . where the peasant is little better than a slave',[27] Herzen saw in the *obshchina* the only possible defence of peasant interests. For him it was a pledge for the future, and would allow some further development after emancipation. Herzen, in fact, accepted—though cautiously—the situation which had arisen in these years. At the same time he tried to bring into it the one Socialist element that was then viable, i.e. the defence of peasant interests in and through the *obshchina*.

And so at this time he again approached the Slavophils, although he smelt in them 'the stink of the police and the seminary'. However, they believed in the *obshchina*, and it was therefore worth signing an 'armistice' with them. He urged them, and the Westerners too, to move rapidly towards politics, and to give up scholarly disputes on the character of Russia and on the historical origins of its institutions. As he wrote in the *Pole Star* in 1857, the Russians did not yet sufficiently realize 'how boring they were, and how fed up everyone was with them'.[28] He summed up his conclusions in a *Letter to Mazzini on the present condition of Russia, February 1857*:

It's no use shouting against the past. True discernment lies in profiting equally from all the features of an existing situation, both those forces that come from the good and those from the bad. It isn't a question of their origin, but of how to guide them ... History and peoples forgive their governments many things, even crimes, even the cruelty of Peter and the dissolute life of Catherine II, but they never forgive a government which does not understand its own mission and is too weak to rise to heights which the situation demands ... We are faced with a huge economic revolution. The government and the nobility no longer conceal this from themselves. The Emperor has hinted at it in a speech to the nobility in Moscow. We are compelled to reorganize the ownership of land fundamentally, and to deal with the great questions of the landowner and the workman, of the rights of the worker to the tools of his trade. For such is the question of emancipation with land ... Hardly was Nicholas dead before an irresistible force drove the government of Alexander II in a different direction from that of his father. Will he take control of this force, master it, and win again for the people what his father made them lose? I do not know. But he cannot stop it. Nicholas, to achieve his evil ends, relied on a limited but inflexible will. Alexander II lacks this quality. They say that he has a good heart. This wins a place in Paradise, but not in history. Alexander II in his manifesto, his ministers in their circulars, journalists in their newspapers, announce that a new era is beginning for Russia. Well, what stops us entering this era? Who should now speak? It's up to them to keep their promises, or we too will say 'No more rhetoric. No more rhetoric.' I know few things more shameful and humiliating than to see a chance of great progress thrown away and some infirmity holding up the movement. The engine is hot, the steam is being used up, and horse-power is being wasted in a roar, and all this because there is no one bold enough to turn the lever and set the engine in motion. What if it should leave without the driver?[29]

But before 1857 was over the long-awaited signal was given. On 5th December an Act was published which engaged the government to free the serfs. A circular ordered the nobles in one of the Western provinces to meet and to prepare a scheme for reform, on the basis of general rules drawn up by the government.

Herzen thought that 'now they cannot turn back again', and he added that it was the most important event in Russia since 14th December 1825.

He must now devote himself to influencing in every possible way these negotiations between the government and the committees of the nobility. For, as was obvious from the first, they would have a decisive effect on the fate of the reforms.

A few months before this he had founded the *Kolokol* (The Bell) a small review, which was at first published monthly, and later, fortnightly. Its first number of 1st July 1857 was called 'a supplement to the *Pole Star*'. One review was no longer enough for the battle which was growing more intense. Two would allow him to leave more general and theoretical discussions to the *Pole Star*, where he could expound his theories on Socialism, and use the *Kolokol* for the discussion of immediate policies. Herzen himself has said that it was Ogarev's idea to start this review. It was founded (we can infer from this) because Herzen was at last no longer alone. He had found a colleague in London to work with—the very man with whom, more than twenty-five years earlier, he had begun his activities with their joint creation of a Saint-Simonist group in Moscow. Ogarev had reached London in 1856, and had brought the first messages assuring Herzen that his work had finally met with a response in Russian intellectual circles. 'It was the first ray of warmth and light after an oppressive nightmare',[30] he said. He had not convinced his friends, but he had shaken them, and the situation was becoming fluid. They were still too pessimistic; they did not realize the important tasks which they were expected to undertake, together with the entire Russian intelligentsia. But their words helped to convince Herzen that he was on the right road.

Ogarev had seen the collapse of his attempts begun in the 'forties to improve the economic situation of his estates, and of the peasants whom he had freed. A fire, apparently lit by the workers themselves, had destroyed his factory. As for the intellectual movement, he had always held himself more or less detached, and expressed what he had to say through his poetry. He nearly always lived out of town, and was entirely preoccupied with the complexities of his private life. He now felt free of all obligations, and was ready to begin his life over again and devote himself to politics. He shared Herzen's ideas, and was bound to him by deep friendship. Personal crises during the following years, which led to his second wife finally living with Herzen, complicated but did not destroy this friendship. He was aware of Herzen's political superiority, and allowed himself to be guided by him in all essential problems. And so their collaboration was complete, and the *Kolokol* was its fruitful product.[31]

The *Kolokol*'s motto '*Vivos voco*' was chosen in memory of their youthful enthusiasm for Schiller. It was politically appropriate for a paper aimed at appealing to all living forces, wherever they were, to support a programme which was now clearly one of social and administrative reforms: freedom from censorship, freedom of the peasants from the landlords, and freedom of non-noble families from corporal punishment.

In the second number, in August 1857, Herzen called his leading article 'Revolution in Russia'. This was a commentary on Alexander II's words to the nobility of Moscow: 'It is better that the changes should come from above than from below.' It was true, he wrote, that they had entered a revolutionary period, but it was not certain that this would develop according to the French pattern. There were other foreign examples which could be followed. For instance, there was the example of England, with which Herzen had become better acquainted, and which influenced his more liberal outlook of these years by convincing him that changes could be brought about by the pressure of public opinion. And then there was Piedmont, whose resistance at the time of the European reaction after 1849 had already impressed him, and which he now suggested to Russia as an example and a model. He wrote:

Under our very eyes Piedmont has been reborn. At the end of 1847 its government was Jesuitical and inquisitorial, without any freedom; indeed, with a political police and a terrible civil and religious censorship, which killed any form of mental activity. Ten years later we can no longer recognize Piedmont. The face of her cities and her people has changed. Everywhere there is a new life, twice the number of people, open faces, activity. And this revolution has been achieved without the smallest clash, merely an unsuccessful war and a series of concessions to public opinion on the part of the government. Professional revolutionaries do not like this method, I know, but that does not concern us. We are convinced that Russia's present situation satisfies no one, and we prefer with all our heart the methods of peaceful human development to those of bloodshed; even though, just as sincerely, we prefer the most stormy development conceivable to the *status quo* of the time of Nicholas I.[32]

This point of view naturally led him to describe the obstacles holding up reforms as mere inertia, rather than organized social forces. They were obstacles which must be denounced and not destroyed: men who must be enlightened and not groups to be swept away. There would not, he said, be any organized opposition from the corps of nobles. He knew, only too well, their traditional lack of independence. Nor did he believe in the 'old Muscovite party', of which the European press was speaking at this time. He had seen this at too close quarters to believe it capable of seriously opposing either any order of the Emperor or any pressure from public opinion.

The *Kolokol*'s efforts therefore were devoted to denouncing individual abuses, particular instances of passive resistance on the part of the reactionaries. It attacked the old officials of the régime of Nicholas I, satirized old-fashioned thinking and gave much of its space to exposing the financial and administrative scandals which were the oppressive legacy of long and arbitrary despotism. Herzen, in common with the most active members of Russian society at the time, demanded 'publicity' even more than 'freedom'. He demanded, in fact, the opportunity to point out the evils of the State, rather than the creation of political organisms which could be permanently guaranteed by freedom. His programme at this stage was to destroy, or at least to restrict, the censorship rather than to seek constitutional guarantees.

This campaign could be developed far more freely abroad than in Russia, though even there 'the literature of public denunciation' was growing in scope. And it was directed by Herzen and Ogarev in a masterly fashion. Any victim of tyranny, anyone trying to assert his rights against the arbitrary power of the State, found in London the public accuser lacking in Moscow or St Petersburg. Letters and denunciations poured in on the *Kolokol*. So much so that as from October 1859 the editor decided to publish a supplement devoted to this aspect of the fight, called *Pod Sud!* (On Trial). In the ministries, in the commissions deciding the fate of the peasants and in local municipalities there was widespread fear of these free voices from London. There is evidence that the Emperor himself sometimes learnt of scandals and abuses from the *Kolokol*. The paper so widened its sources of information (which often included government offices) that it was able to publish secret documents of such importance that even today, after the archives have been opened, the *Kolokol* provides information on Russian life of the period which is not obtainable elsewhere. And so the number of readers doubled and redoubled. They passed it from hand to hand, and increased the circulation to a peak of 2,500. This is a remarkable figure when we remember that the *Sovremennik*, a review published legally in St Petersburg, at this stage had a circulation of 6,000, which was quite exceptional for its time.[33]

It is of course true that this intense but narrow campaign against abuses could in some ways encourage one of the most typical aspects of Russian politics at the time—the tendency of conservative forces to adopt a liberal camouflage. This was fatal, as it meant that reforms, even such important ones as those affecting the peasants, were carried out with all the old tools of government machinery. Liberalism came down from above as an order from the Emperor, and followed the inevitable tendency to confine itself to small details. It thus struck only at secondary features, not at the ones fundamental to a despotic State and to a society divided into rigid castes. Indeed there came from Russia appeals to Herzen to confine himself exclusively to this work of 'public denunciation', which was more administrative and judicial in character, than political. But although he well knew that it was by this means that his ideas spread through Russia, Herzen never confined himself to it, and the *Kolokol* remained a political review.[34]

When, between the end of 1857 and the beginning of 1858, preliminary steps for freeing the serfs were made public, Herzen addressed Alexander II: 'Thou hast conquered, O Galilean.' He gave vent to the joy that had spread throughout enlightened circles in Russia and he promised his support and help 'to those who liberate and as long as they liberate'.[35] Nonetheless, the proposed emancipation was 'without land' and still depended on the decisions of assemblies of nobles in the various provinces, who had been authorized and indeed forced to meet for this purpose.

Because of this, Herzen continued to emphasize the silent menace of the peasants, which so many—among them the Emperor himself—felt was the real motive power of the reform. At the same time he declared himself free of any tie with any section of the ruling class which was bringing about the reform.

Emancipation with land is one of the most important and essential problems for Russia and for us. Whether it comes from above or from below, we will support it. If the peasants are freed by committees made up of sworn enemies of the emancipation, we will thank them sincerely and from our hearts. If the peasants are freed, first by committees and then by all the nobles who have elected them, we will be the first to congratulate them with all our hearts. Finally, should the Tsar order the confiscation of all the possessions of the rebellious aristocracy and deport them all, let us say, to somewhere on the Amur together with Muravev, we will only say 'So be it.' This does not mean that we recommend such means and no others. Nor does it mean that they are the best. Our readers know what we think. But the most important thing is that the peasants should be freed with land. As for the means employed, we have no objections.[36]

The *Kolokol* could later boast that it had been the first to suggest the only way of bringing the reform to a practical conclusion—by agreement between the nobles and the State and possibly the peasants.

The lands farmed by the peasants were to be given to them in return for a redemption fee. Herzen and Ogarev had written about this ever since the beginning of 1858. A detailed plan for reform on these lines was brought over from Russia by V. A. Panaev, and was published both in the *Voices from Russia* and in the *Kolokol*, in time for it to be able to influence the provincial committees of the nobility.

The discussions held by these committees showed that the more liberal nobles—mostly from the north, where the land was poorer and more capable of industrial development—were quite prepared to hand over their land in return for a fee; while a large part of the landlords from the more fertile black soil continued to hold out against this solution, or accepted it only on conditions which were extremely harsh for the peasants. Herzen urged the Emperor not to give way to these proposals. Later, when the central bureaucracy itself took over the reforms and pressed them forward energetically, largely through the work of Milyutin, Herzen ably supported him and his work against his many enemies. Of course he realized that the fee would oppress the peasants, but as Ogarev replied in the *Kolokol* on 1st November 1860, to a correspondent who insisted on the nobles handing over their land fee, 'We do not see any legal basis for the fee, but rather sheer necessity. Given the struggle between the two classes, the peasants will find that paying a fee to the nobles for their land is cheaper than a revolution, and the nobles will find that to give the land which they rightly consider their own for an insignificant fee is more advantageous than to perish in a peasant revolt.'

But this was the problem. Would the fee, in fact, be insignificant? What

4*

would be the quantity of land granted to the peasants, and how much ought it to cost? On this point the *Kolokol*'s vision was not clear. Instead, discussions on the legal problems of emancipation and on the retention for differing periods of a few typical survivals of serfdom—such as the *corvées* and local jurisdiction of the landlord—to some extent diverted Herzen and Ogarev, and indeed a large part of public opinion in Russia, from this vital matter. It is true that this controversy was important, but among the émigrés in London it resulted in concealing the economic and financial kernel of the problem.

Nonetheless Herzen soon realized that things were not going well. In 1860 the *Kolokol* bitterly criticized the government's policy, and this criticism was further sharpened by the long delay which held up the publication of the emancipation decree for more than a year. Though this delay did not cause the loss of any of the fundamental points which had been won earlier, it did give rise to widespread uncertainty and, even in London, encouraged feelings which were more pessimistic than the actual situation warranted.

In the first number of the *Kolokol* for 1860, Herzen compared Alexander II to the *apprenti sorcier*. Elaborating the analogy, he fully brought out the reasons for the delay: fear of the forces in the field—the nobles, peasants and intelligentsia; the same fear in fact that had paralysed Nicholas I, though it had at last forced his successor to take action. Now once more it made the Tsar hesitant and wary. It made him reduce 'publicity' and surround the entire question of emancipation with an air of mystery, and restrict it once again to the higher bureaucracy. Herzen's attacks on this return to the spirit of Nicholas I were particularly striking. In his campaign against it, he began to appeal to the few nobles who had shown not only understanding but above all independence and liberalism.

But now the die was cast. Herzen's arousing of public opinion and his defence of emancipation with land had gone as far as they could in the circumstances. The outcome which he read about in the manifesto of 19th February 1861 did not seem 'all that bad', as he said at first. 'Together with the freeing of Italy, it is perhaps the most important event of the last five years', he wrote to his son.[37]

During these three years of discussions on peasant reform, the *Kolokol* had made enemies within the intelligentsia itself, both on the right and on the left. In 1858 Herzen broke with the more doctrinaire liberals; a year later he clashed with the radicalism of Chernyshevsky and Dobrolyubov, which was just coming into evidence.

The break with the liberals was merely a continuation of the controversy that had begun in the Western group at Moscow in 1846, and which now began to reveal its latent political importance. Chicherin, a historian and jurist, bitterly attacked Herzen at the end of 1858. 'This is the last straw,' noted Herzen, 'an infiltration of enemies within the intelligentsia . . . And surely it is a strange thing that these invaders consist of the pupils of Granovsky, of friends of Korsh, Kryukov, etc.?'[38] Quite apart from his repeated disappointments in the true political nature of his friends—illusions so often contradicted by reality—this was an important symptom. The absolutism which Herzen had accepted purely as a means of advancing towards the liberation of the serfs was now built up by Chicherin into an ideal form of government. This not only disgusted Herzen morally but also complicated, on the political plane, the endless by-play between nobility, bureaucracy and intelligentsia, which constituted the real political issue of the moment. In place of this Chicherin and his doctrinaire followers substituted an idealization of the Tsar. Once more, as at the beginning of the 'forties, the shadow of Peter the Great and the myth of enlightened despotism seemed to be returning. Herzen was convinced that the situation did not demand a Peter the Great but merely a man capable of being guided by public opinion. And so an open break became essential.

Besides, these doctrinaires represented a human type which he found antipathetic. They were the liberal successors, indeed the caricature, of those 'dogmatic ritualists of democracy' against whom he had fought in 1848.

Doctrinaires of the French kind and *Gelehrten* of the German variety, people who institute proceedings and draw up lists and put them in order, people who remain firmly in positive religion and make a cult of positive science, thoughtful people— all these live on into old age, without ever leaving the main road, without ever making spelling mistakes or mistakes of any other kind; but people who fling them- selves into battle are devoured by the passions of faith and doubt, are consumed by rage and anxiety, are soon burnt out, and allow themselves to stumble in the middle of the road and die.[39]

When Chicherin, who was then travelling to London and Paris, read this, he felt it applied to him personally and replied with a long letter, which Herzen published in the *Kolokol* so as to expose what he considered a mistaken attitude.[40] Chicherin's letter was a sort of tract to demonstrate that in politics reason rather than passion was needed. It was written so pedantically that Kavelin and, with him, a group of liberals, wrote to Herzen to deny responsibility for it. Herzen ended by breaking with the liberals but the break took place only gradually with one group after another, beginning with the most typical doctrinaires, and he kept—at least until 1862—contacts and often friendships with the others.[41]

The quarrel with the left, the *Sovremennik*, was, on the other hand, pro- voked by Herzen, with his article 'Very Dangerous!!!' aimed directly at Dobrolyubov and Chernyshevsky. It is true that personal reasons played their part. The director of the *Sovremennik* was Nekrasov, whom Herzen admired as a poet but whom he considered dishonest. On the other hand his comparative ignorance of the financial aspects of the peasant problem made Herzen underestimate Chernyshevsky, who, at this time, saw more clearly than he did the dangers which lay in the government's plan for reform. But these considerations were merely secondary. In his attack on the *Sovremennik*,

Herzen wanted to respond to liberal public opinion, which was alarmed by the growth of a radical trait containing 'nihilist' elements which impressed and worried it. In his criticism of 'these bilious men', as he called them, Herzen tended to confuse the new radicals with his memories of the Petrashevskists. One of these Petrashevskists, in fact, had come all the way to London to collaborate with him and then, out of nervous instability, had suddenly left him. Herzen looked upon them all as psychologically warped and negative characters.

What struck me about them was the ease with which they despaired of everything; the ferocious joy of their denial and their terrible ruthlessness. Despite their excellent spirits and noble intentions, our 'bilious ones' can, by their tone, drive an angel to blows and a saint to curses. They exaggerate everything in the world with such *aplomb* and not as a joke, but out of such bitterness, that they are quite unbearable.[42]

This was the beginning of a long controversy, in which Herzen made great efforts to understand the new generation, and yet always ended by withdrawing into himself. He had no patience with the human and psychological aspects of nihilist Populism and disliked its bitter flavour. Yet this bitterness was to be of great importance in Russian society when the era of liberal hopes and battles for the great reform had drawn to its close.

But though he was critical of these young radicals in private discussion, publically he declared that he did not want to sow discord in the camp of the emancipationists. They differed, he said, over means but not over ends. The *Sovremennik* merely carried opinions of his own to an extreme. When a voice from Russia reproached him with not calling on the peasants to take up their axes, he replied that he would not do this as long as hope prevailed; as long as he could count on a revival of public opinion; as long as he could counter the nobility with the *obshchina*, the weak and hesitant landed aristocracy with peasant resistance. A broom rather than an axe was what was needed.

The manifesto of 19th February 1861 led him to believe that he had been even more correct than he had dared hope. To celebrate the day, he prepared a banquet for all the Russians in London. He drafted a speech, in which he recalled how in 1853, when the first page of the 'Free Russian Press' had been printed, if anyone had said that 'after eight years we should have come together, and the hero of the banquet would have been the Tsar of Russia, we should have thought that he was mad, or even worse.' And yet this was what had happened. True, 'the manifesto of 19th February was only one milestone; the road was still long, and the coach was still in the hands of cruel Tartar and German drivers ... In Russia it is impossible to denounce their intrigues. Speech has not yet been freed, and is still a slave of the censorship.' And so it was necessary to continue working abroad. But the fact remained that serfdom had been abolished in Russia. 'Let us raise our glasses to drink to our brothers who have been freed, and to honour Alexander Nikolaevich, their liberator.'[43]

But this toast was never drunk. The first bloody encounters in Warsaw, a few days after the emancipation, showed that the political oppression of the Russian Empire was still too serious for Herzen to be able to drink freely to Alexander II. 'Our banquet was sad. We lowered our hands. After the blood spilt at Warsaw it could no longer proceed.'[44]

Herzen soon realized that the emancipation of the serfs, as finally carried out, merely brought up all the old problems somewhat aggravated by the reform. The peasants resumed and increased the local protests, which had sprung up at the time of the Crimean War, and which now revealed their discontent at the new situation. The intelligentsia felt that the development of liberal public opinion was no longer enough, and that the positions that it had won must now be consolidated. The more active part of the intelligentsia wanted to put itself at the head of political life in Russia, in an attempt to replace the State and even the Emperor. New problems (chiefly that of the relations between the young intelligentsia and the people) arose, and were widely discussed. The various nationalities contained within the Empire, especially the Poles, began to agitate and try to establish their rights. In fact, all the various problems which Herzen had realized when he had wanted to organize a banquet in London to celebrate 19th February 1861 came to a head during the period that immediately followed, and provided material for the *Kolokol* during the next two years.

Herzen now tried to keep in touch with Russian life and regain the guiding function held by the *Kolokol* when the reforms were being prepared. From the first the task was difficult and it soon grew less and less feasible. An émigré organ found it more and more difficult to direct a complex and stormy movement, and to cope with the various problems raised by the peasant reforms. Herzen and Ogarev were able to suggest a few more ideas which were followed in later years. But their actions were losing unity and efficiency, and were finally crushed by the wave of nationalism that swept through Russia in 1863 when the Polish revolt broke out.

None the less, their efforts deserve close examination. However dispersed and fragmentary, they reveal some of the most significant social tendencies of these years, and reproduce the feeling of the ferment in Russia between 1861 and 1863. Peasant revolts grew more frequent throughout 1861 and were put down with violence and bloodshed. The *Kolokol*, and Ogarev in particular, sensitively reflected the uncertainty and disappointment which prevailed in the countryside; illiterate peasants were faced with an abstruse manifesto— incomprehensible even to the village 'intellectuals', the scribes, bigots of the sects, priests, and merchants. 'A new serfdom' said the *Kolokol* as early as 15th June 1861. 'The Tsar has cheated the people.' But though it expressed the feelings of so many Russian peasants, it could not thereby guide or help them in their distant struggle. The peasants had to grope alone in the dark for a way out of their changed situation.

And it was this situation that convinced Herzen and Ogarev (and their most sensitive compatriots in Russia itself) of their remoteness from the people, its interests and life.

These experiences gave the first stimulus to the movement 'to go to the people'. As early as 1st August 1860 Ogarev had foreseen in the *Kolokol* the need for this—not yet as an autonomous movement, but rather as a necessary complement to the changes which Russian society was undergoing at this time. 'We must train schoolmasters, men who can preach learning to the peasants; travelling schoolmasters, who can spread useful and applied knowledge from one end of Russia to the other.'[45] Herzen and Ogarev were still more concerned with this problem after their break with the government, which grew ever clearer. When disorders broke out and the universities were closed in autumn 1861, the appeal for a movement 'to go to the people' became the *Kolokol*'s battle cry.

Herzen thus pointed out a way which the Populists tried to exploit during the next twenty years. In the meantime the *Kolokol* was trying to guide from a distance the political ferment which the emancipation of the serfs had produced in the nobility, intelligentsia and entire ruling class. In 1861 Herzen still thought that the only chance lay in continuing his tactics of earlier years. Just as he had then helped to create a public opinion favourable to 'emancipation with land', so now he would develop a more urgent feeling which would—with energy and impatience—demand freedom of the press, changes in the structure of the State, and finally, something like a great national assembly.

After reading the manifesto of 19th February 1861, Herzen had written in the *Kolokol*, 'The first step has been taken; now it is freedom's turn.'[46] He still thought of the struggle in the old terms: as a battle against censorship. But soon reactions in Russia convinced him that he must demand much more. Suggestions came to him from St Petersburg. The *Velikoruss*, the first clandestine paper, which had appeared in July 1861, already spoke of the need for a national assembly. Ogarev and N. N. Obruchev wrote an appeal at the same time called *What does the people need?* in language intended to be simple enough for the peasants themselves to understand. This claimed that to guarantee the land—and the peasants had a right to more of this than had been granted to them by the reform—it was essential that 'taxes should be apportioned and collected by the peasants themselves, through leaders elected by them'.[47] The idea of calling such a body *Zemskaya Duma* or *Zemsky Sobor*, in memory of the assemblies which at the beginning of the seventeenth century had put an end to the time of troubles, sprang from various sources. It was circulated in manuscripts and newspapers, and somehow even appeared in the legal press. The term showed the *Kolokol*'s intention of uniting different intellectual trends, from the Westerners, who saw in it a form of constituent assembly, to the Slavophils who were always responsive to memories of the past.

The presence in London of a typical representative of peasant society, Peter

Alexeyevich Martyanov, may have encouraged Herzen to give the *Zemskaya Duma* first place in his propaganda.

'His story is short, but it is a true Russian history', Herzen was to write when Martyanov was later condemned to forced labour.

He was born a serf of Count Guryev. As a young man he showed quite exceptional business ability, and he organized the sale of wheat on a large scale. Count Guryev took him away from these activities and ruined him by seizing a large sum of money almost on the eve of emancipation. This man, who had experienced all the terrible banes of life in Russia, was gifted with exceptional talent. Energetic and deeply emotional, he concentrated within himself the destiny of the entire Russian people. In him was reflected its poetry and religion, love and hatred. Austere and rigidly consistent in his way of life, he made no concessions to himself or others. He somehow combined an element of the rebel Spartacus with the sombre character of our religious sectarians.[48]

Martyanov had a deeply rooted faith in the Tsar, and implored him to free the people from the nobles and the upper classes. To this effect he wrote a pamphlet,[49] and a letter to Alexander II which was published in the *Kolokol*. In it he asked the Emperor to summon a great *Zemsky Sobor* of the Russian people.[50]

Bakunin then took a cue from Martyanov's programme. The main theme of his *The People's Cause: Romanov, Pugachev or Pestel?*, published in 1862 by the Free Russian Press, was the need to summon a national assembly. 'Terrible things will happen in Russia in 1863 if the Tsar does not decide to summon the *Zemskaya Duma* of all the people.'[51] In Siberia, Bakunin had long thought that a dictator was needed to carry out the necessary reforms. After his escape he came to London in January 1861 and was greeted as a brother by Herzen and Ogarev. In this pamphlet he echoed on a larger scale the hesitations that all felt after the emancipation. He was thinking of a Tsar capable of really moving with the people, and a people capable of imposing its will on the Tsar through a national assembly.

The myth of the *Zemsky Sobor* began to take on a certain political coherence at the beginning of 1862, when the more enlightened and educated members of the nobility proposed or voted orders of the day in favour of national representation, and when the *Kolokol* echoed the hope, which was by then widespread, of such a liberal endorsement of the peasant reform.

Ogarev drafted an appeal to the Tsar, which aimed at collecting the signatures and support of all disaffected elements ranging from the nobility to the peasants—all in fact who saw in the future Assembly an opportunity for freely expressing their demands. In view of the uncertainty of public opinion in the summer of 1862 this appeal implied that the public recognized that reforms from above were not sufficient, and that the government alone was unable to guide the forces which had now been set in motion. He said:

The nobility has not been recompensed for its losses. It lacks the means to work, and, let us say so frankly, it lacks the means to live—apart from those nobles who are officials and draw a salary and rewards from the State, all of which fall on the people in the shape of heavy taxes . . . On the other hand, the manifesto of 19th February has made it possible to reduce the peasants' land. They are not convinced that they will be able to keep tomorrow the land that they farm today . . . The redemption fee is crushing, indeed impossible, in the forms decreed by the manifesto. The peasant's situation has become unbearable. Just as before, indeed, even more than before, he looks upon every noble landlord as his enemy, and considers Your Majesty's orders to be cunning plots devised by officials to ruin him . . . Sire, the State cannot be saved without asking the people. Without the *Zemsky Sobor*—the only way of saving the ruined and penniless State—no one will escape unhurt.

He suggested that assemblies from towns and districts should meet to elect deputies. As for the electors they should be chosen 'without discrimination of class, religion or faith; all the categories of the peasants ('with limited obligations', belonging to the State, belonging to the Crown), nobles, merchants, the bourgeoisie, the clergy and people of every profession'. 'To dispel the peasants' distrust', the nobles should not register in any district where they held land; each district (*uyezd*) should elect one deputy. In this appeal, Ogarev also determined an order of the day for the future assembly, which included the most important administrative reforms.[52]

The discussion aroused by this first sketchy plan is of some interest. Turgenev, then in Paris, repeated the criticisms that he had already often made to Herzen. It was wrong to speak badly of the manifesto of 19th February, he said, for with it Russia began 'a new era'. The government knew this, and would not accept criticisms. The peasants too knew it, for however dissatisfied they were with a few of the arrangements, they looked upon it as the charter of their personal liberties, and they would therefore consider all criticisms merely as 'a new attack by the nobility on emancipation'. In Russia, only the educated class was capable of understanding the needs of liberty. Yet the exiles in London, by trying to appeal to the people, were breaking away from this very educated class. 'The revolution, in the truest sense of the word, I could add in the widest sense of the word, exists only in the mind of the intelligentsia.' He suggested an appeal based on these considerations, adding shortly afterwards that it was essential to rely on the government plans, which were just then being discussed, on local self-administration, and on the attempt to create provincial councils representing all classes.

This was the means adopted by the government to satisfy and at the same time evade constitutionalism between 1861 and 1863. The institution of the *Zemstvo*—rather like the *Conseil d'Arrondissement* in France—was a step towards a system of local representation. But it did not in the slightest interfere with the principle of absolutism.

Turgenev was merely expressing the state of mind of the Russian liberals, who trusted in local and partial reforms, without ever carrying the demand for a *Zemsky Sobor* to its logical conclusion. The reasons he had given explain this attitude. The struggle between nobles and peasants was too violent, and suspicion between the various social classes was too bitter for absolutism not to continue to play on them and maintain its own authority, for it was decided not to create constitutional organs which could tie its hands. Even the best and most experienced Russian liberals remained fettered to their conception of the State and their trust in enlightened despotism.

When, at the end of 1862, it became more and more apparent that the Tsar intended to use repression to put an end to the prevailing intellectual excitement, Ogarev, Herzen and Bakunin held that it was less necessary than ever to make concessions to these doubtful liberals. They therefore proposed a new appeal for using the *Zemsky Sobor* still more openly as propaganda against official policies. This last plan, which was once more drawn up by Ogarev, said:

Russia is now in that state of widespread distrust which usually precedes a general upheaval . . . Sire, the people trusts the Tsar, but not the government, or the noble-officials, who compose it. Nor does it trust the noble-landowners from whom it has been freed on terms which it holds to be unfair. If you, Sire, continue to support the régime of officials, the people will soon lose its trust even in you.

Efforts to establish equality between the various social classes in the eyes of the law or local administration were no longer enough. Land was the fundamental problem.

From the very first, ever since the word 'Russia' has lived in the memory of man, the land has been colonized gratis by the people and considered by it as its own . . . By recognizing that the land belongs to the people you, Sire, will destroy the very roots of the difference between the various social classes. This difference is bringing not only Russia but other countries to the verge of ruin.

Faced with reaction from the State and hesitation from the liberals, the London group returned to its original programme of peasant Socialism based on the *obshchina*. This had been at the basis of Ogarev's, Herzen's and, now, Bakunin's ideas.[53] The *Kolokol* of these years expounded more and more definitely this Populist conception of the *obshchina*, and examined its economic, financial and technical aspects. Ogarev gave a particularly precise and interesting account of these ideas in a book called *Essai sur la situation russe. Lettres à un Anglais* which was published in London in 1862.

The campaign for the *Zemsky Sobor* had convinced Herzen and Ogarev that they could place their hopes less and less in the liberals. They now had to appeal directly to the Russian people. How could this be done?

In the summer of 1862 the first attempt at a direct approach had been made if not to the peasants, at least to those groups of merchants, artisans and business men which constituted the Russian third estate. Despite their divisions into corporations, and their caste system, bred by differing customs and traditions, one bond united them all: their adherence to the old faith—

the *Raskol*. On 15th June 1862 the first number of a newspaper addressed to them came out in London, the *Obshcheye Veche* (The Common Assembly). The very word *veche*, recalling the assemblies of all the citizens in mediaeval communes, appealed to a tradition of self-administration which was different from, yet parallel to, that of the peasant *mir*. Ogarev and Herzen thought that it would be possible to reach the villages through these Old Believers, for only some followers of the sects were literate.

The need to contact the religious sects, persecuted by the official church and the government, had already been considered in the 1840s. But only now was the first practical attempt to this effect made in London. Herzen's meeting with Martyanov, the merchant-peasant and an Old Believer, encouraged such a move. And Martyanov was not the only sectarian to visit the Free Russian Press at this time and seek contacts with Herzen and Ogarev. Besides this, they must have realized that the peasant rising at Bezdna, the greatest to follow the emancipation, had been directed by a man of the *Raskol*, and was characterized by its spirit.

A young émigré, V. I. Kelsiev, had been the first in London to urge the possibility of reaching the people through the sects. Sprung from a family of poor aristocrats, he had passionately devoted himself to his studies, chiefly oriental languages, and had become the friend of Dobrolyubov, when he too was a student. 'He is a man who thinks seriously. He has a powerful spirit, and a thirst for action; very developed through his wide reading and deep thought', Dobrolyubov had noted in his diary. But he had added, 'What I don't like about him is his excessive touchiness in personal life. Of course this may be a result of inner impulses which, seeking a proper channel, burst out on every side.'[54] Dobrolyubov's impression was accurate. Kelsiev was a man of remarkable talent and an ability to devote himself enthusiastically to the most difficult studies, but his imaginative, sensitive and hesitant character prevented him from sticking to anything that he started. He was a good example of the forces which were developing in Russian society at the time of the reforms. But he could not stand the test, and after a particularly difficult and painful exile he ended in 1867 by voluntarily going to the Russian frontier and asking to be imprisoned. In prison he wrote a long and detailed *Confession* of what he had done during these years.[55] After his release from prison, he lived the life of a poor man of letters, ostracized by the liberals and yet without the support of the reactionaries; nor indeed did he ever ask for their support.

His *Confession* is rightly named; and even if we read it only as a reflection of his state of mind in 1859 when he wanted to emigrate, it is not without interest.

Forbidden books [which he, like so many of his young contemporaries, was then reading] seemed to us a revelation from above. A new world opened out before us; a fantastic world, perhaps, capable of being realized only in theory; but converts are always enthralled by theories, especially those persecuted by the authorities . . .

Just as ecclesiastical censorship has given rise to the development of every kind of religious sect, in the same way political censorship made inevitable the birth of the party which was later called Nihilist. If one takes into account the passion of the Russian mind, which goes to extremes in all its conclusions and stops at nothing, either affirmative or negative, then Nihilism will appear as a typical and purely Russian symptom. The Russian, say our sectarians, is not like other men, *he seeks the truth*. And indeed, this passion for extremes, for developing every statement to the *nec plus ultra* has led the ordinary people to emasculation for their religion, to voluntary floggings, to enthusiasm, and has driven our schoolboys, seminarists and university students to indulge in abnegations which would not even be dreamt of in the West. Carrying things to their extremes is the characteristic element of our history.[56]

In London he did not find what he was so passionately looking for, until Herzen gave him a large bundle of documents received from Russia. This was an extensive and detailed report on the government policy towards the sects, and a series of *Raskol* texts. Herzen told him to look at them and see if there was anything suitable for the *Kolokol*. It was a revelation.

I didn't sleep all night and carried on reading. I almost went off my head. My life literally split in two, and I became a new man. If Herzen had not given me these documents, I would perhaps have remained a revolutionary and a nihilist. They saved me. Reading them, I felt that I was entering an unknown, unexplored world, the world of Hoffman, Edgar Allan Poe or the *Thousand and One Nights*. Suddenly, in one night, there were revealed to me the emasculates with their mystic rites, their choruses and their harvest songs, full of poetry; the flagellants with their strange beliefs; the dark figures of the 'priestless' sects; the intrigues of the leaders of the Old Believers; the existence of Russian villages in Prussia, Austria, Moldavia and Turkey. One sect after another, one rite after another appeared before me, as in a magic lantern show, and I read on and on and on. My head whirled, I stopped breathing . . . In a flash I saw in front of me the peasants and bearded merchants, so scornfully despised by Europe and our educated classes; ignorant barbarians, sunk in primitive materialism. They were not all that bad, these people who, beneath social oppression and the terrible yoke of the seventeenth and eighteenth centuries, were able to keep awake, unlike the Western *paysan* and *bauer* or the Polish *chlop*. On the contrary they thought, thought of the most important problems that can concern the human soul—truth and untruth, Christ and anti-Christ, eternity, man, salvation . . . The *Raskol* reflects honour on the Russian people, showing that it does not sleep, that every peasant wants to keep a lively independent eye on dogmas, wants to think for himself about truth, that the Russian people *searches for truth*, and then follows what it has found, and does not allow itself to be frightened by floggings or by caves with their entrances blocked up, or by emasculation, or by human sacrifice and cannibalism.[57]

This world of the sects made a deep impression on him. Police action against them offended him and convinced him that he ought to try to know them at closer range and establish contacts with them. Meanwhile, he felt he must protest openly against the lack of religious freedom in Russia.

Using this material of Herzen, and more that he succeeded in getting from

Russia, he brought out four small volumes, 'Recueil de Documents Officiels sur les Dissidents Russes. They were published in London, the first in 1860 and the others in 1861. Two years later, he followed these up with two more containing the laws relating to the Raskol. Taken as a whole, these booklets gave a detailed picture of the problem of religious sects in Russia. The importance of the Dissenters in English history and a close study of similar events in other countries convinced Kelsiev of the value of this mine that he had discovered. He had long discussions with Ogarev, Martyanov and Bakunin about the political lessons that could be learnt from it. For this was the only source, he thought, which could reveal the mentality of the peasants and small townsfolk, and the only means by which they could be reached.

And so the 'Popular Tsarism' which accompanied propaganda for the Zemsky Sobor was inevitably influenced by the deep-seated peasant myth—clearly echoed in some of the sects—of the Tsar who desires to do good but is always prevented by the nobles and government. The very words used to demand an assembly reflect this interest in the religious history of the Russian people, for Sobor is an ecclesiastical term meaning council. Besides, the collectivist character of many of the sects inevitably reinforced the idea of peasant Socialism.

At the end of 1861 a member of the 'Old Believer' clergy came to London and through him Kelsiev was able to establish a first contact.[58] Pafnuty, who was bishop of Kolomna, but travelling with a merchant's passport, was extremely well read in the Scriptures and Fathers of the Church, but not very responsive to the political problems which the London émigrés, including Bakunin, tried to discuss with him. But one item in their programme—freedom of religion—attracted him, and because of this he was prepared to collaborate with Kelsiev.

Kelsiev now went on a secret journey to Russia, to make use of the contacts which Pafnuty had promised to arrange. Armed with a Turkish passport, he visited St Petersburg and Moscow, preparing the ground for the newspaper for Old Believers, which had begun publication in London, the Obshcheye Veche. He arranged for it to be circulated chiefly in the great market of Nizhny Novgorod, where for some time Herzen's works had been sold during the annual fair. He visited some of the most active organizers of Zemlya i Volya, among them N. A. Serno-Solovevich, and above all tried to establish relations with representatives of the Raskol.

In Moscow he was greeted by a group of young merchants as 'a prophet called upon to untie the Gordian knot of their difficulties'.[59] They looked upon him as the agent of a powerful movement, which might bring them freedom. But as soon as he began to discuss politics, difficulties sprang up. 'From the very first words, I realized that they did not understand a thing about it, nor did they know what it was all about.' But it is more than likely that Kelsiev in his Confession cunningly emphasized this negative aspect; for though he always clearly informed the head of the Third Section of his own travels, he tried not to make accusations which could lead to trouble for others, and often obviously falsified their ideas so as to make them more innocent than they actually were. Even the young Moscow merchants were more interested in politics than he claimed. One of them asked him among other things: 'What was to be the date of the revolution in Russia? And who was to be President of the Republic?' None the less, it was difficult to find any common ground between these bigots of the *Raskol* and the young Nihilist, passionately concerned with the history of his country's sects. We know that the greatest obstacle lay in a dignitary of the ecclesiastical hierarchy of the Old Believers, who openly refused to have any relations with the London émigrés; but apart from this we have little information. That there were at least some links is proved among other things by the fact that the money for the publication of the *Obshcheye Veche* was provided by an Old Believer bookseller, K. T. Soldatenkov. He too had only vague political convictions, but he later gave considerable help to persecuted Populist writers, among them Chernyshevsky.

Returning to St Petersburg after his visit to Moscow, Kelsiev was introduced by Alexander Serno-Solovevich to one of those old 'non-clerical' believers, who, in the absence of regular consecration after the schism with the Church in the seventeenth century, had gradually renounced the idea of a clergy. Their eschatological doctrines had often identified the anti-Christ with the Tsar. But for some time they had considered this as a purely spiritual and not a political doctrine. Father Pavel, one of their members, made this clear to Kelsiev, who had hoped that such ideas might provide a basis for developing the *Raskol* on revolutionary lines.

Back in London after this exploratory journey, Kelsiev several times tried to find other contacts with Russian sectarian colonies in the Turkish Empire, especially in the Dobrudja. Through his efforts one of their religious and political leaders was sent to London to meet the editors of the *Kolokol*. This man greatly interested Herzen, but once again it proved impossible to establish permanent political relations.[60]

The problem of the *Raskol*, which Kelsiev raised with such enthusiasm, was to remain a live one for the Populists throughout the 'sixties and 'seventies. During this time the sects made remarkable progress. The development of their dogmas and organization reflected the ferment of the peasants and small townsfolk. But despite many efforts, links between the revolutionary intellectuals and the movement which was springing up in the countryside never proved possible. Though they were both products of the same situation, they were too different in nature and origin to find any point of contact. The leaders of the sects and the revolutionaries met chiefly in prison and in Siberia, where both groups, despite their lack of a common language, were driven together by their struggle and opposition.

The *Obshcheye Veche*, which was edited almost exclusively by Ogarev and published at irregular intervals, discussed, besides the *Raskol*, the same problems as the *Kolokol,* though in simpler language. 'Without the opportunity to live freely, there is no opportunity to believe freely.' Such was the basis of its propaganda, and its most frequently repeated catch-phrase.[61] Its political policy centred on the idea of the *Zemsky Sobor,* the need for which was stressed by Ogarev in an article published both in the *Kolokol* and in the *Obshcheye Veche* called 'What the Clergy must do'. Despite the many efforts that Kelsiev made from the Dobrudja, its circulation remained fairly limited and its main importance is as an example of an unsuccessful attempt to reach the small folk of Russia's towns. It was the first paper addressed, as Ogarev said in the first number, 'to the so-called lower classes, open for anyone to join—Old Believers, business men and craftsmen, peasants and small bourgeoisie, domestic serfs, soldiers, in fact anyone not belonging to the privileged classes'. It was the first visible sign of Herzen's attempts to reach those forces which lay outside the intelli-gentsia after his open break with the liberals and the suppression of the more active centres of radical Populism in the summer of 1862. And it pointed out the road which the Populists were to take during the following twenty years.

But who was to direct propaganda of this kind for the people? Who was to organize the first attempts to found a revolutionary movement in Russia? For a long time Herzen hesitated over this fundamental problem, and his doubts prevented him from becoming leader of the secret movements which were gradually springing up in Russia after 1861, and which eventually led to the formation of *Zemlya i Volya.* Ogarev, on the other hand, was more prepared to move in this direction. The discussions held between these two, and with the various young men who came to visit them in London, showed that they understood the full importance of this problem. As early as August 1860, Ogarev had written to Annenkov:

Public opinion cannot be formed without groups and clubs, either open or secret, depending on circumstances. The important thing is that they must have determined ends, and a determined discipline in their work . . . Methods depend entirely on the outside situation, but such groups are in any case quite indispensable.[62]

His experiences of the émigrés in London convinced him that such an organization must not be international. 'Probably only the Italians are sincere about the problem of national independence.' And so a start must be made in Russia only. At its centre must be a press organ, i.e. the activity which had already been begun and developed in London. But the organization must not be centralized on 'Jesuitical' or 'statist' lines. London must exert only moral authority by issuing ideas and general directives. The final purpose was 'social reform'. But to achieve this Ogarev returned to his plans of twenty years earlier, when he had wanted to devote himself to explaining his ideas to the people and accumulating scientific and technical knowledge. As the fundamental problem was the peasant one, he thought of founding related groups, which should devote themselves entirely to preparing plans and instructions for this purpose. In fact, the dreamt-of secret society was to be a means of obtaining material and examining in detail the conditions and demands of the various popular classes: an attempt, in other words, to understand more fully the country which had been so little studied by modern methods.

The initiative for a secret society more directly political in character was not to come from London, from Herzen or even from Ogarev, but, as we shall see, from the new generation. Its scope was largely determined by N. A. Serno-Solovevich, the founder of the first *Zemlya i Volya*. 'For a long time', Ogarev then observed, 'we have been thinking of the need for an organic concentration of forces, but we thought that the initiative should not come from us abroad, but from Russia itself.'[63] When he finally met with a response, Ogarev devoted himself to providing a programme and chiefly propaganda material for the new movement.

Herzen, on the other hand, always remained suspicious and hostile to the conspiracy which was coming into being. The general tone of the *Kolokol* incited others to protest and take action, but it did not consider its own main task to be to act as a centre for the groups which were being organized. Herzen had no faith in the capacity of these germs to develop rapidly. When the first secret paper, *Velikoruss*, appeared in St Petersburg, he greeted it enthusiastically, seeing in it an important attempt to secure final freedom from the censorship. He then encouraged others to start secret printing presses, without ever fully realizing that such ventures were impossible without an organization. It was not till May 1862 that there appeared in the *Kolokol* the first sign of an agreement between Herzen and the clandestine movement, an appeal for funds 'for the common Cause'.

Herzen continued to hope that the intelligentsia would develop in a liberal direction, even though he found it more and more narrow-minded. Even at the beginning of 1861 he dedicated an article on Owen to Kavelin—one of his works, incidentally, which most clearly reveals the origin of his Socialism. He wrote to tell him of this dedication, and sadly recalled how few still 'remained of the *vieux de la veille*'.[64] For this reason he greeted his distant friends with particular affection. But little more than a year later he had to admit that 'Kavelin has now gone over completely to the supporters of Chicherin',[65] i.e. the doctrinaire liberals, the 'Saint-Justs of the bureaucratic system'.[66] For such were the men who as soon as the peasant reforms were completed did everything possible to help the government put an end to further developments, and had turned into a dogma the Emperor's dictatorship and the compromise with the nobility, against which Herzen had always fought. 'We had thought that our literature was magnanimous and that our professors were *apostles*. We were wrong about them. How painful it all is; it upsets us, as the sight of moral decadence always does.'[67] The government knew how to take advantage of the *Kolokol*'s diminishing influence on the intelligentsia. Its propaganda could no longer present those favourable aspects which the Emperor himself had appreciated at its beginning. Alexander's problem was no longer one of overcoming the resistance of the aristocracy and denouncing the corruption of the bureaucracy. Now he had to make concessions to them. No longer was he concerned to allow (within limits) free public opinion; now he had to curb its most extreme features—the revolutionary consequences to which it had given rise. And so supervision at the frontiers was intensified; police methods were employed; agents of the Third Section were sent to London; and, above all, the press was allowed to attack Herzen and to engage in open controversy with him.

Ever since November 1861 the silence imposed by the censorship had, though unwillingly, acted in Herzen's favour. Because the *Kolokol* was the only Russian periodical able to deal with a whole series of forbidden subjects, it was widely sought after and read. Fear of arousing discussions on forbidden problems had encouraged the government to impose silence. But now, relying on the more moderate liberals and the doctrinaires (who were growing more and more conservative), it thought that the time had come to launch an attack, attacking the *Kolokol* at a moment of crisis while there was still no organization capable of counter-attacking.

The police started the offensive with a pamphlet which printed a letter from Herzen to the Russian Ambassador in London, informing him of anonymous threats on his (Herzen's) life. Ridicule was poured on him for considering himself sufficiently important to believe that his life was in danger. Radicals and students tried in various St Petersburg newspapers to counter this first official attack, which also aimed at deceiving the reading public, by openly displaying Herzen's name in bookshop windows.

But this was only the first skirmish. Among the leading attackers was Katkov, a man of the 'forties, who had grown up in the same atmosphere as Herzen, Bakunin and Granovsky. He was a talented journalist and a careerist. He had been through a phase of English-type liberalism, and had then become the mouthpiece of the more conventional members of the intelligentsia. Soon attacks on the 'London propagandists' became fashionable. Every day the *Kolokol* found it harder to reply from a distance. Its means were limited and its distribution was more and more curtailed. Herzen realized that 'the monologue was gradually becoming a dialogue'.[68] He was soon forced to admit that it was not an easy dialogue. This was obviously not because of the arguments used against him, which were old ones, but rather because of the position in which he was placed. On 13th June 1862, Alexander II noted in the margin of one of Katkov's attacks on Herzen 'Excellent article'. He soon deduced the logical conclusions to be drawn from it. Within the month the *Sovremennik*, the *Russkoe Slovo* and the *Den* were suppressed. These, apart from the *Den*, which was the Slavophil review, represented radical tendencies. At the beginning of July, Chernyshevsky and Serno-Solovevich were arrested on the pretext of their contacts with Herzen. And so began a series of imprisonments and interrogations which affected all the *Kolokol*'s closest allies.[69]

In 1863 the Polish revolt put the finishing touches to Herzen's political influence in Russia.

Since 1853 the liberation of Poland had been a fundamental aim of Herzen's activities in London. It was as much an internal Russian problem as one of international politics, and it had once more confronted Herzen with the reciprocal influence of social and nationalist movements throughout Europe.

From the very beginning the *Kolokol* had amply discussed Russia's foreign policy. It had adopted a consistently pacifist line, holding that war would only delay reforms. As Herzen said to Michelet in April 1859, 'Pour l'accouchement il faut la tranquillité, la guerre fera oublier le travail à l'intérieur.'[70] Besides, Herzen's views on this subject coincided with those of Alexander II, who had little inclination for military adventures, after his experiences of the Crimea. When relations with Austria—regarded with great bitterness by Russia's ruling classes who desired revenge for her policies in 1854—became the main problem Herzen clearly said that:

Russia already has her *own* Austria—all the more dangerous because it is an internal enemy.

A few years later, in 1859 and 1860, Herzen, like all European democrats, turned against Austria and favoured the international movement aiming to free Italy. But, thinking of his own country, he added that Russian intervention would only 'have deepened the hatred of other countries against her, while the peoples [and by this he meant the Western Slavs] would have had nothing to gain from it'.[71] Chernyshevsky, too, bravely supported this attitude against the Slavophil tendencies which at this time (under the growing influence of Russian nationalism) spoke of bringing freedom to the Slavs of Central Europe and the Balkans. Chernyshevsky himself succeeded, despite the censorship, in saying that if the oppressed Slavs wanted to know what Russia would bring them, all they had to do was to look at Poland.

It was this last problem which made it so difficult for Herzen to maintain the *Kolokol*'s point of view. His liberal views on internal politics, his appeals to Alexander II, and his general policies which were aimed at avoiding possible obstacles in the way of reforms finally made him quarrel with the most rigid among the Polish émigrés, who thought that he was abandoning his unconditional defence of the cause of Polish independence.

At this time Herzen often spoke of a federation between Poland and Russia. He countered the repetition of the ideas of 1848 (on nationalism) by maintaining Russia's right to her own internal development; and he claimed that he and others had to understand this new situation. He supported Poland's right to independence, but he claimed that independents desired and hoped for a federation capable of solving the social (i.e. peasant) problems of both countries.

He thus both criticized the idea of nationalism, natural frontiers, etc., and at the same time visualized a federation which would include not only Russia and Poland but also the Ukraine. This solution was to meet with a great response among the Ukrainians, who were beginning to revive after the repression which in 1849 had crushed them too. This response was proved by a letter which he received from the Ukrainian historian, N. I. Kostomarov.[72]

In an article of 1859 called *Russia and Poland* he re-examined the whole problem, starting from the general question of nationalism in Europe. 'In the last decade two ideas have arisen from the shipwreck of the revolution of February 1848. They are *pale* substitutes for the interrupted development from a *political* to a *social* revolution. These two ideas, which are closely associated, consist in the recognition of nationalities as personalities with their own rights, and the tendencies of peoples who come from the same racial roots towards political unity.'[73] Napoleon III was the result of this desire 'to subject the problem of revolution to that of nationalism'. Italy and Germany were realizing this programme, and it was time to be aware of it. He might sympathize with the men who were trying to assert the Florentine tradition against 'the unknown inhabitants of the Alps *al piè del monte* who ruin the Italian language in the *provençal* manner'. But this was merely looking back at the past. Italian unity was the only real problem. As for Germany, 'that unfortunate Œdipus among nations, persecuted by some political curse, unable to assert itself in any way after the suicide of the Thirty Years War and the funeral of Westphalia, unable to find help either in the culture of its people or in science or in art—Germany sees that its weakness lies in its divisions, and with all its energies aims at the barrack-room doctrinaire unity of Prussia, merely because this is one step better than that of Austria, which is made up of vice and corruption and survives only through repeated doses of fortifying medicines. I cannot agree with you', he added, turning to his Polish opponents, 'when you say that Germany constitutes a true federation. The impotent and shapeless Diet of Frankfurt, like an empty plate, only conjures up the possibility of food which at present is lacking.'[74] German unity, too, was a historical necessity.

But though such were the problems of Italy and Germany, why should the Slav world follow the example of these countries? 'You claim that I desire a Slav federation under Russian hegemony, out of glory for Russia and for its power and prestige in Europe. Because this will be sufficient for any patriot, you haven't hesitated to seize on this idea. But you are completely wrong. I am even less a *patriot* than a *liberal*.' While Western Europe was engaged in solving national problems, in Russia the reforms were beginning to raise social problems. To allow these to strengthen, and to be able to save the new seed contained in Russia, he gave second place to the problem of Polish independence and spoke of a federation.

In March 1860 he wrote to Proudhon, suggesting that he translate *Russia and Poland* for his review, and explaining his position even more clearly than he had done in the *Kolokol*.

Pour moi la Pologne représente la *vieille civilisation* dans le monde slave, et cela dans toute sa beauté tragique, avec tous les avantages du malheur, avec des grands souvenirs, avec des aspirations de liberté, de catholicisme (éclairé!), d'aristocratie (radicale!)—tout cela est beau, mais tout cela n'est pas viable. *Nous*, les russes, nous haïssons notre double passé: la tradition moscovite et la *statistique* de Pétersbourg, nous sommes les *gueux* du genre humain, notre race est mêlée avec des Tartares, des Finnois, des peuples thuraniens. La civilisation occidentale nous devient haïssable dès qu'elle hésite à franchir le ruisseau pour entrer dans le socialisme. Le peuple, le moujik, le dissident, l'homme des champs—n'a rien de commun avec Pétersbourg. Notre aristocratie ce sont *des Tartares promus aux rangs d'Allemands*. Le peuple apporte en place du *droit du travail* le droit gratuit *à la terre*, l'organisation communale, le partage de la terre, la possession en commun et les associations ouvrières.[75]

But as early as 1861 the violent clashes between social and national problems, between Poland and Russia, which Herzen hoped and thought could be avoided, arose in all their urgency. On 25th February, a few days after the decree which freed the serfs, there was a demonstration in Warsaw which left five dead on the pavements of the city.

And then, despite his criticisms of nationalism, and although he knew full well how dear it would cost his cause to move the problem from an internal one to one of conflict between peoples, Herzen called his article in the *Kolokol* of 15th March 1861 'Vivat Polonia', and once more resumed his resolute defence of the right of that nation to fight against the despotism of St Petersburg. On 1st May of the same year he clarified his position still further in an article called 'Mater dolorosa', in which, although he expressed his hope that the break could still be avoided, he unhesitatingly took the side of the victims.

Ogarev tells us that when Martyanov, the peasant merchant from the Volga, read this article, he came to Herzen and said, 'Alexander Ivanovich, today you have buried the *Kolokol*. No, you will no longer be able to resurrect it. You have buried it.'[76] Though not immediately true, two years later, on the outbreak of the Polish rebellion, the prophecy was justified, when Herzen, despite heavy doubts, finally made his choice of sides.[77]

The first negotiations between the *Kolokol* and the Polish émigrés who were preparing the revolution were entrusted to Bakunin, who threw himself into them with far more enthusiasm than Herzen and Ogarev; either because these activities seemed to him (and in fact were) a continuation of his activities of 1848 and 1849, after his years of imprisonment and exile in Russia, or because of his revolutionary and conspiratorial temperament.

In 1862 one of the representatives of the 'Reds' came to Paris to meet General Ludwig Mieroslawski. The 'Reds', as opposed to the 'Whites', who were typical exponents of the aristocracy and ultramontane Catholicism, represented the small nobility, the soldiers and above all the lower urban classes. But agreement between Bakunin and Mieroslawski, who was an old fighter for freedom both at home (in 1846 and 1848) and abroad, where he had fought in Sicily for Garibaldi, was impossible, either because Mieroslawski despised Bakunin personally or, more likely, because their social and national ideas did not correspond. Bakunin spoke of the 'Poland of serfs'. He saw the revolution as a peasant war; whereas the General, like many of the Polish 'Reds', although they were prepared to make concessions, did not wish to move too far in this direction. Further, Mieroslawski had only one idea—the re-establishment of Poland within its historic boundaries, i.e. the territorial limits of 1772 which included not only Lithuania and White Russia, but a considerable part of the Ukraine. Bakunin countered with the rights of self-determination, both because he was convinced by this principle and had little respect for historical rights, and because he realized that a return to the situation of 1772 would have made it quite impossible for any section of Russian public opinion—at that time far from hostile to Polish aspirations—to support the insurrection.

Herzen too was worried by this problem. He was even more convinced than Bakunin that the only way to support Poland was by way of propaganda. He had already made concessions in the *Kolokol*. In 1861 he supported the reunion of Lithuania and Poland, driven to this by the extent of the movement of protest against Russian rule in that land.

May Poland thus win with her freedom, heroic struggles, misfortunes and brotherly feeling for her neighbours, everything that the dead despotism of St Petersburg is losing through slavery . . . This is the only way to solve the human problem of frontiers. This solution is stronger than all historic rights or violence of arms.[78]

Herzen's and Bakunin's policy thus consisted in supporting the movement of protest and revolt against Russia where it was really deeply felt, without giving way to the dreams of the émigrés. But although Bakunin made every possible concession to Mieroslawski, no agreement between them could be reached. Besides, it soon became clear that the General represented only one portion and not even the decisive portion of the 'Red' Poles, though he claimed that any agreement with the Russian émigrés ought to be made only through him.[79]

The alliance which Bakunin had tried in vain to reach in the ranks of the émigrés was at this very time being arranged on the spot between the Central Polish Committee of Warsaw and a group of Russian officers linked to *Zemlya i Volya*. One of the organizers on the Polish side was J. Dombrowski, who later became one of the military leaders of the Paris Commune. On the Russian side, there was a young officer Andrey Afanasevich Potebnya, one of the most heroic figures of the clandestine movement of the 'sixties. In June four Russian soldiers were shot as a result of these contacts, but the central core survived. Twice, in summer and in November 1862, Potebnya managed to come to London to make agreements with Herzen. The *Kolokol* was able to publish letters from Russian officers which spoke of the difficulties which they had to overcome and of the suspicion which met them everywhere, but which reaffirmed their intention not to fight against the Poles. They did not conceal the difficulties of their situation, but bravely linked their fate to that of the rebellion.[80]

After these contacts had been made on the spot the émigrés, who were preparing the insurrection and travelling between Paris and Warsaw, began to draw up an agreement with the Russians, using London as a base. At the end of September an agreement was finally reached between the Polish delegates and Herzen, Ogarev and Bakunin.

Herzen himself has told us of the meeting in his memoirs. He did not disregard the fact that the support which they would be able to bring would be small and scarcely organized; it would consist in little more than spreading the ideas of the *Kolokol* in Russian society. Nor did he conceal how inopportune he thought an immediate revolution. As regards the political programme, he insisted on 'a recognition of the right of the peasants to the land they worked, and equal rights for all peoples to decide their own fate'. He fully realized, as he said to Bakunin, that on the Polish side this was a purely formal concession without much practical importance. Herzen remained sceptical about these pacts, but Bakunin insisted on the agreement being signed, and did much to narrow the differences between the Poles and Herzen with a view to overcoming his doubts. Despite all these difficulties, a real agreement was reached. But its terms clearly reflect the uncertainties which had dominated the discussions.

At the end of 1862 Herzen was still telling his Polish friends that he had little faith in the success of the insurrection. The repression in Russia during the summer of that year, which had struck at the *Sovremennik* and all the forces of freedom, inevitably confirmed his view that it would be very difficult to bring practical help from the Russian side.

Si vous avez la moindre sympathie pour la liberté russe—he wrote to a Pole on the 22nd October—et si votre amour pour la liberté polonaise l'emporte sur votre douleur, si vous craignez de faire des victimes inutiles, alors je vous supplie de ne faire aucun mouvement, car il n'aurait aucun succès et mettrait les deux libertés en péril en préparant un nouveau triomphe au cabinet tzarien. Savez-vous pourquoi la réaction triomphe toujours? Parce qu'elle joue en toute sûreté dans toutes les circonstances, tandis que nous, nous jouons au hasard. Avant que M. Ogarew vous écrivit une lettre, nous causâmes longtemps ensemble, ainsi je vous expose ses propres sentiments là-dessus. Croyez à la sincérité de nos sympathies. Mais, songez-y, que pouvons-nous faire si nous ne vous voyons pas en état de remporter une victoire contre votre plus grand ennemi? Remarquez qu'en Russie la consternation règne de nouveau dans les esprits, consternation produite par le faux mirage des réformes et des changements . . .[81]

But though he tried to bring the Poles round to his point of view in private discussions, the *Kolokol* maintained a steady line. It supported and encouraged all the attempts made in Warsaw and St Petersburg to take every possible step in favour of Poland, and above all it protested against the measures of the Russian government. These measures—such as the general mobilization of the young men of Warsaw—were now aimed at provoking rebellion so as to be able to crush it. Herzen maintained this standpoint even when the revolt broke out at Warsaw without the group of Russian officers belonging to *Zemlya i Volya* being warned: a move which led to more clashes and suspicions. None the less, Potebnya and a few of his followers succeeded in joining the insurgents and fighting with them. In April 1863 he fell in an attack on the Russians.

But on the international plane Herzen wanted to make clear his differences of opinion with the Poles. Both in Warsaw and among the émigrés, European support for the revolt was considered certain. Special hopes were placed in Napoleon III. When, on 28th January 1863, Herzen heard the first news of the insurrection, he greeted it with an article, 'Resurrexit', which was a pledge to throw all available forces into the struggle. But, he asked, 'What will Europe do? Will it once more stand aside and do nothing?' His answer was clear: 'Yes, it will stand aside.'[82]

A month later he continued this dialogue, but added, '1863, however, is not 1831. Europe may still be the same, Russia is not.' He then gave the first news of the founding of the secret society *Zemlya i Volya*. The *Kolokol* to some extent became its free spokesman abroad, and Herzen made himself one of its centres of organization. He wrote fairly optimistically about the Polish revolution to Ogarev:

Despite everything, the Polish cause still holds and will soon develop. We must spread propaganda about this, and I utterly disagree with your opinion that we should make known in our press their stupid and disgusting behaviour [i.e. the lack of warning to Potebnya's Russian officers].[83]

Bakunin tried to make the Poles agree to his personally taking part in the revolution. Their unwillingness increased as the Poles realized how small was the help that the Russians could provide. Bakunin's Russian legion remained no more than a project. He left for Stockholm, where he remained about a year, and succeeded in arousing among the Swedes a certain amount of sympathy for *Zemlya i Volya*. Though he certainly exaggerated its importance at this time, he made propaganda about it with all his accustomed energy, even though he had no direct contact with it. He also made some ties with Finland, where he hoped to arouse a movement which would constitute a valuable diversion for the Poles. He took part in the unsuccessful naval expedition which set out to bring a few hundred Polish émigrés from England to Lithuania, and which was eventually intercepted by the Swedish government.

All these brave efforts were unsuccessful. They merely deepened his quarrels with Herzen, and encouraged him to adopt more and more radical conclusions on social questions. Eventually they led to the formulation of his anarchism. When the Polish revolution was almost suppressed in April 1864 he said that he was still convinced that 'only the bloody prologue called *The heroic collapse of the nobles' democracy* is over. Now it is the turn of the Polish serfs, whom the Russian government will never be able to break or to satisfy.' The Polish revolutionaries who survived after the armed struggle, the hangings and the deportations would understand that 'the future of Poland, like that of all the Slavs, depends on the peasants, and there is only one way of salvation for all—the "red" social, geological revolution'.[84]

But meanwhile the Russian government was accompanying its terrible repression with a series of proposals for agrarian reform. These were designed to take advantage of the urban and aristocratic character which the revolution was assuming by satisfying the peasants' ambition for land. Herzen, like Bakunin, was particularly aware of this aspect of the Polish problem, and had done everything possible to persuade the Poles of its fundamental importance. Now, in the *Kolokol*, he spoke of 'His Majesty's Communists' —the Russian troops who with one hand destroyed all liberty, and with the other promised to give land to the peasants. Thus, he said, events had brought about paradoxically and tragically what Martyanov had idealized as the 'Tsar of the land', 'the Tsar and Stenka Razin together', who was to help the peasants to free themselves from the upper classes. 'A *jacquerie* approved of from above!' Such was the strange appearance that the social problem had assumed in Poland.

Although Herzen always countered this with a 'moral principle', and although he deeply felt the shame of his country's policies and vigorously said so, yet in private letters he had his moments of despair. Writing to Bakunin on 1st September 1863, he said:

On whose side are social principles? On the side of Diemontowicz (one of the leaders of the Polish insurgents) or on the side of the St Petersburg satraps, who are giving the nobles' land to the peasants? Of course, one cannot march with Muravev [the 'hangman' who was chiefly responsible for the oppression of Poland]. But sometimes one must immolate oneself and work on calmly. This would not be a *calamité publique*. One must defend one's own cause or not do anything . . . The alliance with the Poles was impossible.[85]

He was saved from despair by his deeply rooted and violent disgust for Russian nationalism, which was then being unleashed throughout the press, and which was really responsible for the government's policies in Poland despite all their 'social' appearances. His finest articles of this time were directed against such 'syphilitic patriotism'.[86]

The *Kolokol* was attacked both by the liberals of earlier years, and by the Slavophils, for whom nationalism provided a new *raison d'être*. 'All the worst in the Russian character, everything that has been corrupted by slavery and the tyranny of the nobles, by the bluster of government services, and the absence of all rights, by the stick and by secret informers—everything has floated to the top, decked out with liberal frills',[87] he said in June, calling his article 'Protest'. In August he added:

Patriotic exacerbation has brought to the top the Tartar, the petty country squire, the sergeant, everything that floated in us like a half-forgotten dream. Now we know how much Arakcheyev there is in our blood, how much Nicholas I there is in our brains . . . The Slavophils can now rejoice, for the national *fond* of the period before Peter the Great is not changed, at least as regards its barbarism, its hatred for the foreigner and its indifference to judicial rights and methods of punishment . . .[88]

By the end of 1863 *Zemlya i Volya* was only a 'myth', and the best of the young officers who had fought for Polish independence were dead. Herzen could only defend the principles which had inspired them to take part in the Polish revolt against the nationalism which he had forecast would arise from the struggle between the two nations.

When this duty had been accomplished he turned to his fundamental faith and to 'defend his own cause' and 'work calmly'. The period of reforms was over, the Polish revolt had been crushed, and Herzen once more returned to the kernel of his political faith, not Bakunin's 'geological revolution' but the *obshchina* of the Russian peasant.

'The social religion of the Russian people consists in recognition of the inalienable right of every member of the *obshchina* to possess a determined part of the land', as he explained to Garibaldi in a letter of 21st November 1863, written in Florence. This letter is the best evidence of Herzen's thoughts at this time. 'We say to the peasant there is no freedom without land, and only add this: land is not secure without freedom. Our banner is very prosaic and sensitive souls and sublime minds consider it very materialistic . . . Yet the fact is that the peasant is a poet all right, but definitely not an idealist.' And he added:

Just when everything was being worked out and in a state of flux; just when a ferment was rising from the very heart of our national life—under the influence, on the one hand, of emancipation and the beginning of an organization, and, on the other, of the concentration of the forces of the minority; just when the troubles of the government were at their worst, and the Winter Palace was hesitating between liberalism and autocracy: in the middle of all this, the Polish insurrection burst upon us. For us, it was primarily a disaster, and only the prostituted government press can accuse us of having tricked the Poles, by promising them that Russia was ready for a revolution. We knew that nothing was ready, that only the seeds were there, that the groups of young officers were only beginning to be formed. We would have given our blood to hold up the Polish revolution for a year or two. But what could we do . . .? In any case, the Poles had the right to decide the time and inevitability of their revolution. We had to accept their decision and stand on the side of justice and freedom, and this is what we did.[89]

5. N. G. CHERNYSHEVSKY

HERZEN CREATED POPULISM; Chernyshevsky was its politician. He provided
Populism with its most solid content, and not only gave it ideas but inspired
its main course of action. This course was modified during the 'sixties and
'seventies, but it undoubtedly originated in the short but brilliant publicizing
activities undertaken by Chernyshevsky between 1853 and 1862.

Even in the history of Populism in which persecution figured so largely,
there were few fates so tragic as that of Chernyshevsky. Few were as aware
of destiny, few so certain that their activities would be brought to such a
rapid end. This awareness was tempered neither by the martyr's religious
exaltation nor that collective power which sustains conspiracies. He was not
even convinced that his own sacrifice would be of any real use to the cause
to which he had devoted himself. He was merely a politician fully conscious
of his own energy and of his intellectual powers. He once said that men such
as Cobden and Bright were his ideal. Yet he knew that he would be capable
of accepting twenty years in Siberia with the same resolution as these English
politicians would accept a parliamentary defeat. He knew that the circumstances were very different; yet against these circumstances complaint was
useless: they merely had to be taken into account when planning his activities. Herein lay the tragedy of his fate. The translation of Populist Socialism
into active politics cost Chernyshevsky his life.[1]

He was born on 28th July 1828 at Saratov, a town on the lower Volga, the
only large centre on the river between Samara and Tsaritsyn.

Saratov was typical colonial territory. It started as one of the wooden
sixteenth-century fortresses which marked the eastward expansion of the
Muscovite State, its victorious struggle against the Tartar hordes, and
the difficult opening of a commercial route with Persia and the East along the
Volga. It was at first colonized by the growing Russian population which
followed this route, and in the eighteenth century by foreign immigrants,
specially Germans. Signs of this remain in the town now called Engels,
facing Saratov across the river, which before the war was inhabited by
peasants of German origin. Even today, Saratov marks the boundary
between Asia and Europe, between the old oppressive Russian colonization
and the world of the Tartars, Kirghiz and peoples of Central Asia. A century
ago this was even more apparent, and when Chernyshevsky was born in the
town, which then contained 50,000 inhabitants, the demarcation between
the Russian State and the social and national forces which lived beyond it

was clearly in evidence. Saratov had been typical Cossack territory, with free peasants who owed allegiance neither to landlords nor to the Tsar, men recruited for his armies or in revolt against him. It was still one of the most characteristic lands of the *Raskol*, the schism in the Russian Orthodox Church which followed the ecclesiastical reforms of the seventeenth century. The *Raskolniki* still had some of their main refuges along the Volga, and these were the most active centres for the creation of new religious sects and beliefs throughout the eighteenth and nineteenth centuries.

Saratov, like all these regions along the Volga, provides one of the most interesting examples of this history of the Russian border. For centuries countless different forces had met here: State centralization; varying races; peasant revolts led by Stenka Razin and Pugachev; the corporative and international interests of the traders with the East. And the basis of this internal colonization was the industry of the patient and stubborn Russian peasant.[2]

In 1863, in the Peter-Paul fortress in St Petersburg, Chernyshevsky began to write of the Saratov he had known as a boy and youth in the 'twenties and 'thirties. He wanted to explain 'the impressions and ideas of that middle-class generation' which had grown up in the old lands of our Mother Russia'.[3] His family chronicle extended its scope, and ended by forming a large fragment of the autobiography which he aimed to write in prison but which he never completed. And twenty years later, in the summer of 1884, in exile at Astrakhan, he turned back to his early youth; but once more he completed only a fragment. In vain he tried to substitute a spurious literary vitality for the genuine inspiration which dried up with his violent removal from political life and direct contact with daily problems. Yet his pages about the primitive life of Saratov are among the finest that he ever wrote. From a mere observer of the slow change of habits between the eighteenth and nineteenth centuries he at times rises to the stature of an historian of the poor society of his own early years, and his Populist outlook throws a new light on the daily life of this provincial city between Europe and Asia.[4]

In these tales an important part is played by the hard daily fight for life, a fight against huge packs of wolves; against bands of brigands and horse-stealers; against the Kirghiz who came to seize the Russian peasants and take them off in slavery to the principalities of Central Asia; against epidemics of cholera; and against the misery which turned men into lifelong drunkards. But it was a world full of humanity, made up of patient resignation, respect even for chronic drunkenness as a terrible necessity, and an instinctive understanding of those who reacted against the oppressiveness of life by becoming 'holy fools' (*yurodivy*). One of these Chernyshevsky described in a portrait that seems remotely autobiographical. He seems to identify himself with one of these men who 'loved the ironical and humorous turns which still further complicated his allegories and embarrassed his hearers who were not quick thinkers. Often they did not know whether he was teasing them or speaking seriously, whether he was praising or blaming. Besides, this is how a *yurodivy* must express himself.' Chernyshevsky well knew that this was the impression that he frequently made on his own listeners, when he expressed himself through paradoxes and when the contrast between his beliefs and surrounding atmosphere was too great. In the poor 'inspired' lunatic he saw a human quality not unlike what so many were to call his 'Nihilism'.

But this was not all. Life on the Russian border included not only a deep religious respect for all the elementary needs of life and a primitive simplification of everything; Chernyshevsky also saw in it the seeds of 'realism'. By this he meant an instinctive rejection of what he called 'the phantasmagoric',[5] i.e. all the rhetorical fantasies which were employed to justify wars and hatred, the useless trimmings of an existence which was basically simple and ruled by elementary needs. Writing of the life of his ancestors at Saratov, he said that it was from them that he drew his conception of history, which was based 'on his personal acquaintance with the life of the masses'.[6]

When in prison, he was amused by the works of English historians on the Crimean War—which spoke of the ambitious dreams of the Russian people, distant visions of the cupolas of Santa Sophia in Constantinople—and he contrasted them with the real interests of his town during this period. He compared what was said of Russian religious fanaticism and the war for Orthodoxy which they were supposed to have launched against the Turks, with the deep-seated popular tolerance for all religious faiths which he had known in his birthplace, where Moslem, Protestant, Orthodox and heretic had lived freely together.

This popular tolerance, based on direct experience of a hard and difficult life, lay at the basis of the lesson in realism which Chernyshevsky recognized in his memories of childhood and youth. 'A simple human glance at each single episode of life was the way things were done in my family; my "old folk" were people of good sense.'[7]

His 'old folk' were all ecclesiastics. For generations they had been priests in the villages round the Volga. When there were no parishes available, they became peasants. When, on the other hand, they had exceptional luck, as did Chernyshevsky's father, they were summoned to one of the churches in Saratov. The lives of these priests were of a patriarchal simplicity, and often not easily distinguishable from those of their peasant parishioners. Chernyshevsky tells us, for instance, that only at the beginning of the nineteenth century did his family begin to use tea and sugar. When his maternal grandfather went from his own parish to Astrakhan, he thought it a good plan to take a sugar-loaf to the Bishop as a sign of respect. He bought this on the journey, making an agreement with the merchant that if the Bishop did not accept the gift, the merchant would take it back again. He himself considered it utterly unnecessary.

Chernyshevsky's father had made striking progress. His library, which mirrored the theological culture of the day, consisted of the lives of mediaeval saints and early eighteenth-century treatises. Among these were, of course, the works of Feofan Prokopovich, the reformer of the age of Peter the Great and the teacher of generations of the Russian clergy. These treatises were in Latin, which had been a window on the West before Russians had learnt to speak German or French. Chernyshevsky, who had been carefully taught Latin by his father, often wrote to him in that language.

Even as a child he was enormously fond of reading. He began by learning the classical languages, much Latin, a little Greek, and a good basis of Hebrew; as well as French, English, German and Polish. He knew these languages, to which he later added Italian, well enough to be able to read with ease, though he was never able to speak them correctly. He also studied Persian, and enough Tartar to allow him to be able to make a detailed inquiry into those names of Tartar origin in the district. Among these he listed Saratov itself, which means 'yellow mountain' or 'beautiful mountain'. His father, a teacher in the town's religious institutions, used his contacts with the small circle of local nobles to borrow non-religious books for him and he soon became interested in these. He then read everything that reached Saratov, from George Sand to Pushkin, from Gogol to Belinsky and Herzen's early works.

In few cases do we have such a vivid picture of the spread of culture to Russia's provincial towns, a spread which was greatly accelerated at the beginning of the nineteenth century. What might (and no pun is intended) be called the cult of culture, a faith in its healing force—which we find so often in modern Russia and its equally important counterpart in the form of Rousseauist and Tolstoyan negation—springs from the spread of culture at the end of the eighteenth century. It was a powerful tool to divert men's minds from their everyday world. Chernyshevsky himself compared this phenomenon to that which occurred in Germany in the eighteenth century, when there had arisen a whole generation of enlightened scholars, born of clerical families. Nor was he wrong in this comparison, though his personal experience emphasizes the more specifically Russian aspect of the phenomenon. In Russia it was more rapid and more revolutionary than in any other part of Europe, because it introduced two distant and different worlds —the culture which came from the West, and the life of the regions round the lower Volga.[8]

After he had completed his theological studies, his father decided not to make him continue his clerical career, perhaps because, even at this stage, he had constant clashes with his superiors. And so he sent him to the university of St Petersburg. Chernyshevsky was always deeply grateful to his father for this decision, for it was in St Petersburg that he found himself.

We can follow his development very closely; indeed, at some periods, daily, for he kept a diary from May 1848 onwards. This is a work of the greatest interest. It contains, for example, a full record of his reactions to the revolution of 1848. It shows the effect that a great historical event could have on a man who was materially and—at least initially—spiritually far removed from it, even in a country like Russia where the dominant desire was to remain isolated and react only to stifle its consequences. Yet Chernyshevsky drew from the European events of these years the faith of his life. His Populist Socialism, like that of Herzen, was born of the experiences and disappointments of these years.[9]

In the capital he led an ascetic life, either through lack of means or on principle. He determined to follow to the letter the moral code he had drawn up for himself; for example, not to know a woman until he was married. These principles, which were chiefly religious in inspiration, remained fundamentally the same even when their clerical significance gradually began to lose importance in his eyes. When in prison ten years later he translated Rousseau's *Confessions*, he was struck by the similarity of his own experiences to those of Rousseau.[10] But his personal life receives less emphasis in his diary than might be expected. Though his ideas on human relationships must have been taking shape at this time, he spoke of them chiefly later, when he came into contact with the new generation of the 'sixties, and described them fully only in his novel of 1863 *What is to be done?* The outstanding features of his university career were his yearning for culture and the initiation of his political life.

'I am a self-taught man', Chernyshevsky once wrote,[11] and what he learnt certainly did not come from his teachers. For, as the revolution in the West struck deeper roots, persecution in St Petersburg grew more severe. The university more and more took on the appearance of a barricade raised by Nicholas I against the spread of Western ideas. In his diary Chernyshevsky speaks of this in cold and detached terms, adopting the attitude which he later maintained when faced with reactionaries. He wished to understand the reasons for their activities, and to try to comprehend them as men and political forces. At the university he viewed the rector 'with hostility, of course, but chiefly with a sort of pity or scorn. There he is, a little old man sitting down; his lips and indeed his whole body seem to have been dropped, as usually happens with old men. This ruin arouses a certain feeling of pity, and yet it is put in a situation where it can guide or suppress the movement of living forces (not really living forces, but at least those that show some sign of not being completely decayed). And so this ruin assumes a threatening and stupid attitude, and shouts, when it ought to be praying to God from an old Voltaire armchair.'[12]

This portrait gives us all Chernyshevsky's views on his university. He merely learnt there how to extend his study of Russian mediaeval documents, which had already begun to enthral him at Saratov, and which he now continued without reaching any conclusion.

But his real preoccupation he described in one of his first letters home in July 1846: the works of the philosophers Schelling and Hegel, and the historians Herder, Niebuhr, Ranke and Schlosser.

He was astounded not to find the complete works of Hegel in the university library, which was 'pretty poor',[13] but it did not prevent him reading this philosopher several times during his years at the university. Eventually he knew him sufficiently well to feel throughout his life that he had belonged to the generation which had based its thought on Hegel. He understood him well enough to be able to appreciate his power and, later, to realize the poverty of thought in the triumphant positivists of his own generation from Comte to Spencer. He revered him as the philosopher who had provided some of his fundamental ideas, and he turned to him each time that he considered the problem of historical development. And yet it cannot be said that he passed through a truly Hegelian period. In one of his notebooks he wrote what he had found essential. 'Hegel is great for the idea of development . . . An eternal struggle, an eternal movement forwards, which in substance is a gain and which in form brings back the end to the beginning';[14] in short, the dialectic. But later he met with an obstacle which prevented him from feeling a real Hegelian. In January 1849, after reading what Hegel had written on ethics and morality, he noted in his diary:

He seems to be a slave of the present situation, of the present organization of society, so that he cannot even make up his mind to reject the death penalty, etc. He draws only modest consequences . . . The characteristic of his philosophy is to avoid stormy transformations, thoughts which dream of perfection, to be *die zarte Schonung des Bestehenden*.[15]

In 1888, in a preface (written in the third person) to one of his own works on aesthetics, Chernyshevsky gave a brief account of his intellectual development. He said that when he was still at Saratov he had come across Hegelianism as interpreted by the Russians (i.e. Bakunin and Herzen), and that later in St Petersburg he had been disappointed when he had been able to read Hegel in the original. He was unable to get over his ponderous style and apparently scholastic mentality.

The Russian interpretations of the system were influenced by the German Hegelian Left, and so when he came across Feuerbach he was already prepared to accept him. 'He then became a follower of this thinker, and until the time when the necessities of his life [i.e. his arrest: the formula used to avoid censorship] put an end to his studies, he read and re-read him closely.'[16] In 1849 he obtained Feuerbach's first book, and he came to know this and others of the same philosopher 'almost by heart', as he wrote in a letter from Siberia in 1873.[17]

Closely related to his philosophical development of these early years was his abandonment of religion. In the first two years of his stay in the capital he had not only remained closely tied to the rites of the Church but, to use the words of one of his contemporaries, 'he was almost a fanatic'.[18] From his diary we can see how fearful he was, even as late as 1848, of following the logical consequences of his philosophic studies and abandoning the religious life which was so closely bound to his family and childhood. He ended an examination of his conscience with the words, 'Thy Will be done, O Lord', as if yielding up his spiritual evolution to God. When he read Feuerbach's *Das Wesen des Christenthums* in March 1849, he was already convinced of the worthlessness of rites and exterior Church forms, but he still believed in the dogmatic kernel of orthodoxy and in 'a personal God, and the possibility and reality of revelation'.[19] Reading Feuerbach, he anxiously wondered once again whether he would be convinced by him or not. He hesitated for about a year. In July 1849 he was no longer clear about his religious ideas; they now seemed to him the result of habit rather than conviction. 'I myself do not know whether I believe in the existence of a personal God, or whether I accept Him as do the pantheists, Hegel or, better, Feuerbach.'[20] At the beginning of 1850 he was still brooding over these doubts: 'If my repudiation was more courageous, I would become a follower of Feuerbach.'[21]

In the course of that year he succeeded, though not without much inner conflict, in overcoming this lack of self-confidence, of which his diaries and even his later writings give us so many examples. From then on he became a follower of Feuerbach. What he had looked for in religion still survived in his constant anxiety about the relation of ethics to life. He worried, too, over the pattern that life would take on for those who dedicated themselves to an ideal. And traces of his old religion reappeared in his description of the 'new men' fighting against the surrounding world as a community of the elect. But from the end of 1850, the content of this religious need was exclusively political and completely detached from the tradition of the Church.

His political development followed a parallel course. He himself has told us when this process began: February 1848, the revolution in Paris.

Before this he had greedily absorbed all the French and English literature which reflected the feelings and social anxieties of the century, from George Sand to Dickens, from Sue to Byron. But, unlike the generation that had immediately preceded his own, he was no longer affected by these writers, For him they were only a sort of preface for his political development. Many of them, indeed, bored him. European romanticism had not had time to mark him deeply, before he was faced with problems of a far greater urgency, of Europe itself in revolution.

He could accept with great meekness of spirit the political lessons which came from the West, chiefly because in his heart he had already utterly condemned the state of affairs in Russia. Even as a boy of eighteen he had come to the conclusion that everything in his own country had to be begun again from the start. He felt—as did Chaadaev and, to a very much lesser extent, Bakunin and Herzen—an attitude of Christian humility towards the Western world. This humility he expressed by admitting the complete worthlessness of Russia's past, and determining to make a clean sweep of the history of his country, so as to create something really new and valuable.

This was partly a result of the effect on his peculiarly sensitive conscience of the contact between the closed and primitive world of Saratov and the world of culture. His development in these years reveals a simple and sincere psychological attitude which is often found in modern Russia; the complete scepticism which is necessary so as to be able to begin everything again. He asked in 1846:

What have the Russians given to Science? Alas, nothing. What has Science contributed to Russian life? Again, nothing. Did not Descartes, Leibnitz, Newton all live in the seventeenth century? What of us? Is our mission just to have an army of a million and a half and the power, like the Huns or the Mongols, to conquer Europe if we so desire? Should we not pity the existence of such peoples? They have lived as if they had not lived. They passed like a storm, destroying, burning, imprisoning, plundering everything—and that is all. Is our mission too to be of this kind? To be omnipotent from the military and political point of view, and nothing as regards any other, superior aspect of national life? In that case it would be better not to be born at all than to be born a Russian, as it would have been better not to have been born than to have been born a Hun, Attila, Genghis Khan, Tamburlaine or one of their warriors and subjects.[22]

In the summer of 1848 he said that his political creed could be summed up as 'admiration for the West and the conviction that we Russians count for nothing compared to them. They are men, and we are children. Our history has developed on other principles. We have had no class war, or it has scarcely begun . . .'[23]

Although later, when he convinced himself that he could do useful work in Russia, this lack of confidence diminished, it still coloured his mind and gave his activities an air of modesty. It prevented him from hoping, with Herzen, in a great future mission for Russia. Indeed, it made him attack all manifestations of this romantic notion, and gave his political activities a clear and exact limitation.

This despair in Russia's past and existing situation gave him the strength to devote himself entirely to his political ideas; and inspired him to look for these ideas in revolutionary Socialism. From afar he saw that this was becoming the popular force in the Paris of 1848; indeed it was the only force capable of completely renewing society. His Socialism prevented him turning this radical lack of faith and repudiation of the past into paradoxical despair, as Chaadaev had done. Thus his initial negative judgment on Russia was transformed into a passion for action and the determination to change completely the political and social structure of his country.

In July 1848 Chernyshevsky wrote in his diary that he: 'was more and more being convinced by the ideas of the Socialists'.[24] Already he felt the need to translate these convictions into Russian. What could the words 'revolution' and 'Socialism' mean in his own country? He answered that the only hope lay in a peasant revolt. 'The only thing that is lacking is unity between the various local risings.' But it was not easy to give unity to these fragmentary and widely dispersed movements. Organization had to begin from nothing. Still full of doubts, he turned to the past and chiefly to Pugachev's revolt which, in the eighteenth century, had shown the force of Cossack and peasant bands but which 'had none the less eventually been crushed'.[25]

A strong incentive to solve these problems was provided by the links he established with some of his school friends and some of the young writers of St Petersburg. Though none too enthusiastic, he eventually found himself on the fringes of the movement which had its centre in the Petrashevskist groups.

In August 1847 he had made the acquaintance of M. Mikhailov, and there is evidence to show that it was he who introduced Chernyshevsky to the problems which were absorbing the intellectuals of the capital.[26] Chernyshevsky formed a close friendship with this young man, who was to make a sensitive translation of Heine and take part in the movement that followed the emancipation of the serfs, and who died in Siberia in 1865, one of the first victims of the reaction.

In December 1848 Chernyshevsky also met one of the first men whom Petrashevsky had converted to Fourierism. This was Alexander Vladimirovich Khanykov, three years older than him, who, as a student, had been dismissed from the university for bad behaviour. He was one of the most ardent supporters of Fourier's theory of the passions, and he spoke of this at a banquet which was held in his honour by the Petrashevskists in April 1849. He was condemned to death and then reprieved and sent to Orenburg as an ordinary soldier in a regiment of the line. In 1853 he died of cholera in the fortress of Omsk. He introduced Chernyshevsky to the works of Fourier, and made him join the group of men who were discussing the possibility of applying Fourier's ideas in Russia. In this circle he also met Debu, the Fourierist who was interested in the peasant *obshchina*. He wrote in his diary of 11th December:

At Khanykov's we spoke chiefly of the possibility and the approach of a revolution in Russia. He showed himself more intelligent than I, pointing out the many elements of disorder which already exist, such as for example the *Raskolniki*, the organization of the peasants in *obshchinas*, the discontent of most of the government officials . . . All this rather worried me, because as Humboldt says of earthquakes 'suddenly the solid and immovable *Boden* on which I was standing upright and which I believed to be absolutely firm began to swell like the sea'.[27]

Chernyshevsky soon absorbed the spirit of this group of young men. Many years later, one of those who had been present at the evenings in Vvedensky's house, a literary friend of his, remembered him 'with his red hair and shrill voice, strongly supporting the fantasies of the Communists and Socialists'.[28] Naturally, the arrest of the Petrashevskists, which he heard about on 25th April 1849, made a strong impression. It constituted the link between his youthful enthusiasm for Socialist ideas and a maturer political conception.

5*

He wrote in his diary that the policemen who had arrested his friends 'deserve to be hanged'.[29] From then on he knew what life held in store for him, and understood that the road he was choosing would lead eventually to Siberia.

At this time he was reading books which the Petrashevskists had shown him, chiefly Fourier, Considérant and a few pamphlets, which popularized this Socialist current. He was interested in Fourier for the same reasons as were many of his contemporaries. For them he was an acute psychologist, and for Chernyshevsky he constituted a touchstone for his own religious ideas. Fourier made him reconsider all his ideas on personal relations, and eventually convinced him, leaving deep and permanent traces on his moral beliefs. But, on the political plane, Chernyshevsky's rationalist spirit was inevitably prompted to criticism. The principle of *association* seemed to him the only solid kernel. Yet he could not help wondering how much this belonged specifically to Fourier rather than to the whole Socialist tradition. What he knew of Louis Blanc seemed to him to be of greater political importance and of the two French Socialists—between whom he was torn in 1848 and the beginning of 1849—he eventually showed a certain preference for the second.

In fact at this time he was undergoing the same experience that was occurring throughout Europe. The various Socialist sects were beginning to flow into wider currents, more in contact with fundamental political and social problems. And the uncertainty that Chernyshevsky felt in choosing between the various 'democratic Socialist parties'[30] was merely a sign of the growth in him of a new vision of Socialism, born of his indirect experiences of the revolution of 1848.

This vision sprang chiefly from the instinctive disgust he felt for the liberalism which, in the France of 1848, had shown itself so incapable of dominating the situation. He noted in his diary: 'I do not like gentlemen who say "Freedom, freedom", and then restrict this word to laws without carrying it into life; who are prepared to abolish laws which speak of inequality but not to touch a social order in which nine-tenths of the population are made up of slaves and proletarians. The problem is not whether there should be a king or not, or whether there should be a constitution or not. It is, rather, one of social relations, and lies in the fact that one class should not suck the blood of another.'[31] He ended with a real prayer: 'O God, grant victory unto Truth.' The disappointments brought on by the increasing reaction, the progress of which he noted daily in his diary, led him during the following months to grow still more scornful of the ruling classes, and to condemn more and more energetically their 'contempt for the lower classes'.[32] More and more he felt that his place was with the latter.

Politically he thought for a moment that the only force capable of establishing true equality lay in dictatorship. Thinking of Russia, he said that any form of dictatorship, even a despotic monarchy, would be of use against the aristocracy.

It must stand above all classes, and is specially created to protect the oppressed, i.e. the lower classes, the peasants and the workmen. The monarchy must be sincerely on their side, must be at their head and protect their interests . . . Its duty is to use all its energies to work for future equality—not a formal equality but real equality . . . To my way of thinking this is what Peter the Great did.[33]

The history of the English and French revolutions, which he was studying in the works of Guizot and Buchez, temporarily confirmed these ideas. Only a dictatorship was capable of 'moving forward'.[34] Only a dictatorship would be able to solve modern problems, especially those raised by Socialism. Reading Lamennais, Proudhon, Louis Blanc and Cabet, he grew more and more certain that they were right and that the only means of realizing their ideas lay in a dictatorship, in absolutism.

So he too had reached that inevitable turning in the road, which had earlier been traversed by the travellers of the preceding generation: the myth of a despotism capable of fighting the serf-owning nobility. He too, in his own way, was passing through the crisis which had turned Herzen and Bakunin into disciples of Blanqui.

But his experiences of the reaction throughout Europe, including Russia, soon led him to the contrary belief. And this he held throughout his life. Nicholas I was far from being on the side of the peasants, and he was imprisoning his Socialist and Fourierist friends. Throughout Europe despotism, whether in traditional or Bonapartist varieties, was the weapon which was destroying the dreams and ambitions of the working classes. Chernyshevsky suffered deeply. He wept when he heard that Robert Blum had been shot in Vienna. 'May his blood fall on their heads, and may their blood be shed for his . . . I have prayed for some minutes for Blum, and yet it is a long time since I prayed for the dead.'[35] These wounds (so deep that for a time they revived the half-forgotten faith of his youth) made him not only a Socialist and a revolutionary but as capable of criticizing the liberals as he remained constant in his love of liberty. Many years later, when serving his sentence of forced labour, he said that on the day the Berlin National Assembly had been dissolved he had wandered, weeping, through the streets of St Petersburg. When a friend had asked him what had happened, he had said, 'I am walking and I do not feel the tears flowing.'[36] In 1849 the expedition against the Roman Republic enraged him, as did the war of Nicholas I against the Hungarian revolution. At the beginning of the year he still thought that France and Germany would at last march together against Russia, but one by one his hopes for a revival of the revolution collapsed.

In January 1850 he again summed up his political ideas. 'The important thing is that power should be given not *de jure* but *de facto* to the numerous and lowest class—the peasants, wage-earners and artisans.' But he had now lost all his illusions in despotism. 'It is merely the peak of the aristocratic hierarchy, to which it belongs body and soul.' As for Russia, 'the sooner it collapses the better'. It was merely holding up the class struggle for the

benefit of the aristocracy. 'We welcome the oppression of one class by
another, for it will lead to a struggle, and then the oppressed will know
who it is who is oppressing them in the present order of things and that
another order is possible in which there will be no oppressed. They will
understand that they are not oppressed by God but by men . . . Far better
anarchy from below than from above.'[37]

All hope of immediate action to this end was only a dream, in view of the
oppressive political and intellectual reaction which prevailed in Russia, a
dream almost as bizarre as the one (of discovering perpetual motion) that
he had secretly cherished in his university days. He was still 'thirsty' for a
Russian revolution, and this aspiration, though violent, was also desperate.
He said that he was prepared to accept a revolution even if 'for a long time,
perhaps for a very long time, it could lead to no good . . . Anyone not
blinded by idealization and able to judge the future from the past, must not
be frightened despite all the evils that revolutions bring at first. He knows
that one can expect nothing else from man, and that peaceful development
is impossible.'[38] But what could be done? He felt himself more and more
alone and isolated. And so when he had completed his studies at the university and was offered a post in a school at Saratov, he returned to his native
town.

In Saratov he continued his studies and discussions with the historian
Kostomarov, who was exiled there for organizing a conspiracy in the
Ukraine similar to that of the Petrashevskists. Some time later he married,
after clearly warning his bride what life held in store for him. 'The people's
discontent with the government, taxes, civil servants and nobles is growing.
Only a spark is needed to set everything alight. Already the number of people
in the educated classes hostile to the existing order of things is growing. So
even the spark which will set this fire alight is ready. The only doubt is when
it will occur. Perhaps within ten years, perhaps earlier . . . And if the fire
starts, despite my cowardly nature, I shall be incapable of not taking part.'
'With Kostomarov?' his bride asked. 'No, he is too noble, too poetic, he
will be afraid of the dirt and the massacres. I am not afraid of dirt, nor of
drunken peasants with sticks, nor of massacres. And how will all this end?
Forced labour or hanging . . . Are you upset by this talk, because I can't
talk of anything else? It will go on for years on end. And what fate can lie
in store for a man who thinks like this? Here is an example for you,
Iskander.'[39] He then told her the story, or rather the legend of Herzen, a
strange mixture of the fates of Herzen and Bakunin, including a demand by
Nicholas I for Herzen's extradition. In 1850 Chernyshevsky said that, 'he
admired Herzen more than he admired any other Russian, and there was
nothing he would not do for him'.[40]

Although he often doubted his own powers of constancy and his courage,
Chernyshevsky cherished the idea of following in Herzen's tracks and exerting
a serious revolutionary influence on his time. He knew that he had acquired

a far wider culture than most of his acquaintances. He also knew that there was only one way open to him if he was to achieve his ambitions: modest literary work in the face of constant oppression by the censorship. The lack of courage of which he spoke—which in fact was chiefly due to the scruples of a sensitive nature—was being transformed into a patient, cold determination to do whatever was possible.

A typically provincial quarrel, provoked by the Bishop of Saratov concerning Chernyshevsky's ideas and teaching methods, though it was fortunately soon stifled, made him decide to return to St Petersburg and in May 1853 he was back in the capital once more. For nearly a year he lived on small literary ventures, preparing his thesis. In 1854 he took up the teaching profession again for a short time, but gave it up as soon as he was able to work with some regularity in one of the principal reviews of the time, the *Sovremennik* (The Contemporary), which had been Belinsky's mouthpiece during the last years of his life. Within a few months he had imposed his own personality and ideas on the review.

We have the distinct impression that he was at first concerned with aesthetics and literary criticism, mainly because it was only in this way that expression was possible. Only thus, and even then with great difficulty, could he find it possible, if not to expound, at least to hint what he was thinking. History, philosophy, economics, not to speak of politics which were completely excluded from the *Sovremennik*, were forbidden ground for anyone like Chernyshevsky—a follower of Feuerbach, a Socialist and a revolutionary.

But the study of aesthetics was the activity for which he was least suited. It was not that he lacked a strong feeling for the humanity which is expressed in poetry or a firm belief in the freedom which the poet needs or the autonomy of his art. But being a politician he was naturally prompted to reason about these matters from the political point of view. He accepted poetry and literature as private nourishment and a support for his activities. He regarded poetry as an influence whose importance for himself and for others he fully appreciated. But he did not see the need of constantly perfecting his judgment. And so he saw in art only the tools of politics or ethics. Or he estimated artists only according to the width and depth of their convictions, according to their greatness as men. And so his judgments often impress us as much by their obvious political bias as by their intelligence and energy, derived, however, not so much from aesthetic intuition as from the vividness of his eye and a sincere and passionate understanding of men.

This is best shown in his fine letter to Nekrasov in September 1856.[41] In it he defended, against the 'civic' tendencies of Nekrasov himself, the freedom of the poet 'which consists in not setting arbitrary bounds to his own gifts, but in writing what is in his own mind. The poet Fet would be helpless if he tried to write of social problems. This would only lead to nonsense . . . Gogol was utterly free when he wrote *The Government Inspector*, because it was the nature of his talent that prompted him to do so; whereas

Pushkin was not free when, under the influence of the Decembrists, he wrote his *Ode to Freedom*.' Chernyshevsky was always convinced of this. Yet he considered Nekrasov (and he told him so) the greatest Russian poet, greater than Pushkin and Lermontov, because he found in his poetry sentiments akin to his own and the ability to create a literary world which was similar in many respects to his own political world.[42]

And so when he decided to choose poetry as the subject for his thesis and wrote a short book on the *Aesthetic Relations between Art and Reality* Chernyshevsky was prompted less by a straightforward interest in art than by the desire to ventilate his own ideas, and in particular those drawn from Feuerbach's philosophy, which he had adopted for himself.

This book, a tardy fruit of the controversy of the post-Hegelian generation, is interesting only as evidence of the changing cultural climate. Chernyshevsky in 1855 was the first writer to turn his back on the tired echoes of Schelling and Hegel which still survived in the official culture of the university. The discussion which his dissertation aroused was a pointer: one of the first symptoms of the intellectual revival which developed rapidly after the end of the Crimean War and the accession of Alexander II. It was important because it was so little concerned with aesthetics and so much with subjects which were really beginning to interest people.

Chernyshevsky himself said this in a criticism of his own work which appeared over a pseudonym in the *Sovremennik*. The review was one of the first causes for his break with men like Turgenev, who were genuinely interested in literary problems. His self-criticism provides a striking example of the particular style of which Chernyshevsky later became a master—the style of a man prepared to use every ingenuity in the battle with a rigorous, stupid and inefficient censorship, and to continue to stimulate the reader, even though he knew it was impossible to say directly what he thought.

'Are aesthetic problems really important?' he asked. 'One may well doubt this, seeing that the author himself is not convinced of it. In fact, aesthetics do present a certain interest in the realm of thought, because the solution of aesthetic problems depends on the solution of other more important ones.'[43] Under the guise of an aesthetic treatise he wanted to encourage men to abandon romantic dreams which always accompany 'a man in a false position'[44] and which had their origin in the fact that 'we are too miserable in real life'.[45] He urged the reader not to be deceived by useless perfection, but rather to create a realistic mentality, 'a practical conception',[46] in other words, to be men before spending so much time on the discussion of literature and poetry.

There was, however, one real issue: 'Literature and poetry have a far greater significance for us Russians than they have in any other country.'[47] This was not merely an observation of the fact that literature flourished because other intellectual activity was impossible. It contained rather an important historical judgment on the part that literature had always played in the formation of the ruling class and the intelligentsia—a part which elsewhere had been played by religion, political ideals, etc. He developed this idea in his *Essays on the Gogol period of Russian literature*. This was not intended to be a history of literature, but rather a demonstration of its importance in the life of the nation from Gogol onwards. It was in short a history of criticism and culture during the last decades.

In fact he was consciously picking up the threads which had been broken after Belinsky's death and the reaction which followed 1848. He was re-examining the problems of relationship with the West, popular traditions and the State. He had now moved beyond the confession of humiliation, which he had made in Russia's name at the beginning of his student life in St Petersburg, when he had claimed that Russia had achieved nothing in the field of ideas. He began instead to write a history of what had actually happened from Gogol onwards, the history of the preceding generation and the spirit of his country. Though he was much distracted by the constant need to discuss immediate issues and so was unable to write a true history, none the less his essays are essential for an understanding of the intellectual discussions of the 'thirties and 'forties.

He looked back directly to the Westerners, seeing in them the one thread of genuine progress in Russian culture. The Westernism to which he referred was still shapeless, before the controversies which split it at the end of the 'forties. As for the Slavophils, he followed Herzen's example. They were merely dilettantes who thought that they could claim originality, whereas in fact all their ideas were derived from European romantic philosophy.

Belinsky's real strength, he said, lay in not having been afraid, as the Slavophils had always been, to take action which would change, or 'spoil', the Russian character by bringing it into contact with the rest of Europe. At the basis of the Slavophil position he saw merely a lack of self-confidence in themselves and in the Russian people. The Westerners had had the great merit of affirming that it was essential to begin not from the traditions of the people but from an imitation of the West; not from the national spirit but from universal ideas. Russian criticism had therefore been right to judge authors by the value of their ideas. Their work lay in education rather than creation.

Chernyshevsky's essay was a careful study of the development of Russian intellectual life but it contained also a programme for the immediate future. Criticism must continue to make writers aware of the exceptional responsibility which historical circumstances had laid upon them. In them 'was concentrated almost the entire spiritual life of the country. In countries whose spiritual and social life have reached a high degree of development, there exists, if we can put it in this way, a division of labour between the various branches of mental activity; whereas with us there is only one—literature.'[48] In a word, Chernyshevsky's critical programme lay in the formula *littérature oblige*.

These ideas underlay all his writing during his first years on the *Sovre-mennik*. For example, in a criticism of a collection of songs of various nations published in Moscow in 1854, he attacked that form of *narodnost* which was a kind of more or less traditional nationalism.

Narodnost develops parallel to general human evolution; but only education gives content and full growth to individuality. Barbarians are all identical, whereas all civilized nations are distinguished by a clearly defined personality . . . The history of all countries shows this. The French character was worked out only when, under the influence of the classical, Italian and Spanish world, general education spread in France . . . The situation is very different when all efforts are concentrated on a content which belongs directly to this or that people . . . We find a typical example of this in a country and period very close to us. We have only to remember the sad story of the Teutomania which did such harm to the rebirth of Germany, which began so brilliantly under the inspiration of the Emperors Joseph II and Frederick the Great, and Lessing, Kant and Schiller . . . A concern with originality kills originality itself, and true independence is only possible for the man who does not even think of the possibility of not being independent. Only the weakling talks of his strength of character. And only the man who is afraid that he will be easily overcome is afraid of exposing himself to the influence of others. Current preoccupation with originality is a preoccupation with form. A man who has any real content will not worry overmuch about originality. Preoccupation with form leads to emptiness and nullity.[49]

He always fought against an excessive cult of folk-lore, patiently explaining what had been its consequences in Germany. He was particularly amused by the example of the Grimm brothers who had started from a national reaction against the French and had then, at the end of their researches, come to the conclusion that German traditions and fables were common to all other European peoples. All his criticism was aimed at encouraging writers to educate the Russian people, fully aware that they could only do this if they were inspired by universal ideas and not by the vain glorification of a national tradition.

To illustrate these ideas, he wrote an extensive biography of Lessing, which was published in instalments in the *Sovremennik*. He explained that in the eighteenth century Germany was two hundred years behind France and England, but that after fifty years of the Enlightenment it had succeeded in laying the foundations of its great literature, which were crowned by the birth of a poetic genius, Goethe. But to achieve this, enlightened despots, even Joseph II and Frederick the Great, had not been enough. What had been needed was the work of an author such as Lessing.

It may well be that almost no one at the time was aware of the German people's sad need to consider literature as its most important asset, in the absence of other direct resources of historical activity. However that may be, for half a century all the best energies of the nation instinctively turned to literature, and in literature the German nation found the springs of a new and better life, and slowly but firmly raised the great edifice whose earliest foundations are in Lessing's *Literary Letters*.[50]

Chernyshevsky did not complete this work, both because, by bringing out the parallel between eighteenth-century Germany and contemporary Russia, he had already made his point, and also because the situation in Russia was now changed. 'The sad need' of speaking only of literature seemed at last to be overcome.

Chernyshevsky often turned back later to the Crimean War, which removed Russia's last chance of remaining in the state of social, political and intellectual paralysis that had marked the final years of the reign of Nicholas I. The war had been the cause of the developments which had led to the period of reforms, and which had made people think and the government act. But what was the real strength of this initial impulse? Was it really as powerful as men thought in the 'fifties? Living through these events in St Petersburg, the problem must have seemed fundamental to him. But we have only indirect evidence of the conclusions he then reached. He returned to this problem in 1863, in the Peter-Paul fortress, when translating and annotating a book on the Crimean War by an English M.P., A. W. King-lake.[51] But this book directed him to international rather than specifically Russian aspects of the war. It was not until he was in Siberia between 1865 and 1868 that he tried to give his impressions of the years that immediately followed the war. This was in the form of a novel, which he thought of calling *Prologue of the Prologue*. This was to show that he planned to look upon the period during which the peasant reform was being prepared as the prologue to the hoped-for revolution, or at least to a revolutionary movement. This autobiographical fragment, his finest work, compared the defeat of Russia in 1855 to that of Prussia in 1806. Both had led to similar profound internal changes and reforms, chiefly in peasant serfdom, the army and government organization. This comparison was a common one at the time, and was made chiefly by the liberals; but Chernyshevsky referred to it primarily to emphasize the differences. 'As if', he said, in an imaginary conversation with a liberal, 'the allies had conquered St Petersburg and Moscow as the French had then conquered Berlin, and the Russian government only held Perm as then the Prussians only held Memel!'[52] It was a mistake to think that the Crimean War had struck such a serious blow at the Russian empire. It forced Alexander II to carry out reforms, but it allowed him to control their size and speed, and left in his hands all the power he needed to counteract the elements of dissolution and change which had been unleashed by the war. These results were far removed from his dreams of 1848 of what would be the consequences of a European war against Russia, and they confirmed his belief that it would still be long before the forces which had been defeated in 1848 could be really revived. It was important not to exaggerate the movement which had been set in motion by the Crimean defeat. This often made him bitterly sceptical of his activities, effective though they were between 1855 and 1862.

At first this realistic outlook made him underestimate the chances of reopening the problem of serfdom. He was convinced that Lessing and Belinsky must for some considerable time continue to be his models and that he must confine himself to literature and polemics. In the autumn of 1857 he still thought that the forthcoming edict would not advance the peasant problem from general discussion to the statute book. He thought that the rights of matrimony would be altered to make serfdom slightly less oppressive, and that the nobles would be asked to sign contracts with their peasants and establish laws to regulate their obligations. 'A continuation in fact of the edict of 1842.'[53] Chernyshevsky was thus even more pessimistic than the situation warranted. When in November 1857 the decree declaring the Sovereign's intention of freeing the serfs was published, Chernyshevsky agreed that 'the principles determined were more liberal than had been expected'.[54]

It is probably this feeling of surprise that explains why he welcomed this promise with such pleasure and deep satisfaction. His article for the second number of the Sovremennik in 1858 is at least as enthusiastic as the one that Herzen published at the same time in London. Once again his prose seems informed with religious feeling—the feeling that as a boy had made him pray when he heard that Robert Blum had been shot on the barricades of Vienna. 'The blessing which is promised to the peacemakers and the humble will crown Alexander II with a joy which has never yet crowned any of the rulers of Europe, the joy of having alone begun and completed the freeing of his subjects.'[55]

So it was really true that 'the great reform' was beginning, the reform which would eradicate what had been considered by all liberals since the time of Catherine II as the root of all evil. The Emperor had had the merit of raising the problem; the question now was the old one of whether the intelligentsia would have the strength to compel the government to carry out the reform with the greatest possible amount of justice to the peasants and in such a way as to encourage the civic and economic development of Russia.

Now was the time to unite. All intellectual forces must be combined, and the old quarrels between Westerners and Slavophils forgotten. The idea of a union between all branches of the intelligentsia was widespread at this time, and Chernyshevsky tried to bring it about in the review which he directed. The Sovremennik was the best and most widely read journal of these years, and largely due to his labours it had acquired a considerable influence on public opinion. And so in 1858, Liberals and Socialists fought together against the conservative and slave-owning nobles who opposed the reform. It was the culminating year of the revival that followed the Crimean War, the Russian risorgimento of the 'fifties.

The rescript of 20th November 1857 had determined the fundamental points of the controversy. The nobles were to continue holding all the land, the peasants would be given their houses only in return for a fee, and would be allowed to hire land in return for a rent either in money or work. All peasants organized in 'rural societies' would be subject to the landlords' police.

Three problems at once came to the fore, problems which conditioned the various currents of opinion among the emancipationists and which took first place in Chernyshevsky's thoughts. Would the emancipation really be 'without land' thus turning the peasants into labourers or tenants of the nobles? If this were not to be the case, what fee would they have to pay? Finally, how would they be administered if they were not prepared to accept a typical relic of serfdom—such as the plan suggested—by continuing to be subjected to the landlord?

Chernyshevsky could not answer these questions directly. Censorship allowed only a truncated discussion during brief moments of tolerance, which it followed with months and sometimes years of silence. All this showed that the government intended to direct the reforms itself, and to complete them— in the words of Alexander II—'from above and not from below'. To do this it was prepared to destroy any possible peasant revolt, and to keep all other social forces such as the various currents of the nobility, the bureaucracy and the intelligentsia firmly bridled. The intelligentsia was to be given the smallest amount of freedom necessary to bring the reforms safely into harbour, and no more.

For Chernyshevsky therefore the problem was to take part in the discussion as far as was possible, concentrating on single aspects of the reform and, at the same time, establishing a few general principles capable of guiding it to a conclusion in line with his convictions.[56]

His answer to the problem was, like Herzen's, a defence of the *obshchina*. Since 1857 he had begun a campaign on these lines, and he continued to develop it during the following years. By defending the *obshchina* he rose above the discussions on Russia's past and established a link with the Slavophils, who were to have appreciable influence on the reforms. In so doing he also indirectly defended the interests of the peasants, by insisting that the emancipation should take place 'with land'. And at the same time he introduced a principle of Socialism into the discussion, by maintaining the superiority of a system of landholding that was at least potentially collectivist in character against those who supported individual tenure. And so in modern terms the *obshchina* represented for Chernyshevsky a means of defending the class interests of the peasants and at the same time a nucleus from which cooperativism and collectivism might develop in the countryside.[57]

His views on the *obshchina* were entirely Western in origin. They were derived from Herzen, of course, and also from Granovsky but not from the

Slavophils. He did not look upon the *obshchina* as a typically Russian institution, a characteristic of the Slav spirit in opposition to the rest of Europe, but only as a survival in Russia of forms of social organization which elsewhere had now disappeared.

Criticizing an article of Granovsky on the subject, he wrote:

Among the Slavs—and specially among the eastern Slavs who turned to agriculture as the fundamental pursuit of their life later than the Germans—traces of collectivism have survived far more than among the Germans. Without realizing that these were only relics of the old pastoral and hunting life, some writers have claimed that the *obshchina* was unknown to the Germans, and that for the Slavs it was not merely a historical phenomenon linked to a certain phase in their development, but rather an innate feature of their character, not to be found in other peoples and enabling the Slavs to achieve the ideal of human life. These people have not observed that with the development of agriculture and civilization, the *obshchina* disappears even among the Slavs, as it has disappeared everywhere, and that it is now far weaker than it was thirty or fifty years ago. We cannot consider here what are the economic ideals of the future. But we are all agreed that it would scarcely be consoling to imagine this future as a reproduction of Europe from the fifth to the tenth centuries. Future ideals will be realized by developing civilization, and not by the futile glorification of the relics of a distant past which is now disappearing.[58]

He had written this in 1855. But two years later the problem of emancipating the serfs made him appreciate the need to defend the peasant *obshchina*. But even then, though he looked upon it far more optimistically and favourably, his Westernism always prevented him indulging in romantic or nationalist enthusiasm. It was he who prompted the Slavophils to consider the economic and administrative aspects of the *obshchina*; neither the Slavophils nor even Herzen were able to convince him of its value as a myth.

His ideas about it began to crystallize when, in 1856, he read an article published in the *Russky Vestnik* by Chicherin, a young historian and jurist.[59] Chicherin maintained that the *obshchina*, far from being a relic of tribal or patriarchal organization, had in fact originated and been developed as a feature of the State and feudal administration of Russia. It had been first a community of peasants on the land of the nobles, and then a product of the fiscal policy of the State. These articles hit their target as a criticism of the Slavophils, and to Chernyshevsky they seemed to refute the power of peasant customs throughout the centuries. Disputing Chicherin's purely juridical view of the situation, Chernyshevsky recalled the stubbornness of agrarian collectivism, the periodical redistribution of the land and the village communities throughout Russian history. 'Into whosesoever's hands ownership of the land passed, the peasants who lived and worked on it went on farming and dividing it according to their old traditions.'[60] The discussion was thus removed from considerations only of the law, and assumed an immediate political tone. The liberals deduced from Chicherin's thesis that just as the

State had founded the *obshchina*, so it could and should dissolve it. Chernyshevsky, on the other hand, posed the problem whether it contained a social force which could be defended and developed along collectivist lines.

In 1857 Chernyshevsky began to insert these ideas on the agrarian community into a comprehensive picture of Russia's economic development. He thought it obvious that his country, following the example of the rest of Europe, would soon begin a phase of rapid industrial and commercial development. Russia was entering the age of capitalism.

Until now a significant proportion of our production has been achieved by almost patriarchal means. Without even talking of agriculture, where this is obvious, the greater part of our internal commerce and even a considerable part of the processing of our raw materials have been carried out by means which are more in keeping with the eighteenth than with the nineteenth century. But this will only last a few years more.[61]

Impressed by the economic revival which followed the Crimean War and the development of foreign trade, the building of railways, the importation of foreign capital, etc., Chernyshevsky seems to have been too optimistic about the pace at which capitalism in Russia would evolve. The example of Western Europe was there for all to see, and he drew a picture of French and English capitalism, chiefly from the point of view of agriculture.

Unlimited competition has sacrificed the weak to the strong, labour to capital . . . The holders of the small strips of land into which France has been divided are unable to use the most suitable methods for improving their fields and increasing their harvests. In England, on the other hand, the farmers possess capital. This means that without considerable capital it is not even worth thinking of becoming a farmer. As people who have a lot of money are always only a small proportion of the population, so the majority of the population in the English countryside is made up of hired labourers whose situation is exceedingly painful. In industrial production all the tools are concentrated in the hands of the capitalist; and for every capitalist there are hundreds of proletarian workmen whose existence is wretched.[62]

Developing these ideas, Chernyshevsky gave the readers of the *Sovremennik* a full and detailed picture of all the social problems that had absorbed European Socialists since the English industrial revolution. At the same time he reviewed the history of the ideas and attempts that had been made to solve these problems. 'A vast revolution is occurring in the West. In France it has already undergone many severe crises.[63] In England it has given rise to Owen and the Chartists. There is no doubt about the eventual success of this cause, because historical necessity imposes it. But it is terrible to think how much time and effort it will require, how much suffering and loss it has already cost and how much more it will still cost.'[64] The entire movement had been guided by one fundamental idea: the association of workmen. This had been expressed in different ways by Owen in England and by the *ateliers nationaux* in France. By its very nature this was an economic and social movement, latent in all the varying political systems of Europe and born of problems that went far deeper than these systems.[65]

'We must not lose the example of the West . . . We still have time to profit from this lesson. Now, while we are still only foreseeing these changes, we must prepare for events and control their development.'

And so the problem which was of such concern to all the Populists began to interest Chernyshevsky. Could Socialism be achieved in Russia before the complete development of capitalism, before the collectivist roots of Russia's traditional country life were utterly destroyed—roots which might ensure a different and less painful economic development than that of Western Europe? In 1857 he still thought that this was possible. He explained to his readers that it would be pointless and harmful to destroy the *obshchina* and then have to re-create it after the victory of Socialism. Attacking a liberal who spoke of a possible and distant 'Third Period' after the pre-capitalist and capitalist epochs, Chernyshevsky said that: 'The rapid movement of modern economic history prompts us to say that we won't have long to wait for this third period.'[66] Not even thirty years, he added, but the figure was too exact for the censor and it had to be removed. None the less, while waiting for this near future, the important thing was to retain the collective elements which already existed in the countryside, and to include them in the general economic development of the country. For the time being the *obshchina* was a promise for the future and a guarantee that development would be achieved more humanely than elsewhere.

He then explained how he visualized the future of Russian agriculture, if the reforms took into account the experiences of the West. Once serfdom was really abolished:

a large proportion of the land will be held as private property, i.e. will be able to be bought and sold according to the laws of competition. And so anyone of enterprising spirit will have a vast opportunity to acquire property for himself and hand it down untouched to his descendants . . . But these private estates will be dispersed like islands of varying sizes in a far greater mass of State and collective properties. This mass of land will be used, as it is already, as an everlasting capital to satisfy the inalienable right of every citizen to have his own strip of land.[67]

The *obshchina* could thus ensure the right to work, and would guarantee bread for whoever wanted it. While capital would find employment in private property—providing an experimental field for the development of means of agriculture which would gradually spread everywhere, even to the peasants in the *obshchina*—collective land would continue to belong to all. 'There are two classes of people', Chernyshevsky said. 'One is particularly gifted and energetic and would willingly stand up to competition and enjoy risks, and the other is made up of ordinary people who only want to live a secure life.'

For the first there is the wide field of private property in which everything depends on money, ability, talent and energy. But the second needs a stable life with means to work, independent of the change of fortune. These people will obtain this through

State property organized in *obshchinas* . . . The fatherland is under an obligation to do no more than guarantee to all its sons the means for a decent existence. But this it is obliged to do. If I have the chance of finding better I can give up my share in the State land and seek my own private property. And if I am unsuccessful, I can turn once again to my mother—the land—and obtain from it what I gave up when hoping for better.[68]

So collective property would constitute the great guarantee against poverty.

But Chernyshevsky did not envisage the *obshchina* merely as a way to realize the *droit au travail*. As he himself pointed out it contained also the germ of an *organization du travail champêtre*.[69] Taking his examples from Haxthausen's book, he showed that the *obshchinas* were generally based on the egalitarian redistribution of strips of land, sometimes every year (though he considered this the worst system because it took away all incentive for improvement), more often at intervals of ten or twenty years. In this funda-mental form, which was more widespread, although the land was held in common it was farmed individually. But there were *obshchinas* in which these two aspects were combined. This was the type he obviously preferred, for it was better adapted, he said, to the use of agricultural machinery and technical progress. 'Certainly there is an immeasurable difference between them. The first merely prevents the growth of a proletariat; the second leads as well to an improvement in production, and so it is much more useful . . .'[70] ' The need to establish this type of management will in time become exceed-ingly great in Russia, as it already is in Western Europe.'[71] So he looked upon the *obshchina* as an elementary and primitive form of cooperative, which could develop into a more modern variety and thence into an agricultural collective.

He hastened to add that such a development of the *obshchina* must be voluntary and follow general economic progress. It was 'still too soon' to speak of agrarian collectivism. 'We must confine ourselves to urging this and pointing out its advantages . . . Our regular readers will not need this information to be assured of what we think about these problems. Without goodwill and voluntary agreement, nothing useful can really be done for the good of man.'[72]

This was the basis of Chernyshevsky's defence of the *obshchina*; his other arguments were concerned with relatively secondary problems. To those who objected that it held up technical progress, he answered that, on the contrary, it was the only way of bringing progress to the countryside and yet avoiding destitution. To those who brought up the example of America, he said that this merely showed that the State ought not to grant land as private property but rather to use land to guarantee food for all. And to those who foresaw an industrial development which would arrest the invest-ment of new capital in agriculture, he answered that Russia would after all remain primarily an agricultural country for a long time to come.

In his *Criticism of philosophical prejudices against the obshchina*[73] of 1859, he puts these ideas in a dialectical form, which was derived from the dialectic of historical philosophy. This revealed his development as typical of the 1848 generation.

We are not followers of Hegel, still less of Schelling, but we must admit that both systems rendered great services to Science through their discovery of the general forms by which the historical process moves. The fundamental result of this discovery lies in the following axiom: In its form, the higher stage of development is similar to the beginning from which it sprang.

He answered those who upheld the belief that progress was a straight line, and that individual property represented a higher stage of historical evolution, by pointing to this constant return of history on itself, 'the spiral of historical progress', as it had been called. He gave many examples based on facts derived from the philosophy of nature and history, from social and political institutions, and claimed that the *obshchina* confirmed this. He gave a detailed picture of the development of land holdings, which had begun from communal tenure and had then grown more complex throughout human development and were now reverting to collectivism.

This would be merely a striking play of the imagination, a brilliant shape to give his political ideas, did it not contain *in cauda* the argument which lay at the centre of his hopes and those of all the Populists. This was the possibility that Russia could benefit from the experience of Europe so as to move directly to a Socialist economy or, as he said, 'skip all the intermediate stages of development or at least enormously reduce their length and deprive them of their power'.[74] In a vivid picture, similar to Herzen's of some years earlier, he said: 'History, like a grandmother, is very fond of its grandchildren. *Tarde venientibus dat non ossa sed medullam ossium*—and when Western Europe tried to get at the marrow it cut its hands badly on the broken bones.'[75] He hoped that history would fulfil the saying that the 'last shall be first'. To bring this about he wanted to use the experience of the West to guide Russia to a more rapid and humane economic development.

As his early hopes that the peasant reform could be achieved radically and fairly declined, Chernyshevsky devoted himself in 1859 to an 'absolute' defence of the *obshchina* as a principle.

It is true that the united campaign of the liberals and the Socialists, directed by Herzen's *Kolokol*, had gained one fundamental point. Contrary to what the rescript of 1857 had said, the emancipation was to take place 'with land'. The peasants were to be given not only their houses but also the land which they had farmed. The reasons for the government's concession were clearly pointed out by Chernyshevsky himself in a memorandum which he sent to Prince Constantine Nikolaevich, a brother of the Emperor and a member of the Central Committee for the peasant problem. He was one of the members of the court who had done most to hasten the emancipation.

The Emperor cannot want disorders in the State; and freeing the peasants who are now serfs of the landlords without land would inevitably lead to serious disturbances. By conviction, the Russian peasant cannot understand or accept such a liberation. If the reform took this line (from which God preserve us—and He surely will through the Emperor's desire) the peasants would attribute this misfortune to the nobles, whom they would accuse of thwarting the Emperor's will, which was favourable to them. They would rise like a man against the landlords to free—so they thought—the Emperor from a conspiracy of evildoers.[76]

Once again the State was faced with the obstacle which had delayed the reforms for so long. But this time the problem had been overcome by looking to public opinion for support, and in various ways compelling the more reactionary landlords to accept the principle of emancipation 'with land'.

But the victory had been bought dearly, so dearly that Chernyshevsky doubted whether it had been worth it. Land would be given to the peasants, but how much, and at what price? Within the limits allowed by the censorship, there was widespread public discussion on these problems: and all classes of Russian society capable of following the events of 1858 and 1859 cogitated upon them in private. The question led to the division of the emancipationists, and to the formation of two currents: Liberal and Populist (or, as it was then called, Radical).

Chernyshevsky succeeded (despite difficulties imposed by the censorship) in explaining to the readers of the *Sovremennik* what he thought about this problem. The peasants ought to pay nothing for the land which they had farmed until then. He claimed that this was the peasants' own opinion and that far from thinking that they would have to pay a fee, they were asking what would be done with the landlords' property. The lands in question were those which had not been divided into strips and granted to them, but which they had, nevertheless, always farmed in their *corvées*. 'Will they still belong to the landlords, or will they too be given to the peasants?'[77] Chernyshevsky knew that the idea of giving all the land to the peasants was not feasible and he only used it as a threat, and a way of making the nobles understand the situation which was developing in the countryside. The immediate problem was that of the peasant lands, and here the landlords had no right to assert themselves. They must recognize the age-old assumption of the peasants that once their servile status was abolished this land would automatically belong to them. This would constitute true emancipation; a fee would merely oblige peasants to buy land which they were convinced was already theirs.

But in 1858 and 1859 Chernyshevsky could not maintain even this second position. He looked upon it sometimes as the target towards which his activities should be directed, sometimes as a scarecrow which was useful to frighten the more conservative landlords. But he knew that no section of Russian society was yet ready to accept such a solution: neither the nobles, the State, nor even the peasants. Indeed the calm and patience with which

the peasants were waiting for the reforms from above was all the more
remarkable in view of the increase in disturbances which had taken place
during the Crimean War.

So instead of discussing the legal and political problem of the peasants'
right to the land, he concentrated on the economic question of how to carry
out the reform in a way that would make the peasants powerful enough to
be able to live on the lands which they were granted, and the landlords
rich enough to free their property of debts; how in fact to make the necessary
improvements and attract enough capital for this new phase of Russia's
development. Once he had put the problem in this way, he clearly understood
in essentials (though he was often mistaken in detail) the economic effects
of the proposed reform. The peasants, oppressed by the fee, would run the
risk of penury; the landlords, just because of the form which their payment
was to take, would not have enough incentive to change the foundations of
Russia's agrarian economy.

He therefore held that the peasants' holdings should not be touched,
although many favoured the reduction of their size: and this latter view
finally prevailed. (It was a view that was specially popular in the more fertile
regions, in the centre of Russia and the districts of 'black land'.[78]) Chernyshevsky carried out a long campaign, especially in his article 'Is Land
Redemption difficult?'[79], against the amount of the fee proposed by the
various assemblies of nobles. Even after their figures had been changed and
often reduced by the Government Commission, he tried to show that they
were still too high. He claimed that the State should bear the main burden
of the transaction and should distribute the weight more equitably among the
various classes of the population, and not let it rest entirely on the peasants.
Such a policy would at the same time leave the landlords sufficient money in
hand to carry out the hoped-for transformations of their estates.

He wished, in fact, to act as mouthpiece for the peasants and, at the same
time, to review the proposed changes from a wider economic angle. It was
no use freeing the peasants and then ruining them economically. To avoid
this the landowning classes would have to reduce the fee and then, in time,
reapportion it in some other way. The economic change which was being
carried out was already entirely to the benefit of the landlords, the industrialists and the businessmen. The State should now intervene to stop this benefit
assuming such proportions that it made Russia's agricultural development
impossible or at least very difficult.

Some of these proposals which were supported by current liberal opinion
were, it is true, included in the final edict, but the economic basis of the
reform remained substantially unaffected. The peasants were made to pay
dearly for the land that they had farmed. As a whole, and taking into account
the differences between the various regions, they had to pay a price higher
than the commercial value of the land which they obtained. In other words
they had to pay a fee to redeem themselves. Annual fees were imposed which,

in the end, came to much the same as they had originally had to pay out to the landlords. As Chernyshevsky himself later said in a bitter attack, it would have been far better never to have made the peasants buy their land: 'Those who had the money could have bought it, but to make the others do this was only condemning them to poverty.'[80]

It was only later that Chernyshevsky drew this conclusion in all its brutality. By 1859 he was already convinced that his campaign in defence of the peasants' interests was lost. He and Dobrolyubov remained isolated from the liberals and emancipationists, at whose side he had fought during the preceding years, and who on the whole were satisfied with the results that had been obtained.

This position brought him once more face to face with the political problem as a whole and aroused again the doubts that he had felt at the end of the Crimean War. In fact, the government bureaucracy had succeeded, despite friction, in holding a balance in the conflict between the various classes of nobles, the intelligentsia and the silent but hopeful peasants, and in imposing its own solution. The reform (which in substance was ready by the end of 1859) was being implemented without affecting the foundations of Russia's political régime. Absolutism emerged, if anything, stronger from the fight against those nobles who wished to retain serfdom. The nobles gained in social power by retaining their estates and carrying through an advantageous economic transaction. The conditions of the peasant masses, as Chernyshevsky had foreseen, were not improved. Finally, the censorship during the final phase of the reform made clear its intention of becoming even stricter than ever before.

Chernyshevsky was among the first to react to this situation, but he was now completely isolated. At the beginning of his campaign to emancipate the serfs, his actions had been in harmony with those of the intelligentsia as a whole. When he had begun to speak of the *obshchina*, he had had supporters among the Slavophils. But now, he had to swim against the tide, taking advantage of the discontent and vague expectation of disturbances prevailing among those sections of Russian society which were unsure how the peasant masses would greet the reform. And because he had to take advantage of the discontent which was the counterpart of the great hopes aroused by the new reign, his radicalism became disillusioned and took on an element of paradox.

As censorship made political writing impossible, he was forced to return to literature. He had to concentrate on the broadest and most theoretical expression of his political and social ideas with no possibility of applying them to the immediate situation. And even then he was often compelled to write of France, England and Italy, as it was difficult to speak clearly of Russia. But despite all these obstacles, he was able to create a strong current of opinion clearly differentiated from the liberals and, of course, from the conservatives. And since his attacks on the latter were almost superfluous, all his blows were aimed at the former, the men who had supported the reforming activities of the State to such an extent that they had been virtually absorbed by it, and become the direct or indirect tools of Alexander II's policies. So it was that around 1859 Chernyshevsky disrupted the unity of the intellectual forces which had been in existence since the new reign. He was convinced that this unity had now served its purpose.

He now had the *Sovremennik* under his control, and could give it the slant he wanted, both in politics and in literature. In a series of disputes, he gradually drove away the writers who could not accept his increasingly radical standpoint. The vague Westernism, which he too had accepted when he had written his *Essays on the Gogol period*, was splitting up internally and giving rise to different currents. Controversies, initiated by Herzen in 1846, were resumed more than a decade later. Feuerbach's philosophy and aesthetic 'realism' alienated pure men of letters and moderate Westerners. Chernyshevsky attempted to follow the tradition of Belinsky against pure literature. That he was successful was partly due to the support of Nekrasov.

The first clash was with Druzhinin, a subtle writer but one interested only in problems of literary form. After reading Chernyshevsky's first articles he said that young men who embraced his ideas 'were thirsting to become the Boernes or Herweghs of Russia, despising all moderation. If we do not oppose them, they will end by doing something stupid, and will ruin literature. And through their desire to become society's schoolmasters, they will bring down persecutions on us and compel us to give up the place in the sun which we have won with blood and sweat.' To this, even Botkin, Belinsky's liberal friend and the man who had defended the bourgeoisie against Herzen in 1847, replied that a writer who took any account of dignity 'had no right to fall back into dreams'.[81]

Druzhinin soon left the *Sovremennik*, but he continued to direct a campaign against Chernyshevsky. He said that reading his articles made him 'smell a smell of unburied corpses'. And he spoke of his 'rhapsodies' as 'scarcely helpful—apart from anything else—from the point of view of the censorship'.[82]

Turgenev had, at first, seemed ready to defend the review from these attacks.

Chernyshevsky saddens me because of his aridity and his dry style, but I don't smell anything corpse-like in him. On the contrary, he has a vital streak, even if it is not exactly what we hope for in criticism. He doesn't understand poetry, but that's not all that terrible . . . He understands—how shall I say this?—the needs of real contemporary life. I think that Chernyshevsky is useful. Time will show that I am right.[83]

This was at a time when the greatest Russian writers were grouped around the *Sovremennik*: Turgenev himself, the playwright Ostrovsky and the young Tolstoy. But this unity of intellectual forces could not last. Tolstoy, in fact, became one of Chernyshevsky's bitterest opponents. His feeling for him was something between aristocratic scorn for an ex-seminarist and a literary pride which forbade the use of letters for immediate political purposes. His attacks on Chernyshevsky were often violent. He said that he smelt of bugs (an allusion to his low social origins) and accused him of 'bad manners, expressed with a subtle and unpleasant tone'. He looked upon him as merely an imitator of Belinsky. 'Among us, not only in criticism but even in literature and society, the opinion is spreading that to be worthless, bitter and nasty is something very beautiful. But I think that it is very disagreeable . . .'[84]

So Chernyshevsky was gradually surrounded by more and more enemies. When the honeymoon period of the reforms came to an end, he wrote of men of letters as 'weathercocks, who turn from side to side as the wind blows. These are the people of whom the scriptures say they should be saved with iron. In literature we still need an iron dictatorship, to make them tremble as they trembled before Belinsky.'[85]

He was struck by the lack of character and political energy of the writers with whom he collaborated. In 1858 he chose one of Turgenev's stories, *Asya*, to exemplify his 'iron dictatorship'. 'The most usual failing of our educated classes', he said, 'does not lie in mistaken ideas but in the lack of any idea; not in mistaken feelings, but in the weakness of any intellectual and moral sense, of any social interest. It is like an epidemic, deep-rooted in our society.'[86]

Turgenev then led the literary opposition against Chernyshevsky and Dobrolyubov, who in turn became more and more closely associated. It was a bitter fight. Turgenev accused the two critics of 'trying to wipe out from the face of the earth, poetry, the fine arts, all aesthetic pleasures, and to impose in their place mere seminarist principles. These men are literary Robespierres; they wouldn't for a moment hesitate to cut off the poet Chénier's head.'[87]

Thinking about this later at the end of his life, when he was exiled in Astrakhan, Chernyshevsky concluded that the world of literature had always been alien to him. Whenever he was asked to write his memoirs of the literary world of the 'sixties, he replied:

My memories of Turgenev and the others are incapable of arousing in me any other feeling than a longing to sleep . . . These people had no interest for me . . . I was a man crushed by work. They lived the usual life of the educated classes, and I had no inclination for that.[88]

These quarrels with men of letters played their part in making Chernyshevsky draw further and further away from the liberals. But this cleavage was only a symptom of a still deeper divergence which was more clearly expressed in his attacks on the jurists and historians of the Western tradition.

The dispute with Chicherin was conducted in courteous terms. He was one of the strictest theorizers of the Liberalism of the time, and was considered by Herzen as a typical incarnation of the doctrinaire. What was the point, said Chernyshevsky, of calling 'a principle of Statehood' what was in fact merely administrative centralism and the oppression of all Russia's social forces? He quoted the example of England and America as evidence of a 'principle of Statehood' which was very different.[89]

With Kavelin, the principal spokesman of the St Petersburg liberals, Chernyshevsky neither wanted to, nor could he, break openly. His opinion of him, however, is clear from the novel that he later wrote in Siberia, *The Prologue*, in which Kavelin appears as one of the leading figures. The same lack of character and political consistency which he had observed in men of letters alienated him from this well-meaning liberal who lacked political realism. Chernyshevsky drew his portrait in a cruel, but intelligent, caricature.[90]

His breach with the liberals became clear, when one day, encountering him, Chernyshevsky in a passion called Herzen 'a Kavelin squared'. In an article 'Very Dangerous!!!', published in the *Kolokol* on 1st June 1859, Herzen accused him of playing the reactionaries' game. He even suggested that the *Sovremennik* was in contact with the censorship, and he said that its editors would meet the fate of those authors who had been paid tools of the Third Section and who had dominated the scene during the reign of Nicholas I. He thought that Chernyshevsky's tactics were those of an *agent provocateur*.

Herzen's article made a vast impression. He seemed to be openly allying himself with the liberals against the only radical nucleus then in existence. The reaction was naturally greatest among the editors of the *Sovremennik*. Dobrolyubov even spoke of a duel, and Chernyshevsky thought that only a personal explanation could make Herzen understand the futility of his charges and, what was more important, the real political situation. At the end of June he came to London. He left after four days. Neither of the two writers has left us an exact account of what was said. Each maintained his own position, except that after the conversation Herzen was convinced of his mistake and at once withdrew his accusations in the following number of the *Kolokol*. 'It would be extremely painful', he said, 'if the irony with which we expressed ourselves were to be considered an insulting allusion.'[91] Immediately after the conversation, Chernyshevsky wrote to Dobrolyubov: 'To remain longer would only have been boring. It is true that the journey was not useless, but if I had known how boring it would be, I should not have come ... My God, I had to say a few things ... He is a Kavelin squared, that is all.'[92]

The most interesting account we possess of the discussions comes from S. Stakhevich, who was later in prison with Chernyshevsky. After having said that the 'literature of public denunciation' (Herzen's policy of emphasizing the shortcomings of absolutism) ran the risk of encouraging absolutism to remain exactly as before, Chernyshevsky added, 'You should have drawn up a detailed political programme, constitutional, republican and Socialist, and then each time you denounced some individual evil, it would seem to confirm the fundamental demands of your programme. You ought to have repeated tirelessly your *coeterum censeo.*'[93] At the very moment when Chernyshevsky was compelled by the situation to expound the general principles of Socialism, he saw Herzen continue his attacks on small details, and he judged this policy useless and dangerous.

That this was Chernyshevsky's position we find confirmed in the pseudonymous 'Letter from the Provinces' which the *Kolokol* published shortly after his visit to London. The author of this article is not known.[94] Although it is far from certain, there is some reason for believing it was Dobrolyubov rather than Chernyshevsky himself, and in any case it was someone obviously well acquainted with the ideas of both men at this time.[95] Speaking of despotism he said:

Remember that you once said that when Russia wakes up again, one danger will threaten her, the danger that the liberals and the people will no longer understand each other, that they will split. This, you said, would lead to a terrible disaster, a new triumph for the authority of the Tsar . . . You are evidently mistaken about the situation in Russia. Liberal landowners, liberal professors, liberal writers, lull you with hopes in the progressive aims of our Government. But not everyone in Russia is taken in by fantasies . . . What is the present position of the Government as far as the peasant problem is concerned? . . . The great majority of regional committees (of the nobles) have fixed upon terrifying sums. The devil knows what the Central Committee is doing. One day it decides on emancipation with land, on the next without . . . While these useless discussions are taking place, the hopes of the peasants are growing . . . And with them grow the mistakes of the Liberals. Everyone hopes in a peaceful solution, which is not unfavourable to the peasants. And so the Liberals go on one side and the peasants on another . . . You have been impressed by the Liberals, and, after the first numbers of the *Kolokol*, you have changed your tone and are now praising the imperial family. You, the author of *From the other shore* and *Letters from Italy*, have begun to chant the song which for centuries has been ruining Russia. You must not forget even for a moment that Alexander II is the Tsar, the autocrat . . . You will soon see that Alexander II will show his teeth, as Nicholas I did. Don't be taken in by gossip about our progress. We are exactly where we were before . . . Don't be taken in by hope, and don't take in others . . . No, our position is horrible, unbearable, and only the peasants' axes can save us. Nothing apart from these axes is of any use. You have already been told this, it seems, and it is extraordinarily true. There is no other means of salvation. You did everything possible to help a peaceful solution of the problem, but now you are changing your tune. Let your 'bell' sound not to prayer but for the charge. Summon Russia to arms.

These where the ideas that Chernyshevsky had gone to London to explain to Herzen.

After this journey Chernyshevsky looked upon the controversy as virtually at an end. He re-opened it not to discuss immediate Russian policies, for he was convinced that here Herzen was on the wrong track, but rather to speak of the distrust of the West which Herzen expressed together with his hopes in Russia's mission in Europe.

The idea that Russia could accomplish a revival of the West, he said, was based on only one piece of evidence and even that was merely a historical comparison: the parallel between the barbarian invasions of the Roman Empire and the modern situation. Not only were allusions of this kind of little use in supporting such arguments, but the event itself was wrongly interpreted. It was not true that the Roman Empire was in a state of decadence when it was invaded. In fact, there were signs of progress in public affairs, communications, administration, etc., i.e. in those fields which particularly affected the masses. On the contrary, it was the fall of the Empire which delayed progress for more than a thousand years. As for the barbarians, their life was a mixture of despotism and anarchy, and could lead to nothing new. Though he pointed out that this was not aimed at the Slavophils, he continued with a savage parody of their nationalism:

Their eyes are so strangely constructed that whatever filth they see, they regard as something marvellous or at least useful for injecting life into moribund Europe. And so they consider that our habit of submitting to all oppression is an excellent one, and that Western Europe is dying through lack of this laudable custom, and that it will only be saved by us when it learns such humility.[96]

Yet he was not so much concerned with the Slavophils as with Herzen, who had been the first to suggest that the *obshchina* was a feature of Russian life which would count in the future development of Europe as a whole. Chernyshevsky too saw a germ of Socialism in the *obshchina*. But it would not be the Russians who would impose it on Europe.

We are far from praising the present social conditions in Europe, but we do say that they have nothing to learn from us. It may be true that Russia has retained, since patriarchal times, a principle which corresponds to one of the solutions at which progressives are aiming; it is none the less true that Western Europe is moving towards the realization of this principle quite independently of us.

The *obshchina* should be revivified and transformed by Western Socialism; it should not be portrayed as a model and symbol of Russia's mission. Such were Chernyshevsky's final conclusions on the subject.

Under pressure from the censorship he now referred to the history of Western Europe to bring home his political ideas to the Russian public and he moved still further from the liberals.

He spoke of Turgot and the enlightened despotism of the French eighteenth century to show that what was needed was not ready-made plans for reform but rather the political energy to bring them into effect. It was true, he wrote, that had Maurepas been able to do everything that he wanted, the French Revolution would have been avoided. But Chernyshevsky's satirical portrait of him was similar to the satire soon to be written by Shchedrin on the Russian liberals, who were so ready to talk of reforms and so incapable of knowing how to bring them into effect.

He referred to the Bourbon restoration to show the aristocratic origin of liberalism and to maintain that there was a great difference in kind between democrats and liberals. Following Louis Blanc, he explained that the monarchy of Charles X had fallen because it did not know how to choose between the liberal and reactionary forces, and because of its ultimate attempt to rely on the latter. Would this also be the fate of Alexander II? That was the question he wanted to suggest to his readers.

The revolution of 1830 had shown that even a revolution would benefit only the middle classes. 'What good did it do to the simple people?' In the July revolution the people 'had fought without demands of its own, without a pre-determined programme, carried away by the gravity of the situation to become involved in problems which were outside its own interests. It had not been concerned with selling its support or making any conditions before taking one side rather than the other, and in the result it got nothing.'[97] This showed the absolute necessity for the people to form an autonomous movement.

He then traced the rise of the democratic and Socialist movements in the July monarchy, and stressed those tendencies which might serve as pointers to the radical movement in Russia. His judgment on both the followers of Saint-Simon and those of Blanqui was unfavourable. The Saint-Simonists had started from 'an idealization of old feudal relations'. In them one could recognize the 'descendants of the aristocrats, the heirs of mediaeval theories',[98] and it was this hierarchical element which repelled Chernyshevsky. Above all they had no real political system, but merely enthusiasm for a sentimental and religious revival. He held that this was especially dangerous for Russia where it was coherence and certainly not enthusiasm that was lacking. He compared the Saint-Simonists to the Slavophils, and regarded them as philanthropists. Of course one must do good for the people. That was not what was wrong with philanthropists. It was rather that they were and always remained men of the upper classes. Their ideas would be of practical value only when they were adopted by 'the more serious classes', i.e. the people itself. As for the followers of Blanqui, who had tried to carry out a republican *coup d'état* in 1839, Chernyshevsky looked upon them as the best example of what to avoid. There was nothing worse than attempting a revolution before the time was ripe. That was obvious once again in the revolution of 1848.

His article on Cavaignac, the best of this series, was devoted to this problem.[99] Victory had been gained in February because the workers and the Socialists had united with the moderate republicans against the July monarchy. But this alliance was a political mistake.

The workers of Paris paid for their alliance with the moderate republicans by starving, by dying in thousands in the fight, and by being sent in thousands to

6+

prison. The moderate republicans paid them back by arousing against them the hatred of all other classes of the population.

Examining the situation in detail, Chernyshevsky suggested a political policy for France which later became that of the radicals under the Third Republic. This consisted in not making enemies on the Left and of giving concessions to the working classes over the heads of the exponents of Socialist theories. He concluded that it was essential for Russia to create an independent radical movement, not allied to the liberals—whom he compared to the moderate republicans of 1848 with their Lamartines and Cavaignacs. 'There is nothing more dangerous in private life, as in politics, than being hesitant in action, pushing aside one's friends and bowing to one's enemies. An honest man who really wants to do something useful must be convinced that he cannot expect support from anyone except those who really share his ideas.' The political force which was to spring up in Russia must also learn from the lessons of 1848 to free itself of the utopian theories which had then deterred the Socialists from action. Such was his detailed and often acute criticism of the heroes of his youth. In this criticism he included Louis Blanc, who, he thought, had acted wrongly in accepting the presidency of the Luxemburg Commission, and who had been quite incapable of guiding the movement.

The international situation in 1859 allowed him to develop these ideas by referring to the contemporary scene without always having to look to the past for his examples. From the beginning of the year he began to discuss European affairs in *Politics*, a special column of his review. 'The last ten years have been very disheartening for the friends of light and progress in Europe',[100] he wrote on the first page. And in later numbers his tone continued to be very pessimistic. Only gradually, and after many doubts, could he be convinced that the ideas which had been suppressed in 1848 had again come to the fore. His doubts were prompted above all by the presence of Napoleon III. His attacks on the Emperor prevented him, for example, from foreseeing and assessing the course of Napoleon's intervention in Italy and alliance with Cavour. His attacks were also due to his fear that Napoleon's policies might lead Russia into a new war, this time as his ally against Austria. He was at this time decisively pacifist, fearing, like Herzen, that Russia's entry into a war would mean the end of the political process which was to lead to increasingly radical reforms.

His pessimism, his insistence on attacking the liberals (even when this seemed to be helping the reactionaries) and the need to write of Western Europe as a means of alluding to Russia—all these led him in 1859 to write an article which aroused a great scandal. In it he justified the long imprisonment which the Neapolitan Bourbons had inflicted on Poerio, Settembrini and their comrades, who had just come to England, celebrated by the entire European press as martyrs in the cause of freedom. Chernyshevsky told the readers of the *Sovremennik* that they had been fairly and logically punished for having believed in the liberal promises of an absolute monarch. Logic had been on the side of their captors, for the liberals, instead of fighting absolutism, had ended by playing its game. There was a bitter Swift-like quality in this paradoxical article: but it expressed one of Chernyshevsky's deepest convictions: a feeling of remorse for his own policies at the beginning of the reforms, perhaps even a premonition of the fate that awaited him. What did it matter, he said, that Poerio and his comrades had been condemned on false evidence? The political necessity of absolutism had demanded that they should be imprisoned. It was up to the revolutionaries to be just as consistent. His words take on a special poignancy when we remember that Chernyshevsky himself was to be condemned some years later on the basis of a false document. 'We must say that neither the honesty of Poerio, Settembrini and the others, nor the eloquence of the English newspapers, can make up for the lack of a clear political vision. This lack we can see both in those who had to suffer in prison and in their defenders.'[101] A political lesson of this kind naturally inflamed a sensitive spot, and it inevitably roused great scandal. But we must remember that the man who wrote these words was prepared to pay for his right to defend logical policies with twenty years in Siberia. Only at this price could he distinguish his voice from that of the Russian liberals, and Chernyshevsky did not hesitate to pay it.

It is in this light that his attacks on Cavour, which played a large part in his column on international affairs, assume their real significance. He prophesied that Cavour would meet with eventual defeat, the defeat which awaits all liberals who try to find support in absolutism.

We say not as a reproach, but in order to clarify the facts, that Cavour has forgotten one thing—the instinct of egoism is so cunning and calculating that the man who is guided only by it can cheat any minister however much of a genius. Sobakevich [the prototype of cunning brute in Gogol's *Dead Souls*] would be able to deceive Machiavelli himself.[102]

And so he foresaw that in the last analysis Cavour would be defeated by Napoleon III. The armistice of Villafranca seemed to justify his prophecy, as he did not hesitate to emphasize. And if Cavour's liberalism seemed to lack coherence, he thought the same of his opponents, the followers of Mazzini. He thought them weak just because they were constantly trying to get an alliance with the liberals and the other conservative forces, whereas they should have tried to found a movement of the people only.

For instance, social conditions in Lombardy seemed to present problems similar to those that concerned him in Russia. The Austrians had maintained a system of land tenure which was unfavourable to the peasants. The new Italian government had done nothing to change the situation, nor were even the revolutionaries who followed Mazzini concerned with it. And yet, he said, if the peasants of Lombardy were wanting a change, it was certainly not a change of government so much as one of social conditions.[103] If Austria wanted to win the next round, all it had to do was to adopt the policies which it had already followed in Galicia in 1846.

If Austria wants to dominate Lombardy once more, and inflict a terrible punishment on the upper classes and citizens for their disloyalty, all it has to do is to promise agrarian reforms to the peasants, and they will rise in a terrible massacre of the landlords, as took place in Galicia . . . This dark mass—virtually dumb, almost dead at ordinary times—is playing no part in the present events in Italy, just as it had no voice in the other political affairs of Western Europe. Its silent aims are so different from the historical aims of educated reformers, moderates and even revolutionaries, that it is rarely that even the latter dare to support the peasants openly. The masses do not find in the plans of the reformers anything that corresponds to what they themselves think, and in general they remain indifferent to them and, indeed, are usually hostile . . . The reforming parties do not even know of the existence of these aims. At least, they do not understand that for the masses only revolutions concerned with the material relations of landownership or the dependence of labour on capital have any importance. The masses do not see their own cause represented and remain apathetic. Eventually they play into the hands of the reactionaries, who at least promise to maintain the outside order which gives them their bread each day . . . This is the situation in Italy as well . . . You, Italians, who long for reforms and freedom, you must know that you will only be able to defeat reaction and obscurantism by making yours the aims of your poor, obscure peasant compatriots, and those of the simple townspeople. You must either demand agricultural changes in your programmes or you must realize that you are doomed to perish through reaction.[104]

This article was badly cut by the censorship, which removed much of the passage here quoted. It is the key which helps us to explain his other articles on the situation in Italy.[105] Chernyshevsky looked upon these articles as a way of expressing his distrust of European politics during these years, and of emphasizing how small a part was played in them by the masses. But above all he wanted to suggest a programme for the movement which he was trying to inspire in Russia. He wanted to tell the younger intellectuals that their future lay in putting themselves at the head of the peasants. They should not be misled by liberal or reforming promises.

At the same time he tried to give a theoretical basis to these new tendencies, and to define the kind of Socialism which would have to guide them. He devoted much of his work in 1860 and 1861 to a consideration of the economic ideas of the English and French Socialists, from which he tried to derive a comprehensive picture of his ideas on the plane of political economy.

This debate with the upholders of a system of *laissez faire* was the natural result of his quarrel with the liberals. He looked upon the followers of Say and Bastiat as apologists for the existing situation, rather than as economists. They had used the scientific principles formulated by Adam Smith and Ricardo to give a superficial description and justification of capitalism out of hatred for Socialist ideas. These men were merely the result of the situation in France that followed the revolution of 1848, and that led to the dictatorship of Napoleon III.

But it was mainly the situation of Russia itself that drove him to clarify and expound his economic ideas. The problems raised by the peasant reform had brought him face to face with the question of State intervention in the economy. In view of what had happened in Russia, all simple theories of *laissez faire* seemed to him to be merely ridiculous. The enormous economic power of the State was a fact; its fiscal, financial and customs policies proved this even at normal times. The great property changes brought about by the reforms showed how great was its power during times of transformation. The question was not whether State intervention in economy was necessary or not, but what its ends and means ought to be. Merely to answer *laissez faire* was meaningless. It was like saying *laissez éclairer, laissez être intelligent. Laissez faire* was not an end but merely a means which should be judged according to political circumstances and intentions.

But such means had now become dangerous. In the European reaction which followed the revolutions of 1848, the ruling classes had had to use force and tyranny to restore order, because they had been brought up on the principles of free trade and did not know how to use the power of the State in any other way. Indeed, they did not even know of other methods or systems of State intervention.

Support for *laissez faire* merely meant accepting as facts of nature, as the fundamental economic laws, what were in fact merely historical situations, often inherited from the Middle Ages. This included all theories about landownership, monopolies and privileges of every kind. In their anxiety to attack State controls, the free-traders had not distinguished between laws which oppress and others which protect and help to develop freedom. The task was to establish the latter, and fight against the former. In England, where, despite appearances to the contrary, the economic power of the State was greater than on the Continent, economists were now appearing who understood the problem of State intervention. Among them was Mill. Compared to them, French economists and the German historical school were merely backward. And so Mill's principles had to be developed.

It was true that a situation could be foreseen in the distant future which would correspond to the ideals of those who supported a free market; but to bring this into being the moment had to arrive when the product of labour would be such that State intervention would no longer be necessary. For the time being the State had to destroy the monopolies which were inevitably created by competition between rich and poor, weak and strong, landowners and those who possessed nothing, capitalists and proletarians. When work was really free, when it was merely a form of pleasure, only then could true *laissez faire* be achieved. But during the existing period of transition the State must intervene where economically necessary and politically just.

Completely free competition was always of its nature a form of oppression; only the law could fight this.[106]

Starting from this basis, Chernyshevsky developed his ideas on State intervention in a series of articles and pamphlets. He was trying to establish the guiding principles, and these could only be drawn from the existing situation by examining class relations in Western Europe and in Russia.

A long time had now passed, he said, since 1789 when 'the followers of Montesquieu had held hands with those of Rousseau, and cheered the people of Paris as they assaulted the Bastille'. Within a few years they were organizing conspiracies to restore the Bourbons. At the time of the Restoration they once more united with the people for a short period, to overthrow reviving feudalism. But from 1830 onwards the division had become final and inevitable. In 1848 the middle classes had ended by acting in alliance with the aristocracy. In England the division was not so obvious to a superficial observer, because the victory of the middle classes over the forces of feudalism was not yet complete. And so the bourgeoisie still needed the help of the people to achieve the parliamentary reform of 1832, and the repeal of the Corn Laws in 1846.

But even in England we see the workmen forming vast unions among themselves so as to act independently in political and especially in economic questions. The Chartists sometimes ally themselves with parliamentary liberalism; and extremist liberal members of parliament are sometimes the spokesmen for the people's demands, if not from the economic at least from the political point of view. But despite these alliances, the middle classes and the workers have for some time, even in England, been acting as different parties with different demands. In France open hatred between the people and the middle classes has led to theories of Communism. The English claim that since Owen, Communism has had no significant literary support, and that this absence of deadly hatred between theorists corresponds to the absence of irreconcilable hatred between the workers and the middle classes. But though there is no English Proudhon, none the less in practice the *Trade Unions* of workers represent something very like those theories that the French call Communist.[107]

As the political economy of *laissez faire* had become the theory of the middle classes, both in their victorious progress and above all in their constant compromises with the feudal past, so the Socialism or Communism of the popular classes, the workers' movements, must now be provided with a rational economic system.

Chernyshevsky tried to formulate this economic system of labour, as opposed to that of capital, in his notes to a translation of Mill which he now published.

He defined his political economy as 'the science of man's material welfare in so far as it depends on the objects and situations created by labour'. This was an attempt to combine English utilitarianism (which his youthful admiration for Helvetius and his general enlightened principles proved to be deeply rooted in him) with the idea of an economy founded on a theory of labour values. On this basis he tried to simplify and organize the ideas of Saint-Simon, Fourier and Owen.

This is not the place to discuss the details of these schemes. They remained fragmentary suggestions designed to encourage State intervention to ensure both equality and the greatest possible economy—by reducing all unproductive activities. It is, however, worth pointing out that Chernyshevsky thought that all this could be achieved through agricultural and industrial cooperatives, protected and eventually run by the State, but economically viable. In other words he saw, through Owen's eyes, what was still the essence of his own original economic vision: the Russian peasant *obshchina*, freely developed along Socialist lines, in a State prepared to act on its behalf.

He ended by pointing out that Communist ideals were simpler and more elementary than Socialist ones, but that the latter were more economically truthful.

To accept Socialism, one must be prepared for combinations of fairly complicated ideas, whereas to accept Communism it is enough to feel for oneself the weight of existing economic conditions and to have a normal human conscience. It is obviously unfair that a man who works and who is prepared to work should not have the necessities of life, while a man who does nothing should enjoy comfort and wealth. But we must have no illusions about the ease with which the masses are attracted by Communist ideas at times of social upheaval. Traditions, customs and ideas essential for the Communist life are far removed from the ideas, traditions and customs of present-day people. At the first attempt to build one's life in accordance with Communist principles, people will find out that those ideas which once attracted them so readily, are in fact not at all suitable for them. To use a popular expression, the masses will quickly think that they have fallen out of the frying-pan into the fire.[108]

Only a slow process, inevitable in its general direction but not in its rate of progress, could lead to Socialism, and perhaps in the more distant future to Communism. For the moment, the only two attempts that had been made in this direction, that of the Chartists in England and the days of June in France, had been defeated. Chernyshevsky, however, was confident in the future of Socialism:[109]

But during our century there will be new battles; we will see with what success. For the rest, whatever the result, we must realize that even if we lose, we merely return to a situation which will inevitably give rise to new battles. And even by winning, not only the first battle—and who knows when that will occur?—but also the second, the third and perhaps the tenth, we still will not have reached final victory, because the interests defending our present social organization are extremely strong.[110]

Having now seen where Chernyshevsky's dispute with the liberals on the literary, legal, political and economic planes had led him, we can turn back for a moment and see what all this meant as a whole, and its significance in his life.

His isolation since 1859 had been a difficult trial. He had lost faith in liberal reforms, and among the mass of peasants he saw only a patient waiting for the freedom which would eventually be granted to them. He had broken with most of the intelligentsia, but had no contact with the peasants.

It is true that the effects of his propaganda were growing. To see this we merely have to look at the circulation of the *Sovremennik*, which grew every year and which eventually reached the remarkable figure of six thousand— far greater than that of all other reviews. He realized the importance of this. He was the first to publish at the end of each year the accounts of his periodical. But the effects of his publicizing activities were still only general. He had as yet hardly begun to gather round him the generation of 'new people' whose numbers grew only in 1861 and 1862.

There was thus reason to think that no political development was possible in the near future and that only the stubborn assertion of his views remained feasible. It was this that gave rise to that mixture of scepticism and irony which was known as his 'Nihilism' and which made such an impression on his contemporaries.

He himself has described in one of his finest works, written in Siberia ten years later, the passion that he put into this attitude. He looked back on himself in this St Petersburg high society, with its liberal intellectuals and aristocrats, all concerned with the problem of their attitude towards the reforms. They had seemed determined to oppose the government with all their strength, and defend their interests and traditions, whether good or bad. These were the same nobles whose unbridled habits had dominated the small towns of the Russian provinces. But, faced with an order of the Tsar and the government bureaucracy, they had been transformed into lambs, pretending to accept liberal ideas and waxing enthusiastic over the reforms.

They quietened down, as if struck with paralysis. Such a transformation was ridiculous and at the same time disgusting to observe. Volgin [the character in the *Prologue* who represents Chernyshevsky] wanted to laugh. He had the habit of turning everything to satire . . . He had not been brought up in well-bred society. He looked back on a rude, primitive life. And he remembered the scenes which had amazed him in his childhood, because even in his childhood he had thought a lot.

He remembered the men pulling the barges along the Volga. There they were at Saratov in the evening, drunk, singing songs inspired by the old local revolts, and claiming to be sons and descendants of Stenka Razin's rebels:

A stranger would have thought, 'the city is in danger, they will attack the shops and the houses, they will loot and destroy everything'. Yet at the sight of an ageing guard's face, shouting from a half-open guard-house door that they were beasts, they ran off. The band of 'Stenka Razin's lads' moved off, mumbling that luckily the guard was a good fellow.

These warriors were really just like the nobles in St Petersburg. 'To be disappointed is not pleasant, even if Volgin did not love nobles in general and magnates in particular. Wretched nation, wretched nation, nation of slaves from top to bottom. They are all only slaves.'[111]

This was the lowest point in his disappointment at the reforms, which had succeeded in arousing a movement neither against absolutism among the intellectuals nor against Russia's social conditions among the people and peasants.

But at the beginning of 1859 international events, especially the example of Italy, began to make him think that a revival was possible. The Italians too had seemed to be a people resigned to the defeats of 1848 and traditional political apathy. And yet in 1860, as he said, 'their activities were astounding all liberal Europe'. But, above all, he felt that the realization that what Russia needed was not just a few single changes, but rather an entire new basis and direction, would eventually sink into men's minds when they finally understood the real nature of the reforms. He was still counting on a collision between the great hopes raised in the past and the situation as it actually was.

When the decree of 19th February 1861 was published, he could see by looking at those nearest to him that he was not altogether wrong. He himself tells us of how he found Nekrasov, who had scarcely finished reading the decree:

On his face there was an expression of grief, his eyes were downcast . . . 'That's liberty, that's what it is' and he went on speaking for two or three minutes in the same tone of voice. 'And what were you expecting? For a long time it's been obvious that this is what we would get', I said to him. 'No, this is not what I was expecting', he answered, and he added that naturally he was not expecting anything extraordinary, but that this went far beyond his expectations.[112]

When the news came of the first peasant disorders these impressions of Nekrasov and a few intellectuals gained wide enough circulation to form a current of public opinion which regarded 19th February as opening rather than closing the problem of social relations in Russia.

Chernyshevsky's position during his last year of free activity was that of a spiritual guide, the intellectual and political pivot of the forces which were gradually beginning to move with his programme, which was summed up by Dobrolyubov in the phrase 'Calling Russia to Axes'. But he wished to act with coolness and dignity, so as not to let himself be carried away and expended too early. He had never had a very high opinion of those whom, when in Siberia, he called 'linear revolutionaries, who do not know or even wish to understand the circumstances of their time and place. At critical moments in the lives of nations, these revolutionaries carry their banners across the theatre of events. They know how to do this. But you can get nothing or nothing much out of them. Saintly boys—saintly, it is true, but boys—and that is equally true.'[113] These 'saintly boys' were springing up

6*

all around him, creatures of immediate circumstances, but also of his own publicizing activities. His policy was to continue providing them with ideas but to avoid being involved with them. He was determined to remain as far as possible on the right side of the law, and emphasize his intellectual activities and position as a writer and editor of an important review.

This policy survived for just over a year, and then collapsed. The difference between the revolutionary movements which were arising and the State's capacity for repression was too great. And his own position as legal head of a movement which was rapidly becoming illegal could not last long. A time of uncertainty had arrived: the old autocracy weakened and all classes of the population were discontented, but not openly rebellious. A single indiscretion would provide a pretext for his arrest, and the punishment in his person of all the rebellious movements of the period.

The *Sovremennik* was beginning to attract the men who were founding clandestine groups, distributing manifestos, trying to guide the student movement and to seek contacts with the peasants. The poet Mikhailov and the writer Shelgunov were among the first of these, and both were associated with the *Sovremennik*. Mikhailov had been a friend of Chernyshevsky since their earliest university years, and Shelgunov was one of the men who shared his ideas on the *obshchina* and the workers' movement in the West. It is even possible that one of the manifestos which they then tried to print and distribute was written by Chernyshevsky.[114] There were three of these manifestos: one addressed to youth, another to the army, and a third to the peasants; and it is possible that the latter was written by Chernyshevsky. Though written in simple language it contained a true statement of his ideas. It replied to the anxious questions that the peasants were asking about the Tsar's decree. It linked their particular problems to the general fight against despotism. The emancipation of the serfs, it said, was closely related to freedom for all. There was even an attempt to explain in simple language the need to look to the West for the renovation of Russian life. 'One can live even with a Tsar, as the English and the French do, but only on condition that the Tsar listens to the people and does not dare to do anything without them and that the people keep a strict eye on him, and as soon as they see him up to any harm, they change him and chase him out of the country as the French and the English do.'[115] It ended with an appeal to the peasants to organize themselves and to discover who among all those who wore uniform (i.e. civil servants and officers) 'would be for the people'. The time for action would come, and until then forces had to be conserved. 'You must not bring down misfortunes uselessly on yourselves. You must keep calm and give nothing away. What is the point of starting the revolt when other villages are not yet ready? That would only mean disaster. The revolt will begin when everyone is ready.' Even if these words were not actually written by Chernyshevsky, they certainly represent his views at the beginning of 1861. It was important not to unleash the movement too quickly. For the time being one must prepare and learn how to act when the moment came.

It was also from people closely associated with the *Sovremennik* that the first attempt was made to start a small clandestine periodical press. This took the form of a leaflet called *Velikoruss*. As we shall see later, it is often very difficult to find out for certain the names of those who took part in these movements. But those we know of were all intimate friends of Chernyshevsky. The ideas of the *Velikoruss* did not exactly correspond to his own, especially as regards constitutionalism. But the very rise of liberal forces—differing in temperament, age and energy from those that he had known in the preceding years—must have seemed to him a symptom of great importance and another indication that the situation was changing.

Plans to transform into a secret society the different intellectual groups associated with the *Kolokol* and the *Sovremennik* came to a head with the earliest attempts to found the first *Zemlya i Volya*. Both Chernyshevsky and Herzen at first opposed this tendency; the latter because he had no faith in secret societies, the former so as to concentrate on his own activities. But it was being strongly endorsed by their closest collaborators. In July or August 1861, for instance, Ogarev complained that Chernyshevsky was still quarrelling with Herzen and did not want the younger generation to take part in conspiracies. He spoke of 'artificial scepticism' and pride. 'Go to St Petersburg and say that this is disgraceful. One really cannot betray Christ (i.e. Truth, and the Cause itself) in this way. That is what Christians call sin against the Holy Ghost.'[116] Quite apart from the personal quarrel, such a state of mind was certainly increasing. Everywhere, with growing insistence, the demand for an organization was growing. And so towards the end of 1861 and the beginning of 1862, Chernyshevsky finally and perhaps somewhat reluctantly found himself at the centre of the groups of *Zemlya i Volya*.

The government crisis had entered a crucial phase. V. A. Dolgorukov, the head of the Third Section, summing up the year of the reform 1861 in his report to the Emperor, was compelled to admit that 'the political situation is extremely tense', and made still more serious by general economic stagnation. He mentioned the revolts in the villages, the 'party of progress', and subversive manifestos. He added that 'it is interesting to see that these have aroused in far-off Europe the joy of the well-known demagogue Mazzini. He has boasted of them in a signed article in a Milan newspaper as evidence of Russia's ripeness for political revolution and the destruction of the reigning dynasty. 'Fortunately', he added, 'Mazzini and his Russian imitators are mistaken in their estimate of our degree of ripeness.'[117] Besides the desire of the peasants to 'get the maximum possible advantage out of the reform', he singled out another source of the widespread discontent: the state of mind of the nobles.

The nobles, though submitting to the necessity of abandoning their ancient rights over the peasants and many related privileges, are in general distressed at their material losses. They consider these unjust and due to the situation of the State finances. For instance, all the weight of the many wise steps taken to prevent a proletariat, the scourge of other European states, now falls exclusively on the Russian nobility, threatening it with collapse. The discontent of the nobles has not yet led the majority of them to open thoughts of a revolution. But individuals among them, especially in the ranks of the liberals, have begun to emerge from the isolation of the countryside and to move into politics. Both in print and in manuscript they are spreading ideas about freedom which go far beyond the intentions of the government.

With the end of the reforms, part at least of the nobility had given political expression to its grievances. It did not demand a return to peasant serfdom, but rather 'a crowning of the edifice', in the words used by Napoleon III in France. By this it meant a series of liberal concessions. Some of the greater aristocrats were thinking in terms of an oligarchy, but the majority were beginning to discuss wider constitutional schemes.

Such tendencies had always made an appearance in Russia at various stages of absolutism—after Peter the Great and Catherine II for instance. In 1730, when the aristocrats had tried to crown the reforms of Peter the Great with a constitution of the Swedish type, they did not aim to restore the *boyar* traditions or demand a simple return to the past; rather they aimed to guide the reforms towards the granting of freedom to the nobles. In the same way the enlightened opposition to Catherine II had drawn strength from a similar aristocratic reaction. Again, in the Decembrist movement, aristocratic tradition and liberal tendencies had merged in the face of absolutism. In prison Chernyshevsky once said that it would have been an excellent thing if these movements had had their way, even in 1730, when they were obviously only of a caste nature. For once in power, even oligarchical constitutionalism would have had to do something for the other classes. Even under a régime of the most restricted freedom, progressive elements would eventually have triumphed. 'The most terrible thing of all is always the Leviathan, the shapeless monster that swallows everything.'[118]

Because of this he was prepared to pay careful and respectful attention to these movements of the Russian nobility, even though he did not share their ideas. With the end of the reforms they were once more following the old traditions of no longer demanding particular and detailed changes in the plans of the bureaucracy, but rather freedom of speech and a free play of political forces. Their attempts were on a small scale and confined mostly to those who owned poor land in the north. For them, the peasants' redemption fee was not enough to allow the development of industry, which was the only economically feasible solution to their difficulties. This helped to make them understand the need to adopt as quickly as possible a more modern and less patriarchal system. In January 1860 the majority of the nobles in the Vladimir region demanded a clear separation of powers, equality of all before the law, and the development of agrarian credit. The heart of this liberal and aristocratic opposition was at Tver. It included men who had taken part in earlier movements, both Decembrists returned from their thirty years' exile in Siberia and Petrashevskists such as A. I. Evropeus and Saltykov-Shchedrin. There were also new men such as A. M. Unkovsky, who was the leading figure and guiding spirit of the movement—especially in its early phases—and Bakunin's brothers. They had already played a large part in hastening and improving the peasant reform and in ensuring that emancipation took place 'with land'. They provided a typical example of the independents on whom the government had relied to bring the reform safe into harbour, when it was under attack from the reactionaries interested in keeping the land and the serfs in their own hands. They had not given up their activities after the emancipation, but had increased their demands. They were now putting themselves at the head of the liberal elements of the Russian aristocracy. At the beginning of 1862 they sent a petition to the Emperor containing a hundred and twelve signatures. It criticized the delays in carrying out the reform and stated

that the changes which are now absolutely indispensable cannot be carried out by bureaucratic methods. We do not, of course, claim to speak for the entire people, although we are in close touch with them. But we are firmly convinced that good intentions are not enough to indicate the people's demands, let alone to satisfy them. We are convinced that the reforms cannot be successful unless they are undertaken after consultation with the people. To summon delegates elected by the entire Russian nation is now the only way of solving satisfactorily the problems which have been raised but not solved by the manifesto of 19th February.

In another document the same nobles from Tver insisted on the need for an independent judiciary, on 'publicity' for all acts of the government and administration, and again spoke of 'an assembly of delegates elected by the country without distinction of class in order to create free institutions'.[119]

In other parts of Russia also the nobility in 1862 came out for administrative autonomy and some form of political freedom. And in Moscow itself these ideas were to meet with a considerable response.

All this convinced Chernyshevsky at the beginning of 1862 that Alexander II might no longer be able to control the situation, and that he might be compelled to allow free play to the forces of society by abolishing the censorship and appealing to the representatives of the nation. A recent event seemed to confirm this prospect: the censorship had been entrusted to apparently more liberal hands. And so in early January he wrote an article weighing up the situation; he called it *Letters without an Address*. Yet the contents made it plain enough to whom they were addressed: the Emperor himself. With great ability and firm dignity he pointed out the only choice which in his opinion remained open. But the result of the test was negative. Not a line was passed by the censorship.[120]

In these *Letters without an Address*, Chernyshevsky explained from the first what he thought was most likely to occur in the long run. The peasants would end by taking the defence of their interests into their own hands. 'No amount of trouble taken by anyone else can produce the results which are given by action for oneself.' But the price would be expensive, very expensive.

The people are ignorant, dominated by primitive prejudices and by blind hatred for anything different from their own barbaric customs, make no distinction between one or the other in the class that wears different clothes from themselves. They will act against them all without exception and will spare neither our science, our poetry nor our arts, will destroy our civilization.

This was the threat, though not for the immediate future. For the moment the masses were still apathetic and their revolts were only symptoms. Political measures were still possible. But even in this field it was important not to have any illusions. The number of people who really supported the Tsar was small, as was the group which was beginning to take a firm stand against official policies, i.e. the group associated with Chernyshevsky himself. A continuation of the duel between these two forces, the only ones which showed any real life at this stage, would lead only to negative results. They could, however, both find one common interest: to increase as far as possible the number of men and classes taking part in political life. The general feeling of discontent showed how necessary this was.

The nobility was beginning to move in defence of its own interests. Many, including Chernyshevsky, had at first looked upon this movement as completely impotent, but the situation of the country as a whole had now given it real weight. The threat of a peasant revolt and the growing radicalism of at least a part of the intelligentsia had drawn together the demands of the nobles and the educated classes. Together they now asked for freedom and political life. The nobles no longer wanted to return to the past; they had now accepted the inevitable, the end of serfdom. They no longer spoke of their class interests but of general interests. There were also of course purely oligarchical movements, but they were of no importance.

In its ideas on a general reform of legislation and the need to base the administration and justice on new principles, such as freedom of speech, the nobility now represents all other classes. It has assumed this position not because these needs are felt more strongly by it than by other classes, but merely because in the present régime, only the nobility has an organization capable of making political demands. If the other classes had legal organs, through which they could express their thoughts, they too would speak about these problems in the same way as the nobility though in even stronger tones. Other classes, even more than the nobility, feel the burden of the general evils of the existing organization of the State.

Although these were only the first symptoms of a general process of growing political consciousness, they were enough to show that problems could no longer be solved, as had been attempted in the peasant reform, by relying for support on the central bureaucracy. The results of a reform which had been planned as purely technical and administrative were now obvious. 'In a bureaucratic régime, the expert knowledge, intelligence and experience of people who are allotted a task are utterly useless. The régime always acts like a machine with no opinions.' And so it was essential to move from this despotic administration to free political discussion. Chernyshevsky began to give examples in the last part of these letters, and explained the difficulties of the situation in which the peasants had been placed by the reform.

At the very beginning of this work he asked himself whether the position he had taken up was not 'a betrayal of the people'. With great firmness and literary skill he answered that it was. Why then had he written the letters? He had come to the conclusion that on the one hand the peasant movement, however widespread, could not lead to a general revolution, and, on the other, that the forces of the 'new people', however limited, would be enough to guide the movement of independent men, if this could be widened and deepened. No longer, as in 1859, must he cut himself off from the liberals. Rather he must be at their head.

He now no longer felt alone. He was struck by the energy, the dedicated spirits and wide human sympathies of the men whom he found immediately around him. Though Dobrolyubov, the only man who shared his ideas, died at this time, the reactions of the new generation, and the growing numbers who followed the current which they had both created, showed him that a new force had emerged. Some years later, in exile, one of the men who joined him at this time said: 'Chernyshevsky, the cold inaccessible Chernyshevsky, rejoiced like a child at every sign of life in Russia, and every action which brought to light conscience and energy.'[121]

But these latest ventures were soon crushed by the repression that now set in. In April 1862 plans were made which, in the summer of that year, led to his arrest and the suspension of the *Sovremennik*. In a report drawn up by V. A. Dolgorukov, Alexander II's Chief of Police, on 27th April, the general political reasons for these measures were clearly given. Liberal concessions had allowed the growth of a movement and state of mind which aimed at seizing the initiative from the authorities. All outstanding problems of the peasant reform must be solved as quickly as possible. It must never be forgotten, said the report, that the discontented nobles were also officers; and that it was from the peasants, who were now revolting, that were recruited the soldiers of the army 'on which the safety of the Empire is founded'. Their discipline must therefore be supervised with particular care. Steps must be taken to put an end to the political significance assumed by the universities, and the freedom of the press must be still further restricted. 'All this is entirely in accordance with what I want', noted Alexander II on the report.[122]

The Emperor's policy consisted in granting tardy concessions of an administrative and social character, without ever going too far and without ever allowing the political problem to be raised. To this policy he remained faithful for the twenty years of his reign, and it was against this that the entire

Populist movement had to fight. They had to attack despotism directly by means of revolts and attempts on the Emperor's life; and at the same time make use of propaganda in order to bring about a situation in which the solitary duel between revolutionaries and authorities could be replaced by the discussion and solution of general problems by all independents of whatever social category. The Populists, therefore, had to create a powerful revolutionary organization and at the same time stress their democratic aims. In his *Letters without an Address* Chernyshevsky had raised the first phase of the problem, at the peak of the wave of discontent and hopes which followed the reform of 19th February 1861. Now the proposed repressive measures were to make him feel for himself how difficult it was to try to widen the movement on a democratic basis.

'Extraordinary measures' were needed, in the words of Dolgorukov, though he looked upon these as even more difficult to take than the situation in fact warranted. 'The smallest error or lack of success in government plans of such great importance can lead to a premature outbreak, whose consequences are unforeseeable.' He drew up a list of fifty people in St Petersburg to be dealt with in various ways. First on the list was Chernyshevsky, and against his name was a note, added in April 1862 (not in Alexander's handwriting): 'This is still necessary.' The authorities were frightened of touching him and wanted to strike at the right moment.

The fires that broke out in the capital during the summer—which were probably merely accidental, but which were used by the entire reactionary press as a proof of revolutionary activities—and the circulation of the manifesto *Young Russia*, brought about the desired psychological climate. The *Sovremennik* was suspended.[123] Only a legal pretext was now needed to arrest Chernyshevsky. This was carelessly provided by Herzen, who, in front of various people, entrusted a letter to a traveller returning to Russia. Among those present was an agent of the Third Section, who immediately telegraphed the news to St Petersburg. The traveller was arrested at the frontier. In one of these letters from Herzen to Serno-Solovevich was found a proposal that he should come and print the *Sovremennik* in London. Serno-Solovevich and Chernyshevsky were arrested.

While Herzen in his memoirs expressed his grief at this fatal lack of prudence, Chernyshevsky never seems to have spoken of it to anyone, even during his long imprisonment. His spirits were extraordinarily resilient in defeat, and besides, he well knew that the letter had only been a pretext.

Ever since the autumn of the previous year he had been under observation, as had all those who frequented his house. His door-keeper was in the pay of the police, and a cook had been sent to him who was 'to report everything possible about the Chernyshevsky family'.[124] But he had been remarkably efficient in concealing his activities. He relied chiefly on his position as a writer. Though his attitude was independent, he had always said that he did not want to take part in conspiracies. It is true that he had often been warned of the dangers which he was running. The campaign against him, which was organized by the reactionary newspapers and which grew fiercer at the beginning of 1859, was an obvious omen. 'As from 1861', he said later, 'the rumour spread that I was to be arrested, either immediately or on the following day.'[125] He received anonymous letters, and so did the police concerning him, but they had their own reasons for not wanting Chernyshevsky to be alarmed.[126] He was encouraged to go abroad, or to accept some academic appointment. And at the last moment the Governor of St Petersburg, Prince Suvorov—who, with some reason, was known as liberal, though not according to Chernyshevsky's definition of the word—sent Chernyshevsky his *aide de camp* to suggest that he should leave Russia. It is true that for some time the police had arranged that he was not to be given a passport, but he was told that even this difficulty could be overcome if he was prepared to accept Suvorov's advice.

But in his fight with the authorities Chernyshevsky wanted to remain at his post to the last—a decision that sums up his whole life. There were many reasons: his almost religious spirit of resignation; the conviction that he was destined for prison; the desire to give himself one more proof of his resolution about which his conscience had been so tormented ever since boyhood; the certainty that he had left no legal evidence of his guilt; possibly even some illusions about the strength of Alexander II's power; and above all his logical position as an intellectual, adhering firmly to his ideals.

He remained in the Peter-Paul fortress from July 1862 to May 1864. The police themselves gave a very simple explanation for this long period of interrogation. 'The Third Section has no legal evidence on which to inculpate Chernyshevsky with having encouraged revolt and aroused subversive activities against the Government.'[127] Even Herzen's letter contained only an invitation; it was political but scarcely legal evidence. And so evidence had to be manufactured. An *agent provocateur* was found from the circle around the *Sovremennik* and induced to provide forged letters to prove that the appeal to the peasants quoted above was written by Chernyshevsky. On this basis a Committee of Senators sentenced him, on 17th February 1864, to fourteen years' hard labour in Siberia and to banishment there for life. Two months later Alexander II confirmed this sentence, but reduced the period of hard labour to seven years.

Chernyshevsky defended himself with intelligence and dignity, fighting in vain against the perjured methods of the Third Section and the crass stupidity of the judges who condemned him. When his friend Mikhailov, who had been arrested in 1861, had made an open profession of faith, admitting all the charges, Chernyshevsky admired him but did not approve of his policy. 'He should not have confessed. He should have done everything in his power to save himself. There are few enough of us already. Why throw ourselves into prison?'[128] He did not repudiate his ideas; not that he was even questioned about them, so certain were the judges on this point. Instead he tried to defend himself mainly on the legal plane.[129] But, as his sentence made quite clear, he was condemned because he was one of the leading editors of the *Sovremennik*. 'Its ideas were mainly materialist and socialist, aiming to deny religion, morality and the law. So much so that the government thought it necessary to suppress this paper. At the same time circumstantial evidence was discovered which made it clear that Chernyshevsky was carrying out activities harmful to the Government.'[130] It was obviously of little enough importance that this evidence was legally insufficient.

In the Peter-Paul fortress he wrote a great deal. His work there, an act of combined faith and despair, was virtually a sequel to his work on the *Sovremennik*. At first, prison made him think that he would be able to resume his philosophical studies, which during the last few years had had to be given up because of his political activities and journalism. This is what he would devote himself to when he was eventually freed.

Then I will be able to find the means of living more easily because eight years' work has given me an established reputation. So I will have time to do what I have dreamed of for so long. My plans are now definitely made. I will begin a *History of the Material and Spiritual Life of Humanity* in a number of volumes. This has never yet been done, because the works of Guizot, Buckle (and even Vico) are conceived on too limited a scale and are very badly executed. Then there will be a *Critical Dictionary of Ideas and Events* based on the history.[131]

And so he continued to draw up plans. In them we feel an exaltation of solitude, and a desire to work which, in his imagination, made up for his inability to act. In the Peter-Paul fortress his daily task of enlightenment was transformed into an encyclopaedic dream. A few drafts of these schemes have remained, but they are of no importance.

But lack of material soon made him turn to other ideas, this time literature.

For a long time I have planned, among other things, to apply myself to literature. But I am convinced that people of my character must do this only in their later years. Earlier than this I would have had no chance of succeeding. Rousseau waited till old age, and Godwin too. A novel is destined for the great mass of the public. It is a writer's most serious undertaking, and so it belongs to old age. The frivolity of the form must be compensated for by the solidity of the thought. So up till now I have only been collecting material for the final stage of my life.[132]

He therefore translated Rousseau, and tried to follow the example of Godwin, who, in old age, had expounded in a novel the Communist and humanitarian ideas of his youth.

Chernyshevsky's words explain clearly enough his conception of the novel. Within these deliberate limits, he was extraordinarily successful in doing what he wanted. *What is to be done?* was soon published in the *Sovremennik* (which was able to resume publication after his arrest) and moulded a whole generation of Populist students and revolutionaries. It became a blueprint of life for the young intelligentsia. Though a novel in form, in fact it recounted the story of their origins; their rise in the years that followed the Crimean War; their moral and personal problems and their disgust at being confined in an uncivilized society of petty interests; their enthusiasms and the formation of their characters through ruthless and paradoxical decisions; their personal efforts to create a different life, which was to include personal freedom and at the same time devotion to the people. It was for this young generation that the book had been written. The answers to the question *What is to be done?* lay in student 'communes' (groups of young men living together and sharing all their possessions), and in cooperatives of production through which these young men could reach the town population. These 'communes' did, in fact, become nests for all the Populist conspiracies of the 'sixties. In the last chapter Chernyshevsky pointed out—in veiled terms, obscure to those who knew nothing of him, but clear enough to those who understood his aims—the revolutionary outcome of these ventures of self-education and social activity. The hero of the novel was a typical revolutionary of the times: a man for whom life's problems are not solved by an affirmation of personal freedom, but by virtue of the task which awaits him and his dangerous and uncompromising opposition to despotism.

The author of *What is to be done?* was no longer the old Chernyshevsky, the man of acute political insight who had somehow aroused and guided the young generation from afar, while he remained personally preoccupied and absorbed in his difficult relations with the authorities. Indeed, in the novel he gave a veiled explanation for the attitude he had adopted before his arrest.[133] Now at last he could say what had not been opportune as long as the chance of further action remained. The novel was a sort of confession; it contained all the moralizing, the introspection which were concealed in his personality and which he had, as it were, buried when he had devoted himself to his work of enlightenment and politics. Even the Socialist ideas which he expounded in the novel were rather those of his youth; they reflected the beliefs of Fourier and not the economic theories that he had formulated after his study of Mill and the problems of State intervention. Even the literary form recalled the romantic literature (chiefly George Sand), from which he had cut himself off with an ironic smile when action and work had been possible. But it was these youthful and sentimental aspects that ensured the novel's success, and which gave it its great influence when reaction set in and hope in the immediate revival of political issues died away. For after the experiences which closed with the arrest of Chernyshevsky, the young generation had somehow to begin again from scratch.[134]

Besides *What is to be done?* he wrote a number of other stories in the Peter-Paul fortress, which he wanted to assemble in a volume. But they are not as interesting as his novel. Only here and there do we come across a vivid page, usually a passage of autobiography. For instance, in a long story called *Alferev*, he put these words into the mouth of a character called Dikarev (a name derived from the word *dikar*, meaning a savage):

He did not want, and in any case he was unable, to publish and go on publishing without a break, as do men of letters. Only for two or three years did he work hard without interruption, but this was a quite exceptional period in his life. He was no longer a young man; his way of thought was now completely settled and did not correspond to any of the ideas which were then in dispute . . . Dikarev was unable to find in contemporary literature any party whose opinions corresponded to even half of his own, but he felt the need to express his own convictions. And so he gave in to this summons which came not from his talent but rather from his conscience, and he worked with passion . . . 'These works were not the result of my will', he said. 'I had no choice in the matter. Nature, which from time to time sends down a thunderbolt, produced them through me. They are not books but phenomena of life and nature. This is why they are strong. I myself have scarcely any strength at all . . .'[135]

His doubts about his character, which had tormented him as a young man, were thus resolved in this faith in his works. He knew that in two or three years' writing he had created something of real importance.

On 19th May 1864, the ceremony of Chernyshevsky's 'civil execution' was performed. A number of his contemporaries have described what was to be his final departure from St Petersburg. Perhaps the description which is most characteristic in its simplicity is that by F. Frey:

Everything showed that something extraordinary was about to happen: another black column with chains; the scaffold surrounded by soldiers, policemen and civil guards all tightly linked to keep the people at the necessary distance; a large number of well-dressed people; coaches; generals going backwards and forwards; and elegant ladies. An old woman offered me a little stool. 'Poor wretches like us have got to earn their bread somehow', she told me. But even if she had asked for fifty rather than ten kopeks I would still have taken the stool, because there was a large crowd in the third row . . . The carriage stopped fifty yards from me . . . The crowd flung itself at it and the guards shouted, 'Back there'. Three men passed rapidly along the ranks of soldiers; they were Chernyshevsky and the two executioners . . . I heard hushed voices saying 'Keep your umbrellas down', and then complete silence. A policeman climbed up on to the stool, the soldiers were ordered to attention, the executioners removed Chernyshevsky's cap and then the condemnation was read. It lasted about a quarter of an hour. No one heard a word of it. Chernyshevsky himself knew it already, and was less interested than anyone. He was apparently looking for someone and kept on staring through the crowd. Two or three times he made a sign with his head on one side. At last the reading ended. The executioners made him kneel down, then broke a sword on his head and put on the chains which were attached to the column. Suddenly it began to rain hard. The executioner put back his hat. Chernyshevsky thanked him and arranged it on his head as far as he could with his hands in chains. And then clasping his hands he quietly waited for the end of the proceedings. In the crowd there was a deathly hush. The old woman who was handing out stools kept on asking me questions. 'Has he got his own clothes on or not?' 'Did he come in a carriage or on a cart?' I tried to swallow my tears so as to be able to give some sort of answer somehow. When the ceremony was over, all the spectators flung themselves on to the coach and broke through the police guard, who had linked hands. Only the efforts of the mounted police succeeded in keeping the people away. Then (I am certain of this, but I did not see it myself) people threw bunches of flowers at him. One woman was arrested. The carriage began to move and, as always happens with prisoners, went at a walking pace. Many who wanted a close look took advantage of this. One of them gave the signal to cheer. It was given by a young officer who took off his hat and shouted 'Farewell, Chernyshevsky'. Others immediately took up this cry, and it was soon mixed with another bolder one, 'Goodbye, Chernyshevsky'. He heard this shout and answered very courteously from the window, nodding his head . . . When they decided to speed up the pace of the carriage, the group which was in front continued to run, shouting and waving their handkerchiefs and hats. The shopkeepers (the carriage was now passing a market) were amazed at this unusual sight. Chernyshevsky understood quicker than anyone else that this group of hotheads would at once be arrested if they left the crowd. He bowed once more with the most cheerful smile (he was obviously leaving in good spirits) and made a warning gesture with his finger. The crowd gradually dispersed, but some hired carriages and continued to follow him.[136]

Only one further detail need be added. During this ceremony, at once so mediaeval and so modern, there was attached to his breast a piece of cardboard on which was written 'State criminal'.

For a time the authorities thought of treating him as Nicholas I had treated Bakunin; i.e. not sending him to forced labour in Siberia, but rather confining him to a fortress, this time at Shlisselburg, where the most dangerous political prisoners were kept between the eighteenth century and 1905. But eventually they decided to carry out the sentence. He was allowed to say goodbye to his wife, his son Alexander, a few friends—among them those who had taken over the *Sovremennik*—and his doctor friend, Bokov, who was the original of one of the characters in *What is to be done?* He left on 20th May; two months later he reached the mines of Nerchinsk, after passing through Irkutsk.

Hard labour (*katorga*) to which State criminals were condemned in fact meant prison. As the Decembrists before him and many Populist and Socialist revolutionaries after, he was a prisoner in various penal settlements, without ever having to work in the mines. For a year he was with Mikhailov, his poet friend, and later with Polish prisoners; then gradually with those condemned for membership of the various Populist groups organized during the 'sixties. After 1866, specially rigid supervision was enforced, because one of the primary aims of the various groups was always to free him. At the end of that year Chernyshevsky was transferred to the Alexandrovsky Zavod, another large penal settlement in the province of Irkutsk.[137] Shortly afterwards he met there many of the men who were condemned following Karakozov's attempt on the life of the Tsar.

When his term of imprisonment came to an end in August 1870, the authorities inquired whether they should free him. A report sent to the Emperor advised that it was better not 'in view of the influence that Chernyshevsky has on subversive parties, and in view of the fact that he might become the centre of revolutionary Nihilism abroad'. The Council of Ministers also thought that it was essential to keep him in Siberia, and the Emperor confirmed this opinion.[138]

And so it was decided to send him to a village not far from the diminutive town of Vilyuysk, several hundred kilometres from Yakutsk. But after another attempt to organize his escape (made by G. A. Lopatin, one of the boldest of the revolutionaries of the time) Chernyshevsky was again put in prison under strict supervision until the end of 1871. He then remained for more than eleven years at Vilyuysk, whose Yakut inhabitants could not even speak Russian. During this period it was only very rarely that he had any personal contact with other deported revolutionaries passing through the district. His main contacts were with a few old peasant 'Old Believers' banished there for their religious beliefs.

For Russians less used to hardship than I am, the climate here is not very good. It's not a question of the cold. There's almost no difference between 20 and 45 degrees . . . It's the climate itself and the air which is bad, except during the cold period. All around there are only marshes, and the ground is always soaked down to a considerable depth . . . Moisture of the air that comes from the earth is not like moisture from rain, and only disappears in winter-time.[139] Vilyuysk is called a town, but it is not really even a village in the Russian sense of the word. It's so deserted and small that there's nothing like it anywhere in Russia. Imagine a small old house in the country in which it is only possible to live because there is a town or large village nearby, with shops where one can buy things. And then you must imagine this house transported into the middle of the desert, seven hundred versts from the nearest market. And even in this market it's often impossible to find even the most essential things. I've been told, for instance, that at Yakutsk it is often impossible to buy a plate, a fork, a knife or even the simplest glass. The ones which were brought last year have all been sold, and we must wait until the end of next summer when others will be brought[140] . . . As for the inhabitants, it is pathetic to see them. I am well acquainted with misery, I know it very well indeed. But looking at these people I find it quite impossible to remain cold and detached. Their misery melts even my hardened heart. I have given up going to the town, so as to avoid seeing these wretched people . . . One wonders what they are, whether people or something little better than stray dogs, animals without even a name. In fact, of course, they are people and not stupid, indeed more gifted than Europeans (apparently the Yakut boys are better at lessons than Russians). But they are poor savages and wild. And the Russians who are here have become very like them. It's impossible to talk to them; they are so nervous that they suspect every word of being some lie that will ruin them. They behave like this not only with me but with each other.

One day he quoted a conversation that he had happened to have with one of the inhabitants.

'Do you often get murders here?' 'No, the people are quite calm; but there are frequent suicides.' 'And why?' 'Because of the loneliness. Almost everyone becomes so melancholy that he finally makes up his mind and hangs himself.' Such is the village, and the region of Vilyuysk. For me it doesn't matter much. I don't have to talk to men, or see them; books replace them for me. But for others it would be impossible to live here.[141]

He stayed there for more than eleven years. In summer 1874 he had refused an invitation of the government which proposed to free him as long as he signed an appeal for mercy.[142] Nor does he appear ever to have thought seriously of flight, partly because his health was gradually giving way, but mainly because of his natural spirit of resignation, which sustained him during these years.

He was only freed from Siberia after secret negotiations between what remained of *Narodnaya Volya* after the assassination of Alexander II on 1st March 1881 and the new sovereign Alexander III. In return for concessions, among them Chernyshevsky's return to Russia,[143] the revolutionaries promised that they would not carry out other acts of terrorism during the coronation ceremony. Simultaneously the steps taken by his family began to have some influence. These had been going on for some time and were supported by a press campaign which included some French newspapers. And so in July 1883 he was able to leave Vilyuysk and was exiled to Astrakhan at the mouth of the Volga. It was only six years later that he was allowed back to his native Saratov. His health was now seriously impaired, and on 17th October 1889 (less than four months after his arrival in his native town) he died.

In Siberia he had tried to continue writing almost exclusively works of literature, but, in fact, the end of his daily political journalism and controversies in St Petersburg meant the end of his true life as a writer. It was only in his autobiographical fragments, especially those that recalled the time of the *Sovremennik*, that he recovered his powers. The *Prologue* which has often been quoted here, and which he wrote when serving his sentence of hard labour, was his finest work of literature, far superior to *What is to be done?* from this point of view. Problems of personal behaviour, like those of politics, take on a paradoxical aspect, as if dominated by Diderot's question *Est-il bon, est-il méchant?* (He read Diderot in the Peter-Paul fortress, and translated one of his stories.) The exciting atmosphere of those times, when words so frequently changed their meaning and only those prepared to be daring in thought and action could find their way about— the atmosphere in fact of the St Petersburg intelligentsia in 1860—all this he interpreted and portrayed with great brilliance, while his satire of the liberals shows some of the political strength of his earlier articles. Rarely do we find anything to compare to this in his other works, which are often incredibly muddled. They were also usually left incomplete, not just because of the circumstances in which he was living but because he himself felt convinced of their uselessness.

At Astrakhan he planned to resume writing, but he was overwhelmed by the work of translation, which he had to undertake to earn a living. The lonely dignity which sustained him throughout his time in Siberia still forbade him to beg, or even re-enter the world from which he had been excluded. Until his last moments, despite ill-health, he had the courage to be himself.

To discover the true Chernyshevsky, we must read his letters, and even then only those written in special circumstances, when political hopes or the need to express his own opinions made him recover his energy of earlier days.

The first chance he had of writing what he thought, without it being controlled by the censor, was in 1871 in a clandestine letter to his wife. He had not given up hope of a Russian revolution.

Throughout Western Europe a new epoch is beginning. When will the results of the German victory have their effect in Russia? . . . All my prophecies about the important problems of Europe and America in the last ten years have been right. And now it should be easy enough to foresee what will happen in Russia within two or three years—or possibly even only one? There is just one thing that I can't see from here—whether there will be a delay of two or three years in the clash between Russia and Western Europe, or whether it has already begun. Poor Russian people, a miserable fate awaits it in this struggle. But the results will be favourable, and then, my dear, it will have need of truth. I am no longer a young man, but remember that our life is still ahead of us . . . I can speak of historical events because I have learnt much and thought much. My turn will come. We will then see whether it is worth complaining about the fact that for so many years I have only been able to study and think. We will then see that this has been useful for our country.[144]

But when he was able to leave Siberia and go to Astrakhan, *Narodnaya Volya* had almost been destroyed at its nerve centre. The oppressive reaction of Alexander III was beginning. The Populist movement to which he had imparted so much width and vigour was now broken. In his letters after 1881, written in Siberia and Astrakhan, he scarcely spoke of politics, because he obviously thought that his letters would be read by strangers. He merely said that he did not believe in the prevailing ideas of his time and that he clung to the beliefs he had held in his days on the *Sovremennik*.

Among these prevailing ideas was positivism, which he had never accepted. General belief in progress aroused his sarcasm. In a letter to his son Alexander he said:

Of all the people I met, young or old, only Dobrolyubov thought in more or less the same way as I did. All the books I read except those of Feuerbach contained stupidities. Feuerbach was not what is generally called a progressive . . . I have always laughed at progressives of all sorts . . . I have always laughed at every form of enthusiasm, except when I thought a serious reproof was needed more than laughter. Enthusiasts are stupid, they are stupid little boys grotesquely contained in an adult body. The majority of them are good people, and we must be indulgent with them. But they are children, tiny children who are leading this century on to stupidities unworthy of grown-up men.[145]

It was not merely general belief in progress that annoyed him but also Darwinism, which was gaining ground in Russia at the same time as positivism. In this he clearly saw the origin of racial doctrines which would exalt the struggle for existence.

The fact is that I am an old man. My ideas of botany and zoology are derived from the eighteenth century and especially Lamarck. Darwinism, where it is correct, is no novelty for me, but Darwin, who was a pupil of Cuvier, did not know Lamarck (a mediocre man, as he himself said). And unfortunately for science it was Malthus who impelled him to these considerations. Now Malthus was a sophist who often said very intelligent things but always for a pessimistic reason, and his ideas have taken root in the theories of Darwin: the results of evil actions are good. Evil gives birth to good and so good is evil and evil is good. This is an absurd, disgusting confusion of words. In Darwin all these stupidities are relatively harmless, because concern with the good of plants and animals does not form a particularly important part of our human consciousness. But when these stupidities are applied to the history of human beings, then it degenerates into bestial inhumanity. It doesn't concern us if a few small trilobites or fossiled ammonites disappear and are replaced by other zoological forms. But supposing the African negroes fight against each other; is that good or bad? According to Malthus and Darwin it is good. And if we whites destroy all the negroes that will be even better? Of course. And this would be true if it wasn't for one thing: when we whites start slaughtering the negroes, we ourselves—just because of these beautiful actions—become barbarians, wild beasts, savages like the negroes . . . We can only keep our present good qualities by avoiding shabby actions and foul behaviour. If we lose our qualities we will end by losing the welfare which we enjoy at present. And so the spreading of our race in Africa can be useful only if we use for it honest and good means . . . Darwin ignored all this . . .[146]

He ended by saying that these theories seemed to be spreading, and to be confirmed by what Schopenhauer and Hartmann were then preaching. He sent long letters to his son from Vilyuysk telling him not to be attracted by the basic theory of all these various kinds of positivism, i.e. the philosophy of Comte. He said in 1876:

This poor fellow who knew nothing of Hegel or even of Kant, nor it seems of Locke, but who had learnt much from Saint-Simon (a thinker of genius but very ignorant), learnt by heart the prefaces of physics books, and thought that he could become a genius and create a system of philosophy. His formula of the three stages of thought (theological, metaphysical and positive) is completely idiotic. It merely means that errors often precede truth, that is all. A theological stage of science has never existed; neither has the metaphysical, as Comte means it, ever occurred.[147]

Eventually he discovered the author who summed up all these positivist elements—Spencer. And for the rest of his life, alone and unheard, he violently attacked him, merely to clear his own conscience, though he was forced to translate him to earn a living. He said that it was all 'nonsense'.[148] Even the language in which it was written lacked form, but, he added, 'the public will find it excellent'.[149] He wanted to write a preface to his translation to explain what he himself thought of it, but he lacked the energy. And so he returned to Spinoza, perhaps his favourite philosopher after Feuerbach.

6. THE INTELLECTUAL MOVEMENT OF THE 'SIXTIES DOBROLYUBOV AND SHCHAPOV

CHERNYSHEVSKY OFTEN SAID that Dobrolyubov was the only man who was really close to him, his only true collaborator on the *Sovremennik*. He added that this friend, who died so young, had been a better man than he was, a more effective writer, nobler and more spirited.

Such an appreciation shows how deep was the friendship between Chernyshevsky and Dobrolyubov, and has given rise to the later opinion that they can be placed on the same plane and considered equally important in the intellectual movement of the 'sixties. But this is a mere legend, however attractive, derived from the admiration spontaneously aroused in all who met him by this boy of genius who by the age of twenty-five was able to make his own effective contribution to the discussion on Russia's spiritual problems. Such indeed was his function: to express with even greater warmth than Chernyshevsky had intended, the feelings, agonies and enthusiasm aroused by the political vision that Chernyshevsky had inspired.

Because of this Dobrolyubov had a great following in the new generation and exercised a remarkable influence on the intelligentsia. It was he who gave shape to Populist psychology. But it must not be forgotten that it was Chernyshevsky who provided the framework within which these feelings and desires were born, and who created the political foundations on which Dobrolyubov's enthusiasm and irony were based.

Dobrolyubov was, so to speak, the first fruit of Populist ideas. He was the first to demonstrate the influence they could have on young men, to show how they could arouse an irresistible desire to follow them and carry them into one's personal and political life.[1]

Dobrolyubov, like Chernyshevsky, came from a family of priests. His father was one of the most cultivated and widely respected clergymen of Nizhny Novgorod, and it was here that Nikolay Alexandrovich was born on 24th January 1836. At the seminary he was a studious and lonely boy, precociously introspective and increasingly preoccupied with the problems posed by the world in which he found himself, by the discipline of his superiors and by association with his school friends. He was very religious and greatly concerned with his everyday behaviour. He kept a diary and noted down his sinful thoughts in a 'Psichatorium'.[2] His very first works were *examens de conscience*.

But reading soon turned him from this exaggerated concern with himself to the sphere of literature and ideas. When, in August 1853, he succeeded in passing the entrance examination to the Teachers' Training School (his parents could not afford to keep him at the university) a new life opened up for him. As he grew up his religious inclinations began to take the shape they later retained—one of constant anguish about the moral significance of all his actions and thoughts, however small or insignificant. For him, as for Chernyshevsky, a reading of Feuerbach marked the end of his Christianity.

He pursued his higher education at St Petersburg during the Crimean War. His discussions with his friends, his quarrels with the authorities of the Institute and his reading—all took on a political flavour, reflecting the general reawakening of Russian society. He soon became one of the most enthusiastic members of a group of students who in September 1855 circulated a lithographed leaflet attacking the entire current political situation. Although the ideas in this pamphlet were not very precise, it showed a hatred for 'military despotism' and a keen desire to be acquainted with the men and ideas that had been in conflict with absolutism since the time of the Decembrists.[3]

Rousseau, Proudhon, Bruno Bauer, Strauss, Belinsky—all led him to a passionate study of the works of Herzen. He began to seek in them 'a concept of honour',[4] and he read enthusiastically his book on the development of revolutionary ideas in Russia and ended by saying:

I am a convinced Socialist. So much so that I am quite ready to take part immediately in a poor society where each member has equal rights and equal property . . . My earthly ideal has not yet been achieved, except possibly in the democratic society spoken of by Herzen when he described the meeting in which he took part in London in 1855.[5]

In 1856 he met Chernyshevsky, who was at once captivated by this young man of twenty, already so well informed and so keen to devote himself to 'an ideal not yet realized on earth'. He hastened his development by bringing him into touch with reality, and emphasizing, not without irony, the true magnitude of the task which awaited him. He also prevented him from getting himself into further trouble with the authorities of the Teachers' Training School. But after reading his first articles and realizing that he had as yet no employment, Chernyshevsky put him in charge of all the literary side of the *Sovremennik*. He was convinced that he had at last found a man whose feelings and thoughts were in sympathy with his own.

Many years later in Siberia, Chernyshevsky described the birth and flowering of their friendship. This was indeed the main feature of the memories so vividly depicted in his novel *The Prologue*. He wrote an imaginary diary of his dead friend, trying to visualize himself as Dobrolyubov must have seen him when they met for the first time. He remembered that he had explained the difficulties of his situation. 'His voice was like a discord in the sweet concert of the Russian liberals.' He remembered too that he had opened his heart to him and revealed his true hopes.

The time for serious things will come. One day in some corner of Europe, most probably in France, the storm will burst which will spread throughout Europe as it did in 1848. In 1830 the storm affected only Western Germany. In 1848 it included Vienna and Berlin. So that we can assume that next time it will reach Moscow and St Petersburg . . . In this or some other way the time for serious things will come. There is no doubt about this. It is proved by our ties with Europe, which are becoming closer and closer. We are too far behind them. In some way or other Europe will drag us forward, pulling us towards itself.[6]

In the meantime they must prepare themselves with patience and growing energies.

For five years Dobrolyubov contributed an enormous amount of work to the *Sovremennik*. He dealt with all the subjects which might in any way help to form a young intelligentsia—an intelligentsia which was to have no illusions about the liberalism which came from above, and which was determined to demand for itself political responsibility in the name of the country. To this end he made use mainly of literary criticism. Through this he could make deep and detailed psychological analyses, and write real sermons on the sins of society and the weaknesses of the intelligentsia. From 1859 onwards he resorted to direct satire in verse and prose, starting a supplement to the *Sovremennik* called *Svistok* (The Whistle). The huge success enjoyed by this helped to create a political atmosphere far removed from the facile enthusiasms of the reformers.[7]

His weak constitution suffered greatly. He developed consumption, and in May 1860 went to Switzerland for a cure. He wandered through France, staying in Paris, Dijon and Rouen. At the end of 1860 he went to Italy, and travelled to Florence, Milan, Rome, Genoa, Naples and Messina. At Naples he thought for a moment of marrying, but in the summer of 1861 he returned to Russia, just in time to hear from his friends the news of the first arrests among the writers. 'I hurriedly told him a few details about this', wrote one of them, 'and he lifted himself up on the sofa where he was lying and looked at me, already with the fixed stare of a God: his magnificent and intelligent eyes were burning; there shone in them the hope and faith in that finer future to which he had sacrificed his years and finest powers.'[8] He died on 17th November 1861 in the arms of Chernyshevsky.

Dobrolyubov's articles in the *Sovremennik* were chiefly concerned with the relationship between the spiritual renaissance of the intelligentsia and the transformation of the entire life of the popular masses. The reforms which everyone considered essential would have some meaning only if the people itself played a part in them, and if they had an effect not just on the administrative machine but also on the customs and mentality of the peasants, the merchants and the immense mass of people still excluded from any share in political life.[9]

And so from the first Dobrolyubov emphasized the inadequacy of the 'literature of public denunciation', that literature of a 'constabulary of satire' hitting out at the superficial scandals and evils of the State, but never touching the one root of all evils, i.e. the relationship between the ruling classes and the people.

It was in the eighteenth century, the age of Catherine II, that he sought the origins of this moralizing criticism which was so ironical about the habits of rulers, but never questioned the right of rulers to exist at all.

Our satirists will attack rudeness, corruption, hypocrisy, illegality, pride, cruelty to the poor, and flattery of superiors. But it is only rarely that such denunciations ever hint that these individual phenomena are the inevitable results of the abnormality of our entire social structure. They will, for instance, attack the corruption of officials as if all the harm was derived from their personal habits of cheating the public. But our satires never extend the problem of bribes into an examination of the general evil of our entire bureaucracy and of the circumstances which are at its origin and which have allowed it to develop.[10]

Even the best examples of the 'literature of public denunciation', such as Saltykov-Shchedrin's *Provincial Essays* were confined to these limits. Saltykov-Shchedrin himself had been far more effective in his stories for the *Sovremennik* written ten years earlier. At that time the Petrashevskists had pointed out the social origins of these bureaucratic evils which he now merely described.

But of course times were different: energies and ideals are not what they were then. That was a vital, a genuine movement, really humanist and not weakened or distracted by legal and economic doctrinairism. In those days to ask why a man becomes a criminal or a thief was to ask why he suffers and is afraid of everything. Bitterly, painfully, men began to examine the pathology of these questions. If this road had been followed, the results would be very much more fruitful. But now our solutions are simple. If people steal, it means the police is carrying out its duty inefficiently. If there are bribes, it means that the director is incompetent . . . But in those days things were different. If a man stole, it meant that he had not found work and was dying of starvation. If an employee pocketed a bribe, it meant that he had a family of fifteen to be fed. From the ethical point of view, the two solutions are very different. One gives rise to human feelings and manful thought. The other leads straight to the police and a legal form of death.[11]

It must never be forgotten that when Dobrolyubov wrote this he knew perfectly well that his words would be supervised by the censorship. So that the mere substitution of the words 'will to solve one's own problems' for 'manly thought' and 'reforming absolutism' for 'legal forms' makes it quite clear what Dobrolyubov meant by referring back to the Petrashevskists and attacking all those who wished to confine changes in the State and society to the surface.

But was there ever any real chance that the transformation that was begun in 1855 could affect the lower classes? Were there any real signs that suggested the birth of a force which might be capable of seizing the initiative from reforming despotism? Dobrolyubov was constantly on the look-out, and careful to note any sign that might confirm these hopes.

In 1859 he published in the *Sovremennik* a long commentary on Ostrovsky's comedies, which he called 'The Kingdom of Darkness'. His article remains a classic spiritual analysis of a society. In it he described the life of the merchants, the Russian bourgeoisie; he spoke of the arbitrary power which prevailed in its families and customs, of the ignorance and traditionalist spirit of that closed caste. 'A purely exterior submission, dull and concentrated grief, capable of going as far as complete idiocy and gloomy depersonalization . . . all these strands are intermingled in "The Kingdom of Darkness" . . . And yet next door to it, on the other side of the wall, there is another life, shining clean, cultivated.'[12] The opposition and the struggle between these two were bitter and violent, but a new force was making itself felt even in the world of shadows. The desire for freedom was not yet dead, even the nightmare of tradition was fading. A year later he read Ostrovsky's new play *The Storm*, and called his article 'A ray of light in the Kingdom of Darkness'.[13] And still later, discussing Dostoevsky's first novels, he ended: 'Our middle classes include many men who are forgotten, reviled and injured, and whose lives are oppressive both spiritually and physically; but despite an outward resignation, they feel grief, they are ready for anger and protest, they long for a way of escape.'[14] Even among the peasants there were signs of a reawakening. Discontent and the search for something new were beginning to replace resignation. 'As many radicals are to be met with among the young peasants as among the sons of other classes.'[15] Though the manner of their protest might be strange, it was none the less significant. Dobrolyubov wrote a detailed article of great interest called *Notes for a character study of the simple Russian people*, and emphasized that 'the fatalism of religious faith and of despair' was now shattered by the promise of emancipation.

There is no longer a corner of Russia where one does not hear how, as soon as the idea of freeing the serfs was discussed, the landlords' peasants met together and sent deputations to the nobles, to the priests, and even to the local authorities, to find out their intentions . . . It is worth remembering too the enthusiasm with which the people burst into the shop in St Petersburg where official publications are sold, as soon as the rumour spread at the beginning of 1856 that the *ukaze* of emancipation was on sale.[16]

The peasants were showing their hatred for serfdom in thousands of ways. They were, for instance, working less, and they were spontaneously starting a temperance movement so as to deprive the State of its revenues from the vodka monopoly. Dobrolyubov referred to this in the *Sovremennik* of 1859, after a battle with the censorship that lasted two months for permission to publish at least part of his article. He seized this occasion to raise the general problem of what was to be expected from the peasants, and he ended:

Yes, among these people there is a force for good, which certainly does not exist in that corrupt and half-mad society which claims to be educated and capable of something serious. The masses are unable to speak eloquently; so they cannot—and do not want to—stick to words, enjoying the sound of their words as they float away in the distance. What they say is never empty. It is expressed as an appeal to facts, and as a condition for immediate action.[17]

But such signs of reawakening were certainly not enough to convince Dobrolyubov of the approach of a deeper revolt. And this belief was largely responsible for his 'bile' as Herzen called it and his 'Nihilism'. Although he always retained his hopes that the movement which had begun with the fall of Sebastopol would go further, he never thought that he personally would see the time when the people would make its own weight and will felt.

So he was acutely aware of the responsibility of the intelligentsia as the only body capable of bringing education to the people, and at the same time representing it. The task that faced the educated classes was immense. They alone could act freely in a society which was dominated by the policy of the State on the one hand, and the oppressive traditionalism of the popular classes on the other. They alone could direct the transformation of Russia and achieve what its people were as yet unable to achieve.

Dobrolyubov therefore devoted much of his work to pointing out the contrast between the intelligentsia's function and its actual position. The sterner, he thought, the duty of the educated classes, the meaner, the more limited, the more hopeless their life and character must have seemed, and the more serious their weaknesses. Emphasizing this contrast, Dobrolyubov finally established an ideal for a Populist intelligentsia which was to have a great influence on the formation of the new generation.

Just as he made use of Ostrovsky's plays to discuss the 'reign of darkness' so now he chose Goncharov's novel *Oblomov* to consider the educated classes, who were incapable of moving from the realm of dreams to that of action. 'The idyll, that is the enemy.' These words sum up his famous article.[18] The inability to have a definite and limited aim in life or even realize that someone could voluntarily devote himself to practical work; the resulting scorn for work; the vague desire for action immediately translated into useless dreams—all this was expressed in Dobrolyubov's *Oblomov*.

In Oblomov is reflected the life of Russia, in him is represented to the life the typical Russian of our times, constructed with implacable severity and exactness. This novel gives us a new and relevant description of our social development, pronounced clearly and firmly, without despair but without childish hopes and with full awareness of the truth.[19]

He compared this 'prototype' with a whole range of other characters in Russian literature, to show that it was the incarnation of that defect in the will which was latent in an entire class, an entire society. From all this was born a sort of monster which had little enough to do with Goncharov's hero, but which acquired the realistic and terrifying intensity of certain distorting mirrors. Everyone could recognize himself in it, each of his readers could identify in that typical face some features of his own. The reformers of the time with their imposing plans to transform Russia could see in it the grimaces of a man beginning to be frightened of the unexpected consequences of his actions and wondering with growing anxiety whether it was really worth throwing over the old habits for a new life. And were not the liberals too Oblomovs of a kind?

If I hear today a country squire talking of the rights of humanity, I know from his very first words that he is an Oblomov. If I come across an official who complains of the chaos and oppression of bureaucracy, he too is an Oblomov. If I hear an officer complaining of the exhaustion of parades and speaking of the uselessness of marching, etc., I have no doubt that he is an Oblomov. When I read in the reviews liberal attacks against the abuses of the authorities or expressions of joy because what was so long hoped for has at last been done, I think to myself that these articles come from the country of Oblomov. When I find myself in the company of educated people who ardently sympathize with the needs of mankind and who for years and years with the same enthusiasm have been repeating stories which are always identical (and sometimes even new) about the corruption of the bureaucracy and oppression and illegality of every kind, then, in spite of myself, I am taken back to the old country of the Oblomovs.[20]

The article ended by clearly explaining why it was essential to attack this mentality 'in all its forms, in every possible disguise'. Only in this way could one find enough strength to pronounce 'an implacable sentence'.[21]

This was a call to action. A long process of development had given the intelligentsia knowledge, hopes and ideals. They must now look upon the time for preparation as over. Dobrolyubov asked in another article:[22]

When will the real day come? What has our society done in the last twenty to thirty years? Until now—nothing. It has educated itself, it has developed, it has stood around listening to the Rudins [one of Turgenev's characters, modelled on Bakunin], and has grieved over their lack of success in the noble fight for ideals. It has prepared itself for action, and done nothing. After the stage in which given ideas are *recognized*, there must come the moment when they are *realized*. Action must follow meditation and talk.[23]

This decisive condemnation of the preceding generation inevitably led to a break with Herzen. But this desire to put thought and action on the same level, this insistence on the vital need for education of character, won Dobrolyubov the new generation.

His entire being was, so to speak, electrified by his ideals . . . He was prepared to sacrifice even his own life to fulfil them. All his thoughts, all his words moved relentlessly to fulfilment in action. But the world in which he lived forbade this.

7+

And the consequent frustration was the reason for his nervous suffering and his moral torments. It was because of this that he constantly burnt himself out in a fever of discontent and even of despair . . . In a letter to a friend he wrote, 'We will die because we have not been able to carry out these activities. Yet we will not die in vain.'[24]

His work in fact was a vigorous protest against 'platonic love in social activity . . . If platonic love of woman is ridiculous, a thousand times more ridiculous is platonic love of country, people, justice.'[25]

He was the first to state uncompromisingly that one's every action, gesture, and taste must be made to correspond with one's ideas, an emphasis which was to be typical of the Populist generation. With him the era which began with the young Bakunin's examination of conscience with eyes reverently fixed on the Hegelian Idea is brought to an end. Now begins instead the period in which love for the people is transformed into the ambition to become a peasant or workman. The aspiration for equality brought into being the student 'communes'; disgust with the hierarchical and oppressed society of Russia led to the young revolutionaries' break with the entire surrounding world. Dobrolyubov was the man who aroused these undetermined energies which were soon to be canalized in the revolutionary movement.

He naturally could not hope that all the intelligentsia, all the educated classes, would be consumed by such extremism. His preaching soon led to a clear break between the great mass of 'well-meaning people' and the few who had to sacrifice everything to 'act'. He himself made this contrast and it exactly defines his meaning.[26]

Dobrolyubov too, like so many contemporaries, saw in this contrast of mentalities a conflict of generations, a clash between 'fathers' and 'sons'. He often idealized 'youth' which he opposed to the liberal intelligentsia, and he did much to create the prototype of the young man of the 'sixties, the 'social type of realistic people with solid nerves and healthy imaginations . . . Looking around at the world, these young men did not indulge in the woolly abstraction and mirages of previous generations. They saw merely the man of blood and flesh in his true relations with the outside world.'[27] His reaction against Oblomov's 'idyll' had put him on the road which was to lead to 'Nihilism', i.e. to that positivist realism which was to be one of the most typical expressions of the barrier between 'sons' and 'fathers'.

But Dobrolyubov was too concerned with political problems to continue further along this road. He always looked upon realism and education of character as tools and not ends in themselves. Not for him the idealization of the free individual surrounded by the crowd of slaves, which occurred in later 'Nihilism'. From this point of view, Dobrolyubov's position lies half way between Chernyshevsky and Pisarev. He was concerned chiefly with the moral and personal problems of the new generation, but was still firmly rooted in the political life of the period which had seen the emancipation of the serfs.

Dobrolyubov rarely tried to give an exact definition of his ideals, most of which he accepted from Chernyshevsky. The article which he devoted in 1859 to 'Robert Owen and his attempts at Social Reform'[28] is enough to show how inferior he was to Chernyshevsky and Herzen when trying to define his Socialist convictions. His articles from Italy, although they are vivid as journalistic reporting, do not have the bitter tang of Chernyshevsky's writing on Poerio and Mazzini's disciples. His point of view is the same but he lacks the energy and the determination to make use of every conceivable means to express his ideas as strikingly as possible. He confines all his powers only to the actual subject under discussion and is too inclined to think that Chernyshevsky's contrivances represented a true interpretation of the Italian situation. And so when making use of them, he goes into too much detail and ends by weakening their original brutality. It is of undoubted interest to observe the discernment with which he scours Italian writings of 1860 and 1861 for anything to confirm or complete the ideas that the editors of the *Sovremennik* had deduced from events in Italy. He quoted widely from Montanelli, Brofferio, Pianciani; he observed the social conflicts of Southern Italy, etc., etc. But his parallel between Cavour and Montalembert has no real significance, from either the historical, political or polemical point of view. He ended by writing a long panegyric of Father Gavazzi whom, of all the politicians who were bringing about Italy's political unity, he found the most congenial. As Antonovich was to say: 'Dobrolyubov dreamt of making and printing speeches and impassioned appeals—like Father Gavazzi in Italy whom he so much praised—of thundering against the public, reawakening it, electrifying it, and leading it into action.'[29] But apart from this curious though significant detail, it is obvious that the most vital element in Dobrolyubov's articles on Italy lies in the passages which he devoted to Mazzini's moral force and the dedicated spirits of the Bandiera brothers and Pisacane, all of whom he contrasted with the 'wisdom' of Cavour. So his travels in Italy did not give him a new outlook, but rather confirmed the passionate longing for action that consumed him and the new generation. This longing was sustained, not by a clearly defined ideology but rather by the single word which was to give its name to the movement. As he wrote in 1860, Mazzini's phrase 'God and the People' was 'half-wrong'. Remove 'God', there remains 'People'.[30]

Dobrolyubov's work thus mirrors the transformations, both psychological and spiritual, which the intellectuals of the 'sixties underwent in their search for a road towards politics and the people. It would be worth while examining the same process among the less important contributors to the *Sovremennik*, and more generally among the widely varied intellectual life of the period. Antonovich, Eliseyev and Shelgunov all considered the same problems that Chernyshevsky and Dobrolyubov had discussed, and each made his personal contribution to the problem of the relationship between the intelligentsia, the State and the masses.

We shall have to consider some of these men when we discuss the first clandestine political groups; others when we examine the quarrels between Populism and Nihilism. But for the moment we will only discuss the man who can be considered at the opposite pole to Dobrolyubov in the culture of the 'sixties.

Shchapov in fact traversed the ground between the intelligentsia and the people in exactly the opposite direction to Dobrolyubov. He did not start from a desire to enlighten and educate the masses and then try to know them, make himself their equal and eventually guide them. He started from the people itself, from its traditions and segregated life, from its religion and political habits, and he then resolutely and ably tried to estimate the value of these traditional institutions and social life in relation to the State, Western culture and the intelligentsia. He ended by being convinced that the intelligentsia had to act as a guide. But before reaching this conclusion, he ardently supported the 'spontaneous' pattern of the people's life, and was the historian of its *mores*. He created that brand of Populism which looked to the village reverently to listen and learn rather than to teach.[31]

Shchapov was a Siberian. His ancestors had fled there at the beginning of the seventeenth century to escape the persecution of the *Raskol*. For generations they had been deacons and sacristans, farming the land like the peasants, and helping the priests in their religious functions. They lived in the village of Anga in the region of Baykal (province of Irkutsk), and they had married into native families. Afanasy Prokofyevich's mother was a Tungus or, more probably, a Buryat. When still young he was given a *bursa*, a kind of compulsory State scholarship to go to the seminary. This elementary school for future priests was famous for its primitive conditions. The pupils were taught in unheated classrooms, and the boys, bundled into their fur coats, were famished and often ill with scurvy. There were no text-books and everything had to be learnt by heart. For this purpose mechanical repetition and whipping were employed. When at last in the 'sixties a realistic description of the *bursa* became possible, it made a deep impression and became the favourite target for all who wanted a complete change in the educational system of the masses.[32]

But Shchapov himself, who was born in 1830, had to go through all the difficult stages in the life of a Siberian ecclesiastic. After the *bursa*, he went to the seminary at Irkutsk, where he was sent in 1846 because his intelligence and retentive memory singled him out from his contemporaries. For many years he was oppressed by the exacting discipline of the seminary and by the contempt displayed by his superiors and companions for the *bursaki*, boys who like himself came from the poorest classes. But he was now firmly on the road to the Ecclesiastical Academy of Kazan, the intellectual centre of the Siberian clergy.

A strange atmosphere prevailed in the Academy, when Shchapov arrived in 1852. The works of Guizot were officially considered 'horrifying'. A

German translation of Gibbon was kept in a secret section of the library; and all Russia's secular literature was described as 'a vast desert'. Yet even this little world, which at first sight seemed to personify hypocrisy and mustiness, contained sufficient energy to respond to the gust of revival that swept through Russia after the Crimean War. Some of the teaching staff spoke of Strauss and of Feuerbach, and very soon manuscripts discussing Russia's fate began to have a wide circulation. As from 1854 the students were allowed to subscribe to newspapers and reviews. There was a revival of interest in the history of the Church. When the valuable manuscripts which were preserved in the ancient fortress of the *Raskol*, the Solovetsky monastery, were evacuated to Kazan, to escape damage or seizure by the English fleet during the blockade, members of the Academy began to study and annotate them, and thus rediscover a whole new phase of Russia's past.

Shchapov flung himself into his studies with a passionate thirst for knowledge. He led an ascetic life, working seventeen hours a day enthralled by every aspect of the life of the Russian people. Greedily, feverishly, he tried to learn the history of the sects and the peasants, and ethnography. He read every book and manuscript which might in any way explain the nature of the Russian people and his own personality as the product of a village in the Baykal region. He looked for the basis and the justification for the dignity and pride with which he bore himself in his daily life, with a sincerity that often bordered on ingenuousness. His superiors and fellow students regarded him as eccentric, almost a *yurodivy* (a 'holy fool'), even though the object of his veneration was no longer Christian mythology but the history of the Russian peasant. In moments of exhaustion and despair he wept over his fate, the difficult road that he had traversed, and the deformation of character which he had had to accept in the *bursa* and the Academy. He wished to become once more, if only for a moment, what he could have been had he not been uprooted from Siberia; and he said to those whom he met in the street: 'I am no better than you are. I, too, come from the peasants.' 'He wept, and on those occasions it was impossible to see him without shedding bitter tears.'[33] His fellow-students wounded him by their mockery of his desire to become an historian entirely devoted to understanding the people. They sneered at his regret at having been forced to taste of the tree of knowledge, his decision to remain (in spite of everything) firmly tied to his origins. 'His warm, boyish heart would flare up with indescribable rage. How was it possible to be so lacking in conscience as to revile Russia's one true strength—the peasant, the backbone of the entire State?'[34]

The first fruit of his studies was a long book published in 1858, *The Schism of the Old Believers*. This resulted in his being made professor in the Academy where he had been a student. His book was not intended to be a purely religious or ecclesiastical history of the schism, so much as a study of the social and political significance of the sects and their development and differentiation in the seventeenth and eighteenth centuries. Shchapov saw in the origins of this process a crystallization of religion into mere formulas, a 'bookish and Judaic spirit'. But this was not what mainly interested him. He was anxious to see how these formulas had been brought to life and translated from the ecclesiastical to the political sphere. At first they served to express a 'clerical ideology of democracy'—the revolt of the clergy against the authority of the Church in the time of Nikon. They had then become formulas of a 'popular secular' rebellion against the Tsar, whose Western reforms from above had met with the most determined resistance from below. In the eighteenth century the *Raskol* 'became deeper, more comprehensive, and ended by taking on a religious, national, and democratic character',[35] by welcoming and absorbing the elements of discontent and revolt which were seething at that time against the empire, local officials and the growing oppression of serfdom.

The State brought into being by Peter the Great's reforms had never succeeded in striking roots throughout the country. Parallel to it, there survived a system of local self-administration dating from mediaeval times with its organized groups of peasants and merchants. This corporate life inherited from the past had been expressed and symbolized in the *Raskol*, and Shchapov therefore devoted particular attention to the geography of this religious movement, its advance along trade routes and the great rivers, and its penetration into the villages. The *Raskol*'s great strength, he said, had consisted in the 'religious and civil democratization'[36] which it had assumed as it increased in numbers and extent.

Shchapov's book received an unfavourable review in the *Sovremennik*[37] and when in 1859 he published an article on the 'Improvement of the situation of the unfree people', defending the work of the Church against the régime of peasant serfdom, Dobrolyubov made great play of the fact that the Church itself had owned peasants.[38] Shchapov was in fact still inclined to discover forces traditionally opposed to the empire and the despotic state all around him even in the most unlikely places. His entire outlook still suffered from a mechanical reversal of the 'Statist' and 'Western' theories of previous historians, and this made him glorify all opposition to the State as 'democratic' and 'popular'.

The *Sovremennik*'s criticism profoundly influenced him and made him reconsider the central argument of his book. From now on he was no longer to be concerned with studying the development of religious expression which had in the past been assumed by resistance to the State. Instead he applied himself to singling out the social and structural elements of this opposition. It was essential to consider not only the sectarian and apocalyptic ferment but also the various popular institutions which had withstood the State's oppression and which could therefore still be employed against it. It was essential also to move from the religious history of the Russian masses to their social history.

His attention was drawn to the *obshchina* by the Slavophil reviews and the

Sovremennik. The studies of Eshevsky, a young historian at Kazan, had already made him reconsider the problem of regionalism and the long struggle of the various 'lands' which made up the Russian empire to preserve their local self-administration. Eshevsky was concerned with the same problems and was then beginning his researches into the provinces of the Roman Empire and their relations with Rome.[39] This theme appealed to Shchapov all the more as he had strong feelings about the autonomy of his native Siberia, and he shared the widespread hopes of the Siberian students at Kazan in a great future for that land.

On taking up the chair of history at the university, he began his course with a lecture which marked the end of the first phase of his studies, and made him the spokesman of a new Populist trend.

I declare from the very start that I bring with me to the chair of Russian history at this University not the idea of the State, nor that of centralization, but the idea of *narodnost* and of regionalism (*oblastnost*). It is now a well-established notion that the fundamental factor of history is the people itself and that it is the spirit of the people which makes history. This idea is no longer a new one . . . But here is another principle which is not yet firmly established in our researches: the principle —please allow the expression—of regionalism. Until now the prevailing idea has been that of centralization; all the variegated strands of provincial history have been swallowed up in the general theory of the development of the State . . . Yet the history of Russia is, more than anything, the history of differing local groups, of constant territorial change, of reciprocal action and reaction, of the various regions before and after centralization.

After referring to the secular struggles of the provinces against Moscow during the Middle Ages, he went on to say that these had been prolonged during the time of troubles in 'that great struggle of the regional communities', and that later they had taken on the character of great 'democratic and native' revolts. He ended by saying that during his course he would study the problem in all its aspects, contrasting it with the development of Russia's internal colonization and the life of the peasants.[40]

His popularity with the students at once became immense. Here at last was a professor who was determined to provide a very different interpretation of Russia's history from the traditional one. Shchapov in turn was overcome by the excitement of his young students. Besides his lectures he held political conversations with them,[41] and when, at Bezdna, not far from Kazan, the most serious upheaval of the peasant revolt against the Manifesto of February 1861 was crushed in blood, Shchapov recovered all the passion that as a boy had made him say, in tears, 'I, too, come from the peasants.' At a solemn requiem mass for the fallen, organized by the students of the university and the Ecclesiastical Academy, he made a speech which recalled that for centuries the peasants of the *Raskol* had protested against 'their grievous situation as serfs. And now there has appeared a new prophet, and he too has proclaimed liberty in the name of God.' Although both he and his disciples had been killed, these victims showed that the Russian people was still capable of political initiative. Their blood would arouse the people to insurrection and freedom. He ended his speech by proclaiming the need for a democratic constitution.[42]

He was arrested on the personal instructions of Alexander II, and taken to St Petersburg. There he faced a political and ecclesiastical investigation, which, after long delays, ended with an order from the Emperor to remove him from the chair at the University of Kazan and to 'subject him to preaching and sermons in a monastery to be chosen by the Holy Synod'. There was a rumour that he was to be confined in the Solovetsky monastery, on an island in the White Sea. But this step was out of keeping with the state of public opinion, and on 19th February 1862 Alexander II ordered that 'he should be pardoned and not sent to the monastery'. He was freed and finally even (for a short time) got a job in the Ministry of the Interior.

In the capital he resumed and extended the historical and political researches which he had begun at Kazan in 1859. He reconsidered the entire problem of the *Raskol* and wrote a short book to show that a regionalist or, as he often said, 'a federal' view of Russian history made even this religious phenomenon far more understandable.[43] The *Raskol* had represented a protest against the State because it expressed the vigorous defence of the 'lands' against centralization. Its character was democratic because it had served to defend the traditional and spontaneous organizations of the Russian people. The chief centre of the *Raskol* in the seventeenth century had sprung up where the tradition of the free lands of Novgorod was strongest. There, had been born the 'democratic doctrine according to which it is not right to pray for the Tsar'.[44] But the movement had been crushed by Moscow. The death of Stenka Razin on the Red Square had put an end to the 'old Russia of the people'. The peasants had been deprived of the right to decide their fate through the free local assemblies which under various names had accompanied the work of ploughing and colonization. The 'brotherhoods' (*bratstvo*), the 'councils' (*soviet*), the 'assemblies' (*skchod*), the 'congregations' (*sobor*), the 'communities' (*obshchina* and *mir*) were no longer masters of their fate, and although they were allowed to survive they were more and more carefully controlled by the State. The *Raskol* had kept their memory alive by basing its own organization on the traditional foundations of the 'lands' and the *obshchina*; and the schismatics had eventually become the 'mythical, religio-anthropomorphic personification of the people's power, the sublimation of the human and spiritual dignity of the peasant, its mythical apotheosis'.[45]

The *Raskol* thus represented the peasants' only culture; the sects were able to adapt themselves to the patterns of the people's life.

While Peter built schools only for the clergy and the aristocracy, the *Raskol* everywhere became a living school for the vast mass of the Russian people, for the peasants, the artisans, the merchants and the soldiers. It took on its shoulders the burden of spreading education among the people. And it chose to do this by the most natural and direct means, those which answered its purpose best; travelling missions and the despatch of preachers throughout the regions, both to towns and villages. These preachers spread the alphabet and their doctrines among the people with far greater success than the government schoolmasters.[46]

It was the *Raskol* which fought against monopolies, against privileges in the use of woods and water, against the formation of 'classes' or 'groups' in the empire of Peter and Catherine, against the corporations being given legal status. The *Raskol* was the main backbone not only of resistance but, here and there, even of the peasant revolts.[47]

Shchapov's studies of the sects thus brought to light the essential element of his political (as well as of his historical) theories. Civic progress in Russia could come only from a revival of the self-administration through which the people's life had expressed itself for centuries. It was not new laws or new theories that were required but the liberation of already existing popular institutions from all the obstacles that held up their development. 'The life of the Russian people is stubborn in its own way; it has its own ethics and its own originality', he wrote in an article called 'The Peasant *Obshchina*' published in 1862, which was the manifesto of his Populist standpoint and 'Socialism of the *mir*'.[48] The only thing needed was a resolute decision to give the people freedom of choice to develop on its own lines. 'The mouth of the people, of the entire people, must be allowed to utter what is necessary.'

It was for this reason that Shchapov devoted such loving care to the forms that the *obshchina*, *soviet* and *mir* had assumed in the past and that he constantly recalled how the time of troubles at the beginning of the seventeenth century had been ended by a summoning of the representatives of all the Russian 'lands'. He pointed out too that 'flight' and 'brigandage' had in the past been the effective means employed by the peasants as a protest against their conditions.[49]

By his repeated contrast of popular institutions and the State; by his appeals for an assembly to give expression to the organic and traditional structure of the Russian people; by his eulogies of even the most extreme aspects of the antithesis between the State and society, Shchapov was preparing the ground to be covered some years later by revolutionary Populism right up to the time of Bakunin.

All this made it easy enough for the government to grasp the conclusions which Shchapov was leading up to. M. N. Muravev, soon to be responsible for the bloody suppression of the Polish revolt, said after reading the *Zemstvo i Raskol*: 'This is authentic Communism, with its constant attack on the boyars and the officials . . . Shchapov has chosen the *Raskol* as a weapon or, rather, as a lever to unleash a new revolt à la Pugachev', and he ended by associating Shchapov's activities with those of the London émigrés, who were also convinced that the religious sects would support a political movement against absolutism.

7*

From this conclusion it was but a short step to implicating Shchapov in the affair of the 'London propagandists', and he was soon trapped in the net which led to the arrest of Chernyshevsky and M. A. Serno-Solovevich. But it appeared that he had had no actual contacts with Kelsiev and that he had played no part in the attempt to create an organization for the purpose of uniting the *Kolokol* and the religious sects. And so for the moment he was able to escape prison and exile. But his fate was henceforth sealed. In the spring of 1864 he was forbidden to live in the capital and, escorted by two policemen, he returned to his native Siberia. His village, Anga, had been chosen as his place of residence, but he was soon allowed to live in Irkutsk.

Here he began to work again. The crisis of 1862 and the collapse of his hopes that the situation might develop in a democratic and revolutionary direction naturally modified his ideas. In the first number of the *Russkoe Slovo* for 1864 he wrote an article called 'Natural Science and Political Economy', which summed up his experiences in St Petersburg.[50]

He had once supported the idea of the *Zemsky Sobor*, and had looked upon a revival of the old assemblies of the Russian lands as the one way of escaping from the crisis in which the State was involved. He was now compelled to see that absolutism had succeeded in retaining all power in its own hands. As he himself said, regional and local autonomy, the *Zemstvo*, had been his *idée fixe*. He could now see just how far this ideal had been realized. The State in fact had succeeded in confining it to a limited administrative sphere, had made use of it for its reforms and had removed all its political power.

All his 'historical-juridical' interpretation had come to nothing. 'Believing in the initiative, in the autonomy of the *Zemstvo*, of the territorial, popular and social forces, I believed not just in local assemblies but in their capacity to open banks, schools, colleges, universities and academies.'[51] Others had held similar ideas. 'Slavophils, classical anglomanes, traditional Russians, in different languages we all made noisy, brilliant and grandiose speeches about self-administration, English self-government, and the need to bring Old Muscovy back to new life. We allowed ourselves to be seduced by the territorial autonomies of the time of Ivan the Terrible; we spoke of Russian "soil" and the organic development of the autochthonous Russian spirit.'[52]

In 1862 ideas of this kind had prevented him agreeing with Chernyshevsky, who had gone to see him one day, in an effort to find some common ground between them, and who, after an entire day of discussions, had had to conclude that their points of view were different. But now, after his experiences of the reaction, Shchapov had to admit that Chernyshevsky was right. It was not legal and traditional forms that were of real importance but 'the economic welfare of all social classes'. No change of institution could of itself lead to an economic improvement, and this was more important than anything else.

Chernyshevsky's ideas have at one blow swept away dozens of legal, organic, Slavophil and classical theories, theories of the Russian soil, etc. Rational economic doctrine shows that it is impossible to get rid of hunger and poverty by purely administrative measures. The economic structure of society can be transformed only by using the one really powerful force capable of bringing about a real change: a rational, scientific-natural economic system and an organization of the working and productive forces . . .[53] At a blow, economic theory has brought us back to the land, to the real world. It has spoken of serious matters, difficult to understand, but necessary and useful ones. It has spoken of bread, work, the working classes, productive and unproductive work, the organization of work, the wages of the worker, income, wealth, poverty, proletariat, the need for economic education, etc., etc.[54]

Seen in this light, the traditional institutions of the Russian people revealed all their backwardness and their reliance on customs and prejudices which hindered a quick economic development. Even Chernyshevsky himself had not seen clearly enough that the root of all evils lay in lack of scientific knowledge. The Russian situation could be changed only after modern technical knowledge had been absorbed. The duty of the intelligentsia lay in bringing these new factors to the people.

At all times and everywhere ignorance of nature has produced only slaves; slaves of nature itself and slaves of all human force, of the force of muscle, brain and intelligence, of the force of deceit and prestige, wealth, power and despotism—in a word, slaves of political, military, economic, bourgeois and religious force . . . Ignorant of the forces, laws and economy of nature, man was unconscious, ignorant, superstitious, poor, impotent . . .[55]

Shchapov threw himself into the natural sciences with the same enthusiasm and tenacity that he had shown as a boy when studying manuscripts of the Russian sects. He developed a complete theory of the relations between geography and history, capable of explaining the objective, natural conditions which had determined the development of the Russian people. His conclusions all too obviously betray his lack of preparation and above all the conditions in which they were carried out. 'In the provinces, in Siberia, intellectual work is real hard labour.'[56] He lacked the means to reconstruct a whole world from this new point of view.

But despite the obvious weaknesses of his work in Siberia, it does contain one vital element: the impassioned search for a new relationship between 'the democracy of ignorance, superstitition, routine, and the aristocracy of thought and knowledge'.[57] Science would give the intelligentsia a tool to reach the popular masses, where the attempts to revive Russia's past had failed.

Between 1866 and 1867 he wrote a long essay, *A general picture of intellectual development in Russia*. In it he traced the different attempts made by men of education to unite theory and practice and to see how science in order to penetrate into the masses had to become a technique. This was the last essay to display the energy so characteristic of his works, however confused or improvised. More and more isolated and lonely, he died at Irkutsk in 1876, exhausting himself in a vain effort to establish a new relationship between the educated *élite* and the peasants.

7. THE PEASANT MOVEMENT

As THE 'FIFTIES drew to a close the intelligentsia was anxiously listening to news from the countryside; the government bureaucracy was completely occupied in planning the reform and putting it into effect; and the nobility was uncertainly discussing the future of its relations with the peasants. But what were the peasants themselves thinking and hoping at this time? A complete answer would naturally require a knowledge of all the economic, legal and political problems of that class that made up the vast majority of the Russian people, at the very time when it was undergoing changes of the greatest importance. Here, however, we only have to consider what weight the peasants could bring to bear in determining, hastening or delaying the general development of events; and to pay special attention to the ways in which the peasants revealed their aspirations and to those aspects of their social life which specially influenced and inspired the early stages of Populism.[1]

Peasant disturbances had been intensified in the 'forties. The timid and partial reforms carried out by Nicholas I had given ground for new hopes in a future emancipation. In the south-west the attempt to establish 'inventories' and thus introduce the State and the law into the relations between landlord and serf had given birth to a series of disorders and protests, which showed that the peasants in these regions intended to have an increasingly influential rôle. There had then followed a period of quiet. In 1849 all reforms from above had been indefinitely postponed and the villages too seemed to have fallen back into silence. There was no large-scale movement between 1850 and 1853, though there were one hundred and thirty-seven cases of insubordination and protest. But the Crimean War marked a turning point for the countryside, as it did for the State and for the intelligentsia.

As before, the initiative came from above rather than below. The peasant movements were a reaction against steps taken by the government and showed again how difficult it was for the authorities to give up their policy of immobility. The response from the peasants was all the stronger this time in that it was no longer some legal change relating to serfdom that was being made, but an appeal to all Russians for the military defence of the national territory. On 3rd April 1854 a Senate *ukaz* announced naval conscription. On 14th December of the same year, and on 29th January 1855, the Tsar proclaimed general mobilization. Every kind of rumour at once began to spread through the countryside. Taking up arms would mean freedom; the edict of emancipation had already been signed; it was being concealed by the local authorities and the clergy. The movement started in the department of Ryazan and then spread to those of Tambov, Vladimir and Kiev. *Corvées* in the landlords' properties were often abandoned. Delegations of peasants were on the move to petition for truth and justice from the Tsar. Entire villages left to join the army and obtain their freedom. The government had to resort to the use of troops to restrain the peasants and suppress the disorders.[2]

Of the nine departments to which the movement spread, eight were in Great Russia and one (Kiev) was in the south-western territories. The discontent, in fact, had now reached even those provinces which had previously been the least affected. Upheavals occurred in the heart of Russia and showed a clear tendency to become rooted in the region of the Volga. All this occurred at the height of the war, when the troops sent to suppress the disorders were needed elsewhere. And so it is not surprising that the movements of 1854, and especially those of 1855, played a large part in persuading the ruling classes that serfdom could no longer be retained as it was. These great disturbances were the last before the emancipation, the introduction of which they considerably influenced.[3]

The unrest was particularly violent around Kiev. The Governor-General, I. Vasilchikov, explained its nature clearly enough in a letter to the Chief of Police on 22nd March 1855.

In many districts the peasants have been enthusiastic about taking up arms in defence of the Holy Church and the Fatherland . . . But this enthusiasm, in view of the typical ignorance of the peasants of this region and their ill-feeling towards their Catholic landlords, has led them to believe that the Tsar has appealed to all in defence of the faith. This has been the case especially in some areas of the department of Kiev which were originally part of the Ukraine and where the memory of the free Cossacks still survives. As they do not trust their landlords, they have compelled the curates to write up the names of these landlords at the head of the lists of enrolment; at the same time they have proclaimed their zeal to take up arms and to go wherever the Tsar orders as long as they are freed from the *corvées* . . . In some districts the peasants did not carry out their duties for a day or two but later they returned to their usual occupations.

Four days later the authorities announced that they had had to resort to the police. The movement, which was complicated, as we have seen, by motives of nationalism against the Polish gentry and of religion against Catholic landowners, rapidly took on a dangerous character. In one of the villages an *ukaz* of 1806 spread from hand to hand and was interpreted by the peasants as an 'appeal to become Cossacks and as a liberation from their duties on the landowners' estates'. They often tried to compel the priest to read the manifesto of emancipation 'which was obviously kept hidden'.

On 10th April about four thousand peasants, coming from all over the district of Tarashchansk, assembled in the village of Tagan. The authorities arrived and drew up troops whom they ordered to advance about forty paces for a parley. The peasants answered that they did not want to work for their landlords. Vain attempts were made to persuade them that there had never been an *ukaz* exempting them from *corvées*. The peasants moved forward, and an officer had his head split open by an axe; the soldiers fired, and left eleven dead and many wounded.

This skirmish was the first to attract a member of the intelligentsia. Three days before the clash the Governor-General announced that an ex-student of the University of Kiev had appeared in the district. He had read a manifesto to the peasants which he claimed to be a letter from the French Emperor and the Queen of England to the Russian people. 'We, a free people, to you our brothers who have groaned under the yoke of Moscow for a century', the message had begun. It had then spoken of the burdens of serfdom and ended by promising 'equality and freedom'. The peasants had at first come to listen but had then grown suspicious and tried to seize the student, eventually carrying the manifesto to the authorities.

The man in question, Yosif-Anton Yosifovich Rozental, succeeded in fleeing to Galicia but was arrested by the Austrian police and handed over to the Russians. In May he was sent to the fortress at Kiev where he said that 'he had acted under the influence of ideas which he had learnt from democratic works from the West and from Polish émigrés'. He had read these books at the University of Moscow where he had also heard of the adventures of Bakunin.[4] He was condemned to be shot together with an accomplice, but the sentence was commuted to banishment to Siberia for life. Dobrolyubov, then a very young man in St Petersburg, gave a somewhat romantic version of his story in a clandestine manuscript newspaper which he and his school friends were then compiling. He also dedicated an enthusiastic poem to Rozental: 'You have aroused the sleeping slaves.'[5] This was something of an exaggeration. For, on later occasions, Rozental showed that he was no fighter. None the less, he was one of the very few who tried to associate himself with the peasant upsurge at the time of the Crimean War. Among others who were pursued and punished as 'instigators' in the affair, the only man who had even the beginnings of a political programme, was a petty official from Kostroma, who incited the peasants not to take up arms and to demand a redistribution of the land. His complete isolation, like that of Rozental, shows that the movements of these years were entirely spontaneous and that an immense gulf still divided the village from the few men who tried to take the side of the serfs.[6]

As soon as Alexander II came to the throne, insistent rumours of an immediate emancipation spread throughout the countryside. Official statistics speak of twenty-five upheavals in 1856, of forty in 1857, and it must be remembered that only the most serious cases were recorded. But more important than numbers (never very accurate) is the character of the more influential movements. In 1856 entire villages of southern Russia were set in motion by a rumour that free land was being distributed in those parts of the Crimea which had been devastated by the war. In the departments of Ekaterinoslav and of Kherson, for example, there was a persistent rumour that 'the Tsar was in the isthmus of Perekop with a helmet of gold and was granting freedom to all who came there, whereas those who did not come or who arrived late would remain serfs of the landlords as before'. 'Influenced by these rumours', reports I. I. Ignatovich, 'the peasants moved with their families and all their goods, sometimes in entire villages, in search of the legendary Tsar, hoping to become free colonizers in the Crimea.' In the vast majority of cases they took leave of the landowners in the most friendly manner, though they seized the cattle they needed and their working tools. Sometimes they went to the landlord to say farewell and to thank him for his care of them. Only in one case, in the department of Ekaterinoslav, was their departure marked by disorders. 'As the peasants left they flung themselves on to the landlord's house and began to loot everything that came to hand, rejoicing that they had killed a steward and threatening the landlord himself. Eventually they took all their goods and their cattle, and after destroying the doors and windows of the house they went off.'[7] Nine thousand peasants set off from the region of Ekaterinoslav, three thousand from Kherson, and many from surrounding districts. Troops had to intervene; there were ten dead, and many wounded.

Meanwhile disturbances increased and spread throughout the Empire. In the first four months of 1858 alone, seventy cases of collective acts of insubordination were recorded, and by the end of the year there were over two hundred. But it is unlikely that the movements had been resumed on a large scale. The very high figure is probably due to the fact that in the decisive period of drawing up the reforms, the central authorities wanted more detailed news, and local officials therefore reported events which in previous years they would not have mentioned. So the unrest continued, spreading throughout all the departments, but without assuming alarming proportions. A report spoke of seventy cases in 1859 and of a hundred in 1860. Impatience for freedom was intense; news from the provinces drew attention to the urgent need to solve the problem of serfdom, but no new facts succeeded in modifying the Emperor's decisions and the despatch of the various Commissions.

The explicit promise of emancipation had had a profound effect on the peasants. It was no longer a question of changing a few details in their relations with the landlords. They now expected complete emancipation. Nicholas I's cautious measures had produced a strong reaction. Alexander II's promises made the peasants think of their own interests, and draw up immediate demands to defend their work and their bread. The most obvious development that can be detected in the villages immediately before 19th February 1861 consists in a passive resistance to the corvées. The peasants carried out these duties, from which they thought they would soon be exempted, more and more slowly and more and more reluctantly. A sort of spontaneous strike, aimed at loosening the bonds of serfdom, and making submission to the local administrative authorities less specific, accompanied, and often partly replaced an open but sporadic refusal to yield to the landlord's will. All this, of course, only took place within the limits possible in a social régime which for the moment was still intact and which still showed itself able to enforce severe repressive measures. There were too some signs of doubt and distrust. 'It would have been better if the Emperor had not promised us freedom, as he is not in a position to control the landowners', the peasants were saying at the end of 1859. These signs of disappointment were all the more frequent in that the landowners were looking to their immediate interests; they often profited from the respite allowed by the slow processes of the law to seize the peasants' land and in general to make as much use of their serfs as they could. But soon the peasants began to hope again. Anyone coming to the village was thought to be the messenger of 'freedom'. Once again it began to be whispered that the edict was already in existence but that the landowners and the authorities were keeping it hidden. In market places excited discussions among the peasants on their future became frequent.[8]

The publication of the manifesto on 19th February brought back in a flash all the hopes, and disappointments, of the peasants. Throughout 1861 the great news of freedom produced a state of passionate excitement. The peasants protested against any aspect of the new situation which did not correspond to their immediate interests or to the notion of freedom that they had already formed. Then in the two following years hopes began to wane; the wave of excitement ebbed. The blow was severe and it left indelible traces on the most sensitive men of all classes. But it did not lead to a political upheaval. The situation which seemed so revolutionary did not end in revolution.[9]

Between 1861 and 1863 eleven hundred cases of disorder, large and small, were reported. Some of them were of considerable size, and though they did not seriously endanger the safety of the State, they showed how bitter was the discontent seething in the masses. From the documents that I have seen it is not possible to classify exactly these disturbances during the three years that followed the emancipation. I. I. Ignatovich has examined three hundred and eighteen cases and concludes that they can be divided in chronological order as follows:

1861	–	–	–	279
1862	–	–	–	35
1863	–	–	–	4

The dates of the remaining cases are not certain. Other documents confirm that this was the general trend of the upheavals which were particularly violent in the summer following the manifesto and then rapidly diminished.

Some of the disorders at least were due to technical errors involved in the publication of the 'Emancipation'. The manifesto and legislative arrangements were drawn up in a complicated, vague and rhetorical style, which seemed calculated to lead to doubts and false interpretation. The Russian administration spent a generation trying to clarify the contradictions in the document and the various circulars which followed. The uncertainty of the peasants in 1861 can easily be imagined. They were almost all unable to read, and were totally incapable of understanding the public reading of such remarkably obscure pronouncements. The documents were not even translated into the different national languages of the various populations who did not speak Russian. The number of copies circulated to local authorities was inadequate. Here and there local governments reprinted them, but this helped to spread the rumour that other manifestos were in existence more favourably disposed to the peasants and had been hidden by the cunning of the authorities.

These technical errors clearly reflected the political and social position of Russia at this time. The muddled style of the decrees mirrored the uncertainty and fears of the ruling classes, which resulted from the compromise so laboriously arranged between the nobility, the bureaucracy and the Emperor. The very difficulties met with in making the edict known showed how great was the lack of any organic connecting body between the State and the great mass of serfs.

The clergy was instructed to read the manifesto from the pulpit, but the village priests were usually so uneducated that they were not even able to do this correctly. Their lack of preparation became all too apparent when during the following months the peasants came to seek further explanations and clarification. In some cases it is obvious that the priests were so close to the peasants both in mentality and interests that they interpreted these peasants' hopes and demands further than the manifesto and were far from being a force on which the government could rely to carry out its reforms.

The case of the clergy was only one of the symptoms of the administrative crisis in the Russian village of 1861. The gentry (*pomeshchiki*) had been the pivot of the *ancien régime*, and Nicholas I well knew that they were the foundations of his empire. This was a dangerous situation which tended to transform any economic struggle between serf and landlord into a revolt against the State. The period of the great reform started when cases of insubordination became more frequent and when it was obvious that the state of mind of the peasants towards their owners was changing. The moment had come to create different relations between the State and the village.

The year 1861 was a time of transition. The nobles had lost their powers but the new local bureaucracy had not yet taken root and the peasant communities had not been brought under the control of the administration. To fill the gap recourse was had to the army, to floggings and repression; and this naturally only embittered the conflict. But meanwhile a new machinery of government was being created. 'Arbitrators' were elected to decide on the relations between the peasants and the landlords, and to determine the size of land granted to the *obshchina* and the amount of the redemption fee. Village administration was reformed, with representatives elected by the inhabitants and controlled by the State bureaucracy. And finally in 1864 the *Zemstvo* took provincial life in hand and created a new basis of collaboration between the nobles and the other classes.

As had occurred while the reforms were being prepared, these changes, willed from above, could only be put into effect through the cooperation of those who were in varying degrees impregnated with the spirit of the intelligentsia. It was men of this kind who were elected 'arbitrators' and who restored to the peasants a minimum of faith in the justice of the ruling classes and the State. It was they who created in the *Zemstvo* a local ruling class which was sufficiently enlightened to appreciate the economic changes which were occurring in the village and to bring some education and help, the lack of which had been so painfully felt in 1861. From the point of view of the revolutionaries and the Populists the final result of the reforms was to 'surround the life of the people with a complete amphitheatre of regulations, each one of which could obstruct the fair development of the people's life. The exclusively noble administration of the time of the serfs has been replaced by an administration made up of officials and gentry', said N. A. Serno-Solovevich, the founder of *Zemlya i Volya*.[10] But this was the only way to restrain and halt the peasant outburst of 1861. It also explains the rapid decline in the number of disorders in the following two years.

Despite this the movement of 1861 had had time to express at least in outline what the peasants expected of an emancipation really corresponding to their ideals and interests. As a rule their protests were not directed against specific details of the new legislation but against its very spirit. I. I. Ignatovich has classified 325 of these disorders as follows:

(1) Protests against the manifesto as a whole	–	1861	192
		1862	26
		1863	2
(2) Protests against particular items	– – –	1861	43
		1862	None
		1863	None
(3) Protests against abuses of the authorities	–	1861	9
		1862	6
		1863	None
(4) Unknown reasons	– – – – –	1861	41
		1862	4
		1863	2

Despite the fact that the three hundred and twenty-five cases here examined are probably the most serious, and that the importance of protests against the manifesto as a whole would probably be less significant if all the risings of 1861 were taken into account, these figures do show the general tendency.

Disorders provoked by the contrasts between 'liberty of the people' (*volya narodnaya*) and 'freedom of the State' (*volya kazennaya*) were particularly severe. Emancipation, it was thought, would mean the complete abolition of existing obligations: no more *corvées*, no more taxes either in kind or in cash; the village would govern itself in accordance with its age-old traditions and customs.

Sometimes the peasants expressed this belief by their desire to belong to the Tsar, to the State, i.e. to move into a better economic situation and escape the direct impact of the owner's authority. In a village in the Vladimir district the peasants interpreted the manifesto as an order by the Tsar to grant them land from the property belonging to the State. 'And they swore together that they would pay nothing more to the landlord.'[11] In 1862 the peasants of the village of Pustoboytov (Poltava) claimed that 'they and their land were free'. If the Tsar had freed them, it meant that they were his peasants and no longer the squire's.[12]

But as a rule their demands were not based on the contrast between their position and that of the State peasants. They made it increasingly plain that they wanted a freedom which would entirely exempt them from any obligation to the gentry or administration. In April a crowd of a thousand peasants assembled in a village in the department of Voronezh and replied to the authorities that 'the Tsar had sent them a most merciful edict, that they were now free and that they no longer intended to pay their *redevances* or carry out their duties on the landlords' property'. When the Governor explained to them that this was not the case, they began to fling their caps in the air and shout: 'We no longer want the landlord. Down with the landlord! We have already worked enough! Now is the time for freedom!' 'These ideas', commented the writer of the report from which these words are quoted, 'spring from almost three centuries of serfdom and cannot be cancelled at a blow.' The movement spread to surrounding villages and was suppressed only by sending troops. The 'instigators' were arrested, but the leading one was able to escape. Alexander II noted on the margin of the report: 'Thank God it's ended like this.'[13]

In the region of Kursk too it was obvious what the peasants felt. 'They are extremely suspicious both of the landlord and of the rural police.'[14] There, too, disorders arose because of their desire to free themselves from both these authorities. In the department of Minsk, risings spread to the shout of: 'Hold fast. Our turn has come.' The peasants were convinced that the Tsar had given them 'freedom and the land' (*volya i zemlya*).[15] In the village of Kadymkor (in the department of Perm) the peasants said that the manifesto which had been read out by the local policeman was a fake, as the real one must of course be written in letters of gold. Two thousand of them assembled to demand an explanation for 'a kind of liberty that leaves us just as before under the authority of the Count our landlord'. They gave in only after two had been killed and eight wounded.[16]

Further examples of such protests could easily be given. The revolt, whether open or concealed, against all local authorities, turned everyone's attention to the distant power that had done away with serfdom—the Tsar. The marshal of the aristocracy in the province of Podolsk gave a vivid description of this state of mind in a report of August 1861:

The Tsar has taken on in their eyes a sort of abstract significance, completely distinct from any executive authority, which, they think, has been sold to the nobility. This sort of idea regarding the supreme power is certainly not new in the history of the masses, but it is always dangerous because it ends by attributing to the supreme power aims which it has never had, and by reducing all executive orders of the State to impotence. The peasants expect everything to come direct from the Tsar, to whom they give the character of a natural force, blind and implacable. They have completely given up believing in the simplest rules of respect for the property of others and for the general economic rules which are laid down in the manifesto of 19th February . . . What they have been granted appears not to correspond to the size of the transformation which they had expected; and so they refuse to believe what is written. According to them, because for once fate has turned the natural force of supreme power to their advantage, they now have the right to expect from it every kind of benefit and generosity . . .[17]

The peasants made frequent attempts to get into contact with a Tsar who was at once omnipotent and simultaneously unable to make his voice felt in their miserable villages. They sent messengers who were of course arrested. They always invoked the Tsar in their clashes with the local authorities, and here and there they ended by believing people who said that they had been sent by the Tsar or members of the imperial family. 'In March 1861 a soldier from the department of Samara, travelling through villages on the Crown lands, passed himself off as Prince Constantine Nikolaevich or the Emperor himself . . . telling the peasants that they too would soon have their freedom.'[18] In the summer of 1862 two 'usurpers' went round villages in the department of Perm 'to see how the gentry were behaving towards their peasants, and to investigate whether they had given a false interpretation of the decree of emancipation', which they said contained a promise of complete exemption from all dues. Troops had to be used to suppress the disturbances which they aroused. The peasants were also convinced that they were to receive not only land but cattle directly from the Tsar.[19]

But these were only sporadic cases. The conviction that the Tsar had granted the peasants 'true liberty' was so widespread that it was not even felt necessary to obtain confirmation by getting into contact with him: it was enough to read the manifesto correctly. It was, of course, easy enough to discover men ready to find in the law just what was wanted, all the more so as the peasants were prepared to pay those able to read the necessary documents. Ex-soldiers, scribes, the odd Pole or Jew in the western territories, priests, bigots of the *Raskol*, all became interpreters of the great hopes which were coursing through the villages and provided the immediate cause of most of the disturbances.

Two districts in the region of Penza, for example, were deeply stirred by the 'interpretation' given by a seventy-year-old soldier, Andrey Semenov Elizarov, who had fought against Napoleon and had been to Paris in 1814. He enjoyed great influence over his fellow peasants whom he made call him 'Count Tolstoy'. In April 1861, dressed in his old soldier's uniform and wearing all his medals, he persuaded them 'to fight for God and the Tsar'. Twenty-six villages refused to go on obeying their landlords and the authorities. A crowd of three hundred peasants flung themselves on the first troops who were sent to disperse them. After a clash in which the peasants lost three dead and four wounded, but also succeeded in taking two prisoners (including a non-commissioned officer), the troops had to withdraw. The movement spread. The news reached Penza that 'ten thousand peasants had rallied to the cry of "Freedom! Freedom!" (*Volya! Volya!*), and were carrying a red flag through the villages, insulting clergymen, beating up the rural authorities and threatening to do the same with the administrative and military leaders, and declaring that the "land is all ours. We do not want to pay the *obrok* [dues] and we will not work for the landlords."' When the troops again advanced the peasants said that they were 'ready to die for God and for the Tsar', and that they refused 'to work for the landlords' even if they were hanged for it, but 'would rather that the last one of them should die'. They held fast in a series of clashes. Two salvoes failed to disperse the crowd. 'We will die but we will not give in', they said. Standing at the head of the peasants, Elizarov shouted to the General in charge of operations, 'We must all support the cause of justice. Why deceive you?' Only after eight dead and twenty-seven wounded had been left on the field and the more determined peasants had been taken prisoner, tried on the spot and flogged, did the disturbance gradually quieten down. Elizarov and another 'instigator' were taken prisoner and exiled to the region of Irkutsk in Siberia.[20]

Another mouthpiece of the peasants' aspirations made his appearance in this rising. Of Leonty Egortsev, an official report said:

He belonged to the sect of the Molokane (milk-drinkers) and he soon succeeded in gaining a great influence over the entire territory. His false interpretations and the special powers of which he boasted inspired such great faith that villages sent him troikas imploring him to come and explain to them the manifesto. They took him by the arm and carried a small bench behind him, made him climb on to it, and so he proclaimed liberty for everyone. So great did his powers become that he even began to collect money and to threaten to hang anyone who disobeyed him as well as those responsible for the repression.

By his threats he convinced the peasants that 'no one even if threatened with death should denounce his own comrades', and that they should pay no attention either to the rural police or to the representatives of the nobility or even to the General in command of the local troops whom he called 'the Tsar's Ambassador' and who had been 'bought by the gentry'. He also went through the villages saying: 'If the troops fire on you, hold fast for three salvoes and then the authorities themselves will give you true freedom.'

It was sectarian preaching of this kind that led to the most serious disturbances of 1861—those at Bezdna.[21]

The region of Spassk between the Volga and the Kama contained twenty-three thousand souls (heads of families). It was not a poor district. General Apraksin, who was responsible for suppressing the revolt, said that its peasants were 'very prosperous'. Although the great majority were of Russian origin, there were also, as throughout the department of Kazan, some Tartar colonies.

When the manifesto was published, the inhabitants began to look around for someone who would interpret it in line with their ambitions. Eventually a peasant from the village of Bezdna, by dint of examining the text succeeded in finding what he was looking for. Anton Petrov was a *raskolnik*. He was able to read and had the typical sectarian veneration for the written word, believing that the printed text *must* contain truth as long as one could succeed in reading it. The mere sight of two noughts [00] used instead of a blank space to indicate a figure which had not yet been decided was enough to convince him that the freedom was 'false'. True liberty would have had the Cross of St Anne, which he recognized in a '10%' printed in another part of the statute. From then on Petrov began to preach his variety of 'liberty'. Serfdom had long been abolished, but the authorities were concealing this from the peasants. They must now be made to read out the authentic text.

He was thought to be a prophet. The peasants rushed to him, not just from the neighbouring villages, but from the surrounding provinces of Samara and Simbirsk. He began to acquire real power over the peasants belonging both to the landlords and the State, over Russians and Tartars.

I told all who came to me that the peasants were free. I told them not to obey the gentry and the authorities. I ordered them not to work the *corvées*; not to pay the *obrok*; and not to do anything when they saw others taking wheat from the landlords' stores. If the water was ruining the mill, it was not up to them to help repair it. I explained that all the land belonged to them and that the gentry would keep only a third of it. I invented all this out of my own head, so as to attract the peasants from my district, assuming that the more of them there were, the sooner they would succeed in obtaining freedom. Many came to me, and I declared them free. To win over still more, I suggested that the *mir* should elect new administrators, whom I sent to other villages to prepare the peasants to receive their freedom.

In many villages new administrators were elected, and they began to demand account books from the local authorities to keep a check on their activities. The peasant communities met together in assemblies and began by deciding on collective abstention from all work on the landlords' properties. At Bezdna and other centres the police were driven away, for, said the peasants, the authorities were lying, and the Tsar had ordered them not to spare the nobles but to cut off their heads.

Gradually a real organization began to take shape, based on Anton Petrov's *izba* at Bezdna. Every kind of rumour began to spread. Constantine Nikolaevich was in prison at Bezdna, and asked the peasants to come and free him. Another prince, Nikolay Pavlovich, had been killed by the gentry. News of true freedom would soon arrive. There was no need to be frightened by the soldiers; even if they did shoot, it was only necessary to hold fast; at the third salvo the authorities themselves would proclaim true liberty.

Anton Petrov continued to preach. One of his speeches has been reported as follows:

You will have true liberty only if you defend the man who finds it for you. Much peasant blood will be spilt before it is finally proclaimed. But the Tsar has given definite orders that you must mount a guard round that man day and night, on foot and on horseback; that you must defend him from all attacks; and not allow either the landlords or the clergy or the officials to reach him; that you must not hand him over, and not remove him from his *izba*. If they burn down one side of the village, do not abandon the *izba*; if they burn down the other side, do not abandon the *izba*. Young men and old will come to you; do not let them reach me; do not hand me over to them. They will cheat you by saying that they have come from the Tsar; do not believe them. The old men will come with smiles; middle-aged men will come; both bald and hairy men will come; and every kind of official; but you must not hand me over. And in due time, a young man will come here sent by the Tsar. He will be seventeen years old, and on his right shoulder he will have a gold medal and on his left shoulder a silver one. Believe him, and hand me over to him. They will threaten you with soldiers, but do not be afraid; no one will dare to beat the Russian, Christian people without orders from the Tsar. And if the nobles buy them, and they fire at you, then destroy with your axes these rebels against the will of the Tsar.

On the night of 11th April, the roads leading to Bezdna were full of peasants on horseback and on foot, all making for the *izba* of Anton Petrov 'who gave freedom and land; who appointed new authorities and said that he would soon give freedom to thirty-four departments'.

On the following morning, General Apraksin arrived at the head of two hundred and thirty soldiers. At the entrance of the village he saw a table with bread and salt on it, and two old men without hats. He asked them: 'Whom have you prepared all this for?' Doubtfully they answered: 'For you, on the orders of the authorities' (i.e. those elected by the rebels). 'I later learnt that this welcome had been prepared for those who came to announce their support for Anton Petrov.'

Facing us at the end of the road, round Petrov's house, was a dense mass of five thousand people. I halted the troops and went forward to about a hundred and eighty paces from them. I then sent on ahead two of the Governor's adjutants to give a first warning to the peasants. But their words were drowned by shouts of 'Freedom! Freedom!' They came back, warning the peasants that if they did not hand over Anton Petrov and if they did not disperse, they would be fired at. I then sent on a priest who held up a cross and called upon them for a long time, saying that if they did not surrender and return to their houses they would be fired at. They went on shouting. Then I myself went forward and explained my orders and commanded them to hand over Anton Petrov and to go away. But this had no effect on their terrible obstinacy. They shouted: 'We do not need an envoy from the Tsar. Give us the Tsar himself. Fire on us, but you will not be firing on us but on Alexander Nikolaevich.' I forced them to keep silence and said, 'I am sorry for you, my lads, but I must fire and I will fire. Those who feel themselves innocent move off.' But I saw that no one moved and that the crowd continued to shout and to resist. So I turned back and ordered one of the ranks to fire one salvo. I then gave them another warning. But the crowd went on shouting. I was then compelled to order a few salvoes. I was forced to do this mainly because the peasants, noting the considerable gap between the salvoes, began to come out from their houses in large numbers shouting to each other to dig up posts and threatening to surround and submerge my small company. Eventually the crowd dispersed and shouts were heard offering to hand over Anton Petrov. He meanwhile tried to flee into an orchard at the back of his house which had been held in readiness for the occasion. Then he came out of the house and went towards the soldiers, carrying the manifesto of emancipation on his head. There he was taken, together with his accomplices, and led under escort to the prison of Spassk. After Petrov's surrender, the corpses were carried off and a search made for the wounded. After confirmation it appeared that there were fifty-one dead and seventy-seven wounded.

From another source we learn that Anton Petrov was 'thirty-five years old; thin, small and white as a sheet, and terribly frightened at the thought that he would be immediately shot'. In fact his spirits remained high even in prison and during the investigations.

When the troops reached our village, I was in the *izba* . . . When the first and second salvoes of guns were fired, I prayed and said nothing. After the third I said to the peasants, 'Do not surrender, lads; it's not time yet. Now they will stop firing and read out the manifesto of freedom.' I said these words so as to hold firm for freedom to the very end. At the fourth salvo I wanted to go away, but while my parents were giving me their blessing, other salvoes were fired. After I had said farewell to my parents, I took the manifesto on my head and went towards the soldiers, thinking that with the Tsar's *ukaz* on my head, they would not fire at me. I did not want to run away . . .

After a quick trial, a military tribunal condemned him to death. His sentence said among other things that the rising he had provoked 'had threatened the entire department of Kazan'. He was shot on 19th April.

Even before he had been executed, the legends began to spread. It was said that he had been clothed in a cloak of gold, given a sword and sent to the Tsar himself by General Apraksin. He would soon return with freedom.

After his death it was said that he was a martyr, that a fire had sprung up on his tomb and an angel dressed in white had announced that he would soon be resurrected. As General Apraksin said in a report of 14th May, the requiem ceremony at Kazan, organized by the students of the university and the Ecclesiastical Academy, including Shchapov, helped to convince the peasants that Anton Petrov was a prophet.

An enormous impression was made by the rising and massacre at Bezdna. The nobles of Kazan spoke of 'a new Pugachev' and put pressure on the authorities to take stronger steps. More troops were stationed in the district of Spassk. Among the intellectuals the salvoes fired at Bezdna aroused varying reactions of reverence, surprise or fear, and helped to deepen growing internal dissensions. In London Herzen was able to give the readers of the *Kolokol* a remarkably full and detailed account of what had happened in that remote corner of the Kazan region. The first news and then Apraksin's reports merely confirmed the exiles' theory that the manifesto of 19th February had imposed a new serfdom on Russia.[22]

Disturbances aimed at finding or applying 'true freedom' continued throughout 1862 and 1863, though on a reduced scale. In the department of Saratov, for example, two villages, Klyuchy and Stary Chirigin, refused to come to any agreement with the landlord to work the land assigned to them, saying that 'Satan had built his house among them, stopped them living, and had put a curse on them.' They called the gentry and officials 'gypsies and mad dogs come to drink their blood'. Two peasant delegates were arrested and then freed because of pressure from their compatriots. The repression was violent and cruel. Women with children at their breasts threw themselves on the soldiers, asking to be flogged in place of their menfolk.[23]

But as time passed the peasants had to concede that the manifesto was in fact the Tsar's law. Their aspirations to 'true liberty' were postponed to the distant future. The decree itself allowed for a transitional period of two years during which the peasants would remain as 'peasants with limited obligations'. Once the peasants' new legal status had been brought into being and the estates had been divided between landlord and community, feudal ties would lapse and the *corvées* would be abolished. Only economic ties would remain between the landed estate and the village. These would be based on the redemption fee, on the renting of the landlords' property and on the use of paid labour. The peasant 'interpreters' repeated this and claimed that the peasants would remain serfs until 19th February 1863. On that day the Tsar would grant a second, the real, freedom. And so they drew the logical conclusion that during those two years of delay it was essential not to sign any contract or agreement. They were frightened of committing themselves too soon, and running the risk that their hands would be tied when their land and freedom became due. Far better, they thought, to continue working in the *corvées* and paying feudal obligations as before. Nothing must be done until the great day.

This idea had gained currency during the last days of the Bezdna rising. 'Brothers, let us wait for the second freedom instead of this wretched one that they have granted us', said the peasants after the repression. Many communities were encouraged by this to refuse to make the agreements envisaged by the law, even when they were in their own interests. The 'arbitrators' often met this additional obstacle in the course of their duties.

In July 1862 the entire village of Olshansk in the region of Kursk was convinced that 'if anyone works the land granted to him before the end of two years, he will remain a serf for ever. On the other hand, those who refuse to work the land granted to them will be freed.' A squadron of Hussars was sent and frightened the peasants, but met with strong resistance when trying to make arrests. A bayonet charge was made, and the peasants fled to the woods and for long refused to surrender.[24] The same sort of resistance, though in different forms, occurred elsewhere. In 1861 eight cases of unrest were recorded, all inspired by the idea of 'a new freedom'. In 1862 there were twenty-one, and another two during the first month of 1863. Hope seemed to grow as 19th February drew near. Finally the Emperor himself thought it advisable to make a public denial of any impending new freedom.

We have now reached the final date of the great peasant movement, and can try to look at it as a whole and grasp its essential characteristics.

Only in extreme cases had the peasants demanded *all* the land, including the landlords' property. Even Anton Petrov thought that the gentry should be allowed to retain a third of their estates. The cry 'All the land is ours' was heard here and there in 1861, but it implied a principle rather than an immediate demand. The landowners' houses were not touched and no attempt was made to seize their estates though the peasants refused to farm them.

What the peasants meant by their dreams of 'true liberty' was mainly the complete separation of their community from the landlord, the breaking of all ties between them and hence the *obshchina* closing in on itself. If they imagined that the Tsar's 'second liberty' was going to grant them the land, it was because they hoped to receive it free, without having to pay the redemption fee, and without having to remain economically and morally bound to the landlord. If they refused so often to make the agreements provided for by the law, it was because they thought that by so doing they were avoiding new taxes which were being imposed on them. The decree of liberation itself allowed for the granting of a reduced strip of land (a quarter of the normal) to anyone not able to pay the redemption fee. The peasants often submitted to this expedient, which was quite insufficient to keep them alive, so as to avoid tying their hands for the future, and falling back into a condition indistinguishable from the serfdom they had suffered for centuries.

But the most violent demonstrations and revolts were not directed against the redemption fee. This was still in the future, too vague and too remote to be seriously alarming. It was only very rarely that the peasants were themselves making the demands that Chernyshevsky was at this time making on their behalf—that the fee should be contributed to by the whole country and not merely by the peasants. Only once do we find among the documents of 1861 the idea of 'the Tsar's redemption', a primitive expression of the idea that the State should compensate the landowners.[25]

Their ambitions were more immediate, and were concerned with the abolition of the *corvées* and other obligations. In other words, they merely expressed with greater violence what they had already made clear before the reform: their refusal to farm the landlords' property for nothing. At first they had confined themselves to a slow and prolonged strike; now they sometimes tried direct refusal. But the law itself provided for these changes, and even the landowners hastened its application, for they were convinced that with the decline in their power and authority it was no longer possible to retain the *corvée*. The revolts and the rebellious state of mind of the peasants, whether open or suppressed, only hastened a process which was latent in events themselves.

From the administrative point of view too, the disturbances of these years had brought to light the peasants' ambition to run their own communities by themselves. Some of the elections provided for by legal decree had to be carried out at the point of the bayonet, in face of a crowd of peasants obstinately insisting on their right to change their leaders when and how they wanted. In the Bezdna rising, for instance, a number of villages, as we have seen, began to create their own administrations and drive out all representatives of the State bureaucracy.

Such symptoms were important in revealing the determination of the villages to live their own lives. But they were only the most obvious aspects of that desire for isolation which inspired the entire peasant class and which led them to face the army's rifles unarmed and impassive, and to 'die for God and the Tsar' while waiting for a mythical 'second freedom'.

8. THE STUDENT MOVEMENT

THE STUDENT MOVEMENTS in the Russian universities which provided Populism with its first human material left their mark on all its activities and even its mode of expression.

Shelgunov called this movement 'the barometer of public opinion', and his expression gained wide currency at the time. Pirogov, for instance, said that 'the students were the most sensitive barometer of the times'. The movement did not, in fact, have any specific aim, ideology or programme. It was vague and indeterminate, and at the time of Nicholas I's death it was ready to assume any shape imposed from outside. Yet within only three or four years the student world was widely and sometimes intensely influenced by revolutionary propagandists and supporters of agrarian Socialism and thorough-going emancipation. This was a factor of the greatest importance for the entire modern history of Russia. All the prevailing currents of thought from liberal to democratic and Socialist fought to gain control over the student body. But the struggle was brief and the final decision quite unequivocal.

The student movement also exemplifies the inadequacy of official policies and the reforms from above. The government tried to give the universities freedom of organization; tried to open their doors to the least privileged classes; and tried to give some dignity to the life of the student. But so confused were these attempts that they led the students to open clashes with the authorities, and the authorities themselves to illogical attempts at reaction.

There are many accounts of university life during the last years of Nicholas I. The situation of the students provides an inexhaustible supply of anecdotes illustrating the organized obscurantism of the State.[1] Relations between professor and student were harsh. Military training was carried so far that it often hindered all other activities. The main virtue demanded of the student was attention to his uniform. Everything was designed to prevent the development of independent thinking.

Platon Vasilevich Pavlov, who was history professor at the University of Kiev in 1847, later described how the Curator of the university, Governor-General Bibikov, one day summoned all the professors and students and made the following speech: 'You professors can meet among yourselves, but only to play cards. And you students remember that I will look with an indulgent eye on drunkenness but that a soldier's uniform awaits anyone who is noted for his free thinking.' And this was the general practice. Violent behaviour was allowed, and even encouraged, as long as the students were interested in nothing else.

But in the last analysis the most serious feature was the difficulty of getting into the university. These obstacles were none the less oppressive for being irregular and constantly changing. In 1853 the number of students in all universities throughout the Russian Empire was less than three thousand. From 1850 onwards preference was given to those who would become government officials. An almost insurmountable barrier was put in the way of sons of peasants, the bourgeoisie, soldiers, merchants of the two lowest guilds, Jews, foreigners and clergy. The philological faculties were specially affected by this policy. In 1856 at St Petersburg University, only 30 out of 429 students belonged to these faculties, and in the following year only one student got a degree in history and philosophy. This, among other things, helps to explain the strictly numerical limitation of the Russian intelligentsia, which was to have a serious effect on the history of these years. The creation of a restricted number of intellectuals only was responsible for a feeling of separation between the *élite* and the masses, a separation which was certainly not desired or looked upon as a privilege.

After the death of Nicholas I changes were comparatively quick and thorough. It is particularly important to note the sequence of events. Even before other aspects of Russia's social life were transformed, even before the fate of the peasants was decided and the organization of justice effected, a start was made to open up the universities. At the same time a collective and free life was allowed, though within limits.

The problem was similar to that of granting freedom to the press, though that too was only relative. In both cases it was the government that allowed the intelligentsia to develop more rapidly than the rest of the nation. Such a development was in any case inevitable, but the government's measures certainly encouraged it. It soon became obvious, however, that the gulf between the intelligentsia and the rest of the Russian people had become wider than had been expected. The filling of this gap was one of the main concerns both of the State and of the intellectuals themselves. The government, in fear, took action through a series of steps designed to control a freedom which seemed already conceded and once more closed access to the universities; while the more active members of the intelligentsia succeeded, after terrible difficulties and struggles, in creating, during the following twenty years, a link with the masses. But this link lay outside and beyond the authority of the State. Only the revolutionary movement in fact was to succeed in filling the gap.

The government's policy towards the universities is worth more detailed examination. It will then be possible to observe the gradual crystallization of this twofold stiffening on the part of the State and of the students.[2]

The students' uniform was soon abolished. Despite all the efforts to retain it, students had already been seen in Kiev dressed in the Polish and Ukrainian national costumes. At Kazan some of the students went around dressed in 'the skins of wild animals and armed with sticks'. At Moscow and St Petersburg some students began to wear peasant folk costumes.

Military training was abolished, and discipline became more humane. A new spirit spread through the university. Soon after 1855 libraries appeared run by the students themselves and sure to include forbidden publications, especially the works of Herzen.[3] At the end of 1857 the first students' friendly society was started in St Petersburg, and this example was soon followed elsewhere. These organizations were the most obvious expression of the sense of solidarity which was growing in the university. Kiev saw the first university tribunal; another, which was instituted immediately afterwards at Kazan, had the right to expel students from the university; and at St Petersburg, where it proved impossible to establish one, its place was taken by a 'comrades' tribunal' which decided, for instance, all questions dealing with the use of taxes. The holding of student meetings (called *skhodki*, the traditional word for peasant meetings in the *mir*) became general, and nearly all questions concerning internal student life were decided by assemblies of the kind.

From 1857 onwards the students in the capital had an academic organ of their own in which they printed university news, as well as historical research, etc. Soon a whole series of manuscript newspapers sprang up, whose titles reveal the students' state of mind. One of them copied Herzen's title page, and under *Kolokol* it added: 'Chronicle of Free Opinion.' In Moscow alone the following were in circulation in 1858: *The Spark, The Living Voice, The Echo, The Unmasker*.[4]

These changes in university life, which led to the introduction of rules similar to those of Western and especially German universities, had not only been allowed, but had often, if not always, been directly encouraged by the authorities. The new Curator at St Petersburg, Prince Shcherbatov, read and approved some of the small manuscript news-sheets as well as the academic review. In Moscow, the students' bank was under the direct protection of the government which among other things gave it a suitable site. In Kiev, under Pirogov's authority, the students obtained wide powers of self-administration and all supervision was abolished.

But the government's really decisive act was to open the universities. This led to a rapid increase in students and to the formation of a 'proletariat of thought', the name given to the large number of poor, sometimes destitute, students. Such students had been exceptional when the university was accessible only to the nobility, but by the end of the Crimean War they became so numerous as to constitute a serious and urgent problem. Further details concerning the origin and number of these new students would be of great interest, but strange as it may seem, no research on these lines has been carried out.[5] The most revealing figure we have is that in St Petersburg three hundred and seventy out of about a thousand students were unable to pay the admission tax which was then about twenty-five roubles. But we have countless examples of the wretched conditions endured by these new students, who, in the capital at least, may have formed a majority. They came, sometimes on foot, from the most distant provinces; they slept two in a cupboard, and, in summer, in the public gardens if allowed to by the police.[6]

The student body thus obtained control over its internal organization and greatly increased in numbers and social range. At the same time it came into increasing contact with intellectual circles, and became the centre of a life of discussion and cultural contacts. The lecture rooms had been reopened to all who wished to come; the audience was large and responsive. And then women entered the university, though this novelty gave rise to prolonged discussions. In St Petersburg, certain faculties had more women than men students, but in Moscow in 1862 a majority of the academic council voted against admitting them.

These growing contacts encouraged meetings between the students and those who were then helping to create public opinion. And the examples at our disposal show that the process was reciprocal. Among the students the atmosphere soon grew such that a contemporary said that 'he did not remember a single one of his companions who did not feel a vocation for some social function'.[7] Writers who wished to influence their times began to take growing account of young university students. Khomyakov, the famous Slavophil, regularly associated with a group of students in Moscow, to whom he persistently explained his ideas; though he was compelled to admit that they had less and less effect or were used to lead to different political conclusions. Similar attempts to reach the new generation were made by some of the amnestied Decembrists who had returned after thirty years in Siberia. Among these was Tsebrikov[8] in St Petersburg. But only one member of the immediately preceding generation, Herzen, succeeded in dominating this new generation. This triumph, which was effected through the *Kolokol* which entered Russia illegally, was deep but by no means complete. Apart from Herzen, it was the men who had been at the university ten to fifteen years earlier, and who were now spreading Populist ideas, who had the strongest influence on the students—Dobrolyubov, Lavrov, Chernyshevsky and Mikhailov. The history of the St Petersburg disturbances in 1861 shows that the contacts rapidly became direct and personal, and were transformed into lasting and coherent guidance.

The triumph of Populist ideas was only possible because those liberal teachers who seemed destined to be the natural guides of this generation (as Granovsky for example had been a decade earlier) were unable to keep the trust or even the respect of their students. At first they (Pirogov and Pavlov, for example) had increased the government's concessions as regards freedom of organization and discussion. But when the first repression set in, they hesitated between the government and the students, and acted more as intermediaries than as comrades or political guides.

So the universities became one of the battlefields of the 'sixties. More openly here than anywhere else was the struggle fought out between official Conservatism, Liberalism and Populism: and more obvious than elsewhere was the victory of Populism. The various student movements of these years, the long and (today) apparently pointless discussions on the position of this or that professor, of this or that type of student organization, take on a new significance when looked at in this light.

A detailed account of these movements is not necessary here. They often lacked political content, and more than anything they betray a disgruntled state of mind, prepared to express itself in the most varying and even contradictory forms and directions. It is not for nothing that 'student stories' became a by-word for trouble.

It is, however, remarkable that the first incidents—in the autumn of 1856—took place in a town where social problems were most acute. This was Kazan. As yet these incidents were confined to clashes with the officers of the local garrison, in defence of student rights—a motive which differentiated this first movement from earlier clashes, frequent enough in a town whose students had a well-deserved reputation for drunkenness and lack of discipline. The few who were punished for these incidents provided some of the first leaders for the clandestine movement in the town. A report on these clashes noted that 'for the first time there could be noted among the students a feeling of corporative solidarity and community of interests'.[9]

A year later a similar story took place in Kiev. It started with a student kicking a dog which belonged to a colonel of the local garrison. A few students were sent to prison, but they were freed by Alexander II in person when he visited the town in October of the same year.

But in Moscow in September 1857 there was a more serious incident. A number of students refused to open the doors of the university to the police until they returned with a member of the faculty. These students were attacked with great violence and some were wounded. Though the Governor of Moscow told the Emperor that there had been a revolt at the university he replied: 'I don't believe it', and eventually, after an inquiry, it was the police force that was punished. The students seemed to have won a right to immunity. Some years later a Committee of Inquiry pointed out that 'it was the first time that a feeling of unity was noted among them'.[10]

The disorders at Kharkov in autumn 1858 would be a mere insignificant repetition of these earlier examples were it not that they marked the end of government protection and the beginning of a reaction. On one of his visits there, Alexander II in person made it quite clear that as far as he was concerned the students were now going too far.

The students had now begun to demand that some of the professors whom they particularly disliked, and rightly considered utterly ineffectual, should be dismissed. At Kazan, in January 1858, Professor V. F. Bervi, who taught physiology, of which he knew very little, received a letter signed by his seventy pupils which politely asked him to give up the chair. 'Please forgive us, professor, if we have been the first to speak of this. Love of science and the desire to be useful to our Fatherland have made us precipitate.' Their request was supported by Dobrolyubov, who published a scathing review of one of Bervi's works in the *Sovremennik*. The request had to be granted, and the professor went. A year later the students decided to show their sympathy for a popular professor. Though applause or signs of disapproval were forbidden during lectures, they demonstrated in favour of a young liberal teacher of history and Russian literature. Eighteen were arrested and dismissed from the university, and even from Kazan itself, unless they lived there with their parents. This had a profound effect on the students, many of whom decided to leave the university in a mass protest against the expulsion of their comrades.[11] So frequent were the demands to leave, that lectures had to be suspended for some time and the students were held back only by threats.

In 1858 the students had their own way even in Moscow, and compelled two professors to resign, one of whom was specially hated for his methods of treating his pupils. So that here, too, desire for a more vivid and up-to-date scholarship was combined with the demand for more dignified treatment. The students won their point but at a heavy cost. One man was expelled and two were temporarily sent down. Yet in the prevailing state of mind such steps seemed if anything designed to strengthen their dedicated spirits and sense of solidarity.

Between 1858 and 1859 it was obvious that a reaction was setting in. A group of professors, among them names well known in liberal circles such as Chicherin, concluded that: 'Russian society has given students a sense of their own importance which does not exist in any other country . . . the student is no longer a pupil but is becoming a master, a guide of society.'[12] Such a state of affairs, said the professors, was not normal. The complaint was, however, really a confession of their own lack of influence.

Access to the university was once more, though indirectly, restricted. In 1859 in St Petersburg only seventy-three out of three hundred and seventy-five who took the entrance examination were admitted; and in Moscow only a hundred and fifty-two out of five hundred. In that year, and still more during the following year, supervision of the students was again entrusted to the police. But these and similar steps were only the preliminaries to a new ruling on internal student life which was then being drawn up. E. P. Kovalevsky, Minister of Public Instruction, tried to make a stand against this reaction; and a few liberal professors, among them Kavelin, tried to anticipate the government's decisions by proposing regulations which, though allowing the students some freedom of organization, would place them under the supervision of their teachers. This was of course an attempt by the liberal professors to win back by administrative means the position which they were

8+

losing in the ideological sphere. But at this stage their mediation was considered superfluous by both sides.

From 1861 the student movement became more political in character and protests against the government's directives were intensified. In St Petersburg, in March, a large university delegation of Russians and Poles took part in the requiem mass to commemorate those who had fallen in the Warsaw disturbances. Three hundred of the students made their presence quite clear by signing the register. At Kazan Shchapov managed to give a distinctly political flavour to the requiem in honour of the peasants who had been shot at Bezdna.

So the problems of nationalism and of the peasants made themselves felt even in the universities. But while most students supported radical solutions to the land problem, on the question of the nationalities in the empire they were divided. At Kiev, for instance, the feeling was against the Poles whereas in Moscow and St Petersburg it was for them. To combine national and peasant liberation, as constantly preached by Herzen and Chernyshevsky, proved a difficult task. It was this problem that drove many students from a purely corporative struggle into the political field. And it was later to become the central issue for *Zemlya i Volya*.

Even the earliest stages of this political trend were enough to convince Alexander II that extreme measures were needed. A commission was appointed to draft regulations which would eliminate virtually all freedom within the university. Its third item forbade 'absolutely any meeting without permission of superiors'. To apply these new directives the Minister of Public Instruction was replaced by an Admiral, E. P. Putyatin. A series of orders very similar to those of Nicholas I's time was then brought into force. The most drastic of these allowed only two students from each department to be exempted from taxes. The significance of this becomes clear enough when it is realized that in St Petersburg in 1859 six hundred and fifty-nine out of a thousand and nineteen students had been exempted. The new ruling meant, in fact, that the poor and lower classes were again to be excluded.

When term began again after the holidays, no one had the courage to give the students a clear account of these decisions. The wildest rumours were allowed to circulate, and when some delegates went to the Curator to ask for an explanation, he told them that 'he was not an orator, and that in any case they would do better to devote themselves to their studies instead of to meetings'. But meetings continued without interruption, and so on 22nd September all empty lecture rooms (where the gatherings were usually held) were closed. On the following day a manifesto—the most typical document of all these student movements—was circulated.[13] 'The government', it announced, 'has thrown down the gauntlet.' The present blow recalled many others, far more serious and painful.

The Russian people has for long been famous for its great patience. The Tartars beat us, and we said nothing; the Tsar beat us, and we said nothing and bowed

down; and now the Germans are beating us, and we say nothing and admire them
... There's progress! ... Only in some distant corner over there in the West there
are still a few fools who are inspired by an empty word: *la gloire*.

In this scathing ironical tone the manifesto continued: 'The essential thing
now is to avoid quarrels among ourselves and not to be afraid of energetic
steps. Put one thing clearly in your head: they will not dare to fire on us, for
the revolt would spread from the university to St Petersburg.' It ended by
praising the Poles and holding them up as an example. 'Energy, energy,
energy', were the last words.

The author of this pamphlet is not known, but a clandestine committee
had now been formed and was beginning to direct the movement. Among
others taking part were E. P. Mikhaelis, brother-in-law of N. V. Shelgunov,
one of the most distinguished contributors to the *Sovremennik*. Mikhaelis
had already helped to circulate the clandestine manifesto *To the Young
Generation*, and was at this time aged twenty. He is recalled by all memoir
writers as 'a typical figure of his time, and a pure Nihilist'. N. I. Utin was
another of the leaders of this movement, and we will meet him again in
Zemlya i Volya, of which he became one of the most active members.[14]
M. I. Pokrovsky, a third member of the committee, was also closely associated
with the *Sovremennik*.

On 23rd September 1861 a crowd of students broke in the door of a closed
lecture-room and held a meeting there. This marked the beginning of a
series of demonstrations which moved from the university to the streets
when the university was closed on the following day. The Curator still
hesitated and refused to give the students a clear account of the new rules.
He even had the crowd of students which had assembled in the courtyard
informed that he was no longer in office. They then began to move in long
files across the bridge over the River Neva towards the part of the town
where he lived. It was an orderly demonstration followed by policemen and
a large crowd of people, but it had one special feature. Never before had a
demonstration taken place in St Petersburg.

A sight like it had never been seen. It was a wonderful September day ... In the
streets the girls who were just beginning to go to university joined in together
with a number of young men of differing origins and professions who knew us or
merely agreed with us ... When we appeared on the Nevsky Prospekt, the French
barbers came out of their shops and their faces lit up and they waved their arms
cheerfully, shouting, 'Révolution! Révolution!'[15]

The Curator had meanwhile hurried home. Amid great shouting and the
danger of a violent clash between the students and the soldiers who were
summoned for the occasion, a delegation at last got him to agree to receive
them at the university. He gave his word of honour that the delegates would
not be touched. The column then marched back along the same way it had
come, with the Curator at its head, for the students did not trust him and

were afraid that he would run away. At the university there were lengthy negotiations. At last the students dispersed, after another threat to use soldiers had had to be made. They thought they had won at least a partial victory.

But during the night numbers of students were arrested, among them the delegates who had been promised immunity. This made a deep impression and won them a halo of sympathy throughout the intelligentsia. On the 27th the students again assembled in front of the university, and with them many artillery officers, encouraged by P. L. Lavrov, who was then a professor at the Artillery Academy and hoped that this would prevent clashes with the troops. The students demanded that their imprisoned comrades should be freed and recalled the Curator's word of honour. The meeting could only be dispersed when the students were threatened with 'not a heroic death but a good beating'. During the following days pickets and platoons were stationed in the most important parts of the town. Arrests continued, sporadic at first and then more and more systematic after the beginning of October.

The authorities tried to enforce at least one of the decisions which had already been made. A special ticket was required to enter the university. But many professors refused to hand these round. 'To take or not to take the ticket' was eagerly discussed by all. About three hundred students submitted, but when on 11th October the university re-opened, the rebels tried to stop the lectures. On the next day even those who had accepted the tickets conspicuously flung them down at the gates of the university, and about one hundred and thirty were arrested. But the students had won their point; the attempt to re-open the university had failed. It is true that the prisoners were beaten, and some even wounded. But their solidarity had been complete. 'Carry me off to prison too', the students shouted to the police. An attempt was made to keep the university open until 20th December, but there were only very few students, and the younger, more liberal professors resigned. And then the gates closed altogether.[16]

The prisoners stayed in the Peter-Paul fortress until the middle of October, and were then taken to Kronstadt. There they were tried by a tribunal. Their sentences were not very heavy, nor had life in prison been excessively hard. Five were exiled to remote territories, thirty-two were excluded from the university but allowed to take their exams as 'external students'; the others were merely solemnly reprimanded.

It is possible that the authorities had hoped to uncover a serious plot, a clandestine organization responsible for the disorders. Mikhailov, who was arrested at this time and who accepted responsibility for drawing up the manifesto *To the Young Generation*, was suspected of having instigated the disorders. From this time onwards the police put a curb on Chernyshevsky, who had supported the students' movement in the *Sovremennik* more openly and vigorously than anyone else. In fact, however, it was the government's own policies that crystallized the atmosphere in which the first clandestine groups sprang up. They were a consequence rather than a cause of the demonstrations at St Petersburg. 'Instead of open meetings, secret meetings took place in some little garret or in private lodgings. The campaign against these secret meetings became more difficult even though it is true they no longer had the wider significance of public meetings',[17] said a contemporary. St Petersburg was covered with a network of centres and clubs which gathered together these students who were 'on strike'.[18]

The effects of the demonstrations lasted a full year, and most of the faculties remained closed until August 1863. During this time an attempt was made to organize a free university with voluntary professors, twenty of whom, including some of the leading ones, agreed to join. The organizing committee invited Lavrov and Chernyshevsky to lecture, but the authorities let it be known that they would not allow this. Others were stopped by the ecclesiastical censorship. Pypin, for instance, could not give a proposed course of lectures on the history of Russian mediaeval literature, while Pobedonostsev—Alexander III's future mentor—who was also invited, said that he would not take part in anything which would mean collaborating with 'a charlatan like Chernyshevsky'.[19] As can be seen, he was well on the way to turning into the pillar of reaction that he became at the end of the century.

The free university lasted only a month, and was brought to an end in a highly significant manner. Platon Pavlov, the Kiev history professor who had been one of the initiators of the liberal movement in the university, was arrested on the night of 5th March 1862. He was sent into exile in the department of Kostroma, and forbidden to give public lectures, for having made a speech which was judged inadmissible on the theme: 'A thousand years of Russian history.' The students demanded that their lectures should be interrupted as a protest. Some professors, however, were opposed to this decision, and one of them, the historian Kostomarov, had his lecture interrupted by insults and shouts of: 'You're just another Chicherin.' And so even those who had once stood out on behalf of the students were joining those liberal professors who had already lost the faith of the student body.[20]

The St Petersburg demonstrations were echoed in the provinces, where they gave rise to similar movements which were similarly repressed. On 2nd September a delegation of students from the capital reached Moscow, with news of the reactions aroused by the closing of the university. In Moscow, too, most of the students decided to defend their right to meetings, and a small secret committee was formed which adopted greater precautions than had been taken at St Petersburg. After a few meetings and threats, on 4th October 1861, Nikolay Stepanovich Slavutinsky, a student who had once helped to found Sunday-schools and whose radical spirit was rapidly becoming known, suggested a demonstration which would give their protests some symbolic significance. A procession was to carry a wreath to the tomb of Granovsky—the historian and friend of Herzen. The entire police force and many soldiers were mobilized on the day and the report said that 'a number of speeches were made, some of them completely lacking in modera-tion'; but there were no incidents.

A demonstration in front of the house of the Governor on 11th October led to very different results. The student delegates who tried to speak to the Governor were arrested and the others were surrounded by the police, and violently beaten. Three hundred and forty were arrested and thirty-nine detained. This was the first time that such a thing had happened in Moscow, and it caused a great sensation, all the more so as the police had not acted alone but had whipped up the small shopkeepers who had taken a prominent part in the attack, hoping for some reward. This was a serious blow, and despite the efforts of the more determined students, a boycott of lectures, as at St Petersburg, proved impossible to organize.[21]

There was a greater degree of uncertainty among the students at Moscow than probably anywhere else. The discussions brought to light two wings: the radicals who were already moving towards political action and soon turned to *Zemlya i Volya*; and the more typical liberals, who insisted on orderly demonstrations and greater faith in possible concessions from the authorities. The historian Gessen has shown that this split corresponded to a social difference: the radicals consisted of students of lower or petit bour-geois origin; the liberals came from the nobility. One of their leaders was N. N. Raevsky, a descendant of typical Decembrist figures. But all sources are agreed that there was a considerable number of students utterly opposed to any movement.

These discussions and differences bring to light even more clearly the limits of the entire student movement: its academic, corporative, 'family' character, in the apologetic words of some of the students themselves. It never broke out beyond these limits, although there were some members who were already determined to push matters on to the end. The disorders were always more a symptom and prelude rather than a real political force. In Moscow there was none of the general sympathy for the movement which was felt by the educated classes in St Petersburg. Indeed, even the professors took up a more negative and, to be precise, cowardly attitude; the clash therefore was mainly between students and police, and so was more violent and brutal. The other forces of society played a less comprehensive rôle than in the capital. There was only one new element in Moscow: the lower classes had been successfully won over by the police.

The year 1863 marks the end of this first phase of the student movement. From then on, though lectures were everywhere resumed, there were no disorders of any importance until 1869; and above all, in that year, the new university regulations, which had given rise to so many discussions, were brought into force. Student corporate life was greatly restricted, almost abolished. In return a concession was made to the educated classes. The uni-versities were granted independence in the choice of professors and internal administration.

Such were the results of the disturbances as far as the government was concerned. In London a different view was taken. Herzen and Ogarev saw in these unsuccessful attempts to organize student strikes and disturbances the first evidence of the Populist call to 'go to the people'. On 15th January 1862 Ogarev published an article in the *Kolokol* called 'The Universities are Closing'. 'Let them close', he said. He considered the moral issues involved, and invited the students to look seriously at their *raison d'être* from the social point of view.

Every rich man, every noble who enters the temple of learning which is closed for the poor and the non-noble would feel that he was a wretch . . . Let them close the universities, this will not make genuine learning perish. Let the young men of the universities scatter through the provinces. Any man worth anything will carry learning with him wherever he goes. Not government learning whose aim is tuition; but vital learning, whose purpose is the education of the people. This learning is universal and knows no distinction of class. We need travelling teachers. The apostles of learning, like those of religion, cannot stay put, shutting themselves up in chapels specially built for them. Their cause is called preaching, their place is everywhere. At first they did not exist, but now, without wanting to, the government has created them. Take advantage of this; do not go to the universities. Let them close; university youth spread throughout Russia will act as a unifying agent between the various classes. To become a free man it is essential to go to the people.

9. THE FIRST GROUPS

HIS MAJESTY HAS been informed that there seems to be in existence in Moscow a secret society whose aim is to introduce a republican régime into Russia. It appears that this may meet with some success as its members are protected by Soldatenkov and other wealthy 'Old Believers' . . . It must be assumed that its members belong to the so-called 'black students', i.e. those who do not come from the upper classes.

So read a letter sent by V. A. Dolgorukov, head of the Third Section, to the Governor-General of Moscow in May 1858. An enquiry was made, and in June the Emperor himself began to take an interest. From denunciations, anonymous letters and the typical workings of the police imagination, it was established that there did in fact exist in Moscow a group of intellectuals, mostly students, who professed Socialist ideas which they were beginning to apply to the situation in Russia. The police reports referring to this movement have recently been published by M. M. Klevensky, who has also collected the little biographical material that has survived. The result is of considerable interest, for we can here observe an early and typically Populist product.[1]

The origins of this movement can be dated between the end of 1854 and the beginning of 1855.[2] At that time there arrived in Moscow University Pavel Nikolaevich Rybnikov, a young man already aged twenty-three, who came from a merchant family of 'Old Believers'. He had travelled abroad, and was remarkably well educated. All those who met him a few years later were astounded by the breadth of his philosophical and literary culture and especially by his wide reading in the works of Hegel, Feuerbach, Stirner, Louis Blanc, Proudhon, as well as Vico and Montesquieu. More than many of his contemporaries, the young Rybnikov combined the ideas which he took from these writers with a keen interest in popular tradition and Russian folk-lore. He was well read in theological literature (especially that of the *Raskolniki*), was interested in their way of life, and had applied himself to studying the day-to-day existence of the Russian peasants. Through this two-fold culture he gradually became one of the leading experts on ancient Russian songs, and one of the most patient and intelligent collectors and commentators on popular literature. In this work he was inspired by a deliberate attempt to draw nearer to the people, and by an effort to establish a contact in the sphere of ideas and values between the intelligentsia and the peasants.[3]

A group of students soon began to collect around him; their organization consisted only in more or less regular meetings held in a small, smoky room, to discuss social and philosophical problems. Closely associated with them was a large number of other young men, chiefly officers and employees, who dropped in at these meetings. The meetings, as will be seen, were similar to those of the Petrashevskists ten years earlier, so much so that the police (and also Klevensky) thought there was a direct connection between them. But the link was probably more one of ideals than of organization. In any case these meetings did resume a movement which had been violently interrupted by the reaction of 1849. 'They discussed the *obshchina*, *narodnost* in scholarship, patriarchal life, etc. . . . And the discussions sometimes touched on Socialist doctrines.' In fact, they raised once again the problem of Russian Socialism, and relations between Western ideas and the collective traditions of the village.

It is interesting to see that these *vertepniki* had already broken with Slavophil ideology. Khomyakov and Aksakov went to the meetings, and so on at least one occasion did Samarin. Rybnikov was the tutor of Khomyakov's sons, and during the summer he lived on his estate. And so these young men had the chance to hear the greatest Slavophil thinkers in person. After constant and often violent discussions, they ended by dissociating themselves from the romantic, religious and traditional elements of their masters' theories. In the religious sphere they were disciples of Feuerbach, and as far as social problems were concerned they followed Proudhon, Louis Blanc and Leroux. The Slavophils merely led them, like Herzen earlier, to an increasing admiration and study of village life.

One of the most ardent speakers in these discussions was Matvey Yakovlevich Sviridenko, who as a member of the group later recalled, had a great influence on his friends 'in turning them [his friends] to Socialism and every kind of emancipation'. He was some years older than the others whom he dominated by his intelligence. By the end of 1858 Sviridenko was passionately trying to get into contact with the peasants. In the words of a police report: 'He did nothing. He visited the peasants and lived with them, treating them all with courtesy . . . He systematically took part in the meetings of the *mir*, and to do this he dressed himself in a peasant cloak.' He went round the villages saying that he himself was of peasant origin and was being persecuted by the police. He took part in their work in the fields. 'In this way', the report continues, 'Sviridenko gained special consideration and had a strong moral influence in the villages. They listened and followed him in everything.' He ended by marrying a peasant woman and lived for some time in an *izba* 'where poverty was visible everywhere'.

Though Sviridenko said that he had come to the peasants to enter into their lives, so as to observe their habits and to describe them, and though he, like these *vertepniki* in general, certainly had a great urge to study, none the less his entire attitude already betrayed a considerable interest in politics.

8*

After living in the *izba,* he soon became a bookseller, and among the most active members of *Zemlya i Volya.* As he stood by the platform on which Chernyshevsky was 'civilly executed' he attracted the attention of the police by asking those present to uncover their heads. He died shortly afterwards, too early to leave a significant mark on the life of these years. But from the recollections of his contemporaries we can see that he was one of the first and most typical young men for whom the break with the Slavophil tradition coincided with a first step on the road to the people. Other *vertepniki* show similar tendencies, in particular A. A. Kozlov, who, before becoming a well known teacher of philosophy, was arrested for propaganda in 1862.

In contact with the Moscow *vertepniki* was a group of Kharkov students who had founded a secret society immediately after the Crimean War.

These two groups were the only illegal and potentially revolutionary political organizations in the period immediately preceding the emancipation of the serfs. Both were weak and temporary, but are none the less interesting mainly as a symptom of the atmosphere of impatience which followed the death of Nicholas I and as the herald of the movement which arose after 1861.

There were appreciable differences between the *vertepniki* and the Kharkov students. While the former were a centre of ideological debates, the Kharkov group was a conspiracy, though as yet indecisive and immature. Political problems and the active struggle against despotism soon took first place in their programme. The strongest tie between the two consisted in the circulation in both of works published by Herzen's 'Free Russian Press'. This provides us with evidence of the great response that Iskander's ideas met with among the young. For while memoirs of the period tell us of the reactions and discussions aroused by Herzen's works in the various strata of the ruling class, we must descend into these, as yet rare, secret 'undergrounds' to find the first repercussions among the students.

The originators of the Kharkov secret society were Yakov Nikolaevich Bekman and Mitrofan Danilovich Muravsky. Both came from the smaller nobility with modest, indeed poverty-stricken, estates. Both later said that the fundamental emotions which had inspired them to found a secret society were shame and discontent at Russia's defeat in the Crimea and the certainty that this showed the absolute necessity for some radical change.[4]

For this purpose they created a nucleus with two other students who were among the poorest of the university, Petr Savelich Efimenko and Petr Vasilevich Zavadsky. The latter was the son of a priest, and later said:

My situation necessarily brought me into close contact with simple folk. I lived their life and their needs were mine also. I was well acquainted with the life of the peasants in my village and I saw its hardships. My family life always left me with a warm feeling for simple folk . . . I saw that they were oppressed and had to put up with much. Yet their songs, their games, and all their life seemed to me full of poetry, and so I looked upon their oppression as even harder.

By November 1856 there were eight members of the society; other students had joined it, among them E. O. Portugalov, the son of a Jewish merchant. These young men were very soon brought face to face with problems of nationality. Portugalov wanted to do something for the rights of Jewish students who were compelled to hide their origin and were persecuted even by their companions. Zavadsky, on the other hand, was convinced that the Russian State was the enemy of the Ukrainian, and so he gave 'a Little Russian' flavour to his opposition. But when he heard of the existence of revolutionary forces among the 'Great Russians', 'he refused to make any distinction between the simple people of the one or the other'.

At the end of 1856 this group combined with another Kharkov group which had been formed unknown to them. This was composed of noble students coming from rich families, and its guiding spirit was Nikolay Mikhailovich Raevsky, who was to die two years later remembered by all who knew him for his remarkable intelligence.

If the first group was a small germ of Populism, the second already contained some typical elements of later 'Nihilism', such as a passionate interest in the exact sciences and a sense of superiority towards the world, which it expressed in the form of irony and bitterness. Indeed the group was known as the *Paskvilny Komitet* (the libellous committee). The two groups together made up a secret society of thirteen and they soon used as a sounding-board a students' literary club which started in spring 1856.

The purpose of the society was clear enough, however general: 'They aimed to arouse a general revolution in Russia beginning with the emancipation of the peasants.'

To achieve this aim did not seem too difficult to us . . . We thought that no real effort would be needed to provoke a general insurrection in Russia . . . We thought that Russia would rise up that very year. All that was needed was to print a few thousand copies of some sort of full programme, to send agents everywhere, give them sufficient means to carry out our plans to the end, and one fine day Russia would have learnt that in all the corners of its territory a violent revolt was in action.

The obvious childishness of such a plan must not prevent us from understanding the significance of these words, which reflect the prevailing fear of a peasant revolt. But for these men the threat was changed into a hope. 'To unleash a revolt seemed all the easier in that not a single one of the social classes was satisfied with the government.'

When after a short consideration the society moved from these great hopes to deciding what had to be done, its members were faced with the problem of drawing up a definite programme. Until then their activities had consisted merely in reading and studying the works of Herzen. They also collected, copied out and circulated any subversive writings that came their way, and their discussions reflected those taking place among the

Russian educated classes, though in a more extremist form. They hesitated between a constitutional monarchy and a republic, and finally chose the latter. They made plans for propaganda among the officers of the Kiev garrison and the peasants, and they probably distributed a few manuscripts drawn up by them for this purpose. They only took one serious step, though this alarmed the local authorities and even engaged the attention of Alexander II himself. This consisted in spreading a handwritten manifesto against the Peace of Paris in April 1856. The manifesto was a parody of the articles of the agreement and the declarations of the Emperor. It cleverly stressed the losses which Russia had had to endure as a result of her defeat. And when the first student movements broke out in Kharkov University, the thirteen conspirators played a prominent part.

But in 1857 the society was already in dissolution. It was not that the authorities, despite many inquiries, had succeeded in discovering the authors of the manifesto which had aroused such a scandal. But lack of means, the huge size of their task and the fact that they had hardly begun to consider how it could be solved, and above all, perhaps, the liberal policy of the government which was promising reforms—all these cut the ground from under their feet. Zavadsky summed up the situation when he said that 'their activities consisted in gossip'. The Kharkov group nevertheless transferred its organizing activities to the University of Kiev and renewed them there in contact with one of the most liberal and open-minded professors of the time, the historian P. V. Pavlov.

In January 1860 its members were affected by a denunciation sent to the authorities, first at Kharkov and then at St Petersburg. The landowner Mikhail Egorovich Garshin called in the authorities to avenge himself against Zavadsky, who after becoming a tutor in his house had persuaded his wife to run away with him, together with his four-year-old son, Vsevolod, later to become a well-known writer. A search for this 'corrupter of souls', as the husband called him, led the police on to the tracks of all the Kharkov student movement. Twenty-two people were involved; five were exiled to small provincial towns, where they were allowed to take part in the local administration; the rest were freed, though kept under police surveillance. The same liberalism from above, which had been one of the fundamental causes of the group's dispersal, was now responsible for the remarkably mild manner of its liquidation.

This early and frail attempt to create a secret society was not without influence in the following years. *A manuscript history of the Kharkov group* circulated among the students and was found by the police in a search at Kazan.[5] Some of these young Kharkov conspirators developed the revolutionary tendencies which they had been the first to try to express in the Russia of the time until these sentiments became the *raisons d'être* for their lives. Bekman himself died in 1863, but he had had time to become an active member of the first *Zemlya i Volya* in the department of Vologda where he had been exiled. In 1862 he was sent to the Peter-Paul fortress and was then exiled to the department of Samara for spreading 'Ukrainian propaganda'.[6] Muravsky became one of the most typical revolutionaries of the next twenty years. In September 1862 he was again imprisoned for letters which he wrote from Orenburg, where he had been exiled and employed in the administration of the Kirghiz tribes. In 1863 he was condemned to eight years' hard labour and banishment for life to Siberia. In the 'seventies he came back to Orenburg and was one of the most active propagandists and organizers in that region. He was involved in the 'trial of the hundred and ninety-three' in 1878, received a sentence of ten years and died in prison a year later.[7]

Attempts at conspiracies were interrupted during the preparatory stages of the peasant reform, but resumed on a very different scale immediately after its final phase, the manifesto of 19th February 1861.

In July 1861 a leaflet called the *Velikoruss* (The Great Russian) was circulated in St Petersburg and later in Moscow. At the beginning of September the second number came out, and two weeks later the third and last. It was written clearly and without rhetoric and addressed to the educated classes. It made no attempt to be understood by simple people. It had no definite political line: indeed it is often difficult to determine how far its clandestine editors were making use of tactical cunning, and how far they were themselves trying to find a solution to their problems. This uncertainty, combined with the desire to consider openly all the fundamental questions of the day, clearly reflects the atmosphere prevailing in educated circles during the summer that followed the emancipation decree.[8]

The very first number of the *Velikoruss* transformed the growing fear of the authorities, as they heard of the reactions of the peasants in the various provinces, into an open threat. 'The government is bringing Russia to a Pugachev revolt. We must re-examine the entire peasant problem and solve it in some other way.' But who could do this? Certainly not the government: 'It is not capable of understanding anything; it is stupid and ignorant.' And so it was up to the 'educated classes' to take political leadership in hand, to 'curb the government and direct it', by imposing their own solutions. This was a suitable moment: 'We are neither Poles nor peasants. They will not fire on us.'

The dilemma was clearly emphasized: either such an action by 'the enlightened part of the nation' or an appeal to the people which the 'patriots' would be compelled to make but whose consequences could only be serious for the intelligentsia as well.

The *Velikoruss* was looking for a solution other than revolution, and in its second number it suggested a new alternative. Most of the peasants wanted all the land which had until then belonged to the gentry. Some, however, would have been satisfied with what they had previously farmed together with the neighbouring woods and fishing rights, as long as they had to pay no redemption fee. The *Velikoruss* maintained that it was vital to support this minority and satisfy its demands. The State itself should assume the burden of the redemption. There were besides other problems which were awaiting solution: Poland should be given freedom, to which it had the right. Such a step would indeed even be to Russia's advantage. Once again, the suggestion was supported by threats: 'If we don't do this, the Poles will in any case soon free themselves.' In the same way it was essential to allow the Ukrainians to express their own will: 'We don't know whether they will want to separate themselves from us or not, but if they want to, let them do it.' Only in this way, by solving the problems of the peasants and the nationalities, would it be possible to obtain freedom in Russia. 'Military despotism', employed against the peasants and the minorities, in fact oppressed all the national territory and all classes. Those of the liberals who wanted intermediate solutions were not aware of the close relation between all these different problems.

In its third and last number, the *Velikoruss* discussed the problem of the relations between the dynasty and the constitution. It did not come out clearly for a republic, and was evidently trying to influence those who were thinking of a constitutional monarchy. But this third number, even more than its predecessors, showed that these tactics were in fact only covering up the uncertainties and hesitations of the editors themselves. For instance, though they ended by giving some practical, if very general, suggestions on how to found a secret society to be based on their ideas, at the same time they published an appeal to Alexander II. It was not just the government, they said, but the entire administrative machinery that was incapable of completing the reforms. This was the obstacle which was crushing the will both of the 'patriots' and of the Tsar. And so they demanded the summoning of an assembly. This would bring the Emperor into direct contact with the nation, above the heads of the incompetent bureaucracy.

These ideas of the *Velikoruss*, and shortly afterwards of N. A. Serno-Solovevich, make it quite clear that we are only at the fringes of a movement. They used threats, pointed out dangers and produced political solutions, but when it came to deciding on the forces to carry all this out they displayed little confidence. And so they had to resort to political action in the Emperor's name and person.

We have no certain knowledge as to who these men were who so faithfully reflected the doubts and aspirations of the time. The police did not lay hands on them, and none of their contemporaries has left us detailed evidence of those who took part in this secret organization.

It has been suggested that the inspiration behind the *Velikoruss* came directly from Chernyshevsky and even that he was its author. But though its ideas and even style are somewhat similar to his own *Letters without an Address* published in 1862, a year later, careful examination shows that it lacks his energy and decision. Above all it lacks his political vision. The *Velikoruss* is far too concerned with dynastic and constitutional problems for us to assume that it corresponds to Chernyshevsky's ideas, which were always exclusively concerned with the political and social forces in the field. And, even more significant, there are too many concessions to that liberal mentality which Chernyshevsky had fought so powerfully for so many years.[9]

It is, however, true that the few names that do emerge from the fog surrounding this episode are all of men who were close to Chernyshevsky. Among them, for example, are the brothers Luginin,[10] of whom Vladimir Fedorovich was described in Chernyshevsky's novel *The Prologue* as the character Nivelzin. He was a sensitive and intelligent man, and his political activities at this time constituted a link between Chernyshevsky and Herzen. The son of an extremely rich landowner from the region of Kostroma, after an excellent education, he took part in the Crimean War, where, among other things, he met Tolstoy. When he returned to St Petersburg, he gave up his military career. He then moved in the circles of the *Sovremennik*, and in 1862 went to the University of Heidelberg to devote himself to his chemistry studies. He remained abroad until 1867, in close contact with the London émigrés. He was one of the men on whom Herzen, Bakunin and Ogarev most counted to launch their campaign in favour of the *Zemsky Sobor*, and for this purpose to maintain relations with liberals such as Turgenev. Luginin could well look upon this as a logical sequel to his campaign in the *Velikoruss*, but his highly critical view of the Tsar soon made him put less and less trust in liberalism and led him to feel rancour for everything Russian. He said that he wanted to spend his entire life in France or England, 'as he had nothing in common either with the peasants or with the Russian merchants. He did not share their beliefs and did not appreciate their principles.'[11] He ended, however, by returning to his country and devoting himself to his studies with conspicuous success.

To return to the *Velikoruss*: the man who suffered most from the repression launched against the paper was Vladimir Aleksandrovich Obruchev. With one of his relations, Nikolay, he too was a frequent visitor to Chernyshevsky's house. Both are good examples of the young men who in 1861 rallied round the *Sovremennik* and were among the earliest members of *Zemlya i Volya*.

At the first obstacle in his military career (his failure to get on the General Staff) V. A. Obruchev had resigned, devoting himself to working as a 'ghost writer' on the editorial board of Chernyshevsky's reviews and in other literary undertakings. When he was twenty-five he accepted an invitation to distribute the second number of the *Velikoruss* and was soon arrested. Though he was questioned at great length, the police got no information from him. After some months in prison he was sentenced to five years' hard labour and banishment for life in Siberia. In May 1862 the Emperor reduced his prison sentence to three years.

At the end of May he underwent the typical ceremony of 'civil execution'. This was remembered by his contemporaries for the hostility with which the people treated him. This was yet another proof of the isolated position of

these young intellectuals and the complete misunderstanding they faced once
they left the world of 'the educated classes'. L. F. Panteleyev says:

The crowd who stood before the platform expressed the bestial desire that Obruchev's head should be cut off, that he should be flogged with the *knut* or at least
tied to the column with his head down, as he had dared to go against the Tsar . . .
The most horrible thing was the savage laugh that ran through the crowd when they
made him put on the convict's clothes and a cloak which covered him up to his
eyes.[12]

But there was another side to the ceremony. The Governor-General of
St Petersburg, Suvorov, went up to him and with an 'alarmed expression'
began to speak to him in French, saying that he knew his father. 'Voyons,
dites-moi, qu'est-ce-que vous êtes allé faire dans cette galère?' But the conversation led to nothing, apart from some easing in Obruchev's immediate
situation. However, its significance is perhaps greater than that of a merely
curious episode, characteristic of the prevailing atmosphere. For Suvorov
had a reputation as a liberal, and rumour tells us that the associates of the
Velikoruss wanted to put him, with his consent or otherwise, at the head of
the movement that they had started. Such a rumour would perhaps scarcely
deserve being reported, did it not show that a legend in the circles of the
Velikoruss linked the paper's fortunes to higher spheres. Whatever the kernel
of truth contained in this tradition, it certainly helps us to understand this
small paper's true significance. It reflected the feelings, hopes and anxieties
of these young men whose banner was the *Sovremennik*, but who were now
ceasing to preach politics—even such intelligent and coherent doctrines as
Chernyshevsky's—in order to engage in more modest, yet practical, tasks.
They were beginning to settle accounts with the political situation as it
really was. Keeping their eyes firmly fixed on the educated classes, the editors
of the *Velikoruss* may well have hoped to find support from above.

The *Velikoruss* now opened what has been pompously called the 'Era of
Proclamations' or 'Manifestos'. Throughout the last months of 1861 and all
the following year it made constant efforts to bring into being a clandestine
press and circulate proclamations which echoed, often violently, the disappointments and hopes of the growing movement. 'Rapid partisan attacks
launched by separate and independent groups.'[13] So they were correctly
defined by Shelgunov, a writer who played an important part in these
activities.

The majority of the intelligentsia was not yet ready for a campaign aimed
to steer the peasant reform into a general political movement. Herzen was
talking of the *Zemsky Sobor*. Chernyshevsky was entirely engaged in his
duel with the authorities. The intellectual *élite* was carried away by great
hopes of immediate freedom. But these 'partisans' had undertaken the task
of saying clearly, free from the reserves imposed by the political struggle
and the censorship, that action was now necessary and that it was time to

raise outstanding problems in all their magnitude. This must be done in a spirit of radical determination.

To this effect Shelgunov and Mikhailov, two typical if minor figures of the period, wrote and circulated a manifesto in the autumn of 1861.

At this time Nikolay Vasilevich Shelgunov was already aged thirty-seven. Though sprung from a family of officers and government servants, he had had to fend for himself. When still a child he was left an orphan, and had to face school life under Nicholas I. He has left us a vivid description of what this meant: discipline, floggings and narrow technical specialization based on a groundwork of complete ignorance of the world, history and above all the political situation. So he had become an expert on forestry and the administrative problems associated with it. In after years, when he was a successful publicist, he always deplored the fact that he had only come into contact late with real culture. He knew the meaning of despotism, and when he said that he was not convinced by eulogies of Louis XIV or Catherine II, he was drawing on his own experiences. The sciences and arts, he said, had been stifled rather than brought into existence by their protectors. Only a free impulse was capable of producing such fruits. In Russia the contrast was naturally even greater than elsewhere. The transition from the régime of Nicholas I to the fervour that characterized the new reign of Alexander II remained the decisive experience of Shelgunov's life. Twenty years later he defended the ''sixties' against all its enemies. His descriptions were perhaps too optimistic, but they were the product of sincere conviction.

At the time of the fall of Sebastopol, Russia seemed to him 'a girl of nineteen who has never left her village. The arsenal of our learning, especially in social questions, was very limited. We knew that in the world there was a country called France, one of whose Kings, Louis XIV, had said, "L'état, c'est moi", and that he had therefore been called "the Great". We knew that in Germany, specially Prussia, the soldiers were well trained in their manœuvres. And finally, the corner-stone of our learning lay in knowing that Russia was the greatest, the truest, the bravest of countries; that it acted as the "granary" of Europe and that if it wanted to it could deprive Europe of bread and in the last resort (if really forced to) it could conquer all its peoples. It is true that after Sebastopol belief in the infallibility of such truths was being shattered, but there were no new ideals with which to replace them. Some had to be found, some created: in a word, the job had to be begun from scratch.'[14] Shelgunov played a large part in this task. Through his travels abroad in Germany and especially in Paris and London, he was able to 'find' what he was looking for. Together with the *Sovremennik* he helped to 'create' the other truths. They took the form of typically Populist ideas.

In 1856 when he crossed the Russian frontier 'he saw for the first time free men who lived without the threat of the stick and without an autocracy, and the difference was that they led a better and wider life'.[15] The peasants' bread was almost white: life was full of intellectual excitement. So he too, like all the Populists, started from a Western standpoint. The Slavophils could make men think about Russia's past, and grow enthusiastic about her people and traditions. But they never provided any stimulus for action; no revolutionary spirit was to spring from their ideas. For what was needed was a break, an essentially youthful determination to begin again from scratch; and this could only be found in a different world. This was the path that Shelgunov too had to tread. If he later returned to the *obshchina*, and accepted Herzen's ideas on the part that a peasant and egalitarian Russia could play in the future renewal of Europe, this was only after he had followed the Westerners' tracks and after he had come into contact with Socialism and brought it face to face with the problems of his own country.

For him, too, Populism was born of his experiences of the revolutionary movements of 1848. He said thirty years later:

Europe, despite its recent failures, had not yet lost either the faith or the great ideas of the end of the eighteenth century. The tradition had not yet been broken as it was later. In France there were still alive stubborn men such as Louis Blanc, Félix Pyat, Ledru Rollin, Blanqui, Barbès. And besides them there was Victor Hugo and the France of the sciences, law and journalism, which had been driven out by Napoleon III but which still in exile remained faithful to its past and did not lose hope of finding support or allies. In London the European émigrés had collected—French, Italian, Polish, Russian, German and Hungarian.[16]

Besides, even in Paris it was not difficult to find circles which kept alive the ideas that had led to 1848. He met, for example, the small world grouped round the *Revue Philosophique et Religieuse* which was inspired by Saint-Simonism.[17] But it was chiefly Herzen, whom he went to see in London, who laid the foundations on which he developed his extensive publicizing activities.

Yet Shelgunov knew that he was bringing from Russia a specific element which made it impossible for him to accept with his whole heart the world he met in Western Europe. True, Herzen was at the peak of his popularity in Russia. His *Kolokol* dominated the minds of all who were really anxious for reforms. Personal contact with him was life-enhancing; even from a distance he had been able to inspire an intellectual and moral renaissance. But despite all this there was something which prevented him from understanding the new generation. Shelgunov clearly saw what it was: 'We had not been through the experiences of 1848 in Europe, and so we still had a faith that he no longer had. We were boiling over, and Herzen had gone off the boil. Naturally events soon showed that he was right, but we believed in ourselves, certain that we were on the eve (of a revolution).'[18] Reconsidering it later, he went to the origins of this gap between them. 'A broadly developed awareness of freedom made any kind of violence intolerable to Herzen . . . He was not democratic enough for barricades, either in his way of life or in his mentality, and he was too aristocratic in his development and his intellectual needs.' It was this that stopped him understanding the 'young émigrés', the representatives of that movement of 1861–62 who, when it was broken up and suppressed, had ended by seeking refuge abroad.

But was the difference between them only one of generations and mentality? Meeting some of the Polish émigrés in London made Shelgunov realize that it went deeper than this. His own social radicalism and longing for equality did not exist among the other revolutionary exiles. He was enlightened one day by a conversation with a Pole who asked him: 'Do you know the difference between us Poles and you Russians?' 'What?' 'We Poles want to turn every peasant into a gentleman, and you want to turn every gentleman into a peasant.' 'These words contained a truth', said Shelgunov, 'which I did not then fully understand, but which became clear to me later in the 'seventies, when the attempt was made to change the sons of the intelligentsia into peasants.'[19] The origins of the movement 'to go to the people' were already present in the most active radicals of the 'sixties.

It was this desire to pursue aims to their inescapable conclusion—to use a phrase which so often expressed the current state of mind—which made Shelgunov think that Russia was on the eve of a social revolution, and that this revolution would help to revive all Europe. At a time when the West was inclined to think that 'bears wandered through the streets of St Petersburg and Moscow, and Siberia began at the Russian frontier', he believed in the *obshchina* as a principle which might well revolutionize social relations everywhere. And as far as Europe was concerned he was thinking mainly of the problems of the proletariat. Indeed his most important article for the *Sovremennik* was an intelligent popularization of Engels' book on the situation of the working class in England.[20]

He now found, in the literary circles of St Petersburg, a friend with whom to share these beliefs. Mikhail Larionovich Mikhailov was a young poet who had been in touch with Chernyshevsky during their early university years around 1847. Mikhailov[21] was no great poet and was aware of his limitations. He nearly always confined himself to translating German, French and English poetry, choosing those works which seemed specially relevant to his own time, and using them to express feelings he was incapable of expressing in words of his own making. He had a literary flair and through it was able to make his personal contribution to the task of 'enlightenment' which constituted the programme of his generation, i.e. to inform the Russian public of the taste of Western Europe round about 1848. His choice of poets was eclectic: Longfellow, Heine, Béranger, Hugo, etc., but his versions were delicate and subtle. Just as he was not a poet so he was not a really original critic or publicist, though he wrote articles on the social and spiritual problems of his time which met with a large response.

He was chiefly a 'witness'. His own life clearly yet modestly revealed the difficulties that still obstructed the formation of the intelligentsia and the strength that it had gained through this fight for existence. In Shelgunov's life we see mainly the rise of Populist ideas and the desire to spread them; but Mikhailov was a more original personality, able to use these ideas not only to create a cultural and political blueprint but also to build up a private world of feeling and activity.[22]

The story of his family in itself showed how difficult it was to break through social oppression and affirm one's personality. His grandfather was a serf, probably of Tartar origin, in the district of Orenburg. He was an able man who managed to accumulate considerable wealth in the hope of redeeming himself. At last he succeeded, only to be told that the decree of liberation for which he had duly paid had not been drawn up correctly. And so he was once more reduced to the status of a serf. He protested, but was imprisoned and sentenced to be flogged as a rebel. His nerve now broke: during the preliminary proceedings he became an alcoholic, and died soon after. But where he failed his son succeeded. He became a zealous official, and was so successful that he was ennobled, married the daughter of a prince, and obtained an estate with several hundred serfs. Enthusiasm for learning had already begun to move him. In his son, Mikhail the poet, this enthusiasm was responsible for putting an end to a comfortable bureaucratic life and bringing him into conflict with the surrounding world. Mikhail too aimed to enter government service. After going to St Petersburg University, he was given an administrative post of some importance at Nizhny Novgorod during the dark years when Chernyshevsky had retired to Saratov, waiting for new possibilities to open up. But the two friends remained in contact through letters, and continued to speak of the ideals aroused in them by 1848. Mikhailov began to make a name with 'realistic' stories and literary studies which were inspired by the Russian Enlightenment of the eighteenth century. At the time of the Crimean War he was already known in St Petersburg as a subtle and elegant writer, highly thought of for his poetic translations. His meeting with Shelgunov and his wife, his travels abroad, the new intellectual life after 1855, all these transformed him into one of the most typical publicists of the *Sovremennik* group.

The age was one, in Shelgunov's words, of 'a complete revolution in family relationships'.[23] The *liaison* between Mikhailov and Shelgunov's wife (who gave him a son) did not in the least affect the deep friendship between the two writers, and is one of the most typical examples of this revolution. The lives of Herzen and Ogarev and the atmosphere of Chernyshevsky's novel *What is to be done?* provide further examples of the birth of this new mentality which, with its problems of personal freedom, accompanied the rise of revolutionary Populism.[24]

It was this problem of woman's freedom which was to interest Mikhailov when, together with Shelgunov, he came into contact with a Saint-Simonist group in Paris. In a series of avidly read articles in the *Sovremennik* he played a large part in bringing about the growth of new customs. Though Chernyshevsky objected that 'the question of women is all very well when there are no other problems'[25] and insisted on raising more fundamental political and social questions, he published Mikhailov's articles, for he well knew that the desire for new standards of personal behaviour derived from a society in transformation. In this way Mikhailov was able to introduce into Russia the debates aroused by the anti-feminism of Proudhon's latest books. He also described life in Paris, in a series of articles whose most vivid feature lay in his curiosity and zest for freedom.[26]

Mikhailov too visited Herzen in London, and returned to St Petersburg convinced that a deep transformation in Russia was now inevitable. The year of doubt and hesitations which preceded the manifesto of 19th February 1861 had made the liberals uncertain, but had driven these younger men to hopes of revolution. He too broke with those well-meaning and moderate writers among whom he had once been numbered. He later described his state of mind in an epigram, called *The Constitutionalist*. 'Even hearing him pronounce the word freedom is disgusting. It's like hearing a eunuch speaking of love.' 'His voice trembled a little', wrote a contemporary, 'when he said that the masses were awakening and ripening, and that the day would soon arrive when he would see them raising their many hydra heads.'[27]

The manifesto of emancipation only confirmed these ideas. Half a century later someone still remembered him in a room in St Petersburg surrounded by students.

They had scarcely finished reading the manifesto aloud and had begun to examine it in detail. No one was satisfied with it. They all condemned its turgid and complicated style. It was the 'seminarist' style of the Metropolitan Filaret. We certainly didn't expect anything of the kind, either in form or content. The most bitter and violent was Mikhailov. He openly said that it was a trap and a fraud, and merely meant a different kind of enslavement for the peasants. His tone and his words showed for the first time that he had now burnt his boats. Besides, he knew very well that since his journey to London he was more than ever looked upon as a member of a revolutionary organization.[28]

These last words show once more how widespread was the impatience for guidance from London and how much men were waiting for Herzen to inspire a secret organization. But the example of Mikhailov and Shelgunov make it clear that the first steps in this direction were taken in Russia, not only without, but actually against, Herzen's advice. Mikhailov may have already belonged to a 'revolutionary organization', but it was he and his friends who were creating it.

It was now that they met V. Kostomarov, a young writer living on translations and debts, who told them that he had the means to print manifestos. They gave him three propaganda manuscripts aimed at the peasants and the army. Of these the first may have been by Chernyshevsky, the other two by Shelgunov. According to at least one piece of evidence this was merely a beginning, which was to be followed by other appeals to different groups and social categories. Shchapov was to have written a manifesto for the *Raskolniki*; Shelgunov and Mikhailov, an appeal to the young generation. If this is true, their attempts are the first example of the propagandist tactics that *Zemlya i Volya* tried to put into practice about a year later.[29]

We know very little of this first attempt to organize a secret press, no longer aimed, like the *Velikoruss*, only at the educated classes but also at the people. Besides, it failed even before it was put into practice, planned as it was on utterly unreliable foundations. Instead of printing the manuscripts quickly, Kostomarov delayed, in the hopes of getting more money. He later entered the service of the Third Section and gave the 'evidence' on which both Mikhailov and Chernyshevsky were condemned.

We have already referred to the manifesto for the peasants which may have been Chernyshevsky's work. Shelgunov's articles too have been found, and they show the extreme importance assumed by the question of the nationalities within the empire and by foreign policy in general in the crisis of 1861.[30] He wrote to the soldiers:

Brothers, do you remember the last war in Poland, do you remember the Hungarian war? You wondered why the leaders made you march. Who found the war necessary or useful? It certainly wasn't us, brothers. Russia didn't come out of it any richer. Are you quite sure that we weren't behaving like bandits in Poland or Hungary?

This was certainly a strange way to write propaganda for the army. Even the manifesto itself recognized that there were few men in the army who had taken part in these two campaigns of 1831 and 1849. In fact the intelligentsia was examining the national conscience and trying in this strange way to bring the people into contact with its own problems. But the remainder of the manifesto showed that its author was firmly convinced of the connection between this repudiation of foreign policy and the social problems raised for the Russian people by the manifesto of 19th February. He told the soldiers:

Brothers, have you heard of the freedom which they have given the people? Talk to the peasants and you will see that it is not true freedom . . . Remember that you were born in those very *izbas* which the landlords are now taking away from the peasants; that you were baptized in the very churches where they are now praying God to free them from evil and violence.

The second manifesto was shorter and more effective and returned to the same theme. It was an appeal to the soldiers not to fire on the peasants who were expressing their aspirations for a very different 'freedom'.

Practical experience showed Shelgunov and Mikhailov the difficulties of a secret press. How could they ensure that their words reach the soldiers and the peasants? But events in St Petersburg in the summer of 1861 were to reveal the only circles to which they could effectively turn. Their new appeal was called *To the Young Generation*. It was aimed not at the real intelligentsia or at the people, but at the students who were demonstrating in the lecture halls and streets of St Petersburg.

The discovery of a suitable field suggested a suitable approach. Despite its obvious uncertainties and generalizations which made it more of a profession of faith than an appeal for action, this work is the most important of the 'Era of Proclamations', and the most typical document of revolutionary Populism in 1861. It was written by Shelgunov and revised by Mikhailov. Together they took it abroad, as they were convinced that they would not be able to print it in Russia. Mikhailov showed it to Herzen, who did not approve of it, both because he had no faith in clandestine activities and thought it would bring ruin on the authors, and for ideological reasons. However, the Free Russian Press printed six hundred copies which were hidden in a trunk with a false bottom and carried back to Russia by Mikhailov. He was imprudent enough to give a copy to Kostomarov before he was able to organize its distribution. When Kostomarov was arrested, the secret was out. However, they took up a bold line and decided to distribute it with the small means at their disposal. Mikhaelis, one of the leaders of the student movement, and A. A. Serno-Solovevich, brother of the founder of *Zemlya i Volya*, circulated it in the capital, despatching it by post and sticking it up on walls. Serno even appears to have flung it on to the Nevsky Prospekt, riding through at full speed. The effect was remarkable. The manifesto was read, discussed, and reached circles far beyond those who saw the few copies that could be circulated. On the following day, 1st September, Mikhailov was interrogated for the first time, but the police remained uncertain. On 14th September he was denounced by Kostomarov and arrested.

The proclamation *To the Young Generation* was based on simple and fundamental political questions.

We do not need either a Tsar, an Emperor, the myth of some lord, or the purple which cloaks hereditary incompetence. We want at our head a simple human being, a man of the land who understands the life of the people and who is chosen by the people. We do not need an Emperor consecrated in the Uspensky Sobor, but an elected leader receiving a salary for his services.[31]

It was time to do with the Tsar what the peasants of an estate in Tambov region had done with the outside administrators whom they had suffered until then. They had followed them out of their village, saying: 'We are very grateful to you, but now, God speed, we no longer need you.' The Emperor's greatest claim to honour—the emancipation of the peasants—closed one epoch and opened a new one. 'Imperial Russia is in dissolution. If Alexander II doesn't understand this and is not prepared to make the necessary concessions freely, so much the worse for him.' But even eventual concessions made by the present government could be a danger for it. 'Young generation, do not forget this.'

The threat was no longer made for tactical purposes. It was a simple statement of fact made before they turned their attention in new directions. Let the dead bury their dead; that was apparently their message.

'We turn to the young generation because in it are the men who can save Russia. You are its real force; you are the leaders of the people. You must explain to the people and the army all the harm done to it by the Tsar's power.' To do this they must realize the extent of the problem which was raised by the emancipation of the serfs. 'This can be the first step towards a great future for Russia or towards catastrophe; towards political and economic welfare, or towards a political and economic proletariat. The choice depends on you.'

Old theories were no longer of any assistance in making this choice. Constitutionalism and political economy led only to conservatism and to the establishment of an absurd *status quo*:

They want to turn Russia into an England and feed us on the experiences of England. But is Russia—in geographical position, natural riches, the conditions of its land, the quality and quantity of its soil—remotely like England? Would the English have developed in Russia in the way that they have done in their own island? As it is we ape the French and Germans enough. Must we now really begin to ape the English too? No, we do not want English economic maturity. It cannot be digested by the Russian stomach.

No, no, our life is another.
We must not carry the cross . . .

Let Europe carry the cross. Who says that we must imitate Europe or the example of some Saxony, England or France . . .? What science has taught him that Europe's ideas are infallible? We know nothing of any science of this kind. We only know that Gneist, Bastiat, Rau, Roscher are merely excavating the refuse to turn the advance of previous centuries into a law for the future. Let a law of this kind serve for others; we will try to find a new one. Who is unaware that Europe, with its hundreds of German states and their kings, dukes and princes, or France with its Napoleons, is astounded when it learns that in America there is an entirely different order? And why should not Russia achieve yet another order, unknown even in America? We not only can but must achieve something different. There are principles in our life completely unknown to the Europeans. The Germans claim that we will reach the point which Europe has now reached. This is a lie . . .

They spoke of the Western bourgeoisie, of the remains of the feudal world and of the revolution of 1848. 'Its failure is a failure for Europe only. It tells us nothing of the possibility of other changes here in Russia.'

We are a backward people and in this lies our salvation. We must thank fate that we have not lived the life of Europe. Its misfortunes and its situation without any way of escape are a lesson for us. We do not want its proletariat, its aristocracy, its governmental principles, its imperial power . . . Europe does not understand and cannot understand our social needs. This means that Europe is not our master in economic problems. We Russians repudiate the idea. And why? Because we have no political past. We are not bound by any tradition . . . That is why, unlike Western

Europe, we are not afraid of the future. That is why we move boldly forward to the revolution, why we long for it. We believe in the forces of Russia, because we believe that we have been destined to bring a new principle into history, to hand on our own message and not haunt the old gardens of Europe. Without faith there is no salvation, and we have great faith in our strength. If to achieve our ends, by dividing the land among the people we have to kill a hundred thousand of the gentry, even that will not deter us. After all, it's not as bad as all that. Do you remember how many men we lost in the wars in Poland and Hungary?

In the same tone the author took up the Saint-Simonist argument: 'Imagine that suddenly, on one single day, all our ministers, all our senators, all the members of our council of state were to expire, and at the same time all our governors, all our officials, Metropolitans, Bishops—in a word, all our present administrative aristocracy—were to die too. What would Russia lose? Not a thing.' The only living forces besides the people were those of the intelligentsia: 'writers, poets, scientists, artists and managers'.

The manifesto ended by suggesting a few general principles for a programme—elections, freedom of speech, self-administration, nationalization of the land and its division into equal holdings.

The land must not belong to the individual but to the nation. Each *obshchina* must have its strip of land. Private farming must no longer exist. Land must not be sold in the same way as potatoes or cabbage. Every citizen must be a member of an *obshchina*, must either join one which already exists or found a new one with other citizens. We wish to retain collective ownership of the land with redistribution at long intervals. This is no concern of the State. If the idea of collective ownership is a mistake, let it die through its own inability to survive and not because it is influenced by Western economic doctrine.

After speaking of soldiers and military service, the manifesto appealed once more to 'Russia's hope: the party of the people made up of the young generation of all classes.' It could not suggest immediate organization, but rather a vast effort at proselytism. 'Get ready for the business which you must undertake; accustom yourselves to this idea, form groups of people who think in the same way; look for leaders who are efficient and ready for anything.'

Herzen's ideas on the future of Russia and Chernyshevsky's on the conservative nature of political economy spring to mind immediately, to mention only two names. The work's originality lay rather in its excessively trustful and enthusiastic tone, and the determination to make its ideas triumph at any price. The authors were prepared to admit doubts on future political organizations or even on the *obshchina*, but they claimed with absolute certainty that to found an egalitarian and free Russia it was essential to wipe out the past; and that the only power able to do this was the people guided by the young generation.[32]

Mikhailov paid for this assertion with his life. After his arrest he denied his share in the matter for some days, but when he learnt of Kostomarov's deposition and was told that Shelgunov and his wife were in danger, he assumed complete responsibility for editing, printing, carrying and distributing the manifesto. He was put in solitary confinement with a few books in the Peter-Paul fortress. There he was greeted in verse by the university students who had been imprisoned after the demonstrations along the Nevsky Prospekt. One of the prisoners, I. A. Rozhdestvensky, wrote:

> The day will come when freely
> We will tell your story.
> We will tell the Russian people
> How you have suffered for them.[33]

Ogarev and Lavrov also wrote poems to him, and his arrest made a vast impression, for he was the first victim among the intellectuals since the emancipation of the serfs. He was known to be poor and in weak health, and a number of efforts were made to ameliorate his conditions and secure his liberation. The shock was all the greater when it was learnt that the Senate had condemned him to twelve and a half years forced labour and banishment for life to Siberia. The Emperor reduced his sentence to six years, and on 14th December 1861 (the anniversary of the Decembrist revolt) the ceremony of 'civil execution' took place in front of a handful of people and with no demonstration from the students or sympathizers.[34]

Even the local authorities were not prepared to treat this 'State criminal' with severity. Suvorov took care to make his journey to Siberia as easy as possible. Once he reached Tobolsk, 'I was treated in the most friendly, almost family way . . . I was surrounded with reviews and books. I was sent newspapers from all sides, as soon as they arrived by the post . . . Each morning at tea I saw excellent cream and sweets. At lunch there were partridges, butter, sweets, etc. They never forgot me, not even for a day.'[35]

But this attitude on the part of Tobolsk society led to changes. During the following years the central authorities were careful to instruct subordinates on how to treat 'State criminals' and in 1866 all who had treated Mikhailov with such kindness were summoned to a tribunal and condemned. For the time being, however, he was able to continue his journey in relatively good conditions. He was even able to meet Petrashevsky, who, like him, was convinced that freedom was near, not only for him but for all Russia. 'See you soon in parliament', he said as he left.[36]

When Mikhailov reached his destination he was not put in prison, but was allowed to live in the cottage of one of his brothers, an engineer in that remote corner of Siberia. A few months later 'friendship and love' arrived in the form of Shelgunov and his wife, who had voluntarily accepted banishment as a sign of solidarity. But this state of affairs did not last long. Shelgunov was suspected of planning his friend's escape, and after a search in his house on 28th September 1862 he was arrested. In January 1863 he was sent to Irkutsk and then to the Peter-Paul fortress in St Petersburg. He was sentenced under administrative law and drifted from exile to exile in one small provincial town after another for the next fifteen years.

Mikhailov was sent to Kadae on the Chinese frontier, in the midst of a vast, unhealthy and almost uninhabited region. This was too much for his health and he died on 2nd August 1865. He was buried alongside the Polish exiles whose fate he had shared during these last years.

He was forgotten except by his closest friends, who were now dispersed, some themselves in prison or Siberia. Only Herzen, from afar, was able to speak of him, and in the *Kolokol* he accused the Tsarist government of having killed this sensitive writer whom in 1861 he had advised not to fling himself into disaster.

Throughout 1862 the secret press and distribution of manifestos continued to flourish. The most important of these, signed *Young Russia*, is of special significance, and will be examined later. Nearly all these now came from 'the young generation' to whom Mikhailov and Shelgunov had appealed. The students were taking a direct part in the struggle and were acting on their own.

The most characteristic of such ventures was Petr Ballod's 'pocket press'. A student of some means, he succeeded in organizing a small press which printed a few leaflets. He reprinted an appeal to officers which had been written by Ogarev and his friends and sent from London. He also printed a pamphlet to defend Herzen from the attacks of the official spokesman Shedo-Ferroti: 'Do you really think', he wrote, 'that you will succeed in wiping out the vast influence of Herzen's works on Russian society?'[37] He asked Pisarev—a young writer of nihilistic tendencies who was then coming to the fore—for an article to develop this defence of Iskander. But he could not publish it as he was soon afterwards arrested.[38]

Pisarev too was arrested and was eventually sentenced in June 1864 to two years and eight months' imprisonment. He was released in November 1866, having been amnested shortly before the end of his sentence. Of Ballod's associates, P. S. Moshkalov and Nikolay Zhukovsky succeeded in fleeing abroad, and the latter became a well-known anarchist in Geneva, and will be frequently referred to. Ballod was sentenced to fifteen years' hard labour and then to banishment for life to Siberia. There he devoted himself entirely to the gold mines and the rough life of the pioneers.

The same tribunal which sentenced these men also struck another small group led by Leonid Olshevsky, aged twenty-three, and Petr Tkachev, aged nineteen. They had succeeded in printing a small manifesto called *What We Want*, in which they claimed:

The most important question is now that of spreading ideas among the people. For this purpose every member of our group must try to find agents in villages and hamlets, in provincial towns and district capitals and convince them as clearly as possible of the need for a speedy revolution. Words are not enough, action is needed . . . If they find a man of the people in difficulties, they must help him at once out of our communal fund. Only in this way will they gain the love of the people; and then success is certain.[39]

Such were the first steps in Tkachev's career. He was destined to become the leading representative of Russian Blanquism. For the time being he got off comparatively lightly—three years' imprisonment. Olshevsky was sentenced to a year.

In summer 1862 Nikolay Vasilevich Vasilev was arrested for having circulated yet another manifesto *To the citizens*. He was also accused of planning to kill the Tsar, and was sentenced to be hanged. On 30th March 1863 this was commuted to ten years' hard labour, and in 1871 he was exiled to Yakut territory. Thirteen years later he was given permission to return to European Russia, but he refused, and stayed in the same wretched village, and there committed suicide on 9th November 1888. One of his comrades, Nikolay Nikolaevich Volkhov, who was also sentenced to hanging and then ten years' hard labour, finally returned to European Russia in 1884.[40]

There were other clandestine manifestos in 1862, but they contain nothing new. Taken together they provide evidence of the varying ventures on which the 'young generation' was spontaneously embarking. It was *Zemlya i Volya*'s function to give these their first organization and first wide significance.

10. THE FIRST ZEMLYA I VOLYA

AN AIR OF MYSTERY still hangs over the first *Zemlya i Volya* (Land and Liberty) society. Though it constituted the first link in a long tradition, and though it popularized a name which was adopted again fifteen years later, it is difficult to enlarge on its activities or narrowly define its purpose and status. Very few of those who took part devoted the rest of their lives to revolutionary organization. Like most of those who joined clandestine groups at this time, the first members of *Zemlya i Volya* failed to survive the wave of repression. Instead, they settled down to research, to literature and, even more often, to business and trade. All this reveals, incidentally, that the movement was already beginning to react on the community and was a formative influence on the new society which emerged after the emancipation of the serfs. But it also blurs the outlines of this early attempt to create a movement inspired by the ideas of Herzen and Chernyshevsky. And so it is difficult to determine the exact contribution of *Zemlya i Volya* to the reforming fervour of these years.

When Herzen met some of the young representatives of *Zemlya i Volya* in exile, he was surprised and unfavourably impressed. He noted their hardness, their sometimes deliberate crudity, and above all their lack of subtlety and intellectual quality. Angry and genuinely disappointed, he concluded: 'No, this is not Nihilism. Nihilism is a great phenomenon in Russia's development. But these people merely combine the officer, the clerk, the priest and the petty provincial noble dressed up as a Nihilist.'[1] If we add to this list the student, with his own special attributes, some idea of the raw material of *Zemlya i Volya* can be gained. Nor is it surprising that these characteristics sometimes reveal themselves beneath the ideals and boldness of spirit of the group as a whole. It is unfortunate that the only two surviving memoirs written by members of the society are by men whose interest in day to day life and gossip is all too obvious. In writing long after the events described, they often resurrect dead controversies and obscure the vitality and interest of these early days.

But we must not forget that besides lesser figures *Zemlya i Volya* attracted men of outstanding nobility and heroism. To avoid unwittingly obscuring the true situation, it will be as well to frame this brief account of the society's fortunes within a biography of the brothers Serno-Solovevich. For their brief and active lives reflect the best in *Zemlya i Volya* which they themselves did most to found, direct and develop.[2]

Nikolay Alexandrovich Serno-Solovevich came from a family of St Petersburg civil servants. His father had been ennobled, thanks to the zeal with which he had performed his administrative duties in the service of the State. Nikolay was born on 13th December 1834 and went to the Alexander School which was the cradle of so many of the new young forces which were springing up. He was twenty when the Crimean War broke out, and his mind was formed in the St Petersburg which was reacting to it.[3] With his brother Alexander he constantly frequented the group of young men who were gathering round Marya Vasilevna Trubnikova. She was the daughter of Vasily Petrovich Ivashov, a Decembrist who had been exiled to Siberia. The freedom of her opinions and actions made her eminently capable of reviving an opposition movement.[4] She had married the editor of one of the many periodicals with weekly literary supplements which sprang up as soon as the war ended—such as *The Shareholders' Review* and *The Banking Courier*. Trubnikov had won the affections of his future wife 'by his liberalism and his quotations from Herzen'[5] and for a long time she helped him to edit his newspapers. But it was not long before she realized that she had in fact married a man without ideals, who soon devoted himself exclusively to his banking and stock exchange activities. She then built up a new life for herself. This consisted of reading and discussion with a small group of friends, of foreign travel (in the course of which she met Herzen) and of active participation in the life of the young revolutionary generation. 'On her chimney-piece', her daughter recalled, 'she had a wax statue of Garibaldi. We wrote poems in his honour and, avoiding the attention of our elders, we recited them to her.'[6] The group round her read mainly Vico, Michelet, Heine, Boerne, Proudhon, Lassalle, Saint-Simon, Louis Blanc and Herzen.[7] These were the authors who formed her mind, and that of the young Serno brothers who were closely associated with her and her sister, and who retained strong ties with them even in later years.

But though the atmosphere of the brothers' early youth was conditioned by the tradition of the Decembrists and the ideas of the French Socialists, the decisive event in their lives was the Crimean War and Sebastopol. Nikolay himself has told us this in a poem written in the Peter-Paul fortress at the end of his brief life as a man of action. It is true that at the beginning of this *Confession* he was careful to write: 'This must not be taken as an account of *my* experience; it is simply a poem.' In fact he was not a poet, and it really was a confession and must be considered such.

> I dreamed in vain for five and twenty years
> But then Sebastopol began to groan
> And this groan outraged everyone.
> I became a citizen of my nation
> From that day my way was different
> The dawn of truth lit up my way
> I shook off my chains

And on the threshold of my Fathers I said
Forward, forward, my sick country
Now I belong to you.
Here is my life.[8]

Earlier in the same poem he said he did not want to belong to the rich and official world. Yet the inception of the reforms made him decide, after a short journey to Germany, Belgium and France, to go into government service and enter the offices in which the means of abolishing serfdom were being considered. The papers of the Committee dealing with the peasant problem passed through his hands, and so he was able to observe the doubts and obstacles which prevailed in the government bureaucracy from the very start.

With a gesture that made Herzen compare him later to Schiller's Marquis of Posa, he then decided to turn directly to the Tsar. He wrote down his ideas on the emancipation of the serfs and 'on the general situation of the State, which was far from excellent', and handed them (in a manuscript which has since been lost) to the sovereign in September 1858 as he was strolling in the garden of Tsarskoe Selo.[9]

His manuscript contained no detailed or concrete proposals, but was essentially an appeal to Alexander to follow the young generation. The Emperor commented: 'In it [the young generation] there is much that is good and really noble. Russia must expect much from it, if and only if it is properly orientated.'[10]

Serno's gesture was not merely romantic. He understood the nature of the Emperor's responsibility ever since he had decided to free the serfs. The entire future would depend on this first act which was opening up a new epoch for his country. Possibilities for the future seemed vast. Absolute power, once on the road to reform, could bring about a real revolution.

Serno had already thought out the general outlines of the plan for the political and social reform to which he wanted to urge Alexander II. He sent a small pamphlet to Herzen for publication. It appeared in that collection of *Voices from Russia*, whose contents, though not always following the *Kolokol*'s line, served to show that the political debate was growing more lively as the reforms were being prepared.[11]

The Tsar must realize, he said, that only Socialist principles could act as a guide for the transformation of Russia. When Nicholas I and Kiselev had propounded to themselves the problem of reorganizing the communities which farmed on the State lands, had they not already raised a Socialist problem? The land had always belonged to the State and to groups of peasants. Only in comparatively recent times had part of it been gradually transferred to private owners. 'The Christian idea, indeed the fair and practical idea, of equal rights to the land has been absorbed so deeply into the mentality of the Russian people that it has become part of its birthright.' It had been to the Slavophils' credit that they 'have been the first to turn their attention to a serious historical study of this problem'. Now the entire reform must be based on this tradition.

Any link which bound the peasant to the landlord must therefore be broken. All land should return to the State, who should hand it over to the peasant *obshchina*. This would create a single agricultural class of State peasants, organized along traditional lines. To bring this about all the nobles' properties must be redeemed. This great task must be undertaken by the government, using methods which Serno described in general terms only but which already reveal that interest in the financial aspects of the problem which he intensified in subsequent years. The entire structure of Russian society would emerge changed. But, he ended, it was essential to realize that: 'On the throne of Russia the Tsar can only be, either consciously or unconsciously, a Socialist.' And if this mission were understood, the experience of Russia would be of general value.

The peoples of the West are already beginning to realize the need to complete with something different what is lacking in their social life. It is this particular element which has been preserved and developed in Russia. Russia will hand it on to the people of the West, receiving in return those rights and laws of the individual which they have especially developed.

Such were Serno's ideas when at the end of 1858 he moved from St Petersburg to Kaluga, a provincial town near Moscow, to take up his post as secretary of the local committee in charge of peasant matters. There he was in direct contact with the immediate problems of the reform, with provincial life and the day to day struggle between bureaucracy and nobility. This experience though it lasted less than a year was of very great importance in his development. His early faith in an enlightened despotism, which was already influenced by a more liberal spirit (Herzen was right to recall Schiller), was now atrophied and finally utterly destroyed as he realized that the machinery wielded by the Tsar was quite incapable of seriously carrying out the reform. We can follow a similar process in all its psychological complexity in the life of Saltykov-Shchedrin, who also moved from an initial trust in the State to a complete break with it. Though we know little of Serno the transition was probably very similar.

Indeed, though Serno was never able to put all his ideas into practice, his life is typical of them. He had asked Alexander II to canalize the younger forces and to interpret their ideals. And in this particular instance the Tsar had taken enlightened and intelligent action. He had given Serno the chance to get to know the real problems. But this very contact with political reality allowed the young 'Marquis of Posa' to comprehend the fundamental flaw in all the hopes of these years. 'We will be unable to make any effective or radical change as long as the bureaucratic structure survives. It is impotent, it is an anachronism, a palpable ruin which destroys and perverts all our best thoughts and plans.'[12]

A group of amnestied Decembrists, representing a tradition of revolutionary liberalism, whom he met at Kaluga must certainly have helped him to digest these experiences. We see this too in his particularly close relations with N. S. Kashkin, one of the most lively representatives of the movement which had been associated with Petrashevsky before 1849.[13] He too had recently been amnestied, and had become one of the leaders of the reforming group at Kaluga which looked for support to the Governor himself, who was among the most open and intelligent administrators of Russia at this time.[14] Serno built up a close friendship with Kashkin, to whom on his return to St Petersburg in 1859 he wrote a series of letters which revealed the ferment of his spirits. 'The time I spent in Kaluga', he wrote on 18th August, 'will never be wiped out from my heart, because of that warm and lively group of people to whom I attached myself by emotions and principles and among whom you were one of the closest.' He continued to give him constant news of 'our business', i.e. the peasant problem, describing the increasing number of commissions and growing obstacles of every kind. 'Our business is moving at a tortoise's pace', he wrote on 18th November. As the months passed these letters became more and more detached: or rather they revealed increasing distrust in the possibility of a result which would correspond to his ideals.

On 25th November Serno told his friend of his decision to give up government service and go abroad, 'not for enjoyment, but simply to learn . . . Of course it is hard for one as interested as I am in the peasant problem to be at the very source of the decisions that are taken, and then go away just when a conclusion is being reached. I confess that I have hesitated for a long, long time. Losing my illusions hurt me. Faith is a very sweet emotion, and it is painful to destroy it. So I clung to every straw and if I am now going, you can be sure that I don't expect anything good for myself. To love the cause and stay here means ceaseless suffering.'

Convinced now that the reform would not succeed, his faith in a revival of Russia took a new direction. 'There's no doubt that things are improving. The old building, if it is not knocked down, will collapse on its own; the pillars are rotten and decayed at their bases. But to put up a new building, much profound experience is essential, and of that we have little.' As he lost hope in a government which could transform Russia's social structure, so it was essential that 'youth' should assume the burden of guiding the movement, and for this a far more detailed programme was needed than the one he had drawn up in 1858. He found in Chernyshevsky a writer who—though he confirmed him in his Socialist ideas—brought the real problems of politics and economics clearly home to him. Besides, Chernyshevsky's life had justified his own aims of being 'completely independent'. There was nothing to keep him in his office any longer, and his resignation and travels abroad merely reflected the decisions he had already reached.

He was anxious to apply himself mainly to questions of financial policy. Already during the last months of his stay in the capital he had studied

9+

economic questions, and had taken part in a discussion on share companies, reaching the pessimistic conclusion that 'shareholders were sheep'. He had written a series of articles on particular problems for the *Shareholders'* *Journal*, and here too his conclusions were pessimistic. Share companies did not work as they should, and the reason for this was to be found in the nation's social and political structure.[15]

His fundamental idea lay in claiming that the State should finance economic development with the real property at its disposal. He wanted it to issue interest-bearing Treasury bonds (*assignats*) backed by Crown property.

Europe has not and cannot have anything of the kind as most European States have already wasted their public domain. Nowhere does there exist a system of agriculture based on the *obshchina* and the principle of the division of the land. This great principle, freed from the bureaucratic harness which completely disfigures its character, is the surest basis for the establishment of a real credit.[16]

He went to the West to try to confirm these ideas and find the technical means for drawing them up into a valid system.

At the beginning of 1860 Serno met Herzen and Ogarev in London. The links then forged and the discussions that took place between the directors of the *Kolokol* and Serno, the most open, intelligent and brave representative of the new generation whom they had yet met, constitute the starting-point of *Zemlya i Volya*.

They laid the foundations of a close friendship as well as political collaboration. Their common ideals immediately affected their personal lives, giving us yet another example of the complete fusion of political problems with those of ethics and custom so characteristic of the intelligentsia in the 'sixties. Serno shared the life of Herzen and Ogarev as early as the end of 1860, only a few months after he had met them. And they confided everything to him, laying bare every detail of their private lives.[17]

The link between them was forged so quickly because Herzen and Ogarev saw with surprise and above all with joy that Serno's own experiences in Russia had led him to the same conclusions as those that they were defending in exile. When Ogarev read Serno's articles on agricultural banks in August 1860, he wrote to Herzen that it was 'a real joy. Our ideas coincide so closely that we speak the same language.'[18]

The special attention that Serno was paying at this time to the financial aspects of the reform and his conviction that the State ought to have shouldered the heavy burden of redeeming the nobles' land were of particular interest to Ogarev who was expounding similar ideas in the *Kolokol*. He soon summed these up in his *Essai sur la situation russe*.[19] Considered from a financial point of view the *obshchina* no longer appeared as a mere agricultural cooperative capable of ensuring that the land should belong to all, but also as an organization of mutual aid on which agrarian credit could be based.

Ôtez ce gouvernement incapable et vous trouverez dans la solidarité communale la vraie garantie du crédit de l'État. Laissez le principe de cette solidarité se développer librement, c'est-à-dire tranquillement, et vous trouverez que, fidèle à soi-même, il se transformera en un système de communes ou sociétés d'assurance mutuelle, en un système de banques communales, propres à créer un crédit social solide . . .

Nor was it necessary to point out the importance of this financial aspect of the problem.

Je me borne à vous faire observer que jamais en Russie la nécessité des banques locales ne s'est faite tant sentir qu'au moment actuel. Jamais il n'y a eu sur ce point tant de projets à bases diverses, tant d'essais et de tâtonnements pour poser et résoudre le problème.[20]

But in his view the only satisfactory solution was to give as much scope as was possible to the cooperative element contained in the *obshchina* by encouraging rural saving and letting it be reinvested by the peasant community itself. So it was essential to lighten the pressure of taxation on the countryside as far as possible, and to substitute for the redemption fee a tax on the nation as a whole. As for the rest, one must 'laisser le crédit s'organiser'.[21]

But Ogarev's and Serno's ideas, which had started from similar bases, did not exactly coincide in this conclusion. Serno was too much influenced by Chernyshevsky to accept a solution of the credit problem which left so much to the spontaneous action of the peasants themselves. He was still convinced of the need for the government to intervene financially in the development of the peasant communities. He demanded not just a reduction in taxation, even if considerable, as Ogarev wanted, but the use of State property to finance the agricultural transformation of Russia.

We lack sufficient material to follow the deepening of this discussion between Herzen, Ogarev and Serno. In fact Serno, though he was passionately interested in economic problems, was mainly a man of action. He had intended to prepare himself for future activities by studying theories of finance. But scarcely had he left Russia before he was again absorbed by the political situation. Very soon the decree of 1861 was published, and he was faced with the question 'What is to be done?'

Action in Russia itself, he must have felt, was now necessary—the more so as his experiences of the West had confirmed his ideas on the situation in Europe. He was still firmly convinced that a Russian move along Socialist lines was possible, though he now went into greater detail and qualifications. Noble dreams were no longer enough. The real situation in Europe had to be examined. In August 1860 he planned to publish a pamphlet in French on Russia's part in the Eastern question. Though his ideas on the subject were appreciated by Ogarev,[22] he soon abandoned these studies of foreign policy.

He was more and more convinced by everything he saw of the weakness of Western institutions. 'All the components of European civilization are moving towards a rapid dissolution.' The plebiscite in Savoy which had seemed to justify Napoleon's tyranny made him pessimistic. He lost his hopes in governments and ruling classes, and looked elsewhere. 'The workers think that the existing order cannot last long. The middle classes, on the other hand, are more satisfied than ever with the situation and are opposed to any change.' In the midst of 'general spiritual decadence' he saw only one bright promise of a new world. 'Garibaldi and the Thousand cannot fail to succeed in their undertaking. Of this I am convinced. All Italy will be free.'

Just because he was so aware of the vital importance that attached to Russia moving towards a revolution, he reacted to the counter-blow of February 1861 with deep pessimism:

Everything is in a state of transformation with us. But because we lack strong and independent personalities, the natural way, i.e. the simplest, is to follow the ground already covered by other countries. This indeed is the direction which the reforms are now taking. According to me, this is one of our greatest misfortunes.

These compromise solutions had been accepted owing to lack of energy. They must be countered with a different programme. Ogarev undertook to write this, and it became the first programme of the groups which later called themselves *Zemlya i Volya*. To the question 'What does the people need?' he answered 'Land and Liberty'. The slogan had been found.

For four years plans for a peasant reform have been drafted and redrafted. At last they have made up their minds and given the people freedom. They have sent generals and officials everywhere to read the decree and to organize services in church . . . The people believed it all and prayed. But when the generals and the officials began to explain the decree, it was seen that freedom had been granted in words but not in fact . . . The *corvées* and feudal dues were still there. And if the peasant wanted to obtain his own land and his own *izba*, he had to pay for it with his own cash . . . The people did not want to admit that it had been so bitterly cheated . . . and it has done well not to believe and not to keep silent . . . The doubtful were convinced with whips, sticks and bullets. Innocent blood flowed throughout Russia. Instead of prayers to the Tsar the groans of martyrs were heard as they stumbled under the lash and bullet and fainted in chains on the roads leading to Siberia.

It was necessary to start again from the beginning and to decide on a programme which really corresponded with the people's needs. Above all it was essential 'to declare the peasants free, with the land that they now possess' and which—organized in *obshchinas*—they would continue to farm. There should be no redemption fee, but a tax equal to that which the State peasants already paid. In accordance with tradition the communities would be collectively responsible for these taxes. As for the landlords, 'the people does not want to harm them' and so would agree to the State's paying them, as compensation for what they had lost, a total of sixty million roubles a year. Taxes would be ample to cover this expense. If need be the government would have to cut down the army and Court expenses. Then 'the people must be freed from officials. To do this, the peasants must administer themselves in the *obshchina* and in the *volost* through their own elected representatives.' The entire country should be governed by delegates who would guarantee these conquests and the State budget. To put this programme into effect it was absolutely essential that the people should find among the educated classes, officials and nobility 'friends', who 'would fight against the Tsar and the landlords for the land, for the freedom of the people and for human truth'.[23]

And so when Serno returned to Russia from London, the manifesto of *Zemlya i Volya* had already been written and printed. It was greeted with great enthusiasm. But it did not convince Herzen of the need to found a secret organization. He was sceptical and remained so until 1863. However it appears to have been Herzen who replied, when Ogarev asked what name the new society should be given, 'Land and Liberty, of course. It is a little pretentious, but it is clear and honest. And that is just what we need in these times.'

We know very little of Serno's organizing activities when he returned to Russia. The St Petersburg committee which was developing round him extended its activities beyond the capital. A. Sleptsov speaks of committees founded in Moscow, Tver, Saratov, Kazan, Nizhny Novgorod and other provincial centres.[24] For the first time since the Decembrists a really widespread organization had come into being. This was of considerable importance. Yet it has left few traces because it was soon stifled at its centre.

A glance at Serno's own activities will explain one reason for this. Much of his energy between 1861 and 1862 was devoted to intellectual and social functions which did, of course, help to conceal his political activities, but which he himself and all his followers considered of such great importance that they gave only second place to any clandestine work.

At the beginning of the winter of 1862, for instance, Serno started a bookshop and circulating library on the Nevsky Prospekt, intending to transform it into a centre for meetings and the distribution of political books. In this he was successful and was thus able to give the first impulse to a centre which even later, after many adventures, played a great part in the Populist movement in St Petersburg. After his arrest the bookshop passed into the hands of A. A. Cherkesov, and was one of the bases of the revolutionary organizations of the 'sixties.[25]

At the same time he wanted to start a 'Society of publishers and booksellers' but the regulations of this could not be discussed because of his arrest. From what we know the proposal seems to have been inspired by the same ideas that had made Novikov found his typographical society almost a century earlier. It aimed to spread education to the provinces and do something to make up for the shortcomings of the Russian government in this field.

The part played by Serno in the short and dramatic life of a cooperative review (in the sense that it belonged to the editors and was produced jointly by them) is more interesting though more obscure. *Vek* (The Century) only lasted from 18th February to 29th April 1862. Among the editors were all the secondary Populist figures of the day, with a few liberals. Serno represented the left wing.[26]

In this review Shchapov wrote a series of articles developing his theory of the historical opposition of regional and autonomous institutions to the centralized and bureaucratic régime. Shelgunov expressed his strong faith in the future development of Russia, to be based on peasant communities and workmen's cooperatives. Serno shared these ideas but unlike Shchapov, Shelgunov and Eliseyev he did not enrich them from the historical point of view and discuss them from all angles: formulate, in fact, the Populist ideal. He introduced a strongly political flavour, and emphasized the need for a firmer organization.

During a debate which grew out of Eliseyev's anti-feminist views and which was held in his house on 27th March, the organization of the review was endangered and the group split up. 'The meeting was stormy and agitated', Shelgunov later wrote in his memoirs. 'The most violent of all was Serno-Solovevich who maintained the need to start a newspaper of his own. When Eliseyev asked him why, Serno replied, "So that it is always ready when needed."' Elsewhere in his memoirs, Shelgunov says that Serno added, 'in case of an insurrection'.[27]

The only article that Serno himself wrote in this review was concerned with the St Petersburg municipal elections and is of no great importance.[28] He had prepared another livelier and very powerful article called 'Thinking Aloud', but it appears to have been rejected by the board of editors and fell into the hands of the police when Serno was arrested.[29] It was a kind of public explanation of the line he had taken during the editorial discussion. 'The time is drawing near', he wrote. The dissolution of the State organization (centralization) and the economic régime (exploitation) was apparent. Like Shelgunov, he too contrasted this building 'founded on foreign models' with 'popular principles'. But it was essential to find men who could make these principles prevail. The privileged classes said that they were acting on behalf of the people, but in fact they were only trying to hide the other aspect of their policies, which consisted in doing 'everything without the people'. They themselves confessed, 'We are not the people.' Liberal reforming policies were incapable of faithfully interpreting the people's opinions and tendencies, nor were the liberals able to communicate their own ideas to the lower classes. Their policies expressed the principles of the privileged classes and the aims of good, well-meaning citizens who were few in number and had no roots in the people. They were, therefore, politically impotent.

It is sad to have to recognize this, but it is necessary. There are many people who, with the best intentions, think that journalism and literature are powerful enough to achieve essential objects. And by looking to such pseudo-power for support they in fact only distract others from practical and effective steps.

Neither liberal currents nor the intelligentsia as a whole could put themselves at the head of the movement. What was needed was a political force that accepted 'popular principles' and remained faithful to them to the very end.

Strange as it may appear, such radically democratic ideas did not conflict with a draft constitution drawn up by Serno at the very same time. Yet this not only looked to the Tsar but even gave him an important rôle in the future machinery of government. Throughout these years any attack in the name of political realism against the vaguely liberal atmosphere of the day almost inevitably led to the problem of an immediate programme as well as the need to create a more active political life. As soon as one wanted to overcome the uncompromising breach between State and people that the revolutionaries had effected; and as soon as one tried to embark on concrete policies, then one was forced—as even Chernyshevsky had been—to try and extend the debate to all elements of society and hence appeal for a National Assembly. Revolutionary organizations were still too weak. Until they could inspire the necessary faith in their abilities to act on their own, it was inevitable that all who did not wish to confine themselves to working out the theory of Populism should try and urge Alexander II to take at least one decisive step on the road leading to reforms.

Serno's plan was even more moderate than the one that Ogarev had drawn up at this time with Herzen and Bakunin, and which had launched the idea of the *Zemsky Sobor*. He spoke of the need for a National Assembly whose electoral basis should be one of status based on nobles, peasants and townsmen. So great was the weight of tradition. But despite this archaic form (which recalled the constitutional plans of the 18th century) he firmly upheld the social conclusions of Populism[30] and also the need for freedom of the press, religion and so on.

This was one of Serno's last works. Increasing attention by the Tsarist police to all contacts between Herzen and his correspondents and friends in Russia soon led to his arrest. The same link that he had forged between the émigrés and the new forces, and that had given the first impulses to the development of *Zemlya i Volya*, now led to the fall of this early nucleus.[31]

An agent of the Third Section sent a warning from London that in July 1862 a messenger would arrive in Russia carrying a number of letters from Bakunin, Herzen, Ogarev and Kelsiev. This man was arrested on the frontier and taken to St Petersburg. But though police measures had improved, the 'London propagandists' had not yet adopted any precautions in their correspondence. On the basis of these letters the police had no difficulty in arresting thirty-two people, and striking the embryonic organization at its heart.

Ogarev was writing to Serno to tell him what he thought of the situation at the time, and to explain his growing disappointment with the Russian ruling classes. He then spoke of new acquaintances, among them the writer and poet M. L. Nalbandyan, founder and guiding spirit of the Socialist and national movement of Armenia. In a short postscript, Herzen suggested that Chernyshevsky's *Sovremennik* should be printed on his press in London or at least that their editorial activities should be associated in some way.

This, of course, led to the arrest of Chernyshevsky, and on the same day, 7th July 1862, Serno too was taken to the Peter-Paul fortress.

As M. Lemke has rightly noted, the fortunes of the many others arrested on that day bring us into touch with a wide cross-section of Russian life in the 'sixties. We find together men of learning and others who could scarcely read or write, believers and atheists, *Raskolniki* of the various sects and men of the army and civil service, together with nobles, peasants, bourgeois, merchants, officials, professional men, men in their sixties and young boys of scarcely eighteen. We find, in fact, a number of figures from differing social classes, all looking for a political centre. But thanks to a few figures, chief among them Serno-Solovevich, these men were gradually being transformed into the first members of an embryonic and ramifying association, which was to leave the capital for the provinces, and build up a new force outside literary and liberal circles. In the person of Nalbandyan it had already touched on the problems of nationalities in the Russian empire; and its attempts to contact the sects had tried to put into practice those ideas on the subversive character of the *Raskol*, which Herzen and Shchapov were then expounding in their books and articles. Shchapov himself was involved in the inquiries and was questioned. So too was Turgenev, who made a statement which is of some interest in showing how far removed he really was from active politics. He spoke with contempt of the Polish revolt and with scorn for Herzen's fanatical ideas.[32]

Bakunin's letters which were seized at this time gave an international background to the situation. The Austrian police collaborated with the Russians in the arrest of Andrey Ivanovich Nichiporenko, who had passed through Lombardy in the summer of 1862 with Italian and Russian newspapers and letters of introduction to Garibaldi from Saffi and Bakunin.[33] But apart from these better-known figures, no other personality of importance was exposed by the inquiry except Nalbandyan and Serno-Solovevich. Serno remained in prison for almost three years (as long as the inquiry lasted) until the beginning of June 1865. At first he refused to answer questions, but later he calmly and bravely expounded his political ideals.[33a] During these three years he had carried on working, reading and thinking as far as he could, though he was sometimes dominated by the feeling that at only thirty years of age his life was already over.[34]

His writings in the Peter-Paul fortress continued the dialogue with Alexander II which had opened with the article he had handed him in the gardens of Tsarskoe Selo. He ended it now with an impassioned but proud request to be allowed to continue working and to own a library. Among his papers were found economic and financial projects, together with confessions, dreams of possible activities, visions of future work, and sporadic reflections on his own hopeless situation. He also translated works by Bentham, Gervinus, Byron, etc.

One of the constant subjects of these reflections was that of Russia's place in Europe. The Polish revolt, and the international tension that accompanied it, soon afforded him an occasion for returning to this theme.[35] Russia, he thought, was weak because she was unable to allow liberty to prevail within her borders and to follow a foreign policy which harmonized with a policy of freedom.

Through the reforms which it has initiated, the State has lost that purely physical power which constituted the strength of Attila, Saladin, Genghis Khan and in general all the great conquerors of the East. But it has not yet acquired that moral strength whose true origin lies in freedom and self-government. This strength constitutes the power of civilized nations.

The Crimean War had been the first defeat after a hundred and fifty years of victories, and it had therefore had a profound effect on men's spirits. And now the Polish revolt was taking Russia by surprise at a time of transformation when already 'faith in the old system was definitely and irrevocably broken', but while everything was still uncertain and undefined. The reaction which was then setting in only weakened Russia's spiritual position still further, and was reflected in her vacillating foreign policies.

Four years ago every officer in our army followed the successes of the Franco-Italian campaign with satisfaction, espousing the cause defended by the latter. But now the officers are called upon to play the same part as the Austrians whom they then so greatly hated.

Hence all Russia's policies in Poland were stultified. Only one solution was now possible: amputation—the treatment for gangrene. He recommended that a decree should be issued announcing that 'Russia has accepted the principle of civil liberty', that an amnesty had been granted and, above all, that an assembly be summoned to decide all internal problems. At the same time the non-Russian nations should be given freedom. The Poles should be allowed to choose between an independent government or a federation of some kind to be decided by them. Lithuania, White Russia and the Ukraine should be invited to send delegates to Moscow or to found local assemblies. The same should be done for the Baltic lands. Finland could become a Grand Duchy allied to Russia. 'Sooner or later Russia will lose Poland, as Austria has lost Italy. Times move too quickly now for such ties to hold. And it is of the greatest importance for us that our neighbour Poland should be an ally and not an enemy.' It only remained to anticipate intelligently and boldly an event that was now inevitable.

Serno-Solovevich returned in this article to the *Zemskaya Duma*. As so

9*

often happens in works of the period, written in deliberately popular and traditional style, there is some doubt as to how far the author really believes in the parallel he draws between Russia's past and his own democratic ideas. How far, for instance, when he speaks of the *mir* in referring to a constituent assembly is he making use of political tactics, and how far does this express a genuine faith in the Russian tradition? Serno's article is one of the best examples of this type of literature. He was trying without popular exaggeration to fuse the requirements of democracy and socialism with those features of collectivism and autonomy which were to be found in the Russian tradition.

A year later, on 7th July 1864, he returned to internal problems. The situation had been brought into being by general ignorance, and he demanded schools. He spoke of the evils of capitalism, which was inevitably linked to the oppression of labour, and he proposed a series of measures designed to create a system of State intervention in the economy. He attacked the Russian tradition of economic tutelage by the State, but, like Chernyshevsky, he was convinced that to bring about the gradual supremacy of *laissez faire* it was essential to pass a series of special measures. This was the only way Russia could avoid the evils from which Western Europe was suffering. Meanwhile he asked Russia to take the initiative in Europe of following a policy of absolute free trade and of allowing complete freedom of colonization for foreigners in Russian territory. 'As soon as the situation in Russia improves the superfluous population of central Europe will pour into us.' He then examined the problems of industrial development. He wanted the railways to be built not by individual capitalists or by the State but by joint-stock companies, to be controlled by the local and provincial authorities and the agricultural or peasant cooperatives. All the State had to do was provide the credit. He thus returned to the central theme of all his economic thought, proposing a series of plans for the alienation of State property which could be used to guarantee the financing of economic development. He quoted the example of America which had had to re-buy for a considerable sum lands which had been given away for nothing. The Russian Government must be more shrewd in the administration of its lands, by making grants of their usufruct, perhaps for life, but continuing to control them. His fundamental intention is clearly stated. This was to start a system of State credit and at the same time give the peasants the chance to acquire new land. 'For they need this far more than is generally believed.'

His articles on the 'new science' (i.e. the science of society) are less lively. They betray the prisoner's desire to plunge back into his researches, to give philosophical expression to his political ideas, and to give himself and others some assurance about the development of human society. His philosophy of history springs here from the need to sum up his faith and to give his own convictions the forms of law. From the little that remains of his writings on this subject, we can say that he was a follower of Buckle, like so many others of his generation. He wanted to paint a picture of universal history whose twentieth and last chapter was to include a few pages of 'practical conclusions'.

On 10th December 1864 Serno-Solovevich was sentenced to twelve years' hard labour and exile for life in Siberia. On 9th April 1865 the Tsar decreed that only the latter part of this sentence should be carried out. On 2nd June the ceremony of 'civil execution' took place. A policeman noted that 'there were a lot of people'.[36]

In November he was at Irkutsk. Here he wrote a letter to his childhood friend V. V. Ivashova, sister of Marya Vasilevna Trubnikova in whose society he had read his first books on political and social subjects. There was no trace of despair in this letter. He entrusted her with his translation of Englander's work on workers' associations and made it clear enough that he was contemplating a daring plan. Documents which have recently come to light reveal that N. A. Serno-Solovevich was one of the organizers of a revolt which was timed to break out in the spring of 1866 among the Polish exiles and the peasants of Western Siberia and which would then have spread throughout Russia. He had already made contact with the Poles and the local elements, had drafted appeals, proclamations and instructions for the insurrection and had played a considerable part in extending and strengthening the web of conspiracy. An informer put an end to the plot. Serno's death on 14th February 1866 spared him from further persecution.

After this account of Nikolay Serno-Solovevich's brief life, we can return to 1862 and consider the groups which had just begun to organize themselves under his inspiration and which were to continue to develop after his arrest.

As we have seen, their original programme was contained in Ogarev's *What does the people need?* which had had a wide circulation. Their principles of organization too were partly derived from the London émigrés.[37] *Zemlya i Volya* was to be composed of a series of groups of five members, each of whom was forbidden to recruit more than five others. The organizer of each group was to be in contact with the leader of another 'five'. So that each man would know the four comrades in his own group and four others in the group which he was obliged to found. This system seems to have been suggested by Mazzini to Ogarev, who passed it on to the young founders of *Zemlya i Volya*.[38] Further techniques such as sympathetic ink also seem to have been suggested by Mazzini through Ogarev.[39] But information on the subject is vague and contradictory. It is, however, certain that Mazzini's name is closely linked to the earliest stages of *Zemlya i Volya*.

But another side of the organization was derived from ideas which were then much in vogue in Russian Populist circles. *Zemlya i Volya* was to represent, even in its structure, the historical differences between the various regions of Russia, with their local and traditional life, contrasting with the government centralization of St Petersburg. It seems possible, though not quite certain, that Chernyshevsky himself had suggested this organization by regions. In any case there is no point in concerning ourselves overmuch with the question of who actually suggested ideas which were current at the time. It is, however, interesting to note which were the large regions proposed in the scheme. Above all there was North Russia, where democratic traditions survived which 'with a few alterations are still of value for the present day'. The intention, as Panteleyev recalled, was to revive the tradition of the *Veche* (citizens' assemblies) which were held in the Middle Ages, mainly in the territories ruled by Novgorod. There certainly was a tradition of this kind, but it was entirely literary and political. Two generations had passed since Radishchev had first looked upon the free status of the Hanseatic city as a symbol, an example and a spur to action. Ever since then this myth had remained a living force in Russian liberal movements, and it now influenced the proposed organization of *Zemlya i Volya*. Secondly, there was the region of the Volga, which in these very years was steadily justifying its reputation for revolutionary traditions, as memories of the past—of Stenka Razin and Pugachev—were recalled by the characteristically bloody revolts of 1861. The third region was to consist of the Urals, which ever since Peter the Great had been the main centre for the employment of slave labour in the factories, and whose history had been one of brutality and revolt. Then there were the regions round Moscow and Siberia. This left the Ukraine and Lithuania, and here the problem became one of nationalism. 'In these parts local groups were to act. The Great Russian organization would naturally have the closest contacts with them, but as an equal with equals.'

The main value of this project was ideological. In actual fact *Zemlya i Volya* acted as a collection of groups, founded at different times, each with its individual characteristics which depended on its founder, and which it was unwilling to surrender. Indeed, their activities and vitality varied directly with their degree of autonomy and when they entered too closely into the proposed scheme, their existence became more one of name than of fact. Even in St Petersburg itself, the heart of the movement, an undisputed central authority was never able to assert itself fully. The truth is that *Zemlya i Volya* was so much the inevitable result of the state of affairs that followed the emancipation of the serfs, and had sprung up so casually from the first network of correspondents and readers of the *Kolokol* or the ideas preached by the *Sovremennik*, that it could never be anything other than a number of different groups in touch with each other.[40]

In St Petersburg the central core consisted at first of the friends of the Serno-Solovevich brothers. It was they who had introduced A. Sleptsov who, after July 1862, tried with varying success to take their place both in respect of duties to the central organization and relations with Herzen and the *Kolokol*. Besides Sleptsov, one of the most active members was N. Obruchev, a relation of the Obruchev who was imprisoned for circulating the *Velikoruss*. *Zemlya i Volya* was in fact beginning to collect the most active forces that had been engaged in earlier attempts to found secret groups. Obruchev took a leading rôle in spreading propaganda among young officers, for whom a manifesto was written and printed in London. *Zemlya i Volya* succeeded in arousing a fairly extensive response in these circles. It found a support in Alexander Fomich Pogossky, who in 1858 began to publish his *Soldatskaya Beseda* (Soldiers' Conversations). The General Staff College seems to have been extensively won over by the secret society. From it, for instance, came Alexander Dmitrevich Putyata, a noble and a colonel, who appears to have been one of the central five of *Zemlya i Volya* along with Chernyshevsky, N. Serno-Solovevich, A. Sleptsov and N. Obruchev.[41]

But students made up the majority of members, particularly after the events of autumn 1861. In that year N. Utin—later to inspire the attempt to found a Russian section of the First International in Geneva—got into contact with the secret movement, together with V. I. Bakst, L. F. Panteleyev, whose memoirs we have already quoted, A. A. Zhuk, A. A. Rikhter, V. Lobanov, etc. At the centre of this nucleus were the literary sets which centred round the *Sovremennik* and the great cultural reviews. But it is difficult to determine the exact part that they played in directing the organization. The most important writers who in varying degrees took part in *Zemlya i Volya* were: V. S. Kurochkin, who translated Béranger and was one of the creators of the political satires in verse which were then in vogue; Blagosvetlov who played a significant rôle throughout the 'sixties in organizing reviews; G. L. Eliseyev and P. Lavrov. The central figure, the guiding spirit of the entire movement, even after his arrest, remained Chernyshevsky.[42]

Outside St Petersburg one of the first groups to approach *Zemlya i Volya* was the 'Library of Kazan Students' which became the source of the entire clandestine movement in Moscow. In about 1859, the university students who came from Kazan had begun to form a group. From the very first their spirit of extremism distinguished them from anything that had yet been seen in St Petersburg. Their state of mind was very largely due to the ideas of Shchapov who had contacts with the Library. When one of its young founders, Yury Molosov, tried to formulate a programme, a prominent proposal was that the Russia of the future should be administered by regions.[43] Closely related to these ambitious views on autonomy was the idea of a radical transformation of the agrarian structure. This was a reflection of the particularly tense situation in the Kazan region, the home of these students. While in St Petersburg the ringleaders were still thinking in terms of increasing the size of the land to be given to the peasants under the reform and of reducing the burden of the redemption fee, here in Moscow, Molosov was already talking of the abolition of private property and the complete nationalization of land which was then to be temporarily leased to the farmer.

The demonstrations against reactionary professors and the consequent punishments inflicted on the students brought new forces to the small original group in Moscow, which also established links with a certain number of officers who shared its ideas. So this group already had some coherence and independence of spirit when in 1861 it began to make its first contacts with St Petersburg.

Sleptsov, one of the creators of *Zemlya i Volya*, travelled along the Volga, founding or making contacts with groups in Astrakhan, Saratov, Kazan, Nizhny Novgorod and Tver. G. N. Potanin, later a well-known traveller and ethnographer, was at the centre of propaganda in the Urals.[44] And Panteleyev has told us of his own attempts to start a group at Vologda and of the difficulties he met with in circles there. He gives us some especially curious information about the state of mind of certain nobles. These men called themselves 'pure Jacobins' merely because the reform had compelled them to give part of their land to the peasants. Already, however, they had given up speaking of national assemblies. For they realized that they could count on the support of the provincial authorities, and above all they had succeeded in removing two unfriendly governors. This trivial example is enough to reveal the weaknesses inherent in the nobles' constitutionalism on which the propagandists had perforce to rely for spreading the idea of a national assembly.

At Kiev Tit Delkevich (a student) circulated *Zemlya i Volya*'s appeals among the officers. He was discovered but succeeded in fleeing to Moldavia. In 1863 he was sentenced *in absentia* to twelve years' hard labour.

At Perm the whole movement was inspired by Alexander Ivanovich Ikonnikov. He had originally been one of Shchapov's fellow students in the Ecclesiastical Academy of Kazan and had then opened a public library in Perm. He was arrested in 1861 for circulating a leaflet, but was then freed. A year later he was banished to Siberia, whence he returned only in 1870.

Scarcely had *Zemlya i Volya* laid the foundations of its organization when, in the winter of 1862, it was confronted with the Polish problem. Polish independence was an essential feature of its programme. But how could the Poles be given effective help? The question was one of choosing the right moment for action. The men of *Zemlya i Volya* were expecting a peasant revolution in 1863, by which time the two years' provisional régime would have elapsed, and the masses would at last be faced with the results of the reform. They therefore implored the Poles not to be too hasty in starting their insurrection but rather to coordinate it with the revolution in Russia. Only then could they give them real support. But the Poles, driven on by the repressive measures taken by the Russian government, were carried away by the momentum of their own situation. They had no hope in a general rising of the Russian peasants, but relied rather on their own forces and on help from Europe.

And so *Zemlya i Volya*, with none of the requisite means, was faced with vast problems which demanded an immediate solution. Negotiations with the Poles were begun in December 1862, when a member of the National Central Committee, Sigismund Padlewski, came to St Petersburg from Warsaw.

He brought a letter of recommendation from Herzen and Bakunin, and asked an officer called Kossowski, head of a Polish group in St Petersburg, to put him into contact with the Central Committee of *Zemlya i Volya*. 'It was a difficult moment', said Sleptsov. There was in fact a group of Russian officers, led by Potebnya, stationed in Warsaw, which was already in contact with Herzen and which was determined to take up arms on the side of the Poles. But the ties between this small body and the centre of *Zemlya i Volya* were very weak. At St Petersburg the members of *Zemlya i Volya* had to rely only on their own forces. The negotiations were entrusted to Sleptsov and Utin, who were forced to admit that 'the revolutionary organization in Russia is still only at its beginnings. It is weak and has no great influence on society. Revolution in Russia is unthinkable before May 1863; if the Poles begin before that the Russians will not be able to give them the slightest help; all they can do will be to try and influence public opinion in Poland's favour.'[45]

Finally they reached an agreement whose fundamental clauses are as follows:

(1) Les principes fondamentaux posés dans la lettre du Comité Central national à MM. Herzen et Bakunin sont acceptés comme bases de l'alliance des deux peuples polonais et russe.

(2) Le Comité Central national reconnaît le Comité de la Russie libre comme le seul représentant de la révolution russe, et le Comité de la Russie libre reconnaît de son côté le Comité Central national comme l'unique représentant de la nation polonaise. Cependant le Comité Central est autorisé à continuer les relations qu'il possède avec le Comité révolutionnaire de Londres.

(3) L'organisation du Comité Central des Ukrainiens comprendra tout le pays situé en deçà du Dniepr . . .

(4) Le Comité Central national reconnaît que la Russie n'est pas assez bien préparée pour seconder par un mouvement insurrectionnel la révolution polonaise dans le cas où celle-ci devrait éclater dans un temps très rapproché. Mais il compte sur une diversion efficace de la part de ses alliés russes pour empêcher le gouvernement du Tsar d'envoyer des troupes fraîches en Pologne.

Il espère aussi qu'une propagande bien dirigée lui permettra de nouer des relations avec les troupes résidentes en ce moment en Pologne. Au moment de l'insurrection cette propagande devra prendre une forme plus arrêtée et amener les troupes à favoriser activement le soulèvement.

(5) Les militaires russes résidents en Pologne qui entreront dans la conjuration, se lieront ensemble en un corps organisé dirigé par un comité qui résidera à Varsovie et auprès duquel l'organisation de la Russie libre aura un représentant. Ce représentant pourra imprimer à cette nouvelle organisation un caractère national dans le sens de la cause de l'indépendance russe.

Jusqu'à nouvel ordre les frais nécessités par cette organisation militaire restent à la charge du Comité Central national.[46]

When the Polish revolt broke out, *Zemlya i Volya* did everything possible to keep faith with this obligation. In January 1863 Sleptsov passed through Warsaw on his way to London to make an agreement with Herzen. While in Poland he sent a long hand-written manifesto to St Petersburg, which was printed after a few corrections, and circulated in February. This was a first gesture of solidarity with the Poles. Official newspapers had adopted a violent attitude towards Poland, and Herzen was able to say that with this manifesto *Zemlya i Volya* 'made a start towards rehabilitating Russia'.[47]

The leaflet was full of admiration for Poland's revolutionary determination, her courage, and even her past. 'Poland has always been superior to us in culture, traditions and civic development. At a time when we considered ourselves happy to be slaves, Poland refused to countenance the shadow of despotism.' There was a close bond between the fate of the Poles and the Russians. 'Why does the government not want to give up Poland? Because it realizes that when Poland is free Russia will be free, and that means that the government itself will be ruined . . . It believes that, by crushing the Polish movement, it will make any movement of the kind in Russia quite impossible.' It was not just a question of the influence of Polish ideas; the movement was powerful throughout Europe. By its policy of prison and exile to Siberia, the Russian government 'itself provides the best propaganda for revolutionary ideas'. The pamphlet then launched a more immediate attack and emphasized the cruelty of the Russian army in Poland: 'The government shoots Polish prisoners just as the Americans of the South shoot negroes.' Sleptsov then defended the idea of the people's war which, he pointed out, was what the Russians themselves had adopted against the Mongols, the Poles and the French: 'It was a people's war that gave rise to Garibaldi. Yet today even those who were most enthusiastic about him now stupidly deny the heroism of the Poles—heroism which is even more worthy of admiration and sympathy than Garibaldi himself. Certainly the Poles have suffered under Alexander II as much as the Neapolitans suffered under the Bourbons.' He ended by appealing to the Russian officers to refuse to fight and to fraternize with the insurgents.

So began a campaign in favour of Poland, into which *Zemlya i Volya* flung all its forces; and sacrificed them all.

Among the Russian troops stationed in Poland great sacrifices had already been made by those directly or indirectly associated with the secret society. The repression had borne heavily on them from the first. 'Some officers, under the guise of developing their soldiers' minds, were reading them books, especially history books, which they explained in such a way as to encourage revolutionary ideas against the Emperor and the government.' Increasingly severe measures were taken. On 24th April 1862 a group of officers was arrested, of whom three, Arngoldt, Slivitsky and Rostovsky, were shot on 16th June.[48] However, the authorities did not realize that this group constituted merely one link in a chain. Andrey Potebnya, the leading spirit in the Warsaw committee, was still in close contact with Herzen and more indirectly with the St Petersburg groups.[49]

Abroad, Sleptsov was searching for new bases from which to organize the printing and distribution of the secret press, and he naturally turned to Herzen who later recalled the strange and depressing impression he had made. He was struck by the pride and arrogance of this youth who had proposed that he, Herzen, should become an 'agent' of Zemlya i Volya.[50] After the arrest of Chernyshevsky and Serno-Solovevich, the younger generation in St Petersburg was obviously inspired by a spirit of pride and exaltation, which is often apparent in memoirs of the period.[51] Such an attitude was encouraged by the magnitude of the tasks which they had assumed and the slender means at their disposal.

But despite their differing mentalities—and an early disagreement—the young delegate of Zemlya i Volya came to an agreement with the London émigrés. It was the Polish revolution which led Herzen to accept and support the organization of Zemlya i Volya, in which he had had so little faith during the two previous years. The Kolokol published a series of appeals for funds. Herzen began intense work in connection with the new Russian press, which V. I. Bakst founded on the Continent in autumn 1862. Bakst was a young man who had taken part in the student demonstrations and earliest clandestine ventures. He had then emigrated to Germany where he played an active part in the quarrels and discussions which split the student colony of Heidelberg. Some of the Russian students from this university had followed their Polish comrades who went back to Warsaw on the outbreak of the revolution. The remainder were divided into two groups: one took the official patriotic line, whereas the other supported Poland. The nature of the relations between these two can easily be divined from the name that the young supporters of Zemlya i Volya gave to their newspaper: 'A tout venant je crache'. In order to develop this campaign, Bakst succeeded, despite many difficulties, in founding a small printing press at Berne, in which Alexander Serno-Solovevich and others collaborated. An attempt was now made to draw up a common policy between this centre and the one in London. As in earlier cases, relations between Herzen and the younger émigrés were not easy. But despite this, the Berne printing press eventually became one of the main centres of propaganda for Russia.

Herzen claimed that these students did not know how to write and that he would do it for them; other works published in Berne were written by Ogarev and Bakunin. But there were only four leaflets in all, addressed to 'the Russian people', 'the Russian armies in Poland', 'the soldiers' and 'the Orthodox people'.[52] These appeals were attempts to explain the connection between the problems of Poland and Russia. For the soldiers, i.e.

peasants in uniform, effective emphasis was given to the fact that only 'a false liberty' had been granted in Russia. The soldiers must help the people to do away with all classes, noble and peasant, leaving a single Russian people able to elect its own administrators after having driven out the thieving officials of the Tsar. In this appeal, as in the one addressed 'to the Orthodox people', the authors were making an obvious attempt to create a popular revolutionary language, made up of a mixture of concessions to current ways of speech and of words to which they tried to give a new import. Besides these four manifestos they printed a collection of 'Free Russian Songs' which, as they wrote in the preface, aimed to be 'the first free collection of Russian songs'. This was largely devised by Ogarev. A considerable effort was made to circulate all this in Russia. Herzen's letters reveal one such attempt. A number of people were to be stationed in towns and other centres in Eastern Europe so as to be able to establish contacts with Russia. But there were never many of these—probably fewer than five, even when the work was at its most intense. In Italy this task was entrusted to Lev Ilich Mechnikov, who had fought with the Thousand and whom we have already met in touch with Chernyshevsky.

Meanwhile efforts were also being made to start a clandestine press in Russia itself.

The main centre of this seems to have been the little town of Mariengauzen. It was organized by Ilya Grigorevich Zhukov, an ex-captain of the General Staff who had been dismissed from the army for spreading propaganda among the troops. He was arrested with a friend on 23rd February 1863, and a year later condemned to the loss of his nobility and ten years' hard labour, which he served in the Aleksandrovsky Zavod in Siberia. Another man who helped in the organization was Mikhail Karlovich Veyde, a noble from Vitebsk and student at St Petersburg. He was arrested in May 1863 and sentenced to fifteen years' hard labour. In 1864 the archives and part of the type-face of *Zemlya i Volya* were being looked after by Nikolay Vasilevich Gerbel. He too had begun his career in the army and had then devoted himself to journalism in touch with Herzen, Mikhailov and Shelgunov. He had been in close contact with the central core of *Zemlya i Volya* from the start.

At the beginning of 1863 two numbers of a small leaflet called *Freedom* were issued in succession.[53]

The first number stressed its ties with 'society' i.e. the intellectual movement that had given birth to *Zemlya i Volya*. The task of the revolutionaries was to 'win over the educated classes to the people's interests'. It also expressed the desire to spread propaganda among the peasants; but a decisive step along these lines was never taken. The authors were still intellectuals, trying to defend the people's interests from within the educated classes to which they belonged. No attempt at propaganda in the villages was promoted by the centre of *Zemlya i Volya*. We have Panteleyev's explicit statement to this effect and we have every reason to accept his word.

The second number of *Freedom* returned to the Polish problem. It laid less emphasis on the right of all nations (including, therefore, Poland) to win their own independence; and spoke at greater length of the danger of war which threatened Russia, and of the country's internal situation which neither allowed nor justified her undertaking an armed struggle against the rest of Europe. The picture it gave of the severities of life in Russia and the persecutions of the last few years was effective enough. But it amounted to no more than instinctive propaganda, typical of a time of reaction and resistance to the government's repressive measures.

The growing difficulties which faced the groups of *Zemlya i Volya* and their increasing isolation explain why its few members who were still active in 1863 depended more and more openly on the émigrés. Indeed a proposed statute which more or less made the *Kolokol* the true centre of *Zemlya i Volya* probably dates from the autumn of that year.

The reaction and discouragement which followed the end of the Polish revolt eventually led to an informal discussion within the central group in St Petersburg. As Herzen said, by the end of 1863 *Zemlya i Volya* was already a 'myth' and as such it survived only in the stubborn, though increasingly unsuccessful, attempts of Ogarev, Bakunin and Herzen to resume some contact with Russia.

But even if they had done no more than create this 'myth' the members of *Zemlya i Volya* would have played an important rôle in history. They had founded the first clandestine movement with any cohesion, a movement which was both a consequence of and an answer to Alexander II's reforms. Their writings, even though most of them were very general in character, had raised some problems which remained fundamental and which were later taken up again. Unlike the *Velikoruss*, they had taken a step forward. They no longer addressed the educated classes merely to warn and threaten them. Instead they told them of the need to represent and prepare to guide the peasant movement. It is true that all this remained purely theoretical. For guidance some sort of contact was necessary, whereas the members of *Zemlya i Volya*, as far as their practical work was concerned, had no direct link with the people. They were already Populists, but still more theoreticians of Populism. It was only the ingenuous and enthusiastic movement to 'go to the people' which succeeded in throwing the first bridge across this abyss.

The first *Zemlya i Volya* in fact owed its life to the determination of a few dozen young intellectuals, students and officers to found a group clearly opposed not merely to the despotism of the State but also to the general ideas of liberalism and reform held by the educated classes. It was this determination that allowed them to overcome the initial cynicism or irony of their teachers and inspirers—Herzen and Chernyshevsky. And it was this determination that both inspired the organization which was now beginning to spread to the provinces, and made the fractional movements which were forming in various parts of the country rally for a brief moment round the central group.

Nikolay Serno-Solovevich has described better than anyone this decision to escape from the world of official politics—politics, moreover, that remained official even when disguised as progressive.

Society will never turn against the Government and will never of its free will give the people what it needs, because 'society' is made up of landlord-officials whose principles and aspirations, whose interests and crimes, are the same as those of the government. A real struggle between them is impossible. There can only be misunderstandings about equal shares and the right to oppress and loot the people. 'Society' is as weak and feeble as the Government which it has always served. As a body it is permeated down to the smallest pores of its organism with petty doctrinairism, servility and corrupt and selfish instincts. Not only is it incapable of reforming Russia; it is incapable of even reforming itself. In 'society' the only vital principle is represented by a small hostile minority. This minority belongs to the people by sentiment, but has no other link with it in reality. That is the source of all the trouble. The good intentions of the minority are useless because of its impotence. The people is courageous—but that is not enough to give the signal to take the initiative.[54]

For twenty years the revolutionary movement was to have two simultaneous aims: a difficult journey of exploration into the real life of the Russian people and an attempt to organize this small minority.

When Alexander Serno-Solovevich became an émigré he tried to develop his brother Nicholas's standpoint. He knew that he was the most gifted and sensitive man of the young generation in exile. He felt too the weight of responsibility which devolved on him as one of the few survivors of *Zemlya i Volya*; for fate had spared him the banishment or silence to which so many of his friends were now condemned.

The path he followed in Switzerland is of considerable interest in the history of Populism; for it shows us the reasons for the break-up of the alliance which had been made (with such difficulty) between the editors of the *Kolokol* and the young generation of exiles at the time of the Polish insurrection. And it is of interest above all because it shows us how the passionate search for the people made by the members of *Zemlya i Volya* found a new expression in Serno's participation in the workers' movement.

Alexander's experiences do much to explain the deepest currents of the Russian movement of the 'sixties. This movement still had countless ties with the aspirations of the liberals. Yet it harboured elements capable of making this young Russian intellectual transplanted to Geneva into a passionate and intelligent adherent of the First International.[55]

Alexander was born in 1838. His childhood was disturbed by conflict with his family and a silent animosity against his mother and schools. Some of the letters he wrote when he was about twenty have been published, and in them we can see how his political opposition sprang out of his stormy adolescence.[56] He joined the illegal movement in St Petersburg in its early stages, and in 1861 he helped to circulate Shelgunov's manifesto *To the young generation*. He then took part in the student movements of the same year, trying, together with his brother, to give them a more obviously political significance. In the spring of 1862 he organized with V. I. Kelsiev a system of transporting illegal newspapers from Koenigsberg.[57] He then became one of the most active members of *Zemlya i Volya*, and began to attract the attention of the police who put an agent on his tracks disguised as a valet. They made a note of him as one of the most highly respected men in the intellectual world of St Petersburg.[58]

Broken by this mode of life and weak in health, he went abroad for a cure, just in time to avoid being arrested with his brother.

Shelgunov, who knew him well, said that: 'The energy of his temperament, the fierce passion of his character, the speed of his intuition, the subtlety and irony of his intelligence and the dedicated spirit which he devoted to the cause without ever thinking of himself—all these put him in a class of his own.'[59]

His life as an exile was hard. Often he had no money, and he inherited a mental illness from his mother which constantly debilitated him and eventually led him to suicide. He was preoccupied with thoughts of his brother and his friends and teachers in prison, and of the crushing of the Polish rebellion. For a time he shared the life of the small group of exiles, taking part in the attempts to found a new Russian printing press in Switzerland, to administer a cooperative bank among the exiles and to publish Chernyshevsky's works, which were banned by the Russian authorities.

At the end of 1866 he read an article in the *Kolokol* which forced him to take up his pen. It was written by Ogarev and dealt with the situation in Poland where the Tsarist government was still persecuting patriots and trying to win over the sympathies of the peasants by giving them land. It reflected the process of self-criticism which had been begun by Herzen and Ogarev immediately after the suppression of the rebellion in 1863–64. At that time they had wondered more and more anxiously where the true defence of the people's interests was to be found.[60] Serno wanted to re-assert Chernyshevsky's views against these doubts, and he now described them more precisely than had yet been done.[61]

Je ne dirais pas aux polonais: 'nous sommes frères', 'donnons-nous la main', 'votre cause est notre cause', et autres belles phrases. Je leur dirais, au contrair, avec une entière franchise, les paroles suivantes: 'Je sympathise avec vous profondément, comme avec une nation de héros, comme avec une nation opprimée, et surtout opprimée par le peuple auquel j'appartiens. Mais, cependant, votre cause n'est pas notre cause, tant que le mouvement polonais se fera sous l'étendard des aristocrates et des prêtres, tant que le mouvement polonais ne deviendra pas un mouvement populaire. Jusqu'à ce jour nous sommes unis uniquement dans une haine commune pour les bâtards allemands, nos maîtres et nos tyrans . . . En tout cas, quelque soit le sort que l'avenir réserve à la Pologne, il faut *d'abord* sa séparation et celle de tout ce qui est polonais d'avec la Russie, et *ensuite*, si celà est possible, une *fédération libre: d'abord* la division—*plus tard* l'union fraternelle . . . Je suis assuré que la jeune génération russe sera avec moi et non avec le 'Kolokol'. Je ne puis croire que la parole puissante et pleine de génie de Tschernyschewski soit tombée en vain sur un sol stérile. Maître, que tu nous manques maintenant! Avec quel bonheur je donnerais ma vie pour t'épargner quelques-unes des souffrances auxquelles te soumettent tes lâches assassins!

And so he called for an open and final break with Herzen. 'Le *Kolokol* n'est plus le drapeau de la jeune Russie. Je comprends autrement le mode de réalisation des théories socialistes et le renouvellement des formes sociales de la vie.'

Serno thus began a controversy which was intensified some months later when Herzen took up a stand against Karakozov's attempt on the Tsar's life—the first act of terrorism organized by the Russian Populist movements. Serno then wrote in Chernyshevsky's name a violent and detailed criticism of Herzen's entire political career. The converging of the *Kolokol* and the *Sovremennik*, which in 1862 had given birth to *Zemlya i Volya*, was now no more than a memory. The defeat of this first clandestine organization now induced the exiles to re-examine the foundations on which it had been developed. This led to an internal conflict which brought to light more clearly than ever before the heterogeneous elements of which it had been composed.[62]

To Serno, Herzen seemed the very incarnation of all the feelings and opinions that Chernyshevsky had warned him to distrust. 'You were beautiful as fireworks are', he said. 'You had a character à la Lamartine, you "deified" the Decembrists instead of criticizing and understanding their political ideas. You allow yourself to be guided by sentiment when for example you praise Orsini's gesture and yet refuse to understand Karakozov's. Chernyshevsky, on the other hand, was *par excellence* a man of logic, of cautious and deliberate thought. You specialize in enthusiasm. Chernyshevsky had a scientific approach; he was a man of objective truth. You have never been able to maintain an exact political course, and so your work is collapsing; whereas Chernyshevsky has founded a real school, has educated men, has given inspiration to an entire phalanx of young men. It is from him and not from you that the young generation has drawn its inspiration—the generation which in word and deed, but mainly in deed— now preaches Socialist theories, and which has sunk its roots so deep in the country that no force will be able to extricate it—the generation, in fact, which has drawn a boundary-line between the Russia which is really young and that which only claims to be.'

Serno's article, though he expressed it in a purely polemical form, did bring to light a real difference between Herzen and Chernyshevsky. Herzen was able to mould public opinion, create a mode of thought and inspire a spiritual revival. Chernyshevsky, through his journalistic activities, was able to vitalize political organizations impelled by the desire for immediate action.

To prove his allegations, Serno looked back to the time when the differences between Herzen and Chernyshevsky had been at their peak, and he recalled the efforts which had been made through his brother Nikolay to effect some agreement and find some common ground between them. 'Chernyshevsky derided these attempts to bring you together, and you have never been able to forgive the ruthless contempt with which he treated your phrase-making. How well he understood you!' Serno recapitulated the history of the union of the *Kolokol* and *Sovremennik* which the new generation had wanted and which *Zemlya i Volya* had momentarily achieved. In doing so, he revealed its artificial elements. 'Between you and Chernyshevsky there was not, there could not be, anything in common. You are two opposing elements who cannot live together, who do not complete each other but rather cancel each other out.'

Not even the Polish question had been able to bring about a real union between the two trends. Even those members of *Zemlya i Volya* who had been closest to Herzen had been scathing about his defects:

Your brother and friend Potebnya spoke of you once in London, during his last journey there, when we were leaving your house together. He spoke of you in anger and told me of your attitude towards the group of officers (the Russian officers in Warsaw). He ended by saying 'Herzen's only use now would be to get himself killed on the barricades, but in any case he will never go near them'.

Herzen, he said, had failed in his true function: that of political education. Whenever possible he had paralyzed the efforts of those 'who wanted to recall society to an independent function, who wanted to build up a force'.

Apart from these purely episodic elements, interesting though they are, Serno's work brought to light the divergence between the elements which were still tied to the liberal tradition and those which were purely Populist. This divergence was taking place simultaneously both in Russia and among the exiles. The unfair estimate of Herzen was merely the form in which this expressed itself. The myth of Chernyshevsky was yet another symptom and at the same time a convenient weapon.

This position led Serno in his last years to take a more and more active part in the Geneva workmen's movement. There he could put into practice his desire for action and could apply himself to purely Socialist activities.

I am tormented by not being able to go to Russia to avenge the loss of my brother and friends. But any revenge I could take would not be enough and would be useless. By working here for the common cause, we will have our revenge on this entire cursed system. The International holds the promise of its complete destruction everywhere.[63]

He expressed this determination mainly in the great builders' strike of March 1868. This strike caused a huge reaction even outside Switzerland,

and it marked an important stage in the history of the Geneva working class movement and the First International.[64] The *Égalité* recalled on 4th September 1869 that Serno had done an immense amount of work on this occasion: 'toujours présent, toujours prêt à receuillir les avis, à les répandre . . . à rédiger les lettres, les circulaires, les affiches, en un mot toujours sur la brèche, il fut l'âme de ce premier combat qui fut si important pour le progrès de l'Internationale à Genève.' He himself wrote to V. Ivashova telling her that he was working fourteen hours a day. He felt that he was doing something useful: 'I am pleased with what I am doing just now', he told her.[65]

He next joined a small newspaper *La Liberté: Journal des Radicaux Progressistes* founded in the autumn of 1867 by a group of dissidents from the old radical party led by A. Catalan for the purpose of carrying out an anticlerical campaign. But the intensification of the strife between employers and workmen had soon led this group to devote itself increasingly to the 'social question' and to adopt a line in support of the strikers of March 1868. The exact part played by Serno in this development is not known. He was certainly in the forefront of the campaign against the *Journal de Genève* in defence of the workmen's demands. And when the strike was over he wrote an article in *La Liberté* which pointed out its consequences both for politics generally and for the organization itself.[66]

La première vérité qui nous semble ressortir des faits et qui ne sera pas contestée, croyons-nous, même par les ouvriers, c'est que cette organisation de l'Association internationale, dont on a fait tant de bruit, est loin d'être aussi complète qu'on s'est plu à dire de tous les côtés.

No steps had been taken to guarantee the financial means necessary to bring the strike to a successful conclusion. Delegates had been sent too late to Paris, Brussels and London to obtain material and moral support. The Central Committee of the Association had never known exactly how many workmen were on strike. In fact, an inquiry into and close study of the situation were essential, followed by a complete reorganization. A considerable effort must then be made to establish societies of mutual aid and cooperative institutions.

Such were the main points in Serno's campaign throughout this period. He had to defend himself, in *La Liberté* itself, against the charge that he had attacked the International, and he explained that 'he only wanted it to be better organized'. He said that he looked upon it as 'la meilleure creation de notre époque' and explained his political ideas. 'Pour nous, non seulement la question économique domine toutes les autres, mais elle sert même de criterium, de règle pour l'appréciation morale des hommes.' For him this implied not merely a belief in economic materialism but above all a typically Populist expression of the desire to achieve (even in his own personal life) a Socialist ideal. And it was on these lines that he followed up this statement.[67]

Although he thus endorsed the final ends and ideals of the International Association, he reserved full rights to criticize its policies:

Nous serons plus méticuleux pour les internationaux qu'envers leurs ennemis, qui sont les nôtres. Et cela parce que nous n'avons qu'un seul but, un unique désir: que l'Internationale devienne une force indépendante, raisonnée et qu'elle ne dresse un piédestal à personne, que ce soit nous, que ce soit MM. Goegg, Fazy [Swiss politicians], Garibaldi lui-même, ou toute autre dieu.

The struggle would be long and difficult. Without 'une force réelle' it would be impossible to keep it up: 'Il n'y a pas à se méprendre: ses adversaires sont sur tous les points beaucoup plus puissants qu'elle.'

In the face of these difficulties the organization had only one advantage: its youth, 'la force de ses jeunes tissus organiques et la jeune volonté à laquelle ne pourront pas résister des tissus desséchés, vieillis, délabrés. L'avenir n'appartient pas à ce qu'est usé, mais à ce qu'est jeune et vigoureux . . .'

It was essential to break away from everything that inhibited this energy: 'L'Utopie, voilà notre plus grande ennemie, dit Proudhon . . .'

Proudhon was right; the International must adopt realistic policies, and rely for support on a serious organization. Did not the Geneva strike demonstrate that the builders had been unable to choose the right moment for dealing the heaviest blow at the employers?

Les sentiments, la bonté ont toujours été nuisibles au peuple . . . Préparez-vous à être maîtres de vous-mêmes et de votre sort. Analysez, disséquez, raisonnez . . . L'histoire nous démontre que tous les bons commencements, tous les mouvements de la classe ouvrière ont avorté parce que précisément dans le moment donné les ouvriers, sentant leur faiblesse et n'ayant ni un but clair et précis, ni un programme bien déterminé, s'en remettent à des archanges qui daignent de temps en temps s'offrir pour les gouverner. Voyez les deux hommes dont l'honnêteté et l'intégrité ne peuvent être mis en doute, Garibaldi et Louis Blanc. Qu'ont-ils fait pour le peuple, quoiqu'ils aient eu la possibilité de tout faire? Absolument rien. Et cela parce qu'on leur a décerné le nom de dieux. L'un a donné les italiens du midi à un roi qui ne diffère en rien de toute cette noble race, et l'autre n'osa rien, alors qu'il avait tout Paris populaire à sa disposition . . . Non, laissez ces questions de fraternité à vos neveux, vous en avez pour le moment bien d'autres à résoudre, beaucoup plus graves et pratiques . . . Avouez-vous à vous-mêmes votre faiblesse. L'avouer, la comprendre, c'est vouloir devenir forts, car, encore une fois, la force ne cède qu'à la force. Il faut donc immédiatement s'organiser et agir. C'est par l'économie politique que la bourgeoisie nous tue. C'est par l'économie politique qu'il faut nous relever.[68]

This was the central problem. 'Ou les économistes théologiens ont raison, ou ils ont tort. S'ils ont raison, pourquoi hurler contre eux? Si l'Internationale ne peut rien créer, inclinons-nous devant la sagesse impotente des maîtres. S'ils ont tort, il faut faire soi-même de l'économie politique et rechercher la formule.' Only this would succeed in providing the International with lucid ideas. The workmen's groups and clubs must be transformed from meeting places and cafés as they were at present into schools: 'A l'étude donc, MM. les internationaux. Créez des commissions.'[69]

In July A. Catalan resumed control of the paper and returned to earlier secular and radical policies, giving only second place to the social problems which had been brought into issue by the strike. So in order to continue his campaign, Serno founded a small paper of his own. Though it only came out twice, these two numbers were enough to clarify his argument.[70] The paper itself was the organ of a minority and it emphasized the right of all members of the International to hold independent points of view and express them freely. Its aim, as Serno said in the first number, was 'secouer enfin, avec toute la force de notre énergie, ce laisser aller de la grande majorité des membres de l'Internationale, cette nonchalance, cette apathie, cette torpeur qui sont incompatibles avec ses buts'. They must now move beyond 'the period of childhood' in which the Geneva section had been living during the two years since its foundation. The first regrouping of the workmen had been achieved; the strikes, even when they had not been altogether successful, had created a communal spirit. 'C'est maintenant le moment du travail qui commence, le moment le plus difficile et, par conséquent, un moment où l'énergie doit être redoublée. C'est maintenant que les Internationaux doivent créer et élaborer l'idée sans laquelle rien n'est encore gagné . . .' Without Socialism, the Association exposed itself to the greatest dangers. It was enough to look at England to realize this. Had there not arisen there 'une nouvelle classe, ou en d'autres termes, la division de la classe ouvrière en deux camps parfaitement tranchés?'

The same danger existed at Geneva, where a large number of the workmen were foreigners, which made the problem of achieving solidarity between them all the more difficult.

These difficulties and defects could only be remedied through organization. 'Sans organisation la marche de l'Internationale est impossible', the second number claimed. This was not just a question of inviting the workmen to take part in festivities and meetings, but also of appointing commissions to study particular problems. This was all the more necessary as the Brussels Congress was soon to meet, and its importance had not yet been fully appreciated.

Ces congrès lient entre eux les ouvriers de toute l'Europe, ce sont eux qui donnent le mot d'ordre, ce sont eux qui disposent, pour ainsi dire, du sort de la classe ouvrière . . . Il suit de tout celà que pour remplir un mandat aussi grave, on doit être préparé. Mais, nous le demandons, est-on préparé pour se prononcer sur une seule des questions? Où est-il ce travail qu'on a fait? . . . Nous n'en savons rien.

The reports they had drawn up contained only vague aspirations. 'Ces réponses de cinque lignes se reduisent à ceci: nous exprimons les vœux que la face du monde tourne. Toujours des vœux! Toujours des songes! . . .' Let them study at least one problem, that of strikes, and try to submit them to international discipline. The general council must be informed a month beforehand of any agitation which was being planned, so as to be able to give them support. And in the meantime they must ask London to explain why it had done nothing during the Geneva strike. 'Oui, que les Anglais disent *pourquoi* il n'ont pas soutenu la grève.'

Serno tried by personal efforts to make up for the deficiencies which he denounced. He became a member of the statistical office and in May he wrote a report on the situation in Geneva and sent it to London.

But he was mainly anxious to translate the experiences gained by the strike and the subsequent discussions to the political plane. At the next cantonal elections the exponents of the International ought to combine with the dissident radicals of *La Liberté* in an attempt to affirm the autonomy of the popular movement in face of the traditional parties. A. Catalan had been one of the members of the Geneva delegation to the Brussels Congress and he had spoken of the strike, emphasizing the freedom of organization which the workmen at Geneva enjoyed. In any case the list of candidates published in *La Liberté* on 10th October could be considered international. The party was called 'Social Democratic' and included J.-Ph. Becker, F. Macmillod and other spokesmen of the workers' movement. Serno had reason to hope that a new party might emerge from the elections.

He soon came into conflict with the Bakuninist wing, which opposed participation in the elections. On 28th October 1868 when the electoral manifesto had already been published, the *Alliance* declared itself against this step. But it was not this departure that led to the party's defeat at elections. The builders, who were the shock-troops of the workers' movement at Geneva, were mostly from other cantons and so did not possess the right to vote.

This episode led Serno into conflict with Bakunin's *Alliance*. He was one of the few Russians who was not a member and was consequently isolated among the exiles as well as among the Geneva working classes. As *Égalité*, which supported Bakunin, said on 4th September 1869: 'Il pensait que la transformation radicale de la société partirait de la minorité intelligente et devouée et manquait de confiance dans la grande force de l'instinct populaire. Il voulait baser la régénération sociale sur l'état, lui-même préalablement régénéré.' This naturally brought him closer to Marx, and he acted as intermediary in an attempt to resume relations between Bakunin and Marx, who sent Serno a presentation copy of *Das Kapital*. On 20th November 1868 Serno wrote him a long letter recounting his experiences in organizing workers, claiming that the strike and the elections, despite their lack of success, had made an important breach in the political life of the country. 'Even to a cold outside observer, the workers' movement as it is at present developing, would still, despite all its defects, be a really impressive sight.' But he was frightened by the lack of preparation which he saw around him.

I have never been so afraid as now of an immediate revolution. I know that on this point I am in disagreement with many people, who think that the only important thing is to provoke a general upheaval at once.

The International like the country itself has absolutely no intellectual forces. With a few microscopic exceptions, the rest understand nothing, absolutely nothing, and are prompted only by the vaguest and cloudiest aspirations. And so the movement may fail through a lack of clear ideas, drowning in a wave of catch-phrases about brotherhood and solidarity which are contradicted by reality at every turn.

He asked Marx to write articles and provide material for a new paper, and spoke of the difficulties of finding people to support it—the more so as it was to be written in French 'and the French in my opinion are colossally ignorant and inexhaustible in their rhetoric'.[71]

In January 1869 he was excluded from the editorial committee of *Égalité*, the organ of the Romance section of the *Alliance*. This led to a final clash. It was only a slight blow, but it was the end of him. He was taken to hospital and told by a doctor that he was incurably ill and that his moments of lucidity would gradually decrease and finally disappear. To escape this fate he committed suicide on 16th August 1869.

11. YOUNG RUSSIA

IN THE SUMMER OF 1862 a clandestine leaflet signed 'Young Russia' was put into circulation. This leaflet differed markedly from the many other publications of the time. It was particularly emphatic about the need to destroy existing political and social relations in Russia, and it raised the problem of contact with the people more energetically than had yet been done elsewhere. This extremism and desire for action succeeded in formulating with surprising clarity the fundamental problems of the relationship between the revolutionary *élite* and the masses. All this was the work of a young man of nineteen, P. G. Zaichnevsky, and a small group of his fellow-students.[1]

Zaichnevsky was born on 18th October 1842 on his father's estate in the province of Orel. His family were small landowners who owned less than two hundred souls. He went to the local secondary school at Orel and was so successful that he was sent to the University of Moscow to study mathematics. By the time he arrived, he was already exceedingly interested in politics. He read Herzen and discovered the word *Socialist* 'almost on every page'. 'I then devoted myself to seeking every possible chance to get hold of books which spoke of this [word].' He studied Louis Blanc, Leroux and Proudhon and read books on history, especially the French Revolution, the Polish Rebellion of 1830 and *Young Italy*. He had discussions with his school friends, and their agreement encouraged him; but 'most of those whom I met held only utterly casual Socialist convictions, because of their inadequate knowledge of the works of Western Socialists'.[2]

And so, when he reached Moscow in 1859 his first concern was to find some means of making the books that had impressed him better known, with a view to developing his fellow-students. Using the methods that were employed to lithograph university lectures, he circulated a small pamphlet by Ogarev which attacked an official book on the Decembrists. He made three hundred copies and sold them with a portrait of Ogarev at 65 kopeks each. He had the satisfaction of seeing this edition sold out in a single day. In 1860 he used the same method to reprint long autobiographical passages from the works of Herzen as well as other articles by him from the *Polyarnaya Zvezda* and the *Kolokol*, and a translation of the *Du développement des idées révolutionnaires en Russie*. In 1861 he followed this up with Feuerbach's *Essence of Christianity* and Büchner's *Force and Matter*. An unfinished manuscript translation of Proudhon's *What is Property?* was found by the police, and only his arrest put a stop to its publication in this series.

As can be seen, for three years Zaichnevsky had been able to carry on working as a clandestine publisher, without the slightest trouble. In fact there was scarcely any control over printing presses. When an inquiry was made, on the occasion of his arrest, it was found that out of a hundred and fifty private presses used in Moscow in 1861, only ninety-six had obtained official authorization. The others were unknown and continued working without any supervision. And so it was easy enough for this little workshop to lithograph pamphlets and escape detection.

Zaichnevsky soon found followers who were prepared to help him work on and distribute these reprints and translations. At first he relied on the group of students who came from the region of Kazan. In their 'library' he must have found at least some of the 'Western Socialists' he was looking for. But even more important, he had found an atmosphere of vitality, and a secret organization capable of long-term survival. Indeed it was this body of students that had given birth to the Moscow branch of *Zemlya i Volya*, and which was later to inspire other movements. It was here too that Zaichnevsky found the man who became his closest comrade, Perikles Emmanuilovich Argiropulo, of Greek descent.

At the beginning of 1861 the two men broke away from the 'Library of Kazan Students' and founded a new group of about twenty young men. The exact reasons for this break are not known, but they were probably political in character. Very soon the group was known as 'The Society of Communists'. Around a central core there were a number of fluctuating members who did, however, take part in the meetings and discussions. Zaichnevsky and Argiropulo knew that they themselves were the most experienced in the group. 'In our society', said Zaichnevsky, in a letter to his friend, 'it's only you and myself that I dare call Socialists.'[3] They divided the work to be done: while Zaichnevsky was chiefly concerned with organization, Argiropulo devoted himself to editorial activities. They went on selling their lithographed works very cheaply, and any money they gained in this way was given to poor students and kept in the students' communal bank of which Argiropulo was treasurer. The students gave all they could to build up an initial fund for the printing. The richer ones gave money, and the poor sold their belongings and earned money by writing articles. The editions were always sold out at once and often fetched far higher prices secondhand.

In view of their success, they thought of founding a real secret printing press, and, at the end of 1861, two Moscow students, Ya. Sulin and I. Sorokov, succeeded in doing so. They called it 'The First Free Russian Press' and they printed Ogarev's pamphlet on the Decembrists with which Zaichnevsky had begun his activities. In February 1861 the book was put into circulation, but the machine which had produced it was so worn during the printing that it had to be abandoned. They then managed to obtain another, which was made this time of metal instead of wood. The police did not discover this in Argiropulo's house when they came in to arrest him; and after he was removed to prison, it was taken to the province of Ryazan, where it was used to print the manifesto *Young Russia*, the climax of all this ferment.

Although Argiropulo devoted most of his time to printing, this was not his sole activity. Both he and Zaichnevsky were looking for other fields which would allow them to leave the academic world and give their activities wider significance. When, some time later in prison, Zaichnevsky was writing his programme he said, 'Our chief hope lies in the young generation.' But he added that to fulfil these hopes the young generation needed a political organization. 'You must understand, young men, that it is from you that the leaders of the nation must spring; that it is you who must stand at the head of the movement; that it is you who are the hope of the revolutionary party.' Everything possible must be tried to bring about the results they hoped for.

The Polish problem offered the first, natural field for their activities.

On 15th February 1861 there was a demonstration in Warsaw in the course of which the population clashed with the troops. Five people were killed. It was this demonstration that prevented Herzen from drinking a toast in honour of Alexander II. In Moscow two days later about two hundred university students went to the Catholic Church to attend a requiem mass for the fallen. Most of these students were Poles, but among them were some Russians.[4] When they came out of the church, Zaichnevsky stood on the steps and made a speech. He asked them all to unite against the common enemy under 'the common banner, red for Socialism and black for the Proletariat'. He ended his short speech with a shout of 'Long live Socialist Poland'. Those present replied that the banner which he had described could not unite the Russians and the Poles. They said:

According to us the time for Socialism has not yet come, because we do not have the proletariat which alone would constitute a reasonable basis and justification for its existence. According to our ideas, Socialism, which for you Russians is a luxury, is indeed almost superfluous, is for us Poles unpardonable . . . Freedom and independence, that is our password.

Zaichnevsky had here already adopted the views which he later expounded in the manifesto *Young Russia*. But he could not hope for support from the Poles. It was the Russian people, the poorest inhabitants of town and country, whom he had to try and reach.

Sunday-schools must have seemed a useful instrument for this purpose. There was at this time a movement among students and intellectuals to teach illiterates.[5] It was soon to be violently dispersed, but it demonstrates the enthusiasm for enlightenment and the intention on the part of embryonic revolutionary groups to make use of the movement for spreading their own ideas. For they were not merely concerned to enlighten the illiterate; they wanted to introduce a new spirit of love and understanding of the peasants, and of criticism of the past and present situation.

The political significance of these Sunday-schools was pointed out by
Prince Dolgorukov, the head of the Russian police, with all the unconscious
irony of bureaucratic language. 'The government cannot permit a situation
whereby half the population owes its education not to the State but to itself
or to the private benefaction of some particular class.' This was why the
schools were closed: any independent action, however small, on the part of
the intelligentsia was in danger of finding a considerable response among the
uneducated. Prince Dolgorukov was only too well aware that the way to the
people, for which the students of Moscow and St Petersburg were so passionately searching, could be found easily enough. And so all centres of voluntary
education were closed.

With the blocking of this first road, Zaichnevsky's group seems to have
spent a fairly long time considering ideas for the formation of a society of
street pedlars to circulate suitable books among the people. And when in
February 1861 the decree freeing the serfs was published some of them,
particularly Zaichnevsky—whose strength and determination as an agitator
was superior to that of all his comrades—thought that the time had come to
start direct propaganda in the country. It was suggested that during the
holidays each man was to return to his native province, distribute works by
Herzen, Ogarev, etc., in the smaller towns and preach Socialism in person to
the peasants.

Some of them actually put this proposal into practice. Two students
founded summer schools for young peasants, and others sold books by the
score. Alexander Novikov wrote an enthusiastic letter from Kharkov. 'If I
had a hundred copies of Büchner with me here, I could soon sell them all.'

At the end of May Zaichnevsky left Moscow on horseback, making for
the south down the road which led to his home. At Podolsk he stopped to
speak to the peasants, and met with a good reception. He attended a meeting
summoned by a landlord to draw up the agreements with his peasants which
the decree of emancipation provided for. 'The peasants surrounded me and
listened to me joyfully. I said that the land belonged to them and if the
landlords did not agree, then the landlords could be compelled by force and
all would go well. But only on one condition: that they gave up hoping in the
Tsar, who had given them such a worthless liberation. And I told them of
Anton Petrov' (the leader of the peasant revolt in Bezdna). He ended by explaining that it was useless to revolt without arms and that it was essential to
obtain them.

When he reached his home in the province of Orel, news of peasant revolts
reached him from all sides. He wrote to Argiropulo that red banners had
already appeared at the head of processions 'which were moving in defence
of the great cause—common ownership of the land'. Whenever he succeeded
in speaking, he had a good reception. One day, during a wedding, he was
listened to with such approval that he wrote to his brother, in the evening,
'the peasants told me that they were ready to give me their last hen'. The core

of his message lay in affirming 'the superiority of communal over private property'.

In the course of the summer, Zaichnevsky decided to conceal his opinions no longer. He revealed them in letters which he entrusted to the ordinary post, and explained them to everyone he met. One of the Senators who later tried him rightly called him 'a preacher and confessor of Socialism'. He was convinced that 'the moment has come to show the gentry that truth is not on their side and that soon the régime to which they belong will collapse once and for all. They themselves are well aware of this. Just as, on the point of death, Christians (especially during the first few centuries) used to see terrible and threatening visions of Hell, so these men now have a confused vision of the new life, whose outlines are gradually growing clearer, and they are frightened for themselves and their sons brought up in their faith.'[6]

His father and his closest friends, even Argiropulo, tried in vain to restrain him and moderate his opinions. A. Novikov who had circulated the secret edition of Büchner's *Force and Matter* at Kharkov said that Zaichnevsky's 'ideas were liberal to the point of madness, and he paid no attention to what he said or did'. In the letters he wrote during this summer of 1861, Zaichnevsky answered these accusations by quoting Mazzini in Italian 'Ora e sempre' [Now and always]. In Russia too all those who wanted to advance Socialism must adopt this password. 'Should we too not adopt this saying of Mazzini and all *Young Italy*? Are we Socialists not bound, everywhere and always, to proclaim those ideas which for the moment are held by a few, a very few people?' Open and constant propaganda was the first unquestioning duty of all who maintained this ideal. It was enough to look around to see how great was the ignorance on this subject. In other countries 'Socialists have even been in the government, but in Russia nothing is known of what they have done. Here everyone from children upwards is frightened by Socialism, which has always been severely persecuted.'

It was true, he added, that essential though it was, preaching was not enough. It prepared the ground for a revolt, it was the necessary condition for a rebellion, but the problems of the revolution could not be solved merely by spreading ideas. He had already told the peasants at Podolsk that an organization was necessary. He now looked at the problem again, seeking for historical examples to help him understand how to move from an open confession of Socialist ideas to real action. Above all it was essential to recognize the right moment. 'The worst enemy of the people could not act differently from the agents of the secret police at Naples at the time of the Bourbons when they provoked a few men to rebel against overwhelming forces . . . I tell the peasants that to lift up their heads so as to offer a target for bullets is stupid and leads to nothing. Arms are needed before anything else.'

His experiences of the various movements that followed the decree of 19th February convinced him that the peasants ought to look for help and

10+

guidance. They would certainly not find this among 'the capitalists or the rich landowners'. The only men capable of 'putting themselves at the head of the movement' would be those 'who in Germany are called "natural proletarians"', i.e. educated people who feel suffocated by the present order of things, and who, though their hands are tied, feel that they would be capable of doing something in different circumstances'.

And I advise the peasants, if they revolt, to make for the towns where they will meet with success and obtain money and arms. I am firmly convinced that if the peasants of some villages revolted and seized a town or sent delegates and messengers to other villages, they would win over to their side the soldiers and the peasants of other centres.

It was the duty of the intelligentsia to provide a movement of this kind with some programme. 'What enormous help we could give if we all got together and wrote a manifesto' and spread it in the villages.

It is not necessary to print an appeal designed to stimulate an armed revolt. We must give the peasants exact ideas on the Tsar, on land and on the people. For the moment the peasants deplore the fact that they know nothing, and they think that the Tsar will do everything for their good. But soon disillusionment will come. Even now, cautiously and hesitantly, it is beginning to destroy this idea.

And so 'a manifesto of this kind, or better still a plan of action from the social party was all the more needed'.

It was not that past experience must be repeated: such as, for instance, preparing a revolt in the army and then dragging in the people, as had been done at Naples. The peasants themselves must act, marching on the towns and seizing everything needed for success, above all arms and money.

There are two different ways of putting oneself at the head of the people's movement; either, like Louis Blanc, by infiltrating into the masses, spreading pamphlets among the workers, denouncing competition, business and everything that both physically and morally oppresses and kills the worker: or, like Barbès, by putting oneself at the head of every movement and making one's name the name of every popular party, so that in time of need the people would turn to us as the men who have prepared the ground. With us in Russia at the present moment Louis Blanc's method is not feasible. That leaves the way chosen by Barbès. It is true that it demands many sacrifices. It demands that those who share these ideas should always be ready for any action, however dangerous. But it is the only way possible, the only one that can lead to victory.[7]

As can be seen, Zaichnevsky had made his choice. At the age of nineteen he had read a few classics of Western Socialism and some history books; and he had been in contact with the peasants fired by the reforms. These experiences were sufficient to turn him to Jacobinism and to attempt to apply the lessons of Barbès to the contemporary situation in Russia.

It is not surprising that when Alexander II got hold of this letter he noted on the margin: 'The content is so criminal and dangerous that I consider it necessary to arrest immediately both Zaichnevsky and Argiropulo and to bring them here with all their papers. I want to know who they are.'

Their activities had in fact provoked a number of denunciations, among them one from the Metropolitan of Moscow. Filaret had written to the Tsar in May 1861, saying that he knew that 'in the University of Moscow, both anti-religious and political works are lithographed and circulated'. He ended by hoping that 'the God of truth will strike down the intrigues of the enemies of the Faith and Fatherland, and will preserve the throne of Your Majesty in peace, strength and glory'.[8]

Zaichnevsky and Argiropulo were imprisoned, and the inquiries that followed led to a few other arrests. They were taken to St Petersburg and then back again to Moscow.

But, despite this, the group that they had founded survived. The original impulse had been strong and its effect lasted, as was shown later by the student demonstrations in the autumn of 1861. The members of Zaichnevsky's group took an active part in the various phases of these disturbances and distinguished themselves by their ruthless support for the campaign launched by Ogarev and Herzen from London. The students, they said, should leave those towns whose universities had been closed, and travel throughout Russia so as to get to know the country and gain recognition. 'To the people, to the people', said the *Kolokol* of 1st November, expressing one of its brilliant general ideas. The idea stirred some deep emotion which might develop in any direction according to circumstances. Everything would depend on how the students of St Petersburg and Moscow greeted the idea. Some of the latter interpreted it as an appeal to leave the university as a demonstration and protest. But when they tried to do this, they saw that it was not easy. The sacrifice was too great; and only about thirty carried the plan through. Their gesture, however, remained an example for the future, This unsuccessful attempt marked the final dissolution of Zaichnevsky's and Argiropulo's group.

The prison to which Zaichnevsky and Argiropulo were sent in Moscow was very much *sui generis*. As was usual in Paris at the time, so in Moscow too, their cell was transformed into a small club, where university students met for discussions. Anyone could come and talk to the two men in prison. Friends brought them flowers, fruit, food, and even the latest papers of interest (including ones published clandestinely) and stayed until nine in the evening and later. Besides this Zaichnevsky left the prison every now and then 'for a bath' accompanied by a guard, in whose company he would go for a walk with a friend. The prison would have been ideal if hygienic conditions had not been so disgusting. Argiropulo soon caught typhus and died.[9]

Such were the circumstances in which the manifesto *Young Russia* came into being, as Zaichnevsky himself explained many years later. The police never knew anything of its origin, and this mystery deepened the impression of horror and fear which it was to produce in conservative and liberal circles when it was put into circulation. The author later said:

We wanted to tell the truth at last, the truth which some were afraid to tell, others could not, and yet others did not want to. Everyone was bluffing, lying, waiting for good from above. All this was so disgusting and oppressive that if we had not acted ourselves, someone else would have done so in our place.[10]

And so he wanted to use his manifesto to express a violent protest. He declared that his aim was 'to make all the liberal and reactionary devils sick'.

It is difficult to be certain who were his collaborators in prison, and it is probable that even his own later recollections are not quite accurate. He said that the young poet I. I. Golts-Miller was responsible for adding to the manifesto everything dealing with the abolition of marriage and the family.[11] Among others who took part were probably members of the student group which was breaking up during the months following the arrests and demonstrations. In any case they were responsible for printing what had been written in the prison cell after they had successfully smuggled it out with the help of a guard. For this purpose the printing press which they had recently bought was taken to the house of a student in the Ryazan province, Pavel Korovin, who had been temporarily sent down from the university. It was decided to distribute the printed copies mainly in St Petersburg so as to divert the attention of the police from Moscow. At the beginning of May 1862 the pamphlets began to circulate, and spread rapidly outside the capital.

'Russia is entering the revolutionary stage of its existence', the manifesto began. This was no longer merely an expression of the growing distrust that Serno-Solovevich had felt for the machinery of the Russian government. It was already an expression of absolute faith in a new force. Revolution was latent in the very order of things; no middle way was possible; there was no more room for reforms or palliatives. There were two social groups, two 'parties' facing each other: the party of the Emperor, made up of all the wealthy and ruling classes, however liberal their ideas; and the party of 'the people' in constant revolt against the authorities, though this revolt might be open or concealed, according to circumstances. 'This antagonism cannot end as long as the present economic régime lasts. Under this régime a small number of people who own capital control the fate of the rest', and 'everything is false, everything is stupid, from religion . . . to the family.' Only one thing could spring from this state of affairs: 'a revolution, a bloody and pitiless revolution, a revolution which must change everything down to the very roots, utterly overthrowing all the foundations of present society and bringing about the ruin of all who support the present order'. The manifesto recalled the revolts of Pugachev and Stenka Razin and the peasant risings of the 'thirties, which, in the Western provinces, 'cut the landowners to pieces', and the most recent one of all, led by 'the noble Anton Petrov.

We do not fear this revolution, even though we know that rivers of blood will flow and that perhaps even innocent victims will perish.'

Compared to this vision, the peasant reform appeared 'idiotic' and the policy of repression merely stupid. 'Give us more banishments and more examples.' All this would only hasten the coming of the revolution.

This was followed by two paragraphs criticizing the *Kolokol*. Zaichnevsky was a profound admirer of Herzen. Indeed he had chosen as a slogan for his 'proclamation' words taken from Herzen's essay on Owen; and it was from Herzen that he had derived his first Socialist convictions. But he now accused him of having deserted his original standpoint and gone over to liberalism.

Herzen's reactionary phase dates from 1849. Alarmed by the failure of the revolution, he lost all faith in violent upheavals. Two or three unsuccessful revolts in Milan; the exile and death of a few French republicans; and lastly the execution of Orsini—finally put out his revolutionary fire. And he set himself to run a review of liberal tendencies and nothing more.

Herzen had of course had a great influence on Russian society, but he had disappointed the younger generation because he had not been able to affirm 'the principles on which the new society must be built'. Zaichnevsky in fact resumed the attack made by Chernyshevsky and Dobrolyubov, contrasting the *Kolokol* with the 'Herzen who was once prepared to greet the revolution of 1848, and reproach Ledru Rollin and Louis Blanc for their hesitation in not seizing the dictatorship when this was possible, and leading France along the road of bloody reforms to the triumph of the workers'. Now, however, he had slid into a purely constitutional position and was discussing reforms with the Tsar.

Zaichnevsky did not conceal the reasons which had led Herzen along this road. His attack was harsh and bitter, but it displays considerable knowledge of Herzen's thought which he had studied and interpreted with a love marred by disappointment. It might be objected, he said, that the history of the West showed that violent revolutions always led to tyranny and that 'every revolution creates its Napoleon'. It might be thought that this was the reason why Herzen had abandoned his original ideas. Yet Herzen himself had explained that the reason for failure of the revolution was very different.

The revolution had ended in failure through a lack of extremism in the men who were at its head. Not for nothing have we studied the history of the West. We will go further, not only than the poor revolutionaries of 1848, but also than the great terrorists of the 1790's.

Zaichnevsky in fact was adopting the views that Herzen had held in 1849 and pushing them to their logical extremes.

The reasons which led him to criticize the *Kolokol* inevitably made him attack the *Velikoruss*. This paper also had had an immense success, which was easy to foresee in view of the social forces which it had represented.

Though it satisfied the needs of our liberal society—i.e. the mass of landowners anxious to oppose the government but fearful of even the shadow of a revolution which might threaten to swallow them—and also those of a large number of utterly talentless writers who are out of date and forgotten (but who in the time of Nicholas were considered progressive), the *Velikoruss* has never been able to create a party around itself. It was read, people spoke of it, and that's where it ended.

Among the revolutionaries it had inspired only 'a smile'. The same could be said of all the other manifestos and proclamations so frequent at the time. They lacked clear principles and gave themselves liberal airs.

Having chased its adversaries from the field, *Young Russia* suggested a positive plan of battle. 'We wish to replace the present despotic régime with a federal-republican union of regions. All power must therefore pass into the hands of national and regional assemblies. We do not know into how many regions Russia will be divided, and which regions will consist of which departments. The population itself will have to solve these problems.' Each region was to be composed of rural *obshchinas*, whose members were all to enjoy the same rights. Everyone was to belong to one of these communities. The *mir* would be responsible for granting everyone a strip of land which could, however, be refused or hired out, thus allowing anyone to live outside the *obshchina*, as long as he paid the levy which it would lay down. Land would not be granted for life, but only for a given number of years, after which holdings were to be redistributed. Other property was to be granted for life and would return to the community only on the death of the tenant.

The national and regional assemblies were to be elected by universal suffrage. Their powers, at least in theory, were to be very wide:

The national assembly will decide all questions of foreign policy and see that they are carried out. It will appoint the regional administrators and will decide the general rate of taxation. The regional assembly will decide questions which concern only the region in whose main town it meets.

The financial system was to be drawn up so that taxes would weigh 'not only on the poorest section of society but on the rich'. The *obshchina* would ensure that this principle was effectively carried out in each village.

Other economic activities would also be governed by similar principles.

We demand the creation of 'social' factories which must be run by people elected by society and must give society an account of the work done in them, within a given time limit. We demand the creation of shops in which the price of goods will correspond to their real worth and not to the whim of a merchant hoping to enrich himself as quickly as possible.

There followed a series of proposals such as free education, emancipation of women, abolition of monasteries, reduction in the length of military service, and increase in soldiers' pay.

Of greater interest was Zaichnevsky's position as regards the problem of nationalities:

We demand the complete independence of Poland and Lithuania which more than any other region have shown their desire not to remain united with Russia. We demand that each region be given the chance of deciding by a majority vote whether or not it wishes to form part of the Russian Federal Republic.

But, even more clearly than he had already done when speaking of regional autonomy, Zaichnevsky now made a distinction between his ideal programme and what could in fact be carried out. He said:

We know that it will not be possible to carry out this part of our programme at once. We are indeed firmly convinced that the revolutionary party, which (if the movement is successful) will be at the head of the government, will have to retain for a time the present system of centralization. This will certainly be necessary as regards politics, if not the administration, in order to be able to introduce as quickly as possible the new foundations of society and the economy. It will have to take the dictatorship into its own hands and stop at nothing. The elections for the National Assembly will have to be carried out under the influence of the Government, which must at once make sure that the supporters of the present régime do not take part—that is, if any of them are still alive. The French National Assembly of 1848 has shown what happens when the revolutionary government does not interfere in the elections; it led to the destruction of the Republic and the election of Louis Napoleon as Emperor.

To achieve this, *Young Russia* intended to base itself mainly on 'the people'. This meant primarily the peasants, and Zaichnevsky had great hopes in the *Raskolniki*. Then there was the army; officers angered at the Court's despotism and the shameful duties imposed upon them—especially that of opening fire on the peasants and the Poles. 'But our greatest hope lies in the young . . . The young generation contains everything that is best in Russia, everything that is alive, all those who are ready to sacrifice themselves for the good of the people.' It was from the younger generation—and this meant from the students and young intellectuals—that the revolutionary party would emerge.

The day will soon come when we will unfurl the great banner of the future, the red banner. And with a mighty cry of 'Long live the Russian Social and Democratic Republic' we will move against the Winter Palace to wipe out all who dwell there. It may be that we will only have to destroy the imperial family, i.e. about a hundred people. But it may also happen, and this is more likely, that the whole imperial party will rise like a man to follow the Tsar, because for them it will be a question of life and death. If this happens, with full faith in ourselves and our forces, and in the support of the people and in the glorious future of Russia—which destiny has ordained shall be the first country to realize the great cause of Socialism—we will cry 'To your axes' and then we will strike the imperial party without sparing our blows just as they do not spare theirs against us. We will destroy them in the squares, if the cowardly swine dare to go there. We will destroy them in their houses, in the narrow streets of the towns, in the broad avenues of the capital, and in the villages. Remember that, when this happens, anyone who is not with us is against us, and an enemy, and that every method is used to destroy an enemy.

And if the revolution does not succeed, if we have to pay with our lives for the bold attempt to give men human rights, we will go to the scaffold without trembling and without fear. And as we lay down our heads or put them in the noose, we will cry our great cry: 'Long live the Social and Democratic Republic!'

This document has been quoted at length because it marks an important phase in the history of the revolutionary movements. The writings of the *Zemlya i Volya* groups had contained many of the fundamental elements of Populism. Here something new seems to emerge, which Zaichnevsky, taking a cue from his reading of history, has called by a most appropriate name—Russian Jacobinism. And it must be added that, while in the works of *Zemlya i Volya* we do not yet find a complete expression of Populist thought, *Young Russia*, on the other hand, for all its intemperance and obvious desire to cause a scandal, does reveal a clear and mature set of beliefs.

This set of beliefs sprang from ground very similar to that which had given birth to *Zemlya i Volya*. Jacobinism was an attempt to answer exactly the same problems. In both systems the protagonists were young intellectuals, and the object was the 'people'. The ideals of community and federation were the same, though more explicit in the Moscow group. But whereas *Zemlya i Volya* had felt only hesitant distrust in the ability of the State to bring about any change in Russian life, *Young Russia* was openly contemptuous. This led Zaichnevsky to two conclusions: on the one hand, nihilism and the ultimate stage of the theories (which had originated in the Enlightenment) directed against the family, religion, etc., and, on the other, a growing faith in a revolutionary party capable of solving all problems through a dictatorship.

In its historical references, terminology and means of expression, *Young Russia* was more 'Western' than the other currents and ideas of its time. It spoke of regions, but did not claim that they were still differentiated by historical traditions. One tradition only was accepted: that of the peasant revolts. And this was accepted because of its revolutionary value as a complete counter to the State. The National Assembly which *Young Russia* envisaged was obviously closer to the Convention than to the revived *Zemsky Sobor* mentioned by Herzen, Ogarev and *Zemlya i Volya*. Even the title of Zaichnevsky's manifesto, *Young Russia*, which he chose as a symbol of his planned Central Revolutionary Committee, was obviously taken from Mazzini whom, as we have seen, he also quoted in his letters. In his declaration to the police, Zaichnevsky said: 'I consider it my duty to affirm before everything else that I have never distinguished the fate of Russia from that of the West, and that when speaking of the need for a social revolution, I have based myself largely on facts provided by Western publicists.' It was from them that he had obtained his central idea, that of a revolutionary dictatorship. His studies of the revolution of 1848 had revealed the figure of Barbès and that of 1789 had shown him Robespierre.

Yet we cannot understand *Young Russia* if it is regarded merely as an imitation of Western doctrines. Zaichnevsky looked beyond these doctrines to see what was really happening in Russia. Mazzini's 'now and always' had provided him with the moral impulse to declare openly his own view of the truth; this was to be characteristic of all the Populists, and eventually it drove them 'to the people'. The Jacobin tradition had helped him to formulate his idea of a revolutionary dictatorship. But the content of this idea was Populist. His social ideal remained that of the *obshchina*, the *mir*, the *oblasty*. His policies were still aimed at the peasants, and even the *Raskolniki*.

Both Populism and Jacobinism sprang out of the revolutionary movement of the 'sixties. *Young Russia* merely proposed a ruthless political method for bringing into effect a programme which was common to all the Populists: communal ownership of the land with redistribution laid down by general rules and carried out by village assemblies. The aim of this Jacobinism was not, in fact, democracy but peasant Socialism. And it was this characteristic —this specific element of 'Russian Jacobinism'—which found such surprising and precocious expression in this manifesto.

And so it was not merely for its juvenile outbursts (which have led a Soviet historian to speak of its 'infantile disease')[12] that this manifesto attracted the attention of its contemporaries. Herzen's reaction is of particular interest. He drew attention to its crude Westernism. 'It is not Russian', he wrote. 'It is a variation on the theme of Western Socialism, a metaphysic of the French Revolution . . . What chance is there of the Russian people rising in the name of Socialism or of Blanqui, to the shout of "Long Live the Russian Democratic and Social Republic" when it will completely fail to understand three of these words?' He then made deeper objections. 'Decentralization is the first condition for a transformation which can come from the fields, from the countryside. The people must be taught not Feuerbach or Babeuf, but a religion of the land which it can understand.' This brought to light the division, which was apparent at its birth, between Populism and Russian Jacobinism. And in his profound criticism of Babeuvism, Herzen propounded a theoretical justification of his standpoint. In *My Past and Thoughts* he contrasted Owen and Babeuf, and made a detailed examination of the documents of the Conspiracy of Equals, so as to emphasize all its tyrannical and statist features.[13]

Bakunin, too, stood out against this new Moscow Jacobinism in his pamphlet *The People's Cause: Romanov, Pugachev or Pestel?* which was published in London at the beginning of September 1862. This was mainly

10*

an appeal for the unity of all those forces which were acting on behalf of the people's cause. They should not pay too much regard to the small minority of young men who had expressed ideas inimical to the feelings of most Russians.

They shout and decide questions as if the entire people stood behind them. But the people are still on the other side of the abyss, and not only do not want to listen to us but are ready to knock us down at the first sign from the Tsar . . . I accuse the writers of *Young Russia* of two crimes. First of a mad and really doctrinaire scorn for the people; and secondly of an attitude which is utterly devoid of tact and which is quite frivolous in face of the great cause of emancipation, for whose success they say they are ready to sacrifice their lives. They are so little used to real action that they move in a world of abstractions.

Some years later Bakunin changed his mind and praised *Young Russia*. But even then he saw it mainly as an expression of a general revolutionary spirit. He always tended to distrust men who were unable to put themselves in unison with 'popular ideas' and the peasants. Bakunin, in fact, felt that this Jacobinism contained a different element both from his reforming Populism of 1862 and also from what was later to be his anarchist Populism.

Chernyshevsky, too, criticized *Young Russia*, mainly from the angle of immediate political considerations. He was at first contemptuous of these exalted young men who made such inopportune statements. He seems to have sent A. A. Sleptsov, one of the most active members of the embryonic *Zemlya i Volya*, to Moscow to give them advice and warning.[14] And then he had a moment of repentance. Would not his attitude discourage the best and most decisive among them? He saw in fact that a detailed reply was needed, and he wanted to call this 'To our Best Friends'. But his arrest prevented him from writing it. Relations between Chernyshevsky and Zaichnevsky combined admiration and hostility. The Jacobin, who spent all his life trying to turn himself into a professional revolutionary, said of Chernyshevsky that he would do better to carry on with his studies. 'He is now turning to a trade which is not his. He is a man of learning. Let him stick to his books. Instead he has begun to collect people in committees. And just look whom he has managed to find—Panteleyev, Zhuk, etc!'[15]

An interesting reply to *Young Russia* was discovered by the police when, on 15th June 1862, they searched the house of a student called Ballod, who, as will be remembered, had organized a small clandestine printing press. This reply gives us our best information about the reaction which *Young Russia* provoked in the circles of *Zemlya i Volya*.[16]

A revolutionary party by itself never has the strength to overturn the State. We have an example of this in the many attempts made by the Paris republicans and Communists, all of which were easily suppressed by a few battalions of soldiers. Revolutions are made by the people . . . We are revolutionaries; this does not mean men who make revolutions, but men who love the people so much that they do not abandon them when (under no pressure from us) they fling themselves into the fight. We implore the public to help us in our efforts to reduce the severity of the revolution which the people are preparing. And, as we pity the educated classes, we implore them not to under-estimate the danger which threatens them.[17]

While the members of *Young Russia* were already thinking in terms of terror to keep themselves in power, those of *Zemlya i Volya* were playing a cat and mouse game with the educated and liberal classes. The latter were more immediately 'realistic'; the former more long-term. But the members of *Zemlya i Volya* had, despite everything, one great advantage over those of *Young Russia.* Their 'love for the people' was leading them to make profounder and more powerful attempts to get into contact with the masses.

As has been seen, *Young Russia* met with a hostile and highly critical reception. Kozmin, however, the historian who has made the most minute study of this period, has published some interesting documents about the circles where the manifesto met with a warm welcome. It was read and discussed by the students at some Sunday-schools. One of these students was even inspired by it to write a political dictionary, one of whose entries was as follows: '*Liberal*—a man who loves liberty, generally a noble; for example, landlords, landed aristocrats. These men like looking at liberty from windows and doing nothing, and then go for a stroll and on to theatres and balls. That is what is called a Liberal.'[18]

Though Panteleyev's memoirs say that 'among the young men in St Petersburg, *Young Russia* did not meet with a warm reception and, if it did circulate, this was merely because young men of the time thought it their duty to spread every kind of proclamation',[19] even in the capital there was a small group which not only accepted Zaichnevsky's ideas but even made them a basis for their own autonomous activities.

At the centre of this group was a university student called Leonid Olshevsky. He had taken part in the demonstrations of 1861 and had been banished to his native district in the department of Kovno, but he had soon returned to St Petersburg. Scarcely had he arrived there before he was denounced and sent to prison on 15th May. His house was searched in vain and he was freed. But a second denunciation led to the discovery of material which he himself had prepared. What he thought of the situation was obvious from a note which was found on him. 'It's absolutely essential that Alexander II should depart for the other world as quickly as possible; otherwise everything will go to the dogs and we will have to pay.' He too was expressing one of the fundamental feelings of this time: the desire to save the educated classes by eliminating the autocracy as quickly as possible. But even more interesting is another work seized from him on this occasion, called *To the Russian People* (*A Tale by Uncle Kuzmich*).[20] When he was questioned he began by saying that this was merely a résumé of what he had read about the events of 1846 in Galicia. Later, however, he admitted that it was a version of *Young Russia* written in simple and often deliberately popular language. He added that these ideas had struck root in his mind when in May 1862 he had been in his department of Kovno and had seen the conditions of the peasants there.

The work was written in the form of a tale told by a peasant (Kuzmich) to other peasants. It spoke of poverty: 'No, brothers, it is not God who has put the landlords above us. It is not He who has made the peasants live their life in such bitterness. But men have done this out of ill-will.' It then spoke of land, of recruits, and of robberies. It followed this with an imaginary dialogue between Kuzmich and a young student, who personified the hopes and desires of these groups of young Populists. 'Some time ago I came across a lad who was neither a landlord nor a merchant. He was dressed as we are in a red shirt, but he did not speak like us. He spoke so gently and well that it was a joy to hear him.' And the dialogue slowly turned on the need for the peasants to cure themselves of the ills which afflicted them. Why not take up their axes? The student said that the land was theirs, that it could not belong to the Tsar, seeing that he was indifferent to the good of the State. And it added that everything that the clergy said was untrue. It looked forward to a time when the people would rule themselves, 'when all will be equal, both peasants and landlords . . . That time is not far off. We just have to wait and think for ourselves and destroy all oppressors with our axes.'

Associated with Olshevsky at this time was P. N. Tkachev, who later became the leader and philosopher of Russian Jacobinism. It is interesting to see that even now he was looking for a road very similar to that pointed out by Zaichnevsky and was probably under his direct influence.

The effect which the spread of these ideas made on society was all the greater in that the proclamation of *Young Russia* coincided with a series of violent fires which devastated St Petersburg and other Russian towns and which the official press was quick to attribute to the work of 'nihilists' and revolutionaries.

One of the most important commercial centres of the capital, the Apraksin Dvor, was burnt to ashes. Throughout May 1862 the fires increased in number. The *St Petersburger Zeitung* was the first to accuse the subversives. Leskov, the well-known writer, acted as spokesman for this campaign, which was inspired by the police. By 25th June, twenty-two people were in prison, and during the following fortnight another fifteen went to join them, generally foreigners, peasants and soldiers. The documents concerning them have been lost except for one case, that of a schoolmaster who was condemned as an incendiary to fifteen years in prison. The treatment that these unfortunate men met with can easily be imagined when it is realized that there were constant proposals in official circles to reintroduce torture.

It is more than likely that these outbreaks of fire were entirely accidental. Such events were not unusual in Russian towns, which were so often built of wood. Some have thought that they were provoked by the government itself. Kropotkin, for example, believed this, and the theory has recently been upheld by a Soviet historian.[21] But the vast majority of orthodox public opinion believed the charges against Herzen, *Zemlya i Volya* and above all the mysterious and violent *Young Russia*. There was, in fact, a wave of panic and a frantic witch-hunt. All this well reflects the atmosphere of anxiety and doubt which led the young generation to believe in an immediate revolution and drove the government along the road of repression.

We must now return to Zaichnevsky who was in prison in Moscow. In December 1862 he was sentenced by a Commission of Senators to two years and eight months' confinement, to be followed by banishment to Siberia. In explanation of this relatively light sentence it must be remembered that the authorities did not know that he was the author of *Young Russia*. He was being condemned merely because of his activities as 'a preacher and confessor of Socialism'. The Tsar reduced the period of confinement to one year. On 10th January 1863 he left for Siberia in secret, as student demonstrations were feared. He lived for some time in the department of Irkutsk and was able to make some contacts with Polish exiles living there or passing through on their way to exile. He remained in Siberia until 1869, when he was allowed to live in the department of Penza in European Russia.[22]

There he was able to resume his work as a conspirator. With great patience and in spite of many difficulties he collected a group of students and soldiers. He tried to approach the local ruling classes so as to influence them and win over those people who he thought could eventually be induced to join a revolutionary party. These activities led to a series of searches and he was transferred to various departments one after another, until in 1872 he reached Orel where he had been born and where ten years earlier he had begun his attempts at direct propaganda.

In the town of Orel he soon became the centre of all the younger revolutionary generation. 'Organization, and still more organization' was still his motto. He was openly against terrorism and public demonstrations. His aim was to teach people how to act when the revolution broke out and immediately afterwards. With this went some contempt for the masses who 'are always on the side of the *fait accompli*'. He was aware that these convictions made him an isolated figure in the world of Populists. But in 1875 he was able to re-form his connections with Tkachev's movement, and he became one of his few supporters in Russia.

Despite his criticisms, he took part in the demonstration in front of the Cathedral of Our Lady of Kazan in St Petersburg, which marked the birth of a public Socialist movement in Russia. Here again he did not hesitate to insist that greater organization was vital. His presence in this demonstration was doubly illegal because he was still compelled to live in the department of Orel. And so he was again banished to Siberia. He went there in 1880, and five years later was once again back in Orel, where he intensified his conspiratorial activities—not without considerable success. He began to evolve an extensive network of supporters which remained intact until 1889, when, almost by chance, his adherents were discovered, arrested and condemned. He himself spent two years in prison waiting for his trial. Then he was sent back to Siberia for another five years; there he was able to contribute to a local paper, *The Eastern Observer*, and for two years, from 1894 to 1895, he wrote articles on foreign policy. His friend, G. N. Potanin, later said that 'Zaichnevsky ran the paper on straight party lines, changing it from a local paper reflecting local interests to an organ of the party to which he belonged in European Russia. Siberian problems vanished from its pages, and were replaced by long articles on the working class movement in Europe, such as the one in Belgium.'

So, until the very end of his life, he remained faithful to his tactical and political Jacobinism and to the ties which, since his earliest youth, had bound him to the problems of Western European Socialism.

He was able to pay one last visit to European Russia. He went to Smolensk on 19th March 1896 and he died there shortly afterwards.

He had managed to educate a number of young men for the coming battle but they often left him to join neighbouring movements. His Jacobinism was too isolated to be able to attract people less intractable than himself. But his preaching left deep marks on these young men. One of his most active followers, Marya Nikolaevna Oshanina, was a member of the Executive Committee of *Narodnaya Volya*.[23] He had considerable influence on Nikolay Sergeyevich Rusanov, the future theoretician of the Socialist-Revolutionary party.[24] Others, such as Vasily Petrovich Artsibushev, M. I. Golubeva, Orlov and Romanov, became Social Democrats. But Zaichnevsky's influence had obviously taken root, for they soon went over to the Bolsheviks.

12. THE KAZAN CONSPIRACY

THE 'Circle of Kazan Students at Moscow University' certainly showed considerable vitality. As early as 1859 it had its own political organization which, by widening and adapting, it was able to retain longer than other groups of the same kind. It has already been mentioned in connection with the earliest activities of Zaichnevsky and Argiropulo, the founders of *Young Russia*. We have seen it too transformed into one of the most active and least disciplined sections of *Zemlya i Volya*. And now it crops up again in the first phase of the tragic episode known in Russian history as 'The Kazan Conspiracy'.

This unsuccessful conspiracy, which was to cost five lives, throws light on the life of the local provincial sections of *Zemlya i Volya*; on the overlapping of the problems of the Russian peasants and Polish nationalism; and on the atmosphere of waiting and fear which followed the emancipation of the serfs.[1]

The 'Library of Kazan Students' had been founded by Yury Mikhailovich Molosov and Nikolay Satilov. They were both of noble origin, and Satilov was four or five years the younger of the two. They had both been dismissed from the university for taking part in disorders aimed at expelling a professor from Moscow in 1858. They had both become railway technicians. In 1862 they entered the Moscow section of *Zemlya i Volya*, and became its leading spirits. But their ideas scarcely harmonized with the Populism, as yet not very different from Liberalism, which inspired the young founders of *Zemlya i Volya* in St Petersburg. The 'Library' therefore maintained an autonomous organization. Molosov's programme has been lost, but it was later summed up by someone who heard him in person: 'Regional administration with a central assembly in St Petersburg and Moscow. All the land must belong to the State and must be let out for a fixed period; private property must be abolished; woman must enjoy the same rights as man.'[2] If this is a true summary, Molosov's programme seems to have been closer to *Young Russia* than to *Zemlya i Volya*. Though we can say that the extremist opinions of these young students were probably due to the particularly bad conditions of the peasants in their native provinces, it is difficult to follow their thought in any detail. Molosov was arrested in 1863 and after a long stay in prison was sentenced on 6th April 1866 to deprivation of all civil rights and banishment for life in Siberia. It is true that in March 1870 he was allowed to return to Saratov in European Russia, but thereafter he took no further part in conspiracies and resumed his life as a railway technician. The fate of his comrade Satilov ran a very similar, indeed parallel, course.

The 'Library' that they founded in Moscow reflected the heated atmosphere of Kazan University. For some years Kazan had been the centre of student disturbances which were probably the most violent, prolonged and varied in kind of all similar movements of the time. The demonstrations had begun early. In 1857 a student called Ivan Umov was sent to the army for three years for having insulted the university authorities. This led to a collective protest on the part of his companions, which was followed by a series of administrative steps aimed against those professors who had been the original cause of the demonstrations.[3] Incidents of this kind soon gave rise to the birth of compact groups of students.

These student groups were inspired by the ambition to administer not only their own lives but the University itself. They were as much organs of self-administration as instruments for imposing their will on the teaching staff and the State. In 1857 a cooperative bank was started followed by a library, which naturally soon began to include forbidden books, such as those of Herzen. A student tribunal was formed which virtually confirmed this increasingly powerful corporate life. From 1859 to 1861 the students demanded the dismissal of professors who, when they would not voluntarily capitulate, were systematically obstructed. Within this organization political groups were formed which held regular meetings and discussed reviews and books.

In the autumn of 1861 the disorders in St Petersburg led to trouble in Kazan. The university was handed over to the military, who kept it closed for some time. Many students were dismissed. Once again such steps only led to new recruits joining the more specifically political movements.

We know little of the exact structure of the clandestine organization which existed at Kazan in 1862 and which now joined *Zemlya i Volya*. It is, however, obvious that here too it consisted of student groups crystallized round the stronger and more influential personalities. We hear, for instance, of a group of fifty, led by a doctor, which included Polinovsky, Sergeyev, Zhemanov, Ivan Orlov, and others. This was called 'the oldest group', and at the time of the conspiracy it was probably the strongest and most active. Despite this its members said that, because of lack of means and military experience, they too were waiting for the word to come from St Petersburg and Moscow. The doctor who led them was probably called Burger. He had been educated at the university and had taken part in the movements of the preceding years. He had then become the university doctor. Though this was the most organized group, the ideological centre of Kazan was to be found in that which derived from the historical-philological faculty. Its members met once a week to read and talk.

Ivan Markovich Krasnoperov, a student and member of these groups, has given us a strikingly vivid picture of the intense, almost feverish, life of a large provincial university at the time. He too, like so many of his friends, came from a clerical family. During his last years at the seminary, he had read only contemporary literature, above all Chernyshevsky and Dobrolyubov. 'In our eyes his [Dobrolyubov's] image was almost surrounded with a halo.'[4] One of his friends, Alexander Alexandrovich Krasovsky, who was later killed in the revolutionary struggle, brought him back news of the two great writers from St Petersburg. The pages which record the impressions of Krasnoperov and his friends in the Vyatka seminary on receiving this news are among the most interesting examples of the enthusiasm with which the younger generation, even in the smallest provincial towns, greeted the *Sovremennik*.

When Dobrolyubov died, the students in the seminary had a Mass celebrated for him and sang the responses with particular enthusiasm. And when during the ceremony the words of the liturgy 'Eternal memory' were spoken, Krasnoperov stood up and made a speech in which he expressed his love for the dead man. 'Let the old insult you and hate you as a corruptor of the younger generation. But this younger generation loves you for your ideas and derides the obscurantists. It is full of pride and faith in itself and in the life which you have pointed out to it.'

A most curious contrast to this atmosphere of youthful enthusiasm is provided by the trouble Krasnoperov got into with the head of the seminary: 'You spoke in church? How dare you defile the temple of God with your pagan words? It is sacrilege.' 'I said nothing wrong, Father Inspector, I only said that Dobrolyubov taught us how to think and that he was a great writer.' 'Oh you stupid, cretinous boys! To learn how to think from society's most dangerous enemies! It is logic which teaches one to think. Read and digest the manuals of logic written by Karpov, Barkhov and Bakhman.'

Krasnoperov was forgiven; but he scarcely had the means to leave the seminary to go to Kazan University. He decided, if necessary, to cover the four hundred *versts* from Vyatka to Kazan on foot. But his friends helped him, and he went to Kazan by boat, taking with him only two books (the Russian translation of Schlosser's *History of the 18th Century* and Feuerbach's *The Essence of Christianity*). When he reached Kazan, he at first had to sleep on the floor. He then gradually took more and more part in the variegated life of the students who lived in 'that temple of the sciences'. They had recently given up the uniform enforced by Nicholas I, and they were dressed in the strangest fashion. They lived in small self-helping communities, often in conditions of complete destitution. Their idol was Shchapov: 'They thought, they lived with his ideas'. They read mainly history books, and Krasnoperov's memoirs show clearly what they were looking for. When he was arrested on 17th March 1863, he was not only accused of having taken part in the conspiracy which will shortly be described, but also of having written a pamphlet called *French Carbonarism*. The content of this work is not known, but its very title is interesting. He and his friends were searching for methods of organization and a revolutionary tradition. That the others were moving along the same lines is proved by a curious piece of information handed on by Herzen, according to which these students had adopted as their regulations those of the 'Illuminati' of Adam Weishaupt.[5] This seems to be true, although there is no confirmation for the story.

In later years Krasnoperov remained faithful to the study of European revolutionary movements. From March 1863 to August 1867 he was in prison, first at Vyatka and then for a longer period in the fortress of Kazan. In that two-storeyed tower he continued the life of reading and discussion that he had led as a free man. The university library provided him with books, and so he was able to read Holbach's *System of Nature*, Cabet's *Voyage to Icaria* and also Fourier, Proudhon, Louis Blanc and Boerne. He read Engels's *Condition of the Working Classes in England* and translated it for his friends. But he was unable to obtain two books which he specially wanted—Louis Blanc's *History of Ten Years*, and the works of Lassalle. One day, after he had saved up his pay for three or four months, he got permission to come out of prison accompanied by a guard. He went to the only foreign bookshop in the town and found the books that he was looking for. He paid for them and took them back to his cell, incidentally giving the German bookseller a bad fright at the sight of the policeman.

In prison he learnt Italian. He used a New Testament to practise on in the absence of other books or a grammar. 'I was extraordinarily interested in the fortunes of Italy . . . the age of Dante, Boccaccio and Petrarch, when the struggle of the bourgeoisie with the people and the Ghibellines was already fully developed. Dante's expulsion and the revolt of the Ciompi in Florence encouraged me to study that period in prison.' He began to write a book called *Florence in the 14th Century*, which was later published in a review.[6]

It has been worth while dwelling on Krasnoperov's memoirs, not because he played a leading rôle in Kazan at this time, but because he gives us the best picture of the discussions and the intellectual interests which animated the crowded, though penurious, meetings of the university students.

But we must now turn to another aspect of this movement. Intense political and conspiratorial experience, nourished by reading books which came in from the West, and a rapid application of their ideas to the situation of the peasants around the Volga, gave rise in Kazan as in Moscow to a typically Russian development—the movement 'to go to the people' and preach directly to it. The students called this the 'apostolate', and the word well expresses the atmosphere of religious enthusiasm which inspired them.

The first 'apostolic' pilgrimages we know of date from March 1863. They were inspired by a student called Ivan Yakovlevich Orlov. He was a Siberian and the son, like so many of his comrades, of a priest. He had been to the seminary at Irkutsk for two years, and there he had met Bakunin. And so when he arrived at the university he was probably already acquainted with ideas which his friends only discovered later. He soon became one of their leaders. He was treasurer of 'the oldest group', and then probably became a member of *Zemlya i Volya*. But their ideas did not satisfy him; he went around telling his comrades that 'some time ago a new society was founded, which has a social programme similar to that of *Zemlya i Volya* but more violent'. Compared to his dreams, even the programme of *Young Russia* might well have seemed feeble.

The main purpose of this society is to found a political-revolutionary sect, and to unleash all the anti-State passions of the people. This new society is in close contact with the followers of Mazzini. It is well-known that these followers do not worry too much about their methods, and in Italy they support, directly or indirectly, both banditry and looting.

Bakunin's young pupil seemed to be overtaking his master. In March 1863 he left Kazan to preach in the countryside. He took with him some of *Zemlya i Volya*'s leaflets, 'Freedom' and others dealing with the Polish problem. He also took a paper printed on the spot which began with the words 'For a long time, brothers, they have suffocated us.' The author of this is not known for certain, but it was very likely written by a student called Umov, who had been among the first to be dismissed from the university in 1857. He had written it at the end of 1862 and a year later had disappeared leaving no trace. He had however had time to give a short account, in a deliberately popular and not ineffective style, of what all his comrades felt about the situation. It was Umov's words that Orlov now prepared to use in speaking to the peasants. Not for nothing did the students say: 'that manifesto's all right, one of us wrote it'.

For a long time now, brothers, they have suffocated us, tortured us with work, beaten us with whips and the knout; for a long time they have carried off your wives and daughters to the gentry. All this you bore. And you hoped that the Father-Tsar would remember you in your poverty and protect you. And look how the Tsar has remembered you: five years ago he wrote a manifesto in which he said 'I want to free the peasants.' We believed the Tsar's words, and from our heart we prayed God for our liberator. But at that very moment the Tsar was summoning committees of landlords, and asking their advice. And now at last he has given us our freedom. Have you read all about this freedom? Have you examined it carefully? Have you thought about it? No one understands what sort of freedom it is. You have become free people, but they haven't given you the land. If you want the land, buy it with money, which is distilled from your blood. You have become free people, and the landlord does not dare touch you, but of course he can refer to the authorities, and they can banish half the village to Siberia.

He then returned to the subject of landlords and cheating officials, reminding his readers that the Tsar had sent his generals against the peasants. 'You will say: In whom can we put our hopes? Hope in yourselves, brothers, and obtain freedom by yourselves.' But this was only possible if there was general agreement. Then at last there would be freedom from landlords and officials. 'Demand free freedom with a single voice . . . The landlords' peasants are twenty-three million, those that depend on the Crown are thirty million. And among those in uniform there are men on the side of the people; it is they who have written this manifesto, and they will warn you of the right moment for rebellion.'

The most keenly felt problem here was the desperate attempt to find a political language which the peasants could understand. As to how this message could be made to reach them, Orlov for the time being could see only 'apostolic' missions. He collected letters of introduction to former students and priests in the towns and villages through which he had to travel. Krasnoperov gave him a letter for his brother who was a priest, which said that a clergyman 'could be of great use to the peasants through his preaching', and recommended him 'to be ready for the great cause of the revival in Russia'.

And so Orlov, accompanied by Mikhail Sulyatnikov, a student who was going home, made for Vyatka, distributing manifestos along the way. He went through the centres of Gladov, Svyatogye, and visited even the small villages to offer them his leaflets. Very soon the authorities began to get news of this strange traveller, and on 17th March, Sulyatnikov was arrested. Krasnoperov's letter of introduction was found on him, and he too was arrested. Orlov succeeded for the moment in escaping the police and reached Kazan.

M. K. Elpidin went on further 'apostolic' missions during this period. He had chosen as his field the region where his father was priest. In one little town he left someone in charge of distributing manifestos to the peasants as they came to market. The peasants were then to carry them back to the villages and have them read aloud by the public reader. Hardly had he got back to Kazan before he was arrested with two other students.[7] In his house the police found not only a number of illegal newspapers but also various manuscripts. Among these was an account of the doctrines of Buddha which 'contained blasphemies and the denial of the dogmas of the faith', in the words of the police report. He was sentenced to five years' hard labour, which was later reduced to two and a half. But a year later he succeeded in escaping abroad. For some years he was one of the most highly regarded of the young Russian exiles in Geneva.

The two students arrested with him were the brothers Evgraf and Ivan Dmitrevich Penkovsky. Ivan still had in his possession a work he had written in 1861 which contained strong views on the 'freedom of the people' (narodnaya volya) and which recalled Pugachev: 'He hanged landlords and seized towns. Now is the time to fight once more for truth, to wait for Pugachev, to follow him with axes in our hands, to strike down the officials and nobles, and to establish the principle of elections.' He ended this manifesto with a poem which demanded that not even the Tsar should be spared. At his interrogation he said that he had taken these lines from a manuscript newspaper written by the Kazan students.

Another member of the same group, Arkady Afanasevich Biryukov, also spent that spring travelling through the countryside. He left for the province of Ryazan with the New Testament, aiming to 'find out if the people was expecting something and see how it would react to an appeal to revolt'. But he returned somewhat discouraged. He had distributed tracts and read the Gospel 'but, I say to my comrades, the peasants listen without saying almost anything so that I do not understand what they are thinking. However, they like listening to the Gospel.' The goal of his second journey was the district of Spassk in which lay the village of Bezdna, centre of the revolt of 1861. But this time Biryukov returned thoroughly distressed. The frightened peasants had not allowed him to spend the night in their houses; in one village they had wanted to denounce him; in another they robbed him. Shortly afterwards he was arrested. He spent four years in prison, and when he finally got out, although he found work on a local newspaper, he was in such a state of despair that he became an alcoholic, and died in the gutter in 1881.

The results of the 'apostolate' were from the immediate point of view thoroughly negative. Compared to the small work of distributing manifestos and the few words spoken in the peasants' houses, arrests had been heavy. Political and sometimes even human contacts had been impossible. Such is the balance-sheet of every movement 'to go to the people'. Yet, taken as a whole, it constituted one of the most important—though still early and naïve—stages in the formation of the revolutionary groups. 'Apostolate' and conspiracy went hand in hand. And now having looked at the ground from which it grew, we must return to the conspiracy itself.

It was to these groups of Kazan students that the men of the Polish National Committee decided to look for help when they learnt that there was little to hope for from *Zemlya i Volya*.

At the beginning of 1863 a delegate of that Committee, Jerome Kienewicz, came to St Petersburg with yet another request for effective support. When he found that agreement with the organizations in the capital was impossible, he decided to act on his own.

His plans seemed to correspond to the peasants' state of mind during the years which immediately followed the emancipation, as the revolutionaries themselves had described it. It would be enough, he thought, to raise the banner of 'peasant liberty' to counter 'the landlords' liberty'.

Kienewicz thought that a false manifesto from the Tsar containing promises of this kind would be the best way to rouse the masses.[8] A manifesto on these lines was drawn up by Yuri Benzenger, a member of *Zemlya i Volya*, a student at Moscow University. During his short life Benzenger gave proof of rare courage. As soon as he had completed his studies in November 1862, he had joined the army and carried out active propaganda among his fellow soldiers. He was discovered and escaped, but soon afterwards was caught. In August 1863 he was leader of a prisoners' rebellion and was sentenced to seventeen years' hard labour by a military tribunal. Scarcely a year later, on 1st April 1864, he sent his superiors a memorandum expounding his 'political outlook'. The views he expressed led to his being immediately sentenced to be shot, but this was later commuted to hard labour for life.[9]

Such was the author of the strange document which promised in the name of the Emperor 'full liberty to all Our faithful subjects' and to the peasants eternal ownership of the land without redemption. He also freed everyone from military service and ordered 'the soldiers of Our army to return to their homes'. He then announced elections for choosing deputies of 'the Council of State which with Our help will rule Russia. This is Our royal will . . . If the army, deceived by its leaders, or if the generals, the governors and the "arbitrators", dare to oppose this manifesto by force, then let all rise in the name of the liberty We have granted and, without pity, enter the battle against anyone who dares to oppose Our will.'

A workman employed in the Senate press stole the necessary type and the proclamation was printed. The work appears to have been done at Friedrich-hamm in Norway and then taken to Russia through Finland. Another source, however, says that it was printed at Vilno.

The author's intention to make use of popular language to correspond to intellectual ideas here found paradoxical expression. Politically this apocry-phal manifesto was the dying hope that the State could be transformed by the Emperor. But as the Emperor had no intention of following the educated classes and the younger generation, the revolutionaries had almost naturally tried to speak in his name.

Two further manifestos were written by Benzenger. They were addressed to the intellectuals and signed with the name *Zemlya i Volya*. One was called *Provisional Government of the People* and the other *Freedom of Religion*. They took up the central theme of the movement: 'Russians, give up all hope in the good intentions of the Tsar.' And they recalled the massacre of Bezdna and other repressive measures. 'Oppressed and sufferers of Russia, arm yourselves against the oppression and injustice which come from the Tsar and his acolytes . . . After we have defeated the enemy, land will be distributed without a redemption fee. Tribunals will be set up, the blood-sucking officials will be tried, and honest and intelligent men will be elected.'

Such was the propagandist and political basis of the plot. Kienewicz hoped to set off the spark at Kazan, where the symptoms were most favour-able and the student movement most active. It was here that the peasants had revolted in 1861, and that the names of Stenka Razin and Pugachev met with most response.

His right-hand man in the execution of this plan was Maximilian Czerniak, a young Polish officer, who had entered the General Staff College in 1860. In St Petersburg, where he had continued his career, he had met two officers, who were soon at the head of the Polish insurrection, Dombrowski (the future general of the Paris Commune) and Serakowski.[10]

Czerniak confirmed Kienewicz's belief that *Zemlya i Volya* was confining its intentions to propaganda and the spread of ideas. The Polish Committee then decided to act on its own initiative and try and unleash a peasant rebellion in Russia. The attempt would at least be of value in diverting some Russian pressure from Poland.

Czerniak set to work. He could look to support from a relative of his in Kazan, another officer on the General Staff, Napoleon Casimir Iwanicki. Of him Krasnoperov wrote that he was a sensitive and amiable young man of about thirty (he had, in fact, been born in Volhynia in 1835) and that he had won over the sympathies of the students by his exceptional talents and boundless devotion to the revolutionary cause.[11] Through him Czerniak was to get into contact with the clandestine groups, and tell them that there had been a schism in the ranks of *Zemlya i Volya* and that one wing led by Bakunin thought that the time had come for a revolution. This would be all the more desirable, as the Polish revolution would have forced the Emperor to cut down his troops within Russia itself. Kienewicz even gave him a letter to this effect with a forgery of Bakunin's signature.

Before he left St Petersburg, Czerniak had written to his relative Iwanicki telling him to prepare the ground for his arrival. Iwanicki was on garrison duty in Spassk, the main town of the district that had witnessed the peasant disturbances of 1861. It was thought that this would certainly assist his activities. He at once went to Kazan, where he began to hold small meetings of students and explain to them his plans in a calm and decided voice 'as if he was getting ready for a hunt'. Although not all sources are in agreement, this was probably the first time that Iwanicki had made contact with the student groups. But he did not find it difficult to get a hearing. He spoke of his experiences with the soldiers and the peasants, and said that he had tried to use parables to explain to them the need for equality. He ended by saying that they must put their greatest hopes in the state of mind which prevailed in the villages.

On 15th March Czerniak arrived and introduced himself as an agent of the Moscow revolutionary committee. Clearer and more detailed explanations were then given. Czerniak openly attacked those who wanted to wait; he said that he belonged to the 'party of action' which had founded a committee for the very purpose of fighting inaction. The revolution must be started at once. Strategically Kazan was the best place. It would be easy to seize the town; the barracks were scarcely garrisoned; all that was needed was to surprise the sentries and hand out the arms, if necessary to the prisoners who were held in gaol. After seizing the Governor it would be possible to hold the town, using it as a centre of support and propaganda for the peasant insurrection. If for some reason or other it proved impossible to hold it, they would have to go to the villages and even possibly to the Urals 'where not even the Devil will be able to find us'. They asked him how he planned to provoke the peasant insurrection. He said that it must be done in the name of the Tsar by using a false manifesto.

It is not clear how the students reacted to this—not just the few at the meeting, but all the small and lively revolutionary groups in Kazan. There were two objections, and though they were different in kind they inevitably ended by overlapping and getting confused. To those who held that the plan was rash, Czerniak and Iwanicki answered that Garibaldi too before landing in Sicily had been considered mad, and that in any case the Poles would begin a revolution in spring. And to those who held that it was not right to turn to the peasants on false pretences, and that they should rather use the propaganda material which was already at hand (such as the manifesto that the students themselves had written), the two officers answered that they would then have to wait for thirty years. 'We know it well enough, that party which first wants to teach the people the alphabet and then to educate it step by step.' In any case, it would be stupid not to take advantage of two favourable circumstances—the Polish rebellion and the widespread wish among the peasants for real liberty.

In the end it seems that two student delegates, Polinovsky and Zhemanov, went to Czerniak on the following morning and said that they would take part in the movement on condition that they received from Moscow: money, thirty men, and above all, arms. He accepted these terms, after having consulted Iwanicki, who was optimistic. He was counting mainly on a few officer friends and on the soldiers under their command. Iwanicki stayed on at Kazan for a few days after Czerniak left, enlarging the number of those who knew about the conspiracy. In the meantime he drew up regulations for the revolutionary army of the future. He also planned to have crosses built of the kind used by the Old Believers (with double arms) with the words 'For land and freedom'.

But he soon met an obstacle. On 25th March the police searched the house of a sergeant called Stankevich, who had been informed of the affair. In fact, this was a pure coincidence as, at this time, the authorities were interested, not in his activities, but only in his ideas. Naturally, however, Iwanicki took precautions and tried to warn Czerniak that it would be dangerous to return to Kazan for the moment.

But the next blow was decisive. In the process of extending his circle of students, Iwanicki met a man who thought that this would be a perfect chance to make money by denouncing him. This he did; first to the Governor, then to the Archbishop of Kazan, and finally to the Third Section. The reaction was overwhelming: the barracks were alerted, the villages on which the conspirators had counted were garrisoned, and a Cossack bodyguard followed the Governor everywhere. Special precautions were taken to protect the administration's safes.

'There was talk', said a contemporary, 'of a vast movement of Russian and Tartar peasants which threatened to repeat the one led by Pugachev.'[12]

Rumours were spread of letters which contained threats to burn down the town. A number of law-abiding citizens took up their belongings and fled.[13]

These precautions and the prevailing atmosphere inevitably made an impression on the conspirators, some of whom were even influenced by the general state of alarm. There were doubts and second thoughts. Some even admitted later that they had been frightened by the proposed peasant revolt, which recalled the terrible Pugachev. Once again the educated classes felt that their presence in the revolutionary forces was a duty not just towards the people but even more towards themselves, in order to avoid the worst excesses of the revolution.

Such reflections were all the more natural in that in the meantime the plan of battle had been changed. There were now too many troops (over a thousand) in the town, and the steps taken by the authorities were too menacing. The conspirators therefore decided to begin in the villages, where they would arouse the peasants, and then march towards the town.

A young Polish student, Osip Yakovlevich Silwand, was sent by Czerniak from St Petersburg to announce this plan. He arrived on 14th April with a large number of manifestos, four hundred roubles and fourteen revolvers. He promised that small groups of revolutionaries would arrive as soon as the rebellion broke out. Four Polish students in St Petersburg had in fact promised to take action when this should occur. A meeting was held consisting of all the inner circle of the conspirators, including the 'apostles' Biryukov, Orlov and other Polish and Russian students and officers, as well as the newcomer Silwand. The discussions grew heated. Those present considered the problem of how to organize supplies for the insurgent peasants and decided to seize the landlords' crops and to mint coins. A series of other plans was made, the few arms were distributed, a command organization was set up, and everyone took away some of the propaganda material.

But when Silwand returned to St Petersburg after the meeting and told Kienewicz how matters stood, the latter became convinced that nothing more could be done. Even if this final decision was correct from an objective point of view, it is obvious that it reflects all the ambiguity which lay at the very roots of the conspiracy. Any hope of creating a diversion to the Polish rebellion in the heart of Russia was lost. And it was this rather than the Russian peasant movement that was the real objective of the Poles.

Kienewicz, however, did not want to abandon entirely the idea of using the apocryphal manifesto. And so he had it stuck up in the villages by the four Polish students who were to have gone to Kazan on the outbreak of the rebellion. Though this led to their arrest, some manifestos did reach the peasants and seem to have given rise to local movements. And apart from this, those university students of Kazan who escaped arrest made use of this material in the same way. A new wave of 'apostolic' journeys was the immediate sequel to the failure of the conspiracy.

On 23rd May Kienewicz left for Paris, taking with him fifty thousand roubles which he had collected for the Polish cause. On 5th June 1863 when he was on the way back to Russia with a false passport to join the Polish movement, he was arrested at the frontier.

In Kazan the situation was now in the hands of an agent of the Third Section, sent to the town on the Tsar's special instructions. Before making any arrests, he wanted to obtain proof. To achieve this he made use of the man who had denounced the conspiracy and who now became a police spy. For these services he later received three thousand roubles from the Minister of the Interior and opened a photographer's shop in St Petersburg.

When sufficient evidence had been obtained, Iwanicki was arrested on 26th April. Brave and rash to the end, he wrote an 'account of a dead man' for the use of the investigating authorities. In this he reasserted his Polish patriotism and assumed responsibility for everything he had done.

Czerniak succeeded in escaping, for the time being at least. He fought under the name of Lado in the ranks of the Polish insurgents; but a year later, in July 1864, he was taken prisoner and sent to Kazan where he shared the fate of his comrades.

All the other conspirators were arrested between April and May 1863. They were taken first to St Petersburg, but in June the Committee of Inquiry had them all sent back to Kazan. At the end of its long and complicated work, the investigating authorities divided the accused into three classes—Polish officers, Polish students, and Kazan students. From the results of the inquiry Kienewicz may have hoped that he had saved his life, as throughout the questioning he had denied all the charges brought against him. But the military tribunal decided otherwise. He was condemned to death together with three others, Iwanicki, Mroczek and Stankevich.

On 6th June 1864 at seven in the morning, they were shot outside the town, on the banks of the river Kazan. The official report describes the scene as follows:

On the road between the fortress and the place of execution, Iwanicki and Kienewicz were laughing, and Iwanicki greeted his acquaintances with great courtesy. Even when the squad turned from the right to the left flank they did not stop smiling among themselves. When the confirmation of Kienewicz's sentence was read out, he turned to all present and quickly moving two steps forward, he said aloud in Russian 'Gentlemen, listen. All this is wrong. All they have written is a lot of muck.' When the order of execution was read out Kienewicz again shouted 'They will not dare shoot me, I am a French citizen.'[14] The other two, Mroczek and Stankevich, were silent the entire time. There was a great crowd of people.

After their corpses had been buried, the soldiers were made to march over their graves. More than a year later on 11th October 1865, Czerniak was brought to the same place and executed.

The third category of accused was condemned by a civil tribunal to sentences ranging from four to ten years' hard labour. But even before this sentence had been confirmed by the Senate in May 1867, the case was closed, and after four years of preventive detention they were all freed under police supervision. In the meantime three of them had succeeded in escaping abroad.

13. POPULISM AND NIHILISM

THE LIQUIDATION of the Kazan conspiracy marked the end of those revolutionary ventures which were carried out in the years immediately after the emancipation of the serfs. The crushing of the Polish revolt put an end to the decade of great changes and great hopes which had opened with the Crimean War. It is true that all the various elements of progress that had emerged during these ten years continued to develop, but they were modified and distorted by the defeat they had undergone and the halt which circumstances now called on the movement of liberation.

A brake was put on the reforming tendencies of the State. A few important steps were taken in the administration of justice;[1] but the problems of censorship and local administration revealed the weaknesses latent in that constant process of compromise which only a few years earlier had allowed the peasant reform to be fulfilled.[2]

With the failure of the campaign to summon a *Zemsky Sobor*, constitutionalism now fled back once more to the bureaucracy and nobility and was transformed into pale and uncertain hopes for a 'liberal' crown to reforming despotism.

'Regionalist' and 'federalist' tendencies were badly hit by the crushing of the Polish rebellion, and made themselves felt only in Siberian demands for autonomy until, in extremist and revolutionary forms, they reappeared in the federalist and anarchist ferment of the 'seventies.

The *Sovremennik*'s Populism survived the arrests of 1862 and carried on the tradition of Chernyshevsky and Dobrolyubov. But it no longer had any faith that its hopes for the complete transformation of Russia would be immediately satisfied. Instead, it turned to satire and criticism of the entire life of the country. The self-confidence of the young intelligentsia of *Zemlya i Volya* had now diminished, and the *Sovremennik* tended to put all its trust in the 'people' and the 'peasant'.

In opposition to this attitude there now appeared on the scene men who re-affirmed the essential rôle that could be played by a 'critically thinking *élite*' which they contrasted with the passive crowd, incapable of revolt. So 'Nihilism' was born. These were the years of Pisarev and the review *Russkoe Slovo* which introduced a new factor, the effects of which will be noticed in the first return to a conspiracy with Ishutin's *Organization*.

But before going back once more to the 'underground' we will have to consider the picture as a whole and follow the development during the 'sixties of all the tendencies here described.

The Polish revolt had already led some members of the higher bureaucracy to think that the time had come to surround absolutism with some sort of constitutional halo. 'Make Russia take a step ahead of Poland—as regards the development of State institutions', said Valuev, the Minister of the Interior, to Alexander II in 1863. There was to be some kind of bureaucratic representation for the purpose of enlarging and giving greater dignity and prestige to the State Council. A scheme along these lines was drawn up and discussed, but remained a dead letter. Obviously in matters of this kind, the first step is also the hardest. Alexander II refused to make even a gesture in the direction of constitutionalism. In January 1865 the assembly of the Moscow nobility sent him an address asking him to 'complete the government edifice which he had created, with a general assembly of delegates from the entire Russian nation to discuss the requirements of the State as a whole'. To this the Emperor replied that 'what he had already done in the past must remain a sufficient pledge for all his faithful subjects', and that none of these had the right to 'anticipate him in his incessant aims for the good of Russia'.[3] In 1861 the nobles of Tver had been arrested, Herzen had flung himself into propaganda for a *Zemsky Sobor* and Chernyshevsky had written his *Letters without an Address*. Now, the movement which had led to all this was reduced to a dialogue in the upper spheres of the bureaucracy or between the Tsar and his nobles.

These were the last rays of a declining movement, quite incapable of affecting public opinion or arousing an interest in constitutional ideas such as might detach the intelligentsia from its growing Populism. Any reform introduced within the system of absolutism naturally conjured up the vision of a liberal solution; but Russian liberalism could find no escape from its innate contradictions. A constitution could only be ceded from above and there was neither the will nor the power to appeal to pressure from below.

Shchapov's 'federalism', the desire for a rebirth of 'historical regions' against State centralization, continued to develop in the 'sixties. But, as was natural in a multi-national State such as the empire of Alexander II, these tendencies soon took the form of national *risorgimenti* against Russian domination. The Ukraine, the Caucasus, Armenia, the regions of the Baltic, and the Lithuanian and the Polish territories, all drew from this 'federalism', as indeed from Populism as a whole, new elements to deepen their own national movements.

The Polish revolt brought these problems violently on to the plane of immediate politics at a time when the other national movements had hardly yet been born. And the suppression of Poland marked a halt for the other movements also and led Alexander II towards a 'Russification' of his empire.

In only one 'historical region' of what can rightly be called Russia was there an attempt to found a movement of independence. Siberia, Shchapov's birthplace, was the most important field of Russian 'federalism'. Although small in scale, the Siberian movement is far from devoid of interest and is worth examining in some detail.

Its guiding spirits were Nikolay Mikhailovich Yadrintsev and Grigory Nikolaevich Potanin.[4] When still very young they had come to study in the capital. For Potanin the road to the university was made easier (or even opened) by Bakunin, who was then an exile in Siberia. Once in St Petersburg, the two men founded in 1860 one of the many regional groups so frequent at the time among the students, by collecting together the Siberians who were scattered in the various higher educational institutes of the capital. Most of them were poor and lived together in communities. The most destitute of all was the young ethnographer Khudyakov, the revolutionary who was to be condemned some years later in the trial of those who organized Karakozov's attempt on the life of the Tsar.

From the start their discussions were lively and ended by dividing the group into two currents: the regionalists, and those who looked upon the federal problem as less important than that of a social and peasant revolution.

The ideas of the regionalists, who were led by Yadrintsev and Potanin, were undoubtedly inspired by Shchapov, although he himself had no direct contacts with the group.[5] The agitation for Ukrainian autonomy also played some part in forming their ideas, and they were further incited by the tradition of the 'Society of United Slavs' and above all the 'Brotherhood of Cyril and Methodius'.[6] They read, for instance, an article by the historian Kostomarov called 'Thoughts on the Federal Principle in Ancient Russia', which was published in 1861 in the Ukrainophil review *Osnova*. The article revived and extended this tradition from the days of the Decembrists and 1848. Kostomarov openly claimed that Russia ought to be divided into sections or *states*: the north, the north-east, the south-east, two *states* of the Volga (upper and lower), two of Little Russia (Central and South), two of Siberia, one of the Caucasus, etc.[7] As will be remembered, *Zemlya i Volya* (at this time beginning to take shape in St Petersburg) took account of similar regional demands even in its structure. While he was a student in the capital, Yadrintsev approached some of the founders of *Zemlya i Volya*. His first works were published in the *Iskra* (The Spark), edited by Kurochkin, another member of this secret society.[8]

The university disturbances and the closing of the lecture rooms led to Potanin's imprisonment. He was then compelled by the police to return to his birthplace. Yadrintsev, too, went back to Siberia in 1863. At Tomsk they both took an active part in public and intellectual life, concerning themselves with peasant problems, and the creation of a Siberian university. They made contacts with the few cultivated and original people in the district, and edited a local paper, etc.

In the spring of 1865 both men were arrested. They were accused of having wanted to overthrow the existing order in Siberia and separate that region from the Russian empire. The words that Yadrintsev used many years later, when he recalled this charge, are still more characteristic: 'Separation of Siberia from Russia and creation of a republic like that of the United States of America.'

The most thorough searches were made and there were many arrests, affecting all the principal towns of Siberia. The main suspects spent as long as three years in preventive detention.

Even today it is difficult to give an exact estimate of the political coherence of the movement. It is not that those involved later repudiated their ideas, but, consciously or otherwise, they tended to give them in retrospect a more innocent appearance. Later historians, even Soviet ones, have paid little attention to this episode as to many other aspects of the Populist movement which were aimed against government centralization.

M. Lemke has almost certainly clarified the background of the problem by pointing out that even in official Siberian circles—such as the Committee of the Geographical Society, inspired by Muravev-Amursky—there was talk in 1861 of Siberia's 'colonial' status and suggestions for the 'separation of Siberia from the metropolis, as the history of all colonies teaches'.[9] The United States of America must have been the obvious example for a movement keen to make propaganda along these lines. Earlier still, among the Petrashevskists, there had been some references to the possibility of Siberia developing autonomously. The period of reforms may have suggested that the time had come to create a Siberian national consciousness. But the repression put an end to the fulfilment of such hopes. 'It was not separatism we were aiming at but the destruction of patriotic tendencies in Siberia', Yadrintsev said later.[10]

Even the prison régime to which the accused were subjected reflects this aspect of the question. For three years Potanin, Yadrintsev and Shashkov[11] were confined in the fortress of Omsk. But Potanin was given permission to work in the local archives, and Yadrintsev to continue his ethnographical researches. The local authorities kept them in prison, but did not want to interrupt their studies completely. Yadrintsev later described his experiences in an extremely interesting book, *The Russian Community in Prison and in Exile*.[12]

The sentences were heavy. Potanin was given fifteen years' hard labour, and Yadrintsev twelve, later reduced to banishment to the region of Archangel. Their health was broken, and the long journey had to be made mostly on foot. But when, in a terrible state, they at last got to Archangel, Gagarin, the Governor, 'a kind of gentleman and aristocrat, a tender and humane administrator', not only treated them as well as possible but read with great enthusiasm a memorandum that Yadrintsev wrote on prison régime. He even went to the hospital where Yadrintsev had been sent and thanked him in person. The memorandum indeed had some influence on the prison reforms of these years. It marked the beginning of a campaign that Yadrintsev carried on for the rest of his life against banishment in general and banishment to Siberia in particular.

All these details throw light on the atmosphere of extreme severity and unexpected humanity so characteristic of the régime of Alexander II. This was a consequence of the disorganization of the State and simultaneously the solidarity which was growing up even in the furthest corners of Russia among the more liberal and independent spirits.

Yadrintsev and Potanin were later transferred to the region of the Volga where they resumed their regionalist campaign in a new guise. They took part in and then edited an independent periodical which was issued in Kazan in 1873: the *Kamsko-Volzhskaya Gazeta*. 'Every Russian region may have its own interests. The outlook of the provincial is different from that of the centralizer in the capital.' Attacks against the bureaucracy in St Petersburg and appeals to local forces were continued throughout 1873. 'The provinces are the future', said Yadrintsev, summing up his programme in a letter of the time.

This was of course a retreat from their position of ten years earlier, when they had dreamed of an independent Siberia. But it also made their regionalist ideas more acceptable. Indeed Yadrintsev, when he was finally freed, began those studies in St Petersburg which made him one of the best known and most quoted authorities on Siberian problems. Thinking over the significance of his regionalism, he wrote a passage which is fundamental for an exact estimate of the points of contact and divergence between this current and Populism.

The Russian intelligentsia which was aiming to move towards the people understood, by activities in the provinces, only activities in the countryside on behalf of the peasants. This withered not only what they did, but the very idea of the Populist movement. But we wanted to reawaken and spread intellectual life in the provinces . . . The problem was, I thought, of enormous importance for the entire development of Russia. It was the problem of the region (*oblast*) and its participation in the life of the nation. It was the same problem that Shchapov had once raised, creating a new historical point of view. To the inhabitant of the capital, the provinces seemed merely a model of immobility and ignorance, governed by the primitive instincts of the masses and the by-now extinguished interests of the serf owners. The provincial intelligentsia was considered wretched and of no importance; the provincial press was looked upon as the kingdom of pettiness . . . No one thought of gathering and holding together the provincial intelligentsia. Populism—in its general, unspecified form—was dominated by a current that sprang from the capital. But how is real Populism possible without the participation of the intellectual and civil life of the provinces?[13]

This analysis is of great interest. The regionalist tendencies of the 'sixties are interpreted as representing a reawakening and the political ideology of the educated classes in the provinces. And when in the 'seventies Populism became revolutionary and terrorist, it came into conflict with this provincialism. The two tendencies which were united at their start diverged more and more thereafter. Potanin lived long enough to try and apply his ideas politically in 1905 and 1917, but he ended alone and submerged by the overpowering wave of the social revolution.

The suppression of the *Sovremennik* and the arrest of Chernyshevsky had, in 1862, deprived Populism of its leading organ and its greatest representative. Some of his closest collaborators succeeded in joining together in a small review called *Ocherki* (Essays), the first number of which came out on 1st January 1863. Shchapov also took part in this, and the very fact of seeing his name next to those of Chernyshevsky's disciples shows how the atmosphere was changing. The political aims put forward in *Letters without an Address* were being replaced by two themes: the exaltation of the community and egalitarian traditions of the Russian village; and the antithesis between the people and the State and Western civilization—all this with some Slavophil flavouring. The leading article of the first number (which was probably written by Eliseyev) spoke of millions of peasants 'who, though they feel the difficulty of their position, are so accustomed to certain forms of life and certain principles that, in spite of wanting something better, they also want something that does not affect their ancestral way of life'. The core of these traditions lay in 'equality, and a life based on the *obshchina* which includes equality of property, rights, ideas . . .' There, and only there, could still be found the germ of 'a social community founded on an ethical principle'. In Western Europe 'despite equality of political rights' there was no principle of the kind. 'Present European organization contains no radical medicine against the misfortunes of humanity.' And so the peasant forces which already existed in Russia must be developed 'by freeing them from foreign elements which were introduced by violence. Destroy all these elements and allow the growth of what springs up naturally, and then you will be on the right road.' A more spontaneous and romantic brand of Populism, less political and more tied to the countryside—such was the initial result of the forcible removal of the more conscious and Westernizing elements which Chernyshevsky had introduced.[14]

When after many months of negotiations and uncertainty, Nekrasov at last got permission to restart publication of the *Sovremennik*, these ideas began to make themselves felt. But they were controlled and guided by the wish to follow in Chernyshevsky's tracks. Besides, the high intellectual standard of the *Sovremennik* tended in itself to balance these ideas against a wider mental and political horizon.[15]

Nekrasov used to describe the board of editors as his 'consistory', composed as it mostly was of the sons of priests—the new intellectual *élite* of the late 'fifties and early 'sixties. Quite apart from Chernyshevsky and Dobrolyubov, such was the origin of Grigory Zakharovich Eliseyev. Eliseyev was a Siberian, a professor at the Ecclesiastical Academy of Kazan, and the author

11+

of books on religious history, before he joined the *Sovremennik*, and became
for twenty years one of the most highly regarded of Populist journalists.[16]
Then there was Maxim Alexeyevich Antonovich who, scarcely had he left the
seminary, began to write articles on philosophy which followed Chernyshevsky's treatment of Feuerbach's 'anthropomorphism'. But Antonovich
interpreted these views in an even more materialist and positivist spirit.[17]
With A. M. Pypin, a relative of Chernyshevsky, these men formed the inner
core of the 'consistory' which controlled the *Sovremennik* between 1863 and
1866. Nekrasov's sincere Populist spirit, no less than his considerable talent
and journalistic and political adaptability, had great weight in the review.
But the main novelty of the new editorship consisted in the presence of
Saltykov-Shchedrin, whose satirical tales and intense publicizing activities
made a profound mark on the first years of the revived periodical.

'In 1863 Russian society had changed to the point of being unrecognizable',
Eliseyev later said in his autobiographical fragments. In this changed situation
the *Sovremennik* tried to maintain its old programme.

The main object was still to cry aloud ceaselessly, that society could prosper only
when it followed the 'divine law' and the 'divine law' means 'one piece for you,
one piece for him, one piece for me'; means, in fact, that even the most insignificant
member of society cannot be disinherited and that each one must have his own
little piece.[18]

But it was one thing to have a programme inspired by good peasant and
egalitarian commonsense and another to be able to apply it; especially during
a time of reaction and under countless difficulties imposed by the censorship
and a public which was less ready and less loyal than in Chernyshevsky's
day. Eliseyev himself has pointed out the review's most serious weaknesses
and obvious mistakes.

Above all, it was not prepared to take a line over the Polish problem.
There were, it is true, some clever references to it by Saltykov-Shchedrin
who, for the occasion, adopted the tactics that Chernyshevsky had employed,
and spoke of Austria when alluding to Russia. But this was not enough. In
the midst of a wave of nationalist passions, the *Sovremennik* was forced to
remain silent or to mumble a few quiet words. It did not want to take useless
risks with its life on this subject. The threat of censorship sufficed to stop it
having any influence on the most important problem of the years 1863 and
1864.

The bonds between the *Sovremennik* and the young generation (i.e. the
students) were weakened. 'N. G. Chernyshevsky had been close to them',
said Eliseyev. 'He had guided them directly and in person and he had
defended them with passion when necessary. He knew what he was doing
and what he was looking for. But when he was arrested all direct and personal
bonds between the *Sovremennik* and the students came to an end.'[19] Chernyshevsky's *What is to be done?* still gave them what they were looking for.

But the youthful and chivalrous Utopianism of this novel was far from satisfying the more critical spirits of the new editor. Saltykov-Shchedrin himself was prepared to make an open attack on *What is to be Done?* within the *Sovremennik*.

In place of this appeal to the younger generation, Saltykov-Shchedrin was able to make use of his marvellous satirical power, which expressed the bitterness that most sensitive spirits felt about the suffocating ugliness of life in Russia. He was able to attack all the various moral, political and social bigotry that was again coming to the fore after the shock of the reforms. But though Saltykov-Shchedrin played an important part in the formation of the intelligentsia between the 'sixties and 'seventies, he had no chance of providing a new political line or a direct spur to the younger generation.[20]

Such encouragement could only come from the West where the working class and Socialist movement was reviving with the formation of Lassalle's party in 1863 and the foundation of the First International a year later. And indeed the *Sovremennik* is full of information and discussions on the subject, and played a large part in making these ideas and currents of thought known in Russia. Yu. Zhukovsky, who emerged as the economist of the group, devoted a detailed article to the 'Historical Development of Workers' Associations in France'.[21] In this he explained the advantages of cooperatives, both of consumption and production, from an admittedly Proudhonist angle. Pypin spoke of the working class movement in England, describing for example 'The Educational Associations of the English Working Classes', and stressing the great usefulness of the popular schools and universities.[22] E. K. Vatson came out strongly against *laissez faire* in his article 'The English Working Classes and the Manchester School'.[23] An attempt was even made to give news of a community based on Communist principles which had sprung up in America and was called *New Times*.[24] News from Germany in particular attracted the *Sovremennik*'s attention. Vatson in his column called 'Politics'[25] repeatedly spoke of the debate between Schulze-Delitzsch and Lassalle.[26] Pypin wrote a biography of Lassalle, a translation of whose article 'On the Relations between the Present Historical Period and the Idea of the Working Class'[27] was given in full in the *Sovremennik*. Despite the evasions and silence imposed by fear of the censorship, it is obvious that the editors' sympathies were with Lassalle's working class politics against the purely reforming and cooperative ventures of Schulze-Delitzsch.

But could these problems of how to organize the proletariat in Western Europe mean anything in Russia? Goncharov, the well-known novelist and author of *Oblomov*, who was at this time mainly occupied in conscientiously fulfilling his duties as censor, wrote in a report dated 18th February 1865:

Articles devoted to these theories are printed in the pages of our reviews with virtually no result. Almost nobody reads them except perhaps a few specialists who in any case prefer to learn of the works of Schulze-Delitzsch and Lassalle in the original. The difference between the situation of the working classes abroad and in Russia, and their different ways of life, make these articles almost incomprehensible to the public.[28]

The repeated 'perhaps' and 'almost' with which Goncharov modified his claim, showed that he himself was not altogether convinced by it. It may have been true that most of the intelligentsia showed little interest in these problems; but there were none the less some who drew inspiration from the articles in the *Sovremennik* to consolidate and perfect their ideas on workers' and artisans' associations—of which they had already caught a glimpse in Chernyshevsky's *What is to be done?* As will be seen later, it was from ventures such as these that Ishutin's *Organization* was developed.

None the less, the problem raised by Goncharov was a real one and was of great concern to the editors of the *Sovremennik*. What lessons could be deduced from the working class movement which could be of help in solving the peasant problem in Russia? Once again it was the ideas of Proudhon (from whom the editors drew inspiration) which acted as a bridge between interest in the workers' movement in the West and Populism in Russia. A censor might accuse Zhukovsky of having written the most vigorous of his articles 'The Problem of the Young Generation' 'in a social-democratic spirit'[29], but it was, in fact, prompted mainly by the spirit of Proudhon.

Zhukovsky envisaged the future economic development of the Russian countryside entrusted to peasant communities enjoying their own credit facilities. He strongly opposed the property of the nobles developing on capitalist lines. He did not deny the need for industrialization, but he claimed that it must be carried out for the benefit of the peasants and not for the nobles and the capitalists. In an article for a periodical which was soon suppressed by the authorities, but which in 1865 attracted the most vital Populist writers, Zhukovsky clearly explained his programme:

Labour is not necessary to help undertakings which well know that they are not able to pay these workmen. Labour is not necessary to cultivate more crops when existing produce is already more than enough for the country. It must not be used in great industries which only enrich the employers or English and foreign merchants. Labour must be employed to provide shoes and clothes, to provide light, houses and civilization for the peasant, who goes without shoes because he works for an English lord, because he has produced superfluous bread and wasted those hours of work which could have been used to give him welfare and comfort. Even the centre of gravity of education must be removed to the countryside; only then will it be possible to write the word 'end' to the age of serfdom. Industrial life must be founded in the world of the peasants. Only then will the people learn, and only then will education become the people's education. This is the way to give solid foundations to the nation's economy.[30]

Zhukovsky in fact was advocating the programme that had already been expounded by Ogarev immediately after the emancipation and which continued to be discussed for two decades, until it finally became the economic vision of all the 'legal Populists'. He also translated Lassalle's ideas on the financial support which the State ought to give to workers' associations into Populist and peasant terms, and suggested an economic policy designed to develop artisan workshops, cooperatives and small local industries.

Zhukovsky once tried to calculate how much total capital the peasant class would need so as to invest it exclusively in economic activities aimed at improving its own situation. The peasants paid about three hundred millions in taxes. If one looked upon this sum as representing an interest of 5% on capital, it could be deduced that they had a capital of six billion roubles. Anyone who observed Russian society could see that this sum was not in fact used for the advantage of the peasants but for the capitalists and the nobles.[31] It is true that the only value of Zhukovsky's calculation was to illustrate roughly what was happening; but it was an effective way of showing the ruling classes that they were living like parasites on the work of the peasants. By contrasting this state of affairs with an economic system exclusively designed to better the peasants' standard of living, he made the intelligentsia aware of the problem of its social justification. It owed a 'debt' to the people; it had a 'duty' to devote itself exclusively to the people's benefit. And so the *Sovremennik* opened up the road to the political outlook that Lavrov was to make his own.

Karakozov's attempt on the life of the Tsar in 1866 found the *Sovremennik* in a critical position. It had already received two 'warnings' from the authorities. In vain did Nekrasov try to ward off a third and decisive blow; in vain did he resort to disavowals and compromises. On 3rd June 1866 the St Petersburg papers carried the news that 'on His Majesty's orders the reviews *Sovremennik* and *Russkoe Slovo* have been suppressed, in view of the pernicious policies that they have pursued for some time'. Such was the epitaph of a review that had had among its contributors Pushkin, Belinsky, Nekrasov, Chernyshevsky, Dobrolyubov and Saltykov-Shchedrin.

Once again, as in 1862, the *Sovremennik* shared its misfortunes with the *Russkoe Slovo*, the organ of Pisarev and 'Nihilism'. 'Every party, every cause, has its *enfants terribles*', said Saltykov-Shchedrin, referring to the editors of the *Russkoe Slovo* who were indeed the *enfants terribles* of Populism in the 'sixties.[32]

Intellectually they represented a positivist and scientific reaction against Chernyshevsky's Feuerbachian 'anthropologism' and Dobrolyubov's moralism. After 1862 similar tendencies had made their appearance even in the *Sovremennik*. Antonovich for example had combined the philosophic culture that he derived from the Hegelian Left with the materialism of Büchner and Moleschott. E. K. Vatson had claimed to be a follower of Comte. Buckle was becoming the idol of the young generation. But Pisarev and his colleagues carried these tendencies, common to European culture as a whole, to the extreme. Aesthetic 'realism' became in their hands a violent repudiation of art; 'utilitarianism' an exaltation of the exact sciences, the only 'useful' kind of human activity; and 'enlightenment' a glorification of the educated classes.

Pisarev found a name for this tendency, welcoming as praise the definition of 'Nihilism' which Turgenev had used as an attack in his novel *Fathers and Sons*.

The word was not new. It had been used in the eighteenth century by F. Jacobi, Jean-Paul Richter and Sébastian Mercier. In 1829 the romantic critic Nadezhdin had used it in Russia, though in a purely negative sense, to mean those who know nothing and understand nothing.[33] Katkov gave it a new meaning, using it to describe someone who no longer believes in anything. 'If one looks at the universe and has to choose one of two extreme attitudes, it is easier to become a mystic than a nihilist. We are everywhere surrounded by miracles.'[34] And so the word as used in the Hegelian Left by Bruno Bauer and Stirner was beginning to assume a philosophical and polemical significance. But it was Turgenev who made it popular and employed it to sum up the spirited attitude and ideas of the young generation of the 'sixties.[35]

It was at once obvious that the word had been badly chosen. The 'Nihilists', more than anyone else, believed—blindly and violently—in their own ideas. Their positivist and materialist faith could be accused of fanaticism, of a youthful lack of a sense of criticism, but not of apathy. Saltykov-Shchedrin was right when he wrote that it was 'a word devoid of meaning, less suitable than any other for describing the younger generation, in which could be found every kind of "ism" but certainly not nihilism'.[36] It would be easy to quote a long list of protests and explanations made by Populists of different trends and different periods in order to point out how little the word launched by Turgenev applied to them. Antonovich thought it necessary to write a long review of *Fathers and Sons* in the *Sovremennik*, which (as was rightly pointed out) passed a sort of legally reasoned sentence on the author for having falsified reality.[37] And even in later years the Russian revolutionaries were amazed and shocked at hearing themselves called 'Nihilists'.

Yet the word stuck and spread, especially in the West, where it became popular and served to express the feeling of mystery which surrounded Russian Populists and terrorists. A glance at the French, English and Italian newspapers of the 'seventies is enough to show how frequently it was used. Seeing it repeated so often inevitably makes us suspect that it had resumed its original meaning, and that it now was used mainly to hide the ignorance of journalists and enemies who wrote about the various Russian movements without understanding their problems or spirit.

If we wish to understand the part played by Nihilism in the development of Russian Populism, we must place it clearly within its historical limits. The expression was at first merely a literary and polemical fashion—a ghost conjured up by fearful liberals and reactionaries, as they saw the deep, violent repercussions that the reforms had induced among the younger generation of intellectuals. It became a political slogan, when Pisarev adopted it for himself, and said that Turgenev had given an exact description of the feelings of the materialist younger generation. By this Pisarev meant that the main function of the revolutionary intelligentsia was one of criticism and corrosion; that the obstacles to be destroyed were so great that even a purely negative function of this kind would be quite enough to occupy the life of his generation.

He made headway because his words appeared at a time when hopes in reform were on the decline and no revolutionary movement had yet arisen to absorb the passions of those who wanted to devote themselves to the cause of the people. Nihilism did not therefore imply scepticism or apathy but, on the contrary, the overcoming of a bitter disappointment and the desire to 'carry things through to the end'.[38]

Politically this led to an important result. The Nihilists on the *Russkoe Slovo* put their trust and hopes mainly in themselves. They refused to believe either in the ruling classes or even in a myth of the 'people' and the 'peasants'. 'The emancipation of the person' (i.e. the formation of independent characters, 'who think critically') was more important than social emancipation. Such emancipation they looked upon chiefly as the diffusion of technical and scientific knowledge. To carry out such a task of enlightenment it was essential to form a class able to think of its existence in modern scientific terms and dispense with sentimentality and romanticism. The Nihilists thus carried to its extreme one aspect of Herzen's and Chernyshevsky's thought. They built up 'egoism' into a theory and exalted economic calculation and utilitarian coldness. These qualities, they hoped, would be capable of giving man a sense of his own individuality and would help to detach him from social discipline and conformity. 'To increase the number of men who think: that is the alpha and omega of social development', said Pisarev.

This 'realism' sometimes led them to accept, with all the enthusiasm of converts, the extreme consequences of the Darwinian 'struggle for existence'. One of them, Zaytsev, one day brought down on his head the attacks and insults of the entire Populist press for claiming that the coloured races were congenitally inferior. Pisarev often praised the strong and able, those who knew how to arm themselves with the modern scientific knowledge required for winning the battle.

All this might easily have become the ideology of the new intelligentsia— the managerial class of technicians—and we often find references and appeals to them in the works of Pisarev. But for all their 'realism' and 'egoism', the editors of the *Russkoe Slovo* were deeply involved with the egalitarian spirit and revolutionary tradition of 1848; they felt bitter scorn and hatred for the bourgeoisie, the powerful and the rich. Their ideology was not absorbed by the new *élite* of orthodox bourgeois which was taking advantage of the situation brought about by the reforms. Instead it was taken up by the 'proletariat of thought', the dissatisfied intelligentsia, which was aware that it constituted the 'critically thinking' element of Russian society. Pisarev's 'realism' provided it with a feeling of pride and superiority, and intensified its desire for autonomy and independence.

A glance at the fate of the leading editors of the *Russkoe Slovo* is enough to show the end of the road they had chosen. Pisarev was already in prison in July 1862 and was only freed on 18th November 1866. A considerable number of his articles were written in the Peter-Paul fortress. In February 1868 he tried in vain to obtain a passport, and on 4th July his corpse was discovered in the Baltic. He had probably committed suicide, unable physically or spiritually to adapt himself to life after imprisonment. His funeral in St Petersburg was the occasion for demonstrations which showed where his readers and admirers were to be found: writers, students and the 'Nihilist youth'. There were many banishments for speeches 'denying the immortality of the soul' or for varying attempts to honour his memory.

Varfolomey Zaytsev was twenty-two when in 1863 he began to write in the *Russkoe Slovo*. His interest in the purely intellectual aspects of Nihilism was less keen than that of Pisarev, who despite all his experiences and the political passion which impelled him, throughout his life remained primarily a man of letters. But Zaytsev was more of a journalist and more concerned with immediate problems. It was not for nothing that when in exile he was called 'the Russian Rochefort'. His articles were scathing and to the point— as far as the censorship allowed—and often took the form of short pamphlets.[39] In the spring of 1866 he was caught in the great net that was cast after Karakozov's attempt on the life of the Tsar. He was freed after four and a half months' detention in the Peter-Paul fortress. Police surveillance increased and the censor no longer allowed him to write. And so there was nothing left but emigration. After many difficulties he succeeded in getting a passport in March 1869. He immediately got in touch with the Bakuninist émigrés in Geneva, and then went for a time to Turin where he founded one of the first cells of the International. He returned to Switzerland and became one of Bakunin's followers. He wrote in the *Bulletin de la Fédération du Jura*, in the *Kolokol* under Nechaev and Ogarev, and later in the *Obshcheye Delo*. He died in exile in 1882.[40]

Another contributor to the *Russkoe Slovo*, Nikolay Vasilevich Sokolov,[41] also became an anarchist and disciple of Bakunin—even more decisively than Zaytsev who always retained a personal standpoint of his own. Sokolov was a *déclassé*. In 1858 he left the General Staff College to begin his career by serving in the Caucasian wars; he was then sent on a diplomatic mission to Pekin. In 1860 he was back in St Petersburg, where he too was affected by the prevailing intellectual ferment. He went to Brussels to meet Proudhon and then to London to see Herzen. Thanks to the sailors of Kronstadt, he succeeded in bringing back with him a load of forbidden books. He became a friend of Obruchev and moved in Chernyshevsky's circle. He then gave up his military career and in 1862 became economic editor of the *Russkoe Slovo*. His Proudhonism was allied to violent hatred for capitalism and all forms of exploitation. He went abroad again between the end of 1863 and middle of 1865 to meet Herzen, Réclus and the Polish exiles; on his return he resumed journalism. One day in a café he read in a French newspaper an advertisement for Vallès' *Réfractaires*. He was so pleased with the title and author that even before reading it, he decided with Zaytsev to publish a translation. But when he found that the book was not what he had expected, he (and possibly Zaytsev) rewrote it in five weeks. When the censor read this, Sokolov was arrested. This was on 28th April 1866, about three weeks after Karakozov's attempt on the life of the Tsar. The book even contained a more or less literary justification of regicide. It is, besides, not altogether impossible that Sokolov was in direct contact with Ishutin's *Organization;* but this the police never found out and they were satisfied with banishing him to the department of Archangel, and then, in 1871, transferring him to Astrakhan. A year later Sokolov fled to Switzerland, where he became one of the strangest and most violent members of the small group around Bakunin.

His booklet *The Refractory Ones* was reprinted in Zurich.[42] It consisted of a number of short essays and portraits collected by him to show that 'the refractory' had always existed and were the salt of the earth:

A professor who throws away his gown; an officer who doffs his uniform for the red shirt of the volunteer; a lawyer who gives up his job to become an actor; a priest who becomes a journalist—all these are refractory . . . So too are calm lunatics, enthusiastic workmen, heroic scholars.[43]

The first Stoics and the first Christians had been 'refractory', and still more so the first Utopians—Sébastien Mercier, Brissot, Linguet and Mably. And even in modern times there had been men who had followed the rule of 'unconditional negation, unconditional refractoriness': Leroux, Fourier and above all Proudhon, 'the prototype of the refractory'.[44]

While Sokolov was drawing up a kind of individualist anarchism on his own, Zaytsev continued to condense this rebellious ferment into his political conception of the relations which ought to exist between revolutionaries and the masses.

Turning to Dobrolyubov, he said that he had been 'the most pure and complete representative of love of the people'. But just because of this there was in him an element of mysticism, an adoration of those virtues which are attributed to the masses. 'This ideal vision sometimes led him into error and made him expect too much from the people.' This was only 1864, but already Zaytsev found all the Populist movement of the age of reforms steeped in useless illusions.[45]

Criticizing a book on Italy in 1848, he had already said that it was essential to banish these myths of democracy. There were countries like France where one really could speak of the superiority of the working classes; indeed in 1848 the workmen of Paris had shown that 'they were the most worthy part of the nation'.

11*

The French workman is always preoccupied with his own fate. He tries to understand the riddle of this sphinx, and neglects no way of developing his mind. We have only to remember that it was from the workers that there sprang the best men of 1848. And so it is natural that the French democrats have the right to summon this class to power; it is incomparably more cultivated than the bourgeoisie and the merchants who have ruled it until now.

But not all countries were in the same position.

Unfortunately, there are countries in which the level of the French worker has been reached only by a few members of the upper and middle classes. The rest of the country, i.e. the so-called 'people', remains in a condition like that of the Kaffirs and the Kurds. How then can one speak of democrats and democracy?

Was not this the situation of the Italians in 1848? And to make clear to whom he was really referring, he went on to speak of the Neapolitans as '*white bears* with King Bomba at their head'. Russia, in fact, seemed to Zaytsev to be a typical example of a country in which it was useless to have any illusions about the people. Progress could come only from a minority in the upper and middle classes.[46]

In fact the 'nihilism' of the *Russkoe Slovo* is at the very source of the stream which flowed both into Russian Bakuninism and into Tkachev's Jacobinism. If we put the emphasis on individual revolt and personal 'refractoriness', we arrive at anarchism; if on the other hand we stress the political function of an enlightened and decided minority, we arrive at Jacobinism and the theory of a revolutionary *élite*. Sokolov and Zaytsev became Bakuninists; Nechaev made a violent and primitive attempt to hold anarchism and Jacobinism in the same harness; and Tkachev, who completed his political education in these circles, came to conclusions that were purely and coherently Blanquist.[47]

14. ISHUTIN'S 'ORGANIZATION' AND KARAKOZOV

THE MOVEMENT which can be personified by the three names of Ishutin, Khudyakov and Karakozov is the most important and significant of any after the dissolution of *Zemlya i Volya*. It was both Socialist and terrorist and—because of the way in which it combined these two elements—it constituted the first typically and purely Populist nucleus.[1]

Nikolay Andreyevich Ishutin was born on 3rd April 1840 at Serdovsk in the department of Saratov. It was from this region of the Volga that Belinsky and Chernyshevsky had sprung, and it was this region that was to give birth to many other Populist revolutionaries. His father was a merchant, 'an honoured and hereditary citizen', and his mother was a noble. At the age of two, he lost both parents, and was brought up by relations of his father, the Karakozovs, in whose family he stayed until the age of eleven. He went to secondary school at Penza, but weak health prevented him completing his studies. In 1863 he went to Moscow to attend the university and 'to finish his education', as he said later when interrogated.

At twenty-three, after an unhappy youth, he began to attract a group of young men, and became the leader of all the students who came from his part of the country, especially those from the department of Penza. He soon showed considerable powers of influence, and the circle of his acquaintances quickly grew.

He came in contact with *Zemlya i Volya* when it was already on the decline. He may have met Sleptsov; in any case, either through him or others, his political education was derived from the legacy of Chernyshevsky's teaching. But it was no longer the Chernyshevsky of brilliant political and economic insight who now impressed the young disciple: instead it was the prisoner, the martyr—a martyr, moreover, who in prison had been careful to express all his dreams and hopes. *What is to be done?* was already Chernyshevsky's best-known book; Ishutin was to be the first real incarnation of the revolutionaries contained in it. 'There have been three great men in the world,' he said, 'Jesus Christ, Paul the Apostle, and Chernyshevsky.' And one of the main concerns of his group was to try to free the writer from his imprisonment in Siberia.

He was a poor speaker and was neither a writer nor, in the narrow sense, an intellectual. Indeed he felt a feeling of superiority and scorn for learning, and shortly after his arrival in Moscow he decided to give up his studies and devote himself entirely to 'the cause'. He regarded completing his studies at the university as 'a little path that led to a bourgeois life'. According to Varlaam Nikolaevich Cherkezov, who joined his group in June 1864, his comrades too were all convinced that an interest in learning was quite useless because people who applied themselves to studying forgot the real needs of life and ended by becoming, whether they wanted to or not, 'generals of culture'. And so they aimed at freeing themselves from any inclination towards learning by devoting themselves exclusively to the people. This was the root of the conflict which divided the revolutionary Populists from the nihilists inspired by Pisarev.[2]

Ishutin's group quickly became strong and active. It was composed mainly of his ex-school and university comrades. Petr Dmitrevich Ermolov, who was younger than he was, and Nikolay Pavlovich Stranden, aged scarcely twenty, and both of noble families, had also come to Moscow for their studies which they had given up of their own accord in order to carry out their ideas. Dmitry Alexeyevich Yurasov, also from Penza, had been through the jurisprudence faculty in 1860, and taken part in the disturbances of the following year, and the demonstrations on the tomb of the historian Granovsky. He too had then given up his studies as an act of voluntary sacrifice. So many, he said, had, because of their rebellious activities, already been excluded from the university; now he would do on his own initiative what the State had compelled others to do. This gesture was a resumption of the movement 'to go to the people', which had also begun with a students' strike. These volunteers were soon joined by others who really had been driven from the university, such as Maximilian Nikolaevich Zagibalov, another pupil of the Penza school who was punished for taking part in the demonstrations of 6th February 1862.

Some of them sacrificed their belongings as well as their career. Ermolov, for instance, whose family was rich, gave the 'circle' all the money that he got from his tutor. And he intended as soon as he reached his majority to sell the twelve hundred *desyatiny* of land that he owned, so as to finance his schemes and those of his comrades.

The desire for self-sacrifice was in fact the dominating idea of the group. Khudyakov, who knew them well, said in his memoirs that Ishutin's circle 'was one of the most remarkable phenomena of these years. They were people who gave up all the pleasures of this life to dedicate themselves to the cause of freeing the people.'[3]

Their renunciation was ascetic in character. Ishutin always went around carelessly dressed, as did the others who, unlike him, had more than adequate means to dress normally. P. F. Nikolaev spoke of 'the severe discipline' that his comrades observed in their private lives. Alexander Markelovich Nikolsky, who, as we will see, took part in the St Petersburg group, looked upon the most elementary needs of life as a luxury and slept on the floor, often without blankets.

Most of their activities were devoted to creating cooperative associations or friendly societies among the workmen, artisans and students, on the lines laid down by Chernyshevsky in *What is to be done?*

Some of the students had real need of such schemes in order to earn a little money; others worked in them and organized them because it was a way of getting into contact with the people, and, above all, of bringing about, to some extent, their ideal of a communal life. In Moscow, for instance, they started a small cooperative business of bookbinders and tailors. But they wanted to do more, and intended to buy a small cotton factory, so as to devote the profits to the revolutionary cause. This ambition however was never realized.

At the same time they tried to urge some employees in a factory to organize themselves, and demand that the factory should be transformed according to the principles of the *artel* and cooperative. One of them, Alexander Kapitonovich Malikov, drew Ishutin's attention to the terrible conditions of the workmen in a glass factory at Lyudinov in the province of Kaluga.[4] These workers had only emerged from serfdom a few years earlier and for them emancipation had meant no reduction in the exploitation to which they were subjected. Malikov did what he could to help them but he was convinced that it would only be possible to achieve anything worthwhile by changing the very foundations of the business. Ishutin came there in person and incited the workers to make disturbances and demonstrations of protest. The owner finally gave them a piece of land and they sent delegates to St Petersburg to ask permission to open a factory to be organized by themselves. But this led nowhere. Malikov tried so hard to bring these plans into effect that he was eventually arrested and banished in 1866. He reappeared in 1874 during the great campaign to 'go to the people', as the founder of a religious 'deo-humanist' current within the Populist movement.

In 1875 Ishutin decided to put himself at the head of a friendly society among the workers of Moscow. He thought that this could be developed so as to include a labour exchange and a professional school for the sons of those workmen who were members of the bank. He went to St Petersburg to get information about the legal position concerning a scheme of this kind, but once again he met insurmountable obstacles.

He was severely reproached for this failure by Fedor Afanasevich Niki-forov, one of the few members of the group who was not a student. He was a small trader and had somehow become a natural intermediary between the workers and students, whom he derisively called 'nobles', accusing them of not working hard enough to start the proposed friendly society.

Efforts to devise a system of education went hand in hand with those dealing with organization. Between autumn 1864 and summer 1865 Ermolov and others founded a boys' school in one of the poorest districts of Moscow. Though they had no faith in the university, which would turn them into 'generals of culture', they did believe in the widespread diffusion of knowledge among the masses. But above all they saw in these schools a way of getting into contact with the people. 'We will make revolutionaries out of these little boys', said Ishutin.

The phrase reveals his true intentions; all his various schemes and those of his group were designed mainly to be the instruments with which to create a revolutionary force. He was not of course the first to try and start schools or cooperative savings banks for this purpose; but he introduced a particularly Machiavellian note. Just as the members of *Zemlya i Volya* had lost faith in the State, so Ishutin could feel nothing but irony for culture. He retained only one passionate belief which was expressed in his determination to fight for the Socialist society of the future. The State was certainly not the best machinery for bringing this into effect; still less so was culture. And so he was completely indifferent about the means to be employed and felt nothing but contempt for any prejudice on the subject.

He soon carried this lack of scruples to extreme limits. Plans were made to rob a merchant and attack the post, thus raising at least in theory the problem of individual expropriation. One member of the group, Viktor Alexandrovich Fedoseyev, thought of poisoning his father so as to be able to give his legacy to the cause. Fedoseyev was the son of a noble from the department of Tambov and lived in Moscow with his mother. His brother, Pavel, had already been a member of the *Young Russia* group and had been sentenced for this. In 1866 both were arrested following Karakozov's attempt on the life of the Tsar. Viktor was found guilty of the plan to rob his family and was banished to Siberia.

This youthful and revolutionary lack of scruples was the kernel around which were crystallized the political ideas that inspired Ishutin and his group. Expectation of a peasant revolution in the near future—within five years, they usually said—was at the very centre of their beliefs. They were in fact merely altering the time predicted by their immediate predecessors of *Zemlya i Volya* and *Young Russia*. As the revolution was to be 'economic' and radical, anything that stood in its way was considered to be harmful to the cause. Thus emancipation in 1861 was only one of the steps aimed at 'delaying the revolution in Russia'. Karakozov, who later was to shoot at the Tsar, firmly believed this, and in general the idea was widely held among them.[5]

This violent opposition to reforms inevitably coincided with the opinions of the most reactionary nobles who had always opposed the emancipation of the serfs and who now continued to criticize it. The members of Ishutin's group knew this and debated whether revolutionaries had the right to make use of this reactionary state of mind against the 'liberator Tsar'. Later,

Bakunin too considered the problem and gave a positive answer. One has the distinct impression that less consciously but perhaps with a greater element of Machiavellism, the young men around Ishutin had already come to the same conclusion.

Certainly they were decidedly opposed to any constitution and liberal concessions. Their attitude was based on the drive to keep intact the collective principle in the life of the Russian peasant, and they were prepared to destroy any obstacle which stood in the way of it developing on Socialist lines. Hence liberalism was the worst enemy of 'popular principles'. In his deposition on 29th July 1866, Ishutin said that when he had heard of a movement that had arisen in St Petersburg whose aim was a purely political revolution, he had told his comrades:

If this party wins, the people in Russia will be a hundred times worse off than it is now. They will invent some sort of constitution and push Russia into the Western way of life. This constitution will find support among the upper and middle classes, as it will guarantee individual liberty and give a stimulus to industry and business, without insuring us against destitution and a proletariat. Indeed, it will rather hasten their development.[6]

Thus Ishutin's terrorism was a compound of revolutionary Machiavellism and extreme Populism. The killing of the Tsar was to be the shock which would incite a social revolution or would at least compel the government to make substantial concessions to the peasants.

However strange it may appear at first sight, if we follow the strand of revolutionary movements from *Zemlya i Volya* onwards, we are inevitably led to conclude that the pistol shot becomes an exact substitute for Serno-Solovevich's appeal to the Tsar (or, after appeal had been proved useless, for the false manifesto used by the Polish revolutionaries to incite the peasants along the Volga). It was when these attempts had failed that the idea of assassination began to take first place. It was both an act of extreme lack of confidence in the State and a confession that the revolutionaries themselves were too immature to replace it with an organization of their own.

It was only when the theories and psychology of anarchism had been consolidated that this tacit confession of immaturity was countered with the declared intention of not wanting a substitute for the State. In other words the anarchists welcomed as an asset what was in fact a symptom of temporary weakness in a developing revolutionary movement.

Around the small group of young men inspired by these ideas there gradually grew up a revolutionary organization which in names and character reflects this psychology of extremism. It was made up of about ten students, who were often extremely poor. Some of them were of peasant stock, but most were the sons of country priests whose way of life bordered on that of the peasant masses. They came from different parts of Russia, but mainly from the Volga, and were students at universities, seminaries and agricultural academies. They had first made each other's acquaintance in a student mutual aid society, whose purpose was to find work for its poorest members, lend them money, etc. Such was the world of which Ishutin had said 'in this pond we will catch our fish'.

And so between 1865 and 1866 a secret society was built up which called itself *Organization*. Its regulations were discussed at length but never completed in time. It was to be an extremely select group. Three members were to stay in Moscow to organize the centre and a library; all the others were to disperse in the various provinces and find work as schoolmasters, clerks, office-workers, etc. Each was to try and build up a library and organize revolutionary activities designed to collect students and above all seminarists. They were then to act on instructions from the centre, forming cooperatives and preaching Socialism among the workers. Their goal was revolution. Ishutin said that he himself intended to go to Uralsk and live among the Cossacks, or to become a supervisor on a railway line, so as to spread propaganda among the workers.

But though this *Organization* might satisfy the requirements of propaganda and agitation, it had not been founded to achieve the group's other aim—terrorism. Within *Organization* there grew up another still more secret cell which took the name of *Hell*. This consisted of a 'commune' of students, i.e. a number of young men who lived together in common. And so the members of *Hell* were more usually called 'the men from Ipatov' (the name of their landlord).

We first hear of this small group of tried revolutionaries at the beginning of 1864. The cell was to remain secret even within *Organization* itself and was to begin work only after it had reached the agreed number of about thirty. In the meantime its members were to keep secret watch on *Organization*, and invisibly guide it. They were also to enter other secret societies to direct and control them. Any member of *Hell* who made a mistake was to pay for it with his life.

Its goal was terrorism aimed at those members of the government and land-owning classes who were particularly hated by the people. Its supreme end was the assassination of the Emperor. The potential assassins were to draw lots to determine who should make the attempt, and the man chosen was to cut himself off from his colleagues and adopt a way of life quite at variance with that of a revolutionary. He was to get drunk, find friends in the most doubtful circles, and even denounce people to the police. On the day of the assassination he was to use chemicals for disfiguring his face, so as to avoid being recognized, and to have in his pocket a manifesto explaining his reasons for what he was doing. As soon as he had carried out his attempt, he was to poison himself, and in his place another member of *Hell* would be chosen to continue the work which he had begun. Even after the outbreak of the revolution, *Hell* was to continue its activities, secretly directing the political forces engaged in the fight and suppressing superfluous or dangerous leaders. Said Ishutin:

A member of *Hell* must live under a false name and break all family ties; he must not marry; he must give up his friends; and in general he must live with one single, exclusive aim: an infinite love and devotion for his country and its good. For his country he must give up all personal satisfaction and in exchange he must feel hatred for hatred, ill-will for ill-will, concentrating these emotions within himself. He must live by feeling satisfied with this aspect of his life.

To complete our picture of this strange mixture composed of intense emotions superficially expressed and of youthful fantasies, we must add that Ishutin said that *Hell* was only the Russian section of a 'European Revolutionary Committee', whose aim was to exterminate monarchs everywhere. When, after Karakozov's attempt to kill him, Alexander II learnt of this Committee, he took it seriously and informed Bismarck, and advised him to organize police supervision on the Russian émigrés.[7]

In actual fact the Committee was primarily a myth launched by Ishutin. His technique of propaganda and proselytism included many elements of deliberate mystification. From the very beginning of his activities in 1864 he had been circulating an article which incited to action and was signed *Zemlya i Volya*, though at the time that body no longer existed. He probably got the idea of spreading the legend of a 'European Revolutionary Committee' from news that Khudyakov had brought from Geneva in August 1865. Khudyakov may have told him of the creation of the International which had occurred the year before, and suggested that he should 'establish close links with it'.[8] This is the most likely explanation, and one that is strongly endorsed by Soviet historians who have recently devoted great attention to this problem; but it is not quite certain. For this European association of terrorists suggests a myth whose character is more in keeping with the followers of Mazzini than with the International. It is even possible that both these legends were fused in Ishutin's propagandist device. Zagibalov, for example, later said that Ishutin had stated that 'in Bukovina there will soon be held a meeting of European revolutionaries who will include Mazzini, Herzen, Ogarev . . .' And he also remembered that Ishutin had often asked him how Orsini's bombs had been made. Others implicated in the trial of Karakozov made similar statements, though in less detail. Stranden said that in 1866 on his way back from St Petersburg, Ishutin had spoken of 'a European Committee' which had already held two meetings in Geneva.

Hell, the 'Committee' and in general all Ishutin's methods of organization were not only aimed at terrorizing the enemy, but also—indeed mainly—at inspiring fear and respect for those who took part in the more secret group. So, too, was the declared policy of amorality. And it was not just a question of words; there was a tense struggle within the groups of the *Organization*, and *Hell* often had difficulty in making itself heard and obeyed. Among

Ishutin's followers there were only a few extremists; most of the young men around him had more faith in resolute propaganda and the organization of schools and cooperatives than in terrorism; most of them believed more in preaching to the people than in revolution, and were less decided in their repudiation of all liberal reforms. They too were active and organized strong opposition within the group; they planned to threaten Ishutin physically so as to compel him to give up his ideas; they wanted to take all possible steps to dissolve the group of students who lived in Ipatov's house. Some they proposed to send to the provinces; others they even thought of having locked up in lunatic asylums. And there was talk of murder. The leaders of *Hell* threatened their opponents in just the same way. Quite apart from the violence, typical of all the movement, this clash of ideas is also of interest from the political point of view. The conflict within the Populist groups—between propaganda and terrorism, between a purely social revolution and political problems—appears here in embryo as a struggle between extremists and moderates. But it already contains those forces which were to lead ten years later to the schism of the second *Zemlya i Volya*.

The best representative of the more political wing of *Organization* was I. A. Khudyakov, a young student of ethnography and folk-lore who made himself the centre of a movement in St Petersburg which at least in part merged with Ishutin's in Moscow. He was one of the most typical figures of the Populism of his time and unquestionably one of the men who best expresses the ideology of the entire movement.[9]

He too was ascetic in temperament and since his early boyhood he had been engaged in activities which were above his strength. Two strands merged in this asceticism: the tradition of his ancestors who ever since the seventeenth century had taken part in the colonization of Siberia and had succeeded in growing rich amidst countless difficulties; and the more immediate precedent of his father, who had started life in poverty, and then after considerable efforts had managed to become a scrupulous and honest official in a world of corrupt ones. Khudyakov himself gives us some idea of the dreadful quality of the schools in which he began his education, though it must be admitted that they were better than the seminaries where some years earlier Shchapov, another Siberian, had suffered so much during his early years. Khudyakov too continued his studies in the University of Kazan.

At that time, although the custom of very heavy drinking which had marked the years before was still not over, atheist and republican ideas were beginning to spread among the students. Besides I myself never took part in these drinking sessions. Herzen's pamphlets and those of other forbidden authors were tirelessly copied out and circulated among all our fellow-students . . . And so I soon became an atheist, and in politics a supporter of a constitution. I broke away from religion without much trouble though I had imagined myself to be strongly tied to it.[10]

A year later, in the autumn of 1859, he went to Moscow. He had with him a letter of introduction to Professor F. I. Buslaev, one of the leading authorities on the traditions, arts and literature of the Russian people, for the study of which he had invented a new technique and aroused a new interest. At about this time (in fact 1861) he was publishing his fundamental work: *Historical Essays on the Art and Literature of the Russian People*.

Khudyakov was soon seized with a devouring passion for this subject. It became the very basis of his political life and his views on the problems of his time. He literally refrained from eating, so as to be able to publish, at his own expense, small volumes of stories and popular proverbs, and so as to be able to buy the books he needed for his researches.[11] During his travels in the countryside he collected peasant stories, copied them out and published them. He promised to write a commentary on them as soon as circumstances (i.e. the conditions of his life and the censorship) allowed.

From the very start, in his first small book which appeared in 1860, *A Collection of Historic Popular Songs of the Great Russians*, instruction was combined with description. His purpose was to extract from the peasants their own mythology and history so as to present these to them in a complete and accessible form. He wanted, in fact, to make up from the various fragments a whole which would represent the soul of the Russian people in all its traditions. His books (by no means devoid of interest for those concerned with Russian folk-lore) thus illustrated an intellectual version of the movement 'to go to the people'. But at the same time they represented an attempt to learn from the masses, to merge with them and to make propaganda by showing the peasants where their own traditions led to in the social field.[12]

Khudyakov maintained Buslaev's theories, according to which popular tales all had an origin in nature and were, in fact, very old transpositions of natural events: the rising and setting of the sun, the moon, the stars, etc. For him too, this idea, besides its value as a scientific hypothesis, was of significance as a romantic myth.

When man was not yet the ruler but the son of nature which surrounded him, when he had scarcely begun to think and observe, the extent of his knowledge was infinitely small. He could not clearly distinguish himself from the beasts, from plants, even from stones; the transformation of men into stones and trees seemed feasible . . .[13]

This feeling of the fusion of men with nature revealed one of the religious roots of Populism.

Among his most successful works was the *Russian Booklet* which was published in St Petersburg. It was a sort of manual containing stories, proverbs, riddles, *byliny*, fables and poems. The first part was made up of traditional material; the second contained works by contemporary authors such as Nekrasov, Uspensky and Pisemsky. The intention seemed to be to bring together, at least in the pages of a book, the peasants and those writers who wanted to speak for them. True, this was only a small anthology, but it had a specific significance, and was well produced. Khudyakov was here following up schemes which had already been made in earlier years. Serno-Solovevich, for instance, had also begun a collection of tales in prose and verse, with the same purpose in mind. Khudyakov's booklet, with its combination of popular traditions and Populist writers, represented the culmination of such ventures.[14]

In his researches into folklore, Khudyakov had to fight against difficulties which give us a vivid picture of the bureaucratic and official obstacles which stood in the way both of the people and the young intellectuals who were turning to Populism. There was first of all the civil censorship. For instance he asked permission to publish a review, called *The World of Fables*; first he showed the authorities what he planned to do, then he obtained the signature of three generals to act as guarantees. Yet after all this, permission was eventually refused.[15] Then there was the ecclesiastical censorship. In his autobiography he has told of the reception he met with when he showed the Archimandrite Sergius a collection of legends which he wanted to publish. The Archimandrite read a traditional version of the story of original sin, decided that it was 'materialist' and eventually refused permission to publish the collection. His argument was as follows: 'They were given permission to write freely on Peter the Great, and you've seen the results!' 'What results?' 'The student disorders of last year.'[16]

Such were the 'various circumstances' he had referred to in one of his books in order to justify the absence of a number of proverbs and stories which he had collected but could not publish. When he was arrested, the policemen of the Third Section spent many enjoyable evenings reading these papers which they had seized and which could not be published 'for moral reasons' (they were considered sinful and pornographic). These circumstances are worth recalling if we want to understand the value of Khudyakov's tenacity, asceticism and dedicated spirit in his attempts to know the people and its traditions, and make known at least a fraction of what he learnt.

In 1865 he published a small volume called *The Self-Teacher*, written for the uneducated 'with the aim of changing the reader's entire outlook on the world'. In it he spoke of the forces of nature, of history and of society. He attacked superstitions and glorified democracy. The United States of America, he said, had the best of all governments.[17] The booklet met with some success; Herzen read it, was very pleased with it and used it for educating his daughter Liza.[18]

This interweaving of Populism and enlightenment ended by making him critical of Buslaev's naturalistic theory of the origin of myths and legends. In an article on his *Stories of the People*[19] Khudyakov was already trying to see how symbols, whose original purpose had been to describe nature, had later been applied to the events of human history. So it was wrong to look upon epics and popular tales merely as an expression of the peasants' state of mind towards the universe. Rather they were a reflection of historical events interpreted from the people's point of view.

Shortly before his imprisonment, he was able to write another small book, *Old Russia*, designed to tell the history of his country from this point of view.

As a student in Moscow he had already been shocked by the methods used by even the greatest authorities to write history. They all adopted the standpoint of the State and looked upon as negative and destructive any forces which the State had not succeeded in crushing and overcoming during during its age-old task of developing absolutism and colonizing Russia. Even S. M. Solovev, the greatest historian of his time, had looked at history like an 'official', unable to visualize the development of civilization except as the systematic enforcement of the will of the State. And if this conception, which was derived from enlightened despotism, was not capable of grasping the history of Russia, just as mistaken were the Slavophils in their praise of the patriarchal monarchy before the reforms of Peter the Great.

And so Khudyakov devoted most of his book to a description of the misery and wars and barbarism of those centuries so idolized by traditionalists. Russians should look only to the future and not to the past. The only traditions that they could and ought to accept were those of the free mediaeval cities and, above all, of the peasant revolts of the sixteenth and seventeenth centuries against the State of Moscow and St Petersburg.

Old Russia was published when Khudyakov was in prison in 1867. It was edited by Lopatin and Volkhovsky, the founders of a *Society of the Rouble*, which aimed to spread culture and Populist ideas among the people. In February 1868 they were arrested, and *Old Russia* was seized.[20] But some copies were saved and proved valuable even in later years. Lavrov spoke of it at the time of the great movement 'to go to the people';[21] N. K. Bukh,[22] L. E. Shishko,[23] S. Sinegub,[24] all refer to the distribution of Khudyakov's book in the 'seventies. And G. A. Lopatin, who had helped to have it printed, explained the reason for its success. 'They may be only little works for popular schools, but in expert hands they can say many things which are most unwelcome to the censor.'[25]

Parallel to his activities in literature and research was the development of Khudyakov's political ideas. While still at Kazan University he had been chosen to organize an illegal students' library. Later in Moscow he had taken part in a demonstration against a professor who was hated for his manner of treating the students. And on 4th October 1861 he had been one of the organizers of the demonstrations at Granovsky's tomb. At St Petersburg he soon came into contact with the most active members of *Zemlya i Volya* and the circles round the *Sovremennik*, above all with Eliseyev.[26] In the spring of 1863 his room was searched by the police, who found nothing compromising. But his writings and the company with which he now associated made him known as a subversive. In the summer of 1865 his *Self-Teacher* was denounced by Muravev, the Minister of the Interior, and seized by the censorship. It had already been on view in the bookshop windows for three months.

Meanwhile a group had gathered round him which began by spreading education among the urban population and then soon became distinctly political in character.[27]

Towards 1864 this group came into contact with the Moscow *Organization*. Ishutin's statement that he had given Khudyakov money to go to Geneva in the summer of 1865 to get in touch with the exiles, is probably true.[28] In Switzerland Khudyakov met everyone from Utin to Bakunin and Herzen, but the impression he formed was mainly unfavourable. He thought that the younger ones could do nothing concrete and the older ones, specially Herzen, shocked him. He, who for years had lived on bread so as to be able to publish his stories of the people, saw Herzen 'living like a gentleman and not applying to his own life those ideas of which he spoke so much. In actual fact all those phrases about sacrifice and service for the good of the public, etc., remained mere phrases as far as he was concerned.'[29] In general Ishutin's movement felt no respect or admiration for Herzen. Like Alexander Serno-Solovevich and so many others of his generation, they condemned Herzen with a bitterness inspired by their own ascetic life and from their scathing nihilist irony.

In Geneva his main activities consisted in writing and printing a small, easily understandable book on politics which could be used for propaganda among the peasants. He called it *For True Christians. A work by Ignatius*. It was composed of maxims often taken from the Bible and especially the Acts of the Apostles, and it formed a small manual of answers to the most varying problems, above all religious and social. It discussed fasts, ikons, the Tsar, wars and cosmology. It was a clever collection, designed to express certain truths dear to Khudyakov's heart, such as 'Any nation which does not elect its own officials and does not keep count of their activities, is the slave of its superiors'; or 'The Bible demands that Kings should be elected. They must be chosen by the people and their power must be limited'; or 'The Lord, when he gave his people land in Palestine, ordered them to farm it collectively and divide it among themselves in equal parts.'

As can be seen the two fundamental themes are the *mir* and freedom. Freedom, indeed, takes first place and this was the difference between Khudyakov's group and Ishutin's *Organization* in Moscow. We must not exaggerate these differences, especially as the documents at our disposal are often unreliable. But there can be no doubt that while Khudyakov was more directly carrying on the tradition of *Zemlya i Volya*, in Moscow the social aspect had already absorbed, and indeed destroyed, any ingredient of liberalism.

Karakozov himself said that in St Petersburg they thought 'that a political revolution should precede the social revolution'.[30] When he was arrested, Khudyakov stressed this aspect of his beliefs not only because it made his position less serious but also because he really felt it to be true. Indeed he spoke of a *Zemsky Sobor* and the need for freedom in Russia. On 11th June 1866, in prison, he wrote a memorandum which, though he had no hopes of it reaching the Tsar, he thought might be of use to the high officials who would read it. It has been rightly pointed out[31] that this is the last work addressed to the Tsar by a Russian revolutionary in an attempt to persuade him to grant liberty. It is in fact the last instance of the example given by Serno-Solovevich. Once more this typical Populist was fired by the idea, or possible the desire, that 'it would be better to anticipate a revolution from below by starting it from above'. He clearly saw what would be the social effects of liberty, i.e. economic, industrial and agricultural development like that of 'the free countries, England and Belgium'. But unlike Ishutin, he seemed prepared to accept even this.

But not all his comrades, even in St Petersburg, shared Khudyakov's views. Nikolsky, for example, translated Owen into Russian; Petr Fedorovich Nikolaev, later one of the founders of the social revolutionary party, was at this time ardently spreading the ideas of Saint-Simon.[32] The more moderate wing, on the other hand, found its most authoritative spokesman in Osip Antonovich Motkov, a man of peasant origins. He said that he wanted to follow 'a slow but sure road', devoting himself chiefly to schools and to education in general. 'The present régime will change when ideas are spread throughout all levels of society. Until that time we must hold back others and ourselves from unleashing a revolution.'

The main centres of *Organization* were in Moscow and St Petersburg, and it never spread much in the provinces. However from the very first a contact was made with Saratov, whence Ishutin attracted the remnants of *Zemlya i Volya*. Alexander Khristoforovich Khristoforov, for instance, the illegitimate son of a noble landowner of that region, had been a member of *Zemlya i Volya* in 1862 and 1863. He had taken part in the university disturbances at Kazan, and had been sent to Saratov under police supervision. There he had devoted himself to Socialist propaganda among the local schoolboys, peasants and workmen, and had founded a series of small producers' cooperatives. In 1864 he was arrested, and after almost ten years' exile in the department of Archangel he managed to emigrate in 1875. In Geneva he started a periodical called *The Common Cause*.[33] Plekhanov later said that as long as ten years after Khristoforov's arrest, he had seen the profound marks left by his preaching at Saratov.

The workmen long remembered him. In 1877 they told us members of *Zemlya i Volya* that among them the small spark of revolutionary thought that Khristoforov had lit had never been extinguished. Even those who had not known him personally looked back on him as their spiritual ancestor.[34]

Apart from this limited attempt to find support in the provinces, and apart from propaganda and barely planned schemes to organize cooperatives,

Ishutin's and Khudyakov's movement set itself the task of trying to free those who had fallen in the fight of *Zemlya i Volya*.

Chernyshevsky still held first place in their thoughts. They wanted to free him so that he could emigrate abroad, and become editor of a periodical. This idea had originated in the St Petersburg group and was enthusiastically welcomed by everyone. Stranden was to carry out the plan. He was to go to Siberia in the summer of 1867 to be as near as possible to the place where Chernyshevsky was imprisoned. Khudyakov, who came from Siberia, had given him information and advice and had got hold of false passports.[35] But the arrests put an end to these plans before they could be put into effect. Another scheme had been devised in 1865. This time Nikolsky was sent from St Petersburg by Khudyakov in order to organize the liberation of M. A. Serno-Solovevich, in conjunction with the Moscow group. And at the same time the Saratov group made lengthy preparations to free Khristoforov.

But their plans were crowned with only one success, though the prisoner in question was a man of the highest importance. This was Dombrowski, a Pole, who was later to be a general in the Paris Commune. He had been arrested at the end of 1864 for his part in the Polish rebellion, and had been put in one of the Moscow prisons. He fled in full daylight, dressed as a woman. Ermolov, Yurasov and Zagibalov hid him for a few days before he was able to get to St Petersburg and flee abroad.[36]

We now turn to another of *Organization*'s interests. The idea of an attempt on the life of the Tsar was probably more widespread than is generally thought. The words of Lincoln's assassin 'Sic semper tyrannis' were fairly well known in Moscow.[37] Moreover both Khudyakov's return from Geneva in 1865 and the news spread by Ishutin of a European Revolutionary Committee helped, in varying degrees, to create the atmosphere. The over-excited and repressed psychology which had gradually developed among the members of *Hell* here acted both as an effect and as a cause. But when it came to the point, the assassination was attempted because a man was found who, overcoming the obstacles imposed even by his comrades, came to the conclusion that action was needed immediately. 'A pale and tired face, hair flowing on to his shoulders; he was noticeable for the carelessness of his clothes.' Such was Dmitry Vladimirovich Karakozov between 1863 and 1864, as remembered later by a professor at Kazan University.[38] It was his second stay there; he had earlier been dismissed for taking part in disorders in 1861. He came from a family of nobles in the department of Saratov, small half-ruined landowners, with about fifty peasants. It was the same family that had taken in the small orphan Ishutin and given him a home during his childhood.

In 1864 Karakozov went to Moscow to study, but a year later he was once more dismissed from the university for not paying his taxes. For two months he tried to work as clerk for a noble, but this experience left him only with a profound hatred of the aristocracy. Ishutin recalled that he always thought of that time with hatred and rage. He always spoke with scorn of the meetings held between landlord and peasants after the emancipation for the purpose of deciding the size of the land to be given to the latter. 'I think that this was the beginning of his hatred for the nobles.' But so far Karakozov's short and disturbed life had not yet revealed the most important element in his character: a quite exceptionally stubborn will and power of concentration.

Like many others, he too began his activities by devoting himself to education and propaganda. He became a master in one of the free schools organized by Ishutin in Moscow, which were named after Pavel Akimovich Musatovsky, a Vladimir noble, who to some extent shared Populist opinions. But these activities only gnawed at Karakozov's conscience. He felt seriously ill, more so than his health really warranted. Weakened by privations and difficulties, he thought of suicide and bought poison. But he then ceaselessly tormented himself with the thought of having to die before doing anything for the people.

In February 1866 he disappeared for a few days, leaving a message that he had gone to drown himself. When he returned, he said that he had been to the monastery of the Trinity and Saint Sergius not far from Moscow. He then told Ishutin, Ermolov, Yurasov, Stranden and Zagibalov of his decision to kill Alexander II. They all tried to dissuade him, but in vain.

At the beginning of March he went to St Petersburg, where, because he had no passport, he was compelled to live in hotels and hired rooms and constantly change his residence. He associated with workmen and students, and met Khudyakov more than once. He had brought a revolver with him, and he now got hold of bullets and gunpowder.

He then wrote a manifesto which he copied out and left where he thought the workmen would be able to find it.[39] From a conspiratorial point of view, this was hardly a very practical move, especially as in it he described his intention of trying to kill the Tsar. But Karakozov felt that such an action was necessary, even if risky. For he was tormented by one problem. Would the people understand what he was about to do, and how would they react? This problem—which was the great void in the terrorist conception, the great gap in the scheme—worried him and Khudyakov uninterruptedly during the days that immediately preceded his attempt. Karakozov had made up his mind. His doubts were not concerned with the deed itself but only with its interpretation. And indeed his proclamation is almost a confession, an attempt to justify himself in the eyes of his 'workmen friends' to whom it was addressed. A strongly personal tone gives this manifesto exceptional originality and power compared to the many others similar in ideas and motives that were drawn up at this time.

The message is simple and inspired by all the fundamental points of the Populist doctrine of the Moscow group.

Brothers, I have long been tortured by the thought and given no rest by my doubts as to why my beloved simple Russian people has to suffer so much! . . . Why next to the eternal simple peasant and the labourer in his factory and workshop are there people who do nothing—idle nobles, a horde of officials and other wealthy people, all living in shining houses? They live on the shoulders of the simple people; they suck the peasants' blood. I have looked for the reason for all this in books, and I have found it. The man really responsible is the Tsar; Russian history shows this. It is the Tsars who through the centuries have gradually built up the organization of the State, and the army; it is they who have handed out the land to the nobles. Think carefully about it, brothers, and you will see that the Tsar is the first of the nobles. He never holds out his hand to the peasant because he himself is the people's worst enemy.

Having thus explained in popular language his idea that the State (and therefore the Tsar) was the fundamental enemy of a revolution in Russia, he spoke of the reforms of 1861 as the most obvious proof that the Emperor was incapable of granting real liberty.

I myself have travelled in various parts of our mother Russia. I have experienced the miserable life of the peasants; they are growing poorer and poorer as a result of the various measures which accompany 'liberty'. Soon even their last wretched clothes will be stripped from their backs. I have felt all the grief and burden of seeing my beloved people die in this way; and so I have decided to destroy the evil Tsar, and to die myself for my beloved people.

And he added, 'If I do not succeed, others will succeed after me.' Only when they had been freed from the main enemy would people see how few and weak were the landlords, the Court dignitaries and the officials.

Then we will have real freedom; land will no longer belong to the idlers but to the *artels* and to societies of the workers themselves; capital will no longer be squandered by the Tsar, the nobles and the Court dignitaries. Instead it too will belong to the *artels* and the workers. With this capital the cooperatives will produce useful works and income will be divided equally among their members. When it owns these means, the Russian people will be able to administer itself even without the Tsar.

Let the workers know that the man who has written this is thinking of their fate and so they must act, with hope only in themselves, to master their destiny and to free Russia from robbers and exploiters.[40]

The authorities learnt of this combined manifesto and confession three weeks before the plot was carried out. On 14th March an anonymous letter signed 'A student' reached the chancellery of the Governor-General of St Petersburg. This letter enclosed a copy of Karakozov's proclamation. The fact that no precautions were taken is a measure of the bureaucratic inefficiency of the time.

It is difficult to determine what the St Petersburg group was doing during the days immediately preceding the plot. During the trial the judges themselves naturally tried to find this out, and at least some of them thought that the leading instigator of Karakozov's action was Khudyakov. Klevensky, the greatest expert on this episode, was for long doubtful about this. In the first edition of his book on Ishutin's group he accepted the 'official' theory that Khudyakov was responsible; but a year later, in the second edition, he rejected this, not without good reasons. In fact it is probable that Khudyakov did not at first welcome the attempt but, when he realized that nothing could be done in view of Karakozov's firm decision, he tried to take advantage of the inevitable, by preparing those around him for the popular rising which he expected. The assassination could be attributed to the nobles who desired to rid themselves of a Tsar who had freed the serfs; the revolutionaries could cunningly encourage this rumour, arousing violence against the nobility and, if possible, inciting the people to lynch the wealthy. Already among the young revolutionaries in St Petersburg, even those not directly in contact with Khudyakov's centre, the conviction had spread during these days that a decisive moment had been reached. This conviction acted like a wave and swept away their plans for long-term propaganda and infiltration among the people, replacing these with hopes of an immediate and drastic upheaval.[41]

There were, of course, some who tried to prevent the proposed assassination. When Khudyakov went to Moscow to tell his comrades of Karakozov's intention, Ermolov and Stranden left for St Petersburg with the specific intention of stopping him; after some searching they found him, and made lengthy efforts to dissuade him. Ishutin himself wrote, telling Karakozov to return to Moscow. He obeyed, and on 25th March silently attended a meeting of *Organization*.

But on 29th he was back in St Petersburg, and on 4th April 1866 while the Tsar was about to get into his carriage, after a walk in the Summer Garden, Karakozov fired at him—and missed; he tried to run away, but was stopped by the police and volunteers among the crowd. To them he shouted, 'Fools, I've done this for you.' He was led to the Emperor, who asked him if he was a Pole. He answered: 'Pure Russian.' When asked why he had fired, he replied, 'Look at the freedom you gave the peasants!'

The shooting made an enormous impression. It put an end to the few remaining traces of collaboration between the Emperor and the liberal intelligentsia in the direction of reforms—a collaboration that had made possible the freeing of the serfs and the subsequent changes in local administration and justice. A wave of indignation and fear destroyed any liberal dreams that still survived after the repression of 1862. And the period of what is traditionally called the 'White Terror' now began. Even men like Nekrasov, who had inherited the spirit of the Tsar's earliest years on the throne, bowed down and tried to save what could still be saved. They added their voice to the chorus of protests against 'nihilism' and joined with the intelligentsia in a mass condemnation of the desperate and violent younger generation. Muravev, who in 1863 had crushed the Polish rebellion in blood, was put in effective charge of internal affairs. He organized a system of repression which aimed to root out the forces of revolution by striking the intellectual tendencies which had given them birth.[42]

The reaction went deep, and even spread to the people. Exact information is difficult to come by, but all sources are agreed that the peasants stood by the Emperor, often violently. In the countryside the legend of a nobles' plot against the 'Liberator Tsar' spread and took root. Only a few witnesses speak of apathy, suggesting that even a plot of this nature was too remote to interest the peasants.

As for the workmen, Z. K. Ralli, who later joined Bakunin but was at this time still in Russia, wrote in his memoirs:

At that time it was dangerous to speak badly of the Tsar in the factories. As a rule the worker does not love the students just because he looks upon them as enemies of the Tsar. The Tsar is for him the personification of truth and justice. In the streets of Moscow they booed and insulted the students, and everywhere they demonstrated their monarchist feelings. The young intellectuals of that time well knew that in Russia the workers and the peasants linked all their hopes in a better future to their faith in the Tsar.[43]

Official circles wished to take advantage of this situation, and a rumour was quickly spread that Karakozov had not aimed badly but that a providential hand had jolted the revolver. For a short time Osip Komissarov, the alleged saviour, became a hero. He was of peasant origin, from the department of Kostroma. The Tsar's life had thus been saved by a toiler of the fields. But the rumour did not last long. Komissarov was in fact a poor artisan given to drink. He was introduced to the Emperor, made a noble, and given an endless series of feasts and banquets. But his behaviour was such that he had to be sent back to the provinces, where he soon died in a state of complete drunkenness.

The episode is significant, but it must not conceal the fact that the attempt on the Tsar's life did show how strong was the alliance between the monarchy and the mass of working classes and peasants. It was a bond which could not be cunningly exploited to incite violence against the nobles, as the revolutionaries had hoped. They must have realized now what an abyss still divided them from the people.

When Karakozov was arrested, he tried to conceal his identity. He was treated with great cruelty and interrogated for hours on end without being allowed to sit or lean against a wall, and was given only bread and water to eat. But the rumour which soon spread that he had actually been tortured was probably only a legend. For several days he said that he was a peasant called Alexey Petrov, whereas the police thought him a Pole. A few days later, however, his real identity was discovered. An hotel keeper where he had stayed reported the disappearance of one of his lodgers. The hotel was searched, and some pieces of paper with an address were discovered. The address was Ishutin's. The entire Moscow group was at once caught. The arrested were taken to St Petersburg.

The atmosphere of reaction and terror in which the inquiries were made inevitably had profound effects on the results. The extent of the arrests, which involved several hundred people, eventually provided the police with a large number of facts. Moreover, the work of the authorities was certainly made easier by ideological differences which existed within the groups in Moscow and St Petersburg. Ishutin, for instance, tried to divest himself of responsibility for the plot. At last the Commission was satisfied that it had all the necessary information in its hands. It is easy to imagine what sufferings the accused underwent from the knowledge that both Khudyakov and Karakozov died insane, and Karakozov, who was not a believer, ended by spending hours on his knees in passionate prayer.

The trial was held in secret in the Peter-Paul fortress, in the very room where the Decembrists had been condemned in 1826. The prosecutor was the Minister of Justice himself. The accused had lawyers who in most cases defended them effectively. And indeed the verdict passed on 1st October was not a pure act of revenge but, within limits, respected the existing laws of Russia.

Karakozov was sentenced to be hanged. When he asked for mercy, Alexander II replied that though as a Christian he could forgive, as a Tsar he could not. At seven in the morning on 3rd October, he was led to the scaffold in front of several thousand spectators. He bowed to the people at each corner, as was the custom, and was hanged. Though the feeling of the crowd was strongly against him, it showed no sign of hatred or derision. 'Among the crowd of people', a contemporary said, 'could be heard the cries and groans of women; and prayers and signs of the Cross were made for the sinful soul of the criminal.'[44] The same reaction was noted by Kostomarov, the historian, in his memoirs:

The public's behaviour was thoroughly Christian in spirit; not a single reproach or accusation was heard. On the contrary, when the criminal was led to the gallows, most of the people present made the sign of the Cross, saying, 'Lord, forgive his sins and save his soul.'[45]

During the following days the police arrested anyone coming to visit Karakozov's burial place.

Ishutin too was condemned to death. Only after he had been led to the scaffold was he told that his sentence had been commuted to forced labour for life. He left for Siberia, but was taken back to the fortress of Shlisselburg, where he remained from October 1866 to May 1868. He was already showing symptoms of madness when he resumed his journey towards Siberia. There he died of consumption in the prison hospital at Novaya Kara on 5th January 1879.[46]

Khudyakov was well defended, and in spite of general expectation he was not sentenced to death; instead he was banished. In February 1867 he was at Irkutsk and from there he was sent to Verkhoyansk. Already at the tribunal and later on at the scaffold, where he was taken with the others for the 'civil execution', he could not control a nervous smile, a symptom of the mental illness which led to his death on 17th September 1876. But in Siberia he still had the time and strength of spirit to devote himself to his ethnographical researches. He collected a series of documents on the popular traditions of the Yakuts among whom he was compelled to live, in one of the most distant and deserted villages of those regions. Part of the manuscript was lost and the remainder was only published in 1890 after passing from hand to hand in a series of strange adventures. For long this considerable work was the only study of popular traditions in those regions and of the relations between the legends of the Yakuts and those of the Russian people.[47]

Thirty other people were tried by the same tribunal. Ermolov, Stranden, Yurasov, Zagibalov, Nikolaev and Shaganov, were sentenced to hard labour and were imprisoned in the Alexandrovsky Zavod in Siberia, where Chernyshevsky was serving his sentence. In 1872 nearly all were freed from prison and scattered throughout the tundra of the Yakuts. They settled in the land and devoted themselves to farming, educating the native children and starting an elementary medical service. They were the first exiles in those regions and their patience and work gradually overcame the distrust and hate with which the Yakuts had originally greeted them. 'From then on the inhabitants of the district recognized them as men of intelligence and as the best among the Russians.'[48]

The repression which followed Karakozov's attempt to kill the Tsar had one immediate and tangible effect. Between 1866 and 1868 there was not a single group in Russia able to carry out clandestine activities or make known its ideas by giving a more general significance to its internal debates. But this does not mean that clandestine groups stopped springing up from the fertile ground of student meetings or that the state of mind which had found expression in Ishutin's *Organization* did not continue to make itself felt underground.

Even the scant information at our disposal does, for instance, allow us to follow the inner life of one of these student circles, the so-called 'Academy of Smorgon'.[49] The name itself considerably mystified the police when they heard of its existence. In fact it was probably an allusion to that Academy of Smorgon* where at the beginning of the nineteenth century gypsies used to train their bears before bringing them to dance in the squares of towns and villages. A member of the group said, for instance, 'our clothes and our activities made us rather like those bears and from them we took our name'.

It was a typical 'commune', a group of students living together in the same house and sharing the expenses. 'On coming back in the evening, one paid about fifty kopeks, and for that sum everyone had the right to take some of the vodka which was on the table and to eat some herrings. When one had drunk, those who could, danced, and the others looked on or talked.' Though this is an extract from a deposition which was evidently designed to

* The name of the woods round a small township in the Urals.

allay all suspicion, in fact the day to day atmosphere of this 'Bears' Academy' must have been very much as described. The group sprang up in 1867 and lasted until March 1869. The police, true to their tradition, thought that these meetings were the scenes of wild orgies and said that a beautiful young 'nihilist' used to sell herself so as to collect money for the 'commune'. In fact the girl in question, whose name was Kozlovskaya, merely organized the board. She was typical of the young girls of St Petersburg at this time— halfway between the feminists who had helped the rise of *Zemlya i Volya* at the beginning of the 'sixties and the terrorist revolutionaries of the following period.

In this 'commune', which sprang up under specially difficult conditions of oppression and reaction, students used to meet whose original bonds lay in a common background of persecution. Many had already had experience of prison during the inquiries that followed Karakozov's attempt. They, too, mostly came from Saratov and the regions of the Volga.

And they too, through this double tradition of region and politics, continued the cult of Chernyshevsky. They were constantly occupied with the prospect of freeing him, so as to let him emigrate and take charge of a revolutionary newspaper abroad. Such aspirations were similar to those of Elpidin, an exile in Geneva, who soon began to reprint the master's works, bringing out in 1867 *What is to be done?*, the book which had had the greatest effect on the new generation.

The 'Academy of Smorgon' made some plans to organize Chernyshevsky's escape, but it soon met with insuperable financial difficulties. Its members did, however, at least want to share in the editing of his works, and with this aim in view they got into contact with the exiles and sent a sum of money which they had collected.[50]

The Academy combined this cult of Chernyshevsky with one of Karakozov, whose example they tried to follow. Indeed there seems to be proof that two of its members tried to blow up a train at Elizavetgrad on which the Emperor was travelling. This is not, however, quite certain as all our information on the subject is based on an anonymous denunciation against two students, Mikhail Petrovich Troytsky[51] and Vasily Ivanovich Kuntusev, who came from peasant stock in Saratov.

In 1867 both were at the university in St Petersburg. At the beginning of 1868 Kuntusev left with a companion for Siberia so as to study the plan to free Chernyshevsky; but lack of money compelled him to make a long detour and he was arrested at Saratov for vagrancy. In 1869 he left Moscow with Troytsky on his way to South Russia, where he planned to circulate leaflets sent by the exiles in Geneva. On 1st November both were arrested on suspicion of planning a terrorist outrage.[52]

The documents at our disposal prevent us being certain how much truth there was in all this; indeed even the police were doubtful. But their journey in itself is enough to show the close bond between motives of propaganda and clandestine organization, the plan to free Chernyshevsky and terrorism.

The only attempt the Academy made to engage in real activities derived directly from legends spread by Ishutin. Remembering that there had been talk of a 'European Revolutionary Committee', they tried to get into contact with it. Although the man they chose for this purpose was a figure of only secondary importance, even he is enough to show, as so often in the lives of these Populists, the reserves of strength, idealism and will-power that inspired the members of this movement.

Ivan Ivanich Bochkarev was born in 1842 in a little town in the department of Tver and came from a family of the small bourgeoisie. He spent some time working for the printing press which his father had left, and also went to university lectures in Moscow and later in St Petersburg. But he was soon fired by the political ideas that he found among his fellow students, and began to take an interest in the 'Slav problem'. In 1866 the revolt of the Croats against the Turks convinced him of the need to act. In St Petersburg he founded an *obshchina*, a group of Serb students who were already allied to the *Omladina*—an organization of southern Slavs whose political tendencies are symbolized in the election some years earlier of Garibaldi, Mazzini, Cobden, Herzen and Chernyshevsky as honorary presidents. Bochkarev then went on a long journey abroad, passing through Geneva, Marseilles, Naples and Rome, where he got into contact with the organization of Serbs and Croats. In 1867 he went to Belgrade, to attend a meeting of the *Omladina*. There he was unable to make the speech he had prepared as the meeting was interrupted because of a political dispute with the Serb government. His notes, however, show that the proposed speech had been inspired by Chernyshevsky's general views on Slav problems.

During this journey Bochkarev tried to carry out his purpose of getting into contact with the Russian émigrés. But his mission was an utter failure. He brought with him a work by Khudyakov, so as to introduce himself to those who had known that author in Geneva some time earlier. Instead it only aroused suspicions. Elpidin and Utin thought him an *agent provocateur*. As the reaction grew in Russia, the exiles became more and more distrustful. Their groups were torn by internal strife and fear. They ended by organizing a search in Bochkarev's room; and he was forced to leave without having done anything. The only result of this attempt to get into contact with the 'European Revolutionary Committee' was his carrying back to Russia the first number of the review *Narodnoe Delo*, written almost entirely by Bakunin. This was a fruitful seed. The students of St Petersburg who slowly, gradually, were reorganizing their forces under the 'White Terror' had been keenly waiting for a stimulus, and S. L. Chudnovsky has described the enormous impression that the review made on them.[53]

On 18th October 1868, Bochkarev was arrested. He defended himself stubbornly and intelligently, but the police managed to get evidence against him. This was given by a man who had recently returned from abroad, where he too had been in touch with the exiles. Unlike Bochkarev, however, I. G. Rozanov was to show throughout his life the pettiness and short-sighted egotism which was so mixed up with the revolutionary movement of these years.

Rozanov's *Confession* is a document of great interest because of its abject sincerity. The poor son of a signalman, he had always been persecuted and crushed by a society too oppressive for him to withstand. His entire education had been derived from 'scientific-drunken' conversations with his acquaintances and mainly from novels. 'I found only one thing in novels: it was my duty to become a hero and to act boldly and openly; and so I often made myself drunk in public.' All his ideas were summed up in a sterile, egotistic 'nihilism'. His favourite author was Pisarev. At Geneva he had for a short time been a member of the local section of the International. When faced with Bochkarev, he managed to persuade the police that he was a dangerous man; as a reward he himself was freed. But his offer to act as an *agent provocateur* was not accepted. He was probably too ill with consumption and syphilis to be of any use.

Bochkarev was condemned to compulsory residence in his native town. He did not remain there long, because he was soon once more in prison after the Nechaev affair. For the time being, thanks to his calm firmness, he escaped without further consequences and returned to devote himself to education in his home town. But the persecutions continued, and he was exiled to Astrakhan. In 1879 he was banished to Archangel on suspicion of having taken part in the murder of an *agent provocateur*. Though he thus spent most of his life moving from exile to exile, he never abandoned his Populist ideas. As an old man he lived near Yasnaya Polyana and became friendly with Tolstoy. Their religious ideas coincided on many points, and the writer felt great respect for him. For many years Bochkarev had been in trouble for refusing to write 'Orthodox' opposite his name on the census form. This naturally won him the sympathy of Tolstoy.

B. P. Kozmin, the historian, has rightly called Bochkarev a vigorous and original searcher for truth. He was unquestionably the most considerable figure to have sprung from the 'Academy of Smorgon' or in general from any of the few revolutionary groups which survived under the White Terror.

15. NECHAEV

◆◆◆

THE REVOLUTIONARY FERMENT that inspired Ishutin and his group produced in Nechaev the very embodiment of violence. He developed the feelings and ideas of *Hell* with a ruthlessness unique among the revolutionaries of the 'sixties.

Nechaev closed the decade that had opened on 19th February 1861. He was the last Populist revolutionary to base his activities on the high hope that the countryside would reject the peasant settlement. When in 1870 the cycle of reforms at last came to an end, and with it the phase of conspiracies based on faith in peasant resistance, the movement 'to go to the people' began, the great attempt to gain by means of propaganda that contact with the villages that *Zemlya i Volya* and Ishutin had lacked, and that Nechaev too never managed to achieve.

Nechaev met with obstacles all the greater in that the failure of Ishutin's *Organization* and Karakozov's unsuccessful *coup*, followed by the 'White Terror', had already convinced many of the Populists that the way he had chosen was mistaken. The only course open, they thought, was one of slow infiltration into the countryside, coupled with a systematic attempt to understand the peasants' conditions and study their problems and mentality. Indeed immediately after Karakozov's gesture in 1866, signs began to appear of the Populism that was to flourish in the early 'seventies. Groups were being organized which in 1874 were to give birth to the movement to 'go to the people'. We shall have to begin by looking at these early groups if we want to understand the atmosphere into which Nechaev injected his overmastering passion for immediate action.

The most important of these groups was the *Society of the Rouble*, which was started in 1867 by Lopatin and Volkhovsky for the purpose of 'getting a closer view of that enigmatic sphinx called "the people"', in the words of one of its founders.[1] To do this they intended to organize a group of young men whose only occupation was to be teaching, and who would travel from one village to the next. All were extremely poor and planned to live on what they were given by the peasants. Yet if for all their asceticism this proved insufficient, they intended to resort to periodical subscriptions from intellectuals who sympathized with them. But they were never to ask for more than a rouble a head; hence the name of the Society. Their teaching, their conversations with the peasants, and their public readings were to be based on books published legally by the Society itself. These schoolmasters were

to be dispersed in various districts according to a general plan so as to be
able to get information from a large number of regions and thus provide
a general picture of the Russian countryside. 'The only illegal thing in our
programme', Lopatin was to say, 'was this very collecting of facts, observations and experiences in order to find out how far the simple people were
accessible to revolutionary propaganda against the government.'[2] The
Society, in fact, was aiming, during a phase of reaction, at exploiting legal
possibilities to the full.

A glance at Lopatin's life will be enough to show that the origins of this
policy of prudence and long-term activity were far from deriving from a
cautious temperament or from fear of persecution. They sprang, rather,
from the desire to find, through detailed and patient preaching, that contact
with the people which conspiracy and terrorism had been unable to achieve.

Lopatin's political outlook was formed at St Petersburg by contact with
Khudyakov's *Organization*. He has left us a portrait of Khudyakov that
clearly reveals the admiration he felt for his indomitable determination to
know the peasants and to love them and devote himself to them, as well as
the equally obvious disgust he felt for his 'fanaticism'.[3] The two elements
that he found in Ishutin's movement, Populism and conspiracy, he looked
upon as contradictory: 'The people was not given much part in the violent
transformation of its fortunes', he said of *Organization*. Indeed, the
revolutionaries appeared anxious to substitute themselves for the people, in
whose name they proposed to act by means of conspiracy and terrorism.
And yet they too had been 'genuine Populists' and had felt 'a real sympathy
for the peasants and tried to spread their ideas at every opportunity'. It
was this side of the movement that Lopatin wanted to develop.[4] He was
opposed to terrorism because he thought that 'under present circumstances
and in the absence of a strong revolutionary organization, the violent death
of the Sovereign would not in fact incite the people to revolution'. The only
result of terrorism would be that the reaction would grow more oppressive.

He therefore avoided the central group of the conspiracy in St Petersburg,
though this did not prevent him being arrested after Karakozov's attempt to
kill the Tsar, and detained in prison for two months. On his liberation,
Khudyakov entrusted him with the job of keeping alive what still survived
of the organization, and taking any conspiratorial measures necessary.

He had scarcely been released from prison, when a chance of action came
his way: 'In 1867 I read in a morning newspaper that Garibaldi had left
Caprera and was moving towards Rome. On the evening of the same day I
left St Petersburg for Italy; but I reached Florence on the very day of the
battle of Mentana.'[5]

He returned to Russia and devoted himself entirely to the *Society of the
Rouble*. He succeeded in publishing the first, and last, book of the proposed
series, Khudyakov's *Old Russia*. In the spring of 1868 he was arrested with
Volkhovsky. After eight months in prison he was banished to Stavropol

whence he escaped abroad. He was destined to become one of the most active revolutionaries of the 'seventies and 'eighties, the friend of Marx and Engels, a translator of part of *Das Kapital* as well as author of the boldest plan to free Chernyshevsky from Siberia. After the events of 1st March 1881, he tried to inject new life into *Narodnaya Volya*, and this cost him twenty years' imprisonment. But he lived long enough to have the joy of seeing the revolution in 1917, and he speaks of this in his notes. The founder of the modest *Society of the Rouble* is, for all his dry unrhetorical manner, one of the most interesting figures of the entire Populist movement.

Volkhovsky was soon released and settled in Moscow, where he joined German Lopatin's brother, Vsevolod. Together they organized a new group, very characteristic of the time. Its members read together, discussed works of science and physiology, and in general followed the trends of the new generation which was more influenced by positivism and the belief in science than its predecessor. It was in fact a typical group of 'self-education' with no specific political purpose. If its members had any plans for their future, they consisted in long patient work among the people. Volkhovsky was employed in Cherkesov's bookshop, which he saw transformed into one of the favourite meeting places of the younger Populists. Among these were many who were later to be implicated in the trial of Nechaev: Petr Gavrilovich Uspensky, his sister Nadezhda and his future wife Alexandra Ivanovna Zasulich. The latter has described these young men as they groped for a new approach and rediscovered the past, after the interruption of the White Terror. 'We were all inexperienced; we read Chernyshevsky's articles in the *Sovremennik* and the works of Lavrov, and we greeted with enthusiasm the appearance of a few back numbers of the *Kolokol* which Uspensky had managed to unearth.'[6]

Other groups, very similar but with greater promise, were springing up in St Petersburg, and in them a considerable number of men who were soon to be among the most active revolutionary Populists of the 'seventies.[7] In October 1869, for instance, there appeared the 'Commune of the Malaya Vulfovaya', named after the street in which it had its headquarters. This was made up of a group of students who collected round M. A. Natanson.

In 1915 Natanson, who became one of the best-known of all Populist and Socialist-Revolutionaries, toyed with the idea of writing his memoirs. For this purpose he made a series of skeleton notes which, far better than many fuller accounts, suggest the outlines of his own life, and that of his group at the end of the 'sixties. He had arrived in St Petersburg in August 1868 and one of his lapidary notes gives his impressions: 'What I had thought of the students (ideal people) and what I found (cards, wine and women).' Within a year he had made friends with all the most remarkable figures who did not belong either to the small wing of constitutionalists or to the circles round Nechaev. He himself has described his own tendencies as being identified with 'seekers' and 'Socialist-Populists'. From the ideological point of view, Fourier and Owen were his favourite authors. 'Then in spring 1869 I first read Marx.' His sympathies lay with long-term policies rather than with that crude desire for immediate action which inspired Ishutin's group and which was soon to find its most typical embodiment in Nechaev.

These feelings were shared by a young man called Mikhail Fedorovich Negreskul, though he was very soon to die. At this time he was an exceedingly active figure both in Moscow and St Petersburg. He introduced the young men in the capital to the spirit of Lavrov, whose disciple he was and whose daughter he married. He had been abroad and had met the exiles. His thought was moving towards an entirely theoretical form of Marxism which was at this time just beginning to enter the world of the Populists without however transforming its fundamental standpoint or spirit. If anything, in fact, it made them reluctant to take immediate action and inspired them with the desire to make a deeper study of social problems. Negreskul was helping to translate Marx's *Zur Kritik* when he was arrested on 28th December 1869. Shortly before this, his friend Lopatin had written from his enforced residence in the Caucasus to ask how far he had got. His letter not only shows that they were already friends but also reveals the similarity of their views on all immediate problems.

These small embryo groups were soon shaken and set in motion by a revival of the student movement, very similar to the one of 1861. Its demands were the same: above all the right to meetings, organization and freedom of speech.[8] But the very fact that these disorders took place after a long phase of reaction, as pronounced in the field of education as in politics as a whole, was of considerable importance. The Minister of Public Instruction, D. A. Tolstoy, viewed with particular disfavour any kind of autonomous student life. He looked upon the increasingly scientific trends of teaching as the origin of all evils and he was starting that classicist reaction which became typical of Russian educational policy for many years. As for the social make-up of the university, the population had not changed much during the last few years. The main statutory restrictions imposed on admission to the universities had affected the Poles, who were not allowed to constitute more than 20% of the student body.

The most important centre of student disorders was the School of Medicine of St Petersburg. This was not under the administrative control of Tolstoy, but of the Minister of War, D. A. Milyutin, the finest representative of what might be called the 'liberalism of the upper government bureaucracy'. Within the school, meetings and libraries had in practice been allowed. When attempts were made to interfere with some of the young students' minor customs, such as the freedom to wear long hair, they were at once followed by violent and well-organized protests. The smallest incident was enough to arouse the entire student body. At this very time an organization was being started to direct the movement, with the purpose, among other things, of sending delegates to other university towns to ask for support and solidarity. These delegates did not meet with a particularly warm welcome in Moscow, though there, too, the poorest students appreciated the need to protest against their conditions, and the exclusion of women was still keenly felt. But as a rule the students of the old capital wanted to confine themselves to expounding these grievances to their academic superiors without resorting to open clashes.

Despite all this, in St Petersburg the movement was to give rise in March 1869 to a protest of considerable size. An incident between a pupil of the School of Medicine and a professor soon became the occasion of a number of meetings. The police intervened; arrests were made. There were some resignations in protest but this only led to further arrests and dismissals. On 15th March the School was closed. The students then organized a demonstration in front of the gates and later along the Nevsky Prospekt. The police tried to put a stop to these meetings and even those that took place in the students' own lodgings. Communal eating was forbidden—a heavy blow for the poorest students. The orders of the police to this effect were so severe that, had they been interpreted literally, they would have virtually prevented any student finding a place to eat. During the next few days demonstrations of solidarity occurred in other institutions, and on 19th March the Technological Institute was closed.[9] On the 20th the university followed suit. All the meetings demanded that the students should be allowed to organize their lives freely and be exempted from police supervision. There were also many acts of individual support. A number of men, for instance, said that they would not go back to their lectures until their fellow students were released. But these protests did nothing to modify the situation. On 24th March the university was compelled to return to normal life, with none of the students' demands satisfied. The repression continued. Altogether eighty-one members of the university were tried by the Academic Council; thirteen were refused entry into any university at all and nineteen were expelled from St Petersburg University; the others got lighter penalties. Six students were permanently, and twenty temporarily, expelled from the School of Medicine.

The conclusions that could be drawn from all this in the academic field were reached by Georgy Petrovich Eniserlov, one of the students whose share in the protests had been among the most vigorous and who had suffered most from the consequences. In a manuscript which circulated among the students Eniserlov wrote: 'We asked to be allowed to escape from our situation by lawful means, and they refused us the opportunity. What do they want us to do? To try illegal methods? Or do they not believe us when we say that our situation has become intolerable?' He then spoke of the attitude of the professors and the poverty of the students: 'The student would like to give all his time to research, but he must earn his bread . . . Without a penny in our pockets we have often come two hundred, three hundred, a thousand versts (there are students who have come on foot from the Caucasus).'

The movement of 1869 was crushed. Compared to the one of some years earlier, its territorial scale had been limited, it had not lasted so long and it had aroused less sympathy and interest in educated circles. It had been a demonstration more specifically concerned with that 'proletariat of thought' whose boundaries had been more clearly defined in the last ten years. Yet though less important in the general history of Russia than the events of 1861, these demonstrations had just as much influence on the development of revolutionary currents, whose human material came from the 'proletariat of thought'.

Many different groups of Populists considered the problem of how far they should keep the student movement within the bounds of the law. But very soon the problem was transformed into a question of absolutes. Was it a good thing, was it *right* to go on studying? Had not the time come to devote oneself entirely to propaganda in the countryside and in general to the cause of the people? In the words of S. L. Chudnovsky, then a student at the School of Medicine:

The problem was raised in a ruthlessly categorical and extremely partial form: learning or work? i.e. was it necessary to devote ourselves, even if only temporarily, to our studies, so as to obtain diplomas and then live the life of the privileged professions of the intelligentsia; or should we remember our duty to the people, recall that all our learning had been acquired only by means provided by the people, who work like condemned men and are always hungry? Should we not rather, we students, give up our privileged position, give up scholarship and devote ourselves to learning a craft, so as to take part as simple artisans or labourers in the life of the people, and merge with it?[10]

Besides those who, under the influence of Lavrov, thought that their duty lay in equipping themselves for propaganda, there also sprang up groups in which Bakunin's demand for a revolution found ready response. We have already mentioned that the first number of the *Narodnoe Delo* which he published in Geneva on 1st September 1868 had seized the imagination of all who read it. At the same time there now came into being a group of medical students inspired not only and perhaps not even mainly by Bakunin. Rather, it was an old book that prompted them to create a secret society. Many of these students later became well-known anarchists, such as Zemfiry Konstantinovich Ralli, Evlampy Vasilevich Ametistov and Mikhail Petrovich Korinfsky. The book that had inspired them was Buonarroti's *La Conspiration pour l'Égalité.*[11]

This ferment found its most powerful expression in Nechaev. 'He was not a product of our world, of the intelligentsia; he was a stranger to us', Vera Zasulich wrote of him many years later, when she sought an explanation for Nechaev's strength and strangeness.[12] And indeed his story was that of a man of the people who was personally acquainted with that coarse, brutal world which so many young Populists were trying to enter; and who, when he had, painfully, deliberately and unaided, finally climbed up to the world of the intelligentsia, absorbed with astonishing speed all its most bitter elements; and then flung himself into action with an energy and ruthlessness which aroused admiration and fear in all around him.

Sergey Gennadevich Nechaev was born on 20th September 1847 in the large centre of Ivanovo. His father was a gilder and painter, his mother the daughter of peasant serfs. She soon died, and the numerous family was brought up by the father with great strictness. Sergey spent his childhood and youth doing various odd jobs and even acted in a little theatre organized by his father. 'He acted very well', his sister was later to say.[13] His father's doubtful social position, somewhere between an artisan, a small merchant and a factotum, must in itself have given him an opportunity to know his township in all its aspects. It was a small provincial centre, deserted, dirty and boring (the three words which appear most often in the letters of his young days), but which had one speciality which distinguished it from all other Russian towns of the kind. Ivanovo was then developing into the largest centre of the textile industry in Russia and was becoming what with some exaggeration was to be called 'the Russian Manchester'.

At the age of nine, Sergey became a messenger boy in a factory, but was soon impelled by an overwhelming passion to escape from the world in which he had been born. He wanted to learn to read and go to the capital and the university. There were very few schools at Ivanovo; but already small private ventures were beginning to give young men such as Nechaev a chance to learn. A writer called Vasily Arsentevich Demetev had started a free school, thus laying the foundations for a small provincial centre of learning, impregnated with love for and research into the life and traditions of the people. Demetev himself wrote stories which were Populist in spirit.[14] Very soon Nechaev got in touch with another writer about ten years older than he was. F. D. Nefedov was the son of comparatively prosperous serfs: he had been able to go to Moscow for his studies and was later to give the best account of life in this part of Russia in a series of polemical writings and ethnographic studies.[15] He was one of the first Russian writers to speak of factory life; and his descriptions of peasants and workmen are of value, both for the sharpness of his observations (for instance on the peasants' thirst for land), and for the typically Populist spirit with which they are informed.

The letters that the young Nechaev wrote to Nefedov inevitably make us think—as is so often the case when we consider the history of these years—of the revolutionary fruit that was to spring from Populism. Nechaev asked his friend in Moscow for books and still more books; he told him of his own progress and gave him bits of local news. Nefedov helped him, and eventually gave Nechaev the opportunity to leave Ivanovo. The correspondence between them would be in no way unusual were it not that already we find traces of Nechaev's passionate determination (which was to mark him for life) to escape at whatever cost from the world in which he had been born. 'Reality without any refinement hits me so hard that I have to leap into the air . . .

Besides this awareness of reality is very useful to me; it does not allow me to sink into apathy and settle down to contemplate the beauties of the world. Constant analysis of my surroundings gives me an exact idea of my own strength.' So he wrote in 1864, at the age of seventeen, to his friend in Moscow who was then writing an essay, *The Devil's Marsh*, which described the lives of the factory owners and merchants of Ivanovo. Nechaev was consumed with passion to leave behind what he regarded as a marsh. 'Nothing new at Ivanovo', he wrote in September, 'only the mud is everywhere; impossible to get through it any more.'

In August 1865 he went to Moscow. Nefedov put him up in a sort of *pension* kept by Pogodin, the well-known publicist. He wanted to become a schoolmaster but failed in his examinations. In April 1866 he went to St Petersburg and became a schoolmaster in the capital. He was there when Karakozov fired at Alexander II, and later he was to say that 'the foundations of our sacred cause were laid by Karakozov on the morning of 4th April 1866 . . . His action must be regarded as a prologue. Let us act, my friends, in such a way that the play will soon begin.'[16] In writing these words he must also have been thinking of himself; for at that time the prologue of his life was ending and the drama beginning.

In the autumn of 1868 he became an external student at the university. He was overwhelmed by the desire to get to know and influence the student body. He had already read much, mostly on politics. At the time he was particularly interested in the French Revolution and Babeuf. But we have few details about his life; he himself spoke as little as possible and at meetings he was generally silent. He got into contact with Ralli's group, which was inspired by Buonarroti, and made friends with Tkachev. Eventually he joined a sort of clandestine committee which they formed to direct the various student movements into revolutionary channels. By now he had clarified some of his political ideas, and was already silently and stubbornly trying to put them into practice. He was convinced that the peasant revolt was not only very near but that its exact date could be forecast. The 19th February 1870 would be the ninth anniversary of the liberation of the serfs. The law had provided that during these nine years the peasants were to farm, besides the holdings granted to them, a strip of land, the rent for which they owed to the landlord. At the end of nine years they could choose between giving back this extra land or carrying on paying for its redemption. This would mark the end of the reforms of 1861. The most authoritative review of the time wrote: 'This is an important moment. Once again millions of people are required to reconsider the entire management of their private lives; and this time there is no guidance; each man must trust only to his own conscience.'[17]

Nechaev was firmly convinced that the peasants would not in fact agree to this seal being set on the reforms of 1861. A revolt, he thought, was certain, and so he made his plans in *A Programme of Revolutionary Action* which he wrote in collaboration with Tkachev. The exact contribution of each man is

12*

not known. In any case the programme reflects the ideas of their little group that had sprung up between 1868 and 1869, and whose aim was to seize control of the student movement and use it for wider purposes.

The *Programme* began with a series of observations on the spiritual impossibility of living in the existing world.

If we think of our surroundings, we must inevitably conclude that we are living in the kingdom of the mad—so terrible and unnatural are people's relations to each other; so strange and unbelievable their attitude towards the mass of injustices, vileness and baseness that constitutes our social régime.

The revolt against this régime is planned in terms which were strongly influenced by Bakunin's articles in the *Narodnoe Delo*; but its content reflects the passion that had filled Nechaev's spirit as a boy in Ivanovo. 'The existing order cannot last for ever.' And so it was possible, indeed essential, to create an organization to hasten its end. 'Union' and 'insurrection' were the two fundamental points of this programme. Its final purpose was 'full freedom for a renewed personality'. The authors were well aware that this was unattainable without a profound social revolution. The revolution seemed to them 'a law of history'. Only by recognizing this would it be possible to act (as far as possible) 'with calm'. But to prepare the revolution it was essential 'to create the largest number of "revolutionary prototypes" and to develop in society the consciousness of an eventual and inevitable revolution as a way of achieving a better order of things'.

The desire to act on the psychological plane ('revolutionary prototypes'), the sense of social history, a realistic view of the need for an organization —these are the main foundations of Nechaev's and Tkachev's movement.

In fact once they had accepted 'the historical law' of revolutions, the authors of the *Programme* were more concerned with the other two features: the psychological moment, and the desire for organization. To these everything was sacrificed. A return was made to the Machiavellism of Ishutin, and no stone was left unturned in order to achieve the necessary organization. The circulation of the clandestine press, illegal meetings, demonstrations and protests—these were of value mainly as 'preventive tests' for indicating suitable men and tying them to the revolutionary group. The group itself was to reflect the principles of the new social order and economic future: 'It must be constructed in accordance with the spirit of decentralization and the law of movement, i.e. its members must change posts after given periods ... Decentralization must be understood in the sense of a weakening of the centre and the granting of considerable scope for action to the provincial centres.' They thus accepted an element of Bakunin's anarchism and then returned to what they held most dear. 'Those who join the organization must give up every possession, occupation or family tie, because families and occupations might distract members from their activities.' In this way they would create 'revolutionary prototypes'. If complete self-sacrifice was not yet demanded, this concession was made in the name of freedom of the person, so as to give the individual the chance to develop.

Nechaev and Tkachev laid down that action must at first be concentrated in the two capitals, where the most important task was to incite the students and populace. The date-line for the formation of this hard core was to be 1st May 1869. In the following summer efforts must be concentrated on the provinces; among the artisans, seminarists and populace of the smaller towns. In autumn and winter they would turn to 'the mass of the people' i.e. the peasants. At the same time they would establish their regulations and 'catechism'. Spring 1870 was to see the outbreak of revolution 'throughout Russia'.

The *Programme* also envisaged a union with all 'European revolutionary organizations', and pointed out how useful it would be to have a centre abroad. This was probably Nechaev's main idea when he crossed the frontier on 4th March 1869 and shortly afterwards reached Geneva.

Reviewing what had been done, he could say that he had laid the foundations of an organization both in St Petersburg and above all in Moscow, where his movement had met with less opposition. Even if he had not been successful in founding a committee controlled by him to direct the student movements, he had at least taken steps in this direction. His venture so far must have convinced him that though there would be much opposition from those who believed in long-term propaganda, it would, however, not be difficult to discover many 'revolutionary prototypes' in the circles in which he moved.

In Moscow he had got into contact with Uspensky's group and he had, so he said, made other journeys to Kiev and Odessa. It must, however, be admitted that Nechaev's political life is, from the first, full of unknown factors and often of deliberate mystifications. At this very time he said that he had been arrested twice, first in St Petersburg and then in Moscow, and that he had succeeded in escaping on both occasions. But these stories had probably been invented with the aim of inspiring an atmosphere of mystery and conspiracy around him which would help to create a model of 'the revolutionary prototype'. In Switzerland at the end of March, even before he met Bakunin,[18] Nechaev issued a proclamation 'to the students of the University, the Academy and the Technological Institute' in which he announced that he had succeeded in escaping 'thanks to a lucky piece of boldness, from the walls of the Peter-Paul fortress and from the hands of the forces of darkness'.[19]

The arrival of this youth of twenty, who had lived at the very centre of the revolutionary circles of Russia and who claimed to be a delegate from a powerful secret society, was obviously considered by the leading Russian émigrés to be a symptom of the greatest importance.

In two appeals which he published in April, Ogarev made known his ideas on the student movement about which Nechaev had brought new and greatly

exaggerated information.[20] He took up the theme which he had launched
ten years earlier with Herzen on the subject of the university strikes, and
spoke of a voluntary withdrawal from the universities so that the students
might devote themselves to propaganda among the people. Bakunin repeated
the same idea in a manifesto to the students.[21] These works of Ogarev and
Bakunin were among the most immediate incentives for the great movement
'to go to the people' of a few years later.

But these instructions were soon set aside by another and more violent
appeal. For the faith in an immediate revolution which had inspired Nechaev,
Tkachev and a few others around them was to find its theorist among the
émigrés. Bakunin, like Ogarev, had been struck by Nechaev's personality;
their impressions were very different from those that the representatives of
Zemlya i Volya had made a few years earlier on Herzen. Nechaev was just
as intellectually narrow and far more fanatical than they had been. But
behind him there was now a revolutionary tradition; Karakozov had fired
at the Tsar; men were in prison and suffering. All this made even Nechaev's
fanaticism appear in a different light. Besides, the older, cultivated and more
complex émigrés now felt a growing disappointment in the history of the
last few years, and increasing disbelief that forces in Russia could develop
along progressive lines. The year 1869 was very different from 1861. All this
helped for a moment to make of Nechaev an exemplary figure in the eyes of
those who saw him as the only (and hence all the more enthralling) exponent
of Russia's revolutionary youth.

Ogarev, urged on by Bakunin, dedicated a poem to him. This was published
in a leaflet and by October was already circulating in Russia, doing much to
build up the fame and legend of Nechaev himself.[22] But it was Bakunin who
turned him into a real hero. He wrote to Guillaume on 13th April 1869:

I have here with me one of those young fanatics who know no doubts, who fear
nothing and who have decided quite definitely that many, many of them will have
to perish at the hands of the government but who will not let this stop them until
the Russian people arises. They are magnificent, these young fanatics, believers
without God, heroes without rhetoric.[23]

By idealizing him in this way, Bakunin turned Nechaev into the 'revolutionary prototype' *par excellence*.

The most interesting result of the collaboration between them was the
Revolutionary Catechism, a small booklet which was published in Latin
characters, in code, and taken back to Russia by Nechaev on his return to
Moscow.[24]

This is indeed a document worthy of the curiosity which it aroused when
it was first made public at the trial of Nechaev's followers. In content, it is
true, it merely expressed feelings and ideas which had developed in the
revolutionary movement ever since Ishutin. But the clear, ruthless style with
which Bakunin expressed these ideas (as yet, hardly whispered in *Hell*)
gives them a new and exceptional power.

It is easy enough to understand how this power was produced. The basic formula was provided by the extremist and personalist interpretation of Fichte's and Hegel's philosophy that Bakunin had first just perceived thirty years earlier. It was an interpretation that turned philosophy into a rule of life, of conscience and of inner psychological analysis. This was the origin of the language which Bakunin used to transform Nechaev's *Programme of Revolutionary Action*. The hatred that both men felt for the entire social situation in Russia—the virulent hatred for the form and substance of the crushing government machine; the hatred, in fact, that had inspired Saltykov-Shchedrin's great satires and which after every repression, with its arrests and persecutions, gave a new impulse to the fight, this hatred was not analysed by Bakunin in political terms but rather expressed in absolute formulas which fused together Hegelian 'negation' and the hatred felt by the poor and the oppressed.

The ideological process at the basis of this *Catechism* may seem strange and obscure. In fact it is not very unlike certain passages in Marx, in which the dialectic becomes the framework for a political analysis of society. Applied here to the world of psychology, it gave grandiose proportions to the idea of the 'revolutionary prototype'.

If we take them literally and ignore Bakunin's formulas, most of the articles in the *Catechism* merely consist of practical advice on conspiracy, and working rules for a clandestine association engaged in a fierce struggle with the surrounding world. The sense of dedication, discipline and rank sprang naturally from the situation in which the revolutionaries found themselves. But each of these rules is carried to its extremes. Loyalty becomes absolute dedication. The desire to carry out an aim is transformed into the repudiation of anything outside it, into scorn, hatred and the determination to destroy. This very ruthlessness provided a source of energy which constitutes the historical novelty of this document. It is violent enough to include even the Machiavellian elements of Ishutin's. The tactical advice on how to make use of others and oneself for the cause, is expressed with such an overwhelming passion for the supreme end that under a thousand different guises it appears almost a repetition of the doctrine, 'omnia munda mundis'.

Paragraph 1. The revolutionary is a lost man; he has no interests of his own, no cause of his own, no feelings, no habits, no belongings; he does not even have a name. Everything in him is absorbed by a single, exclusive interest, a single thought, a single passion—the revolution.

Paragraph 2. In the very depths of his being, not just in words but in deed, he has broken every tie with the civil order, with the educated world and all laws, conventions and generally accepted conditions, and with the ethics of this world. He will be an implacable enemy of this world, and if he continues to live in it, that will only be so as to destroy it the more effectively.

Paragraph 3. The revolutionary despises all doctrinairism. He has rejected the science of the world, leaving it to the next generation; he knows only one science, that of destruction.

Paragraph 4. He despises public opinion; he despises and hates the existing social ethic in all its demands and expressions; for him, everything that allows the triumph of the revolution is moral, and everything that stands in its way is immoral.

Paragraph 5. The revolutionary is a lost man; with no pity for the State and for the privileged and educated world in general, he must himself expect no pity. Every day he must be prepared for death. He must be prepared to bear torture.

Paragraph 6. Hard with himself, he must be hard towards others. All the tender feelings of family life, of friendship, love, gratitude and even honour must be stifled in him by a single cold passion for the revolutionary cause. For him there is only one pleasure, one consolation, one reward, and one satisfaction—the success of the revolution. Day and night he must have one single thought, one single purpose: merciless destruction. With this aim in view, tirelessly and in cold blood, he must always be prepared to die and to kill with his own hands anyone who stands in the way of achieving it.

Paragraph 7. The character of the true revolutionary has no place for any romanticism, sentimentality, enthusiasm or seduction. Nor has it any place for private hatred or revenge. This revolutionary passion which in him becomes a daily, hourly passion, must be combined with cold calculation. Always and everywhere he must become not what his own personal inclination would have him become, but what the general interest of the revolution demands.

The remaining paragraphs deal with his relations with his colleagues. Every decision among true revolutionaries must be taken unanimously. They are given complete freedom and sound economic advice on how to make good use of revolutionaries of the second and third grade, who are to be regarded as capital entrusted to the revolutionary to be spent intelligently on his own initiative and without pity in case of failure.

The *Catechism* then returns to the revolutionary's relations with society, which it divides into various categories. The acute insight which informs this vision can have sprung only from prolonged, calculated hatred and actual experience of the relations between young revolutionaries and the surrounding world. The first category is made up of the intelligent and important. These must be killed by terrorist methods. The second consists of the important and unintelligent. These must be left alive temporarily because their stupid and bestial activities encourage the people to revolt. The third is made up of the great majority of 'animals and high-ranking personalities, neither intelligent nor competent'. They must be blackmailed: 'If possible, we must get hold of their dirty secrets and so make them our slaves.' The fourth class is made up of 'ambitious politicians and liberals of various kinds . . . We can conspire together with them, accept their programmes and pretend to follow them blindly, trying at the same time to get control of them, to get hold of their secrets, to compromise them to the hilt so that it becomes unthinkable for them to turn back and so that they are compelled to overthrow the State with their own hands.' The fifth group is made up of doctrinaires, of revolutionaries who make empty speeches and act only on paper. They must be driven on into real demonstrations where they can get some experience of serious fighting. The majority will then die without leaving a trace and a few authentic revolutionaries will be produced. The final class is that of women, who are of the greatest possible value, if they are open 'in deed and without rhetoric' to real revolutionary understanding but who otherwise must be treated like the third and fourth classes of men.

The final paragraphs give us a clear expression of Bakunin's political programme, which we know too from other documents of the same period.

Paragraph 23.   By 'popular revolution' our association (*tovarishchestvo*) does not mean a regulated movement on the classical Western pattern, which is always kept in check by respect for property, traditions and those social structures called 'civilization' and 'morality'—a movement which until now has always confined itself to destroying one kind of political structure merely to replace it with another by tending to create the so-called 'revolutionary State'. The only revolution that can save the people is one that destroys every established object root and branch, that annihilates all State traditions, orders and classes in Russia.

Paragraph 25.   To do this we must draw close to the people; we must ally ourselves mainly with those elements of the people's life which ever since the foundation of the State of Moscow have never given up protesting, not just in words but in deeds, against anything directly or indirectly tied to the State; against the nobility, the bureaucracy, the priests, against the world of guilds and against the *kulaks*. We must ally ourselves with the doughty world of brigands, who in Russia are the only real revolutionaries.

Paragraph 26.   All our organization, all our conspiracy, all our purpose consists in this: to regroup this world of brigands into an invincible and omni-destructive force.

Having thus determined how the 'revolutionary prototype' was to live and what he was to aim for, Bakunin and Nechaev now applied themselves to preparing propaganda which Nechaev was to use on his return to Russia. They also drew up the political functions of the organization which he was to create and direct, based on the contacts that he had already established in Moscow and St Petersburg.

The revolutionary forces from the 'proletariat of thought' were faced with a huge, grandiose function. In his appeal 'to our young brothers in Russia', Bakunin had already explained what their purpose ought to be in the immediate future. 'The times of Stenka Razin are drawing near . . . Now, as then, the Russia of peasants and workers is rising . . . in expectation of a new and genuine liberty which will no longer come from above but from below . . .' Who was to guide this struggle 'for life and death between the Russia of the people and the Russia of the State'? 'It is unlikely', answered Bakunin, 'that there will be another popular hero like Stenka Razin; his place will be taken by the legions of youth without caste or name, those legions which are already living the life of the people and which have found a powerful cement in the idea and the aim that unites them.' Stenka Razin in fact would no longer be an individual, a single man, but would be replaced by a 'collective and therefore invincible' Stenka Razin.

The student movement and the first ventures at organization would mean something only if they succeeded in creating this collective popular hero. But to achieve this great aim it was essential utterly to renounce all privileged positions and to feel humble towards the people, to bring oneself down to their level, to tie oneself to them, to become one flesh. Said Bakunin:

Go to the people, there is your way, your life, your learning . . . Young men of education must become not the people's benefactors, not its dictators and guides, but merely a lever for the people to free itself, the unifier of the people's own energies and forces. To gain the ability and right to serve the cause, youth must submerge itself and drown in the people. Take no notice of learning in whose name men try to shackle you and strip you of your power. Learning of this kind must die together with the world of which it is the expression. New and living learning will un-doubtedly be born later, after the people's victory, from the liberated life of the people itself.[25]

In another manifesto, called *How the Revolutionary Question presents Itself*, Bakunin pointed out the means and final ends of this movement 'to go to the people', and expounded his anarchist programme. Any venture into 'liberal republicanism' was merely an illusion; any possibility of 'bringing about the economic good of the people without totally destroying the organization of the State in all its aspects' was merely a dangerous dream. Ridiculous were the attempts of the 'Socialist-conspirators, young doctrin-aires, bookish revolutionaries, arm-chair revolutionary-statesmen, and future dictators, who play at revolution but are incapable of making it'. All this was only the result of 'university corruption; . . . the only real school is the people'.

Here then was the justification of Nechaev's conflicts with the 'Socialists' and Natanson's 'Populist seekers'—with all, in fact, who planned to keep student disturbances within the bounds of the law and who had drawn the conclusion from their experiences of Ishutin and the White Terror that what was now needed was a calm and searching investigation of the social conditions which prevailed in the countryside.

To all these 'doctrinaires', Bakunin replied that there was only one possible function: 'to unite the forces for revolt which already exist among the people and which until now have been scattered and disorganized'. It was essential to find these forces wherever they were and in whatever guise. Were these forces fought by the State as brigands, then it was to the brigands that one must appeal.

Brigandage is one of the most honoured aspects of the people's life in Russia. At the time when the State of Moscow was being founded, brigandage represented the desperate protest of the people against the horrible social order of the time which was not yet perfected or transformed according to Western models . . . The brigand is always the hero, the defender, the avenger of the people, the irreconcilable enemy of the entire State régime, both in its civil and its social aspects, the life and death fighter against our statist-aristocratic, official-clerical civilization. An understanding of brigandage is essential for an understanding of the history of the Russian people . . . The brigand, in Russia, is the true and only revolutionary—the revolutionary without phrase-making and without bookish rhetoric. Popular revolution is born from the merging of the revolt of the brigand with that of the peasant . . . Such were the revolts of Stenka Razin and Pugachev . . . and even today this is still the world of the Russian revolution; the world of brigands and the world of brigands alone has always been in harmony with the revolution. The man who wants to make a serious conspiracy in Russia, who wants a popular revolution, must turn to that world and fling himself into it.

It was to this 'revolt of brigands and peasants' that the younger generation must ally itself, 'keeping itself strongly united and collecting together the various peasant upheavals into a single calculated and ruthless popular revolution'.[26]

In another work, *The Principles of Revolution*, Bakunin and Nechaev showed how this task of unifying subversive forces could be achieved. Dictatorship and the preservation of the State even for revolutionary purposes were rejected. 'By revolution', they said, 'we mean a radical upheaval . . . New forms of life can spring only from a complete amorphism.' There was no need for men who occupied themselves with giving orders and devising rules. What was required was something very different, people capable of 'hiding themselves unobserved in the mass and joining one band to another and imposing the same leadership on both. This will give the movement a communal character and spirit.' This was the only point of a secret preparatory organization, in so far as one was required at all. The new men of a true popular revolution would appear as soon as experience had created them and would unite and organize themselves in the course of action.

Bakunin gave a concrete example of what he meant by a popular initiative. 'The Italian peasants have now begun a genuine revolution. When they succeed in seizing a town, they burn all the papers. Destruction of this kind must take place everywhere.' The revolution had a negative function, one of annihilation. Reconstruction could not be undertaken by the same generation that had achieved the necessary work of destruction, because this generation was still under the old influences. It was 'criminal' to try to forecast the 'misty' future.[27]

In this conception two factors were merged: there were, first, the ideas that had prompted Bakunin when he had formed his *Alliance*, the secret group within the International; and secondly the tradition of Ishutin's *Hell*, which had planned to penetrate into the different revolutionary groups, so as to guide them invisibly and continue doing so even after the triumph of the people's movement.

But these two tendencies were very different and they never completely fused. For Bakunin, the emphasis lay on anarchist finality, on the destruction of the State by the spontaneous forces of the people. He counted on a rebellion which would be able to find an organization within itself, as well as its own political and social expression, and even its own new culture. But Nechaev was primarily concerned with the strong organization of those elements which had made their appearance in Ishutin's movement, in the student risings and the general life of the 'proletariat of thought'. Conspiracy, not anarchy, was the most important aim for him. Convinced that the revolution would soon break out, he was above all concerned to build up a powerful nucleus to direct it. His ideas, though strongly influenced by Bakunin, were still inspired by those memories of the French Revolution which had enthralled him in St Petersburg and which Ralli and he had rediscovered in Buonarroti, and Tkachev in the Jacobin tradition.

In these *Principles of Revolution*, the ideas that Nechaev brought from Russia played a powerful rôle. Karakozov was held up as an example. Terrorism, which until then had not formed part of Bakunin's programme, was indicated as one of the methods suitable for preparing the ground for the revolution. The manifesto ended with an appeal 'to all young Russians to unite in brotherhood with those who will act in the same way throughout Europe, and to start work at once on the sacred cause of eradicating evil and cleansing the soil of Russia with sword and fire'. The final object remained Bakunin's 'omni-destruction'; but the means to be used were more like those of the 'European Revolutionary Committee' so dear to Ishutin's fancy.

And indeed Bakunin did not make Nechaev a member of his *Alliance* nor did he include the organization which Nechaev was going to develop in Russia in his *Brotherhood*. Instead he created for him an *Alliance Révolutionnaire Européenne* and a *World Revolutionary Union* with a 'Comité Général' of its own and gave Nechaev a membership card in the name of this fictitious organization. Whatever his reasons, Bakunin obviously intended to let the movement in Russia retain its individual character, though he imposed the imprint of his own ideas on the propaganda which it was to employ.[28]

Nechaev's 'Society' was to be called *Narodnaya Rasprava*. We can translate this as 'The People's Summary Justice', though a more expressive term such as *jacquerie* or *pugachevshchina* interprets the meaning rather better. An even more specific illustration of Nechaev's intentions could be found on the society's official seal: an axe round which were the words 'Committee of *Narodnaya Rasprava* of 19th February 1870'. The organization, in fact, was to be merely the governing committee of a *jacquerie* in action.

Even before Nechaev left for Russia, the first number of the *Narodnaya Rasprava*'s organ was published. There has been much discussion as to who wrote the articles in it. Though by no means denying the part played by Bakunin, we can say that this small clandestine review is rather a reflection of Nechaev's own ideas; under the anarchist externals it clearly reveals that primitive and violent way of thinking that was so indicative of his personality and his origins.

It was dated 'Summer 1869' and began: 'The revolution of all the people, all the tortured Russian people, is drawing near!' This was not the time to start a theoretical or literary review: 'Learning is not our job', i.e. of that section of the younger generation which by one means or another had succeeded in developing: 'We have no time.' Besides, there was no literature in Russia 'but only printed panegyrics and denunciations, no real science but just a kind of sophistry which distorts the past and which has turned the sufferings of the popular masses into an absolute law and laid the necessary foundations for the development of a ruling minority. There is no progress or civilization, only a massive exploitation of the people's energies for the satisfaction of those who have never done anything.' In the name of all who are 'suffocated by the State, . . . we want a revolution of the people and the peasants; . . . everything that is not directed towards this end is foreign and hostile to us.' Doctrinaire theories in any form were just one more obstacle to be destroyed. Only action could be of use.

But not everything that is today called a cause or action really is so. Any secret society which does not have as its aim a series of actions capable of destroying something is a child's toy, a piece of useless furniture: anything must be destroyed, a person, a thing, an institution, anything which appears to stand in the way of freeing the people. Without sparing lives, without stopping in the face of any threat, fear or danger, we must—by a series of personal actions and sacrifices which logically follow a calculated plan, and a series of bold, not to say rash, ventures—fling ourselves into the life of the people, so as to arouse its faith in itself, in its own powers and in ourselves; so as to shake it, unite it, and drive it towards the triumph of its own cause.

Few had been bold enough to propose a programme of this kind. True, Bakunin had suggested something similar in the first number of the *Narodnoe Delo* but, said Nechaev, his tone was too moderate. The final aim was as Bakunin had described, but to achieve it one had to throw away 'the scientific and pseudo-scientific rags' which still covered it. On the other hand, Bakunin's later appeals (i.e. those which Nechaev himself had helped to write), and above all the manifestos urging the younger generation to go to the people, could be fully approved. This was the road, urged Nechaev, that all the émigrés, including the editors of the *Kolokol*, should follow together as brothers. This was, in fact, a call to Ogarev (who had already praised his personality) and Herzen (who always refused to). And so he moved forward a pawn which was to be very useful to him during his second stay in Switzerland, when the *Kolokol* came under his control. Meanwhile the Russian revolutionary committee was to find in the *Narodnaya Rasprava* its own battle organ.

The new review was all the more necessary, said Nechaev, in that Russian revolutionary thought had until then been timid, hesitant and extremely slow in developing. The 'educated class' had shown all its weakness, due mainly 'to lack of popular juices'. It had sunk into a miasma of scepticism, vacuous liberalism and criticisms made out of sheer boredom, and had been unable to come to any decision. 'The people has not been able to find the necessary firmness in those who call themselves its leaders. It can expect no real initiative from them, no drive corresponding to its revolutionary spirit.' One must not, of course, forget the Decembrists. They at least had shown energy and courage. It was true that they had not wanted the complete over-throw of the Tsarist State, that they had not aimed at bringing about real freedom for the oppressed people but had confined themselves to palliatives; it was true that they had been shackled by a whole series of moral prejudices; but at least their 'negation' had been carried out in deeds and not just in words. Among them there had been at least one who had wanted to seize the Winter Palace and exterminate the Imperial family—'If only he had suc-ceeded!' And so the Decembrists remained models of energy. There was only one thing they had lacked: an understanding of the peasant's mentality. Had they appreciated that, they could have led the peasant to what 'in official and bourgeois language is called looting'.

'After the Decembrists, all gave themselves up entirely to theories.' Yet there was no real need for this.

In fact what is usually called Socialism is by no means a novelty. It means only those tendencies which have always and everywhere been present among the masses and through which alone popular revolutions can arise. The peasants have always and everywhere risen up to wipe from the face of the earth the powerful and the oppressors.

They had never had need of theories to learn how to organize their col-lective life in *obshchinas*; they had never needed, indeed they had distrusted, the too many 'unasked-for teachers' who showed all too clearly their inten-tion of 'finding a comfortable place for themselves under the guise of *science* and *art*'. The organization of the Cossacks at Astrakhan at the time of Stenka Razin had realized 'the objective ideal of social equality infinitely better than do Fourier's *phalansteries* or the institutions of Cabet, Louis Blanc and other learned Socialists; better than Chernyshevsky's associations'.

And all the various discussions on individual morality and the family (in the world of literature and 'nihilism') had been of little enough use for preparing real action. The first positive example had been given by the Russian officers who together with Potebnya had sacrificed themselves for the Russian and Polish cause. But real maturity had been reached only with Ishutin and Karakozov. 'The appearance of a group of people prepared to hurl a stone at the face of our filthy society . . . was to have an enormous influence on all future development . . . Anyone who has not lived among Russian youth at that time so charged with significance, can hardly understand its present tendencies . . . With them appeared men of deeds, of action.'

We come from the people, our skins wounded by the teeth of the present régime. We are guided by hatred for all who are not the people. We are devoid of any concept of duty to the State or of honour towards existing society, which we loathe and from which we expect only evil. We have an entirely negative plan, which no one can modify: utter destruction.

'Our immediate predecessors' had not understood this single real need, and at the time of the emancipation had confined themselves to spreading leaflets. At that time it was far easier than now to unleash a general revolution; even 'the inhabitants of the Winter Palace trembled at the results of their fraudulent game with the ignorant people'. But they [these predecessors] had stood still, hand in hand, far from the villages where the people were in rebellion, instead of flinging themselves into whatever disorders were breaking out so as to direct them towards a popular revolution which could destroy everything.

The 19th February 1870, the final stage of the reform, would be a great opportunity, and it was essential not to lose it once more. 'At the striking of the ninth year of its new serfdom, in 1870, in the Jubilee Year of Razin and Pugachev, calculated hatred will burst like a storm over the nobility which wallows in vice and luxury.' The final victim would be kept for a peasant tribunal—Alexander II. He must not be touched until that moment, so that the people's hatred would have time to accumulate. But it was necessary to strike at once at the various classes of exploiters. Nechaev gave a detailed picture of these in a list like that of the *Revolutionary Catechism*. This he illustrated with examples and actual names. Among these were Mezentsov, Trepov and 'other swine', who were indeed soon to be the victims of the daggers and revolvers of *Zemlya i Volya*. There were also a number of reactionary writers, with Katkov at the head of the list, 'who must have their tongues cut out so that we will be freed from systematic lies, and the betrayal of literature and learning as a whole'.

Our task is a great one! We must succeed in carrying it out in time! Let us dedicate ourselves utterly, with all our passion and fire, to the sacred cause of purification, so as to have the right, when the great day dawns, to tell the people as it awakes: 'We are not like our fathers, your tormentors; we have not eaten your bread in vain; we have not been idlers; we have done everything within our power; accept us in your ranks; accept us without doubt or hesitation, so that we go forward together as brothers, in a single body, further along the road of purification towards a new life.

Great is our work!

Ishutin has taken the initiative. And now it is time for us to begin, before his hot tracks have cooled.

In August 1869 Nechaev left Switzerland. He passed through the Balkans, and in Rumania found help and support from the young Bulgarian revolutionaries with whom Bakunin had put him in contact. Once more he succeeded in getting over the Russian frontier.[29]

Within about two months Nechaev had laid the foundations for an organization which despite its short life was to leave an important mark on the Populist groups. There have been many suggestions that *Narodnaya Rasprava* did not in fact exist and was merely one of Nechaev's many myths. But documents prove that such was not the case and that a group of some sort was associated with him.

His activities were centred on Moscow, where, far more than in St Petersburg, he could hope to find listeners and followers. Petr Gavrilovich Uspensky very soon became his right arm, especially in all matters concerning infiltration among the students.

In this world of 'lost men', to use the words of Bakunin's *Catechism*, few characters were as lost and desperate as Uspensky. He came from a family of nobles, once again from the region of the Volga near Nizhny Novgorod. He was born probably in 1847, the same year as Nechaev. He came to Moscow for his education but did not complete his studies. Very soon, however, it became apparent that he was the most educated and mature of the group of young men who collected round him. He was employed, as we have seen, in Cherkesov's bookshop, and succeeded in transforming it into the centre of a vast network of secret retreats. Ever since 1865 he had been in contact with the underground, at first with Ishutin's movement and then with Volkhovsky and Lopatin. In autumn 1869, he founded *Narodnaya Rasprava* with Nechaev. He was condemned to fifteen years' hard labour and banishment for life to Siberia, and in October 1875 tried to commit suicide. On 27th December 1881 he was hanged in prison by his own companions, Yurkovsky and Ignat, on suspicion of being a spy. An inquiry was later made by his murderers and showed that their suspicions had had no foundation.[30]

It was Uspensky who put Nechaev in touch with one of the most turbulent centres of student life in Moscow, the School of Agriculture. He put him in contact with a student from that institute, Nikolay Stepanovich Dolgov, who came from Saratov, and who had already had some experience of fighting, at least on the university level. Dolgov collected a small group of young men (among them Alexey Kirillovich Kuznetsov, Fedor Fedorovich Ripman and Ivan Ivanovich Ivanov); and this together with his work with Nechaev marked the beginning of a long revolutionary career. His companions too carried on the fight throughout their lives. Even during the revolution of 1905, Kuznetsov was a Socialist-Revolutionary organizer at Chita in Siberia. Nechaev certainly had the gift of arousing his 'revolutionary prototypes'.

The organization was made up of groups of five and—according to Bakunin's analysis—it tended to become hierarchical if not exactly centralized. Different elements and groups were considered of differing importance. At the centre was to be the central committee which the various sections were to found when their numbers became sufficient. All members of *Narodnaya Rasprava* were obliged to work among the public, some among students, others among workmen and yet others among peasants.

Most of those whom Nechaev recruited in autumn 1869 were young men, generally students. But there was one remarkable exception. Among those who joined the central core of *Narodnaya Rasprava* was Ivan Gavrilovich Pryzhov, one of the strangest and yet most characteristic figures in this world of rebels.[31]

'My whole life has been a dog's life.' Such are the first words of his 'confession' to the investigating magistrates. Yet his stubbornness and his determination to carry on his ethnographical and historical researches give a suggestion of strength and beauty to the existence of this wretched alcoholic. He provides one of the most vivid examples of the energy and fighting spirit of the contemporary 'proletariat of thought'.

Pryzhov was born in Moscow in 1827, the son of a doorkeeper and clerk, in the same hospital where Dostoevsky's father was doctor, and where Dostoevsky himself spent so much of his youth. Pryzhov's father was a serf who had been liberated after taking part in the war against Napoleon. He had been employed at Srednikovo on one of the Stolypin estates, not far from Moscow. This was a typical neo-classical country house which in the nineteenth century was the home of the future minister. Pryzhov's childhood was 'lulled by the songs of his parents, which spoke of the beauties of being a serf'.[32]

Despite these humble origins, he would have succeeded in completing his studies had he not become due to enter the university in 1848, the very year when Nicholas I decided to make still further restrictions on the number of students in order to combat Western revolutionary influences. And so, excluded by the order, Pryzhov became a clerk, going to lectures when and how he could. But with a heroic, almost monkish resolution, he continued his researches and wrote a number of books and pamphlets. His masters were Buslaev, the authority on popular traditions who had taught Khudyakov, O. M. Bodyansky, and T. N. Granovsky, the historian. But he was more attracted by the love of Slav antiquities of the first two than by the liberalism of the latter. Pryzhov, like many others, drew his Populism from a Slavophil source and became increasingly revolutionary as time went by. He had much in common with Khudyakov, and his position in Nechaev's movement was somewhat like that of Khudyakov in Ishutin's.

For years he travelled through the country around Moscow, taking notes, making comparisons, drawing up theories, but above all opening his eyes to the realities of the people's life which had been more often eulogized than understood by his Slavophil masters. His was a purely individual movement 'to go to the people', inspired by a devouring passion to learn. Although it assumed the forms of science and positivism, this movement was primarily due to a deep understanding and sympathy with the life of the peasants, rather than to any political or intellectual impulse.

There would be no point in dwelling on the circumstances in which Pryzhov carried out his inquiry. It is enough to say that he really did 'lead a dog's life', which ended by turning him into a Bohemian, and to blacker and blacker misery. But his plans were always grandiose. When he was arrested he said he had enough material for a series of studies 'on popular beliefs, on the peasants' way of living (bread and wine), on the *obshchina* and the *bratstvo*, poetry, music, etc.'. He wanted to write a history of 'destitution in Russia' and then a series of studies on the sects and heresies and on Little Russia.

It is this last subject that most clearly reveals the threads which tie his earlier Slavophil erudition to his later political activities. From this interest in the history of the Ukraine he moved to the more immediate aspect of that country's problems. These led him to believe, like so many of his contemporaries, that Russia would be faced with a reawakening of the various historic regions and nations which composed it.

For him too, as for so many others, the idea of regional and national independence destroyed the bonds between *narodnost* (one of the ideological foundations of Nicholas's régime) and absolutism, and made him counter the autocratic State with the concept of the 'people'. Pryzhov in fact may already have drawn the practical consequences of these ideas. He was close to the circles of A. A. Kotlyarevsky, who had been arrested in 1862 on suspicion of relations with the 'London propagandists', but mainly for his Ukrainophil sympathies. At the time Pryzhov too feared arrest and burnt some of his most compromising manuscripts, above all collections of popular anti-clerical stories.

Apart from the problems of the Slav nationalities, he was mainly interested in the people's life in Russia, both among the peasants and—and this is what began to distinguish him from his predecessors—also among the town populace. He tried to publish what he had already written on the subject, but the severity of the censorship prevented the appearance of more than a few fragments. The most interesting of these are *The Life of Ivan Yakovlevich* and *The Twenty-six Yurodivye of Moscow*—vivid descriptions of popular religiosity in the old capital. 'A world of unheard-of fanaticism, ignorance and corruption', so he described the subject of these pamphlets on the destitute, beggarly and 'holy fools' who swarmed round the churches of Moscow. Apollon Grigorev, the well-known writer and critic, thought it his duty to protest against these in the name of 'the old native *Yurodstvo*', i.e. the ancient Russian religious tradition so much beloved, even in its most abnormal features, by the Slavophils, and extolled in the novels of Dostoevsky.[33] In this field too systematic and patient study of the life of the lowest strata of the population had led Pryzhov to an increasingly clear break with tradition.

In 1862 he published a book called *The Poor Folk of Holy Russia*, which was a collection of 'material for the history of social and popular habits in Russia'. But the book which made Pryzhov known, and which remains his most characteristic work, came out in two volumes in 1868. This was a *History of Inns*, a real encyclopaedia of the life of the proletariat at the time.[34] Yet even this did not include all the material he had gathered, either because of the censorship or because he did not want to attract the attention of the government, and hence the police, to the life of the wretched inns of Moscow, 'and thus snatch from the people the last refuge which it still retains in its misfortunes'.[35] The *History*, like all Pryzhov's other works, was transformed as he wrote it into a grandiose description (of which he had long dreamed) of the entire life of the people. Inns were, in his eyes, not just the centre of daily life but 'the centre of every popular revolt, of every rising from Stenka Razin onwards'.

Pryzhov finally came to the conclusion that, if he wanted to spread propaganda, he himself would have to live in these inns. He said, writing of himself in the third person:

Though he knew half Moscow, there was not a single being who was really close to him. He then decided to 'go to the people', in view of the fact, as the proverb says, that even death is beautiful in the community of the *mir*. Each day he would tell his wife that he was going to work, and then go to the remotest suburbs, those inhabited only by factory workers . . . He went into their inns, read the newspapers, drank tea and talked with the workmen . . . There he gathered news of the *kulaks*, who ruled over the people and took the place of the gentry. When he found nothing more to learn from his companions, Pryzhov taught them the general principles of society.[36]

This became his life as well as the source of his scanty income, for the workers used to give him something for his teaching and (sometimes) offered him tea and food.

He was probably living this life even before he met Nechaev. In any case his activities among the workers were interrupted after he had got into contact with *Narodnaya Rasprava* in September 1869. Later he told the tribunal:

The first reason for which I became an ally of Nechaev is that he, like me, came from the people. Anyone who comes from the masses, however little he thinks, is faced with two possibilities: he can either die on the high road . . . or become an agitator. However strange or paradoxical this idea may seem, it is absolutely true. And so I joined Nechaev. I have lived for forty years and I have met many people, but I have never met anyone with Nechaev's energy, nor can I imagine that anyone like him exists.

He was naturally a great asset to the embryonic *Narodnaya Rasprava*, for he was one of the few men who really knew how the people lived. He also had contacts with the petty, poverty-stricken bureaucracy, which were of the greatest use when such things as false passports were needed. And besides this he was well acquainted with student circles, because ever since he had been refused admission twenty years earlier he had constantly associated with them and taken a passionate interest in their various 'stories'. He had possibly also already had relations with Ishutin's group.[37]

In St Petersburg it proved more difficult to spread Nechaev's ideas. He met with the open hostility of those who had clashed with him at the time of the student disturbances of 1869, and who now were not prepared to follow him along a yet more difficult and risky road. However, in the brothers Likhutin and a few others, he found a little group which soon lent itself to his game though not without a suggestion of bravado.

Vladimir and Ivan Nikitich Likhutin were rich nobles from the region of Nizhny Novgorod. Nechaev made use of them mainly to increase his own prestige among his companions in the group. Ivan went back to Moscow with Nechaev, who introduced him to the others as 'an agent of the Geneva International'. He also hoped to get money from them. In St Petersburg Ivan did indeed try to put into effect for the first time a financial scheme on the lines of those that Bakunin had drawn up in Switzerland. His brother Vladimir, disguised as a policeman, succeeded by methods which lay somewhere between farce and blackmail in getting hold of a cheque for six thousand roubles from a rich student who was a member of their own group. Ivan planted on him a secret and compromising document, while the disguised brother threatened him with arrest and forced him to sign the cheque.[38] But the victim very soon discovered the authors of the trick, and after long discussions the cheque was never cashed. As if to put the finishing touches to the farce, the victim shortly afterwards married the sister of the fake policeman, and very soon completely broke with these underground movements to become Minister of Finance in Witte's government between 1900 and 1902. When Nechaev's own ferocious determination was not in control of his methods (which often sounded so romantic when he spoke of them), they easily became ridiculous.

But this note was out of tune, and in fact the atmosphere around Nechaev was one of real tragedy. There is, for instance, the fate of another of his followers in St Petersburg, Alexey De-Teyle, a student at the School of Medicine. He had already been arrested following the demonstrations of March 1869; in December he was sentenced to four months in prison and five years' house arrest. In 1873 Klements organized his escape, but he was recaptured in St Petersburg and finally drowned two years later in a river at Novovchat, where he had been banished.

Narodnaya Rasprava did not last long enough for us to have many details of its inner life. It was, however, certainly dominated by the personality of Nechaev.

He used various methods to recruit his followers, and dominated those who did not submit to his will in this way: he surrounded them, without their realizing, with people who tried to persuade them, by explaining that all had to serve the common cause. This was necessary, they said, even from their personal point of view, as otherwise when the people revolted they, too, would be exterminated. In this way, those who at first did not want to, ended by submitting or at least offering him money, and then found themselves bound by this action. In general Nechaev was extraordinarily efficient at inducing people to join his society. But he used persuasion only when this was necessary to win their allegiance. When he had obtained this, his attitude changed completely—then he gave orders and demanded submission.[39]

All sources agree that such were the methods adopted by Nechaev: it was his determination that kept *Narodnaya Rasprava* alive. Tension and falsity are apparent in all the documents at our disposal. It is true that this violence —so soon to lead to catastrophe—can be explained by the particular nature of Nechaev's character. But the main reason lay in his conviction (which he succeeded in passing on to others) that speed was essential, for the end was near, and the revolution would break out on 19th February 1870. We find the same anxiety in the works of Tkachev. He too was convinced that a peasant revolution in Russia was possible only within the near future and that otherwise development like that in the West (stabilization on bourgeois foundations) would make a real peasant revolution impossible. Unlike Tkachev, Nechaev did not theorize these anxieties. He was a man of action and tried to bring his ideas onto the plane of immediate activity and organization. It is only from this point of view that Nechaev's venture appears desperate, perhaps, but certainly not mad. For he was inspired by a very definite picture of the future.

Though this was the specifically Russian content of Nechaev's movement, it none the less retained—even in Russia itself—that international aspect that had been symbolized by Bakunin's and Nechaev's collaboration. On the Society's seal were the words 'Russian Section of the World Revolutionary Society'. But this was mainly symbolic. Nechaev alone of his companions had some knowledge of the life and ideas of the First International, and he spoke of it from an entirely personal point of view. In Moscow, for example, he said that 'the association had more than four million members', and he added that 'this association contained a more exclusive inner circle which had its own members in nearly all countries. The main object of this association was to organize protests in the form of strikes for higher wages and start friendly societies and cooperatives, etc.' When he was asked who composed 'the inner circle' (by which he obviously meant Bakunin's *Alliance*) he answered more explicitly: 'It is made up of various people; there are also some who are not workers; and the purpose of this inner circle is above all revolutionary and political.'[40]

Some idea of the contacts between Nechaev's followers and the people can be obtained from accounts of the journeys that he made to Ivanovo and the Vladimir region in order to get information about the peasants' state of mind and regain contact with the 'people' from which he had sprung. He seems also to have had another base among the workmen of the Tula munitions factories. Nechaev claimed that they were 'so well prepared that they could blow Tula sky-high at this very moment'.[41]

In the towns they had scarcely begun to infiltrate before they were imprisoned. But we can get some information from F. Ripman's deposition. He had gone to Pryzhov 'to ask for help in getting to know the people'. 'I must admit that before my arrest I did not succeed in drawing close to the people. Besides, even before knowing Nechaev, I had some links with the peasants, but my only aim was to educate them.' Pryzhov had founded a small group in the town which was to try and make other contacts. 'He himself suggested the Moscow markets as the most suitable places. I and Enkuvatov[42] went to one of these . . . I met a few crooks and prostitutes, but I had scarcely any contacts with them, as I still kept to the rule that it was not I who should speak to them but they to me.'[43] It must always be remembered that these are statements made to the police and must therefore be interpreted with care. It is, however, likely that contacts with this world of 'rebels' which Bakunin had described in his *Catechism* were in fact necessarily limited to ventures of this kind.

Narodnaya Rasprava contained a few dozen members when Nechaev suddenly thought that it was faced with imminent danger. One of his earliest followers, Ivan Ivanovich Ivanov, a student who had played an extremely active part in spreading the organization to the School of Agriculture in Moscow, for some reason or other objected to some of Nechaev's instructions. The historian must now inevitably ask himself three questions. Was Nechaev really afraid that Ivanov would actually denounce his companions? Or was he rather merely afraid that his authority had been compromised? Or did he want to put his followers to the test by binding them still closer to him? To none of these can we answer with certainty, even though so many of his contemporaries (including Dostoevsky) thought themselves able to interpret Nechaev's feelings. One thing only is definite. He decided to do away with Ivanov. He summoned the members closest to him and said that the central committee (a theoretical institution to which he often appealed) had in its possession evidence which proved Ivanov's intention of denouncing the Society. He added that in view of the delicacy of the matter such evidence could not be produced. It was unanimously decided to suppress Ivanov.

On the following evening Ivanov was summoned to the garden of the School of Agriculture on the pretext of digging up a typewriter which had been hidden there at the time of the Karakozov affair. There he was killed on 21st November 1869. Nechaev, Kuznetsov, Pryzhov and Nikolaev took part in the murder.[44] When, after the trial, the last three met again on the road to Siberia 'they came to the firm conclusion that there had in fact been no serious basis for carrying out an act of terrorism against Ivanov'.[45]

At the end of November Nechaev left for St Petersburg, and towards the middle of December he crossed the frontier and went abroad.

In the meantime Ivanov's body was discovered. The police thought that the motive of the murder was robbery, but further clues soon put them on the tracks of *Narodnaya Rasprava*. Before the end of the year a large number of people who in one way or another had had something to do with Nechaev were arrested. At the end of the inquiry seventy-nine people were involved to varying extents, and of these about thirty were granted provisional liberty or released under police supervision. About eighty more were questioned by the police and then released. In his fall Nechaev was dragging down even men who had been his enemies. In the files of the police, tried revolutionaries of all the various currents found themselves next to others who had scarcely yet entered underground life, among them Vera Zasulich. The files, in fact, contained much evidence of Populist agitation at the time.[46]

When he reached Switzerland Nechaev published a letter-manifesto which once again reveals his revolutionary spirit and at the same time his extraordinary capacity for mystification.[47] The Russian police at once took steps to seize him, and an entire book has been written (by R. M. Kantor) on the methods that they employed for this purpose.[48] Excessive as this may seem, it must be admitted that the book is of great interest and full of ironical episodes. There is, for instance, the report of one of the leading Third Section agents abroad who, in his efforts to try and find Nechaev, was eventually implicated in the insurrection of Lyons in 1871, and accused by the prefect of being one of Bakunin's followers.

Morally I am dead. I have suffered many injuries. When I was arrested people threw cigarette ends in my face. The temper of Lyons is utterly savage and the government is weak. There is bound to be a revolution. Today I can write nothing more. I am dead—even though after this arrest my relations with the emigration will be better than ever [he had already succeeded in becoming an intimate of Bakunin's] and to think that I have done nine years' service and never harmed anyone.[49]

Despite such resolute efforts, getting hold of Nechaev proved a difficult job. He was in London and Paris during the Franco-Prussian War (though he was not in Paris during the Commune[50]) and then went to London again. In Switzerland he was hidden by some Italian disciples of Mazzini (Zamperini) at St Moritz,[51] and eventually went to Zurich. And there he fell. A Pole, who was acting as a Russian agent, had him arrested by the Swiss police on 14th August 1872. Despite the intervention of a group of émigrés and an attempt to rescue him, Nechaev was handed over to the Tsarist police.[52]

Throughout the disturbed eighteen months of his second emigration, Nechaev had shown once more his iron tenacity. He wrote, he organized, he published leaflets and newspapers, and more and more openly he proclaimed himself leader and sole representative abroad of the Russian revolutionary forces. 'During his second stay in Switzerland', Ralli later said,

'Nechaev's behaviour towards Bakunin no longer showed the modesty of his earlier visit. He demanded that notice be taken of him, as the only person who had a serious organization behind him.'[53] He did not reveal the situation that he had in fact left behind him in Moscow, and tried to impose on the émigrés in general, and on Bakunin in particular, his own methods, mentality and political opinions. This finally led to a break with Bakunin, and thereafter we find in his writings the very core of his ideas, freed from the anarchist forms with which they had been covered.

He opened his campaign with a series of manifestos addressed to all the various social categories in Russia, calling upon them to revolt against the Tsar. He was ready to make use of anything which might incite the revolution. He appealed, for instance, to the national sentiments of the Ukraine and probably used a manifesto which Pryzhov had earlier written in Russia. He wrote leaflets addressed to soldiers and priests. He published a manifesto addressed to artisans and merchants in the name of an imaginary 'Duma of all the free small bourgeois' saying that the towns should be burnt down and turned into fields. 'Why must our brothers have to live in towns? Why must we have officials? Every *muzhik* will be master in his own house.' To women he said that the only escape from their troubles lay in social revolution.

Together with the working classes you must destroy the empire of the gentry. And with it you must destroy all its laws which stifle the people. Only then will the field be open for women to work freely . . . Only by doing away with private property can one do away with the legal family. All land, all factories and work-shops, all working tools, all communications, telegraphs, etc., will belong to the *artels* of the working men and women who are employed in them. These coopera-tives of production will be started according to the geographical and racial con-ditions of each district and will be joined together in federal solidarity . . . Come with us to the people.[54]

Taking up an idea that had already been in the air in Ishutin's time, Nechaev and Bakunin printed and circulated two manifestos addressed to the nobility, which tried to appeal to their feelings of caste against the absolutism of the Tsars. 'The time has now come to return to the stage of Russian history', said the first of these appeals, which was signed 'The descendants of Ryurik and the Nobles' Revolutionary Committee'. 'We must take advantage of the general discontent to replace the absolutism of a single man with the no less solid absolutism of worthy members of our noble classes. We must forestall the popular movement, which is now close upon us. Carried away by dis-turbances in the West, the primitive populace may rise up against the monarchy.' It was the function of the nobility 'to save Russia from the terrible storm which is about to break over Europe . . . And so let us lend a hand to a reasonable upheaval, and we will then be able to lead Russia along the road of progress, and our ranks will act like a wall of granite against any social Utopia.' The second manifesto, most probably written by Nechaev— whereas the first seems mainly the work of Bakunin—stepped up the dose still further. In it the aristocracy boasted of having served Nicholas I, of having destroyed the 'social Utopias' of 1848 and of having given birth to the glorious Muravev ('the butcher'). For this reason, it said, the nobility had the right and the duty to take the fate of Russia into its own hands.[55]

But Nechaev's most typical manifesto of this time was addressed to the 'students of Russia'. He boasted once more of having fled from the police, and continued:

Listen to the screams of those who are dying under torture, and realize your mistakes. We can no longer afford to be wrong. From now on every step we take must be marked by rigid calculation and inflexible logic; every feeling must be stifled in the breast: one single passion alone must live in us: the will to create a collective force. Comrades, believe in yourselves. Too many already have died for the cause of the people. The time has now come to conquer. The students of the West do not understand and will not understand our ideas. They have had their great days and have now left the stage; their rôle in the life of the people is over. The university now only creates Philistines of science and lackeys of the government. But there are in the West other men—new and fresh—and to them belongs the future. The world of workers is not divided by State frontiers or different racial origins: these are the men who will understand us. Our cause—the people's cause—is their cause. Follow the words of Christ, the first revolutionary agitator: 'do not cast pearls before swine'. Do not test yourselves any longer to arouse with the word of truth a dying world which has now had its day. Its end is inevitable, we must act to hasten that end![56]

These ideas were taken up again and developed in the second number of *Narodnaya Rasprava* dated winter 1870. Nechaev spoke mainly of himself, creating another of the countless romances of his life. Here he spoke of his end, of his death at the hands of the police in the region of Perm. He even described the joy of the head of the Third Section when he heard of his end. These curious pages seemed to combine his love of mystification with a desire to complicate the task of those who were on his tracks. Another article was called 'Who is not for us is against us,' and told 'the well-meaning liberals to pass decisively into our ranks or to become spies. There is no point in them remaining in their present position and dying for nothing.' Indeed, he attributed his own death to a liberal, 'a disciple of golden mediocrity'. He insisted with renewed violence on the need for an organization, threatening 'to remove from the number of the living' whoever tried to tamper with its efficiency—obviously a desperate justification of the murder of Ivanov.

The Revolutionary Committee, he said, must be given absolute powers; and he ended by openly announcing that this power as at present constituted would by no means come to an end during and after the revolution. He described his ideal of a Communist and regulated life down to the smallest detail. Bakunin's anarchism was left on one side to reveal the Communist and egalitarian kernel that Tkachev was later to theorize and that Nechaev had perhaps taken from the Babeuvism of some of his Russian companions and from 'Russian Jacobinism'. But it was to Marx, rather than these sources, that Nechaev appealed. 'Anyone who wants a detailed theoretical exposition of our viewpoint can find it in the *Manifesto of the Communist Party* published by us.' He added that his main concern then was 'to explain the practical methods needed to put into effect' the ideas that it contained. The Manifesto was in fact translated by Bakunin and published in Switzerland at this time, and may have helped to turn Nechaev towards a different formulation of his own programme. He again insisted on his primitive and violent Communism in two numbers of a periodical *The Obshchina*, published in London after his break with Bakunin.[57] All this was obviously his most genuine political thought and acts as a link between *Young Russia* and the Jacobinism of Tkachev.

On this basis he tried to collect a small group of followers among the exiles. From America he recalled Sazhin, who had fled there from banishment in the Vologda region, and who arrived in Geneva in July 1870. Other companions were Semen Ivanovich and Vladimir Serebryakov, who helped him to publish his edition of *The Obshchina*. Vladimir soon disappeared in Russia; Semen Ivanovich, however, was the only man to stand by Nechaev when all his other followers passed over to Bakunin and the Russian section of the Brotherhood, the original nucleus of Russian anarchists.

For a moment at least Nechaev succeeded in winning over Herzen's daughter and Ogarev, now an old man. He got money from them and gained control of a new edition of the *Kolokol*. The first number of 'this organ of the Russian emancipation founded by A. I. Herzen' came out on 2nd April 1870, and the sixth and last on 9th May of the same year.

The 19th February, the date on which Nechaev had based all his revolutionary plans, was now past.[58] Even he, despite his desire to act quickly and hasten the revolution, began to modify his extremist views, and think that more extensive propaganda was needed. Besides, his 'Communism' must have shown him the importance of the political aspect of the struggle, which extended beyond the mere antithesis of peasants and State. The *Kolokol* became more moderate in tone and appealed to wider and more varied support in the fight against Tsarism. True, the very fact of having assumed Herzen's mantle must have led him to take up this position, but this was not the only reason. He was moving away from Bakunin; he too was following the pendulum swing of Russian Populism as a whole which was oscillating between social and political problems, between the organization of a revolutionary force and a democratic movement to include all classes.

But on one point Nechaev held fast.

Russia needs not words but deeds. And so the resurrected *Kolokol* will be mainly, indeed we can say exclusively, the mouthpiece of practical action. Enough words have been spent since the death of Nicholas I, but there have been very few deeds. We Russians, influenced by some sort of German-Byzantine education, or perhaps still more by the Tsarist *knout* which has made any kind of individual initiative excessively difficult for us; we Russians have, more than most people, learnt to console, satisfy and intoxicate ourselves with theoretical reasoning and speeches. And so we take fine words for deeds . . . In Russia the capacity and power of the will have not yet been sufficiently developed . . .

This was the task of the young generation, 'the hundreds, not to say thousands, of young men who have had some education and who have no future and no career, nor even the means to eat'. It was they who would provide 'the formula' of the revolution in Russia. It was they who would transform 'disillusionment, the prevailing sentiment of the 'sixties, into a new force'.[59] But until now 'the absence of a plan and of a close organization has paralysed everything . . . These forces must be concentrated and aimed at a single point: the empire. Everything must be directed towards the struggle against absolutism and victory over it.'[60]

Only an organization like this would be able to link together the various kinds of revolt that were appearing in Russia.

One man says we must propagate the idea of a different order of things among our educated classes . . . Another, that we must prepare the young generation . . . A third is convinced of the need 'to go to the people' and sees the only way of salvation in the spreading of the exact sciences which will kill superstition . . . A fourth says that all these ways are wrong and that we must 'go to the people' not so as to educate it but so as to drive it decisively towards a revolt. We must, they say, only 'awaken it' and then the discontented majority will of itself arise and triumph.

The flaw in all these arguments lay in giving them each an absolute value, whereas each was 'only a fraction, devoid of meaning if not joined to all the others'. The schoolmaster, the Populist agitator, the liberal administrator 'will all form part of a common social cause'.[61] Later numbers of the *Kolokol* add little to this extreme attempt (to be resumed at his trial) to appeal for a union of all forces 'from the so-called constitutionalists to the Socialists'.[62]

Bakunin protested against these policies, which, quite apart from any other consideration, he must have looked upon as scarcely consistent with Nechaev's real nature. Such a view was encouraged by the fact that at this very time Nechaev was showing him in somewhat greater detail the means he intended to adopt: threats, blackmail and robbery—perhaps even in Switzerland. When Bakunin became certain that Nechaev had left only a void behind him in Russia, and when he heard the details of Ivanov's murder, he broke with him.

Bakunin had now seen in Nechaev the gruesome incarnation of those ideas and state of mind that he himself had done so much to establish, exalt and theorize. Seeing them before him in flesh and blood, he was filled with horror and disgust. In a carefully considered letter he described the conclusions he had drawn from Nechaev's adventure. His words well describe the significance of Nechaev's overmastering determination to personify the Populist revolt.

13+

Yet it remains true that he is one of the most active and energetic men whom I have ever met. When it is a question of serving what he calls 'the cause', he does not hesitate or stop at anything and is as pitiless with himself as with everyone else. That is the exceptional quality that attracted me and for long drove me to try and keep in touch with him. Some say that he is just an adventurer. That is not true! He is a fanatic, full of dedication, and at the same time an extremely dangerous fanatic. To join with him can only lead to results that are ruinous for all; and this is why: at first he joined a clandestine committee which really existed in Russia, but now this committee no longer exists, as all its members have been arrested. At the moment only Nechaev has remained, and he himself constitutes what he calls the committee. When the organization was destroyed, he tried to create a new one abroad. All this would be absolutely natural and normal as well as extremely useful; but the methods he has used for this purpose deserve every censure. He was terribly affected by the catastrophe of the clandestine organization in Russia, and has gradually convinced himself that, to found a serious and indestructible society, it is essential to build it on Machiavelli's policies and adopt the Jesuit system. For the body—only violence; for the soul—lies. Truth, mutual trust, real solidarity exist only among a dozen people who make up the *sancta sanctorum* of the society. All the rest serve as a blind, soulless weapon in the hands of these dozen men who have reached an agreement among themselves. It is allowed, indeed it is even a duty, to cheat them, to compromise them, and in cases of necessity to have them killed.

He described the system of internal spying which was the result of this policy, and the real destruction of all human personality.

He is a fanatic, and fanaticism has made him change himself into a complete Jesuit, when he is not at certain moments merely stupid. His lying is often naive. But despite this he is very dangerous. He plays at being a Jesuit as others play at revolution.[63]

On 19th October 1872 Nechaev was taken to the Peter-Paul fortress in St Petersburg. A few days later he was transferred to Moscow, where the trial took place in January of the following year. He was sentenced to twenty years' hard labour, to be followed by life-long exile in Siberia.

Nechaev never recognized the charge that he was a common murderer, and did everything in his power to be considered a political criminal.[64] To the tribunal he cried: 'I do not recognize it. I'm an émigré. I do not recognize the Emperor and the laws of this country.'

His political declarations were more 'liberal' than his real convictions. He spoke of a constitution and shouted: 'Long live the *Zemsky Sobor*. Down with despotism!' After he had been sentenced, he protested to the Chief of Police against the way he had been treated, and specially against his flogging. And in his letter he went on to speak of his political ideas.

Leaving aside dreamers and those who believe in Utopias, one must recognize that Russia is now on the eve of a political revolution ... Like a child whose teeth have grown, have inevitably grown, Society, when it reaches a certain level of civilization, unfailingly feels the need for political rights. Russia is on the eve of a constitutional revolution.

This was merely a liberal cover for his real thought, which survived intact. To the end he remained proud of his popular origins. 'I am a son of the people', he repeated after his sentence, and he recalled Pugachev and Stenka Razin, 'who strung up the Russian nobles, as in France they sent them to the guillotine.' These memories he now used to incite the government to make liberal concessions. His letter went on: 'I leave for Siberia in the firm conviction that millions of voices will soon cry "Long live the *Zemsky Sobor*."'

What he really felt about this could be clearly seen some days later, on 25th January, when he was taken out for the 'civil execution'. He refused a priest, and began to shout: 'Before three years are over their heads will be hacked off on this very spot by the first Russian guillotine. Down with the Tsar! Long live freedom! Long live the free Russian people!'[65]

When Alexander II received the report of the 'execution', he wrote in the margin: 'As a result of this we have every right to have him tried again as a political criminal. But I don't think that this would be of much use. It would only stir up passions. And so the more prudent course is to keep him *for ever* in prison.' The Emperor himself underlined these words, and the order was carried out to the letter. This was the sentence that Nechaev served—not the one he had been condemned to by the tribunal.

He was taken back to St Petersburg, after preparations had been taken to conceal his journey, and on 29th January he was locked up in cell No. 5 of the Alexeyevsky dungeon in the Peter-Paul fortress. He was kept completely isolated.

Alone, in the face of the terrible monotony of prison life, he found support only in books which he was allowed to choose. He was refused Louis Blanc's *Histoire de la Révolution Française*, but was given in exchange Proudhon's *La Guerre et la Paix*. In 1875, when a police general came to inspect him, he spoke of revolution. He was threatened with punishment and replied with a blow. Three years later he wrote a letter to the Emperor to protest once more. The answer came: he was to be forbidden to write. He protested: chains were put on his hands and feet. Only after some time were his feet, but not his hands, freed. Finally he was allowed to write again. Memories of Paris, more or less romanticized, stories of his early life, and political works —all have been lost. The few papers which survive still retain the stamp of his ruthless, violent dignity.

But the most remarkable thing of all is that even in the Peter-Paul fortress Nechaev was able to exert that fascination which had been so powerful when he was free. The soldiers who guarded him gradually became his audience, his admirers and often his subordinates.[66] The means he used to win them over show once more the intelligence, psychological insight and cunning that had always marked his activities. For years he was unable to make use of this position that he won among the soldiers in the garrison. He obtained a few newspapers, but he never succeeded in communicating with his companions. In the dungeons there was only one other prisoner, and he was a lunatic.

But on 13th March 1879 another prisoner was imprisoned in the fortress, the first to be sent there after the new wave of the revolutionary movement. This was Leon Mirsky, who had made an unsuccessful attempt on the life of the Chief of Police. He was followed shortly afterwards by Stepan Grigorevich Shiryaev, one of the leading members of *Narodnaya Volya*. Shiryaev was at last able to give Nechaev accurate and detailed news of the outside world and of the new revolutionary groups. Through him Nechaev managed to send a letter to the 'Executive Committee'. In her memoirs, Vera Figner has told of the astonishment that she and her friends felt when they learnt that Nechaev was still alive, that he was not in Siberia, but for years had been a prisoner in the capital itself. At once they thought of trying to free him. The soldiers became more or less regular messengers between the fortress and the 'Committee'. Many plans were examined, the execution of which was postponed only because *Narodnaya Volya* was preparing an attempt on the life of the Emperor. Nechaev himself, from his cell, suggested postponing his liberation and asked that Shiryaev should be freed first. And he also gave advice of another kind. False manifestos should be circulated when the Tsar was killed, all containing the strangest information so as to spread the greatest possible confusion among the population.

The eighteen months of life that remained to Nechaev after the plot of 1st March 1881 were among the most terrible. Many of those who had planned his escape had fallen in the fight. He himself was forced to make new plans, if only because prison régime was daily becoming more unbearable. And so it was decided that he was to be freed by the soldiers who were supposed to be guarding him, for by now the garrison had reached the point of openly reading in their dormitories and guard-rooms the latest numbers of the *Narodnaya Volya*. Some had even taken lessons from Nechaev on how to write letters in code. But after a long period of blindness, explicable only because the Peter-Paul fortress was so impenetrable that it was not supervised even by other State departments, the authorities began to realize what was happening. In November came the first news of Nechaev's proposed flight, which had almost certainly been revealed by Mirsky, and in December sixty-nine soldiers were arrested.

For Nechaev there was now no further hope. Books were forbidden him, and the prison diet soon gave him the scurvy of which he died on 21st November 1882.

16. PETR NIKITICH TKACHEV

In 1861 the ideas expounded by Zaichnevsky and his group in the manifesto *Young Russia* had aroused feelings of astonishment and outrage. And even later, Zaichnevsky—the first to give impetus to this Jacobin trend—was unable for all his stubborn and patient efforts as a conspirator to found an organization of any size drawing inspiration from the ideas of *Young Russia*. It is true that Jacobin elements had been in evidence in the conspiracies of the 'sixties and also in the nihilist ideology of the time. But the conspiracies were stillborn and death prevented Pisarev, the most important 'nihilist' writer, from amplifying such tendencies. Again, the need for a strong organization and the ideal of Communism rather than anarchism had made themselves felt in a primitive, brutal way in the personality of Nechaev and the movement he founded. But the obstacles and opposition that he met— even among the revolutionary students—from the very beginning of his activities, are in themselves proof that, at the end of the 'sixties, Populism was moving in a different direction—a direction opposed to any form of Jacobinism. The feelings of horror and outrage aroused by the way in which Nechaev's organization had collapsed, and the revelation of the methods used by him in his conspiracy and campaign merely emphasized the divergence between the generation that was arising at the beginning of the 'seventies and the Jacobin-tinged conspiracies of the previous decade. Indeed the movement 'to go to the people' was inspired by a desire to start again from utterly changed organizational and ideological foundations. A new era of wider sympathies and far greater numerical participation was opening for the Populist movement. Some years later the need for terrorism and conspiracy—and indeed the very importance assumed by the revolutionary movement itself—compelled the members of *Narodnaya Volya* to consider once more the problems of a centralized organization and the State, and thus revive some of the themes of *Young Russia* and Nechaev's group. But then they were impelled by their own particular requirements; the ground was very different and they were supported by the spread of Populism itself during the 'seventies. The surprise with which they learnt that Nechaev was still alive and in St Petersburg was in some ways a symbol of this merging of the ventures of the last twenty years into the activities of *Narodnaya Volya*. It was only then in the programme of *Narodnaya Volya* that explicit reference was made to those Jacobin ideas which, ever since *Young Russia*, had sprung up here and there on the fringes of Populism.

Only one man other than Zaichnevsky had during the 'sixties and 'seventies tried to give Russian Jacobinism some continuity, an organization and above all a complete ideology. This was Petr Nikitich Tkachev. In Russia he was among the first not merely to make known Marx's historical materialism but also to give it political significance in Populist controversies. He was the only man to give a coherent ideological picture of those primitive demands which had been expressed by Nechaev. And it was he who, in his attacks on the Socialism of Lavrov and the anarchism of Bakunin, had linked the Jacobin impulses which had appeared in Russia during the 'sixties with the Populism of later years and the international current of Blanquism. Though he never succeeded in founding a real movement of his own, his personal activities—isolated, it is true, but sustained by impelling logic—sufficed to shape Russian Jacobinism and to make his Blanquism, if not an immediately effective political force, at least one of the important factors in the political debate of the 'sixties and 'seventies.[1]

Tkachev was the son of an insignificant nobleman from the district of Velikiye Luki. His father died when he was still young. He went to school in the capital, and at once embarked on a life of politics. Twenty years later, when speaking of Chernyshevsky he still said: 'C'est le véritable père et fondateur du parti socialiste révolutionnaire en Russie. Aucun écrivain, en aucun temps, n'eut tant d'influence sur le développement intellectuel de ses contemporains. La partie la plus avancée de la société russe le considérait comme son chef.'[2]

It was thus the *Sovremennik* which gave him the first inspiration. St Petersburg University, which he entered in 1861, was his first contact with the realities of politics. By October of that year he was in Kronstadt fortress, together with many of his comrades who had been arrested in the demonstrations of the autumn.

He was released about two months later, and paid the closest attention to the controversy which had opened between the various political factions; constitutional and Populist, Jacobin and Communist. In the beginning of 1862 he came into contact with a supporter of these latter views: Leonid Olshevsky, one of the very few men who tried to spread in St Petersburg ideas like those of *Young Russia* in Moscow.[3] In the appeal to the peasants which they aimed to distribute at this time and which may have been written by Tkachev himself, one idea predominates—a bold egalitarianism.

He was sentenced to three years' imprisonment, but released before the end of his sentence, and continued throughout the 'sixties to take an active part in the clandestine groups of the time. In 1865 he was again arrested for joining a demonstration organized by the students in a theatre showing a play which attacked 'nihilism'. In the following year, 1866, he was caught in the great manhunt that followed Karakozov's attempt on the life of the Tsar. Once again he was soon released, and kept in contact with the Academy of Smorgon which, as we have seen, was one of the few centres which remained active during the White Terror. In 1869 he tried to give a political slant to the disorders which broke out in the schools, and he launched a small manifesto *To Society*, to make the students' demands more widely known. Together with Nechaev he played an active part in trying to found a conspiratorial movement based on these disturbances. With him he drew up the *Programme of Revolutionary Activities* and laid the foundations for the organization which proposed to put itself at the head of the expected peasant *jacquerie*. But he was arrested on 26th March 1869 and could no longer play a direct part in Nechaev's movement. He had to wait in prison until 15th July 1871 before being tried in the great trial of Nechaev's followers. He was found guilty of having written *To Society* and sentenced to a year and four months in prison. After this sentence he was to be banished to Siberia. Instead he obtained permission to go to his birthplace in the district of Velikiye Luki. There he remained until December 1873, when he succeeded in getting abroad.

Even this brief summary (and further information has not been preserved) shows that Tkachev was in contact with the most active groups of the 'sixties from the University of St Petersburg to Karakozov and Nechaev. He was one of the very few who was able to live a life of continuous conspiracy throughout the period and survive its various phases. When he reached Switzerland he was entitled to regard himself as a typical representative of what he called 'the new youth'. He wrote in 1874:

I myself belong to this generation. With it I have experienced enthusiasms and mistakes, beliefs and hopes, illusions and disillusions. Almost every blow struck by reaction has affected me directly or the persons of my comrades and closest friends. Ever since I first went to school I have known no society other than that of young men devoting themselves to student meetings, taking part in secret conspiracies, starting schools or Sunday reading centres, and organizing *artels* or communes; men in fact dominated by the idea of teaching the people, of drawing closer to them; men who spent their entire lives in conspiracies. I have always been with them and among them; I have been separated from them only by the walls of the Peter-Paul fortress. How could I not know the men whose life, grief and joy I have shared for ten years?[4]

The tone itself shows how deeply Tkachev was attached to his experiences. In the 'seventies he became an isolated figure because he represented an earlier tradition in a movement which had grown and changed. His long period of segregation between the beginning of 1869 and the end of 1873, first in prison and then as an exile, widened this gap. He was always fundamentally concerned with the problem of founding an organization, whereas the Populists were concentrating on the question of getting in touch with the peasant masses, 'going to the people', and even exploiting legal possibilities to the full. Tkachev's clandestine activities in the 'sixties gave him primarily ideas on the technique of conspiracy. This was to be the personal element in his Blanquism. In Switzerland he attacked Lavrov, Bakunin and in general the entire movement which was to lead to the second *Zemlya i Volya*; for he was the lonely heir of the more nihilistic, Machiavellian element which had found its extreme expression in Ishutin and Nechaev, and which had been broken by the government repression and, virtually, buried under the new and wider wave of Populism.

But when he reached Switzerland in 1874, Tkachev was not merely a conspirator who had escaped from the police. For a full decade he had taken part in ideological discussions, and had published a large number of articles on legal, economic and literary problems in the most typical nihilistic reviews, above all the *Russkoe Slovo* and the *Delo*. And even later, as an émigré, he continued to write under various pseudonyms in the Russian press.

These articles provide a typical example of the indirect style of writing which ever since Chernyshevsky had become usual in reviews. Sentences grew longer and longer, in an attempt to imply a meaning that could not be openly expressed; articles took on unusual proportions and were written circuitously round a central subject in order to make the reader aware of their real message; literary problems were treated with an emphasis and violence which show that matters of immediate political concern were really under discussion. Tkachev's writings are typical of the strange mixture of freedom and oppression which prevailed in the Russian press of the 'sixties. When in Switzerland he adopted a very different style. The propagandist clarity of his articles there emphasizes by contrast the closed atmosphere, pullulating with concealed energies, which dominated Russian reviews of the 'sixties. But though arguing within the bounds imposed by the censorship and the *ambience* in which he lived, Tkachev succeeded in expressing in these articles the kernel of his philosophical ideas.

His first articles were written in 1862 and are concerned with legal problems. As early as 1864 such subjects became one of the pretexts through which he expounded his general philosophical ideas, and a means of defining his position among the various tendencies of the time.

He then began his attacks on positivism, which he was to develop in all his later writings. In fact any attempt to apply the methods of the exact sciences to the study of society soon seemed to him both a theoretical mistake and morally and politically harmful. He wrote in 1865:

One can take up an objective, indifferent attitude towards the phenomena of nature. But with the phenomena of social life, one must take up a critical attitude. The phenomena of nature can be reduced to general rules and more or less certain laws; but the phenomena of contemporary life, social phenomena, cannot and must not be reduced to laws; doing this implies justifying a number of absurdities which are transformed into principles thanks to habit and indifference.[5]

Criticizing Herbert Spencer, he said that it was by no means true that society was an organism like living organisms. The idea of organic development which had led to such progress in the study of nature and Darwin's discoveries 'becomes sterile and dead when applied to the science of society' as Spencer had in fact tried to do.[6]

The laws of organic and inorganic development are eternal, uniform, and cannot be modified or avoided; organic and inorganic bodies can exist only on condition that they submit blindly and continuously to them. But, on the contrary, the laws which govern society do not have a single one of these distinctive characteristics; they are always the product of society itself, i.e. the results of human will and human calculation. They are born and die with society.[7]

Confined to the Peter-Paul fortress, he returned to this subject and wrote a long article on Edgar Quinet and the ideas contained in his work *La Création*. Once again he discussed the false analogy between nature and history, and he regarded what Quinet had called 'une science nouvelle' only as the new formulation of an old mistake. In a long essay, *Science in Poetry and Poetry in Science* (only recently published after being concealed in the archives of the Third Section), Tkachev examined the various aspects of this social Darwinism. The idea of the struggle for existence, once it was applied to history, seemed to him to lead only to a justification and not to a criticism of events. Even Quinet, 'an eternal worshipper of freedom and irreconcilable enemy of despotism', was led by this theory to defend the idea that 'Babylon was better and more perfect than Jerusalem because Babylon had defeated Jerusalem'.[8]

In fact there was nothing in common between natural selection and historical selection, even though the comparison had become one of the 'favourite current analogies of contemporary sophists'.[9] It was enough to try to apply it to some concrete historical event to realize how meaningless it was. Only a poet, said Tkachev, can find any similarity between the struggle for existence in the Darwinian sense of the term and the struggle for accumulating capital. This latter struggle leads to no perfecting of the species; it is a purely economic struggle, with no criterion of absolute value; in general 'neither the accumulation of wealth nor the perfecting of production can ever serve as a criterion or be the final purpose of civil progress or the measure of the perfection of a social organization'.[10]

Tkachev considered this problem of the analogy between nature and economy so important that he returned to it in a further article on Spencer which he wrote in prison. In it he clearly drew the inferences implicit in the entire controversy. Society, far from representing the struggle for life, has in fact as its final goal the abolition of this struggle from human existence. Mankind has drawn together for the very purpose of avoiding natural selection. Not that this aim has been reached. The struggle between individuals has been replaced by the struggle for things, for wealth, for possessions. This is a substitute for natural selection which has survived in society but which is contrary to the very purpose for which society was intended. And

13*

so, to speak now of natural selection and to apply Darwinism to human society merely implies a justification of this inner contradiction and support for the economic struggle. The great names of Isis and Nature are used to mask what in fact is only the usurer's passion for accumulating capital. Human progress, far from consisting in natural evolution, can be understood only as a duty, a striving towards the abolition of the inner contradiction inherent in society. Nature is the realm of existence, and therefore also of laws. But in history there are no laws, but only ends or, perhaps, one end, according to which everything can and must be judged.

This is Tkachev's 'formula of progress', and the conclusion to which he was led by his 'realistic' and 'critical' method.

These ideas spring from a double source. On the one side was economic materialism which convinced Tkachev of the second-hand character of ideologies and the so-called 'laws' of sociology; on the other was faith in an egalitarian ideal which provided him with the final aim which alone, so he thought, could explain and illuminate the course of human history.

An article of April 1864 gives the first complete formulation of his economic materialism:

Only during recent years has the science of jurisprudence begun to realize how weak was the ground on which it was based and how false the method which it previously used. The reform began in the methodology of one of its branches, that of civil law. Dankwardt was the awaited and beneficent reformer. He was the first to show or, rather, to point out the close link between the economic and the juridical sphere of social life; he has shown that civil law is only a determined reflex of a people's economic life.[11]

Later Tkachev turned back to Dankwardt's *Nationalökonomie und Jurisprudenz* (published in Rostock in 1859, and in Russian in 1866), thus proving that, at least in part, his economic outlook on history was derived from the researches into the philosophy of law published in contemporary Germany.

But discussions in Russia itself and hints in Russian reviews may have led him to similar conclusions. Tkachev paid particular attention, for example, to the article that Yuly Galaktionovich Zhukovsky had published in 1861–62 in the *Sovremennik* on 'Political and Social Theories of the Sixteenth Century'. This was an attempt to interpret the philosophy of law in economic terms. 'Economic demands', Zhukovsky wrote, 'govern politics and law. It is enough to realize this on one occasion to see afterwards that in each individual case the political activities of the individual and parties reflect their economic interests.'[12] And from this point of view he tried to interpret the more important political theories of the sixteenth century. That period showed 'three fundamental political interests conflicting with each other'.

These were: feudal interests, those of the middle classes and those of the people. All three merely represent three distinct economic interests; those of the landed proprietor, those of the capitalist and those of the worker deprived of land and capital. Each of these interests has its own legal apologists; the first has the scholastics, the second has lawyers, and the third . . . has found defenders in writers such as Machiavelli and More who are able to see the falsity of all juridical interpretations and their dependence on the ruling force. They have utterly rejected all legal forms and destroyed them all, doing away with every kind of system and unmasking general hypocrisy. In a word, these writers are above all parties and are seekers in the name of truth, not in the name of a party . . . Machiavelli rejects the scholastics' natural law, he rejects their mystical morality, and without so many circumlocutions, he introduces the concept of force into law. And so all his activity was directed at making Italy a strong and united monarchy. Machiavelli has in fact understood the real essence of law and in this sense he can be called a genuine realist. [13]

Tkachev accepted this view, but why, he asked, associate More with Machiavelli? It was true that More had understood that the root of evil lay in the economic situation of his time, but he had neither Machiavelli's depth nor his radicalism, and even his political activities had not really been aimed at defending the masses. He had not given his *Utopia* a practical, immediately political character. And so it had ended by being looked upon as a joke. More in fact had been only an 'academic realist'.[14]

This typical passage shows that Tkachev was already concerned to see how the economic interpretation of history is reflected in politics, and he criticized Zhukovsky because he refused to draw the logical inferences. Indeed Zhukovsky later became a critic of Marxism, and in 1877 published an article attacking *Das Kapital*, while Tkachev found in Marxism the fullest expression of his own economic ideas.[15]

In 1864 he still thought that he could find the roots of these ideas in Adam Smith. It is true, he said, that he had never given them clear and categorical expression but they seemed implicit in the *Wealth of Nations*.

But as early as 1865 he was speaking of Marx. The idea of economic materialism was not new, he said: 'It has been transplanted into our press— like everything else worth while in it—from the culture of Western Europe. As early as 1859 the well-known German exile Karl Marx had clearly and exactly expressed it.' To prove this Tkachev translated a passage from *Zur Kritik der Politischen Ökonomie* and added: 'this idea has now become common to all thinking and honest men, and no intelligent man can find any serious objection to it'.[16]

We cannot be certain whether Tkachev already knew this work of Marx earlier or, as seems more likely, read it only in 1865 when he quoted it for the first time. It provided a foundation to his thought and had a considerable influence on him. He spoke of Marx again in later years, for example in 1869, when in an article in the *Delo* he explained his own ideas on economic materialism which had in the meantime grown more precise and clear. 'I maintain that all events in the intellectual and spiritual world correspond in the last analysis to events in the economic world and to the "economic structure" of society, to use the expression adopted by Marx. The development and tendencies of economic principles condition the development and tendencies of political and social relations, and even leave their mark on the intellectual processes of society, on its moral ideas and its political and social conceptions.'[17] As an example he instanced French eighteenth-century philosophy which was an expression of the economic changes of the age.

As if to prove to himself how correct his own view was, he began in 1865 to write a long essay on the history of rationalism which he was unable to complete and which was seized by the police in 1866. This essay was designed to trace the history of the origins of modern thought, bringing it into relation with the development of capitalism.[18] He thought that historians had not yet paid proper attention to the struggles of manufacturing and commercial interests against theological interests, the struggles of the bourgeoisie against Catholicism.[19] From this point of view he found the discussions on usury which had been so frequent during the Renaissance of particular interest; the fight against asceticism and the ideal of poverty was evidence of the correctness of his theories. He entered into the details of theological controversies, describing for example how belief in witchcraft had ended not because scientific discoveries had shown that it was absurd but because economic changes had made it useless. And so he examined the rise of modern rationalism as a reflection of the stabilizing of the rule of the bourgeoisie.

The position of feudal lords and the clergy during the Middle Ages appeared to be sound and safe, but in fact it was completely uncertain and unstable. Their relations with the peasant masses whom they exploited were not determined with exact and scientific clarity with no room for doubt, as were those in the ancient world between lord and slave, or those which would be established in the modern world between the man who buys work and the man who sells it.[20]

And indeed peasant revolts had been frequent and violent. Feudal lords had, as it were, been sitting on a volcano. Only the bourgeoisie was to create exact and precise tools for its own rule and was to fashion the form its economic power would take: rationalism.

In 1867 Tkachev returned to the same problem, confining himself to Germany in a long essay called *German Idealists and Philistines*. Only a study of German economic development could explain the contradictions in the German character; only by studying feudalism in the towns and countryside could one unravel the intricate skein of German ideology.

Such a study would reveal that there was no real contradiction but a deep-seated relationship between the idealism and Philistinism of that country.

Feudalism had already created its idealism of 'sated parasitism'; while the closed and confined life of mediaeval towns had given birth to Philistinism. The only really 'realistic' force had then been that of the peasants.

They are not afflicted with the romantic dreams of the knights, nor with the nebulous dreams of the scholastics. They saw life as it really was. They did not try to beautify it or to turn it into poetry or to give it the value of a law. They looked upon it as an inevitable evil and as such they put up with it. Their common sufferings bound them to each other, compounding their interests to such an extent that they were completely foreign to the petty Philistinism that typified the bourgeoisie . . . The peasants were not bound together in the particular interests of a particular centre or parish. They looked upon themselves as brothers who had to help themselves in all difficulties and necessities, as they were able to show in the so-called peasant war.[21]

Tkachev was very interested in this idea. Between 1865 and 1868 he translated, with V. A. Zaytsev, Zimmermann's work, and wrote a long criticism of it in the *Delo*, when the three volumes of the German historian were published. The defeat of the German peasants was, he thought, the fundamental factor 'on which depended the entire later development and character of European civilization'.[22] It had left the field open to the forces of feudalism and the bourgeoisie, united together against the peasants.

The Reformation had been only the expression or, as Tkachev said, the symbol of the interests of the bourgeoisie. The ideal of Protestantism had expressed far more clearly than reality itself the nature of the new economic principle which was coming into being. Once again, as always happens, it had found first 'an absolute formulation', a symbolic sanction, and only later 'a realization in life'.[23] But the bourgeois advance was held up by fear of revolts in the countryside, and it could only establish its rule by allying itself with the feudal laws. The peasants were defeated and fell back into destitution and so into mysticism and superstition. Thus Germany had not given birth to a society, but only to castes.

In such a situation in what conceivable field could the human spirit obtain material for its thoughts? The interests of surrounding life were too low for thinking man, who could not develop a critical attitude to them, but who grew up under their crushing influence . . . Even before beginning to think, he had become a Philistine. So he could only utterly renounce life and fling himself into the boundless world of metaphysical dreams.[24]

This gap between theory and practice seemed to Tkachev to be at the origin of German idealism. The only ray of light was the work of the eighteenth-century enlightened reformers. But the idealism which was born of it, with its abstract formulas and metaphysical principles, did not comprehend the needs of the German nation and so could not awaken even the smallest response in the masses.

These are the most typical examples of Tkachev's attempts during the 'sixties to apply his economic materialism to history. At the same time he was trying to give this principle a deeper formulation. His original idea of seeking inspiration from Adam Smith widened into a general reflection on the English economists and above all on J. S. Mill. From all this he reached a standpoint which was based on Marx but which always tended to be formulated in utilitarian terms. Not that he was a follower of the utilitarianism of Helvetius, Bentham and Mill: for their ideology too was merely a theoretical reflection of a determined economic reality, that of capitalism. But whenever he tried to escape from a simple repetition of the economic principle of history, he had recourse to formulas which he got from Marxism and expressed himself in utilitarian terms. It might even be said that he was always tending to move from Marxist materialism to its original sources in the eighteenth-century enlightenment.

But Tkachev was more interested in the 'great practical importance' of economic materialism than in a theoretical deepening of it. He noted that this principle was able 'to concentrate the energy and activities of those sincerely devoted to the social cause on really essential points: the vital interests of the people. It guaranteed them the support of the most indispensable forces . . . It was a spur that inspired direct practical action.'[25]

Economic materialism was in fact the political weapon needed to bring about the egalitarian ideal which was the other fundamental element in Tkachev's historical ideas—the final goal towards which all human progress was moving, and the only valid measure by which to judge history and politics.

We cannot be certain whence he derived this ideal. *Young Russia* probably put him on the road, but his own egalitarian ideas were clearer than those of Zaichnevsky, and very likely sprang from Babeuf. The closest student of Tkachev's thought, B. P. Kozmin, has referred to Buonarroti.[26] This is more than likely, though the name never appears in any of his works published in Russia or abroad.

In any case its formula is that 'egalitarianism in deed' understood in its most extreme sense, even more extreme in fact than in Babeuf himself. Tkachev was not only concerned with trying to bring about economic equality accompanied by a levelling of education and culture, but 'physical, organic' equality, as he himself frequently stressed.[27]

This virtually Utopian element in his egalitarianism is certainly the result of the extremist spirit so characteristic of his thought and of Russian Populism in general. But we can throw historical light on it by referring to the French eighteenth-century Utopias, in which this physical, natural element so often goes hand in hand with the ideal of equality. There is unquestionably in Tkachev's thought something that could be called archaic, almost a return to the origins of Socialist ideas during the Enlightenment. The process was common to other Populists who, as we have seen, had attributed great importance to discussions in the spirit of Rousseau on the value of learning in general.

This Utopian element did not figure in Tkachev's conception as a useless ornament, more or less casually superimposed on his political ideas. He himself was concerned to justify and rationalize it, thus emphasizing the importance it evidently had for him. Besides, he had always defended Utopias as the most logically extreme expression of a principle, maintaining that the only true realists were those who had been charged with being Utopians, whereas those who had tried to find compromises and bounds to the logical development of an idea were incapable of seeing things as they were. Speaking of the German peasant war, for example, he said that John of Leyden and Thomas Müntzer had been less Utopian than the moderates of that movement, and he had paid detailed attention to the delaying action of the bourgeoisie in the towns.

Economic reasoning led him to the same results. Once the wage earner was abolished, once all laws of demand and supply in the labour market were radically repudiated,

it will be essential to find a new and a more reasonable criterion to measure the value of the unit of work. But how can this be done? How and with what can one measure the labour value of each individual man at each individual moment...? The fact is that this problem will be solved the more easily . . . as the differences between individuals diminish and their equality from the physical and psychological point of view becomes more absolute. The problem will be solved, the principle achieved, when everyone is unconditionally equal, when there is no difference between anyone either from the intellectual, moral or physical point of view. Then they will all have an exactly equal share in the returns of production, and any special valuation of their work will become utterly superfluous. The reasons which according to backward economists now make the existence of a salary essential will vanish of themselves, and with them will vanish the salary.[28]

And so all attempts to establish reward according to merit or need—in keeping with the formulas of the various Socialist traditions—seemed to him unrealizable, absurd or, worse, the result of a compromise between a capitalist principle of distribution based on demand and supply, and the opposite principles of Socialism. A rational criterion of distribution can exist, he said, when it has become, so to speak, useless, and replaced by a simple, equal sharing between equal people.

The new principle therefore had to be formulated as 'an equality which must by no means be confused with political and legal or even economic equality; but an organic, physiological equality conditioned by the same education and common living conditions'.

This is the final and only possible aim of human life; this is the supreme criterion of historical and social progress; anything that can bring society nearer this aim is progressive; anything that holds it back is retrograde . . . In this way the word progress gets a precise and specific meaning, and the party of progress a fixed and unchangeable banner, a motto which cannot be adapted to double meanings and ambiguities.[29]

It is not therefore surprising that Tkachev was openly critical of the various Socialist currents, though he studied them carefully. Louis Blanc was for him the symbol of the uselessness of all attempts to intervene on behalf of the workers within the capitalist system. In his judgment of Proudhon, Tkachev may have been directly influenced by Marxism. He said that Proudhon's theories were merely a Utopia of the economic relations which already existed in bourgeois society. Though he differed in defining value and put labour as its basis, Proudhon was in fact only returning to the laws of demand and supply. He merely excluded a few of the most extreme consequences of this principle, such as for example bankruptcy and stock jobbing. 'Proudhon is in fact only distinguished from capitalism because he had developed its fundamental principle more logically and more precisely.'[30] Even Proudhon's idea of credit, which was what most interested Tkachev, could function only when the people's bank was in the hands of 'a State which acted clearly on behalf of the workers', a State which really wanted equality. Without this condition, there was not even a hope of any reform. In this criticism he included all the movements which were directly or indirectly inspired by Proudhon, all the varying ideas on associations and cooperatives. To oppose them he emphasized what he thought was a vital streak in the thought of Lassalle: i.e. the idea of having the cooperatives supported by the State. But this, too, thought Tkachev, would work only in the future when the State was no longer in the hands of capitalists.

In 1869—the year, it is worth remembering, that he began his political association with Nechaev—he tried to express his attitude towards the varying Socialist traditions as clearly as the censorship would allow, in a little book which is perhaps the most interesting product of his publicizing activities in Russia. This is a translation of a work by Ernst Becher, *The Problem of the Workers in its Contemporary Significance and the Means to Solve it*, a small work of moderate views and no great importance. But in an appendix Tkachev added Proudhon's plan for a people's bank and the statute of the International, as well as making clear his own point of view in a series of notes to the text.

As he himself wrote in a review as soon as the book was published, he had chosen this work because he thought it could be of tactical use. Its moderate tone would not at once bring the reader face to face with the extreme consequences of the principles which it maintained. In the notes he undertook to develop them himself.

The censor pointed out that Becher in himself contained nothing which need be condemned because he did no more than explain 'the means through which workmen could obtain a fairer share in the product of their work'. But he immediately added that the translator maintained 'purely Communist' ideas and openly said that to bring these into effect 'explicitly revolutionary means'[31] were necessary. The authorities drew the practical conclusions from this judgment. The book was withdrawn from circulation, and on 13th August 1871 Tkachev was sentenced to eight months in prison 'for having repudiated the principle of property with the aim of destroying it or weakening its foundations'. But this relatively light sentence was pronounced only when the book had already had a fairly wide circulation.[32] A remark by the censor may help to explain this comparative indulgence and uncertainty on the part of the authorities. In any case, he said 'the problem of the proletariat and the means to solve it is in no way a Russian problem'.

Despite the repression, Tkachev's tactics could be considered successful. He had made known a book which expressed a generic form of Socialism; he had published documents of fundamental importance in spreading knowledge of the workers' movement in the West; and he had circulated a plan by Proudhon and the statute of the International, and had countered them with his own ideas which were no longer merely 'egalitarian' and 'Communist' but already clearly Jacobin.

The 'social problem' he now considered identical with the problem of the relations between capital and labour. A society must be created composed exclusively of workers. He used Becher to epitomize the results which criticism of the capitalist system in the West had reached so far. It was up to himself to make clear the means required to substitute for it 'the productive association of workmen'.

As he himself said, the model to be followed was that of the 'French Communists and Socialists' who had been able to draw all the inferences from the Socialist principle. 'The more abstract an ideal is, the more logical it is; for by building such a system man is guided only by the laws of pure logic. It can contain nothing illogical, no contradictions. Everything is deduced from an idea, everything is harmonious and balanced.'[33] This was the only way to convince oneself of the impossibility of any reform within the capitalist system.

The entire problem of economic reform can be solved by a government decree granting credit to the workers. We have not the slightest doubt that such a decree, if it were really carried out, would lead to the desired result. We do not doubt that the State has all the means it needs of compelling agreement with its own laws if only it want to, and that it is in a position—if it so desires—to open up the purses of the capitalists to the workmen. But will it so desire? That is the entire problem, and there can be no doubt about the answer. Becher himself maintains that the State is totally dependent on existing economic relations and that these relations determine its essence and the aims of its activities, and that the classes which dominate in the economic sphere always dominate also in the political sphere. Only in one case can the State act and act for the benefit of the workman, and that is when the workers themselves become the dominating class in the political sphere; when the State of Western Europe, the State of the bourgeoisie, becomes the State of the workers.[34]

For this goal alone were movements of association and cooperatives of any value and importance. Historically speaking, Socialist ideas had not begun to have any meaning until they had been placed 'on the economic plane', and had thus become working-class movements. In this way 'abstract Utopia had approached effective reality'. The founders of this movement 'had attracted the strongest and most practical men, uniting under their banner all the workmen, and thus obtaining an immense power for action'.[35] Such was the value of the International. But there must be no illusions; there was no 'natural transition between the old and the new' and 'one must not conceal the fact that there is an abyss between them, that however much one tries to bring them together the abyss remains and it is difficult to bridge it'.[36] The leap was not a fatal one, but it was a leap, and history showed how it could be made. 'To destroy the power of the feudal lords the terrorism of the King's power was required; to destroy the kingdom of Louis XVI the terrorism of the bourgeoisie was indispensable.' A peaceful transition between one social form to the next was only 'one of the non-existent Utopias that humanity has always invented to quieten its conscience and to obscure its vision'.[37]

So however necessary Tkachev thought it to make known the workers' movement of the West; and however much he appreciated the means discovered by the Socialists to bring about the programme of a future workers' State (and chiefly Proudhon's bank, associations of production, and the trade unions), for him the true problem still remained political. From this point of view, universal suffrage would be of no purpose even if it was understood in Lassalle's sense. Political rights could only be enjoyed fully when they were based on economic rights. The central problem was to smash the existing system, even for a short time—the time necessary to nationalize the banks and so finance the workmen's cooperatives. Even the trade union movement was of use only as a tool. The masses, as he was never tired of repeating, were organically incapable of escaping from their position and of transforming a purely economic movement into a revolutionary break. 'Taken as a whole the masses do not and cannot believe in their own strength. They will never on their own initiative begin to fight against the misery that surrounds them.' It was the duty of the intellectual *élite* 'to find in itself, in its own practical knowledge, in its higher mental development, in its spiritual and cultural situation'[38] the first fulcrum for building up a force able to destroy the existing power. Any illusions on the part of this *élite* as to the capacity of the masses to develop themselves and to act for themselves would lead to one result only. It would create a passive attitude towards them and hence deny the revolutionary conception which was at the centre of Tkachev's political ideas.

Was this outlook the result of an already conscious choice in favour of the only revolutionary current in Western Europe which held somewhat similar ideas? For Blanquism was at this very time growing in importance, especially in France. It is true that Tkachev identified himself with it when he was an exile in Switzerland in 1874. But were there earlier links than this —if only in the shape of some knowledge of Blanquist programmes and intellectual support for their ideas? These questions are not easily answered. Blanqui's name never appears in his writings. Was this merely due to the censorship? Our inquiry into Tkachev's thought may prompt us to say with some hesitation that such was not the case. Even if he knew the Blanquist movement, his ideas were based chiefly on *Young Russia* and Russian Jacobinism. They had developed through a collation of Populism, Marxism and the International, into a synthesis which was entirely his own. Only when he was an exile was he in a position to realize that these views largely coincided with those of the Blanquist group. This group he then joined, though he always retained a standpoint of his own.[39]

The Russian Jacobinism of Zaichnevsky and Tkachev is a political pheno-menon born of the discussions of the 'sixties which only later in the 'seventies joined hands with the movement in Western Europe. Its fate is in this respect similar to 'nihilism' which only then came into contact with anarchism and the Bakuninist wing of the International. Tkachev too was a Russian Jacobin before becoming an exiled Blanquist.

This view is confirmed when we turn to his outlook on the state of affairs in Russia. He wrote much about this during the 'sixties, though often in indirect and convoluted forms, being unable to shelter this time behind the comforting idea held by the ruling circles that the problem of the proletariat was of no concern to Russia. Already in an article of 1864 he had recalled 'the insuperable difficulties which face us when we make any personal attempt to draw nearer to the people and to make clear for ourselves—independently, without guidance from outside inspiration and advice—what are their requirements and wishes'.[40] But despite this, Tkachev succeeded in writing a number of articles of great interest on the life and problems of his country, and tried to apply to them the political ideas that he had been developing.

He began with a series of critical analyses of official collections of economic facts and figures. The picture of Russian society that he drew from these had considerable influence on the development of his thought. Facing a hundred thousand landowners were fifty million peasants. He tried to determine how not just the land but above all the produce of agricultural activity was distributed between them. He concluded—using approximate figures, it is true, but ones which obviously indicated the political trend—that while the ratio between the peasants and the landowning class was 234 to 1, the ratio between their lands was 11·5 to 1. 'Whereas each soul has about three and a quarter *desyatiny* of arable land, each noble has about seventy, i.e. twenty times more.'[41] As for income, he calculated that the proportion was 2·5 per cent for the former and 97·5 per cent for the latter. He calculated the average budget of a peasant family, and concluded that a permanent deficit was inevitable. This led to rapid destitution. The fundamental cause of this situation lay in the primitive state of Russian agriculture, the distribution of land, and the crushing weight of taxation. He also examined the industrial side of Russian economy. Quoting the American economist Carey, he said that 'without factories agriculture cannot even exist, let alone flourish'.[42] The technical backwardness of the countryside could only be overcome through the development of industry. But what was in fact the real state of affairs? Inaccurate and missing statistics prevented a full reply. But even so, the facts that he had been able to collect were typical and instructive. Russian coal production represented only one seven-hundredth of what was produced in Western Europe; the percentage per inhabitant of iron and coal production also pointed to great backwardness. It was not possible to get an exact figure of the workers employed, but it was approximately half a million, compared to fifty million peasants. Russian industry, he found, was concentrated in comparatively few factories, with many machines, but those too came from abroad and were paid for by export of agricultural produce. Instead of trying to develop a uniform internal market for wheat, the State had concentrated on a policy of exports, thus making the peasants' situation still worse. In industry wages varied considerably, but even taking account of this fact Tkachev calculated that the workmen received an income of about nineteen millions in wages whereas forty millions went to the factory owners as net income.

Dividing the first figure by five hundred and forty-two thousand (the approximate number of workmen) and the second by eighteen thousand (the approximate number of factory owners and manufacturers) we see that, of the total figure of industrial production, each workman receives about thirty-five roubles a year, whereas each industrialist gets about two thousand two hundred. The workman gets 1·5 per cent of the income, the industrialist 98·5 per cent.[43]

It was enough, he added, to compare these figures (and indeed those of the distribution of income in the countryside) with the incidence of taxation to see the relationship between class exploitation and the policy of the State. The lower classes paid about 22 per cent of the taxes; the upper classes 78 per cent, while they absorbed as a whole about 97 per cent of the income.

The way that this balance was drawn up shows that Tkachev—though he was particularly interested in Russia's industrial situation and in the existence and possible development of a real proletariat—considered class problems from a typically Populist point of view: peasants and workmen on one side, nobles, petit bourgeois and bourgeois on the other. The huge numerical superiority of peasants inevitably prompted him to look upon them as the true force which would allow the development of revolutionary egalitarianism in Russia.

So that if he was Marxist from the ideological point of view of economic materialism (and we have seen that this too had its limits), he was not so from this, fundamental, point of view. He was always particularly attentive to those social phenomena which showed signs of developing on similar lines to the formation of a proletariat in the West. But he always looked at them from within the Populist framework which contrasted all the exploited with the small number of exploiters.

He devoted for example an acute article to destitution in Russia, showing by means of figures that it did in fact exist, contrary to the widespread opinion that everyone in Russia had land and work. He proved that there were hundreds of thousands of destitutes, and that if their problem seemed less acute than in the West, this was merely due to the chaotic state of the various relief systems, the small sums given over to their assistance, and the fact that many were left to private charity.

But he knew that this pauperism did not reveal a modern proletariat so much as a possible germ for one in the future.

In the West, lack of economic security, from being an occasional state of affairs as in the Middle Ages, has become, so to speak, a permanent, normal phenomenon, derived from the very nature of given economic relations. It is in this that lies the radical difference between the proletariat of those days and that of today. As a partial and occasional state of affairs, it could not give rise to serious fears; but as a general and permanent phenomenon it inevitably arouses alarm on the part of all well-off citizens.[44]

But in Russia, on the other hand, destitution was far more than anything a relic of the past, or a result of the existing dissolution of old castes and old social orders. A modern proletariat, in fact, was scarcely in the process of formation.

This only deepened Tkachev's profound lack of faith in the possibility of the exploited masses freeing themselves and starting an egalitarian revolution.

The real fulcrum for overthrowing the existing social situation lay else-where: in the revolutionaries themselves. In Russia they sprang from the intelligentsia to whose social position and ideas they were in origin bound; but they had the energy and the extremism which would enable them to free themselves completely from the bonds which still tied them to the ruling classes. He said in 1868:

Our situation is not as bad and desperate as some people think. Our intellectual development is not as immature as some suppose . . . We must not blame the civilization of our country for the ignorance of our people. We must rather be grateful to that civilization for the healthy thoughts and ideas that have begun to spread during our time among a limited group of our educated classes . . . They are the pledge of our future happiness . . .[45]

In this manner, only general as yet, Tkachev expressed his faith and hope in the germ which was growing in the educated classes. It was true, he added, that there was a marked contrast between 'this minority, which is at the forefront of the European intelligentsia, and the great majority of the population who, through its *forma mentis* and its way of life, is closer to the conditions of the primitives'.[46] This very contrast, 'impressive and astounding' as it was, seemed to him to raise the fundamental problem of Russia's development.

It is therefore natural that Tkachev paid passionate attention to a detailed study of how the intelligentsia had been formed and developed. Before the emancipation of the serfs, it had had its origins in the privileged classes, whose interests and concerns it reflected; but it was now derived 'from another class of people . . . intermediate between those who have a solid economic basis and those who by no means possess one'. These new intellectuals were in an uncertain position. Demand for their work was limited and doubtful, in view of the lean development of Russia's economic life as a whole; their social position compelled them to live entirely on their own work, although they found no guarantees in it.

Here lay the root of the Socialist tendencies which dominated the intelligentsia.

The less a man's position is secure and the more accidental circumstances, independent of his will and anticipation, influence him; the more he feels his dependence on others—then the more strongly and clearly does he feel the need for a complete solidarity of human interests, the more naturally and rapidly does he get the idea that individual happiness is impossible without the happiness of all, that personal happiness is unachievable without that of all society.[47]

But two dangers threatened the development of this Socialist element in the intelligentsia. The first was the widespread conviction—which Tkachev often criticized in his condemnation of positivist ideas in general—that it is men of culture who create progress, that it is they who with their intellectual work transform society. This would lead to a widening abyss between the intelligentsia and the people. And the second was the reverse of this—but an idea that was also deeply rooted in Russia—that the intelligentsia had no duty or value, that it should learn everything from the people. Tkachev never tired of fighting against these two facets of the positivist and Populist mentality. He tried to persuade at least some members of the intelligentsia to become conscious of their essential function—a function that was absolutely necessary, though not in itself sufficient. He tried to convince them that they would in fact be able to become creative and revolutionary only on condition of standing on political rather than purely intellectual or moral ground.

He always dealt particularly severely with positivist theories on the purely intellectual causes or prospects. His satires on intellectual pride are among his most violent works.

'It is we who decide what must remain and what must change', say our masters. 'It is we who make progress, it is we who show humanity the way, it is we who give the tone to everything.' O ingenuous self-adulation! If they carried you into a black pit and told you 'Sing the praises of the perfume of this miasma. Show that what is in black pits is the most healthy and excellent food' you would carry out these orders with cringing humility. *You* show the way of progress! In actual fact you go where you are driven, you are only the echo of life, the reflection of needs, and dreams, of practical action and daily routine.[48]

Escape from this situation was possible only by working out the exact social value of every idea and by becoming aware of the economic element which was implicit in every intellectual point of view. Any general praise of progress only concealed reality.

But his condemnation of that form of Populism which put all its trust in the people was just as clear and highly developed. 'The idealization of the uncivilized masses', he said of Reshetnikov's novels in 1868, 'is one of the most widespread and dangerous illusions.' It was as apparent in the blind faith that the mass can civilize itself by its own efforts as in the exaltation of the purity and absolute morality which it was supposed to contain. 'The people's spirit, the people's genius, the people's principles, are sacred things which the civilized gang dares not touch with its dirty hands, which it cannot analyse and criticize with its corrupt mind.'[49]

In a series of essays he tried to discover the origin and development of these ideas in Russian culture. Even during the time of serfdom idealizing the peasant had been in fashion; sentimentality, the pastoral literary style of the beginning of the century, had been merely the result of adulation aimed at landlords who wished to show themselves satisfied at seeing their peasants happy and prosperous. This literature had transformed 'primitive *muzhiks* into excellent *paysans*'.[50] At the basis of this Arcadia was an apology for serfdom. At the same time another type of idealization, in the opposite direction, had arisen. This had been inspired by desire to win natural rights for the peasants. It had been the idealists who had proclaimed the genius of the people. Somehow or other they had to look for a 'point of light' in the dark 'and as in fact it did not exist, they had invented it'.[51] Already at that time this conception had inspired the Russian idealists with an optimism which freed them from the burdensome duty of acting. From them had sprung 'the doctrines of the so-called Slavophils and liberals who preached *laissez faire*'. In this process of turning the peasant into a god, the Slavophils had gone to the very limit, and the liberals had stopped half-way; but both had helped to create a state of mind which dominated the scene as long as serfdom lasted. As emancipation drew near and as the landlords realized that economically their situation was growing less and less prosperous, and as they became more and more fearful of serf uprisings, so they began to abandon idealizations of the peasant. 'From an excellent, well-behaved and gentle *paysan*, he returned to being the rebellious, ignorant and vicious *muzhik*.'[52] It is curious that Tkachev attributed this satirical or brutal picture of the peasant to those very writers whom Chernyshevsky had welcomed as the first to give a realistic vision of the Russian people—for example, Nikolay Uspensky and in general many of those associated with the *Sovremennik* at the beginning of the 'sixties. A few years had sufficed to change the situation. What was required was no longer a realistic picture of the people's life and the exploration of a newly discovered reality; but rather, as Tkachev said, a complete picture of the Russian countryside, capable of indicating the economic and political problems which had developed in it, and adumbrating the entire problem of the peasant classes.

One of the very few writers to have looked at the peasant masses, not only in the villages but in the factories, with genuinely realistic eyes had been Reshetnikov. Tkachev devoted a long article to him in 1868, drawing from his tales and novels confirmation of his own predictions on the social development of the Russian people. But apart from him and a few other exceptions, the attitude of the intelligentsia to the people remained seriously impoverished by a lack of practical feeling. The sense of compassion that these novels tended to arouse was 'only a feeling of pity for the readers themselves; these writers did not draw near the people, but devoted themselves to self-analysis and self-laceration. Poor, frail characters!'[53] They had great desires and aspirations, but their lives remained petty and mean. Lack of any determination to make a complete break with their social position only gave rise to a false relationship between the intelligentsia and the people.

Tkachev was mistaken in this analysis of the Populist literature of the 'sixties. It was this simple faith in 'the people's principles' and the Russian peasant which was to lead a few years later to the movement 'to go to the people' from which the entire revolutionary movement of the 'seventies was to develop. Such a judgment provides further evidence of the limitations of Tkachev's outlook. He fell back within the bounds of his own experiences as a conspirator to such an extent that he was no longer able to have any serious influence on the ensuing period.

But in spite of this, his assertion of a political spirit outside any idealization of the popular classes was of value and significance. In an article called 'Men of the Future and Heroes of the Bourgeoisie', published in 1868, he drew a portrait of the 'realist'—i.e. the man inspired by a political ideal, similar to what the followers of Tkachev and Nechaev were trying to realize at this very time. In this he tried to establish a model for the intelligentsia and encourage it to take account of its own function. 'Neither ascetics nor egoists nor heroes',[54] this was what he wanted these men of the future to be, men who were outwardly ordinary but who were inspired by one single idea.

Their distinctive badge lies in the fact that all their activity, their whole way of life is dominated by one ambition, one passionate idea: to make the majority of men happy and to invite as many as possible to the banquet of life. The bringing about of this idea becomes the only purpose of their activity, because this idea is completely fused into their conception of personal happiness. Everything is subordinated to this idea, everything sacrificed—if one can even use the word sacrifice.[55]

From this and other similar descriptions by Tkachev, we can say that 'realists' are ascetics without temptation, utterly absorbed by their revolutionary function. They do not fight against themselves but merely follow the dictates of their own nature. And with the same natural simplicity with which they absorb all their passions into the single passion for the happiness of all, they regard morality as relative to their purpose. They are ready to cheat, if that is needed for the triumph of what they consider a higher moral principle—i.e. the principle that inspires them and underlies their entire personality. Their motto could be 'Do not exploit'. They are not prepared to replace this with the traditional one of 'Do not steal' which they attribute to the Philistines 'who preach the untouchability of other people's handkerchiefs, and when they have the chance quietly remove the contents of their neighbour's pocket'.[56] In these assertions we can recognize the ideas so brutally catalogued in Bakunin's *Revolutionary Catechism*, the extreme expression of the realistic nihilism of the 'sixties.[57]

By reading Tkachev we can see how this ideal prototype of 'the man of the future' (or, in language untrammelled by the censorship, 'revolutionary') is derived from the intellectual. The process is one of gradual progression through a repeated stocktaking and soul-searching as to his social position and his function in the economic machinery of society. Tkachev constantly repeats that intellectual activity must be paid for and that its price falls heavily on the shoulders of the peasants. Each page of a review is paid for by the sacrifice of those who will never even read it. Involved in their own immediate surroundings, the intellectuals do not even clearly appreciate the misery of the outside world. Whoever has more than an average income— more than he could expect in an ideally equal society—is eating someone else's bread. Is not this just the position of men of culture? Arguing with a reactionary German writer, Wilhelm Heinrich Rill, whom I. S. Aksakov once called the German Slavophil, Tkachev made some incisive and curious observations on the subject. To understand the true position of the intelligentsia in relation to other classes of society, he said, we must examine the market for intellectual products.

In the market of mechanical and physical work, because of the competition from machines, supply has for long been greater than demand. A natural instinct of preservation therefore makes men move from this market to another, to so-called intellectual and cultural work. This market is dominated by rich men, by landed proprietors, by *rentiers* who, after they have satisfied their real needs, still have a lot of money with which to enjoy and divert themselves. This money goes on to the intellectual market and thanks to it the demand remains fairly high.

Besides, the intellectual worker comes on to this market both as a seller and buyer, and so helps to keep the demand high. Very differently situated is the market for mechanical labour. The workmen of Lyons or Brussels produce silk and satin which they will never use 'whereas the poor man of letters who sweetens the leisure of men who do not work, cannot do without the product of the mental work of his colleagues'. And so the intellectual market enjoys considerable advantages, but they are in part at least vitiated (and Tkachev was obviously thinking mainly of Russia) by the growing number of people who apply themselves to this kind of work. None the less their pay remains higher than that of a workman. 'The worst writer has a higher income than the most efficient and skilled workman.'[58]

Tkachev was well acquainted personally with the position of the intellectuals in the 'sixties, as he had had to make his living by translations and articles throughout this period. They felt themselves dependent on the ruling classes from the economic and spiritual point of view; at the same time they knew that as regards their social position they were nearer the proletariat.

Tkachev saw that this situation was ultimately responsible for the deep-seated discontent felt by the intelligentsia (giving the word its widest meaning so as to include technicians). From this point of view he found one particular instance very revealing: the position of women, who during these years were beginning to take part in cultural and economic activity. They, too, had not been satisfied by the limited and petty work that Russian society could offer them; and for them too, as for all intellectuals, there was only one way of escape: to transform this discontent—these dreams of finding a 'great cause' to which they could dedicate themselves—into a specifically political spirit, a spirit capable of making them conscious of their position and at the same time providing them with the weapons with which to solve it through a revolution. 'Founding cooperatives is a fine thing, but it is fine only because a few women will thus be able to obtain economic independence and practical security.'[59] But how many would be able to achieve this? Only activities aimed 'at attacking the entire structure of society and the solidarity of all human interests'[60] could really satisfy the demands that were now driving young women towards individual and fragmentary activities.

In this way he was returning to the theme of Chernyshevsky's *What is to be done?* He concluded more clearly than Chernyshevsky had done in favour of those who devoted themselves entirely to political action, criticizing any Populist attempt at social activities. Both the two vital elements in Chernyshevsky's novel were now divided in Tkachev's mind. 'The man of the future' was already an idealization of the pure revolutionary.

He considered this all the more necessary as he well knew that the situation was now different from what it had been ten years earlier. The reforms had given an impulse to Russia's economic life which was destined to develop still more quickly in the future. The reforms themselves had brought about the need to build a new administrative and juridical structure. Both from the economic and from the administrative point of view, the foundations had been laid for a new intelligentsia. The number of those resisting the temptation to take part in the economic development of the bourgeoisie or the reformed government administration was growing ever smaller. Many who had been 'repudiators' and 'nihilists' at the beginning of the 'sixties were throwing over their ideas as such practical possibilities opened up before them. 'The demand for the intellectuals' work has increased. The "ruined" and the "enraged" now have the chance to escape from their ruin and to build for themselves a new, definite and secure social position.'[61] The social relations which were being brought about would logically reduce those who continued to maintain revolutionary ideas to a 'small minority'.

The men of the 'forties, said Tkachev, had been in a position where they were unable to realize their 'ideal principles'. Life told them: 'I do not need you; stand aside as your spirit prompts you, but do not interfere in my affairs, in my relations. And they quietly pocketed the fruit of the work of millions and stood aside from a life in which their "ideal principles" had no place.' They were tragic and comic at the same time, but:

The position in which their sons now find themselves is entirely different, and Life speaks to them in very different tones. 'I need you', it says, 'and I will not feed you if you do nothing. Your "ideal principles" do not correspond to the interests which I have created for you. But this does not matter to me. For the development of my principles, I need agricultural foremen, technicians, industrialists, doctors, lawyers, etc. To each one of them I am prepared to give full freedom in the sphere of his own speciality and nothing more. You must help me. Develop industry and trade, rationalize agriculture, teach the people to read, found banks, hospitals, build railways, etc. And for all this I will give you a good and solid reward, and I will do what I can to make your work not too hard. I will create conditions that correspond to your character, and I will give you a feeling of satisfaction with your work and so do away with your melancholy. Those are my conditions.'[62]

How many would withstand such demands made by the 'logic of life'? Their fathers could go on being idealists, because there was no chance of bringing their ideas into contact with reality. But the tragedy of this new situation lay in the fact that these had become realizable, at least in part. In this case 'one can always find a little bridge'[63] built perhaps of indifference, which was 'more dangerous than typhoid and cholera';[64] or of the rationalization of egotism; or of a kind of application of laissez faire to the sphere of morals or still worse of an 'idealism' able to justify such an attitude. As the years passed he was more and more concerned with this state of affairs, and his criticisms of it, especially in the articles which he sent to Russian reviews from Switzerland, became more and more cutting, and his condemnation more and more severe.

All the more intransigent then must be the attitude of the small minority. They must stop being idealists and become realists, i.e. aware of their break with the intelligentsia. They must entirely devote themselves to a policy of revolution.

For a moment he thought that Nechaev was the fruit, now at last ripe, of this process which was forming the 'men of the future'. When the movement which he too had helped to create collapsed, he thought that only abroad could he find an opportunity for openly sustaining his convictions. In Switzerland he did in fact succeed in founding a small centre of Russian Jacobinism. But he ended by paying the price of this determination to isolate the revolutionary élite. He remained alone in the midst of all the other tendencies, and met with no great response in the Populist movement.

In 1874 Lavrov's review *Vpered* was the émigré organ of that branch of Populism which was stirring once again in Russia, thanks to the work of Chaikovsky's group which had helped Tkachev flee from banishment.[65] This review held a discussion on the fundamental problems of propaganda and organization, in which Tkachev wished to take part. As long as he confined himself to writing of the peasants' discontent and social conditions in the region where he had been banished, his collaboration was welcomed.[66] But in the last lines of his short article, he hinted at the political outlook which was soon to lead to his break with Lavrov.

The younger generation must take account of its own forces. Fear today would be criminal; uncertainty, postponement, would be equivalent to a betrayal of the people's cause. The government itself recognizes that the ground is now ready. The right moment must not be missed.[67]

Nechaev's revolutionary impatience, the 'now or never' which had been the basis of his conspiracy, returned to confront Lavrov in the person of Tkachev.

The class of landed nobles is ruined, weak, utterly lacking in power, numerical or political. Our *tiers état* is made up for the most part of proletarians and paupers, and only in a minority of cases are they beginning to form a real bourgeoisie in the Western sense of the word. But we naturally cannot hope that social conditions so favourable to us will last for long. However slowly and weakly, we are moving along the road of economic development and this development is ruled by the same laws and is following the same direction as the economic development of Western states. The *obshchina* is beginning to dissolve; the government is doing everything possible to destroy it once and for all. Among the peasants a class of *kulaks* is growing up, who buy and hire out the land of the peasants and nobles, a sort of peasant aristocracy. The free movement of landed property from owner to owner becomes less difficult every day; the widening of agrarian credit, and the development of monetary transactions, increase each day. The gentry are compelled, willy-nilly, to bring in improvements to their agricultural systems. Such progress is usually accompanied by a development of national industry and an increase in town life. And so in Russia at this time all the conditions are there for the formation on one side of a very strong conservative class of peasants, landowners and farmers; and on the other side a bourgeoisie of money, trade, industry—capitalists in fact. As these classes come into being and grow stronger, the situation of the people will inevitably grow worse, and the chances for the success of a violent revolution will grow more and more problematical. That is why we cannot wait. That is why we claim that in Russia a revolution is in fact indispensable, and indispensable now at this moment. Do not let us allow any postponement, any delay. *Now* or, perhaps, very soon, *never*. Now circumstances are acting in our favour. Within ten or twenty years they will be against us. Do you understand all this? Do you understand the true reason for our haste, for our impatience?[68]

This passage is the vital one for an understanding of Tkachev's standpoint: a cold and realistic analysis of the situation, the result of all his thinking on Russian society, combined with a passionate determination to save the kernel of the Populist conception—the peasant *obshchina*. At the heart of his political viewpoint was the idea that social revolution in Russia was possible only by stopping or interrupting capitalist development. In this way, by means of a revolution, Russia could avoid the road already travelled by the countries of the West. Tkachev's Jacobinism, as indeed his Marxism, are thus used as tools for this central aim. They serve to point out the means or to analyse the situation which can bring it about; they do not change his final purpose and essential aspiration. Tkachev's Jacobinism is Populist and indeed—just because of its tactical originality—it reveals some of the most profound and lasting aspects of Populism itself.

Tkachev developed this idea to the full in his campaign against Lavrov. He had already, in legal reviews, discussed Lavrov's ideas of the historical process. In these he said that it was not moral ideas which allowed one to evaluate the development of history, but one idea only, that of an egalitarian revolution. Now at Zurich he attacked Lavrov for the political consequences of this ideological discussion. His ideas could not possibly become the banner of a revolutionary party.

The wide banner of progress is the most convenient cover for every kind of philosophical-Philistine idea made by every kind of supporter of 'little by little' theories. Beneath it all shades of progressive parties can find a place, beginning with the liberal bourgeoisie and ending with the revolutionary Socialist.[69]

It was for this very reason that revolutionary Socialists could not make use of it—especially when its adherents followed up ideas of progress with the theory that they must prepare themselves and the people, and devote themselves exclusively to political discussions and propaganda. They thus ended by putting all their hopes and trust not in the revolutionaries but in the intelligentsia. And this at the very time when the situation in Russia was in danger of turning intellectuals into egotists and exploiters.

Hope in progress implied a patient waiting for the moment when the masses would at last be educated. But should the revolutionaries wait to persuade the majority? What would then be the purpose of a revolution? A revolution can occur only when 'the minority does not want to wait'[70] and exerts itself to unleash it, trying to bring to a head that feeling of discontent with one's position that always exists, widespread and dumb, among the popular masses.

The revolution that Tkachev visualized did not spring from a growing 'understanding and knowledge' of the masses. Rather it derived from a mechanical accumulation of the discontent that welled up under an increasingly unbearable system of oppression. It was then that the break would come; and then 'the minority will impart a considered and rational form to the struggle leading it towards determined ends, directing this coarse material element towards ideal principles. In a true revolution the people acts as a tempestuous force of nature which destroys and ruins everything in its way, always acting outside all calculations and consciousness. Who has ever heard of civilized people making revolutions?'[71]

'The revolution is made by revolutionaries' in the sense that it is they who give it an aim and an end. The people can always make one, always wants to, and is always ready. But the initiative and guidance must come from the leaders. Their task is not to wait for some historical moment, but to make constant appeals to revolt, fully aware of what to make of this revolt once they succeed in unleashing it.

And so it was essential to tell the young and active members of the intelligentsia who were 'going to the people', not to prepare themselves or devote themselves entirely to propaganda, but rather to fling themselves into disturbances, and do everything possible to increase the general feeling of discontent. To those who were already revolutionaries it was essential to say that their activities must be primarily aimed at building up a solid organization. Everything depended on 'the strong organization of revolutionary forces, the union of single and isolated ventures into a common, disciplined, solid whole'.

'Our practical experience of revolution has already worked out various kinds of activity: political conspiracy, popular propaganda, direct agitation among the people.' This was not the time for discussion. Every way was equally indispensable. Only one answer could be given to the question 'What is to be done?'—start the revolution. To achieve this all ventures were of use as long as they took account of the fact that the fundamental problem remained that of organizing the small revolutionary minority.

Tkachev was still further convinced of all this by his impressions of the workers' movement in Western Europe. What he saw in Switzerland only confirmed the pessimism that he had already felt in Russia.

In a discussion with Lavrov, he said that the idea of waiting for the majority to be ready was all the more dangerous in that if it prevailed 'a bloody and violent revolution would become unthinkable everywhere'. Instead there would dawn the age of 'bloodless revolutions' to the German taste, as dreamt of by Lassalle. The entire workers' movement of Western Europe seemed to have accepted this prospect already. Was it not at the basis of 'the German programme of the International'?[72] So he reproached Lavrov with following the example of the German Social-Democrats, in whom he had no faith. Among other things this would lead the Russian revolutionaries to forget the peculiar conditions of their own country and to fail to see how necessary it was to fight against 'the insensate, blind despotism of autocracy, the revolting and brute force of a rapacious government, our complete lack of all rights, our shameful servility'.[73]

Tkachev summed up these conclusions of his controversy with Lavrov in April 1874 in a pamphlet called *The Aims of Revolutionary Propaganda in Russia*. It was published in London, and in it he explained the reasons that had made him break with the editors of the *Vpered*.

But he did not want to destroy all bridges with the exiles who did not share his ideas. He had not altogether given up the hope of being able to unite around himself other revolutionary groups—possibly even all of what he called 'the party of action'.

It was for this reason that at the end of his pamphlet he said that without exception all experiments and methods were valuable. Indeed he had even made a tactical concession to Lavrov by speaking of propaganda, and above all he had drawn nearer the point of view of the anarchists by emphasizing the idea that the people by virtue of its natural situation is always ready to revolt. The first concession was designed to attract into the world of the revolutionaries some forces which were still enclosed within the intelligentsia; the second answered his need to draw nearer the Bakuninists with whom he had got into contact in Switzerland and with whom he felt that he had so much in common, in spite of his own Jacobin ideas.

This—though more consciously so—was a repetition of what had happened some years earlier in the case of Nechaev. Nechaev had found expressed in Bakunin all his own urges to rebel, but had finally moved away from him, driven by a profound instinct that told him that his own revolutionary tradition did not in fact coincide with anarchism. And it was to Nechaev that Tkachev explicitly referred in this pamphlet, quoting the words of his friend in his review *The Obshchina*.

His pamphlet against Lavrov met with some response. Even Engels referred to it in the *Volksstaat*,[74] confining himself to an attack on the Bakuninist elements in Tkachev's programme which, as we have seen, were not in fact fundamental. In answer Tkachev defended Bakunin, who had become as he said 'the bête noire of the Marxist apocalypse'. But he was mainly concerned to define his own original position.[75]

The discussion is of interest. Engels had used this pretext to attack the isolation of the Russian revolutionary movement in the past and to rejoice in the fact that 'it is now developing in the presence of, and under the control of, the rest of Europe'. He added that the Russian revolutionaries had themselves suffered deeply from this earlier isolation. This was one of the origins of the mad schemes undertaken by Bakunin and his companions. They would now benefit from 'criticism that came from the West, the mutual relations of the various Western movements and the fusion (which is at last occurring) of the Russian movement into the European one'. In this light Engels found Tkachev's ideas particularly crude and primitive. Tkachev replied that the effect of 'such instructive lessons' on the Russians would be like that produced on the Germans by a lesson 'given by a Chinese or Japanese who had by chance learnt German but who had never been to Germany, who had never read anything published there, and who had conceived the idea of teaching German revolutionaries, from the height of his Chinese or Japanese majesty, what they ought to do'. It was in fact the specific elements of the Russian situation which came to the surface as soon as Tkachev tried to give deeper significance to his campaign. Why was Engels not prepared to admit that the Russian revolutionary movement could develop on independent lines? By so doing 'he clearly offended the fundamental principles of the programme of the International'. It had in fact been the Russian revolutionaries themselves who in the past had been the first to hold out their hands to the international movement and to take part in it 'even more actively than their own interests demanded'. But they by no means wanted to follow 'the European Workers' Party' in questions of tactics and practical action.

The position of our country is altogether exceptional. It has nothing in common with the situation of any other country in the West. The means to carry on the struggle which they have adopted are, to say the least, utterly impracticable for us. We need an altogether special revolutionary programme which must differ as much from the German one as the Russian state of affairs differs from that of Germany.[76]

Engels had accused him of ignorance of the problems of the international working-class movement; Tkachev now accused him of not understanding the problems of Russia. 'We have no urban proletariat, we have no freedom of press and no representative assemblies.' So there was no hope of being able to build up, for example, 'disciplined trade unions including all workers, conscious both of the conditions under which they lived and of the means to improve them'. It was essential to remember that in Russia the very fact of intellectuals wanting to draw nearer the people was considered a crime. Anyone wanting to live with the workers had to change clothes and take out a false passport. 'You must admit, my dear Sir, that in a state of affairs like that to dream of transplanting the international association of workers on to Russian soil is worse than childish.'[77] This did not in any way mean that a social revolution was more difficult in Russia than in the rest of Europe. Far from it: 'If we have no urban proletariat, neither do we have a bourgeoisie. Between the oppressed people and the State which crushes it with its despotism, there is no middle class; our workers are faced only with a struggle against political power.' And within the people themselves there were tendencies which acted in the direction of a revolution, above all the *obshchina*. 'They are, if one can put it this way, Communist by instinct and tradition.' The idea of private property could be introduced in Russia, as indeed was happening, only with the bayonet and the whip. He then spoke of the *artels*, the *Raskolniki*, peasant revolts and the social situation of the intelligentsia. These were the classic arguments of Populism which for the first time were openly clashing with those of Marxism.

There was one original feature which still retained the flavour of Bakuninism: this was the bold claim regarding the weakness of the entire Russian governmental machine, a weakness which merely reflected the lack of social coherence among the ruling classes. 'Two or three military defeats, simultaneous peasant revolts in two or three provinces, and an open rising in a town during peacetime will be enough for the government to be completely isolated and alone, deserted by all.'[78] The task of the conspirators was to prepare themselves to take advantage of such a situation. This was indeed what all revolutionaries had done, in Western Europe as well, during times of great oppression. And immediately after the crushing of the Commune, was not something of the kind happening even in the West? Had not the Italians come to the Congress of the International at Brussels in 1874 to say that they were compelled to carry out all their activities conspiratorially? Was not this exactly what the Russian revolutionaries had to do?[79]

Though, as can be seen, Tkachev's ideas grew more precise during this controversy, he had to wait for about a year, from the end of 1874 to the end of 1875, to find an organ in which to advance them. We know little or nothing of his activities during that time; he separated himself more and more from the Bakuninist wing which he had thought for a moment of joining, if only conditionally. Meanwhile he approached various groups among the Polish émigrés, whose ideas he may have found nearer his own.[80] At the end of 1875 he succeeded in organizing a periodical at Geneva, together with a small group of Polish émigrés and some Russians who shared Blanquist ideas, Kaspar Tursky, Karl Yanistky and a few others.[81] Nechaev may already have had some links with them, and Tkachev succeeded in forming from them a small but active political force. This gave birth to the *Nabat* (The Tocsin) which was sub-titled 'Organ of the Russian Revolutionaries'.[82]

Tkachev wrote its programme, which was published in November 1875, and the *Nabat* came out at irregular intervals until 1881. In his many articles, Tkachev did not write propaganda, but always deliberately addressed himself only to the revolutionary minority. He realized that his paper would only have a very restricted circulation; but he was only concerned that his ideas should be known by a small number of people as long as they were the most active in the world of conspiracy and action. One day, writing to a friend, he declared himself satisfied within limits of the work that his paper had done.

I know very well that few in Russia can get hold of this paper. But its existence, its programme and its principles are known in almost all the revolutionary groups. By attacking its ideas in every possible way, by distorting them and slandering them, the anarchists and the followers of Lavrov have ended by spreading them among the younger generation and by preparing their final triumph, a triumph which is shown by the foundation of the party of *Narodnaya Volya*, by the creation of a series of 'executive' and other kinds of committees, by the programme adopted at the meeting of Lipetsk, and finally by a series of successful or unsuccessful attempts on people's lives. The irrefutable truth of the ideas held by the *Nabat* was so obvious to me that I did not doubt for a minute that they would end by prevailing, that they would be put into practice, even though the *Nabat* had not circulated beyond the frontiers of Switzerland and even though we had published only a few dozen copies.[83]

14+

And so, for the time being at least, he did not try to found an organization. He only wanted to point out the means required for the establishment of a really organized force by denouncing the mistakes of the past and present.

He said that the very fact of conspiracy demanded discipline. Neither the bourgeois revolutionaries nor the Bakuninists had been prepared to recognize this, but it would be enforced by the very nature of things. It was essential that the conspiracy should have a plan 'which should be put under the control of a common leadership'. It must be based on the principle of 'centralization of power and decentralization of functions'.[84] Any plan to create a movement on the basis of a federation of independent groups was Utopian and could never constitute an effective weapon. It would be incapable of any speedy and decisive action, and would open the door to discussions and internal dissension, to doubts and compromise. Besides, such an idea of federation had its roots in bourgeois mentality and morality, based as it was on individualism and egoism. The revolutionaries must show, even in their organization, that they knew how to put the collective above the individual.

When Tkachev expounded these ideas, he already knew the results of the movement 'to go to the people'. He then wrote an article to summarize his conclusions. He thought that the entire movement was in a state of crisis. There had been a large number of arrests, the revolutionary forces were dispersed. Instructions 'which were clearly distinguished from those of ten years earlier'[85] had been followed, but the results obtained had not justified this change. It was essential to turn back, above all to the experiences of Nechaev. Nechaev had acted without a prepared field, but at least the ideas which had inspired his movement were clear. Not only had he wanted to start a revolution, but he had wanted to do so at once. Hence he had been concerned with organization. Now the goal must remain the same, and the means to reach it must be improved. The banner of the movement 'to go to the people' had always been very vague and general, so much so that everyone had understood it in his own way. It had been this uncertainty that had disorganized the movement, even though, as Tkachev recognized, it had vastly increased its numbers. But none of the Populists had succeeded in getting into political contact with the true forces of the peasant revolt, the workers and Cossacks. In the 'sixties any means had been adopted as long as the final end was kept in sight. Now they had forgotten the end and were devoting themselves entirely to looking for means. Once again a central organization, able and willing to bring into effect a predetermined plan, had become the fundamental need.

It was therefore essential to fight against the dangerous illusion that a revolutionary movement could spring from 'natural groups' through 'natural evolution'.[86] The seventh issue of the *Nabat* for 1876 ended: 'The unification and coordination of activities is without doubt the first indispensable step for putting the social revolution into practice.' The forces of the revolution were now in the same situation as an army; their position was inconceivable without an organization.

If organization is necessary for a large and strong party, it is undoubtedly even more indispensable for a weak and small party, for a party which is only beginning to be formed. Such is the position of our social revolutionary party, and for it the problem of unity and organization is a problem of life and death . . .[87]

The stage of isolated groups closed within themselves and inevitably hostile to each other must be overcome; all 'fractionalism' could be of use only to the Third Section.

To get rid of this obstacle two things were necessary: to give up all illusions of being a large party, and to determine clearly the function of the minority.

The revolutionaries were indeed few, but they must appreciate the 'intellectual and spiritual power' exercised by a minority over the majority. The revolution in fact consisted in transforming their 'so to speak spiritual' power into 'material' power.

And as in contemporary society in general and especially in Russia, material power is concentrated in the power of the State, a true revolution can be carried out on one condition only: the conquest of the State's power by the revolutionaries. In other words, the first and immediate task of the revolution must consist in conquering this power and changing the conservative State into a revolutionary State.[88]

It was true that the conquest of power was not in itself a revolution, but merely its prelude. The revolution would take place in two phases, the first destructive, the second constructive.

The essence of the first stage is the fight, and therefore violence; the fight can be carried out successfully only on the following conditions: centralization, severe discipline, speed, decision, and unity in action. Any concession or doubt, any compromise, multiplicity of command or decentralization of the forces in the fight, can only weaken their energy, paralyse their work and do away with any chance of victory. Constructive revolutionary activity, on the other hand, though it must proceed at the same time as the destructive activity, must by its very nature rely on exactly opposite principles. The first is based mainly on material force, the second is based on spiritual force; the first relies mainly on speed and unity, the second on the solidity and vitality of the changes it has brought about. The first must be carried out with violence, the second with conviction. The *ultima ratio* of the first is victory, the *ultimû ratio* of the second is the will and reason of the people.[89]

These two different functions must be clearly distinguished. In the one case there must be readiness to be ruthless; in the second elasticity and gradual moves, so as not to fall back into a Utopia. Tkachev thought that to ensure such elasticity in the constructive work, it would be necessary to summon a *Narodnaya Duma* (National Assembly) which would sanction the activities of the revolutionary State, and within limits, even control it. At this stage, propaganda on a huge scale would be of extreme importance. But this propaganda, in which the 'bourgeois pseudo-revolutionaries' had such vain hopes, would be utterly useless while power was still in the hands of the conservatives.

The fundamental rules which this constructive activity would have to obey would be:

(1) The gradual transformation of the existing peasant *obshchina*—founded on the basis of private property limited in time—into a communal *obshchina*, founded on the principle of the collective use of means of production and collective and communal work.

(2) Gradual expropriation of means of production in private hands and their handing over to common use.

(3) The gradual introduction of those social institutions required to abolish the need for any intermediary in the exchange of produce, and to substitute for the principle of bourgeois justice—an eye for an eye, a tooth for a tooth, service for service—the principle of love and brotherly solidarity.

(4) The gradual abolition of physical, intellectual and moral inequality among men, by means of a compulsory system of social education, equal for all and inspired by the spirit of love, equality and fraternity.

(5) The gradual abolition of the existing family which was based on the submission of the woman, the slavery of the child and the egotistic whim of the man.

(6) The development of collective self-administration and the gradual weakening and disappearance of the central functions of State power.[90]

This was to be the programme of the revolutionaries once in power. And this was the method—described by the generic word 'Jacobin'—which he defended in the *Nabat* against objections from all sides.

He told the anarchists in the very first number of the review that it was not just their political outlook but their very ideal that was, if not mistaken, at least incoherent. Even on purely theoretical grounds, he considered anarchism unthinkable and unjustifiable, until absolute equality among men had been brought into being. It would merely lead to the unleashing of selfish instincts. And to bring about equality, the ruthless action of a minority in charge of the conquered State was essential.

From these general principles he descended to a detailed attack in the following numbers of the *Nabat*; above all in a series of notes, under the general title 'Anarchy of Thought', which were published in 1876.[91]

He then made an open attack on the fundamental text of Russian anarchism of the time, Bakunin's work, *Statism and Anarchy*, which, as Tkachev himself admitted, 'has undoubtedly had a vast influence on the thought of our revolutionary younger generation'. He accused Bakunin above all of incoherence. He, Bakunin, who had announced that he did not want to concern himself with politics, was here merely discussing the interplay of the various forces existing within and between the various countries of Europe. And even his ideas on this subject seemed uncertain. His observation that

Italy, Spain and the Slav world were nearer social revolution than the German countries was acute. But what concrete fact could be deduced from such observations? Bakunin praised instinct, which he contrasted with any 'conscious ideal elaborated only by a minority outside the people'.[92] Tkachev replied that the *narodnost* of an ideal is determined by its content; but this content in turn depends on the material with which it has been constructed.

If your man from the minority has taken this material from the life of bourgeois society, from the world of exploitation, business and the stock exchange, his ideals and theories will have a bourgeois, anti-popular character (as for example the ideals and theories of the so-called science of political economy). But if he takes them from the people's life, from the world of work and workmen, then these ideals will by their very nature be popular, anti-bourgeois (for example, the ideals of Communism).[93]

And so there was no point in speaking of instinct. It was true that the minority was not in a position to feel the people's sufferings as it felt them itself, but just because of this the minority understood them better and could behave rationally towards them. It could analyse them and build up an ideal which was not contradictory and confused, as was Bakunin's. To be convinced of this, one merely had to look at the problem of the deepest instincts of the Russian people. The revolutionaries accepted the peasants' conviction that the land belonged entirely to the people, and that the *obshchina* and not the individual must administer it. They even accepted the antithesis of the *mir* and the State. But were they, just because of this, to accept other popular feelings and instincts which were associated with it—such, for example, as religious faith, belief in the Tsar, and in general the patriarchal swallowing up of the individual into village collectivism? Was it not pure hypocrisy to claim to follow 'popular principles' and in fact make a careful choice of these?

The uncertainty of the Bakuninist standpoint was reflected also in the practical hints which its adherents gave to the younger generation. It was true that Bakunin too was against pure and simple propaganda; he was a declared enemy of the position taken up by the followers of Lavrov during the movement 'to go to the people'. Yet, if carefully considered, the objectives he gave to the revolutionaries would reduce themselves to educating the masses rather than a simple appeal to revolution. He told them, for instance, that they must fight against the traditional patriarchal element in the life of the Russian people and that they must do this village by village, district by district, until they created a general peasant movement. But did not this in fact mean postponing the revolution until the ground was ready, as Lavrov advocated?

In this way the Bakuninists vacillated between the Scylla of local risings and the Charybdis of long-term preparation, as the entire Russian Populist movement was still doing. And besides, how could one organize all the

villages by continuing to persuade the peasants that any authority was evil?
This was to demand organization and not want it at the same time.

Any organization presupposes a centre, and instructions of general significance.
Whether it is founded on federal or centralizing principles—i.e. whether it has at
its centre dictators holding all the power or merely delegates representing local
groups with restricted mandates—any organization is always authoritarian and
therefore anti-anarchist.[94]

Tkachev never tired of repeating this in his campaign against the various
brands of anarchism current in the 'seventies. His controversies were conducted mainly with the 'revolutionary Community' founded at Geneva by
some 'young Bakuninists' and with De Paepe, one of the leading exponents
of anarchist ideas at this time.

   With the young Bakuninists he was particularly bitter and sarcastic and
tried to bring to light all the contradictions in the programme which they
published in September 1873.

They demand that there should be no authority. Yet at the very same moment they
plan a federal government of delegates from the *obshchinas* with a pile of every
possible and even impossible ministries. They want these ministries to complete
each other reciprocally and at the same time they want them to be quite independent
of each other.[95]

With De Paepe he was less ironical and brutal. In a detailed examination of
his report on 'The Problem of Social Services in the Society of the Future'
which De Paepe presented and discussed at the (anarchist) Congress of the
International in Brussels in September 1874, Tkachev tried to show him that
in fact an organization of social services of the kind he had discussed in such
detail already had a name. It was called the State.[96]

   Without going into details, which are not devoid of interest, it is worth
emphasizing the central idea that Tkachev had gradually elaborated during
this controversy with the Bakuninist movement.

   He was convinced that the anarchists, by repudiating the State, were in
fact merely theorizing about that 'spiritual power'—of which he had already
spoken and which was inherent in the very nature of the intellectual and
educated minority—and then refusing to transform it into 'material power'.
But this transition was inevitable and had to happen by the laws of history.
All spiritual power contained a germ of material power.

You are driving the Devil out of the door and he will return through the window.
But you are driving out a comparatively harmless Devil from the door (the power
of the State) while a really terrible Devil will come in through the window. The
authority of the State demands the submission of only the outer manifestations
of man's activities; but the authority that you want (if you really want it) subjects
not only man's actions but his intimate convictions, his most hidden feelings, his
mind and his will, and also his heart. Such authority, which is undoubtedly despotic

and autocratic, is really monstrous. Such is the authority of the Church; such is the authority with which the Jesuits founded their fanciful communities in America.[97]

And if the anarchists did not want this, it was merely because once again they were incapable of being logical in their ideas.

The anarchists pictured the revolution as a dissolution of the existing State into the social elements which made it up. 'Every unit, every village, *obshchina* and town will administer its own affairs for itself, determining its relations with others on the basis of mutual agreement.' This might well happen, but it would merely weaken revolutionary activity by splintering it and preventing it from following a single direction. To appreciate this it was enough to realize what would happen to the educated and revolutionary minority in a case like this. 'It would be dispersed into all those little groups, trying to seize spiritual and material power in each of them.'[98] The *élite* would thus fail in its function of guidance. By not wanting the State, the anarchists would end by creating a million States.

Thus, absorbed as he was by the need to expound his Jacobin ideas, Tkachev threw over those elements of Bakuninism which he had earlier adopted. He spoke less and less of the people being always ready for revolt, and instead he emphasized the need for the revolutionaries to do everything possible to weaken the machinery of the State and thus prepare the ground for an upheaval. Speaking of the measures which the revolutionary State would have to take, the model to which he referred more and more clearly was that of Robespierre's dictatorship with its revolutionary tribunals, suppression of hostile forces, control of freedom of the press, etc.

But it is important to note that the Bakuninist and anarchist vision of the State dissolving by means of revolution into its component groups never completely disappeared from his thought. He ended by thinking that such a spontaneous process could become an extremely important tool in the hands of the Jacobin *élite*. He knew perfectly well that revolution was a phenomenon of violent dissolution of State and social structure; the minority would take advantage of this energy, directing it towards those higher ends which it alone knew and incarnated.

The revolutionary minority, by freeing the people from the yoke that oppresses it, and from fear and terror in face of the old authority, gives it the chance to reveal its destructive-revolutionary force, and, basing itself on this force, to direct it cunningly towards the destruction of the enemies of the revolution. In this way it can destroy the strong-points that surround it, and deprive them of all means of resistance and counter-attack. Then, by making use of its force and its own authority it can introduce new progressive-Communist elements into the conditions of the people's life, and free their existence from its age-old chains and bring life to its dried and petrified forms.[99]

Tkachev in fact understood that the Bakuninist element could be and must be inserted into his Jacobin vision of the revolution.

This was the reason he tried to maintain contacts with the anarchists more consistently than with any other movement, even on the plane of tactics. He claimed to be carrying their principles to their extreme and logical conclusion—showing up the contradictions latent in their activities only so as to point out clearly how they could be made to prevail. And so anarchism remained the final aim; the final myth of the social transformation, to achieve which he was only concerned to point out the weapons; the final result of that absolute equality among men which would gradually be introduced from above by the revolution.

His controversy with the Populists of the 'seventies on the other hand merely developed from his discussions with Lavrov. In an article of 1876—'People and Revolution'—he reconsidered the entire problem in detail.[100] Was it true that the people's ideas were really revolutionary? It was essential to take a realistic view of the peasants.

It is true that their social ideal consists in self-administering *obshchinas*, in the submission of the individual to the *mir*, in the right to use the land and not to own it as private property, in solidarity among the members of the *obshchina*—in a word in an ideal with a clearly expressed Communist tinge. Naturally, the forms of life which condition such an ideal are still far from fully developed Communism. It is concealed within them, like, for instance, a germ, a seed. This germ can develop, but it can also die. Everything depends upon the direction taken by our economic life. If it follows the direction along which it is now moving—i.e. towards bourgeois progress—there is no doubt that our *obshchina* (and so also the ideals of our people) will meet the fate of the *obshchina* of Western Europe, and will die out, as it has died out in England, Germany, Italy, Spain and France. But if the revolution arrives in time to build a dyke against the quickly increasing wave of bourgeois progress, if it stops the direction of the current and gives it another, entirely opposite, direction, there is no doubt that in favourable conditions our present *obshchina* will gradually develop into a commune-*obshchina*.[101]

This was a repetition of what the Populists had maintained from the first, and a resumption of the ideas of Herzen and Chernyshevsky. But Tkachev was particularly energetic in making this point and was more precisely aware of the immediate danger that threatened the *obshchina*. Further, he reaffirmed these principles at the very time when many Populist schools of thought were inclined to give the *obshchina* an ideal, absolute value rather than consider its historical *raison d'être*. They exalted its eternal presence in the spirit, and in ways of thinking, in the customs of Russia and Slavs in general, rather than examined the concrete reasons and conditions of its existence.

Tkachev published many articles in Russian reviews under various pseudonyms to attack this vague national myth of the *obshchina*. He attacked those 'legitimate sons of the Westerners' of the preceding generation, who were accepting such ideas which sprang from the opposing intellectual current of the Slavophils. The ideal of the 'soil' which inspired a typically Russian political ideology dear to Dostoevsky was now accepted by those who declared themselves Populists. This led to 'a purely fantastic' picture of the Russian village.[102] Besides, many of the suggestions which they made to improve the peasants' situation were (though they did not realize this) merely means through which capitalism was being introduced into the countryside; schemes which were giving rise to social differences within the *obshchina* and hence leading to its ruin.[103]

Everyone was discussing methods to improve the conditions of the peasants. This merely meant that growing capitalism was trying to infiltrate into the countryside. There was an economic root at the basis of this. As serfdom came to an end, landed proprietors were no longer financially independent and able to stand on their own feet. They had become debtors of the State, to which they looked for help and credit. The reform had certainly not improved their position. But the new economic forces too, the capitalists, found themselves in the same position after the reform, and they too had to look to the State treasury. So both landed and mobile capitalism were constantly looking for support, for a source from which they could obtain help. The peasant alone, the only class of person whose production did not depend on credit, seemed to be such a source, and so they all flung themselves at him, trying to get what they could. But to do this they needed the State, the one instrument capable of getting new riches from the country. Literature merely reflected this state of affairs, even though it may have been tinted with Populist colours.[104]

In the *Nabat*, Tkachev called these Populists 'reactionary revolutionaries' and he attacked them in an article under this title, in the fifth issue of 1876.[105] 'Reactionary revolutionaries' were those who deceived themselves into thinking that they were preparing the revolution—or at least defending the peasants—by founding agricultural cooperatives, workmen's cooperatives, and improving administration or education in the villages. Quite apart from the fact that conceiving trade-union or cooperative organizations on the basis of illegality and secrecy seemed to him merely Utopian, such organizations would in any case lead to a reactionary result by introducing into the Russian village more and more of the features of Western bourgeois society. If these Populists had been logical, they would have given up the countryside and instead have organized the only section of the proletariat which could lend itself to this aim, the proletariat in the factories.

There is no doubt that, when bourgeois progress is able to bring about equality between conditions in the factories and in agriculture, the present organization of the town proletariat in Western Europe will spread also to the country proletariat. But for this, even in the West, a long wait will be needed. And for us in Russia it will be longer still.

So it was useless for the 'reactionary revolutionaries' to think of basing themselves on the *obshchina* and the *artel*. These could only become fighting

14*

organizations for the country and town proletariat when political power passed into the hands of the revolutionary Socialists.

Until that moment, any attempt to transform them locally by acting from within is useless. One must be extremely naive to imagine that the propaganda and agitation of a few dozen young men can maintain and develop institutions which lack economic soil, which are standing in the way of the demands and conditions of bourgeois economy and which contradict the general spirit and direction of economic progress.[106]

The nobility, the liberals, the constitutionalists, the bureaucrats, the *kulaks* were now determined to destroy the *obshchina* at its very roots. Faced with this situation, the Populists had only two courses open to them. They could either wait for a few dozen years until the organization of the proletariat had become possible and natural, or they could boldly adopt the methods of Jacobin conspiracy to seize power as quickly as possible. In the last analysis, any other solution was playing the game of those who were trying to speed up capitalist progress, and meant taking the side of 'the heroes of the day', *kulaks*, stockbrokers, monopolists, etc.[107] These 'heroes' would be able quickly enough to bring to light the real reactionary content that lay beneath so many Utopian demands. The only revolutionary was the one who wanted a revolution at once. 'Even the policemen believe in long-term revolution.'

But, objected Tkachev's Populist adversaries, the revolution he proposed might perhaps be made on behalf of the people but would in any case take place without the people; in other words, it would be political and not social in character. Who would guarantee that the *élite*, once it gained power, would not merely replace the State and become just as oppressive as that which already existed? S. M. Kravchinsky wrote to Lavrov in 1875: 'Tkachev is to publish a review. What he really wants is absolutely disgusting: a political revolution, though naturally dressed up in the trappings of social revolution.'[108]

Tkachev answered that the minority of whom he was thinking must not by any means be made up only of 'repentant nobles', of members of the privileged classes who were 'going to the people'. Part of the minority did of course come from this background but members of the petit bourgeoisie, of the *raznochintsy*, of the peasants, would soon come to complete it. And besides, the social origin of the *élite* was not a fundamental problem. Everything depended entirely on the ideas and principles which would guide its activities.

Why accuse the *élite* of wanting a revolution from above? This could happen if it was inspired by the ideals which prevailed in the upper classes of society and which corresponded to privileged interests. Sometimes 'these ideals may to some extent correspond to purely popular ideals, and it is just these points which are made use of by the upper classes of society' to disguise political movements designed in fact to serve their own purposes.

This explained popular support for revolutions in the world of the bourgeois. But the *élite* that Tkachev wished to bring into being would, on the other hand, be guided only by the ideals of the people.

What are you frightened of? What right have you to think that this minority—partly through its social position, partly through its ideas, and totally devoted to the people's interests—by taking power into its hands will suddenly change itself into a tyrant? You say: Any power corrupts men. But on what do you base such a strange idea? On the examples of history? . . . Read biographies and you will be convinced of the contrary. Robespierre, a member of the Convention, the omnipotent ruler of the destiny of France, and Robespierre an unknown provincial lawyer, are the same—the identical person. Power made not the slightest difference to his moral character or to his ideals and tendencies, or to his private habits.

'The same can be said of Danton, and of any other important characters of the French revolution',[109] as also of Cromwell, Washington, etc.

It was impossible to eliminate power and violence from any revolution. The Jacobins were men who knew how to draw the logical inferences from this truth, men who did not stop when faced with the illusion that there were capacities for revolution latent in the masses, or that other illusion that they could slowly educate them towards a social upheaval by means of propaganda and organization. Such were the essential points that Tkachev made against the Populists.

Bakuninists and Populists or, as he once called them, 'the two fractions of the Populists'[110] were only two particular aspects of the two great tendencies which then ruled the working class movement throughout Europe. They corresponded to the two limbs of the International after the Prague Congress of 1872, the anarchists and the Marxists.

This double and complementary mistake in the way the problem had been raised had in turn influenced the two wings of the Russian revolutionary movement. Was not the anarchist organization of the Belgian sections (and partly of the Swiss sections) a full and solemn consecration of the principle, upheld by the Russian Bakuninists, of 'federative unions' and 'natural groups'? And had not German preaching of a lawful revolution, of the need for peaceful propaganda and the uselessness and immaturity of any violence, of the need for scientific preparation, etc., confirmed the followers of Lavrov in their stand?[111]

Tkachev did not extend the attack to the international plane, absorbed as he was in the fight for a strong organization in Russia itself. This was more than ever the case as the movement in Russia was moving in this direction. It had reacted against the defeats of the movement 'to go to the people', by forming central groups more and more compact in character. Just as after the defeat of the Commune the working-class movement in Europe showed signs of trying to reorganize itself on new and different foundations, so too in Russia the methods of organized conspiracy were beginning to be resumed.

So, at the end of the 'seventies, Tkachev did not confine his overtures for creating a single revolutionary socialist party only to the anarchists. He not only followed with passionate attention the movements of *Zemlya i Volya* and especially *Narodnaya Volya*, but he was ready to accept some aspects of Russian revolutionary Populism which were repugnant to his Jacobin mentality, such as, for example, the policy of terrorism. After a conflict within the *Nabat* group, he ended by admitting the principle of terrorism, though within limits and never very enthusiastically. For a better organization of the revolutionary forces he was ready to sacrifice everything. He wrote in 1878:

It is essential not only in the interests of a more energetic, quick and effective conduct of the campaign, but also in the interests of personal security, in the interests of saving a greater number of forces—it is essential that all our revolutionaries, whatever they call themselves, forget and throw away at the earliest possible moment all federal Utopias and turn once again to the old centralized organization which has been tried more than once. In that lies force, and in that lies salvation.[112]

As if to provide an impulse and an example, he then founded his political organization, *The Society for the Liberation of the People*. This was to advance his views on politics and organization. It was apparently founded when he managed to make contact with the small groups organized by Zaichnevsky in Russia. But *The Society for the Liberation of the People* was always very small and unimportant.[113]

In 1880 Tkachev tried to give it life by taking the printing press of the *Nabat* into Russia. He was, moreover, convinced once again that a revolution in Russia was on the point of breaking out and that the working class movement was reviving throughout Europe. But this effort failed, and the printing press itself was lost.

Tkachev no longer had any reason for staying in Geneva, and he went to Paris to join the organ of the French Blanquists, *Ni dieu, ni maître*, founded at this time. But he had little time left, and his articles were very short. In 1882 he became ill and his state rapidly became extremely serious. He spent the last years of his life in a lunatic asylum and died on 4th January 1886.

17. BAKUNIN AND LAVROV

WE HAVE ALREADY SEEN that in Geneva Bakunin made a short-lived attempt to use the 'young fanatic' Nechaev to influence or even lead the revolutionary movement in Russia itself. And even when this attempt came to nothing, Bakunin did not abandon the idea of organizing the younger generation and spreading his *Alliance* to Russia.

But his efforts along these lines were never successful. On several occasions he succeeded in animating Bakuninist groups among the émigrés, but they were never really faithful to him. An early Russian section of the International which he founded soon passed over to the opposing 'statist' and Marxist wing. Another group of Russian anarchists eventually severed its connections with him and acted on its own account, remaining faithful to anarchism but not to him personally. His only real success was in the influence he gained over considerable sections of the student colony which had grown up in Zurich at the beginning of the 'seventies. It was through these students that his ideas reached Russia where they then played a large part in bringing about the atmosphere which led to the movement 'to go to the people' and the second *Zemlya i Volya*. But even there, the genuinely Bakuninist elements remained few and scattered. He was able to inspire a revolutionary spirit but not an organization.

There are many reasons for these failures. Above all, it was by no means easy to lead from exile a movement which now had its own traditions and sprang out of the problems of the intelligentsia and the Russian State. His adversary, Lavrov, came up against the same difficulties, and, in general, Populism received far less direction from exile than is generally thought. Even when Bakunin reached the zenith of his influence in Russia at the end of the 'seventies, the Populists seized every possible opportunity to emphasize their own specific character and proclaim themselves independent both from the ideological and the political points of view. This state of mind was reflected also in the 'young émigrés' and prevented them being entirely led by Bakunin. Besides, the émigrés were always few, if only for the reason that they were always tempted to devote themselves entirely to organization and propaganda in those sections of the International in which they found themselves, in Italy, Switzerland or France. Their efforts to maintain contacts with Russia were constantly repeated, but scarcely crowned with success. All this made Bakunin sceptical about the Russian émigrés, especially after his painful experiences with Nechaev, and induced him to turn his attention mainly towards France, Italy and Spain.

When the Russian Populists turned to him, they saw primarily the international revolutionary, the leader of one of the two great wings of the working class movement. From him they sought—and obtained—not so much an organization as a conception of the world which had a profound and lasting effect on the entire revolutionary movement.[1]

In 1864, after the crushing of the Polish revolt, Bakunin went to Italy and there he made some Russian contacts. But these men were mostly intellectuals, such as the painter Ge, or the sociologist Vyrubov, and they had no intention of devoting themselves exclusively to the cause. The only exception was L. Mechnikov, whom we have met in contact with Chernyshevsky and Herzen, and who soon became an active figure in the Bakuninist secret societies in Italy, and also in Switzerland and Spain.

Only when in 1866 he heard of Karakozov's attempt on the life of the Tsar could Bakunin hope to resume activities directed at Russia. He had been shocked by what Herzen had written of the attempt, and he found the general attitude of his old friends on the *Kolokol* utterly misguided.

What is the practical standpoint of which you boast? Is it not the same that led Mazzini to neutralize the Republican banner in 1859, to write letters to the Pope and the King, to seek an agreement with Cavour, and, by repeated concessions, to bring about the complete ruin of the Republican party in Italy? Has it not made of the popular hero Garibaldi an unconditional slave of Victor Emmanuel and Napoleon III?

In Russia too it was essential to return to a policy of total opposition, unhampered by the concessions that had been necessary in 1862 when society as a whole was in motion and even the nobles were demanding a *Zemsky Sobor*. And it was essential also to get rid of illusions about the possibilities of a peaceful, gradual development of the peasant *obshchina* towards Socialist and revolutionary forms.

It was time to survey the real situation. The *obshchina* had two advantages. 'One is purely negative, i.e. the absence of Roman law and in general all legal elements; the other is positive, though extremely obscure and instinctive: i.e. the popular idea of the right of each peasant to the land.' But an analysis of this idea would show that in fact it 'by no means includes the right of *all* the people to *all* the land. Instead, in some ways, it includes another very depressing notion, i.e. the attribution of all the land to the State and the Tsar.' It was on this conception that the Emperor relied 'to present the peasants with uncultivated land after having furnished his generals with estates and villages; to drive out entire peasant communities from one place to another without arousing even a protest from the people as long as they had any land at all'. '"The land is ours, and we belong to the *Gosudar*, the Tsar." With ideas like these, my friends, the Russian people will not go far.'

It was enough to look at the history of the *obshchina* to realize this. 'The *obshchina* has been deprived of any real internal development and today is much what it was five hundred years ago. It has had no freedom, and without freedom any social movement is unthinkable.' And now the State was intervening from above; the only effect of this was to bring about the dissolution of those few elements of equality which the *obshchina* did contain. 'Any *muzhik* richer or stronger than the others is now doing everything he can to escape from the *obshchina* which is stifling him.' And so it was no good looking to a gradual evolution of the traditional forms of peasant life. Attention should be paid, instead, to the revolutionary forces contained within Russian society. Only these would be able to destroy the oppression which for centuries had held up all progress. The forces 'of revolt, of Stenka Razin, of Pugachev, of the *Raskolniki*' must be invoked. Had there not appeared among the younger generation elements capable of interpreting these demands? Instead of calling them 'abstract revolutionaries' as Herzen did, they must be regarded as 'the most logical expression of those principles which live and act in the masses'.[2]

And so, when Bakunin returned to Switzerland in 1867, he got into contact with 'the young émigrés' whom Herzen kept at arm's length and who cordially returned his distrust and contempt.

This first Russian colony was settling at Vevey and Geneva. It was made up of young men who had escaped from the police between 1862 and 1866 at the time of the student disorders, the first *Zemlya i Volya* and the Kazan conspiracy. Among them were A. Trusov, N. Zhukovsky, N. Utin, N. Elpidin, A. Serno-Solovevich, and a few others. As early as 1868 Bakunin seems to have tried to collect them into a secret association, the *International Brotherhood*, whose foundations he had laid in Italy.[3]

But he immediately met with opposition. As we have seen. Serno-Solovevich was unwilling to follow his anti-electoral revolutionary policies. As for Utin, after a short association with Bakunin he became his most stubborn opponent.

But this initial contact between Bakunin and the 'young émigrés' was not without results. N. Zhukovsky insisted that a periodical should be started and found the money needed.[4] The first number of the *Narodnoe Delo* (The People's Cause) appeared at the beginning of September 1868. It was almost entirely written by Bakunin; only one article was by Zhukovsky, and it merely reflected the general ideas of the newspaper.

We have already mentioned how, during the White Terror, the young generation at the university greedily devoured this issue when it reached Russia, and we have referred to the passionate discussions that it aroused in their ranks. If we look at the few pages of this first number of the *Narodnoe Delo* it will be easy to understand the reasons for its success. Bakunin resumed the ideological and cultural discussions which had been suspended when the repression set in in 1866 and brought them to a political conclusion.

He pointed out the dangers latent in the positivist currents which now appeared to prevail in the younger generation. By dint of speaking of the superiority of science, they had drawn far away from all political problems, and had ended by 'despising the stupid and ignorant people'. In the eyes of this generation the future presented itself 'as a solitary and melancholy education in science and life, far from the people and from all political and social revolutionary problems'.

In practice, this meant driving the intelligentsia into becoming 'a new class of the aristocracy of thought and learning, a kind of privileged church of the mind and superior education'. In this field it would not be difficult to find a compromise with the State, with absolutism and the other privileged classes. The positivists themselves had already drawn up a formula to equate this compromise with reality. Did they not claim that a positive religion was necessary for the people, that 'the extra-scientific ideal called the Lord God' must be kept for the *muzhiks*?

It was in their opposition to this compromise that the merit of Pisarev's 'nihilists' and the *Russkoe Slovo* lay. By calling themselves materialists and atheists, they had made it impossible for their followers to draw all the conservative consequences latent in their positivist view of the world. They had kept alive those traces of ferment and revolt which still remained after 1863. They had once more raised social and political issues on a wide scale.

But now the 'nihilists' must put aside their contempt for the people and their aristocratic detachment from the ignorant masses. By throwing away all the elements that they held in common with the positivists and the utilitarians, they could develop the ferment of revolt and the socialist spirit which inspired them. Only by throwing itself into revolutionary activities could 'nihilism' thrive.

'Supporters of the revolution, we are enemies not only of religious priests but also of the priests of science.' 'Learned men free themselves from God only through science and within the bounds of science, but not in reality, in life.' It was not Comte but 'the man who made concrete plans for freedom in this world' who ought to be the ideal of the younger generation. It was essential to destroy faith in a heavenly world, and create it *in the people*.

So Bakunin drew up a programme which closely linked 'mental liberation' to 'social-economic liberation'. Indeed he recommended his followers not to give useless offence to the religious beliefs of the people. Only a profound social upheaval could destroy them completely. The revolution must be given first place and all efforts concentrated on it.

He analysed the political situation in Russia so as to convince his readers that things had profoundly changed since 1862, when even he had spoken of the *Zemsky Sobor* and had appealed to all the forces of liberation. The three reforms which were then under way had been carried out and they were 'three tricks'. The peasants had not really been freed. Their vote was not decisive even where it had been given them—in the assemblies of the *Zemstvo*.

'The juridical reform has been far more serious and has in fact greatly improved the situation of the people. Publicity for the tribunals has increased the speed with which justice is administered.' The merits of local judges, who had at last given the people the chance to defend its own rights from time to time, must be recognized. Yet even this, the best of the reforms, had not affected the economic relations between the social classes and hence had not touched the roots of the problem.

It had been 'the logic of class interests' which had now brought the privileged classes and the people into open opposition. Even those nobles who in 1862 had shown a spirit of independence now turned back to the protective wing of the State.

Even that portion of the nobility which has not been completely ruined by the reforms and has been able to restore its estates by the old habit of stealing from the State treasury, finally understands that there is only one way of keeping its privileges: brotherly collaboration with the State and the Tsar, against the people.

And so 'the revolutionary problem' was clarified; the 'extremely harmful confusion' which even shortly before had brought strangers into the revolutionary camp, had come to an end. The end for which the revolutionaries must strive was now obvious: all the land for those who worked it, a campaign for the 'complete destruction of the State and a future political organization made up exclusively of a free federation of free workmen's artels, agricultural, industrial and craftsmen'.

'Above all we must destroy within the hearts of the people the remains of that unfortunate faith in the Tsar which for centuries has condemned them to terrible serfdom.' And this could be done not through a slow infiltration of learning, through schools and preaching, but only 'by reawakening within the people's minds an awareness of its own strength which has slept ever since Pugachev'. The call for a revolt to bring about a social revolution— this was the programme of Russian revolutionaries.

Nor must it be forgotten that their struggle was linked to that of all the peoples of Europe. 'The liberation of many million workers from the yoke of capital, hereditary property and the State' was everywhere a vital problem. It was true that in Russia there were 'many specific historical and economic elements' but 'the cause of the revolution is the same everywhere'. 'We are by no manner of means patriots, like the men of the 'twenties and 'thirties' (i.e. the Slavophils) who had based themselves on the idea of the corruption and decay of the West and Russia's messianic destiny. It was better, rather, to look to the banner which had been raised for the first time at the end of the 'fifties by those 'whose names still live in our hearts' (i.e. Chernyshevsky and Dobrolyubov). They had taught that the Russians 'must learn from the European movement, and Europe must at last get exact knowledge of the essentials of the existing movement in Russia'.

Bakunin was unsuccessful in his attempts to gather the 'young émigrés' into a section of the International based on these ideas. Very soon the *Narodnoe Delo* slipped from his control. The second issue was edited by Utin and at the end was a letter from Bakunin saying that he had nothing in common with the paper. The Russian section, whose regulations he had drawn up, did emerge in Geneva, but, as will be seen, followed its own course in conflict with him.

He then put all his hopes in Nechaev. When these hopes too were wrecked, Bakunin tried in vain to found a new periodical. He wrote of this to Lavrov on 15th July 1870, saying what his programme was to be.[5] He returned to the ideas which he had already expounded in the *Narodnoe Delo*: atheism, the repudiation of any State power, the fight against the bourgeoisie. And to these he added two new elements: chiefly the campaign against 'the authoritarian communism of Marx and the entire German school' and a fight 'against collectivism introduced from above through any revolutionary committee, any central and official authority'. And then—most important of all—he outlined his own point of view on the revolution in Europe. It was now no longer enough to link the Russian movement to that of the West, as he had done in the *Narodnoe Delo*; the differing national problems of revolutionary development could not be put aside. It was not a question of recognizing nationality as 'a principle, a right', but rather of appreciating it as 'a natural, historical' fact which must be taken into account. 'The demands of a social revolution are the same everywhere, but the forms in which they are expressed will be entirely different among different peoples; determined not by the will of individuals or groups but by particular situations and particular historical precedents.' Russia provided proof of this, and it was not the only country in Europe; together with 'some other countries, Slav and non-Slav (Hungary, Southern Italy, Spain) scarcely touched by the industrial and urban civilization of the West', Russia too would see 'the prevalence of peasant Socialism over urban Socialism'.

Such was the intuition which guided Bakunin during the most fruitful years of his political activity. It was thus that he transferred Russian revolutionary Populism to the European plane, and it was on these foundations that his international anarchist movement grew up.

The Franco-Prussian War, the Commune and Bismarck's victory only confirmed him in his ideas and increased his hatred of the Germans. In the work which had most influence in Russia, *Statism and Anarchism*, he expounded his vision of a Europe, dominated by Germany, which would find on its fringes (from Spain to Russia) the forces capable of rebelling against Germany and destroying the oppressive and statist conception at its centre. Of all the revolutionaries it was Bakunin who saw most clearly what Bismarck's victory would mean for the movements and ideas that sprang from 1848 and for all the forces of liberation that had been released. He sounded the alarm and built up a force of violent protest. He tried to harness those energies which still seemed intact, the forces of peasant Socialism in Spain,

Southern Italy, Hungary and Russia. But after 1874 he finally became convinced that Europe had now entered a period of adjustment and slow evolution. Old and tired, he gave up the fight. But meanwhile he had planted, even in Russia, a few vigorous seeds of protest against *Realpolitik*.

He resumed in various forms his campaign against the theories of positivism, which already in the *Narodnoe Delo* he had looked on as the ideology of social conservatism. As science ran the risk of becoming the tool of oppression, it was essential to say clearly that it was more important to devote oneself to an ideal of freedom, to sacrifice all for the 'cause of the people', than to study and become learned, and thus transform oneself into a weapon in the hands of the privileged classes. As science seemed to empty itself of human content, it was essential to fight against all 'doctrinairism', against all claims to restrict freedom in the name of abstract principles. He told the young men in Russia that they must obey their own instincts and their own enthusiasms, throwing themselves 'into the people' before being sullied by the institutions and schools which the State had founded for the very purpose of turning them into its servants.[6]

It was not therefore a question of 'going to the people' in order to bring it doctrines.

That would be stupid. The people know very well what they want. On the contrary, we must learn from them to understand the secrets of their life and strength—secrets which in fact contain nothing mysterious, but which remain unattainable for all who live in so-called educated society. We must not act as schoolmasters for the people, but we must lead them to revolt.

Only by bringing about a social revolution could one avoid the greatest danger, a government of pedants. One must on the other hand open the doors for a social organization which would provide learning for all.

And so good intentions to educate, and attempts to create small kernels of civilized life in the countryside and towns by organizing cooperatives, mutual associations, etc., were useless. He said in 1873:

In Russia today cooperation is even more impossible than in the West. One of the most important conditions for its success, where it really has succeeded best, was private initiative, tenacity and courage. But personality is infinitely more developed in the West than in Russia, where until now the herd instinct has prevailed. Even outside conditions, both political and social, such as the cultural level, are incomparably more favourable in the West than in Russia for the birth and development of cooperatives. And yet, despite all this, even in the West this movement has withered. How could it ever take root in Russia?[7]

Until the Russian State was overturned by a revolution all efforts at local reform, at partial improvements in the situation of the working classes, were useless.

But it was precisely in Russia that there did exist the objective conditions necessary for a peasant revolt. The upper classes were clearly separated from the people; there was no real bourgeoisie; there was no 'privileged working class' as could be seen in Germany or Switzerland. From this point of view too Russia's situation was like that of Italy 'where social revolution is perhaps closer than in any other country'.[8] The peasants felt on their shoulders a feudal yoke, still in many respects like the one that had led to the great peasant revolts in Germany and even Russia. But the reform of 1861 now concentrated all powers of oppression in the hands of the State, and the peasants were learning to see in the State their fundamental enemy.

Even recently their hatred was divided between nobles and officials, and sometimes it even seemed that they hated the former more than the latter . . . But ever since the abolition of serfdom led to the ruin of the nobles who have returned to their origins and are completely identified with government servants, the people have included them in their general hatred for the class of officials.[9]

And so the campaign against the State was bound to take the form of the open antithesis between the people and all the moneyed classes.

'The Russian people is Socialist by instinct and revolutionary by nature', ended Bakunin, in a phrase which recalls how much his viewpoint was derived from Populist ideas.[10] Yet in his hands these ideas had undergone an important modification. The hope that had inspired Herzen and Chernyshevsky that Russia, just because it was the most backward country, would be the first to reach Socialism was now translated by Bakunin into anarchist terms. The Russian peasants, just because they were the poorest and the most backward, would be the first to revolt against the State, destroying it from its foundations.

But Herzen and Chernyshevsky could base themselves on the *obshchina*, on traditional collectivism. What elements could Bakunin find in the Russian village to support his point of view? Obviously the myth of Stenka Razin or Pugachev was not enough, nor could the religious sects in themselves provide proof of this will to revolution latent in the Russian people.

Bakunin re-examined the entire problem of the *obshchina*. In it he saw three positive elements: (1) the conviction that the land, all the land, belonged to the people; (2) the land did not belong to the individual but to the community; (3) 'its almost absolute independence and self-administration and hence the obviously hostile attitude of the *obshchina* towards the State'.[11] But closely linked to these three positive aspects were three negative ones: (1) patriarchalism; (2) the absorption of the individual into the community; (3) faith in the Tsar.

These last three features could only be destroyed by an open revolt. Only a social revolution could destroy the traditional and passive element contained in the *obshchina*. This would leave the positive elements, and especially self-administration and autonomy. The *obshchina* in fact was revolutionary in so far as it was opposed to the State, and reactionary in so far as it was contained within it.

Whereas Chernyshevsky had stressed mainly those technical and economic possibilities which might make the *obshchina* the germ of cooperatives and agricultural communities, Bakunin saw above all the political aspect of a social nexus capable of a life of its own and therefore in a position to resist, fight against, and eventually destroy the State. In fact, the position could be put as follows: 'the Populists looked mainly to the *obshchina*, Bakunin to the *mir*. "Who will ever dare go against the *mir*!" exclaims the Russian peasant.'[12]

The weakness of these cells came from their isolation. The peasant could see only the Tsar above the *obshchina*. Only when they were freely united and joined together would the *obshchina* restore Russia's social fabric. The ideal of a people's and peasants' revolution lay in a free federation of free *obshchinas*.

This opposition to the State by social groups (both economic and administrative) whose final aim would be to destroy the State machinery and fully replace it, had a considerable influence on Bakunin's political conceptions. It was enough to translate it into Western and working class terms to obtain that 'revolutionary syndicalism' which is implicit in Bakunin's anarchism, and which he formulated in his writings, though in fragmentary form. It was not for nothing that, speaking of the positive aspects of the Russian *obshchina*, he at once added 'this ideal corresponds in one of its aspects to what has recently been worked out in the conscience of the proletariat in Latin countries, which are infinitely nearer social revolution than the German countries.'[13]

Syndicalism and his revolutionary Populism met in Bakunin's *Alliance*. He was convinced that in order to effect the transition between the *mir* and anarchism, and to leap from the *obshchina* to a federation of *obshchinas*, some organization was needed to direct the social revolution. Even as regards the working class movement he had said that the International was not enough and that a closer and more secret organization was needed. And so he had never surrendered to pressure from the General Council to dissolve his countless *Brotherhoods*, *Alliances*, etc. The group of true revolutionaries must have its own resources and its own weapons.

Among the Russians too Bakunin recruited his elements from the younger generation of the intelligentsia. For here there could be found men who wanted 'une révolution sociale telle que l'imagination de l'Occident modérée par la civilisation, ose à peine se représenter', as he had written in 1869.[14] The new exiles, the men forced to leave Russia after the student movements of 1869, led him to hope in 1872 that he would at last be able to build up a nucleus capable of inclusion in his international anarchist movement.[15] V. Golsteyn and A. Elsnits, who had been arrested and expelled from Moscow University in 1869, reached Zurich in the summer of 1871. M. P. Sazhin and Z. K. Ralli, who had been in contact with Nechaev, now joined Bakunin, who, after discussions with them, at the end of March 1872 founded *The*

Russian Brotherhood. He drew up regulations for it similar to the other national groups of his *Alliance.* Zurich became the centre of this association, and its press began to operate in the spring of 1873. It printed *Statism and Anarchism* (already mentioned), a collection of articles by Bakunin called *The Historical Development of the International,* and also *Anarchism according to Proudhon,* an account of Proudhon's ideas written in French by Guillaume and translated into Russian by Zaytsev.

In the summer of 1872 Bakunin was living at Zurich among his young Russian comrades. Either through them, or in person, he made contact with the students who had come in large numbers from Russia to attend the university and schools in the town, and who took part in the excitement and ferment of life in the colony. When he left, a woman student noted in her diary: 'The traces he has left are notable. The Russian émigrés have been convulsed, like the sea after the passage of a steamer. They are now divided into two parties, Bakunin's followers and those of Lavrov, bitterly fighting each other.'[16] Many of these men and women students returned to Russia to devote themselves to the cause of the people, and brought back the ferment of revolt and ideas that they had absorbed through personal contact with Bakunin or through reading his works. His myth influenced the movement of 1874 'to go to the people'; his ideas lived in the *Pan-Russian Revolutionary Organization* (which was the first to try and bring the ideas of his international anarchism to the workers of Moscow) and his influence grew stronger as the years passed. At the end of the 'seventies the 'rebels' in St Petersburg and Kiev acknowledged him. But despite all this a genuinely Bakuninist organization was never founded in Russia.

Feofan Nikanorovich Lermontov joined the *Russian Brotherhood* in 1872, returned to Russia to take part in the movement 'to go to the people', and died in prison in 1878. His friend Sergey Filippovich Kovalik came to Switzerland on Sazhin's bidding in 1873 to meet Bakunin, and remained an anarchist throughout his long life.[17] Vladimir Karpovich Debagory-Mokrievich was later one of the 'rebels of the south'. But these are probably the only three men who made definite engagements with Bakunin and acted in his name in Russia. The specifically anarchist current remained a mere stream in the general movement of this time without ever distinguishing itself either through particular activities or through the special stature of its adherents.

Even among the exiles the *Russian Brotherhood* was soon in a critical state. Despite all Bakunin's efforts, personal quarrels quickly divided it, thereby diminishing its activities and efficiency. The character of Sazhin made all further work together impossible. When Bakunin backed him, Ralli, Golsteyn and Elsnits decided to found a movement on their own and to create their own *Revolutionary community [obshchina] of the Russian anarchists,* and to establish a new printing press in Geneva. Their first pamphlet *To the Russian. Revolutionaries* appeared on 1st September 1873.

Their ideas were so like those of Bakunin that with some reason he was able to accuse them of having printed some of the secret regulations of the *Russian Brotherhood*.

The creation of this centre of 'young Bakuninists' seems therefore to have been the outcome of personal quarrels and not of political or ideological conflicts. Yet even this schism was a symptom of what was happening at the same time in Russia, i.e. the fusion of Bakuninist elements into the general Populist current from which sprang *Zemlya i Volya*. It was indeed 'the young Bakuninists' (who were soon joined by N. Zhukovsky) who resumed contact with the clandestine movement, and who printed pamphlets and periodicals which reflected the ideas and needs of those who were working in Moscow, St Petersburg and the villages of Russia. These activities of Ralli and his comrades will be considered when the birth of the working class movement and the underground is described. For the moment only one other aspect of their activities, their entry into the life of the French émigrés in Switzerland (the world of Communards) which played such an important part in the European socialist movement of the 'seventies, will be reviewed.

In 1874 a small book called *The Paris Commune*[18] appeared. It examined the events of 1871 in great detail, in order to show that there had been a clash in the Commune of two opposing currents which had seemed to be complementary but which were in fact inimical. The first 'personified the anti-State idea, the social revolution' and was 'the living negation of dictatorship and government'.[19] For it, the Commune meant 'individual autonomy, autonomy of groups, of *artels*, of corporations'.[20] But for the others the Paris Commune was merely a continuation of the old revolutionary Commune of 1793.

For them it represented dictatorship in the name of the people; a vast concentration of power in the hands of a limited number of persons. Even though they recognized the principle of communal liberty, of the free organization of popular groups, they did this only because this was the revolutionary idea of the time. But in fact many of them scarcely understood or, indeed, completely failed to understand, the true ideal of the proletariat.[21]

The defeat of the Commune was due to the triumph of the second tendency over the first. The revolutionary impulse was halted; the time for construction was confused with that of destruction. Instead of hurling the forces of the proletariat against the institutions of the enemy, instead of proceeding 'with the liquidation of the bourgeois order',[22] there was an ingenuous belief in the possibility of abolishing by decrees the exploitation of the people and of putting an end to bourgeois robbery.[23] Instead of organizing groups of revolutionary *obshchinas*,[24] one or two in each district, and arming them, thus giving power to the insurgents, hopes were pinned to the revolutionary virtues of the State and an improvised government.

And so the Commune's decrees were 'simple palliatives'[25] all the more useless in that 'it was not the function of the Commune to divine the forms of future social life and still less to decree them' but rather to allow the people to fulfil its destructive and negative function. The very concept on which the Commune was founded was false.

The force which drove on the proletariat could not be and cannot be delegated to representatives because once it is so delegated it ceases being a force. J.-J. Rousseau was utterly right when he wrote 'Any people which chooses representatives stops being a free people'.[26]

Only democracy led by organized social groups and revolutionary forces could have saved the Commune. Why had not this happened? In fact:

The hurricane of revolution found the French proletariat unorganized and unready for the fight. The bourgeois organization of the National Guard showed itself unsuitable the day after an unexpected and uncertain victory. The Central Committee, the contriver of this organization, drew back frightened by the storm of the insurrection . . . Not a single member of this Committee, almost none of the members of the Commune, understood the most essential thing. They did not realize that the reconstruction of society must be preceded by the threatening storm of revolution; that a people freed of its chains is gifted with the spirit of destruction; and that before building one must destroy.[27]

It was, therefore, those who continued the Jacobin tradition who had led to the ruin of the Commune.

Inspired by convictions which were worked out during a stubborn fight against the enemies of the people, a fight which for some had lasted throughout their long lives, they unintentionally took to the old beaten track as soon as they were faced with the open field of revolutionary activity. They went on boldly using the old and useless weapons of the past in the middle of a new life and new requirements. They did not understand that in such cases the form swallows up the substance and that, fighting for the freedom of the people, they themselves struck a mortal blow at the people's freedom with their dictatorial and law-making authority.[28]

Even the best of them, even Delescluze, although he 'understood the new programme of the revolution', belonged to the old generation; 'and at a certain age men become more or less incapable of living a life that is not their own'.[29] Even if one excluded those who were poisoned by power, one saw that men of the greatest integrity had shown themselves incapable of escaping from the grooves of a centuries-old tradition.

Ralli knew from his own experiences the source of these Jacobin ideas. He had begun his revolutionary career in Moscow by reading Buonarroti, and he now wished to attack his former mentor in order to explain that Bakunin and the experience of the Commune had convinced him of how mistaken was the road that he too had tried to follow with Nechaev.

He spoke of the period following 9th Thermidor and described how:

There sprang up brave fighters for the freedom of the people, who decided to destroy the bourgeois order and to replace the bourgeois State with a new State:

the Communist Republic. Through the dictatorial authority of one person they wanted to organize the happiness of all. Poor fools! They loved that great people, but they did not understand why it stood by so calmly at the execution of Hébert, Danton, Desmoulins, Robespierre, etc.; why it had allowed the republic to be strangled under its eyes; why it had left the arena of the revolution and withdrawn in silence to the dark, damp Paris suburbs. And the people, which had been cheated so often, did not believe even in them. Such is always the fate of personal initiative and individual undertakings; the common fate of all ideas which are not subjected to collective criticism . . . For them in fact revolution meant the insurrection of the people, by means of which power could be seized, on their own initiative, by men who would hold it in their own hands to create a people's State, the republic of equals. They did not understand that by doing this they merely led to a change of bosses, of gentlemen, of teachers of the people, and that the proletariat would still go on being exploited. The people, with the memory of recent events still fresh in its mind, looked upon their moves as a repetition of the old comedy. It saw no difference between Robespierre and his assassins on the ninth of Thermidor, between Babeuf and his butchers. Was it really worth shedding more blood to have a new boss, a new government . . . ? That is why the people coldly looked on at the death of its friends; who were perhaps sincere, but who did not understand it.[30]

Some years later Ralli again discussed the problem of the Commune, and from it, even more than in 1874, he drew the 'revolutionary-syndicalist' conclusions which were latent in his picture of direct democracy. Once again he said that in 1871 the task was to have a revolution and not to proceed to a new economic organization. Ought they, for instance, to have made laws of nationalization?

Le gouvernement socialiste eut succombé devant cette tâche, comme tout gouvernement en pareil cas, fût-il composé de savants et d'économistes de la valeur de Karl Marx. C'est par la seule action collective de tous les travailleurs organisés, reliés entr'eux par un libre contrat en groupes corporatifs, que la question du travail pourra être tranchée.

Why then had the people not succeeded in setting out in this direction?

Parce que le peuple dé Paris a été pris à l'improviste par le révolution. Son organisation ouvrière n'était pas forte. Ses corporations étaient désorganisées par la guerre, ses sections étaient à peu près anéanties. Aussi remit-il la tâche qui lui incombait entre les mains de ses élus, dont quelques-uns pourtant avaient proclamé que l'émancipation des travailleurs ne peut être que l'œuvre des travailleurs eux-mêmes.

And so they had ended in a 'dictature jacobine'.[31]

Looking back to Russia, Ralli clearly recognized how he had arrived at these conclusions. He was prompted by the entire tradition of Russian Populism, or, as he preferred to say, by the entire history of the Russian people (seen, we may add, through the theories drawn up by revolutionaries of his native country).

La Commune a été le point de départ, le commencement d'une ère nouvelle dans le développement de l'action révolutionnaire en Russie. Et rien d'étonnant à cela.

Aucun peuple ne pouvait avoir plus à cœur le programme de la Commune révolutionnaire, à aucun peuple il n'est aussi essentiellement inhérent. Toute l'histoire du
peuple russe présente de siècle en siècle une lutte perpetuelle du principe communal
contre l'organisation de l'état, un combat sans trève ni merci de la masse ouvrière
contre la minorité privilégiée pour conquérir le sol et la liberté . . . Il est donc
naturel que les révolutionnaires russes soient tous jusqu'au dernier des *communistes
fédéralistes*.[32]

The very vocabulary used by Ralli shows that it was the Russian situation of
which he was really thinking. 'Commune' is both the Paris Commune and
the *obshchina*; *Zemlya i Volya* is translated by 'le sol et la liberté'. This
constant analogy between the problems of Russia and those of the working
class movement in Western Europe, was to be one of the functions of the
small group of young Bakuninists. There was much bitterness and disappointment in their position, and this accounted for their extremism. But the
method helped them to become aware of their own special position.

Le révolutionnaire russe est l'homme le plus indépendant du monde. Qu'est ce qui
pourrait l'arrêter? Le respect de la tradition du passé . . .? Mais il n'a ni tradition
historique, ni passé. Il suit avidement la lutte sociale qui se continue en occident, il
partage la haine des révolutionnaires européens, mais il ne comprend pas leur attache-
ment aux traditions qui leur ont léguées leurs ancêtres—son développement révolutionnaire est achevé. Il ne lui manque que la force! Et voilà d'où vient cette ironie
amère, cette angoisse qui le ronge, cette éternelle recherche d'une issue . . . Homme
sans passé, il se sent étranger dans la grande famille révolutionnaire de l'humanité.[33]

The other small group of men who had broken away from Bakunin—
those who did not, like these 'young Bakuninists', follow in his tracks, but
joined the Marxist wing of the International—was less successful, and soon
faded out. The group never succeeded in making direct contact with the
clandestine movement in Russia. The *Narodnoe Delo*, which after the first
issue had parted company with Bakunin and Zhukovsky, went on printing
in Geneva, but its circulation grew smaller and smaller.

Yet these men were also looking for a point of contact between the problems of Russia and the Socialist movements of the West. Their ideas on the
subject were original, indeed spectacular, but they lacked the energy and
force of Bakunin's intuition. Their political plans seemed wise (and are in
fact intelligent) but they had no effect on the Russian situation, because
they were eclectic and often artificial.

Bakunin once amused himself by satirizing the mentality of Utin, the chief
spokesman of this small group. There is no doubt that he hit his target.

One cannot say that he doesn't work seriously or that he takes a frivolous view of
things. On the contrary, I have met few Russians who work as hard. He is a martyr
to the study of political and social problems . . . but he is gifted with a remarkable
lack of ability to understand, to seize the essence, the real nature of the problem . . .
He runs along behind the thought and the thought scampers on ahead without ever
letting itself be caught.[34]

The disappointing nature of the movement led by Utin and Trusov springs in part at least from the manner of its birth. Its godfather was J.-Ph. Becker, who saw in this small group of Russian émigrés a tool to be used in the factional struggles within the International.[35] Marx agreed to act as a patron for the movement with a similar object in view. He overcame his ironical distrust of the Russians and realized the value of supporting a group which could provide him with useful information on the movement which was dominated by his adversary Bakunin. He also had hopes that it might become a power capable of opposing Nechaev and anarchism.[36]

And so he welcomed the formation of a Russian section of the first International at Geneva in March 1870. Utin and Trusov adopted the regulations which Bakunin had already drawn up, and they changed only a few words. They obviously intended in this way to make the necessary concessions to the mentality of the émigrés and so succeed in planting their ideas.[37] The regulations were indeed drawn up in the most general terms. They dealt mainly with 'the economic oppression of the Russian people . . . which is absolutely identical to the oppression which stifles the entire European and American proletariat'. They then claimed that 'the Russian people has throughout history aspired to the realization of the great principles proclaimed in the international congresses of workers, i.e. the collective possession of the land and tools of work'. 'The principle of the collectivization of land and the fight against capitalist exploitation has already found expression in the organization of working men's unions', they said, proclaiming their faith in the working class movement. In their regulations they proposed:

(1) To use all possible rational methods—the special nature of which derives from the position of the country—to spread the ideas and principles of the International throughout Russia.

(2) To promote the formation of sections of the International among the working masses in Russia.

(3) To collaborate in the forging of a strong link between the working classes of Russia and those of Western Europe, with the aim that, by helping each other, they will reach their common goal of liberation.

They sent their programme and regulations to Marx, asking him for his support and help and imploring him to represent them in the General Council.

Brought up in the spirit of our master Chernyshevsky, we have joyfully welcomed your exposition of Socialist principles and your criticism of industrial feudalism . . . You have had a decisive part in the creation of the International . . . You are tirelessly unmasking the false patriotism of our Demostheneses who preach about the glorious fate ordained for the Slav people . . . So as not to deceive you and to avoid causing you any surprise, we consider it our duty to tell you at once that we have absolutely nothing in common with Bakunin and his few followers . . .[38]

Marx replied with a short letter in which he stressed the work that the Russian revolutionaries would have to undertake in the future for the liberation of Poland.

Russia's conquest of that nation is the disastrous basis and the real cause of the military régime which exists in Germany and therefore throughout the Continent. And so by working to break Poland's chains, Russian Socialists are undertaking an exalted task which contains within itself the destruction of the military régime— an absolutely indispensable preliminary condition for the general liberation of the European proletariat.

He then spoke of Flerovsky, the author of a book on *The Situation of the Working Class in Russia*; and ended by saying that 'works like those of Flerovsky and your master Chernyshevsky reflect great honour on Russia and show that your country too is beginning to take part in the general movement of the century'.[39]

Utin and Trusov were little concerned with Poland's problems, and devoted all their attention to trying to adapt what they knew of Marxism to the situation in Russia.[40] They lacked Nechaev's revolutionary impatience. 'One must recognize', they said, 'that the end, the solution of our struggle, is not for today or even for tomorrow.'[41] There would be time to observe the social forces involved and to see how they developed in the future. As had already occurred for Lopatin and Negreskul, the chief effect of Marxism was to increase their faith in historical development and to stimulate their desire for a full sociological study.

Revolutionary traditions and Messianic dreams looking back to Stenka Razin and Pugachev were not enough. It was necessary to admit that 'the Russian worker, whether peasant or artisan, has not yet reached awareness of himself, and his invincible strength'. All his attention had until then 'been directed towards his interests and the needs of his own village and district' without his being able to see the problem as a whole. But was this not perhaps also the case even outside Russia? 'Even until recent times the Western worker concentrated all his attention on purely local needs and interests. He was only concerned to find locally a cheaper mode of living, a local demand for labour, etc.' The International had given the working classes a fuller degree of awareness. Yet it had to be admitted that internationally minded workers were still a minority and constituted 'the aristocracy of the intelligentsia in the world of the working classes'.

In Russia this minority was already in existence and was just as mature and revolutionary as it was in the West. It must not be sought among the manual workers but rather in 'the proletariat of the brain', the younger generation of intellectuals. Socially, 'by virtue of its formation and all its aspirations, this minority constitutes an element indissolubly linked to the *couches* of the people'. It corresponded exactly to 'the politically advanced proletariat of the International'. Even its history was similar, however paradoxical this appeared at first sight. 'Socialist theories of the nineteenth century undoubtedly have an enormous influence on the advanced workers' proletariat'. In Russia, too, the effect had been no less marked; the Petrashevskists had corresponded to Western Utopianism. The struggle for the right to work had been matched in Russia by the battles sustained by the younger generation for Sunday-schools, and their right to meeting, organization and systems of self-help. Peasant problems had been faced with Chernyshevsky. The entire movement of the 'sixties showed how deeply rooted Socialist ideas were in Russia. Indeed it could be shown that the social and political conditions of the country had led 'the proletariat of the brain' to even more advanced standpoints than elsewhere. In Russia it had reached the same standard as the 'proletariat of muscles' in the West. In Germany, too, social and government oppression had been heavy, but only a small minority of intellectuals had followed the road to the very end. In Poland and in Italy the petit bourgeois atmosphere had often concealed the essence of things, and 'the proletariat of the brain' had allowed itself to be diverted into the field of nationalism. And so it was not wrong to say 'that the same and identical task now faces the proletariat in the West and in Russia'. The working class and intellectual minority would give the working masses, both in Russia and in Western Europe, fuller self-awareness.[42]

For this reason their weapons should be the same. Even in Russia it was not impossible to start cooperatives, mutual aid societies, etc. Even the weapon of strikes was now beginning to be known and used by the Russian workmen. It was in 1870 that there occurred the first abstentions from work in St Petersburg, and the *Narodnoe Delo* spoke of them at length, finding in them proof that its attitude was the right one.[43]

As for the peasants, they already had their own organization, the *obshchina*, which had in the past displayed its powers of resistance. It was now threatened by the formation of a class of richer peasants, but one could be sure that 'it would never give in to the *kulaks*', despite the obvious support given them by the government.[44]

The problems of workers and peasants both showed that the struggle must be at once economic and political. The proletariat in St Petersburg would learn by means of strikes that the State was behind the boss. The peasant *obshchinas* could act in an egalitarian direction against the *kulaks* when the pressure of political authority slackened. It must be the duty of the younger members of the intelligentsia, organized in a 'party of national liberation', to lead the masses of the factories and the fields to this twofold yet identical battle.[45]

This attempt made by the Russian section to bring Russian Populism more in line with the experience of the working class movement in the West was to be resumed some years later on a far greater scale, by Petr Lavrovich Lavrov, a newly emigrated student of philosophical and social problems.

Lavrov was no longer young. He was a reflective character, an introvert by temperament. To his political activities he brought the patience, the attention to detail, and even the tranquillity of the research worker; while his work as an investigator was informed with the same moral passion more openly expressed in the student movements of the Populists. He succeeded in founding the only faction among the émigrés which could really stand up to that led by Bakunin, and even within Russia he was able to influence a small but select group which had a slow but penetrating effect on the entire Populist movement.

His works contrasted the problems of Russia and the West, which had been so roughly and violently treated by Bakunin and Tkachev. They were less passionate and more learned. His point of view could, with reason, be accused of eclecticism. But this was merely the negative aspect, the shadow, as it were, of that attempt to perfect Populist ideas which it was his function to achieve.[46]

Lavrov's development was slow. He was born in 1823 and spent the first part of his life until the end of the 'fifties teaching mathematics in the Artillery College and occupied with minor publicizing activities. Though known only among a small circle of people, he already aroused admiration and respect for his double nature of 'researcher' and 'poet' which—described in various ways—always struck those who met him.

The precise exactitude of the mathematician found expression in a private life of great nobility, in the fearlessness of his scientific thought, in complete intrepidity in the expression of his opinions. Yet he did not have an arid mentality like a scientist, or a hard one like a mathematician. On the contrary, not only was he sensitive to everything that is beautiful and tender, but he himself was a poet . . . He was capable of getting passionately excited and also of controlling himself. So strong was the spiritual element in him that I sometimes really thought that he did not even have a body but only a brain and nerves, completely subject to his soul.

So the poet Benediktov described him in 1853.[47] Lavrov was at this time seeking to express that element of 'poetry' which he felt in himself (and which was in fact a specially delicate response to ethical problems) by writing poems, whose only value lies in their desire for liberty and in the hope that he could one day take part in a Russian society 'where thoughts and words could flow in freedom'.

When, with the death of Nicholas I, men began to think that such a time had at last arrived, Lavrov shared the prevailing optimism, and proclaimed in verse and prose that it was essential to go bravely 'forward'.[48] He played an active part in the student and intellectual movement; he was a member, though on the fringes, of the first *Zemlya i Volya*. But as yet he was not able to make his own contribution to any of these activities. He was looking for his own approach and he had, as Chernyshevsky once told him, the originality to look for it not in one or other of the progressive political doctrines but in the study of philosophy.

His interests are clearly shown by the title of the most important of his works at this time, *An Essay on the Theory of Personality*,[49] which appeared in 1859 and which was republished the following year with the equally significant title of *An Essay on the Problems of Practical Philosophy*. He dedicated it to A.G. and P.P., the initials—deciphered with ease even by his contemporaries—of A. Gertsen (Herzen) and P. Proudhon.

Though Chernyshevsky rightly said that his philosophy was eclectic,[50] it represented none the less an attempt to investigate the widespread discontent of those who read Hegel in search of some indication of 'practical philosophy', some ideal of morality. His reflections on the relations between science and the activities of the individual in society already contained the seeds of what he said some ten years later in the *Historical Letters*, his main work of philosophy.

His eclecticism, even his uncertainty, was just as obvious at this time in his politics as in his philosophy. In 1856 he wrote a letter to Herzen which shows him dubious about the reforms that were being mooted at the time. This was a typical example of a state of mind prevalent among many liberals and moderates. They had waited for so long for the reforms, and were now fearful at the results which would follow from the changes brought about by the State bureaucracy. It was difficult to bridge the gap between general ideas on progress and the actual movement of events. All the more so as Lavrov, by doing so himself, aimed at saving completely what he considered the only vital element in Russia: the intelligentsia in all its aspects. Just as later, when he joined the Socialist movement, he held stoutly to his defence of the value of science and the need to proclaim the vital importance of learning, so now, in face of the proposed reforms of Russian society, he was concerned lest the very sources of the only class concerned with intellectual values should dry up.

The most different currents and ideas meet in the intelligentsia. However much they may disagree, they do converge on one point: the right of free thought, the need for a close study of contemporary problems in general and Russian ones in particular; it is in this that lies the future of Russia . . .

He thought that the peasant reform as planned had not been sufficiently worked out and discussed. It was carried through without the full participation of Russia's intellectual forces. It might also be dangerous for that small nobility which was 'our *tiers état*' and which ran the risk of being ruined by the government decrees. Nor as regards the peasants had the economic aspect of their problem been sufficiently considered. 'It is not merely a question of freeing them from serfdom, but of making them really free and preventing them from being exploited in the future by officials and *kulaks*. It is a peasant who is not to be wretched who must be freed.'[51] His general reforming tendencies and affirmation of intellectual values were already in evidence in this first attempt to adopt a political standpoint.

Nor did Lavrov abandon these ideas in the years that followed, though, like so many others at this time, he quickly jettisoned the element of moderation and fear. At the time when the serfs were liberated he supported a complete reform of society, the overthrow of all the traditional forms of Russian life, and a systematic work of criticism and 'destruction' by the intellectuals. To demand that the changes should be made gradually, 'step by step', was like demanding that first the feet, then the hands, etc., should grow in an organism.[52] 'Social conscience develops gradually; but once it has awoken, then, not step by step, but in a flash it applies its biting criticism wherever it can, and everywhere there springs up a demand for renewal and development which will not be denied.'[53]

This meant in practice taking an ever increasing part in the various schemes which were springing up at the time to spread education and organize the liberal society of the day. So he played an active rôle in editing the *Russian Encyclopaedic Dictionary*, was a member of the committee of the literary fund, of the Chess Club, which was soon suppressed by the police, and of the Society for Women's Work, etc. As regards the latter, for instance, Nikitenko, the professor and censor, noted in his diary in 1864 that 'Lavrov devoted himself to converting the young women and girls to "nihilism", and for this purpose arranged a course in materialist philosophy in his house.'[54]

Looking back later on these years of intense though dispersed activity, Lavrov said that even then he

was aware of the need for a political and social revolution, but that he did not yet see any basis whether for a social transformation or for political action beyond slow preparation . . . For long he had admitted the possibility that there could be a harmony between the interests of someone in the ruling classes and those of the majority of the oppressed classes. He had even been prepared to admit that this could be the case if one were guided only by personal interest and not by moral conviction. This admission had been one of his greatest errors. Though he later repudiated it, it left many traces in his works.[55]

He later said that he had abandoned this earlier view because of the news that he had been able to obtain of the activities of the International in the West. But we have no exact knowledge of how far Lavrov was then acquainted with the working class movement. It is true that by the end of the 'sixties his ideas were developing. He became a Socialist from a theoretical and moral point of view, even before taking a direct personal part in the Russian and European working class movements.

Until 1866 he was able to escape open persecution; but during the days that followed Karakozov's attempt on the life of the Tsar, he—like all the best known 'nihilists'—expected to be arrested from one day to the next. And, indeed, on 15th April 1866 his house was searched, and the poems which he had once sent to Herzen, as well as letters showing that he had been in touch with Chernyshevsky and Mikhailov, were seized. No proof of any link with Ishutin's group was found, nor in fact any document that was really compromising. But despite this, after nine months in prison he was banished 'to one of the inner departments of the empire'. The government obviously intended to put an end to his activities as a writer. The district chosen was Vologda. At the beginning of 1867 he was at Totma, a small centre of that department. And from there he was later transferred to Kadnikov, a poverty-stricken village in the same district, where he remained until the beginning of 1870.[56]

The colony of exiles in the region of Vologda, about five hundred kilometres north of Moscow, reflected, like a small mirror, the varying trends of Populism. Shelgunov, the friend of Chernyshevsky and Mikhailov, was there; some of the students who had taken part in the revival of the university movement at the end of the 'sixties; and, among others, M. P. Sazhin, the future Bakuninist,[57] the writer D. K. Girs, who was guilty of having made a speech at Pisarev's funeral, and a few Poles. All these exiles had met with sympathy and help from the local population, and at Kadnikov, Lavrov was able to make friends with a student who had been to the seminary at Vologda and who was a great admirer of Feuerbach. Indeed, within the Seminary a group had been formed which called itself the 'Chernyshevskyites' and which was made up of men who embraced the ideas of the *Sovremennik* and Feuerbach. These far-off centres heard echoes not only of intellectual life in Russia but even of news from the exiles; the speeches that Bakunin had made at the *League for Peace and Freedom* for example. So that in his banishment Lavrov found himself in direct contact with the world of the Russian underground from which he had until then held himself aloof.

It was to attack the ideas of Pisarev, which he found particularly influential in these circles, that he then wrote his *Historical Letters*. This book marked an important date in the Russian revolutionary movement. For it constituted the manifesto, so to speak, of the revival of the more typically Populist current after the years of 'nihilism'. It was the fundamental ideological document in the attack against the ideas that were later to find expression in Nechaev's venture.[58]

Already in 1865, the year before his arrest, Lavrov had written an article to make a stand against the exclusive passion for the natural sciences which dominated so many of the young generation in Russia. The ingenuous hope of finding a solution to all problems in the study of nature led to a tendency which he described as 'infantile' in the most precise meaning of the word. 'In his earliest years man is near natural life . . .' In his earliest attempts to understand the world that surrounds him, he turns to physical phenomena. But after this initial stage in his education—necessary though it was both for the individual and for the development of Russian culture— it was time to turn to the sphere of ethical and social problems. 'Natural sciences, as they are understood in our society, cannot be used as a guiding rein in the labyrinth of human relations.'[59]

15+

The *Historical Letters* developed these ideas. They were published in stages between 1868 and 1869 in the review *Nedelya* (The Week) and collected in book form in 1870 under the pseudonym of P. Mirtov. Despite the obstacles imposed by the censorship, the book had a huge circulation and lasting success.[60] The works of revolutionaries in the 'seventies which recall the *Historical Letters* as a youthful revelation, as the book which played the largest part in bringing home to them the full extent of the problem which awaited them, are manifold. One of them called it 'the revolutionary gospel, the philosophy of revolution'. Another recalled 'the enormous impression produced on me by reading it'. And yet another recorded that 'our tears of idealist enthusiasm fell on this book, and it gave us an immense thirst to live and die for noble ideas'.[61]

Mirtov's pages have obviously not worn well, and reading them it is sometimes difficult to appreciate the power which they had when they were still fresh. The words of one of Lavrov's followers will, perhaps, convey the vital nourishment that its contemporaries found in it.

Reading this book convinced me that in our present social organization, by the mere fact of birth or other circumstances, independent of the will of its individual components, the members of society itself were inevitably distributed in two unequal groups. One of these, numerically very small, was in a privileged position and able to enjoy—to the detriment of the others—all the good things of life. Whereas the second, which made up the great majority, was destined to eternal misery and to labours beyond the scope of human capacity. Mirtov eloquently pointed out the vastness of the unpaid debt which weighs on the conscience of the privileged group towards the millions of workers of this generation and those of the past . . . I accepted these ideas which were new to me, and felt myself in the position—so much ridiculed at the time—of a 'repentant noble'.[62]

Lavrov, in short, was making a direct appeal to the conscience of the intelligentsia. He did not point out the political advantages that would derive from putting themselves on the side of the people, as had been done at the beginning of the 'sixties. He recalled them to a sense of duty. He spoke of the debt that had been contracted with the peasants and popular classes, and reminded them that it must be paid without delay. So he cut back to their very roots the doubts which had previously weighed on the minds of the intellectuals, torn between the duty of immediate political action and social ideals. To the question 'What is to be done?' he replied by saying that the first, indeed the only thing, to do was to take account of their position as privileged exploiters. It was in this appeal, not political but purely ethical and social, that Lavrov found the message which struck the new generation so forcibly.

This simple and energetic message was not expressed as a sermon or in religious guise. Lavrov worked out his own vision of the philosophy of history. This is the aspect of these *Letters* which has worn least well, but it enabled him to give a rational basis to his appeal. Fighting against the most ingenuous and crude positivism, he maintained that it was not possible to understand the meaning of progress if one did not admit an ethical and intellectual, 'subjective', value which allowed one to evaluate progress itself. The strength of his message did not lie in the rather hesitant and general expression that he gave of this quality; it was to be found in the very fact that he had proclaimed the need for values at all. In his short autobiography, Lavrov rightly recalled the neo-Kantian philosophy, which was then grappling with similar problems in Germany, as one of the sources from which he drew inspiration.

The *Letters* gave the conclusions he had reached in his deliberately 'subjective' evaluation of progress. He no longer looked on progress as the accumulation of wealth and knowledge. Rather, it was an exertion dearly paid for which had gradually developed throughout the centuries. Those who now enjoyed civilization should realize how much they owed to those who had worked, created, sacrificed themselves in order to maintain a privileged class. It was now time to pay the great debt that modern civilization had incurred towards the great majority of people.

Anyone reaching such conclusions should not feel himself isolated or alone for there were many who felt the same way. He described in detail the intellectual development of those groups of 'critically thinking people' who had now grown into 'a party'. And so Lavrov's observations helped to accelerate the transition from small groups to a wider movement which was taking place between the end of the 'sixties and the beginning of the 'seventies.

At the end of the *Letters* he pointed out what ought to be 'the banner of this party':

Critical thought organizes the campaign of united labour against monopolist capital . . . It is guided by an idealization of labour. Previously labour was idealized as a docile tool of capital; as the submission of the workman, a submission latent in the laws of the universe, in the decrees of providence; as a mystical punishment for the sins of our ancestors. But Socialism gives the worker another ideal; the struggle of useful and productive labour against unused capital . . .[63]

The formulation was as yet uncertain but it had the merit of calling attention to Socialism as the only ideal capable of satisfying the consciences of all who fully appreciated the unbearable weight of belonging to the class of exploiters.

When writing these words, Lavrov was already working out plans for putting them into practice. He proposed to escape from the district of Vologda and flee abroad to devote himself to a life of research and propaganda. This was not an easy venture for a man now no longer young and painfully short-sighted. But with the help of G. A. Lopatin, a member of the *Society of the Rouble* and one of the most active revolutionaries of the 'seventies and 'eighties, he was successful. On 15th February 1870 he left Kadnikov, and only two weeks later he reached Paris. His escape was backed in St Petersburg by a group which was beginning to organize itself in opposition to Nechaev. This group was inspired by ideas similar to those expounded in *The Historical Letters*, and included, among others, Lavrov's own daughter and her husband, M. F. Negreskul.[64]

Lavrov reached Paris, certain that he would not remain long in exile and that a rapid change in the situation in Russia would allow him to return shortly to his own country. He thought that to some extent he would be able to combine his activities with those of Herzen; but when he arrived in France Herzen was already dead. He at once envisaged starting a new periodical, and it was perhaps with this in mind that the younger generation in St Petersburg had organized his flight. But for some years he had to postpone this plan. He was absorbed in his work and researches as well as in the events which he witnessed and in which he participated. The urge to consider the problems of Socialism and agitation which he had received from the far-off International when still in Russia, now became immediate and pressing when he was faced with the Franco-Prussian War and the Commune.

Both the Russian wings of the International, the *Narodnoe Delo* on the one hand, and Bakunin on the other, tried to engage Lavrov as collaborator. He ignored the first offer and refused the second.[65] But negotiations with the group at Geneva continued. Elpidin wrote to him again in 1871, but Lavrov was critical of all that side of émigré propaganda that was most blatantly revolutionary. He said that there were two, and only two, ideas which needed dealing with: the increase in workmen's wages and the emancipation of women. And so during this period his contacts with the exiles were only irregular.

He was mainly absorbed in French politics, and took part in the demonstrations which led to the fall of the Second Empire on 4th September 1870. He made contact with the Paris members of the International, probably through the Russian wife of Jaclard, A. V. Korvin-Krukovskaya, who played an active part in the Commune.[66] In autumn 1870 he joined the 'Des Ternes' section of the International. He made friends with Varlin, the Hungarian Leo Frankel, and others. A trip to Brussels gave him the chance to make contacts with those groups around the *Internationale*, an organ edited by Eugène Hins. It was on this visit also that he first established relations with César de Paepe.

When he returned to Paris at the beginning of March 1871, Varlin told him that:

with the new system of electing the commanders of the National Guard, a considerable part of Paris on both banks of the Seine is already in the hands of the Socialists, and within two or three weeks the entire town will be controlled by the Socialist commanders of the battalions. A federation of the provincial Guards, backed by propaganda, will create an armed force of the proletariat throughout France.[67]

This was a few days before the insurrection broke out and the Commune sprang up. 'The workers, having organized their forces, decided to make use of them', as Lavrov himself said.[68]

It was this popular aspect of the movement which struck him most from the very earliest days. The Commune seemed to confirm his Populist outlook. It represented the open struggle of the exploited against the exploiters. Here at last was a social movement after so much useless political agitation. In an article which he wrote for the Brussels *Internationale* on 21st March 1871, Lavrov was one of the first in Europe to emphasize the Socialist aspect of the events then occurring in Paris, and to define the Commune as an instrument of power of the proletariat.

Eh bien! en voilà encore une révolution! Et celle-là ne ressemble guère aux autres. Qui donc est à la tête de tout cela? se demandait-on. Est-ce Blanqui? Est-ce Pyat? Est-ce Flourens? Mais du tout. Pas un seul petit grand nom. Les artistes habituels et connus du public ne prenaient pas part à la pièce. Le rôle de premier révolutionnaire n'était pas occupé. Les grands journaux sont effarés. Ils ne pouvaient se douter qu'une révolution puisse se faire et réussir à Paris sans qu'ils en sachent rien et sans que leurs amis y prennent part. Des gens inconnus! Les épiciers écarquillent leurs yeux en lisant les signatures de ce terrible comité central de la garde nationale qui gouverne maintenant Paris. Des gens tout à fait inconnus! Les concierges font des mines méprisantes, en disant à leurs locataires: mais voyez donc, madame, qu'est-ce que c'est que ce gouvernement là! c'est drôle! des simples gens! des voyous! des ouvriers! Oui, madame, des simples ouvriers.

Sans doute, ce sont des simples ouvriers! et c'est cela qu i fait l'originalité du mouvement des derniers jours. C'est là ce qui le caractérise. C'est là ce qui doit lui donner un intérêt tout particulier aux yeux de tout socialiste, de tout adhérent à l'Association internationale des travailleurs, comme aux yeux de tout penseur sincère, étudiant dans les faits visibles de l'histoire les forces invisibles qui agissent dans les sociétés. Dans le grand écroulement qui s'est fait en France pendant ces derniers mois, la bourgeoisie réactionnaire n'a donné pas un seul homme *nouveau* et toutes ses anciennes gloires se sont montrées au dessous des événements, au dessous de leur renommée . . . Eh bien, ce que n'osaient, ce que ne savaient pas faire les hommes les plus connus de la France, cela s'est fait très facilement par quelques gens honnêtes, intelligents, résolus, mais parfaitement inconnus aux lecteurs des journaux.

He then spoke of the International and of Varlin and his comrades who were 'à la tête du gouvernement des ouvriers'.[69]

On 28th March, in another article for the same paper, he was fairly optimistic about the development of events, and ended by speaking of the universal value of the Commune.

Le penseur socialiste, en étudiant les événements de ce petit nombre de jours, peut affirmer avec plus de certitude encore que cette société bourgeoise qui exploite et démoralise le prolétaire n'a aucune raison d'être. Elle n'a pour elle ni le droit moral, ni la force du nombre, ni même le savoir faire, l'habitude, l'activité sociale, l'influence des conceptions larges et bien conduites, elle n'a pour elle que la routine.

It was true that the situation was still difficult. Would the Commune find real support in France and outside her boundaries? General Socialist sympathies were not enough. 'Peut-on attendre de quelque part un concours actif?' [70]

Lavrov devoted his finest talents to trying to arouse this active help. At the beginning of May he was in Brussels to win support from among the Belgian federation. Shortly afterwards he went to London to go to the General Council of the International. He seems to have taken this step on his own initiative, though it had the agreement and approval of Varlin.

But meanwhile the Commune had fallen. In London he met Marx and Engels, and took part in the earliest discussions on the experiences of the Commune, which were then taking place among the leaders of the International. He soon returned to Paris, but kept in touch with the General Council and above all with H. Jung, to whom he sent news and practical information in an attempt to save those members of the Commune, mainly foreign workers' groups, who had succeeded in escaping persecution.

His conclusions were now absolutely clear. The Commune had represented 'a new kind of State. It had been put into practice for a short time . . . but it had been shown that a workers' government was possible.'[71] He gradually completed a critical study of his experiences. In his letters he often returned to the problems of the Commune; and some years later, in 1879, he summarized his conclusions in a long pamphlet. This is one of the most interesting documents in the endless discussions of the time on the meaning of the Paris movement and the lessons to be drawn from it.

Lavrov was mainly concerned to defend the fundamental importance of theoretical preparation—of ideology. This, he said, would ensure the success of a revolutionary movement. In a detailed preliminary inquiry he ran through the democratic and internationalist press of the period which had preceded the Commune, showing how general, vague and uncertain were the ideas to be found in it. The word 'Socialism', for example, was given the most varying meanings by the press. It was just possible to find 'an odd two or three fragments in the works published at the time by Pyat, Vallès, Lissagaray, which might throw light on the theoretical and practical problems of Socialism '.[72] The tradition of the great French Revolution had continued to dominate men's minds and had prevented them from seeing the new problems. Though this tradition, together with that of 1848, provided the general ideas, the political problems they had raised had not yet been given an adequate theoretical treatment. For example, everyone spoke of individual liberty; but they differed as soon as they raised the problem of a federal system or a centralized State; and the supporters of neither of these two tendencies had been able to give an exact definition of their own programme. Only Millière, in Nos. 23, 29 and 30 of the Marseillaise, had described a plan to organize the 'revolutionary dictatorship of the people'.[73] But the programmes of Delescluze, Vermorel, etc., were still stuck in the grooves of earlier traditions.

A study of the events between September 1870 and March 1871 led to the same conclusion: 'The Socialists were not ready'.[74] Discussions within the International in Paris during the time that immediately preceded the Commune revealed the true cause of this immaturity. The workers' organization had constantly wavered between a purely economic function (the original reason for its existence) and the adoption of a political programme which it had borrowed from different democratic forces. And often there had been no collective and united action on the economic plane, and the individual members of the International each followed their own inclinations in politics. One need only look at the discussions and proposals which had preceded the formation of the National Guard to see that this was so. And even after the Commune had been proclaimed, those at its head were far from bringing about that 'dictatorship of the people' spoken of by Millière.[75] One could not, of course, put the blame only on the Central Committee, which had done everything within its power. 'It was not responsible for the fact that the most advanced parties had taken no trouble or had been unable to organize themselves beforehand.'[76]

So the Commune had been unable to draw the social and economic consequences from the power which had fallen into its hands.

Only a decisive upheaval which would at a single blow have put the proletariat on the same economic level as those who had been its previous rulers, would have given sound foundations for building up a political force able to carry through a revolution on behalf of the proletariat.[77]

Lack of an economic programme allowed the truly Socialist elements of the Commune to be dominated by traditional forces, mainly the *routiniers* of the Jacobinism of 1793.[78]

In this way the movement let itself be deflected from the social field which should have been its only concern. Not one single condition had been realized for moving to an economic revolution, and boldly driving from its ranks all enemies of the proletariat.[79] The very idea of re-adopting the mediaeval principle of a Commune was a mistake as long as there remained within its ranks exploiters and exploited, and as long as it did not become 'the independent Commune of the proletariat'.[80]

That such a policy was possible had been shown by the working of services during the siege and the efficiency of the workers during the insurrection. This was the great lesson of the Commune. Together with the heroism shown by the fighters, it marked out the way for the Socialist movement of the future.

Never, under any circumstances, have the Socialists the right to forget that in the present phase of the historical struggle, the economic problem dominates all the others, and that until an economic revolution has carried out every one of its fundamental points, nothing has been done ... Today there is no field, neither religious, national nor political, in which the proletarian workmen have or can have the moral right to follow the path of the ruling classes in whole or in part.[81]

In decisive moments of history, the masses always follow the banner which proclaims the most precise programme, the most clear, simple and decided objectives. The masses follow those who are ready and do not hesitate. If there is no one in a position to satisfy these demands, if the strongest and most sincere members of the so-called intelligentsia hesitate, then the masses inevitably follow some hint from traditions of the past and draw back from new men. And then even the most heroic actions, even the most disinterested energies will not be able to prevent a return to the old evil, though in somewhat changed form. Our Populists must remember this.[82]

Lavrov did not reach these conclusions immediately after the Commune. He, too, went through a period of discouragement, when he looked upon a revival of the Socialist movement as very far off. The situation in France and the atmosphere of Paris after the crushing of the Commune lay heavy on him as on others. Whereas in all the other countries of Europe, and certainly in Russia, the Commune—despite its defeat—stimulated new energies (which Lavrov studied in a chapter of his book in 1879), the situation in France must obviously have seemed to him far more difficult. None the less, despite this delay in working out the political lessons of his experiences, their essential core was plain from the very first moment. Self-preparation was essential, as was much patient labour to create the future shock troops of the revolution. These, in fact, were the very tasks which the International had not been in a position to undertake effectively.

But how could this be done? Until 1873 he thought chiefly by study and scientific work, both for himself and for the new Russian generation which was growing up. He regarded the function of the intelligentsia as so important and decisive that he resumed his earlier work and tried to write mainly of cultural problems in lawful reviews under a series of pseudonyms. In 1872 he left Paris and settled in Zurich where the colony of Russian students was growing, and gave them lectures on scientific and historical subjects. 'The young generation needs knowledge', he said.

But very soon he too was infected by the atmosphere of political ferment which dominated Zurich. Bakunin, who had been there since June 1872, was once more planning to found a review. Negotiations were started with a view to his editing one with Lavrov, but the programme which Lavrov proposed aroused strong opposition from Bakunin.[83]

Lavrov was driven to take up this position between the end of 1872 and the beginning of 1873 by his hopes of winning the support and collaboration of the Russian intellectuals who were passing through Switzerland in large numbers at the time. They were in many ways the best representatives of the new scientific generation. Lavrov seems to have counted specially on Ivan Vasilevich Luchitsky, teacher at a secondary school in Kiev and soon afterwards at the university there. In later years he became the greatest Russian authority on the problems of agriculture in the eighteenth century, the intelligent historian of the French peasants before and during the revolution, and one of the mentors of present-day historical writing in France, in particular Georges Lefebvre. Luchitsky thus provides one of the best examples of the transference to historical research of the problems raised by Russian Populism. Passing through Zurich with him were V. M. Chekhanovetsky, the professor of political economy of Kiev University, and later the master of Tugan-Baranovsky, the well-known social-democrat economist; M. P. Dragomanov, who was to become the best known of the Ukrainian democratic émigrés; and Nikolay Ivanovich Ziber, soon to become one of the most acute observers of Russian agrarian development of these years, and the first Russian 'legal Marxist'.

Basing himself on this group of intellectuals, almost all of them from Kiev, Lavrov might well have had hopes of founding a particularly strong and important cultural centre among the émigrés. But his plan failed. As a rule, these members of the intelligentsia had no intention of cutting their ties with official Russia, and nearly all of them soon returned to their country.

And from St Petersburg, Lavrov heard from the writer Mikhaylovsky—who was then beginning to take up and develop Lavrov's 'formula of progress'—that he had decided not to emigrate.[84]

In Zurich meanwhile his relations with Bakunin's followers became more and more tense. Lavrov took an active part in the struggles which divided the student colony regarding the control of the communal institutions that had been founded by it and particularly for leadership of the library. These struggles led to Sokolov's (the nihilist writer already mentioned) assault on V. N. Smirnov, an ex-student of the medical faculty in Moscow who had been driven out after the university disorders in 1869 and had become a member of Nechaev's *Narodnaya Rasprava*. In 1871 he had succeeded in getting to Zurich, where he had begun to organize a small press for printing works forbidden in Russia. Lavrov, especially after this attack, became the natural spokesman of those who disapproved of such methods and who in general were moving further and further away from the followers of Bakunin. Smirnov became his most active and faithful collaborator, and organized the printing press for his review. He was, in reality, the leading spirit of the small minority group which was closely attached to the *Vpered*.

As Lavrov himself has told us, as early as spring 1872 he received a request from St Petersburg to found a review reflecting the needs and ideas of the Populists. After giving up his ideas for a cultural review and breaking off his connections with the Bakuninists, Lavrov decided to respond to this appeal. When his proposed collaboration with Tkachev also came to nought, the *Vpered* was started as a review organized exclusively by him and the few young collaborators whom he found among the students and émigrés in Zurich.[85]

Their programme was printed in the first number of the review which appeared in August 1873. It was intended to appeal to all the various

15*

tendencies which were then taking shape, all the currents of 'radical socialist thought', as Lavrov said, excluding only self-confessed Jacobins.

Revolutionary Socialists must give up their old ideas of being able to replace the State—after they have succeeded through a lucky stroke in destroying it by introducing through the processes of law a new organization and making a gift of this to the unprepared masses. We do not want a new constraining authority to take the place of that which already exists, whatever the origin of this new authority may be.[86]

So the function of the Socialists could be summed up as the duty to prepare themselves intellectually and to prepare the masses through propaganda.

The four volumes of *Vpered* which were published at Zurich and later in London under Lavrov's editorship between 1873 and 1876 fully elaborated this position.

But what did 'preparing oneself intellectually' mean? In Russia the review fell mainly into the hands of university students who were leaving their lectures in order to devote themselves entirely to a life of revolution. Lavrov's words were interpreted by them as an appeal to continue their studies, to specialize in some subject and enter one of the careers which were opening up to young intellectuals. And so they generally reacted very bitterly against such an attitude.

Lavrov anticipated a reaction of the kind in the first number of the *Vpered* and replied in an article called 'Knowledge and Revolution'. In this he declared that the exaltation of instinct and scorn for intellectual preparation constituted a real 'mental epidemic which has struck some sections of Russian youth . . . It is one of the most obviously pathological phenomena in the spiritual life of our politically advanced youth.'[87] The Socialists' task must be that of becoming the inspirers, the interpreters, the supporters of the people. How could they undertake this task without having something to give the people? 'Knowledge is the fundamental power of the revolution which is under way and the force essential to carry it out.' It was not a question of starting schools for the people but of laying the foundations so that one day an organization could arise which could really educate the masses. It was not therefore just schoolmastering that was required but a preparation of the intellectual class on whom fell all the responsibility for the social revolution. If they did not clearly realize what was wanted, they were cheating the people, and that was the worst thing possible. Success depended entirely on the faith that the people would acquire in those who wished to draw near to it.

Lack of preparation would compel the revolutionaries to give up the fight at the very moment when they appeared victorious. It was enough to look at the French revolution, which was also popular in character but whose victories lacked solidity. This was proof that 'it is faith that rouses people, and gives them victory, but this victory is purely ephemeral if the ideas which it brings are not based on critical thought'. Even if the 'fanatical religious-revolutionaries' as Lavrov called them, succeeded in winning power, it would have no solidity. A society lacking the active participation of the intellectuals was doomed to become a tyranny. They would then be charged with being 'apathetic'. Indeed from an ethical point of view this charge would be a true one, but historically their attitude would only be the inevitable result of a period when all discussions had taken on a religious and scholastic character. Only a long historical process could gradually bring back the element of criticism to the function of leadership which it ought never to have lost.

As can be seen, Lavrov was trying to lay the foundations of a revolution which was to be radically Populist in form, and completely Socialist from the economic point of view, but which would retain the principle of the part to be played by the intelligentsia. To do this he attacked the summary ethical condemnation of science, which had its origins in Rousseau, and which was widespread in Russia and abroad among Bakunin's followers. It was true, he said, that science could mask privilege; but it was not egotistical per se, it was not one of the advantages which the intellectual must give up to pay his debt to the people. The spirit of Populism and the will to prepare oneself intellectually must be combined in the revolutionary who was springing up in Russia.

Lavrov certainly weakened this position, important though it was, by defining it in eclectic and often vague terms. 'Preparation' meant in turn a technical knowledge of economic, legal, even military problems; and at the same time a defence of the value of learning against denigration in the name of morality or activity.

He explained, it is true, that by 'preparation' he did not mean small local reforming activities, such as creating modern centres or institutions in the Russian countryside. He even said that those who allowed themselves to be taken in by such illusions were 'forces lost for the revolution' unable to see the problem as a whole. He also said that the culture of which he was speaking had nothing to do with the diplomas of the Tsarist universities. But his schemes were not clear enough to prevent his thought being easily misinterpreted, especially by those who could only read his works (which were forbidden in Russia) at irregular intervals. This played an important part in limiting his influence on the Populist movement and confining his followers to small and often ineffectual groups.

The radical rejection of any 'preparation' which inspired so many young Russians at this time revealed a desire for revolt and action which could find no satisfaction in Lavrov's words. He was told this in a particularly intelligent and heartfelt letter by N. V. Chaikovsky, one of the leading spirits of the movement in St Petersburg. Yet Chaikovsky himself could certainly not be suspected of despising culture. In the years immediately preceding he had founded, among other things, a vast organization for spreading books on social and political subjects throughout Russia.[88] Chaikovsky told Lavrov that to demand cultural 'preparation' was useless for those who were already in the movement and realized their responsibilities. On the other hand it was harmful to all those whose ideas were not yet formed, but who were susceptible to the new tendencies. They would inevitably look upon Lavrov's plea as an appeal to remain within the frontiers of a bourgeois existence. There were already quite enough people who—instead of taking action—satisfied themselves by giving purely literary expression to their vague wishes for revolt. This merely encouraged that age-old process of escape into literature which had already too long delayed the birth of an active force.

Obviously you are very well aware that most Russian young men have learnt to know life from the novels of Reshetnikov, the stories of Uspensky, the satires of Shchedrin . . . Before you stands an honourable, enthusiastic man, who lives only in abstract dreams. He has a spirit that believes in justice and the truth of its ideals, and with all his soul he is ready to put these into practice. Do not put obstacles in his way . . . But rather inspire him. Show him that he is morally obliged to bring into his life what he has already elaborated within himself, and what he believes.

He pointed out that as far as practical action was concerned, the first number of the *Vpered* had already created differences within the movement by driving some members to postpone any action until they had completed their studies; and as a reaction by reviving the complete 'nihilist' repudiation of learning which had been growing weaker just as practical and concrete action was beginning to appear on the scene.

But Lavrov's appeal for propaganda and his insistence on the need to draw nearer to the people, to mingle with it and thereby lead it towards Socialism, met with greater response. The movement 'to go to the people' was considerably influenced by his ethical formulation of the political problem. In the *Vpered* in fact he succeeded in resuming and considerably developing the points he had already made in his *Historical Letters*.

The efficacy of Lavrov's formulation of his Socialism at the beginning of the 'seventies was indeed profound. His conception was based on his views on the development of ideas on the subject through the centuries. He wrote a great *History of Social Doctrines*, some of whose chapters were published in the first and third volumes of *Vpered*,[89] and which grew in following years into *An Essay on the History of Thought in the Modern Age*.[90] Naturally the positivist tendencies of his learning, his 'anthropological' interests and in general his studious bent of mind, tended to transform these historical essays into a sociological doctrine. But by 1874 he had already announced that 'true sociology is Socialism'[91] and it was this political perception that lay at the foundations of his most interesting thought.

Meanwhile the ideas which he had expressed in the *Historical Letters*, on the logical and ethical error of looking at progress objectively and evaluating society scientifically, had fully developed. Only by placing the problem of Socialism at the very centre of the inquiry could one interpret adequately the various ideologies which had tried to explain historical development in the past. The rise and growth of Socialist and Communist ideas, he said, was merely an attempt to

discover the laws of the development and structure of society; and on the basis of a knowledge of these laws to clarify the means of practical activity with the aim of eliminating—in a given system of institutions, in a given structure—all those phenomena which stand in the way of progress and the welfare of the masses; to remove those factors which transform the *progressive* development of society into a *circular* process which repeats itself eternally, and finds no way of escape.[92]

Unlike the varying political doctrines, Socialist ones were therefore aimed at eliminating not the symptoms of this recurrent crisis but its deep-seated causes. Naturally those whom Lavrov called 'religious socialists' or 'political metaphysicists' had been unable to assume this rôle. But now society itself had laid the foundations for what he too called 'scientific Socialism', i.e. a notion capable of avoiding the repetitions of history in order to assure harmonious progress.

In this conception Lavrov tried to merge the reforming side of his mentality—the need which he always asserted, for critical thought and hence the value of the intelligentsia—with his Socialist determination to change the very foundations of society and consequently also the rhythm of historical development.

In *Vpered* he applied this conception in detail to an examination of the various ideologies of European Socialism in the 'seventies. Together with Smirnov he wrote a commentary called *News of the Working Class Movement*, which gives us one of the best overall pictures of the development of Socialism published at that time. He showed remarkable curiosity and patience in collecting news from various countries in Europe, and played a considerable part in spreading more exact information in Russia on trade unions, strikes, and the political and intellectual life of workers' groups in the West.

When he began this commentary, the International was already broken. But Lavrov was convinced that the demands which it had expressed would not in the long run be stifled by temporary schisms. Engels described his attitude to the struggle between Marx and Bakunin as eclectic and uncertain. Yet this attitude was deliberate because he was convinced that the unifying force of the working class movement as a whole would end by triumphing. He frequently made concessions on those points which were most bitterly disputed, with the aim of retaining the essentials.

It was true, he said, that to make progress the working class movement would have to solve some fundamental problems; above all it would have to find a formula 'to unite the proletariat with the intellectual part of the bourgeoisie which comes to join its ranks out of sincere conviction'.

It is a remarkable fact that the difficulties of this task are not clearly seen in the ruling circles of either of the parties of the International. The problem arises in the masses. It then comes out into the open, but each time it falls under the blows of the logic of debates. And then once again it is reborn, because it is a living problem which can only be solved by life itself.[93]

Obviously the situation of Populism in Russia made Lavrov feel this problem with particular intensity.

Even more important, the working class movement must bring to an end the controversy which had divided it, and take up a united standpoint toward politics and the State. He then scrutinized with special care the internal conflicts in the anarchist wing of the International, and gave his final conclusions on this in a full-scale essay which constitutes the entire fourth volume of *Vpered* which came out in London in 1876.[94]

The International, he said, had represented an attempt to unite the forces of the working classes into a single organization, into something which aimed to be 'a State without territory'. It was to have a central authority in the General Council. But it had met with obstacles which had finally smashed it to pieces. Above all it had been faced with real existing territorial States. And so there had grown up national workers' parties. These had fought to win power within individual countries when they were governed by the democratic system, or to destroy absolute power in countries where such was the form of government. In either case they had inevitably been absorbed into national politics. Then the International had met with opposition from those within its very ranks who wanted the central power to be more active, and even transformed into the centre of a great conspiracy. Bakunin's *Alliance*, despite its anarchist theories, had aimed to turn the 'State without territory' into an absolute and secret State. On the other hand, others, such as the anarchist followers of Proudhon's mutualism, had ended by repudiating the central authority of the International.

The different factions into which it had been divided represented these different tendencies. The followers of Lassalle had been most for the State and the nation; the federalists had raised the problem of the local authority of the various federations, etc. It was natural that the problem of the State had become the fundamental subject of the controversy; indeed, on the solution of this question depended the organization of the International itself.

In the end it had become clear that everyone, even the anarchists, admitted some statist elements. Lavrov was thinking mainly of De Paepe and his report to the Congress of 1874. In an earlier work Lavrov had pointed out that the real problem of the time was not to drive the workers forward against capitalism (for they were perfectly aware that this was their enemy) but rather to show them their final objective and to make possible its achievement; to foresee the problems of future society and not be too worried by charges of Utopianism.[95] And in this present work Lavrov repeated that only this objective would give 'meaning and significance to the revolutionary activities of Socialists of all countries' and claimed that it should be formulated as follows: 'A society in which the element of the State is reduced to a minimum so insignificant that it can be looked upon as really eliminated.'[96] Anyone who did not admit this principle was not a Socialist. Discussions could be and should be developed on the methods for bringing about this ideal, but the controversy on the State should be about methods and tactics, not principle. Only in this way could they overcome the internal divisions which had destroyed the International.

Lavrov then accepted in the main the idea of a State power which would gradually diminish with the development of 'the communal solidarity of labour', and just because of this it was useless to think that the State could disappear at a single blow, either by destroying it or, worse, by eliminating all central power in the workers' organization.

Organized revolutionary forces must accept some element of control in their ranks, even though they knew that this was a germ of statism. Everything would depend on how the future revolution was managed. It was up to them to leave the doors open for the development of a Socialist society which would be able to eliminate all elements of constriction.

Lavrov thought of this revolution in terms of Russia. It is worth while looking in detail at the description he gives of this, because it is one of the most precise accounts we have of the Populists' view of the revolution for which they were fighting.

A local disturbance on a big enough scale is supported by risings which break out simultaneously in other parts of the country. The army, which has been worked at for some time by propaganda, shows itself to be untrustworthy in the hands of the government. Its defeat leads to the fire spreading quickly over a vast area. Under the leadership of organized members of the Social-Revolutionary Union made up mostly of peasants, groups of people who want a social revolution appear in the villages with instructions to turn all private estates into 'communal, undivided land' and to merge all property 'into a single property of all the workers' . This call, backed by news of the successes of the revolution in other villages, arouses over a vast area the unemployed, the poorest members of the families, destitute peasants, those who now, despite hard work, have no means of feeding themselves every day of the year; and, finally, the majority of workmen and small townsfolk. The terrified *kulaks* and the 'educated' landowners and members of the administration perish in the popular rising or are quite content to hide themselves in face of the storm. In the capital and other centres of the State, the members of the Social-Revolutionary Union (who spring mostly from the intelligentsia) have eliminated or paralysed the organs of government, if not everywhere at least in most places . . . And so the conditions in which the future society of Russia on working class Socialist foundations must be constructed are determined by the development of events themselves. The popular groups organized in the Social-Revolutionary Union constitute the natural kernel of the new organization. They will have nothing new or artificial to invent; they are already members of groups historically formed in the people, of *obshchinas* and *artels*. These groups will continue to exist, but, from now on, there will no longer be heard in the *mir* the voice of the wealthy *kulaks* who previously held the *obshchinas* in slavery. The owner of the inn no longer has any influence; no longer can the policeman's bell be heard in the village . . . no longer is there a place for the recruiting sergeant in the *artel* . . .[97]

But for this society to develop towards communal ownership, work for all and working class solidarity, it was essential to do everything to resist the temptation to fall back into the old forms of administration and government. And the worst of these temptations would be to rebuild the State and the police outside the centre. A central organization would be necessary for essential services, i.e. committees for work, supplies, social security, etc., and to these problems Lavrov devotes much time. If necessary, war would be organized, but it would be mainly a partisan war. Deliverance would come in the form of a preventive agreement with the German and Austrian Socialists to give all possible support to the movement 'in the event of it falling to Russia to begin the struggle before an open clash occurs in other countries'.[98] In any case the important thing was to save those elements which would further the formation of a new society: popular justice, development of schools, freedom of the press. This, of course, must be conditioned by the issue of printing presses to 'local groups', but it must in any case be maintained. Even opponents must have the right to say what they thought, and there must be no limitation of any kind on the controversy between various Socialist currents or, in Lavrov's words, 'Populist currents —a name which can, I think, claim to include all the groups of which we are speaking'.[99]

Such were the ideas and such the programme which received four volumes of theoretical formulation in the *Vpered* and were later spread as propaganda in the more lively newspaper of the same name which Lavrov edited in London between 1874 and 1876; and again in a pamphlet published in 1874 in reply to Tkachev's accusations.[100]

To edit and print his periodical Lavrov had collected a group of Russian exiles in one of the poorer districts of London. The group was made up of a few intellectuals, sailors and workers, who lived a life of Spartan rigour. They lived in isolation, and some could not even speak English. They worked hard and were inspired by the same dedicated spirit which took so many different forms in contemporary Russia itself. Together they built up one of the most interesting Socialist papers in Europe. The *Vpered* was imbued with the studious, sometimes pedantic, spirit of Lavrov himself; it had none of the liveliness of Herzen's *Kolokol*, but it aimed to be and succeeded in being an organ to 'prepare' the Populist spearhead.

It came to an end when Lavrov gave up the editorship, following a meeting of his followers from St Petersburg, Kiev and London, which was held in Paris in autumn 1876. The exact reasons for his resignation are not known.

It is, however, likely that, from what he heard of the reactions that the *Vpered* aroused in Russia, Lavrov felt that it no longer corresponded to the needs of the moment. In Russia a more active phase of the struggle was beginning with the formation of *Zemlya i Volya* and then *Narodnaya Volya*. The *Vpered* had had its day.[101]

What influence had it had in the development of the movement in Russia? The evidence at our disposal is often vague and even contradictory. It would appear, however, that Lavrov's general formulation of Populist thought and his ideas on Socialism had a wide circulation and played a considerable part in shaping the atmosphere of the 'seventies; whereas his direct instructions, advice and practical hints seem to have met with only a limited response and were accepted by a very small number of people. The Lavrovists, in the strict meaning of the word, were few, and played only a marginal part in the development of the movement.

It was not that Lavrov lacked faith in this movement. Though he can be considered the most 'Western' of the theorizers of Russian Populism; though he never stopped stressing the importance of the example of working class organizations in Germany, England and Italy; and though he was the closest of all to Marxism, yet Lavrov cherished a profound hope that Russia would be the country to initiate the social revolution. In 1873, for the centenary of Pugachev's revolt, Lavrov had written an article to draw a parallel between the events of 1773 in America and those which were taking place in Russia at that time. He concluded that despite its crudity, it was the revolt of the Russian peasants and not the beginnings of liberalism in America which pointed to the future. Pugachev's revolt had in fact been a social revolution.

The manifestos of an illiterate Cossack who followed an absurd religious faith, signed with the forged name of an idiot whom nobody knew (Peter III), contained more vital social principles, more solid promises, more threatening and certain prophecies for the future, than those contained in all the humanitarian 'codes' of Catherine II, and even in all the liberal and radical prophecies against throne and altar, that echoed along the banks of the Thames, the Seine and the Delaware.[102]

And now these prophecies were being realized in the Russian revolutionary movement.

Lavrov expressed the same hope in a kind of fable which was published in the second volume of the *Vpered* in 1874. He had tried to write this two years earlier in such a way that it could be published in a Russian review.[103] He imagined a dialogue between a business man, a statesman, a student, a man called the Inquisitor, and a workman called Babeuf.[104] They had a long discussion on political, social and religious problems, which was eventually interrupted by the unexpected and uninvited arrival of a young man of twenty-five looking like a typical Russian revolutionary. Everyone gazed at him suspiciously and fiercely. 'Only Babeuf, from his very first words, felt a feeling of sympathy for the newcomer's open look and his bold and sincere words.' The revolutionary then said that he had carefully studied the books of European authorities, and felt a feeling of solidarity with what the companions and followers of Babeuf had done for the European proletariat. But in Russia things were different. First and foremost the State must be destroyed; it was not even thinkable to turn it into an instrument which could be of use to the masses.

The history of the Russian State is the history of the systematic economic looting, intellectual oppression and moral corruption of our country. Every progressive thing that has been done in Russia has been done against the State, and everything that has come from that source has been harmful to society.[105]

The ideal of the Russian revolutionaries was to attack and destroy it. And to achieve this they could not act with the objectivity which sociologists had adopted towards these problems until then. A real passion for society was essential. Thus the young man expressed his beliefs to the representatives of all the bourgeois and proletarian classes of the West.

But even this declaration of faith contained Lavrov's own special ideas on the need to prepare oneself and above all to develop propaganda. This message—interpreted as an appeal for prudence and patience—restricted Lavrov's followers in St Petersburg in numbers and activity.

The group contained about thirty young men, nearly all students, coming mainly from the School of Medicine, the Technological Institute, etc. One of the most active organizers and leading spirits of this group was Lev Savelevich Ginsburg. In the words of a contemporary he was 'an intelligent and energetic person, extremely cultivated, and very popular among the young men, and in meetings spoke intelligently about the need for propagating Socialist ideas'.[106] It was probably he who came to Zurich to organize in conjunction with Lavrov and Smirnov the publication of the Vpered, and he was in charge of relations with the exiles. He lived in a small students' collective and was often hungry.[107] He had a reputation for being especially lucky in escaping from the police. One day, for instance, during a police raid, he had tried to eat the whole of Tkachev's pamphlet against Lavrov, which he had taken with him to study. Besides him there were many young doctors. One of them, Khudadov, a Georgian, was still active in the revolution of 1905, when he was stabbed to death in the streets of Tiflis. Among the most active technicians was Anton Feliksovich Taksis, of French origin (Taxis), as was also Vasily Egorovich Varzar, the author of one of the most successful propaganda booklets of the time, printed on the Vpered's press.[108] He later became a well-known authority on statistics and wrote important books on factories, strikes and Russia's social problems in general. A similar road was followed by his comrade, Alexander Stepanovich Semyanovsky; but his brother Evgeny met with a very different fate. He too supported 'propaganda', by which he meant chiefly the duty of Russian intellectuals to make known the Socialist movement of the West to the workers and the peasants of their country. 'Propaganda must be as clean and transparent as a crystal; it must clarify and not cloud the people's consciousness.' To those Populists who thought of drawing closer to the people by making use of religious formulas and referring to the *Raskol*, he said that such methods were inadequate and produced harmful results. The very history of religious movements had not yet been studied enough. 'Do not let us look at our historians. They have not yet worked out a scientific working method; we must learn from those in the West.'[109] He was arrested in 1875 for spreading propaganda in the army, and was sentenced by the Senate to twelve years' hard labour at Kara. On 1st January 1881 he committed suicide, leaving a letter to his parents of rare integrity and strength of mind.[110]

The Lavrovists did not extend their organization beyond the capital, though in Moscow they could count on the active support of Alexander Sergeyevich Buturlin. Buturlin sprang from an aristocratic family and was implicated in the Nechaev affair for which he was sentenced to five years' banishment in Western Siberia. He later cooperated with Tolstoy in his religious researches.

There is no need to spend further time on other individual members of the Lavrovist group though it is perhaps worth noting that (together with the man who was to become its most detailed chronicler, N. G. Kulyabko-Koretsky) the great majority of its members came from the south and the Ukraine, generally from Chernigov, Kiev or Kharkov. If we pursue the story of their lives after the 'seventies, we quickly see that these young men turned into well-known doctors and important scholars. Only very rarely did this circle give rise to men who devoted their lives to political and revolutionary activities. Lavrov's propaganda tended to create new intellectual leaders rather than rebels. This was already obvious even when they were still poor students at the time of the movement 'to go to the people' and were only concerned to propagate their ideas. One of the men who took part in the 'trial of the hundred and ninety-three' later said that at the meetings of this time the Bakuninists had a crushing majority whereas the Lavrovists could be counted on the fingers of one hand. 'I remember that they could be recognized by their outward appearance; they were dressed more elegantly, they were better washed, their hair was combed better, they spoke more gently, their hands were white.'[111] And they always insisted on the need to devote oneself above all to intellectual preparation.

For some years they succeeded by means of smugglers in getting the *Vpered* across the frontier and widely distributing it; so much so that towards the end of its existence the number of letters and articles which were received by the editors in London was constantly increasing. Indeed these had become so considerable that they enabled Lavrov and Smirnov to give an ample and detailed picture of life in Russia, in some ways resuming one of the functions of Herzen's *Kolokol*. They had also made some contacts with the workers in the capital; and even if this is one of the least known sides of their activities, there is no doubt that, as we will see, they had considerable influence on the early development of the working class movement in the 'seventies. But their activities could extend no further, and when the *Vpered* stopped its publications in London, the St Petersburg group too decided to liquidate itself at the end of 1879.

The peak of their success had coincided with the discussions that accompanied the movement 'to go to the people'. At that time the problem of propaganda could justly be considered fundamental. But they had no faith in an immediate revolution, and so they did not have the strength to re-form themselves after the repression. They had not tried to find new conspiratorial or fighting tactics. Their reading of the *Vpered* and the news they got from it of the working class movement in the West had driven them to give up working in the villages and to look rather to the factories and urban workers.[112] Lavrov's sociological ideas prompted a calmer outlook and led them to expect social transformation from a development of the economic situation rather than from a revolution. And so they adopted a policy of waiting and of intelligent observation rather than active participation in the strife. Less and less did they believe in the peasant *obshchina* and its capacity for resisting the State and the bourgeoisie.

It would inevitably disappear, to give place to an economic structure of a bourgeois type.

Science itself showed the innate necessity for a dissolution of the patriarchal *obshchinas* which were unable to constitute a rationally organized society. Despite the fact that the *Vpered* constantly told them that for that very reason it was essential to organize the peasants so as to allow them to withstand the pressure of the State and economic development, and to lead them to higher and more perfect forms of association, these followers of Lavrov lost all faith in their chances of realizing a programme of this kind, and confined themselves more and more to their task of educating the workers.

Besides the Lavrovists were never distinguished by any special energy or boldness; in practice their influence became weaker and weaker after 1877.[113]

As Plekhanov later said, some of them at least eventually justified their lack of activity by basing themselves on the inevitable need for capitalism to develop in Russia too. 'We must leave it to the liberals to win political freedom, and only then on the basis of this freedom must we begin to organize the proletariat.'[114] But this was a consequence that few of the Lavrovists drew from their ideological premises, and then only when their movement was already declining. During their active years they had in any case helped to build up an attitude of mind which had distinctly social-democratic characteristics.

18. THE CHAIKOVSKISTS AND THE MOVEMENT 'TO GO TO THE PEOPLE'

THE VIOLENT DISCUSSIONS within the circles which had given birth to Nechaev's group and the deep impression made by his trial were the immediate prelude to the movement that developed during the first years of the new decade.

Few had remained faithful to Nechaev to the very end and there had been considerable opposition to him since his earliest declarations. Still greater numbers turned away from the spirit and tactics that he had advocated when their results were exposed at his trial. The very men who had been his enemies now invigorated the new phase of Populism.

Indeed the Tsarist State itself, by striking at the most advanced elements of the movement and by bringing to light its strangest and most distorted features in the hope of later destroying it whole, in the event merely allowed a far wider movement to develop. Historians who regard the Nechaev affair as a mere isolated incident—an extraneous element in the development of Populism—are only giving historical sanction to a direct result of the repression.

From the point of view of organization Nechaev's followers can be regarded as the last of the provincial groups—bodies which came into being independently, which took action consistent with their own strength and their own ideas, which tried to join up with those who held similar tendencies in other towns, but which had little real chance of development. Here, too, Nechaev had been the true successor of *Young Russia*.

With the beginning of the new decade and the revival of the movement there was a momentary lull in the extremism so characteristic of the eastern regions of Kazan, of the Volga, and of Moscow itself. The movement which was to find its outlet in the plans 'to go to the people' started in the capital. St Petersburg had scarcely been affected by the tendencies of Nechaev's group, and it now resumed the rôle as leader that had been lost with the dissolution of the first *Zemlya i Volya*. New moves towards centralization were to go hand in hand with wider territorial extension of the new organizations. The initiative was no longer to come from the provinces; but these were to be more and more deeply affected and to find their natural place in a general current. Conditions (groups of students, secrecy, etc.) were still the same and led to a decentralization in organization, always leaving a wide field for local initiative, which could be developed into plans for the independence of different groups, etc. But from the very first years of the new decade traces of a current not merely wider but without rivals and with its source at St Petersburg can be found.

This amplification of organization and mental attitude was accompanied and, in some cases, caused by the spread of the component groups. The numbers who joined the movement strikingly increased. The word 'masses' has been employed, and if by this is meant a constantly increasing participation in clandestine organizations, the term is appropriate. There is even something spectacular in this kind of secret levy between 1870 and 1873. A list of those who began their activities at this time includes nearly all who were later to found *Zemlya i Volya* and *Narodnaya Volya*. They were often extremely young, and yet were already sure of themselves and from the very beginning their dedication was complete.

The width and depth of this movement have led many to declare that Populism really began at this time and should be dated from the preparation of the movement 'to go to the people'. Even if this is not historically exact, as I believe earlier chapters of this book may have shown, this period can certainly be considered the real 'springtime' of the movement.

From the point of view of methods of propaganda, too, the atmosphere was now very different from the 'sixties.

We must note that the system at present used by the revolutionary party gives us very few legal pretexts; and, in general, so little appears on the surface that it mostly escapes detection. The methods employed by the police and the administration are today utterly ineffectual in preventing and suppressing the criminal activity of a careful agitator.

So ended a report by General Potapov, head of the Third Section, in March 1875. It is true that these words were written with a view to obtaining more money for the police. But in substance they give a vivid picture of the tactics adopted by the leading movement of these years, i.e. the movement of the Chaikovskists, as it is generally called from the name of one of its organizers.[1]

No formalities were needed to take part in this organization; there were no statutes or written programmes; its ultimate aim was to spread Socialist ideas. For this purpose its members planned to make the greatest possible use of legally printed books.

This was a new kind, rather than a deliberate lack, of organization. There was a group at the helm and it obeyed the rules of conspiracy far more carefully and far more coldly than those earlier groups who had talked and dreamed so much about plots of various kinds. The attempt to make use of legal methods in their propaganda was only one aspect of the Chaikovskists' activities: they too ended by having their illegal printing presses. Their arrest prevented the drawing up of a programme; but their discussions on the subject were frequent. They constantly reconsidered their various ideas and aspirations, and such discussions soon gave rise to a communal spirit which was an adequate substitute for any explicit doctrine.

It was this communal spirit that distinguished them and gave them vitality. It enabled new elements and new groups to join them and afforded Populism the opportunity to develop into a movement of ever wider ramifications. Their very lack of a rigid programme allowed the Chaikovskists to build a platform on which the debate between the followers of Lavrov and Bakunin could be heard. It was the Chaikovskists who laid the foundations of a Populism which, as it absorbed them, modified both the anarchism of Bakunin and the Socialism of Lavrov. The Chaikovskists, in this sense, can be called the first large Populist movement.

But for this very reason, the movement, unlike those that preceded it, has left few documents. Its history lies in the activities of its members and the various propagandist ventures they undertook.

This time, however, after so long, their appeal met with a response. Their propaganda had an effect which had not been experienced since the beginning of the 'sixties, and this profoundly influenced their development. The life of the group was not turned in on itself by the rigid impenetrability of the surrounding world, as had happened at the time of Ishutin and Nechaev. And so we do not find in them the frantic determination to use any means to drag others along with them. Their propaganda could afford to be slower and more systematic.

They no longer needed to indulge in Machiavellian intrigues or the glorification of a revolutionary *élite*. It was enough for their purpose to rely on the idea that guided all their activities: the 'debt' that the educated classes, the intellectuals, owed to the people. So their activities were no longer to be carried out at a special time. They were rather to represent the fulfilment of a duty at all times and in any circumstances. This ethical conception of their political ideal freed them from conspiratorial and revolutionary methods. It was this idea which at last gave them, after so many ventures in the past, sufficient momentum to escape from the enclosed world of sects. As always happens when politics are expressed in moral terms, this conception too may appear ingenuous; in fact, however, it revealed a new source of vitality.

L. E. Shishko, one of the members and a memorialist of the time, has rightly emphasized this:

Undoubtedly every revolutionary movement always contains somewhere within itself some ethical basis, so that from this point of view the movement of the 'seventies was in no way original. But its special characteristic was that here ethical motives played an exclusive rôle. People joined together mainly as a result of the intensity of their subjective state of mind and not out of loyalty to this or that revolutionary doctrine.

And he recalled, as an example of this, that when a potential recruit was under discussion, moral judgment prevailed.[2]

So powerful was this ethical spirit among the Chaikovskists that it was sometimes expressed in religious terms—a religion which gave a more or less simple symbolical form to their aspirations to purity and total sacrifice. But a religious expression of this kind was always only marginal. The Chaikovskists cannot be described in terms of a political manifesto or of a religious credo. Their historical importance lies in the fact that they wanted to live in complete accordance with the idea of a duty to the people.

Despite the name by which they are usually known, Mark Andreyevich Natanson was their real founder. The group which he collected in the School of Medicine, where he was a student, was already inspired by ideas which were to be typical of the new period (even before the formation of the Commune of Vulfovsky Street in October 1869, and the simultaneous birth of Chaikovsky's group). It had a considerable influence in weaning young men from the inspiration of Nechaev. The students had at this time promoted an inquiry among the peasants to see whether they were really ready for an immediate revolution, as Nechaev claimed. The negative result of this inquiry convinced them of the need for the slower measures of propaganda and infiltration.[3]

From the very beginning the group in the School of Medicine, led by Natanson, acted along these lines. It was made up 'of bold, strong and trustworthy *raznochintsy*',[4] V. Alexandrov, A. I. Serdyukov, V. S. Ivanovsky, and others. No other faculty contained students so well organized. Their library was often called the 'Jacobin Club'. This was clearly not intended to imply any special political tendency but rather the general revolutionary spirit which prevailed. And Natanson expressed this spirit more clearly than anyone. All who knew him confirmed S. L. Chudnovsky's judgment. 'He was a man of great energy and initiative and rare organizing ability.'[5] He came from the western provinces of the Russian empire. Already, when still at school, at the time of the Polish revolt of 1863, he had had trouble with the police. 'And later, too, he brought to his activities as a revolutionary some of the conspiratorial ability of the Poles', Chaikovsky was to say.[6] He was a devoted admirer of Chernyshevsky and specially Dobrolyubov, and he said that he was looking for a 'revolutionary ethic' which could give the movement the force of 'theoretical and practical reason'.

He was among the first to fall. As early as 1871 he was arrested and deported to the department of Archangel.[7] So began a long revolutionary career. After his return from banishment, he was again deported in 1877; and in 1890 he became one of the leading organizers of the party called *The Rights of the People*. In 1894 he was again sent to Siberia; he took part in the Socialist-Revolutionary movements; he was present at the Zimmerwald Conference, and sided with the Socialist-Revolutionaries of the Left. He died in 1919 at Berne.

After Natanson's arrest in November 1871, it was Nikolai Vasilevich

Chaikovsky who assured the continuity of the group.[8] At this time he was aged twenty, and made 'an enthralling impression' on Kropotkin.[9] He fused the temperament of a political organizer with that of a constant searcher for inner truth. 'We must be as clean and clear as a mirror', Chaikovsky said at this time; 'We must know each other so well that should there arise difficult times of persecution and struggle, we are in a position to know *a priori* how each of us will behave.' For this reason he called his group 'an Order'.[10] This religious element ended by gaining the ascendancy. After two or three years of intense activity, doubts as to his chances of success became so strong that he welcomed a religious doctrine which was both the expression and caricature of his ideal. This was the religion founded by Alexander Kapitonovich Malikov, one of those involved in the repression which followed Karakozov's attempt on the life of the Tsar. He had been banished to his native region of Orel, and there he had founded his 'deo-humanism' based on the need of each man to seek the God within himself. In the words of Frolenko, who was then beginning his activities and who soon became one of the boldest revolutionaries of *Narodnaya Volya*:

Chaikovsky saw in this preaching a revelation from above. In a flash it solved all the problems which tortured him. It gave him everything he was looking for. It corresponded completely to the demands of his soul, which was so honourable, tender and upright. There was no need for conspiracies, secrecy, revolution and revolts. It was enough to free oneself of shortcomings and vices, to feel oneself a God-man, to believe that one was this. He believed it with absolute faith, and in a flash there fell from his shoulders all the weight of the problems and doubts which tormented him. He won calm and peace of mind. This calm and contentment were reflected even in his physical health. From a thin student he soon changed into a strong well-made man.[11]

He naturally tried, but without success, to convert his friends to his new faith. They continued alone along the road which was to lead them towards the movement 'to go to the people' and the revolutionary organizations at the end of the 'seventies. 'Deo-humanism' had momentarily revealed in religious guise the moral impulse which lay at the basis of the entire movement. Chaikovsky emigrated with Malikov in 1874, and went to live in America in the Communist colony founded by Frey. He later returned to politics and took part in the revival of the Socialist-Revolutionary movement the beginning of this century.

But that feeling of distrust which had detached him as a young man from the group which traditionally bears his name, remained rooted in him. He did not in fact believe in social revolution. In 1917 he told a friend of the 'seventies who asked his opinion on the political situation in Russia: 'naturally we will have a bourgeois democratic republic',[12] and for this reason he fought against the Bolsheviks and became head of the White Government of Archangel.

Between 1871 and 1872 all the most active elements joined the St Petersburg group. We can obtain an impression of the atmosphere which prevailed in the movement at this time from the memoirs of Charushin or those of Sergey Silych Sinegub, which are even more interesting.[13]

At first one is surprised by the strangeness of the atmosphere. There is, for instance, the long chapter in Sinegub's memoirs in which he speaks without a trace of irony of his fictitious marriage, i.e. the marriage which, following a widespread custom of the times, he celebrated to free a young girl oppressed by her family. It is this determination to use the same tone and apply the same point of view when describing their own individual lives and the life of society, their own intimate thoughts and their political activities, that reveals the inner spring of this movement, the utter dedication of these young students. This apparent disappearance of a private life which is transformed into the life of the group and (at least ideally) into the life of the 'people' allows him to speak of himself with the same mixture of naive frankness and detailed seriousness which is typical of these memoirs, as it was of all the ascetic life of the Chaikovskists. It is for this reason that Sinegub's memoirs provide the best and most faithful psychological account of the movement.

It was among the Chaikovskists that Sergey Mikhailovich Kravchinsky began his extraordinary revolutionary career. 'At this time his inner life was completely closed. All his energies were directed to developing his own mind, to preparing himself for that revolutionary function which even then he knew was to be his lot. He already read many languages and had an excellent memory',[14] one of his comrades and friends later wrote of him.

The first illegal publication to pass through his hands was the *Narodnoe Delo* written by Bakunin. It was Kravchinsky who distributed it in the military academy to which he belonged. He thus came into contact with Bakunin's anarchism, and this, together with his passionate desire for self-improvement, led him even in his earliest youth to theorize about revolutionary individualism. A study of the French revolution had convinced him that 'its main purpose had been achieved through the individual energy of its heroes'.[15] In Russia, too, he thought, everything would depend on forming men of sufficient stature for the rôle which awaited them. But this must not just consist in exalting instinct. Knowledge and will must be equally powerful in the man who wanted to devote himself to the people. These were the germs of what was later to be the ideal of *Zemlya i Volya*. Kravchinsky was among the first and most characteristic figures to embody this ideal.

Individualism of this kind can be seen in another whose baptism of fire was undergone among the Chaikovskists. Dmitry Alexandrovich Klements was one of the most fully formed figures in this society and indeed of his times. He was able to fulfil a life and activities of encyclopaedic range in a country where the atmosphere of oppression and official conformity was oppressive in the extreme.[16]

Klements was born in 1848, the son of a landowner from the Saratov region. He sprang from the small nobility which was doing everything possible to maintain its position and keep in contact with the aristocracy, but often slipped right down the social scale like many French nobles before the revolution, who were condemned to lead a life almost as wretched as that of their peasants. Only one right they still retained: that of having themselves fed without working. These tiny landowners had become, as Klements was to say in his memoirs, the greatest curse of the Russian villages. The Crimean War, the call-up which had deprived them of the labour of their serfs, and finally the reforms had made their existence more and more difficult. The peasants hated them but did not know where to find support to defend their own rights, for they had no faith in the authorities of the State, who, they saw, were merely creatures of their bosses. The small nobles, on the other hand, were convinced that the government wanted to ruin them, and their complaints merely confirmed the peasants' belief that 'the manifesto of 19th February was only the beginning of freedom'.[17] Such were the experiences of Klements's youth and they instilled in his mind the ideas of a peasant revolt.

He went to school at Samara, where clandestine literature was still spreading. Herzen's *Kolokol* passed through his hands, as well as those books, such as the works of Büchner, which were typical of the positivist generation. He, too, found Chernyshevsky's *What is to be done?* an important and necessary stage in his development. The future Populists were all reading much the same books at this time, even in the most remote corners of Russia, for there were only very few Russian works to assist their development. Indeed, one of the duties of the Chaikovskists was to provide a more widespread and varied literature.

By 1866 Klements had left school. His father had not the slightest possibility of sending him to the university. However, despite all this, he succeeded in carrying on his studies, but at the cost of joining, like so many others, the 'intellectual proletariat' and eking out a mean existence by small literary works, translations, lessons, etc. At Kazan, the first stage in his university life, he came across the ashes, so to speak, of those earlier movements which had kept the students in a state of ferment. But when he reached St Petersburg he quickly joined very different circles. He got into contact with the Chaikovskist group and became one of its most active members. Some years later, in 1877, he wrote to Chaikovsky:

Yes, brother, I say it truly, in my life I have come across many people . . . but cleaner and better people than those in your group at the time of its flowering I have never seen. In that union which was ours, we were very strong, strong with the moral influence which we exercised on each other.[18]

Klements was at the centre of the work of distributing books on social problems, especially Bervi-Flerovsky's *Alphabet of Social Sciences*. This led to his being harassed by the police, but without consequences. He then devoted himself to working among the workers and peasants. Though his memoirs contain almost nothing about this period of his activities, two lines of conversation which he quotes may throw more light on his state of mind and that of his comrades than many long descriptions: '"Why are you going into the country?" I asked a friend. "We speak so much of the people, but we do not know them. I want to live the life of the people, and suffer for them."'[19] Throughout the summer of 1874 he wandered from the region of Moscow through the departments of Simbirsk and Samara, down along the Volga, 'earning enough to live, through manual work of various kinds'.[20] Morozov described him dressed as a peasant, the very embodiment of the rôle that he had chosen. But as Kravchinsky was to say, 'Under that disguise there was hidden one of the best brains in the ranks of the Russian revolutionary party.' For him, as for so many of his comrades, the preparation and realization of the movement 'to go to the people' were a kind of apprenticeship. He always kept vividly alive this complete, elementary Populism, this youthful wholehearted dedication to the people. But he was able to look upon these experiences with the eye of a politician and, after returning in secret from a temporary residence abroad, he became one of the founders of the second *Zemlya i Volya*.

Kropotkin once said that he had 'always looked upon Leonid Emmanuilovich Shishko as the purest and finest expression of the Chaikovsky group, the highest expression of their moral ideal'. Perovskaya called him 'a man not just pure, but chemically pure', and the works that he has left reflect better than most others of the kind the enthusiasm which filled him and his comrades at the beginning of the 'seventies.[21]

He was born in 1852 of a noble and rich family, and was destined to a military career. By the age of nineteen he had already decided that this was not for him, and so he entered the Technological Institute in St Petersburg, intending to acquire knowledge which could be of use when he devoted himself to the cause of the people. It was Pisarev's articles that prompted him to take up this combined positivist and Populist standpoint. Very soon, however, his friendship with Kravchinsky led to Populism winning the day. He kept up contact with the Artillery Institute, where he had been a pupil, for one reason only: he and Kravchinsky sought out a group of candidates affected by Populist ideas and gave them talks on Lavrov's *Vpered* and the life of the International. He soon gave up the Technological Institute also, hoping to become a village schoolmaster and so find a way to reach the peasants.

His participation in the Chaikovskist group in St Petersburg very soon gave him organizing responsibilities. In 1872 he wrote a propaganda pamphlet which was printed the following year in Switzerland, and which was widely circulated at the time of the movement 'to go to the people': *A few words, brothers, on how difficult it is for our brother to live on Russian soil*.[22] But above all, Shishko wanted Russian history to be used for systematic propaganda among workmen in the towns and peasants in the villages. He returned to the book that Khudyakov had written, to show how and by what means the Russian State had been founded, and he made great use of it. He continued on his own to try and explain the roots of the existing oppression. In St Petersburg and Moscow he was among the first to undertake systematic attempts to win over workmen, as well as start small workshops for young members of the intelligentsia to learn a trade and thus prepare themselves for the life which they planned to live among the peasants. In August 1874 he was arrested and spent four years' solitary confinement in the Peter-Paul fortress before being tried and sentenced to nine years' hard labour. 'After four years at Kara, I was transferred to Chita, then to Tomsk, and finally to Irkutsk. I escaped in autumn 1890 and succeeded in reaching Europe without further hindrance', he said in a brief autobiography. He was one of the first of the generation of the 'seventies to take part in the Socialist-Revolutionary party, and he died in exile in 1910.

He was able to spend only two active years in Russia. Yet when Kravchinsky in 1891 looked back on his work which had so soon been interrupted, he was right to say:

The Chaikovskists were the men who played a remarkable part in creating that moral atmosphere and bringing into effect those rules of conduct which became the code of the following generation of revolutionaries. This was the great merit of the movement which was founded entirely on personal devotion to an idea and the dedicated spirit of its members. In this task of education, Leonid Shishko undoubtedly took part with all his energy.[23]

As these examples show, the Chaikovskists were usually extremely young, on the first steps of their search for a new road. Very few could boast of any revolutionary experience. Only German Alexandrovich Lopatin and Felix Vadimych Volkhovsky came from an earlier organization, i.e. *The Society of the Rouble*, which they had founded after the fall of Ishutin's group.[24]

Lopatin, after his escape from exile in Stavropol, had been arrested during the Nechaev affair, but succeeded in fleeing abroad. In London he met Marx and had translated half *Das Kapital*, but at the beginning of 1871 he had returned in secret to Russia, planning to free Chernyshevsky from Siberia. He gave his comrades detailed information on the situation of the International (he himself had been a member of the General Council) and concerned himself with the publication of *Das Kapital* in St Petersburg. But his true interests were very different. After a series of ventures in Siberia and after two dramatic flights from prison there, he again succeeded in escaping abroad in 1874.[25] His companion, Volkhovsky, who had founded with him *The Society of the Rouble*, was also unable to carry out any large-scale activities among the Chaikovskists, whom he joined in 1873, because he was soon arrested. After four years' confinement in the Peter-Paul fortress, he was deported to the department of Tobolsk. It was not until 1889 that he succeeded in escaping, and it was only abroad that he was able to carry out extensive propaganda which merged into that of the Socialist-Revolutionary party.

Among these young men, there was only one mature personality, though he too had no revolutionary experience. This was Petr Alexeyevich Kropotkin. He was born in 1842, and the circles in which he passed his childhood and youth made it a slow and difficult process for him to break away from the upper ranks of society to which he belonged. His earliest years were spent among the aristocracy and court. 'Do you know where our family springs from?' his father would ask him, before telling him repeatedly that it was one of the highest nobility, and that their ancestors looked back to a period before the formation of the Russian State. The Kropotkins had in fact been one of those aristocratic families which had been left on one side as the Tsars became absolute monarchs, and since the seventeenth century they had held no leading rôle in politics or the administration. Petr's father was merely a typical soldier of the age of Nicholas I, stubborn and violent. His mother was descended from the Cossacks of the Ukraine who for generations had fought against Poles and Russians for their independence. In later years, Petr Alexeyevich was to say that he was 'a Scythian' combining blood from north and south.

Nicholas I in person chose him for his corps of pages, and he grew up in St Petersburg during the 'fifties, a period of high hopes, passionate reading, and ever wider contacts with the culture of the West. He always retained this breadth of view, this spirit of humanity that he had imbibed in his earliest years. The feeling of confinement and oppression which we noted in the minds of the revolutionaries of the 'sixties had no place in him, formed as he was in the intellectual world of Alexander II's early years.

The letters which he regularly exchanged with his brother Alexander are among the best surviving evidence concerning the life of the generation which was then coming to the fore.[26] In them we see a dissatisfaction with all their surroundings, a growing intolerance with the mean, niggardly attitude of the governing class, which was unable to understand and accept the consequences of the peasant reform. But this state of mind was not yet expressed in political terms. Round about 1861 both brothers were absorbed in that generalized liberalism which had not yet assumed precise outlines and which was typical of much Russian society at this time. Alexander found his concerns expressed in the *Velikoruss* and he tried to spread its ideas. But soon he too found himself faced with different prospects. 'All these political reforms', he wrote to Petr on 10th February 1861, 'do not yet have a social character. It may be that they will succeed in Russia. But I foresee a terrible revolution in the West. The proletariat is developing, and in it is growing the need for a better life. The day will come when it will no longer be prepared to remain patient, and then something terrible will begin . . . I do not know who will escape. I have no ideals; I do not believe either in Communism or in Socialism. As regards social life I will act the part of critic; I foresee a tempest, but I will not raise any banner.'[27]

It was Lavrov who, by giving expression to Alexander's interests, drove him to try and clarify them by studying philosophy. He was arrested for having corresponded with Lavrov—with whom he had made friends during a stay in Switzerland between 1872 and 1874—and deported to Siberia. There he committed suicide in 1881, when every hope of getting back his freedom had vanished and he had become convinced that all his scholarly pursuits had been crushed.

Petr, on the other hand, was from the first to choose a life of action, as can be perceived in his earliest letters. He decided to break decisively with the brilliant military career that was opening before him, and to get to know the world and men by divorcing himself from society which, in 1862, was becoming more and more oppressively reactionary in character. Between 1862 and 1867 he travelled in Siberia, taking part in geographical and scientific expeditions and living the hard life of the explorer, soldier and colonizer.[28] He had left St Petersburg as a boy. He returned a fully developed man. Though fired by the enthralling task of drawing conclusions from his scientific and geological observations, his interests turned more and more towards giving some social and political expression to his personal experiences of freedom in Siberia. To this aspiration he was finally driven by contact with the West, and a passionate study of the history of the International and the various Socialist currents which he carried out during a journey abroad. In Geneva he took part in the meetings of the Russian section of the International, but was soon attracted to the group of Bakunin's followers to whom he was introduced by Zhukovsky. He met Guillaume, Malon and other exiled members of the Commune.

I was profoundly influenced by the theories of anarchism which were beginning to be formulated in the Jura Federation, mainly through the work of Bakunin; and also by criticism of State Socialism which threatened to develop into an economic tyranny even more terrible than political despotism; and finally by the revolutionary activities of the Jura workers.[29]

But he was more impressed by the faith of the workers in their movement than by any kind of organization or political ideal. This fervour and trust presented the intellectuals with a fundamental problem. It gave them a moral obligation to devote themselves to spreading Socialist and anarchist ideas. The experiences of Western Europe convinced him that there was nothing more terrible than revolution that was not yet ripe and lacked within itself forces capable of rebuilding on new foundations. The Commune had proved this. The creation of spiritual and constructive forces for the revolution of the future was the duty of all those who were devoting themselves to preparing this revolution. It was a duty that involved him, Kropotkin.

He returned to Russia with a number of forbidden pamphlets and books which he was able to get past the frontier by means of a smuggler.[30] In St Petersburg he met D. Klements. He was already in touch with Chaikovsky, and he now joined their 'family of friends' as he described them in his memoirs. 'Those two years that I lived in the Chaikovskist group will always leave a profound impression on me. Those two years marked the peak of a period of feverish activity.'[31] He was one of the most active in spreading propaganda among the workers and in discussions within the group itself designed to formulate its ideas more exactly. At the end of March he was arrested. After two years in the Peter-Paul fortress he was taken to hospital, and there with the help of some comrades he carried out the masterly escape which he himself has so vividly described in his memoirs.

The Chaikovskist movement could not be described as really complete until in the spring of 1871 it was joined by a small group of women. O. A. Shleysner, who became Natanson's wife, E. I. Kovalskaya, M. P. Leshner and the Perets sisters were all destined to take an active part in the 'underground'. And with them were the Kornilov sisters and Sofya Perovskaya.[32]

Sofya Perovskaya was born in 1853, the daughter of a general who had been governor of the Crimea, of Pskov and eventually St Petersburg. He was dismissed after Karakozov's attempt on the life of Alexander II and then became a member of the Council of the Minister of the Interior. Sofya very soon broke away from her upper bureaucratic family. Indeed, she had no inner struggle, accustomed as she was from her mother's example to live a free and independent life in a distant country estate. This attitude was encouraged by her friendship begun in childhood with the daughter of Poggio, a Decembrist of Piedmontese origin,[33] and by her passion for study. Whatever may have been said on the subject, Sofya never took part in the worldly life of her own home. It passed her by without her even being aware of it, for she was concerned to find in political reading, and later in contact with her friends, truths which she never thought of looking for in the society of her family. Alexandra Kornilova, her intimate friend, has told how Sofya recommended her to read Mikhailov's articles on the proletariat and cooperatives, and Flerovsky's work on *The Situation of the Working Class in Russia*. When some of her comrades suggested organizing a joint reading of Marx's *Das Kapital* 'which for many years was extremely difficult and almost impossible to understand', both the Kornilov sisters and Perovskaya refused, because they thought it was best to study first of all the foundations of political economy. 'We recognized no one's authority, and we did not want to accept as faith, on the word of others, what we could not study for ourselves.'[34]

Sofya soon became the soul of the Chaikovskist group and devoted herself more and more fully to revolutionary activities.[35] Kropotkin writes:

We often met in a suburb of St Petersburg, in a little house rented by Sofya Perovskaya, who was at that time using the passport of a workman's wife. We were excellent comrades with all the female members of our group, but Sofya Perovskaya we all loved. We gave a friendly handshake to Kuvshinskaya and Sinegub's wife when we met; but when we saw Perovskaya our faces always lit up with a broad smile, although she paid little attention to us.[36]

Her life of independence coincided with the beginning of a struggle with the police and with the authorities. She embarked quite instinctively on this struggle: her spontaneity knew no doubts. Her transition from propagandist activities to the deepening struggle and terrorism, which were to lead her to the scaffold, provides the simplest and most direct example of the many who set out along the road with her during these years.

The history of the Kornilov sisters is individually less significant and socially more instructive. Their great-grandfather was a peasant. He had become rich and in 1791 he founded the firm 'Brothers Kornilov', which became one of the greatest porcelain factories in Russia. The family had remained deeply traditionalist, bound to the forms of religion and authority. This was, indeed, the case in the great majority of bourgeois families which had painfully emerged through the cracks in the feudal hierarchy of the Russian State. This state of affairs only began to change in the 'sixties. Only then had this family of great factory owners begun to throw over mediaeval habits. The process was begun by Alexander, one of the sons. He took part in the movement to found Sunday-schools for the people and proclaimed himself a materialist. In the summer he went travelling, dressed in the red shirt of the peasants and the 'nihilists'. He died young, when his sisters were not yet twenty. By the time that they reached this age they were considered by their student comrades to be among the finest representatives of a generation which dedicated itself to the people.

It is difficult to say exactly how many members there were in the St Petersburg group of the Chaikovskists, for they were held together more by friendship and common ideals than by formal rules. In 1928, nearly half a century later, three of the survivors, N. A. Charushin, M. F. Frolenko and A. Kornilova-Morozova, tried to make up an exact list of their comrades between 1871 and 1874. They estimated about thirty active members and fifteen associates.[37]

But to these we must add a group of nineteen in Moscow, eleven in Odessa, eight in Kiev and some in Kharkov, Orel, Kazan and Tula. In each of these towns there occurred, though on a different scale, what had happened in the capital. In each we come across the names of men who were to be among the boldest figures in all the movements of the 'seventies. The levy of the Chaikovskists was decisive in creating the vanguard who later 'went to the people' and joined *Zemlya i Volya* and *Narodnaya Volya*. When we come to speak of these movements and the earlier stages of Populist activity among the workmen, we will have occasion to take a closer look at these groups which were springing up far from the capital and which, as early as 1872, were already in touch with St Petersburg.

Though the Chaikovskists were distinguished by a clearly individual moral

16+

character, politically their outlook was less precise. They sprang from the opposition to Nechaev and the 'Jesuitical system of his organization'.[38] They started from a moderate standpoint which in the first stage seems indistinguishable from that of lawful reformers and even liberal constitutionalists. They only acquired a distinctly Populist and revolutionary outlook after an inner evolution, rapid though this was. Their importance can be understood only by following this development and sharing in their searches.

By 1871 they had already established a fairly large-scale organization for spreading legally printed books intended to provide the foundations of a social and political education. They were thus repudiating in practice the contempt for and rejection of culture which had inspired the more extremist followers of Ishutin and Nechaev. In general, they not only allowed but appreciated education. No one was asked or compelled to leave the university and give up his studies. They made no objections if one of them, such as Perovskaya, for example, gave up propaganda for a given period to complete her own individual preparation. Political education was considered an indispensable way of finding the road that Nechaev had looked for in renunciation and immediate action. 'We want to save the people, and we ourselves know nothing. We must begin by learning', said V. Alexandrov.[39] Even the movement 'to go to the people' often became, because of this spirit of the Chaikovskists, a kind of 'education conferred on the people'.

This propaganda they called *knizhnoe delo*, 'the cause of the book'. It proved to be a success. Some financial support was obtained from the radical liberal circles with which the Chaikovskists maintained connections.[40] Some publishers, such as Polyakov, published on credit the books that they suggested. The Kornilov sisters gave everything they could extract from their family, including their dowries, to the common fund. Books were chosen with care, both for their intrinsic importance and the possibility that the censorship would not realize their significance. Besides all this they bought back from publishers books which were already printed, and distributed these on credit or on the instalment system or below cost, paying special attention to getting them to towns in the provinces.

The most important books in their library were an early volume of the works of Lassalle, Marx's *Das Kapital* which was published in March 1872, Lavrov's *Historical Letters*, a second edition of Bervi-Flerovsky's *The Situation of the Working Class in Russia*, and his *Alphabet of Social Sciences* already mentioned above, and A. K. Sheller's* *The Proletariat in France* and *On Associations*.[41] They also did what they could to spread the classics of 1861 from Chernyshevsky to Shchapov, and made themselves responsible for reprinting and circulating some social novels. They further tried to publish translations of Louis Blanc's *History of the French Revolution*, Lange's *The Working Class Problem* and a history of the Commune. But they were now faced with ever-increasing difficulties. Chaikovsky's house was

* Pseudonym for A. Mikhailov.

searched four times and he himself arrested twice. Natanson was eventually banished to the north of Russia. The exploitation of legal methods had produced good results and had brought into circulation in Russia the fundamental books of Socialist thought in the 'seventies. But its day was now over.

So they now came to the conclusion that only by founding a press abroad and arranging for the books to be secretly conveyed into Russia could they extend 'the cause of the book' and avoid the obstacles of the censorship. At the beginning of 1871 two members of the group were sent to Switzerland and succeeded in starting a small publishing firm. L. B. Goldenberg and V. M. Alexandrov began to publish small pamphlets suitable for propaganda among the people, as well as the works of Chernyshevsky.[42] It was probably Klements who, starting from an adaptation of Chatrian, wrote the *Story of a French Peasant* which became one of the most widely circulated of these booklets.[43] Kravchinsky wrote his *Tale of a Kopek*.[44] But still more typical of the tendencies which now prevailed in St Petersburg were two pamphlets, one (perhaps by S. A. Zhemanov) on Stenka Razin[45] and another on Pugachev.[46] Along with various other pamphlets, among them a *Collection of Songs*,[47] these constituted their main fund of propaganda for the next ten years.

This increasing attention paid to popular editions corresponded to a rapid transformation within the Chaikovskist group itself. Its members now wished to pass over to direct propaganda. The 'Cause of the Book' was very soon replaced by 'The Cause of the Workers'. The Chaikovskists were thus the first to build foundations of any solidity within the factories of St Petersburg. These pioneering ventures will be dealt with when the working class movement of the time is examined.

But these contacts with the workers occasioned the series of arrests which destroyed the nucleus that had been growing ever since 1869 and put an end to their activities. By the winter of 1873, i.e. even before the movement 'to go to the people', the Chaikovskists no longer existed as an organized body.

The arrests also put a sudden end to attempts to clarify their programme which they had been intensifying at the same time. The moral conviction that brought the group into being was no longer enough. They felt too that something more than the practical spirit which had sustained them—and indeed enabled them to become the most efficient Populist organization of all these years—was now needed. Contact with the workers and their first ventures into the villages raised problems which had now to be formulated in political terms. Moreover, their ever-closer links with the émigrés were compelling them to choose between the ideas of Lavrov and those of Bakunin. On his return from Switzerland, Kropotkin hastened the drawing up of a programme.

In November 1873 he proposed a kind of manifesto, the first part of which examined what he called 'the forms and conditions of equality'.[48] He attacked handing over all property to the hands of the State. 'This would merely be a suicide of society.' His ideal was that of a federation of independent agricultural communities. But how could this ideal be realized? He was inspired by the breadth of his humanity—a quality shared by all the finest figures of his generation—to write that the needs of all men were fundamentally identical and that therefore 'the tendencies and hopes expressed by the workers of the West will be accepted with understanding by ours also'. Did not he himself—like all his comrades—read Marx and Lassalle, mentally substituting peasants of the Russian villages or textile workers in St Petersburg for the English and German workmen? The differences between them could not lie in ideals, which were common to Russia and the West, but in tactics.

Kropotkin appreciated the need for revolutionary propaganda but he wanted it to make an advance on what had so far been carried out by his comrades. The movement itself must be fused with the people; the Socialists must adopt the life of the peasants and the workmen, and merge with it. In fact he was giving expression to a demand which they all keenly felt and which led to the movement 'to go to the people'.

From this demand he drew the extreme consequences. He criticized all cooperatives and was against mutual loans banks. 'Any temporary improvement in the life of a small group of people in our present gangster society only helps to keep the conservative spirit intact.' On the other hand, he did suggest that workers' communities should be constituted in which all wages should be put into a common pool. Even strikes and disturbances might be useful in individual cases, but no absolute principle could be established. The main purpose must be to recruit new forces, to organize new elements and to instil a determined state of mind into the workers.

He ended by speaking of the International. Only when a real force had been created among the peasants and the workers in Russia would the problem arise of whether or not to join it. And then they would certainly choose the federalist and not the statist wing. But for the moment there was no problem. The movement must continue on its own road and fulfil its own requirements. 'Here we intend to develop independently.'

Charushin has told how for some evenings his comrades discussed this programme. Kropotkin added various technical points. He proposed the organization of 'armed peasant bands' and called them by the old Russian name of *druzhiny*. Frolenko has told us something of this plan which was known only to a few. Though no attempt was made to put it into practice, it was the prelude to the activities of the 'rebels' in Southern Russia some years later. The plan was to unite 'those fragments of the groups which still survived [already severely denuded by the arrests] and to found an armed band even if it contained only a hundred people; to choose some district where memories of Stenka Razin and Pugachev were still alive; and to move towards Moscow, on the way stirring up the peasants against the gentry and local authorities.'[49]

As can be seen from this, these plans were the result of the disappointments produced by their activities among the workmen which had very soon led to the fall of a great number of their comrades. This disappointment soon took a different shape, when they abandoned the towns and plunged into country life there to resume in other forms their work of propaganda and agitation.

Was Kropotkin's manifesto really accepted as a common statement of policy? Shishko claims this, but others, in an equally good position to know the truth, deny it. In any case, this discussion once more shows the wide, in some senses fluid, character that the organization of the Chaikovskists kept to the very end. Kropotkin's manifesto reflected his comrades' state of mind faithfully enough but it contained an element of extremism and a sympathy for Bakunin's ideas which they were not all ready to share. Lermontov, a member of the *Russian Brotherhood*, had already unsuccessfully tried to make them adopt an anarchist programme and had eventually broken away.

'Here we intend to develop independently', Kropotkin had ended. He was evidently trying to satisfy the wish that prevailed in St Petersburg to avoid an alliance with either of the two wings of the émigrés or, on the ideological plane, with any of the currents of the International.

What was the essential originality of this group, which was felt and expressed in different ways by others of its members also? To this question we may reply that it lay in their unanimous, deeply felt and deliberate repudiation of any expression of constitutionalism. They held the typically Populist conviction that any concessions to freedom would only have made it still more difficult to effect the quick transformation of Russia along Socialist lines. It was not just faith in the *obshchina* and the Socialist development of peasant communities that held this movement together, but rather the translation of this faith into political terms, and its opposition to any liberal tendencies. As Shishko has rightly pointed out, they were not antipolitical because they wanted Socialism to develop in a peaceful, trade-union, cooperative direction or because they closed their eyes to the problem of Tsarist absolutism. They supported a policy of direct contact between the new intelligentsia and the people, above and beyond interference by the State; just as they were then, and were still more some years later, for direct action against absolutism itself.

These beliefs were strengthened by the situation of liberalism at the beginning of the 'seventies. Even in Russia the Paris Commune haunted the imagination of constitutionalists who believed in law and order. One of the Chaikovskists summed up the attitude of his comrades when he said that 'perhaps never, either before or since, was liberalism so weak as in the 'seventies'.[50] Despite their efforts, they never succeeded in establishing any real contact with the left wing and the most radical elements. At the end of 1871, when they were still in the very first phase of their activities, Natanson,

Klements, Volkhovsky, the young Perovskaya and a few others went to a meeting which was held in the house of Professor Tagantsev. About fifty people met there to discuss a report *On the Essence of the Constitution*, based on a work of Lassalle. The objections of the Chaikovskists were summed up by Charushin who was present: 'But among us here in Russia, who will fight for a constitution? Our privileged classes, the bourgeoisie and the aristocracy are weak and will not fight for the constitution. They will prefer to defend their class interests on the quiet and from behind, which in any case they are already doing very successfully. From the point of view of the interests of the people as a whole, a class constitution of this kind (which would be the only one these classes could obtain, even if they wanted to) would be of no advantage and would only increase the exploitation of the great popular masses . . . There is, in fact, only one strand of the population which is really interested in political liberty, and that is our intelligentsia. But it too is weak, and, taken on its own, is materially impotent in the struggle against absolutism. For all these reasons our intelligentsia, which for the most part is socialistically inclined, will not fight for a constitution pure and simple.'[51] Charushin ended by saying that contact with the radical-liberal elements had only made his comrades still more aware of their position and strengthened their will to rely only on the peasant and workers. A year later they tried to consider the problem once more and see whether it would be possible to establish a link with the autonomous provincial administrations of the *Zemstvos*. Once again, however, they came to the same conclusion. In the manifesto quoted above, Kropotkin clearly opposed making any further ventures of the kind. Everyone now considered them to be superfluous and harmful.

At the same time as drawing up a programme, the Chaikovskists tried to start a periodical. Kropotkin spoke of this in the manifesto, declaring that it would be the only way to develop harmoniously those internal discussions which had remained embryonic in the St Petersburg groups but which had grown far more acute among the émigrés. There had already been talk of a periodical in 1871. Like so many of their predecessors, the Chaikovskists thought that Chernyshevsky would have been the ideal editor. Hence Lopatin's attempt to free him. Meanwhile approaches were made to N. K. Mikhailovsky and then to Bervi-Flerovsky, with no results. Practical problems were not easily solved; the review would have to be published abroad, and this naturally made contacts difficult. Mikhailovsky did not want to give up his chances of writing for the conventional press. And though Flerovsky was at this time highly admired by the young revolutionaries, he was undoubtedly a curious character, little suited to the control of such a complex organization.

In 1872 the Chaikovskists helped to organize the flight abroad of the writer Sokolov, who was exiled in the department of Archangel. In December of the same year, they performed a similar service for Tkachev. But for various reasons neither of these met their requirements. Would Lavrov solve the problem?

After discussions which are difficult to reconstruct from the biographical sources at our disposal, it was decided to send Klements to Switzerland for negotiations. When he was prevented from going, he was replaced by M. V. Kupryanov in the summer of 1872.[52] Kupryanov came to an agreement with Lavrov, and entirely ignored Bakunin. But was he, in fact, authorized to take such a step? Kropotkin denies it. Different ideas from his, more immediately revolutionary in character, were now prevailing among the Chaikovskists.[53]

A passage from Charushin's autobiography sums up the real conclusion of this ideological debate.

We were neither Lavrovists nor Bakuninists in the literal meaning of these words. We did not think that it was possible to transfer the revolutionary experiences of Europe on to Russian soil in their entirety. For we maintained that the utterly different conditions of the situation in Russia demanded a search for methods to correspond to this state of affairs.[54]

The writer who proved to be the best interpreter of their ideas, interests and hopes, was Vasily Vasilevich Bervi (Flerovsky). While their organization was in its first phase, Flerovsky was closely associated with it. Subsequently, however, he joined a rival group which was politically removed from theirs. There will later be occasion to discuss this group which was forming around Dolgushin. To be more exact, one can say that it was Flerovsky who inspired the earliest stage of the Chaikovskists' activities at the time of 'the cause of the book' and that it was he who drove them to take action among the workers and peasants. But once they were on this road, to which they had been led by reading his works, they marched on their own, making use of criteria and methods which were born of the experience itself.

Bervi was born in 1829, the son of a professor of English origin at Kazan University who, at the time of the student disturbances, had aroused violent protests for his backward ways of teaching and his antiquated ideas. After reading law at the university, Bervi became in 1849 an official in the Ministry of Justice. Though he began his career in brilliant fashion, his ambitions lay elsewhere. He wanted to teach financial law in a university. His plans were prospering when he attracted the attention of the authorities for taking an active part in collecting signatures in protest against the student arrests of 1861. A year later he heard of the arrest of the nobles of Tver. The single openly liberal step to be taken by the nobility after the emancipation of the serfs had been suppressed. Bervi decided to make an individual protest. He sent a long letter to the Emperor and another to the British Ambassador in St Petersburg. Alexander II's policies, he said, could only lead to strengthening the revolutionary movement, which would draw nourishment from the Emperor's attitude towards the students and the best of the nobles.

Revolutionary sympathies did not represent a real danger during the wretched and shameful reign of Nicholas, because the number of educated people had been reduced to a minimum and the masses were held in barbaric ignorance. But in a State which is in a phase of development, to play with the exasperation of the party of the extreme is a dangerous game. The number of the educated is constantly increasing and the more the people develop, the greater the weight and extent which the party of the extreme will have in it.[55]

When Dolgorukov, head of the Third Section, read this letter, he began by asking 'to be informed of Bervi's mental faculties', and compelled him to undergo six months' psychiatric examination in a lunatic asylum. He eventually drove him out of the Ministry of Justice and banished him to Astrakhan. There Flerovsky established relations with other exiles and tried to propagate his ideas among the peasants along the Volga. He was taken to Kazan for questioning. Though nothing could be proved against him, he was banished to one of the towns in the department of Tomsk in Siberia. He later succeeded in getting transferred to European Russia, and was confined first in Vologda and then in Tver. At last in 1870 he was freed but on condition that he no longer lived in St Petersburg.

These enforced travels throughout Russia led to his most important book, *The Situation of the Working Class in Russia*, which was published in St Petersburg in 1869 under the pseudonym of N. Flerovsky.[56] Its form was that of a series of essays and in it Flerovsky spoke mainly of those regions which he had seen with his own eyes. This helped to give the work a feeling of liveliness and urgency not to be found in his later works. His political and social conclusions sprang from an impassioned description of the ways of life, problems and sufferings amidst which he had lived for so long. The book was not a systematic study of the situation of the working classes in Russia, but rather very full *reportage*. Indeed, despite its five hundred pages of close print and the slow and detailed style, it is a book to be read with bated breath.

The theme appears in the opening words, which are given to a peasant woman in central Russia. 'O, wretched is our life, little our land, great are our taxes, and we do not know what to do.' Though this destitution varied in details, fundamentally it was the same everywhere. It was the result of a situation which crushed the entire Russian 'working class', and by this term Flerovsky meant every kind of worker: peasants, miners and industrial wage earners in the large towns. The book begins by describing the situation of the 'moving labourer' in Siberia and ends with 'the Russian proletariat'. It touches on peasant problems in the poor districts of North Russia, the workers in the Urals, the fishermen of Astrakhan, the gold diggers of Siberia, and the workers in light and medium industry.

The picture he gives is governed by two fundamental ideas. Firstly, all Russian society is backward because the masses are destitute, because they are unable to demand higher wages and a fairer reward for their work, and because they are compelled by their very circumstances to live on the edge of hunger. And, secondly, there is the financial policy of the State with its crushing taxation; and this constitutes the most important of these circumstances. It is the duty of the intellectuals not just to make themselves clearly aware of this state of affairs and to understand it in detail, but also to help the masses themselves to recognize it. And then, taking the *obshchina* and cooperatives as bases, they can start on the road that leads to the realization of his ideal. Though he does not describe this in detail it can be grasped clearly enough from the book. Abstract proposals, he repeats again and again, are not needed. The important thing is to get on to the right road; and it is with this appeal that Flerovsky ends his book.

To understand the situation of the workers in Russia, it was essential to clear the ground of the ideas which had been inherited from the time of Nicholas I, and which, as we have seen, were still firmly held by the ruling class. It was not just that there was no proletariat in Russia in the exact meaning of the word; in fact the position of all workers, peasants and poor artisans included, was worse than that of the proletariat in the West. Speaking, for example, of the northern regions, Flerovsky said:

The English and French think that their own poor have reached the extreme limits of destitution. But here we find a worker incomparably more destitute—the Russian worker. They think that their poor die of hunger, and here we find a wretch infinitely more hungry, the inhabitant of our northern regions.[57]

This comparison which showed the real proportions of the position of the working class in Russia and elsewhere in Europe is repeated again and again so that the reader is always aware of it. It was this contrast that gave meaning to the extension, made by Flerovsky and all the other Populists, of the term 'working class' to include all workers, industrial and peasant alike. The problem was simply this: to bring the workers of Russia, all the workers, to at least the level of the Western proletariat. This, as Flerovsky said, was the only way to turn Russia into a modern country and prevent it from falling into the situation of Asian countries, such as China and India, with their terrible peasant destitution. The fight against poverty was not the concern of only one section of the workers but of the 'working class' as a whole and through it all the nation.[58]

As long as the Russian worker is badly fed, agricultural progress in Russia will be impossible, and even the nobility itself will remain poor ... Neither agriculture nor industry can be based exclusively on the demand of the upper classes. Until the economic demands of the working class can be extended, even the educated parts of society will remain poor and lack initiative ... All parts of society are equally interested in an increase of wages for the working classes ... If, in England, the lord and the merchant are rich, they owe this to the English worker who was intelligent and brave enough to refuse to work for paltry wages.[59]

16*

Naturally the fatal docility and dumb misery of the Russian peasants and workers were not in any way due to defects latent in their nature; though the educated and ruling classes were always saying that these sprang from their character or from vice. Flerovsky took up an argument that Chernyshevsky had used and gave countless examples to show that the peasants were far from being lazy and incompetent. Indeed their drunkenness which so impressed the superficial observer was not as important as was generally claimed. Statistics showed the working classes drank little, and this was one more symptom of their extreme poverty.

Their resignation and docility sprang from very different causes. Their shoulders had to support the burden of the entire State. Of course they were crushed. Russia was passing through a period which, using Marxist terminology, could be called one of 'primitive accumulation' and this was made all the more terrible by the intervention of the State.

In the life of all peoples there is a moment when the social situation of the working classes has no guarantee of any kind against exploitation, when the greatest possible amount of produce is seized from the hands of the worker and when the nation is therefore threatened with extreme impoverishment. In Western Europe this moment coincided with a time of complete political anarchy. And this proved a lucky circumstance for it. The baron was absolute master within the limits of his estates; but outside these his influence was non-existent . . . But Russia went through this economic stage in the middle of the eighteenth century when administrative centralization was already fully developed. Complete calm and order prevailed in the State. The upper classes weighed down on the people no longer as single individuals but as a total mass, which was compact and by now completely organized. That is why it was so difficult for the Russian worker to free himself from this weight, and that is why he has become poor and weak.[60]

The effects of this had been seen a century later when the serfs had been freed. The State had transformed this process into a successful business affair for itself and the upper classes who composed it. The taxes to redeem their own land, which still burdened the peasants, were no less heavy than they had been during serfdom. Indeed they were often still heavier. To pay his taxes the peasant was forced to keep himself and his family at starvation level. Moreover he had no means of protecting the price of his own goods. He had to under-sell to the merchant, and he had to submit to the growing class of *kulaks* who took advantage of his destitution and imposed their own will within the *obshchina*. The intervention of the State in peasant society and the activities of local officials, who were only concerned to collect taxes, not only maintained this destitution but actually increased it by protecting those few elements in peasant society which were in a position to profit from it.

Few observed all this as acutely as Flerovsky. His vivid description of the relations between the *kulaks* and the poor peasants in the villages of Siberia and European Russia gives us some of the best contemporary evidence on the subject. He examines in great detail the varying mechanisms through which the peasant merchant, the *miroed* and the *kulak* were able to accumulate vast riches by playing on their position in the *obshchina* when taxes were distributed within it, and by pitilessly exploiting men and situations. And if this social mechanism was not in itself enough to reduce most of the peasants to starvation, the State intervened directly, with flogging and prison for those who did not pay their taxes. Corporal punishment and prison were the most effective schools to teach the Russian worker his lesson of submission and resignation.

In view of this situation, said Flerovsky, two plans must be followed simultaneously. First the State must entirely do away with the redemption fees which oppressed the peasant and which had been inherited from the régime of serfdom. And, on the other hand, peasant society must defend the *obshchina* against the *kulaks* and those forces which were leading to its internal stratification. To do this it must retain the principle of cooperation and the periodical and egalitarian redistribution of land. These two objectives were closely linked, because, as we have seen, it was the economic policy of the State which led to destitution and this in turn led to the collapse of the *obshchina*.

The first move should be made by the State. On the lands which it owned it should create a class of free and prosperous peasants.

We have now thrown aside the habits of Asiatic barbarism. We are convinced that such ideas were mistaken; we have understood all the advantages to be derived from a class of free peasants unburdened with feudal taxation. Why are we not brave enough to proclaim this . . .? We have freed ourselves from Asiatic ideas only to fall into the Middle Ages . . .

It was up to the State to give the example of real emancipation by doing away with all redemption fees.

But this would not be enough. The position of the *obshchina* demanded that those rules of equality which had been its foundation be re-established. 'The only salvation from exploitation by the insatiable *miroed* lies in the association of work and means.' It was just not true that small holdings led to a class of independent peasants. On the contrary, these peasants were always having to depend on the merchant, the usurer, on a more fortunate neighbour or on the *kulak* who owned the cattle needed to farm their fields and who lent seed in return for labour.

The *obshchina* creates independent workers. That is its fundamental advantage and constitutes its superiority over private, split-up property . . . It is owning land that gives man the chance to interfere in the affairs of others. It deprives the worker of a considerable part of his produce and turns him into a beggar or a rogue, and often both. Sometimes it limits his work so much through outside influences that it makes this work either unproductive or harmful for the nation. The *obshchina* gives the worker full and exclusive rights over the land and makes him entirely independent of everyone else.

Flerovsky was so convinced by this agrarian Socialism that he was led to contrast it with any form of Communism—which he understood as the complete rule of all over the individual. 'Landed property is far nearer communism than the *obshchina*.'[61]

The *obshchina*, then, must be freed from the control of the State, which paralysed even the principle of electing its own administrators, as Flerovsky demonstrated. It must once more be given those egalitarian foundations which were still alive in the hopes and ideas of the peasants. And then it would provide a way for Russian villages to escape from the misery which oppressed them.

His inquiry thus confirmed the conclusions of Populism. The economic policy of the State was the central reason for the misery of the Russian workers. Escape did not mean following the road already pursued by Western Europe, but finding a new one. And this could only be Socialism. Flerovsky wrote at the end of his book:

Of course, to restore a state of affairs which has been earlier spoilt is by no means an enjoyable thing to do. But if we are unlucky enough to have such a fate, the best thing we can do is to accept this fate with dignity, to follow our road without turning aside, openly and dispassionately. As soon as we have the courage needed to take this step, we will see that we not only have the chance to put our affairs in order but also to achieve a great historical function . . . Only that people whose spirit is filled with the highest feelings, and which creates the most perfect ideas, can stand at the head of civilization and lead humanity with it. The great empires, such as those founded by Genghis Khan, Tamburlaine, Cyrus, have vanished without a trace . . .

Russia could follow the tracks already trodden by Europe and could also fall back into barbarism. But it was enough to look at Europe to see that what was needed was the opening up of a new road. 'In the civilization of today, at the head of which stand Europe and the United States of America, we see a radical defect, one of those defects that lead to the graveyard of a civilization . . .'[62] In the very problem which was now facing Russia—in the historical relations between the oppressive State and its 'working class'— the nation contained elements which would solve it in a new way.

We have until now spoken of the peasant problem, which is naturally of prime importance in Flerovsky's inquiry. But his originality lay in not stopping there. Indeed in some of his most brilliant essays he showed how destitution in the villages, starvation, land hunger and above all crushing taxation were giving rise to an ever-increasing proletariat, whose ways of life and mentality he described in great detail.

In Siberia the workers were exploited by the owners of factories and gold mines who took ruthless advantage of the fact that these workers had been driven from their villages by penury, often had no passport and were always liable to be arrested as vagabonds. Their derisory wages were soon reabsorbed by their having to buy essential goods which were in the hands of the very bosses who employed them. The State in fact was keeping these vagabonds in a condition of perpetual dependence on the capitalists. It did not so much persecute them as threaten them with prison and thus throw them, bound hand and foot, into the arms of their exploiters.

In Astrakhan, on the other hand, the capitalists only had to own the tools which were essential for the fishermen for them too to be reduced to penury, as here also labour was plentiful. One after another he examined the various types of fishing contracts, showing that these were not just ruinous for the fishermen but also harmful to production in general, as they contained no incentive to improve techniques.

Can such a state of affairs be considered normal and profitable for the country? It is as oppressive for the workers as it is unprofitable for Russia as a whole. Almost two-thirds of all the fish that is fished in Russian rivers for sale comes from Astrakhan. One must try for oneself to live for half the year on *kvas*, onions and black bread to realize what a great consolation—indeed what an essential necessity —fish means for anyone who is poor in Russia.[63]

Light and medium industry consisted mostly of factories for the preparation of agricultural produce. This was therefore a seasonal industry, and did not guarantee a fixed wage for those employed in it.

The heavy State industry of the Urals (mines, etc.) was organized on archaic lines in a spirit of bureaucracy. By tradition it was the centre of slave-like exploitation.

The picture that Flerovsky gives of the so-called 'industrial zone' (i.e. the regions round Moscow), provides perhaps the best surviving description of the local proletariat as it was coming into being after the emancipation of the serfs. The chance to earn broke through the traditional bonds of peasant society and led to frequent examples of corruption. The new spirit of personal independence expressed itself mostly in violence and arrogance and in habits which combined penury and reckless spendthriftness. Here, for instance, is the conclusion of an inquiry made in the region of Kaluga.

Everyone here wants to hide his rags with a show of well-being. For an *izba* with windows containing well-set and carved wooden frames everyone is prepared to live in the hardest conditions and to let his own children die of hunger. Whereas the peasant in the north and east of Russia remains apathetic for part of the year, without work or the hope of obtaining it, the worker in industrial Russia is never quiet. Here one can hear complaints on all sides that there is no work, that the rewards are not high enough. Here machinery is hated because it lowers wages and gives profits to the capitalists. Here the capitalists are hated when wages go down. Here the mentality and determination of the workers are more highly developed . . . *Artels* are started, there are strikes. Methods are found to fight against the capitalists and increase pay. But though the workers are bolder in their fight to live, the conditions of their lives are even more oppressive.[64]

Flerovsky did not believe in the value of strikes. In this he was influenced either by the tradition of Proudhon or—more probably—of Fourier. His ideal lay in the cooperative which he extended to great industries, for he was convinced that workers could be found capable of administering even the largest factories. They would in any case be more efficient than the bureaucrats of St Petersburg who had to exert remote control over the far-off industries of the Urals. Indeed these industries had been able to function satisfactorily without employers in the eighteenth century, when they had supplied arms to the insurgent peasants at the time of Pugachev's revolt.[65]

When the Third Section finally realized what Flerovsky's book contained, it noted firstly that the book was a serious one and that 'for those who study the life of the people in the various parts of Russia, it could be used as a source in the scientific meaning of the word'. But it added also that 'it very skilfully upheld those Socialist ideas that constitute the programme of the "International Society". There are a few small changes due to the differences between the position of the working classes in Russia and in Western Europe'. The book as a whole, the report continued, was proof 'of the inefficiency of the rules of censorship, which are intended to prevent disturbances, even those which are not crudely expressed'.[66]

Inquiries were made as to who was the mysterious M. Flerovsky. At last it was realized that this was Bervi's pseudonym and the police were put on his tracks. Detailed supervision was kept of his house and his travels; and the most circumstantial and also strange reports were sent to St Petersburg. Supervision was accentuated when in 1871 he published his second book, *The Alphabet of Social Sciences*.[67]

According to the regulations of the Russian branch of the International Society which were found in Moscow during a search of April this year [1871], there are plans to form, among other things, a society and secret groups to publish books dealing with the political sciences. Recently there has been put on sale in St Petersburg a book called *The Alphabet of Social Sciences*. No author or publisher is mentioned on the cover, which only states that the book was printed at the Nusvalt press. We have in our possession reliable information that the book was written by the well-known Socialist writer Flerovsky (Bervi) and published by the same secret group which is made up of people who are under the constant surveillance of the Third Section.

Alexander II himself added a note to this report, ordering that *The Alphabet* 'was not to be put on sale'. When the Third Section had read its five hundred pages and made a summary of them for the Emperor, he noted again 'One must admit, it's a fine tendency!'[68]

The censorship was made stricter still. In 1872 punishment for press offences was once again removed from the hands of the magistrates and entrusted to the Council of Ministers. As we have already seen, the Chaikovskist group was badly affected by this final episode in the 'cause of the book'. Chaikovsky, Klements and Natanson were arrested and the latter was banished. Bervi wrote one more book for the Chaikovskists. It was printed but hacked to pieces by the censorship, even before it could be put on sale.[69]

In October 1873 Bervi, too, was involved in the general repression. He was arrested and implicated in the Dolgushin affair. In May of the following year he was again exiled, this time to the department of Archangel. In 1875 he was given permission to live in the town itself but 'as he exercised a harmful influence on the young boys and girls who were political exiles'[70] it was thought necessary to send him back to a village. He eventually spent many years in Kostroma and later in Tiflis whence he succeeded in escaping to London only in 1893. When he reached England one of his first ideas was to rewrite *The Alphabet of Social Sciences* which had been interrupted twenty years earlier. He published three volumes, but never finished this work, which, as he wrote it, was gradually turning into a universal history. But this second version is one of his weakest and least important works.[71]

Besides, even the edition of 1871 lacked the vigour of his *Situation of the Working Class in Russia*. For us it is of interest only as showing the encyclopaedic thirst of the younger generation in Russia. These young men published and distributed the book at their own risk and peril. In it they found their own beliefs given sociological form and reinforced with countless examples taken from the most varying countries. The author explained that it was not the strong and the wealthy who made civilization, but the weak, united by a sense of solidarity and equality. Strife between workers and capitalists was one of the forms this wider conflict took. To join the side of justice it was not necessary to make plans for the society of the future. Instead a moral ideal must be kept firmly before one's eyes, and in one's heart there must be a strong passion to destroy in oneself and in others the idols of wealth and power. Flerovsky, too, fought against social Darwinism and any application of the struggle for existence to human life. He gave a rough account of what he called 'static civilization', by which he meant a civilization in which struggles of class and nationality have no ideal content. Such a civilization therefore becomes the scene of useless agitation. He was perhaps intending to explain his conclusions more openly in the third part of *The Alphabet*. As it stands, this sociological treatise acquires significance only when read through the eyes of those who published it and who guessed at those thoughts and aspirations which remained half expressed.

On the other hand, in 1873 Flerovsky gave specific details about what to tell the people and how to lay the foundations needed for propaganda among the peasants and workers. These are to be found in a pamphlet called *How one must live according to the Laws of Nature and Truth*, which was secretly published by the group associated with Dolgushin.

This was the most important Populist organization at the beginning of the 'seventies, other than the Chaikovskists. Though it was much smaller in numbers and though it met with less response, it will make us better acquainted with the ideas and state of mind of the young revolutionaries who were preparing to 'go to the people', and it adds a new and original feature to our picture of the period.[72]

Alexander Vasilevich Dolgushin was born in 1848 in a small town in the department of Tobolsk in Siberia. A friend later described him as 'a sanguine personality', and ever since boyhood he showed a rebellious spirit and strong determination. He had the gift of attracting his contemporaries. But he allowed them to see only one side of his personality and retired into himself, fed by an intense faith in his own ideas. In 1866 he went to St Petersburg, in theory to continue his education. In fact, his main purpose was to share in the political life of the university. The group of Siberians which collected round him gives us one of the many examples of the transformation of a 'commune' into a political organization from having been an organization of mutual help, a library and a cultural club. The group at this time contained thirteen young men who at first were mainly concerned to help their fellow students from Siberia, and to collect books and materials for the study of their native land. They appear to have come to the conclusion that the only way to save Siberia lay in separation from Russia. The group therefore represented a revival of the Siberian 'regionalism' which we have already noted in the 'sixties. They made plans to return there and spread propaganda when they had completed their education. They may have already been in touch with groups in Siberia itself. In any case, for them the obligation to 'go to the people' was tinged with local patriotism. A portrait of Chernyshevsky hung in the room where they held their meetings. He was admired both for his ideas and, so to speak, as being a Siberian *honoris causa*.

The group had only just begun to prepare its future activities when Nechaev appeared on the scene. He went under the name of Panin, and in his typically conspiratorial and mysterious fashion tried to spur them on to more intense activities. One of the group, Petr Alexandrovich Toporkov, agreed to join the *Russian Revolutionary Society*, to spread the *Narodnaya Rasprava* and to induce his comrades to join Nechaev's organization. Nechaev was then on a short visit to St Petersburg, and, after the contacts had been made, he soon returned to Moscow. The Siberian group then went through a phase usual with all who were affected by his violent agitation. While some of the group tried to follow him, others were by no means prepared to accept his conclusions. Some, it is true, planned to create a 'band' to attack the nobles. Dolgushin himself began to lay the foundations for a conspiracy. But many hesitated. The programme of the most violent was to 'annihilate or submerge by means of a popular rebellion all the out-dated administrative machine' and to exterminate the entire royal family. This action would begin when the organization numbered two hundred. Except for a few changes in detail, the programme that Dolgushin drew up was a copy of Nechaev's.

Nechaev had sown this seed in St Petersburg during the last days of

November 1869. On 1st January 1870 arrests began in the capital. They struck at the very heart of the group of Siberians, among them Dolgushin himself. However, no proof could be found and even those who confessed later withdrew their confessions at the trial. After a year and a half in prison, they were nearly all acquitted in August 1871.

A year later, in the autumn of 1872, a new group had already formed round Dolgushin. This included members of the Siberian 'Commune' as well as elements who were then for the first time entering revolutionary life. It was called the *Group of the Twenty-two*, that being the number of its members. Besides Dolgushin, the most active were Lev Adolfovich Dmokhovsky, 'a man of strong moral character, like Rakhmetov' [the hero of Chernyshevsky's *What is to be done?*] in the words of a companion, and Viktor Alexandrovich Tikhotsky. Tikhotsky came from a family of Decembrists; he had already spent two years in Zurich but had returned to his country with a view to devoting himself to propaganda among the peasants. Both were then aged twenty-two. With few exceptions Dolgushin's group was made up of typical representatives of the 'intellectual proletariat'. It had by now lost all its regionalist and Siberian character.

Their association with Nechaev's conspiracy had left them with some contempt for those who were concerned to spread education and to publish books. They smiled maliciously when they spoke of 'bookish people' i.e. the Chaikovskists who, because of this, often looked upon them as Bakuninists.[73] In fact their Socialist background was very similar to that of the Chaikovskists and was founded mainly on Lassalle, Marx, and, of course, Chernyshevsky.[74] They derived their specific ideas not from Bakunin but rather from an attempt to reconcile the essential content of Nechaev's preaching on the basis of a wider and more accurate knowledge of the situation of the peasants and workers. This knowledge was based mainly on Flerovsky's book. Thus they believed in the need to prepare a peasant rebellion in the short run instead of a systematic preparation of the masses. But for this purpose they drew up a programme which no longer merely appealed to the revolutionary passion of the most desperate elements in Russian society, but which aimed rather to draw on the fundamental needs and aspirations of the peasants. So they proposed liberating them from the oppressive redemption fees and carrying out an equal redistribution of property.[75]

'Their plan was to found a clandestine press in Moscow and to print appeals . . . They were to spread these booklets throughout the villages over the widest possible area, with the aim of fostering a revolt. For this undertaking, which was to be a speedy revolutionary *coup*, they needed extremely decided members. Dolgushin's small organization was made up of revolutionaries of this type.'[76] So said Shishko, who knew them well. Indeed, he was on the point of entering the organization when Kravchinsky summoned him to the Chaikovskists.

In March 1873 they moved from St Petersburg to Moscow, and then into a small house in the region of Zvenigorod, not far from Moscow itself. There they brought the press which they had succeeded in obtaining, and in the summer of that year they began to print their leaflets. Despite the fact that they soon roused the suspicions of the local peasants (who were convinced that they were 'making cash') and though these rumours soon led to a search, they successfully printed two pamphlets and an appeal which they were able to bring safely to Moscow together with their type faces.

The first work was the one by Bervi-Flerovsky. They had got into contact with him when they had been in St Petersburg and Flerovsky in the district of Vyborg, on the frontiers of Finland. They had taken countless precautions to establish these relations and ask him to collaborate. Although he was under police supervision, Dolgushin himself went to fetch the work from Flerovsky, who was at Nizhny Novgorod.

Flerovsky was impressed by the spirit that fired this new group. He later said:

I was always aware of the comparison between these young men preparing for action and the early Christians. They had not yet begun to take action. They were only preparing themselves and, inspired by their enthusiasm, they were utterly convinced that they would succeed. I, too, was certain that they would give the government trouble. But when I looked at the unlimited field for activities in the midst of the Russian people which was still untouched, I was convinced that success could only be assured when the explosion of enthusiasm among these young men was changed into a permanent and ineradicable feeling. Constantly thinking about this, I grew certain that success was possible only if one path was followed: that of founding a new religion. I wanted to create a religion of equality.[77]

The work which he handed to Dolgushin was the manifesto of this new religion.[78]

'Go to the people', he said, in the first few lines, 'and tell it the whole truth to the very last word. Tell it that man must live according to the law of nature. According to this law all men are equal; all men are born naked; all men are born equally small and weak.' Nature was ready to give its fruits to all equally. All men must enjoy these in equal measure. 'Before you lie the villages and cottages scattered throughout Russia. Around them is the land, and this land is now held in common. There are no longer any landlords—those builders of evil who have enslaved the land, our Mother.' Anyone who is hungry can come and ask for a field to farm. 'They will give equal shares to all without intrigue.' When could this be brought about? When there were no poor, when education for all could be guaranteed from childhood, and above all when those who exploited the work of others had disappeared from the villages. The nobility had made use of every method to secure a position of privilege for itself. In popular and religious language Flerovsky summarized Russia's history, and ended with an appeal for action. 'A curse on the cowardly, on the weakling who will not fight for his brothers.'

Dolgushin assumed the task of translating this appeal into political terms, though he expressed them in forms which were just as inspired and religious. Indeed he used even more quotations from the Gospel; but he also adopted a more specific political line. He spoke of the emancipation of the serfs, but came to the conclusion that even now not everyone in Russia had the same rights. The nobles paid no taxes, and they had the best schools.

Though they work a hundred times more than the landlord, the peasants are incomparably poorer than he is.
The time has come to escape from poverty and darkness.
We, your brothers, we turn to you, the oppressed, and we call on you in the name of eternal justice. Rise up against this régime of injustice, which is unworthy of man and unworthy of the highest moral consciousness of the land. Rise, brothers. We demand the abolition of all dues. This land which we are compelled to redeem has been ours throughout the centuries. On it lived our fathers, our grandfathers and our ancestors. When we were slaves of the noble landlords we farmed this land. The nobles no longer exist. What does this mean? Merely that we have separated from them. Our land has returned to us. Why on earth must we pay for it? Further, we demand a general redistribution of the land, both that which belongs to the peasants as well as that which is owned by the State and the nobles. It must be redistributed among ourselves according to justice, so that each has what he needs.

He then demanded the abolition of military service, which lasted for fifteen years, and the establishment of good schools for all. 'Learning is strength, learning is light; without learning there is slavery.' Passports must be abolished and the heavy taxes which the peasants paid must be controlled. 'The government must spend by our consent.' And this could only happen through elections which would create a government of the people's delegates.

> Like a single man
> All tormented Russia rises.
> Let us free ourselves for ever,
> Our land will be sufficient for all.[79]

Dolgushin had also prepared another short appeal *To the Intelligentsia,* in which he attacked any attempt at local reforms. It was not enough to found small cooperatives, and improve local administration. Any hope of becoming independent through individual as opposed to collective efforts was mistaken. 'All your lives you will be exploiters and parasites.' 'In no rôle will you be of such use as in spreading popular propaganda for a new and better life.' He quoted Proudhon, ending, 'Let us show that we are sincere; that our faith is burning. And then our example will change the face of the earth. Do not think that the Russian people cannot understand you and reject you.'

> Our password is: Freedom and Equality.
> Onward, friends, to arms,
> Death to the enemies of the people,
> The Tsar, the princes and the *boyars.*

As can be seen, they were not just using religion as a tool to make themselves understood by the peasants to whom they intended to turn; religion meant something more than merely the phraseology of the Gospel. But the outlines of this religion of equality had hardly yet been sketched in. It had not become the centre of their thoughts, as it had for the followers of 'deo-humanism', and it was still more a cloak for their political ideas. In the house where they kept the clandestine press, Dolgushin had put some crosses in place of the ikon. On these the following words were written in English, Latin, Italian and French: 'Liberty, Equality and Fraternity'. 'Who cannot be cured with medicine, let him be cured with iron; and who cannot be cured with iron, let him be cured with fire (Hippocrates).' 'Serve only them [the people] because their cause is sacred. The people suffer, and every man who is close to the people has been sent by God.'

They began to spread propaganda among the peasants even before they had finished printing their pamphlets and appeals. These ventures were intensified when they began distributing their books. The books were, of course, free, and this amazed the peasants. The group made many rather incoherent attempts, as if taking soundings in an unknown world, to progress beyond casual meetings to closer links. At once it came up against the greatest obstacle to this 'flying propaganda'. Only few of the peasants were able to read what they had written. Despite all this it managed to organize a few meetings in *izbas*; it held discussions which often left immediate problems for the religious field, so much loved by those peasants who had any glimmer-ings of education. It was able also to circulate publications among the workers of a small industrial centre on a wide scale, through the cooperation of a teacher at an elementary school, which was attached to a factory.

An accidental arrest, however, led to the police discovering their propa-ganda material and being put on their tracks. Some members on the fringes of the movement, and then Toporkov himself, were arrested. There followed a long and careful inquiry designed to paralyse the heart of the movement. In September 1873 Dolgushin was arrested. Eventually twelve people were handed over to the Senate for a trial which lasted from 9th to 15th July 1874. Dolgushin and Dmokhovsky were sentenced to ten years' hard labour, Ivan Papin and Nikolay Plotnikov to five years, Dmitry Gamov (the school-master) to eight years, Anany Vasilev, the peasant who had spread the manifestos to two years eight months, and others to lesser sentences. Alexander II refused to make any reduction in the sentences of those most affected. During the ceremony of the 'civil execution', one of them, Plotni-kov, shouted several times, 'Down with the Tsar, down with the *boyars* and the princes! Down with the aristocrats! We are all equal! Long live liberty!' This led to a demonstration of solidarity among those watching, for the most part students. Thirteen more people were arrested.

There was a long discussion on how to punish Dolgushin's group for this demonstration, and for its generally rebellious attitude during the trial and in prison. It was finally decided not to deport them to Siberia for hard labour but to keep them in the central prison at Kharkov. There they could be kept under greater supervision and there the isolation and living conditions were more severe.

These conditions were indeed terrible. By the autumn of 1875, Gamov was a paralytic lunatic and in April of the following year he died in the prison hospital. Dolgushin succeeded in describing the conditions under which they lived in a manuscript which was smuggled out of the prison at different times. This was probably done by Dmokhovsky's mother, who after many difficulties had at last been able to get permission to make periodic visits to her son. The manuscript was secretly printed in St Petersburg in 1878.[80] On the cover of this, the first issue of a new revolutionary periodical *Zemlya i Volya* was announced for October. Dolgushin's example was at last bringing results. But he himself had to pay for these with his life. In 1880 he was taken to Kara in Siberia for forced labour. Here he succeeded in organizing the flight of some of his comrades. Severe persecution followed. In 1883 he was confined to the prison of Shlisselburg on Lake Ladoga. He contracted consumption and died there on 3rd June 1885.[81] In 1878 Plotnikov began to show the first signs of madness. He was taken to a lunatic asylum in one of the towns on the road to Siberia, together with his other comrades who were making the same journey. Some of these, such as Papin, made a long stay in the asylum.

But despite these personal tragedies, now, for the first time, Populist preaching met with an active response. The propaganda of the Chaikovskists and Dolgushin's followers, and the discussions on the programmes of Bakunin and Lavrov did not—like similar debates in the 'sixties—merely give rise to small groups. This time there followed a real movement, and activities involving several thousand people.

As always happens, even this response seemed unexpected. Witnesses of the time constantly repeat that the movement was 'spontaneous'. And indeed it was so within the limits in which any authentic political movement is spontaneous in respect to the efforts of those who have wanted and prepared for it.

There are, indeed, many spontaneous elements in the movement of 1873 and 1874 'to go to the people'. There was the special freshness and the atmosphere of youthful enthusiasm, indeed recklessness, which struck all observers. Its nobility was so ingenuous that it seemed the very 'springtime' of all the Populist movements. And so it sometimes makes us forget that ideological preparation for it had already been under way for two decades and that the organization itself had been planned for ten years. All the various episodes of the movement still retain, years later, the mark of that impulse and devotion which were at its source. Not by chance was the summer of 1874 called 'the mad summer'.

The movement 'to go to the people' was the answer given by the university students to the appeal of the revolutionary Populists. It was an answer that contributed no new ideological element. The call had already been sounded at the time of Ogarev and Herzen, and since then many others had taken it up. The ideology of the movement was vague, generally far more so than the ideas of the various movements that had gone before. A number of different tendencies met here, and so the critical element contained in each of them was diluted, or rather burnt to ashes, in a great impulse of dedication. When the memoirs of the period tell us that Bakuninist tendencies prevailed over those of Lavrov, they mean that the vaguer and more powerful appeal of Bakunin naturally became the banner of a greater and less specific force.

We must not let our attention be too distracted by the strange, sometimes ridiculous and still more often naive episodes of the movement 'to go to the people'. For they, too, are merely an indication that the impetus was now no longer confined to the closed circles of conspirators but was reaching a movement of the masses.[82]

The Chaikovskists had already made a series of, so to speak, individual attempts to sound the people. They had begun by organizing the workers of St Petersburg, for they hoped to find among these peasants, who had only recently become urbanized, suitable men to take their message to the villages. And later, when the arrests began, some of them were compelled to move into the countryside to try and escape the police. Krylov, for example, went back to his village not far from Tver, determined to found a centre of propaganda there. His comrades promised to send him someone to help him. And at the beginning of 1874 both Kravchinsky and Klements visited him.

Often in the small peasant *izbas*, crowded with listeners, discussions went on until after midnight. The public was overwhelmed by a feeling of solemnity and there rose up the choral singing of one of the revolutionary hymns. Against one's will there came to mind scenes of the first centuries of Christianity and the times of the reforms.[83]

Klements was denounced by the village priest and was very nearly arrested.[84] Krylov was in fact caught by the police. But he was released and continued his pilgrimage among the people, which was put an end to by the authorities on 25th August 1874 at Nizhny Novgorod. He was sent to prison and died there of tuberculosis.

But despite these ventures the Chaikovskists viewed with some alarm the unleashing of the general movement 'to go to the people' as the students began to leave in droves for the country. They tried to guide or to control the movement. In fact they were drawn in its wake.

They often repeated that there would be little value in 'flying' propaganda, i.e., in the words of Kropotkin, 'sowing, in passing, the idea that it was necessary to rebel'. And so they tried to canalize the movement into 'fixed propaganda'. They explained that it was essential to find a trade to exercise in some village so as to carry out a steady propaganda campaign. One of them, A. O. Lukashevich, said, for example:

It is essential that every man learn a trade or some given occupation, and then scatter over a region where easy contact with his comrades is possible. In this way within two or three years all that region will be carried to a high pitch of revolutionary spirit and from it we will draw new energies for other regions.[85]

In other words the more political elements were aiming to create a new village intelligentsia or at least replace the few representatives of one that the countryside contained. In place of the few doctors, midwives, nurses, clerks, etc., young men would come from the university ready to serve the people and inspired by a determination to give Socialist significance to this new social function.

But this idea, which was expressed with varying degrees of coherence by the followers of Lavrov, was swept away by the more spontaneous and revolutionary element which lay at the source of the movement. Renunciation of all privileges, the determination to be freed at last from their 'debt' to the people, the desire for liberty—these were the real forces that drove the students into the country.

Nothing like it had ever been seen before or after. It was a revelation rather than propaganda. In the first cases it was still possible to trace back the book or the individual that had driven such and such a person to join the movement. But after a time this became impossible. It was a powerful cry that arose no one knows whence and that called living souls to the great work of redeeming the Fatherland and the human race. And the living souls, when they heard this cry, arose overflowing with grief and indignation for their past. And they gave up their homes, their riches, honours and families. They threw themselves into the movement with a joy, an enthusiasm, a faith which one can feel only once in one's life and which, once lost, can never be found again . . . It was not yet a political movement. Rather it was like a religious movement, with all the infectious nature of such movements. Men were trying not just to reach a certain practical end, but also to satisfy a deeply felt duty, an aspiration for moral perfection.[86]

Some even converted themselves before leaving for the people. 'I decided to become Orthodox', says Aptekman, who was a Jew; 'I was baptized and felt myself literally renewed . . . So I had drawn near the peasants, among whom I was to live.'[87]

The movement 'to go to the people' was a collective act of Rousseauism. And in Rousseauism political factors are inextricably mixed with the desire to express long-repressed feelings. Here, too, the political content cannot be separated from the desire for a break with the civilization of their fathers, and from the passionate longing for liberation which took as its banner the repudiation of learning in order to find a true, healthy and simple life.

The psychology of this movement will cause no surprise if looked at from this point of view. Here, for example, is how Aptekman, who took part in

it, describes the experience. His enthusiastic style is well suited to the events
it describes.

It is time to go to the people. We must prepare the indispensable, and above all
we must learn physical work. Everyone is starting to work. Some go into workshops and factories where, with the help of trained workmen, they get themselves
accepted and start a job. Their example impresses their comrades and spreads.
Those who cannot follow it, suffer bitterly. Others (and if I am not mistaken they
were the majority) fling themselves into learning a trade—cobbling, carpentering,
cabinet-making, etc. These are the trades which are learnt quickest. And besides,
they will be the most useful when we are banished. We must be ready at once.
In many parts of St Petersburg small workshops are being organized where, under
the guidance of a revolutionary workman, apprenticeship is fairly quick. The need
to learn a trade brings to light some real talent in our younger generation. The
workrooms are all of the same type. At the same time they act as 'communes'.
Let us go into one of them: a small wooden house with three rooms and a kitchen,
in the district of Vyborg in St Petersburg. Little furniture, spartan beds. A smell of
leather. It is a workshop for cobblers. Three young students are working there with
the greatest concentration. At the window is a young girl. She too is absorbed by
her work. She is sewing shirts for her comrades who for days have been preparing
to go to the people. Haste is essential. Their faces are young, serious, decided and
clear. They talk little because there is no time. And what is there to talk about?
Everything has been decided. Everything is as clear as day.[88]

Such were the centres of apprenticeship and propaganda which throughout
the winter of 1873 were multiplying in the leading towns, such as St Petersburg, Moscow, Kiev and Odessa. Lavrov wrote:

The educative and Socialist significance of these centres was enormous. It was no
longer merely cultural activity; no longer just an attempt at intellectual improvement. Ideals were really solved in the supreme principle of social activity and
Socialist propaganda, aimed at the total destruction of the existing economic
organization.[89]

The mass movement began in the summer. Even those contemporaries who
tried in their memoirs to minimize its chaotic nature admit that there was
no central direction. In fact there was no organization of any kind to control
it. If the students concentrated in some regions rather than others this was
because they were responding to the revolutionary literature of the time
rather than obeying instructions. Most of them moved towards the land of
Pugachev and Stenka Razin and towards the South (scene of the peasant
revolts) along the great rivers, the Volga, Don and Dnieper. Often they
merely went to the districts nearest their starting points. Only in those
regions where 'fixed' propaganda prevailed over 'flying' propaganda were
organizations formed so as to maintain contacts between individuals and
groups scattered in the villages. In a few places an attempt was made to
found 'revolutionary shelters'. These were meeting places which generally
took the form of artisan-workshops. The regions of the Volga round Saratov,

Samara and Penza were the best organized. Some of the centres provided money and false passports. Their main purpose was for the exchange of impressions and information.

But despite all this, the majority of students set out individually or in small groups of friends. They dressed as *muzhiks*—sometimes even more poorly than the trade they had chosen would naturally require—and went travelling. They took jobs and tried to make friends with peasants, foresters and boatmen. The physical work was hard and often took up all their energies. But they did not want the peasants to look upon them as parasites. Rather they wanted to show them (and show themselves too) that they were able to earn a living on their own. And so they insisted on digging, sawing wood and living like real labourers. Some could not stand the strain. For others it obviously gave a sporting satisfaction. For many the test constituted the end of any 'normal' life. From the villages they were sent to prison; from prison to exile. All their lives were stamped by the renunciation they made in the summer of 1874.

They wanted to tell the peasants 'the truth'. To lie to the people was a crime. And so often they took no precautions when speaking. They said openly that the land should be held in common and that a rebellion was needed. They wanted to test their own courage. And had not Bakunin said that the people was ready for a revolution? As a result there were a very large number of arrests. Only the cleverest or luckiest were able to escape being denounced. Apart from anything else the movement 'to go to the people' constituted a great lesson on the need for conspiracy and the impossibility of dispensing with it.[90]

And so the Populists went through a political experience which ripened in the following years. They learnt of and shared the misery of the people; they often made their voice heard though they were never able to foster acts of open protest. Here and there they saw the peasants' mentality in a new light not at all as they had imagined. One day, for instance, Aptekman was describing to a crowded group what social life would be like 'when the people owns its own land, woods and waters'. He was interrupted by a peasant who shouted 'That's grand! We'll divide the land and I'll take two workers and then I'll be in a fine position.'[91] N. Morozov too saw for himself how far the patriarchal collectivism and spirit of equality in village life were being undermined by the rise of richer and stronger elements.[92]

Four thousand people were imprisoned, questioned or at least harassed, by the police. The spread of the movement had assumed proportions which seriously worried the government. Thirty departments had, in varying degrees, been affected by propaganda. Nowhere had the Populists been able to arouse a revolt or upheaval. Everywhere the peasants had listened to these strange pilgrims with amazement, surprise and sometimes suspicion. But the government understood that a new revolutionary movement had now been born.

Count Pahlen, Minister of Justice, made this clear in a memorandum when the 'mad summer' was over and the movement of 1874 'to go to the people' had been crushed. Summing up, he pointed out that 770 people had been handed over to justice, of whom 612 were men and 158 women. Provisional liberty had been given to 452 people, and 265 kept in prison. Only 53 had been able to escape. One of the most worrying facts lay in the support and help that the Populists had succeeded in finding among part of the ruling classes. Some landlords had allowed their estates to become nests of propaganda. Judges and local officials had given them hospitality, information and sometimes money. Pahlen realized that the great wave had also shaken and set in motion a portion of the intelligentsia.

Pahlen's report soon fell into the hands of the Populists. It was sent to Geneva and printed on Ralli's press. Ralli himself followed it with a commentary of great interest. These few pages contained the first lesson derived from the movement.[93]

Pahlen was wrong to attribute the development of the revolutionary movement to Bakunin and Lavrov:

It was not Lavrov who created the youth of St Petersburg and Moscow. It was not he who told them that it was time to begin action. On the contrary, it is this youth that has created Lavrov. It has dragged him from his world of transcendental metaphysics, and put him on to a more active and vital road. As for Bakunin and the enormous influence he is supposed to have on Russian youth, here again the report is wrong and sees a highly enlarged picture of what happened. (It is true that fear has large eyes.) We do not want to do anything to diminish the significance of Bakunin as a strong personality and a great agitator, but we must point out that his influence on the Russian revolutionary movement was always fairly weak.

Bakunin had had one great merit. He had clearly said that the time for dictators was past, even in the ranks of revolutionary organizations. 'Russian youth no longer needs them. It knows on its own what must be done.'

No, dear Count Pahlen, it is not to Bakunin or to two or three other people that belongs the exclusive honour for the revolutionary movement in Russia. This honour belongs to all Russian youth, which, with energy, intelligence and courage, has at last—after a desperate fight—been able to build up a menacing revolutionary force. Alone, its initiative has been able to foster the countless groups which you have enumerated in such detail. Alone, it has been able to create the anarchist spirit which inspires them, and ensure that excellent federalist organization which constitutes the invincible force and indispensable condition for any revolutionary task.

19. THE WORKING CLASS MOVEMENT

THE CHAIKOVSKISTS were the first to plant the seeds of a genuine working class organization. It is of course true that the local, unorganized and spasmodic fighting spirit of the workers themselves had sometimes produced spontaneous results. There had also been small cooperative centres founded here and there by the Populists during the 'sixties. But it was the Chaikovskists who provided the impulse for a working class movement which, despite its original limitations and the violence of the persecutions it had to face, always thereafter maintained some measure of continuity, and which grew in scope and influence as revolutionary Populism developed during the 'seventies.

The rise of this current is one of the most important events of the time. From 1871 onwards the problem of the working classes began to count in Russia not merely as a reflection of what was happening in Western Europe or as a theoretical demand on the part of the revolutionaries, but as a concrete fact.

There was no real working class movement during the 'sixties, only a series of protests, disorders and isolated strikes which burst out spontaneously, carrying on a tradition that dated back to the eighteenth century. These disturbances were largely a reflection of the difficulties experienced by workers of peasant origin in adapting themselves to the new conditions brought into being by the manifesto of 19th February 1861.[1]

Between 1860 and 1861 the main strikes were those of miners, road workers and labour engaged on the new railway lines. These strikes were the sequel of the sporadic disturbances which had already broken out during 1859, and which had been more violent than those that followed. A few concessions quickly put an end to nearly all of them. Indeed, it is only by using modern terminology (and at the risk of giving a false impression of the significance of these disturbances) that we can call them real strikes. The most serious cases involved not so much abstention from work as 'flight'—desertion, intended to be irrevocable, by those who had some hope or possibility of obtaining a piece of land and so resuming their normal lives as peasants. Movements of this kind occurred, for instance, among the men digging the New Canal at Ladoga and other similar undertakings. In one case, in 1861, at least fifty workers were flogged for leaving their work. But these were extreme examples of a contemporary phenomenon. When the abolition of slavery did away with the chains that bound the serfs to their factories, they quickly returned to their villages.

507

In 1860 workers in the various industries in course of transformation amounted to 565,000, and of these 135,000 were serfs. In some industries— distilleries and sugar factories for example—the amount of seasonal labour of serf origin was specially great. In the mining industry, serfs were still more numerous. Of a total of about 245,000 men employed in the mines, only 30 per cent consisted of free labour. Most of these interpreted the manifesto of 19th February as an invitation to return to the land.[2]

This rapid decrease in labour led, during the years that followed the reform, to an increase in wages which was only partially arrested by a crisis in the cotton industry. But this lasted only for a short time. Towards 1865 the number of workers was already as high as it had been in 1860. During the following years it grew systematically, though not rapidly. Towards 1870 it was around 800,000 and at the end of the 'eighties nearly a million.

During the 'sixties labour agitation (which was isolated and of no great importance) was still caused by lack of land or the pressure of taxation, and in general by the conditions in which many peasants found themselves after the reform. Once more they were compelled to look to factories, mines and industries for the sustenance that they had hoped to find in the villages. In this respect the disorders that broke out in 1862 among the miners in the Urals were typical. As former serfs they had been given allotments of land, but they were soon forced to realize that these were too small and that taxation snatched the product of their labour. And so once again the Urals became the principal centre of workers' disturbances, as they had been during serfdom. These were caused not so much by problems of wages or working conditions, as by the thirst for land of these worker-peasants. Their demands were combined with a mute resistance to long military service and were often expressed with violence. In 1869, for instance, in a district of the Altai, thirty-nine workers locked themselves in a house and fired on the troops who were sent to pacify the area.

However, even during the 'sixties, strikes accompanied by specific demands with regard to wages were not unknown. They were nearly always defensive in character, and were generally provoked by the employers' failure to pay their wages in time or indeed not paying them at all. In one case, in the industrial centre of Orekhovo-Zuevo, there was a real strike to obtain an increase in wages. It was accompanied by scenes of disorder and drunkenness, which provide some idea of the violent and disorganized mentality of the Russian working class during the 'sixties, even when it was beginning to defend its interests with more modern methods. In any case the disturbances of Orekhovo-Zuevo in 1863, the legal consequences of which lasted till 1869, are worth recalling as the first real strike during the period that followed the reform of 1861.[3]

On the whole we can say that the history of labour disturbances during the 'sixties is not altogether clear. Their only significance is to reveal one of the many symptoms of the difficulties which faced Russian society after the reform. They left no marks on contemporary consciousness. Their numbers were insignificant—about fifty altogether. The newspapers did not mention them, and writers who described the workers' life wrote a great deal about their daily labour and their mentality but very little about these isolated attempts to react and fight. As far as officialdom was concerned, the acceptance of the idea that in Russia there was no proletarian problem meant that the repression was represented purely as an operation of the local police. Only towards the end of the 'sixties do we find the Third Section beginning to spread agents 'in those districts which, because of the character of the population, provide a field more open to disturbances, i.e. in the centres of factories and industry'.[4]

This silence was broken by the strikes which took place in St Petersburg in 1870, and which were accompanied by similar disturbances in the provinces. During the year there were fourteen in all. On 22nd May 1870 seventy-two workers in the cotton mills on the Neva stopped working and demanded an increase in wages; 800 men followed their example. The instigators of the movement were arrested, sent for trial and all except five sentenced to a few days' imprisonment and eventually released. This was followed by a tailors' strike. The Minister of the Interior, angry at the turn events were taking, drew up a circular which announced that, in future, instigators of strikes would be banished—i.e. generally sent back to their place of birth without trial. He added that in the strikes at the cotton mills the influence of instigators could be detected—men who wanted to express their discontent in a way 'which was foreign to the Russian people'. A similar comment was made at this time by the review *Otechestvennye Zapiski*. 'The true significance of the strike is unknown to us, as it does not correspond with the character of the Russian worker.' But this meant denying the evidence. It is not for nothing that an old tradition has described the cotton mill strike in St Petersburg in 1870 as the first strike to take place in Russia.[5] Historically speaking, the tradition is incorrect, but it is none the less significant.

Of course, in the 'seventies the number of strikes was still comparatively small. Using official documents, which are probably incomplete, Korolchuk has listed 225 in the period from 1870 to 1879. A more complete analysis of official reports by Pankratova has brought the figure up to 326. It is true that in only forty-nine of these cases do we find any real desertion from work in any organized way. The rest consist of disturbances, protests, small revolts, etc. Of the 225 general cases of agitation, forty-seven concern metal workers, seventy-five builders and fourteen those engaged on transport, etc. At the beginning of the 'seventies the category most affected were peasants who came to town in search of temporary work, mainly building, digging, etc. At the end of the period it consisted mostly of textile workers—a class of poorer labourers whose mentality was closer to the village, and finally metal workers who represented the most stable form of labour and one which was often not of immediate peasant origin. It was the best paid and already the most typically proletarian in character.

During these years too the nature of the strikes was generally defensive, though the number of offensive ones was greater than during the early period (about 26 per cent of the total number). The years 1874 and 1879 marked the height of these disturbances.

If we look at the curve of the decade, taking both offensive and defensive strikes into account, and compare it with the curve of the development of industry at the same time, we can see that the two curves correspond at the two extreme points. The theory according to which periods of industrial development are marked by an offensive of the working class against capital, whereas periods of crisis are marked by defensive attitudes, is remarkably confirmed by these curves.[6]

From the political point of view the 'peasant' nature that many of these disturbances still retained, and the vital part played in them by problems and mentality inherited from serfdom, were of special importance. 'Flight' was still the means of defence to which the workers sometimes resorted to escape from conditions when they became too oppressive. Whatever spontaneous organization there was in these disturbances was the direct result of 'meetings of the *mir*' which were traditional in the villages. Indeed the word itself was used in the factories, where the workers met together as their fathers or they themselves used to meet in the villages to discuss the problems of the community. In some cases the election of a *starosta* was transplanted from the countryside to the town, as had occurred fairly frequently in previous decades.[7]

These disturbances sometimes sprang from circumstances which were very reminiscent of the time of serfdom. Thus, for example, in 1871 a strike broke out in the Kholunitsky Zavod in the Urals (there had already been disturbances there in 1865), because the management of the industry considered it entirely superfluous to give wages to the workers, on the ground that they all had a bit of land already and it could be assumed that they did not need money. On the occasion of Easter 1871, the workers demanded a wage. The employer refused and then fled in fear to the town. Clashes broke out between the workers and those members of the management who had remained. Before the strike had become fully effective, the 'instigators' were arrested, i.e. the representatives whom the workers themselves had elected. They were forcibly freed by their comrades. Troops had to intervene to take them back to prison. Later they were condemned as agitators. The methods used to maintain discipline were also frequently similar to systems which the gentry had employed for centuries. V. I. Nevsky has described one of the most important strikes of the time, which took place in a workshop owned by an Englishman who, in order to restore order, resorted to flogging and organizing violent clashes between the workers and the rest.[8]

The 'meeting of the *mir*', which was of peasant origin, though it had deeply affected the workers' mentality, remained a purely temporary and casual means of organization. When the workers wanted a firmer and more enduring type of assembly, they generally looked back to the other traditional form, the *artel*. This was a type of association that discharged orders collectively and divided wages among its members.

It was the *artel* that the various groups of Populists first tried to make use of in the 'sixties. They wanted to utilize or develop this nucleus which was already in existence and tried to turn it into a real cooperative. A vast number of books and pamphlets were written on this problem at the time.[9]

A real working class movement can be said to have begun when a move was made away from cooperatives of this kind to attempts at organization on different bases. This was the work of the Chaikovskists. It is of little importance that their ideas were eclectic and that they used the most varied methods in their attempts to unite the workers. It was they who sowed the first seeds of a new organization among the Russian working classes.

Almost against their inclination they had close links with the factories. They were searching among the workers mainly for men to spread propaganda among the peasants. They therefore made contact with those who were least skilled and who were most directly bound to the life and spirit of the countryside. On principle they always chose textile rather than metal workers, for they recognized in them the representatives of what they considered to be the real people.[10] A. V. Nizovkin, one of their most active propagandists, said that the metal workers had already been marked by urban civilization. They dressed better; they no longer lived communally; and the traditions of the *artel* were dying out among them. The textile workers, on the other hand —and in general workers in 'factories' as opposed to the 'workshops' of the metal workers—still dressed in country fashion and retained the habits which were typical of the village—from a communal spirit to drunkenness. Among the working classes of St Petersburg at the beginning of the 'seventies, this was an important distinction. Men employed in the workshops 'considered it degrading to have anything to do with those in the factories, and the latter felt themselves humiliated if the former spoke to them'.

All contemporary evidence confirms this account of the Chaikovskists' attitude. Sinegub, for instance, tells us that his comrades looked upon the textile workers as the best elements because their appearance and spirit were still rustic. At Odessa 'the men in the workshops, spoilt by urban life and unable to recognize their links with the peasants, were less open to Socialist propaganda', in the words of a man who tried to organize them.[11] The same thing was said by Kropotkin in the document which represented the Chaikovskists' most important programme. 'Given the fact that workers in the factories have not in any way broken their links with the village and have made no change in their peasant way of life, it will be all the easier to find among them elements which may become cells for the local groups.'[12] And the lives of some of the most typical propagandists of the period reflect this attitude. Thus, G. F. Krylov, himself of peasant origin, began by devoting himself to propaganda among the workers of St Petersburg, but came to look on this as useless. In his search for alternatives he thought of circulating popular books by passing himself off as a street pedlar, following the example set by the hero in one of Chatrian's novels. After he left the factories he began to sell his books in the suburbs of St Petersburg, and then returned to his village in the department of Tver.[13]

All this of course contained an element of pure idealism—the Populist's desire to devote himself to the poorest and least educated. But this longing for self-sacrifice did reveal a genuine political truth. Only in this way could the Chaikovskists understand the problems of those peasants who were becoming workers and only thus could they make contact with the workers who, in increasing numbers, were coming to the towns.

Indeed, industrial development, which ever since the 'forties had been rapid, was quickly extended in the capital. In 1862 St Petersburg had only about 30,000 workers, but between 1869 and 1881 the population as a whole increased from 668,000 to 928,000. Among these were many workers, whose strength at the end of the decade had already more than doubled.

And so the revolutionary intelligentsia acted as a bridge between the villages and the factories. The intelligentsia had in earlier decades built up theories round the Socialism and collectivism to be found in the *obshchina*. Now they presented this to the workers who came from the countryside, as the ideal towards which their activities should be directed. They later had to admit that it was not easy to make the peasants' ideas acceptable to the working classes, for the latter were already beginning to acquire a different mentality which impelled them to demand something new from the intellectuals. But for the moment Populism enabled them to carry out their task as mediators. Through them, the traditions inherited from the *mir* and *obshchina* began to find new vitality in more modern egalitarian and Socialist aspirations.

Kropotkin has given a vivid picture of the atmosphere in which these first attempts at large-scale propaganda were carried out in the working class districts of the capital.

My sympathies were mainly for the textile workers and in general the workers in the factories. There were thousands of this kind of worker in St Petersburg and every summer they returned to their villages to farm the land. These half-peasants and half-workers brought with them into town the spirit of the Russian country *mir*. Among them revolutionary propaganda met with considerable success. Many of them lived grouped in small *artels* of ten or twelve people who lived and ate together. At the end of the month each bore his share of the common expenses. We began to frequent these communities. Very soon the textile workers introduced us to other *artels* of stone workers, carpenters, etc. In some of these groups our comrades had become part of the family; all night through they discussed Socialism with them. In many districts and suburbs of St Petersburg we had rooms which our comrades had rented for this very purpose. Every evening about a dozen workers came to learn to read and write, and then to chat.[14]

For the first time the Populists were really face to face with workers. For the first time they were no longer speaking to individuals but to important groups. One day when Kravchinsky saw his comrade Sinegub speaking to a large *artel* of builders, he said to him: 'You are a magician. Now I am convinced that we can act on the masses.'[15]

Their propaganda among the workers began in the summer of 1872 in the Vyborg district. A centre of organization made up of the workers themselves was soon formed there and outstanding were: G. F. Krylov, I. A. Abbakumov and N. P. Sabunin. They were among the very first workers to become consciously revolutionary Populists.

This early success convinced the Chaikovskists of the need to create from among their number a specialized group to spread propaganda in such circles. It was made up of about a dozen young men each of whom began by getting into contact with a small group of three to five workers, whom they taught to read and write. They also gave them lessons in geography, history, physics, etc., and organized lectures on a still larger scale. Klements spoke of popular rebellious movements in old Russia; Kropotkin of the International; Alexandra Kornilova of the German working class movement. The work was organized by Sinegub and Charushin. Throughout the winter of 1872 their propaganda grew in intensity. By February 1873 they were in a position to organize a series of 'communes', where the workers whom they had taught could live.

Although throughout this period they were working on virgin political soil, they sometimes came across some seed which had been sown in earlier years. One workman, for instance, said that he had already been affected by propaganda in 1863 (probably by the first *Zemlya i Volya*).

In the Vyborg district their work was broken up at the end of 1873, when a denunciation led to the arrest of Charushin and many others. Spreading propaganda among the workers was indeed to be one of the main charges against the Chaikovskists at the 'trial of the hundred and ninety-three'. Charushin and Shishko were sentenced to nine years' hard labour; Kupryanov to three years and four months. Kropotkin, as is well known, was able to escape. Kokhryakov, the student in whose house the meetings had been held, went mad in prison and died many years later in a lunatic asylum. Krylov, one of the workmen in these groups and, indeed, one of the most active, also died in prison. We have already noted his ambition to bring back to the countryside the ideas that he had come across in town.

In another district of St Petersburg, in the suburbs along the Neva, activities began somewhat later, in July 1873. The work here was for a time inspired by Sinegub, who had returned from his activities in the countryside. 'At that time I had a mass of pupils',[16] he wrote later, looking back at this

17+

period of his life. And, indeed, he soon collected a group of between thirty and forty workers. Sofya Perovskaya managed to establish relations with some workers in the Tortoni factory, with whom another group of Populists was already in contact. These were associated with V. S. Ivanovsky and were perhaps closer to the Lavrovists. A. I. Serdyukov also carried out propaganda there and paid for it with an early death in prison.[17]

Elsewhere in St Petersburg the propaganda of the Chaikovskists was less active. In general their work was so intense and fruitful that towards the end of 1873 they thought of founding a common workers' centre for the entire town. But before the end of the year the propagandists of the Neva district were also arrested, together with a nucleus of workmen.

As we have already seen, cultural and Socialist propaganda were closely related in these activities. A library had been founded for the workers who were ready to pay 2 per cent of their wages towards its upkeep. Kravchinsky insisted that history lessons must be given first place and later he included political economy, based on the works of Marx. In April 1873 a mutual aid bank was inaugurated for the workers in an armaments workshop. This was the first exception made by the Chaikovskists to the preference for spreading propaganda among the less qualified workers. The men in this workshop were relatively well paid and belonged to the highest grade of the working classes in St Petersburg. The mutual aid bank was managed by about twenty of them. At its head was B. P. Obnorsky, who was destined to become one of the most important working class leaders of the 'seventies.

All these activities of the Chaikovskists suffered greatly from the instability of their propagandists who were constantly being distracted by journeys to the provinces and the countryside. This was probably one factor that encouraged a feeling of independence among the men they were organizing, who became dissatisfied with such casual leadership. And the infiltration of propaganda among more skilled forms of labour, such as the metal workers, accentuated this state of mind.

A. A. Lisovsky was the first to try to give political expression to what was becoming a more specifically working class tendency. He was followed by Nizovkin. The expression this tendency took on was still primitive and was prompted mainly by personal ambition and lack of scruples. Exploiting the resentment of the working classes against the intellectuals, Nizovkin succeeded in organizing many small groups, in all about fifty workers. But the contrast between them must not be made to appear too rigid. The workers' depositions do not throw enough light on this episode. Nor can we trust Nizovkin's own statements, which were dictated by the desire to save his own person when arrested and questioned. None the less the movement that he led is of interest. For it was symptomatic of a new state of mind which was growing up among the more skilled workers. They were increasingly unwilling to be used as tools for Populist propaganda in the countryside. They were prompted by a feeling of contempt for the peasants and were convinced that they were now exclusively workmen with their own interests and ideas.[18]

What did this propaganda and organization lead to, by and large? Its duration was short, but we have seen that it tried to make up in intensity what it lacked in permanence and coherence.

For the Populist intellectuals the collapse of their workers' groups acted as a warning, the message of which seemed to be that: 'It was no longer worth wasting time on workers in the towns—rather, immediate preparation must be made to go into the people, and, at least for the moment, leave the workers on one side.'[19] And so the first reaction to the arrests was an intensification of the movement 'to go to the people'. But among the workers themselves the traces of Populist propaganda remained, even though the number of groups founded by the Chaikovskists had never been very great. The first teams had been formed and many of these will be discussed later. They were by no means among the least important. Among others converted by propaganda at this time were B. P. Obnorsky, P. Alexeyev, the brothers A. N. and P. N. Peterson, K. A. Ivanaynen, I. A. Bachin, S. V. Mitrofanov, etc. Each of these was later to have an important and adventurous history.

The spirit of the working class districts in St Petersburg was beginning to reflect the ideas that the Populists had spread. We must certainly not exaggerate the importance of police reports, yet one of these, dated September 1874, is of no little significance. It is worth quoting in detail:

The gross, vulgar methods employed by factory employers are becoming intolerable to the workers. They have obviously realized that a factory is not conceivable without their labour. The employers feed them, but without workers they can do nothing. A realization of this has now given rise to that spirit of solidarity among the workers which has so often been noted these days. Two or three years ago the employers' affairs were no better than they are at present. Then, too, it often happened that the workers did not receive their wages on time. Yet then everything went smoothly. The cunning employer flattered his workers and said good-naturedly that he could not pay them at the right time, and they withdrew in silence, and next day turned up quite normally for work. But now as soon as even the most popular employer holds back wages for only three or four days, the crowd begins to murmur and curse, and strikes often break out. Even in the workshops, where money for wages can never be lacking—as this is a State industry—the spirit of opposition to be found among the workmen has appeared on a scale utterly unknown before. There have been cases of work stopping because the men were not satisfied with an insufficient wage or because of oppression exercised by the management of the workshops. All this, taken as a whole, clearly betrays the influence of the propagandists, who have been able to sow among the workers hatred for their employers and the belief that the forces of labour are being exploited.

Alexander II read this report and wrote on the margin: 'Very sad.'[20]

While the Chaikovskists were at work in St Petersburg an even more characteristic and important piece of organization was being carried out in

Odessa, a city which then contained about 200,000 inhabitants, 30,000 of whom were working men and their families. It centred round the figure of E. Zaslavsky, who directed it for about eight or nine months. *The Union of Workers of South Russia* can be considered the first organization of a typically working-class character to come into being in the Russian empire.[21]

Zaslavsky came from an old noble family living in Saratov. It was far from rich, among other reasons because of its exceptional size. He was born in about 1844 and went to the University of St Petersburg. While still under thirty he 'went to the people' between 1872 and 1873, using Odessa as a centre for his isolated pilgrimages into the countryside. But these experiences eventually made him 'lose his illusions'. He said that it was feasible to approach the peasants both to incite them to revolt and to prepare them for a long-term rebellion, but that both these things were in fact impossible to realize. Besides, he added, the Socialists ought not to put themselves on the same plane as the Carbonari. And so he became convinced of the useless-ness of either propaganda among the peasants or a conspiracy in the country-side. It was these conclusions that drove him to devote all his activities to the workmen of Odessa. In 1872 Odessa already contained some small education centres. A year later Zaslavsky became a teacher in one of these groups, the one concerned with the 500 men in the Bellino-Venderich factory. He gave lectures on political economy and on the history of the proletariat. But his listeners were often incapable of understanding these. Zaslavsky then read Chernyshevsky's *What is to be done?* and explained it to the workers. At the same time he helped to start a small library and cooperative bath, and he worked in a press, which was partly owned by his group and partly by various other Populists. This gave him a chance to print appeals and clandestine leaflets.

At about this time the 350 men in the Gullier-Blanchard factory, among whom were some of his followers, wanted to carry out their plan for a mutual aid bank. They looked to Zaslavsky for help and he transformed this enter-prise into a small but solid workers' organization of about 200 members. It had an internally elected hierarchy, an entrance fee and a weekly sub-scription of twenty-five kopeks. It held regular meetings. This became the nexus of the organization that Zaslavsky had by now succeeded in spreading throughout the factories of Odessa.

The *Union of Workers of South Russia* drew up regulations, of which the following are the fundamental articles:

(1) In view of the fact that the present order does not, as far as the workers are concerned, correspond to the genuine requirements of justice;

and that the workers can get their rights recognized only by means of a violent revolution capable of destroying all privilege and inequality by making work the foundation of private and public welfare;

and that this revolution can only occur: (*a*) when all workers are aware that there is no escape from their present situation; (*b*) when they are fully united;

We the workers of Southern Russia join together in a union which will be called the Union of the Workers of Southern Russia. And we lay down as our aims: (*a*) to propagate the idea of the liberation of the workers from the oppression of capital and the privileged classes; (*b*) the union of the workers in the region of Southern Russia; (*c*) the coming fight against the existing economic and political régime [Skveri says that Zaslavsky proposed to cancel the word 'political'].

(2) The Union has a bank the funds of which are to be used at first to spread the idea of the liberation of the workers, and later to fight for this idea.

(3) Membership of the Union is open to workers of every kind who have close relations with the working class and not with the privileged classes; who feel and act in accordance with the fundamental desires of the working class, i.e. the struggle against the privileged classes in order to win freedom.

(4) The duties of each single member towards the Union and vice versa are determined on the following basis: All for each and each for all . . .

(6) Every member must be prepared for any sacrifice, if such sacrifice is needed for the safety of the Union.

Zaslavsky was in contact with Lavrov and with the *Vpered*[22] and his own personal links were with the Lavrovist and not the Bakuninist group in Odessa. But local conditions, and the actual experiences which this first working class organization underwent, somewhat modified these émigré ideas. It claimed the right to organize itself freely, and above all it emphasized its working class nature. Some of the men even wanted to exclude from their meetings anyone who was not a member of the working classes. This led to internal strife within the organization itself between the followers of Zaslavsky and the Bakuninist elements in Odessa. Eventually there was a schism. Some workers followed the instructions of the anarchist elements or, as they were then called, the 'rebels'. These inner struggles were probably also influenced by the propaganda of Elizaveta Nikolaevna Yuzhakova who had been a member of Nechaev's group and was considered a 'Jacobin', i.e. to have some sort of relation with Tkachev.[23]

And so Zaslavsky's *Union* became a field of battle between supporters of a working class policy, Bakuninists and, possibly, Jacobins. In any case, the literature which was circulated among the workers was of the most varying nature. Chaikovskist pamphlets found a place alongside Ralli's *Rabotnik* and Lavrov's *Vpered*.

The *Union* which had fifty to sixty members in its central organization was able to support two strikes, the first in January 1875 at the Bellino-Venderich factory and the second in August at Gullier-Blanchard's. A manifesto was drawn up and distributed on the second of these occasions. The *Union*'s influence rapidly increased, not just in Odessa but also in other towns along the Black Sea coast. But at the end of 1875 a denunciation enabled the authorities virtually to put an end to its activities and arrest its leaders. And a year later

Naddachin, a workman who tried to resume the interrupted work at Rostov-on-Don, was also arrested.

Some time later, about fifteen admirers of the *Union* were given differing sentences, varying from a short period of imprisonment to ten years' hard labour. Zaslavsky got the heaviest sentence in 1877. He had had to wait for his trial in a prison in St Petersburg, and he seems to have gone half mad. The judges thought that this was a pretence, but it is unlikely. His health was certainly ruined and on 13th June 1878 he died in prison of tuberculosis. Stepan Stepanovich Naumov, who was also involved in the trial, spent twenty years in Siberia before being allowed back home, and died in Odessa in 1905.

Bakuninism, whose appearance in Zaslavsky's *Union* we have noted, prevailed during the following years in those working class centres of Southern Russia which tried on various occasions to resume the work of organization that had been interrupted in 1875. Their development must be followed until the end of the decade before returning to ventures of the same kind in the north.

In 1879 there arose in Kiev a *Workers' Union of South Russia*. This was inaugurated by Pavel Borisovich Akselrod, who ever since 1872 had devoted himself to propaganda among the workers there. The *Union* may also have existed in Odessa.

I decided to adopt the regional name of the Odessa organization of 1875, first for reasons of principle which derive from my federalist ideas, and secondly because I hoped that it would soon be possible to found an organization to embrace the whole of Russia. Later, I thought, such regional unions (of the south, the north, and possibly others) would be able to federate and unite.[24]

This germinal organization sprang from Akselrod's determination to 'let the voice of the working classes be heard',[25] whenever there was a repetition of Solovev's attempt on the life of the Tsar. He knew that this would be soon enough. But besides this element of revolutionary Populism, his plan also contained a social-democratic factor. His programme envisaged a final goal: the transformation of society on anarchist foundations; but it also looked to an immediate objective: democratic freedom, reduction in the hours of work, etc. The two elements remained side by side 'eclectically' as Akselrod himself later said.[26] The regulations were drawn up by Stefanovich.

The life of this organization was short. It disintegrated when its founder left Kiev for St Petersburg to join *Cherny Peredel*, of which the *Union* was in some ways a precursor.[27]

In 1880 the *Workers' Union of South Russia* was reborn in Kiev. This time it was on a very different scale. It was founded by two Populist intellectuals and designed to pursue to the end earlier attempts to bring Bakuninism into the working class circles of the Ukrainian capital.

It was inspired by Nikolay Pavlovich Shchedrin and Elizaveta Nikolaevna Kovalskaya. Shchedrin was the son of an engineer. He had had to interrupt his education when still at secondary school because of his disrespectful attitude to his teachers. He came to St Petersburg in 1876 to follow a university course, and soon joined one of the groups of *Zemlya i Volya*. He was sent to the Saratov region to organize foundations for working among the peasants there, and remained until 1879. When *Zemlya i Volya* split into the two organizations of *Narodnaya Volya* and *Cherny Peredel*, he joined the latter. When the Kiev group fell, he went to that town intending to start a working class organization.[28] He obtained valuable help from Kovalskaya who, ever since the beginning of the 'seventies, had been a member of a revolutionary group in Kharkov and who, in 1879, also joined *Cherny Peredel*.[29]

The experiences that both had undergone led to their losing faith in the possibility of long-term propaganda among the peasants and in political terrorism. Kovalskaya was working in a factory at Kharkov when Solovev made his attempt on the life of the Tsar. She still remembered the comment that she had heard the workers make. 'It's the nobles again, because the Tsar has freed the peasants.' Both Shchedrin and Kovalskaya were therefore convinced that terrorism should be aimed not at the government and the State, but at those who were directly oppressing the workers, such as the employers and the landlords. These tactics they described as 'economic terror' and they were convinced that only by adopting such means would it be possible to bring about a revolution which was not just political but really social. This was to be a revolution carried out not by parties or revolutionary organizations but by the people itself 'which would thus be in a position to show its own capacity for self-administration which it had derived from the traditions of the *obshchina*'.

Inspired by this vision, as Kovalskaya said, 'We worked rapidly, feverishly, well knowing that our days were numbered . . . We wanted to strengthen the *Union* quickly so that it would not disintegrate when we were arrested.' This feverish hurry made them ignore conspiratorial precautions as far as their own persons were concerned; they devoted all their attention to safeguarding the workers they were organizing. They always carried revolvers; they were tireless. As we shall see, their fate was especially terrible, but the method that they employed was effective. At the time of their arrest, the workers' groups were not involved.

In 1880, Shchedrin was twenty-three years old, and was no longer 'in love with the people'. No longer did he want to fuse with them, he only planned to organize them. He was a considerable orator, and used to grow heated and violent. One of the workers who heard him said, 'Like a rope, he lashes with his words. We ourselves do not realize just how much we react where he calls on us.'

He began work in a railway centre. About a dozen railway workers constituted the nucleus of the *Union*, which quickly spread and affected many other categories of workers. These groups varied widely in national content. There were Russians, Poles, Jews, a Frenchman, an Austrian, a Saxon, and remote descendants of Tartars. The majority were Ukrainians. It was therefore natural that problems of nationality were acute. Anti-Semitism was violent among the workers. When the first Jews entered the *Union*, some of the Ukrainians protested, saying 'that they had crucified Christ'. But later, when in prison, Shchedrin and Kovalskaya had the satisfaction of knowing that here too their work had not been in vain. In April 1881, in the course of a pogrom, those workers whom they had organized themselves printed a leaflet which said that they must fight against all the exploiters and not against 'the poor Jews'.

Kiev arsenal, where unrest was developing spontaneously, soon became Shchedrin's centre. He launched a manifesto which threatened the directors with terrorism if they did not satisfy the workers' demands. The move was successful. Working time was reduced by two hours a day. He then held many meetings for workers of the various categories. Generally these took place in the open, outside the town. Sometimes the audience numbered over a hundred. Their *Union*, so we are told by Kovalskaya, contained about 600 men.

Although they met with a great response and round them there was gradually forming a widespread feeling of warm solidarity—a solidarity which was not repudiated even at the time of their arrest—yet they still had to contend with many difficulties. The most important of these was the fact that the workers were still closely tied to the land. For them the noble landowners, rather than factory directors and employers, were the natural enemies. The Tsar, they thought, was inspired by a determination to improve the peasants' conditions, but was constantly being hindered by the bureaucracy and aristocracy. Was it therefore true, the workers often asked, that they ought to fight against any State? They claimed that abroad, outside Russia, there was a tendency to improve the conditions of 'simple people'. Again, religious traditions hindered revolutionary propaganda. The workers spoke of 'visions' and could often be heard saying: 'Pray, and the day of happiness will soon come.'

The *Union*'s programme and the leaflets that it published were intended to overcome these and similar difficulties. The first draft of a plan began by pointing out that in Russia the position of the workers was worse than anywhere else in Europe. A revolution was therefore necessary. But should such a revolution give first place to the granting of political liberty? This was always denied as emphatically as possible.

The science of human society shows without any possibility of doubt that political freedom cannot exist without a preventive economic revolution. Political rights and real power belong only to those classes of society which control economic as well as moral and physical power (the military organization).

The plan referred to the example of the July revolution in France, to show that 'for the workers, political freedom without economic independence is only a dream and a fraud'. It spoke of parliamentary reform in England and of events in Germany. The problem could be solved only when all property passed into the hands of the people. The society of the future would be based on 'the ownership of land, factories and workshops by all the people; on the right of everyone to make use of them; and on production through means of association . . . These steps will lead to the following political changes: personal freedom and freedom of speech, of meeting, of the trade unions and of the press.' As for the army, it would have to be replaced by a militia.

It was useless to hope that an alliance with the bourgeoisie would be of any use for bringing about these ends. The bourgeoisie was the workers' natural enemy. 'One must realize that in Russia the bourgeoisie is very disorganized and cannot therefore stand up against the workers as it does abroad. And so one must recognize that if the bourgeoisie were to become better organized and more united this would be extremely harmful for the workers themselves.'

The workers should not therefore try to find allies among their natural enemies. Rather they should carry on the revolutionary tradition of Stenka Razin and Pugachev in Russia, and of 1830 and 1848 in France. But even here each of these cases had shown what happened when the people had no 'fighting organization' and what happened when the bourgeoisie were left to lead the movement. 'And so the workers' essential task must be to found a fighting organization of their own.' Propaganda pure and simple would be of no use. It would have no effect 'except on the day that Christ returns to the earth'. Even agitation on its own such as strikes and mass protests ought not to be adopted by the workers because 'they only lead to prison'. Rather, the fighting organization should make use of 'factory terrorism'. The Populist party of Ireland had pointed out the path to be followed. Even in England 'during the first half of the nineteenth century, the workers began to burn and loot factories and workshops, and to beat up and kill their employers. By doing this they obtained a series of concessions such as a reduction in hours of work, an increase in wages, the right to strike, trade unions, etc.' The Russian workers too should follow this road. Political terrorism should be a purely subsidiary method and should take the form mainly of agitations designed to arouse or strengthen the revolutionary spirit of the workers.

Manifestos with titles such as 'The Constitution will give the People nothing', 'The Meaning of the International', 'How the Irish fight for their Freedom', were used to spread the fundamental ideas of this programme among the workers. Another manifesto of the *Union* carried a characteristic symbol made up of 'a hammer, an axe and a revolver'.[30]

Shchedrin and Kovalskaya were not in action long enough to be able to put this programme into large-scale practice. Their task consisted mainly of feverishly unleashing a wave of disturbances. They had no time to resort

17*

to the terrorism which they had planned, except for one undiscovered robbery in a church to get funds for their fighting organization. By October 1880 they were already under arrest.

They had been inspired by faith that the revolution could break out within a short time. But when they were in prison, those who took over the organization were less convinced of such a possibility.[31] They continued the work but, under its new leadership, the *Union* underwent a typical change of purpose. It became less aggressive and more trade unionist in character. The new programme which was drawn up in January 1881 reflected this change. It was still directed against purely political parties; it did not modify the ultimate aims and spirit of the *Union*. But it was prepared to admit the usefulness of long-term propaganda and disturbances, such as strikes 'which give hope of positive issue'. The same applied to the manifestos which were distributed at the time. They still spoke of personal threats against this or that factory director, but the main emphasis was on protests against bad working conditions. They demanded 'that the worker should be humanely treated'. They spoke of the need to give the workers good tools, and they stressed fines, the problem of workers arriving late, and other similar matters. They threatened to hand over Colonel Korobkov, director of the Arsenal, to a revolutionary tribunal, and even circulated a manifesto announcing his execution. In fact this was never carried out. Apart from anything else, the workers themselves did not agree to it, through fear that such a move might hamper the position of Shchedrin and Kovalskaya.

When the news of the successful killing of Alexander II on 1st March 1881 reached Kiev, discussions on terrorism were actively resumed in the *Union*. The manifesto which was distributed on the following day reflected the concern within the group. They did not want to arouse too violent a reaction among the many worker-peasants for whom the Tsar was still their emancipator from serfdom. They stressed their anti-constitutionalist position and were mainly concerned to bring agitation on to the field of more immediate requirements.

Even if the new Tsar is better than his predecessor, he will be unable to understand the need and suffering of the people . . . It will be worse still if the new Tsar wants to rule the people with the help of the nobility and merchants. At the moment we can frighten any *miroed*; but when he becomes a *miroed* on a legal basis, when he has power of his own, then the death of some scoundrel will arouse a real storm from all the other *kulaks*, great and small, who will eat our poor worker with the help of the government. We can cope with one Tsar. But with a hundred Tsars there will be nothing that we can do any more.

And so they did not demand a constitution, but: (1) factory legislation which would guarantee the worker against arbitrary rule by the capitalist; (2) freedom of speech and of meeting, and freedom for a workers' press; (3) freedom of Unions and associations; (4) abolition of taxes which oppressed the peasants, and an increase in workers' wages; (5) reduction in the hours of work, and unpaid apprenticeship.

This was the last move made by the Kiev *Union*. In 1881 the second group of Populists to control it was arrested and the greatest venture in working class organization in South Russia during the 'seventies came to an end.[32]

These men who had tried to unleash 'economic terrorism' met with a peculiarly tragic fate. Shchedrin was sentenced to death. This was later commuted to hard labour for life. While still under questioning he had refused to swear loyalty to the new Tsar, Alexander III, who had come to the throne after the assassination of his father on 1st March 1881. He also refused to defend himself or even to take part in the trial. Kovalskaya was sentenced to hard labour for life; and Bogomolets got ten years. All three were taken to Siberia in the same convoy. At Irkutsk, Kovalskaya and Bogomolets managed to escape, but were caught a few days later. A Colonel Solovev threatened to put irons on them and used insulting language. When Shchedrin heard of this he asked to speak to the Colonel and gave him a blow which knocked him down. Local Irkutsk society soon heard of this. In their drawing-rooms 'aristocratic ladies spoke of him as a cavalier, a defender of weak women against the rage of an infuriated colonel'. On the same evening a prison warder gave Shchedrin flowers and a bottle of port, sent to him by the wife of the governor of Irkutsk 'together with her approval of what he had done'. But though she interceded for him, the local tribunal sentenced Shchedrin to be hanged. This time the sentence was changed to one of wearing irons, and so he was tied 'to a wheelbarrow with one wheel like those which are used for unloading in Russian ports. To it was attached a long chain which joined the irons round the prisoner's feet and belt'.[33] He had to remain bound like this throughout the journey, and at Kara, which he reached in 1882, he had to appear like it every time there was an official visit. But he did not stay there for long. He was confined in a particularly terrible prison when Myshkin and other prisoners fled from Kara, and then taken back to St Petersburg, still tied to the wheelbarrow. In the capital he was locked up in the Alexeyevsky dungeon of the Peter-Paul fortress, and then transferred to Shlisselburg. Here his health failed, and he went mad. In 1896 he was taken to the psychiatric clinic of Kazan, where he died many years later in 1919.

In 1884 Kovalskaya again escaped and was once more taken back to hard labour at Kara. In 1888 her prison was changed and then again a few years later. Only in 1903 was she freed. By then she was the only survivor among the leaders of the *Workers' Union of South Russia*. She took part in the Maximalist movement, and lived in Soviet Russia for many years. There she wrote her memoirs of the Kiev organization from which we have frequently quoted.

Sofya Bogomolets served her sentence of ten years' hard labour at Kara and died shortly afterwards of tuberculosis in 1892. She was freed from prison only a few days before her end.

Her sister, O. N. Prisetskaya, was able to return to Russia. Many years later, however, she once again took the road to Siberia, to accompany one of her sons who was banished there; and there she ended her life.

Kashintsev was also sentenced to ten years, but succeeded in escaping from Siberia in 1888. For a time he lived in Bulgaria. He then went to Paris, where he organized a centre for the manufacture of bombs and explosives. He was arrested with several others, sentenced to three years' imprisonment and expelled from France.

Preobrazhensky served his sentence of hard labour and spent the rest of his life in Siberia at Irkutsk. Ivanov made several attempts to escape and died in Siberia of typhus, which he had caught whilst looking after the local population.

Such was the end of those who had tried to give the working class movement of South Russia the character of a terrorist organization. But in Moscow, and specially in St Petersburg, development was different. There the Populists who devoted themselves to the workers were influenced by the solid tradition of propaganda which the Chaikovskists had established. Further, the surrounding conditions encouraged a slower, more systematic and better organized infiltration. Having seen how the Unions developed in the south, the great centres of the north must now be considered.

After the arrests which broke up the workers' groups founded by the Chaikovskists in St Petersburg, and after the great movement 'to go to the people', which had sent all the most active revolutionaries into the countryside, the initiative for reviving propaganda and agitation in the factories had to come from abroad. In various university towns of Europe were to be found colonies of Russian men and women students who had at first centred on Zurich and later dispersed. It was they who in 1875 founded the nucleus of the *Pan-Russian Social-Revolutionary Organization*, whose centre was at Moscow. The organization succeeded in establishing links with other industrial towns and, though it soon failed, it constituted the most important group to take action in the factories between the fall of the Chaikovskists and the rise of *Zemlya i Volya*.[34]

Zurich was the meeting place for many students coming from the Caucasus. Most of these were Georgians; others came from Daghestan and Armenia. They too were seized by the mood of intense political discussion which dominated the Russian colony there. For them, too, Bakunin, Tkachev and Lavrov became the symbols of the various Socialist currents between which they had to choose. But they were faced with a particular problem. Ought they to join the Populist movement and fight with their Russian comrades to overthrow Tsarism, or ought they rather to give first place to the national problem and fight exclusively for 'a federation of Caucasian Republics'? To solve this preliminary problem, they summoned a meeting at Geneva. This proved exceedingly lively. It was held publicly in an isolated house in the suburbs of the town. Among those who came were 'young Bakuninists', such as Zhukovsky; Lazar Goldenberg who was responsible for the Chaikovskist press; Tkachev and also some exiled French Communards such as Lefrançais, Montels and others. The difficulties of the problem under discussion confronted them immediately. What language were they to use? They began with French, but soon realized that most of them were unable to understand, still less to speak it. They then adopted Georgian, but the Armenians and representatives from Daghestan, did not know the language. Indeed, many of the Georgians themselves, who had been educated in Russian schools, were unable to speak even a word of the language of their ancestors. Finally they chose Russian. Despite this significant beginning, the great majority proved to be nationalist, inspired by the idea of restoring Georgia to its mediaeval splendour. On the other hand a minority, made up of Prince Alexander Konstantinov Tsitsianov, Mikhail Nikolaevich Chekoidze, Ivan Dzhabadari and a few others, said that this was the way to turn a great social and political struggle into a petty national conflict. They claimed that the time was still far off when the very varied people who lived in the Caucasus could hope to live together and share a common civilization. There was a risk, they urged, that the meeting would take the path that had already proved so unsuccessful for Poland. This minority therefore concluded that what was needed was an ever closer union between the Georgian and Russian intelligentsia, under the common banner of a social-revolutionary programme.

They therefore demanded a common organization with the Russians. About half a dozen girls then appeared. Dzhabadari writes:

When we expressed our amazement at seeing such a large number of women, they answered, 'We are not all here. Only recently Olga Lyubatovich left with Maria Subbotina to work in Serbia; Vera Filippovna (Figner) is still in Berne, and so are Dora Aptekman and A. Toporkova'.

All these girls were simply and smartly dressed and against our will they attracted our attention. Some were so shy that when we spoke to them they lowered their eyes. They exhaled a country air, perhaps from some distant province. Certainly at least half of these girls had never crossed the threshold of the so-called world . . . Looking at them one would have said that they were a family. And indeed they were a family, not through blood but because they were comrades. One among them stood out for vivacity. She was Sofia Bardina, whom her friends called 'Aunt', although they were all about her age. She was a girl with a large striking head. Her face was not beautiful but very intelligent. She had a large forehead, under which shone a pair of small black eyes, scintillating with irony. For some reason, at first sight this woman's head made one think of the head of Voltaire.

They were called Varvara Alexandrova, Evgenia Subbotina, Vera Lyubatovich, Lydia Figner and Beta Kaminskaya. It was they who, with the Caucasians, constituted the central kernel of the *Pan-Russian Social-Revolutionary Organization.*

Vera Figner, the sister of Lydia, was a member of this group in Switzerland but not in Russia. A few years later, she became one of the most active members of *Narodnaya Volya*. She has described the moral and intellectual upbringing of these girls. In Switzerland they found themselves, so to speak, at the cross-roads of the various internationalist currents of the period. Greedily they devoured Socialist books of every school including, naturally, Marx, who specially impressed them. They listened to Lavrov and Bakunin, and brought into this typically post-Commune atmosphere a new element, an element which she described as 'ascetic and religious'.[35]

We read the *Organisation du Travail*, Cabet's *Voyage en Icarie*, Proudhon's *Plan for a People's Bank*, and everything seemed to us to be practical and feasible. The word 'Utopia' did not exist for us. We saw only 'plans' to bring about a social revolution, and we were equally enthusiastic when we read the speeches of the genius Lassalle, who summoned the workers to conquer the State, as when we read the anarchist pamphlets of Bakunin, who repudiated the State and appealed for the ruthless and implacable destruction of its whole edifice. Most of us thought that this last idea was best suited to the conditions of Russian life. For us parliament did not exist. There was no question of even thinking of universal suffrage and elections and workers' delegates. In Old Russia there had been governments of the people, as Kostomarov had described; there were *artels* which we read about in the works of Flerovsky; there was the *obshchina*, which we knew of through Haxthausen, and the works of Herzen, Bakunin, Shchapov, Yadrintsev. This *obshchina* was the prototype and at the same time the germ of the just organization of future society. All the new ideas of democracy and economic equality seemed to us quite irrefutable from the point of view of logic. And if anyone made any objections to them, we thought that he could only be inspired by motives of egoism and fear.[36]

It was this instinctive and immediate moral judgment that led them to asceticism.

In the world as it then was, during the time of propaganda, when all those in power were hostile to Socialism, when the government offered only persecution, anyone who took this road must be prepared for every kind of material and moral privation. To be up to the task that awaited him, he must prepare himself for all the blows of fate. The asceticism of some who wanted to give up all the goods of the earth achieved the impossible. One day, unawares, the daughter of a landlord from the region of Tambov, called Bardina, admitted that she liked strawberries and cream, and was teased by the group to which she belonged. From that day on Vera Lyubatovich, with perfect sincerity, looked upon her as 'bourgeois'. When this group merged with that of the Caucasians, and the programme of the new revolutionary organization came under discussion, the girls proposed that it should include a renunciation of marriage. The men protested, and the clause was not accepted. Militant Socialism, which promised real liberty, equality and fraternity to the workers and the oppressed; Socialism which refused to recognize the strength and wealth of the powerful, and which was persecuted for the truth which it discovered—this seemed to me a new Gospel . . . Christian concepts and feelings, the ideas of the sanctity of asceticism and sacrifice, all these led me to the new doctrine . . . This was the really apostolic mission of our time.[37]

This state of mind was expressed in the regulations of the *Pan-Russian Social-Revolutionary Organization*. But during the discussions that led to settling the various fundamental points, more and more there came to the fore the political problems and contradictions that were characteristic of Populism and had faced the revolutionaries for more than a decade. They began by taking as their starting point the regulations of the Jura Canton, which appeared to represent their aspirations better than any other. But how could this be applied in Russia? How could they be used in conditions which were so different from those prevailing in Switzerland? As for their final aspirations, what right had they to give an exact, detailed definition of the organization of the society which would one day emerge, even though this change would be partly thanks to their revolutionary activities? Their duty consisted in becoming workers, in merging with the people, in bringing to it a ferment of agitation, and not in deciding *a priori* the forms of future society. And so all their attention was concentrated on drawing up the regulations of their own organization. Its nucleus was to be a community, an *obshchina* as they called it, made up of active elements, i.e. of those who 'would be capable of carrying out at least one of the fundamental principles of revolutionary activity'.[38] Within the *obshchina* there must be the most absolute equality, as also in the relations between the different communities. But this principle must be limited by the requirements of conspiracy and the need to maintain secrecy, etc., and by the discipline which obliged all members to carry out the tasks imposed on them by the collective organization. An attempt was made to avoid a relapse into the atmosphere of Nechaev's conspiracy, which, as Dzhabadari recalled, 'was in the memories of all, and which had shocked everyone, driving people away through its methods', and to avoid any organization of 'a general's type', in the expression of the time. The regulations laid down that all members had an equal right to share in the affairs of the *obshchina*, and also to demand explanations of its activities and to control them. This seemed all the more necessary in that its members not only gave up any political life other than that bound to the community, but also forsook any private life. They were not to own anything, and were to hand over all their property to their comrades.

How could unity of organization be maintained within and between the different communities? This problem they considered with more precision and care than their predecessors, the Chaikovskists, had done. From this point of view they form an intermediate link between the organization that preceded the movement 'to go to the people' and *Zemlya i Volya*. Despite their declared equality of organization, they ended by laying down greater centralization. However, they called this 'administration' rather than government; the very choice of word reflects their concern not to establish a central authority, even though they knew that some organ of coordination was indispensable.

The administration is appointed for the purpose of preventing business in hand coming to a halt just because all the members of the *obshchina* are at work. The administration is exempted from work in the factories and workshops. The members of the administration are not appointed through an election, but in turn, by common agreement of the members. The administration must be made up of members coming from the intelligentsia and working class alike. Each administration is in office for one month.

Despite all these typical precautions, the purpose of the movement, as its name suggested, was to be an organization and not merely a collection of members inspired by the same spirit. In this purpose it was successful.

The experiences of the movement 'to go to the people' had not been in vain. This applied not just to problems of organization. Now the very objective of their activities was changed. In the regulations they spoke, it is true, of 'bands' and 'risings' and they still thought of the people as an undifferentiated mass, made up both of peasants and workers. But in fact all their activities were directed towards a single class, and had a single purpose: the spreading of propaganda and agitation among the working classes.

Propaganda was entrusted to each single member of the *obshchina* as an individual task. Each man was to act at his own risk, infiltrating into the world of the workers on his own responsibility. All methods could be used: conversations, public readings, the founding of banks and libraries, and even the creation of real workers' groups which only then would be recognized by the *obshchina*. The aim of agitation, on the other hand, 'would be to drive people or groups into direct revolutionary activities'. They did not turn down the idea of making use of 'bands' whose main purpose would be loot. Principally, however, they were thinking of something like 'economic terrorism', even though their intentions and programmes on this point remained utterly vague. In any case they repeated that 'the activities of the bands were to be purely social-revolutionary'. Rather than foment new uprisings, they thought mainly of founding an organization which would be able to direct the movements which arose spontaneously here and there. As far as this was concerned, they were still typically Bakuninist. But we must not forget that they, as well as the authorities, used the word 'rising' to include any popular movement including strikes. As will be seen, their idea of concentrating all their efforts on the workers, and their proposal to create a force capable of leading these risings, led them to become more and more interested in this aspect of the struggle.

There was already ample material for propaganda at their disposal when in 1875 they began their activities in Russia. The pamphlets and books which the police found in Tsitsianov's room in Moscow constitute an extensive library of Populist works. It went from Herzen's *Kolokol* and Chernyshevsky's essays on economics to Lavrov's *Vpered*; it included the countless popular pamphlets of the Chaikovskists, Tkachev's pamphlet against Lavrov, and Lavrov's answer. Bakunin was fully represented, as well as the translation of Marx's *The Civil War in France*, which had been published at Zurich in December 1871.

There were, naturally, also works specially published by the movement itself. Before leaving for Russia, the group of Caucasians and the Russian girls had come to an agreement with 'the revolutionary *obshchina* of the Russian anarchists' at Geneva, i.e. 'the young Bakuninists', Z. K. Ralli, N. I. Zhukovsky and A. L. Elsnits. They would circulate the publications which had already been printed by the émigrés and at the same time they would start a periodical for the workers which would to some extent be their periodical.[39]

In 1875 Z. K. Ralli had written and published a small but thick book of 530 pages called *The Sated and the Hungry*. This was a real encyclopaedia of anarchist Populism.[40] He began by explaining that railways and machinery had not improved the situation of the workers. He gave a long description of their position and came to the conclusion that 'all workers in all countries, in all States, have one enemy—the landlord and the government'.[41] But what was the origin of inequality between men? Ralli summed up the whole history of humanity and that of Russia in particular, and then in the last 200 pages described the state of affairs prevailing at that time. This followed the general outlook of the Populist movement and paid special attention to Chernyshevsky, Mikhailov and the first *Zemlya i Volya*. Speaking of Herzen, he attacked the idea of the *Zemsky Sobor*. 'In the free kingdom of life there is no place for the Tsar, the nobles and the merchants.'[42] He devoted some pages to an attack on Nechaev, who was guilty of having believed in 'authority', and he recalled Dolgushin's sacrifice. The book also contained a description of the policies of the International, which he naturally looked at from a Bakuninist angle and discussed in a deliberately and successfully popular style.

The periodical which emerged from these circles was called *Rabotnik* (The Worker) with the sub-title 'A Newspaper for the Workers of Russia'. The first issue appeared in January 1875. It came out once a month throughout the year, except for numbers eleven and twelve which were joined in a single issue. In 1876 another two issues appeared, one of which was a double number. But by then the organization in Russia had already collapsed and the *Rabotnik* too ceased publication. This was the first attempt to found a working class organ in the Russian language. It deliberately echoed the problems and even the language of the workers, who had only recently been urbanized and were still linked by countless threads to the land. Its keynote was summed up in the very first number. 'The cause of the workers and the peasants is one.' It ran parallel to the propaganda of the Caucasians and the young women students who had become workers. But it is difficult to say

how far it corresponded exactly to their ideas. Indeed it is likely that here
too the fact of emigration was responsible for a certain distance between
the *Rabotnik* and the actual experiences that were being undergone in
Moscow. However that may be, the review is full of interest for anyone who
tries to understand the energetic if crude attempt made at the time to link
the problems of the Russian workers to those of the European working
class movement, and to emphasize the points in common and the real
differences between them.[43]

From the very first number the *Rabotnik* came out clearly against any
constitutional or parliamentary tendency. It was true, it said, that many
countries outside Russia contained *dumas*; 'It looks better there than here
with us, but in fact it's the same old mess. Those who have eaten their fill
do not want the hungry to think of their fate. No understanding is possible
between the sated and the hungry.' The Russian peasants who had had to
leave their villages 'through lack of land' and go to work in the factories
well knew that, 'just as the peasants want to take the landlords' estates to
include them in the *obshchina*, so workers in the towns need all the factories
to turn them into workers' *artels*'. It then spoke of recruiting and taxes. From
the first it dealt not with the villages but with industrial centres. There was a
reportage on Odessa.[44] Following numbers appealed more and more clearly
to the workers' campaign. 'A rebellion is necessary, but it must be carried
out in an intelligent way.' True enough, it still spoke of Stenka Razin. But
in longer and more detailed passages it drew inspiration from the experiences
of France in 1848 and above all from those of the International. Number 5
even made an open attack on the myth of Pugachev, in a leading article
called *The Russian State*. Before the State existed, it explained, Russia had
administered itself in free *obshchinas* along the banks of the great rivers.
Every *obshchina* governed itself, and all problems were decided in meetings
of the *mir*. Then gradually the State came into being. Pugachev's great
rebellion had been a reaction against the State. But what would have
happened if he had won? Would the position of the people have been improved? Certainly not. To replace the State of Catherine, Pugachev would
have built his own State, no better than the first. 'Pugachev was not a
champion of freedom for the peasants. He intended to exploit the faith
that the peasants had in him so as to sit on Catherine's throne and rule. Of
course he was against the nobles, of course he promised land and liberty.
But he did not lead the merchants and *kulaks* to the gallows which he built
for the aristocrats.' Alexander II had also promised liberty: 'But the day
will come when the Russian people will win liberty for itself. And this will
happen when the people finally understands that nothing is to be expected
from any of the Tsars. Then the password will be "A curse on the race of
kulaks and *miroeds*".' The translation of class warfare into Russian terminology led to the first criticism of Populist myths. Wanting to attract landless
peasants who were compelled to seek work in the factories, the *Rabotnik*

resorted to more radical slogans, and at the same time tried to hold up the experiences of the West as an example. It published as a serial a *Letter of a French Worker to his Brothers in Russia* by L. Khalin, which spoke of Babeuf and quoted long passages from the manifesto of 'Equals'. These were the things which the Russian workers must know of. The popular booklets which the Chaikovskists had printed were no longer enough; indeed these were attacked in an article in the sixth number dated July 1875. The workers must 'have faith in themselves' and look at what was happening in England, Germany, Switzerland and Belgium.

When a factory went on strike in Moscow, the *Rabotnik* said that 'the Russian workers must follow the example of their foreign brothers'.[45] It then explained how cooperatives were organized in Germany, England and France,[46] and also discussed the trade unions in Great Britain, even though these last showed that: 'It is not by peaceful means that the situation of the workers can be improved.'[47] As the months passed, the *Rabotnik* devoted more and more space to the international working class movement.

The *Rabotnik* was characterized by a rather vague and high-sounding spirit of collectivism. 'The peasants of Great Russia must join together with the other workers into a great *obshchina*, to create a world in which the land belongs to all, everything belongs to all.' Once more the *Rabotnik* raised the banner of Land and Liberty. On the front page of the first issue of 1876 was a drawing which showed a Russian peasant with an axe in one hand and in the other a banner carrying the words *Zemlya i Volya*. He was standing in a village street at the head of a group of peasants armed with pitchforks. Under the drawing was a poem by Ogarev.

The *Rabotnik* published many reports on working class conditions, especially in the early numbers. When the organization collapsed in Moscow, its news from Russia became less and less frequent.

The central core of the movement which spread these ideas in the Russian factories consisted of about twenty people. Its base was established in Moscow, probably for reasons of practical convenience. For St Petersburg had been affected by the recent arrests, and did not offer a field suitable for an immediate revival of activities. Scarcely had the group reached Russia before its members put into practice the article of their regulations which obliged members to hand over their money. As some of them, mainly the Caucasians, came from rich families and sold their goods, the organization was in a far better financial situation than earlier groups had been. It therefore had no need to resort to robbery. Propaganda among the workers was carried out by the girls who came to the factories in turn and applied for work with false papers. They were often able to share the life of the workers. But difficulties arose immediately. The large textile factories of Moscow were very like workers' barracks, with dormitories and rules which regulated the employees' lives down to the last detail. To go into the men's dormitories and read revolutionary books by candlelight was in itself a serious violation of these rules, and naturally attracted the attention of the supervisors. These girl propagandists were soon trapped in the meshes of a world which they did not understand. Besides, even those workers who were drawn into the organization had difficulties enough. They too were at once noticed, and quickly had to give up their jobs. This explains, at least partly, the fact that the first working class groups grew up outside the factories. Illegality transformed these groups into professional revolutionaries, who led a similar life to the Populist intellectuals and students.

Despite these obstacles, which arose in the first instance from a desire to carry out open propaganda, the organization was very soon able to establish fairly solid bonds with all the working class districts and most important industrial centres of Moscow. 'Two months of work', Dzhabadari said, 'led to the most wonderful results. We infected twenty factories and also many small workshops of carpenters, cabinet makers and blacksmiths and also the railway men of the Moscow-Kursk-Kharkov line.' At the same time similar groups were being formed all round Moscow, in the so-called 'industrial region' of Ivanovo-Voznesensk, Serpukhov, Tula, Shuya, etc. Everywhere it was obvious that the workers were paying great attention, though they were still uncertain as to who were these strange men who came to read them revolutionary booklets and newspapers. Everywhere it was clear that the propaganda was not falling in the void.

So the spirit of sacrifice that inspired the young women students of Zurich bore fruit in the first infiltration of propaganda into the working masses round Moscow.

Beta Kaminskaya took advantage of every possible pretext to start discussions with the workers. If she saw a young man holding the book which his employer had given him and which contained the rules concerning the workers' duties, Kaminskaya read it to him aloud, explaining the meaning of each rule and showing the workers how each one of these articles was harmful to them and advantageous only to the employer. She spoke to them of the lives of workers in the West, of their solidarity and their struggle against exploitation by their employers. Gradually as she got deeper into the conversation, she spoke of history, and told them of episodes of the revolution in France and elsewhere. Naturally, the workers were very amazed by these stories. Kaminskaya had said that she was of peasant origins; her seriousness and her culture, which were so unusual in a peasant, made the workers conclude that she belonged to the *Raskol*. For the women of the *Raskol* are indeed the best educated of the inhabitants of Russian villages.[48]

Sofya Bardina took the first opportunity to begin to read a booklet which she had with her, *The Story of the Four Brothers*. The success was enormous. A large crowd collected round her. When she stopped reading, the questions were endless: 'Where do you come from? Who are you? Who has taught you to read so well?' were heard on all sides. Bardina said that she was from the *Raskol*, that as a girl she had been employed as a maid by the gentry and that she had learnt to read. She had gone back to her village, and there had become a devout reader of the scriptures, but now necessity had driven her to try and find work in the factories . . .

From then on Bardina frequently visited the men's dormitories . . . The workers were proud of her, and on their day of rest, in the inns, they turned to her beseeching her to read them the newspapers.[49]

Letters exchanged between the different groups in the Moscow region show that there was general awareness of the danger that such open propaganda could cause to the entire organization. But despite this they saw the possibility of action extending before them. They wrote to each other of the news that there had been a 'rising' of four thousand people at Serpukhov and that the workers had demanded that they should not be made to work on Saturday evening.

They have refused to work. The strike lasted fourteen days, and they have won all along the line. The governor, V. Voeykov, and other swine of the kind intervened; they behaved very politely to the people and praised them to an unbelievable extent. This means that they are frightened. There has also been another rising in the government workshop at Tula. The workers have begun to sabotage their tools. They have been interrogated, but have denied it. They began to rebel when a fine was imposed for all the losses suffered by the industry . . . At St Petersburg, too, there has been a strike against a private employer.[50]

The more their work seemed to grow in extent, the more they felt that they ought to be cautious so as not to lose their more active and strenuous members. But before they could take precautions, the movement failed. The organization was vulnerable. One worker denounced them, and this was enough for the police, helped by a stroke of luck, to strike at the heart of the movement. In many ways their activities among the workers had already followed the road that was soon to be taken by *Zemlya i Volya*. But the mechanism of their conspiracy was always casual and spasmodic. The very impulse that inspired them in their work was to lead to their speedy downfall. During the first few days of April 1875 all the Moscow apparatus collapsed. Before the end of the year the outer centres were also eliminated.

They had to wait three years in prison before the trial took place. But this in itself made their activities far more widely known than anything they had done when free. The police had quickly realized that this was a new force to be reckoned with. When they went to arrest Tsitsianov, they were met with armed resistance, and when they asked him why he had fired, he answered 'for the reason for which one usually fires: to hit the target'. It is true that Tsitsianov failed to hit anyone and it is true that the resistance was improvised. None the less this was the first time that anything of the kind had taken place and it constituted both an example and a precedent. The spirit that inspired Tsitsianov was shared by all his comrades. At the trial they not only defended themselves with vigour and intelligence, but above all they were able to bring their political and moral characteristics clearly to light. Their defence was inspired both by enthusiasm for the 'mad summer' and by a conscious political force. Bardina was perhaps the most typical representative of the movement and, after her speech, the words of Alexeyev echoed in the Hall of Justice; and he was the first Russian worker to proclaim aloud his revolutionary convictions.

Petr Alexeyevich Alexeyev was born in 1849. He was the son of a family of poor peasants, in the department of Smolensk. Since boyhood he had worked as a weaver in a factory. He had learned to read on his own at the age of sixteen or seventeen. For a time he had been in contact with the Chaikovskists in St Petersburg. Desire to learn had driven him to establish links with the group led by Sinegub and Perovskaya. He had gone to work in Moscow, and had allied himself with the Caucasians. He had then devoted himself to intensive propaganda in the factories. His own experiences and those of his family confirmed what they explained to him about the relations between peasants and workers. A small, strong man, he was full of warm and loyal gratitude for the intellectuals who had shown him the way to fight and, at the same time, he had ample faith in himself and in his working-class comrades. Lack of documents prevents us from entering further into the mind of this obviously exceptional man. But all his life is summed up in the speech which he made to the tribunal. He spoke of hard working conditions which did not allow 'the satisfaction of the most essential human needs'.

I know something about the problems of our Western brothers. Their conditions are in many ways different from those in Russia. Over there they do not persecute, as they do here, those workers who devote all their free time and many sleepless nights to reading. Indeed, there they are proud of them, and speak of us Russians as a people of slaves and semi-barbarians. And how else can one speak of us? Have we any free time to apply ourselves to anything? Are our poor folk taught anything in their childhood? Are there any useful and accessible books for the workman? Where and from whom can he learn anything?

After spending much time on the thirst for learning which prevailed among the popular classes, Alexeyev devoted the last part of his speech to the most important political problems.

This peasant reform of 19th February 1861—this reform which was a 'gift'—even though it is indispensable, was not provoked by the people itself, and does not guarantee the peasant's most indispensable needs. Just as before, we were left without a piece of bread, and with a completely inadequate strip of land, and so we passed under the control of the capitalists . . . If we are unlucky enough to be forced again and again to demand an increase in wages which the capitalists are constantly decreasing, they accuse us of striking and deport us to Siberia. And so this means that we are still serfs! If we are forced by the capitalist himself to leave the factory, they accuse us of organizing a revolt and use a soldier's rifle to force us to continue our work, and some are deported as instigators to distant lands. And so that means that we are still serfs! From all that I have just been saying it is obvious that the Russian workman can have hope only in himself, and can expect help only from our young intelligentsia which has stretched out a brotherly hand to us. It has understood in the depth of its soul the meaning and origin of the desperate complaints which come in from all sides. It can no longer look on coldly at the persecuted, oppressed peasant as he weeps under the yoke of despotism. It alone, like a good friend, has held out a brotherly hand, and in all sincerity wants to lift us out of our difficulties and put us on the right road for all the oppressed. It alone is tireless and leads us on . . . and it alone, united with us, will accompany us until the time when the muscular arm of millions of workers will arise and the yoke of despotism, defended by the soldier's bayonet, will fall to pieces.[51]

He was condemned to ten years' hard labour. This was one of the heaviest sentences imposed during the trial, and was the same as that of Tsitsianov and Alexandrov. In 1884, before his sentence had expired, he was banished to the region of Yakutsk in Eastern Siberia. In a letter he speaks of 'the terrible road that implacable fate demands should be trodden by all honest people' and he explains that this 'horrible fate' was incarnate 'in the members of our powerful government'. One day in 1891 he was killed in a wood by tramps or brigands. This was probably pure accident.[52]

At this 'trial of the fifty', many other working men and women besides Alexeyev were sentenced to various punishments, though considerably less than his, 'for having fled from the factory where they were working, fearing as was said the results which would ensue from the spreading of harmful books among the workers'. They were of all trades and often as much artisans as real factory workers. The most typical was one of Alexeyev's friends, Smirnov, who also came from the Tortoni factory, where he had been among the first working class comrades of Perovskaya. After the collapse of the Chaikovskists he had gone to Moscow with a false passport and had found work there. In 1875 he too was arrested. He was deported, and in 1877 fled to Moscow where he was arrested again a year later. In 1880 he was sent to the region of the Enisey in Siberia.[53]

The intellectuals also paid a heavy price for their work as pioneers. Sofya Bardina was sentenced to ten years' hard labour. After some years she was banished to the department of Tobolsk in Siberia. She then succeeded in escaping abroad. But she did not stand the test of exile, and committed suicide in 1883[54]. Only a few of her comrades who were sent to Siberia for varying periods were ever able to resume the fight they had begun in Moscow in 1875. But both L. N. Figner and O. S. Lyubatovich later took part in *Narodnaya Volya*.

The fall of the *Pan-Russian Social-Revolutionary Organization* gave rise to a current of sympathy and admiration for the revolutionaries who had sacrificed themselves in it. Their example helped to intensify the struggle, but no real working class movement was born of their efforts in Moscow. Factory propaganda there was always less lively than in Odessa, Kiev and specially St Petersburg. Till now we have only seen the origins of the working class movements in Southern and Central Russia. To observe the considerable political importance it was assuming we must now turn to the capital.

The arrests of the beginning of 1874, which had struck the Chaikovskists' industrial centres, did not interrupt the infiltration of revolutionary ideas among the workers of St Petersburg. Even after the Populist pioneers had been eliminated, their organizations, the ideas they had launched, and indeed the early friction between workers and intellectuals continued to develop. We know little of this silent process during the years 1874, 1875 and 1876. The documents in our possession obviously represent only fragments of the picture, whose appearance we can guess at rather than grasp as a whole. These documents deal with separate episodes, but they do none the less show that the contact which had been established between students and workers not only survived but indeed was gradually strengthened. After 1874 it was no longer only the revolutionary students who sought contacts in the factories. The workers themselves, once they had been converted by propaganda, took the initiative in tying together broken threads, and repeatedly asking for support and help. Indeed they themselves were now stretching out a 'brotherly hand' to those intellectuals who could give more significance to their dissatisfaction and revolutionary spirit.[55]

The Lavrovists began their propaganda in the winter of 1874. Ya. Tikhomirov was then in touch with Ivan Timofeyevich Smirnov, a worker whose fortunes we already know of, and their group had solid links with the men employed in the arsenal. But very soon the Lavrovists suffered heavy losses in trying to spread propaganda among the troops of a regiment stationed in St Petersburg.

Dyakov and a small group of very young students, all of humble origins, also carried out propaganda during this winter. And we can look upon their work as another example of the attempt to resume the interrupted labour of the Chaikovskists. But in this rapidly developing movement even a single year was of value. New factors are already in evidence in Dyakov's ventures. On the one hand there was a more radical anarchism, and on the other, strange as it may seem, a greater concern with political problems. This was the first symptom of a development which was to be fundamental in the years that immediately followed.[56]

Vyacheslav Mikhailovich Dyakov and Alexey Ivanovich Siryakov both came from clerical families; Dyakov was the son of a deacon, Siryakov of a priest. They had gone together to the seminary in their native Vologda, and in 1874 had entered St Petersburg University. The speed with which the two young men threw themselves into propaganda hardly had they reached the capital astounded the Minister of Public Instruction when they were arrested. 'They arrived in the autumn, and after a few months they were already at work. They could not have had time to be infected by corrupt doctrines there, and there is no doubt that they had been prepared for these ever since their days in the seminary.' An inquiry was made and it confirmed the Minister's impressions. Political exiles in Vologda had 'infected' even the seminary. This was already the case when Lavrov was in the district and the facts show that the ferment he had aroused had not diminished after his departure.

Together with two close friends from the School of Medicine, Dyakov and Siryakov succeeded in making contacts with soldiers and non-commissioned officers of the Moscow regiment of the bodyguard, and above all with workers in a sugar factory, a brewery and other places of the kind.[57] They also made attempts to infiltrate into the munitions factory. They, too, read out popular pamphlets to meetings of about a dozen workers as their usual means of propaganda. 'The harvest is splendid, but there are few to devote themselves to it', said one of the group, as he saw the attention that the audience paid to his words.[58] Dyakov generally began by reading Khudyakov's booklet on *Old Russia*. He showed how the State had gradually come into being and explained the origins of the oppression against which they must now rebel. History for him, like for so many of his Populist companions, was the best field for satisfying the workers' ardent longing for education and simultaneously imbuing them with propaganda. He also taught geography and spoke of French and English history. But the history of Russia was the ground on which he could most easily try and arouse political and social ferment. He naturally emphasized the revolts of Stenka Razin and Pugachev. However, in this group too, as in Moscow, criticism of these peasant myths was beginning. Siryakov explained that 'Pugachev made a mistake when he began to live like a Tsar and forgot the simple people. And so when a revolt breaks out it is essential not to give a single man the absolute power that Pugachev had.'[59] Such was the influence of anarchism and the *Rabotnik*. In general their message was radical in the extreme. The workers certainly interpreted their words in this sense: Seize all the factories from the employers: Eliminate the government: Do away with the gentry: Seize all the land and divide it among the peasants: Do not rebuild any State. That was how they understood the propaganda. The very title of one of the manuscripts which the group read aloud to the workmen pointed out that there was no difference between serfdom in the old days which had been enforced with the stick, and the new serfdom which was based on hunger. It is, however, obvious from the pamphlets that they distributed, and from the few surviving notes of their programmes, that their concern to know and make known the political situation in the countries of Western Europe imposed some limit on this primitive anarchism. Dyakov explained the condition of workers in England and he spoke of their economic problems. Lavrov's publications had a wide circulation. The programmes that they planned make clear that they thought that Russia's economic development might well be similar to that of the West. Their anarchist ideal, by destroying at its very base any absolute faith in the natural tendencies of the Russian people towards Socialism, raised political problems once more.[60]

Dyakov was arrested in April 1875 and his small group fell with him. He was sentenced to ten years' hard labour. Two of his comrades got nine; Siryakov, six; and the others lighter sentences. Dyakov died of tuberculosis in prison on 22nd September 1880. When the records of his trial reached the groups in Moscow which were carrying out—on a larger scale—work parallel to his own, they immediately sent them to Geneva.[61] The eighth number of the *Rabotnik*—dated August 1875—devoted an article to him and pointed him out to the Russian workers as a man who had sacrificed himself for them. As far as we know, this was the only response to the episode at the time.

With the fall of the Chaikovskists, the Lavrovists and those who had tried to follow their tracks, Populist propaganda among the workers of St Petersburg came to a momentary halt. Later it was resumed with the formation of groups which merged into *Zemlya i Volya*. And then it was faced with the first attempt made by the workers themselves to act on their own and found their own organization.

By about 1875 there was already a large number of workers in St Petersburg who were not only extremely keen to learn and to read—typical self-educated men from workshops and factories—but who were also well able to hold their own views on the various political ideas about which they had heard the students speak. They were able, in fact, to contrast Populist propaganda with the events of their own lives. Plekhanov has described some of these workers who were at this time acquiring new personalities through their first experience of political activity. These pages are the most vivid in the book which he published in 1890 about his activities in the working class districts of St Petersburg during the second half of the 'seventies. While some of his judgments on this period are strongly influenced by the social-democratic ideas that he later adopted, these portraits retain the true flavour of authenticity.[62]

Plekhanov gives us a vivid picture of the various problems involved in the process of adaptation to urban life and new conditions of work made by the peasants. We can watch the demoralization which was sometimes brought on by the break in their traditional life; and we see new energies being released which, among the most developed workers, mainly took the form of great thirst for culture. It was on this field that there occurred the first clashes between the workers and the intellectuals. The factory workers were seeking the means to enter the world of learning, and they were no longer satisfied with the booklets published for them by Chaikovskists. They found no organ in the clandestine press which really reflected their problems. It is true that they read the *Rabotnik* with special interest; and the influence of this paper is probably greater than is usually admitted by those who have studied the period. But even this periodical, which was written in popular language, did not give the workers that direct contact with the intellectual life of the educated revolutionary classes which they were beginning to demand. So *The Sated and the Hungry*, that encyclopaedia of anarchist

Populism, became one of their favourite works, just because of its many-sided character. Plekhanov said:

When I asked the workers themselves what exactly they wanted from revolutionary writings, I met with the most varied answers. In most cases each of them wanted a solution to those problems which for some reason were of special interest to my individual hearer at that particular moment. In the mind of the workers such problems were increasing enormously, and each had his favourite questions according-ing to his own tendencies and character. One was particularly interested in the problem of God and claimed that revolutionary literature ought to use its energies mainly for destroying the religious beliefs of the people. Others were interested in historical or political problems, or in the natural sciences. Among my acquaintances in the factories, there was also one who was specially interested in the question of women.[63]

And so the first effect of propaganda among the workers was to separate the most gifted figures from the general mass and to create a small self-educated *élite*. The methods employed in the revolutionary campaign also tended to produce similar effects. We have seen this happening in Moscow, and later events confirm the process. And so the first awakening of the workers tended to bring into being the figure of the workman-revolutionary immediately after that of the student Populist. Indeed this new figure often merged with the other both in mentality and way of life. Thus towards the end of the 'seventies, working class elements, as well as nobles, bourgeois and petit bourgeois, flow into the Populist movement. Tkachev had forecast that a Socialist *élite* made up of varying social classes and united only by the revolutionary ideal would have to take upon itself all the responsibility for the social movement. This now appeared to be happening. Much of the Blanquist influence (in the specifically Tkachevian sense of the word) which we meet in *Narodnaya Volya* derived from this situation.

But alongside this merging into the revolutionary *élite*, there began to appear the first signs of a separation between intellectuals and workers. This came in part from a feeling of exclusiveness which was natural enough as the working classes entered on a life of politics. Bachin, whose tragic life we have mentioned, was perhaps one of the most typical representatives of this state of mind in the middle of the 'seventies. During a journey to Rostov, he explained his point of view to a group of workers who had been assembled by Populist organizers.

He was a man of heated temperament and he began to speak rather bitterly about how the intelligentsia had usurped the position of the worker. He suggested to the workers of Rostov that they should impose some limit on this abnormal situation and should restrict the intellectuals' field of activities to certain given functions. They should be made to understand that the workers' cause ought to be placed entirely in the hands of the workers themselves.[64]

As a rule the workers expressed this state of mind, which is confirmed in other memoirs of the period, by refusing to follow the Populists when they invited them to spread propaganda in the countryside, and thus serve as the instrument for carrying Socialism to the villages. These working class revolutionaries often came from government workshops, and no longer belonged to the *artels* of poor peasants who had been compelled to seek a living in private factories. They had made the effort to become specialized workers, such as mechanics, so as to earn a better living. Now they were being asked to sacrifice themselves for the poorest and most unsuccessful. They had placed all their hopes on getting educated, and now they were being asked to live once more in conditions of patriarchal destitution. Such a sacrifice demanded a Populist consciousness which they had as yet hardly begun to absorb. Some of them, such as Khalturin, were capable of the greatest and most heroic sacrifices; but this was just because they had gradually become revolutionaries pure and simple, linked only to the Populist *élite*, whatever their social origin had been. On close inspection, the refusal to go to the countryside was frequently due to lack of a political conscience and not, as has often been repeated, to the birth of a higher working class consciousness. The Populists, naively perhaps but powerfully and with grandeur, saw the problem of revolution in Russia as a whole; and so they emphasized the bonds between the peasant and the working classes. The workers on the other hand often unconsciously shut themselves into a narrower and smaller world. They were inspired by contempt for those who had not succeeded in winning for themselves some minimum of education or decent conditions. 'The peasants are all sheep,' said Bachin, 'they will never understand the revolutionaries.'[65]

But all these complex reactions towards the intelligentsia were giving birth to a really new movement. This was the creation of a specifically working class mentality. In bringing such a mentality into being, the workers had little to hope for from the students. Nor could they simply 'learn' it from the intellectuals. They had to create it for themselves through the initiative of some of the most intelligent and strongest of their own leaders. It is true that the idea of developing working class agitation on as large a scale as possible, starting from their immediate economic demands, formed part of the programme of the groups which were to constitute *Zemlya i Volya*. It was they who, as we will see, organized the first strikes in St Petersburg at the end of the 'seventies. But the desire to guide these disturbances into an organized force, a '*Union*, came from the workers themselves, mainly as the result of work carried out by Obnorsky and Khalturin. Both were exceptional men, capable even on their own of revealing the energy which was latent in the working masses of St Petersburg.

Viktor Obnorsky was born in the department of Vologda in 1852, the son of a retired non-commissioned officer.[66] His family was poor and numerous. He had, however, had an elementary education in the schools of his district, and had then become a blacksmith and mechanic. In 1869 he went to the armament factory at St Petersburg. There he joined a reading club run by the workers. He then got employment in the Nobel factories in the Vyborg district. In 1872 he got into contact with the Chaikovskists through Mitrofanov who was mixed up in all the workers' movements of the time. He took part in the organization of a small library. This had been founded by the Chaikovskists for the very purpose of entrusting its administration to the workers themselves, for they thought that if they were arrested this small institution would be able to continue on its own. This is, in fact, what happened. In these circles Obnorsky began to speak of a great strike to involve all labour in St Petersburg. This, he said, must be prepared gradually and with great care. At the time of the arrests he succeeded in escaping the fate of many of his companions, and in August 1873 he left St Petersburg for Odessa. This journey seems to have been prompted by the determination, which thereafter always governed him, to obtain personal knowledge of the experiences of other workers and to see for himself what were the real possibilities that were opening up before them. At Odessa, between autumn 1873 and the beginning of 1874 he was in touch with Zaslavsky's organization, the *Union of Workers of South Russia,* and allied himself with G. I. Barantsev.[67] However, the exact nature of his relations with the *Union* is not altogether clear. Some have thought that the internal opposition within the ranks of the *Union* was a reflection of the early antagonism between intellectuals and workers which was already beginning to develop in St Petersburg at the time of Nizovkin. Certainly even at Odessa Obnorsky remained in contact with the capital and among other things asked for financial help. However this may be, it seems difficult to deny that he learnt much from the working class organization at Odessa to which he then belonged in some form or another.

His experiences at Odessa prompted him to look further afield. Getting employment as a ship's stoker at the beginning of 1874, he left in secret for London. From there he went to Paris and travelled in France and Savoy and thence to Basle, Geneva, Lausanne and Freiburg. 'He was prompted by simple curiosity', one of his comrades later told the police when they asked him the reason for Obnorsky's travels. In fact, however, his curiosity was already political. He stopped longer at Geneva than anywhere else, where he was employed as a workman. After returning secretly to Russia, he went to the department of Archangel, probably for some political mission of which we know nothing. It is in any case certain that his organizing ventures, which were to lead to the creation of the 'Northern Union', began towards the end of 1875. It is more than likely that he was then in contact with the Lavrovists, as was also Khalturin whom he met at this time and who became his closest collaborator. In November 1876 Obnorsky again went abroad. He stayed away about a year, getting into contact with Tkachev and above all with the *Rabotnik* group. But at this time his ideas were particularly influenced by German social-democracy. On his return to St Petersburg at the beginning of 1878, he found the situation there specially favourable for his plans. The entire revolutionary movement was growing in intensity and a wave of strikes was beginning to spread through the town. He again went abroad to get hold of a printing press (which he succeeded in buying from the *Nabat* group through V. N. Cherkezov) and also to make some definite political agreement.[68] He had discussions with Akselrod and Lavrov,[69] and asked the former to become editor of the clandestine newspaper which he wanted to start for the workers. As we will see, these plans could only be realized in part. By the time he got back to Russia, the centre of the *Union* had already been destroyed by the arrests.

Stephen Khalturin was born in the department of Vyatka and came from a relatively prosperous family of State peasants.[70] His father knew how to read, and he himself had a good education. The local school was excellent. Indeed it was far better than the classical grammar school, being more technical and scientific, and more in tune with modern life. But in his third year Khalturin had to leave school to begin work. Like Obnorsky, he became a blacksmith and mechanic. When still at Vyatka he had been influenced by Socialist ideas. At the age of fifteen or sixteen he was in touch with political exiles who planned to found with him and others a small cooperative or, as they proposed to call it, a 'commune'. A number of young men from this group were planning to emigrate to America, and at the age of seventeen Khalturin too began the journey. He passed through Moscow on his way to St Petersburg to embark with the others. But when he reached the capital he saw that his friends had left him and had embarked without being able to wait. In Russia as elsewhere the history of the working class movement shows many examples, of which this is one, of the bond between the search for freedom through emigration and the first attempts to organize resistance in the factories.[71] During these years there were many workers who crossed the frontiers of Russia, as did Obnorsky, or who tried to do so, like Khalturin. 'There was at this time among the workers a great longing to go and work abroad', said D. N. Smirnov, one of these men.[72] Ivanaynen and Vinogradov, for instance, worked at Zurich and were arrested on their return and sent to the Peter-Paul fortress. I. I. Medvedev was stopped at the frontier. And there are many more examples.

In St Petersburg, Khalturin got into contact with the Chaikovskists and above all Charushin and Morozov. 'He was a man of few words, but it was obvious that he devoted all his spirit and the greatest attention to our conversations', Morozov recalled.[73] By 1875 and 1876 he himself was already an active propagandist among his workmen comrades.

Young, tall and strong, with a fine complexion and expressive eyes, he impressed us as a splendid fellow . . . But his engaging, and at the same time rather ordinary, appearance did not reveal the strength of his character and his exceptional intelligence. What mostly struck me in his behaviour was his retiring, almost feminine gentleness. When speaking he seemed to grow ashamed, as if he was frightened of offending you by using some word out of place or by expressing his opinions too violently. There was always a shy smile on his lips which never disappeared and which seemed to say to you 'I think like this, but if it does not suit you, please forgive me'. One could only approach him if both of you worked together for this purpose . . . Not that he himself did not want to speak—and not just with his working class comrades but with the intelligentsia also. When his activities were still on the right side of the law, he willingly met students and tried to make their acquaintance, getting every kind of information from them and borrowing books. He often stayed with them until midnight, but he very rarely gave his own opinions. His host would grow excited, delighted at the chance to enlighten an ignorant workman, and would speak at great length, theorizing in the most 'popular' way possible. Stepan would stay there listening. Only rarely did he put in a word of his own. And he would gaze carefully, looking up at the speaker. Every now and then his intelligent eyes would reflect an amiable irony. There was always an element of irony in his relations with the students . . . With the workers he behaved in a very different way . . . he looked upon them as more solid and, so to speak, more natural revolutionaries and he looked after them like a loving nurse. He taught them, he sought books and work for them, he made peace among them when they quarrelled, and he scolded the guilty. His comrades loved him dearly; he knew this and in return gave them even greater love. But I do not believe that even in his relations with them Khalturin ever gave up his customary restraint . . . In the groups he spoke only rarely and unwillingly. Among the workers of St Petersburg there were people just as educated and competent as he was; there were men who had seen another world, who had lived abroad. The secret of the enormous influence of what can be called Stepan's dictatorship lay in the tireless attention which he devoted to each single thing. Even before meetings began, he spoke with everyone to find out the general state of mind; he considered all sides of the question; and so naturally he was the most prepared of all. He expressed the general state of mind.[74]

Politically, Khalturin was the most typical example of the specifically working class mentality, which was forming among the more qualified and best educated workers in St Petersburg. Yet at the same time he was the real symbol of the absorption of the finest of this type into the Populist ranks. Plekhanov recalled that 'compared to those of *Zemlya i Volya*, Khalturin was an extreme Westerner. This Westernism was born and rooted in him thanks to the general situation of working class life in the capital, which alone interested him; and thanks also to various casual circumstances. Indeed, he had been in contact with the Lavrovists before the Populist "rebels", and the Lavrovists were able to stimulate among the workers an interest in the German social-democratic movement.' And yet for all this Khalturin was to become a terrorist and one of the most typical exponents of *Narodnaya Volya*. And his life was to come to a tragic end on the gallows, following an act of terrorism. His story, indeed, contains all the drama implicit in this first stage of the Russian working class movement—torn between an awareness of the specific interests of the workers and growing political and revolutionary consciousness.

The first visible result of the work of organization in the factories and workshops of St Petersburg was the demonstration in the Square of Kazan Cathedral on 6th December 1876.[75] For some time there had been discussions in revolutionary circles in the capital on the possibility of making some public demonstration in one of the central parts of the town. An early plan had suggested a meeting on the Square of St Isaac. There were long discussions and it was postponed from month to month. The funeral of Chernyshev, a student who died in prison, had already led to a demonstration in spring 1876, and it was now proposed to emulate this example on a larger scale. The suggestion that this should be effected by a demonstration of working class groups came from these groups themselves. At this time they were increasing and reorganizing and they claimed that up to 2,000 workers would be prepared to join. Chernyshev, they added, had been buried by the intelligentsia. Now it was to be their turn to display their forces in the centre of the town. The various leaders of the time who were particularly concerned with propaganda among the workers, Lev Markovich Zak, Nikolay Nikolaevich Khazov, Alexander Serafimovich, A. Bogdanovich and Plekhanov, naturally had some doubts about the practical possibilities of bringing such a plan into effect. 'But rebel blood made itself felt in each of us and we agreed.'[76] The Lavrovists were against the move on principle and remained faithful to their programme of long-term propaganda. Zaichnevsky's Jacobins also viewed it with disfavour, but for the opposite reason. They believed in organizing only a ruling *élite*. It was the men who later formed *Zemlya i Volya* who put themselves at the head of this demonstration which the workers had demanded. At a meeting held on 4th December it was decided to summon the workers from the various districts on to the square which opened on to the Nevsky Prospekt and which was surrounded by the semi-circular colonnade of the Cathedral of Our Lady of Kazan, It was planned to give the demonstration an appearance of legality by asking the clergy of the church to arrange a funeral service. Action would then be taken according to circumstances. All the better, they thought, if the demonstration led to a rising.

On the morning of the 6th, the number of workers who collected was far smaller than had been hoped for—200 to 250, possibly 300. None the less it was proof of a new spirit in the organizations in the suburbs. One party from a large industrial undertaking in the port arrived complete. But the crowd was made up mainly of students and revolutionary intellectuals who had not been summoned especially but had heard previously of the plan. The organizers hesitated when they saw that the demonstration was on the brink of failure. Then Plekhanov decided that they must not miss their opportunity. He made a short speech, and ended with 'Long live the Social Revolution, Long live *Zemlya i Volya*'. A red banner with the words 'Land and Liberty' was then unfurled.

Then the guards burst in on the scene to arrest Plekhanov. They were, however, held up by the demonstrators. But when the crowd began to disperse along the Nevsky Prospekt to avoid being arrested individually, real confusion took place. The police meanwhile had been constantly reinforced and were supported by local volunteers, door-keepers, a few merchants, etc. There were many arrests. But they were all made at random and did not touch the real organizers. The men seized were treated with outstanding harshness, both by the police who manhandled them with great brutality, and by the tribunal that tried them. The court, in fact, deliberately sought to make a split between intellectuals and workers. Some of the workers were sentenced to varying periods of retreat and repentance in monasteries. Others were deported to Siberia. But the intellectuals received sentences which were heavy even by the standards of the time.[77] Alexey Stepanovich Emelyanov, who was arrested under the name of Bogolyubov, and who was then twenty-four and had already 'gone to the people', was sentenced to fifteen years' hard labour. His comrades' recollections not only prove that he was not one of the organizers of the demonstration but that he had not even taken any part in it. Indeed he had only arrived on the scene when the meeting had already been dispersed. He belonged to a category of revolutionaries which had been deliberately excluded from the demonstration, as it was engaged on other tasks. 'So as to avoid temptation,' said Emelyanov, 'at the time of the demonstration I had gone to take part in other activities, namely to practise firearms.'[78] But the police thought that they recognized him as a student who had personally distinguished himself in the fight that broke out immediately after the demonstration. In prison he was flogged, and eventually went mad. Two of his comrades got sentences of ten years' hard labour and another six years and eight months. The repressive measures that followed this demonstration were certainly the most arbitrary, the most legally indefensible and the most violent of all those of the time.

The reason for this was evidently to be found in political considerations which this event inevitably aroused in the ruling classes. Although it had not given rise to the great working class demonstration in which the organizers had hoped, its significance was unquestionable. The Populists too were well aware of this. One of them in particular, probably Khazov, made the point very clearly in a report which he wrote in January 1877.[79] 'The important result of the entire affair lies in the union that has now been brought about between the intelligentsia and the people.' This union had been achieved against the more moderate and conventional elements. The liberals were always talking about freedom of speech and meeting, but they had not lifted a finger. Indeed, they had been frightened by what had happened.

The Russian liberals were very learned. They even knew that liberty had been *conquered* in the West. But obviously one ought not to try to apply this knowledge to Russia.

Russia is led along the road to political freedom not by the liberals but by dreamers who organize ridiculous and childish demonstrations; by men who dare to break the law, by men who are beaten, sentenced and reviled.

18+

But reactions among the working class were very different from those in liberal circles. Here sympathy and agreement were complete. The workers of St Petersburg had not caught Oblomov's disease.

The success of their propaganda among the workers must make the revolutionaries themselves think again, the author went on. Was it really true, as was always said, that 'the Russian *people* was more socialist through custom and inclination and less infected by bourgeois conditions and habits than the proletariat of the West, and that therefore it was in Russia that there would occur a profound transformation of the existing order of things, a more rapid transition to a better order?' Did their experiences in the factories and workshops of St Petersburg, which now for the first time had led to a practical result, confirm or deny this traditional point of view? Did not the success they had obtained among the workers contradict these theories? The fact was that the urban workers, as contrasted with the peasants, had shown themselves 'more united and compact because of the equality of their conditions; more developed because of the variety of their impressions of town life and because of their frequent and bitter conflicts with the representatives of the government and the ruling classes; and, finally, more open to socialist propaganda.'

It was true that it must never be forgotten that in Russia the peasant problem remained the central question for anyone who wished to be a Socialist. Experience itself showed that what they had said from the first was not mistaken. The workers themselves would be the most useful and natural carriers of Socialist ideas into the villages. But from now on these policies must be applied in a different way. They must begin by organizing the workers. And to do this quickly they must pass from agitations, from incitement to resistance and revolt to 'political agitation'. Such a policy was demanded by the situation of the urban working classes.

Here the worker is always clearly aware of the injustice of the social régime that oppresses him. Here he can see that the luxury which is the work of his own hands is enjoyed by others. And so his mentality is attuned to demand a fight which will produce immediate results. He does not want to postpone the battle, but he wants to obtain (if not everything he wants) at least as much as possible as can be obtained at that given time. He wants to make at least a breach in that order of things which has become unbearable for him. He wants to be a free man with the right to think and speak openly in accordance with his opinions. In fact he sees that to fight against his economic exploiters he must make use of what is called political freedom. But this freedom he will have to conquer and he will therefore have to enter into conflict with the very essence of our State system. His activities along the road to freedom inevitably take on a political character. The events of 6th December are the result of this state of mind among the most conscious of the working classes.

The demonstrations on the Kazan Square showed that in Russia too 'the movement would follow the same direction as in the West, i.e. from the town to the country and not vice versa'.

This document constitutes the best possible preface to the regulations of the *Northern Union of Russian Workers*, which was given its final, and so to speak official, form almost two years later, in December 1878. The problem of the struggle for political freedom was here raised in the very articles of the statute. This explains the interpretation we must give to Plekhanov's statement that 'the future historian of the Russian revolutionary movement must note the fact that in the 'seventies the demand for political freedom appears in a working class programme before it appears in the programmes of the revolutionary intelligentsia'.[80] Indeed, the statutes of the *Northern Union* were the first public document in which this question of whether to concentrate activities on political activities was answered in the affirmative. But it had been the revolutionary intelligentsia that had raised these problems for the workers in St Petersburg. Some at least of the men of *Zemlya i Volya* had clearly seen, ever since 1876, the political consequences that would result from the formation of the first solid nucleus in the workshops of St Petersburg.[81]

But important progress was necessary before the demonstrators in the Square of Kazan Cathedral could be transformed into members of the *Northern Union*. During the two years that elapsed between these events it required a series of strikes in the factories of the capital in order to make heard the voice not only of the working class *élite* which was by now in a position to raise political problems, but also of the mass of 'grey ones', as the poorest worker-peasants employed in the textile factories of St Petersburg were called. The Balkan War, economic development and the general political ferment of these two years created the atmosphere which brought into being this general revival of the working class movement.

During the same period those revolutionaries who derived from the intelligentsia were also able to show to what extent they had matured. They supported and directed the strikes. They established ever wider and deeper relations with the workers. And, unlike the Chaikovskists and Zaslavsky, they did not collapse during the first stages of the fight. They devised a technique for activities among the workers which assured them relative security. This was all the more remarkable in that the working class organization, as we will see, was very soon infected by *agents provocateurs*. The very fact that the fall of the *Northern Union* had almost no effect on the central nucleus of *Zemlya i Volya* shows that the methods employed were now distinctly superior to those of the past. In practice the technique was based on an increasingly conscious and deliberate division of labour between the organized working class movement and the conspiratorial revolutionary movement. There is no point in examining here these details of clandestine technique. It is, however, worth while emphasizing that at least some of the aspects of the division between intelligentsia and workers that we can see during these years sprang from this deliberate technique rather than from any ideological or political conflict. There was a conflict and it did have historical significance. But in interpreting it we must be careful not to give it more importance than it really had by looking upon circumstantial appearances as actual realities.

In December 1877 there was an explosion in a store of gunpowder in the armaments factory on Vasilevsky Island. Six workers were killed and many more wounded. Ever since 1873 a working class group had been specially active in this factory and the funeral of the men killed in the explosion provided their first opportunity to arouse a collective protest.[82] For the incident had been caused by the criminal negligence of the management. Again and again the men had protested against their unsafe working conditions. In the factory was a small group of working class revolutionaries who were in touch both with *Zemlya i Volya* and with the Lavrovists. They knew that the latter would be against any public demonstration and so they sought and obtained help from *Zemlya i Volya*, who turned up in great numbers on the day of the funeral. Among them was Valerian Osinsky, one of the terrorists of the following period who, less than two years later, was to be hanged at Kiev after using firearms to resist arrest by the police. Khalturin was there, too, though he was not working in this factory at the time. At the cemetery an unknown workman began a speech saying that they had come to bury 'six victims, not of the Turks, but of the fatherly administration of the factory'. The police intervened to arrest him, but the workers not only dragged him away but even threatened the police and won their respect. This was a small but significant trial of strength which had a considerable psychological effect both on the workers and on the intelligentsia. Plekhanov wrote a manifesto which was distributed a week later in the armaments factory. He demanded that the workers should make themselves respected by the management too and that the families of the victims should be given adequate indemnity. His final words, hesitating, so to speak, between town and country, well reflect his own state of mind and that of his comrades.

Workers, now is the time to understand reason. You must not expect help from anyone. And do not expect it from the gentry! The peasants have long been expecting help from the gentry, and all they have got is worse land and heavier taxes, even greater than before . . . Will you too, the workers in towns, put up with this for ever?

In February 1878 disturbances began in the new cotton mills. These led to the most important strike of the time in the capital.[83] It is of considerable interest that the men were textile workers and not mechanics. In fact they were 'grey' ones and not better-paid workers. There were about 2,000 of them, and they were protesting against a reduction in wages of between 4 and 9 per cent. They were mainly demanding a return to the situation as before. The factory already contained a group of workers affected by propaganda, but it had been formed only recently and as yet it lacked experience. It was, however, reinforced by P. A. Moiseyenko, a workman specially sent to this factory by Obnorsky's and Khalturin's organization to spread propaganda and establish bonds with the nucleus of the *Northern Union* which was then being formed. There were also some links with *Zemlya i Volya*. These had been made by Aron Gobst, a junior officer. At the time he was being sought by the police for having spread propaganda among the troops at Odessa, and in June 1878 he was hanged in Kiev. He had settled in a small shop next to the factory, and from here he directed his activities. These were still only in the first stages when the mass of workers was set in ferment.

Plekhanov and Popov soon succeeded in taking over control and made an attempt to direct the movement. But to do this they needed to find someone able to live among the workers and be constantly with them. Such a man they found in Nikolay Lopatin,[84] who at once showed remarkable capacity for making himself heard. The strike was far from easy to organize. The workers were divided into two groups: the bachelors—often very young—who were bolder and more mobile, and the married men who hesitated when faced with the consequences of their actions. There were long discussions between the groups before they stopped work. Besides, during the first few days they were all convinced that the authorities would intervene on their behalf to enforce the original factory regulations. They turned to the chief of police in the district. He promised to help them, but of course did nothing. They finally decided to strike, when one of them shouted: 'Out of the factory, lads. Let the machines work on their own.' Plekhanov introduced himself to them as a lawyer, and made a speech designed to strengthen their determination to defend their rights. He began to sound the possibilities of changing the strike into a demonstration in which all together would carry their demands to the heir to the throne, the future Alexander III. Rumour had it that he was to some extent on the side of the people. The revolutionaries aimed to take advantage of this widespread conviction, so as to give greater political significance to the strike. Plekhanov naturally hoped the workers' demands would be listened to with as much sympathy by the heir to the throne as they had been by the chief of police. The demonstration would then serve to impair the deep and traditional faith in the Tsar which these worker-peasants still retained.

Zemlya i Volya only agreed to these tactics after long discussions. For the first time they were faced with the problem of a large-scale strike. They were of course determined to support and encourage these disturbances. Nothing in their programme, however, seemed to suggest exactly what they ought to do and what ought to be their immediate aim. But from the very first they saw that their influence on the mass of the workers was rapidly growing. They were able to get one St Petersburg newspaper to publish short accounts of the progress of the strike, written by Plekhanov in a spirit favourable to the workers' demands. When Lopatin read out these short articles in the courtyard of the factory, the workmen were deeply impressed by the fact that the newspapers were paying attention to them.[85] The organizers succeeded in collecting large sums to help those families which had been badly hit by the lack of wages. Through these collections they acted as intermediaries between liberal society in St Petersburg, which often supported the strikers, but which was worried by the thought of possible disorders, and the workers themselves, who were amazed and curious about such help which reached them so mysteriously. The organizers also tried to spread the strike to other factories, so as to provide the first great example of working class solidarity. Though here, too, their hopes were not realized, the workers did show remarkable cohesion. The police sent more and more agents round the factory, but they were very soon recognized and then shunned or insulted, whereas the revolutionaries began to inspire great admiration and trust. These men helped them in answering the authorities, and wrote the appeals that they eventually carried in a long and orderly procession through the centre of St Petersburg to the residence of the heir to the throne. The petition explained the situation and ended: 'If our demands are not satisfied, we will know that we have no one in whom we can hope, that no one will defend us, and that we must trust in ourselves and our own arms.' On this occasion there was no incident of any kind. Only later did the police arrest some of the working class leaders, among them Moiseyenko. At last the authorities were cunning enough to make a few promises. These were vague enough, but they were sufficient to induce some at least of the workers to return to work. The rest were driven back by force. And indeed many of their demands were gradually satisfied.

The political aim which Plekhanov had set himself was in great measure achieved. Among the workers and throughout the masses of St Petersburg strange rumours began to spread to the effect that the heir to the throne was bound by close ties to the factory owners. This was, at least, a sign that the blind faith in the State, and above all the Imperial family, which had still been intact in the minds of the workers before the strike, was now disintegrating. They saw that the agitation they had started had been forcefully broken up by the police and that if the strike had been a partial failure, this was due to political and not economic reasons. Much discussion within *Zemlya i Volya* followed these experiences. Plekhanov was led to think more and more about the importance of State intervention in labour conflicts, and so to attach still greater weight to the political campaign and the demand for liberty. Popov, on the other hand, who was here probably more representative of his comrades' views, thought that the strike confirmed the need to pay more attention to the worker-peasants of the factories than to labour in the mechanical workshops. The textile workers were 'both better chaps and more reliable as a power for protest'.[86]

Indeed, the textile workers very soon gave further confirmation of their fighting spirit. Strikes broke out one after another throughout the winter of 1878. The workers were still compelled to work thirteen hours a day, and their wages were extremely low. Once again the younger men put themselves at the head of the disturbances, which were only broken up by massive police intervention, followed this time by many arrests. The workers then made a combined attempt to free their comrades but this was suppressed after a violent clash with the police in the heart of St Petersburg.[87] Many prisoners remained in the hands of the authorities. And then the deportations began. In their demands, the workers openly insisted on the right not to be arrested for striking, and they repeatedly demanded that their comrades should be freed. *Zemlya i Volya* and the *Northern Union of Russian Workers* printed manifestos to appeal for resistance and solidarity in the various factories. Subscriptions for the workers on strike were launched in other factories and met with great success.[88] The police was forced to intervene violently in the strikes and this increased their significance as political protests. And they went on increasing. In November the 200 workers in the König spinning factory stopped work. They too carried a petition to the prince, and they too obtained nothing. In this case the workers themselves sought contact with the students, who until then had had no links with the factory. The police were harsher here than elsewhere. Negotiations with the employer had to be carried out at the headquarters of the Third Section. The police dragged some of the workers there to come to an understanding with the management. But even these steps proved useless and the employer had to resort to the extreme measure of dismissing all the workers. They were helped by subscriptions, and their comrades found new jobs for them.[89] The movement also spread to two cigarette factories, where only women were employed. In both cases violent protests broke out when a reduction in wages was announced. And in both cases labour won the day.

And so less-skilled workers were more and more deeply affected by the waves of strikes and disturbances between 1877 and 1879. During these two years St Petersburg witnessed twenty-six strikes in all. This was more than had ever occurred before; and not till the 'nineties would the figure be reached again.

It fell to the metal-workers, the best educated and prepared of all the workers, to make use of this state of affairs to found an organization directed by themselves, with an exclusively working-class character.

A nucleus had already been formed in winter 1876. Some of its members had scattered throughout the factories of the town, following a plan which aimed to unite all the forces of the working classes. As the strike wave was at its height they drew their conclusions from the work so far achieved and gave their *Northern Union of Russian Workers* its final shape. The programme and regulations were discussed in the course of two sittings, on 23rd and 30th December 1878. Obnorsky and Khalturin were the leading organizers, but among its ranks we find the names of very many of the workers who had already taken part in earlier movements.[90]

Their programme was printed by the clandestine press of *Zemlya i Volya*. After an introductory protest against 'the political and economic yoke which threatens the workers with total material privation and a paralysis of their spiritual forces' they said that they wanted to create 'a *Pan-Russian Union of Workers* which by grouping together the forces of the workers which are now dispersed in the towns and villages, and by enlightening them as regards their own interests, aims and aspirations, will be of real help in the struggle against social injustice and will constitute that internal, organic link which is indispensable for the successful prosecution of the struggle'. They then laid down what were to be the foundations of the organization. 'Members of the Union must be chosen exclusively from the workers.' Thus from the very first they established the condition which gave this organization its fundamental character. The workers who joined, however, were to be selected. One clause laid down that each candidate had to be introduced by at least two members. This was obviously dictated by the needs imposed by secrecy. But other rules were designed to make the *Union* a very select organization. Every member had to know the programme of the organization and 'the essentials of its social doctrine'. There was to be a quota, though in this first manifesto it was not yet determined. Among the functions of the leadership considerable importance was attached to looking after a library, which was to be open even to those who were not members of the *Union*. In general the *Union* revealed its desire for education both in its internal structure and in its political programme.

As in the regulations of all other Populist movements, the nature of the *Union*'s internal structure was determined by the double concern not to create an overpowerful central authority and yet simultaneously to provide an organization which could act quickly in conditions of secrecy. The very terminology used by the authors of the manifesto reflected this state of mind. A central group of ten workers was given the management of the bank, the library, and the responsibility 'only for those activities which are in the immediate interests of all the *Union*'. It was to be controlled by a monthly assembly. But it soon became obvious that the central group as constituted was unable to act quickly enough. Its members were often employed in remote districts of St Petersburg, and they could only meet at irregular intervals. When the second strike in the New Cotton Mills broke out, Khalturin found himself in difficulties and had to wait two days before being able to summon his comrades. The problem of organization was never solved, for arrests prevented the *Union* profiting from these experiences.[91]

The most original feature of the manifesto lay in the ultimate aims of the organization:

The Northern Union of Russian Workers, closely adhering to the social-democratic party of the West as regards its functions, lays down as its programme:

(1) the destruction of the political and economic structure of the State, this structure being completely and utterly unjust;

(2) the establishment of a free popular federation of *obshchinas* based upon com-

plete equality of political rights and complete internal self-government on the basis of the customary laws of Russia;

(3) the abolition of landed property and its substitution by collective agriculture;

(4) the fair organization of labour on the basis of association which gives the worker-producer the products and tools of his work.

As political liberty provides a guarantee for every man of the independence of his convictions and activities, and as it is above all political liberty which guarantees the solution of the social problem, the *Union* must declare the following points to be its immediate demands:

(1) freedom of speech and of the press and of the right to meet and assemble;

(2) abolition of the police spies and of trials for political crimes;

(3) abolition of the rights and privileges of caste;

(4) free compulsory education in all schools and institutions;

(5) a numerical reduction in the standing army or its complete replacement by a people's militia;

(6) the right of the village *obshchina* to decide questions concerning it, such as imposition of taxes, sub-division of the land, and internal self-government;

(7) abolition of the system of internal passports, and freedom of movement;

(8) abolition of indirect taxation and introduction of direct taxation in accordance with income and heredity;

(9) reduction in the hours of work and prohibition of child labour;

(10) creation of productive associations of savings banks and free credit for workers' associations and peasant *obshchinas*.

To achieve these ends, the *Northern Union* gave first place to propaganda. This was 'a sacred duty' for all its members.

This work of propaganda will not be forgotten by posterity, and the glorious names of those who devote themselves to it and to agitations will be inscribed in the annals of history. They are the apostles who spread evangelical truths. They will persecute us, as they persecuted the first Christians; they will beat us and they will laugh at us; but we will be fearless.

After speaking once more of the West and the struggle which the workers were carrying on there, the manifesto ended:

We will renew the world, we will revive the family, we will establish property as it should be, and we will make Christ's great doctrine live once again in brotherhood and equality . . . Workers, your future lies in this propaganda which will save us, and your success depends on your spiritual strength. With it you will be powerful; with it you will overcome the world. Know that you contain all the strength and significance of the nation. You are the flesh and blood of the State. Without you the other classes who are now sucking your blood would not exist; in a confused way you understand all this. But you have no organization, no idea to lead you.

18*

You have not the moral support, which is so necessary to resist the enemy in brotherly union. But we, the workers organized in the *Northern Union,* we are giving you this governing idea, we are giving you this moral support in your attempts to unite your interests; and finally we are giving you the organization which you need. So, workers, you have the last word. On you depends the fate of the great *Union* and the success of a social revolution in Russia.

This manifesto, which certainly does not lack power and energy, is, as it were, a mirror of the experiences undergone by the various workers' cadres which had grown up during the previous ten years in St Petersburg. The fundamental element was still that of the Populists. On it was superimposed the explicit determination to found a class organization and to reaffirm bonds with the working class movement of the West. A considerable part of the programme was directly derived from the resolutions of the congress of Eisenach which they had read in the *Vpered*. This was preferred to the resolutions drawn up at Gotha, which had also been translated by Lavrov.[92] But the most original feature lay in the clear, decided statement of the need to fight for political freedom.

D. A. Klements was right to tell his working class comrades, in an article published in the fourth number of *Zemlya i Volya* on 20th February 1879, 'You are entering the political struggle at a time which could not be better chosen and could not be more to the purpose.' And he was also right to point out that the programme of the *Union* was eclectic. 'The repudiation of the State and the demand for communal autonomy put our comrades in the field of the social revolutionaries. We would like to see the members of the *Northern Union* in this same field, but the last paragraphs of its programme are taken directly from the catechism of the German social-democrats.' The political dangers of such eclecticism were clear to the editor of *Zemlya i Volya*. Would not these general reforming tendencies mean that a radical revolutionary programme would be neglected? As regards the peasants, there was no restatement of the demand for a general redistribution of the land. And as for the means to be used in the fight, what was the point of confining themselves to propaganda and agitation?

The revolutionaries of *Zemlya i Volya* were obviously worried by the prospect of the *Union* slipping back into a Lavrovist position. Klements noted that the programme said not a word of 'propaganda with *facts*, of an active fight'. Avoiding these problems allowed the workmen of the *Union* 'to give a too categorically positive solution of the problem of the influence of political freedom in the struggle between exploiters and exploited'. This was obviously the point in the *Union*'s programme to which the members of *Zemlya i Volya* were most responsive, for they themselves were tormented by the same question at this time. The workmen of the *Union* were once more raising this problem in a particularly clear and harsh way. Their eclecticism had allowed the editors of the programme to bring to light the inner contradictions of the Populist movements during these years.

The *Union* had made up its mind only after much reflection. Among other proofs of this we have the letter that they sent to *Zemlya i Volya* to explain their position in reply to Klements's article. They thanked the editors for the warmth with which their organization had been welcomed. For too long, they said, too many intellectuals had looked upon the workers with a feeling of vague distrust or contempt. They were glad now to be able to talk as equals. (Indeed this psychological element had obviously played a part in the formation of the *Union*.) They then came to the essence of the discussion:

Our logic on the subject is brief and simple. We have nothing to eat and we do not know where to live. And so we demand food and houses. We are taught nothing except swear-words and obedience to the stick. And so we demand that such a primitive system of education should be abolished. But we know very well that our demands will be nothing more than demands, if we stand by with our hands folded. And that is why we unite and organize ourselves and we raise the banner so dear to our heart, of social revolution, and throw ourselves into the fight. But we also know that political freedom can guarantee us and our organization from the tyranny of the authorities and can enable us to develop our conception of the world in the right direction and carry out our propaganda with greater success. And so, wanting to save up our energies and obtain success more quickly, we demand this freedom . . . It will be all the easier to reach this objective in that it coincides with what is dear to the heart of the chatterboxes, the leaders of the future palace of chatterboxes of all Russia. And so it is not all that unlikely that it will come about.

As for the peasant problem, the workers admitted that Klements was right. 'We did indeed allow ourselves to be carried away too much by our situation as townsmen. We were too much influenced by the spirit of the various Western programmes, and that is why our programme gave only very little place to the countryside.' They said that they would fight for the peasants to be able to increase their land-holdings at the expense of the landlords, and for them to pay less taxes. Indeed they ought to pay only those 'necessary for the needs of the peasant *obshchina* and the building of schools and agricultural institutes'.

This discussion between the spokesman of the *Union* (probably Khalturin) and the Populist intellectuals is of great historical significance. The workers, though rather hesitantly, proclaimed themselves even more Westerner than the intelligentsia. They were led to these conclusions by the personal experiences abroad of men such as Obnorsky and the ideas brought into their midst by the German workers who came to get employment in St Petersburg.[93] There was also the influence of the *Vpered* and all the information about the Western working class movement which the Populists had spread. Besides, all the organizers of the *Union* had thought about their own economic and social situation compared to that of other classes in the Russian State and even compared to that of other ranks of the working class in the capital itself. Ahead they saw a working class struggle. They were therefore demand-ing freedom of organization and the chance to make their voice heard, even though they seemed to be wanting to excuse themselves in the light of their own consciences and before the revolutionaries for being on the same plane as the 'chatterboxes' (i.e. the liberals). They hastened to explain that they too stood for a social revolution, and that they too looked upon political freedom purely as a means to that end. The revolutionaries of *Zemlya i Volya* replied that these demands of the working classes must be included in a framework which should cover all the problems of Russia. Above all that they must not forget the greatest of these problems, that of the peasants. It was for this that the intelligentsia was against any concession to the liberals and was reaffirming its Populist standpoint. But within a few years, a few months even, this problem too was open to question again. The workers' stand in favour of a fight with political arms played its part in turning some members of *Zemlya i Volya* on to a new road.

The first months of 1879 constituted the golden age of the *Northern Union*. All the working class districts of St Petersburg had their own organized groups linked to the central body. They could count on about 200 organized men and 200 more in reserve carefully distributed in the various factories. Their library, one of Khalturin's main concerns, was satisfactorily split up among the various clandestine centres, so as not to risk falling into the hands of the police. It was extensively used even by those not affiliated to the organization.

There were good grounds for hoping that the organization could be extended beyond the capital and joined one day to parallel ventures in the south, thus becoming a working class organization for Russia as a whole. Already it had some links with Moscow. M. R. Popov, on the advice of Plekhanov, who showed him the regulations of the *Union*, tried to extend it to Kiev. He was, however, prevented by the arrests.[94] On his return from his last journey abroad, Obnorsky had made agreements with a working class group at Warsaw; 'the first example', said Plekhanov, 'of friendly relations between Russian and Polish workers'.[95]

The *Union* planned to start a periodical of its own to crown its success, and Obnorsky managed to get a press in Geneva. His arrest, however, put an end to the plan. With him fell also Alexey Nikolaevich Peterson, one of the most active members of the 'fighting team' which had grown up alongside the *Union*. He had had very close relations with the 'disorganizing group' of *Zemlya i Volya*, and had several times tried to suppress *agents provocateurs*, spies, etc.[96] The infiltration of a police agent into the group soon led to the fall of some of its most active members. Khalturin, however, escaped arrest and went on to work with the terrorists. The *agent provocateur* was this time suppressed through the direct action of the revolutionary intellectuals, but a large breach had been made. Attempts were made by *Cherny Peredel*, Akselrod and Aptekman, between the end of 1879 and the beginning of

1880, to restore the *Union,* but they were unsuccessful. Its last action was to compile a small leaflet, the *Rabochaya Zarya* (Workers' Dawn), but this was seized by the police in March 1880 before it could be distributed.[97] In any case its propaganda content lacked the *Union*'s earlier political vigour. From now on the organization of the working classes in St Petersburg was to be managed far more energetically and in a very different spirit by *Narodnaya Volya.*

20. ZEMLYA I VOLYA

THE VERY NAME *Zemlya i Volya* (Land and Liberty) implies a programme. No longer, as before, is the revolutionary society called after one of its founders or inspirers. This in itself constitutes a new and important fact and shows us that one is now faced with a real party. The *Zemlya i Volya* of the 'sixties had also tried to become a party, although it was made up of small and barely organized groups. In fact, however, it had been a party of opinion, an intellectual movement which had scarcely begun to crystallize into an organization. The *Zemlya i Volya* of the 'seventies, on the other hand, was a revolutionary party as the term came to be understood in subsequent decades; it was made up of men who devoted themselves to the cause and who did all they could to muster around themselves (and direct) all other revolutionary forces. Indeed, *Zemlya i Volya* was really the prototype of this kind of political organization, and introduced it into Russia. Many currents flowed into *Zemlya i Volya*: the Chaikovskists' dedicated spirit, the religious impulse that had inspired the movement 'to go to the people' and some of the specific elements of Russian Jacobinism. The party further re-elaborated the more genuinely Populist ideas on the relationship between a peasant revolution and an urban movement, and adopted with greater technical skill and on a wider scale the various tactics which had already been tried, such as propaganda, disturbances, public demonstrations, strikes, and finally terrorism. All these currents merged in *Zemlya i Volya* and made it the strongest organization of the 'seventies. All the various elements which made up Russian Populism were here united and worked together.

The historian of *Zemlya i Volya* is faced with two sets of difficulties. The traces left by a conspiracy, even so extensive a one, are always few and details are lacking. They often have to be reconstructed with the help of memoirs written many years later. And a party (and the *Zemlya i Volya* is certainly no exception) is always a combination of fractional groups and differing opinions. Evidence is often conflicting—the reflection of some long distant controversy. But despite all this, for the first time in this history extensive sources are available which provide a many-sided picture of this party, at least in its crucial and final phase. The period about which we know least is that between 1874–75 (when the Chaikovskists collapsed and the protagonists of the movement 'to go to the people' were arrested) and 1876 when close activity was resumed in the capital, and the nucleus was formed round which the new organization was mustered. The reason for this lack of detailed information is not surprising. Extreme secrecy was absolutely essential after the heavy losses suffered by the organization. The thousands of arrests that the Populist movement suffered must not be forgotten if one wishes to understand how the first grouping of what was to become *Zemlya i Volya* came into being.[1]

The tenacity of a few men enabled the threads of the Chaikovskists to be picked up again and it was to their credit that this could be done on a new plane, full of great potentialities. But the rapid and far-reaching effects of their activities can only be understood by re-creating the situation of Russia at the time and the circumstances in which they worked.

The extent of the repression had more or less reassured the authorities. Round about 1875, although they kept their anti-Populist weapons intact, they had some reason for temporarily deceiving themselves into thinking that the danger was over and that the blows they had struck had been decisive. 'Among the ruling classes', a semi-official well-informed historian writes, 'there prevailed the conviction that with the arrest of the majority of propagandists the battle against the State could be considered at an end.'[2]

The events that occurred in this very year in the Balkan Peninsula only confirmed this state of mind. The revolt of Herzegovina and Bosnia against Turkish rule attracted the attention not only of the ruling classes but of an increasingly large part of Russian society. The Slavophils threw themselves into a violent campaign in favour of their 'Slav brothers'. Some at least of the liberals hoped that the reawakening of public opinion would allow them to ask the government openly to introduce into Russia itself those liberal reforms which it was demanding from the Turks. The conservatives and nationalists of all kinds looked upon Russia's intervention in the Balkans as a resumption of her traditional foreign policy—which had been static for the last twenty years, and especially since the agreement between the three Emperors in 1873. Some of these men even thought that they might be able to eliminate all internal danger and stifle the revolutionary ferment by assigning to the Tsar the noble function of liberating Christianity from the Moslem yoke, and more generally by assuring him success in his foreign policy and the war.[3]

But the campaign to enlist aid for the Slavs; the tacit consent and then official encouragement given to the recruiting of volunteers to fight the Turks; and finally the intervention of Russian troops followed by the war of 1877 and 1878, and the liberation of Bulgaria (victories so severely paid for by the Russian soldiers) and the obvious weaknesses shown by the army and the administration during the campaign (soon to be confirmed and aggravated by the diplomatic defeat of the Treaty of Berlin)—in fact these events of the years between 1875 and 1878, far from stifling the revolutionary movement, merely acted as an incitement.[4]

Events in the Balkans had taken Russian Populism unawares in a phase of

weakness and comparative lack of organization. For a time it looked as if
a considerable portion of the forces that had survived the arrests of the
previous year—and some of the new elements which were beginning to
replace them—would be drawn into the patriotic campaign to constitute
a wing (as sincerely revolutionary in spirit as it was ineffective in practice) of
the Slavophil movement which was then rapidly expanding. A certain
number of Populists joined the revolt in Herzegovina as volunteers. Still
more, despairing of the possibility of effective action in Russia, considered
flinging themselves into the venture. But this first impulse was soon arrested.
Not much discussion was needed within the movement to persuade the
Populists to give first place to the fight against absolutism and the desire for
stronger action within Russia. The revolt of the Balkans in fact aroused
energies and hopes which were soon absorbed by the growing *Zemlya i
Volya*.

Indeed from the very first the controversy between the Lavrovists and the
Bakuninists had prevented the current of active sympathy with the southern
Slavs from dominating the field.

From the very first the *Vpered* had conducted a campaign which was
inspired by a purely Socialist and class point of view.

We cannot see without grief the agitation which has developed among the southern
Slavs in the name of old ideals of national independence, State autonomy and the
Christian church. This agitation will only stifle the preaching of Socialism among
our brothers. Whatever the result of the struggle, in either case national hatred will
put obstacles in the way of the brotherhood of the workers; and illusions of
nationalism, state and religion will obscure the true interests of the suffering
masses.[5]

Lavrov's views caused strong protests, even in those circles which had always
followed his guidance. Indeed one, and not the least, of the reasons for
Lavrov's decreasing influence on Russian youth was this attempt to oppose
support for, and personal intervention in, the rebellion of the southern
Slavs. Klements and Kravchinsky, two of the Chaikovskists who had
escaped arrest, went to the Balkans as volunteers. *The Southern Union of
Russian Workers*, led by Zaslavsky, which was close to Lavrov and in touch
with the *Vpered*, took part in the agitation for its 'Slav brothers'.[6] Zhelyabov,
who was never to be a Bakuninist and who was to pass directly from the
propagandists and the Chaikovskists to *Narodnaya Volya*, also took an active
part in the campaign to enlist support for the Serbs, and at one time thought
of joining the war.

The Bakuninist appeal, on the other hand, interpreted the state of mind of
the young revolutionaries and often detached them from Lavrov's influence.
The *Bulletin de la Fédération Jurassienne*, describing the rebellion in Bosnia
and Herzegovina, said that it had taken on the character of 'a social war.
The fight of Christian peasants against the Moslems is a war of the agri-

cultural proletariat against the landowners.'[7] This call was echoed by Ralli's *Rabotnik*:

Many people say that we ought not to assist these rebels because it may happen that the workers, even after victory, will not be in a position to free themselves and that instead of the Turks they will merely choose new bosses. Well, well, this is still uncertain. Who will be able to avoid these new mistakes, if not those who have understood them? We who have living hearts in our breasts, we cannot patiently look on without taking part in the desperate battle of the working class. We say that only activities of the very greatest importance in our own country can justify our not taking part in the fight.[8]

Attacking Smirnov, Lavrov's right arm, a young Russian wrote:

We are leaving as volunteers, above all so as to forge solid bonds with the Slavs, and then so as to return well-trained and expert . . . I admit that even if it was Poland and not Herzegovina, and that even if it was not a question of national independence but, let us say, only the reunion of Poland to Austria, I would go just the same. Because during any movement, however absurd its nature, one can carry on agitation with far greater success than during the best intentioned tranquillity.[9]

M. P. Sazhin (Ross) and Sergey Kravchinsky were the first Bakuninist volunteers. They met in Paris in 1875 and decided to leave together for Herzegovina in the summer of that year. 'I went through Locarno', said the first, 'where Bakunin was living, down to Zagreb; Sergey travelled through Northern Italy . . . At Zagreb there was a committee which provided the volunteers with arms and which helped them to cross the frontier at Ragusa and Cattaro.'[10] Before leaving, Kravchinsky had tried to organize a small band of volunteers and had sent Akselrod to Russia for this purpose.[11] In Herzegovina they were involved in a few clashes, but their military experiences were short lived. Like many other Russian volunteers, they were forced to admit that it was not easy to enter a situation so new for them and adapt themselves to partisan warfare in the mountains of Dalmatia.

By the time they returned they had been completely disillusioned as to the social character of the war. 'Religious fanaticism and love of looting'—this was what they had seen.[12]

From Switzerland two girls of the Zurich group also left for Serbia. Another woman, Anna Pavlovna Korba, who later became a member of the Executive Committee of *Narodnaya Volya*, stayed throughout the war as a voluntary Red Cross worker. Innokenty Fedorovich Kostyurin, one of the Chaikovskists, also prepared to leave for Herzegovina from Odessa. Between 1875 and 1876, like so many others in Southern Russia, he was in process of becoming a 'rebel', i.e. a disciple of Bakunin. However, he was arrested before he had the chance to leave, and was finally tried at 'the trial of the hundred and ninety-three'. The rest of his life was spent in Siberia, and he died at Tobolsk in 1919.[13] 'There was much talk among the radicals', wrote Kostyurin, 'of the need to take part in the movement of the Serbs and Bulgars, both in order to have a "baptism of fire" and to study the mechanism of popular insurrections.' From Kiev, I. Debagory-Mokrievich, the brother of one of the future Southern 'rebels', went as a volunteer. Two Populists, Dalmatov and Balzam, were killed in the Balkans.

As can be seen, the movement in aid of their 'Slav brothers' spread mainly among the Populist groups of Southern Russia, in the Ukraine, at Odessa and Kiev. Adherents of the various groups took part, but the great majority of active volunteers consisted of Bakuninists or those who were now turning to 'revolt' after the failure of the propagandist experiment of the previous years.

Disillusionment, and above all Russia's official intervention, stifled this little movement of volunteering at birth. It had always been insignificant and its only real importance was as a symptom of revival. It was merely one process through which the movement passed on the way to more violent tactics.

Meanwhile the nucleus of men who were soon to fuse these dispersed energies was appearing in St Petersburg. In 1875 they were working deeper 'underground' and it was because of this that their group was known as the 'troglodytes'. 'It was so christened by Klements, who was always fond of nicknames. It was a small group of young revolutionaries distinguished by the fact that no stranger knew where they lived and under what name. Hence he declared they had found refuge in secret caves.'[14]

As is shown by a long report to the Emperor, the police were highly impressed by the nickname, and thought it their duty to explain that 'troglodyte was the name given in ancient times to wild Ethiopian tribes, the inhabitants mainly of present-day Abyssinia. These tribes lived in herds. Women and children were shared. Today, in Africa, the name "troglodytes" is given to races of chimpanzees, extremely intelligent and so well-trained that they can sometimes replace servants, but also extremely irritable, changing quickly from high spirits to ferocity.'[15] In fact, the name of the group, despite this display of erudition on the part of the police, itself revealed characteristics of the new elements. Its members had no intention of flinging themselves into propaganda. Solid organization was the aim.

The founder of this group was once again Mark Andreyevich Natanson. He was the living link between this and previous movements. He had been one of Nechaev's main adversaries and had given the initial impulse to the Chaikovskists. In 1872 he had been exiled to a village in the department of Archangel for publishing and circulating one of Flerovsky's books. But even from there he had kept in touch with his comrades. In 1875 he was transferred, first to Voronezh and then to Finland and had eventually escaped. He was now living illegally in St Petersburg. He soon showed (in the words of Aptekman) that he had 'a remarkable sense of organization'.[16]

He found his greatest help in his wife, Olga Alexandrovna, who had earlier been with him in the Chaikovskist group and in exile, and who replaced him when he was arrested in May 1877. 'She always thought of others before herself, and sacrificed everything for the cause', A. D. Mikhailov said admiringly of her when he was in prison. And he added: 'It fell to her and her husband to be the organizers and leaders of the new current. Mark Natanson was one of the apostles of the Socialist movement, and the father of *Zemlya i Volya*. Olga was his most devoted and energetic support.'[17]

After them came the twenty-two year old Alexey Dmitrievich Oboleshev, who 'had lived through the stormy age of the movement "to go to the people", with all its inevitable errors and its deep wounds. The wounds of his spirit were now healed, but from time to time when touched again they still bled. These terrible "lessons of life" had turned him into an inflexible doctrinaire of revolutionary activities, a fanatic for organization and revolutionary discipline. He was able to control his passionate temperament and stormy nature, but at first sight he gave the impression of being an arid fanatic, as if he were a dogmatic believer in the theories of the sects. It was, however, enough to live a week or two with him and to see him at work, and act with him, not merely to rid oneself of this first impression but to be conquered against one's will and without reservation by this marvellous human being.'[18] Oboleshev was one of the best examples of the transformation which in various ways was occurring among all his comrades: the propagandists were turning into organizers.

Alexander Dmitrievich Mikhailov, on the other hand, was the best representative in this group of the generation which had been born too late to take part in the movement 'to go to the people'. His autobiographical notes are perhaps the best document which we have concerning the inner development of a Populist of the 'seventies. 'From my earliest days a happy star shone above me. My childhood was one of the happiest that a man can have. I can only compare it to a bright spring dawn, untouched by storms or bad weather, or by cloudy days.'[19] This happiness always returns in his writings, when he wants to express the intimate essence of his life. Even when he was already in prison and certain that he would soon be condemned to death 'looking into myself I can say that my life has been quite exceptional for active happiness. I do not know of any man to whom fate has so freely given such happiness. Everything great that has existed in the Russia of our times has passed before my eyes. For some years my most wonderful dreams have come to life; I have lived with the best men and have always been worthy of their love and friendship. That is real happiness for a man.'[20]

In prison, he said that the origins of this happiness lay in his love for nature.

Nature was dear and close to me. In my earliest youth I was a real deist. Even at the moment that I went over to Socialism, Nature played some part in this. At least this conversion occurred in her presence . . . Love for Nature was insensibly transformed into love for man. There arose in me a passionate desire to see humanity as harmonious, as beautiful, as Nature; there arose in me a desire to sacrifice all my energies and all my life for this happiness . . . My heart, which did not seek passions for itself, reserved all its energies for social activities.[21]

This strength—which made Zhelyabov say one day that his friend was 'a real poet of the soul'—was not affected by his first contact with life. The school which he attended seemed to him to be dominated by 'chaos and the German spirit',[22] i.e. that very lack of the harmony and poetry that he felt within himself. He soon broke away from it without difficulty for it was moribund. In the same way from childhood his letters to his parents, brothers and sisters revealed a spirit which was already far removed from 'the reasonable life of the provinces'—the 'petty life' which he very well knew would not be his.[23]

What he was later to call 'a split' was taking place in his spirit. He was becoming aware of 'the secret summons' which he felt arising in himself and which he only confessed openly in a letter written on the point of death.

In my earliest youth, when my character was forming, I realized that two worlds were growing up within me. One tied me down to real life, and to it I reacted with my will, my conscience, my thought and my activities. It was, so to speak, immediately active. The other, which lay deeply concealed within my spirit, was coming into being in contact with the first, and completely and powerfully dominated it. It was the world of ideals and the highest aspirations. This is what always happened in the human spirit. If I grew aware of their appearance so soon, this was because the second was particularly powerful and played an enormous part in my life. In me these two worlds were not confused, were not tied together by reciprocal influences. Their functions, the one as a driving force, the other as a control, were not interchangeable, as often happens.[24]

Something of this conscious split appeared even on the surface when he devoted himself to studying the sects, so as to penetrate their secrets and to find among them forces for the social revolution. So passionately did he fling himself into this religious *ambience* that it is clear that it represented something more to him than a mere political tool. And later he often spoke of religious problems. He brought to revolutionary organization something that made his companions say that 'he was a poet of organization'.[25] But the world of ideals, of religion and poetry, was always deliberately concealed and resolved in action. Mikhailov did not express his religion, but practised it. He was not destined to be a poet, but a revolutionary.

He very soon chose to pass through 'the narrow gate'[26]—a Biblical term used for the sake of his parents. His passion for politics began to make itself felt at school, where he devoured what was by now the classic literature of Russian Populism.[27] He too began by founding one of those 'groups of self-formation' which harnessed so many revolutionary energies at the time. Mikhailov himself one day clearly explained why these 'groups' or 'clubs' were of such importance.

In the vast majority of cases in Russia neither the families of the privileged classes nor schools contain any germ of autonomous activity, which is the fundamental element of progress. And so Russian students, who are surely gifted with spiritual qualities, specially need groups of this kind. In most of their members they stimulate an internal process and make them take their first step towards an autonomous life.[28]

His own formation followed this course, and he soon became the leading spirit of a small centre founded to circulate booklets among the people and collect money to support the propagandists ('although we know about as much about propaganda as about some foreign party'[29]). But the repression severely affected activities even as mild as these. Mikhailov himself escaped persecution fortuitously. Some of his comrades were sent to Siberia, and one was sentenced to two years' imprisonment.

In autumn 1875 he went to St Petersburg to begin his university studies. He had decided to follow these in the Technological Institute, as a protest against the classical direction which Tolstoy, the Minister of Education, had given contemporary Russian education, and which had already disgusted him at school. Very soon he was involved in a student protest and sent back, accompanied by a policeman, to his home in the provinces. Already he was tormented by the doubts of his generation. What was the point of learning and specializing, when 'society and people are, in Russia, in a terribly painful situation? Society is deprived of all rights, and is entirely passive. Its civic spirit has been supplanted by love for the next step on the ladder of career. Narrow and purely individualist instincts triumph. Inclinations of a social character are stifled. People inspired by ideas of freedom are persecuted.'[30]

In December 1875 he was able to settle in Kiev. At once his main concern was to get into contact with 'the world of radicals'. He was faced with the three currents of opinion into which Populism was split at this time. Here these tendencies were specially vital and far more clearly marked than in St Petersburg, where the repression had been more severe and where the Chaikovskists had provided an example of a movement which combined the different ideas on a different, more characteristically Populist plane.

He was closely acquainted with the Lavrovist state of mind, and listened to those who spoke of propaganda as the only possible method of carrying on the fight. 'To open the people's eyes'—this was to be their task; they would:

develop the feeling of solidarity among the people, group together its advanced and boldest representatives . . . To enlighten all the popular masses with hundreds or even thousands of propagandists was, of course, not possible. But for the cause to succeed, only a small minority of the people need become consciously Socialist and in complete unity raise the banner of a social-economic revolution. The situation was so unbearable that an initiative taken by this conscious popular minority would be enough for the giant to awaken, break the chains of centuries and rebuild his life following his traditional aspirations and the initiative of the Socialist minority.

The task of this minority when the revolution broke out would be to direct the people, 'and prevent egoists and careerists from using the victory for their own ends'. 'To go to the people' to make propaganda—such then was the programme of the Lavrovists. But this did not mean giving up Socialist culture:

As a rule, neither disturbances, strikes, nor agitation, aimed to turn passions into immediate action, are of use for preparing the people for the Socialist revolution. In individual cases such means can prepare the ground for propaganda. We must not arouse emotion in the people, but self-awareness.[31]

The Bakuninist 'rebels', on the other hand, attacked the Lavrovists and maintained that emotions and passions constituted the fundamental mainspring of the revolution. The people did not need to be enlightened as regards its own needs. 'The insufficiency of land is so obvious that it finds expression in the expectation of a redistribution which is everywhere widespread . . . By tradition, and through innate feelings, the people recoils from the State, from private property, and the other methods that man uses to oppress man.' The Bakuninist standpoint was expressed in the *Rabotnik*. It lay in an appeal to revolt. A peasant rising was essential, however small and limited. Once this first example had been given, they could unfurl the banner 'of demands which the people itself will understand and feel more closely. These must be as Socialist and federalist as possible. Whatever the result of such a rising, the effect would be to concentrate revolutionary passions and to educate the people.'[32] Mikhailov wondered whether the 'rebels' whom he met at Kiev were anarchists. It is true that they accepted Bakunin's formulas. 'Their economic theory was collectivism, and their political formula lay in a free federation of independent *obshchinas* of production.' But they had turned all their attention to immediate action: the desire to set off the first spark of a peasant movement. For this purpose they were prepared to accept the people's demands, in whatever form they were made, as long as they could set alight the great fire of a revolution. In fact these men were mainly 'rebels', as they themselves claimed. 'For many of them, their theoretical ideals did not constitute more or less immediate ends.'[33]

The very nature of their respective standpoints had to some extent led to the propagandists and 'rebels' dividing functions and representing two different kinds of society as well as two different types of human being. They attacked each other and complemented each other in turn. The Lavrovists in fact comprised the main body of the students, the youngest and most active members of the intelligentsia. Few of them, however, devoted themselves exclusively to revolutionary work. Besides, the arrests had put a brake on their activities. They represented a common state of mind; they carried on the systematic and valuable diffusion of Socialist ideals. But 'they somewhat lacked revolutionary fire'. The 'rebels', on the other hand, 'had fewer points of contact with the students. As a rule they were men who had broken all links with the university and had chosen a tougher and more difficult road. Many of them were being sought by the police.' The central group was made up of 'men who were already well tried and who were unreservedly devoted to the cause'. In fact 'the propagandist was the finest representative of our intelligentsia; . . . the rebel was a complete, immediate nature'.[34]

Tkachev's followers, the Jacobins, had spoken of uniting these 'revolutionary prototypes' into a solid centralized organization. From this they had deduced the need to 'carry out all the transformations demanded by the Socialists, not from below upwards, but the other way round'. 'First the existing government must be destroyed in some way or other. Then a new Socialist government must be created, thanks to the strength of the party. This will then bring about a new order. As the standard of the people's development rises, this government will then hand sovereignty back to the people.'[35] Was this the right answer to the problem? In 1876 Mikhailov was obviously very interested in this view. For a moment it seemed to be the solution to his doubts. 'But I soon saw that the theory and practice of this group did not represent anything solid, and I broke relations with it. They were a very small nucleus. That strong organization, based on the principles which were at the basis of their ideas, was unable to arise owing to lack of serious revolutionary work.'[36] Such were his conclusions after a short attempt to work with the Jacobin group. What attracted him most was the idea of strong revolutionary organization; it was for this reason that he had allied himself with I. Ya. Davidenko, one of the very few men who followed Tkachev's ideas. These experiences made him certain that his faith in organization ought not to remain theoretical as it did with the Jacobins, but should be applied where the movement was most vital.[37]

I was struck by the liveliness and social development of Kiev. But on the other hand it was easy to see that all the movement was splintered. Further, the lack of unity in action and in immediate aims, together with some intolerance, greatly reduced the results obtained by individuals and the movement as a whole. Realization of this important defect drove me to take up the standpoint of an observer. Instinct told me that the centre, the source of the entire movement, would not be found at Kiev. Instinct told me that serious forces and extensive plans would only be found at the centre, where all experience converged, where the best elements were to be found.

And so he gave up the idea of staying in Kiev. 'My dreams floated off towards the distant north, towards St Petersburg.'[38]

In the middle of August 1876 he went to the capital and joined Natanson's group. Plekhanov recalled that Mikhailov used to say that his joining this group (which was about to assume the name of *Zemlya i Volya*) marked the end of the 'nihilist' period of his life. The student who had tried so hard to initiate popular habits was vanishing. Instead 'he changed into a cautious organizer, capable of measuring every step and taking account of every precious minute'.[39] As he himself said, 'The characters and the habits and customs of the most important activists of our society contained many factors which were obviously dangerous and fatal for the development of a secret society . . . Oboleshev and I began a bitter fight against this "generous Russian nature".'[40] And so Mikhailov flung all his spirit into his 'passion for organization'. In him *Zemlya i Volya* found the most powerful of its driving forces.

Mikhailov's development has been followed step by step, because it is typical and because it explains, better than any other evidence, how *Zemlya i Volya* was able to become 'the pan-Russian organization of the energy of the Social Revolutionary Party'[41] which, as he left Kiev, he already boldly envisaged.

During 1875 and 1876 the surviving members of the Chaikovskists had resumed work in the factories of St Petersburg. Plekhanov took part in these activities and, as we have seen, he had become one of those mainly responsible for them. Natanson had developed his group into a 'Society of Friends'. We know little about it. Even the name is probably an invention of the police. It was, however, beginning to acquire some stability and coherence.[42] The original nucleus of 'troglodytes' was attracting the various figures who had been arrested in 1874 and freed during the preliminary investigation, or who had succeeded in hiding in Russia or temporarily escaping abroad.

Another man to join the central group in this early phase was Adrian Fedorovich Mikhailov. He was twenty-three at the time. Ahead of him lay a life of hardships and trouble, which, however, he was able to surmount. He was, in fact, to be one of the few members of *Zemlya i Volya* who did not soon lose his life in the struggle. He was arrested in 1878, and two years later sentenced to twenty years' hard labour. He served this sentence at Kara, and then in exile in the district of Transbaykalia. After the revolution of 1905 he spent yet another year in prison and survived to see the revolution of 1917. He died in 1929.[43] In the two or three years' work which he was able to do in the 'seventies, he proved to be a first-class organizer.

All the men in charge of this group were constantly thinking of their many comrades in prison, who had started the work which they were now determined to continue. They wanted, if possible, to organize their escape and in any case to keep in contact with them. Already in 1876 this motive was a powerful one. Very soon it changed into a determination to avenge them.

In the spring of 1876, the funeral of one of the many men who had died in prison during interrogation provided the first public demonstration of this feeling of solidarity. On 3rd March the student Chernyshev was buried. He had spent three years in preventive detention and died of consumption. The procession assumed such dimensions that we can regard it as the first political demonstration in the streets of St Petersburg since the one organized by the students ten years earlier. But this time a considerable portion of 'society' also took part; professors, soldiers, lawyers. It was a sign that public opinion was reawakening. The priest who followed the bier was so impressed by what he saw all around him that he ran away. Even more amazed were the people in the streets of the capital, as they saw the strange funeral procession without even a priest. The students did everything possible to make the crowd join the demonstration. They said aloud that they were burying a boy 'who had been martyred in prison, and who had borne witness for truth and the people'. The police, too, were greatly surprised. They intervened late in the day and with little enthusiasm. Only one student, who was arrested on the next day, was deported.

In summer 1876 a really remarkable escape was organized. This involved Kropotkin, one of the most notable of the Chaikovskists. A leading rôle in arranging this was played by Doctor Orest Eduardovich Veymar who, though he was never an 'official' member of Zemlya i Volya, took part in many of its boldest activities, and was finally sentenced in 1880 to ten years' hard labour, together with Adrian Mikhailov. He died in 1885 ravaged by consumption. Kropotkin's flight, which took place on 30th July, was one of the most successful feats in which he had a share. Besides Kropotkin's own courage, it revealed the remarkable degree of organization which his friends had now reached in St Petersburg.[44]

The 'troglodytes' were now changing into The Revolutionary-Populist Group of the North, the name they adopted before Zemlya i Volya. During the summer of 1876 they began to organize a real party. At the same time they forged solid links with other groups, especially in Southern Russia. In the winter they drew up their first programme and regulations. On 6th December the red banner of Zemlya i Volya appeared for a moment on the Square of Our Lady of Kazan in St Petersburg, during the workers' and students' demonstration, as if to announce the quick progress they had made during the previous months.

In the summer they established relations with a Populist group in Kharkov whose representatives were O. V. Aptekman and M. P. Moshchenko. They, too, had taken part in the movement 'to go to the people', and they too had had to bear the consequences of its failure. Aptekman, more than most, had retained a naive. religious and, indeed, sentimental faith in the movement. The group which he now led represented the less violent, less 'anarchist' wing of the revolutionary current of the time in Southern Russia. He himself and many of his associates were later to be against Narodnaya Volya and to join Cherny Peredel. Aptekman, like many others in this movement, later became a member of the Russian social-democratic party and a Menshevik. This first agreement between the embryonic Zemlya i Volya and a southern group is characteristic of Natanson's policies and of the tradition of the Chaikovskists. The spirit of the 'rebels' only penetrated slowly into St Petersburg and it never entirely prevailed. The Revolutionary-Populist Group of the North chose its first members from the right wing of the southern movement.

The same is true about its contacts with the Rostov group. But the men who were working there were more decided and of greater personal worth. Characteristic of their general spirit was the life of one of them, by no means the least active. Yury Makarovich Tishchenko was extremely strong physically. 'At the time of the propaganda', says Aptekman, 'he toured half Russia as a labourer, and sometimes as a cobbler; he stoically put up with hunger, with the heat, with prolonged work, and every kind of privation.' Despite all this, and after fifteen hours' physical work a day, he found time to study. 'He read any book that could provide him with ideas on social problems. He never left Marx; in fact he was one of the few who really knew him.' In Rostov he was at the head of the working class movement, and built up one of the largest groups of the time in Southern Russia. Later he presided over the meeting at which *Zemlya i Volya* broke up. Utterly discouraged by this he then went abroad until 1882. He was then sentenced to four years in Siberia. On his return to European Russia, he gave up all revolutionary activities and became one of the most capable leaders of the petrol industry in Baku.[45]

The St Petersburg group also made contacts, as early as 1876, with Odessa and Kiev, the two main centres of the 'rebels'. But these contacts were sporadic and individual, based more on technical collaboration than on a real political agreement.

In Kiev a group of specially bold characters had been driven by disappointment at the outcome of the propaganda campaign to the idea of a peasant revolution. It was no longer enough, they felt, merely to revise their programme or try and approach the people in some different way. This hard core had very soon become united and compact, and could consequently only be absorbed with difficulty into a unified organization. Its guiding figures were Vladimir Karpovich Debagory-Mokrievich, who later wrote his memoirs of the movement;[46] Yakov Vasilevich Stefanovich, the organizer, as we will see, of the only attempt at a peasant revolt which came seriously near success; and Lev Grigorevich Deych, one of the most active revolutionaries of the last thirty years of the nineteenth century and the beginning of the twentieth, and one of the founders of the Russian social-democratic party.[47] With them was a group of women of equal courage and intelligence to those others who fought for *Zemlya i Volya* and *Narodnaya Volya*. One of these was Maria Pavlovna Kovalevskaya (née Vorontsova), sister of the writer who some years later—under the pseudonym V.V.—gave the widest formulation of what can be called 'legal Populism'.[48] She 'was not only one of the most important members of our group, but was one of the most active characters to take part in the movement of the 'seventies as a whole', said L. Deych.[49] She was condemned to hard labour, and died at Kara. Next were: Vera Ivanovna Zasulich, who, with the attempted assassination of Trepov, was destined to bring the spirit of Southern terrorism to St Petersburg and to establish it firmly there by her example; Anna Markovna

Makarevich who, after fighting vigorously in Russia, emigrated and became well known to the Italians under the name of Anna Kuliscioff, the wife of the Socialist leader Turati;[50] and Maria Alexandrovna Kolenkina who was also later sentenced to banishment in Siberia.

In 1875 and 1876 the 'rebels' were not in a bad way. They were always armed, and lived in a kind of 'commune'. The governor of Kiev heard of their retreat, but preferred to keep away, as he feared active resistance. When for the first time a Socialist, Semen Lurye, was arrested, there was still so little tension in the town that he was treated with consideration. The surveillance imposed on him was of a kind that made escape easy enough. The organization was carried out by Deych, who was then an officer. He was imprisoned in Kiev fortress for this, and threatened with a military trial. But on 13th February 1876 he too succeeded in escaping.

The 'rebels' were at this time going through a preparatory phase. They had decided to devote their energies mainly to arousing peasant disturbances. But apart from this, they had few precise ideas. As a whole they accepted Bakunin's view of life. They read little, and their attitude towards theoretical questions was one of fairly deep contempt. The only one in the group to have any complex or articulate conception of politics was Akselrod, who was beginning his long career as a revolutionary. But of one thing they were certain. They would 'not allow themselves to be captured by the police like sheep'. If threatened with arrest they would put up an armed resistance. And as soon as possible they would move over to the offensive themselves and strike those of the authorities who were specially zealous in organizing the repression. Terrorism, in the form it assumed at the end of the 'seventies, sprang from this group.

They were in constant touch with the other centres of Southern Russia, especially Odessa. Mikhail Fedorovich Frolenko was the living symbol of this network of 'rebels'. He himself came from the people; his father had been a sergeant and later a guard in a Kuban mine. His mother, despite the premature death of her husband, had managed to give Mikhail an education. He even succeeded in getting to the Technological Institute in St Petersburg and later the School of Agriculture in Moscow. When still only a student he flung himself into work among the people with a cold and calculated boldness which made him the most formidable of all the revolutionaries of his time. He lived for almost seven years as an outlaw and took part in many of the boldest engagements. He knew, through personal experience, the whole of the Russian underground. Everywhere he brought with him that practical spirit which made him always choose the bravest and at the same time the most effective political policies. For these activities he paid with imprisonment at Shlisselburg from 1881 to 1905.[51]

It was he who in 1876 made contact with St Petersburg. He asked for money to buy arms for a revolt which was being planned in the region of

Elizavetgrad and later in other districts. Assistance was refused; relations with the 'Southern rebels' were still cold.

In Odessa, which he then made the centre of his activities, reorganization was in progress. Though detached from St Petersburg, the group was aiming at something similar to the organization then being achieved by *The Revolutionary-Populist Group of the North*. 'In the winter of 1877', wrote Frolenko, 'in the South too we stopped thinking of mass action in the countryside. People were collecting in the towns. The freeing of prisoners, the establishment of printing presses, the annihilation of spies—these now began to take place.'[52] The theoretical phase of the Kiev 'revolt' was coming to an end, and the terrorist wave of Southern Russia was beginning. Contact with St Petersburg was to be established on this new plane, and Frolenko later became one of the most important members of *Zemlya i Volya*.

This transformation was everywhere taking place in theory as well as in practice. We can say that a transition was being made from Bakuninism to a purer and more conscious form of Populism. At this time the word 'Populism' itself definitely entered political terminology and was adopted as a slogan.

This implied an evident, though not open, dispute with Bakunin himself, who had said that the people was always ready for revolt. Experience had shown that this was not true. Bakunin had therefore 'idealized' the people. The Socialist theories which had been preached till then were too 'abstract'. It was essential to make concessions to the peasants, to listen to their immediate demands, and not speak to them of Socialism in general. And in so doing a political *élite* could gradually be formed. But until this *élite* was formed the revolutionaries themselves must take its place and help to bring it into being. To idealize the revolutionary forces latent in the people led to nothing. It was essential rather to serve its immediate interests and take concrete steps for its liberation. And so it was above all essential to be Populists.

Alexander Mikhailov described this standpoint better than anyone:

The 'rebels' idealize the people. They hope that in the very first moments of freedom political forms will appear which correspond to their own conceptions based on the *obshchina* and on federation . . . The party's task is to widen the sphere of action of self-administration to all internal problems. But as it cannot predict the general form of government, it must leave the solution of this problem to the effective will of the nation.[53]

The party, he added, remained Socialist-federalist.

But in view of the terrible conditions in which the people is placed; and as the people on account of traditions makes demands which once satisfied will constitute a solid basis for further improvement; therefore we do not think it possible to wait for a social-economic revolution until the people is in a condition to bring about a more perfect social order. And so we raise our banner with the people's demands of Land and Liberty. By this we mean (1) from the economic point of view: the passage of land belonging both to the State and to private owners into the hands of the people. In Great Russia this must be done through the *obshchinas*,

and in other regions of Russia according to existing local traditions and requirements. (2) From the political point of view: the substitution of the existing State
by a structure determined by the will of the people; and in any case there must be
wide autonomy for *obshchinas* and regions.[54]

Summing up what he thought on the subject, Mikhailov said that all
'Socialist-revolutionaries' had always accepted the formula 'Social and
economic revolution through the people by means of the people'. The
Populists had added 'and according to its traditional and heartfelt desires'.
This was in fact a concession prompted both by a sincere desire to help the
people and act on its behalf, and by a more reasoned consideration of the
real political and social conditions of the peasants.

Seen in this light, their immediate aims also changed emphasis. The task
of the Populists would be, said Mikhailov, to 'prepare the people for the
struggle to obtain what the State has seized from it in past centuries ... As
history shows, the people has always lacked organization, unity, and the
ability to carry on the struggle. It lacked an intelligent and strong opposition
able to keep the banner of these rights flying from generation to generation,
until circumstances allowed it to enter into open fight with the exploiters.
The creation of such an opposition must be the essential aim of the Populists.'
There were in fact two objectives: 'In the first place to collaborate with all
local resistance to exploitation, oppression and the violence of *kulaks*,
squires and government officials. In the second place, to help the representatives of local opposition and the popular leaders to form and regroup.'[55]

Mikhailov also held clear views on the class nature of the struggle.
'Populists can count mainly on those peasants whose position is about
midway—who have retained their economic independence and have escaped
the vices and defects of the *miroed*.'[56]

To bring all this into effect it was essential to build a real party. In 1876
a programme was drawn up in St Petersburg. The original of this document,
which is still preserved, was written by Oboleshev. Its very wording reveals
the efforts that had been made to achieve these typically Populist standpoints.[57]

We restrict our demand to objectives which really can be achieved in the most
immediate future: i.e. to those claims and demands of the people which exist at
this given moment. According to us, these can be summed up in three essential
points:

(1) The transference of all land into the hands of the agricultural working class
(we are convinced that two thirds of Russia will be cultivated on the basis of the
obshchina). It must be divided into equal shares.

(2) The breaking-up of the Russian empire according to local desires.

(3) The transference of all social functions into the hands of the *obshchinas*, i.e.,
they must be given self-administration. (One cannot, however, say that this demand
corresponds to the will of all the people. There are groups of *obshchinas* which aim
at this; but most of them are not yet prepared for such a moral and intellectual

development, and, according to us, any union of *obshchinas* will give up part of its social functions to the government which they will form. Our duty consists exclusively in reducing this part as much as possible.)

Our demands can be brought about only by means of a violent revolution. The methods to prepare this and bring it about are, according to us: (1) *Agitation*—to be carried out both by word and above all by deed—aimed at organizing the revolutionary forces and developing revolutionary feelings[58] (revolts, strikes; in general, action is in itself the best way to organize revolutionary forces). (2) *The disorganization of the State*. This will give us some hope of victory, in view of the strong organization which will be created by agitations in the early future.

This document contains all the elements of *Zemlya i Volya* in embryonic form, as it were. Here and there we come across formulas which are still typically Bakuninist, but already its Populist substance is clearly apparent. Already, too, 'disorganization' (i.e. terrorism), the germ of the future *Narodnaya Volya*, begins to come to the fore, though as yet and for some time it took only second place. The most immediate task was to put into practice the new tactics among the people, and see what would be the effect of 'agitation', as thus envisaged.

As far as town life was concerned, we have seen that the demonstration of 6th December 1876 raised the entire problem of relations with the working class movement. In the countryside the revolutionaries had to begin from scratch. During 1877 and 1878 *Zemlya i Volya* quickly covered the ground that had already been traversed, before developing to the full the terrorist assumptions contained in the document quoted above.

And so, many members of *Zemlya i Volya* tried to found 'colonies' among the peasants, especially round Saratov, but also near Voronezh and in other districts. A large number of men of high quality were employed in these ventures. There were six or seven groups of ten members each and it was this that Mikhailov referred to as *Zemlya i Volya*. There was also a central group which numbered approximately twenty-five men. This last attempt 'to go to the people' was made with an unimpaired determination to reach the peasant masses.

Fixed centres were established in provincial towns. From them teachers, clerks and doctors radiated out. They were given false passports and often false testimonials, which were necessary if they were to live permanently in small rural centres and make themselves known and respected in village life.

A glance at the map would show that the distribution of the groups was once again based mainly on historical criteria. Hopes were still placed in the lands of Pugachev, Stenka Razin and the Ukrainian revolts.

But this was no longer 1874. This time the centre in St Petersburg was able not only to control but also to lead the movement. However, difficulties too had increased. The first movement 'to go to the people' had surprised the police. Now the authorities in even the smallest corners of the provinces were on the alert, and tended to consider anyone who came to look for work as a propagandist. Plekhanov was among those who experienced this. Despite all his efforts, he finally had to remain at the centre, in the 'commune' of Saratov, where he carried out his duties among the workers and intellectuals of the town.

It is true that the revolutionaries too were now better prepared. Despite Mikhailov's constant concern at his comrades' lack of conspiratorial technique, they were in fact able to act far more skilfully than their predecessors. Their decision never to use printed propaganda and not to distribute popular literature made their task easier. No longer were they 'pilgrims' inspired by impatience and haste. They knew that theirs was a long-term task. Their first duty was to defend the positions that they had gradually won.

Some did succeed in entering into village life and waiting for possible revolutions in the future. In so doing they fulfilled a real social function. They built up, more or less artificially, the small local intelligentsia which alone could act as a mouthpiece for the Russian peasant. Indeed the peasants really longed for this, and often ardently demanded it. These men were to be the most orthodox and determined supporters of pure Populism, even when the will and need to adopt terrorism made themselves felt with increasing strength. They were to be the real basis of *Cherny Peredel*, on the right wing of *Zemlya i Volya*. Their opposition to terrorism was parallel and in some ways similar to that among the working class in the towns, where a similar process was taking place. It was not for nothing that *Cherny Peredel* was to be one of the seed-beds of Russian social-democracy.

Plekhanov was to be the bridge between these two experiences of town and country. He left for Saratov, accompanied by three factory workers of the best-paid and most educated category. It was thought that they could establish contact with the peasants more easily than the intellectuals. But Plekhanov was able to see for himself that this hope was unfounded. One of the workers, Ivan Egorov, was unable to grow accustomed to a countryside which was so different from the one where he had been born and had grown up. 'Literally with tears in his eyes, he asked to be sent into the countryside, but into his own countryside round Archangel.' Another was more quickly assimilated—but into the life of the intellectuals and not of the village. He spoke of general political problems but did not have the strength to return to peasant life. The third, Korsak, was the only one whose physical and moral strength would have enabled him to do what he felt to be his duty; but he was arrested at Saratov.[59] Although both sprang from similar needs, the working class and peasant organizations were very different. From then on, Plekhanov devoted himself entirely to the workers.

Those men who wanted to do everything possible to defend the interests and aspirations of the peasants underwent experiences which convinced them that they were acting usefully and were fulfilling a task which answered the deepest needs of the people. And even those of them who later went over to terrorism never denied this. The doctors were enthusiastically welcomed, and were sometimes even considered to be magicians. The teachers were looked upon not only as benefactors but as the peasants' natural defenders. Deprived of adequate legal safeguards, the village population looked to them for protection from the countless injustices which afflicted them. Very soon the local authorities saw a change in the psychology of the peasants who, encouraged by their teachers' examples, were daring to ask for the barest minimum of justice. Even more did the landowners feel this pressure of the peasants. The peasants wanted land but now they collectively refused to rent even the most indispensable fields when offered at ruinous prices. Agitation, conceived of as the permanent defence of the peasant's smallest interests, was bringing good results, even though these results were, so to speak, experimental. For the agitation was confined to minute islands in the great sea of the Russian countryside and it was surrounded by the stifling world of an agricultural society which was still impregnated with centuries of serfdom. Mikhailov said:

Wherever they lived, in the most differing conditions of life, from country doctors to small business men and cobblers, they established the most sincere and friendly relations with the people. They soon succeeded in making friends among them to whom they confided their plans. These proved to be enthusiastic and active supporters. I know of many cases in which they [the revolutionaries] were accompanied in the most moving way when they left the village to go back to the town, following instructions to enter a new phase in the battle. All the *mir* assembled to ask them to stay, offering them various privileges and money if they went on with the work they had begun. Within a year many of them became literally indispensable to the local population for the disinterested advice and help they gave in every kind of business and difficulty. This is easy enough to understand. How could the people fail to respect and love them, surrounded as it was on all sides by *miroeds* and parasites who sucked its blood? How could the people fail to understand and accept the ideas and explanations [given by the revolutionaries] of all the evils which surrounded it when these ideas opened its eyes to facts which it felt for itself—ideas which were only the generalizations of what it had already thought of for itself? When they left the countryside to take part in the struggle against the government, almost everywhere the Populists left behind them followers whose degree of preparation varied but who would in any case continue the work of building up forces for the popular opposition.[60]

But agitation in the country—when carried out systematically and not just as a diversion between two phases of the struggle in the towns—led the Populists to raise once again the political problem as a whole. They had to consider the question of the State and the fight for freedom. Their very successes, though still only symbolical in scale, led to this. The contrast in size between the work they had undertaken and the forces of the enemy was now becoming all too clear. As they began to defend the peasants, they at once felt ahead of them a huge wall, made up of all the dominating social forces from the *kulak* to the Tsar. And so the need to fight against the State itself became inevitable. The very nature of their agitation made the revolutionaries realize that it was impossible to support the peasants against the administration and landlords without a bare minimum of legal guarantees and political freedom. The Populist movement in the countryside was leading to the same conclusions as the working class movement in the towns. True, the results of this inner transformation and growing conviction were less visible on the surface. There was, for instance, no document like the programme of *The Northern Union of Russian Workers*. But this did not mean that these results were any the less important. Returning from the colonies, individually and in groups, the Populists came to the towns, convinced that a change was necessary. It was they who developed the campaign of terrorism and who wrote the programme of *Narodnaya Volya*.

To see this evolution at work we have only to look at the life of Vera Figner.[61] She belonged to a group of revolutionaries which was close and parallel to *Zemlya i Volya* but not fused with it. It shared the same ideas but wanted to retain the type of organization that prevailed during the first half of the decade. It aimed to be a community of friends rather than a party, and was one of the obstacles that *Zemlya i Volya* met with and had to overcome before achieving an organization based on different and objectively more rational principles. The group was entirely devoted to work in the countryside. Vera Figner was among those of its members who gave most time and loyalty to the 'colonies' along the Volga. And it was these experiences that persuaded her to join *Zemlya i Volya* at the time when its terrorist and political wing, *Narodnaya Volya*, was breaking away from it.

We saw that our cause in the countryside was lost. In us the revolutionary party had suffered a second defeat. And this time it was not because its members lacked experience; it was not because we had an abstract programme which appealed to the people for purposes which did not concern it or for inaccessible ideals; it was not because we had put excessive hopes in the state of preparation of the masses. No, no, we had to give up the stage, knowing that our programme was vital, that our demands met with a real response in the life of the people. What was lacking was political freedom.[62]

The history of the Populist 'colonies' of 1877 is the history of the increasing strength of this new ferment. Intensive propaganda was resumed among the various religious sects of the *Raskolniki* and this too is a symptom of the search for a new approach. The *Raskolniki* had been in existence for centuries and were constantly changing. Would it be possible to direct them into a more active and direct resistance than the mute and all too often passive opposition of the peasants? Saratov had been chosen as centre of the main 'colony' of *Zemlya i Volya* with this hope in mind. Mikhailov put all he had into the venture.

This was one of the finest periods of his life. In the midst of 'nature and her sons'[63] he felt happy. He travelled extensively through the region of Saratov so as to learn its traditions, ideas and the state of minds of its sects. He then settled in a *Raskolnik* village and became a schoolmaster there. He

19+

eventually acquired a knowledge of theological and controversial problems which amazed all his companions.

His experiences convinced him that the sects really did represent a serious social protest. They wanted to separate themselves from the State, and had deep-seated hopes for a better world. Here among these peasants and merchants was the force that the Populists were looking for. But how could it be made use of? For Mikhailov these energies were so close to himself, so akin to his own spirit, that for a time he inevitably had hopes of deriving from them 'a popular and revolutionary religion based on the fundamental demands of the people and its ancient beliefs'. He proposed to deepen his religious studies during his visit to Moscow and St Petersburg by devoting himself to old books and manuscripts. And he foresaw a rationalist and Socialist sect which he would create.

This new world made a deep impression on him.

Coming into the midst of it, one felt in a different State, organized and closed on all sides, with its old laws on faith and collective life, its own customs and ideas. The boundaries all around it are clear, and outside lies the enemy. It is easy to understand why the Old Believers were so willing to follow Pugachev. They had fought against the State even before him, and today they are still fighting against it. From the spiritual point of view the world of the *Raskol* is far higher than that of the Orthodox peasant. Within this world it is easy to arouse moral problems, and the ground is very favourable for these. I felt that there was much that could be done there, but that many other forces would have to be flung in.[64]

But even in this field, where Mikhailov thought the ground more potentially fertile, there was the problem of how to influence millions of people with exceedingly small means. Though he always retained his belief that the attempt should be made seriously on a significant scale, Mikhailov himself was prevented by circumstances from continuing along this road. The struggle against the authorities was too pressing. There lay the centre of those forces which were preventing fruitful contact between the world of the Populists and that of the *Raskolniki*. It was there that the battle must be joined.

Similar attempts were also made in the South at more or less the same time. Viktor Alexandrovich Danilov—later to appear in the 'trial of the hundred and ninety-three'—had succeeded on his way to Kharkov in establishing good relations with the *Molokane* of the Caucasus. Ever since he had been a student at the Zurich Polytechnic, his main idea had been 'to bring the people to revolution through the sects'. It was for this reason that he had discontinued his education. He too was forced to realize that though it was easy enough to enter and join the world of heretics, it was very much more difficult to lead them towards a revolt.[65] Ivan Martynovich Kovalsky, later (in August 1878) to be hanged at Odessa for armed resistance to the police, also devoted part of his activities to propaganda among the *Stundists* and *Molokane* in the Nikolaev region. Together with him, Frolenko too made an attempt to enter these typically rationalising sects and influence them along revolutionary lines. But he concluded that 'it was not even conceivable that they could be brought to open revolution. They were honest, trustful people, but were not suitable as fighters. One could have counted on them for propaganda, but then it would have been necessary to begin again from the start and to come not as "brothers" but as revolutionaries.'[66] Kovalsky was the only one who persisted in this region. Like Mikhailov, he too was attracted by the element of criticism and protest latent in these sects.[67] Even after the end of the 'colonies', there was still much talk of infiltration among the sects, and plans were drawn up to reach the district of Yaroslavl and the problem was frequently raised. But nothing concrete was undertaken.

Instead, the revolutionaries now began to sound the prospects of 'agrarian terrorism' and speak of the need 'to use physical force in the defence of justice . . . Terror of this kind seemed all the more indispensable in that the people was oppressed by economic necessities, was the slave of an arbitrary despotism, and so was not in a position to make use of this weapon on its own.'[68] Once again, similar conclusions were drawn from experiences in countryside and town. At Saratov these ideas remained in the planning stage. But at Kiev they were to be put into effect in *The Workers' Union of South Russia* led by Kovalskaya and Shchedrin.

But the fundamental conclusions of this final movement 'to go to the people' were now different. Terrorism was aimed directly against those responsible for the appalling conditions of the peasants, against those who were preventing the revolutionaries from fighting to abolish this misery. It should even, they said, be directed against the very symbol of this situation, the Tsar himself. Solovev's decision to try to kill the Tsar was made at Saratov in the very midst of those 'Populists' who had left with the firm determination of carrying out a long process of agitation among the peasants.[69]

Tormented by the feeling that they were too few for the work they had undertaken, and caught up in the general trend of the year, which was leading to the creation of powerful urban movements, the members of the 'colonies' had mostly dispersed by the end of 1877. The 'commune' at Saratov was rounded up by the police. Plekhanov was arrested, fortunately by highly inexperienced men. It was Sunday, and after detaining him for some time, they finally told him to come back next day, so that he was able to warn his comrades. With the fall of the centre, nearly all those in the villages returned to St Petersburg. Two other centres met with a similar fate: the one at Samara organized by Yury Nikolaevich Bogdanovich, who later joined *Narodnaya Volya* and took part in the conspiracy of March 1881: and the one at Nizhny Novgorod directed by Alexander Alexandrovich Kvyatkovsky, who later became a member of the Executive Committee and was hanged in November 1880.

These few examples are enough to show the seeds that were germinating in the 'colonies'. We can see the same process in action in the more or less isolated attempts to work among the people made by individual members of *Zemlya i Volya*. The most typical of these was made by Alexander Ivanovich Barannikov in the region of Astrakhan. 'Young, and born of a rich noble family, he threw himself directly "into the people" without any transition or preparation', in the words of Mikhail Rodionovich Popov, who saw a great deal of him at this time.[70] After extensive travels in the South, they made for a region 'where, to judge from the newspapers of September 1876, there had been disorders . . . The village of Nikolskoe was in fact exactly the right sort of ground for the kind of activities indicated in the programme of *Zemlya i Volya*. But there were not enough resources for work of this size.' They asked for help from St Petersburg; but Bogolyubov, the one man who could have done something, had been arrested in the demonstration of 6th December. And so Barannikov too gave up these attempts to work among the people, and joined the Executive Committee. He was sentenced to hard labour and died in Shlisselburg in 1885.

It seemed all the more necessary to move on to a more active and political phase in the struggle, as the activities of the 'rebels' of the South as well as those of *Zemlya i Volya* were now on the decline. Indeed, despite a promising start, the attempted peasant insurrection at Chigirin had been stifled at the beginning of 1877.[71]

The 'rebels'* of southern Russia had not gone 'to the people' with a programme of propaganda or agitation, but exclusively to discover where it would be possible to start peasant rebellions. They were prompted by the Bakuninist idea that any revolt was of value even if immediately crushed, for it was the only way to educate the people in revolution. Indeed preparatory work of any other kind was useless. It was not the peasant masses who had to be prepared, but the small group of revolutionaries which would light the spark. And their preparation must consist exclusively in getting hold of such actual tools as were indispensable for the revolt, i.e., firearms, daggers, saddles and harness, and so on.

It was this way of looking at things that led to their being disillusioned more quickly than in the North. They had not been deterred by the enormous difficulty of finding arms and by the extremely small size of the arsenal they succeeded in collecting, but by the obvious uselessness of their 'colonies' in the villages of the Ukraine. The need for secrecy had prevented them from establishing even those personal and direct relations with the peasants which were being forged in the 'colonies' of the Saratov region. Enclosed within their small groups, they soon realized that in fact all they were doing was to speak of peasant revolutions and dream of the day when Pugachev's example could be followed.[73]

---

* A translation of the Russian *buntary*, derived from *bunt*, a revolt. A more accurate description would be 'supporters of local risings'—so they are described by a close associate.[72]

However, an important episode put an end to these ventures. In the summer of 1876 they noticed that N. E. Gorinovich was beginning to frequent their 'refuge'. Gorinovich had been arrested two years earlier and had denounced all his comrades. They now felt certain that he planned to act as *agent provocateur*. L. Deych and one of his comrades, V. A. Malinka, decided to get rid of him. They took him to Odessa and hit him with a revolver. They then left him for dead, after covering his face with sulphuric acid so as to prevent the police from recognizing him. But Gorinovich was not dead, and though he was seriously wounded and disfigured, he was able to denounce his would-be murderers. It was in fact Nechaev's story all over again, and the results were the same. In 1884 Deych was handed over to Russia by Germany as a common murderer and was sentenced to thirteen and a half years' hard labour. Malinka was hanged in Odessa in 1879.[74] But after this episode, the determination to eliminate spies by physical means, which the 'rebels' had been the first to express since the time of Nechaev, became part of the normal regulations of all subsequent revolutionary movements in Russia. The 'rebels' had not been able to start a peasant revolution, but they had helped to bring about the atmosphere of terrorism of the end of the 'seventies.

Only three of them did not resign themselves to this conclusion and, without paying much attention to methods, really tried to lead the villages to revolt. Between 1876 and the beginning of 1877, after the withdrawal of the groups that had been scattered in the countryside, Deych, Stefanovich and Bokhanovsky succeeded in laying the foundations of a vast peasant conspiracy at Kiev. It was the Chigirin venture that revealed the real state of affairs in the Ukrainian countryside, and showed up in a more brutal light the difficulties and contradictions which faced those revolutionaries who wanted to work among the people.

Ever since the beginning of the 'seventies, serious discontent had smouldered among the peasants round Chigirin on the banks of the Dnieper not far from Kiev. These peasants belonged to the State; the parcels of land which had been assigned to them by the reform had not been sufficient. And, more important, since then this land had gradually become more and more concentrated in the hands of one part of the population, leaving the rest in an increasingly difficult situation. The pressure of government administration had made itself felt, and hatred of the bureaucracy was widespread. The troubles began when the administration began to support the more prosperous section of the population, whose representatives were demanding that the parcels of land that they now owned should be confirmed by official 'acts' to give them full rights of possession. The poorer peasants, on the other hand, demanded 'division according to souls', i.e. redistribution of the land into equal holdings.[75] They had found a mouthpiece in an old soldier and comparatively rich peasant in the village of Sabelniki, called Foma Pryadko, who was convinced that the Tsar was on their side and that one day he would order a redistribution of land. And so he said that they must explain the situation to him and meanwhile stand up against pressure. In 1875 Pryadko left with various other peasants to take a petition to St Petersburg. His fellow-peasants were arrested and sent back to their homes. He himself succeeded in escaping and on his return seems to have said that he had seen the Tsar who had told him that he could do nothing for them as he was surrounded by the *pany*, the gentry. And so he urged the peasants to divide the land among themselves by force, and organize it in *obshchinas* so as to ensure equality between them.[76] In May 1875 the judicial authorities intervened to put an end to this agitation. All those not signing the 'acts' which established the register were to be flogged. Repression set in on a huge scale. Troops were quartered in the peasants' houses. There were floggings (as a result of which two people died) and arrests. And the fields which the peasants had refused to accept were handed over to the inhabitants of other districts on payment of a fee. Many of the inhabitants of Sabelniki and the surrounding villages did not surrender even to these measures. In 1876 the authorities found it necessary to establish permanent garrisons in the villages and deport many hundred peasants to the prisons of Kiev.

Stefanovich soon succeeded in getting in touch with these prisoners. This was made easier by the fact that they were generally allowed to remain free during the daytime so as to be able to work, as long as they returned to their cells at night. Through them he was able to forge links with those who were still carrying on the fight at Chigirin. After getting detailed information about the state of mind prevailing there, he drew up a plan of action with Deych.

In May 1876 he told the peasants that he himself would go to the Tsar to ask for their demands to be satisfied. Having thus adopted the same rôle as that played earlier by Pryadko, he came back bringing with him a *Secret Imperial Charter* and a copy of the *Statutes of the Secret Militia*. He had written and printed these in Kiev with Deych. Some time before they had succeeded in bringing into Russia a small press from abroad. This had been entrusted to a group in Odessa. It had then escaped from their control but for this occasion Deych and Stefanovich had managed 'to capture it', so to speak, and bring it back to Kiev.[77] It was there that they printed the documents which were to prove to the peasants of Chigirin that the Emperor was not only on their side but was actually urging them to take revolutionary action.

The *Secret Imperial Charter* was addressed 'to our loyal peasants' and told them that the Tsar by his decree of 19th February 'had granted liberty despite the will of all the nobility'. At the same time he had ordered that the land should be divided among all his subjects, including all who did not have any 'because God has granted every man the right to enjoy this gift in equal measure'. The nobles should only be left a portion equal to that owned by all the others. 'This is our will. But to our extreme distress the nobles have prevented the execution of our will' and had kept a large quantity of land for themselves. Twenty years had passed since he had come to the throne. During these years he had fought uninterruptedly against the nobility. But now at last he was convinced that 'he had not enough strength to fight against it alone'. And so he was giving instructions for the creation of secret societies and a clandestine militia (*druzhiny*) 'to prepare for insurrection against the nobles, the officials and all the upper classes'. Practical advice followed. They must not talk, they must not confess to the priests who were spies of the gentry; they must keep united and not be discouraged even if he himself were to die. He ended by promising that he would give them all the land without compensation. 'It will be yours like water, like the light of the sun, and all God's other gifts.' At the foot of the *Charter* was the date 19th February, to recall the anniversary of the liberation of the serfs; and it was backdated to 1875, possibly so as to make it coincide in some way with what Foma Pryadko had said earlier.

The *Statutes* consisted of a detailed description of the aims and above all the methods of the 'secret society' which would give the peasants liberty. It was to be led by a Council (*soviet*) of Commissars named by the Emperor himself. They would have the function of choosing the best of the peasants and organizing them into groups of twenty-five militiamen (*druzhinniki*) to make up one *starostvo*. These *starostvos* would in turn make up an assembly (*rada*) with a chieftain (*ataman*) at their head. All were to be armed, even if only with home-made pikes. They were to pay a small monthly contribution, observe military discipline and in general abide scrupulously by the long and detailed oath which the *Statutes* contained. At the foot was a gold seal with the inscription 'Seal of the Council of Commissars' and a drawing of a pike and an axe.

At first this plan met with some distrust from the peasants; but eventually it proved successful. The organization of the *druzhiny* and the recruiting of the militiamen were rapid and extensive. It was the only large-scale conspiracy among the peasants to prove feasible during the 'seventies. The authorities had some hints of the affair, but for a long time they were unable to discover any exact information. For almost a year, between November 1876 and the autumn of 1877, Stefanovich, Deych and Bokhanovsky were able to organize about a thousand peasants in twelve districts. Even after some of these had been arrested, the secret was still carefully kept. A significant part of the district around Chigirin was in the hands of the Commissars. Action was due to begin in October. But in the autumn, before they had the chance to undertake anything definite, careless talk by one peasant led to the organization being discovered. Hundreds of its followers were thrown into prison and some time later the three 'rebels' were arrested. Seventy-four peasants, among them Pryadko, were given varying sentences, among them banishment to Siberia. Stefanovich and his two comrades were put in Kiev prison. From here they were freed by a remarkably cunning trick of Frolenko, who succeeded in getting a job as a prison warder. One night, within a few months of taking on this new profession, he opened the gates and fled with them.[78]

Stefanovich's plan was the logical consequence of those 'concessions to popular ideals' which had led to criticism of the 'policy of propaganda' at the time of the movement 'to go to the people' and to the formation of a more deliberately 'Populist' wing. To achieve this the revolutionaries had to plunge themselves into the psychology of the peasants, to fight with them and alongside them. For this reason Stefanovich had even been prepared to go as far as accepting their faith in the Tsar and trying to make use of it. The 'rebels' now built up theoretical conclusions from these experiences. In 1876 Anna Makarevich came to Geneva with a pamphlet which claimed that the idea of 'usurpation', i.e. a false Tsar, had always been at the basis of Russian popular movements. The revolutionaries ought therefore to make use of these traditions for carrying out their own work in the country.[79] She suggested that the *Rabotnik* should print this pamphlet. The editors hesitated, and after some discussions finally refused. The young Bakuninists were evidently not prepared to accept the consequences of the 'Populist' standpoint. Even Bakunin was opposed to this plan. And the reaction among all the revolutionary currents of opinion within Russia itself was identical when the tactics employed by Stefanovich at Chigirin came to light. Kravchinsky said: 'It was only approved in part by the party, and was not followed afterwards.'[80] And this was among the most indulgent verdicts. The vast majority of revolutionaries severely condemned this attempt to deceive the peasants. Historically speaking there is no doubt that—despite its comparative success—this extremism and Machiavellism only showed that for the moment the road leading towards the peasants was still blocked.

It was the government itself that crystallized this tendency to fight directly against the State, though the revolutionaries had been more and more driven back on it after their failures among the people. By its system of repression and trials, the government turned all eyes towards a more immediate war to be waged in St Petersburg, the real centre of power. The government's policy was clear. It was trying to isolate the revolutionaries from 'society' and from the intelligentsia, by publicly demonstrating that they wanted a social revolution; that they were not in fact liberals but anarchists and Socialists. The State now began to take a part in the complex relationship between the revolutionary movement and the intelligentsia. The roots of this problem had first appeared in the 'forties. Since then it had developed along many different lines, and even at the beginning of the 'seventies it was still at the very heart of all discussions between the various currents of Populism. Now the State was aiming to bring over to its own side at least some of the intelligentsia by frightening it with the spectre of the 'red peril'. Lavrov had insisted on a link always being kept between educated society and the revolutionaries. Tkachev had wanted the revolutionaries to realize that objective circumstances, such as developments in Russian economy and politics, had now broken this link; and he therefore urged the revolutionary forces to build up a closed and separate organization. The government was now trying to use for its own purposes the process which Tkachev wanted to bring about for the advantage of Russian Jacobinism. It was trying to make a final split between the intelligentsia and the revolutionaries.

Such were the tactics that the Committee of Ministers decided to adopt in March 1875. It is worth taking a close look at the considerations that influenced them.

One of the main reasons for the grievous indifference which well-meaning social elements feel for the widespread propaganda of subversive principles—brought to light by recent enquiries—lies in the ignorance which prevails not only among most sections of the public but even among high officials in the government administration (including even the majority of the Committee of Ministers) as to the extent assumed by such propaganda. The Committee is of the opinion that in view of this ignorance, society cannot be directly reproached for not putting up serious obstacles to false doctrines . . . In the majority of cases it is this ignorance which explains the frivolous reproaches made against the government for adopting repressive measures and arresting evilly disposed elements. Such arrests are often attributed only to a whim of the administration, and generally arouse pity for the people arrested or being sought. Yet the Committee is profoundly convinced that the book by one of the leaders of this agitation, in which he traces a picture of the future that the revolutionary propagandists are preparing for the present generation, ought not to arouse any sympathy either among well-disposed social classes or even among undeveloped natures liable to exaltation . . . They themselves say that torrents, rivers—a deluge of blood—are necessary to bring about their ends. The Committee is convinced that these delirious ravings of a fanatical imagination cannot meet with any support. But for public opinion to break away from those who hold such doctrines, their principles must no longer remain unknown.[81]

The great trials of 1877 were an attempt to carry out these directives, but they were badly managed. For the experiment to be a success, it was above all essential that the authorities themselves should not be frightened of the 'red peril' but should cold-bloodedly make use of it as a weapon. In fact, however, they allowed themselves to be prompted by fear and hatred rather than by political considerations. The result was a constant wavering between violence and comparative indulgence. And so they did not succeed either in planting fear among the intelligentsia or—still less—in discouraging the revolutionaries.

Circumstances only made the matter worse. The trials took place at a time when, if only because of the war, the public opinion which they were designed to influence was particularly ready to welcome any protest against the government. The attitude of the accused was nearly always proud and bold, as they skilfully carried out their apostolic determination to bear witness to their own ideas without hesitation or boasting. And so the government's methods acted like boomerangs. The trials merely forged new links between the

19*

intelligentsia and the revolutionaries; and these links were to lead to the development of *Zemlya i Volya* and the birth of *Narodnaya Volya*.

The trial of the demonstrators of the Square of Our Lady of Kazan in St Petersburg took place between 18th and 25th January 1877. We have already seen that it was this trial that made the most impression because of the obviously arbitrary nature of the inquiry and the severity of the sentences inflicted. The violence employed by the police against the crowd and against women who happened to be on the spot; the presence of workers and students standing beside one another in the dock; the repercussions of Plekhanov's speech which referred to Chernyshevsky and others who had been condemned for their ideas—all this merely encouraged the sympathy and pity which the authorities had intended to stifle. One witness described what he had seen as follows: 'There was shown a banner on which was written "Volya" (liberty) and something else which I did not note.' And these words unintentionally expressed the general impression made by the demonstration.[82]

But this was only the first in the series of trials. Far deeper was the impression made in March of the same year by the 'trial of the fifty' in Moscow. Kravchinsky tells us that the spectators at this famous trial kept on repeating the words 'They are saints' with great emotion, and his evidence is confirmed from other sources. Turgenev in his novel *Virgin Soil* and in a prose poem was to write of the young women who had risked everything to spread propaganda in the factories. Ya. Polonsky and Nekrasov dedicated poems to them.[83] Mikhailov watched the trial and was profoundly moved. But he was also able to look at it as a politician and he noted that 'the trial of the fifty had had an even greater influence on society than the one for the demonstration on Kazan Square. In it were people who could be compared to the early Christian martyrs; they were propagandists of pure Socialism, teachers of love, equality and fraternity, the fundamental principles of the Christian *Commune*. But the government did not spare them.'[84]

Already 'the trial of the fifty' was bringing to the fore the element of complete dedication and self-sacrifice which had been at the basis of the movement when it revived at the beginning of the 'seventies. By striking Nechaev, the government had hoped to uproot the element of extreme Machiavellism and violence. Now it was trying to crush the new force which had replaced it. But the attempt failed. Quite spontaneously the propagandists who were called upon to explain their activities gave first place to those general principles of humanity that had driven them to the sacrifice. In Moscow the two main speeches were made by the workman Alexeyev and by Sofya Bardina. And it was thought better not to print them in the account that was published in the *Official Messenger*. The argument *ad deterrendum*, which had driven the government to stage the trials, had now recoiled against it. Sofya Bardina's speech was circulated instead in the *Vpered*. And nothing

could have been of greater use for introducing the Populist socialists to
public opinion in a moderate and at the same time appealing light:

Neither I nor any of the other propagandists preach Communism as something
which forms a compulsory part of our programme. We merely give first place to the
worker's right to enjoy the full produce of his work. How he then disposes of this
produce, whether he changes it into private or communal property, is his own
business . . .

Sofya Bardina then continued in the same spirit to deal with all the other
charges: the repudiation of family and religion and the appeal to revolt.
And she ended:

If the ideal society of which we dream could be brought into being without any
violent revolution, we would be happy in the depths of our souls. I only think that
in certain circumstances violent revolution is an inevitable evil . . . We want to
destroy privileges, the division of men into classes, into those who possess land and
those who do not. We do not want to destroy the individuals who make up these
classes . . . Nor do we (as the charge against us supposes) want to establish a reign
of the working class as a class which in its own turn would oppress other classes.
We are striving for the happiness of all and for equality in so far as it does not
naturally depend on personal qualities such as difference of temperament, sex,
age, etc.[85]

She ended by proclaiming at the top of her voice that the propagandists
did not want any *coup d'état* but merely the triumph of an ideal which could
not be suppressed with bayonets.

If such was really the aim of the revolutionaries, their fate must have
seemed harsh enough to the general public in autumn 1877. Of a hundred and
ten accused, sixteen had been sentenced to hard labour, often for long periods;
twenty-eight had been banished or exiled into distant regions; twenty-one
kept in prison; five sent to disciplinary battalions; only one had been merely
warned; while the other thirty-nine had been acquitted.

It was in this atmosphere that the 'trial of the hundred and ninety-three'
opened in the middle of October 1877. It lasted until 23rd January 1878.
In the mind of the government it was to be the final act of the liquidation of
'revolutionary propaganda in the empire'. This mass trial would put an end
to the movement 'to go to the people'. And indeed such was the result of
the trial. But only in so far as propaganda was replaced by organization, and
agitation by terrorism.

The government was oppressed by the obscure feeling that it had taken
the wrong turning, and at the end of April 1877 the Tsar himself asked for
a new plan of action. A meeting was held at the Ministry of Justice to discuss
this. One of those present has described the meeting, and we can ask for no
better picture of the uncertainty, political incompetence, fear and violence
which prevailed among the ruling classes at this time. No conclusion was
reached and every responsibility was handed over to the bureaucratic machine,

which was, so to speak, left to itself. 'Some evil spirit was weighing down
Russia's internal life',[86] wrote a memorialist. The muddled discussion held
at the Ministry of Justice itself showed that this 'evil spirit' lay in the
incapacity to face the two fundamental problems that beset Russia: the
discontent felt by the peasants at their lack of land, the weight of taxes, etc.;
and the increasing aspirations of 'society' for a free régime, vague though
these were. *Zemlya i Volya*—land and liberty—the two words now took
first place in the minds of the ruling classes as they did in those of the revolutionary underground.

In July the 'Preventive Detention Centre', which contained the prisoners
about to be tried in the imminent 'trial of the hundred and ninety-three',
witnessed a scene which aroused a feeling of deep indignation among the
Populists and made a no less deep impression throughout society as a whole.
One day the Governor of St Petersburg, General Trepov, came to visit the
prison. He already had behind him a remarkable career of brutality. As
Chief of Police in Warsaw he had replied with gunfire to the demonstration
of 25th February 1861. In 1863 the repressive measures he had taken in
Poland had led to an attempt on his life. And after Karakozov's attempt to
shoot the Tsar in 1866, he had been put in charge of the capital. Now, on
his visit to the prison he flew at one of the prisoners who had not taken off
his cap when he passed, and tried to strike him. This took place in the courtyard, while his fellow-prisoners looked on from their windows. An extremely
violent demonstration followed the General's action. After hesitating for a
moment, he went to the Minister of Justice, Pahlen, to ask for authority to
have the prisoner flogged. The prisoner in question was Emelyanov, known
as Bogolyubov. He had been arrested for taking part in the demonstration
on the Kazan Square, and had been heavily sentenced. He was taken off,
and flogged with such violence that he went mad and died a few years later.[87]
The atmosphere in the prison only calmed down when the inmates learnt
that Bogolyubov was to be avenged by those who were still free. From that
day onwards the determination to answer violence with violence rooted
itself in the minds of the prisoners, and among them were to be found many
of the future terrorists of *Narodnaya Volya*. Trepov's brutality was 'the last
straw'. Many of them had been held in preventive detention for as long as
three years in conditions which induced a state of mind very different from
their zeal for propaganda in 1873 and 1874. Trepov's action now showed
them how far their spirits had changed.[88]

We have seen that Trepov had not acted on his own initiative when he
ordered Bogolyubov to be flogged. Nor had Pahlen obeyed his own personal
inclination when he authorized this punishment. Many proposals were now
being made to introduce a law to determine this principle. In the circles close
to the Ministry of Justice this was the type of proposal being made to strike
at the revolutionaries. Pahlen had merely expressed a state of mind made up
of fear and violence which was widespread in the summer of 1877.

And yet when Zhikharev, the examining magistrate at the 'trial of the hundred and ninety-three', announced that everything was ready, there was a moment of uncertainty and doubt in official circles. It was obvious that this was the worst possible moment for a huge political trial. The Russian army in the Balkans had been halted outside Plevna. Casualties were very heavy. A quick victory had been hoped for. Instead a massacre was taking place which was bringing to light all the weakness of the army, the command and the régime itself. Prince Constantine Nikolaevich, brother of the Tsar and President of the State Council, realized that it would be wiser to postpone the trial, and expressed this opinion to Pahlen. But Pahlen, irritated by this intervention in a question which concerned only himself, arranged for justice to follow its course. The Prince did not insist.

All the trial reflected this uncertainty. It was held in private, but there was no lack of guests. The *Official Messenger* promised to give a regular detailed account, but ended by giving such brief notices that St Petersburg was filled with every kind of fantastic rumour. The newspapers were only given the right to reproduce the official version, but many journalists were allowed to watch the proceedings. The defence was carried out by able and often courageous lawyers, in a trial of the most doubtful legality, which included the most varying charges under the term 'propaganda'. At the very moment when the authorities intended to put an end to all propaganda, the trial dragged on for months owing to the large number of prisoners.

From the very first the attitude of the accused revealed the prevailing state of mind.[89] When they were taken into the court room, friends who had not seen each other for years were reunited. An atmosphere of youthful boldness, high spirits and happiness prevailed in the 'Golgotha', as they called the part of the room reserved for them.[90] The Court wanted to separate them again, and decided that on the following day only those directly involved in the questioning would be present at each sitting. This decree divided the accused into two more or less equal sections: those who intended to protest by refusing to take part in the trial, and those who intended to defend themselves. This created a hard core of men determined to protest against the tribunal itself and not collaborate with it in any way, as well as to repudiate all its decrees and judgment. Thus the schism between the world of Populist revolutionaries and the official world became visible and symbolic. Such was the first result of the 'trial of the hundred and ninety-three', and it was a result well worth achieving, even at the cost of dropping the more uncertain and weaker elements or those who just did not want to subject themselves to group discipline.[91]

It was a member of this latter group who emphasized in his statement to the tribunal the importance of what had happened. After having explained his ideas, Myshkin ended:

I am now definitely convinced that the opinion of my comrades was right . . . It is now obvious that not a single word of truth can be spoken here. For every sincere word the accused has his mouth shut. I can now say that this is not a tribunal but a useless comedy; or something worse, something more repulsive, more shameful than a brothel. There, a woman sells her own body out of necessity. Here, senators trade with the lives of others, with truth and with justice; trade in fact with all that is dearest to humanity out of cowardice, baseness, opportunism, and to gain large salaries.

Myshkin was only able to finish his speech because another of the accused obstructed the policeman who had flung himself at him to stop him talking. And this was only the most violent of the many incidents that took place during the trial. Myshkin's words turned him into a symbol and had a wide clandestine circulation. 'After his words the tribunal was annihilated', wrote Kravchinsky.[92]

As far as politics were concerned the trial revealed the transformation not only of psychology but also of ideals that had taken place in the generation that had 'gone to the people'. It marked the consecration of the new phase of Populism which was coming into effect in *Zemlya i Volya*. This Populism included many differing tendencies, temperaments and even ideas. But the trial, by gathering together its varying representatives in a single dock, merely emphasized the element that they all had in common. All the centres affected by propaganda were represented, as well as all the various currents of belief, from the anarchism of Rabinovich and Kovalik to the deo-humanism of Malikov which he defended in a brilliant speech. But the true political force that sprang from all this ferment was described by Myshkin:

The essential task of the social-revolutionary party is to build up on the existing ruins of the existing state-bourgeois régime a social organization which satisfies the demands of the people. These demands have been expressed in the large and small movements that have come from it, and they are present in its consciousness. This organization consists in a land made up of the union of independent productive *obshchinas*. It can be brought about only through a social revolution, because the power of the State prevents any peaceful means being used for this end . . . I believe that our immediate task does not consist in unleashing or making a revolution, but merely in guaranteeing its successful issue. For in view of the desperate situation of the people today, one does not have to be a prophet to foresee that the inevitable result of this will be a general popular revolution. In view of the inevitability of this revolution, our only concern is that it should be as fruitful as possible for the people, by steering it clear of all the various tricks which have been resorted to by the bourgeoisie of Western Europe to deceive the popular masses and take advantage of the blood shed by their own people on the barricades. With this aim in view our practical activities must consist in the union and strengthening of popular forces and revolutionary tendencies, and in the fusion of the two fundamental currents of revolution. One of these—that of the intelligentsia—has only recently emerged, but it has already shown considerable energy. The other—that of the people—is wider and deeper, and has never been exhausted. The work of the revolutionary movement of 1874 and 1875 has been just this: to unite these two elements through the conclusive formation of a social-revolutionary party.

Kravchinsky was right to say that until this speech most people knew of the Russian Socialists only through hearsay, through the attacks of the official press or perhaps even 'through the novels of Dostoevsky'. Now they had a chance to learn their ideas and programme from the voice of a man who was himself one of them.[93]

In contrast to this assertion of political faith, the verdicts of the trial once again brought to light the hesitation of the Senators. Five people were sentenced to ten years' hard labour; ten to nine years; three to five years; forty to banishment; while the majority were freed. This majority contributed what the prosecutor described as the 'background' of the trial. It had been included so that those who were guilty of more serious crimes would stand out in bold relief. Public opinion naturally enough pointed out that, for the satisfaction of creating this 'background', hundreds of people had been sentenced to preventive detention for three or four years.[94] The Senate itself was obviously far from convinced by its verdict. As a footnote it added an appeal to the Emperor to be so gracious as to commute all sentences of detention—except that of Myshkin—to banishment. The authorities had wanted to impress 'society' with the 'red peril'. Now they would give proof of their magnanimity and charity. But the course of the trial itself and the atmosphere in which it had been carried out merely meant that this move was looked upon as a sign of weakness.[95] And so the Tsar thought it advisable to reject the Senators' appeal and confirm the sentences.

The men who were sent to hard labour were really symbolic of a period which was now coming to an end, and of the transition to a new phase in the struggle.

Ippolit Nikitich Myshkin was a son of the people. His father was a soldier, and he had had to fend for himself. He had eventually become a shorthand reporter in the law courts. On coming into contact with the revolutionary movement he flung himself into it with a passion which was exceptional even at the time of the first 'pilgrimage to the people'.[96] He remained rather isolated and on one side, little known to his comrades, who rarely suspected his hidden energies.[97] He started a small press in Moscow, which became the centre of the Chaikovskists in that town, and in 1875 he left for Siberia to organize Chernyshevsky's escape. He was arrested, but escaped, and at Vilyuysk he fired at the Cossacks who were pursuing him.[98] His speech to the tribunal made him the most popular character in the 'trial of the hundred and ninety-three'. On the long road to Siberia and forced labour he thought only of flight. In this he was successful. A month later, however, he was caught in Vladivostok. He was now taken to Shlisselburg. He well knew that from here there would be no escape. This prison would be his tomb. And so he thought only of protesting. He was shot in 1885 for insulting the Governor.[99] Life had given him only two opportunities to say out loud what were the reasons for his existence. He had spoken at the tribunal, and later in the prison church at Irkutsk during the funeral service of Dmokhovsky,

Dolgushin's comrade. His actions spoke the rest. He was not a good conversationalist and he did not enjoy discussion. But he showed himself to be a remarkable orator and above all a fighter whom nothing or no one could crush.

The opposite pole of Russian society was represented at the trial by Porfiry Ivanovich Voynaralsky, who was an illegitimate son of Princess Kugusheva. At the age of seventeen he had been deported to Archangel for taking part in the St Petersburg student movements of 1861. He had then been held in various towns of European Russia, after which he succeeded in getting in touch with Ishutin in Moscow. There he was arrested once more. In 1873 and 1874 he was one of the most active members of the movement 'to go to the people'. He was rich, and had placed all his goods at the disposal of his comrades and the organization.

He was not a theorist by nature. He did have a clear brain which quickly assimilated the essence of every new idea; but he was chiefly interested in the practical side of things and how to bring them about . . . He organized workshops for the intelligentsia, worked in Myshkin's press, founded meeting places, and established shops for the people, and 'refuges' for propagandists. He dreamt of covering the whole of the Volga region (where most of his activities were concentrated) with a net of such 'refuges' all in touch with each other.[100]

The various groups at Saratov, Samara, Penza and Tambov found in him an organizer who was always on the move. In 1874 he was arrested at Samara and taken to the Peter-Paul fortress, and then to the 'Preventive Detention Centre'. He just failed in an attempt to escape which he planned with Kovalik. In prison his gifts as an organizer led to his being elected the *starosta* of his fellow-prisoners. In 1883, at the end of his sentence, he was exiled to the territory of the Yakuts. Here he tried to earn a living by taking to trade and to make a new family for himself by marrying a native. Until 1897 he lived in the primitive misery of Eastern Siberia. He was then able to return once more to European Russia, only to discover that his eldest daughter was far from anxious to see him, for she had been reabsorbed into the aristocratic and reactionary world from which he had broken away in his early youth. It was now too late to resume his activities as propagandist and organizer. He was scarcely able to get into contact with the younger generation before he died, exhausted by the life he had led.

With him there came back to European Russia Sergey Filippovich Kovalik, his companion in prison, flight, and exile. Kovalik was one of the few of the more important accused at the 'trial of the hundred and ninety-three' to be a convinced anarchist. In other words he accepted Bakunin's ideological interpretation of the Populist ferment of these years.[101]

Kovalik's mind was precise and methodical. It is he who gives us our most detailed account of the movement, which, though it reflects his anarchist ideology, is none the less a valuable source of information about his generation.

Dmitry Mikhailovich Rogachev came from the same group of artillery officers in St Petersburg which gave Shishko and Kravchinsky to the revolutionary movement. He had been very close to the Chaikovskists, though he had not been a member of the organization. He was in touch with Nizovkin, who introduced him to a group of workers, whereupon, as he says in his *Confessions to My Friends*:

I came out of the inn as if thunderstruck. I was ready to embrace the whole world; I ran through the street, bumping into two or three people. It so happened that I came across a man who had insulted a woman. I gave him a slap in the face. From that day onwards I decided to devote all my being, all my time, to working among the people.[102]

During the movement 'to go to the people', he travelled between town and country, making contacts and spreading propaganda both among the intelligentsia and the workers and peasants. He worked for a time at the Putilov factory, where he was employed on the heaviest jobs. But he was mainly attracted by a free life, and became one of the barge haulers along the Volga. So great was his physical strength and so like them was he in appearance that his fellow-haulers never suspected that he was a noble and an officer. From the Volga he went to the region of the Don. At Rostov he lived in the 'company of gold', i.e. a kind of organization of beggars who lived by doing unloading work in the port. 'I heard', he later wrote to a friend, 'of the energy with which they defended their position in the labour market . . . Thanks to their solidarity they often succeeded in imposing their conditions on the employers.'[103] But when he tried to urge them to take more decisive steps in protest at their conditions or endeavoured to instil lasting propaganda among them, he met with no success. Yet despite this, Rogachev certainly did not share the views of those who were disappointed by their work among the people.

His conclusions were similar to those of his comrades. He said in his *Confession*:

The peasant reform of 1861 constituted the transition from the servile to the capitalist régime. Besides, at first they allowed the *obshchina* to go on existing, but everything that the land gave the people they carried off as taxes . . . And now the government is aiming at the speedy destruction of the *obshchina* . . . I am convinced that in the near future a proletariat will appear in Russia too, and that—in a word—we will cover the ground traversed by the other countries of Western Europe . . . But the reform and everything that followed from it has had a good influence on the peasant. It has detached and separated him from the landlord. It has brought him face to face with the authorities and the people (of course in its best elements) and has made him understand that he can put his hopes in no one. All he must now do is to make up his mind on what must be done. How can he escape from his situation? Our duty is clear; we must prepare to organize the party of the people. I do not agree with those who maintain that some great movement of the people is possible today. I do not share this opinion because the people has no force round which it can group. And so, I repeat, our essential duty is to organize the party of the people.

This was the road followed by his brother Nikolay, who was one of the most important members of the military organization of *Narodnaya Volya*, and who was hanged at Shlisselburg on 10th October 1884. Dmitry, on the other hand, after a constant series of lucky escapes when on the point of arrest, and after living for a long time among the peasants, was arrested in St Petersburg on 15th August 1876, shortly before the trial in which he was to be sentenced to ten years' hard labour. From this he was never to return, and he died at Kara, aged thirty-three, on 14th January 1884.

A ten years' sentence was also the fate of Mitrofan Danilovich Muravsky, the man who represented at this time the continuity of revolutionary Populism from its origins down to the movement 'to go to the people'. Muravsky was generally called 'Father Mitrofan' by his comrades both because at the age of forty he was the oldest among them, and because to some extent he was their spiritual guide, and had given a religious character to his faith in Populism. We have already met Muravsky at the beginning of his revolutionary career in 1858.[104] He was now once more in prison, having been banished to the department of Orenburg after an earlier stay in prison and Siberia for 'incitement to revolt'. On his return to Orenburg, he had become the centre for the local 'movement to the people'. He was sentenced only after four years' preventive detention, and died exhausted by the life he had led in the central prison of Kharkov.

Among those who received sentences of nine years, were many members of the central group of the Chaikovskist circle, such as S. S. Sinegub, N. A. Charushin, L. E. Shishko. With them was a workman, Ivan Osipovich Soyuzov, 'one of the first representatives of that increasingly large section of the intelligentsia which came from the people', as has rightly been said.[105] He was a craftsman from Moscow. Morozov, who travelled among the people with him at this time, said:

He made an excellent impression on me. His every word and movement showed a naive sincerity like that of a child, a desire to do good and a great thirst for knowledge . . . He was not frightened of showing that he looked upon us as superior to him in culture, and for this very reason when theoretical problems were being discussed, despite his shyness he was not afraid to give his own opinion and then listen carefully. He used odd words less than the other workers and he distorted them less, although he said 'pripaganda' instead of 'propaganda'.[106]

Such was Soyuzov at the beginning of his career. Only a few years later it was he who insisted on the creation of a new organization after the movement 'to the people' had been broken up by the arrests. He served a long sentence of hard labour in Kara and was then able to return once more to European Russia.

In 1878 he was one of the signatories of the letter which put the seal on the moral victory won by the revolutionary Populists at the 'trial of the hundred and ninety-three'. Twenty of these men, though confronted with the sporadic violence of the government, sent to the *Obshchina*, a newspaper printed at Geneva, a declaration which they explicitly asked should be published:

The central authorities have thought it worth while to make us an obvious deterrent to those who belong to the same way of thinking, by hypocritically making differences in the punishments they have imposed, and perhaps by corrupting the weak who are prompted not only by their consciences but also by considerations of personal benefit. This rôle that has been imposed on us compels us to state that no 'condemnation' and no 'pardon' can make the slightest difference in our allegiance to the people's revolutionary party. We are still enemies of the system that exists in Russia. This system is both a disaster and a disgrace for our country: from the economic point of view it exploits labour for the benefit of the greedy parasite and the depraved; and from the political point of view, it hands over labour, possessions, freedom, the life and honour of every citizen, to the hands of personal caprice and whim. We entrust our comrades with the determination to pursue—with our past energy and redoubled courage—the aim for which we have been persecuted and for which we are ready to fight and suffer until our last breath.[107]

This letter, dated 25th May 1878, was published in the *Obshchina*. It constitutes the moral testament of the movement of the first part of the 'seventies.[108]

Before we see how the movement revived it may be of use to reconsider the phase which ended with the 'trial of the hundred and ninety-three'. The figures of the arrests compiled by one of the police departments at the end of 1877 give us a general idea.[109] Between 1873 and 1877, 1,611 propagandists were arrested, of whom 85 per cent were men and 15 per cent women. In fact, the number was probably greater than this, and no account is here taken of the many cases of short imprisonment. However, of these 1,611, 557 were released after varying periods of detention. Of those handed over to the tribunals, 425 were described as 'especially criminal', and these included mostly the young and the very young. Of the 'criminals', 117 were less than twenty-one years old; 199 between twenty-one and twenty-five; 93 between twenty-five and thirty; and only 42 were more than thirty years old. From the class point of view 147 were nobles; 90 came from the clergy; 58 were the sons of high officers; 11 were soldiers; 65 peasants; and 54 bourgeois. In actual fact the two latter categories did not represent two well-defined economic classes. These 'peasants' and 'bourgeois' were for the most part workers and artisans coming from the country and the town, from factories or workshops. There were only 9 real peasants in all. Of the accused, 44 belonged to the mixed category of 'commoners'.* The great majority of these men and women were Russians or Ukrainians; 23 were Jews; 10 Caucasians; and 6 foreigners. If we turn from the men who were classified

* *Raznochintsy.*

by the police as 'especially criminal' to those who were sentenced in the various trials or affected by administrative measures such as banishment, exile, etc., the general picture is still the same. There were 279 nobles, 117 sons of high officers, 33 merchants, 197 sons of priests, 92 'bourgeois', 138 'peasants', 13 soldiers, 27 'commoners', and 68 Jews.

The movement was thus for the most part made up of young men from the upper classes who had passed through school and university to become the most active and sensitive portion of the intelligentsia. But from now on there was a sizeable representation of all classes of the population except the peasants in the villages. Especially important were the clergy. And even the peasants, by emigrating into urban factories, were beginning to take an active part in the limited but extremely vital world of the revolutionary Populists. Tkachev's *élite*, made up of intellectuals capable of integrating those elements that came from the people, had now come into being. And its formation had been due to that very movement 'to go to the people', which he himself had looked upon as a useless waste of endeavour.

And now a considerable part of the *élite* was being released after 'the trial of the hundred and ninety-three', thanks to that shilly-shallying between firmness and indulgence which had already brought about the moral defeat of the authorities. Among those acquitted, to name only two, were Sofya Perovskaya and Zhelyabov, who played a considerable part in organizing the events of 1st March 1881.

On 24th January 1878, the day after the trial ended, a young girl came into the office of General Trepov, governor of St Petersburg, and mixed with the crowd who were going up in turn to hand him requests, petitions, etc. When her turn came she fired at him at point-blank range. She put up no resistance to those who seized her and, after throwing away her revolver, she watched in amazement the confusion that her action had produced. For a time she concealed her name, and then said that she was called Vera Zasulich, and that she had shot Trepov to avenge Bogolyubov, who had been flogged in prison.

Vera Ivanovna Zasulich came from the circle surrounding Nechaev. She had been arrested in 1869, and only came out of prison in 1871, when she was sent into exile. In 1875 she went to Kiev and again joined the revolutionary movement. She had then tried, like so many others, to prepare herself for a peasant rebellion, after which she devoted herself entirely to the task of freeing and avenging her imprisoned comrades.

Another attempt to kill Trepov had been planned at the same time. The governor's steps had already been under observation for some time. Frolenko, Voloshenko, Popko and Osinsky organized the plot which was anticipated by Vera Zasulich. They were waiting until the sentences in the 'trial of the hundred and ninety-three' had been announced so as not to harm their comrades. Vera Zasulich was aware of their intentions, but did not know the details of their plans. She herself had arranged for a double blow to be struck on the same day. One of her comrades was to go to the public prosecutor at the trial, and kill him. But this second assassination failed, because the assassin was refused admittance that morning.[110]

Vera Zasulich's action opened what Klements was rightly to call 'the year of attempted assassinations'.[111] This was not confined to Russia. In 1878 Hòdel Nobiling and Passanante fired at the Emperor of Germany and the King of Italy. Throughout Europe the effect was deeply felt. But Klements himself stressed the great difference in character between these acts of terrorism and those carried out by the Russians in the same year. The former were carried out by isolated individuals inspired by ideals that were often obscure and politically undefined; the latter by a revolutionary movement which had adopted as 'tactics of war' the elimination of those whom it considered 'dangerous' and which was beginning to resort to the armed 'defence' of the 'interests of the party'. The Russian terrorists stand half-way between partisan warfare and the coup of the anarchist. They represented an attempt—at least partially successful—to unleash a political struggle and open up the way to a revolution; they were an expression of 'propaganda through deeds' and not of isolated moves of protest. Russian 'terrorism' in fact is only one aspect of the formation of a revolutionary Socialist party, and the symptom of a general crisis in Russian society.

The example of Vera Zasulich and other attempts made at the same time show that this 'terrorism' came from the South and was brought to St Petersburg by associates of the 'rebels' of Kiev and Odessa. Osinsky had already joined the circles of the *Zemlya i Volya*, but he too came from the Ukraine, as did Popko, Frolenko and Voloshenko. Throughout 1878 armed battles and assassinations were more frequent in Southern Russia than in the North. It was in the Ukraine that terrorism began to take on an organized form, and it was there that the first 'Executive Committee' came into being It was in the Ukraine too that the first political reflections of these 'tactics' made their appearance. By their very nature these tactics removed the issue from the sphere of agitation among the people and raised the problem of a direct 'political' conflict with the authorities. But it was not the South that bore the fruit of this terrorist ferment. For St Petersburg was the seat of a nucleus which already had more political coherence than anything in the South. In 1878 *Zemlya i Volya* took on its definitive shape, and founded a secret periodical press. Here it raised the problem of terrorism within a wider political framework and conducted a passionate discussion of its political consequences. *Zemlya i Volya* became, in short, the organizing centre of the entire revolutionary Populist movement. There were other reasons for this besides the exceptional ability of its leaders. It was in St Petersburg that the crisis of Russian society as a whole was most evident and that the effects of the revolutionaries' campaign were most extensive. And it was in St Petersburg more obviously than elsewhere that the duel between revolutionaries and the authorities which began in 1878 and which came to a halt on 1st March 1881 began.

Vera Zasulich's action 'was, in revolutionary circles, a call to take up a new attitude'.[112] The first example of armed resistance to the police occurred a week later, at Odessa, during a search of Kovalsky's press. Tsitsianov, a member of the *Pan-Russian Social Revolutionary Organization*, had defended himself when about to be arrested in Moscow, but his attempt had been improvised on the spot and had scarcely attracted any attention. Kovalsky and his comrades in Odessa, on the other hand, were the first to put into practice one of the rebels' principles, 'not to allow themselves to be taken like sheep'. As the organ of *Zemlya i Volya* said at the end of 1878, on that day 'a group of Socialists clearly raised the problem of an active fight against the imperial tyranny'.[113]

Indeed the significance of the events of 30th January did not lie only in the courage shown by Kovalsky and his friends, but sprang also from the ideas that inspired the group and their transition from 'revolt' to the 'political struggle', from Bakunin to Tkachev.[114]

As will be remembered, Kovalsky was one of the most ardent supporters of an approach to the sects with a view to spreading revolutionary propaganda among them. He was led into this course of action by his own character. 'He himself was a fanatical sectarian, extremely hard with himself', in the words of one of his comrades, N. Vitashevsky. His poverty-stricken and ascetic life, as well as his inability to adapt himself to day-to-day activity and work out practical plans, have been described in detail by those who knew him. Many of his comrades regarded him primarily as a thinker, a man who tried to understand the problems which were disturbing the spirits of those around him.

But for all this, his chief concern was to put his ideas into practice. He was tormented by the thought that his generation would behave like Turgenev's *Rudin*. 'When we come to action, we halt', he once wrote when considering the habit, which was now widespread in the South, of always carrying arms. Who would provide the example?

His political development is difficult to follow in detail. It is at any rate certain that he too passed from 'propaganda' to 'propaganda with deeds'. In 1874 he was arrested, together with Yurkovsky, for his activities among the *Stundist* sect, but he was freed before the 'trial of the hundred and ninety-three'. In about 1876 he settled in Odessa. Although the society in which he lived was largely dominated by the ideas of the rebels—in 1877 Debagory-Mokrievich and M. Kovalskaya were in Odessa—he none the less formed a group of his own. This lacked a definite organization but had some unity of purpose. Among its members, most of whom were revolutionaries and Populists, were two disciples of Tkachev's *Nabat* who had returned to Russia from Switzerland. Elizaveta Nikolaevna Yuzhakova had joined the Paris Commune with Tursky, whom she had met abroad. She then returned to Switzerland, where she worked with Nechaev and Sazhin, and later joined the group which was at this time beginning to publish the *Nabat*. In 1876–77 she was at Odessa, by this time a convinced Jacobin. The second, N. Vita-shevsky, had in 1877 been to Switzerland, but had not been able to get in direct touch with Tkachev. Instead he had joined two of his followers, Grigoriev and Frenk,[115] and, in his own words, 'had then moved to the "political" programme and to "neo-Jacobinism"'. The *Nabat* was apparently already in contact with Odessa, so that once Vitashevsky arrived there he was able to enter the world of the revolutionaries through information he received from the editors of Tkachev's paper in Switzerland.[116] A third member of the group, Galina Chernyavskaya, also belonged to this wing, and she later joined *Narodnaya Volya*. These three constituted, so to speak, a fractional wing of Kovalsky's group and held separate meetings on their own. Kovalsky himself apparently did not take part. Yet it seems certain that he too had contacts with the *Nabat* and that he even sent articles to Tkachev. He also apparently belonged to the *Society for the Liberation of the People*,[117] whose regulations imposed extreme secrecy and advised its members to infiltrate into other revolutionary movements in order to influence them. It is very likely that Kovalsky, though not openly admitting his Jacobin convictions, had by now been convinced by Tkachev, and was trying to spread his ideas among the 'rebels' of Odessa. Indeed the little that we know of his activities between 1877 and 1878 represents something half-way between Bakuninism and the growing desire for a struggle aimed not only at fostering local revolts, but also at using the forces of the revolutionary movement to attack the power of the State.

The group started a small press on which it printed a manifesto inspired by the execution of a local bandit. The event had impressed the population which was already shaken by the war and the handing over of Odessa (a frontier province) to the military.[118] If someone who had killed for robbery deserved a punishment such as death, said the manifesto, what ought to be the fate of those who robbed and oppressed the people? This was a call to terrorism. As yet, however, it was no more than a call; neither Kovalsky nor his group had done anything to put it into practice.[119] For Kovalsky was entirely concerned with the problem of 'armed resistance' to possible police intervention. 'For the moment, perhaps, the results of such activities are not always successful. None the less if they are repeated and carried to the absolute extreme, it will become clear that the revolutionary atmosphere has ripened to such a point that our words and thoughts are transformed into actions and are becoming objectified into real deeds.'

On 30th January 1878, a strong contingent of police arrived at the house where their press was kept, and Kovalsky now had the chance to put this idea into practice. He defended himself to the end, using a revolver and a dagger. He was helped by his comrades on the spot, who succeeded in taking advantage of the confusion to burn many compromising documents and even to appeal to the crowd from the balcony. Kovalsky almost succeeded in escaping, but he was arrested and tried by a military court which sentenced him to death.

One of his comrades, Svitych, was sentenced to eight years' hard labour; Vitashevsky was awarded six, later reduced to four. Two others received four-year sentences, and two women were deported to Siberia. And the others too, after serving their sentences, spent many years in Siberia.

An attempt was made to free Kovalsky. For this purpose a demonstration (armed, for the first time in Russian revolutionary history) was organized outside the building where the military court was sitting. There were clashes with the police, and two men were killed. But Kovalsky could not be rescued,[120] and on 2nd August 1878 he was shot. His 'armed resistance' and death played a leading part in turning all the Populist movement to terrorism.[121]

By February 1878, Kiev had become the testing ground for this new tendency. It was inspired by Valerian Andreyevich Osinsky, the first man to organize terrorism on a wide scale in southern Russia.[122] He came from a rich family of nobles, which had great influence in his native town of Rostov-on-Don. His brother was president of the local administration, and he himself was for some time secretary of the Rostov municipality. When he too, like so many others, wanted to fling himself 'into the people', his comrades dissuaded him, and told him that he would be very much more useful where he already was. And, indeed, it was partly as a result of Osinsky's work that the atmosphere in Rostov at the beginning of the 'seventies was far more receptive than elsewhere to Populist propaganda. In some factories the management helped those who wanted to get in touch with the workers, and the revolutionaries had many accomplices in the town administration. Some at least of the bourgeoisie in this industrial and commercial town did not view with disfavour some movement of protest and reform. And the workers too were widely influenced by the Populists. Such was the atmosphere when Osinsky first began to work, at a time when he was close to Lavrovist influence. And then, here, too, the break came. He was advised by the authorities to move away. The workshops which the propagandists had founded were searched. Large numbers of workers were arrested, held for long periods in prison, and exiled to Siberia. Osinsky then approached the embryonic *Zemlya i Volya*, and became one of its leading agents in the South.

On his return to St Petersburg (where his plan to kill Trepov had been anticipated by Vera Zasulich) his first thought was to arrange for the suppression of an *agent provocateur*, a workman who had been responsible for the collapse of the extensive movement that had developed at Rostov. On 1st February two of his comrades, Ivan Ivichevich and Rostislav Steblin-Kamensky, successfully carried this out. Posters were stuck up in the streets of Rostov with the warning: 'Such is the fate that awaits every Judas'.[123]

The poster, which was circulated in half a dozen other Russian towns, had at the bottom a stamp on which were shown a crossed axe, revolver and dagger surrounded with the words 'Executive Committee of the Social Revolutionary Party'. And so, for the first time, the 'Executive Committee', later to be so notorious, made its appearance. For the moment it served mainly to instil fear and respect by the use of a mysterious name. But already it was a sign that terrorism was to be organized into a systematic policy. Blows were no longer to be struck by isolated figures, but by an organ set up for the purpose by the revolutionary party. Here, in Southern Russia, the 'disorganizing group' which had been spoken of in *Zemlya i Volya* was really coming into being. But at this stage (early in 1878) it was far from being a definite organization. In practice it was made up of Osinsky and those of his friends who were prepared to make use of terrorism. 'There were many elements in it. There were many men who wanted to undertake duties of the kind', said Frolenko, who was in close contact with Osinsky and organized with him the escape of Deych, Stefanovich and Bokhanovsky from Kiev prison.

Apart from Osinsky, the most typical figure in this first 'Executive Committee' was Grigory Anfimovich Popko. He was a descendant of the Cossacks who had been banished to the Kuban by Catherine II. One branch of his family had made a fortune, but his own relations were poor, and he had lost his father early in life. He went to the seminary at Stavropol and dreamt of starting an agricultural cooperative with four other pupils. He left for Moscow to study agriculture, but he also was caught up by the revolutionary movement. In 1874 he went to Odessa. This was the centre of the group which later carried on Zaslavsky's work after his arrest and the dispersal of most of the *Southern Union of Russian Workers*. It is of interest that the core of the first Kiev terrorists of Osinsky's 'Executive Committee' came from these circles: Ivan and Ignat Ivichevich, Grigory Ivanchenko, the worker, and Popko himself. From their early Lavrovist phase, they moved over to terrorism after passing through the working class movement. The break came in 1876. The groups at Odessa and Kiev had sent two delegates, K. I. Grinevich and Popko, to the Lavrovist meeting at Paris. Although Lavrov later denied this, the dissensions that split this small meeting seem to have been represented as a first skirmish in the conflict between the 'activist' South and the 'propagandist' North. In fact, Kiev and Odessa were beginning to look upon the fight in a new way, though as yet the forms this would take were still uncertain. Popko went to Lvov, Vienna, Geneva and Paris. On his return he devoted another year to working 'among the people', but very soon Vera Zasulich's killing of Trepov drove him too into terrorism.[124]

Alexander Vasilevich Sentyanin, another original member of the 'Executive Committee', developed in much the same way. He had gone to the Mining Institute together with Plekhanov. 'He then insisted on going straight from the school benches to work in a factory.'[125] Much of his work as a propagandist was done among the workers of Rostov-on-Don. We know less of the others in this group, though their names crop up frequently in the various actions of this time: A. F. Medvedev (Fomin), V. Sviridenko and L. K. Brandtner, called 'the German' by his comrades who had a very high opinion of him. 'He was an extremely likeable man, and extraordinarily honourable. By conviction and by taste he was a Populist. He had travelled among the peasants, and went over to terrorism when, like all the others, he saw that "there was no way to act", i.e. that it was impossible to bring the people to revolt.'[126]

On 23rd February 1878, Osinsky backed by Ivan Ivichevich and Medvedev (Fomin) went to the vice-prosecutor of the Kiev tribunal, Kotlyarevsky, who had been particularly intransigent in organizing a series of inquiries during the previous few days, and fired six revolver shots at him. They left him for dead. In fact, however, he was not even wounded, and an attempt to repeat the murder on the following day was unsuccessful.[127]

On 25th May, Popko, after great qualms, stabbed Baron Geyking in the middle of the street. Geyking was the adjutant of the Kiev police; he had won the reputation of being a liberal by closing his eyes to the circulation of popular booklets and indeed to the activities of the Lavrovist and propagandist groups. His inquiries into the Chigirin conspiracy were, however, conducted in a very different spirit. Hence his assassination. Popko was pursued but managed to escape after a series of flights and shootings. That night he merely informed his comrades, 'Carried out'.[128]

After this the activities of the 'Executive Committee' were devoted mainly to attempts to free their imprisoned comrades. In the case of Stefanovich and the others involved in the Chigirin conspiracy these proved successful and many plans were made to snatch the most heavily affected victims of the 'trial of the hundred and ninety-three' from the hands of the police. Myshkin himself was moved too quickly for these to be feasible. But some action was possible in respect of the prison at Kharkov, where most of the others were held. Sofya Perovskaya in particular urged action here. An unsuccessful attempt was made to attack the coach that was transporting Voynaralsky. It was a difficult and risky undertaking, and to carry it out some of the best forces of the Northern and Southern groups had to be employed, here united in action for the first time.[129] There was one casualty—Medvedev (Fomin) who was arrested. In August he tried to escape on his own initiative, but was recaptured. In October two of his comrades, disguised as policemen, went to his prison, but again the attempt failed. In February 1879 he was sentenced to hard labour.

Despite these and other losses, the 'Executive Committee' was able to continue action throughout the first part of 1878. It stuck up posters announcing the sentences it had pronounced, and whenever it struck it managed to save the main body of the organization. It was this work that changed the somewhat fantastic 'Committee' into a real political force. And this transformation was facilitated by the general situation in Kiev.

The political revival as the war drew to an end was far more extensive and apparent in the Ukrainian capital than elsewhere. Here national and social problems were closely entangled. There were, too, the traditional links with Poland and the other Slav countries which were then seething with the desire for liberty, as well as a wide variety of Ukrainophil, Lavrovist, 'rebellious', and constitutionalist currents. All these factors helped to make Kiev the first centre in which the problem of political freedom was raised on a wide scale. With this went a fight whose essential purpose was to destroy the despotism of the empire. 'All Kiev was full of discussions on the constitution', said one of Osinsky's and Popko's companions, summing up the situation.[130] Strangely enough this 'liberalism' was infiltrating even into university circles. In February and March 1878, the students of Kiev were involved in disturbances. There were clashes with the police, and 170 students were driven out of the university and banished. Meetings took place at the same time and included those of 'a constitutional club' of some vitality which had a certain following throughout the younger generation. At the same time the revolutionary Populists were faced with a political problem. The brutality of the police—the flogging of Bogolyubov on Trepov's orders —meant that they too had to consider the problem of whether it was not essential to give first place to winning a minimum of legality. It might, they thought, be indispensable to give up (at least for the moment) 'agitation' among the people, and instead turn to fighting against the repressive organs of the State. The experiment at Chigirin had failed, and all the revolutionaries had to some extent been disappointed at the results of their work among the people. Was not this the time to take advantage of the constitutionalist current in society, and make use of it for the fight against the authorities? Osinsky, Popko, Voloshenko and others considered this plan for a time and then turned it down. They had embarked on terrorism because it gave promise of a 'political' fight, and yet did not simultaneously lead to confusion between the vague, inactive, tendencies of 'constitutionalism' and the revolutionary determination that inspired themselves. They were prepared to fight for political liberty, but with arms, and not merely with propaganda among the educated classes, who seemed—and indeed were—condemned to impotence. These classes did a great deal of talking about a constitution but lacked the spirit to demand one. For those who had such a spirit there was only one way: direct attacks on each individual abuse, and the punishment of all who made themselves the tools of oppression and absolutism. This was the significance of the first 'Executive Committee'.[131]

Throughout 1878 the émigrés and the central group of Zemlya i Volya developed along the same lines as these revolutionaries in the South. Though this development was slower and less spectacular, politically it was more profound and more mature. The more typically Populist positions were transformed or abandoned slowly and thoughtfully, and everywhere possible their supporters tried to find a place for themselves in the changed circumstances. Relations with liberalism were more fully discussed and of greater historical importance. The 'Executive Committee' of the South was a flame which was to be quenched in violence. But the émigrés and the North developed in such a way that *Zemlya i Volya* and later *Narodnaya Volya* were destined to lead the entire revolutionary movement in Russia.

At the beginning of 1878, a new periodical, the *Obshchina*, began publication in Switzerland. This attracted all the most active revolutionaries among the émigrés.[132] Lavrov rightly pointed out that it 'picked up the necessary, fertile project of the periodical press that the Lavrovists had dropped'.[133] In other words it once again discussed the problems of the movement after the end of the *Vpered*. It was the 'rebels'—the Bakuninists—who reopened and enlarged the debate—yet another indication of the importance now assumed by political problems after the disappointment of the movement 'to go to the people' and the failure of the attempts to incite insurrection. These problems sprang from the meeting of the 'young Bakuninists' (Ralli and Zhukovsky) and the émigré Chaikovskists (Klements and Akselrod) who were still under the impression of the great trials. The meeting represented, as it were, a reunion between the 'trial of the fifty' and that 'of the hundred and ninety-three'.[134] The *Obshchina* opened with a long, interesting article on this latter trial. It recognized the transformation (which was now complete) from propagandists into Populists, from men who spread ideas into men who aroused disturbances. It contrasted this development with what had happened elsewhere in Europe. The *Obshchina* was thus widening the scope of the movement just when it was entering on a new phase. Akselrod wrote a long article in several instalments called 'A balance-sheet of the German Social-Democratic Party'. He still maintained his federalist and Bakuninist standpoint, but showed an obvious interest in a working class movement of the masses. V. Cherkezov spoke of the Balkan War;[135] Ralli recalled the lesson of the Commune;[136] Kravchinsky wrote long and admiring articles on the International in Italy.[137]

The first two numbers of the *Obshchina* were still trying to promote an extensive revival of Populist views. However, Vera Zasulich's attempted assassination of Trepov and the consequent revival of public opinion in Russia (and especially St Petersburg), soon compelled the editors to face new problems. The atmosphere was rapidly changing and the results of this were felt when in Switzerland.

The fifth number, in May 1878, asked what was meant by 'The Constitutional Movement in Russian Society' and above all it raised the problem of whether this 'could be reconciled with the demands and traditions of Russian Socialists . . . Must we Socialists take an active part in this movement of "society", or should we stay on one side? Can we hope to prise from it some alleviation in the conditions of our struggle? And if an analysis of this problem leads us to a negative conclusion, what road must we then take?' Most Socialists gave a positive answer to the first question. Yes, they said, 'we must take advantage of every social phenomenon to strike a blow against the imperial system of St Petersburg'. But they must be very careful not to lose their own political and ideological character: 'Is there by any chance anyone in our party who wants to make concessions? . . . What can ally us to our liberals?' Their [the liberals'] constitution could lead to no easing in the situation of the peasants and workers. The positive element of liberalism lay in 'the right of meeting and petition' but even here they must have no illusions. The Second Empire and the Third Republic had shown how any assembly could be cheated: 'And, after all, the liberal constitution of Italy compels our Socialist brothers to hold their meetings in secret.'

While the *Obshchina* was thus cautiously but firmly reasserting the tenets of Socialism, in St Petersburg the men of *Zemlya i Volya* were faced with more urgent and burning problems. For a moment Russian Liberalism seemed to be trying to escape from a purely theoretical rôle to become, instead, a real political force. Vera Zasulich's revolver shots were still echoing in ever-widening circles.

The first impression made by the attempt revealed the irresponsibility of an important section of the ruling classes and at the same time the ferment that was seething in society. Frivolity, malice, and most of all, obtuseness all helped to spread the rumour in official circles that Vera Zasulich had been Bogolyubov's mistress and that the reasons for her action were only personal. This gossip would have been of no importance had it not led the Ministry of Justice to hand over the trial to an ordinary tribunal and not to one of the Senatorial Committees which had always previously been concerned with political cases.

Vera Zasulich was thus to be tried by jury; and a jury was inevitably susceptible to the influence of public opinion. The flogging of Bogolyubov, Trepov's own well-deserved reputation as a murderer and robber, the enflamed atmosphere produced by stories of the suffering inflicted on those who had recently been acquitted in the 'great trial', the publicity of the proceedings (which were carried out with exemplary impartiality) and finally the extremely clever speech of the defending lawyer—all these factors had their effect. Vera Zasulich was acquitted. The jury indeed even denied the obvious fact—that had never been open to doubt and that had, indeed, been admitted by herself—that she had fired at Trepov. The police tried to hold her in prison without judicial authority, but the attempt came too late. When she was freed, a violent demonstration took place. There were clashes with the authorities and one student was killed—either by the police, or— more likely—by himself in order to attract the attention of the guards and thus allow Vera Zasulich to get away. Despite frantic searches, the police were never able to catch her, and she managed to flee abroad.[138] All these events, combined with terrorism in the South, made an ever-wider breach between public opinion and the authorities. By far the greater number of newspapers never stopped praising the jury for a long time after the trial.

Justice, they said, had at last triumphed in Russia, and they underlined this victory of conscience over force. In St Petersburg people spoke of Charlotte Corday, even of the fall of the Bastille. A wave of hope swept the intelligentsia along with it. And an enormous impression was made in Russia as a whole and throughout Europe.[139] 'The acquittal', Deych later reported, 'aroused even greater enthusiasm than the attempt itself and was accompanied by a boundless protest from those who went along with the authorities.'[140] These last used to say quite openly: 'If things go on like this, one will have to flee from Russia.'[141] It was not long before the results made themselves felt. A newspaper which had published a letter from Vera Zasulich was suppressed and others were interfered with. The jury system never recovered from this blow, and a series of decrees considerably restricted its powers.

On both sides, for the intelligentsia as for the authorities, these events acted as a touchstone. Public opinion was waking up again and was therefore agitated, nervous, ready for extremes, and incapable of considering the problems of means and ends. All the 'liberalism' and 'constitutionalism' of the end of the 'seventies was affected by this state of mind which had been brought to light by Vera Zasulich's gesture. The Tsarist government, on the other hand, reacted purely from an instinct of self-preservation. Its reactions were often blind and inefficient, as was shown by the eventual liberation of the terrorist, and as will be seen still more clearly when we discuss the repressive steps which followed.

The revolutionaries of *Zemlya i Volya* at once became aware of the burden which this situation imposed on them. Plekhanov's manifesto, written at this time, makes this absolutely clear.[142]

After almost twenty years of silence, he said, public opinion had woken up again. When Chernyshevsky had been sentenced, there had been no protest. The revolutionaries had been left to their own devices; opinion had been deceived by the mirage of 'the liberation of our Slav brothers'. 'We did not know whether it would ever again make itself heard. But on 31st March and the days that followed, St Petersburg society decided to speak the language of humanity.' At last the abyss between society and the State had been exposed. This break now had to be made conclusive.

In cases like this, who is not for the government must be against it. The whole of society must in one way or another express its protest against an administration that is barbaric. We call upon the boys in our schools, we call upon all parties except the party of the knout and the stick to unite in a general and unified campaign for the conquest of human rights which have been trampled on for so long; for the defence of our freedom-loving fellow-citizens from the hellish cells of the Central Prison and the Peter-Paul fortress; for the defence of the Russian people from misery; for the defence of Russian scholarship and thought from a shameful and inglorious death at the hands of the hangman-censor.

Though Plekhanov was appealing to all currents of thought and to society as a whole, he well knew that the wave of indignation and enthusiasm which was surprising even the intelligentsia was only a 'prologue'. It was only the beginning of 'the great historical drama which is called the trial of the government by the people. The accusation is made up of all Russia's history in the pages of which we find only floggings, beatings, hangings, and the systematic exploitation of the people on behalf of the Tsar's treasury.'

Like all Populist revolutionaries of the time, Plekhanov was impressed by the extent to which public opinion had been roused. But, after this 'prologue', who was now to organize the 'trial'? All responsibility for this obviously fell on the shoulders of the revolutionaries. It was not for nothing that he ended his manifesto by recalling that all peoples had always held sacred the memory of those who were the first to fall 'in the revolution for freedom'. The revolutionary Populists in St Petersburg thus reacted to the events of 31st March by trying to unite and guide 'society' and even more by planning to organize themselves and take action.

A few days earlier a clandestine periodical had begun publication with the aim of expressing this state of mind. It was published by the 'Free Russian Press', which had been organized at St Petersburg in autumn 1877 by A. I. Zundelevich on behalf of Natanson's group. This press had already printed a series of appeals, among them the above quoted one by Plekhanov, and a few pamphlets containing the more important depositions taken at the trials 'of the fifty' and 'of the hundred and ninety-three'.[143] It was, said Mikhailov, important for the Populists to have their own literature of agitation, so as to be able to explain to society and the party the special significance of each important event and to lead them to this or that action, and organize the currents of thought and feeling which were beginning to be defined.[144] Soon these temporary leaflets began to seem inadequate and the Populists planned a regular clandestine periodical. The first move was made by a Pole, Alexander Ivanovich Ventskovsky. In March 1878 with the assistance of various marginal members of the St Petersburg *Zemlya i Volya* (among them Lev Konstantinovich Bukh, later to be a well-known economist, and his brother Nikolay) he began to publish the *Nachalo*,[145] making use of the Free Russian Press. The title itself shows that the paper aimed to be a 'beginning', an attempt to publish a clandestine review in Russia.[146] It was to be the organ of the 'Russian revolutionaries', and from the first it proclaimed its Socialist principles. But seeing that public opinion had turned its attention to the organization of the State, to oppression, and to the lack of freedom, it dealt with the political struggle in preference to social problems.

The *Nachalo* was the first paper to express the standpoint which was to remain fundamental for an understanding of some of the aspects of *Zemlya i Volya*'s policies in 1878, and which can be called 'waiting for a constitution'. About the crisis in the machinery of government there could be no doubt. But as yet, the revolutionaries thought, the forces of the people were not experienced enough for a profound social revolution to be possible. 'We are still at the stage of storing up the revolutionary forces of the people', said the *Nachalo* from the very first.[147] It was therefore possible that the absolutist State might overcome the crisis by making concessions to society and granting a constitution. The revolutionaries, warned the *Nachalo*, must realize this, and understand the nature of the situation. They must then take advantage of it to perform their own specific function and help the people to store up its revolutionary energies, and at the same time draw up a programme of 'Russian Popular Socialism',[148] and organize their own forces. All the more so as the government would certainly not find it easy to embark on the road of constitutionalism. 'The element of anarchism latent in the Russian people and the absence of organic links between it and the State make it difficult, if not impossible, for the government to resort to the lightning conductor of a constitution to avert the storm of the people.'[149] The financial crisis that followed the war would compel the government to weigh down still more on the peasants and thus add new fuel to popular discontent. It was in fact faced with a threat of bankruptcy and a serious crisis. 'The foreign newspapers say that we are on the eve of a revolution.'[150] The revolutionaries must therefore be prepared for all possibilities. In any case it was certain that 'the existing financial and economic situation must lead to the fall of absolutism'.[151]

In May they completed this examination of the situation: 'The most likely thing is that the crisis will lead to a purely political revolution along constitutional lines, though there is nothing definite to exclude the possibility of a general popular movement.' The Socialists must be prepared for either eventuality. Taken in itself, constitutionalism was a matter of complete indifference to them: 'But, if events do not lead to a general revolutionary movement within the people, even a political change must be considered highly desirable by persons who believe in Socialism.' It would in any case be a step forward for society and the people. The Russian bourgeoisie lacked any solid ethical or legal foundations to make it aware of its rights. And so it felt that its position was weak and uncertain. Constitutionalism would not therefore take root in it, and would merely facilitate the people's struggle and make propaganda more feasible and widespread. The Socialists for their part would be able to make use both of the restrictions to which this constitutionalism would be subjected and, on the other hand, the popular movements which would inevitably accompany and follow it. The *Nachalo* concluded with a plea not to support the liberals but rather to adopt a policy of *laissez faire, laissez passer*, trusting in the inevitable development of the crisis. This was all the more important, as the liberals were by no means organized—in itself another reason for persuading the Socialists to concentrate their energies on agitation and the organization of the people.[152]

These views did not altogether correspond to the ideas of the more active members of *Zemlya i Volya*, who very soon resumed control of the periodical press and substituted their own organ for the *Nachalo*, which had only sprung up on the fringes of their organization. The *Nachalo*, however, had obviously expressed the ideas of a significant portion of the various currents of opinion that were gravitating around *Zemlya i Volya*, which was just now widening its ties with 'society' and making its first attempts to direct it. It was easy enough for anyone not wanting to give up his Populist principles and yet anxious to express his own opinions in view of the liberal and constitutionalist ferment, to adopt this Machiavellian policy of *laissez faire, laissez passer*. It reflected the policy of waiting which the Populist movement had been forced to adopt owing to the circumstances of Russian society at the time.

For a time, immediately after Vera Zasulich was acquitted in April 1878, the 'Free Russian Press' even went beyond this position. It allowed its machinery to be used for printing a leaflet written by Mikhailovsky, which not only contained nothing that was specifically Populist but which adumbrated a plan whereby society was to be driven into liberal activities against absolutism. Once again, as during the crisis of the beginning of the 'sixties, there was a call for a *Zemsky Sobor*, a national and a constituent assembly. Starting from the claim that the people was indifferent to political liberty (as indeed to any change which did not affect the social structure), he concluded that the problems of society must be put in the hands of society itself.[153] This attitude was all the more significant in that it was the result of a conversion. Mikhailovsky, a thinker and writer, and a follower of Lavrov, had himself been a convinced Populist until only a few years earlier. As recently as 1873 he had written: 'We do not want these rights, these liberties! A curse on them if they do not give us a chance to pay our debt to the people, if indeed they only increase that debt.'[154]

In the same year he had written that even the idea of political liberty ought to be *sacrificed* to social reform.[155] Now, however, thinking that it was essential to accept the fact that Russia would follow capitalist development, all his hopes were placed elsewhere: liberal public opinion must be consolidated into a political mould. But the uncertainty of this new view is apparent even in the heavy, hesitant style of the leaflet. More than anything else, it was a hope: the same hope that also inspired the editors of the *Nachalo*.

Kravchinsky was among the first to break this psychological pause. From his position as an exile, Vera Zasulich's acquittal must have seemed even more important than it really was. 'Russian absolutism has been killed. The 31st March was the last day of its life.' This only raised once again, more clearly than ever before, the whole problem of the revolution in Russia. 'Beware! Like a flock of crows which smell a rotting corpse, new enemies are arising on all sides. These enemies are the bourgeoisie. In the past all it has been capable of was fear, waiting like a coward for us socialist revolutionaries to destroy what it sprinkled with hatred and incense.' Contempt for these enemies was no longer enough. Taken singly they were incompetent

20+

and cowardly and had always been impotent. But as a mass they might be able to succeed in their plans and the situation might allow them to create a bourgeois world in Russia. And if they did win it was obvious enough what they held in store for the revolutionaries: witness the example of the Paris Commune. 'The same fate awaits us if we give the Russian bourgeoisie time to stifle us.' And so the fundamental problem was to organize the Russian social revolutionary party. 'We are on the eve of great revolutionary events. The future is ours.'[156]

The call 'Now or never' had sounded throughout the history of Populism. Now it was made once again on the eve of the decisive crisis at the end of the 'seventies. The conclusions that Kravchinsky drew from it were to lead to the creation of the strongest Populist organization of the twenty years of Alexander II's reign. But his article in the *Obshchina* represented only a fragment of his thought. The remainder he decided to express in deeds rather than words.

And so he left Switzerland and returned secretly to St Petersburg, where he resumed contacts with the central core of *Zemlya i Volya* and organized an attempt on the life of General Mezcntsov, head of the Third Section.

At about nine o'clock on the morning of 4th August 1878 Mezentsov was going for a walk through the centre of St Petersburg, accompanied by an adjutant. The events which then occurred had been carefully planned by Alexander Mikhailov himself. Kravchinsky and Barannikov walked straight into the General: the former then took out a dagger and fatally wounded him, while Barannikov unsuccessfully fired at the adjutant who tried to seize hold of them. Both men leapt on to a fast coach driven by Adrian Mikhailov, and managed to get away without leaving any traces. Search was made for them and proved useless.

This was the most perfect act of terrorism of the time. Kravchinsky himself justified it in a pamphlet called *A Death for a Death*[157] printed by the Free Russian Press. It was dedicated to the memory of Kovalsky, who had been shot at Odessa two days before the assassination. The killing of Mezentsov had certainly been decided on some considerable time before this execution, but the speed with which the two events followed each other suggested a lightning reply by the revolutionary party, and this increased the impression made by the assassination. Until now only spies, *agents provocateurs* or relatively minor officials, such as Kotlyarevsky and Geyking at Kiev, had been struck down. This time it was the head of the police himself. A manifesto was published to explain that Mezentsov had been killed to avenge all those who had been ill-treated in prison, and all the sentences against the propagandists. The blow, in fact, was the final move in the 'trial of the hundred and ninety-three'.

However, as Kravchinsky explained in his leaflet *A Death for a Death*, the assassination was planned not just to end one epoch, but rather to open a new one. The true enemies of the Socialists had been and still were the bourgeoisie and capitalism. It was a Populist and not a liberal movement that had been responsible for Mezentsov's death. Kravchinsky even went so so far as to ask the government to stay neutral if it could between the revolutionaries and the 'crows which smell a rotting corpse', in the words of the *Obshchina*. The fundamental problem was still to prepare a popular revolution.[158] And indeed after Vera Zasulich's acquittal the main concern of the revolutionaries was to reorganize *Zemlya i Volya*.

Abroad Kravchinsky had (as we have seen) heard this news and returned to Russia. So, in Russia itself, more and more of the revolutionaries were leaving the peasant 'colonies' in 1878 in order to concentrate in St Petersburg. And even those who remained had by now turned their attention and thoughts towards the capital. Alexander Mikhailov, for example, arrived at the beginning of April with a vast scheme for infiltrating into the *Raskol*. A short stay in St Petersburg, however, sufficed to make him turn all his attention to terrorism and problems of organization. In May the group found it necessary to reassert the principles which ought to guide *Zemlya i Volya*, emphasizing the Populist character of all its activities and at the same time revising its organization by introducing greater centralization and discipline. Mikhailov, who was responsible for this revision, succeeded in persuading his comrades that it was indispensable. For now the possibility of a more active and severer struggle for their ideas was opening up before them.[159]

'Among all the various kinds of Socialism in Western Europe', said the programme, 'we have no hesitation in preferring the federalist International, i.e. the anarchists. But we admit that these principles cannot be fully realized today.' After this somewhat formal homage to the Bakuninist tradition, the authors at once turned to their real programme.

The party could be strong only if it relied on the real demands of the Russian people. Its 'fundamental characteristics were so Socialist' that if it was able to win at once, it would lay solid foundations for a further development along Socialist and federalist lines. According to the ideas of the people, the land came from God and belonged to all, and each man had the right to farm it. And so the fundamental point was still to transfer all the land to the 'agricultural working class'. The authors then repeated more or less unchanged the points of their 1877 programme on the 'complete autonomy of the *obshchinas*', and their 'free integration into larger territorial groups' (*volosti, guby, zemli*, etc.) as well as on the need to carry on with the break-up of the nationalities which made up the Russian Empire (such as Little Russia, Poland and the Caucasus) in accordance with local desires. They again stressed the need to bring about this radical revolution 'as quickly as possible'. One reason for speed was that 'the development of capitalism and the increasing injection of the various poisons of bourgeois civilization into the life of the Russian people, due to support from the Russian government, are threatening to destroy the *obshchina* and corrupt popular ideas about the above-mentioned problems'. They were in fact perfectly aware that they were fighting against the tide.

This profession of faith does not seem to have given rise to any important discussions. The real problem lay in the organization of the forces which were to fight for it. Extremely precise and detailed regulations were now drawn up and these marked an important step forward on the road to centralization.

Zemlya i Volya had been and still was an organization of revolutionaries 'of men closely united to each other' (Article 2) of men ready to give 'all their forces, means, bonds, sympathies and dislikes, and indeed their very lives' to the organization (Article 3). They and they alone made up 'the group, the fundamental circle'. The word used (*kruzhok*) again showed the extent to which this 'party' sprang from the 'circles' of university students of the 'sixties and 'seventies. But now the coincidence was purely one of words. The 'fundamental circle' was in fact a party of 'professional revolutionaries', though this is to use a term that only came in later and which sprang from these very experiences. All had the same rights towards the organization but were compelled to submit to its decisions as regards action. Each man was free to choose the field of activity which he preferred, but 'in cases when no one could be found to carry out a given job, the group, by a majority vote, can compel any member to undertake it' (Article 17). Anyone could give up any specific job, but had to ask permission two months before, so that another member of the 'fundamental group' could be found to replace him (Article 18). The secrecy and sense of responsibility which were insisted on sprang naturally from the clandestine nature of the fight in which they were engaged. But the complete absence of private property among the members of the organization was yet another sign of their entire dedication. So also was 'the control of the activities of all the groups and of each individual member' which the regulations established—though this was qualified as follows: 'the private life of each member is under the control of all only in so far as it may be considered important in each individual case' (Article 12). The dedicated spirit of the Chaikovskists was now given objective form in a party of revolutionaries.

But the crystallization of this spirit in the regulations of *Zemlya i Volya* did give rise to much questioning and discussion within the group. Some members stood out against the development, even though they felt it to be necessary and inevitable. A. A. Kvyatkovsky, for instance, wrote a note to say that 'the fundamental group is not the ideal kind of organization. Its conception and triumph represent, so to speak, a necessary evil. It is conditioned on the one hand by the inexperience of a considerable number of Russian revolutionaries, and on the other hand by the difficulties of the situation in which we have to carry on our activities.' This observation was true enough, and we could extend it. It was indeed the weakness of the movement which was led by the intelligentsia and the absence of any wider campaign against the absolutist State which were responsible for saddling the revolutionaries with the full burden of the fight against the authorities. It was possible to overcome the ineffectiveness of some of the revolutionaries in subsequent years; but these circumstances remained fundamental and were always giving rise to parties of 'professional revolutionaries'. In another note, A. D. Oboleshev sought the only possible remedy: 'All the best elements which satisfy our requirements must be given posts of active responsibility in the central group.' In other words they must prevent the party of revolutionaries from closing in on itself, and instead widen it so as to make it representative of all the revolutionary forces in Russia. This improvement was included in the regulations (Article 10) and it was indeed the policy pursued by Zemlya i Volya.

But as against these doubts, scruples and plans, the decisive element in the discussion consisted of the opinion of those who looked upon the organization of the 'fundamental group' as the only solution that was politically correct and that would lead to quick and decisive action. Replying to the two notes quoted above, Mikhailov said:

It is strange indeed to speak of 'a necessary evil' and to define our type of organization as 'evil', when we expect rather the greatest possible good from it and consider that it will save us from the shapeless condition in which the party now finds itself. It springs from our very aim, which is to create a Pan-Russian organization. Relations of a federal nature between the various groups can only be of use in giving mutual help and not in unifying our programme and immediate aims.

Despite some doubts and compromises, the regulations codified Mikhailov's views. Very definite precautions laid down the conditions under which a new member could be admitted into the 'fundamental group' [Articles 2 and 25. 'Rigid appraisal of his personality'; he must be guaranteed by five members; at least two-thirds of the organization must agree]. The internal structure of Zemlya i Volya was to be controlled from the centre, if not exactly centralized. Each member was to belong to a territorial or functional group, i.e. one whose work was to be performed in a given area or concerned with a special activity. 'The groups enjoy complete autonomy as regards their local and internal affairs . . . The internal organization of each single group may be different' (Articles 28 and 29), but they were obliged to follow the programme and to collaborate in the undertakings of the organization as a whole (Article 27). And above all an 'administration' or central 'communion' was set up to coordinate all activities. This word 'administration' recalls the central organ of the Pan-Russian Social-Revolutionary Organization—the Caucasians and women students who had sacrificed themselves in 1875 to spread propaganda in the factories of Moscow. Indeed the state of mind that led to this word being chosen was the same in both cases. But the 'administration' or 'communion' of Zemlya i Volya obtained far more extensive means and powers. It was entrusted with an important political function to 'draw up agreements and federal relations with other organizations and individuals in the name of the fundamental group.' It was obliged, and not merely authorized, to collect 'precise and exact information on the activities of all the groups . . . and to distribute funds at given intervals within the limits of the budget determined by the fundamental group' (Article 37). The 'communion' was elected by a two-thirds majority and made up of three to five members. It was to remain in power for an indefinite period. So that, in fact, the party had created for itself a real system of leadership.

Above this governing body was the congress. During the past few years it had become a custom for those members who were scattered among the people, or at any rate living outside St Petersburg, to discuss common problems once a year, generally in the autumn. This custom was now officially endorsed in the regulations. The 'administration' was to decide the time for the meeting, which was to include all the fundamental group if possible and in any case at least two-thirds of it.

The object of the congress: to draw up a balance sheet of previous activities and—on the basis of these facts—to settle the direction and nature of future activities. The function of the congress: to formulate a rigidly determined programme of practical action; to review and, if necessary, to modify the regulations; to control methods and activities . . . The decisions of the congress must be accepted by all members of the fundamental group (Articles 42 and 43).

An organization of this kind could be effective only if it attracted to itself all the revolutionary energies available. And so the regulations laid down the possibility of entering into 'contractual (federal) relations' with single individuals who could not or would not join the fundamental group. Special tactical rules were laid down for these cases (Articles 31 to 34). They dealt mainly with agreements regarding specific activities. In the same way each member of the party could and indeed was obliged to infiltrate into other organizations to influence and attract them. Even here he was compelled to keep secret his membership of the 'fundamental group'.

A single phrase revealed the spirit which it was hoped would inspire this party of revolutionaries. Article 9 read 'the end justifies the means', and a note added 'excluding those cases in which the use of certain means may harm the organization itself'. This formula inevitably recalled the figure of Nechaev to those who discussed and voted on it. And so the cycle which had opened at the beginning of the 'seventies closed here. Then the revival of the revolutionary movement had been conditioned by disgust at Nechaev's methods. Now his spirit reappeared once more. But here, in the regulations of *Zemlya i Volya*, it was turned into a policy: no longer a weapon to be used in a cold individual revolt but instead the mainspring of an organized struggle.

Such were the regulations of what they themselves called 'a compact and well-arranged organization of prepared revolutionaries springing both from the intelligentsia and the workers'. The next problem was to determine their tactics. These were settled quickly for here they were all agreed. The experiences they had lived through during the last few years indicated what was necessary. First they must 'approach and even merge with those whose religious-revolutionary natures make them hostile to the State'. Secondly they must keep in touch with the conflicts which were endemic in the villages, and eventually put themselves at the head of peasant bands. Thirdly they must 'establish relations and links with those centres where there were large numbers of workers both in workshops and factories'. The universities and the intelligentsia would provide 'the main reinforcements for filling up the ranks of the organization'. Fourthly they must 'establish relations with the liberals, so as to exploit them for our purposes'.

But all this represented only one side of *Zemlya i Volya*'s twofold function. These measures would help to organize new forces; but they also had to 'disorganize the forces of the State'. For this purpose they must forge links with the army 'and specially the officers', to bring them over, in the words of Mikhailov, 'to serve the interests of the people and to prepare the transfer of the army to the party of the people when the decisive moment comes'.[160] Equally great importance was attached to contact with men employed in government service 'so as to paralyse its activities against steps taken by the revolutionary forces'. Last of all was to be 'the systematic annihilation of the most dangerous and important elements in the government'.

For about a year the activities of *Zemlya i Volya* followed these directives. As from the summer onwards, and especially after the assassination of Mezentsov on 4th August, the reaction of the government became increasingly violent. Simultaneously the wave of enthusiasm and hope among the intelligentsia, which had reached its peak at the time of Vera Zasulich's acquittal, began to decline. The State had been slow to react, but it now adopted crushing measures. The energies which were widely scattered throughout public opinion had neither the chance nor the strength to resist.

As early as 2nd April, Pahlen, Minister of Justice, who rightly felt responsibility for the Zasulich case, proposed a series of repressive steps to the Committee of Ministers. The most important of these was to hand over to a military tribunal anyone accused of terrorism, revolt, etc. Men would be dealt with under the laws which were enforced during a state of siege. Women would be dealt with according to the normal code.[161] The idea was welcomed, but considered 'premature'.

Obviously public opinion still had to be prepared. Katkov undertook to break the kind of unanimity which prevailed in the press. It was he who wrote the first and most violent article against 'the madness of the St Petersburg intelligentsia and the Bacchanal of the press in the capital'. Now again, as during the Polish Rebellion in 1863, his words produced an effect, if only because they made it quite clear that the State was determined to defend itself.

What methods it was prepared to make use of soon became clear enough. On 3rd April a group of Kiev students, on their way from one prison to another, passed along the Okhotny Ryad in the centre of Moscow, the street that was inhabited mainly by butchers and small shopkeepers. At the station the group had been welcomed by a demonstration of solidarity from the students of Moscow, who then followed the open cart in which the prisoners had to cross the town. One of them said:

As we drew near the centre, the crowd grew thicker and thicker. It was an impressive demonstration, the meaning of which was known only to the students and the police. The police grew nervous, and here is the splendid system to which they resorted to make up for their stupidity in allowing a procession of the kind . . . It was a fine sunny day, and we felt ourselves to be heroes and looked with interest at the spectacle around us. But suddenly everything changed. As we passed the Theatre Square a number of young men in white aprons and with butchers' knives in their belts, flung themselves at us and began to hit at the students with the utmost brutality. For us the nightmare did not last long. When we reached the Mokhovaya, there were no longer any demonstrators around our cart. But from the next day's newspapers we learnt that the assault had lasted throughout the day and that dozens of seriously wounded students had been taken to the hospitals. This is the way that the police took its revenge on the students and their demonstration.[162]

The *Official Messenger* wrote that the demonstration had been 'the reply of the simple people of Russia to the scandalous demonstration that had greeted the acquittal of Vera Zasulich'.[163]

Katkov praised the violence of the young Moscow butchers, and even the clandestine press had to admit that the students had been attacked 'by what in Europe is called the third estate'. In Russia, however, they should be given another name: *kulaks* and *miroeds*. The State had resorted to them to frighten the intelligentsia, to persuade it that 'its only refuge and safety lay in the State and in the government'. It was true that the execution of this plan had been far from perfect, for the incident had aroused considerable indignation. And yet the Socialists could understand clearly enough from this incident the forces that were concealed under this manœuvre of intimidation. If the Russian third estate was on the side of the police, the intelligentsia was unable to defend itself and the State could thus resume its function of oppression.[164]

The Senate itself had suggested that the sentences it had inflicted in the 'trial of the hundred and ninety-three' should be reduced or cancelled. But now they were confirmed by the Tsar or indeed so changed that in practice they were made more severe. No longer, now, was it 'premature' to appoint a military tribunal and impose sentence of death for terrorism. A law to this effect was decided on 9th August 1878 and accompanied by a declaration in the *Official Messenger* on 20th August which said that 'the patience of the government was now exhausted' and appealed to public opinion to collaborate in suppressing revolutionary intrigues. But the appeal was also a threat. Only by helping the government in the work of repression 'could the Russian people and its finest representatives provide active proof that there was no place among them for such criminals, that they had really repudiated them, and that every faithful subject of the Tsar would help the government in eliminating their common internal enemy with all the means at his disposal'. It was easy enough to see that this official declaration was a sign of weakness. It was appealing to the whole of the Russian people for help in the fight against 'a band of evilly-disposed elements'. Was the government really unable to eliminate this band on its own? Nor did the government seem altogether convinced that it really had the support of the public opinion to which it was appealing. And, most important of all, in return for such cooperation it promised—nothing.

In St Petersburg a clandestine pamphlet was published called *The Government Comedy or the Appeal to Society*, which tried to explain that the only way of salvation lay in active warfare.

Society must understand that it must not get down on its knees and whine for liberty, but conquer it. It must understand this and organize itself for the fight against the government. If it begins to take action in this direction, if it faces this task with real energy, then the Socialists will certainly give it active support because their aim is a common one: to obtain political freedom.

But this was now only the dying echo of the policies sketched out by the *Nachalo* and the Free Russian Press after Vera Zasulich's assassination of Trepov.

The appeal of the revolutionaries did, however, meet with some response in Southern Russia. The *Zemstvo* of the department of Chernigov said that it was absurd to think that repression in itself was enough to defeat ideas, even anarchist ideas. The real causes of the existing state of affairs were the restrictions imposed on schools and universities, the absence of freedom of speech and press, and the lack of respect for law in society. The mass of the intelligentsia was 'depressed, incapable of fight'. How then could it be asked to fulfil an active rôle in the State? It was a bitter admission, and amounted to a refusal to cooperate with the government. The motion was carried on the initiative of I. I. Petrushevsky, who was one of the leading spirits of the constitutional movement founded in the *Zemstva*, and who, twenty years later, became one of the leaders of the constitutional-democratic party (K.D.). But in 1878 this trend was extremely limited, even in the South, which was its centre. Approaches were made with a view to drawing up a common line between these liberals and the revolutionary Populists but came to nothing. On 3rd December 1878, I. I. Petrushevsky and A. F. Lindfors, the leaders of this movement of the *Zemstva*, went in their personal capacities to meet Valerian Osinsky and several other 'terrorists', to ask if 'they were prepared to put a temporary stop to terrorism, so as to give them the time and opportunity to raise an open protest against the policy of the

20*

government in wider social circles and above all in the assemblies of the
Zemstvo'. 'After a long and animated discussion, we did not reach any
specific conclusion', wrote Petrushevsky. He had the impression that 'the
proposal would have had some psychological success and that if it had
succeeded in shaking public opinion from its complete apathy, the terrorists
would have understood the need to put an end to their activities'.[165]

But the following months soon showed that the men of the *Zemstvo* were
in no position to make an open protest, that the terrorists would follow their
own road and the State would resort to repression rather than concessions.

Makov replaced Timashev at the Ministry of the Interior. In place of
Mezentsov, who was buried with full honours in the presence of the Tsar,
Drenteln was appointed head of the Third Section. And in St Petersburg a
police offensive began in grand style. Mikhailov said:

The new head of the police obviously believed in annihilating suspects, using the
word in its widest sense. And as the 'band of evilly-disposed elements' lived in the
world of suspects, uprooting them would do away with it too. But the circles it
moved in were wide and included all the students, some men of letters, lawyers,
etc., and young men with no settled profession.[166]

The forces of the Third Section were far from enough for the job. And so
they were reorganized and special attention was paid to increasing the
number of spies.

In October the police succeeded in striking the very centre of *Zemlya i
Volya*. Olga Natanson, Alexey Oboleshev, Adrian Mikhailov, Leonid Bulanov
and V. F. Troshchansky were arrested. The original group of 'troglodytes'
was now mostly dispersed. Two women, Alexandra Nikolaevna Malinov-
skaya and Maria Alexandrovna Kolenkina, tried to put up armed resistance.[167] The whole organization was now in the most serious danger.
Alexander Mikhailov himself was only able to escape from an ambush
thanks to his exceptional ability and speed, and 'those who were still at large
had neither money nor passports, and had no chance of finding their comrades who were scattered in the provinces, as they did not know their
addresses'.[168]

It was A. Mikhailov who rebuilt the centre. Indeed we can say that his
tireless and intelligent labour almost unintentionally gave rise to a new
organization, the kernel of the future *Narodnaya Volya*.

The arrests had merely hastened a development which was already in
progress. Greater centralization, a more rigid spirit of conspiracy, a concentration of all energies in the towns—these became the principles that
gave life to this final incarnation of *Zemlya i Volya*. It no longer had to take
account of a general feeling of anger and hope in public opinion. Now the
situation was dominated by the reaction of the government which grew more
repressive every day. And withstanding this were only two active elements:
the students and workers of St Petersburg.

Student disorders began in the autumn. The first of them took place in the Veterinary Institute at Kharkov and then quickly spread to other centres. In St Petersburg the most notable activities were those in the Army School of Medicine, though in fact all the faculties and higher educational establishments took part in the movement. On 29th November the students set out in a procession to take a petition to the heir to the throne. This was a further reply to the appeal to society launched by the government after the assassination of Mezentsov on 4th August. It was too easy, said the petition, to attribute everything that had happened to a 'handful of evilly-disposed elements'. In actual fact the situation of young men in Russia was quite unbearable. Police control was oppressive, the students did not have the right to organize cooperative banks or to own their own libraries. 'Admission to institutions of higher education becomes ever more difficult. Soon education will become the privilege of wealth.' On the day following the demonstration the School of Medicine was surrounded by soldiers, Cossacks and police. Clashes took place and the students were beaten and flogged. About 200 were held that day, and the arrests went on for some time afterwards. Many hundreds were eventually sent to different provinces in the north under police supervision.[169]

As for the factories and workshops, we have seen that the winter of 1878 saw some of the most typical strikes of the time and above all the formation of the *Northern Union of Russian Workers*.

And so *Zemlya i Volya*'s most intense activities coincided with the revival of violent student disorders and a strengthening of the working class movement. But in order to take advantage of this situation it was above all essential to rebuild the technical services of the centre. Mikhailov managed not only to do this but even to bring them to a level of perfection that they had never reached before. It is only his work at the end of 1878 that can explain how the clandestine organization was able to survive during the next two years in face of increasingly active police investigations. He was able to establish a whole network of hiding places and lodgings in St Petersburg and he controlled the illegal life of the whole organization down to the smallest details. His knowledge of the town was supreme, and consequently he was one of the most able at avoiding shadowing and pursuit.

But none of this would have been enough had Mikhailov not been able to introduce a spy into the very centre of the Third Section. One day a young man of weak health, who had been a student and had travelled in Russia and abroad, came to him and said that he was prepared to execute any act of terrorism. Mikhailov answered that he was going to ask an even greater sacrifice of him. Would he become a police official? After some hesitation, Nikolay Vasilev Kletochnikov agreed, mainly because he had already been inspired by a feeling of admiration and devotion for Mikhailov. He managed to penetrate into the very heart of police headquarters, and as early as January 1879 he was able to provide detailed lists of spies and *agents provocateurs*. He maintained a regular system of protection for *Zemlya i Volya* and *Narodnaya Volya*, warning them of police moves and future arrests. Mikhailov always kept this precious source of information jealously to himself. Kletochnikov was only discovered in January 1881, and sentenced to death a year later. His sentence was commuted to hard labour for life, but in 1883 he died in the Alexeyevsky dungeon in the Peter-Paul fortress.[170]

These improvements in technique enabled the conspirators once more to gather together in St Petersburg forces capable of replacing those who had fallen. Plekhanov reorganized the 'working class group' and Mikhailov regularly attended its meetings. L. Tikhomirov and Nikolay Morozov joined *Zemlya i Volya* at this time, and at the same time Sofya Perovskaya's group completely merged with what remained of the central organization. The generation of the 'trial of the hundred and ninety-three' took over the most important posts in the 'underground'.

The Free Russian Press was taken over by the central nucleus and transformed into the Free Press of St Petersburg. It was put in an extremely safe place from the conspiratorial point of view, in the very centre of the capital in a flat where every possible care was taken to avoid arousing suspicions. It was Mikhailov who kept contact with it, and it was still organized by Aaron Isaakovich Zundelevich. His own ideas tended more towards German social-democracy than towards Populism, but he gave *Zemlya i Volya* and later *Narodnaya Volya* the most valuable assistance. Better than anyone else he knew the frontiers and the Jewish smugglers who could arrange the escape of those on the run or bring across a load of periodicals.[171] He was an outstandingly able man and the 'technician' of the movement. Indeed he so organized the press that it was able to cope with the regular publication of a large review, *Zemlya i Volya!*[172]

This periodical marked, as it were, the consecration of the fact that a real party had now come into being despite persecution and losses. Mikhailov obviously thought the review of exceptional importance, for he one day said with his usual biting wit that 'the important thing is that some clandestine review should come out. The police looks for it and is unable to find it—that's what strikes the public. It's of no importance what's written inside. I think that the ideal review would be one which had nothing at all printed in it. But unfortunately that's not possible.'[173] Though he thus stressed the value of the review for propaganda and organization, in fact he paid special attention to controlling the work of the editors and discussing with them the articles which were to be published.[174]

The *Zemlya i Volya!* mirrored the inner life of the organization. Its principal editor was Klements, chosen because he was rightly considered the best writer of the group. His main assistants were Plekhanov, Morozov and Kravchinsky.

The leading article of the first number, which was dated 25th October 1878, but in fact came out early in November, was written by Kravchinsky.

It took up a stand on all the problems of the movement. 'The Socialists are the only organized political party in Russia.' They differed above all from those who did not want an open fight; their relations with the liberals were indeterminate because 'Where are the liberals?' Nor had they anything to discuss with the constitutionalists: 'We will see about that when there are any of them.' In any case it was clear that the revolutionary Socialists 'viewed with favour any attempt to fight for the rights of man, and widening the boundaries of freedom of thought'. As for freedom of the press, their reviews were themselves proof that they did not just talk about it, but really put it into action.

Their programme was still one of agrarian Socialism. It was not that they were not well aware of the problems of the workers. But the two things were and must remain closely linked. 'A revolutionary movement which breaks out in the name of the land will inevitably on the very next day realize the need to seize the factories and entirely destroy every kind of capitalism, because, by retaining capitalism, it would dig its own grave.' And the reverse was just as true: 'The Socialist movement in the towns, were it to spring up independently in the villages, would inevitably meet peasant Socialism from the very first.'

And so the immediate problem was not to discuss programmes for the future. What was essential was to start a popular revolution and to start it as quickly as possible because 'one does not have to be a prophet to see that absolutism will collapse and give way to constitutionalism'. This would bring the privileged classes to the fore and give them the power.

So they must not fight only against absolutism but rather prepare the forces of the revolution. In other words they must not accept the point of view of Tkachev's Jacobins. These Jacobins wanted all efforts to be concentrated against something that was not in fact the only enemy. Some of their views, such as terrorism and plans to disorganize the State, could of course be accepted. But the revolutionaries must not let themselves be carried away by terrorism: 'This is not the way by which we will liberate the mass of the people.' 'Against a class, only a class can rebel; only the people can destroy a system.' The terrorists were and must remain no more than cadres of protection. Even if they momentarily succeeded in destroying the absolute power, they would only be helping its passage into the hands of the bourgeoisie and the privileged. Hence their victory would be only a Pyrrhic one.

Kravchinsky therefore clearly raised the problem which was to lead to an increasing conflict within *Zemlya i Volya* and eventually to the formation of *Narodnaya Volya*.

A Populist revolution was possible only if it occurred soon, while the *obshchina* was still safe in the countryside. The penetration of the capitalist system into Russian life was growing more profound, but it was still recent and therefore weak. Success would come if the popular masses could be led to rebel against it soon. But the authorities, the State, the Tsar—these stood in the way of this need to act quickly. To try and eliminate them was dangerous and would bring about the reverse effect, said Kravchinsky. On the contrary, replied the others, it was the only way to open up the road to a revolution which later would no longer be possible.

This was the setting for the controversy for or against terrorism. In view of the problems involved, it is natural enough that it became increasingly violent and the central problem for all the movement.

The rest of Kravchinsky's article and the other articles in the first issue of *Zemlya i Volya!* were attempts to find a way out of this dilemma.

Kravchinsky proposed returning to work among the people. What had been done so far in that direction? 'Little, extraordinarily little.' And yet there was no lack of opportunity. 'The masses are beginning to understand us.' The working class movement proved this if nothing else. The Chigirin conspiracy too, though it had been based on unacceptable principles, had shown 'the possibility of creating a purely peasant and revolutionary organization, starting from local demands and interests'. Past failures must not make them become less Populist. On the contrary they must emphasize their links with purely local and Russian ideas and forces. The time had come to 'strip Socialism of its German and foreign clothes and dress it in the popular blouse of the Russian peasant'.

This was still the faith of *Zemlya i Volya*. But would existing conditions in Russia enable its members to pursue this programme? The very first number of their review had attacked the *Golos* (Voice) for saying that it was useless for the Populists to fight against the bourgeoisie as it did not exist in Russia and that it was useless to want Socialism which could not exist without a bourgeoisie. In reply the Populists said that in actual fact the capitalist system was already established in Russia. The peasant reform of 1861 had taken the decisive step in this direction, and now they must take account of this situation. They recalled Marx's (in fact Engels') attack on Tkachev, and said that they were forced to admit that Marx was right. They accepted his sociological analysis of the situation in Russia. 'There is no slavery, nor serfdom, but a bourgeois system.' And there was no need to wait for this to develop further: 'Nothing is more stupid than to say that Socialism is possible only in a highly developed society', they said. Socialism sprang up wherever inequality and exploitation were to be found.

In fact Russia's situation meant that Populism was still the only brand of Socialism possible. Later numbers of *Zemlya i Volya!* merely defined this outlook more precisely. The editors did not accept materialism, and they did not share Marx's views on the working classes, though they admitted the broad outlines of his examination of the development of bourgeois society. And they did not believe in a Socialism which would come into being when capitalist development reached its end. It was the liberals, they said in a leading article in the third issue, who maintained this idea and who attacked the Populists. It was the liberals who said that society was not yet ripe, indeed that it could not yet even be described as capitalist and that therefore Socialism could not exist in Russia. Was it then to be the function of the Marxists to bring about the necessary economic conditions? It was true that the men of the Enlightenment in Russia had also been gentlemen and owned serfs; it was the situation itself which led to these contradictions. But for this very reason it was essential to be aware of Russia's special situation. Whereas in Western Europe capitalism had developed with the fall of the peasant *obshchina*, and had then re-created 'a collective spirit' in the factories, in Russia this collectivism had not yet disappeared, and was still alive in the villages and the agricultural communities. And so what was progressive in Europe might be retrograde in Russia.

To move from handicraft to factories was a step forwards, but to move from the *obshchina* to capitalism in the countryside was a step backwards. The Populist revolution would pass direct to Socialism. Socialism alone corresponded to the real situation.[175]

Any attempt to give first place to the constitutional problem and fight only for freedom meant that this situation was not understood. Only one reply was possible to 'society' when it complained about the lack of laws, rights, and security for the human being: All this was due to the position of the peasant masses. 'We say, in the interests of liberty itself, "let us hasten to begin a political reform from below so that it is not replaced by a bad substitute from above".' It was useless to hope that the bourgeoisie would fight for liberty. It had already achieved its programme. 'Cheap labour and the freedom to exploit are already with us.' Indeed the bourgeoisie usually added, 'Thank God this has happened without political reforms.' For the moment anyone who wanted freedom must ask for bread and not reforms.

If we carry out a peasant policy, freedom will not be a fundamental aim but an inevitable result. In fact it will be like some natural subsidiary product in a chemical or technical process just as coke is formed during the making of gas or smoke when one lights the stove. Political liberty, the right of the human being to full invulnerability, will come not from demands and petitions on the freedom of the press or the inviolability of the individual—petitions carried to His Majesty's feet or offered on the point of a political revolutionary's bayonet—but from 'laws of God written in the hearts of men'. The free, independent peasant, capable of standing upright and unbowed, will be the only true defender of freedom. Who wants freedom must defend the harmless peasants. That is the way to get freedom in Russia.

Here, then, was the Populist programme in its full extent. It was a programme ready to absorb contributions from Marxism, Jacobinism and liberalism and yet still retain its central faith. It was a programme capable of giving its views on the future development of Russia. But it had not yet explained what should be done in the immediate future. The problems of power, of a political struggle, and of terrorism cropped up whenever the question of the peasants had to be considered.

Far off in Switzerland Akselrod had a clearer view of the problem. He wrote an article called 'Our party's time of transition' which was published in No. 8 (November/December 1878) of *The Obshchina*, the review which the first number of *Zemlya i Volya!* described as 'published by our collaborators and comrades'. 'The revolutionary movement is now passing through a critical moment in its development', said Akselrod:

If circumstances are favourable, existing Socialist currents can develop towards a full, coherent and extensive programme of federalist Socialism, capable of being adapted in practice to the specific conditions of life in Russia. Otherwise these currents may be volatilized and transformed on the one hand into Jacobinism and on the other into constitutionalism. And so the present moment is critical in the highest degree and dangerous for the future destiny of Socialism in Russia.

The revolutionaries must look back and draw inspiration from the origins of the movement. The pilgrimage 'to the people', from which the existing evolution had started, had certainly been a good move. 'Now the Jacobins, who propose to offer the people happiness and prosperity under the leadership of a wise authority, say that to know the popular masses is, if not utterly superfluous, at least of only secondary importance.' This was quite unacceptable to those who, from the very first, had planned to base their activities on the will and initiative of the people. But it was six years since this approach to the people had been made. Why was the 'party of the people' not as extensive as could have been hoped?

The reason for this lack of success was twofold: the rapid spread of capitalism in Russia and the lack of a combative spirit in society. And so something was now happening which had never been seen before. 'That section of the younger generation which has reached the highest spiritual development has taken exclusively on its own shoulders the grandiose task of preparing the working class for a conscious and organized struggle. This leads to objective difficulties and mistakes. Despite the various ideological currents into which the younger generation is divided, such as "rebels", Populists, propagandists, etc.' the very nature of the situation in which it found itself led it 'to incline unconsciously towards Jacobinism . . . There are few logical and coherent Jacobins', but many eventually slipped into it, carried away by events and lacking clear ideas and the ability to examine closely their own consciences.

The mistakes of the whole movement were now clear. '(1) We entered it hoping for speedy and spectacular results. (2) We did not sufficiently specify our duties and so we concentrated entirely on the countryside and left the intelligentsia and workers on one side.' It was now necessary to realize that the fight would be long and that it must be localized and qualified. This, however, did not mean blindly accepting popular traditions and ideals, even when they were collectivist in character. They must never forget that a society made up of *obshchinas* could be extremely reactionary and conservative, 'immobile to an extent existing states cannot even dream of'. It was not by chance that Haxthausen had looked upon the *obshchina* as the citadel of reaction in Russia. And as regards the factories, the Populists must never forget that 'a workers' movement without Socialist ideals is conservative'.

Pure Populism then was dangerous. But it might well be equally dangerous to adopt a 'political' fight. Such a move was, however, inevitable. 'If we must, whether we want to or not, fight absolutism, and therefore, indirectly, win political rights for the bourgeoisie, we must none the less take every possible step to avoid being carried away from our Socialist course: for this would lead to the utter disintegration of such elements of Socialism as exist in Russia.'

Akselrod's analysis of the situation was acute. But he failed to suggest any practical means of solving those contradictions that he himself had pointed out. How could the revolutionaries avoid being consciously or unconsciously drawn towards 'Jacobinism' or 'constitutionalism'—towards a dictatorship or a kind of liberalism incapable of serving the peasant and popular interests that were their own? The little practical advice that Akselrod suggested had already been adopted by *Zemlya i Volya*. Its 'specialized groups' (workmen, peasants, etc.) already corresponded to the need to localize and qualify the fight. Was not their review itself, published secretly in St Petersburg, an expression of that will to seek activities which were to be both 'political and Socialist' which he referred to in his comments on the press?

Even Akselrod's 'self-criticism', which admitted their 'speedy and spectacular hopes', was still only theoretical. Quite apart from the way in which Russian society was developing, the revolutionaries were compelled by the conditions of the struggle to aim at speedy results. They had no time to wait; the repression was growing increasingly severe.

Did the solution lie, perhaps, in the working class movement? Plekhanov, in the leading article of the fourth issue at the end of February 1879, stressed its importance:[176] 'Agitation in the factories is increasing daily: that is the news of the day.' This agitation constituted one of those problems that 'life itself brings to the forefront, its rightful place, despite the *a priori* theoretical decisions of the revolutionaries . . . In the past, and not without reason, we put all our hopes and directed all our forces at the village masses. The urban worker held only second place in the revolutionaries' calculations. Only extra resources were, as it were, devoted to him.' Yet the workers had been quick to absorb the propaganda spread among them: 'Today it is difficult to find a factory, a workshop or even a craftsman's shop which does not contain some Socialist workers.' It was now up to the revolutionaries to move over from propaganda to organization, to concern themselves with wages and not just search among the workers for new elements for the party. Above all, they must stop thinking that the workmen would have only a secondary rôle in the revolution of the future.

Our large industrial centres group together tens and sometimes even hundreds of thousands of workers. In the great majority of cases these men are the same peasants as those in the villages . . . The agricultural problem, the question of the self-administration of the *obshchina*, land and liberty: all these are just as close to the heart of the workers as of the peasants. In a word, it is not a question of masses cut off from the countryside but of part of the countryside. Their cause is the same; their struggle can and must be the same. And besides, the towns collect the very flower of the village population, younger people, more enterprising . . . there they are kept far removed from the influence of the more conservative and timid elements of the peasant family . . . Thanks to all this they will constitute a precious ally for the peasants when the social revolution breaks out.

In order to enable them to achieve this function it was necessary to organize not only the bolder characters but the mass as a whole. A fight in a factory was still a class struggle and a means to educate the workers against the authorities. And they must not let themselves be discouraged by unsuccessful strikes. Agitation must be pressed on relentlessly. 'Let the reader call to mind the history of the Trade Unions of 1824, before the repeal of laws against coalitions; let him remember just how the English workers obtained this repeal.' Plekhanov ended his article by speaking of the 'red terror' which would answer the government's 'white terror'.

Plekhanov was thus concentrating his attention on a particularly important aspect of the situation in the winter of 1878. But by now it was more one of past history than of immediate politics. The *Northern Union of Russian Workers* met its death at this very time, owing to a *provocateur*. And it was only due to information supplied by Kletochnikov, and the sang-froid of two members of *Zemlya i Volya*, that the central organization did not also come to grief. Instead the spy was eliminated in time. The working class movement had already reached its peak. During the following years strikes decreased rather than increased. Plekhanov's ideas led to extensive developments in later decades, but not in the immediate future. *Zemlya i Volya* could not direct its main activities along these lines.

Only one way remained open: the resumption and intensification of terrorism. This was the policy indicated by the government's campaign of repression and by the steps taken by individuals and groups. And so, throughout Russia and especially in the South, the bloody struggle between the authorities and the revolutionaries was resumed after what had seemed like a temporary halt during the summer and autumn of 1878 following the execution of Kovalsky. In November, Sentyanin, one of the members of Osinsky's group, put up armed resistance against the police who came to arrest him at Kharkov. He was accused of being secretary of the 'Executive Committee', but he did not survive until the trial. In May 1879 he died of consumption in the Peter-Paul fortress. Mikhailov, who had known him since his student days, said that 'he was an extraordinarily alive and sensitive person. From his French mother he had inherited a quick talent, nervousness and brilliant irony. Fate did not allow him to survive; he died at the age of twenty-two or twenty-three.'[177]

On 16th December, Konstantin Grigorevich Dubrovin also used arms to defend himself at Staraya Russa. He was an officer who had tried to create a military organization. One day, when talking to M. R. Popov, he had shown him his dagger, on which was written 'Defend yourself with this'.[178] He was sentenced to death on 20th April 1879 and hanged a week later in the Peter-Paul fortress.

Another man, Sergey Fedorovich Chubarov, also fired at the police as they came to arrest him at the end of 1878. He had been a 'rebel', one of the organizers of the Chigirin conspiracy, and then a member of the terrorist groups of *Zemlya i Volya*. He, too, had gone to St Petersburg to see if it were possible to kill Trepov. He had then taken part in the attempt to free Voynaralsky, and subsequently in the demonstration held outside the tribunal which had sentenced Kovalsky to death. He was hanged at Odessa on 10th August 1879.

With him was hanged I. Ya. Davidenko, whose revolutionary career was very similar. He tried in vain to put up armed resistance to the police when they arrested him at Odessa during the demonstration outside the tribunal which sentenced Kovalsky.

Attempts to escape from exile were frequent, especially by those students who had been deported after the disturbances during the winter. Such attempts were often successful. On the other hand S. N. Bobokhov met with a particularly tragic fate. In 1875 he had been driven from the School of Medicine and had been sent first to Saratov and then to the department of Archangel. When in Eastern Siberia among the Yakuts, he fled with two comrades. They were pursued by the police, and he fired. He was sentenced to death, but his sentence was commuted to twenty years' hard labour. He poisoned himself in 1889, unable to overcome the humiliation of having been flogged. He was 'an extreme anarchist in theory, an extreme Populist in practice', according to one of his friends.[179]

Between the end of 1878 and the beginning of 1879 the nucleus of the first 'Executive Committee' in the South came to a violent end. In December, Popko was arrested at Odessa. The police knew of his activities as a propagandist and organizer, but not that he had personally taken part in terrorism. And so he was sentenced to forced labour for life instead of being hanged. He survived until 1885, when he died of consumption at Kara.

In Kiev the position of the revolutionaries was becoming increasingly difficult. Sudeykin, one of the most capable members of the Russian police, took the place of the assassinated Geyking, and during the next few years he acquired a considerable reputation. He succeeded in putting two *provocateurs* on the tracks of Osinsky, who was constantly on the move between Kiev and Odessa and several times made spectacular escapes from the net that was tightening round him. But on 24th January 1879 he was caught, together with Voloshenko, on the road between the two towns. In his house they found Sofya Leshern, one of the most active women among the Southern terrorists.[180]

On the night of 11th February, nearly all the members of their group were taken to prison. Sudeykin came in person with two of his policemen to a house in which were living the two Ivichevich brothers, Ludvig Karlovich Brandtner, a certain 'Rafael' (whose full name is unknown), Veniamin Pavlovich Pozen, Rostislav Steblin-Kamensky and Natalia Alexandrovna Armfeld.[181] The first of these used their revolvers and one policeman was killed in the clash. Sudeykin himself seems to have escaped, thanks only to the breastplate that he was wearing. The two Ivicheviches were fatally wounded. Brandtner and 'Rafael' were less seriously injured and tried to escape as the policemen withdrew. But they fell down and were arrested. Meanwhile Pozen and Armfeld managed to burn all their compromising papers before they too fell into the hands of the police.

Immediately afterwards, during the same night, an attack was made with arms and blank shots that led to the arrest of a second group. Debagory-Mokrievich (who subsequently wrote his memoirs) and a few others were taken prisoner. Two men, Vladimir Sviridenko (Antonov) and Dicheskul were arrested on the road. Both fired in an attempt to escape, but only Dicheskul was successful.

They were all tried together at the beginning of May 1879. During the trial Osinsky said, 'I know for certain that not a single member of the "Executive Committee" is among those arrested. I know that this has not put an end to its activities as it will soon show.' He thus set an example which was followed in similar circumstances by members of the Executive Committee of *Narodnaya Volya*. When accused of having admitted immoral characters among his comrades, he answered: 'The public prosecutor, with his morality, or rather immorality, could find no place among us.'[182] A sentence of death was given to those who had put up armed resistance, and fourteen years and ten months' hard labour to all the others. But later on this system of uniform punishments was somewhat modified. Antonov, Sviridenko, Brandtner and Osinsky, however, went to the scaffold on 14th May 1879.

On the previous evening Osinsky had managed to dictate to Sofya Leshern a testament in code for his comrades in *Zemlya i Volya*. Osinsky had done more than anyone to have terrorism adopted as a fundamental weapon in the fight and he now said that though the results so far had been negligible, terrorism was still the road to follow.

We have no regrets at having to die. We die for an idea, and if we do have any regret it is only that the significance of our deaths lies merely in the shame it puts on the dying monarchy and not something better, and that before our death we have not done what we wanted to do. I send you wishes, my dear friends, for a more profitable death than ours. This is the only, the best of all wishes that we can give you. And again; do not throw away your precious blood in vain.

We have no doubts that your activities will now be aimed in one single direction. Even if you had not written this, we could do it together. According to our way of thinking the party cannot physically undertake anything else. But for real terrorism we need people and means.

There followed some technical advice. Finally he briefly recalled the dissensions that had been stimulated among his comrades by his ideas and personality, all burning with the desire for terrorism. Now he asked them to forget all this and he embraced them farewell. Osinsky's appeal was then published in the sixth issue of the *Listok Zemli i Voli* as evidence of the terrorist spirit which was now constantly increasing in power among the revolutionaries.[183]

At the beginning of 1879, another successful assassination was carried out in the South. On 9th February Grigory Davidovich Goldenberg shot Kropotkin, the governor of Kharkov. This man was a cousin of the well-known anarchist, and although he enjoyed the reputation of being a liberal, it was he who was responsible for the severe conditions which prevailed in the central prison at Kiev. His assassination was yet another gesture of protest and self-defence against the repressive policies of the government.

Meanwhile in St Petersburg another incentive to terrorism was provided by the accidental arrest of Klements, who had been denounced by one of his servants. For Klements, who had been running the review during this period, had kept it firmly to the Populist line, and was more directly in touch with 'society' than many of his comrades. Indeed during his last days of freedom he had intended to spread propaganda in the *Zemstvo* of Nizhny Novgorod, whose members included his friend Petr Alexandrovich Alexandrov, who was arrested with him.[184] But now his removal from the scene made Tikhomirov and Morozov the most important editors of *Zemlya i Volya!* And both were resolute supporters of terrorism. On 12th March the first number of the *Listok Zemli i Voli* to be edited by them made its appearance.

'Life does not wait', it began. 'A monthly review cannot report as quickly as it should the events which follow one another in battle. And so this leaflet will fill an indispensable need.' The leaflet, in fact, was a war communiqué which announced acts of terrorism and armed resistance. It also exalted them, built them into theories and looked upon them as the very centre of the party's activities. Morozov was the leading editor and man responsible for this leaflet. It virtually replaced the review itself, of which only one more number appeared, whereas five communiqués announced the various stages of the battle until June 1879.

The second number of the *Listok* was already able to announce that the road pointed out by Kravchinsky on 4th August had been resumed. On 13th March 1879, Drenteln, the new head of the police, had been shot at while driving in his carriage along a central street of St Petersburg. The would-be assassin had been on horseback and had managed to escape. The determination to aim high and move over to the offensive was obvious. A manifesto was published and the name 'Executive Committee' now made its appearance in the North. St Petersburg was inheriting the mantle of Osinsky.[185] 'A political assassination', said the *Listok*, in its report, 'is above all an act of revenge, the only means of defence in the existing situation, and at the same time one of the best weapons of agitation.' It was essential to aim at the centre 'so as to make the entire system quake'. It recalled that in the *Kolokol* of 1st April 1864 Herzen had spoken of those groups of revolutionaries 'who in underground caves had joined together in indissoluble communities of "holy fools", whom neither the savage barbarity of the one nor the traditional civilization of the others had been able to crush'. Had they adopted the system of terrorism, these revolutionaries would have become terrifying. At present this system was 'the realization of the revolution . . . The authorities feel an abyss opening beneath their feet. That is why we look upon political assassination as one of our most important weapons against despotism.' The future would be the time for mass movements, and it would be the terrorists who had opened the road for these movements. They were the last representatives of conspiracy and the first of revolution.

The shots at Drenteln had been fired by Leonid Filippovich Mirsky. He had been prompted both by ideas of the kind quoted above and also by a measure of adventurous romanticism. Of Polish origin, he had already been arrested and had only left the Peter-Paul fortress two months earlier. He belonged to the exclusive world of St Petersburg rather than to the 'indissoluble communities' of the revolutionaries. Mikhailov had influenced him. Shortly afterwards he was arrested and sentenced to death in October 1879. His spirits failed and he asked forgiveness, and even betrayed Nechaev's plans for escape. His bitter experiences now made him into a fighter for the rest of his life. Later he was again sentenced to death and only just avoided being shot during the revolution of 1905.[186]

Mirsky had fired and missed on 13th March. By this time Alexander Konstantinovich Solovev had already firmly made up his mind to try to kill the Tsar. In February 1879 he was in St Petersburg where he met Mikhailov, whom he had known for two years and who was his closest comrade among those then in the capital. He also got into contact with Alexander Alexandrovich Kvyatkovsky. But he did not ask for help, as he wanted to take independent action. He did not even ask Mikhailov to agree with his plans. He had made up his mind to act in any case.[187]

The situation was now somewhat similar to that which had existed more than ten years earlier in Moscow, when the underground had learnt that Karakozov had decided to fire at the Tsar. But this time Solovev found support from the hard core of terrorists in *Zemlya i Volya*. Mikhailov wanted to inform his comrades of what was about to happen, both through political loyalty and so that they might take the necessary security measures against the inevitable reaction of the police and the government. An exceedingly violent discussion took place, which brought to light the schisms in the party which were now evident. Some members even recalled Komissarov, who had been credited with saving the life of Alexander II in 1866: 'If there are Karakozovs among us, there may also be another Komissarov, who is not prepared to accept your decisions', M. R. Popov (soon to become one of the leaders of *Cherny Peredel*) is reported to have said. 'If you are a Komissarov, I will kill you myself', answered Kvyatkovsky.[188] Plekhanov was on Popov's side; and theirs was probably the majority opinion. Mikhailov, however, held firm. The assassination, he said, had to be reckoned with, as Solovev had made up his mind, and so it was useless to discuss it any further. In any case, no agreement was reached. As a compromise it was decided that every individual member of the organization could collaborate in the assassination, but that he would do this on his own initiative without involving *Zemlya i Volya*.

Solovev even found a rival claimant for the function he had taken upon himself. This was Goldenberg, who had killed Kropotkin at Kharkov. And so a meeting was held with Mikhailov, Zundelevich, the two candidates, and Ludvig Kobylyansky, a Pole. As a result of this, Solovev assumed full responsibility for the undertaking.

On the morning of 2nd April while Alexander II was taking his usual walk in the grounds of the Winter Palace, Solovev fired five times at him with his revolver. None of his bullets hit the target. The Tsar ran off, stumbled and fell, but was unhurt. The many policemen who were accompanying him flung themselves at Solovev, who defended himself and wounded one of them. He then swallowed the poison that he carried with him, but was given immediate medical treatment and revived. Meanwhile Mikhailov was able to watch the whole scene from some way off.

Solovev was tried and explained the reason for what he had done. He was, however, able to conceal his movements, which would have put the police on to the tracks of his friends. In his deposition he wrote that he was perfectly well aware of the fact that many young men were able to embark on a career when they left the university. This, however, had not attracted him. 'I wanted to devote myself to serving the people, poverty and the needs of those who are close to my heart ... And so I began by sharing the ideas of the Socialists.' He had become a schoolmaster, but had become convinced that this too was of no use to the people. 'My school was attended only by the sons of the bourgeoisie and government officials.'[189] And so he had 'gone to the people' and lived as a workman and railway carpenter. Although he did not say it in his deposition, he had in fact lived longer than most among the people, having worked and spread propaganda for three years in succession. In October 1876, for instance, he had been in the departments of Vladimir and Nizhny Novgorod 'where work on the railways had been developed and it was easier to find a job'. Besides, he was attracted by these districts because exploitation by the *kulaks* was making the position of the

local peasant artisans more and more desperate. The land was burdened with
unbearable taxes and no longer gave any produce. He had spent the winter
and spring going from village to village in search of work. Unfortunately for
him, the diplomatic tension with Europe and the mobilization which seemed
to presage war had their effects even here. The employers were closing down
factories and dismissing the workers. Thousands of penniless, homeless men
were wandering throughout the countryside offering their labour for a hunk
of bread. Solovev soon came to the end of his resources and found himself
in the same situation as these wretches. 'Hunger, nights spent in the winter
cold, in empty shelters or in unheated *izbas* on damp, dirty straw, all this
made my position nearer and nearer that of these unfortunate men, while
my health was gradually ruined.' After several months he returned to St
Petersburg, and told Mikhailov of the misery that he had seen and shared.
He then resumed his life as a worker in the department of Saratov. Even in
1879 when he had already decided to kill the Tsar he still spoke 'of his faith
in the possibility of working among the people'. Yet this hope was dying.
He confided to Mikhailov that his plan to kill the Tsar was justified mainly
'because of the benefit it would bring to the peasants . . . I could think of no
more powerful means of bringing the economic crisis to a head. Desires and
impatience were now obvious everywhere. The discontent of the people was
extremely strong.'[190] Now was the time to begin an open battle. In the words
of his deposition: 'We revolutionary Socialists have declared war on the
government.' He had never been a good subject; but ever since he had become
'a convinced revolutionary Socialist' he had looked upon the Tsar as 'an
enemy of the people'. Although the idea of avenging his fallen comrades
was a very real one to him, the fundamental reasons for his action were very
different. His was the first really political act of terrorism since Karakozov.[191]

On 28th May he was hanged in front of a large crowd, which included the
correspondents of the *Figaro* and the *Monde Illustré*.

The measures that were now taken by the government, the discussions
that the attempted assassination gave rise to among the revolutionaries, the
increasingly serious schisms within *Zemlya i Volya*—all these opened a new
chapter in the history of the movement, and belong to the story of *Cherny
Peredel* and *Narodnaya Volya*.

21. NARODNAYA VOLYA

THE GOVERNMENT'S REPLY to Solovev's attempt on the life of the Tsar was to impose a state of siege. An *ukas* of 5th April handed over those regions of the Empire where the revolutionary movement had been strongest to generals who had distinguished themselves in the war against the Turks. St Petersburg was given to General Gurko; Odessa to Totleben;[1] Kharkov to General Count Loris-Melikov. These changes extended a régime which had already subjected the regions of Moscow, Kiev and Warsaw to 'governor-generals', and their powers were now increased. Every aspect of civil administration, including public order, came under their control. They were given power to hand over anyone to a military tribunal, to arrest and banish in cases where they considered it necessary, and also to suppress any newspaper or review. In fact a régime of terror was set up, made more severe by the fact that the power of the State was carved up and entrusted to six regional military dictators. Solovev's action revealed both the determination of the State to act against the *kramola* (subversive forces) and the inability of the central organs of government to assume control of the fight against the revolutionaries.

The Emperor himself left St Petersburg and withdrew to his residence at Livadia in the Crimea. Before his departure he appointed a special Commission of Ministers under the leadership of Valuev to inquire into the reasons for the rapid spread of 'subversive doctrines' among the new generation and to propose measures for combating them. At first the Commission did not show much enthusiasm for the task, and tried to avoid it. But Alexander II was insistent, and finally, in June 1879, Valuev submitted the conclusions reached by the Commission to the Committee of Ministers. Its picture of the situation was hardly optimistic. It had to admit that the appeal to the intelligentsia, which had been launched after Kravchinsky's assassination of Mezentsov, had met with no response.

Specially worthy of attention is the almost complete failure of the educated classes to support the government in its fight against a relatively small band of evildoers . . . Most of these people are anxious. Though taking no part in the struggle and though not acting on behalf of the government, they are to some extent waiting for the result of the battle. Generally they do not take a favourable view of the government's measures, which they consider to be sometimes too weak and sometimes too strong.

Was the position any better as regards the 'masses who do not think much'? It was true that when a revolutionary was being arrested or a demonstration resisted, the masses intervened on the government's side; but their help was 'disordered, violent, always verging on the arbitrary, and consequently too dangerous to be relied upon'.

In the meantime these masses are easily accessible to ill-intentioned rumours or interpretations, and promises referring to the granting of new improvements and material benefits . . . In general, among all classes of the population there is evident a certain vague dissatisfaction which preoccupies all minds. Everyone is complaining about something and waiting for a change.[2]

After this analysis of the situation, the Special Commission proposed a series of repressive measures: the strengthening of the prestige and power of the police, supervision of the *Zemstvo*, and restriction of the press. Further, the peasants should be clearly told that there was no question of giving them more land. Finally the government should rely for support on the 'private and hereditary landholders' and should be more tolerant of the *Raskolniki* as a reward for their imperviousness to propaganda, and also make some concessions to the Poles who had not provided 'ground suitable for revolutionary agitation'.

As regards schools, discussions within the Commission had been so lively that no unanimous conclusions had been reached. The contradictions which had existed here for over twenty years still survived, despite all the repressive steps and palliatives adopted in the 'seventies. The desire of the government to allow a growing number of students from the poorer classes to enjoy higher education meant that among the students there were many men who had to fight against difficult and often terrible economic conditions. The economic development of Russia was tending to break down the rigidly classicizing (or rather, archaeological) framework within which the minister Tolstoy had wanted to confine education. And recent disorders, especially those in the capital, had shown that the students' *esprit de corps* was still a powerful and active force. The Commission could do no more than emphasize that it was 'positively harmful in Russia to arouse by artificial means the desire to pursue higher education'.[3]

Only a fraction of the measures proposed were put into practice quickly. Only those concerning the police were seriously enforced, and on 16th June 1879 a circular was sent out to explain to the peasants that they must cherish no illusions about the land.[4] But the Commission, despite its apparent practical ineffectiveness, had none the less pointed out the true situation and drawn up the main lines of what was to be the government's policy during 1879. The educated classes kept aloof; the popular classes were showing obscure signs of not wanting to support the government without receiving something in return and had their eyes on the property of the gentry and the State. And so it was obviously not advisable to appeal to them. This left only one choice: the apparatus of government must take on the fight with the revolutionary organizations.

The circumstances of the case—which had driven the Populists to assume the burden of the struggle and had commended the use of terrorism—now led the State to rely entirely on its own resources for eradicating the revolutionary ferment, and drove it to adopt methods of pure police repression.

At Kiev and Odessa the first task of the new governor-generals was to put the final legal touches to the liquidation of the 'rebels'' activities, whose centres had already been hit by the arrests of the beginning of the year. On 14th May, Osinsky, Brandtner and Sviridenko were hanged at Kiev, and on 18th June Yosif Bilchansky, Gorsky and Aron Gobst.[5] In Odessa, Sergey Chubarov, Yosif Yakovlevich Davidenko and Dmitry Andreyevich Lizogub went to the scaffold on 10th August. On the next day, in connection with the trial of these latter, S. Ya. Vittenberg and I. I. Logovenko were hanged at Nikolaev.

These executions were due partly to the 'armed resistance' which some of the revolutionaries had put up, and partly to the discovery of preparations for killing Alexander II. A plan had been made to blow up a street in Nikolaev while the Emperor was on his way through. The police discovered the machinery in Vittenberg's house, and he, together with the sailor Logovenko, was the main organizer of the plot. They were arrested, but the dynamite which had already been prepared was rescued from the Nikolaev police and taken to Davidenko's house in Odessa. When he too was arrested the explosives were once more saved and handed over to Gobst at Kiev. Finally he too fell and the police laid their hands on the dynamite.

Even these secondary figures from among the Southern 'rebels' showed the spirit that inspired the whole movement. On the day before the executions, Salomon Vittenberg wrote a letter to his friends:

Naturally I do not want to die. To say that I am dying willingly would be a lie. But this fact must not cast a shadow on my faith and on the certainty of my convictions. Remember that the highest example of honour and sacrificial spirit was without doubt shown by the Saviour. Yet even he prayed 'Take this cup away from me.' And so how can I not pray also? And yet I too, like Him, tell myself, 'If no other way is possible, if it is necessary that my blood should be shed for the triumph of Socialism, if the move from the present to a better organization can only be made by trampling over our bodies, then let our blood be shed and flow to redeem humanity; let it serve as manure for the soil in which the seeds of Socialism will sprout. Let Socialism triumph and triumph soon. That is my faith.

In a postscript he told his friends to give up any idea of avenging him. 'Forgive them, for they know not what they do.' And he ended: 'Even this is a sign of the times. Their mind has been obscured; they see that a new epoch will soon begin and they do not know how to prevent it.'[6]

This faith was expressed with more than usual purity in the life of yet another man who was hanged at this time, Dmitry Andreyevich Lizogub, who was executed with Chubarov and Davidenko.[7] 'This is not of course the first example we have had of the heroic courage with which our comrades are meeting their deaths', wrote the first number of the *Narodnaya Volya*, 'Lizogub, however, is a figure of quite outstanding spiritual grandeur.' And the issue which appeared shortly before the plot of 1st March 1881 contained another long article devoted to his memory, as if intended to let his spirit act as an encouragement to the revolutionaries at this decisive moment in the struggle.

This 'ascetic' Socialist came from one of the richest families in the Chernigov region in the Ukraine. He had had an aristocratic education, partly in French, partly in Ukrainian. His family still retained vivid memories of the poet Shevchenko who had lived in their house and had been arrested there, and also of the historian Kostomarov, both of whom were the creators of mid-century Ukrainophilia. At the age of eleven he had gone with his family to live at Montpellier. The *Narodnaya Volya* said:

His education in France kept him far removed from those conditions which develop the slavish instincts which survive so long in the Russian. Hence Lizogub's nature lacked a feature which is characteristic of the people of our country: i.e. involuntary fear in the face of authority. When speaking with a superior, the Russian involuntarily gives his voice a particular inflection and adopts a respectful look and attitude. These reflections of spiritual alignment were unknown to Lizogub.

On his return to Russia this independence of character was soon allied to the spirit of complete dedication which he also inspired in the comrades with whom he came into contact at St Petersburg. From the very first he gave up any idea of a career. He repudiated marriage, for he thought that the revolutionary should not have to look after a family, and indeed he was distressed every time he saw one of his comrades marrying. 'Lizogub never loved a woman in his life, and no woman loved him . . . He carried his convictions to their extreme, mathematically logical conclusions, and therefore looked on love as an obstacle on the road along which he had embarked.'

At the beginning of 1877 he got into contact with the Populists in St Petersburg.[8] They gave him important duties, which included trying to secure contacts abroad. For this purpose he went to London to see the editorial board of Lavrov's *Vpered*.[9] His large family estates became a centre for propaganda among the peasants, and a kind of 'colony'. From this 'colony' came Nikolay Nikolaevich Kolodkevich, one of the members of the Executive Committee of *Narodnaya Volya*, who died in 1884 in the Peter-Paul fortress. Lizogub planned the systematic liquidation of these estates, so as to hand over the proceeds to the organization. Legal difficulties, however, delayed the realization of these plans, and the actual money he was able to give to *Zemlya i Volya* was not much compared with the value of his inherited property, though still considerable when compared to the budget of the secret society. He always lived a life of complete poverty, so as to avoid taking advantage of this property, which he looked upon as no longer belonging to him. Mikhailov has told how Lizogub considered that he was doing no more than applying the rule which obliged members of the group to 'sacrifice all their private possessions: property, sympathies, friendship, love, and very existence'.

While sharing in the life of *Zemlya i Volya*, he too underwent the mental and political development of his comrades. He was by no means sentimental. Indeed he was able to gauge the consequences of his situation with implacable logic. 'He too was convinced after the movement "to go to the people" that it was essential to unite all the splinter groups of Russian Socialism into a single party, pledged to an active struggle against the government. For him, too, partisan warfare replaced peaceful propaganda.' Hardly had he time to embark on this new adventure when he was arrested.

Everything now seemed to collapse around him. He had entrusted his property to a friend, instructing him to administer it, sell it and then hand over the proceeds to *Zemlya i Volya*. This man at once proposed to the police that he should divulge to them something he knew, on condition that he was allowed to become the sole owner of the property. He managed to put Lizogub in a desperate situation, and helped to have him sentenced to death. Indeed he succeeded in damaging the organization as a whole, and very nearly had Mikhailov himself trapped in an ambush. But he himself was eventually betrayed by the Third Section and handed over to a military tribunal. Even in prison, Lizogub came across an *agent provocateur*. Yet never for a single moment did his faith waver. Even when sentenced to die at the scaffold (to the great surprise of his comrades, who expected that he would follow the many propagandists then on the way to Siberia), he managed to smile.

The morning of 10th August was a fine one. Behind the square of troops round the scaffold there was a great crowd of people. In front stood the carriages of the rich citizens of Odessa; the women with their binoculars and lorgnettes, were sitting on the drivers' seats . . . A mood of curiosity and complete indifference prevailed. Occasionally one could hear a few words spoken by kindly souls shaken at the sight of the gallows. Spies were moving around everywhere. The thick crowd of people did not dare to give outward expression to sentiments of humanity. It was dangerous to utter anything other than brutal sentiments . . . And now along the road came the cart containing Lizogub, Davidenko and Chubarov. As they came through one side of the square of troops which opened up to let them pass, Dmitry Andreyevich looked at the gallows and then at the crowd and smiled and said something to Davidenko. The drums were rolling, and it was impossible to hear what he said.

The death of Lizogub closed an epoch. In him the self-sacrificial spirit of the movement 'to go to the people' found its last symbol. He was the only man to be hanged because he wanted to surrender everything that he had to the revolutionary movement, and even before becoming an organizer and terrorist. At his death Osinsky had urged his comrades to follow a new line. Lizogub showed by his death that it was now impossible to follow the old one.

These death sentences, which had been demanded by the governor-generals, and especially Totleben at Odessa, created the atmosphere that drove the revolutionaries to organize terrorism and form the Executive Committee of *Narodnaya Volya*. This atmosphere was still further exacerbated by the measures that accompanied these sentences and directly affected the educated classes. Even those who were by no means prepared or inclined to take armed action were now struck down. In Odessa searches were carried out in all the newspaper offices and inquiries were made about every single editor. Gertso-Vinogradsky was found guilty of flirting with liberalism in the *feuilletons* that he wrote under the name of 'Baron Iks', and banished. So too was Sergey Nikolaevich Yuzhakov, whose sister's revolutionary activities we have already referred to, and who subsequently became a well-known Populist writer. The schools were invaded, and a dozen teachers and professors arrested. The administration of the town was affected and two municipal officials, Gernet and Kovalevsky, were seized by the police. Many of the relations of those sentenced to death were sent to prison, including Vitashevsky's sister. As was to be expected, the number of students and workers removed from circulation was specially large:

It was as if a dark cloud was oppressing the town. Everyone felt it; everyone was loaded with an oppressive nightmare. Everywhere one could hear the cry—no longer stifled, but violent and insistent—that 'one could no longer go on living, it was essential to find some escape'. People who until then had hardly even heard of the revolutionary movement were now on the move looking out for radicals, pointing out the way of escape, offering themselves for work, and suggesting that the best, indeed the only, way to put an end to this suffocation was to kill the Tsar,[10]

wrote Frolenko. He was living in Odessa at this time, and tried, though in vain, to organize an attempt on the life of General Totleben.

Things in other parts of the South were much the same. In Kiev, however, the police acted more calmly after having liquidated the central group of terrorists. And at Kharkov, Loris-Melikov wanted to retain more humane and legal forms, so as to win the reputation of being a more liberal governor-general than the others. Indeed, on one occasion he apparently had a revolutionary sentenced to death for the very purpose of pardoning him.[11]

The centre of the repression was still Odessa. The hanging of Lizogub made such an impression that it compelled the government to cancel the governor-generals' right to confirm death sentences inflicted by military tribunals. From now on these had to be countersigned in St Petersburg. But this did not stop the execution of three more revolutionaries in Odessa

on 7th December 1879: Victor Alexeyevich Malinka, Ivan Vasilevich Dro-
byazgin and Lev Osipovich Maydansky, all of whom were implicated in the
unsuccessful attempt to kill Gorinovich, whom they suspected of being a
government spy.

There is other evidence besides that of Frolenko to show that it was public
opinion, in its reaction against the policy of repression and executions,
which encouraged the revolutionaries to make plans for the assassination of
the Tsar and concentrate all their forces against the centre of the system of
oppression. There is no doubt that the formation of this public opinion
favourable to regicide was a considerable factor in the political development
of summer 1879.

If we look closely, we will see that this state of mind only confirmed the
analysis which both the government and the revolutionaries had made of
the situation from opposing points of view. 'Society' was politically passive,
the people was silent. So the only active forces were the State and the Populist
organizations. Consequently these organizations had to bear the burden of
the day. Now by suggesting terrorism as 'the best, the only way out' even
the most active section of society was merely throwing responsibility for the
struggle onto the shoulders of the revolutionaries. For theirs would be the
only organization capable of carrying out such an undertaking. The intelligentsia was unable to suggest a programme for itself; it could only urge the
Populists on towards terrorism. It might perhaps help them, but the initiative
would still remain in their hands. At the time of the Southern Executive
Committee, terrorism had been an early symptom of the increasing 'political'
bent of Populist and Socialist tendencies. Now in the Executive Committee
of *Narodnaya Volya* it became the very symbol of the individual combat
between revolutionaries and authorities in a social and political situation
where no room for further manœuvre was left.

It was some months before these reactions and hints produced a determination not merely to carry out a series of assassinations, but rather to
pursue a systematic policy of terrorism. From 2nd April, when Solovev
fired his revolver, to 26th August, when the guiding spirits of *Narodnaya
Volya* decided to organize the systematic suppression of Alexander II, the
entire revolutionary movement went through a phase of internal rearrange-
ment. There were intense discussions, splits and regroupings on new
foundations. Throughout this period the movement was in a state of ferment.
Mikhailov said later:

The spring of 1879 was the most favourable moment for trying to create a wider
organization. Circumstances themselves suggested this idea to all of us. The government's repression had weakened the party as far as numbers were concerned, but
had helped to make it five times stronger from the point of view of quality. It had
created a remarkable unity of spirit and aims. Everywhere the majority had only
one desire; a bloody fight with the government. But there are people who are more
influenced by theory than by the logic of events, and they did not share this state of

mind. These people had their representatives in the Populist organization, and so the organization, despite the determined efforts of the other side, could not change direction without the problem being discussed collectively.[12]

The fifth issue of the *Zemlya i Volya!*, which came out in the middle of April. clearly reveals these differences. By now, Solovev had fired at the Tsar and there had been violent discussions to determine whether or not support should be given to this move. Yet the organ of the party still had no clear ideas on the problem of terrorism. The leading article reaffirmed the line of Populist agitation: 'More than anything else it is essential to turn ourselves into the people and live within the people; to become a force not only capable of acting in the people's interests, but with sufficient resources to hold firm for itself and the people. We must put the revolutionary party in the place that the mythical Tsar now holds in the eyes of our citizens.' This could be done by organizing protests, avenging the peasants for the abuses of the authorities, carrying out partisan operations to free them when they were arrested, and forming armed bands. 'Mazzini was able to arm up to seven thousand men, a complete army.' The fight in the towns only went to show that by now the State was unable to deprive the revolutionaries of their arms.

In other words the *Zemlya i Volya!* was trying to inaugurate a campaign of economic terrorism in the countryside instead of an offensive against the central offices of the State. It reported Solovev's attempt on the Tsar with detachment. Society, it said, had been taken by surprise. Everyone was saying that 'something ought to be done' though no one knew exactly what. 'Only the revolutionary Socialists know the answer', it continued, in words which were threatening in tone but really concealed inner uncertainties. The 2nd April showed that something new was coming into being, something vague, which was still not coherent or concrete. 'It is the threatening *memento mori* announced by a future arising out of an order of things which now belongs to the past.'[13]

On the other hand, the *Listok Zemli i Voli*, which between April and June 1879 was gradually replacing the review itself, openly justified terrorism. The most explicit article on the subject was published in the third issue and written by Nikolay Morozov.

Though Morozov was in fact responsible for the *Listok*, it reflected not only his own ideas, but also those of a section of *Zemlya i Volya* which came into being immediately after 2nd April, and which assumed the name of *Liberty or Death*. We know little of this group, if only because it had neither the time nor the opportunity to display itself in action. It was only a link between that wing of *Zemlya i Volya* which had been prepared to support Solovev and the Executive Committee of *Narodnaya Volya*. Its early members were Morozov, Mikhailov, Alexander Kvyatkovsky, Zundelevich and Stepan Grigorevich Shiryaev. Shiryaev was a revolutionary returned from exile. He had been a physics student and had already helped to spread propaganda among the workers of St Petersburg. He had then 'gone to the people', after which he had continued his studies in Paris. He now returned to put his technical knowledge at the disposal of the movement. According to Morozov he was virtually the head of the *Liberty or Death* group.[14]

At first the group seems to have been purely technical in character, assembling those men who were determined to plan the methods for a policy of terrorism. From these foundations it rapidly increased in size and weight and became the centre of all those who were determined to break out beyond the bounds imposed by the programme of *Zemlya i Volya*.

The presence of Alexander Alexandrovich Kvyatkovsky at the very heart of this group showed what progress had been made by terrorist ideas in one who only shortly before had been the most enthusiastic of travellers and propagandists among the people. During the early 'seventies, Kvyatkovsky had helped to organize a forge in the Kostroma region with his brother, who was then sentenced to hard labour at the 'trial of the hundred and ninety-three'. In 1877 he had joined the 'colony' at Nizhny Novgorod, and a year later had travelled with Popov from one market to another in the lands of Voronezh. Here he had made ties with the peasants, admiring their strength of mind and their work. He flung himself wholeheartedly into all these experiences. They seemed to be bringing to light elements of 'protest' and latent revolt in the countryside. Popov has left us a particularly vivid description of their joint activities among the people and their enthusiasm at finding among the peasants those demands and hopes for which they were looking. But in autumn 1878 he was recalled to St Petersburg by Mikhailov. There, in the words of Popov, who joined him in the capital shortly afterwards, he became 'a convinced terrorist'.[15] He was certainly a man of fighting spirit, as he had shown during the attempt to free Voynaralsky. Popov explained his transformation by saying that the will for an immediate fight triumphed in him. Later, looking back at the problem, he added that, 'Kvyatkovsky was sincere when he told the tribunal which was about to condemn him (as, indeed, he was always sincere) that his convictions were those of a *narodnik*, a Populist.'[16] So even terrorism did not affect the foundations of his belief in a peasant revolution. Besides, Kvyatkovsky was not the only man in this position. Even Zhelyabov had to find a pretext for his Populist conscience so as to be able to move from faith in the people to terrorism. In actual fact both these elements always survived, though in varying proportions, in Kvyatkovsky, in Zhelyabov and in all the other members of the Executive Committee.

The originality and power of *Narodnaya Volya* lay in just this: the attempt to make a synthesis out of, on the one hand, an armed conspiratorial, political struggle, and, on the other, the all-pervading desire for a social revolution capable of setting the people against all the ruling and privileged classes.

21+

The inner evolution of another of the members of this new group is more difficult to follow. Though Nikolay Ivanovich Kibalchich was one of the most brilliant of all these revolutionaries, he too had once been a propagandist. However, the decision to supply his comrades with dynamite (the most perfect of all weapons), and to make use of it under the particular circumstances which would condition partisan warfare against the Tsar, must have moved him to join the terrorists. Of Ukrainian origin, he had at first had some sympathy with the national movement in that country. Between 1875 and 1878 he was under preventive imprisonment for circulating clandestine newspapers. And then at 'the trial of the hundred and ninety-three' he was sentenced to a month in prison. When he came out he went over to the 'outlaws'. Popov recalled:

Prison had had its effect on him. I can see two Kibalchiches in front of me, one before and the other after prison. True, he had never been a cheerful youth, and he was always a systematic person. But before prison he loved taking part in discussions; perhaps he dreamed of guiding the others. Afterwards I remember nothing of him except handshakes and a friendly and affable smile . . . Even the jokes of his friends he answered only with a smile . . . He studied chemistry in a small scientific laboratory and had one firm purpose: to provide the Russian revolution with dynamite.[17]

He was a real scientist; his head 'was extraordinarily inventive'. He did not enjoy political discussions or factional disputes; 'his character was against every kind of diplomacy'.[18] But he proved to be a remarkable theoretician in politics as well as in technique, and he wrote one of the most interesting articles to be published in the Narodnaya Volya. He managed to lead an extraordinarily active life, and in summer 1879 he and Shiryaev began to build a laboratory in St Petersburg in order to prepare nitro-glycerine and dynamite.

Using an improvised laboratory, whose organization was absolutely primitive and in constant danger of being discovered by the police and blown up with the house, these brave comrades prepared some ounces of dynamite. They had never been technically trained for the purpose, and had to work by trial and error and were liable to be killed at any moment.[19]

Among those recruited for the laboratory were men who later became leading members of Narodnaya Volya. Like Kvyatkovsky, Shiryaev and Kibalchich, they represented the new group which had been recruited by the terrorist wing of Zemlya i Volya in St Petersburg. Two women, Anna Vasilevna Yakimova[20] and Sofya Andreyevna Ivanova, came from the 'trial of the hundred and ninety-three'. And Grigory Prokofevich Isaev[21] and Ayzik Borisovich Aronchik came from student circles. Both these men later became typical members of Narodnaya Volya, prepared to carry on the party's work even after 1881 when its founders perished in the struggle.

In May 1879 Lev Tikhomirov, editor of the Zemlya i Volya!, went over to the group. This decision was of great importance despite the hesitation, doubts and a certain scepticism with which he always pursued his revolutionary activities and which did not desert him now.

Despite all this, however, with Klements out of the battle and Kravchinsky back among the émigrés, Tikhomirov was the outstanding spokesman among his comrades. He could express the driving force that inspired them all in a politically comprehensive form whereas Morozov looked upon 'neo-partisanship', as he called it, mainly as a fight in the manner of William Tell or Charlotte Corday against tyrants. He stressed the purely political aspect of the duel with absolutism. He was gradually abandoning his Populist ideas and the problems of a social revolution in order to concentrate all his attention on the conquest of political freedom through the assassination of the tyrant. Even the name (*Liberty or Death*) of the group which he helped to found was a clear indication of political rather than social extremism. Tikhomirov, on the other hand, helped to create that synthesis of a political and social revolution which was to be characteristic of *Narodnaya Volya*. He looked to Tkachev and the Jacobin tradition for the elements to make up this synthesis; and he included in the programme of the 'Executive Committee' those general problems of a revolution in Russia that the political radicalism of Morozov's variety was in danger of forgetting. And finally he gave expression to that bond between Populism and terrorism which remained so strong for most of those who made up the more combative wing of *Zemlya i Volya*.[22]

The existence of a secret society within the ranks of a secret society could obviously not last for long. Very soon the party would have to be reorganized on entirely new lines or there would be a schism. Further, only a general meeting of members would be in a position to decide the future of *Zemlya i Volya*. This solution had already been proposed at the time of Solovev's attempt on the life of the Tsar, and it was now unanimously agreed upon. The terrorist wing took immediate steps to win over all members dispersed throughout the country, and especially the few figures who had survived the repression in Southern Russia. Among these the most significant was M. F. Frolenko. He had been in contact with *Zemlya i Volya* for some years and at this time was living in Odessa, where he was preparing an attempt on the life of the governor-general, Totleben. But by now the atmosphere that prevailed there had convinced him that it was wrong to waste energy on what were relatively side issues, and that instead all efforts should be concentrated against the Tsar. And so he came to St Petersburg. There the first task he was given was to get in touch with Alexander Ivanovich Barannikov. Barannikov had taken an active part in the 'colonies' of Nizhny Novgorod and Voronezh, as well as in the attempts to free Voynaralsky and the assassination of Mezentsov. He had then gone to live in the Orel region on the estates of his wife, Maria Nikolaevna Oshanina. 'They lived with false passports; and, as they had been unable to make any contacts in the district, they were terribly bored. And so they welcomed the invitation to resume a life of activity 'as a liberation from the yoke of the Tartars'.

Barannikov was a soldier (he had been to the Military College). He had an honest and combative nature which desired open clashes with the enemy without tricks, conspiracies, etc. He was no good at propaganda, and did not much like speaking. For all these reasons he immediately agreed to take part in armed assaults. For this sort of work he was perfectly suited, being cold-blooded, of extreme physical strength, able and brave.[23]

His wife, on the other hand, was interested in politics. She too had for long been in contact with *Zemlya i Volya*, and of all the group she was the only one who did not come from the propagandists or the 'rebels'. She had become a revolutionary after meeting Zaichnevsky, the Jacobin of *Young Russia*, who had been banished to Orel ever since the 'sixties. She always remained 'a centralist'—the word then used to describe those who were convinced that power would have to be seized by a conspiracy which would then make use of the machinery of State to direct the social and political revolution from the centre. She had only disobeyed Zaichnevsky's advice and taken part in the activities of *Zemlya i Volya* because of her longing for action. She was determined not to let herself be trapped by a dream of the perfect conspiracy; for such had been the fate of Zaichnevsky, the only true Jacobin living on Russian soil, a man unable to influence the real progress of the movement, and confined within a sect that scarcely even existed. And so she had made ties with the most active elements in St Petersburg, though remaining, so to speak, in a 'technical' position, without sharing their federalist or 'rebellious' standpoint. When Frolenko explained the situation that was developing in St Petersburg and told her of their discussions and plans for the future 'she at once understood that the time for isolated *coups* was over. Something new was coming into being. This might give rise to an altogether new line, something closer to what was dear to her heart.'[24] And so Maria Oshanina entered *Narodnaya Volya*, the only consciously Jacobin member to do so.[25] With her came her two sisters, Elizaveta and Natalia,[26] who were also exceptional women, though they did not possess that over-powering energy and political consciousness that Maria revealed throughout her life, from the day when she became Zaichnevsky's most brilliant pupil, until, with Tikhomirov in Paris, she came to represent the tradition of the *Will of the People*.

While exploring in the South, Frolenko had attracted a figure of even greater importance; and he now summoned to the meeting of the terrorist wing a young man from Odessa called Andrey Ivanovich Zhelyabov, who as yet was little known but who was soon to become the very soul of *Narodnaya Volya*.[27] Zhelyabov had neither been a member of *Zemlya i Volya*, nor had he associated with the 'rebels'. Instead he had embarked on an independent approach, pursuing with a vigour which revealed his political spirit his own way among the various propagandist, Populist and liberal tendencies of

Odessa. He came from a peasant family in the Feodosia region, and after going to school in Simferopol, he went to the university at Odessa. He was a born orator, and soon acquired a great influence over his fellow students. He was always trying 'to remove the narrowly professional aspect from student problems, so as to give them a wider social significance'.[28] At the age of twenty-one he was expelled from the university for organizing a protest against Professor Bogisich, a particularly vulgar man from the Balkans who had been welcomed by Russia so that she might show her interest in the problems of 'her Slav brothers'. This helped to give the incident a political flavour, so that when Zhelyabov and one of his comrades were expelled in 1872, a noisy demonstration took place in the town.[29]

Zhelyabov now began to spread propaganda among the workers and intellectuals. In this he was supported by the expanding wave of discontent which at this time was sweeping through Odessa, gathering up Ukrainophil and liberal sympathies in its train. His political life began in those constitutionalist circles, whose most advanced and pugnacious wing consisted of the young men who were more or less allied to the Chaikovskists. In 1871 he went to St Petersburg to make contact with them, and on his return he began to work in the group organized by Volkhovsky, Makarevich and others. But the distinction between liberals and Populists which was already so clear in St Petersburg was as yet hardly apparent in Odessa or other towns in the South.[30] 'Society' as a whole seemed to be united in a general political revival. The factor of Ukrainian nationalism helped to bring about this atmosphere and give a uniform colouring to the various tendencies.

In autumn 1874 Zhelyabov's work as a propagandist led to his imprisonment, and he was released only in March 1875. On his return to Odessa he was able to see for himself the growing split between the revolutionaries and the intelligentsia. Indeed his own private life was affected by the break. Some time before he had married the daughter of Yakhnenko, the mayor of Odessa. This man had the reputation of being a liberal and was related to the Simirenko family who had turned their sugar factories into a centre of Ukrainophilia and constitutionalism.[31] Zhelyabov now asked his wife to engage in the life of the people and to work with him and share his ideas, which were becoming increasingly hostile to the bourgeoisie. This was too much for the marriage, which broke up. Later, when he was hanged, his wife resumed her maiden name and agreed that their son Andrey should also abandon the name of a State criminal.

It was a symbol of two different worlds which for a moment had come together only to discover that they really stood for opposing things. Later Zhelyabov wrote to Dragomanov, the intellectual leader of the Ukrainian democratic movement:

It was the winter of 1875, the prisons were crammed with people. Hundreds of lives had been shattered. But the movement did not halt. The only thing to change was the nature of our tactics. The revolutionaries had by now learnt from experience and instead of propaganda for scientific Socialism they gave first place to agitation in word and deed, basing themselves on the demands of the people . . . Let us take just one corner of the battle, Odessa. I saw the flowering of the local *Hromada* (the Ukrainian organization) and its vigorous beginnings. Slowly but surely the two revolutionary currents, the Russian and the specifically Ukrainian, began to merge. Real unity, even more than a federation, was now near. And then suddenly . . . everything collapsed. The old, enticed by the advantages to be derived from keeping on the right side of the law, were slow to abandon their sheltered nests. Excellent men perished. Initiative died.[32]

This was Zhelyabov's first important political experience. He saw for himself that the attempt to create a compact movement designed to include both the younger generation of revolutionaries and the intelligentsia had foundered. The crucial problems had been two. First, should the movements be federated or merged? And, secondly, were they to accept the idea of a conspiracy and all its consequences? These had been the touchstones which showed who were the real revolutionaries. In his heart Zhelyabov decided for conspiracy, battle, and a centralized organization.[33]

The insurrection in the Balkans soon raised other vital problems. He was among the most ardent supporters of the view that society, and the revolutionaries themselves, should take independent action on behalf of 'their Slav brothers'. The government must be driven to free the Balkans; above all, volunteers must be recruited, and funds collected. He became the leading spirit in the committee for doing this which was founded, more or less illegally, in Odessa. Events soon proved that this road led nowhere; but it served to show him the extent of the political questions connected with this movement, which had appeared to be prompted only by an impulse of solidarity for the independence of other countries.

The Slav rebellions once again raised the problem of Poland. Zhelyabov was led to wonder why the Poles did not join the Russian Populist movement, and why there was no current in Poland to correspond to the revival of activity in St Petersburg, Kiev and Odessa. In any case Poland too had the right to independence, as he insisted in his conversations with Dragomanov. In view of the complexity of these problems he must have grown increasingly convinced of the inadequacy of a Populism devoted only to propaganda and agitation.

Zhelyabov did not choose the road taken by the 'rebels'; nor did he want to establish relations with Valerian Osinsky. His own road, he felt, was different. Only a real organization would enable him to give his full measure. He then began a phase of concentration and meditation. He cut himself off more than ever from society and became increasingly convinced of the need for a radical revolution. Shortly before the 'trial of the hundred and ninety-three', he was once more arrested and tried before a Committee of Senators. In January 1878 he was acquitted.[34] He had left his comrades with the impression that he was a convinced Populist, capable of following the road to the people, and insisting on the need to live among the peasants, and to work with them. They considered, in fact, that he was 'orthodox'—the name given, round about 1878, to those who held that the right course was to follow the road already begun. Yet he too had not been left untouched by experience. He explained this at the end of his life to the tribunal which was about to sentence him to death, in a brief but significant phrase: 'On leaving the countryside, I understood that the authorities were the main enemy of the party of Socialists who loved the people.'[35]

And so when Frolenko got in contact with him at Odessa, Zhelyabov said at their very first meeting 'that he was fully prepared to take part in the action against Alexander II'. Yet even now the Populist in him still spoke. Frolenko writes:

Later on in the conversation I explained to him in great detail the aims of the meeting which was being prepared. I told him of the opinions and intentions of the St Petersburg members to organize, if possible, a group of regular shock troops and to develop terrorism on a systematic basis without confining it to a single *coup*. Zhelyabov saw that other *coups* might follow, and then his comrades might compel him to join in. As if withdrawing, he said in a single breath that he gave his word for a single *coup* and that he would remain until it had been carried out; afterwards he would feel himself free from any further obligation. Indeed, he wanted an assurance that he would then be free to leave the organization or to stay, whichever he thought best, naturally committing himself to secrecy. This assurance was of course given, though in any case it was not our custom to hold back a member by force. Zhelyabov knew this, but I think that he felt it essential to reassure his Populist conscience. He imposed his condition so that he would have the right to say: 'In any case I have not given up Populism, even though I have agreed to one single act of terrorism.'[36]

Even if Frolenko's guess as to what was in Zhelyabov's mind at the moment when he chose the path of terrorism is not exactly correct, he is none the less right when he refers to the two attributes which he possessed: the will to fight directly against the authorities and the will to prepare a Populist revolution. Both these were vital elements and constituted Zhelyabov's personal force within *Narodnaya Volya*.[37]

The development of the various men who, in the summer of 1879, formed what was really a new revolutionary group—though 'officially' it was still only a section of *Zemlya i Volya*, has now been considered. This study will have shown that the policy of terrorism united many very different characters and mentalities. Terrorism in fact was the cement that joined Morozov's radicalism, Oshanina's Jacobinism, Barannikov's and Frolenko's aggressive spirits and Kibalchich's and Shiryaev's desire to apply modern technique to the armed struggle. It was also the junction for all the different roads that led from propaganda to political warfare, from agitation to the organized battle against Tsarist despotism. Systematic terrorism, aimed at the centre of the autocratic power, offered an immediate, concrete programme, and attracted the greatest energies that had been aroused and put to the test by the activities of previous years.

The programme that those who opposed this new tendency now suggested, was vaguer and above all less immediate and practical. Inevitably they were compelled to take up a standpoint limited to pure opposition confined to criticism and repudiation, without offering any new advance. This led them to seek refuge in 'orthodoxy', and maintain that the only thing to do was to go on following the programme and spirit of *Zemlya i Volya*; and indeed to turn it into a model and a myth, by doing away with those differences of forces and opinions which had met and clashed within its ranks, and which had made it living and vital. This 'orthodoxy' of what we might call 'the right wing' was both a symptom of its political impotence and the reason it remained sterile, even when it inspired the new current which emerged in *Cherny Peredel*. Like so many other political orthodoxies, it managed to preserve certain spiritual and historical values which the new fighting force was compelled to destroy and even to repudiate. But this preservation was of significance for the distant future, not for the immediate political struggle.

This intrinsic weakness soon revealed itself even on the tactical plane, in the day-to-day discussions which led to the schism. Instead of raising general problems and demanding a re-examination of the situation as a whole, the right wing was led, by this desire to carry on existing activities, to raise secondary and to some extent technical problems.

In St Petersburg, the opponents of political terrorism grouped themselves round Plekhanov and Popov. Both these men had earlier put themselves at the head of the majority which had stood out against Solovev and Mikhailov, mentor of the would-be assassin. They now turned for support to the men who were still in the 'colonies', ('country folk' as they were humorously called).[38] These men, they hoped, might be induced to oppose the urban elements who always had less respect for the general discipline of the movement and showed a greater readiness to act unilaterally. Among other things these town workers were absorbing increasingly large sums of money and neglecting their fellow-revolutionaries who worked among the people. And so, thought the 'orthodox' Popov, the best way to resist the advancing terrorist wing and bring it to terms was to set 'country folk' against 'townsmen' and demand a new division of funds.[39]

But the initiative was no longer in their hands. Instead it was Mikhailov who directed the political operation which led to the reorganization of the whole movement. Having agreed to the need for a general meeting, the 'innovators' had no intention of letting themselves be surprised. They would hold their own preliminary meeting and build up a definite organization. Once united, they would then engage in a trial of strength with the 'country folk'. The first meeting was to be held at Lipetsk, a bathing resort near Kiev, where the arrival of members would not arouse surprise. It was agreed that the general meeting on the other hand would be at Tambov, but when a piece of carelessness prejudiced its safety, Voronezh was chosen instead.[40]

Between 17th and 21st June, the most representative members of the St Petersburg group met at Lipetsk. These were Mikhailov, Tikhomirov, Morozov, Shiryaev, Kvyatkovsky, and those summoned by them from other towns: Frolenko, Zhelyabov, Kolodkevich, Goldenberg, Barannikov and Oshanina.

They were all 'outlaws' and 'professional revolutionaries'. The meetings were made to look like excursions into the country made by people whose only interests were boating, and picnicking among the trees.

The discussion at once revealed that they were far more united than even they themselves had believed. It soon became obvious that the thing to do was to register what they all already felt and embark on a series of practical steps. There was no need to reconsider general problems. Besides, they still intended to act as part of *Zemlya i Volya*, so as not to prejudice the chances of wider agreements. The important thing was to settle the fundamental issues. In Frolenko's words: 'The goal was to create a strong fighting organization and to give it the chance of acting independently, by finding the people and funds required.'

It is, however, obvious that they could not be unaware of the political consequences implicit in this goal. A draft programme was read out. According to Morozov he himself was the author, whereas Frolenko says that it was written by Mikhailov and Tikhomirov. In any case the text was lost and was reconstructed from memory by Morozov several years later. This programme deals exclusively with the fight against absolutism. The social 'Populist' element makes virtually no impression. It is only an appeal to destroy the tyrant. True enough, this expressed one aspect of the meeting's feelings: their wish to take up arms against Alexander II. But quite plainly it could not satisfy the Populist conscience which still animated Zhelyabov and many of the others. And so when the programme of *Narodnaya Volya* was drawn up, this first draft was rejected as inadequate.

It is, however, worth reproducing for, though it was not really representative of the Lipetsk meeting, it does nevertheless reflect the will to wage 'political warfare' which prevailed.

In view of existing social conditions in Russia, we see that no activity aimed at the good of the people is possible, given the despotism and violence which here reign supreme. There is no freedom of speech or freedom of press, which would allow us to act by means of persuasion. And so any man who wants to go in for progressive social work must, before anything else, put an end to the existing régime. To fight against this régime is impossible without arms. And so we will fight with the means employed by William Tell until we achieve those free institutions which will make it possible to discuss without hindrance, in the press and in public meetings, all social and political problems, and solve them through free representatives of the people.

21*

Until that has been achieved, we will consider as friends all those who agree to our ideas and help us in this fight, and as enemies all those who help the government against us.

Seeing that the government in this fight against us resorts not only to banishment, prison and death, but also confiscates our goods, we consider that we have the right to repay it in the same coin by confiscating its own means on behalf of the revolution. The goods of private people and of society, as long as they do not take part in the government's fight against us, we will regard as inviolate.[41]

Of far greater importance than the discussion on the programme, was the approval given to the statutes.[42] For here, though not without difficulty, the principle of a centralized, hierarchical, disciplined organization won the day. This put an end to the repeated attempts which had been made in the past to choose a kind of leadership designed to take account of the variety of Populist tendencies and groups; and then to try and reproduce in its structure the ideal of anarchistic freedom which inspired them. The statutes adopted were closer to the model 'conspiracy' which Tkachev and Zaichnevsky had conceived than to the earlier ones of *Zemlya i Volya*. The conditions imposed by clandestine warfare, the special needs of a group of shock troops, the very logic of terrorism whose target was the heart of the State—all these factors led to this conclusion. But it was clear enough that these technical aspects of the problem, which by now had been accepted and discounted, were no longer the fundamental ones. This conspiracy raised the problem not merely of the blow to be dealt at absolutism but of the later developments which were latent in such a policy. The party's function would no longer be limited to 'disorganizing' the State. It would also have to destroy it. And then what? The 'conquest of power'—in the Jacobin sense—became a real problem, if not in the practical immediate sense, at least in that of politics and ideology. The delegates at Lipetsk were not as yet called upon to make a decision on these problems; but their existence was now real enough. 'Conspiracy, revolutions, the conquest of power so as to hand it over to the people—all this we talked of and discussed', said Frolenko, even though prospects of this kind were taken into consideration mainly because they proved that 'with a strong fighting organization even things like this could be achieved . . . One could agree or not with these ideas, they were not made obligatory.'[43] In fact, these ideas were finally systematized only in the programme of *Narodnaya Volya*.

'The strong fighting organization' which they wanted to build was to adopt the old name of 'Executive Committee'. And so, having been a symbol, it now became an organized reality. Only one trace of its past survived. Anyone who was arrested and tried was to call himself not a member but an *agent* of the Committee, and indeed, a *third class agent* so as to suggest the existence of an invulnerable organization beyond the reach of the authorities. Later events showed that this move succeeded, at least within limits, in building up an atmosphere of terror and myth around the Executive Committee.

Besides, these agents really did exist, and this was one of the most important novelties introduced into the statutes and approved at Lipetsk. The equality of all members before the organization had been one of the characteristics of previous groups, and had been retained by *Zemlya i Volya* even after it had transformed itself into a party. Henceforward this equality was to be abandoned. The clause which now divided the members of the Committee into different categories proved to be difficult to apply, and there were never very many *agents* (scarcely more than a dozen). Their egalitarian and individualist consciences hindered this form of organization, which had been imposed by circumstances. Frolenko says:

The Russian revolutionaries found it difficult to assimilate the idea of submission. Eventually, however, sheer necessity and a more serious attitude towards the cause compelled many of them to see how important this was, and they agreed, realizing that a large fighting organization was unthinkable if based only on the personal relations between friends and comrades. Against an organized army only an even better organized army can take action. All this entered only slowly into practice, but it went increasingly deep.[44]

On the other hand, within the real Executive Committee, all members naturally had the same rights (Article 2) although they were 'unconditionally subject to the majority' (Article 3). 'All for each and each for all' was their motto (Article 5). 'Any private friendship or animosity, all the forces and the very lives of the Committee's members, must be sacrificed to achieve its ends. The duties that members owe to the Executive Committee are far greater than any other kind of private or social obligation' (Articles 7 and 8). The principle upon which their organization was founded was described as 'elective centralization', and this was considered 'the best principle for fighting' (Article 9). As will be seen, they now no longer had to resort to moral considerations of the end justifying the means, as even *Zemlya i Volya* had still done. The political aim had now won the day and they did not think that any purpose would be served by discussing this once more and comparing it with any other aim in life.

The Executive Committee was deliberately assigned the rôle of ruling body of the whole revolutionary movement. 'It must be the centre and the government of the party, in achieving the aims determined by the programme' (Article 1). It recognized only one authority, that of a 'general assembly' of the members of the Committee itself, whose functions and attributes were minutely determined. Among these were 'the exclusion of members and sentences of death' (Articles 11, 12 and 13). The 'Rules for accepting and dismissing members' were as follows:

Article 44: A candidate for membership of the Executive Committee must be:

(a) In complete agreement with the programme, principles and statutes of the society.

(b) Autonomous in his convictions.

(c) Tenacious, experienced and practical in action.

(d) Utterly dedicated to the cause of liberating the people.

(e) Before his admission he will have to spend some time as a second class agent.

He had to be recommended by five members and was admitted only after an open ballot in which each negative vote was equal to two positive ones (Article 45). An earlier ruling (Article 11) laid down that 'Every member obliges himself to remain in the society until its ends have been achieved, i.e. the existing government has been destroyed. Until then the resignation of members, and the conditions under which they can be accepted, depend entirely on the decisions of the Committee itself.'

Around the Executive Committee were to be grouped the bodies directed by it.

In the first place there were to be 'the generically revolutionary groups' (which were to be given a series of tasks other than those of terrorism). They would be sub-divided according to their relations with the centre, into 'tributary' groups and 'allies' (Article 56). The first type was considered the better and was to be governed by second class members and members of the Executive Committee, all of whom were obliged 'to follow completely the rulings of the Committee and to put at its disposal a given amount of their own forces' (Article 59). Every 'tributary' group was to include no more than fifteen people (Article 63) and was to have in turn other centres depending on it. The 'allies' were considered to be only an expedient and accepted only when they could not be dispensed with.

In the second place there were to be 'fighting groups' sub-divided into those 'dependent on the Committee', 'allies' and 'temporary'. Naturally the first of these categories was preferred, and was to be made up of elements of the Committee, agents and outsiders (in a minority). They were 'obliged to carry out all terrorist actions indicated by the Committee, and at the time of the political revolution are to appear together as a whole at the request of the Committee' (Article 65).

The statutes laid down that an 'Administration' consisting of five members and three candidates was to be elected. The choice of this governing body already had a certain political flavour, and tended to exclude those who did not represent general opinion. Morozov was not elected, probably so as to show that his purely political, radical interpretation of terrorism was not fully accepted. Nor was Zhelyabov made a member; at Lipetsk he had already played a leading rôle, but he still had to be absorbed into the group which he now joined. Mikhailov represented the element which had been most consistent in supporting within *Zemlya i Volya* itself those new political ideas and new forms of organization which had now triumphed. Frolenko represented the Southern tradition and the living link between the 'rebels' and *Zemlya i Volya*. Tikhomirov, despite some opposition, was also elected as the movement's ideologist.

The division of labour which already existed within the ranks of *Zemlya i Volya* was reproduced within the Executive Committee. Morozov and Tikhomirov were confirmed as editors, and others took over responsibility for the first practical step concerning assassinations, etc.

The third and last meeting of the Lipetsk assembly [said Morozov] was devoted to discussing the society's future activities. During the course of it Alexander Mikhailov made a long speech attacking the Emperor Alexander II . . . This was one of the most powerful speeches that I have ever heard, even though Mikhailov was not a natural orator. He recalled and gave a clear sketch of the positive side of the Emperor's activities; he referred to the peasant and judicial reform. He then went on to describe his reactionary steps, among which he gave first place to the sub-stitution of the dead languages for living science in the schools, and a series of other laws drawn up by his ministers . . . He said that during the second part of his reign, the Emperor had nullified nearly all the good that he had allowed the progressives of the 'sixties to accomplish under the blow of the defeat at Sebastopol . . . He ended this remarkable speech with a detailed account of the political persecution of the last few years, during which there passed before our eyes the long ranks of young men banished to the tundra of Siberia for love of their country, the suffering faces incarcerated in prison, and the unknown tombs of those who had fought for liberation. And he ended by asking: 'Must we forgive, because of two good deeds carried out at the beginning of his reign, all the evil that he has since done and will do in the future?' To this everyone present answered with the single cry of 'No'.[45]

When the Lipetsk gathering came to an end everyone who had taken part went to Voronezh for the general meeting. Only Goldenberg failed to go. His presence at Lipetsk had already aroused some surprise. He was known to be a man incapable of formulating any political programme, and anxious to make himself appear important. Yet he had assassinated Kropotkin, the governor of Kharkov, and had volunteered to replace Solovev in the plot to kill Alexander II. Motives of terrorism had prompted him to be invited among the founders of the Executive Committee. Now, however, he was not considered suitable for the second meeting which was to be more political in character. It was this obvious weakness and unreasonableness which later led him to denounce all his comrades, when he was arrested.

On the basis of the decisions which had been reached at Lipetsk, the Executive Committee was now faced with two alternatives. 'Either the Populist organization recognized the need to fight against the State', said Mikhailov, 'in which case it would assume the burden of carrying the struggle to a conclusion. Or, if this were not so, it would become necessary to split up the two organizations.'[46] Instead, a compromise solution was reached which kept *Zemlya i Volya* alive (though more or less only in form), for some months more.[47]

A number of different groups attended the Voronezh meeting. There were, first, Plekhanov and Popov; then there were Aptekman and Tishchenko, the 'provincials' of the first *Zemlya i Volya*, who had allied themselves to the 'troglodytes', who were the product of Lavrovism and propaganda in the South. Mikhail Vladimirovich Debel and Alexander Abramovich Khotinsky who had remained in the 'colonies' of Saratov also came to the meeting. Other members were expected from the 'colonies', but they thought it better not to relinquish their posts and entrusted their votes to Popov and Preobrazhensky, who were on the side of the 'country folk', though they themselves came from St Petersburg. Others from the capital were Isaev, who was allied with the terrorists, and three women, Vera and Evgenia Figner and Sofya Perovskaya, whose main purpose was to fight for the unity of the movement.[48]

When the meeting took place on 24th June, it was at once obvious that there was a general feeling of repugnance at the idea of a break. Plekhanov was the only man who openly raised the question of terrorism. He read out the article that Morozov had published in the *Listok Zemli i Voli*, and asked in shocked tones, 'Have you heard me? Is this your programme?' But contrary to what he had expected, no one else shared his indignation. The real 'country folk' were few, and even they were well aware of the problems that had forced their comrades to abandon the villages: how could they continue slow penetration among the peasants while the reaction grew increasingly powerful? The others proposed to include the new ideas in the old programme. And so Plekhanov's attack was greeted in silence, and in the short discussion that followed no one supported him. He 'got up and left the meeting . . . "There's nothing more for me to do here", he said as he went away.' Vera Figner, who reported this, added that she got up to hold him back, but Mikhailov told her 'Let him go'.[49]

With the removal from the scene of the man who represented the extreme wing of the 'country folk', any prospect of a schism seemed over. This was even more than Mikhailov had expected. Thinking that he would be faced with a hostile meeting, he had decided on a break. Now, however, a compromise seemed to be advantageous, for it would serve to attract all the more active elements into the Executive Committee. This is in fact what happened. Vera and Evgenia Figner and Sofya Perovskaya, the very women who were most keen on agreement, went over to *Narodnaya Volya*.

The programme of *Zemlya i Volya* was read out, article by article, and left unaltered. Zhelyabov particularly insisted on the need for a political fight, as he had already done at Lipetsk. Years later his ideas were summed up by Tikhomirov as follows:

The function of the social-revolutionary party does not include political reforms. Such reforms ought to be exclusively the task of those who call themselves liberals. But here in Russia these people are utterly impotent. Whatever the reasons, they are quite incapable of giving Russia free institutions and guarantees for rights of the individual. Yet such institutions are so indispensable that all activity becomes impossible without them. And so the social-revolutionary party must take on itself the function of destroying despotism and giving Russia the political forms within which a 'struggle of principles' will become possible. And so we must make it our immediate goal to put freedom on solid foundations and for this purpose to unite all those elements who have shown themselves capable of political activity.

This account (given by Tikhomirov) of Zhelyabov's ideas is probably accurate enough. At Voronezh it earned him the title of 'pure constitutionalist'. To this he replied violently that his opponents were 'indeed fine revolutionaries'.[50] But he too agreed to endorse the old programme of Zemlya i Volya, on condition that the party continued to base itself on the popular masses and the peasants, and not on the more or less liberal elements of the bourgeoisie. Like all the others, he was still a convinced Populist, but he wanted to be a revolutionary. He wanted to make use of tactics and manœuvres to open the way for a 'fight of principles'. This was why he gave a clear political interpretation to terrorism and wanted to embrace an immediate objective— the destruction of absolutism.[51]

The formula concerning 'the elimination of those agents of the government who are harmful to the organization' was replaced by one that gave terrorism a more obviously offensive goal, thus opening the door for anyone who planned to carry on where Solovev had left off. When put to the vote, a suggestion to plan the assassination of the Tsar was carried, though it was understood that the problem of principle implicit in such a move would remain an open one and would be discussed at a future meeting. This was a temporary compromise, but it clearly showed on whose side political initiative and the desire for action were to be found.

A decision was reached on the future distribution of funds which seemed, however, to put in doubt the victory that Mikhailov had obtained. A third of the funds at the disposal of the revolutionaries was to be used to support terrorist activities, while the rest would be assigned to work among the people in the countryside. But when accounts were settled at the time of the schism, it became clear that even this decision had been a concession to the terrorists. From 31st October 1878 to 14th August 1879 Zemlya i Volya had spent 5,994 roubles 95 kopecks. Of this only a quarter had gone to terrorism, though it was true that the St Petersburg centre had absorbed a third of the total sum, even without the funds for secret lodgings, clothes, etc. When it came to the point, it was found impossible to grant the 'colonies' the two thirds laid down at Voronezh. An active centralized organization by its very nature easily absorbed most of the petty funds at Zemlya i Volya's disposal.[52]

The election of Frolenko, Mikhailov and Tishchenko to the 'Administration' clearly reflected the results at Voronezh. The new tendency had a majority. A 'countryman', who was not even one of the leaders, represented the 'orthodox'; Tikhomirov and Morozov were to continue as editors and were later joined by Tishchenko.

By now *Zemlya i Volya* might well seem reconstructed and reorganized. At the last session, however, three new members, returned émigrés, appeared to bring unhoped-for support to those policies which had been absorbed and neutralized rather than defeated at Voronezh. These were Stefanovich and Deych, the two leading inspirers of the Chigirin conspiracy, and Vera Zasulich. Their intervention soon showed how unstable was the balance that had been reached after the discussion on fundamental issues had been left on one side. Their joining the 'country folk' showed in fact that the question was not whether or not arms should be used (after all, the first two were rebels, and Zasulich had been responsible for starting the wave of terrorism) but whom they should be used against: those responsible for the repression or the Tsar himself. It was these extreme 'rebels' who did not accept the line later adopted by *Narodnaya Volya*. They insisted on the need for economic terrorism to be closely linked to the immediate agitation and demands of the people. This terrorism should be inspired by revenge, by protest, by the need to protect the revolutionary organization, perhaps even by plans to 'disorganize' the central authority. But it should not, because of this, concentrate all its forces against the head of the State. Here, at last, was a programme of action which seemed to offer a real alternative to the Executive Committee. The 'rebels' said that they had hopes of being able to resume work at Chigirin by picking up the threads of the abortive peasant insurrection. Now, they said, there would be no need to resort to false manifestos and false agents of a mythical Tsar imprisoned by the nobility. Experience had taught the peasants to count only on their own forces and those of the revolution.

This programme—which when it came to the test proved to be a vain hope—induced many of the revolutionaries, once they were back in St Petersburg, to reassert the point of view that they had abandoned at Voronezh. Popov, who had not followed Plekhanov at the Congress, now insisted on a break, and tried to organize the faction which was later called *Cherny Peredel*.

In St Petersburg the discussions lasted two months. In the provinces they were less lively. Sometimes there were none at all. Far from the centre the main desire was often to keep the whole of 'the social-revolutionary party' united. In the capital this state of mind merely meant that the schism took place in a friendly spirit. Cordial relations were maintained between the respective comrades and reciprocal help promised in the fight which was still a common one. But from the political point of view it was obvious that their roads were now different. On 26th August the Executive Committee formally condemned Alexander II to death. On 12th September it proclaimed itself 'a secret society entirely autonomous in its activities'. It only remained to divide the legacy of *Zemlya i Volya*.

Maria Konstantinovna Krylova, who was responsible for the printing press, declared for the 'country folk'.[53] And so they took over the old printing machinery and prepared to start a new periodical, the *Cherny Peredel*. The other organizers and type-setters went over to the innovators. Sofya Ivanova and Nikolay Bukh, supported by Zundelevich and Mikhailov, were able to found a masterpiece of efficient clandestine technique providing the Executive Committee with a new and perfect printing press.

It was decided to divide the funds into two equal parts. The money involved, however, was little enough, for Lizogub had been hanged before he had had the chance to hand over his property. It proved to be far more important to look for new supplies than divide what little there was in hand. Here, too, the 'terrorists' soon showed their greater resolution and cunning. It is true that the greatest attempt made at 'expropriation' during the summer had been a failure. After managing to make a tunnel under the Kherson treasury and seizing the coffers, they had not been able to hide the money quickly enough, and it soon fell into the hands of the police.[54] But various sources made up for this: there was a secret fund specially destined for acts of terrorism, which Lizogub had handed over to Zundelevich; money was brought in by the Yakimovs, and subscriptions proved to be comparatively large. Clearly the political slant was meeting with some response and increasing the Executive Committee's opportunities to take action.

It was agreed that neither of the two sections should use the old name *Zemlya i Volya*. One of these groups now adopted as its symbol the fundamental demand of the peasants that all the land should be divided up equally and that it should be partitioned among the labourers who had been serfs and classed for centuries as 'blacks' (i.e. slaves) because they did not belong to the so-called privileged classes. This group, therefore, called the party's organ *Cherny Peredel* (Black Partition). The other group wanted to emphasize its determination to fight for the realization of the will of the Russian people, so that after the destruction of absolutism it might at last become the master of its fate. They therefore called the political organ of the Executive Committee *Narodnaya Volya* (The Will of the People).

It was said that of the old name *Zemlya i Volya*, the land remained with the first group, the freedom and will with the second. It was one of those polemical contrasts like 'country folk' and 'townsmen' which both concealed and revealed the complexity of the political problems involved in the schism. But this play on words itself emphasized that the break had now gone deep and was final.

Cherny Peredel was born under an evil star. An attempt was made to resume contact with the peasants round Chigirin but it soon became clear that the police were on the alert and that the repression had left serious scars in the villages. Though some of the victims had shown a desire to carry on the fight when detained in the prisons of Kiev, an atmosphere of anxiety and fear reigned on the spot. Besides, in St Petersburg itself, the energy required to resume the long and difficult work in the 'colonies' could no longer be found. The central group remained in town, devoting itself to propaganda among the students and the intelligentsia. But even here one failure followed another. Very often the groups they succeeded in forming went over to the side of *Narodnaya Volya*, where the fight was more lively and the political prospect wider.[55] And in January 1880, scarcely four or five months after the schism, the central body itself, of about twenty or perhaps fewer members, suffered a severe blow. A traitor put the police on to the group's printing press, which was seized while the first number of the *Cherny Peredel* was being published on 29 January 1880. On 5th February the traitor was killed by the revolutionaries but the blow had been too severe, and the movement proved unable to survive it. Once again the leaders emigrated. 'It can be said that, with the departure of Plekhanov, Stefanovich, Deych and Vera Zasulich, the party was liquidated' as Aptekman rightly pointed out. There remained those members who were still dispersed in the provinces, above all Popov, who was extremely active at Kiev. But he was working for a re-unification with the local members of *Narodnaya Volya*, and his policies in the working class movement and the revolutionary organization did not contribute any really specific factor. This tendency towards unity found further expression in the attempt that Akselrod made during 1881 to restart *Zemlya i Volya* in Kiev. About this we know little except that it was one of the last steps taken to try and galvanize *Cherny Peredel*. The second number of the review had to be printed abroad; and though the third was once more published on Russian soil, its repercussions were few.[56] The fourth and fifth again had to be printed in Switzerland,[57] and in 1881 Stefanovich too joined *Narodnaya Volya*.

Though *Cherny Peredel* did not succeed in taking root as a revolutionary organization and though not much took place under its auspices, this does not mean that the ideas that it represented were lacking in interest or historical importance. Far from it.[58] It was like a shadow that followed *Narodnaya Volya*, a sort of Cassandra which pointed out its limitations, shattered hopes, and impractical visions. Its very insistence on 'orthodoxy' and continuity, its appeal to resume work among the people whatever the circumstances—all this ended in the long run by establishing a link between the Socialist preaching of the 'seventies and a resumption of the movement in social-democratic form during the subsequent decade.

Cherny Peredel began by maintaining that even ideologically it was essential to go back to origins. It was not enough for its members to reassert solidarity with the ideas expressed in the five numbers of the clandestine organ of *Zemlya i Volya*. Rather they must return to the Bakuninist sources of Populist thought. The 'federalist' element which had been overshadowed by the rise of new political problems, the contrast between the peasant masses and the State, memories of Stenka Razin and Pugachev—all these had been characteristic of the early stages of the movement and now returned in the pages of the new review as an open reproach to those who had deviated from the principles and the emotional fervour of the movement 'to go to the people'. Plekhanov wrote in the first number of the *Cherny Peredel*:

According to us, the inner history of Russia consists only in the long tragedy-filled tales of the struggle to the death between two forms of collective life which are diametrically opposed: the *obshchina* which springs from the people and the form which is at the same time statist and individualist. This struggle becomes bloody and violent like a storm when the masses are in movement during the revolts of Razin and Pugachev. And it has never stopped for one moment, though taking on the most varying forms.[59]

Even now the struggle was still a living one. It was not for nothing that Makov, the Minister of the Interior, had thought it necessary to distribute a circular to explain to the peasants that there would be no re-partitioning of the land, that the State did not, in fact, intend to go on with a *Cherny Peredel*. This great hope had always been alive in the heart of the peasants. They shook their heads and said that it had been the same before emancipation: the State had said that it intended to maintain serfdom, and yet serfdom had come to an end. So now, land hunger and the unfair distribution of fields would also come to an end. The only real revolution that the peasants demanded was an agrarian revolution. The revolutionary party could not and must not have any other goal. It was not for nothing that Makov himself had attributed these rumours in the villages to Populist propaganda. But the minister was flattering the Populists; they had not been as successful as that. On one point, however, they must admit the justice of what he said: the *raison d'être* of Populism lay in this widespread, deep-rooted desire of the Russian peasants.

In a *Letter to my ex-comrades* published in this same first number, Aptekman deduced with characteristic ingenuity that the conflict between the two tendencies could be summed up as follows:

One of the two sides put all the emphasis on the war with the government, which it considered to be the problem of the day; while the other, through a reaction, which was natural enough in the circumstances, absolutely denied the need for an immediate war of this kind and was convinced that all forces should be concentrated in the people. And so the debate was based on a question of principle: You propose giving first place to the political, we to the economic war.[60]

But though Aptekman was prepared to stop at this contrast between politics and economics, Plekhanov was not satisfied. The road, he felt, led nowhere; or, rather, it was going back to where they had started from. Assuming this position, therefore, meant moving backwards, even from the points he had made in the *Zemlya i Volya*! He had adopted Marxist sociology and was convinced that economics were at the basis of every problem. When he analysed the situation, he spoke in economic terms. But how did the situation in the Russian countryside appear when seen from this point of view, leaving aside the mythology of Razin and Pugachev? He said:

The present situation of our agriculture, with its predominance of extensive farming, does not favour collective exploitation of the fields. The instrument most in use is the plough which, as is well known, can be employed only by a single labourer. Sub-division of work is impossible given the use of such tools; nor would cooperative work increase produce. We must find the solution to the problem, which may seem strange at first sight, as to why our peasants, who are used to organization by *artels*, do not apply this principle to work in the fields . . . Socialization of agricultural work can be a natural consequence of property based on the *obshchina* only when a certain level of agricultural technique has been reached.

Plekhanov was here merely repeating an argument that had always been raised by the Populists: the move from the *obshchina* to an agricultural collective would be accompanied by the introduction of machinery and a transformation of the technical level of the countryside. The Russian Fourierists and Chernyshevsky had already spoken of this. But this point was leading Plekhanov to different results, because he was looking more and more at the situation in the West. There, capitalism had brought about the socialization of production; there the transformation of labour which the Russian *obshchina* was unable to carry out had occurred in the factories. Was it not, perhaps, 'capitalism itself which prepared the road to Socialism and was its indispensable precursor?' He remained convinced that in Russia the road could very well be a different one: i.e.—that of a development along Socialist lines and not that of the capitalist dissolution of the *obshchina*. He was still, in other words, a Populist; but a different road was more and more clearly coming into view.[61]

Until now the victory of the State has been complete. It has enclosed the people within the iron circle of its organization. By making use of its prerogatives, it has been able to stifle not only all risings of the people, both large and small, but every manifestation of its life and thought. It has put its heavy hands on the Cossacks; it has maimed the *obshchina*. It has made the people pay for what has always been its own, i.e. the land, and has demanded a fee which is even greater than the price of the fields. Labour as a whole is dominated by the State. The land hunger that it has created by seizing the people's property has given rise to that crowd of manual workers artificially snatched from their houses and fields, which constitutes the labour in our factories and workshops. It imposes heavy taxes and thus compels the peasant to find extra work with which to pay them. In this way it forces the peasant to submit to economic exploitation. It supports the *kulaks* and the capitalism of the extortioners in the villages, thus undermining the forms of the people's life in those very places which are most dangerous to it.[62]

His examination of the relations between the various forces as they then stood in Russia thus led him to pessimistic conclusions. In the age-old struggle between State and peasants, it had been the latter who had got the worst of it. It was impossible for the Populists really to penetrate into the world of the peasants. And the forms of communal property would scarcely be able to develop along Socialist lines on their own, without the intervention of different techniques and policies. The vitality of the *obshchina* was one of ideal rather than of fact. The State was intervening more and more in peasant society which was splitting up internally. The *kulaks* and capitalism were developing under the protection of the State. Such, then, were Plekhanov's conclusions. But were not these the very reasons that were driving the members of *Narodnaya Volya* into political warfare? Were not these the reasons that had suggested that the State was the enemy to be destroyed, and destroyed at once, for otherwise it would become more and more unlikely that Russia could develop along non-capitalist lines? Were not these the very reasons that had led them to reconsider Tkachev's Jacobin ideas?

To see instead, as Plekhanov did, an essential importance in economics could only mean accepting the natural development of events. It meant, too, a refusal to provoke the break that *Narodnaya Volya* wanted, and the submission to a longer-term struggle, or rather, to propaganda and Socialist agitation while capitalism developed at increasing speed.

His sociological outlook had prepared him for this conclusion: 'Nature does not jump', he used to repeat. Even when he stressed that it was essential to be radical, he saw this radicalism purely in economic terms. 'The revolutionary must be able to generalize the individual causes of popular discontent and bring them to the common denominator of an economic revolution; he must give support to the resolution and energy of the masses who protest. How far this will succeed in each single case it is impossible to foresee; the masses are not always equally ready for a radical solution of their own problems', he concluded in the second number of the *Cherny Peredel*.[63]

And so the concessions made by the *Narodniki* to 'popular demands' now came to the fore again: but this time in the form of a long and systematic study and acceptance of the economic needs of the masses.

In the third number of the *Cherny Peredel*, which came out in March 1881, at the same time as the assassination of Alexander II, Plekhanov wrote a letter summing up his conclusions: 'If the people's forces are not organized and their consciousness and autonomous activities are not stimulated, then even the most heroic fight put up by the revolutionaries will prove advantageous only to the upper classes, i.e. for those very strata of existing society against which we must arm the disinherited working masses. The liberation of the people must be the work of the people itself.'[64] He had already made it clear that this translation of Marxist formulas into what was still a form of Populism, implied the recognition of an urban, working class content. 'The agrarian problem is the central factor in the revolution in Russia. But while we carry on our work, Russian industry is not standing still. Poverty snatches the peasant from the land and drives him into the factories and workshops. The centre of gravity of the economic problem is shifting towards industry.'[65]

He now drew the political inferences from this situation. He repeated that it was necessary to make a stand against the constitutionalists, but he added that 'an organized class that fights for economic liberty cannot support political slavery', and that the revolutionaries must therefore win those elementary rights that would allow them to regroup and become aware of their own strength. 'We attribute the greatest importance to organizing the people's forces. In this way we are choosing a road which may be long but which is sure . . . It demands not momentary and gigantic impulses, but a concentrated and inflexible energy.'[66]

At Voronezh Plekhanov had abandoned his comrades and repudiated the idea of political terrorism. Now this policy was bearing its full fruits. His refusal to accept the 'now or never' of the Executive Committee had put him on the road that was to lead him to a position of social-democracy. By 1881 he had still not reached this conclusion—and this was only because he still retained many elements of Bakuninist and federalist 'orthodoxy'. But these were now reduced to formulas, to the tired repetition of well-worn themes. Obstinately, almost pedantically, he countered the idea of the *Zemsky Sobor* (the assembly of the Russian land) with the formula of federalism. He rejected the idea of a policy of Socialism to be carried out by an advanced party, and appealed instead to the peasants and workers to seize the land and factories. He opposed the idea of State centralism, which was gaining ground in *Narodnaya Volya*, and proclaimed instead the right of all the nations that made up the Russian Empire to dispose of their own fates.

All these elements constituted the capital that had been accumulated by the Populist movement for many years. They remained indeed fundamental for the future development of Russia, but here in *Cherny Peredel* they were like scattered limbs that lacked a central system. They had no political prospect. In other words, Plekhanov was countering the synthesis of *Narodnaya Volya* with the elements from which it had arisen and which it was trying to absorb and unite around a single centre. It is true that in the course of these attempts *Narodnaya Volya* finally emptied them of their content; for it was making use of them purely as the weapons of its political policies. 'We are living on capital', Zhelyabov once said, and this was indeed the case. *Narodnaya Volya* wanted an immediate success, and in its will for a revolution it was spending the capital of ideas, passions and hopes that had been stored up by the Populist movement. *Cherny Peredel*, on the other hand, was trying to retain and perpetuate this capital. But it was not destined to succeed. For political ideas cannot be preserved in this way. When he took stock, Plekhanov himself realized that though his adversaries might have spent their capital, his own cash in hand was rapidly losing value. So he left Populism for Marxism. The experiences he had been through left him with a certain tendency to 'orthodoxy' and a sociological approach to political problems which lent weight to his social-democratic ideas.

While Plekhanov was passing through this ideological development, his comrades, likewise, were going through a political evolution. The *Cherny Peredel* was never tired of repeating that this was not the time for an insurrection, and that neither the revolutionary party nor the people was ready for this. True, the economic situation in the countryside was deteriorating and hopes in a social revolution were widespread. But this did not mean that the peasant masses would support revolutionaries in their struggle against the central power. The revolutionaries would be compelled, even if successful, to act on their own and to carry out the revolution from above. Such would be the result of putting political functions before social ones and concentrating efforts on 'conspiracy' rather than the organization of the masses.

Even when the battle had been won, and a National Assembly could be summoned, the great majority of representatives would (contrary to the expectations of *Narodnaya Volya*) be made up of the privileged classes and would act in furtherance of their own interests. 'You are relying on agitation at the time of the elections', said Aptekman, addressing himself to his ex-comrades in the first number of the *Cherny Peredel*. 'You are counting on deputies to represent the peasants. Such hopes are vain and this is the reason: when the revolution from above takes place, the people will be taken by surprise.'[67] Akselrod repeated this again in 1881:

The people is unorganized, not just as a mass, but even as regards its most active elements. The consciousness of the people has not been affected by revolutionary work. It is not in any way ready for political revolution. The crowd of get-rich-quick business men, still in their peasant blouses or already wearing the townsman's jacket, educated and uneducated alike, will soon organize themselves and will constitute a weighty foundation for an intelligentsia of their own . . . If we go on completely ignoring the people, this prospect seems to me to be so inevitable that, if it becomes a question of choosing between political inaction and centering all our efforts exclusively on the privileged classes, Socialists should in my opinion choose the first of these policies.[68]

In other words the fundamental danger of what *Narodnaya Volya* was doing was this: its isolation from the people would lead to its replacing the State rather than destroying it. 'The policemen of the Imperial department will be replaced by the policemen of the *Zemsky Sobor*, and "order" will be re-established to the satisfaction of all who are interested in preserving it.'[69] In the long run the revolutionaries would be working only for the triumph of the bourgeoisie and capitalism. Even 'Robespierre and Danton', said Aptekman, 'did not give their lives for the people, but for the one and indivisible republic, i.e. for the old principle of the State'.[70]

If, therefore, as Akselrod and Plekhanov maintained, political action was dangerous in any case, or if, at best (in the opinion of those who were too close to the *Narodnaya Volya* in St Petersburg to be able to escape its fascination), it could only indirectly 'educate' the masses, then only one course remained: to devote themselves entirely to organization, and to prepare for a slow development, in which Socialism would be the goal—and no longer the economic aspect of an immediate revolution capable of diverting the natural course of society and the State.

These ideas were frequently drawn up in broad outline. The second number of the *Cherny Peredel*, published in September 1880, printed a 'Programme of the North Russian Society of *Zemlya i Volya*', probably written by Akselrod. In April of the following year, a second version, the 'Programme of the Popular Party' was published as a leaflet. The leading article of the third number of the review commented on and paraphrased this second version.[71]

The authors reaffirmed their Socialist-federalist principles, and then emphasized the 'agrarian revolution' and the equal redistribution of land. They knew that this was not in itself Socialist in character, but they immediately added that 'it would constitute a stage towards the transformation of society on Socialist lines'.[72] Plekhanov had already stated that this programme represented a minimum in respect of the functions and demands of Socialism, and that it would be 'the starting point for agitation among the people'.[73] The 'Programme of the Popular Party' established this idea that it was 'a first step towards reaching the final goal'.[74] Hence there arose that clear distinction between a minimum and maximum programme, which was to be characteristic of social-democracy, and the sub-division into successive phases of a movement that *Narodnaya Volya* wanted to keep united in a single Socialist and Populist, economic and political nexus.

Cherny Peredel still retained its hopes in a peasant revolution; but it was willing to consider, though reluctantly, the possibility of 'a constitutional movement'. Should this take place, their duty was to 'make use of the natural excitement that would accompany it to weaken the people's faith in the significance of peaceful and lawful moves. For example during the electoral campaign the "party" too might present its candidates with its own social-revolutionary programme. The reaction of the vast majority of parliament would serve to illustrate the claim that the people's only hope lay in revolution'.

This faith in the capacity of disappointment to educate, which was so maximalist in character, was however tempered by an increasingly careful study of the problems of the workers. 'In view of the fact that the desire to revolt is not so widespread among them as among the peasants, agitation on the basis of individual causes of discontent (such as strikes, wage problems, working hours) must be considered specially important.'[75] The 'Programme of the Popular Party' also considered this problem and concluded:

As regards the urban workers, a considerable portion is made up of a mobile element which has not yet succeeded in definitely establishing itself in the towns and differentiating its own interests from those of the peasants. At given intervals, this portion of the workers emigrates from the towns back to the countryside and *vice versa*. All its thoughts and hopes tend towards the fundamental idea of the peasant masses, i.e. land and liberty. The party must make use of these workers as a powerful tool with which to act on the consciousness of the peasant masses and as a weapon for creating an organization aimed at them. On the other hand, the other portion of the urban workers has already differentiated itself from the peasants as regards its interests and ideals. This social stratum, because of its size and the strategical significance of industrial and administrative centres, constitutes a very considerable force in the general mass of the Russian people. Agitation and organization must be accompanied by the introduction among these men of the broad ideal of collectivism. To do this we must make use of the limited claims which are beginning to make themselves felt.[76]

This detailed account of the development of *Cherny Peredel* may have served to throw more light on the specific and original element contained in *Narodnaya Volya*.[77]

By the end of 1879 the Executive Committee had managed to set its hand to a terrorist operation in the grand manner and at the same time provide it with a political basis. Three numbers of the review came out one after the other as from October. Between 2,500 and 3,000 copies were printed, and they had a wide circulation. Through them, the 'fighting organization' which had been created at Lipetsk assumed the features and importance of a party. The Executive Committee and *Narodnaya Volya* always remained one and the same body from the point of view of organization. But by thus publicly affirming its ideas and directives, the wing that had broken with *Zemlya i Volya* lost the character of a group of terrorists, and became instead the most active force of revolutionaries in Russia.

In January 1880 the press which had printed the first three numbers fell into the hands of the police and the review had to be temporarily suspended. It was replaced till the end of the year by three 'leaflets of *Narodnaya Volya*'. These summed up the political situation but had no room to discuss ideas. The fourth number of the review came out at the end of December, and the fifth at the end of February 1881, just before the final and successful attempt to kill Alexander II. In these issues the ideas that had led the Executive Committee to this decisive clash were discussed more fully than in the first issues, but brought no important change to the programme, whose essential features had been determined since 1879. *Narodnaya Volya* continued to appear after 1st March 1881, and the last number (11–12), was published in October 1885. But it is not necessary to refer to these last numbers in order to understand the ideas of the Executive Committee. They remained faithful to the original spirit, but tended to crystallize it and to harden its formulas and feelings in a situation which by now had changed. Though it was sometimes expressed with greater precision and clarity after 1st March 1881, the ideology of *Narodnaya Volya* by then lacked that impulsion which had been its source of strength between 1879 and 1881.[78]

The very first number of *Narodnaya Volya* confirmed that Populism had now reached maturity after its long voyage. During that summer of 1879 the passionate discussions within the movement and the constant clash of ideas and tendencies precipitated a process which had long been in preparation. Illusions fled, leaving behind them the energy and force of men determined to act. They wanted to be realistic:

A party which claims to have a future must base itself above all on an absolutely real relationship with life. The most rosy of ideals is not only useless but positively harmful, if by its nature it cannot be realized in life, and consequently deflects forces and labour from a reform which may be less grandiose but which is feasible . . . A party of action must give itself concrete, realizable objectives which are of immediate use to the people. It must choose the most effective means at the right moment.[79]

They looked back to the previous years as a time of rosy hopes and facile enthusiasms. Even shortly before, a prisoner had been flogged in prison and as a result 'there had almost been a revolution. All St Petersburg was agitated, and when Vera Zasulich's pure soul fired on the shame of her Fatherland, the whole of Russia unanimously applauded her heroic action.'[80] But now beatings, shootings, hangings were all taking place in complete silence. They looked back down the years and marvelled at the noble impulse of those who had spread propaganda among the people. Now, their own experiences helped to show that 'it is unfortunately the mark of all our social programmes to indulge in political illusions'.[81] Public opinion was dumb, the battle had become ferocious.

Vast, covered in impenetrable darkness, ahead of us there lies the marsh of Russian life; and far off like some will o' the wisp there float the illusions which seduce the inexperienced to come to a warm, light corner. But these illusions only lead to some cold, dark pit.
Political illusions ruin peoples and are ruining our parties.[82]

And so one real force remained: the revolutionaries themselves, their will to fight, their capacity to make an exact analysis of the situation and to lay bare the roots of public apathy and the mistaken illusions of everyone else.

The Populists were framing this more mature policy while the government's reaction grew in intensity. *Zemlya i Volya* had been formed when it became clear that the revolutionary Socialists would have to shoulder the whole burden of a movement of public opinion which had not been able to find an outlet in organized political opposition. *Narodnaya Volya* had to bear this burden at a time when it appeared that the State had succeeded in stifling the forces of revolution and stabilizing the situation by the vigour of its repression.

But how much strength of purpose was there really behind this reaction? That was the fundamental question. Events would show that this repression had in itself isolated the government, which could now rely only on its own resources. 'We are living in a moment of history that is extremely oppressive, and at the same time extraordinarily interesting for the probable results it will give rise to.'[83] The government's policies were in themselves a confession of its own impotence. By acting as it had done, it had ended by saying:

that in Russia no one respects it, considers it, or thinks it of any use; that the courts—not just those depending on juries but any which show the slightest signs of independence and honesty—are in no position to defend it; that because of the general discontent it is unable to fight against groups of revolutionaries (described in its own words as insignificant) without setting a policeman on every single inhabitant; that any thought, freely expressed and sincerely stated, is infallibly directed against it, and that it can therefore only endure by utterly crushing every thought and destroying any organ which expresses the will of the people, and by a policy of terror. In bringing into effect a whole system inspired by this mission, the government is denying the right of the people to the land, the rights of the towns and the *Zemstva* to administer their own business, the right of any section of the population to take part in government administration. That is the real, the only meaning of all the government's recent steps and declarations, of all the governor-generals, military tribunals, scaffolds and banishments, of Makov's circulars, of clarifications on the administration of the towns and the *Zemstva*, of the temporary regulations for universities and other bodies. Such a moment in history—when the whole of the existing régime with the government at its head openly declares its lack of solidarity with the interests of any single part of the population—is a fatal moment for the State and for all the parties of opposition, and the touchstone of their political maturity.[84]

The important thing was to understand that this situation did not arise from some whim or deliberate wickedness of the Russian State. The State only acted according to its own nature. Under the blows of the revolutionaries, it had shown itself for what it really was.

The Russian State was very different from Western States. How was it possible to describe it as 'a commission of the plenipotentiaries of the ruling classes'? In fact, of course, it was an independent organization, hierarchical and disciplined, 'which would hold the people in economic and political slavery even if there were no privileged class in existence'.

It was a real monster, like those in fairy-stories, which can, they say, only be destroyed by the intervention of divine forces. Political and economic power were both inextricably merged in its fabric. 'Our State owns half Russia as its private property and more than half of the peasants are tenants on its lands.'[85] It was in addition 'the greatest capitalist force in the country',[86] not only because taxation absorbed most of the population's income, but because the system of capitalist exploitation was organized by the State. For centuries the history of Russian industry had only been an application of this principle. Tariffs had allowed industries to arise which could only survive because they were protected. The State had always put its powers at the disposal of private business men, assuring them the profits. 'Whole sets of feudal prerogatives have been created for those who own the mines. For

centuries the peoples of the Urals have been handed over like slaves to the
capitalists, who are unable to manage their businesses even as efficiently as
the workers ran them in Pugachev's time.' The events of the last twenty years
had only confirmed these policies on an even vaster scale. 'The building of
railways in Russia provides a spectacle that is unique anywhere in the world;
they are all built with the cash of the peasants and the State which, for no
apparent reason, hands out hundreds of millions to the various business
men.'[87] 'The pennies of the peasants flow into the pockets of stockbrokers
and shareholders by means of the State treasury.'[88] A few years later
Tikhomirov summed up:

La science économique a une expression, accumulation primitive, qui s'applique
au moment de la vie économique où la richesse provient moins de la *production*
que du vol plus ou moins franc. La classe industrielle russe, il est impossible de
le taire, se trouve actuellement dans cette phase de l'accumulation primitive.[89]

This was the reason why the industrial class was forming an increasingly
close alliance with the State and finding support from it. Such had been—
and indeed still was—the economic function of the State. It was useless even
to recall the part it had played in the spiritual development of the country.
'The history of Russian thought can scarcely provide a single instance of a
man who has contributed to the development of Russia and who (when he
was alive) was not considered to be a State criminal.'[90]

This was the monster which *Narodnaya Volya* wanted to fight. It was
deliberately putting aside the ideological problem—so real throughout
Europe in the 'seventies—of the relations between the Socialist movement
and the State. 'We ask the reader to remember that when we speak of *State*
we always mean the existing Russian State.'[91] How could a Socialist movement, which had to live in a country dominated by such a system of exploitation and oppression, be purely political?

Hence the Bakuninist arguments on the function of the State in Russian
life came to the fore once again. But they were no longer now expressed as
mythological and sociological discussions on the eternal contrast between
the peasant masses and the machinery of government, but rather as elements
in an analysis with a view to action.[92] And indeed, even *Narodnaya Volya*'s
analysis of Russia's social problems and its description of the various classes
of the population sprang from its ideas on the State.

Its spokesmen began of course by considering the peasants. Local administration, the fiscal system, the government's whole policy were, they thought,

literally planned with the aim of generating the *kulak*. An intelligent, energetic
man, who feels the need for a personal life, can find no way of escape if he belongs
to the peasant world. He must either perish with the community or himself become
a rapacious exploiter. As a man of the *mir* he is a wretched creature despised by
all, a man who must put up with everything. As a rapacious exploiter he raises himself to a special category which is not foreseen by the law but which is recognized in

practice. The *kulak-miroed* not only gets the chance to live decently from the material point of view, but becomes a man and even a citizen. The authorities and the priests respect him. They will not hit him in the face, they will not insult his personal dignity. The law begins to exist for him; . . . and so the *kulak* is born. Then the peasant is driven by his hopeless situation to depend on this *kulak*. Whose fault is this? Who else's if not that of State oppression, the economic oppression which the State exercises specially so as to bring the masses down to the level of destitution and at the same time deprive them of any chance to fight against exploitation? Who else's if not that of the spiritual oppression exercised by the State which enforces civil and political misery on the masses and which demoralizes the people and stifles its energies? Remove this oppression, and, at a single blow, you will remove nine-tenths of the likelihood of a bourgeoisie being formed.[93]

Here, too, an analysis of the situation led to the fixing of a political goal. At the same time it singled out the forces which the revolutionary movement might hope to arouse and which in turn would give it support. As will be remembered, Mikhailov had spoken of the peasants whose situation was about average. Zhelyabov too thought that the future of the Russian countryside would lie with these more energetic elements after absolutism had been destroyed and they were no longer driven to exploit their fellows under governmental protection. It was not for nothing that he himself was a peasant by origin.

I know of many intelligent and socially energetic peasants, who today keep themselves apart from the activities of the *mir*, because they have been unable to develop, because they have no strong social ideal and do not want to end as martyrs for trifling causes. They are people who work, who are healthy, who understand the beauty of life, and do not want to be deprived of everything it contains for petty causes. A constitution would give them the chance to act without the danger of becoming martyrs, and then they would energetically set themselves to work. And then they would fashion for themselves a great social ideal, clear and palpable, unlike the present cloudy one, one that would give the impulse for a great cause, and they would stop at nothing. They will be heroes, as the sects have sometimes shown. This is how the people's party will come into being.[94]

Fighting against the State meant opening up this possibility. It meant bringing about the conditions necessary for society to reverse the direction along which it had been moving with growing intensity for the twenty years that had passed since emancipation. The villages had seen the rise of the *kulaks*; the towns of an industrial class. Both had been wanted and brought into being by the policies of the State. United they formed what could be called the Russian bourgeoisie. The bourgeoisie and nobility together (and they were increasingly merging) made up the privileged classes. They too bore the stamp of their origins.

We saw how helpless the nobility was in defending its rights in 1861, and the passivity with which it watched its own degradation and ruin. And now our society is just as weak in putting up with the most revolting tyranny of the administration. Neither the spate of banishments, nor the violation of personal rights, nor its outrageous subjection to the control of police, guards and doorkeepers, has aroused any collective resistance from society. A few miserable petitions, full of servile humiliation: that is all that it has been able to do. We do not mean that society is made up of stupid, timid people, unable to understand or to fight. No; this society has produced the most resolute of opponents, men ready for anything. It has shown itself able to produce as many Kropotkins, Lizogubs, Osinskys, Solovevs as you want. But it has not been able to find the strength necessary to maintain the most insignificant administration or rights. Our wealthy and educated classes are obviously not aware of the fact that they constitute a certain 'position'. They have no idea of communal action, and they recognize themselves to be incapable of carrying this out. Our nobles, merchants and bourgeoisie are only tied to their class by formal links. Men of education and craftsmen alike completely ignore any social problem. And if then one of them suddenly catches a spark of God, he becomes a Socialist and a revolutionary; he refuses to recognize any religion other than the people, its interests and its rights. The same can be said of our embryonic bourgeoisie. Of course, with time, it may become a class, but at the moment where can we find any expression of its class ideas? Where does it show its solidarity, its unity? Nowhere. Only the people, the peasants and the workers, constitute a body that is really united, a body with certain ideals. Only they are able to understand not just what Ivan or Makar or Sidor wants but what they all want as a body.[95]

Naturally this organic weakness of the ruling classes was reflected in the State. The monster, whose economic and political activities seemed so powerful, was in fact devoid of any social content. Its policy of centralization had prevented the rise of any autonomous force in the privileged classes. Its concentration of all powers had stifled initiative. Its system of oppression had crushed thought.

The logic of this analysis led the members of *Narodnaya Volya* to believe that, whatever happened, the State would be unable to find within itself the strength to overcome the crisis which now faced it. It would either try to sink its roots in society by granting concessions, or it would be broken by the revolutionary movement. But whatever happened it could not remain as it was.

Life today is so differentiated that this antediluvian State no longer has the strength to dominate it . . . It is spending more and more of its means to preserve itself. And even now the amount that it drags out of the people scarcely covers its expenses. For some time it has been trying to find support among the people; support, of course, in harmony with its own character—i.e. among the exploiters. In the past it dragged up the nobility but was unable to do anything with it. Now it is trying to get support from the bourgeoisie and like the most zealous midwife it is doing whatever it can to arrange for the little monster of the people to have a happy delivery. This time, naturally, its efforts have been crowned with success, and the bourgeoisie will soon develop.

But even this was a danger for the State. Very soon the time would come when the bourgeoisie would be unable to support the monster that had fed it and which no longer corresponded to what it wanted. The sort of régime the bourgeoisie itself was planning was not difficult to guess.

When it takes over power into its own hands, the bourgeoisie will of course be able to keep the people in slavery to a far greater extent than happens today. And it will find more efficient methods for paralysing our activities than the present government, which is unable to go beyond prison and the gallows.

What, then, should the revolutionaries do? Give up the political struggle and devote themselves entirely to organizing the forces of the people so as to improve its conditions? Or lead the people to a conclusive revolution against the State and the privileged classes? This was the double road, the minimum and maximum programmes between which the founders of *Cherny Peredel* were doubtfully oscillating. Should they then come to an agreement with the State so as to 'crush the bourgeoisie in the bud'? This, said *Narodnaya Volya*, was 'the most stupid solution, devoid of any meaning, not worth even a moment's consideration'. But it may be added that it was an idea that had followed Populism like a shadow ever since its birth, appearing in the most varied guises. It had come to the fore repeatedly in the myths of a Russia immune from the proletariat, and a Tsar who defended the interests of the people against the privileged classes. And it had most recently found expression in Kravchinsky's suggestion that the State should remain neutral in the battle between the revolutionaries and the bourgeoisie.

But these prospects were rejected. Only one was left. It was the most difficult but it was also the only one that responded to immediate tasks: 'the fight against the State, but a calculated, serious fight with a determined goal'. They must strike the State in such a way that it was prevented from handing over power to the bourgeoisie. The revolutionaries must intervene at the very moment when the State had not yet been able to find enough support from the new privileged class, but when the danger that power would fall into the hands of this class was at its height. If the revolutionaries managed to take advantage of this moment, they would be able to hand over power to the people and prevent the Tsar from giving it to the bourgeoisie. But there was no time to be lost. They must act before 'it is too late, while there is a real possibility that power can in fact pass to the people—Now or never; that is our dilemma'. So ended the leading article in the second number of the *Narodnaya Volya*.[96]

Delenda est Carthago! The war against the State would be decisive. Any chance of introducing Populist Socialism would depend on the methods with which it was waged, the ideas which inspired it, and the successes which attended it. The call to arms, the glorification of heroism, the extreme tension of revolutionary endeavour—all these expressed not just the state of mind of a small group of terrorists, but the very basis of their political convictions as derived from their analysis of the situation. They knew that they were isolated, but they knew too that the State was isolated. The bourgeoisie might be behind the State, but behind the bourgeoisie were the Russian people, the peasants and the workers. Their function was to engage in a duel with the authorities. The people would then be able to defeat its own enemy.

Narodnaya Volya thus made the call for an immediate battle one of its leading themes. 'We must fight, we must act. An honest man has now no right to stand aside with his arms folded.' There was no need to point out that the only road open was that of revolution. Experience had demonstrated this.

Social reform in Russia is the revolution. With our existing régime of despotism and complete rejection of all the people's rights and wishes, reform can only assume the character of a revolution. Everyone fully understands this. And this is why our revolutionaries have always had the sympathy of all. The only men against us are those who, consciously or unconsciously, are aiming to enslave the people ... Our cause now is not that of a party but of Russia itself.

Everyone therefore was in duty bound to join it. All this was an attempt to mobilize the intelligentsia, whose sentimental sympathies were with the Populists. The intelligentsia was responsive to the themes of a political fight against absolutism. And so the revolutionaries were launching an appeal to those of its members who were in a position to contribute solid assistance; and the appeal was all the more urgent in that the revolutionaries had no illusions about the possible duration of the war. The 'now or never' which rang like a bell through all their discussions was no longer only an aspect of a tactical problem, as it had been in the controversy between Tkachev and Lavrov. It told men rather that their days were numbered.

We would like all the social party and all the friends of liberty in Russia to look at things directly, without beautifying events and without allowing themselves to be seduced by hope. True, the Executive Committee is carrying out a really heroic fight, and in the midst of the desperate efforts of the government, is managing to develop forces which the State itself could scarcely even have suspected. But the State, too, is not standing still with its arms folded. We repeat, this situation cannot go on for long; either the government explodes or the Committee and all the party will be suffocated.[97]

The passivity of society—the reasons for which the revolutionaries found in Russia's history and position—meant that they had now reached the very limits of their activity. They were asking for help where they knew they would meet with only a very limited response. And so here too they were trying to adopt bold tactics to smash the obstacle which stood in their way, by undertaking activities which would arouse enthusiasm and energy. One aspect of the history of *Narodnaya Volya* was to be the story of the unavoidable conflict between the means that they had chosen—terrorism—and the limitations which this weapon imposed on spreading their movement within the intelligentsia.

This conflict was already apparent in the first numbers of the review, and it naturally increased after a series of unsuccessful acts of terrorism and above all when the consequences of 1st March 1881 became clear.

But there was no way out: it was up to the revolutionaries of the Executive Committee to open up the road. No popular insurrection could be expected shortly; it was useless to wait for the masses to move spontaneously. Nor was there even any hope that the intelligentsia as a whole would give them active support, even though it believed in liberty and was orientated towards Socialism. 'The party must take the initiative of a political revolution on itself.'

Did this mean that they ought to give up their policies based on the fundamental demands of the peasants and abandon the traditions and programme of Populism so as to concentrate all their forces on winning political liberty and a constitution? When *Narodnaya Volya* came into being, some of its members did indeed demand such a policy, and insisted that emphasis should be put more on political than on social radicalism. Morozov and Olga Lyubatovich represented this tendency. They suggested that the Executive Committee should not draw up a new programme, but that the brief declaration already approved at Lipetsk should merely be confirmed. As will be remembered, in this declaration terrorism was urged in the name of William Tell; and the winning of political freedom was said to be the essential, if not the only, aim of the struggle. Three things, however, prevented this tendency from winning the day: the bonds which tied *Narodnaya Volya* to the entire preceding Populist movement were still too strong; the controversy with the 'orthodox' members of *Zemlya i Volya* was still too near; and the new movement was too well aware of the relations that existed between the State and the people. A new programme was drawn up by Tikhomirov, and was accepted after a short discussion. Morozov's brief declaration was not even taken into account. He was left in isolation and soon left Russia for Switzerland, where he tried to give an ideological form to what might be called pure terrorism.[98]

For Morozov's other comrades a 'blow at the centre' meant an insurrection capable of handing over the State to the people. They did not want to give terrorism any theoretical value or to establish a doctrine of 'conspiracy' and 'the conquest of power'. This, they felt, would merely be to halt at one of the stages of a process in course of development. They did not want to follow Morozov, still less Tkachev. Both of these had singled out one aspect, one moment of the fight. To separate these aspects, to turn any particular one of them into the only goal, would be to fall into doctrinaire errors. Once it was decided that at this particular moment all the forces of the revolutionary party should be hurled against the State, the fundamental point had been made. The rest could only depend on circumstances.

22+

In the preparatory phase, they said, 'conspiracy' was an indispensable weapon which must make use of all the means at its disposal to destroy the existing State. For this was its essential function. But *Narodnaya Volya* always refused to make any theoretical choice between the alternatives open to it. Should the war be waged as a series of partisan actions designed to disorganize the power of the State? Or should there be a 'plot' aimed to seize the central power, even perhaps a military *coup d'état*? *Narodnaya Volya* refused to commit itself. If it concentrated its forces on the first policy—though trying to adopt the second simultaneously—this was only because it had to act at once and had no other resources available at the time. It was not just reasons of secrecy which discouraged it from the item in the Executive Committee's programme which concerned the 'organization and achieving of the revolution'. The problem was a technical one; the party had assumed all the weight of the battle at the most difficult moment, and it intended to solve this problem on its own and take full responsibility for its solution.

As for the 'conquest of power', they often repeated that even an insurrection could only be fruitful if it represented 'the first stage in a popular revolution or an episode in it' and that it must therefore be dictated by circumstances.

We will give an example to show more clearly what we mean by the decisive function of the party. We implore the reader not to look upon this example as a real plan of action. Only doctrinaire revolutionaries draw up plans ten years in advance. The true, genuine revolutionary only has one plan; to apply his fundamental idea to circumstances and carry it out according to them. We are giving this example only for the sake of greater clarity. Let us suppose, then, that the party has organized enough forces, and, anticipating a general movement of the people, has seized the central power. What must it then do? Create a new structure for the State and decree the reforms which are indispensable? We say no. Only in the most unfortunate case, only if the body of the people were to show not even a spark of life, could such a step be considered necessary. In normal times the party would be obliged to use the power and means it had won so as to upturn the whole of Russia and to appeal everywhere to the people to realize its century-old demands. It would have to help the people with all its forces and retain control of the central power only so as to help the people to organize itself.

This, then, was how the revolutionaries visualized the 'conquest of power'. This was how they replied to the charges that they had returned to the Machiavellism of Nechaev or the Jacobinism of Tkachev and had betrayed the very spirit of Populism. Besides, they were well aware of the dangers of their position. It evoked a spectre that had horrified an entire generation of Populists, the spectre of a revolution decreed from above, of reforming and revolutionary absolutism in Jacobin guise. The members of *Narodnaya Volya* itself called this 'a despotic Utopia'[99] and they always attacked it.

Indeed the very essence of their function was trying to empty the mythical content from Tkachev's conception of the revolutionary State, to repeat that power itself was and must remain a tool and only a tool. It should be used to allow the people to express itself, to build up its own political consciousness, and become a force capable of acting independently and winning its own rights and forms of communal life. The Populist content of the revolution was still deeply rooted in their minds, it was still blood of their blood, flesh of their flesh. And therefore they could only conceive of the revolution as the conquest by the peasants of their *obshchinas*, and local, independent systems of administration. For them these were not only weapons for destroying local power but the true objectives of an autonomous social and political transformation.

But the same will and energy which now drove them to assume responsibility for destroying the existing system and waging war against the State would certainly not desert them when they finally succeeded in winning power. And this too they understood very well. We have seen that they advanced two hypotheses and claimed that should the worse of these prove true and a spontaneous movement fail to appear, this would not prevent them acting from above in order to transform Russia. At this stage in the argument they were still on the upgrade and only at the beginning of the battle. When blows began to rain and when the horizon became ever darker, this decision to act at any cost, even without active popular support, was emphasized. Their desperate and yet steady revolutionary spirit drove them to write in the eighth issue of the review:

The very fact that our State is the strongest capitalist force in Russia will considerably simplify the solution of the social problem on the day when power is in the hands of the revolutionary party. If circumstances should become less favourable, the provisional revolutionary government will carry out an economic revolution at the same time as it frees the people and creates new political institutions. It will do away with the right of private owners to the land and to the tools of heavy industry. And then the true representatives of the people, freed now of their political and economic bondage, will answer the summoning of the *Zemsky Sobor*. And the life of the people itself will be impregnably based on the will of the people.[100]

The author of this was V. D. Lebedeva, and she was faithfully reflecting the ideas of Vera Oshanina, the member of *Narodnaya Volya* who sprang directly from the Jacobin tradition. In fact, Tkachev's and Zaichnevsky's ideas seemed to represent the extreme position. The revolutionary party would not hand over power to the representatives of the people until the revolution had been achieved. Until that time they would keep it firmly in their own hands and resist anyone who tried to snatch it from them.

The central nucleus of the Executive Committee always clung to these ideas and many of the formulas which we meet in the first numbers of the *Narodnaya Volya* show that they penetrated deeply. But for all that, the

Committee intended to do what it could to make the Russian revolution pursue a different course. Vera Lebedeva herself had said that an economic revolution of this kind, enforced only by the central power, would be the result of hard necessity due to unfavourable circumstances. About this all the revolutionaries were agreed: 'Only in the most unfortunate case, only if the body of the people does not show even a spark of life, would we resort to such a step', Tikhomirov had written. If, on the other hand, the more satisfactory alternative were realized, the *Zemsky Sobor* would have to sanction a political revolution. This was an essential, but not in itself sufficient, preliminary for a social 'upheaval' which would be carried out by the popular masses themselves and by an assembly of their representatives; not by the central power and the party, or, rather, not only by them.

It was now time, the revolutionaries thought, to translate into politics Populism's central tenet: that, in Russia, the survival of the *obshchina* had predisposed the vast masses of the people towards Socialism. On the day when the revolutionary power (or even the old State under the pressure of terrorism and the revolutionary activity of the Populists) appealed to the people and summoned a real *Zemsky Sobor*, (i.e. a constituent assembly which at last represented the peasants), the vast majority of those elected would be Socialists. The free will of the people would thus be expressed by electing deputies determined to carry out 'that social upheaval' which was not 'a despotic Utopia' but the very expression of the whole of Russia's historical evolution.

In a constituent assembly, created autonomously or by a summons from the government, and supplied with the mandates of its electors (such as the *cahiers* of the Assemblée Constituante) ninety per cent of the deputies will be peasants. And if we assume that the party acts cleverly enough, they will belong to the same party. What will such an assembly decide? It is exceedingly likely that it will completely reverse the whole economic and governmental system. We know how the people has always organized itself, wherever it has been freed from government oppression. We know the principles that it developed, on the Don, on the Yaik, in the Kuban, on the Terek, in the sectarian colonies of Siberia, wherever it has been able to organize itself freely and follow only its own tendencies. We know the true password of popular movements. The right of the people to the land, local independence, federation—these are the principles which remain permanent in the people's outlook on the world. And in Russia there is no power other than the State which has any possibility of blocking the road to these principles.[101]

It was the conviction that, in the last analysis, power would remain with the revolutionaries which led *Narodnaya Volya* to launch the idea of a constituent assembly. Kibalchich, for example, said: 'When government centralization has been finally smashed by the wave of the popular movement, what social elements will show that they constitute real forces? Who will govern the course of events? Not the privileged classes, of course, for they are not united. Not the lawful parties, because they are disorganized. Only the people and the social-revolutionary party will constitute those fundamental forces on which the social and State organization of the future will depend.'[102]

Naturally this conception too had its Jacobin aspect: the *Zemsky Sobor* under discussion was really the Convention. The rôle to be played by the party in its relations with it was obviously that of the French Jacobins. But Populism contributed a new element—the spontaneous organization of the people in 'local autonomies'. And the special transformation of Russia was to depend on these. The function of the assembly would be to 'sanction' them and give them not only legal significance but the political significance that they could not assume for themselves. The people would provide the 'principle' on which to found the new society. And there need be no fear concerning lack of energy to develop this principle and give it strength.

We can say that when a revolution breaks out in Russia the talents, the energies and even the egotistical interests of private individuals will be directed to serving the people, exactly as at the time of Mirabeau and Sieyès they acted on behalf of the bourgeoisie. Given the circumstances, only one idea will be found at the basis of the future organization of the State: the idea that lives in the masses. No other idea exists.[103]

This was why the Executive Committee had chosen to adopt the principle of a Constituent Assembly. 'Naturally', its programme stated, 'this is not the ideal form in which the will of the people can show itself. But, in practice, at this moment, it is the only one possible. We therefore consider it essential to adopt it.' They thus rejected both the anarchist policy of destroying the State and establishing a federation, and the extremist plans of Russian Jacobinism: to enforce a dictatorship of the revolutionary party. In actual fact, even Nechaev had spoken of a *Zemsky Sobor*. Even he considered that pure power in the hands of the 'conspirators' would be, if not a 'despotic Utopia', at least a 'Utopia'. Complete anarchism and revolution by decree were two ghosts which never really existed. They merely signposted two opposite extremes between which *Narodnaya Volya* sought its own road. And so its members determined on a Constituent Assembly.

The question then was: What would be the position of the party in relation to the Assembly? The Executive Committee expressly declared its intention 'of submitting to the will of the people'. But this of course would not or could not exempt it from having its own programme 'which it would support in the electoral campaign and defend in the Constituent Assembly'. This programme was as follows:

(1) Permanent representation of the people . . . with full powers on all problems concerning the whole of the State.

(2) Wide regional self-administration to be guaranteed by the election of all the administrations, the autonomy of the *mir*, and the economic independence of the people.

(3) Autonomy of the *mir* as an economic and administrative unit.

(4) The land to belong to the people.

(5) Measures to hand over factories and workshops to the people.

(6) Complete freedom of conscience, speech, press, meeting, association and electoral agitation.

(7) Universal suffrage, with no limitations of class or income.

(8) The standing army to be replaced by a territorial army.[104]

Though not a minimum programme—it included all the essentials in *Narodnaya Volya*'s policies—it was still an electoral programme. But if we want to find out what rôle the party was expected to play in the revolution, we will have to look elsewhere for the answer. This was given by Tikhomirov on the eve of 1st March 1881. He took as his starting point the psychological situation of the peasants.

The man who despairs in his struggle with the natural phenomena which surround him and the generally hostile conditions of life, and feels the need for a beneficent force from above to come and defend him, ends by creating this force. He then turns to this divinity with the firm conviction that it will not abandon him. If he did not have this way of escape, he would have to resign himself to dumb despair and suicide . . . The same process takes place among the peasants, with the only difference that they cannot resign themselves to suicide . . . And so the people's mind and fantasy have created a divinity in the heavens. On land, too, the people seeks support, someone to act on its behalf. This support it finds in the person of the Tsar . . . Obviously we must not look for the source of this faith in the benefits which the Tsars have given it, nor in their historical function. The origin lies, rather, in the circumstances of the people's spirits—the need it feels to have a strong ally in its fight against the enemy. This is an instructive lesson for us. We must create a force which goes boldly forwards to meet the people and we must show that that force is capable of bringing it help.

Such then would be the function of the social revolutionary party: 'to become that outside force which the people needs'. The party was to be the true successor of Stenka Razin and Pugachev, stripping those myths of their outer garments and adapting them to a world 'of railways and telephones'. It had not been founded to arouse small local rebellions destined to be quickly crushed, but to organize a collective force capable of replacing the Tsar; both the authentic one of the day and the usurpers of the past.[105]

Here, too, *Narodnaya Volya* had translated Populist ideology into politics. The great Socialist majority which it envisaged in the future assembly would have behind it a party capable of producing the Pugachev of the nineteenth century.

Tikhomirov's article was followed by one of the few signed works in the *Narodnaya Volya*: 'The Political Revolution and the Economic Problem.' Anonymity was an old tradition which went back to Chernyshevsky and had always been retained in Populist publications, which were designed to represent groups and tendencies rather than individuals. This article, however, was signed by A. Doroshenko, which was naturally a pseudonym. In fact, it was written by N. I. Kibalchich, the technician who had supplied *Narodnaya Volya* with dynamite. It was the most important theoretical article that the review had published, the only one to draw the ideological consequences of the political position assumed by the Executive Committee.

The goal chosen by this Committee, wrote Kibalchich, was more complex than anything in the past.

Together with our fundamental, social-economic objective, we also have to assume that of destroying political despotism. In other words, we have to do what has already long been done everywhere else in Europe, not by Socialist parties, but by the bourgeoisie. For this reason there is not a single Socialist party in Europe which has to wage so oppressive a war as we do and offer up so many victims.

But it was impossible to escape this responsibility. Both the political and the social battle had to be faced. The fight against the State would indeed be 'a powerful means for bringing closer the economic revolution (or at least the agrarian one) and for making it as profound as possible'.

This standpoint brought Kibalchich to the theoretical problem of the value of political institutions for social-economic development. Here the ideas of the Socialists had frequently changed. They could be summed up in three 'typical categories . . . The first was made up of those who thought political institutions were by far the most important. They granted them the force to produce any economic transformation that was wanted, only by using power from above and the submission of subjects and citizens from below.' Such were the 'Jacobins', the 'Statists', the followers of the *Nabat* and Tkachev. The second category, on the other hand, was made up of those Socialists who thought that the political factor was negligible. 'They denied that political institutions had any influence, positive or negative, on economic relationships'. This opinion was held by *Cherny Peredel* (or, rather, part of it, as Kibalchich rightly pointed out).

And finally, there is the synthesis of these two unilateral opinions. This recognizes the close link and reciprocal action of economic and political factors. It claims that the social revolution cannot be carried out without certain political trans-formations; nor, *vice versa*, can free political institutions be maintained without some historical preparation in the economic sphere.

This was the position of *Narodnaya Volya*.

It was useless to counter this view with the theories of Marx, 'who in his *Kapital* has shown that the economic relationships of any country are the basis of all its other social, political, and legal institutions. This has led some people to deduce that any transformation in the economic system can only be the result of a struggle in the economic sphere, and that therefore no political revolution can either delay or start an economic revolution.' But those who interpreted Marx in this way went 'far beyond their master. His thesis is true in substance, but they infer consequences which are absurd in practice.' Kibalchich did not specify the name of his opponent, but he was probably thinking of Plekhanov. He refuted this economic interpretation of Marxism, and referred him to the *Civil War in France* and what Marx himself had said of the Paris Commune. He suggested too that his opponent should think again about what Lavrov, Louis Blanc, Lassalle and Cherny- shevsky had written on the subject. After all, did not the economic trans- formations carried out by the Convention during the French Revolution show that the repudiation of politics was absurd? Was not Russia itself the living example of the importance of the State in economic life?

Our State provides an example of the enormous negative significance that a political system can assume when it remains backward as regards the economic demands of the people. In Europe, political progress precedes the social-economic problem. With us, our ever-oppressive political system puts a brake on the economic, legal and political reorganization, which would inevitably take place were this system to collapse and were the revolutionary initiative of the people given the chance to manifest itself freely.[106]

Kibalchich thus drew up a theory of that 'complete merging of the political and social revolution[107] . . . the utterly indissoluble fusion of the elements of political radicalism and Socialism',[108] referred to by his comrades in other pages of the review. He probably based this theory on the doctrine of E. Dühring. His references to political and economic factors and his positivist language both suggest this source. Tradition also tells us that the men of *Narodnaya Volya* were interested in this writer, who maintained the vital importance of politics in historical development.[109] But this question is only of secondary importance. Kibalchich's synthesis was not the produce of any doctrinaire view. It was rather the fruit of all the experiences undergone by the Executive Committee.

An examination of what was happening in the countryside would, he said, provide confirmation of his views:

Turn your attention to the occasions which have provoked the various peasant insurrections, large and small. They have always been of a political and legal nature. They have always originated within the sphere of the State or the administration: a false Tsar, a usurper, a mythical 'golden charter', some violation of a law (as understood by the people), the example given by an urban revolt. There has never been a case of a village or land revolting without an extraneous reason, or without having some example to follow. No village has ever revolted merely because it was hungry. In order to revolt, the people must either be conscious that its rights have been violated, or have hopes in the success of an insurrection. Naturally, the fundamental condition of nearly all these popular revolts has been material suffer- ing. But the actual occasion has always been some violation of the law (real or false) by the authorities, or a revolutionary initiative taken by an organized nucleus close to the people and its interests.

This conclusion was important, for it marked the final defeat of the mentality of the 'rebels'. And at the end of his article Kibalchich named the one organized association which could provide an 'occasion' for a peasant revolt. He said:

Today neither the *Raskolniki*, who have lost most of their former fighting spirit, nor the Cossacks, who represent a privileged class when compared to the peasants, appear to be able to give the signal for a popular insurrection. Only the social-revolutionary party, which has strong roots in the urban and working classes and which has gained a firm foothold among the peasants, can constitute the ferment which is indispensable for provoking a movement in the town and countryside.

Peasant movements would be crushed too easily by the government, and could not therefore act as foundations. The signal must come from another source:

In view of the greater development and mobility of the urban population, and the larger numerical results obtained there than in the countryside by the party's activities, it appears that the first signal for a revolution will come from the town and not from the village. But once success has been achieved in town, this will raise the banner of revolt for millions of starving peasants.

These discussions on the relations between the economic and political 'factor' had not been useless. They had clarified *Narodnaya Volya*'s ideas on the rôle of the party towards the State, the people and the National Assembly of the future. They had led to a greater part being given to the town than to the countryside and, even, from now on, to the factory workers than to the peasants. This was the conclusion to which the Executive Committee was led by the eighteen months of warfare that preceded 1st March 1881.

The first phase of the Committee's activities, in the autumn and winter of 1879, saw the adoption of terrorism as the supreme goal of all its efforts. It will be remembered that Alexander II had been sentenced to death on 26th August and plans to put this decision into effect had already been made. The Emperor was at Livadia in the Crimea and it was assumed that on his return to St Petersburg he would travel by sea to Odessa and then go on by rail. Alternatively he might take the train that passed through Kharkov and Moscow. It was therefore planned to mine the track at three points.

The dynamite was already prepared, but as there was not enough, the revolutionaries had to carry it around from one place to another and travel more than should have been necessary. Though this was not the reason why their plans failed, the constant movement gave the police the chance to lay their hands on Goldenberg, and he finally told them all he knew about the revolutionary organization.[110] It is, however, true that none of the Executive Committee's nerve-centres was damaged by this confession for some time, and this gives us some idea of the high level of technique that had now been reached.

The three points chosen for the dynamite were Odessa, Alexandrovsk and Moscow. The Odessa trap was organized by Kibalchich, Kvyatkovsky and Vera Figner, who laid the foundations, and by Kolodkevich, Frolenko and Tatiana Lebedeva, who prepared to carry it out. At first they considered

22*

putting the dynamite directly under the tracks not far from the town, but very soon they realized the practical difficulties that stood in their way. The solution was found by Vera Figner. Elegantly dressed as a society lady, she visited the head of the local railway system to ask him to employ 'her porter whose wife suffered from tuberculosis and needed good air outside the town' as a guard. In this way Frolenko and Lebedeva (who were naturally soon given false passports) became signalmen about a dozen *versts* from Odessa. Everything would have gone perfectly if Goldenberg had not come from Moscow for some more dynamite, and above all, if they had not begun to have doubts that bad weather would compel the Emperor not to take the sea route and come to Odessa by boat. This is in fact what happened, and so it was necessary to cancel the undertaking.[111]

The second trap was organized by Zhelyabov. He went from Kharkov—which had been chosen as headquarters for the three ambushes—to Alexandrovsk, a small town on the railway line between the Crimea and Kharkov and called at the town hall with a passport guaranteed by an imaginary Yaroslavl merchant. He asked and obtained permission to open a small business, and then summoned two workmen who were friends of his, Ya. Tikhonov and I. F. Okladsky. He was helped by Presnyakov, Kibalchich, Isaev and M. V. Teterka.

Zhelyabov was inimitable in his work as a merchant manufacturer. Besides, he liked his new fellow-townsmen, and was interested in these descendants of the Cossacks of the Zaporog, among whom were some whose names were those of famous leaders of the past. He made friends with them quite sincerely, he ate and drank with them and meanwhile he applied himself to his job. Later, he was often amazed that he had not been blown up with all his comrades. Along the roughest roads, they used to sit on the dynamite in a simple cart, and even then they would drive the horses for all they were worth. And to think that the books say that dynamite explodes when shaken![112]

These men dug a hole under the railway line, and hid two cylinders of explosives there. On 18th November they were ready to detonate them. 'Okladsky lifted up the two hidden wires which led to the mine, and handed them to Zhelyabov. As the Emperor's train passed above the explosive, there was a shout of "Fire!" and he joined the wires. But for some unknown reason the explosion did not take place, and the Emperor's train passed by these criminals without anything happening. Immediately afterwards they left Alexandrovsk.'[113] So read the accusation in 1882. An inquiry was made by the members of *Narodnaya Volya*, and it was found that Zhelyabov had made a technical mistake in assembling the electrical battery which was to set off the spark.[114]

The third attempt in this series designed to blow up the Emperor was made on the following day, 19th November. It very nearly proved successful. Alexander Mikhailov had bought a house adjoining the railway line, three *versts* from Moscow station. For this he had paid a thousand roubles, and had then mortgaged it for six hundred. The expenses for this base were not therefore very heavy. Lev Gartman and his 'wife' Sofya Perovskaya had gone to live there with false passports. They then claimed that the house was in need of fundamental repairs, and used this excuse to get rid of the tenants. After this, they began to dig a tunnel leading from the cellars to the railway line. Besides Lev Gartman and Sofya Perovskaya, the others involved in this operation were Mikhailov, Isaev, Morozov and later Shiryaev, Barannikov, Goldenberg and Aronchik. The work proved long, difficult and tiring, but when the time came everything was ready. The execution of the venture was entrusted to Sofya Perovskaya and Shiryaev. They knew the approximate time that the train was due to pass, for the Emperor was supposed to reach Moscow between 10 and 11 in the evening. So when he heard a train coming rather too early for this schedule Shiryaev thought that it was only a testing coach 'which sometimes preceded the Imperial carriage'. He therefore set the battery as a second train passed through. This was derailed and destroyed. But it was soon learned that it contained only Alexander's servants and retinue. The Emperor had reached Moscow unharmed.[115]

On 20th November at the gates of the Uspensky Sobor, within the Kremlin, the Emperor told the representatives of the various classes who had come to pay him homage that 'he hoped with their collaboration to divert erring youth from the ruinous road along which they were being driven by ill-disposed elements'.[116] The impression made by the news of the attempt on his life soon showed whether such hopes were justified. The *Narodnaya Volya* maintained that there had been a certain apathy, a remarkable coldness even in Moscow, 'neither emotion nor anger, or even any special interest'.[117] Whether or not this claim was true (official sources, of course, said quite the reverse) it none the less showed what the revolutionaries thought of the position. Lack of success must not discourage them; the duel with the authorities must be continued.

Besides, though so far their plots had not met with success, neither did the government have much reason for satisfaction. For a year it had pursued a policy of terror; the governor-generals had imposed a state of siege; every precaution had been taken, yet the Executive Committee emerged virtually intact from its first and threefold battle. Only Gartman, the owner of the house adjoining the railway line, had to flee abroad. Despite great pressure, Russia was unable to get France to extradite him as a common criminal.[118] In November, moreover, the police were still unaware that there had been two other similar plots besides the one at Moscow, and they knew very little about the other terrorists. The organization had stood the test.

This did not, of course, mean that the battle had become any the less bitter or that sacrifices had grown fewer. A few days after the explosion at Moscow, Kvyatkovsky was arrested in St Petersburg. His comrades heard from their disguised agent in the Third Section that his house was about to be searched when it was already too late to take action. When Olga Lyubatovich went to warn him, the police were already in the house and only her own cunning and that of her husband, Morozov, enabled her to trick the police and escape in safety. Kvyatkovsky, however, was caught. The police also found explosives and a mysterious plan of the Winter Palace with a cross marking one of the rooms. He always denied that it was his, and it was some time before the police discovered the significance of the plan. But when the attempt was made to blow up the Winter Palace, Kvyatkovsky had to pay the price. He was included in the 'trial of the sixteen', and sentenced to death. About a year after his arrest, on 4th November 1880, he was hanged. Vera Figner's sister, Evgenia, who lived with Kvyatkovsky, fell at the same time and was sentenced at the same trial to fifteen years' hard labour in Siberia. She only returned to European Russia in 1900.[119]

At the end of 1879, Zundelevich, the tireless 'technician' of *Zemlya i Volya* and *Narodnaya Volya*, and the founder of their various clandestine presses, was arrested. On 4th December 1879, S. G. Shiryaev fell into the hands of the police. His part in the Moscow plot was revealed by Goldenberg and he was sentenced to death in October 1880. The commutation of this sentence to hard labour for life merely prolonged his existence by about a year. On 18th August 1881 he died of consumption in the Alexeyevsky dungeon in the Peter-Paul fortress.[120]

Even if no consideration were given to the possible loss of whole groups in the future, this process of attrition must have ended by rapidly exhausting the Committee. Its members knew that they were saying no more than the truth when they wrote in their review, 'Either the State will explode or we shall'.

In January 1880 it was the turn of the press. It had been organized by Kvyatkovsky and Mikhailov. Nikolay Bukh and Sofya Ivanova, using passports that declared them to be husband and wife, had taken rooms which were ideal from the conspiratorial point of view. They were in a central part of the town, inhabited by thoroughly respectable people. This family of 'officials' naturally had a servant, who was in fact a student, Maria Gryaznova. 'She acted her rôle as cook to perfection . . . Her value lay in the fact that she did not look like a conspirator, and behaved like an ordinary mortal.'[121] The printing equipment was arranged in such a way that it could easily be hidden. The rooms had a completely innocent air and they contrived to exhibit them in this state as often as possible to their neighbours, etc. Two printers lived in the same house. They had not declared their residence and were therefore obliged to hide themselves and remain indoors. One of them, Abram Lubkin, came from the press of *Zemlya i Volya*; the other, Leyzer Tsukerman, had arrived in St Petersburg at the end of September 1879. 'He was a Jew from the western regions of Russia. His family was so bound by Jewish prejudices, and he had lived in such bad conditions, that in his earliest boyhood he had fled abroad, where he had spent half of his life. He had no means, had become a compositor, and had worked in the

German presses and those of the Russian émigrés. But he wanted to return to Russia, and when he was invited to come to St Petersburg and work in a clandestine press, he had no need to think twice, but left at once.'[122] Zundelevich had arranged his clandestine journey across the frontier.

It was a small piece of carelessness that led to the discovery of the press. A house belonging to one of the members of *Narodnaya Volya*, who had nothing whatever to do with the press, was searched by the police. During their investigations they discovered, among the many false documents and other materials of the kind, a model passport which had been used for practice in forging one for Bukh. This document, which the revolutionaries had forgotten to destroy, contained the name under which Bukh was inscribed in the police register. When it fell into the hands of the police they did not think it very important. An inquiry was made as a matter of routine, without much hope of discovering anything serious. To avoid disturbing the Third Section, this job was entrusted to the municipal police. Hence Kletochnikov, the revolutionaries' spy, knew nothing of it and could not warn his comrades.

On the night of 17th January 1880, the bell of the flat was violently rung and woke all the inmates. Sofya Ivanova did not open the door, but began instead to collect all the papers, which after a long process she successfully managed to destroy. The others engaged the police in an armed battle.

The rooms were in complete darkness. The reason was as follows. We had agreed that should a search be made, we would break the panes in all those windows which could be seen from the road, so as to warn our comrades who were to come to us . . . We carried out this arrangement with such good-will (trying to break even the ribs of the windows) that the wind in the flat blew out all the lamps.

The police went to the military for help and attacked the barricaded revolutionaries. After firing to the end, they all went to one room and decided to surrender. Abram Lubkin went off, said farewell to the others, and committed suicide with the last bullet; the other four were taken to the Peter-Paul fortress. But on the next day Mikhailov was warned by the broken windows and consequently managed to avoid the close supervision kept by the police on the flat and all round the house.

At the 'trial of the sixteen', Zundelevich was sentenced to hard labour for life and Nikolay Bukh and Maria Vasilevna Gryaznova to fifteen years. All three survived. In 1906 Zundelevich was able to return from Siberia and emigrate to England, where he died in 1924.

Narodnaya Volya later managed to set up another printing press. But at the beginning of 1880 this was not its main concern. For it had already prepared another great plot, which, if successful, would make up for its failures to blow up the Emperor's train.

In September 1879 a cabinet-maker went to the Winter Palace, the Emperor's residence in St Petersburg, and was taken on as a workman. The false passport he produced concealed his real name, Stepan Khalturin. This was the man who had founded the *Northern Union of Russian Workers* with Obnorsky, and who had been one of the most active and intelligent members of the working class movement in the capital. He knew his trade to perfection, and was proud of it; he had already given proof of his ability when repairing the Imperial yacht. The collapse of the working class organization which he had founded, and the obstacles which the police and government oppression put in the way of any trade union development, had now led him to terrorism. One day while at work he met the Emperor alone in one of the rooms of the palace. For a moment he thought that the best solution would be to kill him with his axe. But his comrades in *Narodnaya Volya* persuaded him to adopt a different plan. This was to put a sufficient quantity of dynamite under the ceiling of a room which the Emperor used to frequent. Kvyatkovsky was told to keep in contact with Khalturin and provide him with explosives. After Kvyatkovsky's arrest, Zhelyabov took his place. Meanwhile, the mysterious plan of the Winter Palace, which had been found in Kvyatkovsky's house, had aroused the suspicions of the police and they began to keep a careful watch. But Khalturin was one of the regular staff, and he lived in a dormitory in the cellars of the palace itself. And so when he came back to the palace in the evenings, he could bring in the dynamite bit by bit in a basket. Searches were made, but proved fruitless. Meanwhile the dynamite was methodically stored up next to Khalturin's small folding bed. In the evenings he used to discuss with Zhelyabov how much would be required. Zhelyabov thought that it was important to press forward the execution of the plot without too much delay, fearing that the police would sooner or later succeed in laying hands on Khalturin. Besides, the revolutionaries wanted to restrict the number of victims which the explosion would inevitably produce. The problem now was to put the dynamite and fuse in place without being seen. Each evening Khalturin went out, and passing next to Zhelyabov he would whisper: 'It's not been possible', or 'Nothing'. But on the evening of 5th February he told him: 'It's ready.' Very soon a tremendous explosion confirmed his words. A room was blown up, and eleven people were killed and fifty-six wounded. The Emperor was in the dining-room, just above the scene of the explosion. The room was severely shaken, but not nearly enough for the floor to collapse. When Khalturin heard that he had not been successful, 'he never forgave Zhelyabov for what he called his mistake'.[123]

The wildest legends soon began to spread; some even said that the conspiracy had been organized by the Court. The first *Listok Narodnoy Voli* to appear after the explosion said:

We hold it necessary to say that this famous carpenter who is so much talked about is in fact a workman both by origin and by craft . . . He finds newspaper gossip that he is an aristocrat by origin extremely disagreeable, and he has asked the editors of the *Narodnaya Volya* to confirm the fact that he is of pure working class stock. We are happy to fulfil this request.[124]

Khalturin had stood next to Zhelyabov in the square in front of the palace and had watched the mysterious and terrifying results of his work. He was then taken to the rooms of one of the conspirators, and thus escaped detection.

For the fourth time Alexander's life had been put in danger, this time in his own residence. And still the revolutionaries were at large. The Executive Committee had become a threatening and powerful force. The government itself had helped to create this halo of glory and danger, by issuing an official communiqué that the assassination was to be the signal for an immediate revolution. For some days patrols marched through the streets of St Petersburg, and a state of siege was imposed.

This time, political consequences were inevitable. There was no one to punish, as there had been with Karakozov and Solovev. Pathetic speeches were no longer enough, as after the explosion in Moscow. Yet something had to be done.

The political crisis of February 1880 is of great interest, if we wish to understand the limits within which the revolutionary movement was compelled to fight. These limits it tried heroically to destroy by using terrorism; in the end, however, they constituted the impregnable barricade against which it was shattered.

In many ways the crisis was very like the one that was to open about a year later, after the successful assassination of Alexander II. Again, some of its fundamental features are similar to those of the crisis which began in 1861 after the peasant reforms, and which ended with the outbreak of the Polish revolts. In each of these three crises, in 1861–63, in 1880 and in 1881, the reaction of Tsarism followed an inner logic which was latent in its structure. The problem was this: to encourage the most educated, progressive classes in Russia to participate in the life of the State; to insert the developing forces of the bourgeoisie within the political as well as the administrative and economic sphere and to find a place for the intelligentsia within the framework of absolutism. Each time, autocracy began by thinking of more or less constitutional reforms, and by drawing up more or less plausible plans for consultative assemblies. And each time, under the impulse of some revolutionary event such as the Polish revolt, Khalturin's dynamite or Sofya Perovskaya's terrorist activities, it was forced to realize that these plans were all dreams, that the circle could not be squared and that only one solution remained: to give direct satisfaction to some at least of the demands of 'society' by using the tools of absolutism itself. And so autocracy continued in its own way; the intelligentsia remained extraneous and hostile; the people, distant and repressed; and the revolutionary movement more and more convinced that only the complete destruction of the State could lead to true reforms in Russia. And so a new cycle opened again.

In 1879, then, as the revolutionary movement developed in power, the Tsar was advised to create some organism for including the representatives of public opinion within the administration of the State—though only on the fringes and as little as possible. On this occasion, the advice was given by Valuev, one of the very few intelligent men among the high officials of the time. He took out from his files the memorandum that he had already presented to Alexander II in 1863. It now seemed relevant once more. At the same time he wrote in his diary: 'Everything is going to pieces, every-thing is going to the dogs. One feels the earth shaking, the building is threatening to collapse, but people do not seem to be aware of this.'[125] It was no longer enough to appeal to public opinion for help. There was no point now in trying to frighten it, as had been done at the 'trial of the hundred and ninety-three'. The State had not found the support it had asked for; the intelligentsia did not seem to be terrorized by the 'red peril'. The only thing to do was to summon from the provinces some representatives elected by the Zemstva and include them in the Council of State. This would mean a Zemsky Sobor, reduced to its narrowest limits, and a constitution 'which did not give the least genuine rights to the representatives from the provinces'. Yet in order to produce even this, Valuev himself thought that the State edifice would have to suffer still greater shocks. He argued—it is worth noting—very like the men of Narodnaya Volya, though of course from the diametrically opposite point of view. 'Perhaps, in order to move to a different order of ideas and events, it is necessary that the earth should tremble even more beneath our feet.'

This was the conclusion he had come to at the end of January 1880. By now his 'constitutional' ideas, after frequent ministerial discussions in the presence of the Tsar, had been rejected and put back in the archives. Some support, though conditional and hesitant, had come from Constantine Nikolaevich, the Tsar's brother. He, too, had once again produced an old memorandum of 1865 in favour of a consultative assembly. But the other councillors who had been summoned to examine these plans had been hostile. The discussion had been very muddled, and personal jealousies and conflicts had naturally joined the fears and prejudices of these great bureau-crats. Valuev's estimate of one of these men could have been applied to all: they were merely ruminating on the ideas of the 'sixties, trying to find some spark from the time of reform, trying to grasp at any foothold which might give the State the chance of action.

Despite their vagueness, the arguments used during the debate explained how this situation had been brought about. Valuev said that the steps he had proposed were important chiefly because they were designed to 'restrict the passivity of the majority of right-thinking people and give the government itself the chance to counter-attack and refute the revolutionary principles which were being preached everywhere.' His leading opponent, the heir to the throne and future Alexander III, replied that they ought to do nothing, as the representatives of the social classes who would be summoned under the proposed constitution would only be 'incompetent chatterboxes, lawyers, etc.' In vain everyone swore again and again that 'le mot constitution ne devait même pas être prononcé'; in vain Constantine Nikolaevich proposed that lawyers and any other body professionally associated with the law courts should be excluded from the future assembly; in vain they recalled the differences between Russia and the West. The dilemma between Valuev's and the Crown Prince's views remained unresolved: to repose (even the smallest) trust in elected representatives or to regard them as useless chatterboxes.

Despite its extremely primitive form, the discussion was not without historic interest. Anyone who planned any step, however slight, in the direction of liberalism, did this only for a Machiavellian purpose: to try and snatch forces from the revolution, to allow the State to resume the offensive, and to break up the prevailing apathy. These arguments were repeated exhaustively during the last years of Alexander II's reign, both inside and outside the Winter Palace, in newspapers and in ministerial sessions. In the last analysis, it was this tactical game, this concern with a double purpose, which weakened the 'constitutionalism' of the time, for it was always compelled to show itself 'right-thinking' and indeed *plus royaliste que le roi*.

And even in this guise, constitutionalism could not be accepted by absolutism. Absolutism might reform from above, but it had no intention of creating any autonomous body, even if only for consultative purposes, for this inevitably ran the risk of becoming an organ of opposition. The heir to the throne had a good hand, and he ended by winning the game when he said that the representatives of the *Zemstva* would end by opening their mouths and pleading some cause other than that of absolutism.

All this was merely an extremely vulgar form of the same debate which had been conducted—on a far more highly developed and subtle plane—by the revolutionaries. Some of them too had thought of the orthodox liberals as potential weapons, without having any real faith in them; while others objected that a constitution would only help to reinforce the governing classes by giving legal sanction to their economic and social predominance.

Besides, it was not by chance that the two debates had these common features. The problem that they each had to solve was the same: the political apathy of the whole of Russian society. Until that was broken, the duel still involved only the autocracy and the revolutionaries.

Ten days after the ministers had finished their discussions on the 'constitution' the explosion in the Winter Palace made 'the ground tremble even more beneath their feet'. The future Alexander III, who maintained the doctrines of absolutism, loudly proclaimed his victory.

The discussions of the preceding weeks had leaked out among the public. It was said that a constitution was to be granted on 19th February, the 25th anniversary of Alexander II's accession to the throne. The foreign press reported these rumours, and even the *Narodnaya Volya* spoke of them. There followed, instead, Loris-Melikov's 'dictatorship of heart and mind'. The heir to the throne had no difficulty in showing that this only involved

a rather better organization; it was not a radical change in the régime. When
the Tsar had summoned his ministers, the opinions expressed 'had introduced
nothing new. They remained within the sphere of those half measures which
had already been proposed by the ministers during earlier sessions. Everything possible, they realized, had already been done to fight the subversives.
Governors-general had been appointed, and given almost limitless powers;
the authority of other governors had been reinforced; all political criminals
had been handed over to military tribunals; all the springs of the most
rigorous police supervision had been brought to their maximum tension.
What remained to be done?' As usual, an educational reform was suggested.
But that could hardly be considered adequate at that particular juncture.
Constitutional plans had been rejected. Now, said the heir to the throne,
they must realize that 'the fundamental evil, the main hindrance to the
government's putting any real force into the fight against the subversives,
did not lie in a lack of measures—there were already more than enough—
but in disagreement among the various departments and lack of solidarity
among them.' Everything must be put under the control of a single leader,
to be responsible to the Tsar for re-establishing order.[126] What was required,
in fact, was not a series of concessions to 'society' but a more efficient
organization of the absolutist régime.

The man chosen to carry out this programme was the governor-general of
Kharkov, Loris-Melikov. His first task was to concentrate the various rulings
that had been piling up as the repression grew more severe. He had to overcome a number of obstacles. Even once he was in charge, the other governor-
generals still kept a wide range of autonomy and his authority was most
effective in St Petersburg. Yet despite this strong resistance from entrenched
positions, he eventually found himself at the head of a Ministry of the
Interior which was stripped of its many cumbersome accretions and capable
at last of exerting control over the various police forces. The Third Section
passed under his control and changed its name. The police in the capital took
their orders directly from him. It became obvious that many of the methods
which had so far been used to enforce the repression were utterly inadequate.
Loris-Melikov not only concentrated the services of public order, but
modernized them and made them more rational.

The porters who had been recruited by the police to act as spies cost more
than a million roubles a year in the capital alone, and had produced no
result. They merely irritated the population, without discovering a single plot.
Loris-Melikov therefore dissolved this body of porter-policemen. The
system, which was extensively used for suspects, of imposing special supervision, had merely tampered with the personal liberty of a large number of
people, without in fact putting any brake on the revolutionary movement.
It was a bureaucratic abuse whose only result was to drive the more decided
members of the public into becoming 'outlaws'. The files of the Third Section
recorded 6,790 people supervised for political reasons, and 24,362 for other

causes. Loris-Melikov made no change in the substance of the system, but ordered the files to be carefully revised. Banishment had been so much abused that it was said that the organization of exiles 'would soon become a State problem'. Here, too, some limit had to be put on the arbitrary methods of the police, by separating the more dangerous figures from those who had been sent to exile without justification. The hesitation of the government in choosing tribunals for judging State criminals, and the slowness of inquiries, meant that hundreds of people had to wait in prison sometimes for years on end before being tried. When Loris-Melikov came to power, 197 people were in this situation in St Petersburg alone. The 'dictator' tried to speed up the judicial machinery. Searches had become extremely frequent, and were carried out with arbitrary and illegal methods. He insisted that here too some order should be established.

As will be seen, all these policies were aimed primarily at perfecting the system of repression by avoiding useless irritation to the public. This was to be done by isolating the revolutionaries and striking at them, and, if possible, only at them. In Loris-Melikov's own words, he was trying to 'show the power of the State, and detach the hesitant from the revolution'.[127]

The new minister, however, could not be satisfied with merely being more efficient than his predecessors. Even government circles clearly understood, as the discussions on the 'constitution' had shown, that a political problem lay behind the problem of public order. It was not for nothing that Loris-Melikov's rise to power had been accompanied by talk of 'a dictatorship of heart and mind'. The 25th anniversary of Alexander II's reign, with its ceremonies and speeches, seemed almost specially designed to recall that the reasons for the existence of the revolutionary movement were far from superficial. First there had been the peasant reform; this had then been followed by the administrative and judicial reforms. But as soon as the intelligentsia had requested that the 'edifice be crowned' with a constitution, the process had come to a halt at the very bounds beyond which absolutism seemed incapable of going. Very cautiously, with a full expenditure of bureaucratic phraseology, Loris-Melikov pointed out to the Tsar that there was only one way out of the impasse: the reforms must be resumed. After taking all the precautions necessary, he must let himself be guided by the spirit that had inspired his government in the 'sixties. It was essential, in fact, that Alexander II should himself carry out the reforms that public opinion was expecting from its elected representatives.

This attempt to seek inspiration from earlier years was only an illusion. We only have to read a list of the reforms suggested by Loris-Melikov to realize how relatively unimportant they were, and how incapable of affecting the heart of the political problem. It was necessary, for instance, to raise the moral standard of the clergy and so some steps were taken in this direction, but they only handed over control of the Holy Synod to Pobedonostsev, the man who became the mainstay of Alexander III's obscurantist régime. It was necessary also to 're-establish the relations between managers and workmen'. Later, indeed, some working class legislation was passed in Russia; but the motives that drove Khalturin to carry dynamite into the Winter Palace would scarcely have been affected by it. Tsarism showed itself unable even to give freedom to the *Raskolniki* until 1905.

There was much to be done; autocracy still had many transformations to undergo; but in 1880 the central problem remained that of giving some rights to the emerging ruling classes. Loris-Melikov wrote memoranda to say that no advance must be made along constitutional lines: 'Such steps would seem to be taken under the pressure of circumstances; that is how they will be interpreted both in Russia and abroad.' Public opinion would be satisfied with concessions made from above, by attempts not to irritate it, and constant appeals for its collaboration against the subversives. 'I am convinced that Russia is today living through a dangerous crisis and that it can be rescued from this only if the Tsar shows a determined autocratic spirit. Today, as after the Crimean War, which left Russia in an even more tense situation than the present one, all attention, all the hopes of thinking and loving Russians are turned to Your Majesty's sacred person.'[128] 'To trust' public opinion, but not to give it any rights; to control the government machinery (even to send 'inspectors' into the provinces as in the time of Nicholas I), but to change nothing essential, let alone interfere with the principle of autocracy: such was Loris-Melikov's plan.

It can be understood why the conservatives accused him of 'playing for popularity' and that he was often judged to be 'more an actor than a statesman'. The game of appearing to be liberal without taking any step to establish liberal rights, seemed to them risky and dangerous in the presence of a revolutionary party, which though it might be small in numbers nevertheless had a clear picture of the situation and was determined to use arms. But for one moment, six months after he had taken power, Loris-Melikov deceived himself into thinking that his game had succeeded. He had, he thought, stabilized the situation.

Then he was once more caught up by the train of events. He too, like Valuev in 1863 and 1879, began to speak of a 'constitution' and to make plans for admitting deputies from the town *Zemstva* into the Council of State. Once again a revival of reforms gave rise to the demand for some organization of liberty, however limited in scale. To proceed along the road which had been opened up in 1861 became impossible unless those 'chatterboxes and lawyers', fear of whom had brought him to power, could be given some share in the administration. Loris-Melikov, too, was once again going through the cycle of Alexander II's absolutism. And once more the game was interrupted by an intervention of the revolution. On 1st March 1881 *Narodnaya Volya* carried out its sentence of death on the Emperor, and liberal plans collapsed for an entire generation.

Faced with Loris-Melikov's policies, the Executive Committee did not hesitate, even though, on his accession to power there was a moment's pause, as though the explosion in the Winter Palace had forced the government to make some concession. The revolutionaries had known Loris-Melikov ever since he had been governor-general of Kharkov. The *Narodnaya Volya* had already spoken of his 'astute and double-faced' policies, and his 'semi-liberal phrases' which had made the comfortably situated inhabitants of Kharkov call him 'an angelic soul'.[129] But when, on 20th February 1880 a young man, whose name was later found to be Ippolit Osipovich Mlodetsky, unsuccessfully fired at Loris-Melikov, the Executive Committee did not accept responsibility for the plot. They honoured Mlodetsky's memory when two days later he was hanged; they called him a 'social-revolutionary', but they made it known that his action had been entirely personal.[130]

Pure love of truth was not the only motive that prompted the Executive Committee to make this declaration. More probably the reason was one of political logic. *Narodnaya Volya* intended to concentrate all its terrorism against the Tsar. It did not want to deviate from this plan, or to allow its political campaign to be diverted. Loris-Melikov was only a product of existing circumstances, of the duel between the revolutionaries and the authorities, and it was not up to them to kill him. Their task was to continue along the way they had chosen, noting the effects of their activities on the 'dictator'. 'It will be interesting to see if he is able to keep his balance between the two stools for long.' Would he succeed in 'dividing the liberals from us' and winning over the sympathy of the students by making concessions? The Executive Committee was ironical at Loris-Melikov's expense. He 'intended to divide the radicals into two factions, one more dangerous and the other less dangerous, and he was beginning to protect the more peaceful revolutionaries'. But the revolutionaries could not avoid seeing that his manœuvres were dangerous.

At bottom it's by no means a stupid policy! To concentrate the forces of the government; to divide and weaken the opposition; to isolate the revolution and to stifle all his enemies in turn—all this is by no means stupid. Will the policies of the Armenian diplomat succeed? [The 'dictator' came from Armenia.] This will naturally depend on the amount of intelligence and civic sense that the Russians possess. Loris-Melikov's policy is entirely based on the stupidity and selfishness of society, of the young generation of the liberals and of the revolutionaries. We very much hope that his calculations will prove to be mistaken.[131]

To reply to these tactics, the revolutionaries deepened their relations with the intelligentsia; they not only showed it that in Russia the only reform could be a revolution, but, above all, they made specific bonds with its most vital representatives. They called on these to join, if not the Executive Committee, at least *Narodnaya Volya*, which would thus become the political and intellectual fighting core.

But in this field they met with only comparatively limited success. They soon had to admit that the revolutionary party aroused admiration rather than active support. The very clarity of the revolutionaries' standpoint, and the maturity which they had now reached, discouraged all hesitant and sentimental forces. The mixture of white terror and flattery which was at the basis of Loris-Melikov's policies, made it even more difficult to choose 'the narrow way'. Virtually the only man, other than professional revolutionaries, to collaborate with *Narodnaya Volya* was Mikhailovsky. He wrote two articles which echoed the views of the Executive Committee in somewhat vaguer language, though he made reservations on some important points. He was the only well-known publicist on whom they could count, the only one to whom they could turn for inspiration and support.[132] This situation showed how much things had changed from previous years. Populism had been born under the inspiration of 'those teachers of life', Chernyshevsky, Dobrolyubov, Lavrov. Now it was the revolutionaries who were expressing the clearest ideas and who were creating those theories of which 'legal Populism' was only a weak echo.[133]

In view of these objective difficulties which prevented intellectuals joining the revolutionary group, some members of the Executive Committee tried to make their opinions known in the legal press and to write in the great reviews which influenced the more advanced public opinion. In 1881 Tikhomirov published a few articles in the *Delo* and the *Slovo*. He sometimes signed these with the initials I.K. which, as was whispered in well-informed circles, coincided with the seal of the Executive Committee (*Ispolnitelny Komitet*). In 1880 and 1881 Kibalchich published some articles in *Mysl* and the *Slovo* under the pseudonym Samoylov.[134] Others made great friends with Gleb Uspensky, the leading Populist man of letters of the time.[135] There was always a divan in his house on which they could pass the night when the fortunes of battle deprived them of any other refuge, and it was there that they met to wait for dawn on 1st January 1881 and to welcome in the new year. Among his most constant visitors and friends were Zhelyabov, Kibalchich, Perovskaya, Vera Figner and Tikhomirov.[136] Their terrorist activities aroused profound admiration and sympathy in the minds of other writers and men of letters. Garshin threw himself at Loris-Melikov's knees to try and save Mlodetsky's life; Shelgunov, Chernyshevsky's friend and one of the survivors of the 'sixties, followed them with bated breath and a determination to act for their common ideas as soon as the opportunity presented itself.[137] And other names could be added to the list. But there were never more than a few. The intelligentsia as a whole did not stir and was not up to making itself heard on those aims which were common to it and the revolutionaries (freedom of press, meeting, etc.).

Narodnaya Volya, like all earlier Populist movements, tried to appeal above all to the young intelligentsia and the students, hoping to find in them the energy and revolutionary enthusiasm which it had not succeeded in arousing in the educated class as a whole. In St Petersburg University Zhelyabov founded a group which was allied to the Executive Committee.

Some young recruits from these circles soon became professional revolutionaries and were given delicate assignments involving conspiracy and terrorism. But it proved to be impossible to create a new wave of the student movement, or to arouse strikes and protests. *Zemlya i Volya* had still been able to find a place in a great university agitation; *Narodnaya Volya* tried in vain to provoke one. Loris-Melikov had anticipated the revolutionaries. Count Tolstoy, the hated Minister of Public Instruction who represented the classicist reaction, had been removed in April 1880 and replaced by Saburov, a man of more liberal principles and broader views. Some of the revolutionaries suggested making an attempt on his life and thus striking a representative of the government's 'hypocritical policies', but this plan was soon rejected.[138] Instead they decided to foment an incident, in the hope that this would arouse a general movement of all the students. On 8th February 1881 the minister was presiding at a solemn ceremony in the University of St Petersburg. An account of the academic year was being read out to an audience of four thousand, when suddenly a student called L. M. Kogan-Bernstein began to shout: 'We will not allow ourselves to be cheated by the government's lying policy. They want to stifle us with deceit as well as with violence. Saburov will soon find someone in the intelligentsia itself to avenge it.' In the middle of the turmoil aroused by these words, a student called P. B. Podbelsky came up to the minister and gave him a slap on the face. Meanwhile, in the back of the hall, Zhelyabov, Vera Figner and other members of *Narodnaya Volya* tried to heat up the atmosphere. But the demonstration was only half successful. Many protests were made against the men who had disturbed the ceremony and insulted the minister. Five hundred students later said that they supported the idea of some kind of protest, but only eighty-two said that they agreed to the form that it had taken. When it described these events, the *Narodnaya Volya* had to admit that there was a strong 'Bonapartist' current in the ranks of the students. It had to admit, too, that 'Saburov's system, which consists only in advice to "wait" and "be reasonable", has begun to demoralize the students and has allowed the young-old men and careerists to make themselves felt'.[139] The 'central university group' which was inspired and controlled by the revolutionaries was soon faced with a right-wing organization, which was also secret. This organization kept an eye on the activities of its opponents and hindered any collective movement.[140] And so the climax of *Narodnaya Volya* coincided with a time of apathy and inaction among students.

On the other hand, the Executive Committee's political standpoint allowed the members of *Narodnaya Volya* to penetrate into circles which ten years earlier had been scarcely touched by revolutionary propaganda. It was now the turn of the army.

As will be remembered, at the beginning of the 'sixties the groups of *Zemlya i Volya* had been able to attract young officers into their ranks both in St Petersburg and in Moscow. The name of Potebnya, who had fallen at the side of the Polish insurgents, still survived as a symbol of the effect produced in the Russian army by the ideas of Chernyshevsky and Herzen. But there had been far fewer officers in those conspiracies which took place after the crushing of the Polish revolt. Some of the Chaikovskists had been soldiers, but their desire to communicate with the people and to merge with it had soon led them to give up their uniforms, freeing themselves from a life which no longer corresponded to their convictions. Dyakov had spread propaganda among the soldiers but not the officers. Only the revival of a situation, which in so many ways recalled the period between 1861 and 1863, now encouraged some in the army to resume that rebellious tradition which the Decembrists had turned into a distant and glorious legend. The fight against the State, the idea of a 'conspiracy' designed to destroy the government and hand over power to the revolutionaries, inevitably once again raised the problem of how the armed forces would behave. They could serve either as a tool of absolutism or a weapon for the revolution. The task of the revolutionaries was no longer to tell the officers not to fire on the peasants and invite them to throw over their careers in order to show solidarity with the people. Rather, these officers must understand their rôle in the future political and social revolution, and retain their uniform so as to carry out the orders of the Executive Committee. Besides, the technical, scientific element contained in the plans of *Narodnaya Volya*—that passion that inspired Kibalchich, Zhelyabov and their comrades to make use of all the most modern weapons and inventions for the triumph of the cause—all this might also appeal to the mind of young officers and attract them into the ranks of *Narodnaya Volya.*

The foundations of the 'military organization' were laid by Zhelyabov in the autumn of 1880. The central core was at St Petersburg and was made up of N. E. Sukhanov, a particularly well-educated and brave young officer, A. P. Shtromberg and N. M. Rogachev, brother of one of the most typical 'pilgrims to the people'. They formed a group which took its orders from the Executive Committee. The links between them were at first maintained by Zhelyabov himself and Kolodkevich. Others helped them to spread propaganda.

Rogachev was an artillery officer, and his regiment was stationed in the department of Vilna. He could not therefore count on acting directly on his unit. But the other two were naval officers; Shtromberg was serving at Kronstadt, and Sukhanov had recently been detached from the fleet to enable him to follow university lectures at St Petersburg. And so he retained a great number of links with the officers of the naval base. Kronstadt soon became one of the strongest bases on which the *Narodnaya Volya* could count. One of the first officers in Kronstadt to join the organization, Sergey Degaev, enabled the revolutionaries to form another group among the artillery officers in the garrison on the island. The members of *Narodnaya Volya* found the ground already well prepared. *Zemlya i Volya* had had followers among the naval officers and had extended its activities to various institutions and military academies. By as early as 1879, about a hundred sailors had been affected by the propaganda which reached them through their officers. But this very desire of the officers to influence their subordinates had put the authorities on the tracks of the organization. An inquiry had been made, which ended with a series of very light sentences, obviously aimed to suppress the scandal. But now *Narodnaya Volya* had no intention of exposing itself to such danger again. The officers of the organization were ordered not to spread any propaganda among the soldiers under their command. All they had to do was to behave humanely towards the sailors and soldiers, and show themselves to be able leaders. They must make themselves respected and loved, without uselessly risking their position; this would be too precious on the day of the revolution, when their prestige would be enough to win over their men. The officers also counted on the natural grievances of their troops. N. I. Rysakov, for example, said in his deposition that he had often met soldiers who had been dismissed after the Balkan campaign. 'They had solved the problem of the political situation by themselves—in the same way as that preached by *Narodnaya Volya*.'[141]

Sukhanov was confident that the 'military organization' would soon lead to important results. 'I remember that in one of the meetings (shortly before 1st March 1881)', Oshanina later said, 'Sukhanov explained his plan for the Kronstadt fleet to bombard St Petersburg. He obviously had great faith in his plans, and he replied to a sceptical objection, "Give us time, a year or two, and you will see".'[142]

At St Petersburg, *Narodnaya Volya* founded a group of officers, of whom the two best were N. G. Senyagin and A. V. Butsevich. A few members of *Narodnaya Volya* could also be met with in the garrisons of other Russian towns, though the real military groups of Odessa, Nikolaev and Tiflis only arose after 1st March 1881.

After this period the 'military organization' was to play a leading rôle in all the history of *Narodnaya Volya*. In practice it replaced the Executive Committee, which was destroyed by the repression and which at this stage was represented only by Vera Figner. She alone carried on the fight in a situation which can more truthfully be described as desperate than difficult. The officers managed to keep functioning all that remained of the party. They even expanded the organization and created new centres and deeply influenced some units in the army, such as those at Tiflis. All in all we can name about seventy officers who were in *Narodnaya Volya*, without of course counting the many soldiers who were shaken by the propaganda and agitation of these extremely active elements.

But another very different man was also to come from these circles. Degaev, an officer from Kronstadt, played a double game with the police, and spread a series of hallucinating stories of false escapes and of murders carried out to redeem himself, which ended by making it impossible for

Narodnaya Volya to pursue an organized existence. His activities marked the lowest point in the curve of the Executive Committee, which had found its climax in the plot of 1st March 1881.

The first core of the 'military organization' paid for the energy with which it had infiltrated into the army with its life. Sukhanov was shot at Kronstadt on 19th March 1882. On 10th October 1884, Shtromberg and Rogachev were hanged in the Peter-Paul fortress after being tried with Figner in the 'trial of the fourteen'. Butsevich was condemned to hard labour for life in 1883. Shortly afterwards many others followed him on the same road.[143]

The idea that the army could play a leading rôle in the proposed revolution had first arisen in the 'military organization'. Zhelyabov on the other hand put his hopes mainly in the *druzhinas* (the workers' combatant militia). The army would support and follow their movement.[144] It was for this reason that he attributed so much importance to propaganda and organization in the factories. In 1880 he directed a considerable part of the Executive Committee's activities into this sphere.[145]

Here, too, *Narodnaya Volya* was compelled to swim against the tide. By now the *Northern Union of Russian Workers* had been struck at its very heart, and the little that still survived of Obnorsky's and Khalturin's work was lacking in spirit and initiative. It is, however, symptomatic that even so it did not approach *Cherny Peredel*. Instead it followed *Narodnaya Volya*, for it was there that it found those elements of the political objectives which it had been the first to include in its programme. The weakness of the working class organization and the desire of its leaders to fight against the State meant that these leaders were soon absorbed into the party and devoted much of their activities to terrorism and conspiracy. Khalturin naturally provides the most significant example of this. But there are other names which can be added to his.

A. K. Presnyakov had been one of the most active organizers of the working class groups in St Petersburg in 1876 and 1877. The meeting which, in December 1877, had decided to hold the demonstration on the Square of Our Lady of Kazan had been held at his house; since then he had devoted himself to armed warfare against spies and provocateurs. He had been arrested, but, helped by Kvyatkovsky and Khotinsky, he had succeeded in escaping in 1878. He had then gone for a year to France and England. On his return he had become a member of the 'Executive Committee' at the Lipetsk meeting. He was given a leading rôle in organizing the working class districts of the capital. He always travelled with a revolver, and when the police arrested him in the street on 24th June 1880, he fired. He was hanged on 4th November 1880.

P. L. Antonov, an engineer from Kharkov, had organized a strike in that town in 1878. He got in touch with members of *Narodnaya Volya* at Poltava, where he was employed in the railway workshops. He, too, then moved over from 'propaganda' to 'terror', and became one of the most active members of the Executive Committee. He was sentenced to death in 1887, but this was commuted to hard labour, which he served at Shlisselburg until the revolution of 1905.

Mikhail Fedorovich Grachevsky had a similar history. He was the son of a deacon in the Saratov region, and for a time he became an elementary schoolmaster. He then took a job as a railway machinist. By 1873 he was already in prison for reading one of Dolgushin's booklets. On being freed he got in contact with the Chaikovskists, and devoted himself to propaganda among the workers, getting employed for a time in workshops in St Petersburg. He was imprisoned again in 1875, but was acquitted at the 'trial of the hundred and ninety-three' after many years of preventive detention. He was then banished to the department of Archangel, but escaped in 1879 and joined *Narodnaya Volya*. He became a member of the Executive Committee. In June 1882 he was again sent to prison and in his deposition he described the experiences that had turned him into a revolutionary. As a boy, he had had a father 'who was religious to the point of fanaticism, and a tyrant in family life' but 'adored by the peasants'. He had then had to study in exceedingly difficult circumstances owing to lack of means and books. The life of his fellow peasants was dominated by the power of the *kulaks* 'who always found support in representatives of the State' and who therefore always flourished in their fight against the peasants, when they had the 'fantastic idea' of trying to defend their property. Everything that was happening in the countryside seemed to be 'the result of an incomplete reform'. But it had been his work as a railwayman that had finally opened his eyes. 'After long sleepless nights, after deep moral suffering, Russian life itself' had led him to adopt revolutionary conclusions. 'The railways, the pearl of Russia's modern industry, gave me such a mass of facts to explain our social and economic situation.' After forced work in the workshops and railway engines, sometimes with only three or four hours' rest in every twenty-four, and despite exhaustion' Grachevsky read and thought. 'Before my very eyes the curtain rose on the real situation of our police, military, capitalist and State régime.' He took part in many of the boldest terrorist ventures of *Narodnaya Volya* and, when sentenced to hard labour, he committed suicide by burning himself alive in one of the cells in Shlisselburg fortress.[146]

This transition of the most skilled workers, from attempts to agitate in defence of their own interests to politics and terrorism, was also due to the economic situation of the working classes in 1880. That year was one of crisis and unemployment. 'In St Petersburg dismissals were constant. For every workman employed, nine were trying to find work outside the factory doors. Some factories stopped production. The conditions of those men who had no work was very hard', said Rysakov in his deposition on 20th March 1881. And he added that the labour force therefore had to depend entirely on the employers, and did not dare to contradict them, still less to speak of strikes.

They saw that, situated as they were, it was impossible to withstand the exploitation of the factory owners; and at the same time they saw that the employers had no restraint. These employers bullied the men with fines, for no reason at all, and shamefully oppressed them. On the other hand, the workers knew that they could not appeal to the law, and that no help was to be expected from that quarter, in view of the very nature of factory legislation.[147]

The economic crisis and the impossibility of fomenting strikes thus helped to emphasize the political character of *Narodnaya Volya*'s activities among the workers. Besides, the workers' ideas on the State and society in Russia had already prepared them to choose this road. 'In Russia every strike is political', Zhelyabov used to say. Both he and his comrades looked upon any attempt to detach economic problems from those involved in the fight against absolutism as absurd. The working classes everywhere, not only in St Petersburg but in the provinces too, formed 'a stratum of the population which was very well aware of the régime which obtained in Russia' and which had shown that it was 'easily inflammable'. An insurrection in the capital would give the signal to the smaller towns and the countryside. The workers would take action because 'they had met the Socialists and had been persuaded by the idea of a new life and were convinced that this could be brought about.' In a revolution their rôle would be that of an élite.[148]

The *Programme of the Working-class Members of the Party of the Narodnaya Volya*, which was published in 1880, laid the foundations for the organization which it was intended to carry out in the factories.[149] This programme, which is one of the Executive Committee's fundamental texts, took as its starting point the Socialist and Populist ideal that *Narodnaya Volya* held in common with *Zemlya i Volya* and *Cherny Peredel*.

(1) Land and the tools of work must belong to all the people, and every worker has the right to use them.

(2) Work must be done collectively (in *obshchinas*, *artels*, associations), and not singly.

(3) The produce of communal work must be divided among all the workers after consultation between them and according to the needs of each.

(4) The structure of the State must be based on a federal pact of all the *obshchinas*.

(5) Every *obshchina* will be fully independent and free in everything that concerns its internal affairs.

(6) Every member of the *obshchina* will be completely free in his opinions and in his private life. His freedom will only be restricted should he use violence against members of his own or other *obshchinas*.

The *Programme* then insisted on collective work, explaining that only in this way would it be possible 'to make extensive use of machinery, inventions and the discoveries of science' both in industry and in agriculture; only in this way could real welfare and freedom be achieved.

Freedom of the *obshchina*—i.e. its right and the right of all other federated *obshchinas* to concern themselves with affairs of State and to guide the State according to common desires—will prevent the establishment of State oppression and make impossible the concentration of power in the hands of those unworthy figures, who, in the guise of governors and officials, are now ruining the country.

In other words, the 'Socialist-federalist' ideal remained intact, but it did not now, on principle, repudiate the very existence of the State. The communities of workers were envisaged as the organs of a system of democratic control permanently exercised on the new machinery of government which would emerge from the social revolution.

But, as a whole, the *Programme* was devoted more to showing how to achieve the society of the future than to discussing its finer details.

We are profoundly convinced that such a social and political order would ensure the good of the people. But from the experiences of other peoples we also know that it is not possible to obtain full freedom and solid happiness at a single blow and in the immediate future. Ahead of us lies a long and resolute fight against the government and the exploiters of the people, and a gradual conquest of civil rights.

The oppression of centuries and the situation in which the masses still found themselves would not allow this ideal to be realized at once. The important thing was to fight every day to bring it into being.

'We consider that the function of our life is to help the Russian people to find its road towards freedom and a better life.' First it was essential to clarify who were their enemies and who friends. The fight must be directed against 'all who live on the backs of the people: the government, the landlords, the factory owners, the merchants and the *kulaks*.' It was obvious that these would never give up their positions without fighting. 'The working classes must count on their own resources; their enemies will certainly not help them.'

But the people can always count on one faithful ally, the social-revolutionary party. The members of this party come from all classes of the Russian State; they devote their lives to the cause of the people; and they think that all will be free and equal and that there will be a just system of government only when the country is ruled by the working class, i.e. the peasants and workers in the towns. Because the other classes, even if they achieved freedom and equality, would do so only for themselves and not for all the people.

Apart from the social-revolutionary party, the working classes could find other allies in 'a few individuals of the educated classes'—not because these were concerned with their fate but because they had a common enemy: government oppression.

The people, naturally, would have everything to gain from a slackening of this oppression. Everyone would become freer. Every man's mind would function with greater energy. Education would become accessible to all. The number of those who want the good of the people would increase. And, most important of all, the people itself could build up an organization and unite. And so, the working class must not reject these allies. It is to its own advantage to obtain an extension of freedom by working together with them. It is only essential that the workers do not forget that their cause does not stop there; that soon they will have to break away from these temporary friends and go ahead united only with the social-revolutionary party.

The *Programme* ended by expounding the immediate political goals.

(1) The power of the Tsar will be replaced by a government of the people, i.e. a government made up of representatives (deputies) of the people. The people will appoint and recall them . . . demanding a full account of what they have done.

(2) The Russian State, in view of its situation and the character of its population, will be divided into regions (*oblast*) which will be autonomous as regards their internal affairs but allied in a Pan-Russian Federation. Regional administration will regulate internal affairs, and the Federal Government those which concern the State as a whole.

(3) Peoples which have been annexed to the Russian State by violence will be free either to abandon the Pan-Russian Federation or to remain within it.

(4) The *obshchinas* (of countryside, village, hamlet, and the factory *artels*) will decide their affairs in meetings of their members and will entrust them to elected representatives to be carried out.

(5) All the land will be handed over to the working classes and will be considered as the people's or national property. Every single region will entrust the land at its disposal to the *obshchinas* or to single individuals on condition that they work it in person. No one will be authorized to have a larger amount than he can farm. On the request of the *obshchinas* the redistribution of the land (*peredel*) will be carried out.

(6) Factories and workshops will be regarded as belonging to the people (or the nation) and will be entrusted to the factory and workshop *obshchinas*. Tools will belong to these latter.

Other articles envisaged labour legislation, decided the basis of universal suffrage, and established freedom of opinion, religion, meeting, speech and press, etc. Education was to be free and universal. The army was to be supplanted by a militia. 'A State bank will be established with branches in the various regions of Russia, in order to help the creation of industrial and agricultural economic activities, and, in general, for every kind of *obshchina*, *artel* and union of production and education.'

The rest of the *Programme* consisted of practical advice on how to spread propaganda among the workers by creating libraries and meeting places, where necessary, by 'organizing strikes against factory owners, by preparing the workers for the battle against the police and the government (which always support the employer)' and above all by organizing clandestine groups able to develop into real 'working class unions'. 'At this stage it is impossible to divine the circumstances in which these will have to take action.' In any case the important thing was never to forget that 'to obtain anything at all the workers must constitute a force able to oppose the government and, if necessary, ready to back their claims by force of arms. Whether or not blood is shed, in either case it is essential to prepare some force; the more ready this is, the more likely our enemies will be to surrender without a struggle.'

'To have any hope of victory, an attack against our enemies can only be undertaken by the social-revolutionary party as a whole, of which the working class organization constitutes only one part. The party collects from the people and society those forces which are capable of carrying out a revolution; it creates unions among the peasants and the workers, in the army and in other bodies.' The party draws from its ranks 'a fighting union which attacks the government, shakes and disorganizes and disconcerts it. In this way the party makes it easier for all those who are dissatisfied—for the people and the workers and all those who desire their good—to arise and carry out a general revolution. Once an important revolt has been started either in the town or in the country, the party must support it with all its resources and make its own demands known. It must unleash similar disorders in various districts and thus unite the entire movement into a general insurrection throughout Russia. For the success of the cause it is extremely important to gain control of the larger cities and keep them in our own hands.' To do this the party would at once proclaim a government of workers. 'The workers will closely follow the activities of this provisional government and will compel it to act on behalf of the people.' The insurrection would hand over 'the land, workshops and factories to the people'. It would entrust the authority of the State to locally elected administrations, and destroy the army and replace it with a militia. Then the people would elect deputies to the Constituent Assembly. This would meet when the revolution was over 'to sanction the people's conquests and to draw up the laws of the Federation as a whole'.

If, on the other hand, the government gave in and granted a constitution 'the workers' action must not change. They must show their power and demand large concessions. They must send their own representatives to parliament and, if necessary, back their claims with demonstrations and mass risings.' By putting pressure on the government in this way, and by organizing the forces fighting against it, 'Narodnaya Volya will be waiting for the right moment. When the old order shows itself unable to resist the people's demands, it will carry out the revolution with every hope of success.'

As can be seen, the Executive Committee's ideas were extremely clearly formulated when, in 1880, it began to give first place to the problem of working class politics. Starting from the ideals of Zemlya i Volya it drew up a policy that left the door open to any circumstances that might arise, trusting in its iron determination to bring about a social revolution. A wide strategic outlook allowed considerable tactical elasticity.

All *Narodnaya Volya*'s plans now hinged on the social-revolutionary party. This, it was thought, could manage to guide the army and temporary allies, such as the liberals and constitutionalists as well as the workers' natural associations such as *obshchinas*, unions, etc. It could then lead all these forces to a revolution which was to be both political and social.

Zhelyabov clearly saw that, if all this was to be achieved, some basis had to be established in the working classes. In the summer and autumn of 1880 much of his activity was aimed at forming a group of about thirty students capable of spreading propaganda through speeches and leaflets among the working classes. On 15th December the first number of the *Rabochaya Gazeta* made its appearance. In order to print this a special clandestine press had been started. It was kept by a workman called M. V. Teterka and by Gesia Gelfman. The latter had already been in contact with the Moscow girls who in 1875 had flung themselves into the propagandist movement in the factories of that town.[150] It was edited by Zhelyabov himself, by N. A. Sablin, A. S. Boreysha and a few others. The second number came out at the end of January 1881. It was written in a deliberately simple and popular style which sometimes still echoed the propagandist methods of the Chaikovskists (for instance, stories with a social background, descriptions of the difficulties of working class life, poems, etc.). The second number contained a vivid account of the unemployment, dismissals, fines and reduced wages in various factories in St Petersburg. It told how the police constantly intervened in the factories and struck down the most resolute workers. 'The State felt that they were beginning to awake.' A short article at the end of the second number explained how the revolution had liberated the French workers from the kings and their worst oppressors.[151]

At the same time *Cherny Peredel* was also trying to spread propaganda in working class districts. In December 1880 the first number of the *Zerno* (The Seed) came out and the second was later distributed as a lithograph. Four other issues were printed at Minsk. The tone and ideas of this review were very similar to those of the *Rabochaya Gazeta*.[152] Its exact circulation is hard to determine; but we do know that though the *Gazeta* was published in a limited impression, it was widely read in St Petersburg. Zhelyabov and Sofya Perovskaya, for instance, gave Rysakov a hundred copies, all of which he distributed within a week or two. 'Even in inns the workers were ready to circulate it, and they often read it in the factories.'[153] The propaganda affected all the districts of St Petersburg and succeeded in uniting two or perhaps three hundred workers who were to some extent allied to the group of students.[154]

In 1880 similar work was begun in Moscow. Ever since 1875 the working class groups there had been very few and far between, and in general the revolutionary movement had remained very quiet. Obnorsky's efforts and those of the *Northern Union* had remained almost entirely fruitless. The revival at the end of 1880 was organized by *Narodnaya Volya*, under the leadership of Petr Abramovich Tellalov. A year later he was replaced by Khalturin. At the end of 1881 the third number of the *Rabochaya Gazeta* was printed in Moscow. At that time the organization could count on about thirty fixed bases and a hundred followers. At the beginning of 1882 the repression tore to shreds the network of workers' circles that *Narodnaya Volya* had succeeded in spreading in various parts of the town. At the centre were some of the elements of the Executive Committee, among them M. N. Oshanina. The group had become so strong that it was second only to St Petersburg. Indeed shortly before 1st March 1881 Zhelyabov placed all his hopes on Moscow, and relied on it giving rise to a revival of the movement after the losses that the revolutionaries were bound to suffer.

At Odessa, the working class group was at first organized by Vera Figner and N. N. Kolodkevich. 'At that time there were still to be found in the factories and workshops men who had been educated by Zaslavsky', the founder of the first *Southern Union*. Here too the main problem was to pick up the threads of an organization that had already been begun and to extend it by fighting against difficult economic conditions. In 1880 the working class group passed under the control of Mikhail Nikolaevich Trigoni, who came from a rich, cultivated family of Greek origin. His father was a soldier and his mother was the daughter of an admiral 'but ever since his youth he had had liberal ideas. In his souvenir-album photographs of Herzen and Garibaldi held the place of honour.' Mikhail Nikolaevich had been a school friend of Zhelyabov's, and in 1875 he had begun to spread propaganda. He had joined *Narodnaya Volya* and had devoted himself to making contacts with the educated classes. Now he was entrusted with the working class group of his native town. He was summoned to St Petersburg in 1881. There he was arrested and served a sentence of twenty years' hard labour.[155]

In Kiev, *Narodnaya Volya*'s labours clashed with the work of Shchedrin, E. N. Kovalskaya and their followers who had succeeded in giving life to the *Southern Union*. These early organizers countered the idea of using terrorism only against the 'centre' (i.e. the Tsar and the State), by maintaining the need for 'economic terrorism' and 'factory terrorism', directed against the immediate enemies and exploiters of the people. The tradition of the 'rebels', the economic policies of *Cherny Peredel*, and the liveliness of the working masses, helped to keep alive this opposition to the purely 'political' views of the Executive Committee. Later, too, *Narodnaya Volya* was constantly faced with this 'economic' deviation of its policy and, according to circumstances, tried either to fight it or to absorb it.

But this was only one aspect of the opposition that the Executive Committee had to overcome everywhere in order to impose its increasingly terrorist policies on working class groups. During the last months of 1880 and the first of 1881, Zhelyabov and his comrades were faced with an

23+

increasingly harsh and tragic dilemma. Propaganda among the workers was giving good results, but these were slow and small when compared to the enormous size of the duties that confronted the revolutionaries. To divert men, energy and money to this field would mean giving up, or at least postponing, the fundamental aim of the Executive Committee: the destruction of the Tsar. The forces at the Committee's disposal were limited and in constant danger. These forces all had to be flung into the operation which it was hoped would open the door to a wider movement. They would prize open that breach in the system within which the entire revolutionary movement ran the risk of remaining confined.

The revolutionaries therefore decided to close the press which published the *Rabochaya Gazeta*. Sablin and Gesia Gelfman would instead be put in charge of one of the clandestine refuges needed for planning the execution of the Tsar. Zhelyabov and Sofya Perovskaya were to concentrate all their activities on preparing the blow. In Moscow, Tellalov was convinced that it would be a mistake to kill the Tsar before the revolutionaries had at their disposal a force powerful enough to rebel, and an organization capable of taking advantage of the confusion which would be caused by the bombs. Khalturin was constantly divided between his zeal for terrorism and his duties as a workers' organizer. He gave vent to his feelings by saying that the intellectuals compelled him to start again from scratch after every act of terrorism and its inevitable losses. 'If only they gave us a bit of time to reinforce ourselves', he said, on each occasion. But then he too was seized by that thirst for immediate action which drove on his comrades to terrorism and which led him to the scaffold with them. Trigoni had to leave Odessa to go and discuss the decisive blow in St Petersburg, and was arrested shortly afterwards.

The activities of the 'working class groups' of *Narodnaya Volya* were in fact subordinated to the execution of the political plan drawn up in the *Programme*. These activities had already been restricted by the situation of the Russian working class in 1880. The Executive Committee now concentrated all its best resources.

The Executive Committee's desire to reach a final decision was all the greater in that Khalturin's attempts to blow up the Emperor had been followed by two other failures of a similar kind.

In the spring of 1880 Sofya Perovskaya and Sablin left for Odessa, armed, of course, with false passports. There they opened a shop in one of the leading streets, the Avenue of Italy, where they lived during April and May. When the dynamite was ready, they began to dig a tunnel from the back of the shop. They knew that the Emperor was intending to travel through Odessa, and it was planned to blow up the tunnel as he passed by. Unexpectedly, however, the Emperor arrived earlier than the date they had foreseen, and the work therefore had to be given up after only three days. The police did not hear of these preparations till long afterwards, when most of those who had taken part were already dead or in prison.[156]

In the summer of the same year Isaev, Langans, Barannikov and Presnyakov devised a plan to blow up a bridge over which the Emperor usually passed on his way from the Winter Palace to take the train for Tsarskoe Selo.[157] Two *pud* of dynamite wrapped up in gutta-percha were dropped from a boat at the bottom of the canal which passed under the bridge. Zhelyabov and Teterka were to let off the fuse. But on the appointed day Teterka, who was a workman, failed to turn up, apparently because 'he had no watch'. Alexander II had meanwhile left for the Crimea, and the attempt could not be repeated. They tried in vain to fish out the dynamite which remained in the canal until the police found it a year later. The fuse had been so well placed that it was still dry and usable.

Again, as had already happened in the winter of 1875, though their plans had come to nothing, none of the revolutionaries had been arrested. Boldness seemed to make them invulnerable; their losses were due not to their terrorist activities but to the wear and tear of the day-to-day campaign.

At the end of May, eleven members of *Zemlya i Volya* were put on trial, among them some who had been the first to revive the movement after 1875, such as Oboleshev, Olga Natanson, Adrian Mikhailov, Troshchansky, M. A. Kolenkina and Dr. Veymar (who had organized Kropotkin's escape). Oboleshev and Mikhailov were sentenced to death, which was commuted to hard labour for life. All the others served long years of hard labour, except for Olga Natanson, who soon died of consumption. As the *Listok Narodnoy Voli* rightly pointed out, the government was here punishing opinions rather than deeds. This showed how restricted was the 'liberalism' of the dictator Loris-Melikov.

In July twenty-one people were handed over to the military tribunal at Kiev. Two revolutionaries, M. R. Popov and I. K. Ivanov, were sentenced to death but later pardoned; while all the others received fifteen or twenty years' hard labour, though some of these sentences were later reduced. The men concerned were generally half-way between *Narodnaya Volya* and *Cherny Peredel*, and were caught in the traps laid by Sudeykin, the cleverest policeman in the service of the Minister of the Interior. The Kiev movement was not destroyed, but here, too, as at St Petersburg, the trial marked the end of one phase in its existence. Ivanov died at Shlisselburg; Popov was not released until 1905.[158]

On 25th October the 'trial of the sixteen' began in the capital. Five were sentenced to death, and in two cases the sentence was carried out. Kvyatkovsky and Presnyakov were hanged in the Peter-Paul fortress on 4th November 1880. Shiryaev, who was also a leading party man, got a reprieve but this merely meant a year's agony in the Alexeyevsky dungeon, where he died on 18th August 1881.[159]

The first number of the *Narodnaya Volya* to appear after the fall of the press began by announcing the hanging of these two 'revolutionary-socialists'. The short commentary that followed was a declaration of war. *Narodnaya Volya* had never believed that Loris-Melikov was carrying out a more liberal policy. Now he had issued a challenge by hanging those members of the Executive Committee whom he could lay hands on. 'Brothers, do not allow yourselves to be carried away by a desire for revenge! Be guided by calculated reason. Save and accumulate your forces. The hour of judgment is not far off.'[160] Thus the 'trial of the sixteen' played its part (a not insignificant part) in persuading the Executive Committee to concentrate all its forces on striking the Tsar.

On 28th November 1880, Alexander Mikhailov was caught by the police. Mikhailov was the finest politician in *Zemlya i Volya*. He had laid the foundations of *Narodnaya Volya* and, both morally and technically, he embodied the spirit of the entire revolutionary movement at the end of the 'seventies. One day, he went into a photographer's shop on the Nevsky Prospekt to order photographs of his two hanged comrades, Kvyatkovsky and Presnyakov. The owner of the shop was a police agent. When his wife saw the two photographs, she looked in amazement at the customer, and put her hands round his neck as if to explain that he too would be hanged. Mikhailov went back and told this strange story to his comrades. They reproached him for risking his life for photographs, and implored him to leave them there where they were. But on the following day he could not resist the temptation. He entered the shop and was at once arrested. And so the man who had taught the technique of conspiracy to all his comrades fell through an act of imprudence. He had been a great organizer and he died to honour the memory of two fallen comrades.

On 25th February 1882 he was sentenced to death, and on 17th March, Alexander III commuted his sentence to hard labour for life. But Mikhailov never saw Siberia. The Minister of the Interior suggested to the Tsar that he should be detained for life in the Peter-Paul fortress. Alexander gave orders to this effect and Mikhailov died there on 18th March 1884.

Just before his trial he wrote letters to his comrades, in which he said: 'Do not let yourselves be carried away by the desire to avenge or free your comrades . . . Do not be carried away by fine theories. There is only one theory in Russia: to acquire freedom to own the land'; and he added, 'There is only one way to do this: fire at the centre.'[161]

22. 1st MARCH 1881

FOR MANY MONTHS the revolutionaries had been keeping a very close watch on the Tsar's movements, and they were now well acquainted with the streets through which he used to pass on leaving the Winter Palace. Every Sunday he went to the stables, and he often walked towards the Catherine Canal, where his morganatic wife, Princess Dolgorukova, had her residence. In either case he almost always went through the Malaya Sadovaya. A close examination of these two itineraries made it clear that if Alexander II was attacked at two stages on the road he had to pass through, he would at last fall under the blows of the Executive Committee. A tunnel would therefore have to be dug under the Malaya Sadovaya, to explode as he passed. And in case this did not work, four revolutionaries armed with bombs would wait for him further on. If this too should prove unsuccessful Zhelyabov would intervene with a dagger and a revolver. The plot had now assumed the proportions of a military operation, designed to succeed at all costs.[1]

To this effect, Yu. Bogdanovich and A. V. Yakimova, with passports that described them as a married couple called Kobozev, went to see the proprietor of No. 56 Malaya Sadovaya. They asked to rent a shop from him as they planned to start a small cheese business. As soon as this had been arranged, they began to fill the shop with boxes of various kinds and to serve customers. But soon the neighbours began to grow suspicious: the new traders seemed uninterested in making money and they were curiously ignorant about the various kinds of cheese. A shopkeeper grew anxious about possible competition and denounced them to the police. Under the pretext of a sanitary inquiry, a search was organized. In one corner of the shop there was a little pile of fresh soil which seemed suspicious, but Bogdanovich succeeded in persuading the police that it was used to keep the dairy produce fresh. (Later when telling his comrades how he had escaped, he jumped with joy.) Sukhanov, the man responsible for the 'military organization', just managed to leap on to his horse as he saw the police arriving. Had the latter looked a little more carefully behind the pile of earth, they would have seen a tunnel that was daily growing longer and deeper. Already it had reached the Malaya Sadovaya. It had been dug by the two 'shopkeepers' and by Sukhanov, Zhelyabov, Frolenko and others. The long and difficult work had used up much energy and precious time, but within a few days of the search, the tunnel was ready to take the dynamite.

On 27th February the Executive Committee suffered a terrible blow.

Zhelyabov was arrested. Ever since the action had been decided upon, he had divided his time between practical organization (such as supervising the smallest details of the plot and choosing the men who were to take part, etc.) and working out what would be its political consequences. It was obvious that *Narodnaya Volya* was not strong enough to organize the destruction of the Tsar and a revolution simultaneously. All available energies had been absorbed in practical details: preparation of the bombs, digging the tunnels, daily contacts, the subtle and delicate network of clandestine refuges, and safety precautions. Even admitting that all went well and that losses were not higher than expected, Zhelyabov well knew that the Executive Committee would not be in a position to man the barricades on the day after Alexander II's death. Indeed, years later, when Vera Figner looked back at the situation, she came to the conclusion that the authorities would not even have needed to employ the army in order to disperse any demonstrations that *Narodnaya Volya* might have organized. The police, and even doorkeepers and volunteers, would have been enough on their own, as had happened in the Square of Our Lady of Kazan on 6th December 1876. It was, therefore, all the more important to maintain an organization which would be able to make its voice heard after the explosion and to take advantage of the unknown situation which would follow. The repercussions might be so great that they would put the problem of political forces in an entirely new light. The explosion might reawaken the intelligentsia and convince the working classes that the revolutionary party was powerful. And so it was essential to save as many as possible of the revolutionaries in the capital. This being the case it might be necessary to employ the younger men for the actual assassination. True, they had less experience than the others: but their political importance was also less. At all costs it was essential to maintain continuity. But each day that passed, each new problem that the operation brought to light, showed Zhelyabov how difficult it was not to throw all available forces into the furnace. And so he ended by putting all his hopes in the provincial organizations, in Moscow, Odessa, etc. It was from there that the party would be reborn after the great test. 'Everything will depend on Moscow', he said one day at a meeting specially summoned to discuss these problems and the political preparations for the attempt. Delegates from other Russian cities came to St Petersburg to keep in contact with the centre at the decisive moment and to receive orders.[2]

On the evening of 27th February, Zhelyabov went to meet Trigoni, who had arrived from Odessa. Trigoni was one of the very few members of *Narodnaya Volya* whose status was not 'illegal' and though he knew that he was under police supervision, he trusted in his ability to escape being shadowed. He had already frequently changed his lodgings, and he was now settled in a *pension* on the Nevsky Prospekt. Coming into his room, Zhelyabov said to him, 'I have a feeling that there are policemen in your corridor.' Several years later Trigoni described the scene that followed.

'Wanting to find out what was the matter, I at once went out. I scarcely had the time to say to the maid, "Katya, bring in the samovar", before I was seized on all sides by a mass of people who came out from a neighbouring room. They led me in there and searched me immediately. At the same time they arrested Zhelyabov in my room.' Zhelyabov was taken to the police. Later he just managed to say a few words to Trigoni. 'As soon as I came in the vice-prosecutor said, "Zhelyabov, it's you". I didn't think there was any need to deny this. He knew me from my time at Odessa, when I was involved in the "trial of the hundred and ninety-three".'[3]

As soon as his comrades heard that Zhelyabov was in the enemy's hands, they forgot the problems that he had felt to be so crucial. Action was essential; immediate action. The plans that he had made must be fulfilled. Sofya Perovskaya, his friend, would take his place. Day after day, for months on end, she had accompanied him as he visited the houses of those who were destined to be sacrificed. She knew every detail of the organization and her abilities were up to the task. The Tsar, it was decided, would be killed on the following Sunday, 1st March.

Kibalchich was to prepare the bombs. He had invented them, and at the trial the experts who were called to examine them were amazed at their ingenuity. Two crossed tubes containing nitro-glycerine were surrounded by a metal covering. They were so placed that they would explode whatever the position of the bomb when it struck its objective. It was calculated that their effectiveness could be guaranteed within a radius of about a metre. It was essential, therefore, that they should be thrown very carefully and from a very close range. The assassin had not the slightest chance of escaping death or capture; but if his aim was good, the number of useless victims would be cut down to the minimum.

Number 1 'thrower' (to use the word that they then adopted) was Nikolay Ivanovich Rysakov, a young man aged nineteen whom Zhelyabov had introduced into the workers' *druzhinas* (militia) and who had taken an active part in spreading propaganda in the factories of St Petersburg. 'Thrower' Number 2 was Ignaty Yoakimovich Grinevitsky. He came from a family of nobles and was a student at the Technological Institute. He was now aged twenty-four, and entirely dedicated to the revolutionary cause. He too belonged to the working class organization of the Executive Committee.[4] The third and fourth assassins were Timofey Mikhailovich Mikhailov, a workman, and Ivan Panteleymonovich Emelyanov, a student in touch with the revolutionary movement. All four had volunteered for the work. At his trial, Zhelyabov said that the number of men to reply to the appeal had been huge, and that he had had to choose among the many volunteers. Though this was certainly an exaggeration, designed to emphasize the power of the Executive Committee, the fact remains that the number of volunteers had in fact been considerable. The spirit of terrorism had penetrated deeply into *Narodnaya Volya*, absorbing and consuming every other political idea or feeling.

Zhelyabov's choice of 'throwers' did, however, show that he had 'social' intentions: the Tsar was to be killed by those elements who were closest to the factories. The original plan seems to have been that Timofey Mikhailov, the only real working-man among them, would throw the first bomb.[5]

On the night of 28th February the bombs were feverishly prepared in the 'conspirators' rooms' occupied by Vera Figner and Isaev. Early in the morning of 1st March Sofya Perovskaya took two of them to the house occupied by Gesia Gelfman and Sablin, which had been transformed into the headquarters of the operation. Shortly afterwards Kibalchich arrived with the other two.

Everything was now ready. On the Malaya Sadovaya, Frolenko was waiting to set the electric fuse which would blow up all that part of the street which lay in front of the shop as the Tsar passed by. Frolenko himself would most probably remain buried under the debris. Vera Figner watched him take a bottle of red wine and a piece of salami out of his pocket and begin quietly eating. She was amazed as she observed 'such materialist inclinations in a man who was soon to die' and told him so with an air of reproach. But Frolenko objected that 'in such matters a man must be master of all his resources'.[6]

Sofya Perovskaya meanwhile had met the 'throwers' in a café and had handed them the packages containing the bombs. If the Emperor did not pass along the Malaya Sadovaya, or if, for some reason, the mine failed to work, they were to attack at a signal which she would give with a white handkerchief.

The question now was: would the Emperor go out on that Sunday to review the troops as usual? During the Saturday Loris-Melikov had told him of the arrest of Zhelyabov and of the results of his interrogation. Zhelyabov had refused to answer any of the questions and had merely said that whatever happened the party would make an attempt on the life of the Emperor. Loris-Melikov told the Tsar that it was up to him to decide whether or not to go out on the following day, assuring him, however, that all the necessary security measures had been taken. Alexander II was so worried by what the Minister of the Interior had told him, that his morganatic wife noticed his concern and asked him if he was going to the review on the following day. 'Why not?' he heard himself answer. She then advised him not to pass along the Nevsky Prospekt but to follow the road that went along the Catherine Canal.[7]

Sofya Perovskaya saw the Emperor following this route, and assumed that he would come back the same way. She had time to place the 'throwers' along the railing of the canal, and then she herself went to the other bank. From there she would be able to get the first view of the Emperor's sleigh as it turned the corner and came along the bank.

At a quarter past two the Emperor's convoy passed at full speed. Rysakov was warned by Sofya Perovskaya's handkerchief and threw the first bomb.

Alexander II was alone in his sleigh, which was followed by two others, with a police dignitary and two officers. They were surrounded by a squadron of Cossacks. The bomb blew up the back of the Emperor's sleigh, wounded a number of people, among them a Cossack and a boy who happened to be passing by, but left Alexander II quite untouched. He gave orders to halt, and went on foot to where the bomb had exploded. Meanwhile a crowd had assembled and Rysakov had been seized by some soldiers. An officer failed to recognize the Tsar, and asked him if the Emperor had been hit. 'Thanks be to God, I am safe. But what of him? . . .' and he pointed to a wounded man who was groaning on the ground. Rysakov looked at the Emperor and said, 'It may still be too early to give thanks to God'. He was asked if he was the man who had thrown the bomb and what was his name. He agreed that he was and gave a false name. The Emperor then turned to go back to his sleigh. He had only gone a few steps when there was a second violent explosion which lifted up a cloud of smoke and snow. The second 'thrower', Grinevitsky, had come up, and had thrown the bomb at his feet from only a pace away. When the smoke began to disperse, Alexander II was seen lying on his back by the canal, scarcely breathing. He was losing blood, and said only, 'Help me, help me', and, 'Cold, cold'. Next him was Grinevitsky, fatally injured. Alexander II was quickly taken to the Winter Palace and died about an hour later. Grinevitsky died at the hospital during the evening, without even admitting his name. About twenty people had been more or less seriously wounded in the two explosions; of these three died within a few hours.

All the evidence agrees that the impression made by these events in the capital was one of amazement, anxiety and dumb expectation. The revolutionary party had shown its temerity and strength; the blow had been terrible. What would it do next? Some members of the intelligentsia were now convinced that *Narodnaya Volya* was master of the field, and that it could dictate laws and impose its will. 'This time it's the revolution', Mikhailovsky had already said some days earlier. Shelgunov was less optimistic, but he was the only one of his group who did not share the general enthusiasm and hopes.[8] In the suburbs the workers asked Sofya Perovskaya what to do. They were prepared to follow her at a sign.[9] Everywhere else a feeling of fear prevailed. This was enough to prevent monarchist demonstrations, but it also made impossible any act of solidarity with the revolutionaries. *Narodnaya Volya* had assumed the task of fighting the authorities; now, this responsibility had come to weigh like a heavy burden on its shoulders.

Repercussions in the provinces were even more muffled than in the capital itself. At Moscow on 2nd March, small groups of students stopped passers-by 'to show their pleasure at the killing of the Tsar'; others refused to subscribe to a collection for a wreath, and this gave rise to a great scandal. 'In university circles many showed how happy they were at what had happened on 1st March.' But for the most part public opinion was reactionary

23*

Loris-Melikov and even Prince Constantine Nikolaevich were blamed because their liberal tendencies had opened up the road for the revolutionaries.[10]
In the provinces there were a few scattered signs of approval. Some sons of
clergymen, artisans and school-teachers said that Alexander II had been
killed because 'he had done evil'. In the Voronezh region some maintained
that 'the gentry wanted a republic like in France'; others that, 'If the new
Emperor does not give liberty, they will smash him too.' In the province of
Vladimir, someone said, 'What we want is no Tsar at all and the people to
govern on its own.' This opinion was obviously fairly widespread in the
district, and the authorities were seriously alarmed that there would be
strikes. Reports reaching St Petersburg from other provinces spoke of 'a
dark and oppressive state of mind in society at Ryazan and other towns'.
In the countryside it was nearly always the gentry and the nobles who were
thought to be responsible for the assassination. But even these rumours were
not altogether reassuring for the governors and the Minister of the Interior.
A report from Ryazan on 9th March stated that 'the people are convinced
that those guilty are the landlords who had no intention of obeying the
Tsar's will that they should hand over their lands to the peasants without
any redemption fee'. It was said in Pskov that the Tsar had been killed
'because he had done away with serfdom'; but it was added that 'if something
should happen to the new Emperor as well, or if they make us serfs again, we
will go and cut off the heads of all the nobles'. At Poltava the peasants were
convinced in some districts 'that they could take the gentry's lands and
divide them . . . by doing this we will all be equal'. Real disturbances took
place only in the regions of Voronezh and Tambov. 'It is said among the
peasants that the new Tsar has ordered them not to harvest the landlords'
and merchants' lands for less than fifty or sixty roubles a *desyatina*.' 'Energetic action by the officials was needed to suppress this agitation.'[11]

Cherny Peredel's policy to redivide the land was thus still a live issue in
the countryside. But by now the revolutionaries were in no position to base
their future activities on it. In St Petersburg, during the days that followed
the assassination, they were engaged in a desperate fight to try to keep the
organization alive. For the counterblows of the authorities were now
shaking the foundations of the Executive Committee.

Rysakov was questioned day and night, and finally gave the names of his
accomplices and the addresses that he knew. The safety precautions that the
conspirators had taken when Zhelyabov had begun to make his plans had
been very strict; but during the feverish days that preceded the operation,
they had been fatally relaxed. Rysakov knew little, but even that was enough
to affect several vital centres.

On the night of 3rd March the police burst into the rooms belonging to
Gesia Gelfman and Sablin. The latter put up an armed resistance as long as
he could, and on seeing that he was lost he shot himself. Gesia Gelfman was
arrested. The police discovered the two bombs that had not been used on

1st March, and waited in the flat. At ten o'clock on the following morning, Timofey Mikhailov, the third 'thrower', came to the door. When he saw the police, he took out his revolver and fired six shots, wounding three of them. Finally he was forced to surrender. On 4th March the shop belonging to the 'Kobozevs' was discovered. All those employed there had time to get away; but two *pud* of dynamite and the battery, etc., fell into the hands of the police. The government was greatly struck by this further proof of the extent of the revolutionaries' preparations. From Goldenberg's confession the Ministry had some idea of the small number of men involved in the revolutionary movement, no more than a few hundred. Yet the vigour of the Executive Committee's measures was all too obvious. At first Loris-Melikov thought of handing Rysakov over to a military tribunal and having him hanged as quickly as possible, as he had done with the young Mlodetsky, who had fired at him less than a year before. But the discoveries that the police were now making suggested that a political trial to be held by a Committee of Senators would be more satisfactory. Rysakov could be made the chief witness. He was young, uneducated and inexperienced. Fearing for his life, he would adopt a repentant attitude. When Zhelyabov understood this manœuvre, designed to reduce the political significance of the assassination, he had not a moment's hesitation. He wrote a letter claiming that he alone had been responsible for the whole operation, and he implored the judges to try him at the same time as the 'throwers'.[12]

This move made a profound effect on the spirits of those of Zhelyabov's comrades who were still free, and gave them strength and hope in the midst of their increasing feeling of suffocation as the circle closed around them. The only action that they could seriously think of was: to begin again on the same road, to prepare a new plan to assassinate the new Tsar, and so give another battering to the State edifice which had stood firm at the death of Alexander II. This was Zhelyabov's own opinion. He was convinced that Alexander III would not 'take a step' to satisfy the demands of the party 'and that it is therefore necessary to do away with him'. In his cell in the Peter-Paul fortress, Alexander Mikhailov came to exactly the same conclusion and wrote it to his comrades as soon as he had the chance. And some of those who were still at large suggested beginning work at once. But the blows they had suffered were too severe, and the anxiety they felt too widespread for this to be possible. Discipline and precautions were relaxed. Sofya Perovskaya implored the Executive Committee to use all its remaining resources to try to free Zhelyabov, who had signed his own death sentence by admitting responsibility for the operation. She had always scorned precautions of any kind[13]: now she seemed to be looking for death. On 10th March, she was arrested by a policeman who recognized her as she went along the Nevsky Prospekt. A week later Kibalchich, who had made the Executive Committee's dynamite and bombs, fell into the hands of the authorities.

During the terrible days that followed 1st March, *Narodnaya Volya* succeeded in carrying out only one political gesture. But this had been well-calculated and it had vast repercussions in Russia and abroad. It marked the end of the twenty-year period which had opened with the reforming enthusiasms of the 'fifties.

Once more the revolutionaries were seized by the logic of terrorism. The bombs had perhaps not succeeded in provoking a general revolt but they would at least serve to persuade autocracy that its policies had entered a blind alley; the duel between the revolutionaries and the authorities would carry on inexorably until all categories of the population were called upon to take part in the life of the nation. Freedom and a constitution: such was the only road that lay open for Alexander III, if he wanted to avoid getting caught up in the fatal circle that had led to the death of his father.

In order to affirm these ideas, *A Letter from the Executive Committee to Alexander III* was published on 10th March 1881. It was then extensively circulated. It had been written by Tikhomirov, and discussed and somewhat modified by his comrades who finally approved it. Mikhailovsky was entrusted with re-reading it and making a few changes, almost only formal in character. The letter read:

The bloody tragedy which took place along the Catherine Canal was not just the result of chance and was not unexpected. After everything that has been happening for the last ten years, it was inevitable . . . Only someone utterly incapable of analysing the life of peoples can explain it by speaking of 'the criminal intentions of single individuals' or even of a 'band'. Despite all the severe persecutions, despite the fact that the government of the ex-Emperor sacrificed everything—freedom, the interests of all classes, the interests of the economy, and even its own dignity—in order to suppress the revolutionary movement, we have seen that during the last ten years it has gone on obstinately developing and growing. It has attracted the finest elements in the country, the most energetic men and those capable of the greatest sacrifices, and it has reached the hoped-for partisan warfare that it has been carrying out for three years against the government. You know, Sire, that the government of your father can certainly not be accused of having lacked energy. In Russia, innocent and guilty alike were hanged; the prisons and lands of exile were filled with people; dozens of so-called 'chiefs' were persecuted and hanged. They died with the courage and resignation of martyrs. But the movement did not stop; it grew and was constantly reinforced. Yes, Sire, the revolutionary movement does not depend on individuals; it is a process of the national organism . . . Revolutionaries are created by circumstances: the general discontent of the people, the desire of Russia to bring it towards a new social system. It is impossible to exterminate all the people or to do away with discontent by enforcing repression; indeed, this will only make it grow. And it is this that makes new elements rise from the people in ever increasing numbers to take the place of those who have been killed; and it is this that gives life to ever more energetic and violent passions.

Tikhomirov then showed how they had moved from propaganda to terror and recalled the names of those who had marked a step forward in the evolution of the movement; Kovalsky, Osinsky, Lizogub. He went back over the terrible ground that had been covered, and said,

What is the origin of this sad necessity for a bloody fight? It springs, Sire, from the fact that we have no authentic government in the real sense of the word. The government, by its very nature, should express only the forces of the nation and the people; it should realize the will of the people. And yet, here with us—please forgive the expression—the government has degenerated into a pure camarilla and (far more than the Executive Committee) it deserves to be called a 'usurping band'. Whatever the intentions of the government, they have nothing in common with the desires of the people.

The State was suspended in the air, based only on the exploiters and the misery of all.

'There can only be two ways to escape from such a situation: either revolution, which is absolutely indispensable and which no death sentence can stop; or, the voluntary transference of supreme power to the people.' (Tikhomirov used the word *obrashchenie*, the Russian word corresponding to revolution and conversion, thus making it clearly understood that the voluntary transference must be complete and entire.) 'In the interests of the fatherland and so as to avoid those terrible evils which always accompany a revolution, the Executive Committee turns to Your Majesty, with the advice to choose the second road.' Should he take this advice, the revolutionaries undertook to put an end to all terrorist activity and to 'devote themselves to cultural work for the good of the beloved people . . . The peaceful struggle of ideas will replace violence, which is more repellent to us than to your servants, and which we practise only out of sad necessity.'

The letter recalled the two fundamental conditions that were required for this to happen:

(1) A general amnesty for all 'political criminals', in view of the fact that their actions were not criminal but merely the fulfilment of their civic duties.

(2) The summoning of representatives of all the Russian people in order to reconsider the existing system of the State and social life and in order to rebuild them in accordance with the desires of the people.

This second clause would be of significance only if elections were carried out in absolute freedom, and so it was indispensable that:

(1) The deputies must be elected from all classes and categories without distinction, proportional to the number of inhabitants.

(2) No restriction must be imposed on the electors or the delegates.

(3) The electoral campaign and the elections themselves must be carried out in complete freedom. And so, as a temporary measure, the government must ensure: (*a*) full freedom of the press; (*b*) full freedom of speech; (*c*) full freedom of assembly; (*d*) full freedom for the electoral programmes.

This was the only way which would allow Russia to continue along the road of fair and peaceful development. 'We solemnly declare before our beloved

Fatherland and the entire world that our party will of its own accord un-conditionally submit to the decisions of a National Assembly.'[14]

Fate decreed—or it may have been the logic of events—that this letter should reach the Winter Palace at the very moment that discussions were proceeding about a decree which Alexander II had signed just before his death. This decree had at last sanctioned Loris-Melikov's constitutional pro-posals.[15] The importance of this decision certainly did not lie in the legal forms which embodied the liberal tendencies of the last two decades. Loris-Melikov's plans were particularly elaborate and envisaged the summoning of two Commissions—one economic and administrative, the other financial. These were to consist of officials and men coopted for their ability. Both these Commissions were to be controlled and coordinated by a general Commission in which the plans to be submitted to the Council of State would be discussed by men chosen from the *Zemstvos* and some of the leading towns. The importance of the plan did not lie in all this, but rather in the value that Alexander II himself attributed to it. 'I have given my approval, but I do not hide from myself the fact that it is the first step towards a constitution.' Throughout February it had been discussed in high govern-ment circles, though nothing had leaked outside the Winter Palace. *Narod-naya Volya* did not even suspect that Loris-Melikov's policies were coming to harbour and that his year-old attempt to include part of the intelligentsia and the bourgeoisie in the machinery of government was about to be estab-lished by law. The debate had been as ambiguous as the one that had pre-ceded and followed Khalturin's attempt to kill the Tsar. But this time the Emperor had finally made up his mind. On the morning of 1st March he had signed the document, although he had reserved the right to submit the proposal to be examined by the Minister of the Interior and discussed by the Committee of Ministers which was to be summoned for this purpose on 4th March.

Hardly had Rysakov's and Grinevitsky's bombs exploded before Loris-Melikov understood that his fate was sealed. For Alexander III would certainly bring about the triumph of those Slavophil and obscurantist tendencies, which he had derived from his mentor Pobedonostsev, from his admiration for writers like Aksakov, and above all from his utter scorn for public opinion, the press, and the 'chatterboxes' of St Petersburg and the provinces. A decision was reached on 8th March. Loris-Melikov insisted that the dead sovereign's will should be put into effect. Even now he managed to get a majority by looking for support to Prince Constantine Nikolaevich, Milyutin and in general those who still retained something of the spirit which had brought about the peasant reform twenty years earlier. But he clashed with the Tsar's advisers, who were urging him not to give in to the ferment of the intelligentsia, and to remember that he was the autocrat. The new Emperor began to say that 'he too feared that Loris-Melikov's plans marked the first step towards a constitution'. He was afraid of making even a gesture which might lead him to the road pointed out by the Executive Committee. So he chose absolute power and embarked on the policy of reaction which characterized his entire reign. The fight between the liberal and the reactionary groups continued until April, but now its conclusion was no longer in doubt.

The revolutionary party kept silent. It was no longer in a position to strike and to shake the government edifice. A manifesto of 29th April consecrated Pobedonostsev's victory. 'It is a demonstration of the Sovereign's firm determination to maintain and defend the autocracy . . . It contains a kind of legal summing-up and threats, but there is not a single word which can satisfy either the educated classes or the simple people. It has had a profoundly depressing effect on society', wrote Peretts in his diary. He himself had urged a liberal solution to the crisis.[16]

It was left to Zhelyabov and his comrades to reassert in the face of death those values which the State appeared to be trying to wipe out from the soil of Russia. They did this in a way that won admiration even from liberal bureaucracy, and that sowed a seed that no repression could crush.[17] The trial began on 26th March 1881, and ended four days later. Zhelyabov said that the prosecutor had been perfectly right to declare that the operation of 1st March was not just a simple fact but 'history'. Not only all the accused but the entire party took responsibility for this. It corresponded to the ends and means that *Narodnaya Volya* had declared to be its own in all its proclamations and in the review that it had published. Zhelyabov did not theorize a terrorist revolution, as Morozov had done, but he recognized that the battle was the logical consequence of the movement's whole development, and he summed up the history of his generation.

We have tried in several different ways to act on behalf of the people. At the beginning of the 'seventies we chose to live like workers and peacefully propagate our Socialist ideas. The movement was absolutely harmless. But how did it end? It was broken only because of the immense obstacles in the form of prison and banishment with which it had to contend. A movement, which was unstained by blood and which repudiated violence, was crushed . . . The short time that we lived among the people showed us how bookish and doctrinaire were our ideas. We then decided to act on behalf of the interests created by the people, interests which were inherent in its life and which it recognized. Such was the distinctive character of Populism. From metaphysics and dreams we moved to positivism, and kept close to the soil . . . Instead of spreading Socialist ideas, we gave first place to our determination to reawaken the people by agitation in the name of the interest that it felt; instead of a peaceful fight we applied ourselves to a fight with deeds. We began with small deeds . . . It was in 1878 that the idea of a more radical fight first made its appearance—the idea of cutting the Gordian knot. The roots of 1st March must be looked for in our ideas of the winter of 1877. The party had not yet seen clearly enough the significance of our political structure for the destiny of the Russian people, though now all its forces drove it to battle against the political system.

At Lipetsk, the revolutionaries had decided to fight in this way, and they had worked out the methods required to bring about 'a violent revolution by means of a conspiracy. This was to be achieved by organizing the revolutionary forces in the widest meaning of the word . . . After the Lipetsk meeting, I joined the organization whose centre was the Executive Committee, and I worked to widen it. In this spirit I did what I could to found a single centralized organization, made up of autonomous groups but acting according to a common plan in the interests of a common purpose.'[18]

Sofya Perovskaya, Kibalchich, Gesia Gelfman and Mikhailov, all confirmed the ideas for which they had sacrificed their lives. Sofya Perovskaya was outstandingly brave. Kibalchich revealed his true worth, and showed himself a man of genius, always concerned with the technical problem of the relations between ends and means. In his prison cell he went on designing a plan for a flying machine, which he regretted not being able to finish before he was hanged. Only Rysakov said that he was a peaceful Socialist and that he felt remorse for his terrorist activities.

They were all sentenced to death, but Gesia Gelfman was not hanged because she was pregnant. Her existence and that of her newborn child in the Peter-Paul fortress outraged Europe, and aroused violent protests in Socialist and democratic circles. Her baby died in a foundlings' home on 25th January 1882. Five days later she too died.

At 9.50 in the morning of 3rd April 1881, Rysakov, Zhelyabov, Mikhailov, Kibalchich and Sofya Perovskaya climbed the scaffold. With the exception of Rysakov they all embraced for the last time. Then they were hanged.

NOTES

The standard system of transliteration of Russian words, modified in the text to conform to accepted usage, has been adhered to in the notes.

◆◆◆

CHAPTER 1

1. His complete works have been published with abundant notes and subsidiary documents: M. K. Lemke, '*Polnoye sobranie sochineniy i pisem*' (*Collected works and letters*), P., 1915–25, 22 volumes. This publication is a virtual encyclopaedia of the intellectual and political movement of Herzen's time. From now on it will be referred to in this chapter simply by volume and page. Among the most important additional publications are: '*A. I. Gertsen. Novyye materialy*', pod redaktsiey N. M. Mendel'sona (*New material*, edited by N. M. Mendel'son), M., 1927; 'Literaturnoye nasledstvo', nos. 7–8, M., 1933, pp. 56 ff. and pp. 280 ff. of the same issue where a list of lesser works from reviews, miscellanies, etc., not included in the *Complete works*, can be found in *ibid.*, nos. 39–40, and also nos. 41–2, M., 1941, in which, on pp. 632 ff., is a bibliography of Herzeniana for the period 1934 to 1940. See too nos. 61–3, '*Gertsen i Ogaryovi*'. A corpus of still unpublished material, which had remained in the Herzen family, was given by them to the Russian Archives in Prague; after the war the Czechoslovak Government gave it to the Soviet Government. Of a new edition of Herzen's works (*Sobranie Sochineniy v tridstati tomakh*, M., 1954) 16 volumes have now appeared. A complete bibliography up to the year 1908 appeared as an appendix to the important book by C. Vetrinsky, '*Gertsen*' (*Herzen*), Spb., 1908. Among later studies the most outstanding are: G. V. Plekhanov, '*A. I. Gertsen. Sbornik statey*', s predisloviem V. Vaganyana (*A. I. Herzen. Collected articles*, with a preface by V. Vaganyan), M., undated (but 1924); the publication, with preface and notes by L. Kamenev, of '*Byloye i dumy*' (*My past and thoughts*), M.-L., 1932, 3 vols.; and Ya. El'sberg, '*A. I. Gertsen. Zhizn' i tvorchestvo*' (*A. I. Herzen. Life and work*), M., 1948; in French, Raoul Labry, *Alexandre Ivanovich Herzen, 1812–1870, Essai sur la formation et le développement de ses idées*, Paris, 1928; in English, E. H. Carr, *The romantic exiles*, London, 1933. '*Gertsen v vospominaniyakh sovremennikov*' (*Herzen in contemporary recollections*) in '*Seriya literarurnykh memuarov*' (*Collection of literary memoirs*), M., 1956, is useful.
2. XII, 59.
3. XII, 54.
4. XII, 74.
5. *Ibid.*
6. This recurring remark is taken from A. Kizevetter, '*F. V. Rastopchin*', in '*Istoricheskiye otkliki*' (*Historical echoes*), M., 1915, p. 100.
7. This element of disinterestedness and voluntary sacrifice which inspired the Decembrists is also proved by the fact that hardly anyone among the peasant masses at the time understood their gesture. The conspiracy of nobles was indeed often interpreted as contrary to peasant interests, and to the monarchy's supposed intention to abolish serfdom. See the interesting article by I. I. Ignatovich, '*Krest'yanskiye volneniya 1826 g. v svyazi so slukhami o vole i o 14 dekabrya 1825 goda*' (*Peasant risings of 1826 in relation to rumours of emancipation and*

to 14th December 1825) in 'Bor'ba krest'yan za osvobozhdenie' (The peasant struggle for freedom), L.-M., 1924.

8. See principally V. I. Semevsky, 'Politicheskiya i obshchestvennyya idei dekabristov' (The political and social ideas of the Decembrists), Spb., 1909.

9. S. S. Mil'man, '"Prakticheskiye nachala politicheskoy ekonomii" P. I. Pestelya' (Pestel's 'Practical principles of political economy') in 'Krasnyy Arkhiv', 1925, no. VI.

10. P. I. Pestel', 'Russkaya Pravda, Nakaz Vremennomu Verkhovnomu Pravleniyu' pod red. P. Shchegoleva (Russian law, an instruction for the Supreme Provisory Government, edited by P. Shchegolev); and I. M. Lubin, Zur Charakteristik und zur Quellenanalyse von Pestels 'Russkaya Pravda', Hamburg, 1930.

11. Op. cit., pp. 203–5.

12. V. I. Semevsky, op. cit., p. 536. Semevsky thinks it likely that Filippo Buonarroti was in touch with the Decembrists. In Paris, towards the end of his life, he knew N. I. and A. I. Turgenev. The latter, in his article 'Paris (A Russian's chronicle)', published in 'Sovremennik', 1836, no. I, p. 275, speaks of him. See also 'Ostaf'evskiy arkhiv knyazey Vyazemskikh' (The Ostaf'yev archive of the Vyazemsky family), vol. III, p. 323. The brochure by the Abbé Antoine de Cournaud, De la propriété ou la cause du pauvre plaidée au Tribunal de la Raison, de la Justice, et de la Vérité, Paris, 1791, is a project for the equal distribution of real property in France. It contains none of the elements characteristic of Pestel''s Russian Law.

13. Op. cit., p. 205.

14. N. S. Rusanov, 'Vliyanie evropeyskogo sotsializma na dekabristov i molodogo Gertsena' (The influence of European Socialism on the Decembrists and the young Herzen), in 'Minuvshiye gody', 1908, no. XII.

15. 'Plan gosudarstvennogo preobrazovaniya grafa M. M. Speranskogo' (Count M. M. Speransky's plan for the reform of the State), M., 1905, p. 59.

16. The most recent examination of the problems underlying these discussions is found in F. M. Morozov, 'Razlozhenie krepostnicheskoysistemy khozyaystva v Rossii i ekonomicheskaya politika v pervoy chetverti XIX veka' (The dissolution of the servile system and Russian economic policy in the first quarter of the 19th century), in 'Voprosy istorii narodnogo khozyaystva SSSR' (Problems of Russian economic history), M., 1957.

17. Quoted by V. I. Semevsky, op. cit., p. 613.

18. Ibid., p. 532, note 2.

19. For the controversy in Western Europe, see I. V. Luchitsky, 'Istoriya krest'yanskoy reformy v zapadnoy Yevrope s 1789 g.' (The history of peasant reform in Western Europe from 1789), in 'Universitetskiya Izvestiya', Kiev, 1879. In Russia, interest in the organization of the peasant obshchina, its usages and customs, began in the eighteenth century, particularly in the second half of the century, when it ran parallel to the work of codifying the administrations of great estates in noble ownership which was then in progress. See the interesting documents published by M. V. Dovnar-Zapol'sky, 'Materialy dlya istorii votchinnogo upravleniya v Rossii' (Material for the history of administration of estates in Russia), in 'Universitetskiya Izvestiya', Kiev, 1903, no. 12; 1904, nos 6–7; 1905, no. 8; 1909, no. 7; 1910, no. 11. It was about this time also that Catherine, in various acts of legislature, defined the corporative rights of the obshchina on Crown land. For a discussion of the whole problem see V. I. Semevsky, 'Krest'yanskiy vopros v Rossii v XVIII i pervoy polovine XIX veka' (The peasant problem in Russia in the eighteenth and first half of the nineteenth century), Spb., 1888.

20. It was published with other writings in N. A. Bestuzhev, '*Stat'i i pis'ma*', redaktsiya, vstupitel'naya stat'ya i primechaniya I. M. Trotskogo (*Articles and letters*, edited, with introductory article and notes, by I. M. Trotsky), M.-L., 1933, pp. 91 ff.

21. *Op. cit.*, pp. 248–9.

22. *Op. cit.*, pp. 267–8; and M. Yu. Baranovsky, '*Dekabrist Nikolay Bestuzhev*' (The Decembrist Nicholas Bestuzhev).

23. S. Gessen, '*Dekabrist o kommunizme*' (Neopublikovannaya stat'ya M. A. Fonvizina 'O kommunizme i sotsializme') (*A Decembrist speaks about Communism* [an unpublished article by M. A. Fonvizin, 'On Communism and Socialism']), in 'Krasnyy Arkhiv', 1927, no. IV; and N. G. Bogdanova, '*Iz perepiski M. A. Fonvizina*' (*From the correspondence of M. A. Fonvizin*), in 'Pamyati Dekabristov' (*In memory of the Decembrists*), 1926, no. III. V. I. Semevsky, '*M. A. Fon-Vizin. Biograficheskiy ocherk.*' *Obshchestvennyya dvizheniya v Rossii v pervuyu polovinu XIX veka.* Tom I. *Dekabristy : M. A. Fon-Vizin, Kn. E. P. Obolensky i bar. V. I. Shteyngel'* (*stat'i i materialy*). Sostavili: V. I. Semevsky, N. Bogucharsky, i P. E. Shchegolev (*M. A. Fonvizin. A biographical sketch*, in Social movements in Russia in the first half of the 19th century. Vol. I. The Decembrists : M. A. Fon-Vizin, Prince E. P. Obolensky and Baron V. I. Shteyngel' [articles and documents], compiled by V. I. Semevsky, V. Bogucharsky and P. E. Shchegolev), Spb., 1905, pp. 77 ff.

24. XX, 324.

25. XXII, 78.

26. VI, 255.

27. X, 96.

28. This fragment was printed for the first time in 'Zven'ya', 1936, no. VI, pp. 339 ff. It was thought to have been written by Herzen; but cf. Vol. I. of the new edition of his Works (Moscow, 1954), p. 478.

29. These words, written in 1856, were published in 'Literaturnoye nasledstvo', nos. 39–40, M., 1941, p. 358.

30. I, 117. Compare XII, 348, his remark to the police on arrest: 'The followers of Saint-Simon have not achieved what Saint-Simon wished'.

31. Elsewhere he mentions the *Introduction à la science de l'histoire* by Buchez (XII, 364). On the atmosphere of intellectual enthusiasm at this time, compare an article by Sazonov—the third of the three young men whom Ogarev mentions in his verses—published in 1860, and reprinted in B. Koz'min, '*Iz literaturnogo nasledstva N. I. Sazonova*' (*N. I. Sazonov's literary inheritance*), in 'Literaturnoye nasledstvo', nos. 41–2, M., 1941. There he speaks of Schelling, Oken, Böhme and Balzac, and describes the impact of the romantic movement on the generation of Russians that followed the Decembrist movement.

32. In a literary work, *Encounters* (1836), Herzen imagines himself talking to Cloots 'who promised I should meet a great man who, in his opinion, excelled all men, and disowned not only any form of political organization but also the right to hold property. Afterwards I learnt that this was Hébert' (I, 288).

33. See I. Berlin, *The marvellous decade*, in 'Encounter', nos. 21, 26, 27, 32, London, 1955–6.

34. I, 370.

35. II, 223.

36. II, 424.

37. III, 35.

38. III, 362.

39. III, 352.

40. III, 145–6.

41. III, 220.

42. III, 221.

43. III, 224.

44. XIII, 16.

45. III, 38.

46. III, 88.

47. III, 22–3.

48. Reprinted in P. V. Annenkov, '*Literaturnyye vospominaniya*' (*Literary memoirs*), with preface by N. Piskanov, L., 1928, pp. 159 ff.

49. *Op. cit.*, p. 216.

50. For this aspect of his activity, see P. Sakulin, '*Russkaya literatura i sotsializm. Chast' pervaya. Ranniy russkiy sotsializm*' (*Russian literature and Socialism. Part One: Early Russian Socialism*), M., 1924; and also '*Sotsializm Belinskogo*'. Stat'i i pis'ma. Redaktsiya i kommentarii P. N. Sakulina (*The Socialism of Belinsky*. Articles and letters edited and with comments by P. N. Sakulin), M., 1925. For a refutation see S. E. Shchukin, '*V. G. Belinsky i Sotsializm*' (*V. G. Belinsky and socialism*), M., 1928.

51. VI, 275

52. III, 319.

53. III, 141.

54. III, 332.

55. III, 361.

56. III, 448.

57. III, 24.

58. III, 91.

59. III, 57.

60. III, 57.

61. A. S. Khomyakov: '*Polnoye sobranie sochineniy*' [*Complete works*], M., 1904, vol. I, p. 636.

62. Yu. F. Samarin, '*Sochineniya*' [*Works*], M., 1877 onwards, vol. I, p. 40.

63. See N. S. Derzhavin, '*Gertsen i slavyanofily*' (*Herzen and the Slavophils*), in 'Istorik-marksist', 1939, no. I. On the importance of the Slavophils see R. Hare, *Pioneers of Russian thought*, Oxford, 1951.

64. III, 117.

65. August von Haxthausen had developed in a typically Romantic environment; he collaborated with Arnim, Brentano and the brothers Grimm on the periodical 'Wünschenruthe'. He remained on terms of the closest friendship with the Grimms. His ideas on agricultural relations sprang from the romanticism of *Volkstum*. Everything he wrote is of the greatest interest. See, for example, *De l'abolition par voie législative du partage égal et temporaire des terres dans les communes russes*, Paris, 1858, in which he re-examined the agrarian problems of Russia and Western Europe after the events of 1848.

66. A Slavophil, A. I. Koshelev, remarked on this, not without some bitterness: 'A German, visiting our country, pointed out the way for our "learned men" to a serious study of things which they had not taken seriously before ...', '*Obshchinnoye pozemel'noye vladenie*' (*The communal ownership of land*), in 'Russkaya beseda', 1858, no. VIII, p. 108. The discussion about who first 'discovered' the *obshchina* still survives in Soviet historiography. See, for example, V. M. Shteyn, '*Ocherki razvitiya russkoy obshchestvenno-ekonomicheskoy mysli XIX–XX vekov*' (*Essays on the development of Russian economic and social thought in the nineteenth and twentieth centuries*), L., 1948, pp. 111 ff.

67. III, 111.
68. A. Haxthausen, *Studien über die inneren Zustände, das Volksleben und insbesondere die ländlichen Einrichtungen Russlands*, 3 vols., Hanover, 1847; Berlin, 1852. It was not translated into Russian for some years, and then only partially, by L. I. Ragozin in Moscow in 1870.
69. In 1846, N. I. Nadezhdin, one of the most interesting critics of Russian romanticism, gave a lecture at the Russian Geographical Society—founded the previous year to encourage the 'collection of data about the common man'—in which he drew attention to 'those remnants of communal life where the force of time and other influences have not wiped out all traces of the primitive organization of the life of the people'. P. P. Semenov, '*Istoriya poluvekovoy deyatel'nosti Imp. Rus. Geograficheskogo Obshchestva, 1845–1895*' (*History of the Imperial Russian Geographical Society in the first half-century of its activity, 1845–1895*), Spb., 1896, pp. 38–9.
70. See IV, p. 451, footnote.
71. P. V. Annenkov, '*Zamechatel'noye desyatiletie*' (*The remarkable decade*), *op. cit.*, p. 463. On the Westerners in Moscow, see B. N. Chicherin, '*Vospominaniya. Moskva sorokovykh godov*'. Vstupitel'naya stat'ya i primechaniya S. V. Bakhrushina (*Memoirs of Moscow in the forties*. Introductory article and notes by S. V. Bakhrushin), M., 1929, pp. 35 ff.
72. See the interesting and controversial article by M. N. Pokrovsky, '*Otkuda vzyalas' vneklassovaya teoriya razvitiya russkogo samoderzhaviya*' (The origin of the supra-class theory of the development of Russian absolutism), in '*Istoricheskaya nauka i bor'ba klassov*' (*The science of history and the class struggle*), M.-L., 1933, vol. I, p. 167.
73. XII, 184 ff.
74. '*P. V. Annenkov i ego druz'ya. Literaturnyye vospominaniya i perepiska 1835–1885 godov*' (*P. V. Annenkov and his friends. Literary memoirs and correspondence from 1835 to 1885*), Spb., 1892, p. 538.
75. P. V. Annenkov, *op. cit.*, p. 429.
76. Letter to Annenkov of 12th October 1847, quoted in P. V. Annenkov, *op. cit.*, p. 492.
77. III, 303. At the same time he observed that the Slavophils 'remember what the people forgets'.
78. Herzen often repeated these lines, which were a symbol of his hope for Russia. In 1851 they were the opening words of one of his most important works: *Du développement des idées révolutionnaires en Russie*. There his own translation runs: 'Dans ton existence, pleine de sève et de vie, tu n'es troublée ni par d'inutiles souvenirs, ni par de vaines discussions'. V, 300.
79. V, 133.
80. V, 165.
81. Letter dated 30th January 1848, V, 178.
82. See especially the *Letters from France and Italy*, letters V–VIII, of which the different versions were published by Lemke. In Rome, Herzen was in close contact with radical opinion. In one letter from Paris he wrote: 'In Rome I had very friendly relations with the editorial staff of "Epoca", particularly Spini and Gonzales of Milan. I helped—don't laugh—to give "Epoca" a republican tinge'. '*A. I. Gertsen. Novyye materialy*', pod red. N. M. Mendel'sona (*A. I. Herzen. New material*, edited by N. M. Mendel'son), M., 1927, p. 56. Compare what Herzen said about 'Epoca' in V, 606. Even if none of its issues, directed by M. Pinto and L. Spini, which first appeared on 16th March 1848, contain articles signed by Herzen, there are many suggestions of his influence. For instance, throughout April Poland and Russia are often mentioned. 3rd

April: 'The Polish movement is invincible.' 16th April: 'From letters which arrived yesterday from St Petersburg, it seems that the proposal put forward by the Tsar is coming up again. We do not know how far this report can be trusted, since the sentiments of the Russian government towards Poland are well known, as are the rigid measures which are already in force and particularly the autocratic spirit, which is certainly not very capable either of generous actions or of liberal thoughts, or of the recognition of the true rights of the people. Perhaps God, Who can soften the hearts even of tigers and Who has performed many miracles in recent times, can bring about the easy redemption of all Poland, and consequently a change for the better in Russia too. . . .' Perhaps it was Herzen also who persuaded 'Epoca' to concern itself with the German groups. A proclamation bearing G. Herwegh's signature, and dated 21st March 1848, was printed on 6th April: '. . . with France against Russia! This cry explains the profound conviction of the German people that the last war was necessary and inevitable, a war between two worlds. . . .' On 28th April, the *Manifesto del poeta Herweg a nome della legione democratica tedesca formata a Parigi*, was reprinted from a German review. On 26th April 'Epoca' discussed the internal politics of Russia: 'An *ukaz* gives the serfs the right to buy immovable property. This would be a social revolution in Russia, were it not an astute move by the government to put into circulation money belonging to serfs, which they now conceal for fear that their masters should take it from them.' Later, M. A. Tuchkova referred to Spini in a letter to Herzen (see '*Arkhiv Ogaryovykh*') (*The Ogarev archives*), in 'Russkiye propilei', M., 1917, no. IV, p. 90. In fact not only Herzen but also several other members of his circle in Italy at that time were connected with 'Epoca'.

83. VI, 62.
84. VI, 62–3.
85. VI, 73.
86. VI, 622.
87. V, 128 ff.
88. VI, 623.
89. '*A. I. Gertsen. Novyye materialy*' (*A. I. Herzen. New material*), *op. cit.*, p. 46.
90. The meeting between Herzen and de Tocqueville in the streets of Paris is particularly curious: Herzen looked upon de Tocqueville as a symbol of the impotence of the liberal movements of the time. XIII, 302.
91. VI, 655.
92. XII, 382.
93. VI, 655.
94. VI, 641.
95. VI, 87.
96. VI, 90.
97. See R. Labry, '*Herzen et Proudhon*', Paris, 1928. Herzen's letters to Herwegh in 1849 give some interesting glimpses of his connection with Proudhon. They are published in 'Literaturnoye nasledstvo', nos. 7–8, 1933, pp. 64 ff. Herzen criticized Proudhon for a position he considered to be too moderate. See also vol. 62, M., 1955, p. 492 ff.
98. V, 290.
99. V, 286.
100. VI, 121.
101. On the whole question see Herzen, *From the Other Shore and The Russian people and Socialism*, with an introduction by Isaiah Berlin, London, 1956.
102. VI, 118.

103. V, 414–15.
104. V, 419.
105. '*A. I. Gertsen. Novyye materialy*' (*A. I. Herzen. New material*), *op. cit.*, p. 125.
106. V, 422.
107. V, 425.
108. VI, 563.
109. V, 289.
110. This appeal was not printed until 1941, when A. Ivashchenko published it in 'Literaturnoye nasledstvo', nos. 39–40, M., 1941, p. 165.
111. '*A. I. Gertsen. Novyye materialy*' (*A. I. Hertzen. New material*), *op. cit.*, p. 54, note.
112. V, 390.
113. V, 391.
114. V, 299–300.
115. V, 314.
116. VI, 142.
117. V, 314.
118. Herzen used this expression when trying to persuade Mazzini not to ally himself with the defeated democrats in other European countries, VI, 141.
119. VI, 124–5. For this period of Herzen's life, cf. F. Venturi, *Esuli russi in Piemonte dopo il '48*, Torino, 1959.
120. Even leaving out of consideration Bakunin—whose life we shall follow in the next chapter—Herzen was not the only Russian to draw similar conclusions from the 1848 revolution. It is true that N. Turgenev, the émigré Decembrist. had nothing but good liberal intentions to suggest. In his pamphlet, '*La Russie en présence de la crise européenne*', Paris, 1848, he tried to find a *juste milieu* between the hatreds and hopes which his native country had aroused at that time. 'La Russie', he wrote, 'ne mérite ni cet excès d'honneur, ni cette indignité' (p. 8). And he continued: 'Ou pourrait en établissant un régime constitutionnel et réprésentatif dans l'Empire de la Russie' (p. 39) . . . achieve countless wonderful things, culminating in the consoling spectacle of 'tous les slaves confondus dans un embrassement fraternel' (p. 46). But others began to advance problems more concrete and more connected with Russian intellectual and social traditions. Sazonov, a friend of Herzen and Ogarev, took part in the 'Club de la Fraternité des Peuples' at Paris, and in the 'Tribune des Peuples' made a stand which has much in common with Herzen's. He defended the *obshchina* and spoke of its possible relationship with Western Socialist movements. When he emigrated to Switzerland, he continued to think in Socialist terms and was in touch with Marx. [D. Ryazanov, '*Karl Marks i russkiye lyudi sorokovykh godov*' (*Karl Marx and the Russians of the forties*), P., 1918, pp. 13 ff.] In a letter to Herwegh, Sazonov mentions what he said to Marx: 'I, a barbarian, appreciate you and love you more than any of your fellow-countrymen': published by B. Nikolaevsky in 'Letopisi marksizma', 1928, no. VI.

Another émigré, Ivan Golovin, who had previously supported aristocratic and constitutional ideas simultaneously, was moved to Populist ideas by the revolution. Already in his pamphlet of 1846, '*Des économistes et des socialistes*', he had spoken at length about Fourier and Louis Blanc and had concluded: 'Dans la masse d'idées excentriques qui ont été jetées dans le monde, une seule les domine toutes et forme le fil de ce labyrinthe, c'est l'association' (p. 30). Some years later he wrote in his book, *L'Europe révolutionnaire*, Paris, 1849, p. 443: 'Puisqu'on ne veut pas de réformes en Russie, on aura une révolution, mais une révolution sociale, une jacquerie en permanence, une

Saint-Barthélemy des propriétaires. La moyenne officielle des nobles tués par leurs serfs s'élève déjà a 67 par an. Les ouvriers russes entrent pour peu dans l'élément révolutionnaire. Ce sont pour la plupart des paysans qui, l'été, travaillent à leurs champs, et l'hiver aux fabriques. Leur salaire, quelque minime qu'il soit, ne leur sert qu'à se griser les jours de fêtes. Leur existence est assurée et la misère les stimule peu à se révolter; leur intelligence, d'ailleurs, est obscurcie. Mais les licenciés, ces soldats aguerris qui rongent leur frein et traînent une vie oisive, en attendant l'occasion de se battre contre le gouverne-ment plutôt que pour lui; mais les enfants de troupes, dont on compte jusqu'à 280,000 dont 200,000 sont auprès de leurs mères; les ecclésiastiques manqués; les employés subalternes qui couvent une vieille rancune contre une société privilégiée; les petits nobles qui ne peuvent assouvir leur ambition; les mécon-tents de toute espèce, voilà la classe révolutionnaire qui, dans les mains d'un Pougatscheff éclairé, peut faire sauter en l'air cet échafaudage d'incapacité pretentieuse, de fourberie élevée à l'état de système, qui s'appelle le gouverne-ment russe. . . . Une constitution n'est guère probable ni désirable pour la Russie. Si jamais il s'élevait une guerre entre la couronne et le peuple, il n'y aurait ni armistice, ni paix. Les chartes ne sont que des mensonges, grâce à la bonne foi royale. Le gouvernement des rois est le despotisme, celui des peuples la république. . . . La commune russe est régie d'une manière démocratique. La bourgeoisie n'a pas pu se former malgré tous les efforts du gouvernement et l'existence de la noblesse elle-même n'est pas dans l'esprit des institutions slaves.' Other observations in this book are not without interest. Some verses of Herwegh's, which are on the cover, show that Golovin expressed similar ideas to those of the Herzen circle. Golovin was to be a witness in the High Court of Justice at Bourges at the trial of Blanqui ('Tribune des Peuples', 24th March 1849) and to write for that paper. He even fulfilled Herzen's plan to set up a Russian press in Paris, though on a much reduced scale. There he pub-lished in 1849 a *Catechism of the Russian People*, which spread propaganda for a free system of government in Russia (G. Bakalov, '*Pervaya revolyutsionnaya broshyura russkoy emigratsii: "Katekhizis russkogo naroda" I. G. Golovina, 1849 goda*' (*The first revolutionary pamphlet by a Russian émigré:* '*Catechism of the Russian People*' *by I. G. Golovin, 1849*), in 'Zven'ya', 1932, no. I.

CHAPTER 2

1. The basic work for his life up to 1861 is M. A. Bakunin, '*Sobranie sochineniy i pisem, 1828–1876*', pod redaktsiey i s primechaniyami Yu. M. Steklova (*Complete works and letters, 1828–1876*, edited and with notes by Yu. M. Steklov): vol. I (*Pre-Hegelian period, 1828–37*), M., 1934; vol. II (*Hegelian period, 1837–40*), M., 1934; vol. III (*Period of the first visit abroad, 1840–9*), M., 1925; vol. IV (*Prison and deportation, 1849–61*), M., 1935. The subsequent volumes have not yet been published. From now on in this chapter this work will be referred to by volume and page. See especially A. A. Kornilov, '*Molodyye gody M. A. Bakunina*' (*The youth of Michael Bakunin*), P., 1915; '*Gody stranstviy M. A. Bakunina*' (*M. A. Bakunin's years of travel and research*), P., 1925; Yu. Steklov, '*Mikhail Alexandrovich Bakunin. Ego zhizn' i deyatel'nost'*' (*M. A. Bakunin. Life and activity, 1814–1876*), enlarged second edition, in three volumes (in fact made up of four), the first about the period 1814–1861, M., 1926–7; V. Polonsky, '*Mikhail Alexandrovich Bakunin. Iz istorii russkoy intelligentsii*' (*M. A. Bakunin. From the history of the Russian intelligentsia*), second edition, 2 vols., the first devoted to Bakunin as a romantic

(1814–61), M.-L., 1925; and Benoît P. Hepner, *Bakounine et le panslavisme révolutionnaire*, Paris, 1950; E. H. Carr, *Michael Bakunin*, London, 1937.

2. Eugene Pyziur, *The doctrine of anarchism of Michael A. Bakunin*, Milwaukee, 1955.

3. See, as a curiosity, an article, 'Alexandre de Bacounin', in the *Memorie della R. Accademia delle Scienze di Torino*, 1778–9, vol. IV.

4. V. Polonsky, *M. A. Bakunin, op. cit.*, vol. I, p. 9.

5. III, 250.

6. I, 52.

7. I, 154.

8. I, 175.

9. I, 178.

10. I, 180.

11. See the new study by Edward J. Brown, *The Circle of Stankevich*, in 'The American Slavic and East European Review', vol. XVI, no. 3, October 1955.

12. He died in Rome whilst still a young man. His literary remains are collected in '*Sochineniya*' (*Works*), edited by A. I. Stankevich, M., 1890, and, principally, his letters in '*Perepiska Nikolaya Vladimirovicha Stankevicha, 1830–40*' (*Letters of N. V. Stankevich, 1830–40*), also edited by A. I. Stankevich, M., 1914. See also M. O. Gershenzon, '*N. V. Stankevich*', in '*Istoriya molodoy Rossii*' (*History of young Russia*), second edition, M.-P., 1923; the portrait of Stankevich is, however, altogether too moralized and superficial.

13. '*Perepiska N. V. Stankevicha*' (*Letters of N. V. Stankevich*), *op. cit.*, p. 450.

14. *Ibid.*

15. *Ibid.*, p. 649.

16. *Ibid.*, p. 578.

17. *Ibid.*, p. 598.

18. *Ibid.*, p. 606.

19. *Ibid.*, p. 607.

20. I, 184.

21. I, 221.

22. I, 257.

23. I, 417.

24. I, 246.

25. II, 306.

26. III, 87.

27. '*Perepiska N. V. Stankevicha*' (*Letters of N. V. Stankevich*), *op. cit.*, p. 582.

28. *Ibid.*, p. 486.

29. *Ibid.*, p. 624.

30. *Ibid.*, p. 672.

31. See footnote, II, 456.

32. '*Pis'ma M. A. Bakunina k A. I. Gertsenu i N. P. Ogaryovu*'. Pod red. M. P. Dragomanova (*Letters from M. A. Bakunin to A. I. Herzen and N. P. Ogarev*. Edited by M. P. Dragomanov), Geneva, 1896, pp. 244–5.

33. '*Perepiska N. V. Stankevicha*' (*Letters of N. V. Stankevich*), *op. cit.*, p. 638.

34. Bakunin himself quoted this phrase to explain his own passing from the search for God to the search for God 'in people, in liberty, in revolution', January 1849, III, 370.

35. III, 147.

36. III, 148.

37. 'They are now completely beyond my memory', he said about his Russian friends in November 1842 (III, 170): a very different attitude from Herzen's, who emigrated a few years later; Herzen's Populism sprang from the constant

comparisons he made between Russia and the West, whereas Bakunin's owed its origin to his experiences of the West which he applied to his knowledge of Russia. Turgenev was struck by Bakunin's personality, although he caricatured his negative aspects in *Rudin*. Chernyshevsky protested violently: 'Instead of a portrait he has made a caricature; as if a lion was a proper subject of caricature.' Turgenev himself said that in *Rudin* he had wanted to portray Bakunin, but had not been successful. 'Rudin was at once superior and inferior to him.' This episode is interesting as an example of how often Russian literature at the time was bound up with political realities, and of how little, on the other hand, we can use it for the real history of these men and movements.

38. V. Fleury, *Le poète Georges Herwegh (1817–1875)*, Paris, 1911.

39. III, 180.

40. III, 223.

41. III, 229.

42. III, 230.

43. In his *Confession* to Nicholas I he was to give a long list of these friends, IV, 113.

44. See an article by Yu. Kamenev in 'Vestnik Evropy', 1914, no. IV, on this interesting member of the German democratic movement. Herzen once called him the most intelligent of his opponents; he was friendly both with Herwegh and Bakunin.

45. III, 237.

46. III, 235.

47. Quoted by Yu. Steklov, *op. cit.*, vol. I, p. 189.

48. D. Ryazanov, '*Karl Marks i russkiye lyudi sorokovykh godov*' (*K. Marx and the Russians of the forties*), P., 1918, in which the author's assertions about Tolstoy need correction: he confused him with a man of the same name, an agent of the Third Section. Regarding G. M. Tolstoy's connections with Belinsky see V. Evgen'ev-Maksimov, '"*Sovremennik*" v 40–50 gg. ot Belinskogo do Chernyshevskogo' ('Sovremennik' in the forties and fifties from Belinsky to Chernyshevsky), L., 1934, pp. 32 ff.

49. Quoted by Yu. Steklov, *op. cit.*, pp. 192–3. Even Herwegh, then as much the friend of Marx as of Bakunin, 'was always hostile' to Proudhon, III, 317. It was Bakunin on his own who had made his choice between Marx and Proudhon, against the opinion of the circle in which he was living at that time. Later he agreed with Herzen on this point, when they met in Paris in 1847.

50. Quoted by Yu. Steklov, *op. cit.*, p. 199.

51. III, 460.

52. A. I. Gertsen, '*Polnoye sobranie sochineniy*' (*Complete works and letters*), III, p. 449.

53. We know of these plans from the memoirs of a Russian woman writer, Avdot'ya Panaeva, who was at that time visiting Paris with her husband. See '*Vospominaniya, 1824–70*' (*Memoirs, 1824–70*), M.-L., 1933, p. 203.

54. '*Pis'ma*' (*Letters*). Edited by E. A. Lyatsky, vol. III, p. 328.

55. III, 57.

56. III, 265.

57. III, 276.

58. Sazonov speaks of this celebration in a letter dated 29th November 1853, published in C. H. Ostrovsky, *Lettres slaves (1833–1857)*. Orient, Pologne, Russie, 3rd ed., Paris, 1857, p. 219.

59. III, 282.

60. III, 286.

61. This speech was not printed. It is very likely that he expressed himself with some force on the possibilities of a revolution in the Slav world. In any case he asserts this in his *Confession*, IV, 119. He wrote in a letter that he was intending to take a step, 'serious, full of thought, touching on all the most difficult aspects of the question', III, 286.

62. A. I. Gertsen, '*Polnoye sobranie sochineniy i pisem*' (*Complete works and letters*), XIV, p. 424.

63. IV, 122.

64. III, 296.

65. III, 298.

66. Yu. Steklov, '*M. A. Bakunin*', *op. cit.*, vol. I, p. 267.

67. The recent study by B. Hepner, *op. cit.*, suffered from this defect.

68. III, 301.

69. III, 346 ff. On page 329 is given an interesting first draft of this appeal.

70. III, 349.

71. III, 370.

72. III, 315–16. With reference to the bond between Italy and the Slavs, Bakunin was again to remember in his *Confession* how at that time in Rome 'the Italian democrats were talking of the Slavs as possible and desirable allies'. IV, 176.

73. III, 367–8.

74. III, 317–18.

75. IV, 153.

76. IV, 172–3.

77. III, 339 ff., see the interesting article by B. Nikolaevsky, *Vzglyady M. A. Bakunina na polozhenie del v Rossii v 1849 godu* (*Bakunin's ideas on the Russian situation in 1849*), in 'Letopisi marksizma', 1929, nos. IX–X. This pamphlet is mentioned in *Russland unter Alexander II*, by Iwan Golowin, Leipzig, 1871, p. 246. See letter to Emma Herwegh, 26th October 1849, from Geneva, published in E. H. Carr, *Some unpublished letters of Aleksandr Herzen*, Oxford *Slavonic Papers*, vol. III, 1952, p. 98.

78. III, 385.

79. III, 399.

80. III, 408.

81. III, 415.

82. III, 416.

83. IV, 155.

84. See I. Berlin, 'Herzen and Bakunin on individual liberty', in *Continuity and change in Russian and Soviet thought*. Edited with an introduction by E. J. Simmons, Cambridge, Mass., 1955, pp. 473 ff.

CHAPTER 3

1. See chiefly V. I. Semevsky, '*Krest'yanskiy vopros v Rossii v XVIII i pervoy polovine XIX veka*' (*The peasant problem in the eighteenth and the first half of the nineteenth century*), Spb., 1888; '*Krest'yanstoye dvizhenie, 1827–1869*. Podgotovil k pechati E. A. Morokhovets' (*The peasant movement, 1827–69*. Documents edited by E. A. Morokhovets), M.-L., 1931, vol. I (1827–1860); and N. M. Druzhinin, '*Gosudarstvennyye krest'yane i reforma P. D. Kiselyova*' (*The State peasants and the reforms of P. D. Kiselev*), 2 vols., M.-L., 1946, 1958.

2. N. M. Druzhinin, *op. cit.*, vol. 1, p. 207.

3. I. I. Ignatovich, '*Bor'ba krest'yan za osvobozhdenie*' (*The peasants' struggle for*

freedom), L.-M., 1924, p. 193. See also Yu. I. Gerasimova, '*Krest'yanskoye dvizhenie v Rossii v 1844–1849*' (The peasant movement in Russia in 1844–9), in 'Istoricheskie Zapiski', no. 50, 1955, pp. 224 ff.

4. V. I. Semevsky, *op. cit.*, vol. II, p. 582.

5. One of the most typical examples was provided by the disturbances on State property which continued from 1833 to 1838 in the surroundings of Izhma (Archangel region). See the account in D. N. Khon'kin,'*Volneniya izhmenskikh krest'yan*' (*Peasant disturbances in Izhma*), Syktyvkar, 1941. See also '*Rabocheye dvizhenie v Rossii v XIX veke. Sbornik dokumentov i materialov*' pod red. A. M. Pankratovoy, vol. I, Part I and II, M., 1955.

6. For a detailed study of the large peasant risings on State land in the region of Perm and Orenburg, 1834–5, see N. M. Druzhinin, *op. cit.*, pp. 224 ff. This was the land of Pugachev and the situation in 1834 was not very different from the situation which preceded the great revolt of 1773, though naturally on a smaller scale.

7. S. Gessen, '*Kholernyye bunty (1830–1832)*' (*The cholera disturbances*, 1830–2), M., 1932.

8. '*Krest'yanskoye dvizhenie, 1827–1869*' (*The peasant movement, 1827–1869*), *op. cit.*, vol. I, p. 15.

9. N. M. Druzhinin, *op. cit.*, vol. I., p. 285.

10. These reports are quoted by E. V. Tarle, '*Imperator Nikolay I i krest'yanskiy vopros v Rossii, po neizdannym doneseniyam frantsuzskikh diplomatov, 1842–1847*' (*The Emperor Nicholas I and the peasant problem from French diplomatic reports, 1842–1847*), published in '*Zapad i Rossiya. Stat'i i dokumenty iz istorii XVII–XX vekov*' (*The West and Russia. Articles and documents relating to history from the seventeenth to the twentieth centuries*), P., 1918, p. 17, and p. 27, note 7.

11. V. I. Semevsky, '*Krest'yanskiy vopros v Rossii v XVIII i pervoy polovine XIX veka*' (*The peasant problem in Russia in the eighteenth and first half of the nineteenth century*), *op. cit.*, vol. II, p. 136.

12. N. M. Druzhinin, *op. cit.*, vol. I, p. 276.

13. *Ibid.*, p. 182.

14. *Ibid.*, p. 480.

15. *Ibid.*

16. E. V. Tarle, *op. cit.*, p. 18.

17. A. Haxthausen, *Studien über die inneren Zustände, das Volksleben und insbesondere die ländlichen Einrichtungen Russlands*, 3 vols., Hanover, 1847; Berlin, 1852; Russian translation by L. I. Ragozin, M., 1870, vol. I, p. 72.

18. Quoted by I. I. Ignatovich, *op. cit.*, p. 30.

19. N. Barsukov, '*Zhizn' i trudy M. P. Pogodina*' (*The life and work of M. P. Pogodin*), Spb., 1895, vol. IV, p. 303. Other evidence to the same effect in V. I. Semevsky, *op. cit.*, vol. II, pp. 187 ff.

20. A. Nifontov, '*1848 god v Rossii. Ocherki po istorii 40-kh godov*' (*1848 in Russia. Essays on the history of the forties*), M.-L., 1931, and a second edition, enlarged and corrected, 1949, pp. 128 ff., which quotes many documents concerning the nobles' state of mind at the time.

21. V. S. Pecherin, '*Zamogil'nyye zapisky*'. Podgotovil M. O. Gershenzon, pod red. L. Kameneva (*Memoirs from beyond the tomb*. Edited by M. O. Gershenzon and L. Kamenev), M., 1932, p. 115. Herzen has left a vivid portrait of him: XIV, pp. 54 ff. See M. Gershenzon, '*Zhizn' V. S. Pechyorina*' (*Life of V. S. Pecherin*), M., 1910, and V. Frank, '*Ein russischer Exulant im 19. Jhd. W. Petscherin*', in '*Schriftenreihe Osteuropa*', No. 3, 1957.

22. V. S. Pecherin, *op. cit.*, p. 109.

23. M. A. Bakunin, '*Sobranie sochineniy i pisem*'. Pod red. Yu. M. Steklova (*Collected works and letters*. Edited by Yu. M. Steklov), vol. II, p. 186.

24. N. P. Ogarev, '*Zapiski russkogo pomeshchika*' (*Memoirs of a Russian land-owner*), in 'Byloye', 1925, vols. XXVII–XXVIII, p. 15.

25. Reprinted in 'Zven'ya' by N. Mendel'son, 1933, no. II, p. 346 ff. See too N. P. Ogarev, '*Izbrannye sotsial'no-politicheskie i filosofskie proizvedeniya*'. Pod obshchey red. M. T. Iovchuka i N. G. Tarakanova (*Selected works on socibl, political and philosophical questions*. Edited by M. T. Iovchuk and N. G. Tarakanov), vol. I, M., 1952, p. 90.

26. See details in '*P. V. Annenkov i ego druz'ya. Literaturnyye vospominaniya i perepiska 1835–1885 godov*' (*P. V. Annenkov and his friends. Memoirs and literary correspondence 1835–1885*), St Petersburg, 1892, pp. 72 ff. See M. O. Gershenzon, '*N. P. Ogaryov pomeshchik*' (*N. P. Ogarev as a noble land-owner*), in '*Istoriya molodoy Rossii*' (*History of young Russia*), M., 1908, 2nd edition, M.-P., 1923.

27. See also the later project (1868) published in 'Literaturnoye nasledstvo', vol. 61, p. 572.

28. '*P. V. Annenkov i ego druz'ya*' (*P. V. Annenkov and his friends*), *op. cit.*, p. 104.

29. N. I. Sazonov's letter, published by Ya. Z. Chernyak, in 'Zven'ya', 1936, vol. VI, p. 345, quotes these words.

30. M. O. Gershenzon, *op. cit.*, p. 285.

31. See his important letters to Herzen, in 'Literaturnoye nasledstvo', vol. 61, pp. 703 ff.

32. His main works are collected in V. A. Milyutin, '*Izbrannyye proizvedeniya*' (*Selected works*), with preface by I. Blyumin, M., 1946.

33. *Op. cit.*, p. 162.

34. *Ibid.*, p. 39.

35. *Ibid.*, p. 40.

36. *Ibid.*, p. 350.

37. *Ibid.*, pp. 339–41.

38. Sources for this movement have been collected in '*Petrashevtsy v vospominaniyakh sovremennikov*'. Sbornik materialov. Sostavil P. E. Shchegolev s predisloviem N. Rozhkova (*The followers of Petrashevsky in the recollection of contemporaries*. A collection of material compiled by P. E. Shchegolev, with a preface by N. Rozhkov), M.-L., 1926. All other accounts derive from the voluminous records of the Commission of Inquiry which brought them to trial in 1849. Before the revolution these papers were re-copied entirely by the historian, V. I. Semevsky, who based on them a number of articles which were then published in various reviews. Some of them were republished, posthumously, in his book, '*M. V. Butashevich-Petrashevsky i petrashevtsy*' (*M. V. Butashevich-Petrashevsky and his followers*), Part I (the only part), M., 1922. V. Vodovozov, the editor, provides in the preface a complete bibliography of Semevsky's researches. A selection of the material has been published in '*Petrashevtsy*', edited by P. E. Shchegolev, two volumes, a sequel to the collection mentioned at the beginning of this note, M.-L., 1927–8. Complete records of the trial are in '*Delo petrashevtsev*' (*The case of the Petrashevskists*), edited by V. R. Leykina, E. A. Korol'chuk and V. A. Desnitsky, M.-L., vol. I, 1937; vol. II, 1941; vol. III, 1951. Poems written by the members of this movement have been collected in '*Poety-petrashevtsy*' (*Petrashevskist poets*), edited by V. L. Komarovich, L., 1940. See too '*Filosofskie i obshchestvenno-politicheskie proizvedeniya petrashevtsev*, (*The philosophical, social and political works of the Petrashevskists*), M., 1953; V. R. Leykina,

'*Petrashevtsy*', M., 1924; L. Raysky, '*Sotsial'nyye vozzreniya Petrashevtsev*' (*Social ideas of the Petrashevskists*), L., 1927; and G. Sourine, *Le fourierisme en Russie*, Paris, 1936.

39. N. Shchedrin (M. E. Saltykov), '*Brusin*', in '*Polnoye sobranie sochineniy*', pod red. V. Ya. Kirpotina i dr. (*Complete works*, edited by V. Ya. Kirpotin and others), vol. I, 1941, pp. 294–6.

40. A. S. Nifontov, '*Rossiya v 1848 godu*' (*Russia in 1848*), M., 1949, p. 153, for other Slavophil reactions.

41. Even the 'Tribune des peuples', for instance, to which Sazonov and Golovin were contributing, wrote on 4th June 1849, at the time when the Petrashevskists were arrested: 'D'après ce que l'on dit l'empereur devait être assassiné à la grande revue de la garde impériale. . . . Pendant un séjour à Moscou le nouveau palais a été miné. Mais ces deux conspirations ont été découvertes avant que le mouvement n'éclatât.' It is true that it was corrected a day later: 'La conspiration russe découverte à Saint-Pétersbourg n'est nullement une conspiration contre la vie de Nicolas et de toute sa famille. Elle était basée sur une révolution radicale, ayant pour but un changement complet du système gouvernemental' (5th June).

42. Quoted by A. Dolinin in his article '*Dostoevsky sredi petrashevtsev*' (*Dostoevsky and the Petrashevskists*), in 'Zven'ya', 1936, vol. VI, p. 512.

43. Quoted in '*Petrashevtsy*', *op. cit.*, vol. I, p. 57.

44. '*Delo petrashevtsev*' (*The case of the Petrashevskists*), *op. cit.*, vol. I, p. 29.

45. *Ibid.*, p. 449.

46. *Ibid.*, pp. 559 ff.

47. *Ibid.*, p. 421.

48. *Ibid.*, p. 353.

49. *Ibid.*, p. 358.

50. Quoted by I. V. Semevsky, *op. cit.*, p. 171.

51. '*Delo petrashevtsev*', *op. cit.*, vol. I, p. 91.

52. '*Petrashevtsy*', *op. cit.*, vol. I, p. 115.

53. '*Delo petrashevtsev*', *op. cit.*, vol. I, p. 183.

54. *Ibid.*, pp. 515 ff.

55. *Ibid.*, p. 514.

56. *Ibid.*, p. 30.

57. *Ibid.*, p. 82.

58. *Ibid.*, p. 522.

59. *Ibid.*, vol. II, p. 209.

60. On the Debu brothers, see the article by V. I. Semevsky in the '*Entsiklopedicheskiy slovar' Granat*' (*Granat Encyclopaedia*), vol. XVIII, M., 1914, and an article by the same author, '*Petrashevtsy. Kruzhok N. S. Kashkina*' (*The Petrashevskists. Kashkin's group*), in 'Golos minuvshego', 1916, vols. II–IV.

61. A. P. Milyukov, '*Literaturnyye vstrechi i znakomstva*' (*Literary meetings and friendships*), Spb., 1890, p. 180.

62. Good arguments in support of this have been put forward by A. Dolinin, *op. cit.*

63. N. F. Bel'chikov, '*Dostoevsky v protsesse petrashevtsev*' (*Dostoevsky at the trial of the Petrashevskists*), M.-L., 1936, pp. 91–2.

64. N. F. Bel'chikov, *op. cit.*, p. 142.

65. Quoted by Semevsky in '*Petrashevtsy*', *op. cit.*, p. 134.

66. V. Leykina, '*Petrashevtsy*', *op. cit.*, p. 40.

67. '*Delo petrashevtsev*', *op. cit.*, vol. I, pp. 47, 68.

68. *Ibid.*, vol. II, p. 360.

69. It is not easy to understand exactly what he intended these words to mean.

They may refer to a book by T. Dézamy, which he had owned in St Petersburg and which was taken away from him when he was arrested: *Le Jésuitisme vaincu et anéanti par le socialisme ou les constitutions des jésuites et leurs instructions secrètes, en parallèle avec un projet d'organisation du travail*, Paris, 1845. This is one of the polemical works directed against the Jesuits which were widespread in the 'forties, the writings of Quinet and Michelet being the most famous examples. It summarized 'le bilan de la doctrine des jésuites et des actes qu'elle a enfanté', and concluded: 'Jésuitisme ou socialisme. Choisissez!' The author, a well-known follower of Babeuf, took the opportunity of attacking all those who 'ne voient d'unité légitime que dans une dictature républicaine aux mains d'une convention nationale', who 'vantent l'excellence d'un pouvoir théocratique, hiérarchiquement organisé'. In his attacks on the Jesuits, T. Dézamy was also fighting against the introduction of an authoritarian spirit into Socialism. And so it is likely that Speshnev intended to refer not to Dézamy but to Barruel. He used to make his friends read the works by this famous Jesuit against the French Revolution. In it—he said—a detailed description could be found of the conspiracy of the 'Illuminati' founded by Weishaupt, which he put forward as a model. His friend, Mombelli, said that it was 'the most dangerous book there is, as methods are found in it which otherwise would never have come into people's minds' ('*Petrashevtsy*', *op. cit.*, p. 87). Speshnev was always very interested in the various forms of conspiracy. Abroad, Christianity interested him as a conspiracy which came off! The proposed regulations which he put forward involved the blind obedience of the flock to the leaders, and the duty of bearing arms when they commanded it, etc. See '*Obshchestvo propagandy v 1849 godu*' (*A propaganda society in 1849*), Leipzig, 1875, p. 63.

70. V. I. Semevsky, *op. cit.*, p. 185.
71. '*Delo petrashevtsev*' (*The case of the Petrashevskists*). *op. cit.*, vol. I, p. 418.
72. *Ibid.*, p. 470.
73. *Ibid.*, p. 476.
74. V. I. Semevsky, *op. cit.*, p. 115.
75. '*Delo petrashevtsev*' (*The case of the Petrashevskists*), *op. cit.*, vol. I, p. 93.
76. *Ibid.*, p. 533.
77. Speshnev was, as we have seen, much appreciated by Herzen as well as by Bakunin, and also apparently by Dobrolyubov. On Speshnev's return from Siberia in 1860, A. N: Pleshcheyev said to Dobrolyubov 'he was perhaps the most remarkable personality in our whole group' (see N. M. Chernyshevskaya, '*Letopis' zhizni i deyatel'nosti N. G. Chernyshevskago*' (*Annals of the life and activity of N. G. Chernyshevsky*), M.-L., 1953, p. 182). Like many other Petrashevskists, Speshnev later dedicated himself body and soul to agrarian reform, 'taking the part of the peasant very strongly', as an official report of the period says. Afterwards he retired into private life and died in 1882.

CHAPTER 4

1. A. I. Gertsen, '*Polnoye sobranie sochineniy i pisem*' (*Collected works and letters*), VII, 9.
2. VII, 142–3.
3. VII, 192.
4. A particularly useful pamphlet on Herzen's publishing activity in London is *Desyatiletie Vol'noy Russkoy Tipografii v Londone. Sbornik ego pervykh listov, sostavlennyy i izdannyy* L. Chernetskim (*Ten years of the Free Russian Press in London. A collection of its first issues, compiled and edited by L. Chernetsky*), London, 1863, reprinted by the Soviet Academy of Sciences,

M.-L., 1935, with the addition of a second valuable volume, '*Bibliografi-cheskoye opisanie izdaniy Vol'noy Russkoy Tipografii v Londone, 1853–1865.* Sostavil P. N. Berkov' (*Bibliographical description of the publications of the Free Russian Press in London, 1853–1865.* Compiled by P. N. Berkov).

5. VII, 206.

6. VII, 186.

7. Granovsky's letters to Herzen of this period were partly published by Herzen in the fifth number of his review, 'Polyarnaya zvezda'. But he did not print the most important of them all, the one which most clearly reflects the state of mind of the Moscow intellectuals in 1851. It has been published in 'Zven'ya', 1936, no. VI, pp. 355 ff. Annenkov's memoirs confirm the impression that Herzen's book produced in Russia. He quotes a remark of the Head of the Third Section, Count Orlov: 'If we wanted to, it would be easy enough for us to pass from the dead, whom Herzen has named, and get on the tracks of the living.' N. Lerner, '*Dve zimy v provintsii i derevne. S yanvarya 1849 do avgusta 1851 goda. Iz vospominaniy P. V. Annenkova*' (*Two winters in the provinces and in the countryside. From January 1849 to August 1851. From the memoirs of P. V. Annenkov*), in 'Byloye', 1922, vol. XVIII.

8. V. Evgen'ev-Maksimov, '"*Sovremennik*" v 40–50 gg. *Ot Belinskogo do Chernyshevskogo*' (*The 'Sovremennik' in the forties and fifties from Belinsky to Chernyshevsky*), L., undated (but 1934).

9. For these writings, which had a wide circulation in Russia before they were printed by Herzen or in later publications, see A. A. Kornilov, '*Obshchestven-noye dvizhenie pri Aleksandre II (1855–1881). Istoricheskiye ocherki*' (*The movement of Russian society in the time of Alexander II [1855–1881]. Historical essays*), M., 1909, chapter I.

10. VII, 250.

11. VII, 253.

12. VII, 252.

13. VIII, 90.

14. VII, 263. This saying, attributed to Pugachev, involved a play upon words: *Voron*, crow; *Vor*, thief, and in old Russian: bandit, rebel.

15. VII, 276.

16. VII, 277.

17. VII, 296.

18. VII, 298.

19. VIII, 67 ff., where some letters of Mazzini's, referring to this manifesto, are printed in Russian.

20. VIII, 46.

21. VIII, 57.

22. VIII, 131. It was, he said, a movement that was 'tranquille, morne, silencieux mais obstiné, mais persévérant et aimant l'étranger (tolérés comme les filles publiques par le gouvernement, détestés par les classes aisées, les refugiés sont aimés par les chartistes)'.

23. VIII, 142.

24. VII, 325.

25. VII, 323.

26. VII, 313.

27. VII, 322.

28. VIII, 485.

29. VIII, 402 ff., in which the Italian text published by Mazzini is given. See too *Lettres de Mazzini à Herzen*, in Bulletin of the International Institute of Social History, Amsterdam, 1953, no. 1, pp. 16 ff.

30. VIII, 276.
31. B. Koz'min, '*Iz publitsisticheskogo naslediya N. P. Ogaryova*' (*From documents of N. P. Ogarev*), in 'Literaturnoye nasledstvo', M., 1941, nos. 39–40, pp. 298 ff; N. A. Tushkova-Ogareva, '*Vospominaniya*' (*Memoirs*), edited by S. A. Pereselenkov, L., 1929. (The memoirs of Ogarev's wife, although full of inaccuracies, give an idea of the tormented and complex life of the little group of émigrés in London, which not only politically but in its private life constituted a typical example of the life of the Russian intelligentsia in the 'sixties.) Documents concerning the life of the Herzen-Ogarev group have been published by M. Gershenzon in 'Russkiye propilei', M., 1917, no. IV, and in '*Arkhiv N. A. i N. P. Ogaryovykh*' (*The archive of N. A. and N. P. Ogarev*), edited by V. P. Polonsky, with notes by N. M. Mendel'son and Ya. Z. Chernyak, M.-L., 1930. Number V of the 'Byulleteni gosudarstvennogo literaturnogo muzeya' (Bulletins of the State Literary Museum), M., 1940, includes: '*Gertsen, Ogaryov i ikh okruzhenie. Rukopisi, perepiska i dokumenty*. Redaktsiya B. P. Koz'mina' (*Herzen, Ogarev and their circle. Manuscripts, letters and documents*. Edited by B. P. Koz'min). Contains an interesting *catalogue raisonné* of the numerous documents and photographs of documents in the Literary Museum at Moscow. Ya. Z. Chernyak, '*N. P. Ogaryov, Nekrasov, Gertsen, Chernyshevsky v spore ob Ogaryovskom nasledstve*' (*The litigation of N. P. Ogarev, Nekrasov, Herzen and Chernyshevsky for Ogarev's inheritance*), L., 1935, deals in this case not with his literary inheritance, but with the complicated discussion about Ogarev's property which involved a number of Russian writers and which was one of the chief causes for Herzen's continuous hostility towards Nekrasov. See too new documents published in vols. 61, 62, 63, 'Literaturnoye nasledstvo', M., 1953, 1955, and a new collection of Ogarev's writings in two volumes, '*Izbrannyye sotsial'no-politicheskie i filosofskie proizvedeniya*'. Pod obshchey redaktsiey M. T. Iovchuka i N. G. Tarakanova (*Selected works on social, political and philosophical questions*. Edited by M. T. Iovchuk and N. G. Tarakanov). The first volume was published in Moscow in 1952, the second in 1956, the latter containing an interesting collection of letters of Ogarev and his various friends: Herzen, Bakunin, Ketcher, Annenkov, Satin, Luginin, Lavrov, etc.
32. IX, 2.
33. It is very difficult to draw up an exact list of the 'Kolokol's' correspondents, for Herzen received a great many anonymous contributions. See the careful list reconstructed by M. Klevensky, '*Gertsen izdatel' i ego sotrudniki*' (*Herzen the publisher and his collaborators*), in 'Literaturnoye nasledstvo', M., 1941, nos. 41–2, pp. 572 ff.
34. A useful general picture is given in Z. P. Basileva, '"*Kolokol*" *Gertsena* (1857–1867)' (*Herzen's 'Kolokol'* [*1857–1867*]), M., 1949. Also very useful: '"*Kolokol.*" *Izdanie A. I. Gertsena: N. P. Ogaryova. 1857–1867 gg.*' ('*The Bell*'. Edited by A. I. Herzen and N. P. Ogarev. 1857–1867), Moscow, 1957, with detailed indexes of names of persons, places, etc.
35. IX, 128.
36. IX, 363.
37. XI, 35.
38. IX, 388.
39. IX, 363.
40. See the whole of the interesting correspondence in IX, 406 ff.
41. '*Pis'ma K. D. Kavelina i I. S. Turgeneva k A. I. Gertsenu.*' S obyasnitel'nymi primechaniyami M. Dragomanova (*Letters of K. D. Kavelin and I. S. Turgenev to A. I. Herzen*. With explanatory notes by M. Dragomanov), Geneva, 1892.

24+

42. IX, 419.

43. The outline of this speech was published for the first time in Z. P. Basileva, *op. cit.*, p. 105.

44. IX, 67.

45. '*Pis'mo k sootechestvenniku*' (*Letter to a fellow-countryman*), 'Kolokol', 1st August 1860.

46. XI, 59.

47. XI, 144.

48. XVII, 6–7.

49. '*Narod i gosudarstvo*' (*People and State*), London, 1862, especially for his curious attempt to look upon merchants and artisans as intermediate between State and people.

50. The letter to Alexander II was published in 'Kolokol' on 8th May 1862. On Martyanov, see M. Lemke, '*Delo P. A. Martyanova*' (*The case of P. A. Martyanov*), in 'Byloye', 1906, no. VIII, and in '*Ocherki osvoboditel'nogo dvizheniya "shestidesyatykh godov"*' (*Essays on the liberation movement of the sixties*), second edition, Spb., 1908, p. 333 ff. When Martyanov returned voluntarily to Russia in the spring of 1863 he was arrested and imprisoned in the Peter-Paul fortress, and condemned to five years' hard labour for his collaboration with the 'Kolokol'. In September 1865 he died in the prison hospital at Irkutsk.

51. Ogarev confirms, in a letter to Bakunin, that the latter was inspired by Martyanov. It is quoted by Yu. Steklov, '*M. A. Bakunin, ego zhizn' i deyatel'nost*' (*M. A. Bakunin, his life and work*), vol. II (1861–68), M.-L., 1927, p. 40. It was, moreover, due to Martyanov's insistence that this pamphlet by Bakunin was published.

52. This first project and the documents of the discussion are given in XV, 484 ff.

53. For two other projected appeals, parallel to this one and also by Ogarev, at the end of 1862, see '*Nuzhdy narodnyye*' (*The needs of the people*) and '*Adres tsaryu ot gosudarstvennykh krest'yan*' (*Appeal to the Tsar by the State peasants*), published by B. Koz'min, in 'Literaturnoye nasledstvo', 1941, nos. 39–40, pp. 328 ff. See too 'Literaturnoye nasledstvo', vol. 61, pp. 502 ff.

54. N. A. Dobrolyubov, '*Polnoye sobranie sochineniy*', pod obshchey redaktsiey P. I. Lebedeva-Polyanskogo (*Complete works*. Edited by P. I. Lebedev-Polyansky), vol. VI, M., 1939, p. 459.

55. '"*Ispoved*'" *V. I. Kel'sieva*' Podgotovka k pechati E. Kingisepp. Vstupitel'naya stat'ya i kommentarii M. Klevenskogo ('*Confession*' of *V. I. Kelsiev*. Edited by E. Kingisepp, introductory article and notes by M. Klevensky), in 'Literaturnoye nasledstvo', M., 1941, nos. 41–2, pp. 253 ff. The other works on him are mentioned and a list is given of his own works.

56. *Ibid.*, p. 270.

57. *Ibid.*, p. 285.

58. For information about him see XV, 342 ff., as well as Kelsiev's *Confession*.

59. '*Ispoved*'' (*Confession*), *op. cit.*, p. 321.

60. For his mission to Turkey see P. G. Ryndzyunsky, '*V. I. Kel'siev—Gertsenu i Ogaryovu*', in 'Literaturnoye nasledstvo', vol. 62, pp. 159 ff.

61. See, for example, the issue of 10th July 1863.

62. A. I. Gertsen i N. P. Ogarev, '*Pis'ma k P. V. Annenkovu*', publikatsiya i predislovie V. F. Pokrovskoy, pod redaktsiey i s primechaniyami N. Mendel'sona (*Letters to P. V. Annenkov*, published with a preface by V. F. Pokrovskaya, edited and with notes by N. Mendel'son), in 'Zven'ya', 1934, nos. III–IV, and '*Zapiska o taynom obshchestve*' (*Memoir on a secret society*), published by B. Koz'min, in 'Literaturnoye nasledstvo', 1941, nos. 39–40, pp. 323 ff.

63. '*Otvet* "*Velikoruss*"' (*Reply to* '*Velikoruss*)', 'Kolokol', 10th September 1861.
64. XI, 102.
65. XV, 194.
66. XIV, 374.
67. XI, 241.
68. XV, 226.
69. See the detailed study of this repression by M. Lemke, '*Protsess 32-kh*' (*The trial of the thirty-two*), in '*Ocherki osvoboditel'nogo dvizheniya* "*shestidesyatykh godov*" ' (*Essays on the liberation movement of the* '*sixties*'), second edition, Spb., 1908, pp. 18 ff.
70. IX, 551.
71. X, 9.
72. See IX, 473. See too, for Herzen and Poland, I. M. Belyavskaya, '*A. I. Gertsen i pol'skoye natsional'no-osvoboditel'noye dvizhenie 60-kh godov XIX veka*' (A. I. Herzen and the Polish national liberation movement of the 1860s), M., 1954.
73. X, 68.
74. X, 238–9.
75. X, 266.
76. For his own words, see XI, 83.
77. It is curious to note that, after Herzen had made his stand in 1861, he received two letters, one of congratulation, the other warning him against defending Polish aspirations. The first was from Garibaldi in Turin, written on 13th April: 'Il n'y a pas longtemps que la parole d'émancipation des serfs en Russie fut saluée en Europe avec admiration et reconnaissance. Le prince, initiateur de cette grande œuvre, se posa par ce seul fait à côté des plus illustres bienfaiteurs de l'humanité. Aujourd'hui, je le dis avec douleur! . . . l'œuvre de bienfaisance a été souillée par le sang répandu d'une population innocente, et c'est le devoir de ceux qui applaudirent au bienfait de jeter la voix de malédiction sur la consommation du plus détestable des crimes. Que votre journal, justement apprécié dans ce grand empire, porte un mot de sympathie de la nation italienne à la malheureuse et héroïque Pologne, un mot de gratitude aux braves de l'armée russe qui comme Popoff ont brisé leurs sabres plutôt que de les tremper dans le sang du peuple—et un cri de réprobation des nations sœurs de l'Europe contre les auteurs de l'effroyable massacre.' The other letter was from Proudhon. He stressed his ideas on nationality and threatened 'de dire de vous ce que je dis depuis six mois de votre ami Garibaldi: grand cœur, mais de cervelle point . . . quant à la Pologne, la connaissez-vous donc si mal que vous croyez à sa résurrection? La Pologne a été de tous temps la plus corrompue des aristocraties et le plus indiscipliné des états. Aujourd'hui, elle n'a encore à offrir que son catholicisme et sa noblesse, deux belles choses ma foi! . . . Prêchez-lui la "liberté", l' "égalité", la "philosophie", la "révolution économique", à la bonne heure! aidez-la à obtenir les libertés constitutionnelles civiles, qui sont le caractère de l'époque; préparez-la par là à une révolution plus radicale, qui fera disparaître, avec les grands états, toutes ces distinctions désormais sans fondement de nationalité. En poussant les Polonais dans cette voie, poussez les Russes, voilà le vrai chemin'. Herzen published the first letter, but though he shared many of Proudhon's ideas, he did not follow his advice. For the Garibaldi letter, see XI, 85, where the Russian translation of Proudhon's letter can also be found. It was published in *Correspondance de P. J. Proudhon*, Paris, 1875, vol. XI, pp. 22 ff.
78. XI, 234.
79. See Yu. Steklov, '*M. A. Bakunin, ego zhizn' i deyatel'nost*' (*M. A. Bakunin*,

Life and work), op. cit., vol. II, pp. 172 ff., for the translation of an interesting passage from the memoirs of Mieroslawski, published in Warsaw in 1924, which reveals his extravagant spirits.

80. A list of the officers, Russian and Polish, who took part in this organization was brought to London, probably by Potebnya, and is published in 'Literaturnoye nasledstvo', vol. 61, M., 1953, pp. 515 ff. It is not entirely without interest to notice that the father of Lenin's wife, N. K. Krupskaya, took part in this clandestine military organization.

81. XV, 533.
82. XVI, 27.
83. XVI, 69.
84. Yu. Steklov, *op. cit.,* p. 272.
85. XVI, 492–3.
86. XVI, 404.
87. *Ibid.*
88. XVI, 441–2. See M. B. Petrovich, *Russian Pan-Slavists and the Polish uprising of 1863,* in Harvard Slavic Studies, vol. I, 1953, pp. 219 ff., and generally Hans Kohn, *Panslavism: History and Ideology,* Notre-Dame, 1953.
89. XVI, 530.

CHAPTER 5

1. After his arrest in 1862 his works, which had almost all appeared in the *Sovremennik,* could not be generally republished in Russia until the revolution of 1905. The numerous editions produced by the exiles abroad, especially in Geneva, show the great importance which the new generation attributed to his writings, but they do not claim, nor indeed have they, any scholarly value. The earliest and most significant of them are listed in ' *Russkaya podpol'naya i zarubezhnaya pechat'. Bibliograficheskiy ukazatel'. Tom I.* ' *Donarodovol'cheskiy period'.* 1831–1879. Vyp. I. Sostavlen M. M. Klevenskim, E. N. Kushevoy i O. P. Markovoy, pod red. S. N. Valka i B. P. Koz'mina (*The clandestine press in Russia and abroad. Bibliographical survey,* vol. I, *The period before* '*Narodnaya Volya*', 1831–1879. Pt. I. Compiled by M. M. Klevensky, E. N. Kusheva and O. P. Markova, edited by S. N. Valk and B. P. Koz'min), M., 1935, pp. 135–8. The first publication to give a true idea of Chernyshevsky's activity, and in which many unpublished works were printed, was edited by his son, '*Polnoye sobranie sochineniy*' (*Complete works*), Spb., 1906, 11 volumes. This was reprinted without alteration in 1919. After this date many more unpublished works, letters and documents appeared in reviews and miscellanies. The chief collection is N. G. Chernyshevsky, '*Literaturnoye nasledie*' (*Literary inheritance*), M.-L., vol. I: '*Iz avtobiografii. Dnevnik, 1848–1853 gg.*'. Pod red. i s primechaniyami N. A. Alekseyeva, M. N. Chernyshevskogo i S. N. Chernova (*From the autobiography. Diary, 1848–1853.* Edited and with notes by N. A. Alekseyev, M. N. Chernyshevsky and S. N. Chernov), 1928, vol. II: '*Pis'ma*', pod red. i s primechaniyami N. A. Alekseyeva i A. P. Skaftymova (*Letters,* edited and with notes by N. A. Alekseyev and A. P. Skaftymov), 1928, vol. III: '*Pis'ma*', sost. N. A. Alekseyevym i N. M. Chernyshevskoy-Bystrovoy, pod red. i s predisloviem L. B. Kameneva (*Letters,* collected by N. A. Alekseyev and N. M. Chernyshevskaya-Bystrova, edited and with preface by L. B. Kamenev), 1930. The result of twenty years' study of Chernyshevsky's texts is the publication '*Polnoye sobranie sochineniy*' v pyatnadtsati tomakh, pod obshchey redaktsiey V. Ya. Kirpotina, B. P.

Koz'mina, P. I. Lebedeva-Polyanskogo, N. L. Meshcheryakova, I. D. Udal'tsova, E. A. Tsekhera, N. M. Chernyshevskoy (*Complete works*, in fifteen volumes, edited by V. Ya. Kirpotin, B. P. Koz'min, P. I. Lebedev-Polyansky, N. L. Meshcheryakov, I. D. Udal'tsov, E. A. Tsekher, N. M. Chernyshevskaya), M.; the first volume came out in 1939 and the last in 1951. From now on in this chapter it will be referred to by volume and page. Apart from previously unpublished texts it has the merit of giving, whenever possible, Chernyshevsky's text before it was passed to the censor, and of indicating the passages which then had to be left out. Among the selected editions, the following are particularly useful: '*Izbrannyye sochineniya*' v pyati tomakh (*Selected works*, in five volumes), M.-L., vol. I, edited by M. N. Pokrovsky, with an introductory article by V. Nevsky, 1928, containing the historical works; vol. II (in two parts), edited by I. D. Udal'tsov, 1935 (the works on economics); vol. III (not yet published), vols. IV and V, edited by A. V. Lunacharsky, 1931, (the critical and literary works); also '*Izbrannyye ekonomicheskiye proizvedeniya*' (*Selected works on economics*), in three volumes (the third in two parts), edited by I. D. Udal'tsov, 1948-9, place of publication not given (but M.).

There are many studies of Chernyshevsky. The most important are: the writings about him at various times by G. V. Plekhanov; collections in his '*Sochineniya*', pod red. D. Ryazanova (*Works*, edited by D. Ryazanov), M.-P., undated, vols. V, VI; Yu. M. Steklov, '*N. G. Chernyshevsky. Ego zhizn' i deyatel'nost'. 1828-1889*' (*N. G. Chernyshevsky. His life and work. 1828-1889*), second edition, M.-L., 1928, two volumes; G. Berliner, '*N. G. Chernyshevsky i ego literaturnyye vragi*', pod red. L. B. Kameneva (*N. G. Chernyshevsky and his literary enemies*, edited by L. B. Kamenev), M.-L., 1930; N. M. Chernyshevskaya, '*Letopis' zhizni i deyatel'nosti N. G. Chernyshevskogo*' (*Annals of the life and activity of N. G. Chernyshevsky*), M., 1953; A. Skaftymov, '*Zhizn' i deyatel'nost' N. G. Chernyshevskogo*' (*Life and work of N. G. Chernyshevsky*), second edition, Saratov, 1947, mainly useful for the extensive, though incomplete, bibliography of the period 1917-47, on pp. 96 ff.

2. T. M. Akimova and A. M. Ardabatskaya, '*Ocherki istorii Saratova*' (*Historical essays on Saratov*), Saratov, 1940, with extensive bibliography.

3. I, 567.

4. His writings about Saratov and about his family, of which the most interesting is '*Vospominaniya slyshannogo o starine*' (*Recollections of what I have heard about old times*), are collected in I, 566-713.

5. I, 646.

6. I, 643.

7. I, 684.

8. The most interesting recollections of this period of Chernyshevsky's life are by a relative, A. N. Pypin, the famous historian of Russian literature: '*Moi zametki*' (*My observations*), edited by V. A. Lyatskaya, M., 1910. Other accounts have been carefully assembled in '*N. G. Chernyshevsky v Saratove. Vospominaniya sovremennikov*'. Sostavleno N. M. Chernyshevskoy (*N. G. Chernyshevsky at Saratov. Accounts by his contemporaries*. Collected by N. M. Chernyshevskaya), Saratov, 1939.

9. The diary was full of abbreviations and other literary devices which made it very difficult for the police to read when it was confiscated after Chernyshevsky's arrest. The part which could be read was, however, enough to provide further confirmation of the suspicions of the authorities. His son published a small part in 1909 in vol. X of the '*Polnoye sobranie sochineniy*' (*Complete works*), *op. cit.* The most important part, from the years 1848-51,

was published for the first time in '*Literaturnoye nasledie*' (*Literary inheritance*), *op. cit.*, vol. I, and in a separate publication edited by N. A. Alekseyev, M., 1931–2, in two volumes. A third edition, revised and recorrected from the difficult manuscript, is in I, 29–565. See Peter Scheibert, 'Der junge Chernyschewsky und sein Tagebuch', in Jahrbücher für Geschichte Osteuropas, vol. 5, nos. 1–2, 1957.

10. Fragments of his translation of the *Confessions* and notes for a biography of Rousseau, written in the Peter-Paul fortress, have been published in N. G. Chernyshevsky, '*Neizdannyye materialy*' (*Unpublished material*), Saratov, 1939. These notes are of little interest, except as an indication of his personal preoccupation with Rousseau's character.

11. Letter written from Vilyuysk of 11th April 1877, XV, 21.

12. I, 145.

13. XIV, 56.

14. Quoted by E. Lyatsky, '*N. G. Chernyshevsky i uchitelya ego mysli: Gegel', Belinsky, Feyerbakh*' (*N. G. Chernyshevsky and the men who influenced his thought: Hegel, Belinsky, Feuerbach*), in 'Sovremennyy mir', 1910, nos. X–XI.

15. I, 232.

16. '*Polnoye sobranie sochineniy*', *op. cit.*, vol. X, part II, 190.

17. XIV, 543.

18. These words are taken from an anonymous pamphlet published in Geneva in 1865 by the 'young émigrés', those who considered themselves to be the closest followers of Chernyshevsky. The pamphlet was in memory of the poet M. L. Mikhaylov, who died in Siberia. It was reprinted by E. Kusheva, in 'Literaturnoye nasledstvo', 1936, nos. 25–6, pp. 293 ff.

19. I, 248.

20. I, 297.

21. I, 358.

22. XIV, 47–8.

23. I, 66.

24. I, 59.

25. I, 67.

26. N. V. Shelgunov, '*Vospominaniya*'. Redaktsiya, vstupitel'naya stat'ya i primechaniya A. A. Shilova (*Memoirs*. Edited, with introduction and notes, by A. A. Shilov), M.-P., 1923, p. 95.

27. I, 196. See also ' *Delo petrashevtsev*' (*The case of the Petrashevskists*), *op. cit.*, vol. III, M., 1951, pp. 15 ff.

28. Quoted by Yu. M. Steklov, *op. cit.*, vol. I, p. 33.

29. I, 274.

30. I, 357.

31. I, 110.

32. I, 115.

33. I, 122.

34. I, 134.

35. I, 171.

36. V. E. Cheshikhin, '*N. G. Chernyshevsky (1828–89)*' (*N. G. Chernyshevsky, [1828–89]*), P., 1923, p. 61.

37. I, 356–7.

38. I, 357.

39. I, 419.

40. I, 381.

41. XIV, 311 ff.

42. Yu. Steklov, *op. cit.*, vol. I, p. 170, note I, quotes a curious incident which shows how this judgment on Nekrasov—which Chernyshevsky was the first to formulate—was accepted by all his generation of Populists. At Nekrasov's funeral, Dostoevsky gave a funeral oration. As he was saying that the poet was not inferior to Pushkin, one of the bystanders said: 'He was greater, he was greater!' It was Plekhanov, who was a young man at the time and a member of *Zemlya i Volya*.

43. II, 94–5.

44. II, 97.

45. II, 96.

46. II, 117.

47. II, 94.

48. III, 303.

49. II, 294.

50. IV, 136–7.

51. This work was published for the first time with the title of '*Rasskaz o krymskoy voyne po Kingleku*' (*Story of the Crimean War, taken from Kinglake*), with introductory preface and notes by N. A. Alekseyev, A. N. Straukh and Kh. N. Kantor, M., 1935.

52. N. G. Chernyshevsky, '*Prolog*'. Podgotovka teksta A. P. Skaftymova i N. M. Chernyshevskoy-Bystrovoy. Kommentarii A. P. Skaftymova. Stat'ya N. V. Vodovozova (*Prologue*. Text edited by A. P. Skaftymov and N. M. Chernyshevskaya-Bystrova. Comments by A. P. Skaftymov. Introductory article by N. V. Vodovozov), M.-L., 1936, p. 164.

53. XIV, 350.

54. '*Prolog*' (*Prologue*), *op. cit.*, p. 232.

55. '*Izbrannyye ekonomicheskiye proizvedeniya*' (*Selected works on economics*), *op. cit.*, vol. I, p. 417.

56. Cf. N. M. Sikorsky, '*Zhurnal* " *Sovremennik*" *i krest'yanskaya reforma 1861 g.*' (*The* '*Contemporary*' *and the agrarian reforms of 1861*), M., 1957.

57. Of outstanding interest for the understanding of the discussions which the economic problems of the period aroused is N. A. Tsagolov's '*Ocherki russkoy ekonomicheskoy mysli perioda padeniya krepostnogo prava*' (*Essays on economic thought in Russia at the time of the collapse of the serf system*), M., 1956.

58. Article published in *Sovremennik*, vol. IX. Reprinted in II, 735 ff.

59. Reprinted in his book '*Opyty po istorii russkago prava*' (*Essays on the history of Russian law*), M., 1858, p. 1 ff.

60. Article of April 1856, published in *Sovremennik*, cf. III, 642 ff.

61. IV, 303–4.

62. IV, 739.

63. IV, 738.

64. IV, 742.

65. IV, 746.

66. IV, 750. In another article he returned to this idea: 'Within twenty or thirty years the *obshchina* will offer our peasants another and greater advantage, by giving them a great opportunity to create agricultural societies for farming the land...' i.e. cooperatives and collective enterprises. '*Izbrannyye ekonomicheskiye proizvedeniya*' (*Selected works on economics*), *op. cit.*, vol. I, p. 489.

67. IV, 329.

68. IV, 438.

69. IV, 413.

70. IV, 414.

71. IV, 347.
72. IV, 328.
73. '*Izbrannyye ekonomicheskiye proizvedeniya*' (*Selected works on economics*), *op. cit.*, vol. I, pp. 689 ff.
74. *Ibid.*, p. 718.
75. *Ibid.*, p. 727.
76. This was published for the first time by N. A. Alekseyev in 'Krasnyy arkhiv', 1939, no. V.
77. '*Izbrannyye ekonomicheskiye proizvedeniya*' (*Selected works on economics*), *op. cit.*, vol. II, p. 261.
78. An interesting survey of these reductions in peasant holdings in different regions is published in the appendix to the '*Istoriya SSSR, tom II, Rossiya v XIX veke*', pod red. M. V. Nechkinoy (*History of the USSR*, vol. II, *Russia in the XIXth century*, edited by M. V. Nechkina), M., 1940.
79. Published in *Sovremennik*, 1858, no. V, and reprinted in '*Izbrannyye sochineniya*', v pyati tomakh (*Selected works*, in 5 vols.), *op. cit.*, vol. 1, pp. 1 ff.
80. '*Prolog*' (*Prologue*), *op. cit.*, p. 226.
81. Quoted from V. Evgen'ev-Maksimov, ' "*Sovremennik*" pri Chernyshevskom i Dobrolyubove' (The '*Sovremennik*' in the time of Chernyshevsky and Dobrolyubov), L., 1936, pp. 24–5.
82. Letter to Turgenev, 13th October 1856, published in the collection '*Turgenev i krug "Sovremennika". Neizdannyye materialy. 1847–1861*' (*Turgenev and the 'Sovremennik' circle. Unpublished material. 1847–1861*), M.-L., 1930.
83. *Ibid.*, p. 196.
84. Quoted by Yu. Steklov, *op. cit.*, vol. II, p. 20.
85. XIV, 333.
86. '*Russkiy chelovek na rendez-vous*' (*The Russian at the rendez-vous*), in *Sovremennik*, 1858, no. III, reprinted in '*Polnoye sobranie sochineniy*' (*Complete works*), vol. I, p. 90.
87. These words are quoted by Avdot'ya Panaeva, '*Vospominaniya 1824–1870*' (*Recollections, 1824–1870*), fourth edition, with notes by K. Chukovsky, M.-L., 1930, p. 421.
88. XV, 431.
89. III, 568 ff.
90. Kavelin was equally critical of Chernyshevsky. The difference between them is all the more characteristic in that for a long time they maintained good relations; but it reflects a deep-rooted political dissension. Kavelin wrote to Herzen on 6th August 1862, when Chernyshevsky was arrested with Serno-Solovevich: 'These arrests do not amaze me, nor, I confess it, do they seem revolting. It is war: win or lose. The revolutionary party maintains that all ways are good to overcome the government, and the latter defends itself with its own methods. This was not the meaning of the deportations and imprisonments under that animal Nicholas. Then people died for what they believed, for their convictions, their faith and their word. I would like to see you in the government and what you would do against a party which started to work against you openly and underground. I like Chernyshevsky very much, very much, but I have never seen such a *brouillon*, a man so lacking in tact and so full of self-confidence.'
91. Gertsen, X, 61.
92. XIV, 379.
93. Quoted in Gertsen, X, 20.
94. See a convincing article, which denies that Chernyshevsky was author, by B. Koz'min, '*Byl li N. G. Chernyshevsky avtorom pis'ma "Russkogo cheloveka"* k

Gertsenu' (*Was Chernyshevsky the author of the letter from 'A Russian' to Herzen?*), in 'Literaturnoye nasledstvo', 1936, no. 25–6, p. 576.

95. The arguments in favour of attributing it to Dobrolyubov have been collected by M. V. Nechkina, '*N. G. Chernyshevsky v gody revolyutsionnoy situatsii*' (*N. G. Chernyshevsky in the years of the revolutionary situation*), in 'Istoricheskiye zapiski', 1941, no. X, pp. 3 ff. See too E. A. Bushkanets, '*K voprosu ob avtore pis'ma Russkogo cheloveka*' (*On the question of the authorship of the letter from 'A Russian'*), in Izvestiya Ak. Nauk SSSR. Seriya istorii i filosofii, 1951, no. 2.

96. '*O prichinakh padeniya Rima (Podrazhaniye Montesk'e)*' (*On the causes of the fall of Rome [in imitation of Montesquieu]*), in *Sovremennik*, 1861, no. V, reprinted in '*Izbrannyye ekonomicheskiye proizvedeniya*' (*Selected works on economics*), *op. cit.*, vol. II, pp. 572 ff.

97. '*Bor'ba partiy vo Frantsii pri Lyudovike XVIII i Karle X*' (*Party conflict in France in the time of Louis XVIII and Charles X*), published in *Sovremennik*, 1858, and reprinted in '*Izbrannyye sochineniya*' (*Selected works*), *op. cit.*, vol. I, pp. 228 ff.

98. '*Iyul'skaya monarkhiya*' (*The July monarchy*), published in *Sovremennik*, 1858, and reprinted in '*Izbrannyye sochineniya*' (*Selected works*), *op. cit.*, vol. I, pp. 316 ff.

99. Published in *Sovremennik*, 1858, and reprinted in '*Izbrannyye sochineniya*' (*Selected works*), *op. cit.*, vol. I, pp. 454 ff.

100. VI, 5.
101. VI, 153.
102. VI, 342.
103. VI, 368.
104. VI, 369–70.
105. The fact that Chernyshevsky took advantage of the events in Italy, to state his own political ideas more clearly, ought not to make us forget the sympathy and interest with which he followed the development of Italian affairs. Generally speaking the last phase of the Risorgimento attracted the attention of all the liberal democratic elements in Russia. *Sovremennik* was, at that time, the mirror for this interest. P. I. Bibikov, for instance, took the opportunity of an historical study on *Italy at the time of the first French Revolution* to speak at length about Mazzini. It published in serial form Ruffini's novel *Lorenzo Benoni*. The central censorship committee, in a report of September 1861, pointed out that the novel was particularly dangerous at that time, when the student movement in St Petersburg, Moscow, and other Russian cities was increasing in strength. 'The translation of *Lorenzo Benoni* tells the reader of the author's revolutionary education, in the kingdom of Sardinia, at the beginning of the movement in that country, under the autocracy of Carlo Alberto. The revolutionary activities of the students against their professors and masters already foreshadow—according to the author of this novel—the future significance of this movement. He himself then began to come to the fore not just because of his success in work, but also for his early anti-government tendencies. The author does not fail to refer every activity at his college to a general conception of revolution and conspiracy . . . The author brands with particular passion the closing of the universities of Turin and Genoa.' (Quoted from V. Evgen'ev-Maksimov, '"*Sovremennik*" *pri Chernyshevskom i Dobrolyubove*' (*The 'Sovremennik' in the time of Chernyshevsky and Dobrolyubov*), *op. cit.*, pp. 497–498). The censor protested again when the novel appeared in a separate edition (*ibid.*, p. 505). It is interesting to note, in connection with this, that among the books read by Chernyshevsky in the Peter-

24*

Paul fortress was a novel by Ruffini, *Vincenzo*, in English (XIV, 489). Again, in 1885, when he was in prison in Astrakhan, Chernyshevsky remembered the articles which Gallenga had published in *The Times* during the war of 1859, 'which were very exact and very well written', and he thought of translating the memoirs, which had been published in England. The *Sovremennik* did not have a proper correspondent of its own in Italy at that time, nor did any other review or periodical in Russia. But Dobrolyubov wrote numerous articles during his journey in Italy which followed Chernyshevsky's political line [cf. E. V. Tarle, '*Stat'i Dobrolyubova ob ital'yanskikh delakh*' (*Dobrolyubov's articles on Italian affairs*), in the eighth volume of '*Polnoye sobranie sochineniy Dobrolyubova*', pod red. E. V. Anichkova (*Complete works of Dobrolyubov*, edited by E. V. Anichkov), M., 1913]. In 1862 the *Sovremennik* published two articles by Leone Brandi (the pseudonym, or rather the translation, of the name of a Russian follower of Garibaldi, L. Mechnikov), *Caprera* (no. III), and *The last Doge of Venice* (on the 1848 revolution in Venice), no. IV. Just before he was arrested, Chernyshevsky received a letter from Mechnikov, dated 20th June 1862, with an article on Mazzini, and the promise of an immediate sequel. On 12th July, from Siena, he told him how he had been turned out of the *Flagello*, for which he had been working, and proposed the following series of articles for the *Sovremennik*: '(1) Manin—Venice in 1848 and 1849; (2) Mazzini—the leader of the movement in Rome in 1849; (3) Cattaneo—Lombardy in 1848; (4) Three landings—Bandiera, Pisacane (episodes very little known in Russia) and Garibaldi; (5) V. Gioberti; (6) C. Balbo; (7) Cavour (the last three were to be on the Piedmont government in relation to Italian unity, the constitution and nationalism); (8) Piedmont in 1849; (9) Naples in 1848 (the minister, Troya, the radicals, Poerio, etc.); (10) Sicily in 1848; (11) Leopardi and Giusti; (12) the Tuscan triumvirate (Guerazzi, Montanelli, Mazzini); (13) Southern Italy in 1862 (the party of action and the party of the status quo).' The general ideas which he proposed to expound were: 'Italy cannot find her salvation in a bourgeois-Christian world, she must *rise* (*risorgere*), join the new element, the Slav, and start a universal federation with this which would sweep away all the illegitimate elements of Christian feudalism and bourgeoisie, which are so flaccid and lifeless that they have to hide under the abstract idea of the greatness of the State, and that other abstract idea—society' (N. G. Chernyshevsky, '*Literaturnoye nasledie*' (*Literary inheritance*), op. cit., vol. III, pp. 672 ff.). It is clear that Mechnikov looked at Italy from a point of view similar to Herzen's, as well as similar to Bakunin's, during his stay in that country.

106. This fundamental treatment of the subject, noteworthy for its clarity and acuteness, is contained in '*Ekonomicheskaya deyatel'nost' i zakonodatel'stvo*' (*Economic activity and legislation*), in *Sovremennik*, 1859, no. II, and reprinted in '*Izbrannyye ekonomicheskiye proizvedeniya*' (*Selected works on economics*), op. cit., vol. II, pp. 127 ff.

107. '*Kapital i trud*' (*Capital and labour*), in *Sovremennik*, 1860, no. I, and reprinted in '*Izbrannyye ekonomicheskiye proizvedeniya*' (*Selected works on economics*), op. cit., vol. II, pp. 300 ff.

108. '*Ocherki iz politicheskoy ekonomii*' (*po Millyu*) (*Essays on political economy [after Mill]*), in '*Izbrannyye ekonomicheskiye proizvedeniya*' (*Selected works on economics*), op. cit., vol. III, part II, p. 656.

109. *Ibid.*, p. 658.

110. Marx, who criticized everything in Chernyshevsky's economics which was different from his own, felt and appreciated the strength of his Socialist convictions. See B. Nikolaevsky, '*Russkiye knigi v biblioteke K. Marksa i F.

Engel'sa' (*Russian books in the libraries of K. Marx and F. Engels*), in '*Arkhiv K. Marksa i F. Engel'sa*', pod red. D. Ryazanova, (*The archive of K. Marx and F. Engels*, edited by K. Ryazanov), M.-L., 1929, no. IV, pp. 356 ff.

111. '*Prolog*' (*Prologue*), *op. cit.*, pp. 237–8.

112. I, 747.

113. Quoted by S. G. Stakhevich, '*Sredi politicheskikh prestupnikov*' (*Among the political delinquents*), in the miscellany, *N. G. Chernyshevsky*, M., 1928, p. 82.

114. This is one of the most debated questions among students of the life of Chernyshevsky. The one proof in favour of his authorship is Shelgunov's evidence in his memoirs. But even this, written many years later, is open to doubt. Shelgunov said that he no longer remembered the theme of the manifesto and he gave it a different title from that of the text we possess. There is a manuscript in Mikhailov's handwriting. This may be just a copy. When it fell into the hands of the police it was one of the weightiest pieces of evidence against Chernyshevsky, but only because a *provocateur* said that he was certain that Chernyshevsky was the author. Chernyshevsky always denied it. It must be said, however, that in his depositions the *provocateur* quoted phrases of Chernyshevsky's which have an authentic ring. The problem, however, may not be as important as it has seemed to recent Soviet historians, who have been anxious to make Chernyshevsky not only an intellectual and political revolutionary, which indeed he was, but also a conspirator. Here we are encroaching upon the realms of hagiography. About this whole question, see Yu. Steklov, *op. cit.*, vol. II, pp. 182 ff., and M. V. Nechkina, '*N. G. Chernyshevsky v gody revolyutsionnoy situatsii*' (*N. G. Chernyshevsky in the years of the revolutionary situation*), *op. cit.*, pp. 6 ff.

115. '*Barskim krest'yanam ot ikh dobrozhelateley poklon*' (*To the peasants of the landlords from one who desires their well-being, greetings*), reprinted in '*Izbrannyye ekonomicheskiye proizvedeniya*' (*Selected works on economics*), *op. cit.*, vol. II, pp. 606 ff.

116. The letter is reprinted in '*Protsess N. G. Chernyshevskogo. Arkhivnyye dokumenty*'. Red. i primechaniya N. A. Alekseyeva (*The trial of N. G. Chernyshevsky. Material from the archives.* Edited and with notes by N. A. Alekseyev), Saratov, 1939. As to whether it was addressed to Obruchev, see Ya. Z. Chernyak's contribution in 'Literaturnoye nasledstvo', vol. 62, p. 420.

117. Report published in '*Protsess N. G. Chernyshevskogo*' (*The trial of N. G. Chernyshevsky*), *op. cit.*, p. 11.

118. V. N. Shaganov, '*N. G. Chernyshevsky na katorge i v ssylke. Vospominaniya*'. Posmertnoye izdanie E. Pekarskogo (*N. G. Chernyshevsky. Hard labour and deportation. Recollections.* Posthumous publication by E. Pekarsky), Spb., 1907, p. 29.

119. Reprinted in Herzen's '*Kolokol*', and often elsewhere. See, for example, B. B. Glinsky, '*Revolyutsionnyy period russkoy istorii (1861–1881 gg.). Istoricheskiye ocherki*' (*The revolutionary period in Russian history [1861–1881]. Historical essays*), Spb., 1913, part I, pp. 146 ff. On the spirit of this opposition, cf. G. Dzhanshiev, '*A. M. Unkovsky i osvobozhdenie krest'yan*' (*A. M. Unkovsky and the liberation of the peasants*), M., 1894. Cf. S. G. Svatikov, '*Konstitutsionnoye dvizhenie pri Aleksandre II*' (*The constitutional movement under Alexander II*), no place, no date.

120. They were not printed till some years later in London by Lavrov, in 1874. See '*Izbrannyye ekonomicheskiye proizvedeniya*' (*Selected works on economics*), *op. cit.*, vol. II, pp. 617 ff.

121. A. A. Serno-Solov'evich, '*Nashi domashniye dela*' (*Affairs at home*), Geneva, 1867.

122. 'Protsess N. G. Chernyshevskogo', op. cit., p. 18.

123. M. V. L'vova, 'Kak podgotovyalos' zakritie "Sovremennika" v 1862 g. (Preparations for the closure of the 'Sovremennik' in 1862), in 'Istoricheskie zapiski', 1954, no. 46.

124. A. Shilov, 'N. G. Chernyshevsky v doneseniyakh agentov III Otdeleniya' (N. G. Chernyshevsky, from the reports of the agents of the Third Section), in 'Krasnyy Arkhiv', 1926, no. I, in which 113 police reports on him are examined, from 2nd October 1861 to 7th July 1862.

125. Letter from prison, 20th November 1862, to Prince A. A. Suvorov, in 'Protsess N. G. Chernyshevskogo', op. cit., p. 78.

126. See his visit to General Potapov of the Third Section, 16th July 1862, described from unpublished documents in N. M. Chernyshevskaya, 'Letopis' zhizni i deyatel'nosti N. G. Chernyshevskogo' (Annals of the life and activity of N. G. Chernyshevsky), op. cit., p. 260.

127. 'Protsess N. G. Chernyshevskogo', op. cit., p. 27.

128. Quoted by N. Ya. Nikoladze, 'Vospominaniya o shestidesyatykh godakh' (Memories of the sixties), in 'Katorga i ssylka', 1927, no. IV, p. 30.

129. The most detailed studies of this trial are by M. Lemke in 'Politicheskiye protsessy v Rossii 1860–kh godov. Po arkhivnym dokumentam' (Political trials in Russia in the sixties. Documents from the archives), M.-P., 1923, p. 161.

130. 'Protsess N. G. Chernyshevskogo', op. cit., p. 321.

131. Letter to his wife, 5th October 1862, XIV, 456.

132. 'Protsess N. G. Chernyshevskogo', op. cit., p. 295.

133. He imagines that the young Rakhmetov, the revolutionary in his novel, insults him for refusing to take part in conspiracy. And he comments: 'I in fact had not told him what I was thinking, and he had the right to call me a liar. Yet his words could not seem in the least offensive to me; they were even a compliment "in this case", as he said, because this itself was "the case". In reality he was able to preserve his initial trust and even his respect for me.' XI, 205.

134. What is to be done? was begun on 4th December 1862 and finished in a few months. It was given to the prison authorities and by them to the commission of inquiry. Both put so many seals on the manuscript that when it arrived at the censor's office he never read it, thinking that it had already been examined. It was passed to the Sovremennik. Nekrasov lost the manuscript on the Nevsky Prospekt, and only found it when, after putting an advertisement in the police journal of St Petersburg, it was handed to him by a poor clerk who had picked it up. It went to press in February 1863 and came out in serial form. It aroused great enthusiasm and also much criticism—not only of its artistic nullity, which was only too evident, but also of its political and social ideas. See V. Evgen'ev-Maksimov and G. Tizengauzen, 'Posledniye gody "Sovremennika", 1863–1866' (The last years of the 'Sovremennik', 1863–1866), L., 1939; and Avdot'ya Panaeva, 'Vospominaniya' (Memoirs), op. cit. The opinion of other circles in the State is shown by Muravev's proposal to recall Chernyshevsky from Siberia to question him. Muravev 'the butcher' was head of the Committee of Inquiry that was appointed after Karakozov's attempt on the life of the Tsar. He had noticed that at the end of the last chapter (which foresaw the revolution) Chernyshevsky had put a date, 4th April 1863. Muravev seemed to think that this had some connection with the date of Karakozov's plot, 4th April 1866. Alexander II had to intervene in person to put an end to the idea.

Chernyshevsky's contemporaries at once saw that What is to be done? was a roman à clef and it is not very difficult to identify the various characters.

Rakhmetov, the revolutionary, for example, was based partly on a young nobleman from Saratov, who in 1861 went to London and left all his money to Herzen for the cause. He then set off for the Pacific, planning to found a Communist colony. After this, nothing more was heard of him.

It is interesting to remember that A. Tveritinov, a follower of Chernyshevsky, devoted himself to making his personality and sufferings known in Western Europe in the 'seventies. In 1875, together with Malon and Guesde, émigrés from the Paris Commune then in Milan, he prepared a translation of *What is to be done?* It was printed at Lodi on the press belonging to Bignani's *La Plebe*. Tveritinov encouraged Eugenio Cameroni, editor of *Pungolo*, to write an article on Chernyshevsky, which was published in *Il Sole, La Plebe, La Capitale*, and a Neapolitan journal. See A. Tveritinov, '*Ob ob'yavlenii prigovora N. G. Chernyshevskomu, o rasprostranenii ego sochineniy na frantsuzskom yazyke v zapadnoy Evrope i o mnogom drugom*' (*The reading of his sentence to N. G. Chernyshevsky, the spread of his works in French in Western Europe, and many other things*), Spb., 1906.

135. This remained in the police archives until 1906, the year in which it was partially published in '*Polnoye sobranie sochineniy*' (*Complete works*), *op. cit.*, vol. X. It has been published complete at Moscow in 1933 and reprinted in XII, 5 ff.

136. '*Russkaya starina*', 1905, no. II. Also interesting for the eye-witness account by M. P. Sazhin (Ross), '*O grazhdanskoy kazni N. G. Chernyshevskogo*' (*The civil execution of Chernyshevsky*), published for the first time in '*Russkoye bogatstvo*', 1909, no. XII, and republished in '*Vospominaniya*' (*Memoirs*), M., 1925, pp. 16 ff.

137. P. F. Nikolaev, '*Lichnyye vospominaniya o prebyvanii N. G. Chernyshevskogo na katorge (v Aleksandrovskom zavode), 1867–1872 gg.*' (*Personal memories of N. G. Chernyshevsky serving sentence of hard labour at Alexandrovsky Zavod, 1867–1872*), M., 1906; V. N. Shaganov, '*N. G. Chernyshevsky na katorge i v ssylke*' (*N. G. Chernyshevsky, hard labour and deportation*), *op. cit.*

138. The documents in question have been published in 'Byloye', 1924, no. XV.

139. Letter to his wife, 2nd December 1872. XIV, 524.

140. Letter to his wife, 3rd April 1872. XIV, 516.

141. Letter to his wife, 17th May 1872. XIV, 518–19.

142. V. Ya. Kokosov, '*Rasskazy o kariyskoy katorge*' (*Accounts of hard labour at Kara*), Spb., 1907.

143. N. Ya. Nikoladze, '*Peregovory " Svyashchennoy druzhiny" s partiey " Narodnoy Voli"*' (*The discussions between the 'Holy Company' and 'Narodnaya Volya'*), P., 1917, p. 29.

144. Letter of 12th January 1871. XIV, 505.

145. XIV, p. 551.

146. XIV, 643–4.

147. XIV, 651.

148. XV, 465.

149. XV, 479.

CHAPTER 6

1. There are many publications of Dobrolyubov's works, but the most complete is N. A. Dobrolyubov, '*Polnoye sobranie sochineniy*' v shesti tomakh, pod obshchey redaktsiey P. I. Lebedeva-Polyanskogo (*Complete works*, in six volumes, under the general direction of P. I. Lebedev-Polyansky), L., 1934–9. There is a comprehensive bibliography in the prefaces and notes. From now on in this chapter it will be referred to by volume and page only. For books

on him, see V. Polyansky (P. I. Lebedev), '*N. A. Dobrolyubov. Mirovozzrenie i literaturno-kriticheskaya deyatel'nost'*' (*N. A. Dobrolyubov. His conception of the world and his work as a literary critic*), M., 1933; and '*Letopis' zhizni i deyatel'nosti N. A. Dobrolyubova*'. Pod red. S. Ya. Reyzera (*Annals of the life and work of N. A. Dobrolyubov*. Edited by S. Ya. Reyzer), M., 1953. On the cultural atmosphere of this town see the important and curious article of Pierre Pascal, *Un centre intellectual provincial au XIXe siècle: Nijni-Novgorod*, in Revue des études slaves, Paris, 1954, nos. 1–4.

2. Curious extracts in VI, 389 ff.
3. This small paper, *Slukhi* (*Voices of today*), is reprinted in full in IV, 429 ff. Accounts of the political life of the Institute have been assembled by S. Reyzer, '*Materialy dlya biografii N. A. Dobrolyubova*' (*Material for a biography of N. A. Dobrolyubov*), in 'Literaturnoye nasledstvo', 1936, nos. 25–6.
4. Diary, 6th January 1853. VI, 382.
5. Diary, 15th January 1857. VI, 453. This refers to the meeting for the anniversary of the 1848 revolution.
6. N. G. Chernyshevsky, '*Prolog*' (*Prologue*), M.-L., 1936, p. 298.
7. The name of this periodical was most probably taken from the famous *Fischietto* published at Turin. See, with reference to this, the notes by V. N. Knyazhin in '*Polnoye sobranie sochineniy*' (*Complete works*) of Dobrolyubov, edited by E. V. Anichkov, Spb., 1912–13, vol. IX, p. 528.
8. N. V. Shelgunov, '*Sochineniya*' (*Works*), Spb., 1895, vol. II, p. 684.
9. See the interesting analysis by Nestor Kotlyarevsky, '*Kanun osvobozhdeniya*' (*On the eve of emancipation*), P., 1916, pp. 196 ff.
10. '*Russkaya satira v vek Ekateriny*' (*Russian satire in the age of Catherine*), II, 139.
11. II, 381.
12. II, 56.
13. II, 310 ff.
14. II, 404.
15. II, 269 (the phrase was suppressed by the censor).
16. II, 271.
17. IV, 138.
18. '*Chto takoye oblomovshchina?*' (*What is an Oblomov mentality?*), II, 5 ff.
19. II, 10.
20. II, 30.
21. II, 35.
22. II, 206.
23. II, 211.
24. M. A. Antonovich, '*Iz vospominaniy o N. A. Dobrolyubove*' (*From recollections of N. A. Dobrolyubov*), in '*Shestidesyatyye gody*'. Vstupitel'nyye stat'i, kommentarii i redaktsiya V. Evgen'eva-Maksimova i G. F. Tizengauzena (*The sixties*. Edited, with introductory articles and notes by V. Evgen'ev-Maksimov and G. F. Tizengauzen), L., 1933, p. 140.
25. II, 256.
26. '*Blagonamerennost' i deyatel'nost'*' (*Good intentions and actions*), II, 241 ff.
27. IV, 60.
28. IV, 3 ff.
29. M. A. Antonovich, '*Iz vospominaniy o N. A. Dobrolyubove*' (*From recollections of N. A. Dobrolyubov*), op. cit., p. 142.
30. IV, 157.
31. An important body of his writings has been collected in A. P. Shchapov, '*Sochineniya*' (*Works*), Spb., 1906–8, 3 vols. See also A. P. Shchapov, '*Neizdan-*

nyye sochineniya', s predisloviem i primechaniyami E. I. Chernysheva (*Unpublished works*, with preface and notes by E. I. Chernyshev), Kazan, 1927; and A. P. Shchapov, '*Sochineniya'*, dopolnitel'nyy tom k izdaniyu 1906–1908 (*Works*. Supplementary volume to the 1906–1908 edition), Irkutsk, 1937. The two most important biographies are: N. Ya. Aristov, '*Afanasiy Prokof'evich Shchapov (Zhizn' i sochineniya)*' (*A. P. Shchapov [Life and works]*), Spb., 1883; and G. A. Luchinsky, '*Afanasiy Prokof'evich Shchapov. Biograficheskiy ocherk*' (*A. P. Shchapov. A biographical essay*) which is at the beginning of vol. III of the '*Sochineniya'* (*Works*), previously mentioned. See the article on Shchapov by G. V. Plekhanov, published in '*Vestnik Narodnoy Voli*', no. I, and reprinted in '*Sochineniya'*, pod red. D. Ryazanova (*Works*, edited by D. Ryazanov), M.-P., undated, vol. II, pp. 10 ff.; M. N. Pokrovsky, '*A. P. Shchapov (k 50-letiyu so dnya ego konchiny)*' (*A. P. Shchapov: On the fiftieth anniversary of his death*), in 'Istorik-marksist', 1927, no. III, reprinted in '*Istoricheskaya nauka i bor'ba klassov*' (*The science of history and the class struggle*), M.-L., 1933, vol. II, pp. 165 ff.; A. Sidorov, '*Melkoburzhuaznaya teoriya russkogo istoricheskogo protsessa (A. P. Shchapov)*' (*A petit bourgeois theory of the historical development of Russia [A. P. Shchapov]*), in '*Russkaya istoricheskaya literatura v klassovom osveshchenii. Sbornik statey*' (*Russian historical literature from the class standpoint. A miscellany*), vol. I, M., 1927; E. Chernyshev, '*Revolyutsionnyy demokrat-istorik A. P. Shchapov*' (*A. P. Shchapov: revolutionary democrat and historian*), in 'Voprosy istorii', 1951, no. 8.

32. N. G. Pomyalovsky, '*Ocherki bursy*' (*Essays on the 'bursa'*), Spb., 1865.
33. N. Aristov, '*A. P. Shchapov*', *op. cit.*, p. 38.
34. *Ibid.*, p. 10.
35. A. P. Shchapov, '*Sochineniya*' (*Works*), *op. cit.*, I, p. 225.
36. *Ibid.*, p. 200.
37. '*Chto inogda otkryvaetsya v liberal'nykh frazakh*' (*What one can often find under liberal phrases*), 1859, no. IX. Often attributed to Dobrolyubov, but in fact by M. A. Antonovich. Cf. M. A. Antonovich, '*Izbrannyye stat'i*' (*Selected articles*), L., 1938, p. 488.
38. IV, 318 ff.
39. Fragments of these researches were published in S. V. Eshevsky, '*Sochineniya*' (*Works*), Spb., 1870. See the biography written by K. N. Bestuzhev-Ryumin in S. V. Eshevsky, '*Sochineniya po russkoy istorii*' (*Works concerned with Russian history*), M., 1900.
40. Quoted by G. A. Luchinsky, '*A. P. Shchapov. Biograficheskiy ocherk*' (*A. P. Shchapov. Biographical essay*), *op. cit.*, p. XXXI.
41. See, for example, a conversation 'On the constitution', in A. P. Shchapov, '*Neizdannyye sochineniya*' (*Unpublished works*), *op. cit.*
42. There are several different versions of Shchapov's words. All must be regarded with caution, but the general sense of his speech is unmistakable. See '*Rech A. P. Shchapova posle panikhidy po ubitym v sele Bezdne krest'yanam*' (*A. P. Shchapov's speech after the requiem ceremony for the peasants who were killed in the village of Bezdna*), in 'Krasnyy arkhiv', 1923, no. IV.
43. '*Zemstvo i raskol*' (*The zemstvo and the schism*), Spb., 1862, reprinted in A. P. Shchapov, '*Sochineniya*' (*Works*), *op. cit.*, vol. I, pp. 451 ff.
44. *Ibid.*, p. 461.
45. *Ibid.*, p. 464.
46. *Ibid.*, p. 502.
47. '*Beguny*' (*The fugitives*), *ibid.*, pp. 505 ff.
48. *Ibid.*, pp. 760 ff.

49. '*Russkiye samorodki*' (*The self-made men of Russia*), in 'Vek', nos. 9–10, quoted in B. Koz'min, '*Artel'nyy zhurnal "Vek"*' (*The cooperative review 'The Century'*); '*Russkaya zhurnalistika*'. I. '*Shestidesyatyye gody*', pod red. i s predisloviem Valer'yana Polyanskogo (*Russian reviews*. I. *The sixties*, edited and with a preface by V. Polyansky), p. 41.

50. A. P. Shchapov, '*Sochineniya*' (*Works*), *op. cit.*, vol. II, pp. 154 ff.

51. *Ibid.*, p. 158.

52. *Ibid.*, p. 159.

53. *Ibid.*, p. 160.

54. *Ibid.*, p. 162.

55. *Ibid.*, p. 170.

56. *Ibid.*, p. 154.

57. *Ibid.*, p. 156.

58. *Ibid.*, pp. 481 ff.

CHAPTER 7

1. Geroid Tanquary Robinson, *Rural Russia under the old régime*, second edition, New York, 1949; and Hugh Seton-Watson, *The Decline of Imperial Russia, 1855–1914*, London, 1952.

2. M. Lemke, '*Krest'yanskiye volneniya 1855 goda (po neizdannym materialam)*' (*The peasant disturbances in 1855 [from unpublished documents]*), in 'Krasnaya letopis'', 1923, no. III; Ya. I. Linkov, '*Krest'yanskiye dvizheniya v Rossii vo vremya Krymskoy voyny*' (*The peasant movement in Russia at the time of the Crimean War*), M., 1940; and A. Shapiro, in 'Bor'ba klassov', 1936, no. 10.

3. I. I. Ignatovich, '*Osnovnyye cherty krestyanskikh volneniy pered osvobozhden-iem*' (*The fundamental nature of the peasant disorders which preceded the liberation*), in '*Bor'ba krest'yan za osvobozhdenie*' (*The peasant struggle for freedom*), L.-M., 1924, pp. 189 ff.; E. Kots, '*Pobegi pomeshchich'ikh krest'yan v nikolaevskuyu epokhu*' (*Peasant escapes in the time of Nicholas I*), in 'Arkhiv istorii truda v Rossii', no. V; E. Kots, '*Volneniya krepostnykh v nikolaevskuyu epokhu*' (*Serf disturbances in the time of Nicholas I*), in 'Russkoye proshloye', 1923, no. II.

4. M. Lemke, '*Krest'yanskiye volneniya 1855 goda*' (*The Peasant disturbances in 1855*), in *op. cit.*

5. N. A. Dobrolyubov, '*Polnoye sobranie sochineniy*', pod obshchey redaktsiey P. I. Lebedeva-Polyanskogo (*Complete works*, edited by P. I. Lebedev-Polyansky), vol. IV, pp. 439 ff.

6. L. A. Ayzenberger, '*Svedeniya o polozhenii krest'yan k kontsu krymskoy kampanii*' (*Accounts of the peasant situation at the end of the Crimean campaign*), in 'Arkhiv istorii truda v Rossii', 1923, no. X.

7. I. I. Ignatovich, '*Osnovnyye cherty krest'yanskikh volneniy pered osvobozh-deniem*' (*The fundamental nature of the peasant disorders which preceded the liberation*), *op. cit.*, p. 207.

8. A careful study of the documents has now qualified and corrected the assertion that the peasants awaited the will of the monarch with patience and trust. This legend has been very difficult to disprove since it was put abroad in the 'sixties, by the progressives who were fighting against the reactionaries. The latter's opinion was that the liberation would be accompanied by grave disorders, hence they concluded that nothing ought to be changed. See A. A. Kornilov, '*Krest'yanskaya reforma*' (*The peasant reform*), Spb., 1905, pp. 104 ff.

9. Of the extensive documentation on the subject, consisting generally of local and of detailed studies, the principal works are: I. I. Ignatovich, '*Volneniya*

pomeshchich'ikh krest'yan ot 1854 do 1863 goda' (*The risings of peasants who belonged to landlords, from 1854–1863*), in 'Minuvshiye gody', 1908, nos. VII–XI; A. Popel'nitsky, '*Kak prinyato bylo polozhenie 19 fevralya 1861 g. osvobozhdyonnymi krest'yanami*' (*How the freed peasants received the manifesto of 19th February 1861*), in 'Sovremennyy mir', 1911, nos. II–III; P. A. Zayonchkovsky, '*Provedenie v zhizn' krest'yanskoy reformy 1861 g.*' (*The enforcement of the peasant reform of 1861*), M., 1958. The most important publications of documents relating to this subject are: '*Krest'yanskoye dvizhenie v 1861 godu posle otmeny krepostnogo prava.* Podgotovil k pechati E. A. Morokhovets (*The peasant movement in 1861, after the abolition of serfdom.* Edited for publication by E. A. Morokhovets), M.-L., 1949; and '*Otmena krepostnogo prava. Doklady ministrov vnutrennykh del o provedenii krest'yanskoy reformy 1861–1862*' (*The abolition of serfdom. Reports of Ministers of the Interior on the application of peasant reforms, 1861–1862*), edited by S. N. Valk, M.-L., 1950. On all this period, see the collective work, '*Velikaya reforma*' (*The great reform*), by A. K. Dzhivilegov, S. P. Mel'gunov and B. I. Picheta, M., 1911.

10. N. A. Serno-Solov'evich, '*Okonchatel'noye reshenie krest'yanskogo voprosa*' (*The final solution of the peasant problem*), Berlin, 1861, p. 64.

11. '*Krest'yanskoye dvizhenie v 1861 godu*' (*The peasant movement in 1861*), op. cit., pp. 35–6.

12. I. I. Ignatovich, '*Volneniya pomeshchich'ikh krest'yan*' (*The risings of peasants who belonged to landlords*), op. cit., no. VIII.

13. '*Krest'yanskoye dvizhenie v 1861 godu*' (*The peasant movement in 1861*), op. cit., p. 46.

14. *Ibid.*, p. 117.

15. *Ibid.*, p. 116.

16. 'Kolokol', 1862, no. 134.

17. '*Krest'yanskoye dvizhenie v 1861 godu*' (*The peasant movement in 1861*), op. cit., p. 174.

18. The annual report of the Third Section published in '*Krest'yanskoye dvizhenie, 1827–1869*'. Podgotovil k pechati E. A. Morokhovets (*The peasant movement, 1827–1869*. Edited for publication by E. A. Morokhovets), M.-L., 1931, vol. II, p. 3.

19. I. I. Ignatovich, '*Volneniya pomeshchich'ikh krest'yan*' (*The risings of peasants who belonged to landlords*), op. cit., no. VIII.

20. '*Krest'yanskoye dvizhenie v 1861 godu*' (*The peasant movement in 1861*), op. cit., pp. 142 ff.

21. I. I. Ignatovich, 'Bezdna', in '*Velikaya reforma*', op. cit., vol., V, pp. 211 ff.; M. Nechkina, '*Vosstanie v Bezdne*' (*The insurrection in Bezdna*), in 'Krasnyy Arkhiv', 1929, no. IV; M. Nechkina, '*Iz istorii krest'yanskikh vosstaniy protiv "voli"*' (*From the history of peasant insurrections against the 'liberation'*), *ibid.*, 1929, no. V; E. I. Ustyuzhanin, '*Bezdnenskoye vosstanie 1861 g.*' (*The insurrection at Bezdna in 1861*), in '*Uchyennyye zapiski Kazanskogo Pedagogicheskogo Instituta*', 1941, no. IV; and '*Bezdenskoye vosstanie 1861 g.*' Sbornik dokumentov. Obshchaya redaktsiya A. I. Yampol'skoy i D. S. Gutmana (*The insurrection at Bezdna in 1861.* Collected documents, under the general editorship of A. I. Yampol'skaya and D. S. Gutman), Kazan, 1948.

22. 'Kolokol', nos. 98–9, 100, 101, 122–3, 124 and 125.

23. I. I. Ignatovich, '*Volneniya pomeshchich'ikh krest'yan*' (*The risings of peasants who belonged to landlords*), op. cit., no. IX.

24. *Ibid.*, op. cit., no. X.

25. The peasants of the village of Karasin in Volhynia began a revolt in 1862 which they kept up until 1867; they refused to come to terms, saying 'we will wait for the Tsar's redemption'. Ignatovich, *op. cit.*, no. VIII.

CHAPTER 8

1. See principally I. Solov'yov, '*Russkiye universitety v ikh ustavakh i vospominaniyakh sovremennikov*' (*The Russian universities from their statutes and from the memoirs of contemporaries*), Spb., no. I, 1914. Also of interest, S. Mel'gunov, '*Iz istorii studencheskikh obshchestv v russkikh universitetakh*' (*The history of student societies in the Russian universities*), no place of publication given (but Moscow), 1904.

2. The best chronicle of the student movement is by S. Ashevsky, '*Russkoye studenchestvo v epokhu shestidesyatykh godov*' (*Russian students during the sixties*), in 'Sovremennyy mir', 1907, nos. VI–XI. A different interpretation is to be found in Sergey Gessen, '*Studencheskoye dvizhenie v nachale shestidesyatykh godov*' (*The student movement at the beginning of the sixties*), M., 1932, with unpublished documents and an extensive bibliography.

3. See, for example, I. A. Shvinyn, '*Vospominaniya studenta shestidesyatykh godov za 1862–1865 gg.*' (*Recollections of a student in the sixties, 1862–1865*), Tambov, 1890, p. 8. He found the 'Kolokol' inside the university news sheet, as well as a large number of pictures of Iskander. 'Imagine my terror', says the author of this stupid but curious little book.

4. See some of the short passages given in the appendix to S. Gessen, *op. cit.*, pp. 124 ff. For example, no. I (1858) of the 'Living Voice' said: 'The aim of our paper is to spread ideas about the reform of serfdom', and it eulogized the atmosphere of freedom which was gradually coming into being in Russia. 'The Unmasker' originated from discussions between a group of two hundred elementary school masters and a group of university students. The latter felt compelled to lay bare and criticize their own shortcomings. See Il'ya Petrovich Verkhachev, '*Vospominaniya o studencheskoy zhizni*' (*Recollections of student life*), published in the collection '*Iz moskovskikh studencheskikh vospominaniy*' (*From the recollections of Moscow students*), M., 1899, p. 232.

5. S. Gessen, *op. cit.*, p. 12.

6. Compare S. V. Eshevsky, '*Moskovskiy universitet v 1861 godu*' (*The University of Moscow in 1861*), in '*Sochineniya po russkoy istorii*' (*Works concerned with Russian history*), M., 1900; and S. Ashevsky, *op. cit.*, nos. VII–VIII, p. 32.

7. S. Ashevsky, *op. cit.*, nos. VII–VIII.

8. He is remembered by two writers: V. Ostrogorsky, '*Iz istorii moego uchitel'stva*' (*About the story of my life as a master*), Spb., 1895; and V. Sorokin, '*Vospominaniya starogo studenta*' (*Recollections of an old student*), in 'Russkaya starina', 1906, no. XI.

9. N. A. Firsov, '*Studencheskiye istorii v kazanskom universitete 1855–1863*' (*Student disorders in the University of Kazan from 1855 to 1863*), in 'Russkaya starina', 1888, nos. III, IV, VI–VIII.

10. Quoted from S. Gessen, *op. cit.*, p. 18. Cf. V. I. Orlov, '*Studencheskoye dvizhenie moskovskogo universiteta v XIX stoletii* (*The student movement in Moscow University during the nineteenth century*), M., 1934 and P. S. Tkachenko, '*Moskovskoye studenchestvo v obshchestvenno-politicheskoy zhizni Rossii II-oy poloviny XIX veka*' (*Moscow students in Russian political and social life in the latter half of the 19th century*), M., 1958. On the cultural background and the student movement in Moscow, see N. M. Druzhinin, '*Moskva i*

reforma 1861 goda' (*Moscow and the reform of 1861*); and S. M. Levin, '*Obshchestvennaya zhizn' Moskvy v 60-kh godakh*' (*Social life in Moscow in the sixties*) in '*Istoriya Moskvy v shesti tomakh*' (*History of Moscow in 6 volumes*), vol. IV, M., 1954, pp. 13 ff., 291 ff.

11. A manuscript poem in circulation at the time said:

> 'Let us go away together like a group of brothers
> My friends let us leave these walls
> Where pettiness suffocates us
> Where there is nothing but spying and betrayal.'

Quoted by S. Gessen, *op. cit.*, p. 128. The idea of voluntarily going down from the university was in the air even before the 'Kolokol' suggested it to the students.

12. S. Ashevsky, *op. cit.*, no. IX.

13. S. Gessen, *op. cit.*, p. 129.

14. See S. Gessen, '*Peterburgskiy universitet osenyu 1861 g.*' (*Po neopublikovannym materialam iz arkhiva A. V. Nikitenko*) (*The University of St Petersburg in autumn 1861 [from unpublished material from the archives of A. V. Nikitenko]*), in '*Revolyutsionnoye dvizhenie 1860-kh godov*'. Sbornik pod red. B. Goreva i B. P. Koz'mina (*The revolutionary movement of the sixties. Miscellany edited by B. Gorev and B. P. Koz'min*), M., 1932, p. 11.

15. V. Sorokin, '*Vospominaniya starogo studenta*' (*Recollections of an old student*), *op. cit.*

16. See the interesting comment on these events by K. D. Kavelin, published in the Kolokol, no. 119–20.

17. I. A. Shvinyn, *op. cit.*, p. 9.

18. The most comprehensive and intelligent interpretation of the student movement at St Petersburg—among the many in the memoirs of the period—is probably by N. V. Shelgunov, '*Vospominaniya*'. Redaktsiya, vstupitel'naya stat'ya i primechaniya A. A. Shilova (*Recollections. Edited and with preface and notes by A. A. Shilov*), M.-P., 1923, pp. 122 ff.

19. S. Ashevsky, *op. cit.*, no. X; M. Lemke, '*Ocherki osvoboditel'nogo dvizheniya 60-kh godov*' (*Essays on the liberation movement of the sixties*), Spb., 1909, p. 7; and 'Byloye', 1907, no. IV, p. 21.

20. N. I. Kostomarov, '*Neizdannaya glava iz avtobiografii*' (*An unpublished chapter from my autobiography*), in 'Golos minuvshego', 1918, nos. V–VI.

21. B. P. Koz'min, '*Iz istorii studencheskogo dvizheniya v Moskve v 1861 godu*' (*From the history of the student movement in Moscow in 1861*), in '*Revolyutsionnoye dvizhenie 1860-kh godov*' (*The revolutionary movement of the sixties*), *op. cit.*, p. 22. An interesting letter (author unknown), which is published in this book, comments as follows on the clash with the police: 'To see boys fighting with bears is horrible, but I must add that it is the first time that I have seen either the people or the educated classes in agreement with the police.' There is also an important handwritten manifesto which was distributed by V. N. Lind at the time and copied out about twenty times. Lind defended his fellow-students from accusations which the police were spreading: among others that they 'wanted the peasants to return to serfdom'. The police cunningly spread these rumours to turn public opinion against the students.

CHAPTER 9

1. M. M. Klevensky, *Vertepniki*, in 'Katorga i ssylka', 1928, no. X

2. The meaning of the name *Vertepniki*, which was adopted by this group, was not understood even by its contemporaries. A police report said: 'These

meetings are called, no one knows why, vertep (puppet theatre and den, place of evil doings), but the members also call themselves socialists.'

3. '*Pesny sobrannyye P. N. Rybnikovym*' (*Songs collected by P. N. Rybnikov*), second edition., M., 1909, 3 vols. In the first volume there is an interesting account of the author by A. E. Gruzinsky. See A. P. Razumova, '*Iz istorii russkoy fol'kloristiki*'. *P. N. Rybnikov, P. S. Efimenko* (*History of Russian folklore. P. N. Rybnikov and P. S. Efimenko*), M.-L., 1954.

4. All the basic documents concerning this episode were published for the first time by B. P. Koz'min, in '*Khar'kovskiye zagovorshchiki 1856–1858 godov*' (*The Kharkov conspirators of the years 1856–1858*), no place of publication given, undated (but Kharkov, 1930). See A. Z. Barabov, '*Khar'kovsko-kievskoye revolyutsionnoye taynoye obshchestvo 1856–1860 gg.*' (*The secret revolutionary society of Kharkov and Kiev in 1856–1860*), in 'Istoricheskie zapiski', 1955, no. 52, which emphasizes this group's link with Herzen.

5. N. A. Firsov, '*Studencheskiye istorii v kazanskom universitete*' (*Student disturbances in the University of Kazan*), in 'Russkaya starina', 1889, no. 64.

6. N. F. Bunakov, '*Moya zhizn' v svyazi s obshcherusskoy zhizn'yu*' (*My life in relation to the life of the Russian society*), Spb., 1909, pp. 50–3.

7. E. Breshkovskaya, '*Iz moikh vospominaniy*' (*From my memoirs*), Spb., p. 21. M. Muravsky, '*Ssylka i katorga v 1860-kh godakh*' (*Deportation and hard labour in the sixties*), in 'Byloye', no. IV, 1903; and the literature on the 'trial of the hundred and ninety-three'.

8. The three numbers of '*Velikoruss*' have often been reprinted. Soon after they came out, they were republished abroad in 'Letuchiye listki' (*Leaflets*), Heidelberg, 1862. 'The significance of these pages is so great, in view of the state of affairs in Russia, that no justification is needed for reprinting them', according to the anonymous preface, dated 1st December 1861. See also in M. Lemke, '*Protsess "Velikorusstsev"*' (*The trial of the authors of the '*Velikoruss*'), in '*Ocherki osvoboditel'nogo dvizheniya shestidesyatykh godov*' (*Essay on the liberation movement of the 'sixties*), second edition, 1908, pp. 359 ff. See the interesting article by N. N. Novikova, '*Komitet "Velikorussa" i bor'ba za sozdanie revolyutsionnoy organizatsii v epokhu padeniya krepostnogo prava*' (*The committee of 'Velikoruss' and the struggle to establish a revolutionary organization in the period of the decline of serfdom*), in 'Voprosy istorii', 1953, no. 5, which tends to exaggerate the importance of this episode.

9. Yu. M. Steklov, '*N. G. Chernyshevsky. Ego zhizn' i deyatel'nost'*' (*N. G. Chernyshevsky. Life and activity*), second edition, M.-L., 1928, vol. II, p. 248, in which there is a collection of evidence for and against this opinion; the author decides that Chernyshevsky had no share in the '*Velikoruss*'. In my opinion, Steklov is right, even if some of the arguments he uses are invalid (it is not true, for example, that he always maintained the necessity of giving *all* the noblemen's estates to the peasants).

10. I. Trotsky, '*Avtobiograficheskoye pis'mo P. D. Balloda*' (*An autobiographical letter by P. D. Ballod*), in '*Revolyutsionnoye dvizhenie 1860-kh godov*'. Sbornik pod red. B. Goreva i B. P. Koz'mina (*The revolutionary movement of the sixties. Miscellany edited by B. Gorev and B. P. Koz'min*), M., 1932. It is confirmed also by L. F. Panteleyev in '*Iz vospominaniy proshlogo*'. Redaktsiya i kommentarii S. A. Reyzera. Vstupitel'naya stat'ya V. I. Nevskogo (*Recollections of the past. Edited, and with comments, by S. A. Reyzer. Introductory article by V. I. Nevsky*), M.-L., 1934, p. 310. See 'Literaturnoye nasledstvo', vol. 62, pp. 413 ff.

11. B. P. Koz'min, '*Gertsen, Ogaryov i "molodaya emigratsiya"*' (*Herzen, Ogarev and the 'young emigration'*), in 'Literaturnoye nasledstvo', 1941, nos. 41–2.

12. L. F. Panteleyev, '*Iz vospominaniy proshlogo*' (*Recollections of the past*), *op. cit.*, p. 241.
13. N. V. Shelgunov, '*Vospominaniya*'. Redaktsiya, vstupitel'naya stat'ya i primechaniya A. A. Shilova (*Recollections. Edited, with introductory article and notes, by A. A. Shilov*), M.-P., 1923, p. 135.
14. *Ibid.*, pp. 166, 167.
15. *Ibid.*, p. 71.
16. *Ibid.*, p. 83.
17. *Ibid.*, pp. 72, 103. Cf. L. P. Shelgunova, '*Iz dalyokogo proshlogo*' (*From the distant past*), Spb., 1901, p. 69.
18. N. V. Shelgunov, *op. cit.*, p. 34.
19. *Ibid.*, p. 110.
20. '*Rabochiy proletariat v Anglii i Frantsii*' (*The proletarian worker in England and France*), in *Sovremennik*, 1861, nos. IX, X, XI.
21. M. L. Mikhaylov, '*Polnoye sobranie stikhotvoreniy*'. Redaktsiya, biografi-cheskiy ocherk i kommentarii N. S. Ashukina (*Collected poems. Edited, with biographical essay and comments by N. S. Ashukin*), M.-L., 1934; and '*Sobranie stikhotvoreniy*'. Pod red. Yu. D. Levina (*Collected poems. Edited by Yu. D. Levin*), L., 1953.
22. M. L. Mikhaylov, '*Zapiski. 1861–1862*'. Redaktsiya i vstupitel'naya stat'ya A. A. Shilova (*Memoirs. 1861–1862. Edited and with an introductory article by A. A. Shilova*), P., 1922.
23. N. V. Shelgunov, '*Vospominaniya*' (*Recollections*), *op. cit.*, p. 122.
24. T. A. Bogdanovich, '*Lyubov' lyudey shestidesyatykh godov*' (*Love in the sixties*), L., 1929, with many letters and accounts of this 'revolution' in the circles of the *Sovremennik* and *Zemlya i Volya*.
25. N. V. Shelgunov, *op. cit.*, p. 105.
26. In almost every number of the *Sovremennik* there is an article by Mikhaylov on the question of women. They are collected in M. L. Mikhaylov, '*Zhensh-chiny, ikh vospitanie i znachenie v sem'ye i obshchestve*' (*Women, their education and importance in the family and society*), Spb., 1903.
27. P. V. Bykov, '*Siluety dalyokogo proshlogo*' (*Portraits from the distant past*), M.-L., 1930, p. 149.
28. P. D. Boborykin, '*Za polveka*' (*Fifty years after*), M., 1929, p. 173.
29. The few and contradictory accounts of this first nucleus have been transcribed and collected by Yu. M. Steklov in '*N. G. Chernyshevsky. Ego zhizn' i deyatel'nost*' (*N. G. Chernyshevsky. Life and work*), second edition, M.-L., 1928, vol. II, pp. 282, 295.
30. The two appeals are reprinted in N. V. Shelgunov, '*Vospominaniya*' (*Recollections*), *op. cit.*, appendices II and III, pp. 303 ff.
31. The whole of this document is printed in N. V. Shelgunov, '*Vospominaniya*' (*Recollections*), *op. cit.*, appendix I, pp. 287 ff.
32. Not without cause, F. Raskol'nikov calls this 'the first manifesto of Populism', in '*Iz istorii russkoy revolyutsionnoy mysli 60-kh godov*' (*About the history of revolutionary thought in the sixties*), in '*Molodaya gvardiya*', 1924, no. IV.
33. M. L. Mikhaylov, '*Polnoye sobranie stikhotvoreniy*' (*Collected poems*), *op. cit.*, appendix, p. 641.
34. M. Lemke, '*Politicheskiye protsessy v Rossii v 1860-kh godakh* (*Po arkhivnym dokumentam*)' (*Political trials in Russia in the sixties* [*based on documents from the archives*]), second edition, M.-L., 1923, pp. 55 ff.
35. M. L. Mikhaylov, '*Zapiski*' (*Memoirs*), *op. cit.*, p. 109.
36. M. L. Mikhaylov, *op. cit.*, p. 139.

37. This and other pages of the 'pocket press' are reprinted in M. Lemke, '*Politicheskiye protsessy v Rossii 1860-kh godakh*' (*Political trials in Russia in the sixties*), *op. cit.*, p. 503 ff., where there is a careful study of the whole incident. See P. I. Valeskaln, '*Revolyutsionnyy demokrat Petr Davidovich Ballod*' (*The revolutionary democrat P. D. Ballod*), Riga, 1957.

38. See B. P. Koz'min, '*Pisal li D. I. Pisarev stat'yu pod nazvaniem "Russkoe pravitel'stvo pod pokrovitel'strom Shedo-Ferroti*"' (*Is D. I. Pisarev the author of the article 'The Russian government under the protection of Szedo-Ferroti'?*), in '*Izvestiya Akademii Nauk SSSR. Serya istorii i filosofii*', vol. VIII, no. 4, July–August 1951, pp. 364–5.

39. M. Lemke, *op. cit.*, p. 578.

40. Their sentences are reprinted in V. Bogucharsky, '*Gosudarstvennyye prestupleniya v Rossii v XIX veke*' (*State crimes in Russia in the nineteenth century*), Spb., 1906, p. 119. See M. Lemke, *op. cit.*, pp. 647 ff.

CHAPTER 10

1. A. I. Gertsen, '*Polnoye sobranie sochineniy i pisem*', pod red. M. K. Lemke (*Complete works and letters*, edited by M. K. Lemke), P., 1912–23, vol. XIX, pp. 331–2.

2. Most of L. F. Panteleyev's memoirs have been collected in '*Iz vospominaniy proshlogo*'. Redaktsiya i kommentarii S. A. Reyzera. Vstupitel'naya stat'ya V. I. Nevskogo (*From Recollections of the past*. Edited and with comments by Reyzer. Introductory article by V. I. Nevsky), M.-L., 1934. The memoirs of Aleksandr Aleksandrovich Sleptsov were left unfinished by the author and have never been published complete. M. K. Lemke, however, has quoted from them and used them extensively in a digression on '*Zemlya i Volya*' included in his edition of the works of Herzen, vol. XVI, pp. 70 ff. See also the memoirs of Sleptsov's daughter, M. Sleptsova, '*Shturmany gryadushchey buri (Iz vospominaniy)*' (*The pilots of the advancing storm [From recollections]*), in '*Zven'ya*', vol. II. A series of letters and a detailed commentary are to be found in articles by B. Koz'min, '*Gertsen, Ogaryov i "molodaya emigratsiya"*' (*Herzen, Ogarev and the 'young emigration'*), and by E. Kusheva, '*K istorii vzaimootnosheniy A. I. Gertsena i N. P. Ogaryova s "Zemlyoy i Volyey" 60-kh godov*' (*On the history of the connections of A. I. Herzen and N. P. Ogarev with 'Zemlya i Volya' in the sixties*), both in '*Literaturnoye nasledstvo*', 1941, nos. 41–2, 61–3, 67. The principal work is by V. I. Nevsky and E. Safonova, '*"Zemlya i Volya" shestidesyatykh godov*' ('*Zemlya i Volya*' in the sixties), M., 1930, which, however, I have not been able to see.

3. The most recent studies on him are by I. Volodarsky, '*N. A. Serno-Solov'evich, vydayushchiysya deyatel' russkoy revolyutsionnoy demokratii*' (*N. A. Serno-Solovevich, an eminent political figure of Russian revolutionary democracy*), in '*Voprosy istorii*', 1946, no. X; and V. I. Romanenko, '*Mirovozzrenie N. A. Serno-Solov'evicha*', s.l., (but L.), 1954.

4. See the interesting memoirs by her daughter, O. K. Bulanova-Trubnikova, in '*Tri pokoleniya*' (*Three generations*), M., 1928. These were: Decembrist, Liberal-Populist and Social-revolutionary.

5. *Ibid.*, p. 72.

6. *Ibid.*, p. 146.

7. *Ibid.*, p. 74.

8. N. Bel'chikov, '*Iz naslediya revolyutsionnoy poezii 60-kh godov. Neizdannyye stikhotvoreniya N. A. serno-Solov'evicha*" (*From the legacy of the revolutionary*

poetry of the sixties. Unpublished poems by N. A. Serno-Solov'evich), in 'Literaturnoye nasledstvo', 1936, nos. 25–6.

9. See two accounts by contemporaries, although they do not agree about the details, published by M. Lemke, '*Ocherki osvoboditel'nogo dvizheniya "shestidesyatykh godov"* ' (*Essays on the liberation movement of the 'sixties'*), Spb., 1908, second edition, p. 43. He himself was to speak of this act in his deposition, when he was arrested, *ibid.*, p. 144.

10. E. Safonova, '*K biografii N. Serno-Solov'evicha*' (*For a biography of N. Serno-Solov'evich*), in '*Revolyutsionnoye dvizhenie 1860-kh godov*'. Sbornik pod redaktsiey B. I. Goreva i B. P. Koz'mina (*The revolutionary movement in the sixties. Miscellany edited by B. I. Gorev and B. P. Koz'min*), M., 1932, p. 72. Serno's letter to Alexander II from prison, 16th December 1863. In it Serno replied to the Tsar's comment: 'But in order to give that guidance, one must give these people room for their activity and thoughts, room to correspond to their fortitude and honourable intentions.'

11. '*Ob osvobozhdenii krest'yan*' (*On the liberation of the peasants*), in 'Golosa iz Rossii' (*Voices from Russia*), 1858, no. V. Serno-Solov'evich's authorship of this pamphlet is confirmed in the obituary by his brother, Aleksandr, published in 'Narodnoye delo', 1869, nos. 7–10. This periodical was edited by friends of the brothers in a position to know the truth. The copy of this pamphlet, which is preserved in the International Institute of Social History in Amsterdam, has a note, evidently of an early date, which makes the same attribution.

12. N. A. Serno-Solov'evich, '*Okonchatel'noye razreshenie krest'yanskogo voprosa*' (*The definitive solution to the peasant problem*), Berlin, 1861; quoted in M. Lemke, '*Ocherki osvoboditel'nogo dvizheniya "shestidesyatykh godov"* ' (*Essays on the liberation movement of the 'sixties'*), op. cit., p. 45.

13. I. Trotsky, '*Pis'ma N. A. Serno-Solov'evicha k N. S. Kashkinu*' (*Letters from N. A. Serno-Solov'evich to N. S. Kashkin*), in '*Revolyutsionnoye dvizhenie 1860-kh godov*' (*The revolutionary movement of the 'sixties'*), op. cit., p. 103.

14. See the collection of articles and recollections dedicated to him, '*Viktor Antonovich Artsimovich*', Spb., 1904.

15. On his part in the discussions on the share companies, which were very heated at that time, see Dobrolyubov's article in *Sovremennik*, 1859, no. XII, reprinted in '*Polnoye sobranie sochineniy*', pod red. P. I. Lebedeva-Polyanskogo (*Complete works, edited by P. I. Lebedev-Polyansky*), M., 1934, vol. IV, pp. 158 ff.

16. '*Razbor trudov komissii dlya ustroystva zemskikh bankov*' (*Examination of the work of the commission for setting up agricultural banks*), in *Sovremennik*, November 1860; and '*O proekte preobrazovaniya zemskikh povinnostey*' (*Concerning a plan for reform of local taxation*), in *Sovremennik*, November 1861.

17. '*Arkhiv Ogaryovykh*'. Pod red. M. O. Gershenzona (*The Ogarev archives. Edited by M. O. Gershenzon*), in 'Russkiye propilei', 1917, no. V, pp. 260 ff.; and a letter from Serno to Ogarev, published by S. Pereselenkov, in 'Literaturnoye nasledstvo', 1941, nos. 41–2.

18. '*Arkhiv Ogaryovykh*' (*The Ogarev archives*), op. cit., p. 230.

19. London, 1862.

20. *Ibid.*, p. 25.

21. *Ibid.*, p. 119.

22. '*Arkhiv Ogaryovykh*' (*The Ogarev archives*), op. cit., p. 232. This pamphlet never appeared, as far as I know, and has been lost.

23. This programme is given in A. I. Gertsen, '*Polnoye sobranie sochineniy i pisem*' (*Complete works and letters*), op. cit., vol. XI, pp. 38 ff.

24. *Ibid.*, vol. XVI, p. 76.
25. N. Chernyshevskaya, '*Neopublikovannaya perepiska S. N. i E. N. Pypinykh*' (*Unpublished correspondence of S. N. and E. N. Pypin*), in 'Literaturnoye nasledstvo', 1936, nos. 25–6, from which one can gather how highly Pypin and his family, who were related to Chernyshevsky, valued this enterprise. For general information about Serno's bookshop, see the anecdotes related by N. V. Shelgunov, '*Vospominaniya*'. Redaktsiya, vstupitel'naya stat'ya i primechaniya A. A. Shilova (*Recollections*. Edited, with an introductory article and notes, by A. A. Shilov), M.-L., 1923, pp. 113 ff.
26. B. P. Koz'min, '*Artel'nyy zhurnal "Vek"*' (*The cooperative review 'The Century'*), in '*Russkaya zhurnalistika. Shestidesyatyye gody*' (*Russian reviews. The sixties*), M.-L., 1930, and reprinted in *ibid.*, '*Ot devyatnadtsatogo fevralya k pervomu marta*' (*From 19th February 1861 to 1st March 1881*), M., 1933.
27. N. V. Shelgunov, '*Vospominaniya*' (*Recollections*), *op. cit.*, p. 146; cf. '*Zapiski imperatorskogo russkogo geograficheskogo obshchestva*' (*Proceedings of the Imperial Russian Geographical Society*), Spb., 1862, no. 2.
28. 'Vek', nos. 13–14, partially reprinted in M. Lemke, '*Ocherki osvoboditel'nogo dvizheniya "shestidesyatykh godov"*' (*Essays on the history of the liberation movement of the 'sixties'*), *op. cit.*, p. 486. Lemke thought that it had never been published.
29. M. Lemke, *op. cit.*, p. 60.
30. This was his formula: 'Every Russian living permanently in Russia has the right to possess 4 *desyatiny* of land.'
31. M. Lemke has made a study of this in '*Delo o litsakh obvinyaemykh v snosheniyakh s londonskimi propagandistami*' (*Documents concerning the people accused of being in touch with the London propagandists*), in the review, 'Byloye', 1906, nos. IX–XII; and later with some additions in his previously mentioned book, pp. 17 ff. N. Nalbandyan, '*Izbrannye filosofskie i obshchestvenno-politicheskie proizvedeniya*' (*Selected works on philosophical, political and social questions*), published and edited by A. B. Khachaturyan, s.l., (M.), 1954.
32. M. Lemke, *op. cit.*, p. 162 ff.
33. *Ibid.*, p. 86. See P. C. Masini e G. Bosio, '*Bakunin, Garibaldi e gli affari slavi 1862–1863*', in 'Movimento operaio', 1952, no. 1, p. 78 ff.
34. Letter to his mother, from I. Volodarsky, '*N. A. Serno-Solov'evich, vydayushchiysya deyatel' russkoy revolyutsionnoy demokratii*' (*N. A. Serno-Solov'evich, an eminent political figure of the Russian revolutionary democracy*), *op. cit.*, p. 40. On 3rd April 1865 he wrote: 'I am determined and full of courage. I am as tranquil in mind as none of those who persecute me can be. This hard school has taught me many things. I have found within myself the strength to understand my many errors and to admit them. But on going over all my convictions, I have remained faithful to them.'
35. His article of 15th April 1863 has been published by E. Safonova, '*K biografii N. Serno-Solov'evicha*' (*For a biography of N. Serno-Solov'evich*), *op. cit.*, p. 53.
36. Quoted by I. Volodarsky, *op. cit.*, p. 42. See 'Literaturnoye nasledstvo', vol. 62, pp. 561 ff.
37. The part played by Herzen and Ogarev in the inception of 'Zemlya i Volya' has recently been the subject of numerous and extended discussions. See Ya. I. Linkov, '*Rol' A. I. Gertsena i N. P. Ogaryova v sozdanii i deyatel'nosti obshchestva "Zemlya i Volya"*' (*The function of Herzen and Ogarev in the creation and operation of the 'Land and Liberty' organization*), in 'Voprosy istorii', 1954, no. 3, which assembles a great deal of material to prove the weight of initiative displayed by the émigrés and '*Kolokol*' in the establishment and development of the clandestine groups. S. A. Pokrovsky, '*O roli*

Chernyshevskogo i Gertsena v sozdanii revolyutsionnoy organizatsii' (*The role of Chernyshevsky and Herzen in the creation of a revolutionary organization*), *ibid.*, 1954, no. 9, tries to maintain a balance between the role of '*Kolokol*' and '*Sovremennik*'. In spite of indications to the contrary contained in these and a great many similar articles, it does not seem that documents of Ogarev, recently published in 'Literaturnoye nasledstvo', vol. 61, pp. 459 ff., throw much new light on the matter, though they enrich impressions already formed. See the introductory article of M. Nechkina, '*Novyye materialy o revolyutsionnoy situatsii v Rossii, 1859–1861 gg.*' (*New materials on the revolutionary situation in Russia, 1859–1861*), which deals with other recent articles on this question. A more careful examination of the texts will be necessary to reach a conclusion. For an example of a critical reconsideration of a text, see V. N. Shul′gin, '*K rasshifrovke "Stranichki iz dnevnika" N. A. Dobrolyubova*' (*On deciphering 'A Page of a Diary' by N. A. Dobrolyubov*).

38. According to Sleptsov. A. I. Gertsen, '*Polnoye sobranie sochineniy i pisem*' (*Complete works and letters*), *op. cit.*, vol. XVI, p. 75.

39. L. F. Panteleyev, '*Iz vospominaniy proshlogo*' (*From memories of the past*), *op. cit.*, p. 258, where he quotes Sleptsov, though without much confidence, which seems to be confirmed by an observation by Sleptsov himself in 1862: 'always use Mazzini's ink.' Ya. Chernyak, '*Neizdannye i nesobrannye proizvedeniya Ogaryova*' (*Unpublished and uncollected works of Ogarev*), in 'Literaturnoye nasledstvo', vol. 61, p. 556.

40. This aspect of the 'Zemlya i Volya' movement has been rightly emphasized by N. I. Utin in an article, '*Propaganda i organizatsiya*', in 'Narodnoye delo', October 1868, nos. 2–3.

41. M. Sleptsova, '*Shturmany gryadushchey buri*' (*The pilots of the advancing storm*), *op. cit.*

42. R. A. Taubin has collected some useful material in '*K voprosu o roli N. G. Chernyshevskogo v sozdanii "revolyutsionnoy partii" v kontse 50-kh—nachale 60-kh godov XIX veka*' (*On the problem of Chernyshevsky's role in the creation of a 'revolutionary party' from the end of the fifties to the beginning of the sixties*), in 'Istoricheskie zapiski', 1952, no. 39, pp. 59 ff. He tends to exaggerate his role as chief conspirator and fails to distinguish propagandist activity from organizing activity, and does not recognize to what extent the initiative of the clandestine groups derives from the younger elements, and above all from Serno-Solov′evich.

43. B. P. Koz′min, '*Kazanskiy zagovor 1863 goda*' (*The Kazan conspiracy of 1863*), M., 1929, p. 19.

44. See the article by L. F. Panteleyev, '*Iz lichnykh vospominaniy o G. N. Potanine*' (*My personal recollections of G. N. Potanin*), in 'Birzhevyye vedomosti', 21st September 1915.

45. A. I. Gertsen, *op. cit.*, vol. XVI, p. 87.

46. J. Witrowski, '*Powstanie 1863 roku i rosyjski ruch rewolucyjny poczatku 1860-ch lat*' (*The insurrection of 1863 and the Russian revolutionary movement in the sixties*), Minsk, 1931, p. 151.

47. A. I. Gertsen, *op. cit.*, vol. XVI, p. 150; and '*Wydawnictwo materyalow do powstania 1863–4*', Lwow, 1888–94, vol. IV, p. 76 ff.

48. A. A. Shilov, '*Delo Arngol′dta, Slivitskogo, Rostovskogo i Shchura 1862 g.*' (*The Arngol′dt, Slivitsky, Rostovsky and Shchur affair of 1862*), in '*Muzey revolyutsii. Sbornik I*' (*Museum of the Revolution. Miscellany I*), P., 1923.

49. S. Skord, '*Zhertva pol′skogo osvobozhdeniya (Andrey Potebnya)*' (*A victim of the Polish liberation [Andrey Potebnya]*), in 'Katorga i ssylka', 1931, no. IV; 1933, no. II; 1934, no. II.

50. A. I. Gertsen, *op. cit.*, vol. XVI, p. 444.

51. Panteleyev relates that Sleptsov was even thinking of forming a Provisional Government, *op. cit.*, p. 290.

52. E. Kusheva, '*K istorii vzaimootnosheniy A. I. Gertsena i N. P. Ogaryova s "Zemlyey i Volyey" 60-kh godov*' (*On the history of the connections of A. I. Herzen and N. P. Ogarev with 'Zemlya i Volya' in the sixties*), *op. cit.*

53. The first number is reprinted in B. Bazilevsky, '*Materialy dlya istorii revolyutsionnogo dvizheniya v Rossii v 60-kh godakh*' (*Material for the history of the revolutionary movement in Russia in the sixties*), Paris, 1905, p. 89. The second is given in 'Byloye', 1906, no. VIII.

54. 'Kolokol', 15th September 1861.

55. See the article by B. P. Koz'min, '*A. A. Serno-Solov'evich v I Internatsionale i v zhenevskom rabochem dvizhenii*' (*A. A. Serno-Solov'evich in the First International and in the Geneva working-class movement*), in 'Istoricheskiy sbornik', 1936, no. V, pp. 77 ff., which must, however, be completed by researches into Genevan papers of the period.

56. M. Lemke, '*K biografii A. A. Serno-Solov'evicha*' (*For a biography of A. A. Serno-Solov'evich*), in '*Ocherki osvoboditel'nogo dvizheniya "shestidesyatykh godov"*' (*Essays on the liberation movement of the 'sixties'*), *op. cit.*, p. 233.

57. In his *Confession* Kel'siev has given a detailed account of their experiences in the extensive and well-organized smuggling ring of that city. Cf. 'Literaturnoye nasledstvo', 1941, nos. 41–2.

58. B. P. Koz'min, '*N. G. Chernyshevsky v III Otdelenii*' (*Chernyshevsky in the Third Section*), in 'Krasnyy arkhiv', 1928, no. 29.

59. N. V. Shelgunov, '*Vospominaniya*' (*Recollections*), *op. cit.*, p. 158.

60. 'Kolokol', 1st November 1866.

61. *Question polonaise. Protestation d'un russe contre le 'Kolokol'* (*La Cloche*), no place, no date. This short pamphlet, not even paginated, was bound together with another article entitled: '*Protestation des polonais contre la russification dans le "Kolokol"*.' Evidently, Serno had some connection with an unidentified group of Polish émigrés. A Russian translation of Serno's pamphlet, by F. Freydenfel'd, is published in 'Literaturnoye nasledstvo', 1941, nos. 41–2.

62. A. Serno-Solov'evich, '*Nashi domashniya dela. Otvet g. Gertsenu na stat'yu "Poryadok torzhestvuet"*' (*Affairs at home. Reply to Herzen with regard to his article 'Order triumphs'* ['*Kolokol*', no. 233]), Vevey, 1867 (dated 9th March).

63. From his obituary in 'Narodnoye delo', 1869, nos. 7–10.

64. J.-Ph. Becker, *L'Association Internationale des travailleurs et la grève génévoise en mars-avril 1868*, traduit par Fréd. Kohn, Geneva, 1868; and the numbers of the 'Journal de Genève' for those months, which well reveal the apprehension of the ruling classes.

65. A. A. Serno-Solov'evich, '*Pyatnadtsat' neopublikovannykh pisem*' (*Fifteen unpublished letters*), in 'Zven'ya', 1935, no. V.

66. 'A l'Internationale', 25th April 1868.

67. *Ibid.*

68. Continuation of the preceding article, 2nd May 1868.

69. *Ibid.*, 23rd May 1868.

70. 'L'Internationale'. The first number was dated 5th August, the second 12th August 1868. Both were published at Geneva.

71. '*Perepiska K. Marksa i F. Engel'sa s russkimi politicheskimi deyatelyami*' (*Correspondence of K. Marx and F. Engels with Russian political figures*), L., 1947, pp. 22 ff. Cf. MEGA, *Dritte Abteilung*, vol. IV, pp. 132, 134, 138, 141, 147, 231, 233; and Marx and Engels, *Scritti italiani a cura di G. Bosio*,

Milan-Rome, 1955, p. 61, where Marx, on 23rd May 1872, recalls *Affairs at home* by Serno-Solov'evich in order to criticize the "socialist dilettante Herzen".

CHAPTER 11

1. The basic works are by B. Koz'min, '*K istorii "Molodoy Rossii"*' (*For a history of* '*Young Russia*'), in 'Katorga i ssylka', 1930, nos. V, VI; '*Kruzhok Zaichnevskogo i Argiropulo*' (*The Zaichnevsky and Argiropulo group*), ibid., 1930, nos. VII, VIII–IX; '*P. G. Zaichnevsky na katorge, poselenii i ssylke*' (*P. G. Zaichnevsky, hard labour and exile*), ibid., 1931, nos. VIII–IX; and '*P. G. Zaichnevsky v Orle i kruzhok "Orlyat"*' (*P. G. Zaichnevsky at Orel and the* '*Eaglets*' *group*), ibid., 1931, no. X. These studies have been assembled in a shortened and more popular form in a small book, also by B. Koz'min, '*P. G. Zaichnevsky i "Molodaya Rossiya"*' (*P. G. Zaichnevsky and* '*Young Russia*'), M., 1932. At the end of this last study, on pp. 171, 172, there is a virtually complete bibliography.

2. '*Delo Zaichnevskogo*' (*The Zaichnevsky case*), in the historical miscellany '*O minuvshem*' (*The past*), Spb., 1905. In their search made in 1861 the authorities found, among other books, *De la justice dans la révolution et dans l'église*, by Proudhon, *Révélations historiques*, by Louis Blanc, and *L'Humanité*, by Leroux.

3. V. P. Alekseyev, '*P. G. Zaichnevsky*', in 'Krasnyy arkhiv', 1922, no. I.

4. For interesting details of the clandestine organization of Polish students, see I. M. Belyavskaya, '*A. I. Gertsen i pol'skoye natsional'no-osvoboditelnoye dvizhenie 60-kh godov XIX veka*' (*Herzen and the movement for national liberation in Poland in the sixties of the nineteenth century*), M., 1954, pp. 57 ff.

5. Ya. V. Abramov, '*Nashi voskresnyye shkoly*' (*Our Sunday-schools*), Spb., 1900.

6. V. P. Alekseyev, '*P. G. Zaichnevsky*', in 'Krasnyy arkhiv', op. cit.

7. A. Smirnov, '*K biografii P. G. Zaichnevskogo*' (*For a biography of P. G. Zaichnevsky*), in 'Krasnyy arkhiv', 1936, no. III, which publishes the whole of this letter to Argiropulo (1st July).

8. M. Lemke, '*Politicheskiye protsessy v Rossii 1860-kh godov*' (*po arkhivnym dokumentam*) (*Political trials in Russia in the sixties.* [*From documents in the archives*]), second edition, M.-L., 1923, p. 3.

9. For the life of this young Greek, who died so soon and who left a deep impression on all who had known him, see V. Lind, '*Vospominaniya o moey zhizni*' (*Recollections of my life*), in 'Russkaya mysl'', 1911, no. VIII.

10. M. Lemke, '*Politicheskiye protsessy v Rossii 1860-kh gg.*' (*Political trials in Russia in the sixties*), op. cit., p. 521.

11. About him, see '*Poet-revolyutsioner I. I. Gol'ts-Miller*'. Sostavili B. Koz'min i G. Lelevich (*The poet-revolutionary I. I. Gol'ts-Miller.* Compiled by B. Koz'min and G. Lelevich), M., 1930; the article by N. Gavrilov, '*Zabytyy revolyutsionnyy poet*' (*A forgotten revolutionary poet*), in 'Katorga i ssylka', 1929, no. XII; and I. Yampol'sky, '*Neizdannyye stikhotvoreniya I. I. Gol'ts-Millera*' (*Unpublished poems by I. I. Gol'ts-Miller*), in 'Literaturnoye nasledstvo', 1936, nos. 25–6.

12. F. Raskol'nikov, '*Iz istorii russkoy revolyutsionnoy mysli 60-kh godov*' (*From the history of Russian revolutionary thought in the sixties*), in 'Molodaya gvardiya', 1924, no. IV.

13. A. I. Gertsen, '*Polnoye sobranie sochineniy i pisem*' (*Collected works and letters*), op. cit., XIV, pp. 495 ff.

14. M. Lemke, '*Politicheskiye protsessy v Rossii 1860-kh gg.*' (*Political trials in Russia in the sixties*), op. cit., p. 527.

15. '*N. G. Chernyshevsky. Sbornik*' (*N. G. Chernyshevsky. Miscellany*), M., 1928, p. 116.

16. B. Koz'min, '*P. G. Zaichnevsky*', *op. cit.*, p. 125, puts forward some good arguments against M. Lemke's opinion, for attributing this to the group which was centred around N. I. Utin.

17. B. Koz'min, '*K istorii "Molodoy Rossii"* ' (*For a history of* ' *Young Russia*'), in 'Katorga i ssylka', 1936, no. VI.

18. B. Koz'min, *op. cit.*

19. L. F. Panteleyev, '*Iz vospominaniy proshlogo*'. Redaktsiya i kommentarii S. A. Reyzera. Vstupitel'naya stat'ya V. I. Nevskogo (*From recollections of the past. Edited and with notes by S. A. Reyzer. Introductory article by V. I. Nevsky*), M.-L., 1934, p. 242.

20. This has never been published in its entirety, but B. Koz'min has summarized it at length in '*P. N. Tkachev i revolyutsionnoye dvizhenie 1860-kh godov*' (*P. N. Tkachev and the revolutionary movement of the sixties*), M., 1922, p. 35.

21. S. Reyzer, '*Peterburgskiye pozhary 1862 goda*' (*The fires in St Petersburg in 1862*), in '*Katorga i ssylka*', 1932, no. X.

22. On this period of Zaichnevsky's life, see the curious memoirs of V. Bystrenin, '*Ukhodyashchiye*' (*Those who have vanished*), chap. X, '*Prosvetiteli*' (*The enlighteners*), in 'Golos minuvshego', 1922, no. II.

23. She wrote what was probably the fullest and most interesting article on Zaichnevsky, at the time of his death, in '*Materialy dlya istorii russkogo sotsial'no-revolyutsionnogo dvizheniya*' (*Material for the history of the Russian social-revolutionary movement*), Geneva, 1896, no. X, notes 6–7. She said of him that 'he was, as one said at that time, a "centralist". All revolutionary activity must be perfectly planned beforehand by a "centre", made up of people who are dedicated body and soul to the revolution, and superior to the average in quality'.

24. N. S. Rusanov, '*Na rodine*' (*In my native land*), M., 1931, p. 98. 'On looking back at my conversations with Zaichnevsky, I tend to think that he believed even less than Tkachev—of whom he spoke with great understanding—in the possibility of the *obshchina* becoming the point of departure for socialist development.' According to these memoirs, Zaichnevsky was against the distribution of the gentry's lands to the peasants—at least at the end of his life: 'It will take some years of revolutionary government to teach our peasants how they should farm the land and generally how to develop the productive forces of agriculture. Otherwise nothing will succeed.' These words are quoted by B. Koz'min in '*P. G. Zaichnevsky v Orle i kruzhok "Orlyat"* ' (*P. G. Zaichnevsky at Orel and the* '*Eaglets*' *group*), *op. cit.* He makes this comment: 'In the seventies and eighties Zaichnevsky fundamentally maintained the same point of view that he had held as a young man, when he wrote *Young Russia*.' This is true, but above all it is interesting to note how his Jacobinism had, with the passage of time, gradually worn down and almost completely destroyed the Populist core of his youthful manifesto. Only Jacobin dictatorship remained.

25. See '*Vospominaniya o Zaichnevskom*' (*Recollections of Zaichnevsky*), in 'Proletarskaya revolyutsiya', 1923, nos. VI–VII.

CHAPTER 12

1. The two best studies are: A. Ershov, '*Kazanskiy zagovor 1863 g.*' (*The Kazan conspiracy of 1863*), in 'Golos minuvshego', 1913, nos. VI, VII; and B. Koz'min, '*Kazanskiy zagovor 1863 goda*' (*The Kazan conspiracy of 1863*), M., 1929, which has a comprehensive bibliography.

2. See Andrushenko's depositions (1865) which were originally published in the 'Kolokol', nos. 208, 210, of 1865, and nos. 211, 215, of 1866, and reprinted later in B. Bazilevsky, '*Materialy dlya istorii revolyutsionnogo dvizheniya v Rossii v 60-kh godakh*' (*Material for a history of the revolutionary movement in Russia in the sixties*), Paris, 1905, p. 109 ff.

3. N. Firsov, '*Studencheskiye istorii v kazanskom universitete, 1855–1863 godov*' (*Student disorders in the University of Kazan in the years 1855–1863*), in 'Russkaya starina', 1889, nos. 61–4.

4. Krasnoperov's memoirs have been published in 'Mir Bozhiy', 1896, nos. IX, X; in 'Vestnik Evropy', 1905, no. XII; and also in 'Minuvshiye gody', 1908, no. XII. They were partially reprinted with a preface by B. Koz'min, under the title '*Zapiski raznochintsa*' (*Memoirs of a* déclassé), M.-L., 1929. Unless it is stated to the contrary, all references are to this last publication.

5. A. I. Gertsen, '*Polnoye sobranie sochineniy i pisem*', pod red. M. Lemke (*Complete works and letters*, edited by M. Lemke), XVI, 201. It is probable that these students came across the ideas of Weishaupt and the 'Illuminati' in Barruel's book on the Jacobins. It had been translated into Russian in 1805, and had already interested some of Petrashevsky's followers as a hand-book for conspirators.

6. 'Istoricheskaya biblioteka', 1869, no. I ff. This essay, based on Sismondi and Quinet, was very critical of Capponi; it quoted Veselovsky's studies on the *Villa Alberti*, and *Teste e figure, studi biografici*, by Alberto Mario. He rapidly sketched in the social struggles of the Florentine republic, and came to the conclusion that there was an inherent despotism in the municipal character of Florence itself and in the straitened circumstances of a number of its citizens. He ended by discussing the national unity that Italy had now achieved, but added that the welfare of the Italian people was still only a 'pious wish'.

7. B. P. Koz'min, '*Revolyutsionnoye podpol'ye v epokhu "belogo terrora"*' (*The revolutionary underground at the time of the 'white terror'*), M., 1929, pp. 11 ff.

8. Evidently the same idea was in circulation among the Polish revolutionaries. In March 1863 they distributed another apocryphal manifesto: 'The golden charter, addressed to the peasants in the name of the Father, the Son and the Holy Ghost,' quoted in '*Russkaya podpol'naya zarubezhnaya pechat'*'. Bibliograficheskiy ukazatel', sostavlen M. M. Klevenskim i dr. (*The clandestine press of the Russian émigrés*. Bibliographical guide edited by M. M. Klevensky and others), M., 1935, no. I, p. 116.

9. '*Delo ryadovogo Benzengera*' (*The case of the soldier Benzenger*), in 'Byloye', 1906, no. VII; and A. I. Gertsen, '*Polnoye sobranie sochineniy i pisem*' (*Complete works and letters*), op. cit., vol. XVII, pp. 109 ff.

10. I. M. Belyavskaya, *op. cit.*, p. 61.

11. A. I. Gertsen, *op. cit.*, vol. XVII, p. 94.

12. P. I. Zhudra, '*Kazanskiye pozhary 1863 g.*' (*The fires at Kazan in 1863*), in 'Istoricheskiy vestnik', 1891, no. III.

13. For the atmosphere of those days, see I. D. Shestakov, '*Tyazhyolyye dni kazanskogo universiteta*' (*Difficult days in the University of Kazan*), in 'Russkaya starina', 1896, no. XII.

14. This was probably true, as he was the son of a Polish émigré. The French ambassador at St Petersburg tried to do something for him. But Alexander II wrote on a report: 'I am absolutely against allowing such intervention.'

CHAPTER 13

1. '*Sudebnaya reforma*', pod redaktsiey N. V. Davydova i N. N. Polyanskogo (*The judicial reform*, edited by N. V. Davydov and N. N. Polyansky), M., 1915, 2 vols.
2. M. Lemke, '*Epokha tsenzurnykh reform, 1859–1865 godov*' (*The period of the reforms in the censorship, 1859–1865*), St Petersburg, 1904.
3. A. A. Kornilov, '*Obshchestvennoye dvizhenie pri Alexandre II (1855–1881). Istoricheskiye ocherki*' (*The movement of Russian society in the time of Alexander II [1855–1881]. Historical essays*), M., 1909, pp. 106, 172–3.
4. Their political and scientific activity was extensive, and there are innumerable books and articles about them. For the early stages, see B. Glinsky, '*N. M. Yadrintsev*', M., 1895; M. Lemke, '*N. M. Yadrintsev*', St Petersburg, 1904 (the most comprehensive essay with a vast bibliography); I. I. Popov and N. M. Mendel'son, '*Iz vospominaniy o G. N. Potanine* (*From recollections of G. N. Potanin*), in 'Golos minuvshego', 1922, no. I.
5. See Yadrintsev's words recorded by M. Lemke in '*N. M. Yadrintsev*', *op. cit.*, p. 48.
6. V. Semevsky, '*Neskol'ko slov v pamyat' Yadrintseva*' (*Some words in memory of N. M. Yadrintsev*), in 'Russkaya mysl'', 1895, no. I.
7. V. Semevsky, '*N. I. Kostomarov*', in 'Russkaya starina', 1886, no. I.
8. Besides this federalist tradition there was also probably in this some recollection of Bakunin's ideas. For Potanin, see '*Pis'ma M. A. Bakunina k A. I. Gertsenu i N. P. Ogaryovu*' (*Letters from M. A. Bakunin to A. I. Herzen and N. P. Ogarev*), St Petersburg, 1907, p. 268.
9. M. Lemke, '*N. M. Yadrintsev*', *op. cit.*, p. 69.
10. His manuscript autobiography, in M. Lemke, *op. cit.*, p. 56.
11. Serafim Serafimovich, who came from an ecclesiastical family, studied in the University of Kazan, from which he was expelled for having taken part in the *requiem* in honour of the peasants of Bezdna. He went to St Petersburg where he took an active part in the Siberian group. In autumn 1863 he opened a school at Krasnoyarsk, but the authorities closed it. In 1864–5 his public lectures were one of the most typical and important manifestations of 'Siberian patriotism'.
12. '*Russkaya obshchina v tyurme i ssylke*', Spg., 1872.
13. His autobiography, quoted by M. Lemke, '*N. M. Yadrintsev*', *op. cit.*, pp. 96–7.
14. S. Breytburg, '*K istorii gazety "Ocherki"*' (*For a history of the weekly 'Essays'*), in '*Russkaya zhurnalistika. Shestidesyatyye gody*'. Pod redaktsiey i s predisloviem V. Polyanskogo (*The Russian press in the sixties*. Edited with a preface by V. Polyansky), M.-L., 1930, pp. 53 ff.
15. V. Evgen'ev-Maksimov and G. Tizengauzen, '*Posledniye gody "Sovremennika" 1863–1866*' (*The last years of the 'Sovremennik', 1863–1866*), L., 1939.
16. L. M. Kleynbort, '*Grigoriy Zakharovich Eliseyev*', P., 1923.
17. '*Shestidesyatyye gody*'. M. A. Antonovich, '*Vospominaniya*'. G. Z. Eliseyev, '*Vospominaniya*'. Vstupitel'nyye stat'i, kommentarii i redaktsiya V. Evgen'eva-Maksimova i G. F. Tizengauzena (*The sixties*. M. A. Antonovich. *Recollections*. G. Z. Eliseyev. *Recollections*. Introductory articles and comments by V. Evgen'ev-Maksimov and G. F. Tizengauzen), M.-L., 1933.
18. *Ibid.*, p. 290.
19. *Ibid.*, p. 298.
20. See Kyra Sanine, *Saltykov-Chtchédrine. Sa vie et ses œuvres*, Paris, 1955; and *Les 'Annales de la patrie' et la diffusion de la pensée française en Russie (1868–1884)*, Paris, 1955.

21. 1864, nos. IV and VI.

22. 1865, no. II.

23. 1864, nos. VIII, IX.

24. 1865, no. VIII.

25. 1865, nos. I, II, XI–XII.

26. 1865, no. VIII.

27. 1865, no. IX.

28. Report quoted in V. Evgen'ev-Maksimov and G. Tizengauzen, '*Posledniye gody "Sovremennika"*' (*The last years of the 'Sovremennik'*), *op. cit.*, p. 87.

29. *Ibid.*, p. 150. Zhukovsky's article is in the *Sovremennik*, 1866, nos. II, III.

30. '*Narodnaya letopis'*' (*Annals of the people*), no. 8; quoted in B. Koz'min, '*Gazeta "Narodnaya letopis'"*' '(*The review 'Annals of the people'*), in '*Russkaya zhurnalistika. Shestidesyatyye gody*' (*The Russian press in the sixties*), *op. cit.*, p. 96.

31. '*Zapiski sovremennika*' (*Notes of a contemporary*), in the *Sovremennik*, 1865, no. IX.

32. '*Nasha obshchestvennaya zhizn'*' (*Our social life*), in the *Sovremennik*, 1864, no. III.

33. '*Sonmishche nigilistov. Stsena iz literaturnogo balagana*' (*The meeting of the nihilists—a scene of the literary fair*), in 'Vestnik Evropy', 1829, no. I.

34. Review of S. Tolstaya's works in '*Otechestvennyye zapiski*', 1840, no. XII.

35. Benoît-P. Hepner, '*Bakounin et le panslavisme révolutionnaire*', Paris, 1950, 192 ff.

36. '*Nasha obshchestvennaya zhizn'*' (*Our social life*), in the *Sovremennik*, 1864, no. III.

37. '*Asmodey nashego vremeni*' (*The Asmodeus of our time*), in the *Sovremennik*, 1862, no. III. Cf. G. Z. Eliseyev's comment on this review in '*Vospominaniya*' (*Recollections*), *op. cit.*, pp. 272 ff.

38. A. Coquart, *Dmitri Pisarev (1840–1868) et l'idéologie du nihilisme russe*, Paris, 1946, with an exhaustive bibliography.

39. The most important of these pamphlets are collected in V. A. Zaytsev, '*Izbrannyye sochineniya*' v dvukh tomakh. Tom I (1863–1865). Pod redaktsiey i s predisloviem B. P. Koz'mina. Vstupitel'naya stat'ya G. O. Berlinera (*Collected works*, in 2 volumes. Vol. I (1863–1865). Edited and with a preface by B. P. Koz'min. Introductory article by G. O. Berliner), M., 1934. (The second volume has never been published.)

40. See his wife's recollections, '*V. A. Zaytsev za granitsey*' (*V. A. Zaytsev abroad*), in 'Minuvshiye gody', 1908, no. XI, and particularly his obituary published in 'Obshcheye delo', no. 47, May 1882.

41. A. Efimov, '*Publitsist 60-kh godov: N. V. Sokolov*' (*A publicist of the sixties: N. V. Sokolov*), in 'Katorga i ssylka', 1931, nos. XI–XII.

42. N. V. Sokoloff, '*Die Abtrünnigen, Les réfractaires, Otshchepentsy*' (*The Refractory Ones*), no place of publication given, 1872, second edition (after the one suppressed by the censor).

43. *Ibid.*, p. 2.

44. *Ibid.*, p. 208.

45. '*Belinsky i Dobrolyubov*', in 'Russkoye slovo', 1864, no. I; reprinted in '*Izbrannyye sochineniya*' (*Selected works*), *op. cit.*, pp. 159 ff.

46. A review of the Russian translation, published in 1863, of '*Storia d'Italia dal 1846 al 1850*', by Diego Soria, in 'Russkoye slovo', 1863, no. VII; reprinted in '*Izbrannyye sochineniya*' (*Selected works*), *op. cit.*, pp. 90 ff.

47. See principally B. Koz'min's interesting article, '*Raskol v nigilistakh. Epizod iz istorii russkoy obshchestvennoy mysli 60-kh godov*' (*Schism among the*

nihilists. An episode in the history of Russian social thought in the sixties), in '*Ot devyatnadtsatogo fevralya k pervomu marta*' (*From 19th February 1861 to 1st March 1881*), M., 1933, pp. 39 ff.; in it he makes a close study of the controversy between the '*Sovremennik*' and the '*Russkoye slovo*' between 1863 and 1865. Dostoevsky called this controversy a 'schism among the nihilists'. Koz'min justly remarks on the pre-Blanquist element in the position taken up by '*Russkoye slovo*'; he has a tendency to attribute this principally to Pisarev, whereas I consider that it is more conscious and pronounced in his collaborators, above all, Zaytsev. Pisarev's article, '*Pchyoly*' (*The bees*), on which Koz'min bases his argument, is largely a plagiarism from Karl Vogt, as A. Coquart has shown in his article, '*Pisarev et Karl Vogt*', in Revue des études slaves, 1945, no. XXII.

CHAPTER 14

1. The writer of the first pamphlet on this episode was N. A. Vorms, but it was published anonymously. The author was well informed but did not wish to go into details which might be dangerous for those who were in prison or who had not yet emigrated from Russia. For this reason it does not add much to the archive sources which have been published later: '*Belyy terror ili vystrel 4 aprelya 1865 goda. Rasskaz odnogo iz soslannykh pod nadzor politsii*' (*The white terror or the pistol shot of 4th April 1865 (sic). Told by one of the exiles under the supervision of the police*), Leipzig, undated (but 1867). The two basic volumes are those by M. M. Klevensky and K. G. Kotel'nikov, '*Pokushenie Karakozova*' (*The attempted assassination by Karakozov*), in the series '*Politicheskiye protsessy 60–80 gg.*', pod red. V. V. Maksakova i V. I. Nevskogo (*Political trials from the sixties to the eighties*, edited by V. V. Maksakov and V. I. Nevsky), vol. I, M., 1928; vol. II, M.-L., 1930, in which the trial in the summer of 1866 is published. In no. XVII of 'Krasnyy arkhiv', 1926, M. M. Klevensky published the material of the Commission of Inquiry. He also wrote another short but interesting study: '*Ishutinskiy kruzhok i pokushenie Karakozova*' (*The Ishutin group and the attempted assassination by Karakozov*), second edition, M., 1928. See also A. Shilov, '*D. V. Karakozov i pokushenie 4 aprelya 1866 goda*' (*D. V. Karakozov and the attempted assassination of 4th April 1866*), P., 1920.

2. The two most interesting accounts of this first conflict between the Populists and the nihilists are by P. F. Nikolaev, published by V. E. Cheshikhin-Vetrinsky, '*N. G. Chernyshevsky*', P., 1923, p. 175, and by V. Cherkezov, published by E. E. Kolosov, in '*Molodoye narodnichestvo 60-kh godov*' (*Young Populism in the sixties*), in 'Sibirskiye zapiski', 1917, no. III. B. P. Koz'min discusses this in '*Ot devyatnadtsatogo fevralya k pervomu marta*' (*From 19th February 1861 to 1st March 1881*), M., 1933, pp. 78 ff.

3. I. A. Khudyakov, '*Opyt avtobiografii*' (*Autobiographical essay*), Geneva, 1882, p. 45.

4. For members of the working class in touch with the early Populist groups, see '*Rabocheye dvizhenie v Rossii v XIX veke*'. Pod red. A. M. Pankratovoy (*The workers' movement in Russia in the nineteenth century*. Edited by A. M. Pankratova), vol. II, part I, 1861–74, M., 1950, pp. 221 ff.

5. M. Klevensky, '*Iz vospominaniy Z. K. Ralli*' (*From the recollections of Z. K. Ralli*), in '*Revolyutsionnoye dvizhenie 60-kh godov*'. Sbornik statey pod red. B. Goreva i B. P. Koz'mina (*The revolutionary movement in the sixties*. Collection of articles edited by B. Gorev and B. P. Koz'min), M., 1932.

6. Quoted by M. Klevensky in the preface to '*Pokushenie Karakozova*' (*The attempted assassination by Karakozov*), *op. cit.*, vol. I, p. x.

7. See the detailed and interesting article by M. Klevensky, ' "*Evropeyskiy revolyutsionnyy komitet*" *v dele Karakozova*' ('*The European revolutionary committee*' *in the Karakozov affair*), in '*Revolyutsionnoye dvizhenie 60-kh godov*' (*The revolutionary movement of the sixties*), *op. cit.*, pp. 147 ff.

8. Quoted from an article about I. A. Khudyakov in 'Vperyod', no. 15, of 15th December 1876.

9. I. A. Khudyakov, '*Opyt avtobiografii*' (*Autobiographical essay*), *op. cit.*, reprinted in 'Istoricheskiy vestnik', 1906, nos. X–XII, with the title, '*Iz vospominaniy shestidesyatnika*' (*From the memoirs of a man of the sixties*), and later, in book form, with the title, '*Zapiski Karakozovtsa*' (*Recollections of a Karakozovist*), M., 1930. There is a French translation: I.-A. Khoudiakoff, *Mémoires d'un révolutionnaire. Mœurs russes*, Paris, 1889. The translator says, very rightly, that it is 'one of the most precious documents for the study of nihilism'. M. M. Klevensky, '*I. A. Khudyakov, revolyutsioner i uchyonyy*' (*I. A. Khudyakov, revolutionary and scholar*), M., 1929. An article by E. E. Kolosov is interesting for what it says of him: '*Molodoye narodnichestvo 60-kh godov*' (*Young populism in the sixties*), in 'Sibirskiye zapiski', 1917, no. II. He describes Khudyakov as the first 'man to spread Populist ideas in the sixties'.

10. I. A. Khudyakov, '*Opyt avtobiografii*' (*Autobiographical essay*), *op. cit.*, p. 24.

11. His publisher, E. P. Pechatkin, who was first arrested in 1861 in the student agitations at St Petersburg, was again thrown into prison a year later for the affair of Ballod's 'pocket press'. In 1866 a third arrest brought the cooperative press which he had organized to an end.

12. For the scientific aspect of these researches, see E. Bobrov, '*Nauchno-litera-turnaya deyatel'nost' I. A. Khudyakova*' (*The scientific-literary activity of I. A. Khudyakov*), in 'Zhurnal ministerstva narodnogo prosveshcheniya', 1908, no. VIII.

13. I. A. Khudyakov, '*Osnovnoy element narodnykh skazok*' (*The fundamental element of folk-stories*), in 'Biblioteka dlya chteniya', 1863, no. XII.

14. '*Russkaya knizhka*' (*Russian booklet*), Spb., 1863.

15. The programme of the review, taken from the censor's archives, has been published by M. M. Klevensky, '*I. A. Khudyakov*', *op. cit.*, p. 28. It was to have included: (1) Studies of popular mythology and poetry; (2) Mediaeval Russian texts, legends, etc.; (3) folk-poetry of other nations; (4) a bibliographical section.

16. I. A. Khudyakov, '*Opyt avtobiografii*' (*Autobiographical essay*), *op. cit.*, pp. 78–9.

17. '*Samouchitel' dlya nachinayushchikh obuchat'sya gramote*' (*The self-teacher for those learning to read and write*), Spb., 1865.

18. A. I. Gertsen, '*Polnoye sobranie sochineniy i pisem*' (*Collected works and letters*), vol. XVIII, p. 337.

19. 'Zhurnal ministerstva narodnogo prosveshcheniya', 1864, no. III.

20. F. Volkhovsky, '*Druz'ya sredi vragov*' (*Friends among enemies*), Spb., 1906, p. 4.

21. P. L. Lavrov, '*Narodniki-propagandisty*' (*Populist-propagandists*), L., 1926, p. 37.

22. '*Vospominaniya*' (*Memoirs*), M., 1928, p. 52.

23. '*Sobranie sochineniy*' (*Complete works*), M., 1919, vol. IV, p. 207.

24. '*Vospominaniya chaykovtsa*' (*Memoirs of a follower of Chaykovsky*), in 'Byloye', 1906, no. XI, pp. 113–14.

25 +

25. 'German Aleksandrovich Lopatin. Sbornik', pod red. A. Shilova (German Aleksandrovich Lopatin. Miscellany, edited by A. Shilov), P., 1922.

26. L. F. Panteleyev, 'Iz vospominaniy proshlogo'. Redaktsiya i kommentarii S. A. Reyzera. Vstupitel'naya stat'ya V. I. Nevskogo (From recollections of the past. Edited and with comments by S. A. Reyzer. Introductory article by V. I. Nevsky), M.-L., 1933, p. 299.

27. Here is an example of a dictation lesson, found among the police files and published by M. M. Klevensky, op. cit., p. 72: 'Where is it best to live? In the United States. Where are the honest people? In Siberia. When will it be best to live? When there is no Tsar. Who are the most vile and stupid people in the world? The generals.'

28. 'Pokushenie Karakozova' (The attempted assassination by Karakozov), op. cit., vol. I, p. 53.

29. Ibid., p. 303.

30. 'Krasnyy arkhiv', 1926, no. IV.

31. M. M. Klevensky, 'I. A. Khudyakov', op. cit., p. 68.

32. M. M. Klevensky, 'Iz vospominaniy Z. K. Ralli' (From the memoirs of Z. K. Ralli', in 'Revolyutsionnoye dvizhenie 1860-kh godov' (The revolutionary movement of the sixties), op. cit., p. 139.

33. On his activity at Saratov, see the article by V. Sushitsky, 'Iz istorii revolyutsionnoy deyatel'nosti A. Kh. Khristoforova v Saratove' (For a history of A. Kh. Khristoforov's revolutionary activity at Saratov), in 'Katorga i ssylka', 1924, no. IV; also N. Volkov (I. Maykov), 'Iz zhizni saratovskikh kruzhkov' (On the life of the Saratov groups, Spb., 1906; and K. Vinogradov, 'Odna iz pervykh stranits rasprostraneniya kommunisticheskikh idey sredi saratovskogo proletariata' (One of the first pages in the spreading of Communist ideas among the working classes at Saratov), in 'Izvestiya I.K.S.D. Ryaz.-Ur. zh-d.', (News-sheet of the Executive Committee of the Soviet of Deputies from the Ryazan—Ural Railway), 1918, no. 18; and A. Khristoforov, '"Obshcheye delo". Istoriya i kharakteriistika izdaniya' ('The common cause'. History and nature of this periodical), in 'Osvobozhdenie' (Liberation), no place of publication, 1903, no. I, pp. 24 ff.

34. G. V. Plekhanov, 'Russkiy rabochiy v revolyutsionnom dvizhenii' (The Russian working-man in the revolutionary movement), in 'Sochineniya', pod red. D. Ryazanova (Works, edited by D. Ryazanov), M., undated, vol. III, p. 194, note.

35. M. M. Klevensky, 'Materialy ob I. A. Khudyakove' (Material on I. A. Khudyakov), in 'Katorga i ssylka', 1928, nos. VIII–IX.

36. M. M. Klevensky, 'Pobeg Yaroslava Dombrovskogo' (The flight of Dombrowski), in 'Krasnyy arkhiv', 1927, no. III; and A. Chernov, 'K istorii pobega Yaroslava Dombrovskogo' (For a history of the flight of J. Dombrowski), in 'Katorga i ssylka', 1931, no. I.

37. Ralli recalls this in his memoirs, published in the collection entitled 'Revolyutsionnoye dvizhenie 1860-kh godov' (The revolutionary movement of the sixties), op. cit.

38. I. D. Shestakov, 'Tyazhyolyye dni kazanskogo universiteta' (Difficult days in the University of Kazan), in 'Russkaya starina', 1898, no. XII.

39. It has been published by A. Shilov in 'Iz istorii revolyutsionnogo dvizheniya 1860-kh godov. Proklamatsiya "druz'yam rabochim!" D. V. Karakozova' (On the history of the revolutionary movement of the sixties. The proclamation, 'To my worker friends!', by D. V. Karakozov), in 'Golos minuvshego', 1918, nos. X–XII.

40. Shilov has tried to see an original element in the insistence with which he kept on returning to the *artel* in this manifesto, and he believed that it dated back to the spread of Owen's ideas in the Moscow group. Certainly this working-class interest is a very marked characteristic, but similar ideas had already been expressed by *Young Russia*. The similarity of all the social ideas of this manifesto to those of *Young Russia* has rightly been emphasized by V. Cherkezov, quoted in the article by E. Kolosov which has already been mentioned.

41. '*German Aleksandrovich Lopatin*'. Sbornik (*G. A. Lopatin. A miscellany*), op. cit., p. 139.

42. This wave of repression had a profound effect on the young generation. It rooted in them the idea of a duel to the death between the State and the revolutionaries. See the interesting pamphlet by Nikifor G. (N. Ya. Niko-ladze's pseudonym), '*Pravitel'stvo i molodoye pokolenie*' (*The government and the young generation*), Geneva, 1866. For the reaction of a typical liberal like Kavelin, see P. A. Zayonchkovsky, '*Zapiska K. D. Kavelina o nigilizme*', in 'Istoricheskiy arkhiv', M.-L., 1950, vol. V, p. 323.

43. M. Klevensky, '*Iz vospominaniy Z. K. Ralli*' (*From the memoirs of Z. K. Ralli*), op. cit., p. 143.

44. Letter, 10th November 1866, by M. I. Semevsky (a well-known historian of the period), published by B. Koz'min, '*Sovremenniki o karakozovskom protsesse*' (*Contemporaries on the Karakozov trial*), op. cit.

45. *Ibid*.

46. E. Breshkovskaya, '*Iz moikh vospominaniy*' (*From my recollections*), Spb., 1906, pp. 4 ff., tells how she met Ishutin in prison, completely eaten up with disease. He was 'thin and pale', and criticized the simple peasant dress worn by Breshkovskaya, talking to her at great length about theatres, and other amusements in Moscow. 'It was painful and terrible to hear such talk coming from his mouth . . .'

47. See V. Kubalov, '*Karakozovets I. A. Khudyakov v ssylke*' (*The follower of Karakozov, I. A. Chudyakov, in exile*), in 'Katorga i ssylka', 1926, nos. VII–VIII. Verkhoyansk had a total population of 164 Yakuts; and one policeman, one priest, and one nurse making up the Russian population.

48. E. Breshkovskaya, op. cit., and V. Nikoforov, '*Karakozovtsy v ssylke i ikh vliyanie na yakutov*' (*The followers of Karakozov in exile and their influence on the Yakuts*), in 'Katorga i ssylka', 1924, no. III.

49. On all this period, see B. P. Koz'min, '*Revolyutsionnoye podpol'ye v epokhu "belogo terrora"*' (*The revolutionary underground at the time of the 'white terror'*), M., 1929; it contains and comments upon many documents previously unknown.

50. Max Nettlau mentions this in his obituary of Cherkezov, published in the anarchist periodical, Plus loin, 1925, nos. VII–IX. B. P. Koz'min, op. cit., p. 118, quotes documents from the archives which prove this (i.e. Cherkezov's own deposition in 1870).

51. Arrested for the Nechaev affair, he spent the first part of his exile in Penza, and afterwards at Saratov. 'He was to be the creator of the group of *Narodnaya Volya* at Saratov.' (I. I. Maykov, '*Saratovskiy semidesyatnik*' (*A man of the seventies from Saratov*), in 'Minuvshiye gody', 1908, no. IV). Arrested in 1882, he was to die mad in his cell after a long imprisonment.

52. See B. Nikolaevsky, '*V. I. Cherkezov*', in 'Katorga i ssylka', 1926, no. IV.

53. '*Iz davnikh let*' (*From years long past*), in 'Byloye', 1907, no. IX.

CHAPTER 15

1. '*German Aleksandrovich Lopatin (1845–1918)*', P., 1922, in which A. A. Shilov has collected Lopatin's letters, writings and documents. There is a comprehensive bibliography, p. 9.
2. *Ibid.*
3. *Ibid.*, p. 135.
4. *Ibid.*, p. 137.
5. *Ibid.*, p. 9.
6. A. Uspenskaya, '*Vospominaniya shestidesyatnitsy*' (*Memoirs of a woman of the sixties*), in 'Byloye', 1922, no. 18.
7. The most detailed study of this subject is by B. P. Koz'min, '*N. G. Nechaev i ego protivniki v 1868–69 gg.*' (*N. G. Nechaev and his adversaries in the years 1868–69*), in '*Revolyutsionnoye dvizhenie 1860-kh godov*'. Sbornik statey pod red. B. I. Goreva i B. P. Koz'mina (*The revolutionary movement of the sixties. A collection of articles, edited by B. I. Gorev and B. P. Koz'min*), M., 1932, pp. 188 ff. See also A. L. Reuel', '*Russkaya ekonomicheskaya mysl' 60-70-kh gg. i marksizm*' (*Russian economic thought in the 1860s and 1870s and Marxism*), M., 1956.
8. S. G. Svatikov, '*Studencheskoye dvizhenie 1869 goda (Bakunin i Nechaev)*' (*The student movement of 1869 [Bakunin and Nechaev]*), in 'Istoricheskiy sbornik. Nasha strana' (*Historical miscellany. Our country*), Spb., 1907.
9. One of the organizers of the agitation at this institution, M. P. Sazhin, was destined to become Bakunin's right-hand man in exile. He adopted the pseudonym of Armand Ross. He was the son of a small business man in the region of Kostroma, and had been brought up in St Petersburg on the works of Chernyshevsky, at the time of the most flourishing intellectual period in the 'sixties. In 1865, at the age of twenty, he was prosecuted for having lithographed Büchner's *Force and Matter*, in a Russian translation. He was expelled from the Technological Institute and banished to the department of Vologda for his active participation in the student demonstrations. M. P. Sazhin, '*Vospominaniya 1860–1880-kh gg.*'. S predisloviem V. Polonskogo (*Recollections. 1860–1880*. With a preface by V. Polonsky), M., 1925, pp. 14–19 ff. See M. Sazhin's obituary by V. Nevsky, in 'Katorga i ssylka', 1934, no. II.
10. S. L. Chudnovsky, '*Iz davnikh let*' (*From years gone by*), in 'Byloye', 1907, no. IX.
11. Z. K. Ralli, '*S. G. Nechaev*', in 'Byloye', 1906, no. VII.
12. V. Zasulich, '*Nechaevskoye delo*' (*The Nechaev affair*), in 'Osvobozhdenie truda', no. II, 1924, p. 69.
13. See her own words taken down when she was very old, and published in 1922 in 'Katorga i ssylka', 1925, no. I.
14. N. F. Bel'chikov, '*S. G. Nechaev v sele Ivanove v 60-e gody*' (*S. G. Nechaev in the centre of Ivanovo in the sixties*), in 'Katorga i ssylka', 1925, no. I, which quotes several letters of the period. On the Ivanovo artisans, see B. V. Zlatouskovsky, '*Bibliograficheskiy ukazatel' materialov dlya izucheniya istorii rabochego i professional'nogo dvizheniya v Ivanovo-Voznesenskom rayone (1813–1921)*' (*Bibliographical guide to the study of the labour and union movement in the area of Ivanovo-Voznesensk [1813–1921]*), Ivanovo-Voznesensk, 1927, and P. M. Ekzemplyarsky, *Istoriya goroda Ivanova* (*A history of the town of Ivanovo*), vol. I, Ivanovo, 1958.
15. A. V. Smirnov, '*F. D. Nefedov*', in 'Trudy Vladimirskoy uchyonoy arkhivnoy komissii' (*Proceedings of the scientific and archive commission of Vladimir*), 1917–18, no. XVIII.

16. 'Narodnaya rasprava', 1869, no. I.
17. N. Kolyupanov, ' *Devyatnadtsatoye fevralya 1870 goda*' (*19th February 1870*), in 'Vestnik Evropy', 1869, no. X; quoted from B. P. Koz'min, '*S. G. Nechaev i ego protivniki v 1868–1869 gg.*' (*Nechaev and his adversaries in the years 1868–1869*), *op. cit.*, p. 174.
18. An unpublished letter from Ogarev to Herzen proves that this was written on 1st April 1869, and is quoted in '*Russkaya podpol'naya i zarubezhnaya pechat'*'. Bibliograficheskiy ukazatel'. Tom I: '*Donarodovol'cheskiy period 1831–1879*'. Vypusk I. Sostavlen M. M. Klevenskim i dr. (*The Russian press: clandestine and published abroad*. Bibliographical list. Vol. I: *the period before* '*Narodnaya Volya*', *1831–1879*, no. I, compiled by M. M. Klevensky and others), M., 1935, note 98, p. 170.
19. Given in S. Svatikov, *op. cit.*, p. 228.
20. The first, 'Oh Russian students, the police is beating you . . .', has been reprinted by S. Svatikov, *op. cit.*, p. 223; the second, 'Appeal to the Russian students', has never been reprinted. See A. I. Gertsen, '*Polnoye sobranie sochineniy i pisem*', pod red. M. Lemke (*Collected works and letters*, edited by M. Lemke), vol. XXI, p. 374.
21. 'A few words to our young brothers in Russia', printed at Geneva on 1st April 1869, reprinted in *Volksstaat* on 5th May, and later in *La Liberté*, which was published at Brussels, and in *La Réforme* of Vermorel.
22. Given in S. Svatikov, *op. cit.*, p. 225, and in an article by Yu. G. Oksman, '*Sud'ba odnoy parodii Dostoyevskogo*' (*The fate of a parody by Dostoevsky*), in 'Krasnyy arkhiv', 1923, no. III.
23. Quoted from A. Gambarov, '*V sporakh o Nechaeve. K voprosu ob istoricheskoy reabilitatsii Nechaeva*' (*Discussions on Nechaev. On the problem of the historical rehabilitation of Nechaev*), M.-L., 1926, p. 85.
24. For the problems concerning the discovery of this *Catechism* by the Tsarist police, its deciphering, etc., see A. A. Shilov, '*Katekhizis revolyutsionera (K istorii nechaevskogo dela)*' (*The revolutionary catechism* [*For a history of the Nechaev affair*]), in 'Bor'ba klassov', 1924, nos. I–II; which gives in the appendix a critical edition of this text. The discussion as to who was the author, which had already begun at the time of the trial, has been taken up by B. P. Koz'min, '*P. N. Tkachev i revolyutsionnoye dvizhenie 1860-kh gg.*' (*P. N. Tkachev and the revolutionary movement of the sixties*), M., 1922. He produces good arguments to back up his conclusion that Bakunin was responsible for it.
25. This manifesto of May 1869 is given in S. G. Svatikov, '*Studencheskoye dvizhenie 1869 goda (Bakunin i Nechaev)*' (*The student movement of 1869* [*Bakunin and Nechaev*]), in 'Istoricheskiy sbornik. Nasha strana' (*Historical miscellany. Our country*), Spb., 1907, p. 233.
26. This appeal is given with others in a miscellany, ' "*M. A. Bakunin*": *Stat'ya A. I. Gertsena o Bakunine*'. Biograficheskiy ocherk M. Dragomanova, rechi i vozzvaniya ('*M. A. Bakunin*': *an article by A. I. Herzen on Bakunin*. Biographical essay by M. Dragomanov, speeches and appeals), no place of publication, 1906, p. 235.
27. Given in '*M. A. Bakunin*', *op. cit.*, pp. 245–51.
28. For the complex and obscure history of the connection between Bakunin and Nechaev, apart from the works by Nettlau already mentioned, see Yu. Steklov, '*Mikhail Aleksandrovich Bakunin. Ego zhizn' i deyatel'nost'*' (*M. A. Bakunin. His life and activity*), M.-L., 1927, vol. III, pp. 418 ff.
29. See the article by G. Bakalov, '*Khristo Botev i Sergey Nechaev*', in 'Letopisi marksizma', 1929, nos. IX–X; a careful inquiry which shows that Nechaev's

'Communist ideas' (the word is used by one of Botev's friends) had some influence on the political evolution of the Bulgarian poet and revolutionary. The
contacts between the young Bulgarian émigrés and Bakunin—at the very time
when Nechaev was with him—constitute an important episode in the history
of the spread of Socialist ideas in the Balkans. In July 1869 a committee of
Bulgarian émigrés went to consult Mazzini, Garibaldi, Herzen and Bakunin.
Nechaev used the links this committee made with Bakunin to hide himself and
continue his activities during his second period abroad. In this period he hid
his identity under the name Ivan Ivanovich, and very probably Frolenko
also.

30. About his death, see V. Kolosov, 'Rasskazy o kariyskoy katorge' (Stories of
    forced labour at Kara), Spb., 1907, pp. 302 ff.; and ibid., 'Kara i drugiye tyur'my
    nerchinskoy katorgi' (Kara and other hard labour prisons at Nerchinsk), M.,
    1927. In the already-quoted memoirs by his wife, Aleksandra Ivanovna
    Zasulich, the sister of Vera, there are some simple and intelligent comments on
    Nechaev. Even if they do not give the key to his personality, they are a useful
    and efficacious antidote to false literary interpretations: 'It made me laugh'—
    she says—'when I heard people talking of him later on as if he had been an
    austere and gloomy fanatic, or when I saw him represented on the stage of the
    Arts Theatre, in a drama based on Dostoevsky's novel, The Demons . . . In
    fact he was nothing like it, nor had he ever been in the least similar; it was
    nothing but a stupid caricature of Nechaev and of all of us in general. Nechaev
    was a simple Russian boy, rather like a workman in looks, a little unsure of
    himself in city life. He pronounced "o" as they do in the Vladimir region. He
    never gave himself airs. He loved to joke and laugh.' Nechaev gave her the
    impression of being an intelligent man, extremely energetic, utterly dedicated
    to the cause. He made a similar impression on her husband and on all those
    who met him in Moscow.
31. See principally his 'Ispoved'' (Confession), published in 'Minuvshiye gody',
    1908, no. II; M. S. Al'tman, 'I. G. Pryzhov', M., 1932; and above all, I. G.
    Pryzhov, 'Ocherki, stat'i, pis'ma'. Redaktsiya, vvodnyye stat'i i kommentarii
    M. S. Al'tmana (Essays, articles and letters. Edited with introductory articles
    and comments by M. S. Al'tman), M.-L., 1934.
32. 'Ispoved'' (Confession), op. cit.
33. A. Grigor'ev, 'Plachevnyye razmyshleniya' (Sad reflections), article reprinted
    in his 'Vospominaniya' (Recollections), edited by Ivanov-Razumnik, L., 1930,
    pp. 349 ff.
34. 'Istoriya kabakov v Rossii v svyazi s istoriey russkogo naroda' (A history of
    inns in Russia, in relation to the history of the Russian people), Spb., 1868,
    reprinted, no place, no date (but Kazan, 1914).
35. 'Ispoved'' (Confession), op. cit.
36. Ibid.
37. See Cheshikhin-Vetrinsky, 'N. G. Chernyshevsky', P., 1923, p. 177. The
    character of Tolkachenko in Dostoevsky's Demons was based on Pryzhov, as
    M. S. Al'tman has shown, op. cit., pp. 192 ff.
38. See I. Likhutin's deposition published in 'Nechaev i nechaevtsy'. Sbornik
    materialov. Podgotovil k pechati B. P. Koz'min (Nechaev and his followers.
    Collection of material. Edited by B. P. Koz'min), M.-L., 1931, pp. 129 ff. A
    useful collection of documents which gives the report of the Minister of
    Justice on the Nechaev affair, the depositions of many who were arrested,
    several letters from the defendants and police reports of the trial.
39. A. Kuznetsov's deposition, 7th January 1870, in 'Nechaev i nechaevtsy'
    (Nechaev and his followers), op. cit., p. 108.

40. P. Prokorenko's deposition, 2nd February 1870, *ibid.*, p. 118.
41. B. Koz'min, '*S. G. Nechaev i tul'skiye oruzheyniki*' (*Nechaev and the workmen of the Tula arms factories*), in 'Katorga i ssylka', 1930, no. 3. When V. A. Cherkezov was arrested, a kind of propagandist guide was found on him. It indicated the state of mind of different villages in the Tula region, points to stress and so on.
42. P. A. Enkuvatov, student at the School of Agriculture, was condemned to a year in prison, and five years supervision. He escaped from Odessa in 1877 to take part in the revolt of Herzegovina. On his return, his own brother, who had also been involved in the Nechaev trial, killed him in a fit of jealousy.
43. '*Nechaev i nechaevtsy*' (*Nechaev and his followers*), *op. cit.*, p. 112.
44. Ivanov was the illegitimate son of a Moscow bourgeois. As a boy he lived for a long time in Nechaev's native town where he worked in a factory. When he met Nechaev at Moscow, he was guard in a prison where, with the permission of the authorities, he had started a workshop for the inmates. He gave Nechaev his own passport when the latter fled abroad the first time and for this reason he himself had to hide for a time at Tula.
45. See Kuznetsov's interesting autobiography published in '*Entsiklopedicheskiy slovar' Granat*' (*Granat Encyclopaedia*), vol. 40, *s.v.*
46. The account of the trial is reprinted in V. Bogucharsky, '*Gosudarstvennyye prestupleniya v Rossii v XIX v*' (*State crimes in Russia in the XIXth century*), Spb., 1906, pp. 159 ff. There is a police report of 21st December 1871 on the 'civil execution' of the three ringleaders, Uspensky, Pryzhov and Kuznetsov, published in '*Nechaev i nechaevtsy*' (*Nechaev and his followers*), *op. cit.*, p. 184. 'The ceremony took place very quietly. There were a good many people there, but principally merchants from the working-class district. On the way back, when the criminals were being taken back to prison in the cart, fifteen "nihilists" emerged from the crowd and accompanied them right to the prison. By some inexplicable chance, the waggon was drawn by a very poor old horse which was so obstinate that it stopped every two steps . . .' In the last months of 1872 they arrived in their respective penal settlements; Kuznetsov and Uspensky at Kara, Pryzhov in the area of Transbaikalia.
47. In the Brussels 'Internationale', 20th February 1870. 'La foule des grands dignitaires de l'empire, craignant pour la propre existence et poussée par la peur, s'est jetée avec une férocité digne des tigres sur tout ce qui est jeune et énergique . . .' He spoke of the 'gouvernement tartaro-allemand' and made up a fantastic story about the killing of Ivanov, saying he was the object of 'la plus éhontée' accusation. 'Le défunt Alexandre Herzen n'as pas été accusé par le gouvernement d'avoir pris part aux incendies en Russie?' It was reprinted in 'Volksstaat' on 26th February 1870. There is another letter from Nechaev in the same paper (14th May and 4th June 1870).
48. '*Na pogone Nechaeva*' (*In pursuit of Nechaev*), L., 1925, second edition corrected and annotated.
49. *Ibid., op. cit.*, p. 107.
50. B. Nikolaevsky, '*Pamyati poslednego yakobintsa, G. M. Tursky*' (*In memory of the last Jacobin, G. M. Tursky*), in 'Katorga i ssylka', 1926, no. II, suggests that Nechaev sowed the first seeds of Russian Jacobinism, during his stay in Paris. These were then later developed by Tkachev.
51. M. P. Sazhin, '*Vospominaniya 1860–1880-kh godov*'. S predisloviem V. Polonskogo (*Recollections of the sixties to the eighties*. With a preface by V. Polonsky), M., 1925, p. 14. 'They had an excellent organization', said Sazhin, speaking of the émigré followers of Mazzini.
52. 'Byloye', 1906, no. VII; and the admirable contribution that has been devoted

to these matters by J. M. Meijer, *Knowledge and Revolution. The Russian colony in Zürich (1870–1873). A contribution to the study of Russian Populism,* Assen, 1955.

53. Z. K. Ralli, '*Mikhail Aleksandrovich Bakunin*', in 'Minuvshiye gody', 1908, no. X.

54. '*Ot russkogo revolyutsionnogo obshchestva k zhenshchinam*' (*To women, on behalf of Russian revolutionary society*).

55. B. P. Koz'min, '*K istorii nechaevshchiny*' (*For a history of the Nechaev affair*), in 'Krasnyy arkhiv', 1927, no. III, in which both the manifestos are reprinted in full.

56. B. P. Koz'min, '*Proklamatsiya S. G. Nechaeva k studentam*' (*A manifesto to the students by Nechaev*), in 'Krasnyy arkhiv', 1929, no. 33.

57. I have been unable to see this periodical of Nechaev's.

58. He speaks of it again in the 'Bulletin russe' (Supplement du 'Kolokol') ('La Cloche'), no. I, 2nd April 1870. 'Le peuple agricole de la Russie, c'est-à-dire l'immense majorité de la population de l'empire, se voit frustrée dans ses dernières espérances. Ainsi des soulèvements partiels et chaque jour plus fréquents ont-ils déjà lieu sur tous les points de l'empire ... Pour peu que tous les mouvements locaux se donnent la main, le gouvernement est perdu.'

59. '*K russkoy publike ot redaktsii*' (*To the Russian public from the editor*), in 'Kolokol', no. 1, 2nd April 1870.

60. 'Kolokol', no. 2, 9th April 1870.

61. 'Kolokol', no. 3, 16th April 1870.

62. The issues of 'Kolokol' which were edited by Nechaev have been reprinted by V. Nevsky and I. Teodorovich, with notes by E. A. Morokhovets, M., 1933.

63. Quoted in Yu. Steklov, '*M. A. Bakunin*', *op. cit.*, vol. III, p. 542.

64. There is a very detailed article by P. E. Shchegolev on Nechaev's whole period in prison, '*S. G. Nechaev v raveline, 1873–1882*' (*S. G. Nechaev in the dungeon of the Peter-Paul fortress*), in '*Alekseevskiy ravelin*' (*The Alexeyevsky dungeon*), M., 1929, pp. 188 ff.

65. '*Obryad publichnoy kazni nad S. G. Nechaevym*' (*The ceremony of Nechaev's civil execution*), in 'Krasnyy arkhiv', 1922, no. I.

66. For the last period of Nechaev's life, see also Tikhomirov's article in 'Vestnik Narodnoy Voli', Geneva, 1883, no. I.

CHAPTER 16

1. Most of Tkachev's works have been collected in '*Izbrannyye sochineniya na sotsial'no-politicheskiye temy*', v chetyryokh tomakh, redaktsiya, vstupitel'naya stat'ya i primechaniya B. P. Koz'mina (*Selected works on social-political themes*, in four volumes, edited and with an introductory article and notes by B. P. Koz'min), M., 1922–3. This includes his writings from 1865–80. Later there was a plan to increase the number of volumes from four to seven under the same editor, but only two more were published: vol. V in 1935, and vol. VI, undated but 1937, covering Tkachev's articles from 1864 to 1877. This publication also includes many of his writings which had never been published previously, because they had been seized in police raids or suppressed by the censor. On page 449 of vol. IV there is a 'List of Tkachev's works', which gives everything he was able to publish, whether signed, anonymous or under different pseudonyms. From now on these volumes will be referred to simply by their number and page. The two most important writings on Tkachev are

both by B. P. Koz′min: '*P. N. Tkachev i revolyutsionnoye dvizhenie 1860-kh godov*' (*P. N. Tkachev and the revolutionary movement of the sixties*), 1922, a small and reliable little book containing numerous archive documents, and the article, '*Tkachev i Lavrov*' (*Tkachev and Lavrov*), which appeared in the miscellany 'Voinstvuyushchiy materialist' ('The Militant Materialist'), vol. I, M., 1924, and was later reprinted in '*Ot devyatnadtsatogo fevralya k pervomu marta*' (*From 19th February 1861 to 1st March 1881*), M., 1937, pp. 107 ff.

2. 'Ni Dieu, ni maître', 21st November 1880, foreword to the translation of Chernyshevsky's *What is to be done?*
3. See chapter XI, pp. 251.
4. III, 58.
5. I, 69.
6. V, 300.
7. V, 302.
8. II, 106.
9. II, 110.
10. II, 114.
11. V, 24.
12. Zhukovsky's articles were reprinted in one volume, Spb., 1866, p. 157.
13. *Ibid.*, p. 158.
14. I, 73.
15. When in exile Tkachev was to protest against Zhukovsky's anti-Marxist standpoint and to speak of his 'shameful article on "*Das Kapital*" in which he makes use of scientific *escamotages* to defend the capitalists', 'Nabat', 1878, p. 92.
16. I, 70. This is the first mention of Marx's book in the Russian press. But it seems that it had already had a wide circulation—as Marx noted with amazement not long after it had been published: 'My book has aroused great interest in Russia, and a certain Moscow professor has even lectured on it. I have even received friendly letters from Russia on account of it.' This was written to Lassalle on 15th September 1860. Also the 'Gazette du Nord' of 5th May 1860 had made Marx's name. It is possible that Zhukovsky knew this work, although he does not mention it. See the introductory article to the Russian edition of *Zur Kritik* (translated by I. Rubin), by D. Ryazanov, M.-L., 1929, p. xxxii, nos. XXIII–XXV, of the 'Biblioteka marksista' (The Marxist Library).
17. I, 445.
18. Published for the first time by B. P. Koz′min in 'Literaturnoye nasledstvo', 1933, nos. VII–IX, and reprinted in V, 104 ff.
19. V, 114.
20. V, 149.
21. I, 131.
22. I, 134.
23. I, 138.
24. I, 170.
25. I, 70.
26. B. P. Koz′min, '*Ot devyatnadtsatogo fevralya k pervomu marta*' (*From 19th February 1861 to 1st March 1881*), *op. cit.*, p. 138.
27. II, 207.
28. I, 427.
29. V, 206.
30. I, 99.
31. Report quoted in I, 418.

25*

32. Again, in 1871, a police report noted that this book, 'in spite of being banned by the tribunal, has had a wide circulation by means of clandestine sales'. Document quoted by O. V. Aptekman, '*Vasily Vasilyevich Bervi-Flerovsky*', L., 1925, p. 63.
33. I, 415.
34. I, 410.
35. I, 407.
36. I, 411.
37. I, 428.
38. I, 368–9.
39. B. Nikolaevsky has arrived at similar conclusions in '*Materialy i dokumenty. Tkachev i Lavrov*' (*Material and documents. Tkachev and Lavrov*), in 'Na chuzhoy storone', 1925, no. X. However, it ought not to be forgotten that Tkachev himself on one occasion attributed the origin of his ideas to Blanqui, even if only in very general terms. But this claim was made on an occasion when historical exactitude is not customary—a funeral oration on the death of Blanqui. 'À lui, à ses idées, à son abnégation, à la lucidité de son esprit, à sa clairvoyance, nous devons la grande partie du progrès, qui s'accomplit chaque jour dans le mouvement révolutionnaire de la Russie. Oui, c'est lui qui a été notre inspirateur et notre modèle dans le grand art de la conspiration' (words from a speech which Tkachev would have delivered had he not been prevented by his state of health, and which appeared in 'Ni Dieu, ni maître' on 9th January 1881). On the same occasion Tursky added: 'C'est justement parce que le gouvernement du czar comprend la signification universelle des principes que représentait, si éminemment, Auguste Blanqui, qu'il avait interdit en Russie de prononcer même son nom. . . .'
40. V, 42–3.
41. V, 273.
42. V, 241.
43. V, 295.
44. V, 359.
45. I, 275.
46. I, 277.
47. I, 282.
48. V, 178.
49. I, 326.
50. I, 328.
51. I, 329.
52. I, 330.
53. II, 251.
54. I, 181.
55. I, 174.
56. I, 208.
57. This comparison has already been made by B. P. Koz'min in '*P. N. Tkachev i revolyutsionnoye dvizhenie 1860-kh godov*' (*P. N. Tkachev and the revolutionary movement of the sixties*), *op. cit.*, pp. 90–8, 179–205.
58. V, 355.
59. I, 319.
60. I, 322.
61. I, 343.
62. I, 348–9.
63. I, 357.
64. VI, 297.

65. B. Nikolaevsky has formulated the likely hypothesis that it was Kupryanov who had organized his escape as an inducement to him to contribute to 'Vpered'. '*Materialy i dokumenty. Tkachev i Lavrov*' (*Material and documents. Tkachev and Lavrov*), *op. cit.* For Kupryanov, see chapter XVIII, p. 487.

66. 'Vpered', no. III, 1874, reprinted in II, 49.

67. III, 54.

68. III, 69–70.

69. III, 78.

70. III, 64.

71. III, 65.

72. III, 65.

73. III, 80.

74. Nos. 117, 118 of 1874.

75. *Offener Brief an Herrn Fr. Engels*, Zürich, 1874. Russian translation in III, 88 ff.

76. III, 89.

77. III, 90.

78. III, 93.

79. III, 95. Engels replied to this *Open Letter* with an article in 'Volksstaat', in 1875, '*Soziales aus Russland*'. It is reprinted in the collection of his articles entitled *Internationales aus dem* Volksstaat, Berlin, 1894. Marx also read the *Open Letter* and in a note written on its jacket advised Engels to 'drauf hauen in lustiger Manier' (quoted in *Karl Marx. Chronik seines Lebens in Einzeldaten*, M., 1934, p. 350).

80. This is also proved by the translation he made, together with M. Elpidin, of a pamphlet published in Zürich in October 1874, '"*Die polnische Fälscherbande" und die russischen Staatsräthe und deren Agenten*'. The Russian version was published at Geneva in the following year. Tkachev was then also in touch with a 'cercle slave' at Zürich which had emerged at the beginning of the 'seventies. On the Poles in Zürich, see J. M. Meijer, *Knowledge and Revolution. The Russian colony in Zürich (1870–1873). A contribution to the study of Russian Populism*, Assen, 1955. There Tkachev found Blanquist elements. The 'cercle slave' had, for example, published the Russian translation of *L'Internationale et la révolution* in 1873 as a litho-printed pamphlet. This was the protest of French Blanquists (Edouard Vaillant, F. Cournet, and others) against the Prague Congress. Tkachev and Tursky were to print this pamphlet a few years later in 1876 at Geneva. The litho-printed brochure of 1873 is mentioned in P. L. Lavrov, '*Izbrannyye sochineniya na sotsial'no-politicheskiye temy*' (*Selected works on social-political themes*), M., 1934, vol. II, p. 387. On the 'Slav section' of the 'International' at Zürich, see Yu. Steklov, '*Mikhail Aleksandrovich Bakunin. Ego zhizn' i deyatel'nost*' (*M. A. Bakunin. His life and activity*), M.-L., 1927, vol. IV, pp. 233 ff.

81. On Tursky, see B. Nikolaevsky, '*Pamyati poslednego yakobintsa*' (*In memory of the last of the Jacobins*), in 'Katorga i ssylka', 1926, no. II. Tursky's ideas are expounded in the pamphlet '*Idealizm i materializm v politike*' (*Idealism and materialism in politics*), signed with the pseudonym, A. Amari, and published at Geneva in 1877 by the 'Nabat' press. This is particularly interesting for the sources of the ideas of the Russian Jacobins, which Tkachev rarely spoke about. It opens with a quotation from Saint-Just and all the first part is an exaltation of the traditions of the French enlightenment. It speaks there of the 'very fine work of Mably' (p. 36), and defends 18th century utilitarianism. 'The proletariat . . . instead of concealing egoism recognizes it as the principal quality of human nature.' The aim of the revolution was to reinstate 'equality

among men and to bind the interests of the individual closely to that of the community, through the strength of a revolutionary state' (p. 31). As regards the French revolution, K. Tursky looked solely to the followers of Robespierre. 'Those principles which were fruitful in the hands of the latter acted against the interests of the people when, after the fall of Robespierre, they fell into the hands of the *Cordeliers*' (that is to say, the followers of Danton) (p. 41). He did not hide his sympathy for Machiavelli, 'this great thinker and excellent judge of human nature whom our contemporaries slander . . .' (p. 48).

The pamphlet was mainly a polemic against the anarchists. 'In the socialist party there exists a group of imbeciles and people paid by the police who tell the workers not to concern themselves with politics . . . such propaganda is very useful to the bourgeoisie who have nothing to fear so much as the development of a political sense among the masses . . .' (p. 60). And like Tkachev he also underlined the contradiction between liberty, understood in an anarchist sense, and equality: 'The anarchist section of the International wants the complete destruction of the bourgeois order, and wants to set up in its place the principle of absolute individual liberty—a principle purely bourgeois in essence, on which the present order is founded. But their metaphysic does not limit itself to this sort of mess: whilst proclaiming the principle of absolute individual liberty, they also desire equality. But if to obtain this equality it is indispensable that individual liberty be curtailed it is obvious that there must be some force capable of setting the limit. Whether this force arises from a mutual contract, or whether it is imposed by a minority, will depend on the circumstances that accompany the revolution. But in one way or another it is still necessary to have a force which maintains equality between the strong and the weak . . .' (p. 62).

He remembered how Blanqui and his friends had tried to take the International along the path of revolution at the Geneva congress of 1866; he went back over the story of the Blanquist minority, and the story of what he considered to be the degeneration of the International, now reduced 'to a sort of *Club des Cordeliers*, to an association of individualists and dilettantes, very like the one which curbed the great revolution of the Jacobins . . .' (p. 64). One of the few anarchists to arouse his sympathy was 'the Italian Malatesta, who in 1876 had proposed to give up all discussion of the society of the future and to devote himself to *révolution en permanence*' (p. 65).

The development of Tursky's ideas in the 'eighties is also very interesting; the primordial importance of the political problem drove him, like the French Blanquists, along the path of a version of radicalism which ended by demanding a republic and liberty before all else. He sought to influence the Russian intelligentsia in this respect and tried to push it into the struggle against absolutism. See his journal 'Svoboda' ('Liberty') which came out in Geneva in 1888. Speaking, for example, of *Narodnaya Volya* he said that 'the last heroic phase of the struggle of the advanced members of the Russian intelligentsia against tsarism, despite its mistakes and failures, was of inestimable value to our native land, allowing, as it did, a place of such importance in its programme to the *political* struggle' (no. 5, April 1888).

82. This review had an international flavour right from the start, publishing articles by Polish and French Blanquists and socialists. In 1878, it listed the following as its agents: G. Tursky and F. Cournet at Geneva, E. Vaillant in London, Grakch in Paris, and in 1879 it published articles by E. Granger and F. Cournet whose interesting account of the Marseilles congress appears in nos. 3–5. In 1881, when it came out in London, it was directed by P. T. Grezko, P. T-A (?) and G. Tursky. It referred to E. Granger as its Paris agent. 'The following people

have promised to collaborate—E. Vaillant, E. Granger, F. Cournet, E. Eude, B. Limanowski, Z. Schultz' (no. I). 'Nabat' is, as we shall see, an interesting source for the whole history of the French Blanquists in exile and their international ramifications, a history that would be worth the trouble of writing. As far as we know, the only other Russian connected with 'Nabat', apart from Tkachev, was P. V. Grigor'yev who was only a secondary figure; for an account of him, see M. Lemke, '*K biografii P. N. Tkacheva (Po neizdannym istochnikam)*' (*For a biography of P. N. Tkachev [From unpublished sources]*), in 'Byloye', 1907, no. VIII. These international links explain how it was that Russian Jacobinism found a greater echo in the Western socialist press in the 'seventies than its limited influence on the revolutionary movement in Russia itself would have warranted.

83. '*K biografii P. N. Tkacheva*' (*For a biography of P. N. Tkachev*), in *op. cit.*
84. III, 228.
85. III, 233.
86. III, 240.
87. III, 286.
88. III, 224.
89. III, 225.
90. III, 327.
91. Nos. 1–4. They were collected, together with an article on a related subject: *The anarchist State*, in a pamphlet, '*Anarkhiya mysli*'. Sobranie kriticheskikh ocherkov P. N. Tkacheva. Izdanie zhurnala 'Nabat' (*The anarchy of thought. A collection of critical essays by P. N. Tkachev. A 'Nabat' publication*), London, 1879. It is reprinted in III, 303 ff.
92. III, 311.
93. *Ibid.*
94. III, 310.
95. III, 321.
96. '*Anarkhicheskoye gosudarstvo*' (*The anarchist State*), in 'Nabat', 1876, nos. 5, 6, reprinted in III, 338 ff.
97. III, 254.
98. III, 255.
99. III, 266.
100. 'Nabat', 1876, no. IV, reprinted in III, 262 ff.
101. III, 263.
102. '*O pochvennikakh noveyshey formatsii*' (*The most recent type of adherents of the 'soil' theory*), published in 'Delo', 1876, no. II, reprinted in IV, 5 ff.
103. '*Pomozhet li nam melkiy zemel'nyy kredit?*' (*Can small agrarian credit be of advantage?*), in 'Delo', 1876, no. XII, reprinted in IV, 32 ff.
104. '*Muzhik v salonakh sovremennoy belletristiki*' (*The peasant in the literary salons of today*), in 'Delo', 1879, no. 3, 6–9, reprinted in IV, 180 ff.
105. III, 269 ff.
106. III, 272–3.
107. III, 275.
108. Letter published in 'Byloye', 1913, no. XIV. B. Nikolaevsky has corrected the date, proving that it was written in the autumn of 1875, even before the first number of 'Nabat' came out. '*Materialy i dokumenty. Tkachev i Lavrov*' (*Material and documents. Tkachev and Lavrov*), *op. cit.*
109. III, 250. It is characteristic that the name of Danton should have disappeared from this phrase when this article was republished in the pamphlet, '*Oratory-buntovshchiki pered russkoy revolyutsiey. Na temu: neobkhodimo pristupit' nemedlenno k taynoy organizatsii, bez kotoroy nemyslima politicheskaya bor'ba*'

(*Rebel-orators faced with the Russian revolution. On the subject: It is indispensable to move at once to clandestine organization, without which the political struggle is unthinkable*) Geneva, 1880. In it the names of Marat and Saint-Just were substituted for Danton's. In 1876 Tkachev was still outside the battles which raged over the names of Danton and Robespierre, and which were particularly heated among the various factions of the French revolutionary movement, especially the Blanquists. His view of the French revolution was a general one, and it had not seemed to him to be necessary to take sides among the different Jacobin factions. This same Jacobinism seemed to him at that time to be able to draw strength even from the much earlier examples of Cromwell and Washington. A few years later these names were also cancelled.

110. III, 289.
111. See how much 'Nabat', for example, has to say on Bismarck's anti-socialist laws: 'The German socialist party had a vast official literature, an official organization, official representatives even in parliament, it counted hundreds of thousands of people among its members: one would have thought it a *force* capable of fighting the police government of the Iron Chancellor on *legal grounds*. Well? Simply a stroke of the Chancellor's pen and this *force* has shown itself to be nothing at all.'
112. III, 403.
113. Some years ago there was a discussion on the real importance of Tkachev's organization in the review, 'Katorga i ssylka'. E. N. Kusheva maintained not only that the *Society for the Liberation of the People* really existed, but also that it carried on a certain amount of activity, see '*K istorii Obshchestva narodnogo osvobozhdeniya*' (*For the history of the* 'Society for the liberation of the people'), 1931, no. IV. M. F. Frolenko replied: '*Obshchestvo narodnogo osvobozhdeniya*' (*The society for the liberation of the people*), 1932, no. III. He maintained the opposite thesis, and brought forward as proof the fact that none of the people directing *Narodnaya Volya* had ever met a representative of Tkachev's organization in Russia. As we shall see, there were Jacobins in Russia but, apart from the small Zaichnevsky group, there was never a true and proper Tkachev organization. Its failure was of an ideological and moral nature. Ol'ga Lyubatovich has summed the situation up particularly well in '*Dalyokoye i nedavneye*' (*The distant past and the recent past*), M., 1930, p. 57. She recalls how Kravchinsky used to say that 'Men of all sorts are good for the revolution except Jacobins and absolutists'.
114. See 'Nabat', 20th June 1881, note I.

CHAPTER 17

1. M. Nettlau, *Bakunin und die russische revolutionäre Bewegung in den Jahren 1868–1873*, in 'Archiv für die Geschichte des Sozialismus und der Arbeiterbewegung', 1915, no. V.
2. Letter of 26th June 1866, in '*Pis'ma M. A. Bakunina k A. I. Gertsenu i N. P. Ogaryovu*'. S prilozheniem ego pamfletov, biograficheskim vvedeniem i ob'yasnitel'nymi primechaniyami M. P. Dragomanova (*Letters from M. A. Bakunin to A. I. Herzen and N. P. Ogarev*. Together with his 'pamphlets', and a biographical introduction and explanatory notes by M. P. Dragomanov), Geneva, 1896, pp. 170 ff.
3. Z. K. Ralli, '*Mikhail Aleksandrovich Bakunin*', in 'Minuvshiye gody', 1908, no. X.
4. '*Intrigi gospodina Utina*' (*The intrigues of Mr. Utin*), in '*Materialy dlya biografii M. Bakunina*'. Redaktsiya i primechaniya V. Polyanskogo. Tom III: '*Bakunin*

v pervom Internatsionale' (*Material for a biography of M. Bakunin*. Edited and with notes by V. Polyansky. Vol. III: *Bakunin in the First International*), M.-L., 1928, p. 409. A letter written at the end of September 1867 by Zhukovsky to Ogarev reveals the development of his thought. 'Literaturnoye nasledstvo', vol. 62, p. 136.

5. This letter in German translation appears in the great litho-printed biography written by Nettlau (note 4025), and also in his article, '*Bakunin und die russische revolutionäre Bewegung in den Jahren 1868–1873*', *op. cit.* To my knowledge the Russian text has never been found.

6. This is the theme of the appendices to his pamphlet, *Statism and Anarchism*, which Bakunin added in the first edition: '*Gosudarstvennost' i anarkhiya*', no place (but Zürich and Geneva), 1873, and which were not reprinted in the edition edited by V. Cherkezov, M., 1922. Bakunin had also alleged this in his '*Nauka i nasushchnoye revolyutsionnoye delo*'. Vypusk I (*Science and the essential revolutionary cause*), no. I (the only one), Geneva, undated (but 1870).

7. '*Gosudarstvennost' i anarkhiya*' (*Statism and Anarchism*), no place (but Zürich and Geneva), 1873, p. 246.

8. *Ibid.*, p. 7.

9. *Ibid.*, p. 258.

10. '*Istoricheskoye razvitie Internatsionala*' (*The historical development of the International*), 1873, p. 355, quoted in Yu. Steklov, '*M. A. Bakunin*', *op. cit.*, vol. III, p. 312. We have not succeeded in finding this pamphlet of Bakunin's.

11. '*Gosudarstvennost' i anarkhiya*', p. 250.

12. *Ibid.*, p. 255.

13. *Ibid.*, p. 251. Marx's notes and critical comments on *Statism and Anarchism* have been translated and published by D. Ryazanov, in 'Letopisi marksizma', 1926, no. III.

14. 'L'Egalité' of 7th April.

15. Z. K. Ralli, '*Iz moikh vospominaniy o M. A. Bakunine*' (*My recollections of M. A. Bakunin*), in '*Istoricheskiy sbornik. O minuvshem*' (*Historical miscellany. On the past*), Spb., 1909, pp. 287 ff.; and Yu. Steklov, '*Mikhail Aleksandrovich Bakunin. Ego zhizn' i deyatel'nost'*' (*M. A. Bakunin. His life and activity*), M.-L., 1927, vol. IV (1870–6), pp. 205 ff.

16. E. El' [E. F. Litvinova], '*M. A. Bakunin v Shveytsarii*' (*M. A. Bakunin in Switzerland*), in 'Severnyy vestnik', 1898, no. IV, quoted in Yu. Steklov, '*M. A. Bakunin*', *op. cit.*, vol. IV, p. 211. See J. M. Meijer, *Knowledge and Revolution. The Russian colony in Zurich (1870–73). A contribution to the study of Russian Populism*, Assen, 1955.

17. I. I. Popov, '*Sergey Filippovich Kovalik*', in 'Katorga i ssylka', 1926, no. IV.

18. Z. K. Ralli, N. I. Zhukovsky, A. L. El'snits, '*Parizhskaya kommuna, n. 2. Revolyutsionnaya obshchina russkikh anarkhistov*' (*The Paris Commune, no. 2. The revolutionary community of Russian anarchists*), no place (but Geneva), 1874. The no. 2 indicated that this book followed on after the pamphlet, *To the Russian Revolutionaries*, of which we have already spoken.

19. Z. K. Ralli, N. I. Zhukovsky, A. L. El'snits, *op. cit.*, p. 61.

20. *Ibid.*, p. 44.

21. *Ibid.*, p. 61.

22. *Ibid.*, p. 74.

23. *Ibid.*, p. 63.

24. *Ibid.*, p. 71.

25. *Ibid.*, p. 95.

26. *Ibid.*, p. 75.

27. *Ibid.*, p. 41.

28. *Ibid.*, p. 62.

29. *Ibid.*, p. 65.

30. *Ibid.*, p. 7 ff. Ralli then gave the first eleven articles of the *Manifesto of Equals* from Buonarroti's book, saying that 'with us so little is known of the road along which revolutionary thought in the West has moved and developed; it is so difficult for Russia to perceive a sane and vital idea' that he thought it a good moment to reproduce part, at least, of the *Manifesto*.

31. *La révolution du 18 mars, par un socialiste révolutionnaire russe*, in 'Le travailleur'. Revue socialiste révolutionnaire paraissant tous les mois. Comité de rédaction: N. Joukowsky, A. Oelsnitz, C. Perron, Élisée Réclus, Geneva, 1878, no. III.

32. Z. Ralli, *Le socialisme en Russie*, in *La Commune. Almanach socialiste pour 1877*, by Élisée Réclus, Arthur Arnauld, Alexandre Oelsnitz, Paul Brousse, Adhémar Schwitzguébel, Adolphe Clémence, Elie Réclus, C.-F. Gambon, Z. Ralli, etc., Geneva, 1877, pp. 70 ff. In this same almanac there is an article on Sten'ka Razin by A. El'snits (or, as he signed himself, A. Oelsnitz), pp. 61 ff.

33. Z. Ralli, *op. cit.*

34. '*Intrigi gospodina Utina*' (*The intrigues of Mr. Utin*), *op. cit.*, p. 412. For Utin's political development from 1863-9, see his letters to Herzen and Ogarev, 'Literaturnoye nasledstvo', vol. 62, pp. 607 ff.

35. The 'Narodnoye delo' publicly acknowledged this connection with Becker, 'the friend and faithful collaborator of Marx'. 'The good start of our cause owes a great deal to his experience and to his wide contacts', it said in the first number of the second year, issued on 15th April 1870.

36. '*Drôle de position* für mich, als Repräsentant der junge Russie zu funktionieren! Der Mensch weiss nie, wozu er es bringen kann, und welche *strange fellowship* er zu untergehn hat', wrote Marx in a letter to Engels, 24th March 1870, 'MEGA', *Dritte Abteilung*, vol. IV, p. 296. See the letter of 14th September of the same year, which Marx ironically signed 'Secretary for Russia', *ibid.*, p. 387. But this did not stop him following with close attention the conflict between the different parties among the Russian exiles and among the sections at Geneva. 'Es ist mir das schon gleich aufgefallen, dass der Outine sich albereits bei den Genfern in eine Position zu setzen gewusst', *ibid.*, p. 313.

37. Z. K. Ralli, '*Mikhail Aleksandrovich Bakunin*', *op. cit.*

38. Letter from Geneva dated 12th March 1870; the Russian translation can be found in '*Perepiska K. Marksa i F. Engel'sa s russkimi politicheskimi deyatelyami*' (*The correspondence of K. Marx and F. Engels with Russian political figures*), no place (but L.), 1947, pp. 26 ff.

39. *Op. cit.*, pp. 28-9. This volume also includes subsequent letters. These, however, are interesting more for the history of the conflicts in the ranks of the International than for that of the Russian section. The first letter to Marx was printed in 'Narodnoye delo', 1870, no. I, of 15th April.

40. V. A. Gorokhov, '*Pervyy Internatsional i russkiy sotsializm. "Narodnoye delo". Russkaya sektsiya Internatsionala. 1864–1870*' (*The First International and Russian socialism. 'Narodnoye delo'. The Russian section of the International. 1864–1870*), M., 1925, and especially B. P. Koz'min, '*Russkaya sektsiya I-go Internatsionala*' (*The Russian Section of the First International*), M., 1957.

41. 'Narodnoye delo', 1868, nos. 2–3, October.

42. '*Russkoye sotsial'no-revolyutsionnoye delo v ego sootnoshenii s rabochim dvizheniem na Zapade*' (*The Russian social-revolutionary cause in its connections with the workers' movement of the West*), in 'Narodnoye delo', 1869, nos. 7–10, November.

43. '*Internatsional'naya assotsiatsiya i Rossiya. Bunt, stachka i revolyutsiya*' (*The International and Russia. The rising, the strike and the revolution*), in 'Narodnoye delo', 1870, no. 3, of 31st May.

44. '*Krest'yanskaya reforma i obshchinnoye zemlevladenie*' (*The peasant reform and communal landholding*, 1861–1870), in 'Narodnoye delo', 1870, no. 2, of 7th May.

45. A resolution which summarized this was put before the London Conference of the International by Utin on 22nd September 1871. The text has been lost. Marx supported it, saying that 'he had great hopes of the Russian social movement. There the students, most of whom are very poor, are very close to the people and will give a strong impetus to the working class. In Russia secret societies are not necessary, there one could perfectly well create an organization of the International. Among the workers the spirit of cooperation and solidarity is very strong'. '*Londonskaya konferentsiya pervogo Internatsionala 17–23 sentyabrya 1871 g.*' (*The London Conference of the First International, 17th–23rd September 1871*), no place (but M.), 1936, p. 101.

46. The most important comprehensive study of Lavrov is by I. Knizhnik, '*P. L. Lavrov, ego zhizn' i trudy*' (*P. L. Lavrov, his life and works*), L., 1925; second edition, M., 1930. For the future we shall refer to the first edition. Many accounts of him can be found in '*Materialy dlya biografii P. L. Lavrova*', pod redaktsiey P. Vityazeva (*Material for a biography of P. L. Lavrov*, edited by P. Vityazev), no. I, P., 1921, in '*P. L. Lavrov. Sbornik statey. Stat'i, vospominaniya, materialy*' (*P. L. Lavrov. Collected articles. Articles, memoirs and material*), P., 1922. There is a large bibliography of Lavrov's works in Knizhnik's book, *op. cit.*, on pp. 106 ff. Soon after the 1917 revolution a group of his admirers, centred on the publishing house 'Kolos' at Petrograd, started the publication of '*Sobranie sochineniy P. L. Lavrova*', pod red. N. Rusanova, P. Vityazeva i A. Gizetti (*The works of P. L. Lavrov*, edited by N. Rusanov, P. Vityazev and A. Gizetti). The works were not arranged chronologically, but grouped according to subject matter. Nos. II and VI of series I: '*Stat'i po filosofii*' (*Articles on philosophical subjects*), came out in 1917–18 and 1918; no. VII of series II: '*Stat'i sotsial'no-politicheskiye*' (*Social-political articles*) in 1920; nos. I, II, V, VIII of series III: '*Stat'i nauchnogo kharaktera*' (*Articles of a scientific nature*) in 1917–18; nos. I, VII, IX of series IV: '*Stat'i istoriko-filosofskiye*' (*Historical-philosophic articles*) in 1918; and one number of series V: '*Stat'i po istorii religii*' (*Articles on the history of religion*) in 1917–18. As well as this incomplete collection of Lavrov's works, other writings were published separately at the same period. These are the most important: '*Parizhskaya kommuna 18 marta 1871 goda*' (*The Paris Commune of 18th March 1871*), P., 1919; '*Sotsial'naya revolyutsiya i zadachi nravstvennosti. Starye voprosy*'. S primechaniem P. Vityazeva (*The social revolution and the functions of ethics. Old problems.* With a note by P. Vityazev), P., 1921; '*Iz istorii sotsial'nykh ucheniy*' (*From the history of social doctrines*), P., 1919; '*Komu prinadlezhit budushcheye?*' (*To whom does the future belong?*), P., 1917; '*Ocherki po istorii Internatsionala*'. S predisloviem i primechaniyami P. Vityazeva (*Essays on the history of the International.* With preface and notes by P. Vityazev), P., 1919; '*German Aleksandrovich Lopatin*' (*G. A. Lopatin.* With a preface by P. Vityazev, and with additional material for a bibliography on G. A. Lopatin, collected by A. A. Shilov), P., 1919; '*Etyudy o zapadnoy literature*'. Pod red. A. A. Gizetti i P. Vityazeva (*Studies on Western literature.* Edited by A. A. Gizetti and P. Vityazev). In 1934, in the edition *Classics of revolutionary thought in the pre-Marxist period*, the publication began of '*Izbrannyye sochineniya na sotsial'no-politicheskiye temy*' v vos'mi

tomakh. Vstupitel'naya stat'ya i redaktsiya I. A. Teodorovicha. Podgotovka k pechati, kommentarii, primechaniya, biograficheskiy i bibliograficheskiy ocherk I. S. Knizhnika-Vetrova (*Selected works on social-political problems* in eight volumes. Introductory article and compilation by I. A. Teodorovich. Edited with comments, notes and biographical and bibliographical essays by I. S. Knizhnik-Vetrov). The first volume includes Lavrov's writings from 1857 to 1871, the second and third, those from 1873 to 1874; the fourth, those from 1875 to 1876. The first three were published in Moscow in 1934, the fourth in 1935, also in Moscow. The other volumes planned never saw the light. This publication from now on will be referred to by volume and page. On the Lavrovist movement in Russia and in exile, the fullest and most detailed document is the memoirs of N. G. Kulyabko-Koretsky, '*Iz davnikh let. Vospominaniya lavrista*' (*From years gone by. Recollections of a Lavrovist*), M., 1931. The Lavrov archives, preserved partly in the Marx-Engels-Lenin Institute of Moscow and partly in the International Institute of Social History at Amsterdam, have not yet been published.

47. From E. A. Stakenshneyder, '*Dnevnik i zapiski (1854–1886)*'. Redaktsiya, stat'ya i kommentarii I. N. Rozanova (*Diary and memoirs (1854–1886)*. Compilation, preface and notes by I. N. Rozanov), M.-L., 1934, p. 361.

48. A poem of his written in 1857 was in fact called *Forward!* Lavrov may have remembered this fifteen years later when he was choosing a name for the socialist review which he was about to publish in Switzerland; for he called it 'Vperyod' (Forward).

49. 'Otechestvennye zapiski', 1859, nos. XI and XII.

50. '*Antropologicheskiy printsip v filosofii*' (*The anthropological principle in philosophy*), in '*Polnoye sobranie sochineniy*' (*Complete works*), Spb., 1906, vol. VI, pp. 183 ff.

51. This letter to Herzen, one of the group published in 'Golosa iz Rossii' (Voices from Russia), no. IV, London, 1857, is reprinted in I, 108 ff.

52. He was writing this about 1862–3 in an article which was seized from him at the moment of his arrest in 1866. It was published for the first time by P. Vityazev in 'Kniga i revolyutsiya', 1922, no. VI. It is reprinted in I, 128 ff.

53. *Ibid.*, p. 131.

54. A. V. Nikitenko, '*Moya povest' o samom sebe*' (*The story of myself*), Spb., 1905, vol. II, p. 181.

55. '*Biografiya-ispoved''* (*Biography-confession*), written by Lavrov in the third person in 1885, I, 103.

56. On the atmosphere of the intellectual world of St Petersburg at the time of Lavrov's arrest, an atmosphere typical of the reaction which followed Karakozov's attempt to assassinate the Tsar, see E. A. Stakenshneyder, '*Dnevnik i zapiski*' (*Diary and memoirs*), *op. cit.*, pp. 374 ff. On Lavrov's sentence, see V. N. Nechaev, '*Protsess P. L. Lavrova 1866 g.*' (*Lavrov's trial in 1866*), in the '*Sbornik materialov i statey*' (*Miscellany of material and articles*), published by the 'Glavnoye upravlenie arkhivnym delom (General Administration of Archives), edited by the 'Istoricheskiy arkhiv', 1921, no. I, pp. 45 ff.

57. M. P. Sazhin (Arman Ross), '*Vospominaniya 1860–1880-kh gg.*'. S predisloviem V. Polonskogo (*Recollections from the sixties to the eighties*, with a preface by V. Polonsky), M., 1925, p. 20.

58. The Vologda intelligentsia 'went mad at that time over the works of Pisarev', says one student who was imprisoned the year after Lavrov, as a result of the University disorders. N. A. Ivanitsky, '*Zapiski*' (*Memoirs*), in 'Sever', 1923, no. II.

59. '*O publitsistakh-populyarizatorakh i o estestvoznanii*' (*The popularizing publicists and the natural sciences*), published under the pseudonym of A. Ugryumov in *Sovremennik*, 1865, no. IX. There is some doubt about the attribution to Lavrov. See I, 134 ff.

60. On the rather half-hearted obstacles put in its way by the authorities, see S. A. Pereselenkov, '*Ofitsial'nyye kommentarii k* "Istoricheskim pis'mam" *P. L. Lavrova*' (*Official comments on Lavrov's* 'Historical letters'), in 'Byloye', 1925, no. II. They were often reprinted in Russian. There are translations into German and French: *Lettres historiques par Pierre Lavroff*, traduit du russe et précédé d'une notice bio-bibliographique par Marie Goldsmith, Paris, 1903. They are reprinted in I, 161 ff.

61. O. V. Aptekman, '*Obshchestvo* "Zemlya i Volya" *70-kh godov*' (*The society* '*Zemlya i Volya*' *in the seventies*), P., 1924; P. B. Aksel'rod, '*Perezhitoye i peredumannoye*' (*Things seen and reflected*), Berlin, 1923, vol. I, p. 88; N. S. Rusanov, '*Sotsialisty Zapada i Rossii*' (*Western and Russian socialists*), second edition, Spb., 1909, p. 227.

62. N. G. Kulyabko-Koretsky, '*Iz davnikh let*' (*From years gone by*), *op. cit.*, p. 24.

63. I, 287.

64. D. G. Venediktov Bezyuk, '*Pobeg P. L. Lavrova iz ssylki*' (*P. L. Lavrov's escape from exile*), in 'Katorga i ssylka', 1931, no. V. While Negreskul was soon to die in prison, Lavrov's daughter was able to carry on with her political activity for a long time. The socialist group to which Kalinin, the future President of the Supreme Soviet of the USSR, belonged in 1904 had been organized by her. See P. Dorovatovsky, '*K biografii M. I. Kalinina*' (*For a biography of M. I. Kalinin*), in 'Katorga i ssylka', 1933, no. II.

65. The editors of 'Narodnoye delo' sent him at that time the collected numbers of their review, which may have had some influence on determining his political standpoint in the following years. On this point, see I. Knizhnik-Vetrov's introduction to vol. I, 54 ff. Bakunin's letter of 15th July 1870, asking him to join the editorial staff of a review he was planning to bring out, has already been referred to in note 5 of this chapter.

66. For a study of this woman revolutionary, the friend of Dostoevsky, see I. Knizhnik-Vetrov's interesting book, '*A. V. Korvin-Krukovskaya (Zhaklar)*', M., 1931.

67. P. L. Lavrov, '*Parizhskaya Kommuna 18 marta 1871 g.*' (*The Paris Commune of 18th March 1871*), *op. cit.*, p. 68.

68. I, 66.

69. 'L'Internationale', 26th March 1871.

70. *Ibid.*, 2nd April 1871.

71. Letter to Stakenshneyder of 10th October 1871, quoted in I, 71.

72. P. L. Lavrov, '*Parizhskaya Kommuna 18 marta 1871 g.*' (*The Paris Commune of 18th March 1871*), *op. cit.*, p. 31.

73. *Ibid.*, p. 42.

74. *Ibid.*, p. 45.

75. *Ibid.*, p. 76.

76. *Ibid.*, p. 78.

77. *Ibid.*, p. 109.

78. *Ibid.*, p. 118.

79. *Ibid.*, p. 141.

80. *Ibid.*, p. 166.

81. *Ibid.*, p. 211.

82. *Ibid.*, p. 216.

83. Already, on 27th May, Bakunin had written from Locarno: 'In the programme

there is too much said about the necessity for scientific preparation, which is indispensable to revolutionaries. What, are you thinking of setting up a university in exile? A fine thing it would be no doubt, but it is none of our business. Let Colonel Lavrov look after that, I in the meantime will busy myself with the cause of the revolution . . .' Letter given in Zamfir Ralli, '*Iz moikh vospominaniy o M. A. Bakunine*' (*From my recollections of M. A. Bakunin*), *op. cit.* When Bakunin arrived in Zürich, his controversy with Lavrov soon led to a definite break.

84. In 'Minuvshiye gody', 1908, no. I, and reported in V. Bogucharsky, '*Aktivnoye narodnichestvo semidesyatykh godov*' (*Active Populism in the seventies*), M., 1912, p. 120. See J. H. Billington, *Mikhailovsky and Russian Populism*, Oxford, 1958.

85. On the pre-history of 'Vperyod' (which is often uncertain), see the recollections of Z. Ralli just mentioned, and M. P. Sazhin, '*Vospominaniya*' (*Memoirs*), *op. cit.* See, above all, N. G. Kulyabko-Koretsky, '*Iz davnikh let*' (*From years gone by*), *op. cit.*, who discusses in great detail, from a Lavrovist's point of view, the Bakuninist accounts; and also by N. G. Kulyabko-Koretsky, in 'Materialy dlya istorii russkogo sotsial'nogo revolyutsionnogo dvizheniya', 1893, no. V; also P. L. Lavrov, '*Narodniki-propagandisty 1873–1878*' (*Populist-propagandists 1873–1878*), second edition, L., 1925; and finally a letter from Lavrov to G. N. Vyrubov, 30th March 1873, in which he describes his preparations for the publication of 'Vperyod'—this can be found in B. Modzalevsky, E. Kazanovich and V. Karenin, '*Pis'ma Lavrova*' (*Lavrov's letters*), in 'Byloye', 1925, no. II. For Lavrov's connections with the Zürich students and the Populist elements in Russia, see J. M. Meijer, *Knowledge and Revolution. The Russian colony in Zürich (1870–1873). A contribution to the study of Russian Populism*, Assen, 1955.

86. II, 31.

87. II, 67.

88. This letter of 1st January 1874 was published, naturally unsigned, in volume III of 'Vperyod', pp. 146 ff. It is not reprinted in II, 89 ff., where, instead, Lavrov's reply is to be found.

89. They are reprinted in II, 143 ff.

90. Published in eight parts at Geneva from 1888 to 1894.

91. II, 182. Lavrov derived this idea from L. Stein, *Der Sozialismus und Kommunismus des heutigen Frankreichs*, Leipzig, 1842, p. 130.

92. II, 144.

93. II, 320.

94. '*Gosudarstvennyy element v budushchem obshchestve*' (*The statist element in the society of the future*), reprinted in IV, 207 ff.

95. Preface to the Russian translation of *Social services in the society of the future*, by César De Paepe, which was published in 1875 and reprinted in IV, 7 ff.

96. IV, 347.

97. IV, 304–5.

98. IV, 334.

99. IV, 376.

100. '*Russkoy sotsial'no-revolyutsionnoy molodyozhi. Po povodu broshyury "Zadachi revolyutsionnoy propagandy v Rossii*". Redaktora zhurnala 'Vperyod' (*To the social-revolutionary youth of Russia. On the pamphlet 'The task of revolutionary propaganda in Russia'. From the editor of 'Vperyod'*), London, 1874, reprinted in III, 335 ff.

101. On this Paris meeting, see principally N. G. Kulyabko-Koretsky, '*Iz davnikh*

let' (*From years gone by*), *op. cit.*, pp. 200 ff. In the autumn of 1875 'Vperyod' had been criticized particularly severely by S. M. Kravchinsky-Stepnyak in two letters to Lavrov. Extensive extracts from the first one have been published by V. Bogucharsky in '*Aktivnoye narodnichestvo semidesyatykh godov*' (*Active Populism in the seventies*), *op. cit.*, reprinted in 'Byloye', 1912, no. XIV, and the second has been published by B. Nikolaevsky, '*Materialy i dokumenty. Tkachev i Lavrov*' (*Material and documents. Tkachev and Lavrov*), in 'Na chuzhoy storone', 1925, no. X. Amongst other things he said: 'You are terribly wrong in thinking that your review is guiding our revolutionary party. I am not giving you my impressions, but facts which I know very well. Only a completely insignificant number of our young revolutionaries are satisfied with your review. The vast majority are opposed to it. You desire social revolution in the fullest and widest sense of the word, in its most *scientific* sense. You await the moment when the Russian people will be able to rise in the name of a programme of which they are fully aware . . . Thus propaganda is the word written on your banner and on every page of your review. All revolutionary activity is comprised, according to you, of propaganda (and naturally of its work of preparation). In short, for you the panacea of all ills is chatter. You propose nothing else . . . We believe in neither the possibility nor the necessity of the sort of revolution you are waiting for. Never in history has there been an example of a revolution which began clear-headedly, consciously, scientifically . . .' For Lavrov's reactions, see J. M., *Lavrov at the end of 1875*, in 'Bulletin of the International Institute of Social History', Amsterdam, 1952, no. 2, pp. 110 ff.

102. II, 135.
103. This first version, detained in the archives of the censorship, has been published by B. P. Koz'min in 'Zven'ya', 1932, vol. I.
104. '*Komu prinadlezhit budushcheye? Razgovor posledovatel'nykh lyudey*' (*To whom does the future belong? A conversation among logical people*), reprinted in III, 79 ff.
105. III, 124.
106. O. V. Aptekman, '*Obshchestvo "Zemlya i Volya" 70-kh godov*' (*The society of 'Zemlya i Volya' in the seventies*), *op. cit.*, p. 112.
107. N. G. Kulyabko-Koretsky, '*Iz davnikh let*' (*From years gone by*), *op. cit.*, pp. 44, 98, 126.
108. '*Andrey Ivanov. Khitraya mekhanika. Pravdivyy rasskaz, otkuda i kuda idut den'gi*' (*Andrey Ivanov. The astute mechanism. A truthful account of where the money comes from and where it goes to*), M. (in fact Zürich), 1874. It was reprinted in London in various forms and with titles just as characteristic: '*Kto i kak dyoshevo dobyvat' den'gi. Rasskaz byvalogo cheloveka*' (*Who and how to obtain money cheaply. The story of an expert*), Spb. (in fact London), 1876; '*Chudesnaya skazka o semi Semyonakh rodnykh brat'yakh*' (*The amazing story of the seven Simeon brothers*), M. (in fact London), 1876; '*O tom, chto takoye golod i kak sebya predokhranit' ot ego gibel'nykh posledstviy. Soch. F. R. . . . Obshchedostupnoye chteniye*' (*On the nature of hunger and how to guard against its ruinous consequences. The work of F. R. . . . To be read by all*), Spb. (in fact London), 1876.
109. O. V. Aptekman, '*Obshchestvo "Zemlya i Volya" 70-kh godov*' (*The society of 'Zemlya i Volya' in the seventies*), *op. cit.*, p. 113.
110. To be found in '*Kalendar' russkoy revolyutsii*', pod red. V. L. Burtseva (*The calendar of the Russian revolution*, edited by V. L. Burtsev), P., 1917, p. 324.
111. Words reported by P. L. Lavrov, '*Narodniki-propagandisty*' (*Populist-propagandists*), *op. cit.*, pp. 165–6.

112. Plekhanov, who at that time was a Populist, was to say later on that the Lavrovists' propaganda 'was probably more reasonable than ours. The Lavrovists were at least good in this respect, that they did not distort the workers' movement in the West. Under the influence of what they said, the Russian worker was able to be clear in his own mind about the task which awaited him. If, in the programme of the *Northern Union of Russian Workers*, formed in the winter of 1878–9, a strong social-democratic note could be detected, this must be attributed very largely to the influence of the Lavrovists'. '*Russkiy rabochiy v revolyutsionnom dvizhenii*' (*The Russian worker in the revolutionary movement*), G. V. Plekhanov, '*Sochineniya*' (*Works*), M., undated, vol. III, pp. 140–1. N. S. Rusanov is of a similar opinion: 'The Lavrovists were very successful among the workers, who learned in greater detail from them of working-class problems in the West, and the lives, rights and demands of the workers in Europe and America.' '*Iz moikh vospominaniy. Kniga I. Detstvo i yunost' na rodine*' (*From my recollections*). Book I. *Childhood and youth in my native country*), Berlin, 1923, p. 152.

113. From the article on the Russian revolutionary movement by P. B. Aksel'rod, published in 'Jahrbuch für Sozialwissenschaft und Sozialpolitik', year II, 1881.

114. Letter of 23rd February 1903, published in '*Perepiska G. V. Plekhanova i P. B. Aksel'roda*'. Redaktsiya i primechaniya P. A. Berlina, V. S. Voytinskogo i B. I. Nikolaevskogo (*The correspondence of G. V. Plekhanov and P. B. Aksel'rod*. Edited and with notes by P. A. Berlin, V. S. Voytinsky and B. I. Nikolayevsky), M., 1925, vol. II, p. 190. In this letter Plekhanov denied that this mentality could be attributed to all the Lavrovist movement in Russia, as Aksel'rod had maintained in the article mentioned in note 113. See, however, N. S. Rusanov, '*Iz moikh vospominaniy*' (*From my recollections*), *op. cit.*, pp. 15 ff., in which he claims that the Lavrovists, and Ginsburg himself, had thought it would be necessary even in Russia to pass through capitalism, or 'at least some phases of it'.

CHAPTER 18

1. Potapov's report is summarized and quoted in N. Asheshov's article, '*P. A. Kropotkin i russkoye pravitel'stvo v 1875 godu*' (*P. A. Kropotkin and the Russian government in 1875*), in 'Byloye', 1922, no. 17.

2. L. Shishko, '*Sergey Mikhaylovich Kravchinsky i kruzhok chaykovtsev (Iz vospominaniy i zametok starogo narodnika)*' (*S. M. Kravchinsky and the Chaykovskist group [From the recollections and notes of an old Populist]*), Spb., 1906, p. 13. Naturally these words are not to be understood solely in the sense that there was at that time a group of really exceptional people in St Petersburg, though this is true enough. They imply above all that these men were to find in this ethical grounding a more assured basis for their revolutionary activity. This left a profound mark on many of those who took part in the movement, as for example Kropotkin. What he wrote on the Russian revolution in 1918, a little before his death, is a distant but clear echo of the world of his youth at the beginning of the 'seventies: 'Unfortunately'—he wrote— 'despite the wonderful acts of sacrifice of the Russian revolutionaries in the period of preparation, despite the high social ideal that inspired them, we see that now it has ended in the supremacy of a doctrine which has crept into our life these last few years, the doctrine of economic materialism. This doctrine is not understood in the sense in which the Blanquist organization in France understood it when they called themselves communist-materialists. By communism they meant not that of monastic groups, of Paraguayan Jesuits, or

colonies of slaves, but communism *de facto*, which was to give not only comfort to everyone, but also spiritual independence ... That was considered Utopian, and it was replaced by the idea of a social revolution understood in the sense of the unleashing of the individual passions of supermen, either Stirnerians or Nietzschians. In this lack of a higher and more inspiring ideal lies all the difference between the Russian revolution and the ones that preceded it. Only one thing is left, only one hope for life, and that is that the revolution has assumed this character under the pestilential influence of the recent years of absolutism, and that the sane mind of the Russian people may gain the upper hand, saving itself from that evil which threatens to sap the strength from the very revolution and to make it sterile.' P. Kropotkin, '*Ideal i revolyutsiya*' (*Ideal and revolution*), in 'Byloye', 1922, no. 17.

3. B. P. Koz'min, '*S. G. Nechayev i ego protivniki v 1868–1869 gg.*' (*S. G. Nechaev and his opponents in the years 1868–1869*), in '*Revolyutsionnoye dvizhenie 1860-kh godov*'. Sbornik statey pod red. B. I. Goreva i B. P. Koz'mina (*The revolutionary movement of the sixties*. Collection of articles edited by B. I. Gorev and B. P. Koz'min), M., 1932, pp. 168 ff.

4. O. V. Aptekman, '*Obshchestvo "Zemlya i Volya" 70-kh godov*' (*The society 'Zemlya i Volya' in the seventies*), P., 1924, p. 61.

5. S. L. Chudnovsky, '*Iz davnikh let. Vospominaniya*'. Podgotovil k pechati V. S. Alekseyev-Popov. Redaktsiya M. A. Braginskogo (*From the distant past. Recollections*. Text revised by V. S. Alekseyev-Popov, edited by M. A. Braginsky), no place (but M.), undated (but 1934), p. 276.

6. '*Cherez pol-stoletiya*' (*After half a century*), in 'Golos minuvshago na chuzhoy storone', 1926, no. III.

7. Aleksandr Stepanovich Prugavin was arrested and deported at the same time; he was to become a famous student of Russian sectarian movements. He remained exiled in various parts of European Russia for nine years.

8. Chaykovsky has described the rise of this group in a long letter. It was published in '*Cherez pol-stoletiya*' (*After half a century*), op. cit.

9. P. A. Kropotkin, '*Zapiski revolyutsionera*'. Podgotovka teksta k pechati i primechaniya N. K. Lebedeva. Predislovie P. P. Paradizova (*Memoirs of a revolutionary*. Text and notes edited by N. K. Lebedev. Preface by P. P. Paradizov), no place (but L.), 1933, p. 187.

10. '*Nikolay Vasil'evich Chaykovsky. Religioznyye i obshchestvennyye iskaniya*'. Stat'i M. A. Aldanova, E. K. Breshko-Breshkovskoy, Dioneo, B. A. Myakotina, D. M. Odintsa, T. I. Polnera i '*Vospominaniya*' N. V. Chaykovskogo, pod obshch. red. A. A. Titova (*N. V. Chaykovsky. Religious and social researches*. Articles by M. A. Aldanov, E. K. Breshko-Breshkovskaya, Dioneo, B. A. Myakotin, D. M. Odinets, T. I. Polner, and *Recollections* by N. Chaykovsky edited by A. A. Titov), Paris, 1929, p. 55.

11. M. F. Frolenko, '*Malikov i malikovtsy*' (*Malikov and his followers*), in '*Sobranie sochineniy*' (*Works*), M., 1932, vol. I, pp. 208–9.

12. N. A. Charushin, '*O dalyokom proshlom*' (*On the distant past*), M., 1926, vol. I: '*Kruzhok chaykovtsev. Iz vospominaniy o revolyutsionnom dvizhenii 1870-kh godov*' (*The Chaykovskist group. From recollections of the revolutionary movement of the seventies*), p. 94.

13. Collected under the title of '*Zapiski chaykovtsa*' (*Memoirs of a follower of Chaykovsky*), M.-L., 1929, with a preface by I. Glavnen.

14. L. Shishko, '*S. M. Kravchinsky i kruzhok chaykovtsev*' (*S. M. Kravchinsky and the Chaykovsky group*), op. cit., p. 5. His writings are collected in S. M. Stepnyak-Kravchinsky, '*Sobranie sochineniy*.' Red. S. Vengerova (*Works*, edited by S. Vengerov), Spb., 1906–8, in six volumes; reprinted in seven

volumes in P., 1919, and 'Sochineniya v dvukh tomakh' (Works, in two volumes), M., 1958.

15. Ibid., p. 9.
16. See his unfinished autobiography, published in 1910–11 in the 'Russkie vedomosti', and reprinted with an interesting introductory article by I. I. Popov under the title 'Iz proshlogo. Vospominaniya' (From the past. Memoirs), L., 1925. S. M. Levin published a very detailed study on him, with a comprehensive bibliography, 'D. A. Klements. Ocherki revolyutsionnoy deyatel'-nosti' (D. A. Klements. Essays on his revolutionary activity), M., 1929.
17. Klements's own words from his autobiography, op. cit., p. 79.
18. 'N. V. Chaykovsky. Religioznyye i obshchestvennyye iskaniya' (N. V. Chay-kovsky. Religious and social researches), op. cit., p. 54.
19. Ibid., p. 123.
20. S. M. Levin, 'D. A. Klements', op. cit., p. 41.
21. Kropotkin's and Perovskaya's words are given in the pamphlet, 'Pamyati Leonida Emmanuilovicha Shishko' (In memory of L. E. Shishko), no place, 1910, pp. 107 ff.; it consists of a biography of Shishko with documents, and an incomplete bibliography of his works. Later most of these were published in four volumes in M. in 1918, with the title 'Sobranie sochineniy' (Works).
22. Published in Geneva in 1873 and often reprinted in the following years, always under the title 'Chtozh-to, brattsy, kak tyazhko zhivyotsya nashemu bratu na russkoy zemle!'.
23. 'Free Russia, organ of the Society of Friends of Russian Freedom', London, 1891, November.
24. See chapter XV.
25. On the spread of Marx's works, see principally a letter addressed to him by N. F. Daniel'son in St Petersburg, 11th May 1871. In it he spoke of Lopatin and said that Das Kapital 'was in great demand'. Daniel'son was sending him, at Lopatin's suggestion, Chernyshevsky's works on economics. This letter is to be found in 'Perepiska K. Marksa i F. Engel'sa s russkimi politicheskimi deyatelyami' (The correspondence of K. Marx and F. Engels with Russian political figures), no place (but L.), 1947, p. 54.
26. 'Perepiska Petra i Aleksandra Kropotkinykh'. Predislovie I. Smigli. Redaktsiya, primechaniya i vstupitel'naya stat'ya N. K. Lebedeva (The correspondence of Petr and Aleksandr Kropotkin. Preface by I. Smigla. Edited and with notes and an introductory article by N. K. Lebedev), M.-L., 1932–3, two volumes. For Kropotkin, see too George Woodcock and Ivan Avakumovic, The Anarchist Prince, London, 1950.
27. Ibid., vol. I, p. 213.
28. This period of his life is recorded in great detail in 'Dnevnik P. A. Kropotkina'. S predisloviem A. A. Borovogo (Diary of P. A. Kropotkin. With a preface by A. A. Borovoy), M.-L., 1923.
29. P. A. Kropotkin, 'Zapiski revolyutsionera' (Memoirs of a revolutionary), op. cit., p. 117.
30. The list of publications found by the police in his house at the time of his arrest has been printed in 'Dnevnik P. A. Kropotkina' (Diary of P. A. Kropotkin), op. cit., p. 291. It consists mainly of works on the Commune.
31. P. A. Kropotkin, 'Zapiski revolyutsionera' (Memoirs of a revolutionary), op. cit., p. 193.
32. E. Koval'skaya, 'Iz moikh vospominaniy' (From my recollections), in 'Katorga i ssylka', 1926, no. IX, in which she speaks of the initial resistance to the amalgamation of the two groups of men and women.

33. See F. Venturi, *Il moto decabrista e i fratelli Poggio*, Turin, 1956.

34. A. Kornilova-Morozova, '*Perovskaya i kruzhok chaykovtsev*' (*Perovskaya and the Chaykovsky group*), M., 1929.

35. On this period of her life, see O. V. Aptekman, '*Obshchestvo* "Zemlya i Volya" *70-kh godov*' (*The society* 'Zemlya i Volya' *in the seventies*), *op. cit.*, pp. 70 ff. Naturally all the memoirs of the Chaykovskists refer to her.

36. '*Zapiski revolyutsionera*' (*Memoirs of a revolutionary*), *op. cit.*, p. 194.

37. A. Kornilova-Morozova, '*Perovskaya i kruzhok chaykovtsev*' (*Perovskaya and the Chaykovskist group*), *op. cit.* For some modifications of this list, see N. A. Charushin, '*O dalyokom proshlom*' (*On the distant past*), *op. cit.*, vol. II, p. 88.

38. N. V. Chaykovsky, '*Otkrytoye pis'mo k druz'yam*' (*Open letter to my friends*), in 'Golos minuvshego', 1926, no. III.

39. I. E. Deniker, '*Vospominaniya*' (*Recollections*), in 'Katorga i ssylka', 1924, no. IX.

40. N. A. Charushin, '*O dalyokom proshlom*' (*On the distant past*), *op. cit.*, vol. I, p. 88. But it was not always as easy as this to find money. Charushin himself tells how one of the members of the group, whom he does not name, tried at one time to start a scheme for counterfeiting money. Chaykovsky forbade him to do so, as he was utterly opposed to resorting to 'nihilistic' methods, *ibid.*, p. 91.

41. '*Proletariat vo Frantsii. 1789–1852. Istoricheskie ocherki*' (*The proletariat in France. 1789–1852. Historical essays*), Spb., 1869 and 1872. '*Assotsiatsii. Ocherk prakticheskogo primeneniya printsipa kooperatsii v Germanii, v Anglii i vo Frantsii*' (*On Associations. Essay on the practical application of the co-operative principle in Germany, England and France*), Spb., 1873. Although the latter book was obviously intended to be popular, it gives a vast panorama of the working-class movement in the West. It speaks at length of the trade unions, saying: 'This is the peaceful road, which has hardly begun to be followed, but which will probably lead the west European working classes to prosperity, as long as some act of violence does not force them into another open fight for their very existence' (p. 111). 'Certainly'—said Mikhaylov—'even the trade unions can only achieve partial results. Complete emancipation of the proletariat must also be political.' Later he speaks of the cooperatives, the housing problem and so on, giving a great many facts and a large bibliography (which includes even Marx). Despite the title, he also talks a good deal about Russia. On the housing problem, he noted that no one made much attempt to improve conditions for the workers: 'They sleep in factories and workshops, under the machines and even out in the open' (p. 126). On the other hand he noted the first signs of a cooperative movement (pp. 224 ff.).

42. L. B. Gol'denberg, '*Vospominaniya*' (*Recollections*), in 'Katorga i ssylka', 1924, nos. III–V. Despite the excessively self-complacent tone, these memoirs give useful information about this foreign centre of Chaykovskists. After he had started a small press at Geneva, Gol'denberg amalgamated with Lavrov's much larger concern and in 1874 they transferred to London where they both worked on 'Vperyod'. There they reprinted some Chaykovskist pamphlets, and published many more for the first time which had been written by members of the St Petersburg group. Aleksandrov did nothing more after the tragic suicide of Katerina Ivanovna Grebnitskaya. She was the sister of Pisarev, the famous 'nihilist' writer, and she was married to Grebnitsky, although only in name. She worked in the printing press. Aleksandrov persuaded her to sell herself to an old man and give the money to help the press. She obeyed, but finally killed herself in July 1875.

43. 'Istoriya odnogo frantsuzskogo krest'yanina. Kniga siya napisana odnim frantsuzskim krest'yaninom v znak bratskoy lyubvi k russkim krest'yanam' (Story of a French peasant. This book has been written by a French peasant as a sign of his brotherly love for Russian peasants), Geneva, 1873.

44. 'Skazka o kopeyke. Soch. F. . . .' (Tale of a kopeck. Written by F. . . .), Spb. (in fact Geneva), 1874. It is reprinted in S. M. Stepnyak-Kravchinsky, 'Sobranie sochineniy' (Works), op. cit., vol. III, and 'Sochineniya' (Works), op. cit., vol. II.

45. (Geneva), 1873.

46. [L. A. Tikhomirov and P. A. Kropotkin], 'Emel'yan Ivanovich Pugachev, ili bunt 1773 goda' (Emel'yan Ivanovich Pugachev, or the revolt of 1773), M., 1871 (in fact Geneva, 1873).

47. 'Pesennik', (Geneva), 1873.

48. 'Dolzhny li my zanyat'sya izucheniem ideala budushchego?' (Ought we to think about examining the ideals of the future?). It was seized by the police at his arrest and mentioned in the 'trial of the hundred and ninety-three'; later it was published in 'Byloye', 1921, no. 17.

49. M. F. Frolenko, 'Sobranie sochineniy' (Works), op. cit., vol. I, p. 218.

50. S. F. Kovalik, 'Revolyutsionnoye dvizhenie semidesyatykh godov i protsess 193-kh' (The revolutionary movement of the seventies and the trial of the 193), M., 1928. This posthumous publication of his writings includes the Autobiography given in vol. 40 of the Granat Encyclopaedia, the memoirs already published under the pseudonym of 'Starik' in 'Byloye', 1906, nos. X–XII, and an article, 'Revolyutsionery narodniki' (Revolutionary Populists), which had appeared in 'Katorga i ssylka', 1924, no. IV.

51. N. A. Charushin, 'O dalyokom proshlom' (On the distant past), op. cit., pp. 101–2. For this episode, see also I. E. Deniker, 'Vospominaniya' (Recollections), in 'Katorga i ssylka', op. cit.; and I. I. Popov, 'Minuvsheye i perezhitoye. Vospominaniya za 50 let. Sibir' i emigratsiya' (Things past and endured. Recollections of fifty years. Siberia and exile), L., 1924, p. 120, in which the author quotes what Natanson had told him about the subject, when they were both deported to Siberia.

52. Kupryanov was one of the most promising hopes of the Chaykovskist group, but we know little of him, for he died tragically in prison. In 1873 he was one of the most active working-class organizers in St Petersburg. Together with Charushin, he founded a library for workers, and he engineered Tkachev's escape from prison in 1874. He too led a very ascetic life and was one of the most cultured and reflective members of the group. One day, V. K. Debagory-Mokrievich, taking up a Bakuninist theme, spoke to him of the 'revolutionary instinct'. Kupryanov replied that 'he had no faith in temperament, he believed only in a sense of duty' (V. K. Debagory-Mokrievich, 'Vospominaniya' (Recollections), Spb., 1906, p. 89). He was probably the most Marxist of the Chaykovskists. This seems to have been the reason for his backing Lavrov against Bakunin. S. L. Chudnovsky met him at this period in Vienna where Kupryanov had come to buy a printing press on behalf of his comrades in St Petersburg and said: 'I was literally stupefied by his exceptional mental energy. He concerned himself with and read (or rather studied) only the basic works on political economy and social science, he was never remotely interested in literature or art, and when he opened a magazine he only stopped to read the fundamental and most serious articles. When he was seventeen or eighteen he knew (and how he knew) the tremendous œuvre of K. Marx almost by heart. For hours together he would explain to me the various aspects of Marx's theory, impressing me with the extraordinary acuteness of his analysis and by

the powerful logic of his conclusions ...' S. L. Chudnovsky, '*Iz davnikh let*' (*From years gone by*), *op. cit.*, p. 43. He was arrested in 1874, and died before the 'trial of the hundred and ninety-three', after a long illness, in the Peter-Paul fortress on 18th April 1878.

53. P. A. Kropotkin, '*Vospominaniya o P. L. Lavrove*' (*Recollections of P. L. Lavrov*), in '*P. L. Lavrov. Stat'i, vospominaniya, materialy*' (*P. L. Lavrov. Articles, recollections, material*), P., 1922, pp. 436 ff. It makes clear that Klements had been chosen just because 'he occupied an intermediate position between the two tendencies'. The discussion took place in St Petersburg in May 1872. 'The first number of "Vperyod" deeply disappointed us with the exception of very few people ...' The programme of 'Vperyod', which Charushin took to Kiev, also disappointed young Aksel'rod, who was then just beginning his activities. P. B. Aksel'rod, '*Perezhitoye i peredumannoye*' (*Things seen and reflected upon*), Berlin, 1923, vol. I, p. 101.

54. *Granat Encyclopaedia*, vol. 40, under Charushin.

55. Given in O. V. Aptekman, '*Vasiliy Vasil'evich Bervi-Flerovsky po materialam b. III Otdeleniya i D.G.P.*' (*V. V. Bervi-Flerovsky from the documents of the ex-Third Section and the Department of State Police*), L., 1925, pp. 29–30. This study is the best source for the life of Bervi, together with his own autobiographical writings, published in 'Golos minuvshego', 1915 and 1916, and collected in V. Bervi-Flerovsky, '*Zapiski revolyutsionera mechtatelya*' (*Recollections of a revolutionary dreamer*), M.-L., 1929. There is not much of interest in '*Ekonomicheskiye vozzreniya V. V. Bervi-Flerovskogo*', [M.], 1952.

56. '*Polozhenie rabochego klassa v Rossii*'. Nablyudeniya i issledovaniya N. Flerovskogo (*The situation of the working class in Russia.* Observations and researches by N. Flerovsky), Spb., 1869. The publisher was N. P. Polyakov, who also published Marx's *Das Kapital* and several other socialist works. In 1872 there was another edition of this book, revised and augmented with new material. It was, however, stopped by the censor. The quotations which follow refer to the 1869 edition. See L. Dobrovol'sky, '*Zapreshchyonnyye i unichtozhennyye knigi V. V. Bervi-Flerovskogo*' (*Books by V. V. Bervi-Flerovsky which were forbidden and destroyed*), in 'Literaturnoye nasledstvo', M., 1933, nos. VII–VIII, and V. V. Bervi-Flerovsky, '*Izbrannyye ekonomicheskiye proizvedeniya*' v dvukh tomakh s predisloviem G. Podorova (*Selected works on economics* in two volumes, with an introduction by G. Podorov), M., 1958.

57. '*Polozhenie rabochego klassa v Rossii*', *op. cit.*, p. 108.

58. 'We should remember that two paths open in front of us: one could lead us to the forefront of civilization, the other holds out the same fate as India, China, Spain', *ibid.*, p. 120.

59. *Ibid.*, p. 12.

60. *Ibid.*, p. 225.

61. *Ibid.*, p. 248.

62. *Ibid.*, pp. 452 ff.

63. *Ibid.*, p. 126.

64. *Ibid.*, p. 357.

65. On 24th March 1870 Marx wrote to the Committee of the Russian section of the International: 'Some months ago I was sent Flerovsky's book from St Petersburg. It is a real discovery for Europe. In it the "Russian optimism", which is spread over the continent even by so-called revolutionaries (i.e. Bakuninists), is pitilessly unmasked. The worth of the book will not suffer if I add that some passages do not altogether stand up to criticism from a strictly theoretical point of view. It is the book of a serious observer, a dispassionate scholar, a critic without prejudices, a powerful artist and above all a man

enraged by every form of oppression, incapable of backing national anthems of any kind and one who shares deeply in all the sufferings and all the aspirations of the productive-classes.' The book had been sent to him on 30th September 1869 by N. F. Daniel'son. Through Daniel'son, Flerovsky himself wrote to Marx sometime later, in 1871, and spoke to him of his work. See '*Perepiska K. Marksa i F. Engel'sa s russkimi politicheskimi deyatelyami*', pp. 28 and 53. Cf. Jenny Longuet (Marx's daughter) to Kugelmann, in G. Del Bo, '*Nuova luce sulla vita di Marx da un carteggio inedito della moglie e della figlia Jenny*', in 'Movimento operaio', no. 2, 1955.

66. O. V. Aptekman, '*Vasiliy Vasil'evich Bervi-Flerovsky*', op. cit., p. 55.

67. '*Azbuka sotsial'nykh nauk v tryokh chastyakh*' (*Alphabet of the social sciences in three parts*), Spb., 1871. In fact only two parts came out.

68. O. V. Aptekman, '*Vasiliy Vasil'evich Bervi-Flerovsky*', op. cit., p. 61.

69. '*Issledovaniya po tekushchim voprosam*' (*Researches on the problems of the day*), Spb., 1872. It consisted of a collection of studies on *The philosophic basis of the right to collect taxes, Our press and the Nechaev trial, The school and the intellectual movement: their significance and present situation.*

70. O. V. Aptekman, '*Vasiliy Vasil'evich Bervi-Flerovsky*', op. cit., p. 112. See E. Breshkovskaya, '*Ippolit Myshkin i arkhangel'skiy kruzhok*' (*I. Myshkin and the Archangel group*), no place, 1904, p. 9.

71. N. Flerovsky, '*Azbuka sotsial'nykh nauk*' (*Alphabet of the social sciences*), vol. I; '*Greko-rimskaya tsivilizatsiya*' (*Graeco-Roman civilization*), vol. II; '*XVII i XVIII veka sovremennoy zapadnoy evropeyskoy tsivilizatsii*' (*Civilization in the 17th and 18th centuries in western Europe*), vol. III; '*XIX vek sovremennoy zapadnoy evropeyskoy tsivilizatsii*' (*Nineteenth-century civilization in western Europe*), London, 1894. In England he also wrote '*Tri politicheskiye sistemy*' (*Three political systems*), London, 1897; and even a novel, '*Na zhizn' i smert'. Izobrazhenie idealistov*' (*For life and for death. Portrait of idealists*), London, 1898. None of these works contains anything of much interest about the 'seventies. Nevertheless there are many traces of the spiritual and cultural atmosphere of that period, principally in *Three political systems* which contains a great deal of autobiographical material.

72. A. A. Kunkl', '*Dolgushintsy*', s vstupitel'noy stat'yoy B. P. Koz'mina (*The Dolgushin group*, with an introductory article by B. P. Koz'min), M., 1931.

73. L. E. Shishko, '*K kharakteristike dvizheniya nachala 70-kh godov*' (*For a characterization of the movement of the early seventies*), in '*Sobranie sochineniy*' (*Works*), op. cit., vol. IV, p. 202.

74. As well as *Das Kapital*, which Dolgushin often referred to when talking, they also knew Marx's *Manifesto* in a lithoprinted Russian translation. For Marx's connections with the Russian movement of these years, see A. L Reuel', '*Russkaya ekonomicheskaya mysl' 60–70-kh godov XIX veka i marksizm*' (*Russian economic thought in the 1860's and 1870's and Marxism*), M., 1956.

75. I. Teodorovich, '*Chem zhe nakonets byli Dolgushintsy*' (*Who were, in fact, the Dolgushinists?*), in 'Katorga i ssylka', 1933, no. II. In discussion with B. P. Koz'min, the author underlines Dolgushin's debt to Nechaev and the *political democratic* character of his group. Nevertheless he does not take enough account of the influence exerted on him by Flerovsky.

76. L. E. Shishko, '*K kharakteristike dvizheniya nachala 70-kh godov*' (*For a characterization of the movement of the early seventies*), op. cit., p. 202.

77. N. Flerovsky, '*Tri politicheskiye sistemy*' (*Three political systems*), op. cit., p. 305.

78. A first version was published in Switzerland by Dmokhovsky—who had gone there for that purpose—with the title, '*O muchenike Nikolaye i kak dolzhen*

zhit' chelovek po zakonu prirody i pravdy' (*On the martyr Nicholas and how one must live according to the laws of nature and of truth*); a second version, the one printed by Dolgushin's clandestine press, is given in A. A. Kunkl', '*Dolgushintsy*' (*The Dolgushin group*), *op. cit.*, pp. 205 ff.

79. Dolgushin's appeal is to be found in A. A. Kunkl', '*Dolgushintsy*' (*The Dolgushin group*), p. 212.

80. '*Zazhivo pogrebyonnyye. K russkomu obshchestvu ot politicheskikh katorzhnikov*' (*Buried alive. From the political prisoners to the society of Russia*), Spb., 1878. Reprinted L., 1921.

81. See the article devoted to him in '*Gallereya shlissel'burgskikh uznikov*', pod red. N. F. Annenskogo, V. Ya. Bogucharskogo, V. I. Semevskogo i P. F. Yakubovicha (*A gallery of the Shlisselburg prisoners.* Edited by N. F. Annensky, V. Ya. Bogucharsky, V. I. Semevsky and P. F. Yakubovich), Spb., 1907, vol. I, pp. 72 ff.

82. Few other episodes of Populism have attracted so many anecdotes and memoirs as this. Apart from books referred to above, see A. I. Ivanchin-Pisarev, '*Iz vospominaniy o "khozhdenii v narod"*' (*From recollections of the movement* 'to go to the people'), Spb., 1914, reprinted M. in 1929; T. A. Bogdanovich, '*Khozhdenie v narod*' (*The movement* 'to go to the people'), P., 1917 (a short pamphlet); '*Khozhdenie v narod*', pod red. F. Raskol'nikova (*The movement* 'to go to the people', edited by F. Raskol'nikov), M.-L., 1926, a pamphlet which assembles a series of recollections.

83. Krylov's obituary in 'Vperyod', no. 43, 1876.

84. On Klements's travels at this period, see Sh. M. Levin, '*D. A. Klements*', *op. cit.*, particularly pp. 34 ff., which gives a very interesting letter, written in 1874. This is an account of his journey which characteristically alternates between observations on the social system, brief ethnographic notes and comments on what ground is best suited to propaganda. Together with more or less open expressions of joy at being able to wander around at liberty, these are the themes which are constantly repeated in other documents of the movement 'to go to the people'.

85. This was repeated at the 'trial of the hundred and ninety-three'. See B. Bazilevsky, '*Gosudarstvennyye prestupleniya v Rossii v XIX veke*' (*State crimes in Russia in the nineteenth century*), Spb., 1906, vol. III, p. 154.

86. S. M. Stepnyak-Kravchinsky, '*Podpol'naya Rossiya*' (*Underground Russia*), in '*Sochineniya*' (*Works*), *op. cit.*, vol. I, p. 380.

87. O. V. Aptekman, '*Obshchestvo "Zemlya i Volya" 70-kh godov*' (*The society* '*Zemlya i Volya*' *in the seventies*), *op. cit.*, p. 168.

88. *Ibid.*, pp. 132–3.

89. P. L. Lavrov, '*Narodniki-propagandisty*' (*Populist-propagandists*), 1925, p. 174.

90. In this connection, the notes of A. O. Lukashevich are particularly interesting. They were written in 1877 and published by V. Nevsky, '*K istorii khozhdeniya v narod*' (*For a history of the movement* 'to go to the people'), in 'Krasnyy arkhiv', 1928, no. II.

91. O. V. Aptekman, '*Obshchestvo "Zemlya i Volya" 70-kh godov*' (*The society* '*Zemlya i Volya*' *in the seventies*), *op. cit.*, note 172.

92. N. Morozov, '*Povesti moyey zhizni*'. Red., vstupitel'naya stat'ya i primechaniya I. A. Teodorovicha (*Stories from my life.* Edited and with introductory article and notes by I. A. Teodorovich), M., 1933, vol. I, pp. 276 ff.

93. '*Zapiska ministra yustitsii grafa Palena. Uspekh revolyutsionnoy propagandy v Rossii*'. Izdanie gazety 'Rabotnik' (*Memoir of the Minister of Justice, Count Pahlen. The successes of revolutionary propaganda in Russia.* Published by the journal 'The Worker'), Geneva, 1875, pp. 17 ff.

CHAPTER 19

1. On the period before the emancipation of the serfs, the basic work is '*Biblio-grafiya po istorii proletariata v epokhu tsarizma. Feodal'no-krepostnoy period*'. Pod red. M. V. Nechkinoy. Bibliograficheskaya redaktsiya A. A. Borovskogo, M.-L., 1935: Vyp. I, '*Knizhnaya literatura*'; Vyp. II, '*Zhurnal'naya literatura A–Z*' (as far as we know these were the only numbers to appear) (*Bibliography of the history of the proletariat under Tsarism. The feudal-serf period*. Edited by M. V. Nechkina, bibliographical editor A. A. Borovsky, M.-L., 1935: pt. I, *Books*; pt. II, *Articles A–Z*) is important for this period and for the following ten years; so is the '*Bibliograficheskiy ukazatel' po istorii fabrik i zavodov*' (*Bibliographical guide to the history of factories and workshops*), M., 1932. On the events of 1861: M. Nechkina, '*Rabochiye volneniya v svyazi s reformoy 1861 g.*' (*Working-class agitations connected with the reform of 1861*), in '*Istoriya proletariata SSSR*', pod red. P. O. Gorina, E. P. Krivoshenskoy i dr. (*History of the proletariat in the USSR*, edited by P. O. Gorin, E. P. Krivoshenskaya and others), M., 1930, no. I, pp. 90 ff. On the 'sixties the fol-lowing works are still important, despite the publication of many collections of documents since: M. Balabanov, '*Ocherki po istorii rabochego klassa v Rossii*' (*Essay on the history of the working class in Russia*), 3 vols., Kiev, 1923, M., 1926; and B. P. Koz'min, '*Rabocheye dvizhenie v Rossii do revolyutsii 1905 g.*' (*The working-class movement in Russia before the 1905 revolution*), M., 1925; also Yu. Gessen, '*Istoriya gornorabochikh v SSSR*'; tom I: '*Istoriya gornorabochikh do 60-kh godov XIX v.*', M., 1926; tom II: '*Vtoraya polovina XIX veka*', M., 1929 (*History of the miners in the USSR*; vol. I: *History of the miners before the sixties of the nineteenth century*, M., 1926; vol. II: *Second half of the nineteenth century*, M., 1929); and A. El'nitsky, '*Rabocheye dvizhenie v Rossii*' (*The working-class movement in Russia*), Kharkov, 1925; '*Rabocheye dvizhenie v Rossii v XIX veke*'. Sbornik dokumentov i materialov. Pod redaktsiey A. M. Pankatovoy, (*The labour movement in Russia in the 19th century*. Collection of documents and material. Edited by A. M. Pankratova), vol. II, part I (1861–74); and part II (1875–84), M., 1950. On the general history of Russian industry, see the classic work by M. I. Tugan-Baranovsky, '*Russkaya fabrika v proshlom i nastoyashchem*' (*The Russian factory—past and present*), seventh edition, M., 1938; A. M. Pankratova, '*Propaganda idey sotsializma sredi rabochikh Rossii v 70-80-kh godakh XIX v.*' (*Socialist propa-ganda among the Russian working-class in the 1870's and 80's*), in '*Iz istorii sotsial'no-politicheskikh idey. Sbornik statey k 75-letiyu akademika Vyacheslava Petrovicha Volgina*' (*From the history of social and political ideas. Miscellany in honour of the 75th birthday of Academician V. P. Volgin*), M., 1955, pp. 702 ff. Cf. also Roger Portal, *La Russie industrielle à la veille de l'emancipation des serfs*, in 'Etudes d'histoire moderne et contemporaine', Paris, 1953, vol. 5, p. 147; and *Das Problem einer industriellen Revolution in Russland im 19. Jahrhundert*, in 'Forschungen zur Osteuropäischen Geschichte', Band I, Berlin, 1954, pp. 205 ff.

2. A. G. Rashin, '*Formirovanie promyshlennogo proletariata v Rossii. Statistiko-ekonomicheskiye ocherki*' (*The formation of the industrial proletariat in Russia. Statistical-economic essays*), M., 1940, pp. 93 ff.

3. N. P. Shakhanov, '*Pervaya stachka rabochikh v Orekhovo-Zuyeve*' (*The first workers' strike at Orekhovo-Zuyevo*), in 'Katorga i ssylka', 1929, no. X, which prints many official documents. These show, among other things, that this strike took place in 1863 and not in 1865, as is often said. On the development

of the movement in that area, see a work by the same author, '*Ocherki po istorii rabochego dvizheniya v Vladimirskoy gubernii v 70-kh godakh proshlogo stoletiya*' (*Essays on the history of the working-class movement in the department of Vladimir in the seventies of the last century*), Vladimir, 1929.

4. Report quoted by B. P. Koz'min, '*Rabocheye dvizhenie v Rossii do revolyutsii 1905 g.*' (*The working-class movement in Russia before the revolution of 1905*), *op. cit.*, p. 35.

5. The quotation from the 'Otechestvennye zapiski' is taken from N. Baturin, '*Ocherki iz istorii rabochego dvizheniya 70-kh i 80-kh godov*' (*Essays on the history of the working-class movement of the seventies and eighties*), second edition, corrected, 1925. Though this is a pamphlet, it is written by an authority on the Russian working-class movement. See also his '*Sochineniya*' (*Works*), M.-L., 1930. The basic studies of the working-class movement of the 'seventies as a whole are those by V. I. Nevsky, '*K voprosu o rabochem dvizhenii v 70-e gody*' (*On the problem of the working-class movement in the seventies*), in 'Istorik-marksist', 1927, no. IV; Yu. Gessen, '*K istorii stachek sredi fabrichnykh rabochikh v nachale 70-kh godov XIX veka*' (*For a history of the strikes of the factory workers at the beginning of the seventies*), in 'Arkhiv istorii truda v Rossii', 1922, no. III; E. A. Korol'chuk, '*Rabochee dvizhenie semidesyatykh godov. Sbornik arkhivnykh dokumentov*' (*The working-class movement of the seventies. Collection of archive documents*), M., 1934; and E. A. Korol'chuk and E. Sokolova, '*Khronika revolyutsionnogo rabochego dvizheniya v Peterburge*', tom I (1870–1904 g.) (*Chronicle of the revolutionary working-class movement in St Petersburg*, vol. I (1870–1904)), L., 1940 (the second volume has never been published); and A. M. Pankatova, *op. cit.*, vol. II, part I, pp. 35, 45.

6. E. A. Korol'chuk, '*Rabocheye dvizhenie semidesyatykh godov*' (*The working-class movement of the seventies*), *op. cit.*, Introduction, p. 18.

7. K. A. Pazhitnov, '*Polozhenie rabochego klassa v Rossii*'; tom I: '*Period krepostnogo truda*' (*The situation of the working-class in Russia;* vol. I: *Period of serf labour*), second edition, L., 1925, pp. 297 ff.

8. '*K voprosu o rabochem dvizhenii v 70-e gody*' (*On the problem of the working-class movement of the seventies*), *op. cit.*

9. For a list, see V. I. Mezhov, '*Bibliograficheskiy ukazatel' knig i statey otnosyashchikhsya do obshchestv osnovannykh na nachalakh vzaimnosti, arteley, polozheniya rabochego sosloviya i melkoy kustarnoy promyshlennosti v Rossii*' (*Bibliographical guide to books and articles on societies founded on the principles of mutual association, artels, the situation of the working-class and small artisan industries in Russia*), Spb., 1873. Typical examples of such literature are: M. L., '*Arteli rabochikh dlya osnovaniya fabrik ili masterskikh*' (*Workers' associations for the creation of factories and workshops*), Spb., 1862, and second edition, Kiev, 1870. (This pamphlet was often circulated among Populist groups along with the clandestine press); and P. S-ky., '*Istoricheskiy ocherk kooperativnykh uchrezhdeniy v Rossii*' (*Historical essay on cooperative institutions in Russia*), in 'Otechestvennye zapiski', 1871, nos. 11, 12.

10. On this, one of the most interesting aspects of the activity of the Chaykovskists, see the article by Sh. M. Levin, '*Kruzhok chaykovtsev i propaganda sredi peterburgskikh rabochikh v nachale 1870-kh godov*' (*The Chaykovskist group and propaganda among the workers of St Petersburg at the beginning of the seventies*), in 'Katorga i ssylka', 1929, no. XII. There are also the memoirs of Charushin, Sinegub, Kropotkin, etc., already quoted.

11. P. L. Lavrov, '*Narodniki-propagandisty*' (*Populist-propagandists*), L., 1925, p. 191.

12. 'Byloye', 1921, no. XVII.

13. L. Shishko, '*S. M. Kravchinsky i kruzhok chaykovtsev* (*Iz vospominaniy i zametok starogo narodnika*)' (*S. M. Kravchinsky and the Chaykovskist group* [*From recollections and notes of an old Populist*]), Spb., 1906, p. 28.

14. P. A. Kropotkin, '*Zapiski revolyutsionera*'. Podgotovka teksta k pechati i primechaniya N. K. Lebedeva, predislovie P. P. Paradizova (*Recollections of a revolutionary*. Text and notes edited by N. K. Lebedev. Preface by P. P. Paradizov), no place (but L.), 1933, p. 199.

15. L. Shishko, '*S. M. Kravchinsky i kruzhok chaykovtsev*' (*S. M. Kravchinsky and the Chaykovskist group*), op. cit., p. 153.

16. Letter to Lev Tikhomirov of 1896, published in 'Katorga i ssylka', 1925, no. IV, p. 84.

17. 'Obshchina', 1877, nos. 6–7.

18. The attitude taken up by I. A. Bachin and his tragic fate provide an interesting example of this state of mind. He was one of the most active among the factory workers at that time, and was employed in an armaments factory. He is reported to have said: 'You must take books from the students, but when they begin to teach you nonsense, you must knock them down.' Arrested in September 1874—i.e. later than his companions—he was in prison until 1876. When he came out he said to Plekhanov that 'he was ready, as before, to work for revolutionary propaganda, but among the workers'. 'I don't want to go into the country on any account. The peasants are sheep, they will never understand revolutionaries.' And he went back to work, not only in St Petersburg, but also in the cities of southern Russia. He was one of the organizers of the Northern Union. For reasons which are not very clear, he somehow ended up in Siberia in 1880 and 1881. There he was faced in his private life with the problem that had always occupied him—his relationship with the intelligentsia. In exile he married Elizaveta Nikolaevna Yuzhakova, a revolutionary who had been a student at the University of Zurich. Life with this typical representative of the revolutionary intelligentsia proved to be impossible; he killed her, and committed suicide soon afterwards at the beginning of 1883. See G. Golosov, '*K biografii odnogo iz osnovateley* "*Severo-russkogo rabochego soyuza*"' (*For biography of one of the founders of the 'Northern Union of Russian Workers'*), in 'Katorga i ssylka', 1924, no. VI.

19. M. F. Frolenko, '*Sobranie sochineniy*' (*Works*), M., 1932, vol. I, p. 200.

20. From Sh. M. Levin, '*Kruzhok chaykovtsev i propaganda sredi peterburgskikh rabochikh v nachale 1870-kh godov*' (*The Chaykovskist group and propaganda among the workers of St Petersburg at the beginning of the seventies*), op. cit.

21. '*Yuzhno-Rossiyskiy Soyuz Rabochikh*'. Sbornik statey i materialov pod red. N. M. Osipovicha (*The Union of Workers of South Russia*. Collection of articles and material, edited by N. M. Osipovich), Nikolaev, 1924. Some of the articles in this miscellany have been reprinted, together with others in '*Yuzhno-russkiye rabochiye soyuzy*'. Sbornik statey pod red. i s vstupitel'noy stat'yoy M. Ravicha-Cherkasskogo (*The workers' unions of South Russia*. Collection of articles with an introductory article by M. Ravich-Cherkassky), Kharkov, 1925; V. Dembo, '*Pervaya massovaya organizatsiya rabochikh v Rossii. K 50-letiyu* "*Yuzhno-rossiyskogo soyuza rabochikh*" (*1874–1875*)'. S predisloviem R. Yakubova (*The first mass workers' organization in Russia. On the fiftieth anniversary of the 'Union of Workers of South Russia'*. With a preface by R. Yakubov), M., 1925; '*Yuzhno-russkiye rabochiye soyuzy*'. Sbornik materialov i statey pod red. V. V. Maksakova i V. I. Nevskogo. S vstupitel'noy stat'yey V. I. Nevskogo (*The workers' unions of South Russia*. Collection of material and articles edited by V. V. Maksakov and V. I. Nevsky. With an introductory article by V. I. Nevsky), M., 1924

(particularly the article beginning on p. 35: V. K-ov, '*Yuzhno-rossiyskiy rabochiy soyuz*' (*The Union of Workers of South Russia*), which prints the Union's statutes (p. 101); B. Itenberg, ' " *Yuzhnorossiyskiy soyuz rabochikh*"—*pervaya proletarskaya organizatsiya v Rossii*' (*The Union of Workers of South Russia—first proletarian organization in Russia*), M., 1954; Yu. Bocharov, '*E. O. Zaslavsky, osnovatel' " Yuzhno-rossiyskogo soyuza rabochikh*" ' (*E. O. Zaslavsky, founder of the 'Union of Workers of South Russia*'), M., 1926. The trial was not published in the official journal, but the case for the prosecution can be found in 'Vperyod', no. V; it is reprinted in '*Gosudarstven-nyye prestupleniya v Rossii v XIX veke*'. Sbornik sostavlen pod red. V. Bazilevskogo (V. Bogucharskogo) (*State crimes in Russia in the nineteenth century*. Collection edited by B. Bazilevsky [V. Bogucharsky]), Rostov on Don, undated, vol. II, pp. 334 ff. Other details can be found in a pamphlet by a member of this movement, an 'Italian subject' as he himself says, though he was born at Odessa, the son of an Italian who emigrated to Russia in the 'forties and was employed there in the Gullier-Blanchard factory: Mikhail Petrovich Skveri, '*Pervaya rabochaya sotsialisticheskaya organizatsiya v Odesse*' (*The first socialist workers' union at Odessa, 1875*), Odessa, 1921. See an article on him by P. Vladychenko, '*M. P. Skveri*', in 'Katorga i ssylka', 1925, no. I.

22. The letter from Odessa in number 20 is by him. See B. Itenberg, '*Dey-atel'nost' " Yuzhno-rossiyskogo soyuza rabochikh*" ' (*The activity of the 'Union of Workers of South Russia*'), in 'Voprosy istorii', 1951, no. I. He speaks of a strike in February 1875. See J. M., *Lavrov at the end of 1875, op. cit.*, for a letter from Lavrov to N. G. Kulyabko-Koretsky in October/November 1875 which throws light on his relations with the Union and the importance he attributed to the working-class groups in Odessa.

23. See J. M. Meijer, *Knowledge and Revolution. The Russian colony in Zürich (1870–1873). A contribution to the study of Russian Populism*, Assen, 1955; see index, *s.v.* Juzhakova.

24. P. B. Aksel'rod, '*Perezhitoye i peredumannoye*' (*Things seen and reflected upon*), Berlin, 1923, vol. I, p. 327.

25. *Ibid.*, p. 330.

26. *Ibid.*, p. 331.

27. K. Koval'skaya, in '*O proiskhozhdenii " Yuzhno-russkikh rabochikh soyuzov*" ' (*On the origin of the 'Workers' Unions of South Russia*'), in 'Katorga i ssylka', 1926, no. IV, has denied that Aksel'rod's movement extended to Odessa and in general has stressed the weakness of this organization.

28. M. R. Popov, '*Nikolai Pavlovich Shchedrin*', in 'Byloye', 1906, no. XII, an article included in his '*Zapiski zemlevol'tsa*', pod red. I. Teodorovicha (*The memoirs of a member of* 'Zemlya i Volya', edited by I. Teodorovich), M., 1923, pp. 333 ff.

29. E. N. Koval'skaya (Solntseva), '*Yuzhno-russkiy rabochiy soyuz*' ('*The Union of Workers of South Russia*'), in '*Yuzhno-russkiye rabochiye soyuzy*'. Sbornik materialov i statey ('*The workers' unions of South Russia*'. Collection of material and articles), *op. cit.*, pp. 179 ff.

30. These ideas led to conflict between the organizers of the *Union* and the members of the *Narodnaya Volya* of Kiev. The latter thought that the scarcely conspiratorial methods adopted by the leaders of the *Union* would lead to the downfall of their own centres which included workers. And they added that 'economic terrorism' would prevent the liberals from giving the support and money for which they had hoped. Zhelyabov 'thought local disturbances and "economic terror" positively harmful'. On his negative attitude towards the

26+

Union, see P. B. Aksel'rod, '*Perezhitoye i peredumannoye*' (*Things seen and and reflected upon*), Berlin, 1923, vol. I, p. 361.

31. These were Georgy Nikolaevich Preobrazhensky, once an active participant in the workers' movement of 'Zemlya i Volya' in St Petersburg, Sofiya Nikolaevna Bogomolets (born Prisetskaya), her sister Ol'ga, Ivan Nikolaevich Kashintsev and Pavel Ivanov.

32. R. M. Kantor, '*Razgrom " Yuzhno-russkogo rabochego soyuza", 1880–1881*' (*The fall of the 'Union of Workers of South Russia', 1880–1881*), in '*Krasnyy arkhiv*', 1928, no. V.

33. M. R. Popov, '*Zapiski zemlevol'tsa*' (*Memoirs of a member of* 'Zemlya i Volya'), *op. cit.*, p. 335.

34. The fundamental document on this organization is the official account of the trial of its members in 1877. It is known as 'the trial of the fifty', from the number of those involved. It was first published in 'Pravitel'stvennyy Vestnik', and reprinted in V. Bogucharsky, '*Gosudarstvennyye prestupleniya v Rossii v XIX veke*' (*State crimes in Russia in the nineteenth century*), *op. cit.*, vol. II, pp. 128 ff. Only one of the members of this organization has left us any memoirs, but they are very detailed and interesting: I. S. Dzhabadari, '*Protsess pyatidesyati* (*Vserossiyskaya sotsial'no-revolyutsionnaya organizatsiya*)' (*The trial of the fifty* [*The Pan-Russian Social-Revolutionary Organization*]), in 'Byloye', 1907, nos. VIII, IX, X. Cf. the chapter devoted to this movement by Sh. M. Levin, in '*Istoriya Moskvy v shesti tomakh*' (*History of Moscow in 6 vols.*), M., 1954, vol. IV, pp. 355 ff.

35. V. Figner, '*Studencheskiye gody (1872–1876)*' (*Student years (1872–1876)*), M., 1924.

36. *Ibid.*, pp. 85–6.

37. *Ibid.*, pp. 97–8.

38. These regulations were produced at 'the trial of the fifty'. They are given in V. Bogucharsky, '*Gosudarstvennyye prestupleniya v Rossii v XIX veke*' (*State crimes in Russia in the nineteenth century*), *op. cit.*, vol. II, p. 155.

39. P. B. Aksel'rod, '*Perezhitoye i peredumannoye*' (*Things seen and reflected upon*), Berlin, 1923, vol. I, p. 140. Two years later Ralli said: 'Le journal ouvrier le "Rabotnik" (Le Travailleur) a publié dans l'espace de deux ans 127,000 feuilles imprimés': Z. Ralli, *Le socialisme en Russie*, in *La Commune. Almanach socialiste pour 1877*, Geneva, 1877.

40. '*Sytyye i golodnyye*', izd. gazety '*Rabotnika*' (*The sated and the hungry*, published by the 'Rabotnik'), Geneva, 1875.

41. *Ibid.*, p. 10.

42. *Ibid.*, p. 415.

43. 'Rabotnik' sprang not only from a meeting between the group of Caucasians and women students of Zürich and the 'young Bakuninists' of Geneva, but also from an agreement—of which very little is known—with those Chaykovsk-ists still at liberty in St Petersburg after the arrests. On its origin, see N. Morozov, '*Povesti moyey zhizni*'. Redaktsiya, vstupitel'naya stat'ya i prime-chaniya I. A. Teodorovicha (*Stories from my life*. Edited and with an introductory article and notes by I. Teodorovich), M., 1933, vol. II, pp. 149 ff., although this is mainly of value for its anecdotes. Morozov was a Chaykovskist sent to Geneva to help in the editing of this working-class paper. It has been reprinted: '*Gazeta "Rabotnik", 1875–1876*' (*The journal* 'Rabotnik', *1875–1876*), M., 1933.

44. '*Kak zhivyotsya kochegaram na chyornomorskikh parokhodakh*' (*How the stokers live on the boats in the Black Sea*).

45. "Rabotnik": '*Stachki*' (*Strikes*), no. 4.

46. *Ibid.*, no. 7.
47. *Ibid.*, no. 10.
48. *Obshchina*, 1878, nos. 8–9.
49. Quoted in V. Bogucharsky, '*Aktivnoye narodnichestvo 70-kh godov*' (*Active Populism in the seventies*), M., 1912, p. 226; and for the living conditions in a Moscow factory at this time and its evidence of a spontaneous working-class movement, cf. K. S. Vasilenko, in '*Istoriya Moskvy*' (*History of Moscow*), *op. cit.*, vol. IV, M., 1954, pp. 397 ff.
50. Letter produced at the trial, given in V. Bogucharsky, '*Gosudarstvennyye prestupleniya v Rossii*' (*State crimes in Russia*), *op. cit.*, vol. II, p. 204. On these events, see a long and interesting correspondence in 'Rabotnik', no. 8. See also E. Korol'chuk, '*Pis'ma G. F. Zhdanovicha*' (*G. F. Zhdanovich's letters*), in 'Krasnyy arkhiv', 1927, no. I.
51. V. Bogucharsky, '*Gosudarstvennyye prestupleniya v Rossii*' (*State crimes in Russia*), *op. cit.*, vol. II, p. 331.
52. M. M. Klevensky, '*Pis'mo rabochego P. A. Alekseyev*' (*Letter from the worker P. A. Alekseyev*), in 'Katorga i ssylka', 1931, no. I. In 1890 Plekhanov reprinted his speech with a preface in which he somewhat artificially tried to make Alekseyev out as the first champion of working-class policies which conflicted with those of the intelligentsia. The preface is reprinted in G. V. Plekhanov, '*Sochineniya*', pod red. D. B. Ryazanova (*Works*, edited by D. Ryazanov), M., undated, vol. III, pp. 112 ff. For the controversy which this preface aroused among German social-democratic journals, see Ryazanov's preface to this volume. Alekseyev's speech has often been reprinted and republished as a pamphlet. There are some new documents in S. Piontkovsky, '*K biografii Petra Alekseyevicha Alekseyeva*' (*For a biography of P. A. Alekseyev*), in 'Proletarskaya revolyutsiya', 1924, nos. VIII–IX. The two following works are essentially popular: M. Mishev, '*Stepan Khalturin i Pyotr Alekseyev*' (*S. Khalturin and P. Alekseyev*), M.-L., 1928; and N. Tsvilyanev, '*Revolyutsionnyy rabochiy P. Alekseyev*' (*The worker-revolutionary P. Alekseyev*), M., 1928; N. S. Karzhansky, '*Moskovskiy tkach Pyotr Alekseyev*' (*The Moscow textile worker Peter Alekseyev*), M., 1954, is also useful. The most interesting and comprehensive articles about him are still those by Yu. Steklov, '*Russkiy tkach P. A. Alekseyev, 1849–1891*' (*The Russian textile worker P. A. Alekseyev, 1849–1891*), in '*Bortsy za sotsializm*' (*Fighters for socialism*), M., 1911; E. K. Pekarsky, '*Rabochiy Pyotr Alekseyev*' (*The worker P. Alekseyev*), in 'Byloye', 1922, no. XIX; and N. Baturin, '*P. A. Alekseyev (1849–1891)*', in '*Ocherki iz istorii rabochego dvizheniya 70-kh i 80-kh godov*' (*Essays on the history of the working-class movement in the seventies and eighties*), M., 1925. For his end, see M. Krotov, '*Ubiystvo Petra Alekseyeva (po arkhivnym materialam)*' (*The assassination of P. Alekseyev [from archive documents]*), in 'Katorga i ssylka', 1928, no. X; M. Ya. Struminsky, '*Pyotr Alekseyev v yakutskoy ssylke*' (*Peter Alekseyev in exile in Yakutsk*), Yakutsk, 1940.
53. R. Klenova, '*Ivan Timofeyevitch Smirnov (1850–1896)*', in 'Katorga i ssylka', 1930, no. VII.
54. '*Sofia Illarionovna Bardina*', Geneva, 1883.
55. The most detailed study of this period is by E. Korol'chuk, '*Iz istorii propagandy sredi rabochikh Peterburga v seredine 70-kh godov*' (*From the history of propaganda among the workers of St Petersburg in the middle of the seventies*), in 'Katorga i ssylka', 1928, no. I, with many documents from the archives.
56. B. V. Titlinov, '*Molodyozh' i revolyutsiya. Iz istorii revolyutsionnogo dvizheniya*

*sredi uchashcheysya molodyozhi dukhovnykh i srednikh uchebnykh zavedeniy.
1860–1905'.* S predisloviem i pod red. E. E. Essena (*Youth and revolution.
From the history of the revolutionary movement among the students in ecclesiastical institutions and secondary schools. 1860–1905.* With a preface and
edited by E. E. Essen), L., 1924, p. 23.

57. For the state of mind of these workers, see the memoirs of one of them who
was affected by Dyakov's propaganda at this time, and was sentenced to nine
years' hard labour. 'In the factory confused rumours circulated among us
about the socialists; that they were the followers of a certain German, Marx;
that they incited people to kill, burn, steal and destroy.' They believed in the
emperor 'anointed by the Lord', etc. D. A. Aleksandrov, '*Vospominaniya*'
(*Recollections*), in 'Katorga i ssylka', 1926, no. IV.

58. Fragment of a letter produced at their trial. The account of this trial, which is
one principal source as far as their activities are concerned, is reprinted in V.
Bogucharsky, '*Gosudarstvennyye prestupleniya v Rossii*' (*State crimes in
Russia*), *op. cit.*, vol. I, pp. 318 ff. The charge, which was not printed in
'Pravitel'stvennyy vestnik', has been published in 'Byloye', 1906, no. XI.

59. V. Bogucharsky, *op. cit.*, p. 301.

60. They were up to date on the internal discussions within the International.
Among the books found in a raid on the house of one of them were the following pamphlets: *Die Bakounisten an der Arbeit* and *Les prétendues scissions
dans l'Internationale.*

61. See a reference in a letter written in September 1875, published by
E. A. Korol'chuk, '*Pis'ma G. F. Zhdanovicha*' (*G. F. Zhdanovich's letters*),
op. cit.

62. '*Russkiy rabochiy v revolyutsionnom dvizhenii*'. *Po lichnym vospominaniyam*
(*The Russian worker in the revolutionary movement. From personal recollections*).
Reprinted in G. V. Plekhanov, '*Sochineniya*' (*Works*), *op. cit.*, vol. III, pp.
121 ff.

63. *Ibid.*, p. 143.

64. M. R. Popov, '*Iz moyego revolyutsionnogo proshlogo*' (*From my revolutionary
past*), in 'Byloye', 1907, nos. V, VII, reprinted in '*Zapisky zemlevol'tsa*'
(*Memoirs of a member of* 'Zemlya i Volya'), *op. cit.*, p. 85.

65. G. V. Plekhanov, '*Russkiy rabochiy v revolyutsionnom dvizhenii*' (*The Russian
worker in the revolutionary movement*), *op. cit.*, p. 135.

66. V. O. Levitsky, '*Viktor Obnorsky, osnovatel'* "*Severnogo soyuza russkikh
rabochikh*"' (*Victor Obnorsky, founder of the 'Northern Union of Russian
workers'*), M., 1929.

67. V. I. Nevsky, '*Pervaya klassovaya sotsialisticheskaya organizatsiya rabochikh
v Rossii*' (*The first class and socialist organization of workers in Russia*), in
'*Yuzhno-russkiye rabochiye soyuzy*' (*The workers' unions of South Russia*),
op. cit., in which he speaks at length of Obnorsky's stay in Odessa.

68. B. I. Nikolaevsky, '*V. N. Cherkezov*', in 'Katorga i ssylka', 1926, no. IV.

69. See Shiryaev's letters to Lavrov, October 1878, which speak of Obnorsky.
They are given in V. Burtsev, '*Severnyy soyuz russkikh rabochikh*' (*The
Northern Union of Russian Workers*), in 'Byloye', 1906, no. 17, p. 172, note I;
and P. B. Aksel'rod, '*Perezhitoye i peredumannoye*' (*Things seen and reflected
upon*), Berlin, 1923, vol. I, p. 209, in which Aksel'rod describes this meeting with
Obnorsky.

70. N. Baturin, '*Ocherki iz istorii rabochego dvizheniya 70-kh i 80-kh godov*'
(*Essays on the history of the workers' movement in the seventies and eighties*),
op. cit., pp. 31 ff.; and M. Mishev, '*Stepan Khalturin i Pyotr Alekseyev*' (*S.
Khalturin and P. Alekseyev*), *op. cit.*

71. The idea of creating a Populist centre, a Russian 'commune', in America flourished among the intellectuals also at this period. We have already noted Malikov, the creator of 'deo-humanism'. For other examples, see B. B. Glinsky, '*Revolyutsionnyy period russkoy istorii (1861–1881)*' (*The revolutionary period of Russian history (1861–1881)*), Spb., 1913, vol. II, p. 36.

72. D. Smirnov, '*Na trubochnom zavode v proshlom*' (*In a munitions factory in the past*), in 'Krasnaya letopis'', 1928, no. II.

73. N. Morozov, '*Povesti moyey zhizni*' (*Stories from my life*), op. cit., vol. IV, p. 147.

74. G. V. Plekhanov, '*Russkiy rabochiy v revolyutsionnom dvizhenii*' (*The Russian worker in the revolutionary movement*), op. cit., pp. 195–6.

75. E. A. Korol'chuk, '*Pervaya rabochaya demonstratsiya v Rossii. K pyatidesyatiletiyu demonstratsii na Kazanskoy ploshchadi v Peterburge 6/18 dekabrya 1876 g.*' (*The first workers' demonstration in Russia. For the fiftieth anniversary of the demonstration in the Kazan Square in St Petersburg, 6th/18th December 1876*), L., 1927.

76. G. V. Plekhanov, '*Russkiy rabochiy v revolyutsionnom dvizhenii*' (*The Russian worker in the revolutionary movement*), op. cit., p. 149.

77. See the accounts of this trial in V. Bogucharsky, '*Gosudarstvennyye prestupleniya v Rossii v XIX veke*' (*State crimes in Russia in the 19th century*), op. cit., vol. II, pp. 1 ff.

78. M. R. Popov, '*Zapiski zemlevol'tsa*' (*Memoirs of a member of* 'Zemlya i Volya'), op. cit., p. 79.

79. It was published for the first time as an appendix to the article by E. Korol'chuk, '*Iz istorii propagandy sredi rabochikh Peterburga vo vtoroy polovine 70-kh godov*' (*From the history of propaganda among the workers of St Petersburg in the second half of the seventies*), in 'Istoriko-revolyutsionnyy sbornik', no. III. It is also reprinted as an appendix to E. Korol'chuk, '*Pervaya rabochaya demonstratsiya v Rossii*' (*The first workers' demonstration in Russia*), op. cit., pp. 64 ff. D. Kuz'min (E. Kolosov's pseudonym), in '*Kazanskaya demonstratsiya 1876 g. i G. V. Plekhanov*' (*The demonstration in the Kazan Square in 1876 and G. V. Plekhanov*), in 'Katorga i ssylka', 1928, no. V, has tried to prove that this report is by G. V. Plekhanov. His arguments, however, are not very convincing. Certainly Khazov corrected it in his own hand and in all probability it represents his views. But whoever the author was, this manuscript reflects the ideas of those members of the future 'Zemlya i Volya' who had been especially engaged in organizing the workers in St Petersburg. Khazov had been a member of revolutionary groups from the beginning of the 'seventies. In 1874 he had been arrested, and in 1876 freed on condition that he did not live in the capital. He had stayed in St Petersburg despite this, and had been one of the most active propagandists in the working-class districts. Arrested again in 1877 he was exiled to Siberia. There he died in 1881, in the town of Verkhoyansk.

80. G. V. Plekhanov, '*Russkiy rabochiy v revolyutsionnom dvizhenii*' (*The Russian worker in the revolutionary movement*), op. cit., p. 186.

81. Distant echoes of these intense discussions on the question of the workers can be traced in some letters to L. M. Zak, written in the spring of 1877. They are published in E. A. Korol'chuk, '*Severnyy soyuz russkikh rabochikh*' (*The Northern Union of Russian workers*), L., 1946, pp. 136 ff. See also N. S. Rusanov, '*Iz moikh vospominaniy*'. Kniga I. '*Detstvo i yunost' na rodine*' (*From my recollections. Book I. Childhood and youth in my native land*), Berlin, 1923, p. 152, in which he speaks of this group as one which was already looking ahead to social-democracy.

82. G. V. Plekhanov, '*Russkiy rabochiy v revolyutsionnom dvizhenii*' (*The Russian worker in the revolutionary movement*), *op. cit.*, p. 155. The manifesto distributed on this occasion is reprinted in '*Literaturnoye nasledie G. V. Plekhanova*', pod red. A. V. Lunacharskogo, F. D. Kretova, R. M. Plekhanovoy (*The literary heritage of G. V. Plekhanov*, edited by A. V. Lunacharsky, F. D. Kretov, R. M. Plekhanova), M., 1934, vol. I, p. 380.

83. This strike is described in G. V. Plekhanov, '*Russkiy rabochiy v revolyutsionnom dvizhenii*' (*The Russian worker in the revolutionary movement*), *op. cit.*, p. 159; in M. R. Popov, '*K istorii rabochego dvizheniya v kontse 70-kh godov*' (*For a history of the working-class movement at the end of the seventies*), in 'Golos minushvago', the only number for the years 1920–1, and reprinted in '*Zapiski zemlevol'tsa*' (*Memoirs of a member of* 'Zemlya i Volya'), *op. cit.*, p. 167; and in P. A. Moiseyenko, '*Vospominaniya. 1873–1923*' (*Recollections. 1873–1923*), M., 1924. Moiseyenko became a famous working-class organizer in the 'eighties.

84. N. Lopatin was to be arrested and exiled in the department of Archangel. In 1878 he attempted to escape and was sent back to Siberia. In 1881 he escaped from Verkholensk and found refuge abroad.

85. These articles were published in the journal 'Novosti', and reprinted in G. V. Plekhanov, '*Sochineniya*' (*Works*), *op. cit.*, vol. III, pp. 421 ff.

86. From a note written at Shlissel'burg in 1902, published in 'Katorga i ssylka', 1923, no. VI, and reprinted in '*Zapiski zemlevol'tsa*' (*Memoirs of a member of* 'Zemlya i Volya'), *op. cit.*, p. 187.

87. There is a detailed account of this episode by Plekhanov, in 'Zemlya i Volya!', no. IV, of 20th February 1879, and reprinted in G. V. Plekhanov, '*Sochineniya*' (*Works*), *op. cit.*, vol. I, pp. 44 ff.

88. One manifesto is reprinted in '*Literaturnoye nasledstvo G. V. Plekhanova*' (*The literary heritage of G. V. Plekhanov*), *op. cit.*, vol. I, p. 382. He also mentions the close links between the problems of the workers and those of the peasants: 'Bitter necessity, heavy taxes, drive you from the villages into the factories and workshops; you look for a job to satisfy the local tax collectors who collect them with a whip. The worker can find no protection anywhere. The police always join in on the side of the boss. The bosses are happy when the workers are not friendly among themselves ... As long as the workers will not understand that they must help each other, as long as they act separately, they will be the slaves of their employers. When they unite, when after a strike in one factory workers in other factories help, then they will have nothing to be afraid of, neither their employers, nor the police. United you are a power, isolated any policeman can finish you.'

89. See the article by G. V. Plekhanov, in 'Zemlya i Volya!', no. III, of 15th January 1879, reprinted in G. V. Plekhanov, '*Sochineniya*' (*Works*), *op. cit.*, vol. I, pp. 37 ff.

90. V. L. Burtsev, '*Severno-russkiy rabochiy soyuz. Stranitsa iz istorii rabochego dvizheniya v Rossii*' (*The Workers' Union of Northern Russia. A page in the history of the working-class movement in Russia*), in 'Byloye', 1906, no. I; and principally E. A. Korol'chuk, '*Severnyy soyuz russkikh rabochikh*' (*The Workers' Union of Northern Russia*), *op. cit.*

91. G. V. Plekhanov, '*Russkiy rabochiy v revolyutsionnom dvizhenii*' (*The Russian worker in the revolutionary movement*), *op. cit.*, p. 183.

92. The Eisenach programme is in no. I of 1873, that of Gotha in no. 7 of 1875.

93. For specific cases, taken from police records, see E. A. Korol'chuk, '*Severnyy soyuz russkikh rabochikh*' (*The Workers' Union of Northern Russia*), *op. cit.*, pp. 195 ff.

94. M. R. Popov, '*Zapisky zemlevol'tsa*' (*Recollections of a member of* 'Zemlya i Volya'), *op. cit.*, p. 235.

95. G. V. Plekhanov, '*Russkiy rabochiy v revolyutsionnom dvizhenii*' (*The Russian worker in the revolutionary movement*), *op. cit.*, p. 186. See the documents published by I. Volkhovicher, '*Nachalo sotsialisticheskogo rabochego dvizheniya v byvshey russkoy Pol'she*' (*The beginnings of the working-class socialist movement in former Russian Poland*), M.-L., 1925, pp. 75 ff.

96. See Peterson's autobiography in 'Katorga i ssylka', 1924, no. III. He was to become a member of the Socialist-Revolutionary party and to die in 1919.

97. A. Shilov, '*Poslednyaya stranitsa iz zhizni "Severnogo rabochego soyuza" v Peterburge*' (*The last page in the life of the* '*Northern Union of Russian Workers*' *in St Petersburg*), in 'Krasnaya letopis'', 1922, nos. II–III.

CHAPTER 20

1. O. V. Aptekman, '*Obshchestvo* "Zemlya i Volya" *70-kh godov*' (*The society* 'Zemlya i Volya' *in the seventies*), P., 1924. This is a muddled book but it contains a great deal of information. The author belonged to the *Chyornyy peredel* wing, which was opposed to the terrorism of 'Narodnaya Volya'; this must be taken into consideration when reading the book. E. Serebryakov, in '*Ocherki po istorii* "Zemli i Voli" ' (*Essays on the history of* 'Zemlya i Volya'), in 'S rodiny i na rodine', 1894, no. IV, and afterwards in book form, Spb., 1906, makes one of the first attempts to see the movement as a whole. The essay is interesting above all for this reason. A. A. Kunkl''s pamphlet, '*Obshchestvo* "Zemlya i Volya" *70-kh godov*' (*The society* 'Zemlya i Volya' *in the seventies*), M., 1928, adds little, but it does contain some unpublished documents. The two basic collections of documents are '*Revolyutsionnaya zhurnalistika semidesyatykh godov*', pod red. B. Bazilevskogo (*Revolutionary journalism in the seventies*, edited by B. Bazilevsky [V. Bogucharsky]), Paris, 1905; and '*Arkhiv* "Zemli i Voli" *i* "Narodnoy Voli" '. Podgotovili k pechati V. R. Leykina i N. L. Pivovarskaya. Redaktsiya i predislovie S. N. Valka (*The archive of* 'Zemlya i Volya' *and* 'Narodnaya Volya'. Edited by V. R. Leykina and N. L. Pivovarskaya. Preface by S. N. Valk), M., 1932. The vast number of memoirs will be referred to individually from time to time.

2. S. S. Tatishchev, '*Imperator Aleksandr II. Ego zhizn' i tsarstvovanie*' (*The Emperor Alexander II. His life and reign*), Spb., 1903, vol. II, p. 593.

3. B. H. Sumner, *Russia and the Balkans, 1870–1880*, Oxford, 1937.

4. V. Bogucharsky, '*Aktivnoye narodnichestvo 70-kh godov*' (*Active Populism in the seventies*), M., 1912, pp. 262 ff.

5. 'Vperyod', no. 16, of 1st November 1875. Lavrov's journal always maintained this standpoint. For instance, when war broke out it said: 'Among the southern Slavs it will inevitably bring together the economic and political exploiters and the masses whom they exploit. Political problems will be stifled and economic problems postponed indefinitely. The propaganda and the organization of the social revolution will lose much of their ethical basis . . .', no. 44, November 1877.

6. B. Itenberg, in '*Deyatel'nost'* " *Yuzhno-rossiyskogo soyuza rabochikh*" ' (*The activity of the* '*Union of Workers of South Russia*'), in 'Voprosy istorii', 1951, no. 1, publishes a police report on this disturbance, and on Zaslavsky's connections with the Bulgarian émigrés at Odessa, etc.

7. No. 35 of 29th August 1875.

8. '*Bunt v slavyanskikh zemlyakh*' (*The revolt in the Slav countries*), in 'Rabotnik', no. 9 of September 1875.

9. Quoted by B. Nikolaevsky, '*Materialy i dokumenty. Tkachev i Lavrov*' (*Material and documents. Tkachev and Lavrov*), in 'Na chuzhoy storone', 1925, no. X.

10. From one of M. P. Sazhin's letters, quoted in V. Bogucharsky, '*Aktivnoye narodnichestvo semidesyatykh godov*' (*Active Populism in the seventies*), *op. cit.*, p. 287.

11. In Russia he met with some resistance to this plan to take part in the Balkan struggles. 'To my comrades in St Petersburg these plans seemed groundless inventions of the émigrés, who were inadequately informed of the real state of things.' P. B. Aksel'rod, '*Perezhitoye i peredumannoye*' (*Things seen and reflected upon*), Berlin, 1923, vol. I, p. 155.

12. 'Bulletin de la fédération jurassienne', 10th October 1875.

13. M. F. Frolenko, '*Sobranie sochineniy*'. Pod red. i s primechaniyami I. Teodorovicha (*Works*. Edited and with notes by I. Teodorovich), M., 1923, vol. I, pp. 213 ff.

14. N. Morozov, '*Povesti moyey zhizni*'. Red., vstupitel'naya stat'ya i primechaniya I. A. Teodorovicha (*Stories from my life*. Edited with an introductory article and notes by I. A. Teodorovich), M., 1933, vol. IV, p. 44. This explanation is more plausible than the one given by Tikhomirov, according to whom 'Klements called the Populists "troglodytes" because they despised the sciences and culture'. '*Vospominaniya L'va Tikhomirova*', predislovie V. I. Nevskogo, vstupitel'naya stat'ya V. N. Figner (*Memoirs of Lev Tikhomirov*, preface by V. I. Nevsky, introductory article by V. N. Figner), M.-L., 1927, p. 87.

15. Quoted by A. A. Kunkl', '*Obshchestvo "Zemlya i Volya" 70-kh godov*' (*The society* 'Zemlya i Volya' *in the seventies*), *op. cit.*, pp. 10–11.

16. O. V. Aptekman, '*Obshchestvo "Zemlya i Volya" 70-kh godov*' (*The society* 'Zemlya i Volya' *in the seventies*), *op. cit.*, p. 205.

17. '*Pis'ma narodovol'tsa A. D. Mikhaylova*'. Sobral P. E. Shchegolev (*Letters by A. D. Mikhaylov of* 'Narodnaya Volya'. Collected by P. E. Shchegolev), M., 1933, pp. 227–8.

18. O. V. Aptekman, '*Obshchestvo "Zemlya i Volya" 70-kh godov*' (*The society* 'Zemlya i Volya' *in the seventies*), *op. cit.*, pp. 243–4.

19. The most complete of these autobiographies, and the one from which these words are quoted was published in the review 'Na rodine', Geneva, 1883, no. III. It was reprinted in A. P. Pribyleva-Korba and V. N. Figner, '*Narodovolets Aleksandr Dmitrievich Mikhaylov*' (*A. D. Mikhaylov of Narodnaya Volya*), L., 1925, p. 35. This book is a valuable collection of documents and recollections. See M. M. Klevensky, '*Aleksandr Dmitrievich Mikhaylov*', M., undated (but 1925).

20. A. P. Pribyleva-Korba and V. N. Figner. *op. cit.*, p. 53.

21. *Ibid.*, pp. 40–1.

22. *Ibid.*, p. 41.

23. '*Pis'ma narodovol'tsa A. D. Mikhaylova*' (*Letters by A. D. Mikhaylov of Narodnaya Volya*), *op. cit.*, pp. 31, 80.

24. *Ibid.*, p. 250.

25. Zhelyabov's definition.

26. *Ibid.*, p. 247.

27. In 1876 he gave his brothers and sisters a complete reading list. This list is highly characteristic of the books which were to form the opinions of all his generation. *Ibid.*, p. 110.

28. Mikhaylov's depositions of 1880, in A. P. Pribyleva-Korba and V. N. Figner, '*Narodovolets Aleksandr Dmitrievich Mikhaylov*' (*A. D. Mikhaylov of Narodnaya Volya*), *op. cit.*, p. 93.

29. *Ibid.*, p. 42.

30. *Ibid.*, p. 86.

31. *Ibid.*, p. 90.

32. *Ibid.*, p. 91.

33. *Ibid.*, p. 92.

34. *Ibid.*, pp. 93–4.

35. *Ibid.*, p. 96.

36. *Ibid.*

37. Davidenko was twenty years old at that time, and was to become one of the boldest and most active revolutionaries of the following years. In Odessa he was allied with Koval'sky and more or less secretly associated with Tkachev's 'Nabat'. When Koval'sky was condemned to death, Davidenko took part in the armed demonstration and fired at the police who arrested him. He in his turn was condemned to death and hanged on 10th August 1879. He had at one time been very close to the Jacobins, but was later 'disillusioned'. Apart from this little is known of his political ideas. The evidence of Mikhaylov shows how Jacobinism infiltrated into the 'rebels' of South Russia, and also explains why it never won the day.

38. A. P. Pribyleva-Korba and V. N. Figner, *op. cit.*, p. 98.

39. Plekhanov's article on Mikhaylov was published in the review 'Na rodine', 1883, no. III, and reprinted *ibid.*, p. 62.

40. *Ibid.*, p. 45.

41. *Ibid.*, p. 43.

42. E. A. Korol'chuk, '*Iz istorii propagandy sredi rabochikh Peterburga vo vtoroy polovine 70-kh godov*'. Prilozheniya: '*Zaklyuchenie prokurora Peterburgskoy sudebnoy palaty po delu "Obshchestva druzey"*' (*From the history of propaganda among the workers in St Petersburg in the second half of the seventies. Appendix: The summing up of the prosecutor of the St Petersburg Tribunal on the affair of the 'Obshchestvo druzey'*), in '*Istoriko-revolyutsionnyy sbornik*' (*Historical-revolutionary miscellany*), vol. III.

43. His own autobiography in the *Granat Encyclopedia*, vol. 40.

44. P. A. Kropotkin, '*Zapiski revolyutsionera*' (*Memoirs of a revolutionary*), edited by N. K. Lebedev and with a preface by P. P. Paradizov, no place (but L.), 1933, pp. 236 ff.; and A. I. Ivanchin-Pisarev, '*Pobeg P. A. Kropotkina*' (*The escape of P. A. Kropotkin*), in 'Byloye', 1907, no. I.

45. O. V. Aptekman, '*Obshchestvo "Zemlya i Volya" 70-kh godov*' (*The society* '*Zemlya i Volya*' *in the seventies*), *op. cit.*, pp. 246 ff.

46. '*Vospominaniya*' (*Recollections*), Spb., 1906, reprinted with the title '*Ot buntarstva k terrorizmu*', s predisloviem S. N. Valka (*From revolt to terrorism*, with a preface by S. N. Valk), M.-L., 1930, in 2 volumes.

47. For this period of his activity, see his own writings: '*Pochemu ya stal revolyutsionerom*' (*Why I became a revolutionary*), in 'Golos minuvshago', 1919, nos. V–XII; '*Yuzhnyye buntari*' (*The 'rebels' of the south*), in 'Golos minuvshago', 1920–1, the only issue; '*Zagovor sredi krest'yan Chigirinskogo uyezda*' (*The conspiracy among the peasants of the Chigirin district*), in '*Sbornik materialov i statey*'. Glavnoye upravlenie arkhivnym delom. Redaktsiya zhurnala 'Istoricheskiy Arkhiv' (*Collection of materials and articles. Central administration of archives. Editorial board of the review 'Historical Archive'*), M., 1921, no. I, later collected in '*Za polveka*' (*Over half a century*), P., 1922, in 2 volumes.

26*

48. 'Sud'by kapitalizma v Rossii' (The fate of capitalism in Russia), Spb., 1882. Plekhanov wrote a whole book against him: A. Volgin (G. V. Plekhanov), 'Obosnovanie narodnichestva v trudakh g-na Vorontsova (V. V.). Kriticheskiy etyud' (The foundations of Populism in the works of Vorontsov [V. V.]. A critical study), Spb., 1896.

49. 'Yuzhnyye buntari' (The 'rebels' of the south), op. cit., p. 50.

50. F. Venturi, L'attività rivoluzionaria della Kuliscioff in Russia (The revolutionary activity of Anna Kulishov in Russia), in 'Movimento Operaio', 1952, no. 2.

51. M. F. Frolenko, 'Sobranie sochineniy', v dvukh tomakh, pod redaktsiey i s primechaniyami I. Teodorovicha (Works, in two volumes, edited and with notes by I. Teodorovich), M., 1932.

52. Ibid., vol. I, p. 168.

53. A. P. Pribyleva-Korba and V. N. Figner, 'Narodovolets Aleksandr Dmitrievich Mikhaylov' (A. D. Mikhaylov of 'Narodnaya Volya'), op. cit., p. 106.

54. Ibid., p. 108.

55. Ibid., p. 145.

56. Ibid., p. 145.

57. First published with a commentary, in 'Arkhiv "Zemli i Voli" i "Narodnoy Voli"' (The archives of 'Zemlya i Volya' and 'Nardodnaya Volya'), op. cit., pp. 53 ff.

58. The best ways to achieve this goal are: combining with already existing popular organizations of a revolutionary nature, and grouping revolutionary elements together which are now separate, for instance 'men of the mir', the leaders of the peasant mir. [Note from the original text.]

59. O. V. Aptekman, 'Obshchestvo "Zemlya i Volya" 70-kh godov' (The society 'Zemlya i Volya' in the seventies), op. cit., p. 265.

60. A. P. Pribyleva-Korba and V. N. Figner, 'Narodovolets Aleksandr Dmitrievich Mikhaylov' (A. D. Mikhaylov of 'Narodnaya Volya'), op. cit., pp. 147–8.

61. Her writings have been collected in V. Figner, 'Polnoye sobranie sochineniy' v semi tomakh (Complete works, in seven volumes), M., 1932.

62. Vera Figner, 'Zapechatlyonnyy trud' (Work concluded), M., 1933, vol. I, p. 120.

63. 'Pis'ma narodovol'tsa A. D. Mikhaylova' (Letters from A. D. Mikhaylov of 'Narodnaya Volya'), op. cit., p. 120.

64. A. P. Pribyleva-Korba and V. N. Figner, 'Narodovolets Aleksandr Dmitrievich Mikhaylov' (A. D. Mikhaylov of 'Narodnaya Volya'), op. cit., p. 120. See p. 149, where Mikhaylov lists the occasions at the time of the movement 'to go to the people' when revolutionary and social influences had affected the various sects of the Volga, and where he speaks of those confessions which were closest in mental attitude to those of the Populists (the fugitives, the taciturn, etc.).

65. Starik (S. F. Kovalik), 'Dvizhenie semidesyatykh godov po Bol'shomu protsessu' (The movement of the seventies in the great trial), in 'Byloye', 1906, no. XI.

66. M. F. Frolenko, 'Sobranie sochineniy' (Works), op. cit., vol. I, p. 120.

67. He wrote an article on the sects which was published in 'Otechestvennye zapiski', 1878, nos. III, IV, signed with the pseudonym Emel'yanov.

68. Vera Figner, 'Zapechatlyonnyy trud' (Work concluded), op. cit., vol. I, p. 120.

69. 'Pokushenie A. K. Solovyova na tsareubiystvo 2 aprelya 1879 g.' (A. K. Solovyov's attempt on the life of the Tsar, 2nd April 1879), in 'Byloye', 1918, nos. I–II.

70. M. R. Popov, 'Zapiski zemlevol'tsa'. Predislovie I. Teodorovicha (Memoirs of a member of 'Zemlya i Volya'. Preface by I. Teodorovich), M., 1933, p. 75.

71. 'Dokumenty k chigirinskomu delu' (Documents on the Chigirin affair), in 'Byloye', 1906, no. XII; Lev Deych, 'Zagovor sredi krest'yan chigirinskogo

uyezda' (*The conspiracy amongst the peasants in the district of Chigirin*), *op. cit.*; '*Protsess 17-ti narodovol'tsev v 1883 godu*' (*The trial of the seventeen members of* 'Narodnaya Volya' *in 1883*), in 'Byloye', 1906, no. X.

72. P. Aksel'rod, *Russia*, in 'Jahrbuch für Sozialwissenschaft und Sozialpolitik', Zürich, 1881, no. III.

73. V. Debagory-Mokrievich, '*Vospominaniya*' (*Recollections*), *op. cit.*, pp. 156 ff. Despite the literary tone of these memoirs, and despite the superior attitude of the author who seems to look back with a smile on his youthful follies, there is no doubt that he gives a true picture of the discouragement which overwhelmed the *buntari*, and the reasons for it.

74. M. F. Frolenko, '*Sobranie sochineniy*' (*Works*), *op. cit.*, vol. I, pp. 221, 228.

75. 'Rabotnik' had already spoken of this disturbance in no. 9 of August 1875.

76. See the article, '*Pervoye chigirinskoye delo*' (*The first Chigirin affair*), in 'Nachalo', no. I, March 1878, reprinted in '*Revolyutsionnaya zhurnalistika semidesyatykh godov*' (*Revolutionary journalism in the seventies*), edited by B. Bazilevsky (V. Bogucharsky), Paris, 1905, pp. 27 ff.

77. M. F. Frolenko, '*Sobranie sochineniy*' (*Works*), *op. cit.*, p. 189.

78. *Ibid.*, pp. 241 ff.

79. See Aksel'rod's article, p. 272, in the 'Jahrbuch für Sozialwissenschaft und Sozialpolitik'. This was probably the group which even decided, without his knowledge, on the man to be chosen for the role of 'usurper'. This was the revolutionary, Rogachev, who was to receive a particularly heavy sentence in the 'trial of the hundred and ninety-three'. Starik (S. F. Kovalik), '*Dvizhenie semidesyatykh godov po Bol'shomu protsessu*' (*The movement of the seventies in the great trial*), in 'Byloye', 1906, no. XII.

80. Stepnyak, *La Russia sotterranea* (*Underground Russia*), Milan, 1898, p. 49.

81. S. S. Tatishchev, '*Imperator Aleksandr II*' (*Emperor Alexander II*), *op. cit.*, vol. II, p. 595.

82. '*Gosudarstvennyye prestupleniya v Rossii v XIX veke*'. Sbornik sostavlen pod redaktsiey B. Bazilevskogo (V. Bogucharskogo) (*State crimes in Russia in the nineteenth century*. Collection compiled by B. Bazilevsky [V. Bogucharsky]), Spb., 1906, vol. II, p. 47.

83. Polonsky's poem '*Uznitsa*' (*The girl prisoner*) was published complete in 'Byloye', 1906, no. I; Nekrasov's poem, which Alekseyev himself was able to read in prison immediately after the trial, was first printed in the émigré journal 'Obshcheye delo', 1882, no. III.

84. A. P. Pribyleva-Korba and V. N. Figner, '*Narodovolets Aleksandr Dmitrievich Mikhaylov*' (*A. D. Mikhaylov of* 'Narodnaya Volya'), *op. cit.*, p. 112.

85. V. Bogucharsky, '*Gosudarstvennyye prestupleniya v Rossii*' (*State crimes in Russia*), *op. cit.*, pp. 329–30.

86. A. F. Koni, '*Vospominaniya o dele Very Zasulich*', s predisloviem I. Teodorovicha (*Recollections of the affair of V. Zasulich*, with a preface by I. Teodorovich), no place (but L.), 1933, pp. 18 ff.

87. On his last days, see V. Svitych, '*Nadgrobnoye slovo Aleksandru II*' (*Funeral eulogy of Alexander II*), in 'Vestnik Narodnoy Voli', 1885, no. III.

88. This psychological transformation is particularly vividly described by one of the prisoners, N. Morozov, '*Povesti moyey zhizni*' (*Stories from my life*), *op. cit.*, vol. III, pp. 290 ff. His account is confirmed by all the others. See S. S. Sinegub, '*Vospominaniya chaykovtsa*' (*Recollections of one of the Chaykovskists*), in 'Byloye', 1906, no. X; D. M. Gertsensteyn, '*Tridtsat' let tomu nazad*' (*Thirty years ago*), in 'Byloye', 1907, no. VI. For the impression made on society, see N. S. Tagantsev, '*Perezhitoye*' (*Things lived through*), vol. II. P., 1919, pp. 21 ff. Even abroad these events at once brought the problem of

terrorism into the foreground again; this can be seen from the title of a pamphlet by Z. K. Ralli, '*Bashi-Buzuki Peterburga. Posvyashchaetsya pamyati Dmitriya Kazakozova, pytannogo v 1866 godu v zastenkakh Petropavlovskoy kreposti*' (*The bashi-bazook of Petersburg. Dedicated to the memory of D. Karakozov, tortured in 1866 in the torture chambers of the Peter-Paul fortress*), Geneva, 1877, published by 'Rabotnik'.

89. '*Pis'ma uchastnikov protsessa 193*' (*Letters from the participants in the 'trial of the hundred and ninety-three*') are very interesting documents illustrating this state of mind. They were published by R. M. Kantor in 'Krasnyy arkhiv', 1923, no. II.

90. For this atmosphere, see the satirical poems of the day which parodied the public prosecutor's speech in V. Bogucharsky, '*Aktivnoye narodnichestvo semidesyatykh godov*' (*Active Populism in the seventies*), M., 1912, pp. 307 ff.; and in 'Krasnyy arkhiv', 1929, no. III.

91. V. Bogucharsky, '*Gosudarstvennyye prestupleniya v Rossii*' (*State crimes in Russia*), *op. cit.*, vol. III, which is entirely devoted to the 'trial of the hundred and ninety-three'.

92. 'Obshchina', 1878, no. 2, leading article on the 'trial of the hundred and ninety-three'.

93. *Ibid.* On Myshkin, and the movement of the 'seventies as a whole, see the lively memoirs of V. G. Korolenko, '*Istoriya moyego sovremennika*' (*History of a contemporary of mine*), M., 1948, in two volumes.

94. A. F. Koni, '*Vospominaniya o dele Very Zasulich*' (*Recollections of the affair of V. Zasulich*), *op. cit.*, p. 58.

95. See interesting accounts of the reactions of official circles in Sh. Levin, '*Final protsessa 193*' (*The conclusion of the 'trial of the hundred and ninety-three'*), in 'Krasnyy arkhiv', 1928, no. V.

96. M. Bel'skich, '*Yunosheskiye gody I. N. Myshkina*' (*The early years of I. N. Myshkin*), in 'Katorga i ssylka', 1924, no. V.

97. Starik (S. F. Kovalik), '*Dvizhenie semidesyatykh godov po Bol'shomu protsessu*' (*The movement of the seventies in the great trial*), in 'Byloye', no. XI; and E. Breshkovskaya, '*Ippolit Myshkin i arkhangel'skiy kruzhok*' (*I. Myshkin and the Archangel group*), no place, 1904.

98. M. Aleksandrov, '*Arest I. N. Myshkina*' (*The arrest of I. N. Myshkin*), in 'Byloye', 1906, no. X; and Sh. L., '*Pis'mo I. N. Myshkina iz yakutskoy tyur'my k bratu*' (*I. N. Myshkin's letter to his brother from the prison of Yakutsk*), in 'Krasnyy arkhiv', 1923, no. II. On 22nd August he wrote: 'Fate obviously wants to play a joke on me. I, the enemy of all privilege, have ended up in a privileged position; apart from me, no one else went to prison.'

99. M. Chernavsky, '*I. N. Myshkin (po vospominaniyam katorzhanina 1870–1880-kh gg.)*' (*I. N. Myshkin [From the recollections of a man condemned to hard labour in the 1870s and 1880s]*), in 'Katorga i ssylka', 1924, nos. I, V; 1925, no. III; and above all the striking recollections of Shlissel'burg by M. R. Popov, '*K biografii Ippolita Nikiticha Myshkina*' (*For a biography of I. N. Myshkin*), in '*Zapiski zemlevol'tsa*' (*Recollections of a member of* 'Zemlya i Volya'), *op. cit.* pp. 307 ff.

100. Starik (S. F. Kovalik), '*Dvizhenie semidesyatykh godov po Bol'shomu protsessu*' (*The movement of the seventies in the great trial*), *op. cit.*; and, by the same author, '*K biografii P. I. Voynaral'skogo*' (*For a biography of P. I. Voynaral'sky*), in 'Katorga i ssylka', 1924, no. I.

101. O. V. Aptekman, '*Dmitriy Rogachev v ego "Ispoved' k druz'yam" i pis'makh semidesyatykh godov*' (*'Dimitry Rogachev in his "Confession to his friends" and letters of the seventies'*), M., 1928.

102. O. V. Aptekman, 'Dmitriy Rogachev v ego "Ispoved' k druz'yam" i pis'makh rodnym (Po materialam arkhiva byvshego III otdeleniya)' (D. Rogachev in his 'Confession to my friends' and in his letters to his parents [Material from the former Third Section]), in 'Byloye', 1924, no. XXVI.

103. S. S. Sinegub, 'Vospominanyia chaykovtsa' (Memoirs of one of the Chaykovskists), in 'Byloye', 1906, no. IX.

104. Chapter IX, p. 234.

105. A. O. Lukashevich, 'V narod!' (To the people!), in 'Byloye', 1907, no. III.

106. N. Morozov, 'Povesti moyey zhizni' (Stories from my life), op. cit., vol. II, p. 11.

107. 'Obshchina', 1873, nos. 6–7.

108. 'Iz-za reshetki. Sbornik stikhotvoreniy russkikh zaklyuchyonnykh po politicheskim prichinam v periode 1873–1877 gg., osuzhdyonnykh i ozhidayushchikh "suda"' (From behind bars. Collection of verses by Russians detained for political reasons in the period 1873–1877, including those already condemned and those awaiting 'judgement'), published by 'Rabotnik' in Geneva, 1877, also constitutes an interesting document of the psychology of the movement developed in the 'trial of the hundred and ninety-three'. The preface (by Lopatin?) makes violent attacks on Russian writers such as Turgenev and Dostoevsky (who is described as 'the great Russian slave in the kingdom of slaves') for their political weakness.

109. N. P. Sidorov, 'Statisticheskiye svedeniya o propagandistakh 70-kh godov v obrabotke III Otdeleniya' (Statistical data on the propagandists of the seventies as estimated by the Third Section), in 'Katorga i ssylka', 1928, no. I.

110. M. F. Frolenko, 'Sobranie sochineniy' (Works), op. cit., pp. 130 ff.; A. Yakimova, 'Pamyati M. A. Kolenkinoy-Bogorodskoy' (In memory of M. A. Kolenkina-Bogorodskaya), in 'Katorga i ssylka', 1927, no. II.

111. 'Zemlya i Volya!', no. II, 15th December 1878, in 'Revolyutsionnaya zhurnalistika semidesyatykh godov' (Revolutionary journalism of the seventies), op. cit., p. 171. From now on this periodical will be quoted from this reprint.

112. M. R. Popov, 'Zapiski zemlevol'tsa' (Memoirs of a member of 'Zemlya i Volya'), op. cit., p. 93.

113. 'Zemlya i Volya!', no. II, 15th December 1878, op. cit., p. 201.

114. N. A. Vitashevsky, 'Pervoye vooruzhyonnoye soprotivlenie—pervyy voennyy sud (protsess Koval'skogo)' (The first armed resistance—the first military tribunal [the trial of Kovalsky]), in 'Byloye', 1906, no. II; M. F. Frolenko, 'I. M. Koval'sky', in 'Katorga i ssylka', 1924, no. V, and reprinted in 'Sobranie sochineniy' (Works), vol. II, pp. 90 ff.; G. Koff, 'K delu o pervom vooruzhyonnom soprotivlenii v Odesse v 1878 g.' (On the first armed resistance at Odessa in 1878); and C. Martynovskaya, 'I. M. Koval'sky i pervoye vooruzhyonnoye soprotivlenie v Odesse' (I. M. Koval'sky and the first armed resistance at Odessa in 1878), both in 'Katorga i ssylka', 1929, nos. VIII–IX. See also the novel (or rather recollections barely disguised as a novel) written in the Shlissel'burg prison by F. N. Yurkovsky, 'Bulgakov', predislovie V. I. Nevskogo, vstupitel'naya stat'ya i kommentarii E. E. Kolosova (Bulgakov, preface by V. I. Nevsky, introductory article and notes by E. E. Kolosov), M.-L., 1933; in it Koval'sky appears under the name of Kovalenko. For the general atmosphere, see A. Shekhter, 'Revolyutsionnaya Odessa v 1877–1878 gg.' (Revolutionary Odessa in 1877 and 1878), in 'Katorga i ssylka', 1923, no. VI. The propagandist followers of Lavrov were dominated by the idea that 'Constitutions don't feed the people'. But they too were soon to be involved in terrorist activity and the 'political' struggle.

115. For an account of them, see F. Pokrovsky, '*Russkaya revolyutsionnaya emigratsiya. Zapiska Ya. V. Stefanovicha*' (*Russian revolutionary émigrés. A memoir of Ya. V. Stefanovich*), in 'Byloye', 1921, no. XVI.

116. A. Vitashevskaya, '*N. A. Vitashevsky (Beglyye vospominaniya)*' (*N. A. Vitashevsky [Brief recollections]*), in 'Katorga i ssylka', 1924, no. IV.

117. E. N. Kusheva, '*Iz istorii "Obshchestva narodnogo osvobozhdeniya"*' (*From the history of the 'Society for the Liberation of the People'*), in 'Katorga i ssylka', 1931, no. IV. The 'Nabat', nos. 1–2, of 1879, announced the publication of two pamphlets: *The trial of Koval'sky, with an editorial preface*, and a reprint of an article of Koval'sky's on the religious sects of South Russia 'with a preface by one of his friends'. To the best of my knowledge these two pamphlets never actually appeared. Nonetheless, they bear witness to the 'Nabat's' interest in Koval'sky.

118. The 'Nabat' asserted that this 'was a volunteer in the Slav rising against the Turks and also a member of Garibaldi's bands. He seems to have been a man with ideas, and not just a simple bandit'. His name was Lukyanov. 'Nabat', 1878, nos. I–II.

119. A report from Odessa in the 'Nabat' (probably from this group) describes the state of mind in which the news of Zasulich's plot was received. 'They have fired at Trepov! The first thought that came into our minds when we heard the news was: "At last! What a pity they did not think of it sooner!" The second thought was of gratitude.' *Ibid.*, 1878, nos. I–II.

120. S. I. Feochari, '*Vooruzhyonnaya demonstratsiya 1878 g. v Odesse (sud nad I. M. Koval'skim)*' (*The armed demonstration at Odessa in 1878 [The trial of I. M. Koval'sky]*), in 'Katorga i ssylka', 1924, no. I; and 'Zemlya i Volya!', nos. II, V, *op. cit.*, pp. 201, 415.

121. 'C'est l'agitation par le *fait* qui accompagne désormais la propagande orale ou imprimée', commented D. Klements, in 'Le Travailleur', 1878, no. 2, February–March.

122. '*Biograficheskiye zametki o Valeriane Osinskom*' (*Biographical notes on V. Osinsky*), in 'Narodnaya Volya', no. 2, 1st November 1879, in '*Literatura partii "Narodnoy Voli"*' (*Literature of the 'Narodnaya Volya' party*), M., 1906, p. 52.

123. The manifesto has often been reprinted; for instance, 'Obshchina', 1878, nos. 3–4, and 'Nabat', 1878, etc.

124. Rostislav Steblin-Kamensky, '*Grigoriy Anfimovich Popko*', in 'Byloye', 1907, no. V.

125. M. R. Popov, '*Zapiski zemlevol'tsa*' (*Recollections of a member of* 'Zemlya i Volya'), *op. cit.*, p. 60.

126. Lev Tikhomirov, '*Vospominaniya*', pod red. V. I. Nevskogo (*Recollections*, edited by V. I. Nevsky), M.-L., 1927, p. 108.

127. The manifesto, which was published on this occasion, and which (according to V. Debagory-Mokrievich, '*Ot buntarstva k terrorizmu*' (*From 'revolt' to terrorism*), M., vol. II, p. 14) bore the stamp of the 'Executive Committee' on some copies, was reprinted in 'Obshchina', 1878, nos. III–IV.

128. Rostislav Steblin-Kamensky, '*Grigoriy Anfimovich Popko*', in 'Byloye', 1907, no. V. The poster, which bore the stamp of the 'Executive Committee', also announced the violent death of a working-class comrade and the flight of Stefanovich, Deych and Bokhanovsky from prison. It is reprinted in Yu. Ber, ' "Zemlya i Volya" *na rozdorizhzhi*' ('Zemlya i Volya' *at the cross-roads* [in Ukrainian]), in 'Za sto lit', 1929, no. IV.

129. M. F. Frolenko, '*Popytka osvobozhdeniya Voynaral'skogo 1-ogo iyulya 1878 g.*' (*The attempt to free Voynaral'sky on 1st July 1878*), in 'Katorga i

ssylka', 1929, no. IV; and in '*Sobranie sochineniy*' (*Works*), *op. cit.*, vol. I, p. 276.

130. Rostislav Steblin-Kamensky, '*Grigoriy Anfimovich Popko*', *op. cit.* See other accounts collected in V. Bogucharsky, '*Aktivnoye narodnichestvo 70-kh godov*' (*Active Populism in the seventies*), *op. cit.*, p. 323. These accounts must, however, be appraised cautiously. Obviously those Populists, such as Debagory-Mokrievich, who took part in the movement at that time but who subsequently became liberals, have a tendency to transfer their later ideas to the period of their youth.

131. See O. V. Aptekman's analysis in '"*Chyornyy peredel*". *Organ sotsialistov-federalistov 1880–1881*'. Predislovie V. I. Nevskogo ('Chyornyy Peredel'. *The organ of the federalist-socialists, 1880–1881*. Preface by V. I. Nevsky), M.-P., 1923, pp. 5 ff.

132. The 'Obshchina' was very close to 'Le Travailleur', the review edited by Zhukovsky, Ch. Perron and É. Réclus, which was first published at Geneva in May 1877. Klements was one of the Russians who contributed to it, with many interesting reports on the 'trial of the hundred and ninety-three' and on Populist ideas. 'Selon nous la propriété collective, telle qu'elle existe actuellement en Russie, est la première étape vers une jouissance collective du sol, plus complète et plus parfaite, qui ne se réalisera qu'après une confiscation générale au profit de tous et par l'abolition de toute propriété individuelle. Cette confiscation sera le premier pas de la révolution russe', he wrote in no. 4, August 1877. In the same report he discussed the problem of the State: 'Il peut se faire que les socialistes allemands réussissent à concilier l'inconciliable, à trouver une solution à l'antagonisme de l'État et du peuple sous forme de *Volksstaat* (État du peuple). Peut-être leurs tentatives se font-elles avec une foi profonde dans le succès, mais je dois avouer que la majorité des socialistes russes ne possèdent pas cette foi ... Qui s'est fait l'apôtre des idées anti-étatistes en Europe? Bakounine, un russe. Loin de moi de faire une question de mérite national entre les socialistes des divers peuples, je veux seulement démontrer que ce n'est pas le hasard qui a poussé un russe à propager l'anarchie, tandis que d'autres penseurs ont laissé de côté des idées pour s'occuper du mutualisme, des banques du peuple, etc. Loin de moi aussi l'intention de créer une doctrine du socialisme russe, mais qu'il me soit permis du moins de résumer les aspirations populaires qui se traduisent par une puissante tendence à l'abolition de la propriété individuelle et par conséquent à l'abolition d'une classe privilégiée de propriétaires ... La question des industries et fabriques est résolue par les socialistes russes de la même façon qu'en Occident ...'

133. His article, '*Russia*', in 'Jahrbuch für Sozialwissenschaft und Sozialpolitik', 1879, no. I.

134. P. B. Aksel'rod, '*Perezhitoye i peredumannoye*' (*Things seen and reflected upon*), Berlin, 1923, vol. I, p. 201.

135. No. I.

136. Leading article, nos. 3–4.

137. Report from Italy in no. I. After speaking of the Calabrian paper, 'Anarchia', he said: 'At the root of the Calabrian peasant's ideal is the dream that one day the period of the "peasant republic" will dawn at last. But the followers of Mazzini are not pleased about it—this is not the republic which they are trying to bring about. It is a republic of land and liberty, in which there is no place for masters and gentlemen.' And he goes on in a similar vein, mentally drawing a parallel between Calabria and Russia. Of course, no one in the huts of Calabria could read, 'but every one of those peasants knows the best way

to use a gun and a knife'. No. 2: 'The attempt at Benevento' (a detailed description of the insurrection in which he had played a part in 1877). In no. I there is also a detailed report, *From Italy*, signed Antonio, which discusses the 'Plebe' ('published, as everyone knows, by Malon . . . and whose programme is not completely identical with that of the German social-democrats, although it is statist'). It also refers to the Italian revolutionary tradition, Romagna, the Neapolitan bandits (who are 'the most faithful and cooperative allies of the priests'), the Forli congress, Costa's letter ('interesting, but I am not in full agreement with him'). The author's political conclusion is that in Italy 'the bourgeois revolution is dying out and socialism is not yet sufficiently developed to create its own advancing phalanx of competent fighters'. This crisis is general throughout Europe, but is particularly serious in Italy, 'in view of the strong tradition of Mazzini and Garibaldi, and the newness of socialism'. Another report from Italy, in nos. 6–7, quoted, among other things, a manifesto of the Neapolitan Federation which ended: 'Long live the band of the Matese.' In the same number there is an unsigned article, perhaps by Kravchinsky, on the *Activity of the Italian people in the struggle against the bourgeoisie and the government*. For the revolutionary activities of Kravchinsky in Italy, see: E. Conti, *Le origini del socialismo a Firenze*, Rome, 1950, p. 268; F. Della Peruta, *La Banda del Matese e il fallimento della teoria anarchica della moderna jacquerie in Italia*, in 'Movimento operaio', 1954, no. 3; and A. Romano, *Storia del movimento socialista in Italia*, vol. III, no place (but Rome), 1955, chap. 6.

138. A. F. Koni, '*Vospominaniya o dele Very Zasulich*' (*Recollections of the Vera Zasulich affair*), *op. cit.* Koni was the president of the tribunal which acquitted her. This book gives one of the most lively, accurate and interesting pictures of the period 1877–8. In the notes there is a very detailed account of the various individual events in this affair. Also: Vera Zasulich, '*Vospominaniya*', podgotovil k pechati B. P. Koz'min (*Recollections*, edited by B. P. Koz'min), M., 1931; A. A. Kunkl', '*Vystrel Very Zasulich*' (*The revolver shot of Vera Zasulich*), M., 1927. See also A. F. Koni, '*Izbrannyye vospominaniya*' (*A selection from the memoirs*), M., 1956.

139. 'Quarante-huit heures durant, l'Europe a tout oublié, la paix, la guerre, M. de Bismarck, lord Beaconsfield, le prince Gortchakov, pour ne s'occuper que de Vera Zassoulitch et de l'étrange aventure judiciaire dont cette inconnue a été l'héroïne', wrote G. Valbert in the 'Revue des Deux Mondes', May 1878.

140. L. Deych, '*V. I. Zasulich*', in 'Golos minuvshago', 1919, nos. V–XII.

141. A. F. Koni, '*Vospominaniya o dele Very Zasulich*' (*Recollections of the Vera Zasulich affair*), *op. cit.*, p. 231.

142. *To Russian society*, reprinted in '*Literaturnoye nasledie G. V. Plekhanova*', pod red. A. V. Lunacharskogo, F. D. Kretova, R. M. Plekhanovoy (*The literary heritage of G. V. Plekhanov*, edited by A. V. Lunacharsky, F. D. Kretov, R. M. Plekhanova), M., 1934, vol. I, p. 382.

143. In a letter addressed to B. I. Nikolaevsky, on 14th February 1923, the founder of this press, A. I. Zundelevich, described the difficulties which he encountered, and his poverty and that of his companions at that time; he also spoke of M. K. Krylova, one of the women workers at the press, of a young Bulgarian called Kozlovsky and of Vera Zasulich, who all helped to get the press going. The letter is published in '*Perepiska G. V. Plekhanova i P. B. Aksel'roda*' (*The correspondence of G. V. Plekhanov and P. B. Aksel'rod*), *op. cit.*, vol. I, p. 212.

144. A. P. Pribyleva-Korba and V. N. Figner, '*Narodovolets Aleksandr Dmitrievich Mikhaylov*' (*A. D. Mikhaylov of* 'Narodnaya Volya'), *op. cit.*, p. 123.

145. N. K. Bukh, '*Vospominaniya*'. Predislovie F. Kona (*Recollections*. Preface by F. Kon), M., 1928.

146. Only four numbers came out, between March and May of 1878. They are reprinted in '*Revolyutsionnaya zhurnalistika semidesyatykh godov*' (*Revolutionary journalism in the seventies*), *op. cit.*, to which the following pages refer.

147. March 1878, p. 3.

148. *Ibid.*, p. 5.

149. *Ibid.*, p. 4.

150. *Ibid.*, no. 2, 15th April 1878, p. 47.

151. *Ibid.*, no. 3, April 1878, p. 66.

152. *Ibid.*, no. 4, May 1878, p. 88.

153. Reprinted in '*Revolyutsionnaya zhurnalistika semidesyatykh godov*' (*Revolutionary journalism in the seventies*), *op. cit.*, p. 67. Rusanov remembered that this leaflet of Mikhaylovsky's was 'considered by the revolutionaries to be the work of the liberals who had worked up some courage and had become quite bold. On the other hand most liberals considered it to be too vigorous and too full of concessions to the revolutionaries'. N. S. Rusanov, '*Iz moikh vospominaniy*'. Kniga I: '*Detstvo i yunost' na rodine*' (*From my recollections. Book I: Childhood and youth in my native land*), Berlin, 1923, p. 238.

154. Quoted from the introductory article by O. V. Aptekman, in '*Chyornyy peredel*' (*The black partition*), *op. cit.*, p. 24.

155. B. Gorev, '*N. K. Mikhaylovsky*', M., undated, p. 41.

156. '*Obshchina*', nos. 3–4.

157. It was reprinted, with an introductory article by V. Petrovsky, in Petrograd in 1920. It provides curious evidence of the contradictions between which the whole Populist movement was oscillating at the time; of the accumulation of political and social issues; and of the desire to hit out directly at those responsible for the sufferings of the socialists in prison. So strange is this document that abroad it was taken to be the work of a *provocateur*. V. Zaytsev wrote in 'Obshcheye delo', 1878, no. 16, an article with the characteristic title of '*New tricks of the spies*'. He had welcomed the assassination itself very differently. 'In ordinary society the killing of a spy, like the killing of a spider, is the most common thing in the world and attracts no one's attention. So in Italy, in the time of the Bourbons, they killed them off like flies without regarding their importance or lack of it, and no one took any notice except the spy himself', no. 14, August 1878.

158. Regarding his state of mind at this period, see E. A. Korol'chuk, '*Iz perepiski S. M. Kravchinskogo*' (*From the correspondence of S. M. Kravchinsky*), in 'Katorga i ssylka', 1926, no. VI; this includes a letter to Vera Zasulich, which is against both Kropotkin (propaganda) on the one hand, and Stefanovich (too many concessions to the peasant mentality) on the other, and advocates deliberate and active Populism.

159. The original manuscript in A. D. Oboleshev's own hand has been preserved, '*Arkhiv "Zemli i Voli" i "Narodnoy Voli"*' (*Archives of 'Zemlya i Volya' and 'Narodnaya Volya'*), *op. cit.*, pp. 70 ff., which includes various additions, modifications and other documents referring to this discussion.

160. S. P. Pribyleva-Korba and V. N. Figner, '*Narodovolets Aleksandr Dmitrievich Mikhaylov*' (*A. D. Mikhaylov of 'Narodnaya Volya'*), *op. cit.*, p. 109.

161. This proposal is reprinted in a note by A. F. Koni, '*Vospominaniya o dele V. Zasulich*' (*Recollections of the Vera Zasulich affair*), *op. cit.*, p. 536. This session, and those immediately following, in which it was decided to abolish trial by jury for political offences and in which the foundations of the legislation concerning juries began to be undermined, found an echo in a work, apparently

by Plekhanov, which was clandestinely published by the 'Free Russian Press' in April. The title was *Two sessions of the Council of Ministers*, and it is reprinted in '*Literaturnoye nasledie G. V. Plekhanova*' (*The literary heritage of G. V. Plekhanov*), *op. cit.*, vol. I, pp. 386 ff. This shows that the 'Zemlya i Volya' circle was pretty well informed about the government's activities, and it proves what hopes they still placed, in April, in public opinion. 'The Russian social conscience, awakened by the Zasulich affair, will arouse itself still more at each new blow of the whip.'

162. A. N. Bakh, '*Zapiski narodovol'tsa*'. Predislovie P. Anatol'eva (*Recollections of a member of* 'Narodnaya i Volya'. Preface by P. Anatol'ev), no place (but L.), 1931, pp. 18–19.

163. Quoted by V. Bogucharsky, '*Aktivnoye narodnichestvo 70-kh godov*' (*Active Populism in the seventies*), *op. cit.*, p. 318.

164. 'Nachalo', no. 2, April 1878, *op. cit.*, p. 48.

165. I. I. Petrushevsky, '*Iz zapisok obshchestvennogo deyatelya. Vospominaniya*'. Pod red. Prof. A. A. Kizevettera (*From the notes of a political figure. Recollections*. Edited by Professor A. A. Kizevetter), in '*Arkhiv russkoy revolyutsii*' (*Archive of the Russian Revolution*), Berlin, 1934, p. 100. See V. Ya. Bogucharsky, '*Iz istorii politicheskoy bor'by v 70-kh i 80-kh godakh XIX veka. Partiya "Narodnoy Voli", eyo proiskhozhdenie, sud'ba i gibel'*' (*From the history of the political struggle in the seventies and eighties of the nineteenth century. The party* 'Narodnaya Volya', *its origins, its destiny and its downfall*), M., 1912, pp. 401 ff.

166. A. P. Pribyleva-Korba and V. N. Figner, '*Narodovolets Aleksandr Dmitrievich Mikhaylov*' (*A. D. Mikhaylov of* 'Narodnaya Volya'), *op. cit.*, p. 124.

167. The former went mad in prison before the trial, the latter was sentenced to ten years' hard labour, which she served, until 1886, at Kara. She was then exiled to the department of Irkutsk.

168. G. V. Plekhanov, '*Vospominaniya o A. D. Mikhaylove*' (*Recollections of A. D. Mikhaylov*), in '*Sochineniya*' (*Works*), *op. cit.*, p. 163.

169. See the manifesto of the 'Free Press of St Petersburg'—edited probably by Plekhanov—*To the students of all the institutions of higher education*, with the motto 'Who is not with me is against me', and also an appeal for resistance. Reprinted in '*Literaturnoye nasledie G. V. Plekhanova*' (*The literary heritage of G. V. Plekhanov*), *op. cit.*, vol. I, p. 384.

170. L. Tikhomirov, '*Vospominaniya*' (*Recollections*), *op. cit.*, p. 129. '*Protsess 20-ti narodovol'tsev v 1882 g.*' (*The trial of twenty members of* 'Narodnaya Volya' *in 1882*), in 'Byloye', 1906, no. I; A. P. Pribyleva-Korba, '*Pamyati dorogogo druga N. V. Kletochnikova*' (*In memory of my dear friend N. V. Kletochnikov*), in '*Arkhiv "Zemli i Voli" i "Narodnoy Voli"*' (*Archive of* 'Zemlya i Volya' *and* 'Narodnaya Volya'), *op. cit.*, p. 40. She describes him as a small, modest, good-natured man, who regarded Mikhaylov and the other members of 'Zemlya i Volya' as being infinitely above himself; like giants, models for the whole human race. He always remained something of a provincial. Only once in his life did he protest: when it was proposed that he should enter the Third Section. But he got used to the idea later on and carried out scrupulously the task entrusted to him. His reports are still preserved intact in the archives of 'Zemlya i Volya'. They were published in part in 'Byloye', 1908, no. VII; and 1909, no. VIII.

171. On the group of 'propagandists' at Vilna, from which he came, see B. Sapir, *Liberman et le socialisme russe*, in the 'International Review for Social History', 1938, no. III.

172. In the autumn of 1878 the press had published a leaflet asking for financial

support. It had already been functioning for two years and promised to increase its activity in the future. This leaflet, which has never been fully reprinted, is quoted in '*Russkaya podpol'naya i zarubezhnaya pechat'. Bibliograficheskiy ukazatel'. I. Donarodovol'cheskiy period 1831–1879*'. Vyp. I. Sostavlen M. M. Klevenskim, E. N. Kushevoy i O. P. Markovoy pod red. S. N. Valka i B. P. Koz'mina (*The clandestine press in Russia and abroad. Bibliographical guide. I. The period before* 'Narodnaya Volya', *1831–1879*. No. I, compiled by M. M. Klevensky, E. N. Kusheva and O. P. Markova, under the direction of S. N. Valk and B. P. Koz'min), M., 1935, p. 194.

173. L. Tikhomirov, '*Vospominaniya*' (*Recollections*), *op. cit.*, p. 133.

174. For a politically vague description of the inner life of 'Zemlya i Volya', see N. Morozov, '*Povesti moyey zhizni*' (*Stories from my life*), *op. cit.*, vol. IV. pp. 177 ff.; and above all G. V. Plekhanov, '*Sochineniya*' (*Works*), *op. cit.*, pp. 165 ff.

175. The article is by Plekhanov. It is reprinted in '*Sochineniya*' (*Works*), *op. cit.*, vol. I, pp. 56 ff.

176. Reprinted in '*Sochineniya*' (*Works*), *op. cit.*, vol. I, pp. 67 ff.

177. A. P. Pribyleva-Korba and V. N. Figner, '*Narodovolets Aleksandr Dmitrievich Mikhaylov*' (*A. D. Mikhaylov of* 'Narodnaya Volya'), *op. cit.*, p. 110.

178. M. R. Popov, '*Zapiski zemlevol'tsa*' (*Recollections of a member of* 'Zemlya i Volya'), *op. cit.*, p. 107.

179. (Anonymous), '*S. N. Bobokhov*', in 'Byloye', 1900, no. I.

180. For an account of her, see E. K. Breshko-Breshkovskaya, '*Iz vospominaniy*' (*From recollections*), in 'Golos minuvshago', 1918, nos. X–XII. As the daughter of General Leshern von Gertsfel'd, she had been brought up in a wealthy and cultured environment. She was one of the Chaykovskists and was principally connected with the group of F. N. Lermontov, one of the men who moved from propaganda to 'the rebels'. She was arrested in 1874 and set free after the 'trial of the hundred and ninety-three'. She went straight to Kiev to take part in terrorism there. At her trial, the prosecutor said of her that 'she was not a woman, but a monster, a sort of hermaphrodite' and asked for the death penalty, which was afterwards commuted to hard labour for life. She remained at Kara until 1894, then she was exiled in the Baikal area.

181. *Ibid.* She too was a particularly well educated woman. She had interrupted her studies in mathematics at the University of Heidelberg to take part in the revolutionary movement at Moscow. She was arrested six times and eventually exiled in the department of Kostroma. Later she worked at Kiev and was condemned to fourteen years' hard labour.

182. '*Protsess sotsialistov Valer'yana Osinskogo, Sofii Leshern von Gertsfel'd i Varfolomeya Voloshenko. Kratkiy otchyot zasedaniya Kievskogo Voennookruzhnogo suda 5 maya*' (*The trial of the socialists V. Osinsky, Sofya Leshern von Gertsfeld and V. Voloshenko. A brief account of their trial by the military tribunal of the district of Kiev on 5th May 1879*), no place (but Geneva), 1879, p. 12. Sofya Leshern said 'that she had nothing to say except that she utterly despised the tribunal and the governor', *ibid*.

183. L. Deych, '*Valer'yan Osinsky*', in 'Katorga i ssylka', 1929, no. V.

184. L. Tikhomirov, '*Vospominaniya*' (*Recollections*), *op. cit.*, p. 134. This standpoint of Klements's was eventually reflected in his sentence—deportation to Siberia—at a time when hangings and the *katorga* were the order of the day.

185. 'Zemlya i Volya!' had not spoken of the 'Executive Committee'. 'Listok' had published, for the first time in the North, a communiqué signed in this way when the spy, Reynshteyn, was killed, 'guilty of having brought the *Northern Union of Russian Workers* to its downfall'.

186. N. Morozov, '*Povesti moyey zhizni*' (*Stories from my life*), *op. cit.*, vol. IV, pp. 206 ff.; and P. E. Shchegolev, '*Alekseyevskiy ravelin*' (*The Alexeyevsky dungeon*), M., 1929, pp. 263 ff.

187. A different opinion from this, and from all the other accounts, is expressed by Zundelevich in a letter published in 'Sbornik. Gruppa "Osvobozhdenie truda"', no. III, p. 207. Zundelevich himself conducted the negotiations with Solovyov in the days before his attempted assassination of the Tsar. What he wrote in any case confirms the fact that Mikhaylov and Kvyatkovsky did nothing to stop him.

188. V. Figner, '*Zapechatlyonnyy trud*' (*Work concluded*), *op. cit.*, vol. I, p. 129; and M. R. Popov, '*Zapiski zemlevol'tsa*' (*Recollections of a member of* 'Zemlya i Volya'), *op. cit.*, p. 202.

189. '*Pokushenie A. K. Solovyova na tsareubiystvo 2 aprelya 1879 g.*' (*A. K. Solovyov's attempted assassination of the Tsar on 2nd April 1879*), in 'Byloye' 1918, nos. I, II.

190. A. P. Pribyleva-Korba and V. N. Figner, '*Narodovolets Aleksandr Dmitrievich Mikhaylov*' (*A. D. Mikhaylov of* 'Narodnaya Volya'), *op. cit.*, pp. 109, 127.

191. There is an anonymous pamphlet (in fact by P. Kropotkin) which is interesting for its assessment of Solovyov's gesture, *La vie d'un socialiste russe*, Geneva, 1879. 'La bourgeoisie se sent ennuyée de ce règne, commencé par des promesses si belles et finissant par l'incapacité, l'oppression, l'arbitraire des gendarmes, la banqueroute, la terreur. Pétersbourg, cette capitale si servile autrefois, témoigne une indifférence frappante le jour de l'attentat, et devient morne, triste, le jour de l'exécution de Solovieff. Les villes murmurent. Et là-bas, dans ces vastes plaines, arrosées par la sueur du laboureur resté esclave, dans ces sombres hameaux où la misère tuait toutes les espérances, les coups de revolver de Solovieff deviennent la cause d'une sourde agitation: l'insurrection, précourseur des révolutions, fait déjà entendre son grondement. Le 1793 du paysan russe se sent dans l'air.'

CHAPTER 21

1. See N. Shilder, '*Graf Eduard Ivanovich Totleben. Ego zhizn' i deyatel'nost'. Biograficheskiy ocherk*' (*Count Totleben. His life and work. Biographical essay*), Spb., 1882.

2. S. S. Tatishchev, '*Imperator Aleksandr II. Ego zhizn' i tsarstvovanie*' (*The Emperor Alexander II. His life and reign*), Spb., 1903, vol. II, p. 606.

3. *Ibid.*, p. 613.

4. 'Narodnaya Volya', no. I, 1st October 1879, in '*Literatura partii* "Narodnoy Voli"' (*Literature of the party* 'Narodnaya Volya'), M., 1907, p. 23.

5. *Ibid.*, p. 29. On the journey from prison to gallows, the condemned men tried to shout to the crowd from their carts that they were dying on behalf of the people. Before his head was pushed into the hood (the custom with those about to be hanged), Bil'chansky managed to say: 'Long live the revolution! Long live the poor!'

6. *Ibid.*, p. 8. See A. Semyonov, '*Salomon Vittenberg (Materialy i biografiya)*' (*S. Vittenberg* [*Material and biography*]), in 'Byloye', 1925, no. VI. He was born in 1852 of a poor Jewish family; after finishing his studies he went to Vienna for a time. In 1877 he spent three months in the fortress at Nikolaev for spreading propaganda among the sailors. When he came out, he went off to Odessa as a workman and took part in the demonstrations following the

Koval'sky trial. 'Throughout that terrible night I stayed in the streets. . . . A terrible night, but beautiful . . .'

7. *Ibid.*, no. 5, 5th February 1881, p. 182. S. Yastremsky, '*D. A. Lizogub (Tri vstrechi)*' (*D. A. Lizogub [Three meetings]*), in 'Katorga i ssylka', 1924, no. IV; and E. Khir'yakova, '*Vospominaniya i nekotoryye svedeniya o Dmitrii Andreyeviche Lizogube*' (*Recollections and some information about D. A. Lizogub*), in 'Zven'ya', 1932, no. I.

8. A. P. Pribyleva-Korba and V. N. Figner, '*Narodovolets Aleksandr Dmitrievich Mikhaylov*' (*A. D. Mikhaylov of* 'Narodnaya Volya'), L., 1925, p. 131.

9. P. L. Lavrov, '*Narodniki-propagandisty 1873–1877 gg.*' (*Populist-propagandists in the years 1873–1877*), in '*Materialy dlya istorii russkogo sotsial'no-revolyutsionnogo dvizheniya*' (*Material for a history of the Russian social-revolutionary movement*), Geneva, 1895, no. X, p. 75.

10. M. F. Frolenko, '*Sobranie sochineniy*', v dvukh tomakh, pod. redaktsiey i s primechaniyami I. A. Teodorovicha (*Works*, in two volumes, edited and with notes by I. A. Teodorovich), M., 1932, vol. II, p. 33. For the ideas of S. N. Yuzhakov, see T. H. Von Laue, *The Fate of Capitalism in Russia. The Narodnik Version*, in 'The American Slavic and East European Review', 1954, no. 1.

11. 'Narodnaya Volya', no. 3, 1st January 1880, *op. cit.*, p. 105.

12. A. P. Pribyleva-Korba and V. N. Figner, '*Narodovolets Aleksandr Dmitrievich Mikhaylov*' (*A. D. Mikhaylov of* 'Narodnaya Volya'), *op. cit.*, p. 135.

13. '*Revolyutsionnaya zhurnalistika semidesyatykh godov*' (*Revolutionary journalism in the seventies*), Paris, 1905, pp. 399 ff.

14. Nikolay Morozov, '*Povesti moyey zhizni*'. Redaktsiya, vstupitel'naya stat'ya i primechaniya I. A. Teodorovicha (*Stories from my life*. Edited with an introductory article and notes by I. A. Teodorovich), M., 1933, vol. IV, p. 284. On Shiryaev, see R. M. Kantor, '*Avtograficheskaya zapiska Stepana Shiryaeva*' (*Autobiographical memoir by S. Shiryaev*), in 'Krasnyy arkhiv', 1924, no. VII, which publishes his deposition. He was the son of a serf in the Saratov region, and had started off as a follower of the ideas of Pisarev, a 'nihilist'. But before long he gave them up, 'because I realized their falsity and narrow egoism, and I saw my moral obligation to be a useful member of society'. His spiritual evolution was typical of his generation, influenced as he was by the writings of Dobrolyubov, Flerovsky and Chernyshevsky. He, too 'almost went as a volunteer to Serbia'. In Switzerland he was in touch with the émigrés. He sided with the Bakuninist party against Lavrov, and above all against the new policy of 'Vperyod' and the St Petersburg followers of Lavrov, who trusted only in propaganda and the development of Russian economy: 'The Swiss anarchists were the first to talk about *propagande par le fait*.' For his connections with Lavrov, see his letters to him written in 1878, from May to October, which were published by V. L. Burtsev in 'Golos minuvshago na chuzhoy storone', 1927, no. V. In these he discussed his programme of action before returning to Russia: 'To struggle against the factory owners, against the *pomeshchiki* and the *kulaks* in the villages, against the police, the judges, the apathetic . . . to be at the head of those whom the Tsar and the nobility have offended, to be at the head of the workers who have been reduced to despair by the will of their bosses, to be at the head of the religious sects . . .' This programme was typical of a *narodnik* of 'Zemlya i Volya', yet no sooner did he get to St Petersburg than he was caught up by terrorism and put himself at the head of those who supported such a policy.

15. M. R. Popov, '*Zapiski zemlevol'tsa*'. Redaktsiya I. A. Teodorovicha (*Recollections of a member of* 'Zemlya i Volya'. Edited by I. A. Teodorovich), *op. cit.*, M., 1933, p. 200.

27+

16. *Ibid.*, p. 222. See S. Valk, '*Avtobiograficheskoye zayavlenie A. A. Kvyatkovs, kogo*' (*A. A. Kvyatkovsky's autobiographical deposition*), in 'Krasnyy arkhiv'-1926, no. I. He came from Tomsk in Siberia, and was a cousin of Bakunin's wife.

17. *Ibid.*, p. 94.

18. '*Nikolay Ivanovich Kibal'chich*', Geneva, 1882, second edition, 1889, p. 6. See '*N. I. Kibal'chich*'. Red. F. Delova, N. Maksimova, S. Nechetnogoy i A. Rudina (*N. I. Kibal'chich*. Edited by F. Delov, N. Maksimov, S. Nechetnoga and A. Rudin), Spb., 1906. His depositions have been published in 'Byloye', 1918, nos. X–XI.

19. Vera Figner, '*Zapechatlyonnyy trud*' (*Work concluded*), M., 1933, vol. I, p. 132.

20. She was one of the few members of this group to survive the suppression of 'Narodnaya Volya'. She published some of her recollections: for instance, '*Iz dalyokogo proshlogo. Iz vospominaniy o pokusheniyakh na Aleksandra II*' (*From the distant past. Recollections of attempts on the life of Alexander II*), in 'Katorga i ssylka', 1924, no. I.

21. Vera Figner, '*Grigoriy Prokof'evich Isaev*', in 'Golos minuvshago', 1917, nos. IX–X.

22. It is not easy to reconstruct the stages of Tikhomirov's development, principally because he himself has covered over the traces in his recollections (or rather, notes for the memoirs he intended to write) by editing them when he became a reactionary and a violent opponent of all the ideals of his youth. The fact remains that the leading article in the last number of 'Zemlya i Volya!' was by him. It was not terrorist in tone, in the political sense that this word was soon to assume. He spoke of economic terrorism, not of the 'blow at the centre'. He wrote the article, it is true, in place of a projected article by Plekhanov who cared for terrorism even less than he did; but he had not yet taken the decisive step. He confined himself, as always, to explaining standpoints which he had accepted rather than created. But by continuing along this road, he found himself side by side with the founders of 'Narodnaya Volya'. He followed this course without inner struggle, guided by outside influences rather than by any inner change of conviction. This is confirmed by Vera Figner's comment: 'Tikhomirov was a man without will and without character'. It was just that which, combined with his undoubted intelligence, enabled him to reflect the general state of mind better than anyone else. Lev Tikhomirov, '*Vospominaniya*', pod redaktsiey V. I. Nevskogo. Vstupitel'naya stat'ya V. N. Figner (*Memoirs*, edited by V. I. Nevsky. Introductory article by V. N. Figner), M.-L., 1927, pp. xxxvi, 120; D. Kuz'min (pseudonym of E. E. Kolosov), '*Narodovol'cheskaya zhurnalistika*'. S poslesloviem V. Figner (*The journalistic activities of* 'Narodnaya Volya'. With a final note by V. Figner), M., 1930, p. 214. (For the attribution to him of the leading article in 'Zemlya i Volya!', no. 5.)

23. M. F. Frolenko, '*Sobranie sochineniy*' (*Works*), *op. cit.*, vol. II, pp. 13–14. See V. N. Figner, '*Narodovolets A. I. Barannikov v ego pis'makh*' (*A. I. Barannikov of* 'Narodnaya Volya', *from his letters*), M., 1935.

24. *Ibid.*, vol. II, p. 14.

25. One comes across her under different names in the memoirs and documents of the period. She was born Mariya Nikolaevna Olovennikova, which she later changed either by marriage or for purposes of conspiracy to Oshanina, Barannikova and Koshurnikova. When she lived in Paris she went under the name of Marina Nikanorovna Polonskaya. Her notes on the history of 'Narodnaya Volya', published under the title, '*Pokazaniya. K istorii partii "Narodnoy Voli"*' (*Depositions. For a history of the party* 'Narodnaya Volya'),

in 'Byloye', 1907, no. VI, give an interesting account of her political ideas, as well as being an important source for the history of the whole movement.

26. A. Yakimova, *'Pamyati Natal'i Nikolaevny Olovennikovoy'* (*In memory of N. N. Olovennikova*), in 'Katorga i ssylka', 1925, no. I.

27. D. Footman, 'Red prelude. A Life of A. I. Zhelyabov', London, 1944.

28. P. P. Semenyuta, *'Iz vospominaniy o A. I. Zhelyabove'* (*From recollections of A. I. Zhelyabov*), in 'Byloye', 1906, no. IV.

29. V. N. Pisnaya, *'Studencheskiye gody Zhelyabova'* (*Zhelyabov's student years*), in 'Byloye', 1925, no. IV.

30. In 1873 Zhelyabov amazed the young Aksel'rod and other Chaykovskists at Kiev by saying that 'Choice of profession was of little importance for the revolutionary. He could be a doctor, a professor, etc.'. 'I did not agree', added Aksel'rod, 'as I thought that a privileged position, even that of a teacher, would not have helped us to come near to the people, but, on the contrary, would have alienated us and at the same time would have weakened our revolutionary state of mind.' P. B. Aksel'rod, *'Perezhitoye i peredumannoye'* (*Things seen and reflected upon*), Berlin, 1923, vol. I, p. 103.

31. For a detailed description, see in I. P. Belokonsky, *'Dan' vremeni. Vospominaniya'* (*The tribute of time. Recollections*), M., 1918, pp. 83 ff.

32. Letter of 12th May 1880, published by Dragomanov himself with some small alterations (for conspiratorial reasons), and reprinted complete from the original by L. Peretts, in 'Zven'ya', 1935, no. 5.

33. M. Dragomanov is of special interest as regards this period of his life: *'K biografii Zhelyabova'* (*For a biography of Zhelyabov*), in *'Sochineniya'* (*Works*), Paris, vol. II.

34. V. N. Pisnaya, *'K biografii Zhelyabova (Materialy doznaniya po delu 193-kh)'* (*For a biography of Zhelyabov* [*Documents dealing with the investigation of the* '*hundred and ninety-three*']), in 'Katorga i ssylka', 1924, no. IV.

35. *'Delo 1-ogo marta 1881 g. Protsess Zhelyabova, Perovskoy i dr. (Pravitel'stvennyy otchyot)'*. So stat'yey i primechaniyami L'va Deycha (*The affair of 1st March 1881. The trial of Zhelyabov, Perovskaya and others* [*Official account*]. With an article and notes by Lev Deych), Spb., 1906, p. 92.

36. M. F. Frolenko, *'Sobranie sochineniy'* (*Works*), op. cit., vol. II, pp. 16–17.

37. For Zhelyabov's desire to form a close union between the social and political fight, see P. B. Aksel'rod's interesting account, *'Perezhitoye i peredumannoye'* (*Things seen and reflected upon*), Berlin, 1923, vol. I, p. 320.

38. A characteristic programme of a group of 'country folk', in this case L. N. Gartman, M. V. Debel', Aptekman and Tishchenko from Tambov, has been published by B. P. Koz'min, in *'K istorii "Zemli i Voli" 70-kh godov'* (*For a history of* 'Zemlya i Volya' *in the seventies*), in 'Krasnyy arkhiv', 1926, no. VI.

39. This polemical and tactical opposition of 'country folk' to 'townsmen' was later adopted by Plekhanov as an historical criterion for understanding the internal struggle that divided 'Zemlya i Volya'. This risks falsifying the very basis of the debate. See, for instance, his preface to the Russian translation of Alphons Thun, *Geschichte der revolutionären Bewegungen in Russland*, published at Geneva in 1906.

40. An interesting discussion about these meetings was restarted many years later, when the few who had escaped the gallows or death in prison were able to write their impressions and recollections. M. R. Popov, ' *"Zemlya i Volya" nakanune Voronezhskogo s'yezda'* ('Zemlya i Volya' *on the eve of the congress of Voronezh*), in 'Byloye', 1906, no. VIII, reprinted in *'Zapiski zemlevol'tsa'* (*Recollections of a member of* 'Zemlya i Volya'), op. cit., p. 191 ff.; N. A. Morozov, *'Vozniknovenie "Narodnoy Voli"* (*Iz vospominaniy o Lipetskom i*

Voronezhskom s'yezdakh)' (The origin of 'Narodnaya Volya' [*From recollections of the congresses of Lipetsk and Voronezh*]), in 'Byloye', 1906, no. XII, reprinted with additional material in *'Povesti moyey zhizni' (Stories from my life), op. cit.,* vol. IV, pp. 267 ff.; M. F. Frolenko, *'Kommentarii k stat'ye "Vozniknovenie 'Narodnoy Voli'"' (Comments on the article* [by N. A. Morozov, just mentioned] *"The origin of* 'Narodnaya Volya'"), in 'Byloye', 1906, no. XII; and *'Lipetskiy i Voronezhskiy s'yezdy' (The congresses of Lipetsk and Voronezh),* in 'Byloye', 1907, no. I, both reprinted in *'Sobranie sochineniy' (Works), op. cit.,* vol. II, p. 9 ff.

41. N. A. Morozov, *'Povesti moyey zhizni' (Stories from my life), op. cit.,* vol. IV, p. 285.

42. In his book, Morozov repeats these statutes from memory with serious inaccuracies; they have since been published from an original which fell into the hands of the police in 1882, by B. I. Nikolaevsky, *'Ustav Ispolnitel'nogo Komiteta "Narodnoy Voli"' (The statutes of the Executive Committee of* 'Narodnaya Volya'), in 'Na chuzhoy storone', 1924, no. VII. They were drawn up by Morozov, and completed by Mikhaylov, Kvyatkovsky, Zhelyabov and Tikhomirov. They were later confirmed without modifications when 'Narodnaya Volya' was formed.

43. M. F. Frolenko, *'Sobranie sochineniy' (Works), op. cit.,* vol. II, p. 21.

44. *Ibid.,* p. 46.

45. N. A. Morozov, *'Povesti moyey zhizni' (Stories from my life), op. cit.,* vol. IV, pp. 290–1.

46. A. P. Pribyleva-Korba and V. N. Figner, *'Narodovolets Aleksandr Dmitrievich Mikhaylov' (A. D. Mikhaylov of* 'Narodnaya Volya'), *op. cit.,* p. 135.

47. To the recollections of the Lipetsk conference mentioned in note 42, Vera Figner's *'Zapechatlyonnyy trud' (Work concluded), op. cit.,* vol. I, pp. 132 ff., should be added.

48. Other sources show some divergencies from this list but not enough to alter the essential character of the meeting.

49. Vera Figner, *'Zapechatlyonnyy trud' (Work concluded), op. cit.,* vol. I, p. 134.

50. *'Andrey Ivanovich Zhelyabov',* London, 1882. In the above-mentioned preface to the Russian translation of A. Thun's work, Plekhanov says that this pamphlet was written by Tikhomirov. He also adds that it was approved by the 'Executive Committee', that is to say, by what was left of it after the arrests in 1881. The most essential parts have since been reprinted in 'Byloye', 1906, no. VIII.

51. Vera Figner gave a different interpretation of this discussion at Voronezh. She attributed Zhelyabov's attitude to his inexperience of the circle into which he had only just entered. But his words seem to have contained the core of a fundamental political viewpoint which he was to develop from then on throughout his activity.

52. *'Arkhiv "Zemli i Voli" i "Narodnoy Voli"' (The archives of* 'Zemlya i Volya' *and* 'Narodnaya Volya'), M., 1930.

53. 'She was an extremely typical product of the 'sixties.' A sense of duty towards the people, the problems of the freedom of the individual in general and of women in particular lay at the very heart of her personality. She was the daughter of an ignorant, provincial nobleman, and on coming to Moscow to study she began to work with the revolutionary movement right from the time of the Ishutin and Karakozov groups. Later, in Geneva, she worked in one of the émigré printing presses. On her return she was exiled in the trial of Nechaev's followers. But she always remained a 'propagandist'. See E. K.

Breshko-Breshkovskaya, '*Iz vospominaniy*' (*From recollections*), in 'Golos minuvshago', 1918, nos. X–XII.

54. The man who arranged this *coup* was Fedor Yurkovsky, one of the boldest and most picturesque of the 'rebels' of the South. Under the name of 'Sasha the engineer' he became a legend at that time for his courage and ability. When he was condemned to hard labour, he wrote his own account of his exploit: '*Podkop pod khersonskoye kaznacheystvo*' (*The tunnel under the Kherson treasury*), which was published in 'Byloye', 1908, no. VII. Frolenko, who also took part, added his recollections in the same number; they are reprinted in '*Sobranie sochineniy*' (*Works*), *op. cit.*, vol. I, pp. 288 ff. On 'Sasha the engineer', see E. E. Kolosov's detailed notes to his edition of Yurkovsky's autobiographical novel written at Shlissel'burg, '*Bulgakov*', M.-L., 1933.

55. V. I. Nevsky, '*Ot "Zemli i Voli" k gruppe "Osvobozhdeniya truda"*' (*From 'Zemlya i Volya' to the group* 'Osvobozhdenie truda'), M., 1930, pp. 180 ff.

56. N. Sergievsky, '*Chyornyy peredel i narodniki 80-kh godov*' ('Chyornyy peredel' *and the Populists of the eighties*), in 'Katorga i ssylka', 1931, no. I.

57. All the literature of this movement has been reprinted in ' "*Chyornyy peredel*". *Organ sotsialistov-federalistov 1880–1881 g.*' Predislovie V. I. Nevskogo. Vstupitel'naya stat'ya O. V. Aptekmana ('Chyornyy peredel'. *The organ of the federalist-socialists. 1880–1881*. Preface by V. I. Nevsky. Introductory article by O. V. Aptekman), M.-P., 1923.

58. I. A. Teodorovich, '*Sotsial'no-politicheskaya mysl' chyornoperedel'chestva i eyo znachenie v nashem proshlom*' (*The social and political thought of* 'Chyornyy peredel' *and its significance in our past*), in 'Katorga i ssylka', 1933, nos. IV–V.

59. G. V. Plekhanov, '*Sochineniya*' (*Works*), *op. cit.*, vol. I, p. 111.

60. ' "*Chyornyy peredel*". *Organ sotsialistov-federalistov*' ('Chyornyy peredel'. *The organ of the federalist-socialists*), *op. cit.*, p. 122.

61. G. V. Plekhanov, '*Sochineniya*' (*Works*), *op. cit.*, vol. I, p. 120.

62. *Ibid.*, pp. 113–15.

63. *Ibid.*, p. 129.

64. *Ibid.*, p. 134.

65. *Ibid.*, p. 131.

66. ' "*Chyornyy peredel*". *Organ sotsialistov-federalistov*' ('Chyornyy peredel'. *The organ of the federalist-socialists*), *op. cit.*, pp. 250–1.

67. *Ibid.*, p. 136.

68. 'Vol'noye slovo', 1881, no. 19.

69. G. V. Plekhanov, '*Sochineniya*' (*Works*), *op. cit.*, vol. I, p. 125.

70. ' "*Chyornyy peredel*". *Organ sotsialistov-federalistov*' ('Chyornyy peredel'. *The organ of the federalist-socialists*), *op. cit.*, p. 125.

71. N. Sergievsky, '*Narodnichestvo 80-kh godov*' (*Populism in the eighties*), in '*Istoriko-revolyutsionnyy sbornik*' (*Miscellany on revolutionary history*), vol. III.

72. ' "*Chyornyy peredel*". *Organ sotsialistov-federalistov*' ('Chyornyy peredel'. *The organ of the federalist-socialists*), *op. cit.*, p. 197.

73. G. V. Plekhanov, '*Sochineniya*' (*Works*), *op. cit.*, vol. I, pp. 129–30.

74. ' "*Chyornyy peredel*". *Organ sotsialistov-federalistov*' ('Chyornyy peredel'. *The organ of the federalist-socialists*), *op. cit.*, p. 185.

75. *Ibid.*, p. 198.

76. *Ibid.*, p. 186. The ideas behind 'Chyornyy peredel' are also reflected in its attitude towards the international labour movement. After proclaiming its loyalty to the tradition of the anarchist International, it showed some reserve about the activities of J. Most, the most important anarchist in Western Europe at the time, on account of his violent opposition to social-democracy

(*ibid.*, no. 2, pp. 216 ff.). It showed great interest in the social-democratic congress at Zürich (*ibid.*, no. 2, pp. 230 ff.), and criticized the congresses held by the French socialists at Lyons and Marseilles in 1878 and 1879, as well as 'Le travailleur' for its too favourable attitude towards them. Yet the spread of the socialist movement in France obviously aroused the sympathy and interest of 'Chyornyy peredel' (*ibid.*, no. I, p. 179; no. 2, p. 227). Another characteristic was its friendly respect for Lavrov. For the general development of the working-class movement in this period, see Leo Valiani, *Dalla prima alla seconda Internazionale, 1872–89*, in 'Movimento operaio', 1954, no. II, pp. 188 ff.

77. The memoirs on 'Narodnaya Volya' published abroad by émigrés from 1880 right up to the revolution of 1905 form an important body of material, rich in critical and interpretative insight. But they belong to the realm of political, polemic and apologetic literature. Although they lack historical vision, they are an indispensable source. A *catalogue raisonné* would cover the ideological formation of Russian social-democracy and of the various socialist-revolutionary currents. The same is true of the numerous publications which appeared in Russia after 1905, when it was possible to speak openly on the subject of 'Narodnaya Volya', and now the distance in time gave an added breadth and complexity to personal recollections. The first attempt at a comprehensive picture of all the material was made by V. Ya. Bogucharsky, '*Iz istorii politicheskoy bor'by v 70-kh i 80-kh godakh XIX veka. Partiya "Narodnoy Voli", eyo proiskhozhdenie, sud'ba i gibel'*' (*From the history of the political struggle in the seventies and eighties of the nineteenth century. The party* 'Narodnaya Volya', *its origins, its destiny and its fall*), M., 1912. The opening of the police archives provided another series of new documents. The fiftieth anniversary of 'Narodnaya Volya' in 1929 was the occasion for one of the most interesting discussions held by Soviet historians. Political and social problems were treated with great heat, showing the importance and vitality of the subject. The writers of the documents listed below were interested in extracting whatever had a bearing on Soviet politics in those decisive years. But here we are interested in the positive contribution that this debate made to the interpretation of 'Narodnaya Volya': M. Pokrovsky, '*Ocherki po istorii revolyutsionnogo dvizheniya v Rossii XIX i XX vekov*' (*Essays on the history of the revolutionary movement in Russia in the nineteenth and twentieth century*), M., 1924; idem., '*Po povodu yubileya "Narodnoy Voli"*' (*On the occasion of the jubilee of* 'Narodnaya Volya'), in 'Istorik-marksist', 1930, no. XV; and also '*Ocherednyye zadachi istorikov-marksistov*' (*The tasks of Marxist historians today*), in 'Istorik-marksist', 1930, no. XVI; I. Teodorovich, '*Istoricheskoye znachenie partii "Narodnoy Voli"*' (*The historical significance of* 'Narodnaya Volya'), in 'Katorga i ssylka', 1929, nos. VIII–IX; idem., '*K sporam o "Narodnoy Voli"*' (*The disputes on the subject of* 'Narodnaya Volya'), ibid., 1930, no. I; idem., '*O "Narodnoy Voli"*' (*On the subject of* 'Narodnaya Volya'), ibid., 1930, no. III; idem., '*Pervoye marta 1881 goda*' (*The first of March 1881*), ibid., 1931, no. III, and reprinted in book form, M., 1931; idem., '*Ot bakunizma k babevizmu*' (*From Bakunism to Babeuvism*), M., 1933; V. I. Nevsky, '*Ot "Zemli i Voli" k gruppe "Osvobozhdeniya truda"*' (*From* 'Zemlya i Volya' *to* 'Osvobozhdenie truda'), op. cit.; V. Malakhovsky, '*Na dva fronta (K otsenke narodovol'chestva)*' (*On two fronts [Towards a judgment on* 'Narodnaya Volya']), L., 1930; V. Levitsky (V. O. Tsederbaum), '*Partiya "Narodnoy Voli". Vozniknovenie, bor'ba, gibel'*' (*The party of* 'Narodnaya Volya', *origin, struggle and fall*), M.-L., 1928; M. Potash, '*Narodnicheskiy sotsializm*' (*Populist socialism*), M., 1930; Dmitriy Kuz'min (pseudonym for

E. E. Kolosov), '*Narodovol'cheskaya zhurnalistika*'. S poslesloviem V. Figner (*The journalistic activities of* 'Narodnaya Volya'. With an appendix by V. Figner), M., 1930; '*Diskussiya o "Narodnoy Voli" v Obshchestve istorikov-marksistov*' (*The discussion on* 'Narodnaya Volya' *in the Society of Marxist Historians*), in 'Istorik-marksist', 1930, no. XV. The interest aroused led to the publication of a whole series of collections of documents; the most important is '*Trudy kruzhka narodovol'tsev pri Obshchestve politkatorzhan i ssylko-poselentsev*', pod red. A. V. Yakimovoy-Dikovskoy, M. F. Frolenko, I. I. Popova, N. I. Rakitnikova i V. V. Leonovicha-Angarskogo (*Works of the group of members of* 'Narodnaya Volya' *in the Society of Political Prisoners and Exiles*. Edited by A. V. Yakimova-Dikovskaya, M. F. Frolenko, I. I. Popov, N. I. Rakitnikov and V. V. Leonovich-Angarsky), M., 1930–1, in five volumes.

78. There have been three reprints of the publications of 'Narodnaya Volya'. We shall refer to '*Literatura partii "Narodnoy Voli"*' (*The literature of the party* 'Narodnaya Volya'), M., 1906. Although it includes some additional material, the reprint edited by A. V. Yakimova-Dikovskaya, M. F. Frolenko and others, M., 1930, is neither complete nor very accurate.

79. 'Narodnaya Volya', no. I, *op. cit.*, p. 6. The article has been attributed both to Kvyatkovsky and to Morozov.

80. *Ibid.*, no. III, p. 78. The article is by Tikhomirov.

81. *Ibid.*, no. I, p. 6.

82. *Ibid.*

83. *Ibid.*, p. 4.

84. *Ibid.*

85. *Ibid.*, p. 6.

86. *Ibid.*, no. III, p. 84. From the 'Programme of the Executive Committee' published there.

87. *Ibid.*, no. II, p. 41. The article is by Morozov.

88. *Ibid.*, no. I, p. 6.

89. L. Tikhomirov, *La Russie politique et sociale*, Paris, 1886, p. 206.

90. 'Narodnaya Volya', no. I, p. 6.

91. *Ibid.*, no. II, p. 41.

92. In no. VI, pp. 201 ff., G. G. Romanenko gives a more detailed description of the Russian state, which is, however, even more anecdotal and less penetrating than the few but telling allegations published in the first numbers of 'Narodnaya Volya'.

93. 'Narodnaya Volya', no. II, p. 41.

94. '*Andrey Ivanovich Zhelyabov*', London, 1882, p. 26.

95. 'Listok Narodnoy Voli', no. 3, 20th September 1880, *op. cit.*, p. 136. The article is by Tikhomirov.

96. 'Narodnaya Volya', *op. cit.*, pp. 43–4.

97. *Ibid.*, no. III, *op. cit.*, p. 81.

98. Details of the conflict between Morozov and the others are given by O. S. Lyubatovich, in '*Dalyokoye i nedavneye. Vospominaniya iz zhizni revolyu-tsionerov 1878–1881 gg.*' (*The distant past and the immediate past. Recollections of the life of the revolutionaries, 1878–1881*), in 'Byloye', 1906, nos. V, VI. These memoirs were reprinted in M. in 1930, and form one of the most lively documents of the period. For Morozov's activity in Switzerland, see S. Valk, '*G. G. Romanenko (Iz istorii "Narodnoy Voli")*' (*G. G. Romanenko* [*From the history of* 'Narodnaya Volya']), in 'Katorga i ssylka', 1928, no. XI. Romanenko came from the Odessa group of Koval'sky, Malinka and Voloshenko; he left Russia in December 1879. When Morozov met him in Switzerland, he realized that they had many ideas in common. 'When talking we found ourselves in com-

plete agreement in thinking that the Russian situation is extraordinarily sad. The party which is in action now runs the imminent risk of having no ground on which to stand', he wrote to Lavrov in May 1880, when announcing their intention of publishing a new review. Its policy was to have been based on the one means that they considered efficient and capable of development: terrorism. The review was never published, but they expressed their ideas in two pamphlets: Nikolay Morozov, 'Terroristicheskaya bor'ba' (The terrorist struggle), London (but in fact Geneva), 1880, and reprinted in 'Da zdravstvuet "Narodnaya Volya". Istoricheskiy sbornik' (Long live 'Narodnaya Volya'. Historical miscellany), Paris, 1907, pp. 17 ff.; and V. Tarnovsky (G. G. Romanenko), 'Terrorizm i rutina' (Terrorism and 'routine'), London (but in fact Geneva), undated. Morozov, in his pamphlet, justified terrorism on the grounds of the disproportionate size of the State forces compared with those of the revolutionaries. This position must be recognized and all its positive aspects appreciated. Up to that time everyone had understood terrorism in his own way. Now its theory must be formulated. It was 'the struggle of knowledge and science against bayonets and the gallows'. It was technically and morally superior to its adversary, it was a more perfect and modern instrument than bloody and confused 'mass revolutions', in which the people ended up by 'killing its own sons'. 'But the terrorist revolution only punishes those who are to blame', and therefore it is 'the fairest of all forms of revolution' (original edition, pp. 7–9). It would stop as soon as it has won sufficient freedom to spread propaganda for socialist ideas, those ideas which have been characteristic of the whole Russian movement' (p. 10). Romanenko also came to the same conclusions, after having drawn a brief and effective picture of the situation in Russia: 'The poison of bourgeois relationships has entered the economic life of the countryside, whilst the political structure has preserved all the arbitrary nature of an Oriental despotism. It is no wonder that this morganatic union between West and East has led to the impoverishment of all classes, and all categories, and above all, of the productive class, where misery has now become unending hunger' (p. 4). Against this situation he too saw only one weapon: terrorist revolution. And he was pleased at the definition given by a Frenchman to whom he had expounded his ideas: 'C'est une révolution scientifique' (p. 19). He, too, denounced the 'horrors of a popular revolution', as an argument in favour of terrorism and drew up a wide programme of political liberty (p. 24). As far as social matters went he remained a Populist. He edited a Russian edition of Schäffle's Essence of Socialism and used the notes and preface to make his own views clear, views which he discussed in a letter to Morozov of 22nd September 1880: 'Marx and Engels say that Socialism will result from capitalism developed to its extreme. Many have shown that this is not a compulsory road for us to travel, and the best among them was Chernyshevsky. Now I wish to show that Marx's way is simply impossible everywhere.'

On the basis of these ideas Morozov and Romanenko tried to come to an agreement with 'Nabat', and to make a political and financial agreement between Tkachev's 'Jacobins' and the 'Executive Committee' of 'Narodnaya Volya'. Tursky conducted the negotiations on behalf of 'Nabat'. Tikhomirov's reply, on behalf of himself and his companions in St Petersburg, was negative; his letter was dated 13th/25th May 1880. 'Tell the Anabaptists that we are very grateful for their offer, but at the moment we have no particular need of money.' As for the printing press that was offered, here too they would manage on their own. 'We cannot make concessions of principle.' 'As for temporary connections, let them give first thought to making their programme known and say what they intend to do, how they want to do it and with what means. We have no idea.' When he told Tkachev of this rebuttal, Morozov added that he was very embittered. But later, when he attempted to start a review with Tursky, Tkachev and Romanenko—to be called 'Narodnaya zashchita' (*The defence of the people*)—he soon understood that in fact 'to be sincere' his scientific terrorism 'had nothing in common with Jacobinism'. In January 1881 he returned to Russia and was arrested. He remained in the Shlissel'burg fortress until 1905. Romanenko went back to Russia in the summer of 1881, and by November was already in prison.

99. 'Narodnaya Volya', no. III, *op. cit.*, p. 80.
100. *Ibid.*, nos. VIII–IX, p. 247.
101. *Ibid.*, no. II, p. 42.
102. *Ibid.*, no. V, p. 172.
103. 'Listok Narodnoy Voli', no. 3, *op. cit.*, p. 136.
104. 'Narodnaya Volya', no. III, *op. cit.*, pp. 84–5.
105. *Ibid.*, no. V, pp. 167–8.
106. *Ibid.*, pp. 169 ff.
107. *Ibid.*, no. II, p. 42.
108. *Ibid.*, no. VII, p. 229.
109. Plekhanov tells how one of the important members of the 'Executive Committee' had said to him: 'We in fact have nothing against Marx, but we think that our programme is closer to Dühring's theory'. '*Sochineniya*' (*Works*), *op. cit.*, vol. XIII, p. 28. Lavrov also said: ' "Narodnaya Volya" inclined towards Dühring's sociological conception of the determining influence of the political-legal element on the economic element'. '*Vzglyad na proshedsheye i nastoyashcheye russkogo sotsializma*' (*A glance at the past and the present of Russian socialism*), in '*Kalendar'* "*Narodnoy Voli*" *na 1883 g.*' (*The calendar of* 'Narodnaya Volya' *for 1883*), Geneva, 1883, p. 109.
110. R. M. Kantor, ' "*Ispoved'*" *Grigoriya Gol'denberga*' (*The 'confession' of G. Goldenberg*), in 'Krasnyy arkhiv', 1928, no. V.
111. V. Figner, '*Zapechatlyonnyy trud*' (*Work concluded*), *op. cit.*, vol. I, pp. 154 ff. On Tatiana Lebedeva, see E. K. Breshko-Breshkovskaya, '*Iz vospominaniy*' (*From recollections*), in 'Golos minuvshago', 1918, nos. X–XII; and M. F. Frolenko, '*Tatiana Ivanovna Lebedeva-Frolenko*', in 'Katorga i ssylka', 1924, no. II, reprinted in '*Sochineniya*' (*Works*), *op. cit.*, vol. II, pp. 109 ff.
112. '*Andrey Ivanovich Zhelyabov*', London, 1882, p. 30.
113. '*Protsess 20-ti narodovol'tsev v 1882 godu*' (*The trial of 20 members of* 'Narodnaya Volya' *in 1882*), in 'Byloye', 1906, no. 1.
114. V. Figner, '*Zapechatlyonnyy trud*' (*Work concluded*), *op. cit.*, vol. I, p. 158.
115. A. P. Pribyleva-Korba and V. N. Figner, '*Narodovolets Aleksandr Dmitrievich Mikhaylov*' (*A. D. Mikhaylov of* 'Narodnaya Volya'), *op. cit.*, p. 142. He gives this version, which is the account of the organizer himself. Other versions in the recollections of other members of 'Narodnaya Volya' differ only in a few, comparatively unimportant, details.
116. S. S. Tatishchev, '*Imperator Aleksandr II*' (*The Emperor Alexander II*), *op. cit.*, vol. II, p. 618.
117. 'Narodnaya Volya', no. III, *op. cit.*, p. 98. This report from Moscow claimed that the words attributed to the Emperor and printed in the papers at the time were never spoken. Instead the Tsar was said to have confessed that the very foundations of the State had been shaken. When faced with the representatives of other social categories, so the report said, he merely wept in silence.
118. Russian émigrés, and French democrats and socialists (including Victor Hugo), interceded on his behalf. He was expelled and went to England. For an account

27*

of him, see: '*Iz vospominaniy L'va Gartmana*' (*From the recollections of Lev Gartman*), in '*Vospominaniya russkikh revolyutsionerov*' (*Recollections of Russian revolutionaries*), Berlin, 1904. He had worked at Rostov with M. R. Popov and Tishchenko, and had known Osinsky there. After a long pilgrimage 'to the people' in the Caucasus, Volga and Kuban, he joined Vera Figner's group at Saratov and then 'Narodnaya Volya'. However, he stayed in touch with 'Chyornyy peredel' and, in exile, he wrote an article on Ireland for the movement's review. A curious letter he wrote to Chaykovsky tells of his attempts to found a weekly paper in England so as to make known the problems of the Russian revolutionary movement. It was to be written in English and among the contributors were to have been many of the most prominent émigrés—Lavrov, Kropotkin, Deych, Stefanovich, Morozov, Plekhanov, and so on. Zasulich was to have been the editor. He spoke of the plan to Marx, who viewed it favourably and promised his collaboration. The title was to have been 'The nihilist', 'a word which intrigues the West and for this reason a good one to use', as Gartman himself said. Dioneo, '*V emigratsii*' (*In the emigration*), in '*N. V. Chaykovsky. Religioznyye i obshchestvennyye iskaniya*'. Stat'i M. A. Aldanova, E. K. Breshko-Breshkovskoy i dr. Pod obshchey redaktsiey A. A. Titova (*N. V. Chaykovsky. Religious and social researches. Articles by M. A. Aldanov, E. K. Breshko-Breshkovskaya and others, edited by A. A. Titov*), Paris, 1919, p. 173.

119. O. S. Lyubatovich, '*Dalyokoye i nedavneye*' (*The distant past and the recent past*), *op. cit.*; V. Figner, '*Evgeniya Nikolaevna Figner*', in 'Katorga i ssylka', 1924, no. II.

120. '*Protsess shestnadtsati terroristov*', pod red. Burtseva (*The trial of the sixteen terrorists*. Edited by V. Burtsev), Spb., 1906.

121. Sof'ya Ivanova-Boreysha, '*Pervaya tipografiya "Narodnoy Voli"*' (*The first printing press of* 'Narodnaya Volya'), in 'Byloye', 1906, no. IX.

122. P. B. Aksel'rod gave a detailed account of him in '*Perezhitoye i peredumannoye*' (*Things seen and reflected upon*), Berlin, 1923, vol. I, p. 58.

123. '*Prebyvaniye Khalturina v Zimnem Dvortse*' (*Khalturin's stay in the Winter Palace*), in '*Kalendar' "Narodnoy Voli" za 1883 g.*' (*The calendar of* 'Narodnaya Volya' *for 1883*), Geneva, 1883, pp. 40 ff.

124. 'Listok Narodnoy Voli', no. I, *op. cit.*, p. 118.

125. Quoted by P. Shchegolev, '*Iz istorii konstitutsionnykh veyaniy v 1879–1881 gg.*' (*From the history of the* '*constitutionalist*' *currents in the years 1879–1881*), in 'Byloye', 1906, no. XII.

126. S. S. Tatishchev, '*Imperator Aleksandr II*' (*The Emperor Alexander II*), *op. cit.*, vol. II, p. 631.

127. *Ibid.*, p. 635.

128. *Ibid.*, p. 641.

129. No. III, *op. cit.*, p. 104.

130. A. Engel'meyer, '*Kazn' Mlodetskogo*' (*The execution of Mlodetsky*), in 'Golos minuvshago', 1917, nos. VII–VIII.

131. 'Listok Narodnoy Voli', no. I, *op. cit.*, p. 121.

132. Yu. Gardenin (V. Chernov), '*Pamyati N. K. Mikhaylovskogo*' (*In memory of N. K. Mikhaylovsky*), no place, 1904. For the activities of this writer, see the accurate and intelligent inquiry of James H. Billington, *Mikhaylovsky and Russian Populism*, Oxford, 1958, which perhaps over-emphasizes Mikhaylovsky's importance in the Populist movement but which provides invaluable material for the understanding of this controversial matter.

133. D. Kuz'min (E. E. Kolosov), '*Narodovol'cheskaya zhurnalistika*' (*The journalism of* 'Narodnaya Volya'), *op. cit.*, exaggerated the importance of the part

played by Mikhaylovsky in the editing of the review. Vera Figner, in her appendix to this book, '*Po povodu issledovatel'skoy raboty D. Kuz'mina*' (*About D. Kuz'min's research*), claims that Mikhaylovsky had *nothing* to do with the editing and had only sent in the articles. The two in charge, Tikhomirov and Morozov, had indeed asked him not to write on questions of 'principle'.

134. I. Yasinsky, '*Roman moyey zhizni*' (*The romance of my life*), M.-L., 1926, pp. 134, 156.

135. See G. I. Uspensky, '*Polnoye sobranie sochineniy*' (*Complete works*), M., 1952–4, in 14 vols.

136. V. Cheshikhin-Vetrinsky, '*Gleb Ivanovich Uspensky*', M., 1929, pp. 248 ff.

137. N. R. (N. Rusanov), *Sobytie pervogo marta i N. V. Shelgunov*' (*1st March 1881 and N. V. Shelgunov*), in 'Byloye', 1906, no. III.

138. V. Ya. Bogucharsky, '*Iz istorii politicheskoy bor'by v 70-kh i 80-kh godakh XIX veka*' (*From the history of the political struggle of the seventies and eighties of the nineteenth century*), *op. cit.*, p. 167.

139. No. V, *op. cit.*, p. 187. For the fate of the two student members of 'Narodnaya Volya' who had carried out the protest, see '*Yakutskaya tragediya 22 marta 1889 g.*' Sbornik vospominaniy i materialov pod red. M. A. Braginskogo i K. M. Tereshkovicha (*The tragedy in Yakutia on 22nd March 1889*. Collected memoirs and documents edited by M. A. Braginsky and K. M. Tereshkovich), M., 1925. Arrested shortly after their first excursion into illegal activities, the two students spent long years in prison and in exile. Podbel'sky was shot by the police in a prison revolt in 1889 and Kogan-Bernstein, who was wounded on the same occasion, was hanged a little while later.

140. A. V. Tyrkov, '*K sobytiyu 1-go marta 1881 goda*' (*On 1st March 1881*), in 'Byloye', 1906, no. V. Tyrkov was one of the student members of 'Narodnaya Volya' who played an active part in the life of the revolutionary party. He considered, nevertheless, that the demonstration against Saburov was useless and harmful, and took no part in it; this too was an indication of the students' state of mind in the winter of 1880–1.

141. S. Valk, '*Iz pokazaniy N. I. Rysakova*' (*From the depositions of N. I. Rysakov*), in 'Krasnyy arkhiv', 1926, no. VI.

142. M. N. Polonskaya, '"*Pokazaniya*". *K istorii partii "Narodnoy Voli*"' ('*Depositions*'. *For a history of the party of* 'Narodnaya Volya'), *op. cit.*

143. N. N. (E. A. Serebryakov), '*Vospominaniya o Sukhanove*' (*Recollections of Sukhanov*), in 'Vestnik Narodnoy Voli', 1886, no. V; E. A. Serebryakov, '*Revolyutsionery vo flote*' (*Revolutionaries in the fleet*), in 'Byloye', 1907, nos. II, III; N. Yu. Ashenbrenner, '*Voyennaya organizatsiya "Narodnoy Voli" i drugiye vospominaniya*' (1860–1904). Pod red. N. S. Tyutcheva (*The military organization of* 'Narodnaya Volya' *and other recollections* [*1860–1904*]. Edited by N. S. Tyutchev), M., 1924; and the records of the official inquiry (1883–4) into the infiltration of 'Narodnaya Volya' into the army, which are published under the title, '*K istorii narodovol'cheskogo dvizheniya sredi voyennykh v nachale 80-kh godov*' (*For a history of the activities of* 'Narodnaya Volya' *in the armed forces in the early eighties*), in 'Byloye', 1906, no. VIII.

144. S. Valk, '*Iz pokazaniy N. I. Rysakova*' (*From the depositions of N. I. Rysakov*), *op. cit.*

145. V. Levitsky (V. Tsederbaum), '"*Narodnaya Volya" i rabochiy klass*' ('Narodnaya Volya' *and the working class*), in 'Katorga i ssylka', 1930, no. I.

146. S. Valk, '*Avtobiograficheskiye pokazaniya M. F. Grachevskogo*' (*M. F. Grachevsky's autobiographical depositions*), in 'Krasnyy arkhiv', 1926, no. V.

147. S. Valk, '*Iz pokazaniy N. I. Rysakova*' (*From the depositions of N. I. Rysakov*), *op. cit.*

148. Rysakov, who said this, was obviously repeating ideas current among the working-class organizers of the 'Narodnaya Volya'.

149. '*Literatura partii "Narodnoy Voli"*' (*Literature of the* 'Narodnaya Volya' *party*), *op. cit.*, pp. 439 ff.

150. R. M. Kantor, '*Ges'ia Mironovna Gel'fman*', M., 1930.

151. The two numbers of 'Rabochaya gazeta' are reprinted in '*Literatura partii "Narodnoy Voli"*' (*The literature of the* 'Narodnaya Volya' *party*), *op. cit.*, p. 419 ff.

152. '"*Zerno*". *Rabochiy listok*'. S predisloviem V. I. Nevskogo ('Zerno'. *The workers' leaflet*. With a preface by V. I. Nevsky), in '*Istoriko-revolyutsionnyy sbornik*' (*Miscellany on revolutionary history*), 1924, no. II.

153. S. Valk, '*Iz pokazaniy N. I. Rysakova*' (*From the depositions of N. I. Rysakov*), *op. cit.*

154. See, for instance, the account of a heavy industrial workshop, in '*Iz rabochego dvizheniya za Nevskoy Zastavoy v 70-kh i 80-kh godakh. Iz vospominaniy starogo rabochego*' (*From the history of the workers' movement in the Nevskaya Zastava district in the seventies and eighties. From the recollections of a veteran workman*), Geneva, 1900, pp. 5 ff.

155. V. Figner, '*Mikhail Nikolaevich Trigoni (1850–1917)*', in 'Golos minuvshago', 1917, nos. VII–VIII.

156. '*Protsess 20-ti narodovol'tsev v 1882 g.* (*The trial of 20 members of* 'Narodnaya Volya' *in 1882*), in 'Byloye', 1906, no. I, gives the charge against those who helped Sofia Perovskaya and Sablin, including Isayev, Yakimova, Zlatopol'sky, and others.

157. *Ibid.*

158. M. R. Popov, '*Voyennyy sud v Kieve v 1880 godu (Iz moikh vospominaniy)*' (*The military tribunal at Kiev in 1880* [*From my recollections*]), in '*Zapiski zemlevol'tsa*' (*Memoirs of a member of* 'Zemlya i Volya'), *op. cit.*, pp. 261 ff.

159. '*Po povodu protsessa 16-ti*' (*On the trial of the sixteen*), in 'Byloye', 1903, no. III; and '*Protsess shestnadtsati terroristov*'. Pod red. V. Burtseva (*The trial of the sixteen terrorists*. Edited by V. Burtsev), no place, 1906.

160. No. IV, 5th December 1880, in '*Literatura partii "Narodnoy Voli"*' (*The literature of the* 'Narodnaya Volya' *party*), *op. cit.*, p. 145.

161. '*Pis'ma narodovol'tsa A. D. Mikhaylova*'. Sobral P. E. Shchegolev (*Letters by A. D. Mikhaylov of* 'Narodnaya Volya'. Collected by P. E. Shchegolev), M., 1933, pp. 101–2, 194.

CHAPTER 22

1. On this first plan, see M. F. Frolenko, '*Sobranie sochineniy*' (*Works*), vol. II, p. 63.

2. V. Figner, '*Zapechatlyonnyy trud*' (*Work concluded*), M., 1933, vol. II, pp. 200 ff.

3. M. N. Trigoni, '*Moy arest v 1881 godu*' (*My arrest in 1881*), in 'Byloye', 1906, vol. III.

4. '*Biografiya Grinevitskogo*' (*Biography of Grinevitsky*), in 'Na rodine', no. I.

5. A. V. Tyrkov, '*K sobytiyu 1-go marta 1881 goda*' (*On 1st March 1881*), in 'Byloye', 1906, no. V.

6. This incident was to be remembered in 1928 on 30th December, when Frolenko's eightieth birthday was celebrated in Moscow; Frolenko survived all the events of the 'seventies and more than twenty years in prison at Shlissel'burg. M. F. Frolenko, '*Sobranie sochineniy*' (*Works*), *op. cit.*, vol. I, p. 23.

7. V. Ya. Bogucharsky, 'Iz istorii politicheskoy bor'by v 70-kh i 80-kh godakh XIX veka. Partiya "Narodnoy Voli", eyo proiskhozhdenie, sud'ba i gibel' ' (From the history of the political struggle in the seventies and eighties of the nineteenth century. The party of 'Narodnaya Volya', its origin, its destiny and its fall), M., 1912, pp. 86 ff.

8. N. R. (N. Rusanov), 'Sobytie 1-go marta i N. V. Shelgunov' (1st March 1881 and N. V. Shelgunov), in 'Byloye', 1906, no. III.

9. A. V. Tyrkov, 'K sobytiyu 1-go marta 1881 g.' (On 1st March 1881), op. cit.

10. K., 'Moskva v marte 1881 goda' (Moscow in March 1881), in 'Krasnyy arkhiv', 1926, no. 1, gives the police reports for the first few days of March, from which the sentences quoted here have been taken.

11. S. Valk, 'Posle 1-go marta 1881 g.' (After 1st March 1881), in 'Krasnyy arkhiv', 1931, no. II, and various studies on the events of those days collected in '1 marta 1881 goda', podgotovleno k pechati literaturnoy komissiey kruzhka narodovol'tsev v sostave A. V. Yakimovoy-Dikovskoy, M. F. Frolenko i dr. (1st March 1881, compiled by the literary committee of a group of members of 'Narodnaya Volya' consisting of A. V. Yakimova-Dikovskaya, M. F. Frolenko and others), M., 1933.

12. This letter was published in 'Byloye', 1906, no. III.

13. 'Sof'ya L'vovna Perovskaya', London, 1882, p. 22.

14. 'Literatura partii "Narodnoy Voli" ' (The literature of the party 'Narodnaya Volya'), M., 1907, pp. 451 ff.

15. 'Konstitutsiya Loris-Melikova' (Loris-Melikov's constitution), London, 1893; F. Volkhovsky, 'Chemu uchit "konstitutsiya" gr. Loris-Melikova?' (What is the lesson of Count Loris-Melikov's 'constitution'?), London, 1894; P. Shchegolev, 'Iz istorii konstitutsionnykh veyaniy v 1879–1881 gg.' (From the history of the 'constitutionalist' tendencies in the years 1879–1881), in 'Byloye', 1906, no. XII; N. Golitsyn, 'Konstitutsiya gr. Loris-Melikova' (The constitution of Count Loris-Melikov), in 'Byloye', 1918, nos. IV–V; E. A. Peretts, 'Dnevnik (1880–1883)', s predisloviem E. A. Presnyakova. Text podgotovil k pechati A. A. Sergeyev (Diary (1880–1883). With a preface by E. A. Presnyakov. Text edited by A. A. Sergeyev), M.-L., 1927; 'Konstitutsionnyye proyekty nachala 80-kh godov XIX veka' (Constitutional projects in the early 1880s), in 'Krasnyy arkhiv', 1928, no. VI; Yu. V. Got'e, 'Bor'ba pravitel'stvennykh gruppirovok i manifest 29 aprelya 1881 goda' (The fight between groups within the Government and the manifesto of 29th April 1881), in 'Istoricheskiye zapiski', 1938, no. II; D. A. Milyutin, 'Dnevnik'. Redaktsiya, biograficheskiy ocherk i primechaniya P. A. Zayonchkovskogo (Diary. Edited and with a biographical essay and notes by P. A. Zayonchkovsky), M., 1947–50, in four volumes, volume IV covering the years 1881–2.

16. E. A. Peretts, 'Dnevnik' (Diary), op. cit., p. 69.

17. 'K 25-letiyu 1881–1906 gg. Delo pervogo marta 1881 g. Protsess Zhelyabova, Perovskoy i dr. (Pravitel'stvennyy otchyot)'. So stat'yey i primechaniyami L'va Deycha (For the twenty-fifth anniversary of 1881. 1881–1906. The affair of 1st March 1881. The trial of Zhelyabov, Perovskaya and others [Official account]). With an article and notes by Lev Deych), Spb., 1906.

18. Ibid., pp. 333 ff.

BIBLIOGRAPHICAL NOTES

THE READER will have seen that I have noted only those books, pamphlets, articles, etc., which directly concerned specific problems as they arose. It has not been my aim to provide a complete bibliography: the works already quoted will have given some idea of the large number of studies devoted to particular aspects of the Populist movement. Had I tried to complete this list I would certainly have had to weigh down still further a book which is perhaps already too bulky and detailed.

I must now add those general works which I have not referred to on specific occasions, as I would have had to quote them each time. This book owes at least as much to them as to individual studies and articles. By compiling them in this note I hope to express my gratitude to their authors and at the same time provide a short bibliography of the Populist movement as a whole.

For all material concerning the literary, political and social history of Russia between 1848 and 1881 I refer the reader to the researches of scholars such as E. Lo Gatto and W. Giusti, in whose work he will find extensive bibliographies in Russian and other languages. I am especially indebted to the writings of Leone Ginzburg, in whom the spirit of the *narodniki* found a new and original incarnation.

For a general view of nineteenth-century economic discussions, see J. F. Normano, *The Spirit of Russian Economics* (London, 1949). A wide selection of writings by the first generation of Populist thinkers will be found in *Il pensiero democratico russo del XIX secolo—Scritti di Bielinski, Herzen, Cernicevski, Dobrolinbov*, a cura di G. Berti and M. B. Gallinaro, intr. di G. Berti (Florence, 1950).

For the more specifically philosophical background to the Populists' ideas, see Alexandre Koyré, *Etudes sur l'histoire de la pensée philosophique en Russie* (Paris, 1950), with an extensive bibliography.

For the history of the European Socialist movement of the period, see Leo Valiani, *Storia del movimento socialista*, vol. I: *L'epoca della Prima Internazionale* (Florence, 1951); and G. D. H. Cole, *A History of Socialist thought*, vol. I: *The Forerunners, 1789–1850* (London, 1953), and vol. II, *Marxism and Anarchism, 1850–1890* (London, 1954).

The first history of the Populist movement is A. Thun's *Geschichte der revolutionären Bewegungen in Russland* (Leipzig, 1883). This is strikingly well informed if we consider when it was written, and twenty years after its publication the Russian Socialists still found it worth translating and commentating on. Two editions appeared in 1903: A. Thun, '*Istoriya revolyutsionnykh dvizheniy v Rossii*', s predisloviem G. V. Plekhanova (*History of the revolutionary movements in Russia*, with a preface by G. V. Plekhanov), (Geneva); and A. Thun, '*Istoriya revolyutsionnogo dvizheniya v Rossii*', pod red. i s primechaniyami L. E. Shishko (*History of the revolutionary movement in Russia*, edited and with notes by L. E. Shishko) (Geneva). Both editions are valuable—the first for Plekhanov's preface, the second for L. E. Shishko's comments. The editions are complementary: in one case the material is seen from a social-democratic viewpoint, in the other from a socialist revolutionary angle—though it must be remembered that each was designed for propaganda and controversy. In 1890 a large volume of 700 pages was published in St Petersburg: *Chronique du mouvement socialiste en Russie, 1878–1887, rédigée sous la direction de l'Adjoint du Ministère de l'Intérieur, General Schébeco.* Only a hundred copies 'for official use' appeared of this book, which tells the story of revolutionary Populism from the angle of the police.

A *Geschichte der russischen Revolution,* by Ludwig Kulczycki, was published in three volumes in Gotha in 1910. Part of the first and all of the second volume are concerned with the period dealt with in this book. Kulczycki was able to use the vast amount of material which came to light during and immediately after the revolution of 1905. Though the book does not lay enough stress on the ideological problems of the movement as a whole, it is still the best non-Russian work on the subject.

No special bibliography lists the extensive material which was published in the years just before and after 1917. As from 1924 reference can be made to the careful catalogues by R. S. Mandel'stam, '*Revolyutsionnoye dvizheniye v Rossii XVIII–XIX vv. Sistematicheskiy ukazatel' literatury vyshedshey v 1924 godu*' (*The revolutionary movement in Russia in the 18th and 19th centuries. Systematic index of the literature which appeared in 1924*), in collaboration with B. P. Koz'min (Moscow, 1924). The bibliography for 1925 was published in Moscow in 1927, that for 1926 in 1928; for 1927–8 in 1929; for 1929–31 in 1933. These are pamphlets which appeared as appendices to the review, 'Katorga i ssylka'. They have not, as far as I am aware, been published in book form. This review, which provides a mine of information on Populism, has published detailed indices of the individual revolutionaries referred to in its pages and of the articles it has published: R. M. Kantor, '*Imennoy i sistematicheskiy ukazatel' k istoriko-revolyutsionnomu vestniku* "Katorga i ssylka"' (*Systematic name index of the historical-revolutionary review* 'Katorga i ssylka' *for 1921–1925*) (Moscow, 1928); and *idem.*, '"Katorga i ssylka" *za desyat' let (1921–1930), sistematicheskiy i predmetnyy ukazatel'*' ('Katorga i ssylka' *for ten years (1921–1930), systematic subject index*) (Moscow, 1931).

Studies and researches completed during the fifteen years after 1917 have been summarized in that indispensable source for all investigations on the Russian revolutionaries: A. A. Shilov, B. P. Koz'min and others, '*Deyateli revolyutsionnogo dvizheniya v Rossii, bio-bibliograficheskiy slovar'*' (*The exponents of the revolutionary movement in Russia. Biographical and bibliographical dictionary*) (Moscow, 1927–33). The first volume contains two parts, the first of which goes up to 1855, while the second includes the 'sixties (1855–69). Volume 2 contains four parts, all of which are devoted to the 'seventies (1869–79). Volume 3 has one part devoted to 'Narodnaya Volya'; Volume 4 two parts concerned with the social-democrats (1883–1904). Volumes 3 and 4 are incomplete and no more have appeared.

An important bibliography (with references to the French, Dutch, Swiss and Italian libraries in which the works quoted can be found) has been published by Eugène Zaleski: *Mouvements ouvriers et Socialistes* (*Chronologie et bibliographie*), *La Russie*, Tome I, 1725–1905 (Paris, 1956), p. 31 ff. Chapter II, *Le mouvement populiste* (1851–84).

No comprehensive modern book deals with the repercussions abroad of the Russian revolutionaries and the discussions provoked by their ideas in the Western socialist and democratic press. There are many valuable references in I. Rubanovich, '*Inostrannaya pressa i russkoye dvizhenie*' (*The foreign press and the Russian movement*), in 'S rodiny i na rodinu', 1893. This is a field in which research might well be particularly fruitful and provide new material for the study of the movement in Russia itself—which has been my only concern in this book.

Since the Italian edition of this book, significant new works which have appeared include James H. Billington, *Mikhaylovsky and Russian Populism* (Oxford, 1958); and *Harvard Slavic Studies*, vol. IV, 'Russian thought and politics' (The Hague, 1957).

CHRONOLOGICAL TABLE

1825	Decembrist revolt.
1834	Herzen, Ogarev and other members of the St Simonist group in Moscow arrested.
1840	Bakunin emigrates.
1847	Herzen emigrates.
1848–9	Herzen takes part in the revolution in Italy and France, and Bakunin in France, Bohemia and Germany.
1849	Petrashevsky and his Fourierist groups arrested in St Petersburg.
1853	First publication of the 'Free Russian Press in London' organized by Herzen.
1853–5	Crimean War.
1855	Death of Nicholas I. Accession of Alexander II.
1857	First appearance of the *Kolokol* (The Bell), edited in London by Herzen and Ogarev.
19th February 1861	Alexander II's edict freeing the serfs.
April 1861	The riots at Bezdna.
July 1861	Circulation of the first secret leaflet, the *Velikoruss* (Great Russian).
September 1861	Circulation of *To the young generation.* Student demonstration in St Petersburg.
1862	Chernyshevsky's *Letters without an Address.*
Summer 1862	*Young Russia.*
7th July 1862	Arrest of Chernyshevsky and N. A. Serno-Solovevich.
1862–3	*Zemlya i Volya* (Land and Liberty).
1863	Polish insurrection.
1864	The Kazan conspiracy.
1864–5	Alexander II's administrative (*zemstvo*) and judicial reforms.
1864–5	Yadrintsev's and Potanin's Siberian plot.
1864–6	Ishutin's *Organization.*
4th April 1866	Karakozov's attempt on the life of the Tsar.
1866–8	The 'white terror'.
1867	The *Society of the rouble.*
1867–9	The *Smorgon Academy.*
1868	First number of the *Narodnoe delo* (The People's Cause), edited by Bakunin.
1869	Student disorders in St Petersburg and Moscow. The *Commune* of the *Malaya Vulfovaya.* Origin of Natanson's group.
1868–9	Serial publication of Lavrov's *Historical letters.* Nechaev's and Tkachev's groups. *Programme of revolutionary activities.*

March 1869	Nechaev's first departure from Russia and collaboration with Bakunin. *The revolutionary's catechism.*
August–November 1869	*Narodnaya rasprava (The people's summary justice).*
21st November 1869	Nechaev's killing of Ivanov.
1869–72	Nechaev again out of Russia.
1869	Publication of Bervi-Flerovsky's *Situation of the Working Class in Russia.*
1870	Russian section of the First International in Geneva. Lavrov emigrates. First strikes in St Petersburg.
1870–3	'Chaikovsky's group' in action.
March 1872	Bakunin's *Russian Brotherhood* in Zürich.
1873	Chaikovskist action among the working classes in St Petersburg.
Summer 1873	Dolgushin's group.
August 1873	First number of Lavrov's *Vpered* (Forward) in Zürich.
1874	Tkachev emigrates.
1875–81	Tkachev publishes *Nabat* (The Tocsin).
1875	Zaslavsky's Union of Workers of South Russia at Odessa. Pan-Russian Social Revolutionary organization in Moscow. *Rabotnik* (The Worker) in Geneva. Natanson's 'troglodytes' in St Petersburg.
1875–6	Movement for Russian volunteers in the Balkans. Revival of activities among the St Petersburg working classes. Dyakov. The *Society of Friends.* Formation of the group of 'rebels' in the South.
3rd March 1876	Demonstrations break out in St Petersburg during funeral of student Chernyshev.
Summer 1876	Escape and emigration of Kropotkin. Formation of the *Northern revolutionary populist group.* First contacts with southern groups. Formulation of first programme (Mikhailov-Oboleshev).
6th December 1876	Demonstration in the Square of Our Lady of Kazan in St Petersburg.
1876–7	Attempted peasant revolt at Chigirin.
1877–8	Populist attempts to found 'colonies' at Saratov, Voronezh, etc. Russo-Turkish war in the Balkans.
January 1877	Trial of those who took part in the demonstration in the Square of Our Lady of Kazan (Emelyanov-Bogolyubov).
March 1877	Trial of the Fifty in Moscow (Bardina, Alexeyev, etc.).
October 1877–January 1878	Trial of the Hundred and Ninety-three.
24th January 1878	Vera Zasulich's attempted assassination of General Trepov.
30th January 1878	Kovalsky's armed resistance at Odessa.
1878	Osinsky's *Southern Executive Committee.* Attempts on the lives of Kotlyarevsky, Geyking and others.
February–March 1878	Student demonstrations in Kiev.
31st March 1878	Acquittal of Vera Zasulich.
March 1878	First number of *Nachalo* (The Beginning) at St Petersburg.
May 1878	Programme of *Zemlya i Volya* (Land and Liberty).
2nd August 1878	Shooting of Kovalsky.

4th August 1878	Kravchinsky's assassination of Mezentsov.
9th August 1878	Government statement about 'band of evildoers'.
October 1878	Nucleus of 'troglodytes' arrested.
	First number of *Zemlya i Volya* (Land and Liberty).
November 1878	Student disorders in St Petersburg.
1878–9	Wave of strikes in St Petersburg. Formation of *Northern Union of Russian Workers*.
3rd December 1878	Meeting between representatives of the *zemstva* and the Southern terrorists.
Beginning of 1879	Liquidation of the Southern Executive Committee.
9th February 1879	Goldenberg's assassination of Kropotkin, governor of Kharkov.
13th March 1879	Mirsky's attempted assassination of Drenteln.
2nd April 1879	Solovev's attempt on the life of Alexander II. Conflicting tendencies within *Zemlya i Volya*. Birth of the group *Freedom or death*.
Spring–Summer 1879	Many southern terrorists hanged.
17th–21st June 1879	Lipetsk meeting. Formation of the Executive Committee.
24th June 1879	Voronezh meeting.
26th August 1879	Executive Committee votes for the execution of Alexander II.
	Formation of the *Narodnaya Volya* (The People's Will).
18th November 1879	Zhelyabov tries to assassinate Alexander II at Alexandrovsk.
19th November 1879	Mikhailov tries to assassinate Alexander II near Moscow.
January 1880	First number of *Cherny Peredel* (Black Partition).
	Printing press of *Narodnaya Volya* (The People's Will) discovered.
5th February 1880	Khalturin tries to assassinate Alexander II at Winter Palace.
February 1880	Loris-Melikov's 'dictatorship'.
May 1880	Trial of Oboleshev, Olga Natanson, Veymar and others.
October 1880	Arrest of Schedrin and Kovalskaya, founders of the *Workers' Union of Southern Russia*.
25th October 1880	Trial of the Sixteen (Kvyatkovsky, Presnyakov, etc.).
Autumn 1880	*Narodnaya Volya*'s 'military organization'.
28th November 1880	Arrest of Alexander Mikhailov.
15th December 1880	First number of *Rabochaya gazeta* (Workers' Gazette) in St Petersburg.
February 1881	Demonstration of members of the *Narodnaya Volya* against Minister of Public Instruction.
27th February 1881	Arrest of Zhelyabov.
1st March 1881	Assassination of Alexander II.
10th March 1881	Letter of *Executive Committee* to Alexander III.
3rd April 1881	Hanging of Rysakov, Mikhailov, Kibalchich, Zhelyabov and Perovskaya.

INDEX